Handbook of Public Information Systems

Second Edition

PUBLIC ADMINISTRATION AND PUBLIC POLICY

A Comprehensive Publication Program

Executive Editor

JACK RABIN
Professor of Public Administration and Public Policy
School of Public Affairs
The Capital College
The Pennsylvania State University—Harrisburg
Middletown, Pennsylvania

Assistant to the Executive Editor
T. Aaron Wachhaus, Jr.

1. *Public Administration as a Developing Discipline,* Robert T. Golembiewski
2. *Comparative National Policies on Health Care,* Milton I. Roemer, M.D.
3. *Exclusionary Injustice: The Problem of Illegally Obtained Evidence,* Steven R. Schlesinger
5. *Organization Development in Public Administration,* edited by Robert T. Golembiewski and William B. Eddy
7. *Approaches to Planned Change,* Robert T. Golembiewski
8. *Program Evaluation at HEW,* edited by James G. Abert
9. *The States and the Metropolis,* Patricia S. Florestano and Vincent L. Marando
11. *Changing Bureaucracies: Understanding the Organization before Selecting the Approach,* William A. Medina
12. *Handbook on Public Budgeting and Financial Management,* edited by Jack Rabin and Thomas D. Lynch
15. *Handbook on Public Personnel Administration and Labor Relations,* edited by Jack Rabin, Thomas Vocino, W. Bartley Hildreth, and Gerald J. Miller
19. *Handbook of Organization Management,* edited by William B. Eddy
20. *Organization Theory and Management,* edited by Thomas D. Lynch
22. *Politics and Administration: Woodrow Wilson and American Public Administration,* edited by Jack Rabin and James S. Bowman
23. *Making and Managing Policy: Formulation, Analysis, Evaluation,* edited by G. Ronald Gilbert
25. *Decision Making in the Public Sector,* edited by Lloyd G. Nigro
26. *Managing Administration,* edited by Jack Rabin, Samuel Humes, and Brian S. Morgan
27. *Public Personnel Update,* edited by Michael Cohen and Robert T. Golembiewski
28. *State and Local Government Administration,* edited by Jack Rabin and Don Dodd
29. *Public Administration: A Bibliographic Guide to the Literature,* Howard E. McCurdy
31. *Handbook of Information Resource Management,* edited by Jack Rabin and Edward M. Jackowski

32. *Public Administration in Developed Democracies: A Comparative Study,* edited by Donald C. Rowat

33. *The Politics of Terrorism: Third Edition,* edited by Michael Stohl

34. *Handbook on Human Services Administration,* edited by Jack Rabin and Marcia B. Steinhauer

36. *Ethics for Bureaucrats: An Essay on Law and Values, Second Edition,* John A. Rohr

37. *The Guide to the Foundations of Public Administration,* Daniel W. Martin

39. *Terrorism and Emergency Management: Policy and Administration,* William L. Waugh, Jr.

40. *Organizational Behavior and Public Management: Second Edition,* Michael L. Vasu, Debra W. Stewart, and G. David Garson

43. *Government Financial Management Theory,* Gerald J. Miller

46. *Handbook of Public Budgeting,* edited by Jack Rabin

49. *Handbook of Court Administration and Management,* edited by Steven W. Hays and Cole Blease Graham, Jr.

50. *Handbook of Comparative Public Budgeting and Financial Management,* edited by Thomas D. Lynch and Lawrence L. Martin

53. *Encyclopedia of Policy Studies: Second Edition,* edited by Stuart S. Nagel

54. *Handbook of Regulation and Administrative Law,* edited by David H. Rosenbloom and Richard D. Schwartz

55. *Handbook of Bureaucracy,* edited by Ali Farazmand

56. *Handbook of Public Sector Labor Relations,* edited by Jack Rabin, Thomas Vocino, W. Bartley Hildreth, and Gerald J. Miller

57. *Practical Public Management,* Robert T. Golembiewski

58. *Handbook of Public Personnel Administration,* edited by Jack Rabin, Thomas Vocino, W. Bartley Hildreth, and Gerald J. Miller

60. *Handbook of Debt Management,* edited by Gerald J. Miller

61. *Public Administration and Law: Second Edition,* David H. Rosenbloom and Rosemary O'Leary

62. *Handbook of Local Government Administration,* edited by John J. Gargan

63. *Handbook of Administrative Communication,* edited by James L. Garnett and Alexander Kouzmin

64. *Public Budgeting and Finance: Fourth Edition,* edited by Robert T. Golembiewski and Jack Rabin

65. *Handbook of Public Administration: Second Edition,* edited by Jack Rabin, W. Bartley Hildreth, and Gerald J. Miller

66. *Handbook of Organization Theory and Management: The Philosophical Approach,* edited by Thomas D. Lynch and Todd J. Dicker

67. *Handbook of Public Finance,* edited by Fred Thompson and Mark T. Green

68. *Organizational Behavior and Public Management: Third Edition,* Michael L. Vasu, Debra W. Stewart, and G. David Garson

69. *Handbook of Economic Development,* edited by Kuotsai Tom Liou

70. *Handbook of Health Administration and Policy,* edited by Anne Osborne Kilpatrick and James A. Johnson

71. *Handbook of Research Methods in Public Administration,* edited by Gerald J. Miller and Marcia L. Whicker

72. *Handbook on Taxation,* edited by W. Bartley Hildreth and James A. Richardson

73. *Handbook of Comparative Public Administration in the Asia-Pacific Basin,*
    edited by Hoi-kwok Wong and Hon S. Chan

74. *Handbook of Global Environmental Policy and Administration,*
    edited by Dennis L. Soden and Brent S. Steel

75. *Handbook of State Government Administration,* edited by John J. Gargan

76. *Handbook of Global Legal Policy,* edited by Stuart S. Nagel

78. *Handbook of Global Economic Policy,* edited by Stuart S. Nagel

79. *Handbook of Strategic Management: Second Edition,*
    edited by Jack Rabin, Gerald J. Miller, and W. Bartley Hildreth

80. *Handbook of Global International Policy,* edited by Stuart S. Nagel

81. *Handbook of Organizational Consultation: Second Edition,*
    edited by Robert T. Golembiewski

82. *Handbook of Global Political Policy,* edited by Stuart S. Nagel

83. *Handbook of Global Technology Policy,* edited by Stuart S. Nagel

84. *Handbook of Criminal Justice Administration,* edited by M. A. DuPont-Morales,
    Michael K. Hooper, and Judy H. Schmidt

85. *Labor Relations in the Public Sector: Third Edition,* edited by Richard C. Kearney

86. *Handbook of Administrative Ethics: Second Edition,* edited by Terry L. Cooper

87. Handbook of Organizational Behavior: Second Edition, edited by
    Robert T. Golembiewski

88. *Handbook of Global Social Policy,* edited by Stuart S. Nagel and Amy Robb

89. *Public Administration: A Comparative Perspective, Sixth Edition,* Ferrel Heady

90. *Handbook of Public Quality Management,* edited by Ronald J. Stupak and
    Peter M. Leitner

91. *Handbook of Public Management Practice and Reform,* edited by Kuotsai Tom Liou

92. *Personnel Management in Government: Politics and Process, Fifth Edition,*
    Jay M. Shafritz, Norma M. Riccucci, David H. Rosenbloom, Katherine C. Naff,
    and Albert C. Hyde

93. *Handbook of Crisis and Emergency Management,* edited by Ali Farazmand

94. *Handbook of Comparative and Development Public Administration: Second
    Edition,* edited by Ali Farazmand

95. *Financial Planning and Management in Public Organizations,*
    Alan Walter Steiss and Emeka O. Cyprian Nwagwu

96. *Handbook of International Health Care Systems,* edited by
    Khi V. Thai, Edward T. Wimberley, and Sharon M. McManus

97. *Handbook of Monetary Policy,* edited by Jack Rabin and Glenn L. Stevens

98. *Handbook of Fiscal Policy,* edited by Jack Rabin and Glenn L. Stevens

99. *Public Administration: An Interdisciplinary Critical Analysis,* edited by
    Eran Vigoda

100. *Ironies in Organizational Development: Second Edition, Revised and
     Expanded,* edited by Robert T. Golembiewski

101. *Science and Technology of Terrorism and Counterterrorism,*
     edited by Tushar K. Ghosh, Mark A. Prelas, Dabir S. Viswanath,
     and Sudarshan K. Loyalka

102. *Strategic Management for Public and Nonprofit Organizations,* Alan Walter Steiss

103. *Case Studies in Public Budgeting and Financial Management:
     Second Edition,* edited by Aman Khan and W. Bartley Hildreth

104. *Handbook of Conflict Management,* edited by William J. Pammer, Jr.
     and Jerri Killian

105. *Chaos Organization and Disaster Management,* Alan Kirschenbaum

106. *Handbook of Gay, Lesbian, Bisexual, and Transgender Administration and Policy,* edited by Wallace Swan

107. *Public Productivity Handbook: Second Edition,* edited by Marc Holzer

108. *Handbook of Developmental Policy Studies,* edited by Gedeon M. Mudacumura, Desta Mebratu and M. Shamsul Haque

109. *Bioterrorism in Medical and Healthcare Administration,* Laure Paquette

110. *International Public Policy and Management: Policy Learning Beyond Regional, Cultural, and Political Boundaries,* edited by David Levi-Faur and Eran Vigoda-Gadot

111. *Handbook of Public Information Systems, Second Edition,* edited by G. David Garson

112. *Handbook of Public Sector Economics,* edited by Donijo Robbins

113. *Handbook of Public Administration and Policy in the European Union,* edited by M. Peter van der Hoek

114. *Nonproliferation Issues for Weapons of Mass Destruction,* Mark A. Prelas and Michael S. Peck

Available Electronically

Principles and Practices of Public Administration, edited by Jack Rabin, Robert F. Munzenrider, and Sherrie M. Bartell

Handbook of Public Information Systems

Second Edition

edited by
G. David Garson
North Carolina State University

Taylor & Francis
Taylor & Francis Group

Boca Raton   London   New York   Singapore

A CRC title, part of the Taylor & Francis imprint, a member of the
Taylor & Francis Group, the academic division of T&F Informa plc.

Published in 2005 by
CRC Press
Taylor & Francis Group
6000 Broken Sound Parkway NW
Boca Raton, FL 33487-2742

© 2005 by Taylor & Francis Group, LLC
CRC Press is an imprint of Taylor & Francis Group

No claim to original U.S. Government works
Printed in the United States of America on acid-free paper
10 9 8 7 6 5 4 3 2 1

International Standard Book Number-10: 0-8247-2233-7 (Hardcover)
International Standard Book Number-13: 978-0-8247-2233-3 (Hardcover)
Library of Congress Card Number 2004059361

Library of Congress Cataloging-in-Publication Data

Handbook of public information systems / edited by G. David Garson.–2nd ed.
    p. cm. – (Public administration and public policy; 111)
  Includes bibliographical references and index.
  ISBN 0-8247-2233-7 (alk. paper)
   1. Public administration–Information technology. I. Garson, G. David. II. Series.

JF1525.A8H36 2005
352.7'4–dc22

2004059361

Taylor & Francis Group
is the Academic Division of T&F Informa plc.

Visit the Taylor & Francis Web site at
http://www.taylorandfrancis.com

and the CRC Press Web site at
http://www.crcpress.com

CONTENTS

Preface xiii
Editor.. xv
Contributors.. xvii

Part I: Introduction

Chapter 1   Public Information Systems in the 21st Century 3
G. David Garson

Chapter 2   Bridging the Gap between Information Technology Needs in
the Public Sector and in Public Administration Graduate Education.......................... 11
Mary Maureen Brown, Jeffrey L. Brudney, and William L. Waugh, Jr.

Chapter 3   Public Information Technology and e-Government:
A Historical Timeline 27
G. David Garson

Part II: Organizational Research

Chapter 4   Using Strategic Information Systems to Improve Contracted Services
and Assess Privatization Options 43
Steven Cohen and William B. Eimicke

Chapter 5   Interorganizational and Interdepartmental Information Systems:
Sharing among Governments.. 59
Bruce Rocheleau

Chapter 6   Implementing e-Government Projects: Organizational Impact and
Resilience to Change 83
Mila Gascó

Chapter 7   Understanding Large-Scale IT Project Failure: Escalating
and De-escalating Commitment 93
Mark R. Nelson

Chapter 8   Revisiting Virtual Locals and Cosmopolitans "In and As" Electronic
Governance: A Comparative Analysis of the Social Production of an Academic
Community.. 107
Lynn M. Mulkey, William L. Dougan, and Lala Carr Steelman

Chapter 9   Information Technology Investment and Organizational
     Performance in the Public Sector 127
Pamela Hammers Specht and Gregory Hoff

Chapter 10   Electronic Data Sharing in Public-Sector Agencies 143
Irvin B. Vann

Chapter 11   Governance in the Era of the World Wide Web: An Assessment
     of Organizational Openness and Government Effectiveness, 1997 to 2001 155
Todd M. La Porte, Chris C. Demchak, and Christopher Weare

Part III: Policy Issues

Chapter 12   Social Stratification and the Digital Divide 173
Kenneth R. Wilson, Jennifer S. Wallin, and Christa Reiser

Chapter 13   Intellectual Property for Public Managers 185
Roland J. Cole and Eric F. Broucek

Chapter 14   Cybersecurity Considerations for Information Systems 203
Cynthia E. Irvine

Chapter 15   Information and Terrorism Age Militaries 219
Chris C. Demchak

Chapter 16   e-Rulemaking 237
Stuart W. Shulman, Lisa E. Thrane, and Mark C. Shelley

Chapter 17   Citizen Participation and Direct Democracy through Computer
     Networking: Possibilities and Experience 255
Carmine Scavo

Chapter 18   Internet Tax Policy: An International Perspective 281
Dale Nesbary and Luis Garcia

Chapter 19   Taking Advantage of the Information Age: Which Countries
     Benefit? 299
Shelly Arsneault, Alana Northrop, and Kenneth L. Kraemer

Part IV: Case Studies

Chapter 20   The Role of Information Technology and the
     New York State Legislature 321
Antoinette J. Pole

Chapter 21   Managing e-Government in Florida: Further Lessons from
     Transition and Maturity 335
David H. Coursey and Jennifer Killingsworth

Chapter 22   Exploring Internet Options: The Case of Georgia's
    Consumer Services.. 353
Gregory Streib and Katherine G. Willoughby

Chapter 23   The Virtual Value Chain and e-Government Partnership:
    Nonmonetary Agreements in the IRS e-File Program 369
Stephen H. Holden and Patricia D. Fletcher

Part V: Applications

Chapter 24   Computer-Based Training in the Public Sector 391
Genie N. L. Stowers

Chapter 25   Issues in Contracting and Outsourcing Information Technology 407
Jay D. White and Ronnie L. Korosec

Chapter 26   Management Information Systems and an Interdisciplinary Budget
    Model.. 427
George B. K. de Graan

Chapter 27   Analysis and Communication for Public Budgeting 463
Carl Grafton and Anne Permaloff

Chapter 28   Public Finance Management Information Systems 489
John W. Swain and Jay D. White

Chapter 29   Statistical Analysis Software in Public Management................................ 505
T. R. Carr

Part VI: E-Government

Chapter 30   Enacting Virtual Forms of Work and Community: Multiwave Research
    Findings across Individual, Organizational, and Local Community Settings 521
Thomas Horan and Kimberly J. Wells

Chapter 31   E-Government: The URBIS Cities Revisited... 545
Alana Northrop

Chapter 32   Agency Internets and the Changing Dynamics of Congressional
    Oversight.. 559
Julianne G. Mahler and Priscilla M. Regan

Chapter 33   Privacy Considerations in Electronic Judicial Records:
    When Constitutional Rights Collide 569
Charles N. Davis

Chapter 34   Information Technology and Political Participation:
    A Comparative Institutional Approach 581
Juliet Ann Musso and Christopher Weare

Chapter 35   E-Government Performance-Reporting Requirements 599
Patrick R. Mullen

Chapter 36   Assessing e-Government Innovation 615
Jonathan D. Parks and Shannon H. Schelin

Chapter 37   E-Democracy and the U.K. Parliament 631
Stephen Coleman

Chapter 38   Emerging Electronic Infrastructures: Exploring Democratic
    Components 643
Åke Grönlund

Part VII: Conclusion

Chapter 39   Information Systems, Politics, and Government:
    Leading Theoretical Perspectives 665
G. David Garson

Index 689

PREFACE

Because of the fast-evolving nature of technology and the issues and opportunities faced by public-sector managers as they wrestle with the information age, it is perhaps not surprising that this second edition of the *Handbook of Public Information Systems* contains approximately two thirds new material, including a whole new section on e-government. I wish to thank all those in government service, schools of public administration, and elsewhere who contributed to this volume, either directly or as reviewers. Without their generous contribution of time and energy, this volume would not be possible.

It is appropriate that the study of information technology (IT) is assuming a central place in public administration curricula and, perhaps more important, that the inadequacy of narrowly technocratic approaches to IT management is increasingly recognized in government. There is good reason to study and better understand the implementation of IT projects. More often than not, IT projects are late, over budget, do not achieve their functional objectives, or are even simply canceled, as has been reported by organizations such as the Gartner Group, Meta Group, and the Standish Group.

There are several theories about IT failure, each emphasizing different themes found in this volume. Some have noted that the greater the number of stakeholders (and the public sector tends to proliferate stakeholders), the more complex the requirements and the higher the risk of project failure. IT projects fail because of lack of commitment from the organization's stakeholders; consequently, the project manager must spend much time mobilizing stakeholders, leaving IT technology issues largely to the tech team. Time is spent, for instance, getting agency leadership to figure out what they really want and to realize that they didn't have the time or resources to do it. The organization's executive leadership is the prime stakeholder, whose active support is critical to implementation success.

Others have stressed that senior management lacks understanding not only of the technology, but also of the general systemic nature of their organizations, and particularly lacks an understanding that technological change means change of the organizational culture. Lack of a participative approach is commonly cited as a cause of IT failure. Without participation, IT initiatives often fail to capture important social relationships, which may undermine the technical logic of the IT system.

Then, too, technology projects often fail because of poor business plans. To be sustainable, the technology project must make economic sense to the principle stakeholders. Thus there must be an economic model that accompanies the technology model. Project managers must focus on business needs first, technology second. When the solution is selected solely on technological grounds, ignoring business requirements, failure often ensues. The Gartner Group finds that as many as three quarters of all IT projects fail because of old-fashioned, poor planning. Failure to invest in planning the project within the organization, and buying a prepackaged outside "solution" instead, has been cited as one of the leading reasons for IT failure.

IT projects fail because the underlying assumptions about a program are unrealistic. IT projects fail because conventional and inappropriate methods traditional to the organization are forcibly used in new IT project implementation initiatives. IT projects fail because of unrealistically short time horizons, sometimes encouraged by IT consultants who seek/need to close and go on to new projects. In the public sector, expending an agency's entire budget before the end of the fiscal year is a common pattern, designed to demonstrate need so as to assure the following year's budget will be at least as large. This strategy, however, can result in undue acceleration of IT projects. This is compounded when the strategy is implemented at the end of the year, under an even more compressed time schedule.

In general, the more rapid the rate of change in the environment, the more disordered and uncoordinated the implementation of technology initiations, the more likely the system failure. Under these circumstances, IT projects fail because of inadequate support, training, and incentives for end users. Lack of user input may lead to an inappropriate technology design. An important part of IT implementation is mobilization at the workgroup level. This may involve participative planning, training, and individual or group rewards for IT success. Lack of communication and understanding between top management, the technology team, and end users is a major factor in the failure of IT projects. IT training must be about more than technology. IT training must take a holistic approach to organization development in the context of constant performance pressure associated with implementing new technology.

The prevalence of failure to deliver IT projects on time and within budget, and to do so while also providing for such values as privacy, security, and accountability, is as important a public management challenge as any in our time. The chapters in this book address different aspects of a systemic whole but the unifying theme is that technology is too important to leave to the technocrats. To do so is not only to leave democratic values in peril, but also to fail to apply to IT what students of public administration have found to be wise management practice in its more traditional domains of strategic planning, policy development, and the mobilization of human capital.

G. David Garson
Raleigh, NC
March 2005

EDITOR

G. David Garson is full professor of public administration at North Carolina State University, where he teaches courses on geographic information systems, information technology, e-government, research methodology, and American government. In 1995 he was recipient of the Donald Campbell Award from the Policy Studies Organization, American Political Science Association, for outstanding contributions to policy research methodology, and in 1997 of the Aaron Wildavsky Book Award from the same organization. In 1999 he won the Okidata Instructional Web Award from the Computers and Multimedia Section of the American Political Science Association, in 2002 he received an NCSU Award for Innovative Excellence in Teaching and Learning with Technology, and in 2003 he received an award "For Outstanding Teaching in Political Science" from the American Political Science Association and the National Political Science Honor Society, Pi Sigma Alpha.

He is editor of *Public Information Systems: Policy and Management Issues* (2003); coeditor of *Digital Government: Principles and Practices* (2003); coauthor of *Crime Mapping* (2003); author of *Guide to Writing Quantitative Papers, Theses, and Dissertations* (Dekker, 2001); editor of *Social Dimensions of Information Technology* (2000), *Information Technology and Computer Applications in Public Administration: Issues and Trends* (1999), and *Handbook of Public Information Systems* (1999, 2004); author of *Neural Network Analysis for Social Scientists* (1998), *Computer Technology and Social Issues* (1995), and *Geographic Databases and Analytic Mapping* (1992); and is author, coauthor, editor, or coeditor of 17 other books and author or coauthor of over 50 articles.

He has also created award-winning American government computer simulations, CD-ROMs, and six websites for Prentice-Hall and Simon & Schuster (1995–1999). For the last 20 years he has also served as editor of the Social Science Computer Review and is on the editorial board of four additional journals. He is currently principal investigator for the North Carolina Governor's Crime Commission on "Using Neural Network Analysis and GIS to Model Crime Data" (2001–2004) and two other crime-related grants. Professor Garson received his undergraduate degree in political science from Princeton University (1965) and his doctoral degree in government from Harvard University (1969).

CONTRIBUTORS

Shelly Arsneault, California State University, Fullerton, CA
sarsenault@fullerton.edu

Eric F. Broucek, DHL Express

Mary Maureen Brown, University of North Carolina, Chapel Hill, NC
brown@iogmail.iog.unc.edu

Jeffrey L. Brudney, University of Georgia, Athens, GA
jbrudney@arches.uga.edu

T.R. Carr, Southern Illinois University, Edwardsville, IL
tcarr@siue.edu

Steven Cohen, Columbia University, New York, NY
sc32@columbia.edu

Roland J. Cole, Barnes & Thornburg, Indianapolis, IN
rcole@btlaw.com

Stephen Coleman, Oxford Internet Institute, Oxford, UK
Stephen.Coleman@oii.ox.ac.uk

David H. Coursey, Florida State University, Tallahassee, FL
dcoursey@garnet.fsu.edu

Charles N. Davis, University of Missouri, Columbia, MO
daviscn@missouri.edu

Chris C. Demchak, University of Arizona, Tucson, AZ
demchak@u.arizona.edu

William L. Dougan, University of Wisconsin, Whitewater, WI
douganw@uww.edu

William B. Eimicke, Columbia University, New York, NY
wbel@columbia.edu

Patricia D. Fletcher, University of Maryland–Baltimore County, Baltimore, MD
pfletcher@umbc.edu

Luis Garcia, Suffolk University, Boston MA
lgarcia@suffolk.edu

Mila Gascó, International Institute on Governance of Catalonia, Barcelona, Spain
mila.gasco@iigov.org

George B.K. de Graan, Road and Hydraulic Engineering Institute, Den Haag, Holland
g.de.graan@hccnet.nl; G.B.K.dGraan@dww.rws.minvenw.nl

Carl Grafton, Auburn University, Montgomery, AL
graftonpermaloff@worldnet.att.net

Åke Grönlund, Örebro University, Örebro, Sweden
Ake.gronlund@esi.oru.se

Gregory Hoff, University of Nebraska at Omaha, NE
ghoff@mail.unomaha.edu

Stephen H. Holden, University of Maryland–Baltimore County, Baltimore, MD
holden@umbc.edu

Thomas Horan, Claremont Graduate University, Claremont, CA
Tom.horan@cgu.edu

Cynthia E. Irvine, Naval Postgraduate School, Monterey, CA
Irvine@nps.navy.mil

Jennifer Killingsworth, Florida State University, Tallahassee, FL
ikillingsworth@earthlink.net

Ronnie L. Korosec, University of Central Florida, Orlando, FL
rkorosec@mail.ucf.edu

Kenneth L. Kraemer, University of California, Irvine, CA
kkraemer@uci.edu

Todd M. La Porte, George Mason University, Washington, DC
tlaporte@gmu.edu

Julianne G. Mahler, George Mason University, Fairfax, VA
jmahler@gmu.edu

Lynn M. Mulkey, University of South Carolina, Hilton Head, SC
mulkey@sc.edu

Patrick R. Mullen, U.S. Government Accountability Office, Washington, DC
mullenp@gao.gov

Juliet A. Musso, University of Southern California, Los Angeles, CA
sppd@usc.edu

Mark R. Nelson, Lally School of Management and Technology, Rensselaer Polytechnic Institute, Troy, NJ
nelsom@rpi.edu

Dale Nesbary, Oakland University, Rochester, MI
nesbary@oakland.edu

Alana Northrop, California State University, Fullerton, CA
anorthrop@fullerton.edu

Jonathan D. Parks, Raleigh, NC
parksnc@earthlink.net

Anne Permaloff, Auburn University, Montgomery, AL
graftonpermaloff@worldnet.att.net

Antoinette J. Pole, The City University of New York, NY
apole@gc.cuny.edu

Priscilla M. Regan, George Mason University, Fairfax, VA
pregan@gmu.edu

Christa Reiser, East Carolina University, Greenville, NC
reiserc@mail.ecu.edu

Bruce Rocheleau, Northern Illinois University, Dekalb, IL
brochele@niu.edu

Carmine Scavo, East Carolina University, Greenville, NC
scavoc@mail.ecu.edu

Shannon H. Schelin, University of North Carolina, Chapel Hill, NC
schelin@icgmail.iog.unc.edu

Mark C. Shelley, Iowa State University, Ames, IA
mshelley@iastate.edu

Stuart W. Shulman, Drake University, Des Moines, IA
Stuart.Shulman@drake.edu

Pamela Hammers Specht, University of Nebraska, Omaha, NE
pspecht@unomaha.edu

Lala Carr Steelman, University of South Carolina, Columbia, SC
steelman@sc.edu

Genie N.L. Stowers, San Francisco State University, San Francisco, CA
gstowers@sfsu.edu

Gregory Streib, Georgia State University, Atlanta, GA
gstreib@gsu.edu

John W. Swain, Governors State University, University Park, IL
j-swain@govst.edu

Lisa E. Thrane, Iowa State University, Ames, IA
lthrane@iastate.edu

Irvin B. Vann, North Carolina State University, Raleigh, NC
ibvann@unity.ncsu.edu

Jennifer S. Wallin, RTI International, Raleigh, NC
wallin@rti.org

William L. Waugh, Jr., Georgia State University, Atlanta, GA
wwaugh@gsu.edu

Christopher Weare, University of Southern California, Los Angeles, CA
weare1001@yahoo.com

Kimberly J. Wells, Claremont Graduate University, Alexandria, VA
kjwells@prodigy.net

Jay D. White, University of Nebraska–Omaha, Lincoln, NE
jwhite@neb.rr.com

Katherine G. Willoughby, Georgia State University, Atlanta, GA
kwilloughby@gsu.edu

Kenneth R. Wilson, East Carolina University, Greenville, NC
wilsonk@mail.ecu.edu

PART I

INTRODUCTION

1

PUBLIC INFORMATION SYSTEMS IN THE 21ST CENTURY

G. David Garson

North Carolina State University

CONTENTS

I. Organizational research 4
II. Policy issues.. 5
III. Case studies 6
IV. Applications.. 7
V. E-government 8
VI. Conclusion 10

Public-sector information systems have become a pervasive part of the life of agencies at all levels of government. As indicated by Mary Maureen Brown and coauthors in Chapter 2, textbooks and graduate instruction in the field of public administration are struggling to keep up with the rapid pace of change and to prepare students and practitioners alike for public service in the "information age." It is hoped that the present volume will make some modest contribution to the preparation and career readiness of public administration students and practitioners new to information and communication technology (ICT). This collection of original essays presents the historical, institutional, legal, organizational, functional, policy, and theoretical background that we believe constitutes ICT literacy for the public service.

The chapters that follow are divided into several broad categories. In Part I, historical background is presented, in the form of a timeline of technological, legislative, and judicial events pertaining to ICT. Part II on organizational research lays out the implications of information technology (IT) for the ways organizations may adapt to change in a wide variety of organizational dimensions, ranging from the details of implementation to the strategies involved in political considerations. Part III synopsizes a variety of policy issues, including issues of equity, intellectual property, public participation, and international issues. This is followed in Part IV by a small number of case studies, after which Part V describes federal-level applications of IT to training, contracting, budgeting, public finance, and other areas. Part VI is a new section, focusing on e-government examples and issues from several perspectives. Part VII contains an essay by the editor, discussing the theoretical context of public information systems.

I. ORGANIZATIONAL RESEARCH

Steven Cohen and William Eimicke, in "Using Strategic Information Systems to Improve Contracted Services and Assess Privatization Options" (Chapter 4), trace how government officials look to contracting out and privatization as means to a more effective public sector. They explore the theory and practice of performance measurement and IT in the context of outsourcing public service delivery and discuss the use of government strategic planning and information-based performance management to plan and manage private contractors performing public tasks. While information systems are critical to the management of in-house organizational units, the authors believe they are even more important in managing the work of contractors.

Bruce Rocheleau, in "Interorganizational and Interdepartmental Information Systems: Sharing among Governments" (Chapter 5), examines the types of sharing of IT resources that take place among governmental organizations. He studies sharing relationships among local governments, between state and local governments, between the federal and state governments, and other complex relationships that include private organizations. A wide variety of examples of sharing are drawn from available resources in order to identify the types of sharing that exist and the key factors that influence its success.

In "Implementing e-Government Projects: Organizational Impact and Resilience to Change" (Chapter 6), Mila Gascó discusses technological innovations in the public sector that have led to digital administration and government programs that have not always been successful. To understand why requires analyzing the organizational and institutional setting where the transformations that are related to ICT adoption in the public sector occur. The adoption of new technologies has given rise to important organizational change processes but it has not necessarily been accompanied by needed cultural alterations or institutional changes. Those factors that produce resilience to technological change are not different from those related to other public administration transformations, the author argues.

Mark R. Nelson, in "Understanding Large-Scale IT Project Failure: Escalating and De-escalating Commitment" (Chapter 7), notes that large-scale IT projects are particularly prone to failure. Moreover, in the public sector, IT failure may be cumulative and even have a domino effect. Increasing commitment to success yields subsequent project iterations that are both increasingly costly and increasingly less likely to succeed. Nelson looks at how commitment to large-scale IT projects in the public sector escalates and de-escalates repeatedly over time. The consequences of such cycles are discussed, including specific concerns and recommendations that are made for public-sector managers of large-scale IT projects.

In "Revisiting Virtual Locals and Cosmopolitans 'In and As' Electronic Governance: A Comparative Analysis of the Social Production of Academic Community" (Chapter 8), Lynn M. Mulkey, William L. Dougan, and Lala Carr Steelman shift the focus to academia. Building on Robert Merton's theory of "locals" and "cosmopolitans" for understanding the governance of virtual academic organizations, the authors address whether virtual communities have the same essential characteristics as those typically observed in face-to-face communities to which the local–cosmopolitan dichotomy was originally applied. The authors explore how norm construction in public access data obtained for previous research — faculty at a large state university — compares with observations on a sample of electronic communications among members of the American Society of Public Administration (ASPA). The authors find that virtual communities appear especially amenable to self-selection and exclusivity of normative orientations for fulfilling the functions of academic institutions and they trace implications for public administration.

Pamela Hammers Specht and Gregory Hoff, in "Information Technology Investment and Organization Performance in the Public Sector," focus on determining what will be measured or tracked to accurately represent investment and performance within public and private agencies. The authors offer a framework for public-sector managers to use in developing appropriate performance measures and guidelines based on the literature are presented to aid in the formulation of business cases containing IT investment to organization performance.

In "Electronic Data Sharing in Public-Sector Agencies" (Chapter 10), Irvin B. Vann distinguishes information sharing and data sharing, examining both concepts as found in public administration literature and proposes some clarifications between them. IT is viewed as one of the solutions for reducing the information "collection burden" on citizens and businesses. Using technology, information sharing between government agencies is frequently proposed as the method to efficiently use the vast amounts of information collected by government but this widely accepted goal confronts numerous obstacles.

Todd M. La Porte, Chris C. Demchak, and Christopher Weare, in "Governance in the Era of the World Wide Web: An Assessment of Organizational Openness and Government Effectiveness, 1997 to 2001" (Chapter 11), contend that bureaucratic openness, administrative efficiency, and increased public participation are separate but potentially linked aspects of increasingly reliance on electronic networked information systems, principally the Internet. This chapter updates their earlier report on a systematic long-running research program, supported by the National Science Foundation, to survey and analyze these trends. They analyze the effects of these digital government efforts, and relate them to several government performance measures, including standard economic growth rates, government performance data, and data on democratic institutions.

II. POLICY ISSUES

Kenneth R. Wilson, Jennifer S. Wallin, and Christa Reiser, in "Social Stratification and the Digital Divide" (Chapter 12), note that while recent studies have shown that the size of the digital divide has been shrinking for many groups, the authors explore whether socioeconomic factors explain the racial, geographic, and gender divides. Rural, minority, and female respondents were found to be less likely to have home computers or to be connected to the Internet. Controlling for socioeconomic variables, the effects of rural residence and gender disappeared but African Americans were still less likely to have home computers or Internet access.

In "Intellectual Property for Public Managers" (Chapter 13), Roland J. Cole and Eric F. Broucek set forth some of the history of the concept of intellectual property, then discuss its four major types. The authors discuss the special legal rules surrounding the federal government's acquisition and creation of intellectual property, then the role of the states (in this context, local governments are similar to states). Finally, the authors conclude with a table summarizing some of the major legal aspects of each type of intellectual property.

Cynthia E. Irvine, in "Cybersecurity Considerations for Information Systems" (Chapter 14), notes that as the value of the information stored electronically increases, computer systems become targets for abuse and attack. To ensure continued public confidence in these systems, managers need to understand the impact of security shortcomings in their automated systems. A high-level taxonomy of threats to information systems is presented to provide a basis for security requirements. Fundamental concepts of computer security are reviewed. The costs and benefits of investment in cybersecurity will be introduced. The concept of organizational information policy, mechanisms for its enforcement, and the value of assurance and the notion of costs and benefits of investment in cybersecurity are presented.

In "E-Rulemaking" (Chapter 16), Stuart W. Shulman, Lisa Thrane, and Mark C. Shelley present and assess the debate about the future of e-rulemaking. They examine the impact of electronic enhancements to the collection and synthesis of public commentary. Focus group data are presented to highlight a number of the competing values that are at stake as public managers implement e-government. The authors speculate about the next steps that might culminate in a public information system for e-rulemaking that is technologically robust, applied in the most appropriate ways possible, and a genuine enhancement to both the regulatory and the democratic processes.

Carmine Scavo, in "Citizen Participation and Direct Democracy through Computer Networking: Possibilities and Experience" (Chapter 17), examines the potential of ICT to be a democratizing force, citing the generally positive track record of computer networking experience of various levels of government in the U.S., the work of various nongovernmental organizations, and the theoretical formulations of various analysts and researchers.

In "Internet Tax Policy: An International Perspective" (Chapter 18), Dale Nesbary and Luis Garcia show how new forms of electronic commerce have led to concern and interest on the part of governments, business, and individuals about the collectivity of taxes on Internet transactions, downloads, and access. The authors examine Internet tax policies of the U.S., Canada, Australia, England, and European Union nations, and they offer recommendations for a model Internet tax policy.

Shelly Arsneault, Alana Northrop, and Kenneth L. Kraemer, in "Taking Advantage of the Information Age: Which Countries Benefit?" (Chapter 19), address the issue of technological advance by reviewing the factors that led countries to computerize at high rates during the 1990s and by asking which countries have been most likely to take advantage of the Internet as it gains wide popularity at the start of the 21st century. The authors find that the profusion of information infrastructure was a key mediating force determining the likelihood of a nation-state making use of computers in the early 1990s, and the Internet early in the 21st century. To fully participate and gain the economic, political and social benefits of computers and the Internet, nations are advised to expose their citizens to earlier generations of mass information mediums and to provide them an extensive information infrastructure.

III. CASE STUDIES

In "The Role of Information Technology and the New York State Legislature" (Chapter 20), Antoinette J. Pole explores the role of computing technology in the New York State Legislature during the past two decades. She looks at how technology has transformed constituency correspondence, the tracking of legislation, the process of redistricting, and how policymakers and their staff use the Internet. In addition, the author assesses the level of collaboration, efficiency, and acceptance toward new technologies in these areas. Overall, she finds a greater degree of efficiency across the board but acceptance of new technologies is not universal. Increased collaboration in the areas of tracking legislation and the Internet, in particular, is found to have greatly altered policymaking.

David H. Coursey and Jennifer Killingsworth, in "Managing e-Government in Florida: Further Lessons from Transition and Maturity" (Chapter 21), discuss reasons why the state of Florida was the leading state government in e-government in the mid-1990s. Explanations include political leadership and competition, innovative personnel practices, and entrepreneurial leadership. With a change in the governor's office in the 1998 election from a moderate Democrat to a firmly antigovernment conservative Republican, the state became one of the first to experience the influence of a dramatic government transition in e-government management philosophy. This chapter primarily reflects on the state's experience under Jeb Bush and whether commonly asserted public information management ideas are supported. Evidence tends to support the importance of factors such as political leadership, personnel arrangements, and institutional structures on innovation.

In "Exploring Internet Options: The Case of Georgia's Consumer Services" (Chapter 22), Gregory Streib and Katherine G. Willoughby examine citizens' perspectives about service delivery options of a state agency that specifically compares traditional means of delivery (like in-person office visits) with web-based ones. The authors present data from a yearlong series of four statewide polls that examined attitudes toward the services provided by Georgia's Office of Consumer Affairs and citizen assessment of different service delivery options, including electronic communication methods. Their findings show a strong preference for in-person communication. Their work throws light on the hurdles that public administrators face as they seek to find ways to benefit from new communication technologies.

In a fourth case study, Stephen H. Holden and Patricia Diamond Fletcher, in "The Virtual Value Chain and e-Government Partnership: Nonmonetary Agreements in the IRS e-File Program" (Chapter 23), trace how a new form of collaboration emerged in the Internal Revenue Service (IRS) e-file program in 1999 and what dimensions helped to make it a success. The IRS e-file program, one of the largest and most successful U.S. e-government programs with tens of millions of users each year, experienced dramatic changes in its long-standing partnership with the tax preparation and related software development industries in 1999 and 2000. The authors show, using the concept of the virtual value chain, how the IRS rethought its relationship with its private-sector partners. A combination of conditions in the marketplace, in U.S. society, within the IRS, and among the private-sector partners helped to make this new model of collaboration quite successful. The chapter concludes by examining how the dimensions of partnership in the IRS e-file case and the concept of the virtual value chain might enable other public organizations to reconceptualize their e-government partnership arrangements with the private sector with a new model of collaboration.

IV. APPLICATIONS

Genie N. L. Stowers, in "Computer-Based Training in the Public Sector" (Chapter 24), discusses the various technologies involved in computer-based training and provides a special emphasis on online training. Computer-based training can be provided just-in-time and allows participants to have more flexibility in their learning experiences.

This chapter reviews these options, including the fast-changing online training opportunities. The existing evidence suggests most types of computer-based training are just as effective, if not more so, than traditional forms of instruction.

In "Issues in Contracting and Outsourcing Information Technology" (Chapter 25), Jay D. White and Ronnie Korosec find contracting out technology and outsourcing information services in the public sector is fraught with many financial risks and project failures. They provide an overview of some major issues in contracting and outsourcing IT in public organizations and examine the risks and failures of large-scale IT projects, outlining some of the things that management can do to deal with risks and failures in contracting and outsourcing deals.

George B. K. de Graan, in "Management Information Systems and an Interdisciplinary Budget Model" (Chapter 26), argues that management systems in the U.S. and European public sectors suffer from the lack of adequate measures of efforts for efficiency and effectives and the retrospective-oriented management information. By styling the causal relationships of the transformation process from inputs to outputs independently of the traditional administration and on a strongly prospective-oriented way, this information can be used to reinforce the strategic planning (effectiveness) and the management control process (efficiency). A budget model can be described as a quantitative and a qualitative goal to be achieved on the basis of parameters that have been estimated by statistical methods or experts. Management information systems (MISs) play a vital role in providing relevant information to the different management layers for efficiency and effectiveness.

In "Analysis and Communication for Public Budgeting" (Chapter 27), Carl Grafton and Anne Permaloff discuss how relatively inexpensive and common computing tools permit budgeting and analytical techniques to be used quickly, accurately, and less expensively than would have been the case only a few years ago. Computer tools also permit great improvements in the production and dissemination on the Internet of budgetary information transparent to the public and their legislative and news media representatives. The authors discuss important lessons learned in relation to the budgetary techniques.

John W. Swain and Jay D. White, in "Public Finance Management Information Systems" (Chapter 28), define key terms, describe the application of IT to accounting in the public sector, and explain the barriers to the fulfillment of ICT promises. These authors also assess developments in public finance in relation to ICT. Likewise, T. R. Carr, in "Statistical Analysis Software in Public Management" (Chapter 29), examines the role of statistical packages as a management tool in the public sector. Carr discusses the use of statistical packages in improving the quality of information available to decision-makers.

V. E-GOVERNMENT

Thomas Horan and Kimberly Wells, in "Enacting Virtual Forms of Work and Community: Multiwave Research Findings across Individual, Organizational, and Local Community Settings" (Chapter 30), examine how digital technologies are affecting work and community. They focus on virtual forms of telework and community technology applications as pursued in the state of Minnesota. Reporting three waves of data collection, the authors find that the success of virtual activities depends on the surrounding activities by local organizational and community networks. The community focus groups' findings highlighted the extent to which community success with technology deployment is in significant part due to the extent to which community participants collaborate to develop "action-oriented" forums for deployment. These results provide confirmation that virtual activities do not occur in isolation, but rather should be seen as part of a broader knowledge-sharing enterprise occurring in organizations and communities.

In "e-Government: The URBIS Cities Revisited" (Chapter 31), Alana Northrop discusses ICT in the 42 U.S. cities that had been the subject of a $1.9 million NSF-funded series of studies in 1975 and 1988. Northrop returns to the URBIS cities and explores their use of e-government, with contrasts with several other data sets: Government Technology magazine's Best of the Web 2001 and 2002 city winners, ICMA's 2002 city/county survey, Brown University's Taubman Center's 2002 municipal survey, and Scavo's 2002 survey of city/county websites in each state. Focus is on how up to date the websites are, common features across websites, number of clicks on home page, and online transaction features.

Julianne G. Mahler and Priscilla M. Regan, in "Agency Internets and the Changing Dynamics of Congressional Oversight" (Chapter 32), focus on the effects of the increasing digital capacity of federal agencies on congressional oversight. They explore the impact of expanded online agency offerings on the number and type of requests for casework; on the focus, duration, and number of investigative hearings; and on the detail and specificity with which program legislation is written. This research is based on interviews with committee staff, with jurisdiction over two agencies with a strong Internet presence and two with a weak presence.

In "Privacy Considerations in Electronic Judicial Records: When Constitutional Rights Collide" (Chapter 33), Charles N. Davis addresses the growing trend toward electronic judicial records and the policies various states have enacted addressing the issue of privacy. By examining the results of a much-anticipated working group studying issues of e-government and information access, the author examines the challenges posed by electronic records and proposes a more proper balance between the public's right to know and other competing interests.

Juliet Ann Musso and Christopher Weare, in "Information Technology and Political Participation: A Comparative Institutional Approach" (Chapter 34), consider whether new information and communication technologies have significant effects on citizen participation by evaluating the development of a major innovation in electronic governance. They analyze the creation of an electronic system in Los Angeles to provide stakeholders a warning of upcoming political decisions and an opportunity to furnish feedback. The authors find that technology can positively affect individuals' capacity and motivations. Nevertheless, it is not a panacea, because, by itself, technology does not overcome the complex of political, institutional, and behavioral impediments that have limited previous participatory reforms.

In "e-Government Performance-Reporting Requirements" (Chapter 35), Patrick R. Mullen discusses several U.S. laws that contain IT and e-government performance-reporting requirements, including the Paperwork Reduction Act, the Computer Security Act, the Clinger–Cohen Act, the Government Information Security Reform Act (GISRA), and the e-Government Act. For each, the author reviews the legislative history and then focuses on the specific requirements for reporting to the Congress, the Office of Management and Budget (OMB), and the agency heads. The author concludes that OMB's new Office of Electronic Government needs to evaluate whether performance requirements could be improved through (1) consolidation, thereby providing a more comprehensive discussion of agency IT and e-government issues and (2) addressing broader issues, such as an across-government focus on both national and international IT issues.

Jon Parks and Shannon Schelin, in "Assessing e-Government Innovation" (Chapter 36), offer a theoretical framework for understanding e-government and examine two alternative assessment methodologies for gauging e-government capacity. The authors empirically test several hypotheses about policy innovation at the local level and discuss implications and questions for future research.

In "e-Democracy and the U.K. Parliament" (Chapter 37), Stephen Coleman notes how representative institutions are slowly adapting to the digital world. In 1996 the U.K. Parliament established its own website. Although a highly informative resource, of particular value to journalists and those familiar with the parliamentary system, Coleman finds that the site is designed to promulgate official knowledge rather than facilitate interactive communication between citizens and legislators.

Åke Grönlund, in "Emerging Electronic Infrastructures: Exploring Democratic Components" (Chapter 38), discusses how the components of a democratic society are treated as they are built into the emerging electronic infrastructures dealing with services and dialogues pertinent to the functioning of the public sector and tries to find emerging patterns. Grönlund opens a discussion on the nature of the emerging infrastructures by reviewing four implementations of local "e-democracy" and putting them into the context of the global e-government development, in particular the EU development of "eEurope." He finds that the cases represent different models of democracy, models that are only partially explicit. The development is governed more by gradual implementation of ICT tools than a general political agenda. This means local actors have great influence and hence e-democracy is not deterministic but rather can come in many shapes.

VI. CONCLUSION

In "Information Systems, Politics, and Government: Leading Theoretical Perspectives" (Chapter 39), G. David Garson focuses on recent theorists who have addressed the core concern of social science theory: the modeling of long-term trends to postdict the past and predict the future of the impact of ICT on society. Such theories are pertinent to many fields and are central to public administrationists' concern for policy development and pragmatic efforts to reconcile the potential of ICT with societal needs as we enter the 21st century. The theorists discussed in this chapter are grouped in four broad camps. The decentralization/democratization school emphasizes the progressive potential of ICT in government, business, education, the home, and almost all spheres of life. The critical theory school emphasizes the internal contradictions of information systems and promulgates a cautionary counter to the enthusiasm of the decentralization/democratization theorists. The sociotechnical systems theory school discussed in this chapter is one of the oldest and best established, which combines elements of the first two, but at the expense of predictive theory. The global integrationist school transcends the optimism–pessimism duality of the first two schools and is critical of both while still laying the basis for predictive theory. Theorists and writers in this school focus on the globality of worldwide information networks as a transformative socioeconomic force.

2

BRIDGING THE GAP BETWEEN INFORMATION TECHNOLOGY NEEDS IN THE PUBLIC SECTOR AND IN PUBLIC ADMINISTRATION GRADUATE EDUCATION

Mary Maureen Brown
University of North Carolina

Jeffrey L. Brudney
University of Georgia

William L. Waugh, Jr.
Georgia State University

CONTENTS

I.   Introduction 12
II. The growth of IT in the public sector 12
     A. The need for instruction in software application 13
     B. The need for instruction in IT management 14
III. Methodology and data collection 16
     A. Findings on instruction system application use 17
     B. Findings on instruction in IT management 22
IV. Conclusion 24
References 25

ABSTRACT

The information technology (IT) revolution in the public sector has been slowed by shrinking budgets and expanding expenditures for security and other concerns, but the promise of greater efficiency and effectiveness continues to encourage investment in new technologies. A continuing obstacle, however, has been the gap between public-sector IT needs and the skills of public employees. Master of Public Administration (MPA) programs have tried to address the need for IT skills, but much still needs to be done to meet agency needs. This chapter focuses on the IT skills currently being taught in MPA programs and the perception that they do not fully address public-sector needs. On the basis of a survey of the National Association of Schools of Public Affairs and Administration–affiliated MPA programs, the authors conclude that greater attention needs to be paid to effective IT management, including the concepts identified by the Clinger–Cohen Act, in order for public managers to be able to use IT effectively to meet organizational imperatives.

I. INTRODUCTION

While the IT revolution in government has been bogged down by budget deficits and, at least partially, by greatly increased expenditures for security, the growth of e-government is gaining momentum. In some measure, IT applications are still viewed as a means of reducing expenditures, making government more efficient (Harris, 2003: 6), and, at the same time, making it more effective in addressing societal needs. Digital government, e-commerce, Internet and intranet networks, and other IT applications are changing the very nature of the relationship between citizen and government. However, progress has not been without major mishaps.

Governments have invested heavily in computer technology over the past two decades, but these investments have not always fulfilled management expectations. Project failures in the Internal Revenue Service in the early 1990s, for example, cost taxpayers an estimated $50 billion per year (Anthes, 1996). The primary reason for the high failure rate is a lack of knowledge in software utilization and information technology (IT) management. In 1986, the National Association of Schools of Public Affairs and Administration (NASPAA) promulgated general guidelines for curricula in computers and information systems in graduate programs in public affairs and administration (Kraemer and King 1986). In 1996, Congress passed the Clinger–Cohen Act (CCA) intended to reform and improve information management in the federal government. This chapter examines the extent to which schools and departments of public administration provide instruction on software application use and IT requisite to these two challenges. The study focuses on the extent to which MPA and Master of Arts in Public Administration (MAPA) graduates receive instruction that will prepare them for the dramatic changes in IT under way in the federal, state and local governments.

II. THE GROWTH OF IT IN THE PUBLIC SECTOR

When NASPAA made its original recommendations in 1986, it recognized formally what had become obvious: the need for students to become computer literate. In the decade following the NASPAA report, the federal government spent roughly $200 billion on IT (GAO/AIMD-94-115). In 1994 alone the federal government obligated more than $23.5 billion toward IT products and services — about 5% of its total discretionary spending (GAO/AIMD-96-64). A 1997 General Accounting Office (GAO) report concluded, "nearly every aspect of over $1.5 trillion in annual federal government operations depends on information systems" (GAO-AIMD/GGD-97-60: 3).

Expenditures for IT continue to increase. From 2000 to 2003, state and local government expenditures for IT rose from $56 billion to $81 billion, and federal expenditures rose from $35 billion to $52 billion. On the basis of RFPs, the Center for Digital Government estimates that 19% of recent expenditures are for computing, 18% for administrative systems, 18% for telecom/wireless technologies, 17% for consulting, 13% for networking, 4% for videoconferencing, 4% for e-commerce, 3% for public safety, 2% for records management, and 2% for GIS (*Government Technology*, September 2003: 10).

Across the gamut of government operations, IT is used in virtually every function: criminal justice and law enforcement, taxation and finance, human services, transportation, accounting, budgeting, personnel, payroll, procurement, inventory control, and so forth. Public managers look to IT to streamline work processes, enable easier access and retrieval of information, provide better products and services, save money by avoiding workforce expansion, speed up transactions such as payroll and billing, facilitate adherence to government regulations, and provide greater data security.

Despite the substantial level of investment in computer technology, as will be discussed below, IT has not usually met the high expectations of managers for improvements in productivity, performance, and decision-making (Attewell and Rule, 1984; Keen, 1986; Drucker, 1995). As the next section of the chapter shows, information system benefits are not easily achieved, and large investments in computing do not guarantee success (Brown and Brudney, 1998). Skill deficits in software use and system management detract from benefit attainment. In 2002, for example, the Brainbench Report estimated that the performance gaps between government and private-sector IT service workers was 17% in entry-level technology skills, 17% in programming language skills, 16% in database skills, 12% in networking skills, and 10% in Internet skills. Government workers were more skilled than their private IT counterparts by 8% in Microsoft applications skills and 5% in Microsoft technology administration skills (*Government Technology*, October 2002: 11). In other words, government workers are more skilled in basic word processing, spreadsheet, and other office applications and less skilled than private-sector workers in more sophisticated IT applications.

This chapter evaluates how instruction on IT in graduate programs in public administration and policy has evolved over time, and whether MPA and MAPA students receive instruction requisite to the computing demands of government agencies.

Focusing on changes that have taken place over a 10-year time frame, the analysis below examines the evolution of curricula in software application utilization in schools and departments of public administration. The analysis reports data from the fourth in a series of national surveys of MPA programs on topics related to preparation and instruction in quantitative and computer skills. The analysis also examines the extent to which public administration departments and schools incorporate concepts relating to system management and implementation. To promote a more effective and efficient use of IT, Congress has enacted several legislative reforms to control and monitor IT adoption and implementation practices in the federal sector. Using the goals of the Clinger–Cohen Act of 1996 as a benchmark, the research examines the degree to which masters of public affairs and administration programs have met recommendations for instruction on pivotal issues and practices in IT.

A.   The Need for Instruction in Software Application

The literature on public administration has amply documented the expanding use of ITs in pubic agencies and the need for public administration graduates to have basic computer skills (Brudney et al., 1993). According to Kraemer and Northrop (1989), basic computing tasks, such as record keeping, record searching, and word processing, are so common across public-sector positions that they should be included in most MPA courses, including those in the core. While the professional and academic communities have come to accept as a given the increasing use of computer technologies in public agencies, they have reached far less consensus on the impacts of that use, or how graduate education in public affairs and administration should prepare students for careers in government. The 1986 NASPAA guidelines recommended that students receive computer instruction in courses in public management, including accounting, finance, budgeting, and personnel. In addition, NASPAA institutional accreditation standards state the expectation that MPA programs are to present students with management training in "information systems, including computer literacy and applications" (NASPAA, 1988: 3). Other scholars, too, have provided guidance on the particular computer competencies that ought to be part of the public affairs and administration curricula and the methods for integrating those skills into substantive courses (Bretschneider, 1990; Bergin, 1988).

Yet, some evidence exists that during the 1980s, masters degree programs in public affairs and administration adapted only slowly to the impacts of the computer and ITs on agencies, tasks, and jobs in the public sector (Waugh et al., 1985; Kiel, 1986; Norris and Thompson, 1988; Garson, 1993; Kraemer and Northrop, 1989) and revised their curricula in response. At issue is the level of computer literacy that students should achieve as ITs proliferate and the nature of public administration adapts to the technology changes. What software skills are necessary now, and, more importantly, what skills will be necessary in the next 5 to 10 years? How does one identify the basic software skills that are needed for entering the public-sector workforce, and how does one find the crest of the technological wave and anticipate the skills that will be needed in the future? The findings below provide insight on the changes in software application instruction in schools and departments of public administration since 1995.

The debate concerning which techniques and technologies should be included in public administration curricula has continued. A recent study of the top 20 MPA programs, for example, concludes that programs have tended to emphasize research methodologies, management science, or management decision-making and their related technologies. The authors suggest that a management decision-making approach emphasizing problem-solving skills, such as policy analysis, performance measurement, program evaluation, and cost–benefit analysis, would be a better choice for MPA programs. In terms of computer applications, they argue, "[g]enerally, computer applications are not worthy of credit at the graduate level" and go on to suggest that students learn the applications in training workshops (Aristigueta and Raffel, 2001: 166).

B. The Need for Instruction in IT Management

The failure of computer technology to achieve the organizational benefits anticipated is a recurrent problem. In 1982, Turner wrote, "After more than two and a half decades of experience in implementing computer application systems a surprisingly large number of them still end in failure" (Turner, 1982: 207). Similarly, in an early study of the implementation of information systems, Thayer et al. (1982) found that over 30% of a sample of 60 large public- and private-sector computer projects were abandoned during the implementation phase.

In a more recent study of public- and private-sector organizations, the Standish Group (1994) validates these earlier findings. The responses of 365 public- and private-sector IT executives suggest that fully one third of all IT projects were canceled before completion. Only 16% of the projects were successfully completed on time and on budget. Over 50% of the projects exceeded their original cost estimates by almost 200%, and roughly one third of the projects experienced schedule delays of 200 to 300%. The Standish Group estimates that American companies and government agencies spent a staggering $81 billion on canceled IT projects in 1995 alone. In another study, Cats-Baril and Thompson (1995: 563) claimed that 20% of all IT projects are scrapped before completion; 80% of those that are completed finish behind schedule, over budget, and with lower functionality than originally anticipated.

While the past two decades have witnessed the proliferation of computer technology throughout government, studies indicate that technology benefits are neither guaranteed nor automatic. For many public agencies, dysfunctional systems that impede productivity and thwart effective service delivery are too often the rule rather than the exception. Several GAO reports show that IT efforts are plagued by unusually high project failure rates (GAO/AIMD-94-115, 1994b; GAO/OIMC-96-46, 1996a; GAO/OIMC-96-64, 1996b). One GAO report remonstrates, "Despite spending more than $200 billion on information management and systems during the last 12 years, the government has too little evidence of meaningful returns. The consequences — poor service, high costs, low productivity, unnecessary risks, and unexploited opportunities for improvement — cannot continue" (AIMD-94-115: 7).

Poorly performing computer systems plague state and local governments as well. Many state agencies are hampered by information systems that are incompatible, overly complex, and substandard. For example, a 1996 study found that every human service agency in New York has its own eligibility assessment system, its own way of monitoring services, its own billing system, its own audit system, and its own client tracking system (Gurwitt, 1996). Similarly, in North Carolina incompatible computer systems across agencies with similar functions, such as the State Bureau of Investigation, the Department of Criminal Investigation, and the Administrative Office of the Courts, make sharing information exceedingly cumbersome.

The dollars squandered on such problems are significant. Disturbed by the news that states failed to collect more than 80% of delinquent child support payments in 1980, the federal government provided funds to state agencies to develop computer systems to track noncomplying parents. Nearly two decades and $2 billion later, 35 states and 60% of the nation's child support cases are still not computerized. States fail to collect more than 80% of overdue child support, with past due accounts now topping $32 billion (Mazzarella, 1997). As a result of these setbacks, the California State Legislature has scrapped development of a statewide child support collection system, at a sunk cost of $260 million, and is starting over with the development of a new system (Kavanaugh, 1997a).

Local governments suffer from many of the same problems with computer systems. For example, frustrated by continued IT failures despite a $268 million cash infusion, Los Angeles Mayor Richard Riordan proposed creating an office of technology implementation within the Los Angeles Police Department. Riordan recommended the appointment of a chief information officer to overcome the lack of coordination and leadership that has resulted in system failure, project setbacks, and cost overruns (Kavanaugh, 1997b). The appointment of a CIO has now become a common practice in federal, state, and local government agencies, as well as in private and nonprofit organizations.

Other municipalities are also confronted with poor system performance that spills over into daily work operations. In 1984, Attewell and Rule (1984: 1184) were puzzled that "people remain so willing to speak and write as though the overall effects of computing technologies were a foregone conclusion". Two decades later, others in the field continue to document the gap between investments in and outcomes from computing. Keen (1986: 83) insists, "claims about the almost deterministic relationship between investing in office technology, personal computers, and information systems and getting improved productivity have produced too few proven results. It is as if there is some missing ingredient". Scholars such as Davenport (1993) and Drucker (1995) have identified the gap: they argue fervently for the need to build capacities in attendant organizational and management practices to span the chasm between information system investment and performance.

So great have the problems of IT failures become in the public sector that the U.S. Congress has seen fit to take action. Congress has passed a series of legislative acts to address the organizational and managerial challenges of information system adoption and implementation. Five pieces of legislation have been directed at ameliorating the risks associated with IT adoption: The Clinger–Cohen Act of 1996, the Paperwork Reduction Act of 1995, the Federal Acquisition Streamlining Act of 1994, the Government Performance and Results Act of 1993, and the Chief Financial Officers Act of 1990 [Brown and Brudney (1998) discuss the legislation in depth]. Here we focus on the most recent legislation, the CCA, which aims to lower the rising rate of IT failures experienced by federal agencies. In an earlier report, then Senator William Cohen (1994) worried that "poor information management, is, in fact, one of the biggest threats to the government treasury because it leaves government programs susceptible to waste, fraud, and abuse."

With the goal to prevent computer system failures, the CCA seeks to reform IT management practice. The law requires the Office of Management and Budget to report on the net program performance benefits achieved as the result of major capital IT investments and to examine the relationship between these benefits and the achievement of agency goals. The act addresses the policy, management, and integration aspects of aligning IT with the operation and performance of public agencies. In sum, the CCA proposes that the remedy for IT failures lies in legislative and policy requirements that will dramatically affect the leadership, management, and oversight of new technology in the federal government.

The chapter now turns to the efforts made in master's degree programs in public affairs and administration to meet the demands for managing IT in the public sector. While the pace of technology, management, and policy initiatives in IT has escalated, to what degree have graduate programs in public administration made necessary accommodations? The research evaluates the extent to which departments and schools have implemented the 1986 NASPAA recommendations on computing and show evidence of preparing MPA graduates in computer system use and management. To do so, the study monitors the degree to which instruction on system application use periodically over the past decade. In addition, it assesses whether schools and departments of public administration provide instruction on the concepts identified in the CCA as critical to successful IT adoption and operation.

III. METHODOLOGY AND DATA COLLECTION

To ascertain the degree to which graduate programs in public administration provide instruction in software application use and IT management, the research relied on a nationwide survey of all MPA and MAPA granting schools and departments conducted in 2003. The sample was drawn from NASPAA's Directory of Programs; questionnaires were mailed to all 218 principal representatives of MPA institutions affiliated with the NASPAA. Repeated mailings yielded a response rate of 50%, or 106 completed surveys.

The survey probed two areas: use of computer technology and instruction on the management of IT adoption and implementation. The later items explored the concepts set forth by the CCA. The questions focused on project management issues, including planning and coordinating IT adoption and implementation, information system life cycle, evaluating IT outcomes, developing IT policies, integrating TI across organizational boundaries, and coping with the legal ramifications of IT.

A. Findings on Instruction System Application Use

Table 2.1 contains data from our 1995 survey (Brown et al., 2000) and indicates that the methodological training of entering MPA students did not change significantly between 1989 and 1995. There were slight decreases in the percentages of entering students who had taken research methods and advanced mathematics courses. Those slight declines may be attributable to the increased numbers of students entering MPA programs with undergraduate degrees in disciplines outside of the social sciences, but the difference was too small to infer much change. What does stand out in the 1995 data is the 44.1% of students who had taken microcomputer courses. According to respondents, nearly two thirds (65.1%) of entering students were familiar with microcomputer usage. Common wisdom would suggest that more and more entering MPA students have some formal exposure to microcomputer usage and some may well have rather sophisticated skills in this domain. Since the 1995 survey, microcomputers and other IT technologies have become more common in homes and schools and there is every reason to expect that students entering MPA programs have even more sophisticated skills.

Table 2.2 provides further details on the number and kinds of microcomputer courses offered by the NASPAA-accredited schools. For comparative purposes we report in Table 2.2 and the tables following the analogous data from a 1995 survey of NASPAA institutions conducted previously by the authors ($n = 106$ completed surveys).

The findings in Table 2.2 show that virtually all of the NASPAA-accredited schools and departments — 96% — integrate microcomputer skills into coursework. Thus, the MPA programs seem to have heeded the recommendation of the NASPAA Ad Hoc Committee on Computing in Public Administration Education for the integration of microcomputing

Table 2.1 Methodological Training of Entering MPA Students (Mean Responses, in Percent)

Prior Coursework	1978	1984	1989	1995
Research methods	22	23	34	31
Data processing	10	9	20	21
Basic statistics	36	45	51	50
Advanced mathematics	*	*	11	7
Computer programming	6	5	14	11
Philosophy of science	*	2	8	11
MISs	*	*	9	9
Operations research	*	*	6	5
Microcomputer usage	*	*	36	44

*Denotes items not mentioned in that survey

Table 2.2   Microcomputing in MPA Curricula, 1995 and 2003 (in Percent)

	1995	2003
Number of reporting schools and departments	(n = 106)	(n = 90)
Integrate microcomputer skills into coursework	70	96
Have required course on microcomputers in MPA curriculum	56	32
Microcomputing competency required for graduation	19	38
Offer a series of courses on microcomputer applications	31	44
How many courses are offered in the series	(n = 28)	(n = 40)
One course	18	13
Two courses	36	22
Three courses	36	31
Four courses	4	11
Five courses	4	7
Six courses	4	7
Seven courses	0	7
Students that complete the series (mean response)	55	49
Number of required computer courses		
One course	66	58
Two courses	27	24
Three courses	5	15
Four courses	2	2
How do students gain access to microcomputers?		
University computing lab	35	91
School or department lab	36	71
Individually owned	38	92
Computers in student workspace	3	65
Other department computer lab	1	25

into substantive coursework. Perhaps for this reason, the percentage of MPA programs requiring a *separate* course on microcomputers has actually dropped from over half in 1995 (56%) to just a third in 2003 (32%). Or, it may also be the case that entering MPAs bring with them greater computer competency, thus mitigating the need for a required course. Nevertheless, the percentage of schools and departments requiring microcomputer competency for graduation doubled from 19% in 1995 to 38% in 2003. Forty of these programs or 44% offer a series of courses on microcomputer applications. Consistent with other MPA "concentrations," the number of courses in the microcomputer applications series is most often three (31% of MPA programs that have a series), yet the percentage of schools in the fortunate position of being able to offer four or more courses in this area has grown dramatically from just 12% in 1995 to 32% in 2003. The mean response from all 40 programs that offer a series of courses on microcomputer applications shows that about half of the students in the program (49%) complete the series.

In concert with the findings that show greater integration of microcomputer skills into public administration coursework and generally more courses available in the MPA curriculum in microcomputer applications, the findings from the 2003 survey demonstrate much greater student access to microcomputer facilities. Microcomputer access seems to have grown substantially in the NASPAA-accredited institutions since the 1995 survey. Results of the 2003 survey show that the percentage of programs reporting that students gain access to microcomputers through university computer labs (91%), labs in the school or department (71%), computers in student workspace (65%), and through labs in other departments (25%) have all at least doubled since 1995. In addition, access through student ownership of microcomputers has grown tremendously over the past decade or so, reported by more than 90% of the departments and schools in the 2003 survey (92%) compared to just 38% in the 1995 survey. The lower cost of this technology, combined with the greater need to integrate it into instruction, is perhaps responsible for the large increase.

Table 2.3 shows the integration of microcomputing applications into MPA courses in the 1995 and 2003 surveys. The table presents the applications in descending order according to the number of programs in which they are taught in the 2003 survey. In both surveys, the top two applications by frequency of use are statistics and spreadsheets, taught by 90% or more of the reporting schools and departments in 2003. The integration of microcomputer packages in required statistics analysis courses remains the most common usage in MPA programs (reported by 97%).

Budgeting is the next most common area for microcomputing applications, although the percentage of MPA programs claiming to use microcomputers in this domain is much less (58%). The responses suggest relatively frequent integration of microcomputing applications in pubic personnel administration courses (for example, data management, database management, and record search) and in budget and finance courses (for example, spreadsheets and financial management). With the exception of microcomputing applications in cost–benefit analysis (which might also be found in courses in

Table 2.3   Applications Taught in Required Courses, 1995 and 2003 (in Percent)

	1995	*2003*
Statistics	88	97
Spreadsheets	85	90
Budgeting	64	58
Word processing	36	57
Data management	63	52
Database management	63	43
Graphics	55	40
Financial management	57	40
Cost–benefit analysis	64	35
MIS	27	33
Electronic communications	29	32
Record searching /data entry	47	28
Data processing	49	27
GIS	14	27
Time series	47	25
Economic forecasting	34	20
Decision support systems	18	20
PERT/CPM	30	12
I/O modeling	11	12
Econometric modeling	23	10

research methods or program evaluation), economics courses seem to have fewer such applications (for example, microcomputing applications in economic forecasting and econometric modeling are apparently used infrequently). These results are generally consistent with the findings of a 1989 study of NASPAA member programs. They continue a trend noted in the 1995 survey in Table 2.3 for significantly greater use of microcomputers in personnel and related courses.

Another noteworthy trend in these findings is that relatively few MPA programs integrate microcomputer applications such as PERT/CPM and I/O modeling into management science courses. Relatively few schools and departments offer these courses, and fewer still require them for students (see Waugh et al., 1994). Management science techniques are taught in relatively few programs (and the number is declining slowly), and the same holds true for microcomputer-based management science techniques. By contrast, relatively high percentages of the MPA programs teach word processing, graphics, and electronic communications.

One reversal in trend noted between the 2003 and 1995 surveys is the apparent growth in the number of programs that teach geographic information system (GIS) applications (27% of reporting programs in 2003 compared to 14% in 1995). Still, GIS remains much more popular in urban and regional planning programs, and can be a high-maintenance operation (Waugh, 1995).

Table 2.4 presents the results over time pertaining to faculty and staff support for microcomputer usage in MPA programs obtained from surveys conducted in 1989, 1995, and 2003. As expected, the percentage of faculty members with a microcomputer in their office has increased to include all reporting institutions (99%). The increase demonstrates the essential role that microcomputers play in academic programs. To the degree that the increased access to microcomputers has an impact on the number and variety of computer applications taught in MPA and MAPA programs, the increase is even more important.

The percentage of MPA programs with a staff person responsible for microcomputers continues to hover around 50 to 60%. Given the labor-intensive nature of computer setup, support, maintenance, connectivity, and so forth, it is surprising, and even troubling, that a large percentage of MPA programs apparently lack a staff member dedicated

Table 2.4 MPA Faculty and Staff Support for Microcomputing, 1989, 1995, and 2003 (in Percent)

	1989	1995	2003
Faculty (mean) with microcomputer in office	70	93	99
Programs that have staff responsible for microcomputers	60	52	56
Difficulty of recruitment of microcomputer staff			
Not difficult		66	57
Somewhat difficult		23	35
Very difficult		11	8
Programs having faculty with specialized microcomputer skills		75	75
Difficulty of recruitment of faculty with specialized microcomputer skills			
Not difficult		80	47
Somewhat difficult		19	41
Very difficult		1	12

to microcomputing. A remedy for this problem may not be close at hand either: even if the monetary resources become available, a larger percentage of the MPA programs reported difficultly recruiting a staff person in microcomputing in 2003 than in 1995, 43 to 34%. Perhaps in some way compensating for this gap, in the 2003 survey as in the 1995 survey, three fourths of the reporting MPA programs claimed that they have faculty with specialized microcomputer skills (75%). However, whereas 80% of programs said that it was *not* difficult to recruit such a faculty member in 1995, just below half gave this response in 2003; the remainder said that it was somewhat (41%) or very difficult (12%).

Table 2.5 turns to the issue of the appropriateness of the computer skills taught in MPA and MAPA programs. Over 80% of the programs (84%) report that they ask practitioners what kinds of skills are needed in their fields, and about two thirds ask about the appropriate hardware and software. Ninety percent also indicated that the students use the same or similar hardware as practitioners, and 80% said that students use the same or similar software. Virtually all programs (98%) report that students use microcomputing skills in papers, research, and other assignments. Most of these percentages emanating from the 2003 survey reveal marked increases over the 1995 survey. Overall, then, the MPA and MAPA programs represented in the surveys seem to be responsive to the use of microcomputers in the public administration workplace.

Much lower percentages of the programs reported in both 1995 and 2003 that their microcomputer facilities made it easier to recruit and retain students (39% and 46%, respectively) or faculty members (51% and 53%, respectively). The reported effects of computer skills on job placement of students is another matter, however: nine in ten

Table 2.5 MPA Students and Microcomputing, 1995 and 2003 (in Percent)

	1995	2003
Do you or other faculty members meet or talk with public administrators to determine the kinds of computing skills they need on the job? (Yes)	79	84
Do you or other faculty members meet or talk with public administrators to see what types of hardware and software they use on the job? (Yes)	70	67
What percentage of students use the same or similar hardware that public administrators use?	78	90
What percentage of students use the same or similar software that public administrators use?	72	80
What percentage of students use microcomputing skills in papers, research, and other assignments?	81	98
Have microcomputer facilities made it easier to recruit and retain students? (Yes)	39	46
Have microcomputer facilities made it easier to recruit and retain faculty? (Yes)	51	53
Have microcomputing skills gained by students in your MPA program assisted in placing students in jobs? (Yes)	89	96
Does your program teach the full range of microcomputing skills students will need for jobs in the public and nonprofit sectors? (Yes)	38	44

programs (89%) judged that computer skills helped students find jobs in the 1995 survey, and that figure grew to 96% in the 2003 survey. The comparable figure in the 1989 survey was only 77% (Brudney et al., 1993). Evidently, computer skills are becoming more essential to the placement success of MPA and MAPA students.

Notwithstanding the attention to the kinds of microcomputer applications and the specific hardware and software that students may encounter in the workplace, fewer than half of the program representatives felt that their MPA or MAPA program teaches the full range of microcomputing skills students will need for jobs in the public and nonprofit sectors (44%). Although that percentage has increased somewhat from the 1995 survey (38%), it still falls short of what might reasonably be expected from a terminal master's degree program. This rather sober assessment may be indicative of a number of factors, which will be revisited in the concluding section.

B. Findings on Instruction in IT Management

The data analysis now turns to the instruction provided by MPA and MAPA schools and departments on the concepts derived form the Clinger–Cohen Act of 1996 (CCA). Table 2.6 displays the percentage of programs that claim to provide coverage of the six main CCA concepts according to surveys conducted by the authors in 1995 and 2003.

The data in Table 2.6 suggest greater penetration of CCA concepts into MPA and MAPA curricula. The percentage of programs reporting coverage of each concept shows an increase between the 1995 and 2003 surveys. For the most part, the increases appear to be substantial (10 percentage points or more), although one is very modest (just 4 percentage points for coverage of information system life cycle concepts). In the 1995 survey about one third of the programs (32% on average) reported covering these concepts, whereas in the 2003 survey about half reported doing so (49% on average). According to the results of the later survey, over half of the responding MPA and MAPA programs provide coverage of planning and coordinating information system concepts (57%), evaluating information system outcomes (57%), and developing information system policies (55%). Program coverage of two more concepts, legal implications of information system technologies (45%) and integrating information systems across organizational boundaries (44%), approaches half of the programs; the latter is instrumental to "e-government" initiatives. Comparatively fewer programs, but still more than for any of the other CCA concepts in the 2000 survey, report coverage of information system life cycle concepts in the 2003 survey (36% of responding programs).

Table 2.6 Programs that Cover CCA Concepts, 1995 and 2003 (in Percent)

	1995	2003
Planning and coordinating information system concepts	32	57
Information system life cycle concepts	32	36
Evaluating information system outcomes	33	57
Developing information system policies	30	55
Integrating information systems across organizational boundaries	34	44
Legal implications of information system technologies	30	45

In sum, the data in Table 2.6 suggest that schools and departments of public administration and affairs have made some headway in integrating the Clinger–Cohen concepts into the curriculum. These practices are mandated by the CCA and were foreshadowed by the NASPAA (1986) recommendations issued nearly two decades ago. Roughly half of the MPA and MAPA programs, on average, report coverage.

Table 2.7 displays the percentage of students exposed to the CCA concepts by responding public administration schools and departments in the 1995 and 2003 surveys. For all the six concepts, the percentage seems to have increased, with substantially fewer schools reporting exposure to no, or zero, students in each instance in the later survey compared to the earlier one.

Nevertheless, the percentage range that tends to show the largest, most consistent increase in student exposure across the two surveys is also the one that indicates that the fewest students are involved, 1 to 25%. The 51 to 75% range also demonstrates consistent increases, but the number of schools falling into this percentage range is less. Table 2.7 also reveals that between 1995 and 2003, the percentage of schools in which at least 50% of MPA and MAPA students are exposed to CCA concepts has increased. Overall, though, in less than half of the schools and departments did reported student exposure reach this level. If these findings provide any guide, a growing, but still relatively modest percentage of the total MPA and MAPA student population may be exposed to appropriate instruction in areas affecting the ability of public agencies to realize advantages from advances in IT.

As reflected by the passage of the CCA and other legislation (see above), recognition of IT concepts in government seems well ahead of implementation in the curriculum of MPA granting institutions. The signs are optimistic, however, that instruction in these computing concepts will increase in the 5-year time frame. Although only a small proportion of the sample provided core course instruction on the CCA concepts, more than 70% believed that students should be taught these concepts (73%) — up from 64% of the MPA and MAPA programs in the 2000 survey. In addition, among the schools that are not currently providing instruction in these areas, 58% indicated that they hoped to provide instruction within the next 5 years — again up from the 53% that gave this response in 1995. Schools and departments of public administration and affairs play a critical role in instilling the knowledge needed by managers to reap the benefits of IT in government. While these institutions appear to have responded over the past decade to the curriculum recommendations in computing forwarded by NASPAA in 1986, considerable work lies ahead to integrate the more ambitious concepts derived from the CCA.

Table 2.7 MPA Students Exposed to CCA Concepts, 1995 and 2003 (in Percent)

Percentage of Students	Planning and Coordinating		Life Cycle Concepts		Evaluating Outcomes		IT Policies		Integrating IT		Legal Implications	
	1995	2003	1995	2003	1995	2003	1995	2003	1995	2003	1995	2003
0	41	20	44	28	38	20	38	16	35	25	40	24
1–25	26	42	30	41	23	34	28	38	26	38	29	43
26–50	11	13	12	12	14	11	14	10	12	10	9	4
51–75	1	18	0	9	3	10	0	11	0	8	0	8
76–100	20	8	14	12	23	26	21	26	26	20	23	21

IV. CONCLUSION

There are a number of important questions that were not addressed in the surveys discussed above that should be considered in future research. Not the least of these are questions concerning the use of the Internet. It is difficult to anticipate changes in technology that may be important to MPA programs. Indeed, NASPAA's Ad Hoc Committee on Computing (1986) recommended a goal of computer literacy because of the need for students to be prepared for technological change. The use of Internet and other e-mail communications processes for advisement of students, disseminating program information, accessing databases, contacting experts outside of the university, and collaborating with other students or faculty on projects certainly requires some assessment.

While the surveys did seek to assess the depth of instruction provided by MPA and MAPA programs in computer utilization with respect to the number of courses and specific applications covered, breadth and depth of instruction are difficult concepts to measure. A better measure may be the level of knowledge about the applications that students acquire. Some attention should also be paid to the way that the courses are taught. Klay's (1994) analysis of how public employees learn to use computers strongly suggests that the social context of the learning, for example, interaction with others using or learning the same technologies, is more important than formal training programs, and that problem-solving tasks may be better learning experiences than more abstract step-by-step progress through users' manuals or textbooks.

The implications of technological change for MPA and MAPA programs should also be examined. The surveys reported here have suggested that MPA faculty tend to teach the techniques that they use themselves. The fact that more than 90% of public administration faculty have microcomputers in their office bodes well for the integration of microcomputers into MPA and MAPA classes. In addition, providing access to management information systems (MISs) for student records, geographic information systems or econometric modeling software for faculty research, or spreadsheets for internal budget analysis may facilitate integration of these techniques into graduate courses in the MPA and MAPA curricula.

The changing skill levels of entering students also have important implications for MPA and MAPA programs. We can expect that students will increasingly have their own microcomputers with modem access to university and departmental facilities. Though this increases accessibility to computer resources, it also limits the social interaction that Klay's study suggests is conducive to learning, although self-teaching was also considered an effective approach. Student versions of software, too, permit students to take their work home and work on it alone. Some attention should be paid to the possibilities of interactive learning processes, such as team projects using electronic communications.

The smaller problems may be how to deal with faculty who prefer to work at home and use e-mail to communicate with colleagues and students. Such faculty may be more accessible than they might otherwise be if there were to spend more time on campus. Yet, the collegiality and support that colleagues and students desire is often lost. There are also practical issues such as whether hard copies are necessary when students e-mail examinations and research reports to instructors. Some departments already have problems paying for paper when students fax their work to instructors.

The issue of why public administration faculty, or perhaps their NASPAA principal representatives, feel that their students are not getting all the IT training that they may need is intriguing. One answer may be that the perception is that students are not being taught the skills required or at least used in the most technologically advanced agencies. That is, faculty may be focusing on the agencies that are the most innovative. To keep up with the skill demands in such agencies may be unreasonable. Another answer may be that MPA and MAPA programs are lagging behind public agencies in the adoption of new IT or new applications of older technologies. A third answer may be that, just as high-end users tend to dominate university decision-making on technology adoption, high-end users are evaluating the skills currently taught, and they are dissatisfied with how fast new technologies and applications are being implemented. In short, we may be too critical of MPA and MAPA programs for not reaching the cutting edge of technology soon enough.

The pervasive nature of IT and its ability to support virtually every organizational function calls for a core curriculum that should focus on the critical emerging issues. These include: (1) increasing the productivity, efficiency, and service delivery efforts of government employees through the use of IT, (2) planning, adopting, and implementing IT effectively within a government framework, (3) developing government policies to promote benefit attainment and minimize negative impacts resulting from the widespread use of IT, and (4) facilitating the strategic management of information resources in government and nonprofit settings.

With the passage of IT-related legislation such as the CCA, the need for students of public administration to be well versed in issues surrounding the implementation and management of computer resources/technology has never been greater. The failures of information systems encountered too frequently in the public sector are not grounded in limitations of technology but in attendant issues of management — domains where schools and departments of public administration could and should make a difference. These educational programs must broaden their course offerings to educate public managers regarding the bridge between technical capabilities and operational, mission-driven needs. In no small part, failures in IT have occurred because public managers and staff have not been actively involved in shaping the direction of IT efforts according to organizational and operational imperatives. With respect to computing, the challenge to schools and departments of public administration is to support instruction in critical areas of IT management.

REFERENCES

Anthes, G., IRS project failures cost taxpayers $50 billion annually, *Computerworld*, 30, 1–30, 1996.

Aristigueta, M.P. and Raffel, J.A., Teaching techniques of analysis in the MPA curriculum: research methods, management science, and "the third path," *J. Pub. Aff. Educ.* 3, 161–169, 2001.

Attewell, P. and Rule, J., Computing and organizations: what we know and what we don't know, *Comm. ACM*, 27, 1184–1192, 1984.

Bergin, T.J., 1986 survey on computers in public affairs and administration. Proceedings of the Tenth Annual Conference on Teaching Public Administration, George Washington University, Washington, D.C., 1988, pp. 27–42.

Bretschneider, S., Management information systems in public and private organizations: an empirical test, *Pub. Adm. Rev.*, 50, 536–545, 1990.

Brown, M.M. and Brudney, J.L., Public sector information technology initiatives: implications for programs of public administration, *Adm. Soc.*, 30, 421–442, 1998.

Brown, M.M., Brudney, J.L., Hy, R.J., and Waugh, W.L., Graduate education in information technology in the public sector: the need and the response, in *Handbook of Public Information Systems*, Garson, D., Ed., Marcel Dekker, New York, 2000, pp. 9–25.

Brudney, J.L., Hy, R.J., and Waugh, W.L., Building microcomputer skills in public administration graduate education: an assessment of MPA programs, *Adm. Soc.*, 25, 183–203, 1993.

Cats-Baril, W.L. and Thompson, R.L., Managing information technology projects in the public sector, *Pub. Adm. Rev.*, 55, 559–566, 1995.

Cohen, W., *Computer Chaos: Billions Wasted buying Federal Computer Systems*, Report to the senate Governmental Affairs oversight of government management subcommittee, 1994.

Davenport, T., *Process Innovation: Reengineering Work through Information Technology*, Harvard Business School Press, Boston, 1993.

Drucker, P., *Managing in a Time of Great Change*, Truman Talley Books/Dutton, New York, 1995.

Garson, G.D., Human factors in information systems, in *Handbook of Organizational Behavior*, Golembiewski, R.T., Ed., Marcel Dekker, New York, 1993.

GAO (General Accounting Office), *Executive Guide: Improving Mission Performance through Strategic Information Management Technology*, Government Printing Office, Washington, D.C., 1994b (GAO/AIMD-94-115).

GAO (General Accounting Office), *Information Technology Investment: Agencies Can Improve Performance and Produce Results*, Government Printing Office, Washington, D.C., 1996a (GAO/OIMC-96-46).

GAO (General Accounting Office), *Information Technology Investment: Agencies Can Improve Performance, Reduce Costs, and Minimize Risks*, Government Printing Office, Washington, D.C., 1996b (GAO/OIMC-96-64).

GAO (General Accounting Office), *High Risk Areas: Actions Needed to Solve Pressing Management Problems*, Government Printing Office, Washington, D.C., 1997 (GAO/AIMD/GGD-97-60).

Gurwitt, R., The new data czars, *Governing*, December, 52–56, 1996.

Harris, B., Beyond budget deficits, *Gov. Technol.*, May, pp. 6, 47, 2003.

Kavanaugh, J., Child support system in trouble. *Gov. Technol.*, 10, 8, 1997a.

Kavanaugh, J., LAPD technology office proposed, *Gov. Technol.*, 10, 10, 1997b.

Keen, P., *Competing in Time*, Ballinger, Cambridge, MA, 1986.

Kiel, L.D., Information systems education in masters programs in public affair and administration, *Pub. Adm. Rev.*, 46 (Special Issue), 590–594, 1986.

Klay, W.E., How Public Employees Learn to Use Computers, paper presented at the Southeastern Conference on Public Administration, Lexington, KY, Oct. 8, 1994.

Kraemer, K.L. and King, J.L., Computing and public organizations, *Pub. Adm. Rev.*, 46 (Special Issue), 488–496, 1986.

Kraemer, K.L. and Northrop, A., Curriculum recommendations for public management education in computing: an update, *Pub. Adm. Rev.*, 49, 447–453, 1989.

Kraemer, K., Thomas, B., Stuart, B., George, D., Thomas, F., Wilpen G., Alana, N., and Naomi, B.W., Curriculum recommendations for public management education in computing, *Pub. Admin. Rev.*, 46, 595–602, 1986.

Mazzarella, D., $2 billion search fails to catch deadbeat parents, *USA Today*, July 28, 1997, p. 12A.

National Association of Schools of Public Affairs and Administration. Ad Hoc Committee on Computers in Public Management Education, Curriculum recommendations for public management education in computing, *Pub. Adm. Rev.*, 46 (Special Issue), 595–602, 1986.

National Association of Schools of Public Affairs and Administration. *Guidelines and Standards for Professional Masters Degree Programs and Public Affairs/Administration*, NASPAA, Washington, D.C., 1988.

Norris, D.F. and Thompson, L., Computing and public administration: practice and education, *Soc. Sci. Comput. Rev.*, 6, 548–557, 1988.

Standish Group, Chaos, 1994
http://www.standishgroup.com/chaos.html

Thayer, R.H., Pyster, A., and Wood, R.C., Validating solutions to major problems in software engineering project management, *Computer*, 15, 65–77, 1982.

Turner, J.A., Observations on the use of behavioral models in information systems research and practice, *Inf. Manage.*, 5, 207–213, 1982.

Waugh, W.L., Utilizing geographic information systems: the case of disaster management, *Soc. Sci. Comput. Rev.*, 13, 422–431, 1995.

Waugh, W.L., Hy, R.J., and Brudney, J.L., Quantitative analysis and skill building in public administration graduate education, *Pub. Adm. Q.*, 18(2), 204–222, 1994.

Waugh, W.L., Hy, R.J., and Nelson, P.B., Microcomputers in public administration graduate education, *Manage. Sci. Policy Anal. J.*, 2, 9–19, 1985.

3

PUBLIC INFORMATION TECHNOLOGY AND E-GOVERNMENT: A HISTORICAL TIMELINE

G. David Garson
North Carolina State University

ABSTRACT

The history of public information technology (IT) is traced from the 1895 Depository Library Program through to the CAN-SPAM Act of December 2003, in the form of a timeline chronological listing of relevant events drawn from a wide variety of governmental and other sources.

1895   The Depository Library Program (44 USC 1902) is taken over by the Government Printing Office. Originating in the 1840s, the Depository Library program promotes the practice of agencies making their publications available via the U.S. Superintendant of Documents. A century later, in the 1990s, the Office of the Superintendant of Documents moved increasingly toward electronic publication formats.

1943   Colossus, used for code-breaking, is an early computer funded and run by the British government.

1944   Vannevar Bush, Director of the Office of Scientific Research and Development, authored a report at the request of President Roosevelt entitled *Science, The Endless Frontier: A Report to the President*. It called for promotion of interchange of scientific knowledge, long before NSFNET. In July 1945, Bush published the article, "As We May Think" in the *Atlantic Monthly*, describing a desktop "memex," with functions similar to the modern Internet.

1942–1946 The ENIAC computer is developed by J. Presper Eckert and John W. Mauchly at the University of Pennsylvania for the U.S. Army, which needed it for ballistic calculations.

1946 The Administrative Procedures Act required hearings and public participation in regulatory rulemaking. In the late 1990s this became a legal basis for electronic public participation in e-rulemaking.

1950 Federal Records Act of 1950 (amended 1964) mandated that each agency head preserve "adequate and proper documentation of the organization, functions, policies, decisions, procedures, and essential transactions of the agency." Combined with the 1966 Freedom of Information Act and the 1996 Electronic Freedom of Information Act, the Federal Records Act is the legal basis for the mandate that federal agencies make information available online.

1951 Remington Rand sells the first UNIVAC computer to the Census Bureau and subsequently to five other clients. The first private-sector purchase was by General Electric 3 years later in 1954. UNIVACs weighed 8 tons and had a speed of 1000 instructions per second. The UNIVAC was phased out 6 years later.

1952 IBM sells the 701 computer for the U.S. government for defense purposes connected to the Korean War. The 701 marks the advent of widespread mainframe computing in the federal government.

1957 In response to the Russian launching of Sputnik-1, the Earth's first artificial satellite, the U.S. government established the Advanced Research Projects Agency (ARPA) within the Department of Defense to promote defense technology. Twelve years later, ARPANET goes online, the predecessor of the Internet.

1958 Semi-Automatic Ground Environment (SAGE) was installed at the McGuire Air Force Base in New Jersey. Used for air defense, the SAGE and the related Whirlwind project involved major advances in data communications technology.

1960 President Eisenhower placed NASA in charge of communications satellite development. Echo, NASA's first satellite, was launched on August 12 and functioned to reflect radio waves back to the Earth.

1962 The Communications Act of 1962 combined the efforts of ATT, NASA, and the Department of Defense to create Comsat on February 1, 1963. In 1964, led by Comsat, a consortium of 19 nations formed IntelSat with the purpose of providing global satellite coverage and interconnectivity. IntelSat in 1965 launched the Early Bird satellite, the world's first commercial communications satellite, serving the Atlantic Ocean region. Global satellite coverage is achieved by IntelSat 7 years later, in 1969.

1965 In a precursor to the Internet, ARPA sponsors a study about a "cooperative network of time-sharing computers" at MIT's Lincoln Lab and the System Development Corporation (Santa Monica, California), directly linked via a dedicated 1200-bps phone line. A DEC computer at ARPA was added later to form "The Experimental Network."

1966 The Freedom of Information Act of 1966 (FOIA; Public Law 89-554) established the right of public access to government information. Agencies were required to make information available through automatic channels or upon specific individual requests. The law specified certain exemptions, including classified defense and foreign policy matters, internal agency personnel rules and practices, information protected by other laws (e.g., many contractor bids), commercial trade secrets and financial information, documents, normally privileged in the civil discovery context, personal information affecting an individual's privacy, investigatory records compiled for law enforcement purposes, information that might reasonably be construed to interfere with law enforcement or deprive a person of a fair trial, information revealing the identity of a confidential source, information needed to protect the safety of individuals, records of financial institutions, and geographical information on oil wells.

1969 ARPANET, the predecessor of the Internet, went online with four nodes and reached 15 nodes by 1971.

1972 e-Mail comes to ARPANET.

1972 The Technology Assessment Act of 1972 created the Office of Technology Assessment (OTA), later disbanded as other IT agencies emerged. The OTA along with the Congressional Research Service (reconstituted and expanded by the Legislative Reorganization Act of 1970) and the Congressional Budget Office (created by the Budget Impoundment Act of 1974) became major users of FOIA to access executive agency data.

1972 The Federal Advisory Committee Act (FACA) was an elaboration of the 1966 FOIA legislation. It required timely notice in the *Federal Register* of advisory committee meetings. FACA also required agencies to allow interested parties to appear or file written statements, mandated that advisory committees keep detailed minutes (to include a record of the persons attending, documents received, documents issued, and documents approved by committees). These materials and all other advisory committee minutes, transcripts, reports, and studies were required to be available for public inspection.

1973 The first international connections were added to ARPANET, from University College of London (England) via NORSAR (Norway).

1973 Bob Kahn started the "internetting" research program at ARPAKahn and Vint Cerf developed many of the fundamental concepts on which the Internet rests.

1974 IntelSat activated a "Hot Line" for direct telecommunication between the White House and the Kremlin.

1974 Telenet is started as the first public packet data service. As such, Telenet is the first commercial version of ARPANET.

1974 The Privacy Act of 1974 (Public Law 93-579; 5 USC 552a) protected the privacy of individuals identified in information systems maintained by federal agencies. The collection, maintenance, use, and dissemination of information were regulated. The Privacy Act forbade disclosure of any record containing personal information, unless released with the prior written consent of the individual. Agencies were also mandated to provide individuals with access to their records.

1974 The Office of Federal Procurement Policy Act created the Office of Federal Procurement Policy (OFPP). In 1979 OFPP set up the Federal Procurement Data Center as a computerized repository of detailed information on all purchases over $25,000, and summary details of smaller ones. OFPP came under the GSA in 1982.

1975 ARPANET initiated online discussion lists.

1976 The Government in the Sunshine Act was an elaboration of the 1966 FOIA. It established the principle that the public is entitled to the fullest practicable information regarding the decision-making processes of federal agencies.

1977 The University of Wisconsin established TheoryNet, which provided e-mail to over 100 researchers.

1978   The Presidential Records Act changed the legal ownership of the official records of the president from private to public, further expanding public access to federal information.

1979   USENET was established. It soon became the umbrella for hundreds of online discussion groups (lists).

1980   ARPANET suffered its first viruses, grinding the network to a complete halt on October 27 because of a status message virus that was introduced accidentally.

1980   The Paperwork Reduction Act of 1980 (PRA) mandated an Information Resources Management (IRM) approach to federal data. This represented the first unified policy framework for information resource management at the federal level. The director of the OMB was given responsibility for developing an IRM policy and for overseeing its implementation. A major revision of the PRA in 1995 mandated strategic planning for IRM.

1981   BITNET, the "Because It's Time NETwork," was initiated as a cooperative network at the City University of New York. BITNET provided e-mail, file transfer, and listserv functionality. ARPANET, BITNET, and NSFNET were the three immediate precursors of the Internet.

1984   The domain name system (DNS) was established, allowing users to employ mnemonic Internet addresses instead of number addresses.

1986   The National Science Foundation funded NSFNET, a long-haul backbone network with a speed of 56K bps.

1986   The Computer Fraud and Abuse Act imposed fines and imprisonment up to 20 years for various types of unauthorized computer access and fraud. A 1996 amendment extended coverage to all computers involved in interstate commerce and communications.

1986   The Rehabilitation Act Amendments of 1986 (sometimes called the Rehabilitation Act of 1986) added Section 508 to the Rehabilitation Act of 1973. Section 508 required federal agencies to establish guidelines for disability-accessible IT. Agency accessibility evaluations were mandated and the attorney general was charged with compliance evaluation. The deadline for agencies to have accessibility standards in place was extended to August 7, 2000.

1987   NSF signed a cooperative agreement to manage NSFNET in cooperation with IBM, MCI, and Merit Network, Inc. By the end of 1987 there were 10,000 Internet hosts.

1987   The Computer Security Act (CSA) mandated that the National Institute of Standards and Technology (NIST) develop security standards and guidelines for federal computer systems. The CSA also required that all federal agencies and their contractors establish computer security plans.

1988   The Computer Matching and Privacy Protection Act was an amendment to the Privacy Act of 1974, which extended Privacy Act protections to most forms of computer matching of individual records across agencies.

1989   The number of Internet hosts reached 100,000.

1990   ARPANET was phased out, eclipsed by NSFNET.

1990   The Chief Financial Officers Act (CFOA) focused on improving federal financial management and reporting practices but also called for: (1) complete and timely information prepared on a uniform basis and which is responsive to the financial information needs of agency management; (2) the development and reporting of cost information; (3) the integration of accounting and budgeting information; and (4) the systematic measurement of performance. These four objectives required development of a financial information system and networked access to it, as well as a computerized performance tracking system.

1991 The High-Performance Computing Act (HPCA) authorized the president to create a "National High-Performance Computing Program" for high-speed networking and established the National Research and Education Network (NREN). The OMB was given authority to review department budget requests for this program. The HPCA is sometimes called the "Gore Act" due to the activism and leadership of Vice President Al Gore.

1992 Tim Berners-Lee developed the World Wide Web and Mosaic software was released to surf the Web. The number of Internet hosts reached 1 million.

1992 The first White House home page was launched on the Web.

1992 In *Quill Corporation v. North Dakota*, the Supreme Court explicitly upheld the precedent of its *Bellas Hess (1967)* case. These principles prohibited Internet sales taxation, overruling a North Dakota Supreme Court finding that technology had made the 1967 ruling obsolete. The tax prohibition applied to vendors with no physical presence in the state.

1992 Up to 1992, access to the Internet backbone was limited by the NSF's "Acceptable Use Policy." This restriction of the National Science Foundation Act prohibited commercial traffic on the Internet. Up to 1992, all Internet traffic had to be educational, scientific, or research-oriented. With the support of Congressman Rick Boucher (D, VA), Chairman of the Science Subcommittee of the House Committee on Science, Space, and Technology, legislation was passed and in November 1992, President Bush signed new legislation that repealed the Acceptable Use Policy, replacing it with language which permitted commercial traffic on the Internet backbone.

1992 The Information and Technology Act promoted technology development in public education, health care, and industry and called on NSF to fund efforts to connect K-12 classrooms to NSFNET.

1993 The National Information Infrastructure Act mandated funding priority in federal research and development efforts be given to accelerated development of high-performance computing and high-speed networking services.

1993 Federal funding of the Internet ended as the Internet became a private-sector entity. Routing began through private providers in 1994. NSFNET reverted to being a limited research network.

1993 National Performance Review (NPR) was established on March 3. NPR represented the Clinton administration's emphasis on information technology as a tool to reform government, under the leadership of Vice President Al Gore. The NPR report, *Creating a Government that Works Better and Costs Less: Reengineering through Information Technology*, illustrated that the reinventing government movement, which originated with a focus on decentralization/devolution, had come to see e-government as major reform thrust. NPR was later renamed the National Partnership for Reinventing Government (NPRG).

1993 The Government Information Technology Services Board was created to help implement NPR in IT areas.

1993 The Government Performance and Results Act (GPRA) required agencies to prepare multiyear strategic plans that described agency mission goals and approaches for reaching them. The act required agencies to develop annual performance plans that OMB was to use to prepare a federal performance plan that is submitted to the

Congress along with the President's annual budget submission. The agency plans must establish measurable goals for program activities and describe the methods by which performance toward these goals are measured. The act also required agencies to prepare annual program performance reports to review progress toward annual performance goals, which, of course, included IT goals.

1993 Executive Order 12862: Setting Customer Service Standards. This executive order mandated that all agencies, including IT agencies, identify their customers, customer needs, and set standards and benchmarks for customer service. Customer orientation became a keystone of e-government policy later in the decade.

1993 The Government Information Locator Service (GILS) was announced on February 22. GILS was established as an Internet index to federal materials. It reflected a decision of the Clinton administration to support direct agency release of electronic information, reversing a Reagan-era policy which held release should be contracted through private third parties.

1993 The White House established public e-mail to the president and vice president.

1994 The Commerce Department's National Telecommunications and Information Administration (NTIA) report, "Falling Through the Net," brought widespread public attention to the issue of the "digital divide."

1994 The Federal Acquisition Streamlining Act (FASA) required agencies to define tolerance standards for and to monitor cost, time schedule, and performance goals for federal acquisition programs, including IT projects. If a program falls out of tolerance, FASA required the agency head to review, take necessary actions, and, if necessary, terminate the program.

1995 The 1995 amendment to the Paperwork Reduction Act of 1980 (PRA; this amendment is sometimes called the Paperwork Reduction Act of 1995) established strategic planning principles for information resources management, including setting IT standards, applied life cycle management principles, mandating cross-agency information technology initiatives, and setting technology investment guidelines. The PRA designated senior information resources manager positions in major federal agencies and created the Office of Information and Regulatory Affairs (OIRA) within OMB to provide central oversight of information management activities across the federal government. OIRA was mandated to "develop and maintain a governmentwide strategic plan for information resources management." The OIRA director became, in principle, the main IT advisor to the director of the OMB. The PRA also called on agencies to "ensure that the public has timely and equitable access to the agency's public information," including electronically. Agency use of GILS (the Government Information Locator Service, an Internet index to federal information) was mandated.

1996 The Telecommunications Act of 1996 provided for a Universal Service Fund fee (a telephone tax, also known as the "e-rate" fund or fee), part of which became used on Clinton administration initiative to provide modem-based Internet access to schools, libraries, Indian reservations, and other "digital divide" target groups.

1996 The World Trade Organization, meeting in Singapore, reduced tariffs on information technology trade items, thereby encouraging global information and communication technology (ICT) development.

1996 The Electronic Freedom of Information Act Amendment of 1996 (EFOIA) extended the right of citizens to access executive agency records to include access to electronic formats and online opportunities for access information. EFOIA officially defined a "record" in very broad terms. Release of information had to be in a format convenient to the user, not agency option, as previous case law had held. Agencies wee required to make "reasonable efforts" to search electronic databases for records. Electronic reading rooms were mandated to include "policy statements, administrative rulings and manuals, and other materials that affect members of the public."

1996   The Communications Decency Act (CDA) prohibited Internet distribution of "indecent" materials. A few months later a three-judge panel issued an injunction against its enforcement. The Supreme Court unanimously ruled most of the CDA unconstitutional in 1997.

1996   The Federal Acquisition Reform Act (FARA) made purchasing of IT more flexible than under the prior Brooks Act. FARA gave the GSA a powerful oversight role, but they function more like an "IT commodities broker" than as an "IT policeman."

1996   OMB Circular A-130 implemented the Paperwork Reduction Act of 1980 and 1995 amendments by establishing governmentwide uniform information resources management practices. It mandates life cycle information management planning and work process redesign. The Department of Commerce is also mandated to improve federal telecommunications systems. Circular A-130 is revised and re-issued periodically.

1996   The Federal Financial Management Improvement Act (FFMIA) required agency financial management systems to comply with federal financial management system requirements, applicable federal accounting standards, and the *U.S. Government Standard General Ledger* (SGL). To the extent that federal accounting standards specify IT aspects, the FFMIA requires uniformity of IT accounting across the federal government.

1996   The Clinger–Cohen Act of 1996 (originally named the Information Technology Management Reform Act of 1996, an amendment to the Paperwork Reduction Act of 1980) established a chief information officer (CIO) in every federal agency, making agencies responsible for developing an IT plan that relates IT planning to agency missions and goals. The Clinger–Cohen Act also mandated top management involvement in IT strategic planning, using IT portfolio management approaches. The oversight role of the director of the OMB was strengthened. The Clinger–Cohen Act

1. Encouraged federal agencies to evaluate and adopt best management and acquisition practices used by private- and public-sector organizations.
2. Required agencies to base decisions about IT investments on quantitative and qualitative factors related to costs, benefits, and risks, and to use performance data to demonstrate how well the IT expenditures support improvements to agency programs through measures like reduced costs, improved productivity, and higher client satisfaction.
3. Streamlined the IT acquisition process by ending the General Services Administration's central acquisition authority. It placed procurement responsibility directly with federal agencies and encouraged adoption of smaller, more modular IT projects.

Later, when e-government became a priority, the existence of the CIO strategic planning structure was an important element facilitating e-government implementation at the federal level.

1996 President Clinton issued Executive Order 13011, a companion to the Clinger–Cohen Act. EO 13011 sought to improve management through an alignment of agency technology goals with strategic organizational goals and through interagency coordination of technology applications. EO 13011 created the CIO Council, an advisory body from 28 federal agencies plus senior OMB/OIRA personnel. The CIO Council was intended to be the central interagency forum for improving agency IT practices. EO 13011 represented the presidential "seal of approval" for e-government. In practice, the CIO Council was eclipsed by initiatives from the OMB itself and did not become a major generator of Bush administration IT initiatives.

1996 The Personal Responsibility and Work Opportunity Reconciliation Act (PRWORA), also known as welfare reform, required interstate and intergovernmental coordination of information technology systems to ensure that no individual exceeded the allotted 5-year lifetime cap on assistance.

1997 The U.S. Department of Agriculture (USDA) became the first federal agency to engage in e-rulemaking, soliciting web-based comments on rules for organic foods. This initiative won the 1998 Government Technology Leadership Award.

1998 Virginia, then Colorado, became the first state to have a cabinet-level secretary of information technology.

1998 The Digital Millenium Copyright Act extended copyrights to digital media, but the "Fair Use Doctrine" was retained to promote the rights of universities, libraries, and other occasional users of intellectual property. The act also prohibited removal of "copyright management information" from electronic media, outlawing the circumvention of antipiracy access controls.

1998 The 1998 Amendments to the Rehabilitation Act of 1973, signed by President Clinton on August 7, required federal agencies to make their electronic information available to people with disabilities, including their Internet pages. This strengthened the Section 508 disability access standards mandated by the 1986 amendments to the Rehabilitation Act. Federal agencies were exempted from Section 508 implementation where the disability initiative in question would constitute an "undue burden."

1998 The presidential memorandum of May 14, 1998: Privacy and Personal Information in Federal Records. This memorandum directed federal agencies to review their compliance with the Privacy Act of 1974. Each agency was to designate a senior official for privacy policy. Each agency was required to conduct a Privacy Act compliance review.

1998 Presidential Decision Directive 63: Protecting America's Critical Infrastructures. Based on recommendations of the President's Commission on Critical Infrastructure Protection, this directive set the goal of establishing an integrated, secure IT infrastructure by 2003. A national center to warn of infrastructure attacks was established in the National Infrastructure Protection Center. Agencies were required to establish performance measures of website security.

1998 The Government Paperwork Elimination Act of 1998 (GPEA, signed into law on October 21) authorized the OMB to acquire alternative information technologies for use by executive agencies (Sec. 1702), provided support for electronic signatures (Secs. 1703–1707), and provided for the electronic filing of employment forms (Sec. 1705). Electronic filing of most forms had to be in place by October 21, 2003. The GPEA was the legal framework for accepting electronic records and electronic signatures as legally valid and enforceable and also represented congressional endorsement of the e-government strategy.

1998   The Federal Activities Inventory Reform (FAIR) Act required agencies to inventory and report to the OMB all their commercial activities. The FAIR Act then established a two-step administrative challenge and appeals process under which an interested party may challenge the omission or the inclusion of a particular activity on the inventory as a "commercial activity." While the FAIR Act did not require agencies to privatize, outsource, or compete their commercial activities, subsequent OMB guidelines required that nonexempt commercial activities undergo a cost evaluation for a "make-or-buy" decision. Each time that a federal agency head considers outsourcing to the private sector a competitive process is required. FAIR puts pressure on agencies to outsource IT operations. Though "core operations" were not to be outsourced, CIOs sometimes felt the core was encroached upon and that it was difficult to establish effective performance standards with vendors.

1998   IRS Restructuring and Reform Act of 1998 (RRA). Section 2001c promoted electronic filing of tax returns. Section 2003d required the IRS to establish that all forms, instructions, publications, and other guidance be available via the Internet. Section 2003e provided for tax return preparers to be authorized electronically to communicate with the IRS. Section 2005 provided taxpayer electronic access to their account by 2006.

1998   The National Archives and Records Administration (NARA) Bulletin 98-02: Disposition of Electronic Records. This reminded agencies of their obligations under federal law to provide documentation of agency activities, including website pages and records.

1998   The Postal Service launched e-commerce, selling stamps via the Web.

1998   The Internet Tax Freedom Act of 1998 (ITFA) imposed a 3-year moratorium on state and local taxation on Internet access.

1999   The presidential memo of December 17, Electronic Government, reflected Clinton's endorsement of the concept of a federal governmentwide portal (FirstGov.gov). Clinton announced 12 steps agencies can take, including getting forms online by December 2000, posting online privacy policies, posting e-mail contact information, identifying e-government "best practices," and more.

1999   The Trademark Cyberpiracy Prevention Act outlawed "cybersquatting," giving businesses protection against those who register well-known domain names as a means of extorting fees from the true owners of existing trademarks.

1999   FY 1999 National Defense Authorization Act required the Department of Defense to establish a single electronic mall system for procurement.

2000   The President's Management Council adopted digital government as one of its top three priorities.

2000   On June 24 President Clinton made the first presidential Internet address to the nation, calling for the establishment of the FirstGov.gov portal.

2000   FirstGov.gov was launched September 22 as a Clinton management initiative. It was the official U.S. government portal, designed to be a trusted one-stop gateway to federal services for citizens, businesses, and agencies. At launch, it was a gateway to 47 million federal government web pages. FirstGov.gov also linked state, local, DC, and tribal government pages in an attempt to provide integrated service information in particular areas, such as travel. It was managed by the Office of Citizen Services and Communications within the General Services Administration.

2000 President Clinton asked Congress for $50 million to provide computers and Internet access to the poor, and requested $2 billion in tax incentives for the same purpose. The Universal Service Fund Fee, a telephone tax created in 1996, paid for these incentives.

2000 In Election 2000, both candidates (Gore and Bush) advocated digital government expansion.

2000 The Electronic Signatures in Global and National Commerce Act (ESIGN) made digital signatures legal in all 50 states, essential for the expansion of e-commerce.

2000 The OMB revised Circular A-130 to include a mandate for IT portfolio management, a management which requires a strategic approach to IT investment and risk.

2000 The Government Information Security Reform Act (GISRA; located within the FY 2001 Defense Authorization Act) amended the Paperwork Reduction Act of 1995 by enacting a new subchapter on "Information Security." Sometimes called the "Security Act," this legislation required the establishment of agencywide information security programs, annual agency program reviews, annual independent evaluations of agency programs and practices, agency reporting to OMB, and OMB reporting to Congress. GISRA covered programs for both unclassified and national security systems but exempted agencies operating national security systems from OMB oversight. The Security Act is to be implemented consistent with the Computer Security Act of 1987.

2001 *The President's Management Agenda*, issued in August, commits the Bush administration to five major management objectives, one of which is electronic government.

2001 In June the OMB created the position of associate director for information technology and e-government. This gave the OMB a "point man" to give higher priority to IT initiatives, particularly the goal of creating a "citizen-centric government." In essence, this position was given a mandate to provide leadership to all federal IT implementation, including a special emphasis on e-government. The associate director also directed the activities of the CIO Council. Mark Forman was the first incumbent.

2001 Information Quality Act (IQA) is Section 515 of the Treasury and General Government Appropriations Act for FY 2001, passed as a "rider." Section 515 charged OMB with the task of developing governmentwide guidelines to ensure and maximize the quality of information disseminated by agencies. These guidelines were published in October 2002. Under the guidelines, agencies must have a data quality control policy; quality control procedures must be applied before information can be disseminated; and each agency must develop an administrative mechanism whereby affected parties can request that agencies correct poor quality information (that is, an appeals process was mandated).

2001 Executive Order 13231: Critical Infrastructure Protection in the Information Age. It was issued in October, following 9/11, creating the President's Critical Infrastructure Protection Board. The board is the central focus in the Executive Branch for Cyberspace Security. It comprises senior officials from more than 20 departments and agencies.

2001 The USA Patriot Act became law on October 26. It gave government investigators greater authority to track e-mail and to eavesdrop on telecommunications. In September 2002, the Court of Review interpreted the USA Patriot Act to mean that surveillance orders under the Foreign Intelligence Surveillance Act could apply to criminal as well as terrorist cases.

2001 President Bush signed the Internet Access Taxation Moratorium on November 28, extending the 1998 ITFA to November 1, 2003. At this point, online spending was expected to account for 15% of holiday 2001 spending. The moratorium on Internet taxation was seen by the Bush administration as an economic stimulus as well as a promotion of Internet industries, but state governments feared significant revenue losses.

2002 The first chief technology officer (CTO) for the federal government was appointed. This officer was to oversee the implementation of e-government initiatives. Casey Coleman, heading up the GSA's Office of Citizen Services, was appointed on July 25.

2002 The OMB issued the document *e-Government Strategy* on February 27. This document sets forth Bush administration's e-government principles: citizen-centric, results-oriented, market-based. It also called for increased cross-agency data sharing. Some 34 specific projects are identified for funding, including the 22 initially announced in the "Quicksilver Initiative" in October 2001:

I.   GOVERNMENT TO CITIZEN

1. USA Service (GSA)
2. EZ Tax Filing (Treasury)
3. Online Access for Loans (DoEd)
4. Recreation One Stop (Interior)
5. Eligibility Assistance Online (Labor)

II.   GOVERNMENT TO BUSINESS

1. Federal Asset Sales (GSA)
2. Online Rulemaking Management (DOT)
3. Simplified and Unified Tax and Wage Reporting (Treasury)
4. Consolidated Health Informatics (HHS)
5. Business Compliance One Stop (SBA)
6. International Trade Process Streamlining (Commerce)

III.   GOVERNMENT TO GOVERNMENT

1. E-vital (SSA)
2. E-grants (HHS)
3. Disaster Assistance and Crisis Response (FEMA)
4. Geospatial Information One Stop (Interior)
5. Wireless Networks (Justice)

IV.   INTERNAL EFFECTIVENESS/EFFICIENCY

1. E-training (OPM)
2. Recruitment One Stop (OPM)
3. Enterprise HR Integration (OPM)
4. Integrated Acquisition (GSA)
5. E-records Management (NARA)
6. Enterprise Case Management (Justice)

2002   The Homeland Security Act established a CIO for the new Department of Home-
       land Security. The CIO was to oversee the largest consolidation of federal data-
       bases in U.S. history. Other provisions of Title 2 (the Information Analysis and
       Infrastructure Protection title):

       *Section 201. The Office of Under Secretary for Information Analysis and Infra-
       structure Protection was created to receive and integrate security information;
       design and protect the security of data; issue security advisories to the public.
       *Section 202. Transferred these units: the National Infrastructure Protection Center of
       the FBI (other than the Computer Investigations and Operations Section), the Na-
       tional Communications System of the Department of Defense, the Critical Infrastruc-
       ture Assurance Office of the Department of Commerce, the Computer Security
       Division of the National Institute of Standards and Technology, the National Infra-
       structure Simulation and Analysis Center of the Department of Energy, and the
       Federal Computer Incident Response Center of the General Services Administration.
       *Section 203. Access to information. This section established the Secretary of Home-
       land Security's entitlement to receive intelligence and other information from agencies.
       *Section 204 of the Homeland Security Act allowed the federal government to
       deny FOIA requests regarding information voluntarily provided by nonfederal
       parties to the Department of Homeland Security.

2002   Acting on a February 2002 recommendation from the federal CIO Council, the
       OMB established the Federal Enterprise Architecture Program Management Office
       (FEAPMO) on February 6, 2002. In 2002 FEAPMO issued "The Business Reference
       Model, Version 1.0," which created a functional (not department-based) classifi-
       cation of all government services with a view to its use by OMB for cross-agency
       reviews to eliminate redundant IT investments and promote reusable IT compon-
       ents. A Performance Reference Model (fall, 2002) set general performance meas-
       urement metrics. Data and Information Reference Model data needed to support
       enterprise architecture. Overall, this was reminiscent of 1960s PPB: functional not
       line item budgeting, emphasis on empirical measurement of performance,
       strengthening top-management oversight capabilities.

2002   The OMB called for a uniform protocol for e-rulemaking by the end of 2003.

2002   The General Services Administration (GSA) and the Office of Federal Procurement
       Policy (OFPP), with involvement from DOD, NASA, and NIH, advanced e-pro-
       curement by establishing the Past Performance Information Retrieval System
       (PPIRS) to give online access to past vendor performance records.

2002   President Bush issued a "Presidential Memo on the Importance of e-Government"
       in July, stating, "My Administration's vision for government reform is guided by
       three principles. Government should be citizen-centered, results-oriented, and
       market-based."

2002   The OMB issued a revision of OMB Circular A-16 in August, setting guidelines for
       standardizing GIS data collection records. This laid the basis for its Geospatial One-
       Stop portal, one of the eventually 24 OMB e-government "Quicksilver" initiatives.
       Circular A-16 was originally issued in 1953 to give OMB authority over surveying and
       mapping.

2002   The OMB issued a revision of OMB Circular A-76 in October, replacing lowest-cost
       acquisition with best-value acquisition, a goal long sought by CIOs. The circular
       also encouraged outsourcing, in line with the Bush administration's goal to
       outsource 15% of "noninherently governmental jobs."

2002 The Cyber Security Research and Development Act (CSRDA), passed as part of the Homeland Security Act, enacted November 27, authorized funding for new computer and network security research and grant programs. It also shielded ISPs from customer lawsuits when they reveal customer information to law enforcement authorities.

2002 The Federal Information Security Management Act (FISMA), enacted December 17, permanently authorized and strengthened the information security program, evaluation, and reporting requirements of federal agencies.

2002 The Dot Kids Implementation and Efficiency Act, passed December 4, created a new domain, similar to .com and .edu. The .kids domain was to be a child-friendly space within the Internet. Every site designated .kids would be a safe zone for children and would be monitored for content and for safety, and all objectionable material would be removed. Online chat rooms and instant messaging were prohibited, unless they could be certified as safe. The websites under this new domain would not connect a child to other online sites outside the child-friendly zone.

2002 The Electronic Government Act of 2002 was passed by Congress on November 15 and signed by the president on December 16. The act was sponsored by Senator Joe Lieberman (Democrat, Connecticut) and was intended to promote e-government in all federal agencies. In essence, the EGA formalized much of what had been done by the OMB's Associate Director for IT and e-Government.

*The EGA established an Office of Electronic Government within the Office of Management and Budget. The head of this office was to be appointed by the president and report to the OMB director. In essence, this formalized the administrative setup established by the OMB in 2001 under Mark Forman, making the OEG head the federal CIO and the new Office of Electronic Government the overseer of setting cross-agency standards, including privacy standards, and assuring new e-government initiatives were cross-agency in nature. As such the EGA represented a direct attack on the agency-centric "stovepipe" approach to IT of prior years.

*The EGA required regulatory agencies to publish all proposed rules on the Internet and to accept public comments via e-mail as part of "e-rulemaking."

All information published in the *Federal Register* was now to be published on the Web also.

*The federal courts were required to publish rulings and other information on the Web.

*Privacy protections were added, prohibiting posting of personally identifiable information. Privacy notices are required, codifying a 3-year-old OMB directive to agencies.

*The EGA also promoted better recruiting and training of federal information technology officers. Each agency head was required to establish an IT training program. Public–private employee exchange programs were also authorized.

*Share-in-savings IT contracting was authorized and Federal Acquisition Regulations (FAR) was changed accordingly.

*Common standards for GIS information were mandated.

*The OMB's prime role in overseeing IT security was reaffirmed, to be coordinated with the NIST's role in setting security technical standards.

*The EGA authorized $45 million available to the OMB for e-government projects in the current FY 2003, $50 million in FY 2004, and $250 million in FY 2005 and in 2006. However, actual appropriations deleted $40 million of the authorized $45 million, forcing the OMB to implement e-government strategy from mostly departmental budgets. Subsequent appropriations were also far lower than originally planned. *The GSA was also authorized $8 million for digital signatures and $15 million for maintenance and improvement of FirstGov.gov and other portals. FirstGov.gov will be improved by adding a subject directory so pages can be accessed by topic rather than by agency.

2002 Regulation.gov was launched as a new one-stop Web portal in late 2002, part of Bush administration e-government initiatives. It was designed to encourage citizens to participate in federal rulemaking. On this site, one can find, review, and submit comments on federal documents that are open for comment and published in the *Federal Register*. The url is http www.regulations.gov.

2003 President Bush dissolved the Critical Infrastructure Protection Board on February 28, placing its function in the new Homeland Security Council, which is charged with coordinating cybersecurity policy. Early strategy emphasized public- and private-sector best practices and downplayed enforcement of security policies.

2003 The OMB announced "Round 2" of its e-government initiatives in March, looking beyond the initial 24 "Quicksilver" initiatives. Round 2 was to focus on data and statistics, criminal investigations, financial management, public health monitoring, and monetary benefits to individuals. The OMB sought to force joint projects (e.g., Justice, Treasury, and EPA) to have one criminal investigation system instead of three separate ones.

2003 The OMB required privacy assessments as part of the FY 2005 budget process, for the first time. Agencies were required to submit privacy assessments of major IT systems as part of their annual business case submissions. This implemented privacy provisions detailed in the e-Government Act of 2002, which included privacy assessments and website privacy statements.

2003 Funding of e-government initiatives for FY 2004 was cut to $1 million, far short of the $50 million over 5 years initially announced. OMB's head of the Office of Electronic Government, Mark Forman, quit, departing for the private sector. Future growth of e-government was called into question, at least temporarily.

2003 The Check Clearing for the 21st Century Act was passed in October, allowing the substitutability of electronic images of checks for physical transfer of printed checks among banks. It did not mandate electronic check clearance but made it legally equivalent.

2003 The 2003 Amendment to the Fair Credit Reporting Act strengthened laws to prevent identity theft, improve resolution of consumer disputes, improve the accuracy of consumer records, and make improvements in the use of, and consumer access to, credit information, and for other purposes.

2003 The Controlling the Assault of Non-Solicited Pornography and Marketing Act (CAN-SPAM) was passed in December, giving the Federal Trade Commission, state attorneys general, and ISPs the power to enforce rules requiring senders of marketing e-mail to include pornography warnings, to offer opt-out methods, and to not use false or deceptive information in e-mail subject lines. The law became effective January 1, 2004 and authorized the FTC to impose fines up to $250 per e-mail, with a cap of $2 million for initial violations and $6 million for repeat violations (these caps do not apply to e-mail using false/deceptive subject lines). There were also criminal penalties including up to 5 years of prison. The FTC was mandated to develop a plan for a national do-not-spam registry and is authorized to launch the list after filing its report.

PART II

ORGANIZATIONAL
RESEARCH

4

USING STRATEGIC INFORMATION SYSTEMS TO IMPROVE CONTRACTED SERVICES AND ASSESS PRIVATIZATION OPTIONS

Steven Cohen
Columbia University

William B. Eimicke
Columbia University

CONTENTS

I.   Introduction 44
II. Organizational networks and organizational management 44
     A.   The influence of changing technology on organizational form and
          function 44
     B.   Management challenges posed by organizational networks 45
     C.   Performance management 46
     D.   Performance management and contracting out 46
     E.   Performance management and information needs 47
     F.   The use of performance measurement systems to respond to network
          management problems 48
     G.   Performance measures and IT 49
III. Measures of performance 49
IV. Case studies of efforts to utilize performance measurement systems to
     manage contracted operations 51
     A.   New York City Department of Parks and Recreation 51
          1.   Measuring park outcomes: objective indicators 52
          2.   Measuring park outcomes: subjective indicators 53
          3.   Impact of the outcome measures 54
     B.   New York City Department of Homeless Services 55
          1.   The Performance Investment Program 55
          2.   Analysis 56
V.   Conclusions 57
VI. Acknowledgments 57
References 57

ABSTRACT

Government officials are looking to contracting out and privatization as means to create a public sector that works better and costs less. This new approach to public service delivery is evident in the welfare to work reforms of the 1990s, low- and moderate-income housing construction and management, homeless services, economic development and job training, and the charter school movement. Contracted services require a whole new set of skills for government workers, including contract design, negotiation, monitoring, and evaluation. Sophisticated information systems are crucial to performance management and evaluation systems that are essential to effective contract management. This chapter explores the theory and practice of performance measurement and information technology (IT) in the context of outsourcing public service delivery. It discusses the use of government strategic planning and information-based performance management to plan and manage private contractors performing public tasks. While information systems are critical to the management of in-house organizational units, we believe they are even more important in managing the work of contractors.

I. INTRODUCTION

Government officials are looking to contracting out and privatization as means to create a public sector that works better and costs less. This new approach to public service delivery is evident in the welfare to work reforms of the 1990s, low- and moderate-income subsidized housing programs since the 1980s, homeless service programs, job training, the business improvement district initiative, and the charter school movement. Contracted services require government workers to develop a whole new set of skills, including contract design, negotiation, program monitoring, and evaluation. Sophisticated information systems are also needed to provide the performance measures and evaluation programs that are essential to effective contract management.

This chapter explores the theory and practice of performance management and information technology (IT) in the context of outsourcing public service delivery. It discusses the use of government strategic planning and information-based performance management to plan and manage private contractors performing public tasks. While information systems are critical to the management of in-house organizational activities and units, we believe they are even more important in managing the work of contractors.

II. ORGANIZATIONAL NETWORKS AND ORGANIZATIONAL MANAGEMENT

A. The Influence of Changing Technology on Organizational Form and Function

The need for vertically integrated, hierarchically controlled organizations has been reduced as technology has made it easier to communicate ideas and information and transport goods around the world (Cohen and Eimicke, 1998, 2002, 2003): satellite communication, cellular telephones, handheld computers, wireless Internet access, containerized shipping, and multinational organizational networks make it possible to create goods and services in a variety of locations. These goods and services can be assembled throughout the globe, from components made all over the world, and can be tailored for use in a particular location or market.

The creation of a worldwide system of production means that organizations must constantly ask and then reexamine the "make-or-buy decision." Should we do this task in-house or hire a consultant or another firm to do this work for us? The correct answer to this question is not necessarily to increase the amount of contracting out. In today's world, yesterday's decision to buy something can be today's decision to make it. Technology alone can change the basis for such a decision. Perhaps the most dramatic recent example of changing dynamics is the decision of the U.S. government to take airport security back from the private sector in the aftermath of terrorist attacks of September 11, 2001. Access to information about individuals and groups available only to public law enforcement instantaneously on a global basis is essential to airport security and cannot be shared with private vendors. In 2003 and 2004 the military discovered that some vendors refused to perform contracted tasks during the war with Iraq because they refused to put their workers in danger. The military discovered they could not outsource bravery — some functions such as food service and construction needed to remain in-house if they were to be performed on or near a battlefield. The work that each organization does can change rapidly as do the organization's structures that support that work.

Organizational form is therefore far less stable in well-managed organizations than it once was. Organizational function changes rapidly as well. There are three basic questions that organizations must ask: (1) What should we do? (2) How should we do it? and (3) Who should do it? In the past, these questions could be answered definitively and for a long period. Bureaucratic hierarchies and standard operating procedures could be built on the answers to these questions. Today, these questions must be raised constantly in a global struggle to keep current with technology and competition.

Some might wonder who is government competing with? For the most part, government has a monopoly, or at least a shared monopoly, with other levels of government within distinct functional areas. However, the best managers understand the importance of the cost of government as an element in a nation's (or region's) ability to have its goods and services compete in a global economy. Governments do not directly compete, but their cost, efficiency, and effectiveness affect a nation's or a region's economic well-being. Therefore, well-managed organizations are always asking and responding in different ways to the aforementioned three questions. This means that organizational function and form are constantly in flux.

B. Management Challenges Posed by Organizational Networks

Although well-managed, dynamic organizations find themselves undergoing constant change, one factor does not change — the need for management direction and the demand for accountability. While mayors and commissioners might try to blame a bad result on an inadequate contractor, that argument is generally not accepted by the public — especially over the long term. When programs are implemented by a variety of organizations that form a network, issues of communication, coordination, and direction are generated.

Organizations within the network need to learn what tasks they are to perform, when they should perform them, the objectives they are attempting to achieve, the customers they are being asked to serve, and the information they must provide to the agency they are working for. This requires extensive contact and information exchange. The agency contracting for the work does not perform the tasks in question, but it should determine what tasks must be performed, by whom, at what time, and for what purpose. The agency must learn whether the tasks have been performed and what outputs and outcomes the tasks have generated. It must coordinate the actions of numerous contractors and, where contractors must interact, ensure that the interaction is working as designed.

Organizational networks, when they run well, can be more efficient and effective than vertically integrated hierarchical organizations. However, they must be managed, and such management is not cost-free or easy. It requires a new type of management that relies on creativity and innovation to fuel new mechanisms for communicating to and influencing the behavior of external organizations. Often, contract instruments must be used to exercise influence: for example, linking payment schedules and bonuses to performance. To receive these incentives, vendors must perform in certain specific ways and they must also provide the lead agency with information on their performance.

C. Performance Management

A number of researchers have noted the trend over the past decade for state and local governments to contract out, or outsource a substantial number of the services previously delivered by civil servants to private and, particularly, nonprofit organizations (Butcher, 1995; Forrest, 1995; Sclar, 2000; Cohen and Eimicke, 2002). Forrest (1995: 51) notes that agencies have thus been transformed "from direct providers to monitoring, regulation, and contract-enforcing agencies." He emphasizes the importance of new management skills necessary to guide these organizations that now have a networked contractor structure, rather than the traditional hierarchical service delivery structure. Forrest regards the increase in emphasis on performance monitoring as part of the process of contract specification and oversight necessary in these new structures.

Martin and Kettner (1996) cover the process of performance measurement in human service agencies and programs in some depth. They define performance measurement as the regular collection and reporting of information about the efficiency (inputs/outputs), quality, and effectiveness (outcomes) of programs (p. 3). They argue the chief reason to adopt performance measurement in human services is to improve the management of those programs by supplying agencies with information about who their clients are; their demographic characteristics; their service requirements; the amount, quality, and level of service received; and the outcome of receiving the service. Performance measures keep managers informed about how their program is doing and assist in oversight.

Performance measures may be used to monitor the delivery of contractors' services in the same way that they can be used to monitor agency performance. The advantage, according to Martin and Kettner (1996), is that once performance measures are in place, the agency can move to performance-based contracting, in which contractors are paid for meeting certain performance-based criteria. For example, payment to a job training and employment contractor is based on the number of people they actually place in a job, not on the number of people they are currently training.

D. Performance Management and Contracting Out

Management of interorganizational networks and contracts means that leaders cannot depend on traditional hierarchical controls to influence the behavior of subordinates who are responsible for performing particular tasks. This means that management cannot use organizational culture, personnel promotion, demotion, termination, or authoritative command structures to influence behavior. In our view, many of these tools are of declining usefulness anyway. Given that public employees are entitled to due process rights, it is increasingly difficult to fire someone. In the professionalized environment characteristic of most government agencies, few professionals are responsive to direct command. They are more likely to behave as management requires in response to persuasion and positive incentives. Merit pay and other bonus systems can be effective in rewarding good performance, but few techniques are available to government to effectively punish poor performance.

In contrast, contractual relationships with private and nonprofit firms provide the surest way to punish poor performance: contract termination. While there are limits to the use of this technique — it is difficult to terminate contracts in midterm — it does send a message that is clearly understood by the people who work in the organizations holding the contract. Competition and the intense work environment it engenders can be created through contracting. Systems can be established with competing vendors, and contracts can be signed with incentive and penalty clauses. When the term of the contract is over, new bids are sought and a poorly performing contractor can see the contract simply come to an end. In this sense the contractor has some of the same attributes as an employee on a renewable term appointment.

One example of a contractual mechanism to enhance contractor performance was used in a New York City subway track repair project. The contractor renovating the tracks on the city's number 2 and 3 lines received a $30,000 bonus for each day the project was finished ahead of schedule (and could have been fined $30,000 for each day it was late). The project was completed about 3 weeks ahead of schedule and the contractor was paid a bonus of more than $600,000. To develop this incentive and disincentive clause in the contract the government needed to know: (1) a reasonable deadline; and (2) the appropriate level to set the reward/punishment. They also needed an operational definition of "complete project" to put in the contract. Finally, they needed to find a way to confirm when the project was completed. These extensive information requirements place new demands on government managers that must be addressed if the contract mechanism is to work.

The challenge to management is to develop contract clauses that provide them with tools to influence the behavior of the organization under contract. It is also important to ensure that the vendor does not develop a monopoly over the function it is performing. If the contractor is the only organization capable of performing the task, threats of termination can be easily ignored. We have seen this result frequently in military procurement and ironically, in the purchase of IT hardware, software, and contracting services. In our view, functions that cannot generate competitive bids should be directly performed by government wherever feasible. If sole-source contracting is unavoidable, government managers must ensure that performance criteria are clear, well-publicized, easily measured, and understood, and that penalties for missing performance targets are severe.

E. Performance Management and Information Needs

Contract management requires that government receive timely, accurate information. When possible, contracts must be developed that require vendors to report input, process, output, and outcome measures on a frequent basis. However, self-reporting, while necessary, is not sufficient. When services are provided directly to the public, citizen service complaints and complements can serve as a useful barometer of contract performance. It is also important to have all contract performance measures and payment generation actions verified and audited by third parties that are independent of the contractor. This can be done directly by a government agency's performance measurement unit, or can be done under contract to a consulting firm, think tank, or university.

Some members of a program's implementation network are organizations that are not under direct contract to the government. Examples of these actors include nonprofit organizations and private firms with a similar mission. The private insurers of underground oil and chemical storage tanks help the Environmental Protection Agency (EPA) enforce tank standards, but do not work for EPA. Recently, the insurance industry was credited by the federal government for the automobile industry voluntarily accelerating compliance with government requirements for passenger protections in the case of vehicle collisions.

Similarly, a nonprofit organization that advocates for the government protection of abused children may also provide shelter for such children. The nonprofit is thereby part of a city's network for protecting and providing foster care for children, but they may not be a government contractor. In these cases, collection of important performance data may be difficult if not impossible. Despite these difficulties, information about performance must be collected if the government hopes to manage the program being implemented by the interorganizational network.

F. The Use of Performance Measurement Systems to Respond to Network Management Problems

The managers of government programs that utilize networks of organizations to perform critical tasks must obtain information about the performance of these organizations if they are to effectively manage these programs. This requires strategic thinking about what information they need and how they might obtain that information. When dealing with private firms, government must overcome the issue of proprietary information. Some firms are reluctant to tell you what they are doing, as they consider their work processes and outputs to be part of the competitive edge they have over other organizations. If they are under contract to you, it is possible to use the contract as leverage to collect information. If the firm is simply in a related business to yours, information collection may be difficult, and may require substantial effort to obtain.

However difficult collection of information might be, the key first step is to decide what information is needed. This should be guided by the management needs of the program. What is the definition of success? What direct or surrogate measures can be used to determine if progress is being made? The definition of success and the appropriateness of measures to that definition is critical. One cannot manage a program unless one can measure its performance. Without a way to measure performance you cannot tell if your actions are leading you toward or away from success. You have no way of knowing if you are moving forward or backward.

Decisions on performance measures are critical management decisions. They are the ground-level, operational definition of policy. They provide real-world specificity to abstract ideas and policy and are therefore of great consequence. The information collected on performance must be an integral part of an agency's strategy for implementing a program. If the goals of a program change, the measures must change as well.

Once the information necessary to manage the program is known, a strategy is needed for collecting the information. A fundamental principle of management information systems (MISs) is that people and organizations are more likely to provide accurate information to a system if they utilize the data themselves and they see a benefit to cooperation. If the organizations providing information think its provision can help sell the program and help them obtain additional resources they will be more cooperative than if the data are used to monitor and punish poor performance. The problems of collecting timely, accurate information can be overcome if care and strategic thought are given to developing and maintaining the performance measurement system. Information retrieval is not an automatic, mechanical process. It is a political process requiring the buy-in of those providing information.

Performance measurement is critical to overcoming the management challenges faced when using an interorganizational implementation network. The construction of a system of measurement is an important early task for a program's managers. It should not be off-loaded to a consulting firm or the organization's MIS shop. It is leaders that create partnerships and networks, not technical experts. As such, it should be treated as a subject worthy of formal negotiations and either a contractual agreement or a memorandum of understanding (written or tacit) agreement. Below we discuss, in conceptual terms, the types of measures that should be included in these performance measurement agreements.

G. Performance Measures and IT

While the nature of the system being managed is a key issue in establishing methods of performance measurement, IT itself is an influence on the feasibility, timeliness, and accuracy of performance measurement systems. Computer, communication, and transportation technology make it possible to implement public programs through interorganizational networks. This same technology makes it possible to track and manage the work of these networks (Henderson, 2003). However, technology is never cost-free and new technology is never glitch-free.

IT is crucial to the implementation of an effective performance management program (Carter, 1989; Cohen and Eimicke, 2002: 157–186) Technology must be accessible and user-friendly to ensure that data entry is accurate (Barrett and Greene, 2000). Turnaround of reports to management must also be rapid to ensure that indicators are available when management decisions are made (Buntin, 1999).

Muid (1994) discusses issues in managing the vendors that provide IT services. A key issue is the development of sufficient in-house expertise to manage technically sophisticated computer hardware, software, and management system vendors. Without sufficient in-house expertise it is impossible for the government to be an intelligent consumer of IT and its related services. While IT capacity remains essential, it is also true that simple, off-the-shelf systems are increasingly available and capable of performing more functions. Even as state-of-the-art information systems become more and more complex and expensive the price of computing power and basic systems comes down. This means that even the smallest community-based nonprofit contractor can be asked to submit performance data electronically. As recently as 5 years ago this was not the case.

III. MEASURES OF PERFORMANCE

Most performance measurement systems incorporate four types of measures — inputs, process, outputs, and outcomes. Traditional, budget-based performance measurement systems focus primarily on inputs: What are the resources available to address the priority problems faced by the organization? Input measures are relatively easy to identify and collect. Commonly used input measures include dollars appropriated, person-hours committed, equipment purchased, space provided, and the length of time committed to the problem or the project. Less common but other very relevant input indicators are: other funds/other organizations involved or leveraged as a result of the initial organization's actions or decisions; capital funds directly or indirectly committed as a by-product of the operating budget commitment; and external staff and consultant time dedicated to the preparation, operation, monitoring, and evaluation of the program being launched.

Input measures are frequently criticized because they tell you only how hard you are trying to do something about a problem or the extent of your commitment to reach a particular goal (e.g., how much are we willing to spend to find a cure for AIDS?). Input measures tell you very little about how well you are doing in reaching the objective — they measure effort much better than they assess results. But input measures should not be ignored. They provide an important barometer of the scope of activity, the present and future demand on overall resources, serve as surrogates of the organization's priorities, and often reflect the organization's customer preferences as well.

The process of producing work is an increasing focus of performance management systems and indicators. Total quality management's lasting contribution to management practice may be its attention to the work steps involved in producing goods and services. Measurement of these activities facilitates organizational learning and improvement. Process measures include the delineation and definition of specific work steps, measures of the amount of time it takes to perform specific tasks, error rates, and similar indicators. Requiring organizational units to report process measures can signal government's concern for the quality and efficiency of an organization's internal operations and can compel attention to these fundamental management issues.

Output measures are the third type of performance measurement indicators. Output measures seek to quantify the amount of work accomplished with the input/resources provided. Output measures can seek to measure quantity, quality, or both aspects of the work performed. Typical output measures include: customers/clients served; facility condition and cleanliness; miles of road paved; numbers of applicants trained; tons of garbage collected; wages earned; course work completed; certificates or licenses acquired; or number of products sold. In simple terms, output measures gauge the volume of activity generated by inputs. As with input measures, some outputs are more important than others. Utilizing a select number of indicators that have a direct impact on performance (particularly for customers and funding agencies) leads to a successful performance measurement system.

Since World War II, most successful performance measurement systems have been output-based. However, in the 1990s, many experts have written about the weaknesses inherent in output-based systems. Output systems tend to measure and reward work accomplished on a milestone basis. For example, interim payments are doled out as a contractor achieves preestablished targets along the way toward a completed assignment or full service to a customer.

On the surface, output measures seem to provide exactly what senior management should want — simple categories designed to encourage staff to accomplish the work desired by paying for milestones actually achieved. The key weakness of an output-based system is that it often "pays" more for the process toward the desired outcome than the outcome itself. The ultimate objective ends up being underemphasized. For example, in the welfare to work reform efforts over the past decade, we found that by the time employment and training programs are paid for outputs, such as training, certification, resume preparation, and job interviews, only a small percentage of the contract amount remains to reward the contractor for actually placing clients in a job, keeping them employed, or assisting them up the employment ladder (Cohen and Eimicke, 1996, 1998, 1999).

This leads us to outcome or impact measures. Performance measurement experts are seeking to tie input and output measures to more meaningful program impacts and goal achievement (Eisenberg, 2003; Kaestner et al., 2003). For example, the performance of a police department is not best measured by the number of officers on the payroll (input), how many people are arrested (output), or even the reduction in the overall crime rate (output), but rather how safe people feel and how safe they actually are (outcome). In New York City, a private think tank has constructed a "Quality of Life" index to measure the overall performance of its hometown city government (McMahon, 2003).

An initial review might lead to the conclusion that properly designed outcome indicators are all a good performance management system requires. In practice, outcome measures have significant weaknesses. First, outcome data are usually the most difficult to identify and expensive to collect. Frederickson (2000) argues that because performance measures are quantitative representations of some reality, they are necessarily never as neutral and objective as they are presented. Rather, program supporters will use the same measures as program critics to come up with diametrically opposite conclusions regarding the efficacy of the initiative. In Washington, D.C., Mayor Anthony Willliams initiated an extensive system of agency scorecards that even cynics agreed produced positive results. However, with persistent problems, such as unsafe streets, high homicide rates, and poorly performing schools, critics questioned the importance of the scorecard improvements (Scott, 2002).

Second, outcomes are ongoing and the long-term impacts, both positive and negative, often do not evolve quickly. So, while in theory outcome measures are supposed to measure long-term impact, annual budget cycles and biennial elections often lead to very short-term definitions of long term. Third, it is often difficult, if not impossible, to determine the independent effect of a program or government activity on a particular outcome (Eisenberg, 2003). Fourth, even outcome measures fail to answer the question of maximum potential — "How well are we doing? Compared with what?" Some sort of comparative benchmarking exercise is required to assess how well a program or organization is performing compared with other entities doing similar work (Morley et al., 2001).

Finally, in the early 1990s, creators of the so-called balanced scorecard argued that existing performance management systems were far too limited and failed to adequately account for the need for continuous improvement, innovation, and the needs and wants of customers (Kaplan and Norton, 1991, 1993, 1996; Kaplan, 2002). The balanced scorecard sets goals and measures from four perspectives — financial, internal business operations, innovation and learning, and customers. The challenge for managers is how to create a set of measures that is comprehensive and still limited enough to focus the organization on what is most important.

IV. CASE STUDIES OF EFFORTS TO UTILIZE PERFORMANCE MEASUREMENT SYSTEMS TO MANAGE CONTRACTED OPERATIONS

A. New York City Department of Parks and Recreation

The New York City Department of Parks and Recreation (DPR) maintains a municipal park system of more than 28,600 acres, including approximately 1500 parks, 950 playgrounds,

800 athletic fields, 570 tennis courts, 63 swimming pools, 14 miles of beaches, 36 recreation centers, 13 golf courses, 6 ice rinks, 9 nature centers, 4 zoos, 4 major stadia, and 2000 "greenstreets." DPR also manages 22 house museums, 1100 monuments and markers, and 2.5 million trees.

Since 1984, DPR has made extensive use of performance measurement to achieve its core mission to "maintain a green, clean and safe park system for all New Yorkers." Over the past two decades, parks have used a variety of measures to measure their performance, including the number of crews conducting park cleanups, the number of park benches and playgrounds renovated, and the public's satisfaction with the city's parks (as measured by a random sample of park users). The DPR has also collected two sets of outcome data on the overall condition and cleanliness of an ever-larger number of its park facilities and playgrounds. While the DPR's performance measurement system, known as the Parks Inspection Program (PIP), was and is not specifically designed for measuring contractor performance, it is used citywide to measure the performance of both governmental and nongovernmental organizations involved in the maintenance and management of DPR properties.

The DPR has dramatically increased its use of contractors over the past decade. Through "requirements contracts," it uses private firms to replace playgrounds, fences, and park benches throughout the city's park system. Under these contracts, vendors bid to replace a specific number of facilities in a given period. They do not know in advance where they will be asked to work and are called on during the time the contract is in effect by parks management to install facilities in particular places. The DPR has also turned over day-to-day management of several parks to nonprofit organizations. Two of the city's most famous parks, Bryant Park and Central Park, are managed by nonprofit organizations. As contracting increases, the DPR's performance measurement system has become a critical tool of program management.

1. Measuring park outcomes: objective indicators

A key strategy utilized by New York City Parks Commissioner Adrian Benepe is the use of park inspections to increase the day-to-day accountability of on-site park managers. Similar to the Compstat program utilized by the New York Police Department (NYPD) to achieve dramatic reductions in crime (Buntin, 1999), Parks Commissioner Benepe consults parks inspection data to target problems and to direct the activities of his staff. Trained inspectors from DPR's division of Operations and Management Planning used handheld computers and digital cameras to perform 4949 inspections in fiscal 2002–2003.

The expansion of the Parks Inspection Program became feasible through the use of handheld computers to record inspection data. These handheld computers, which inspectors utilize during on-site inspections, facilitate the swift compilation of inspection results. In 1992, 1993, and 1994 combined, 1400 park inspections were filed on paper and later manually entered into the program's database. With the introduction of direct data entry of inspector reports into handheld computers, the 1995 inspection total reached 2000 and has accelerated to the current year total by 600 inspections, as parks staff completed 2000 inspections that year alone.

The increased use of performance data remains an operational imperative at DPR. Every inspected park, playground, and "greenstreet" is given an overall rating of "Acceptable" or "Unacceptable" for overall condition and for cleanliness. The overall ratings are the composite of as many as 16 separate park features. Some additional park elements are inspected and tracked but do not figure into the overall rating of a site. Hazards are noted as needing "Immediate Attention" and must be corrected with two inspection rounds following its issuance. An immediate attention finding can fail a feature or even an entire site.

Inspections occur in 2-week cycles, with 205 sites selected at random. Park managers do not receive advance warning about inspections. Results of the inspections are presented to the commissioner, deputy commissioners, and borough commissioners at regular senior-staff meetings. The results are also posted on a bulletin board located outside the parks commissioner's office.

Site managers of inspected parks also receive inspection data on a regular basis. In addition to the general inspection rating, park managers get detailed lists of deficiencies and Polaroid photographs of their site taken at the time of the inspection. The inspection report also assesses the seriousness of each deficiency and advises what corrective action is required.

The program also has a built-in method for correcting maintenance and cleanliness problems. Any unacceptable measures from the original inspection are reinspected after 8 weeks. The results of these second inspections are presented to the first deputy commissioner and Commissioner Stern. The first deputy commissioner's staff independently track deficiencies involving potential safety hazards.

2. Measuring park outcomes: subjective indicators

An important step in the measurement of DPR's performance was the development of outcome measures. The views of park users are a critical measure of departmental performance. While it can be argued that understanding the views of nonusers is also important, if the focus of the measure is improving the facility itself, the users of those facilities are the best judges of their subjective quality. While customer surveys are not a regular element of the department's performance measurement system, DPR seeks information on customer satisfaction when it is available, affordable, and verifiable. So, during the summers of 1996 and 1997, the DPR cooperated with a pilot test and a full-scale survey of park users as a means of enhancing the performance measurement system.

A team from Columbia University and the New York City Parks Council conducted random surveys of 374 park users in ten New York City parks in the summer of 1996. In the summer of 1997 a full-scale random sample survey of 1086 park users in 19 parks was completed. The survey data indicated that the public is generally satisfied with the quality of New York City parks. In the survey we conducted in 1997, nearly 76% of park users rated the quality of the park that they were visiting as either good or excellent. Most park users were reasonably satisfied with the parks; the most common response to our question asking respondents to rate the park they were visiting was good (50%).

Central Park received the highest rating of any park. No one rated it poor, and half of those interviewed in the park gave it a rating of excellent (this park is managed under contract with a private, nonprofit organization, The Central Park Conservancy). Only one other park (Clove Lake) was rated excellent by a majority of its visitors.

If we combine ratings of good and excellent as positive ratings and fair and poor as negative ratings, 18 of the 19 parks surveyed were perceived positively by their users. This included 14 parks viewed positively by 70% or more of those interviewed. Park users were satisfied with their parks in both high- and low-income neighborhoods. In parks neighboring lower-income census tracks, 71% were rated good or excellent. While this is slightly lower than the 79% positive rating given to parks in higher-income areas, it is notable that this positive rating of parks was universal throughout the city.

Recently, New York City established a citywide 311 Information Call Line to handle citizen inquiries, requests, and complaints and free its 911 Emergency Line for true emergencies. An unexpected benefit of the 311 Citizen Service Center is that it provides continuous public feedback on how well city agencies such as DPR are meeting the needs of the citizens, as citizens see those needs. Beginning in fiscal 2002–2003, the New York City Mayor's Management Report includes 311 data for every agency.

For the first period for which 311 data were available (March through June 2003), the 311 Citizen Service Center received 8769 DPR inquiries. Among the top five categories of inquiries for DPR, three related to emergency tree/branch removal or dead tree removal (17.8% of all inquiries), about 10% represented general information requests, and 7% concerned information on DPR special entertainment events.

3. Impact of the outcome measures

The Parks Inspection Program has evolved into a highly effective performance management tool for DPR. The inspections inform park managers about what operational areas require improvement and establish their maintenance priorities. The program also provides site managers with performance incentives. Ultimately, inspection results help assess the effectiveness of park managers, borough offices, and the contractors they manage. Park managers and their vendors compete with one another for ratings and ratings improvements, and the five boroughs compete to have the best-maintained parks. Perhaps most importantly, the inspection program communicates the park's quality standards to park personnel and contractors and evaluates how well they uphold these quality standards.

Citywide, overall condition ratings increased from 39% acceptable in the spring of 1994 to 43% acceptable in the spring of 1995. They improved again to 69% acceptable in the spring of 1997 and 80% in the spring of 1998. Since then, overall acceptable ratings have been no lower than 85% and reached 87% for 2003. Despite these excellent results, like many performance measurement systems, PIP could itself be improved, and over the past several years the authors have worked with the New York City Parks Council and the Parks Department to do so. DPR has also aggressively pursued expansion of the PIP to new areas by raising its own performance targets.

The inspection system is conducted at the places used most frequently by park users. These sites only comprise a relatively small percentage of the system's total acreage of 28,600 acres. Natural areas, trails, ball fields, and other less utilized facilities were not inspected. In the summer of 1998, we worked with the New York City Parks Council and the Parks Department to develop a methodology for inspecting these other park resources and conducted a pilot test of the new system. We found that 56% of the facilities we inspected were of acceptable quality, as compared with 80% in the areas of the park that were traditionally inspected. We also found that personnel resources tended to be allocated to the areas that were inspected. Both these findings demonstrated the impact of performance measurement on management decision-making and organizational performance. Inspected facilities got more personnel and were in better shape.

Despite our own work in developing subjective outcome measures, there is little question that the most important performance measures are those output data on condition and cleanliness that the DPR collects regularly. They provide a check on all contracted and government-performed activities and have a direct impact on management decisions. In addition, the system has led to tangible improvements in the quality and condition of the most heavily utilized park facilities.

B. New York City Department of Homeless Services

The New York City Department of Homeless Services (DHS) provides and oversees the provision of shelter-based services to homeless people in New York City. The population served consists of both single individuals and families, so a variety of services are offered through different types of shelters. Three broad categories of shelter reflect a continuum of care: (1) basic drop-in shelters without beds that provide shelter for a night and minimal counseling services; (2) more structured shelter programs providing beds, counseling, and referral services; and (3) single-resident occupant (SRO) and commercial hotels providing a more independent experience of living. The DHS seeks to move its clients through this continuum of care, with the ultimate aim of moving them into their own public or private housing (Cohen and Eimicke, 1995).

When Mayor Michael Bloomberg appointed Linda Gibbs to become the commissioner of DHS, she was aware that she was inheriting a department that was in transition and still struggling to deal with its prime objective — alleviating the levels of homelessness in New York City. When Gibbs ended up taking office in January 2002, the rate of homelessness in New York City was at an all-time high, as more than 30,000 men, women, and children were in shelters. The rising cost of housing, coupled with the unemployment in the wake of the attacks of September 11, 2001, were the main causes of this. It did not help that New York City itself was in an economic recession, thereby subjecting every city agency to massive budget cuts.

Out of all those who were homeless, the largest subdivision was composed of homeless families. While New York was scrambling to find solutions to this problem, the number of homeless families was rising while the housing facilities in which they were to live were filling up. Rather than being in the shelter system for a short period of time before moving on to some sort of permanent housing, homeless families were now facing stays of up to 10.5 months in the system. It cost the city an average of $28,657 per year for each family in the system, whereas if they were put into permanent housing, the annual housing subsidy provided by the city would be $12,000. Rather than depleting the DHS of its already stringent budget, Gibbs determined to help solve this problem in a way that would rapidly increase the number of permanent housing facilities for the city's homeless families and at the same time tackle the problem of homelessness. What she proposed was the Performance Investment Program (PIP), which would reward non-profit city contractors for the number of people moved out of homelessness into permanent housing. Gibbs hoped that this system would expedite the permanent housing opportunities available to homeless families.

1. The Performance Investment Program[1]

The DHS was created under Mayor David Dinkins, and showed results before being severely curtailed by the administration of Mayor Rudolph Guiliani. During Guiliani's tenure, the department suffered budget reductions and a policy created by the Guiliani Administration that tried to discourage homeless people from requesting city services. However, a major facet of the DHS that Guiliani did carry on from the era of Dinkins

---

[1] This section of the chapter is based in part on original research conducted by Columbia University MPA students. See "New York City Department of Homeless Services: A Comprehensive Case Study of the Performance Investment Program (PIP)" by Diana Glanternik, Dana Krieger, Amy Shefrin, and Hong Yin, Unpublished Manuscript, December, 2003.

was to continue the process of privatizing homeless shelters through the use of nonprofit vendors. The city actively pursued a contracting strategy which resulted in a system of increasingly cost-effective service delivery. The goal of the Performance Investment Program (PIP) was to add a performance-based element to this contracting process.

The PIP pilot program began in June 2002. It was to be based on two main factors — housing targets and result cards. Housing targets were assigned to shelter providers, with the targets based on historic statistics compiled by policy analysts at DHS. The agency's annual target was to move a total of 9250 families into permanent housing. The result cards were used to measure each shelter's population and performance data. Overall, the goal of PIP was to move more homeless families into homes. Once evaluations were completed, each shelter would be given a grade out of a maximum of 100 to determine whether they would receive bonuses based on their performance. If they failed to reach their target they would be penalized. Such an incentive helped to rally the shelters to increase the number of homeless families they placed into homes, as it would benefit the shelters as well as the city.

Result cards were issued monthly. They reflected each shelter's population and relevant statistics. The way in which DHS tracked each client's basic identifying information was through its main computer database, the Client Tracking System (CTS). Once a client was input into DHS's system, DHS would search for that name in the Human Resources Administration's (HRA) database to find out whether the client received public assistance. However, the system contained some level of inaccurate data. DHS began to work with shelter providers every month to identify discrepancies between data sets and to verify correct information. The CTS would then be updated. PIP forced the agency to better ensure the accuracy of its data, and to reconcile it with that of the shelter providers.

Although the main goal of PIP was specifically geared toward getting housing for families, it functioned as a tool to improve DHS as a whole. It made the shelters accountable for their clients through housing targets and result cards. These helped DHS focus on the common goal of permanent housing. The development of a hard-data, performance-based system helped to dramatically improve the services offered by shelters as well as the overall way in which the DHS functioned. Constant evaluation helped DHS to gauge what measures needed to be implemented in order to fix specific problems. Placement rates had reached a low of 2943 in 2001 and 3531 in fiscal 2002 but with PIP, 5289 families were placed in permanent housing in 2003 (DHS website, Office of Policy and Planning). While this still fell short of the goal of 9250, it demonstrated a remarkable turnaround and highlighted the fact that a program of strategic planning coupled with performance-based contracting could be effective.

2. Analysis

The case of homeless services in New York City indicates the importance of strategic thinking when contracting services. DHS set a clear strategic goal of placing homeless people into permanent housing. They worked with their contractors to focus their attention on the ultimate goal of moving people out of the homeless system. As a result, we see dramatic improvement in outputs from 2001 to 2003 The small improvement from 2001 to 2002 is greatly accelerated in 2003. While we do not have definitive proof that this is a result of PIP, it is difficult to see what else would have caused this change.

V. CONCLUSIONS

The two local government agencies discussed in this chapter have begun the process of measuring the performance of services delivered with the assistance of contractors. In the case of the New York City DPR, this effort is simply folded into their overall performance measurement system. In the case of the DHS, it focused on a performance-based reward system that required contractors to provide data and evidence of goal-oriented performance.

What is striking about these cases is the degree to which computer-based information systems are now fully integrated into the standard operating procedures of these municipal agencies. Even paper forms are now e-mailed and the use of standard spreadsheets that are easily downloaded into off-the-shelf data systems has significantly reduced the costs of collecting, reporting, and analyzing data. Performance data are now routinely and rapidly collected from vendors and when connected to a tangible reward system are considered a central tool of contractor management.

Performance is measured and incentives are beginning to be based on the reports of performance. In the case of community-based, nonprofit organizations, the issue of staff capacity and resources used to limit the ability of government to require participation in a particular electronic performance measurement system. Today, those limits have virtually disappeared in even the smallest nonprofit organization.

As the technology of personal computers, networked both locally and through the Internet, expanded through society, ease of access to these systems had made their use more commonplace. It is increasingly easy to construct performance measurement systems that connect and track the accomplishment of all the organizations involved in implementing a particular program. This in turn has increased the tendency for organizational networks to be constructed to deliver services such as parks and homeless services in New York City.

ACKNOWLEDGMENTS

The authors gratefully acknowledge the assistance of Laura Sullivan of the New York City DPR for kindly making available information on the Parks Inspection Program used to develop the DPR case study.

REFERENCES

Barrett, K. and Greene, R., Powering Up: How Public Managers Can Take Control of Information Technology, Congressional Quarterly Press, Washington, D.C., 2000.

Buntin, J., Assertive Policing, Plummeting Crime: The NYPD Takes on Crime in New York City, Kennedy School of Government Case Program, Cambridge, MA, 1999.

Butcher, T., *Delivering Welfare: The Governance of Social Services in the 1990s*, Open University Press, Buckingham, 1995, pp. 107–136.

Carter, N., Performance indicators: "backseat driving" or "hands off" control?", *Policy and Politics*, 17, 131–138, 1989.

Cohen, S. and Eimicke, W., Managing Reinvention: Contracting with Non-profits in New York City's Homeless Program, paper presented at the Annual Research Meeting of the Association for Public Policy Analysis and Management, Washington, D.C., 1995.

Cohen, S. and Eimicke, W., Assessing the Cost Effectiveness of Welfare to Work Programs, SIPA Occasional Paper, Columbia University, New York, 1996.

Cohen, S. and Eimicke, W., *Tools for Innovators: Creative Strategies for Managing Public Sector Organizations*, Jossey-Bass, San Francisco, 1998.

Cohen, S. and Eimicke, W., The Indianapolis Independence Initiative, The Rockefeller Foundation, New York, 1999.

Cohen, S. and Eimicke, W., *The Effective Public Manager*, Jossey-Bass, San Francisco, 2002.

Cohen, S. and Eimicke, W., The Future of E-Government: A Projection of Potential Trends and Issues, 36th Annual Hawaii International Conference on System Sciences (HICSS'03) January 6-9, Big Island, Hawaii, 2003.

Eisenberg, D., Evaluating the effectiveness of policies related to drunk driving, *Journal of Policy Analysis and Management*, 22, 251–274, 2003.

Forrest, R., Contracting housing provision: competition and privatization in the housing sector, in *Markets and Managers: New Issues in the Delivery of Welfare*, Taylor-Gooby, P. and Laws, K., Eds., Open University Press, Buckingham, 1995, pp. 38–53.

Frederickson, H.G., Measuring performance in theory and practice, *PA Times*, 23, 8, 2000.

Henderson, L., The Baltimore CitiStat Program: Performance and Accountability, IBM Endowment for the Business of Government, Arlington, VA, 2003.

Kaestner, R., Korenman, S., and O'Neill, J., Has welfare reform changed teenage behavior?, *Journal of Policy Analysis and Management*, 22, 225–248, 2003.

Kaplan, R., *The Balanced Scorecard and Nonprofit Organizations*, Harvard Business School Publishing, Cambridge, MA, 2002.

Kaplan, R. and Norton, D., The balanced scorecard — measures that drive performance, *Harvard Business Review*, 1, 71–79, 1991.

Kaplan, R. and Norton, D., Putting the balanced scorecard to work, *Harvard Business Review*, 5, 134–142, 1993.

Kaplan, R. and Norton, D., Using the balanced scorecard as a strategic management system, *Harvard Business Review*, 1, 75–85, 1996.

Martin, L.L. and Kettner, P.M., *Measuring the Performance of Human Service Programs*, Sage, Thousand Oaks, CA, 1996, pp. 3–10.

McMahon, E., City journal's quality-of-life index, *City Journal*, 13, 82–85, 2003.

Morley, E., Bryant, S., and Hatry, H., *Comparative Performance Measurement*, Urban Institute, Washington, D.C., 2001.

Muid, C., Information systems and new management — a view from the centre, *Public Administration*, 72, 113–125, 1994.

New York City' Department of Homeless Services Web Site: Data on Placement of Families into Permanent Housing.

Sclar, E., *You Don't Always Get What You Pay for: The Economics of Privatization*, Cornell University Press, Ithaca, NY, 2000.

Scott, E., Mayor Anthony Williams and Performance Management in Washington, D.C., Kennedy School of Government Case Program, Cambridge, MA, 2002.

5

INTERORGANIZATIONAL AND INTERDEPARTMENTAL INFORMATION SYSTEMS: SHARING AMONG GOVERNMENTS

Bruce Rocheleau
Northern Illinois University

CONTENTS

I.   Introduction 60
II. Previous research on interorganizational information sharing in government 61
III. Methodology 63
IV. Findings 64
     A. Sharing among local governments 64
     B. Criminal justice sharing efforts: local–local and state–local efforts 66
     C. State–local (including private providers) systems 67
     D. State to state and interdepartmental sharing within states 68
     E. Federal–state intergovernmental sharing 70
     F. Informal sharing 74
V.   A framework for studying sharing relationships 75
VI. Conclusion 77
References 79

ABSTRACT

This chapter examines the types of sharing of information technology (IT) resources that take place among governmental organizations. It adopts a broad definition of sharing, including formal and informal sharing of resources. It studies sharing relationships among local governments, between state and local governments, between the federal and state governments, and other complex relationships that include private organizations. A wide variety of examples of sharing are drawn from available resources in order to identify the types of sharing that exist and the key factors that influence its success.

I. INTRODUCTION

There are many reasons why today's computerized information systems can achieve more sharing in government than ever before. Over the last decade, an increasing emphasis has been placed on taking an enterprise-wide view of governments in order to replace "stovepipe" systems that focus on one department's needs with integrated systems that would allow users from any department to access information they need to achieve their jobs. This ability to share information across departmental boundaries has become accepted as one of the basic goals of modern information management in government. One of its key precepts is that data should only be input once into a system and any user (with a valid need) can use that information from anywhere at any time in a variety of forms.

The implications of this enterprise-wide approach are visible when one studies the requirements to establish standards that facilitate sharing within and possibly between governmental organizations. Information technology (IT) standards generally require that each department's new applications be compatible with the organizational network and its major platforms and these requirements are aimed at ensuring compatibility as well as saving money on IT support.

There are other developments that facilitate sharing between organizations, including the development of data warehousing, the World Wide Web, and software developments such as extensible markup language (XML). The purpose (Weinman, 2002: 10) of XML is to enable better interactivity between websites and databases. Data warehousing refers to the combination of hardware and software that allows an organization to set up a database that can integrate information from a wide variety of sources, such as legacy applications on mainframes, and allow for sophisticated analyses. Governments have made use of data warehouses and data marts to integrate data to meet the demands of the new welfare reform (Newcombe, 2000a). The World Wide Web allows easy sharing of information and the development of XML standard enhances this capability even further and has been explored as a device for sharing of parks' data in an experimental project entitled Government Without Boundaries (2003). A major advantage of XML-based sharing is that it does not necessarily require major changes to legacy and mainframe-based systems and thus is affordable in times of budget stress (Peterson, 2003). Thus it enables governments with disparate and even antiquated information systems to suc-cessfully exchange information in a manner that is minimally intrusive or disruptive.

In addition to the Government Without Boundaries (GWoB) project, there are efforts by other organizations to encourage shared systems and shared data among governments. For example, the National Association of State Chief Information Officers (NASCIO) has focused many of its efforts on achieving integration. In the human services, the U.S. General Accounting Office (U.S. GAO, 2002a) has encouraged efforts to integrate human services, such as to welfare recipients through integration of information systems of the agencies that provide services for them. The criminal justice area has long emphasized sharing and the online National Crime Information Center Computerized Criminal History (NCIC-CCH) was proposed in 1968 and the number and size of CCH record systems in criminal justice continue to grow (Laudon, 1986a; O'Shea, 1998). There are numerous other efforts at sharing criminal justice information, such as the Regional Information Sharing Systems (RISS) Program that has been funded by U.S. Department of Justice to share intelligence across jurisdictional boundaries (http://www.iir.com/riss/).

The growth of geographic information systems (GISs) also helps to spur sharing of information. Federal, state, and local governments have established numerous on-site sharing systems that organizations can use due to the existence of common geographic identifiers that serve as the "foreign keys" (common identifiers that allow the joining of two separate tables of data) to integrate all kinds of information from governmental organizations and the private sector. There is now an Open GIS Consortium (OGC) that is aimed at making sharing more effective. There are several examples of long-standing multiorganizational sharing of GIS data (e.g., Bamberger, 1995). The growth of so-called "open standards" makes sharing much easier. But the sharing that is done may be of a limited nature or, as one critic said, "low-level, stripped-out, dumbed-down conversion" (Robinson, 2003). Indeed, the most promising sharing is enabled by agreements between major private vendors due to commercial reasons (Robinson, 2003). The GIS movement has also spurred some of the most advanced examples of meta-data (information that describes key characteristics of data such as its source, date of creation, etc.) that assist users in finding data that meet their needs (Douglas, 2003) such as a "Geospatial One-Stop" where agencies can access data from other organizations throughout the U.S.

In short, the last few years have made the vision of almost universal, seamless, integrated information systems appear to be imminent. However, despite these strong forces that enable shared systems and data, there remain many forces that make sharing difficult and that is why I am writing this paper. First, we review research that has developed conceptual frameworks and theoretical models or propositions concerning sharing of IT in government. Then we study examples of sharing by organizing them into categories by types of organizations involved or by the type of sharing. Finally, we propose a new conceptual framework on sharing in government IT to guide future research. In studying sharing, I define the term broadly to include all significant forms of sharing related to IT, whether formal or informal in nature.

II. PREVIOUS RESEARCH ON INTERORGANIZATIONAL INFORMATION SHARING IN GOVERNMENT

I found little theoretical research that has focused on sharing of information between governmental organizations outside of the GIS area — the Onsrud and Rushton (1995) volume has several analytical chapters proposing frameworks concerning the sharing of GIS data. One major set of studies have been conducted by researchers at the Center for Technology in Government (CTG) at Albany, New York. These researchers have published a number of reports that we employ in our analysis below, with most of them focusing on sharing between state and local governments. The CTG researchers have developed a framework that identifies the obstacles to sharing as well as several prescriptions on how sharing can be enhanced. They identify key environmental factors that constrain effective state–local systems such as variation in state–local relations and local conditions (Dawes et al., 1997: 2). They point out that these factors can lead to inconsistent local participation, a tendency to create stand-alone systems and uneven participation in efforts to share. Their work (Dawes et al., 1997: 10) identifies the following set of barriers to state–local sharing:

1. A general lack of education and information about both technology and programs
2. Lack of a shared, reliable computing, and network infrastructure
3. Goals that are too ambitious for the resources available to achieve them
4. Human and organizational resistance to change
5. Unrealistic time frames

6. Organizational, programmatic, technological, and legal complexity
7. Changing priorities
8. Overlapping or conflicting missions among the participating organizations

The CTG researchers (Dawes et al., 1997: 21) have developed a number of prescribed "best practice" recommendations on how to facilitate sharing relationships between state and local governments, including the following:

1. The system is designed to integrate with the related systems and business processes of the affected organizations.
2. Standard definitions of key data need to be used by all participants.
3. Built-in safeguards assure system security and the confidentiality of sensitive or personal information.
4. The design adheres to commonly accepted industry standards and does not rely on proprietary technologies.
5. The design takes into account the current technical capabilities of the participating organizations.

They go on to identify user support features that would characterize the "ideal system" such as continuing user training and support as well as provision for local modification of the systems based on local needs (Dawes et al., 1997: 21). They identify a number of other "best practices" such as identifying existing models, use of a prototype approach to test out possible solutions, and frequent communication with stakeholders (Dawes et al., 1997: 11–12).

Brown and O'Toole (1998) compared the success of GISs in government, including single-unit operations with multidepartmental and interinstitutional arrangements at the local level. Their research was aimed at testing hypotheses as to whether shared systems were more expensive and less successful than single-unit operations. Their findings showed that the shared arrangements were not more expensive than single-unit GIS systems but that the interinstitutional systems did not achieve as high a level of success.

Laudon (1974: 143) conducted case studies that emphasized the importance of political obstacles to sharing, such as the fact that organizations seek to control information in order to serve "as an important boundary-maintaining device against potentially disruptive external inquiries." This author (Rocheleau, 1995, 1996) reviewed the literature on interorganizational and interdepartmental information sharing. Based on this review, I identified facilitating forces that encourage sharing, such as common goals and functions, legal mandates to share, political pressures to share, funding, and individual-reward incentives. I identified obstacles to sharing, including technological incompatibilities, privacy and other legal restrictions, and asymmetry of benefits. If there is perceived to be a substantial asymmetry, in which one unit benefits and another unit does not, then the less enthusiastic organization may resist or sabotage (e.g., by poor quality of data entry) the shared effort (see examples in Rocheleau, 1996). My review turned up examples of organizations that desire to maintain autonomy over their information due to "survival" and other political reasons similar to those discovered by Laudon (1974). In an empirical study of sharing of municipal data (Rocheleau, 1995) between the police department and other municipal departments, I found that sharing took place less often than expected among departments that shared some functions and common goals, such as police and fire. The research discovered that police shared most frequently with those departments that had the most formal authority and influence over them such as the central manager office and the finance department.

What can the public sector learn about sharing from research that has been conducted in the private sector? The work of Michael Porter (e.g., Porter and Millar, 1985) encouraged the view that information and information systems can help an organization to achieve a strategic advantage over competitors. This view would support a reluctance of organizations to share, at least with organizations that they view as competitors. Indeed, there are examples of companies where their technology has been integral to their success (e.g., Amazon) and consequently they refuse to share details about their information system. By way of contrast, governments do not have the same incentives to keep information about their successes private and thus this is one reason why the willingness to share information among governments may be greater than that of the private sector (Rocheleau and Wu, 2002). In addition, government information is subject to Freedom of Information Act and other laws (e.g., sunshine laws) that create a sense of living in a "fishbowl." Bozeman and Bretschneider (1986) noted the fishbowl quality of government information as being one of its key contrasts with private-sector information management in their model of public management information systems (MISs).

However, there is research to show that even competitor private organizations can and do share information and systems under certain circumstances. Carr (2003) has recently argued that, although technologies have been used to provide a competitive advantage at first, later on the technology (e.g., electricity) became more valuable when it was shared rather than used in isolation. Meier and Sprague (1991) point to several areas where sharing of information has become a strategic necessity, such as in the health care and travel industries. Likewise, Clemons and Knez (1988) point to the automated teller machines (ATMs) area as an example where it is more advantageous for private for-profit organizations to share than compete. However, research on private-sector interorganizational systems shows that they too encounter many obstacles (e.g., Boddy, 2000) and that in areas like community health (Payton, 2000), competition can be an important obstacle in some cases, though it varied from situation to situation. Kumar and Dissel (1996) identify different kinds of interorganizational systems (pooled information resources, value-supply-chain, and networked) that are related to the kind of interdependency relationship that exists among the organizations. They also point out that the successes of interorganizational systems are affected by the quest for dominance, clash of personalities, and organizational cultures (Kumar and Dissel, 1996: 289). The term interoperability (Institute of Electrical and Electronics Engineers, 1990; Landsbergen and Woken, 2001) has traditionally been referred to as the "engineering and technical requirements" used to design systems so they can work together effectively. However, previous research shows that neither in the public nor in the private sector are technological advancements and the emphasis on interoperability sufficient conditions to establish interorganizational sharing. Personal and organizational priorities often take precedence.

We will return to the research issues at the conclusion as we attempt to synthesize the results of our literature and identify the most promising research and theoretical approaches to sharing government IT.

III. METHODOLOGY

I conducted a broad literature review employing both traditional library searches as well as the use of Internet search engines to identify examples of interorganizational and intergovernmental information sharing. In addition to these literature searches, I also put out queries that contain a broad variety of government IT executives to an association: the Governmental Management Information Sciences (GMIS) organization. These queries resulted in several communications about sharing relationships in which they were involved and I have included these in the analysis below. I have also used some material based on semi-structured discussions with government employees who were guaranteed anonymity in order to encourage candor.

IV. FINDINGS

A. Sharing among Local Governments

The ultimate form of sharing occurs when the IT systems of two separate organizations merge to become one. One example is the city of Auburn, Alabama, where the city of Auburn provides all IT services for the school system as well as for the city (Buston, 2003). James C. Buston, Director of Information Technology for Auburn, puts the case for integration as follows:

> Whenever I talk about shared infrastructure, I use the following analogy. If you were the city and if I were to come to you and tell you that I needed separate roads. One road to go to schools only and one road to the city facilities only, you would tell me I was crazy. If I were to further request separate water systems and separate electrical system for schools and city buildings, you would know I was crazy. However, if I come to you and tell you that we need to provide separate data infrastructures, one for the city and one for the schools, you would hardly raise an eyebrow.

One of the few detailed descriptions of a governmental integration effort is provided by Hall (2001) in her description of an intergovernmental agreement in which the city of Douglas, Douglas County, and the Omaha/Douglas Public Building Commission con-tracted to purchase a shared enterprise resource planning (ERP) system. The initiating forces were the need to upgrade the financial systems in view of the upcoming Y2K crisis and the fact that ERP systems are very expensive and require substantial resources and that sharing would lighten the burden of acquiring and implementing such a complex and expensive system. The case study acknowledges conflict, such as the fact that the county IT director opposed any sort of outsourcing, and Hall describes the "politics" as being "intense" but the steering committee (made up of the heads of the different governments) decided to proceed anyway. In a recent note to me, Hall (2003) states that the two IT shops "formally merged under the umbrella of a non-profit corporation whose governing board reports to the County Board, City Council and Mayor."

Another model of integration is exemplified by the Local Government Information Systems Association (LOGIS) system that has served a number (24 in 1995) of munici-palities and certain other organizations in Minnesota. The cities and other agencies signed a "joint powers agreement" in which IT is controlled by a board of directors containing one representative (a nonelected official) from each organization (Norton, 1995: 43). An executive committee elected by the board has overview responsibility for the system while an executive director manages the organization on a daily basis (Norton, 1995: 43). LOGIS has a wide range of software applications that it offers, including financial, GIS, utility billing, human resources, among others. Members can choose which applications they want to use and they only pay for those they employ. Hardware, support, and training support are provided by the organization. What effect does LOGIS have on the need to have local IT staff? In a communication with this author, Garris (2003), the executive director of LOGIS, said that typically cities with a population of over 50,000 have three IT staff, those with 25,000 to 50,000 have two IT staff, and one IT coordinator suffices for those from 10,000 to 25,000. The role of the local IT staff is to support their local personal computers (PCs) and troubleshoot office applications, deal with printer problems, and do some of the city service administration tasks. LOGIS staff do work that requires network (e.g., Microsoft and Cisco) certified training and help to maintain the LOGIS wide area network (WAN) as well as the city servers. LOGIS application specialists provide help for financial, utility billing, public safety, and other applications. LOGIS allows a great deal of flexibility for participating organizations. LOGIS members can share via use of central-site or distributed processing. In 1995, the smallest municipality in LOGIS was Farmington with a population of 8000 and the largest population was Coon Rapids (59,945).

The above arrangements involved major forms of integration in which the IT units give up substantial degree of their autonomy over a wide range of applications. Another approach is sharing that involves more specific functions, specific applications, or hardware systems. For example, a group of northwest suburbs of Chicago have formed a GIS Consortium (http://www.giscon.org/). The key purposes of the consortium are to reduce risk and reduce costs (Thomey, 2003). The initial setup of the organization (GIS Consortium) heavily involved top administrators and it was definitely a "top-down" solution but they also have heavy involvement of a "second-tier" staff such as program directors or coordinators who are involved in consortium activities on a more regular basis (Thomey, 2003). The consortium has contracted with a private IT consulting firm that provides GIS technical staff to the participating municipalities. The cost sharing is based on a formula related to population size and density. The municipalities involved are generally small in size and most could not afford GIS staff on their own.

Indeed, the growth of GIS systems has spurred many data-sharing arrangements among state and local governments. Sharing of GIS information is not new by any means. Bamberger (1995) reports on the San Diego Regional Urban Information System (RUIS) that was established in 1984 to share costs among the city, county, and other governments and also private organizations that had overlapping interests in GIS data. For example, instead of spending huge amounts of money to build their base map, RUIS contracted to obtain the data from the San Diego Gas and Electric Company (SDG&E) in exchange for providing SDG&E with all updates and enhancements as well as a share in any sales of base map products to the private sector (Bamberger, 1995: 129). Bamberger points out that this agreement and other aspects of the sharing occurred only after a substantial degree of politics and pressure took place. RUIS initially adopted a decentralized approach to base map maintenance because it was the "path of least resistance" and would not upset "existing organizational structures" (Bamberger, 1995: 130). A more recent example is the Minneapolis–St. Paul's Metro GIS, which is a geodata collaborative (Landkamer, 2003). The metropolitan council, a regional agency responsible for collecting and treating wastewater and for the oversight of land use planning, spurred the effort to develop a regional GIS that includes public-sector, nonprofit, and private-sector organizations. The Metro GIS has a 12-member policy board made up of officials from key local governments and a policy board whose 25 members come from a variety of organizations (Landkamer, 2003). Landkamer (2003) points out that the structure of the agency is unusual in that it has "no formal legal standing" and participation is voluntary but that options to move toward a more formal setup have been rejected in favor of the *ad hoc* arrangement.

In some cases, local governments can use their combined market to develop more favorable contracts with IT consulting firms than would otherwise be possible. For example, in one case, several small municipalities have developed a contract with a consulting firm in which the firm gives it a favorable price for IT consultants. Several of these municipalities lack any IT staff at all and the joint contract has provided better access to needed expertise. This is an example of the sharing of resources to leverage a better contract but the local IT systems remain independent of one another.

There are many examples of sharing arrangements limited to specific functional areas such as computer-aided dispatch systems where local governments provide funding for shared operations. In many cases, the IT department of one unit of government will provide Computer Aided Despatch (CAD) and other systems to other units of government. For example, the city of Reno provides a computer-aided dispatch and other systems (e.g., police records management) to other units of government such as the Washoe County (Vandenberg, 2003). In the GIS area, in addition to the city of Reno and the Washoe County, a private-sector company, the Sierra Pacific Power Company, cooperates in obtaining orthophotos and parcel database maintenance. There are many examples of sharing of data centers, such as has occurred in Mecklenberg County, North Carolina, and the city of Charlotte. Their partnership began with colocation of a common facility in 1988, progressed to a shared mainframe in 1993, and a consolidated mainframe data center under the county in 1996, and then progressed to competitive bidding in 1999 as forced by the city (Pinkard, 2003). Perlman (2001) describes how Palo Alto, California, performs six services for East Palo Alto, a smaller city with fewer resources. Palo Alto has hired additional staff and is interested in becoming a "government service provider" and developing contracts with other agencies. Of course, this sharing is voluntary and I know of cases where small local governments have approached larger governments and been refused. We lack longitudinal studies of these types of arrangements. It will be interesting to compare such "government service provider" arrangements with the success of private vendor services to local government.

B.   Criminal Justice Sharing Efforts: Local–Local and State–Local Efforts

1.   Criminal justice agencies have been sharing information for decades in a variety of intergovernmental relations. A NASCIO (2003: 22) report identifies different types of sharing that take place among criminal justice agencies:

1.   Query (and receive a response) local, regional, state, and national databases.
2.   Push operational information from one agency to another based on actions taken regarding subjects or cases by the sending agency.
3.   Pull operational information from another agency based on actions the other agency has taken regarding subjects or cases.
4.   Publish operational information on key transactions and events regarding subjects, events, cases in traditional (e.g., paper and electronic) media.
5.   Subscribe/notify key transactions and events regarding subjects, events, and cases.

Thus push and pull technologies are useful ways for governments to share information with others as well as with their customers without engaging in spam. For example, in the push technology approach, a citizen will register to receive certain types of information such as through e-mail or phone (Hibbard, 1997; Poulakos, 2002).

Sharing in the criminal justice area appears to take time to develop and formal sharing is preceded by much informal sharing. For example, sharing in Harris County, Texas (includes the city of Houston), began in 1977 by creating the Harris County Justice Information System and it grew incrementally and now has a board that includes members of all county agencies and courts. The conclusion of the CTG's (1999) study of criminal justice information systems is as follows:

> In many cases, informal networking forms a key component of integration. There are many potential interested parties in any integration initiative. Their collaboration requires much communication and ongoing opportunity for interaction. Informal networks and other opportunities for joint effort are often necessary and effective in moving integration forward.

A study by O'Shea (1998) examined sharing of information between police officers of the Chicago Police Department; the communities they police echoes the CTG studies' conclusions with regard to the importance of trust. With regard to community policing, O'Shea cites one officer who said that some police officers tried to develop a trusting relationship with community residents while other police officers tried to maintain a distance. This officer (O'Shea, 1998: 91–92) found that trust was the key to gaining information from community residents:

> I know people on my post by their first name and they know me. I'm not out there looking for information from them. I sit and visit . . . .They're looking for someone they can trust to help. Once they see you as a person who cares and isn't just passing through you get more information than you can use.

As for sharing among police officers themselves, the willingness to share depends on whether the officers who share information will get credit in the official personnel system for sharing. If they do not, then no more information will be shared as one officer described it (O'Shea, 1998: 91):

> They are not going to tell us anything that might screw up their pinch. The only way to get anything is to get it from someone that trusts you and you make sure his name goes on the arrest report. But screw him once and that's the last you'll get from him.

Laudon (1986b) found that police had more confidence in local than in state or federal systems and the importance of people-to-people communications. Laudon also points out that the justice information systems lacked the "self-correcting" nature of financial systems in which outside auditors as well as customers studying their bills provide mechanisms for identifying and correcting poor quality data.

C.   State–Local (Including Private Providers) Systems

The CTG studied the attempt to build a homeless information system in New York City that included a variety of state and local government agencies as well as many private nonprofit organizations that delivered the actual services to the homeless. The original plan had been to use a "canned commercial system" but that plan was abandoned because the information from such a system would not be useful to the case managers (CTG, 2000). The nonprofit providers were concerned that the Bureau of Shelter Services would set performance goals unrealistically high. Indeed, it was found that agreement had to be negotiated even on key concepts such as "admit date" of the client because these basic terms were open to different interpretations and different actors had an interest in how they were defined. CTG researchers concluded that contextual knowledge was crucial and that the system designers need to understand how data were collected, again implying the sharing of informal, qualitative information in order to understand how the system "really works." The CTG researchers' major conclusion is reflected in the title of their publication, *Building Trust before building a system: the Making of the Homeless Information Systems*. It is necessary for the organizations engaged in sharing the information to "trust" one another if the system is to work. Thus technical issues such as whether to use an "SQL server or data warehouse" were set aside for the time being in order to achieve this trust.

Dawes et al. (1997) outline several sharing arrangements that exist between New York State and its local governments concerning state–local information systems. Based on the description of Dawes et al. (1997) it appears that in several of their cases such as the Aging Network Client Based Service Management System, the Probation Automation Project, and the Real Property System, the systems are essentially state systems with active efforts to solicit input from local governments at the start of the projects and to provide for ongoing communications thereafter. The state realized in cases such as the Local Social Services Imaging Project that the system needed to integrate with the systems at the local level and they attempted to accomplish this task by making sure that the system was compatible with "as many mainstream hardware and software standards as possible" (Dawes et al., 1997: 62). Thus this form of sharing involves giving input opportunities as to the goals and needs of local organizations so that the state system may be more responsive as well as attempting to facilitate by use of standard platforms. It is undoubtedly the case that much sharing of informal information (e.g., about organizational and political issues and obstacles) takes place as a result of these consultation efforts. For example, Dawes et al. (1997: 52) discuss the automation by the state of probation information. County probation directors provided guidance for the design of the state system but these local officials had problems finding money in their own budgets to travel to the meetings so the state paid travel expenses and received the benefits of the expertise of these officials and also undoubtedly helped to cement local support for the state project and spur the kinds of informal communication necessary to build trust and the willingness to share crucial information.

D. State to State and Interdepartmental Sharing within States

Many states are attempting to build more integrated systems that avoid information silos among their departments. Information silos refer to the situation in which each department organizes its information for its internal use and does not give attention to other outside users, thus making sharing of information difficult. Utah has developed an e-government council to set priorities for major IT projects and one of the goals is to encourage cross-agency IT projects (Perlman, 2003). Governor Leavitt's approach was to use his power to push a top-down solution. One of their first major projects involved the creation of unified systems for dealing with eligibility determinations concerning

Temporary Assistance to Needy Families (TANF), Medicaid, child care, and Food Stamps. The three state agencies involved established a written agreement on what resources as well as staff they will contribute (Perlman, 2003). The initial funding of the system was simple because it used TANF funds, which is a block grant that the state is able to use in a flexible manner, but the article notes that agreement from other federal agencies is difficult when monies from different programs (e.g., Food Stamps) are mixed together because it requires efforts to trace how monies are used and to trace if they are used for the purposes intended by that particular program. Such interagency systems also may require the approval of several legislative committees and the project must be sold to all of these committees as making business sense — it is not just a simple IT matter (Perlman, 2003).

Perlman (2003) also points to *shallow solutions* employed by presenting web pages of information to users that give the impression of integrated information while the data actually reside on separate backend servers. Pennsylvania uses this approach in their website to allow businesses to fill out one form to register with three different agencies (Perlman, 2003). The U.S. GAO (2002a: 2–3) likewise found states using *integration by screens* to assist in integration efforts:

> To enhance service integration, the state initiatives are making data from different programs available to case managers and, in some cases, to program applicants using a single computer screen. For example, New Jersey's One Ease-E Link initiative provides hardware and software to counties so they can create county-level networks comprised of a multitude of public and private service providers, including nonprofit agencies. The Internet-based system enables these providers to share recipient information using case management software and assess applicants' program eligibility by using an eligibility-screening tool.

The shallow solution appears to avoid many difficult organizational problems because the databases do not actually have to be merged (hence the term "shallow" integration) and these shallow approaches may become more prevalent with the development of XML.

Some states (and other governments) are sharing applications and code. Swope (2003) describes a case in which Kansas used a program to manage grants to school districts by using code that Missouri had given them. In this particular case, the Missouri application did virtually everything that was needed by Kansas, with only a few gaps (Swope, 2003). Kansas hired the same vendor that had developed the Missouri system to fill in these few gaps (Swope, 2003). According to Perlman (2001), Arizona is now running Hawaii's Medicaid information system, with the Hawaii data residing on the computers in Arizona. Hawaii paid Arizona $11 million for the initial system and will also pay for processing time. Hawaii will share in the cost for modifications of the system as well (Perlman, 2001). There is a proposal to create a nationwide software component sharing system for governments (Perlman, 2001).

There are also examples of where the borrowing of systems has led to problems. There are examples from the child support mandate by the federal government that states replicate systems created by other states. Perlman (1998) cites an example of North Carolina modeling its system on Virginia's but discovering that the processes underlying the system differed and led to basic problems, such as the inability to reconcile bank records with the state database (Perlman, 1998). Likewise, a study of children's information systems by U.S. GAO (2003: 40) found that Iowa did not save any money by borrowing because the maintenance of the borrowed systems "takes just as much money as building them."

E. Federal–State Intergovernmental Sharing

Human services is an area where a potentially large number of organizations are often involved in serving one consumer or a family unit. Consequently, the potential for information systems sharing among various human services systems (e.g., Medicaid, Food Stamps, TANF, and job training) is great. Most of these programs are intergovernmental in nature, with the federal government providing funding and setting certain rules and guidelines and the state governments administering the programs on a day-to-day basis. The realization of the potential for information sharing is not new. Indeed, the idea to use information systems to help integrate human services dates back to the 1970s, when the movement for integrated human services first developed and there were attempts to make the information system a key force for integrating these services so that consumers of human service programs would receive better services such as through integrated intake processing. But a recent assessment of integration efforts by Ragan (2003a: 62) concluded that "human service information systems are more often viewed by local staff as a barrier" to integration.

It is instructive to look at some selected areas of human services to identify the reasons why the growth of successful sharing has been so difficult. The nature of these intergovernmental systems is that each state has a unique human services system. Indeed, over the past generation, the general movement of intergovernmental programs has been to devolve more and more authority to the states, and thus it is impossible for the federal government to set up a single system for any of these programs. Certainly, the idea that it is impossible to implement a single system that "fits all sizes" for complex intergovernmental programs like TANF is true. Yet, the federal government does need to gather aggregate data about overall TANF program and monitor the program's successes and failures. Thus the federal government must create a hybrid system at the federal level by integrating data from the 50 states. How does the federal government design a system that will meet its own needs when there is so much state-to-state variation in both the programs and the information systems? The approach of the federal government is to require that the states provide data and meet standards and requirements set by the federal government.

The TANF program established by the 1996 Welfare Reform illustrates the complexity of intergovernmental information systems. In this program, the federal government set rules and guidelines for the program but the program is decentralized and run by state governments on a day-to-day basis. States have extensive control over the program and devolution meant that the states have responsibility for design of many key elements of the program. There are general federal rules that must be adhered to such as the 5-year time limit that individuals can be on total welfare and the requirement that TANF recipients cannot be in the program for more than 2 consecutive years, though states can implement more rigorous time limits if they wish. The predecessor program, Aid to Families with Dependent Children (AFDC), had no such time limitations and the focus of the previous information system was structured around a yearly time frame. Thus the changeover to the TANF system requires that state systems now be able to provide a longitudinal analysis of clients, which makes for a major change in the structure of the information system. Likewise, the federal requirements necessitate that states gather information on clients who have moved from other states to learn how much total time and for how many consecutive months they have been receiving TANF benefits. Thus interstate sharing is required.

The federal government also sets goals for the hours of work and the percent of recipients who will be engaged in work-related activities. The federal government requires that the states provide information on state compliance with these rules. The federal government also provides incentives to states that excel on certain performance indicators, and states must report to the federal government their success on these measures. The TANF program also has complex relationships with other programs such as Medicaid, Food Stamps, and "support services" for TANF clients such as transportation and child care. Indeed, the relationship between the TANF program and these other programs proved problematic as there was concern that many citizens incorrectly lost both Medicaid and Food Stamp benefits as a result of initial implementation of the reform and the inadequacies of the state information systems (U.S. GAO, 2002a: 7).

The limitations of the older IT state systems are revealed by the fact that many states had to revert to "manual processes to prevent eligibles from losing Medicaid coverage" (Ragan, 2003b). The persistence of this problem, as Ragan (2003b) notes, is indicated by the fact that 5 years after the reform, the federal government is still sending states guidance on this issue. In such an intergovernmental system, what ability does the primary funding agency (the federal government) have over the recipients of funding (the state governments) to ensure that they take corrective actions. Basically, there are three methods (Ragan, 2003b):

1. They can provide positive enticements to the states by providing enhanced funding for the development of better systems.
2. The federal government can employ on-site reviews that can identify weaknesses and require improvements.
3. The federal government can rely on legal cases brought by advocates against the state government's handling of cases.

But, as Ragan and others (e.g., Derthick, 1975) have noted, the federal government is generally very reluctant to cut off funding for such programs so threats are used sparingly and are not enforced often.

Although the picture painted by GAO and Ragan suggests that the federal government is lax in its implementation of federal standards for information systems, some view the states as being unfairly penalized by inflexible federal standards. For example, the federal government denied funding to the North Carolina system because it was not *statewide* but North Carolina argued against the federal definition of statewide because some wealthy counties did much more than the minimum required by the state or the federal government. Cox (2001) of North Carolina argues that the federal role should be oversight in setting strategic objectives but letting the states decide how to meet these.

An interesting point made by another GAO report is that systems developed at the state level often do not meet the needs of local officials (U.S. GAO, 2000; Nathan and Ragan, 2001). Similarly, the attempt to build a statewide child welfare system in California was resisted by the local governments and many argued that it was not "feasible" to build a centralized system but rather they needed "a variety of systems that" could "interface with one another" (Daniels, 1997). A study by Hahm et al. (1995) of a Texas State property inventory system found similarly that the system was designed for a particular set of end users and that the needs of people who are viewed as the "primary users." Another study of 15 states conducted by the U.S. GAO of welfare systems (Sherill, 2001) asked to what extent state and local managers were able to obtain needed to perform their jobs. Sixty-seven percent (10 of 15) of state mangers vs. only 40% (6 of 15) of local managers agreed that the system provided most or all of the information required. The general implication from these experiences appears to be that the level of government that controls the design of the system fashions it to meet its own needs and pays less attention to the need of other organizations involved. This is supported by a U.S. GAO (2003b: 11) study of GIS sharing that explains why local governments have little interest in spending money and effort to share with the federal government:

> Existing commercial products using a variety of formats are already meeting the needs of states and localities in providing … information. Hence these organizations are likely to have little incentive to adopt potentially incompatible federal stands that could require substantial new investments. According to Arizona's state cartographer, many local governments currently do not comply with FGDC [Federal Geographic Data Committee] standards because most of their GIS applications were created primarily to meet their *internal* [emphasis added] needs, with little concern for data sharing with federal systems.

A related finding of Sherrill (2001) is that different data needs exist among different categories of users. Case managers need information on individual clients and it has to be "real time" if it is to be effective (Sherrill, 2001: 8–10). Program oversight officials need aggregate data on program performance. So sharing may be successful in meeting one group of users but fail to meet others' needs. Although the terms intergovernmental and interorganizational information systems would seem to imply that at least some of the needs of all parties are met to some degree, the actual degree to which information systems fulfill needs of users is an open question. When some governments are participating solely due to legal issues or funding pressures, important needs may not be met.

The job training programs initiated by the Workforce Investment Act (WIA) illustrate another attempt by the federal government to use information systems to integrate services and spur better performance by state and local agencies. A primary vehicle used to achieve better performance is to provide "one-stop shopping" for consumers that state information systems gather and report performance to the federal government (Department of Labor in this case). In order to be successful, this popular one-stop shopping approach requires service coordination and sharing of information. But the U.S. GAO (2002b: 28) in a review of WIA found that gathering and reporting information had the opposite effect on the program:

> The system's narrow focuses on program outcomes for a limited number of participants misses a key requirement of WIA to support the movement toward a coordinated system. In fact, the measures may focus the opposite — a siloed approach that encourages competition and limits their cooperation.

Consequently, the shared accountability information had some undesirable goal displacement effects, leading some programs to ignore certain groups of consumers (e.g., those that would result in poor performance results) and also leading to competition among local programs for desirable recipients and less willingness to refer consumers to other more appropriate programs. Thus the sharing of information between levels of government may or may not lead to the achievement of better integrated services, depending on how the key actors (usually the local service providers) react to these information requirements.

Federal government monitoring of nursing homes provides a third example of intergovernmental human services information systems. The states collect data on nursing homes but these data are fed into a federal Medicaid case-mix reimbursement system that determines the amount of funding that will be received by the states and nursing homes (U.S. GAO, 2002c). The GAO found that the states were not accurately recording harm done to patients and that one of the reasons was the lack of clear definition of harm that federal guidance on this key definition contributed to the problem (U.S. GAO, 2002b). The GAO found that separate on-site interviews were important to assuring accuracy of data and that interviews with nursing home personnel familiar with the resident provided valuable information. But most states did not conduct such reviews but relied on "off-site" data provided by the nursing homes. GAO also reported that the timing of the nursing home reviews was crucial (U.S. GAO, 2002b). If state reviews were too predictable, the facilities were able to hide problems. Finally, GAO reports that the Health Care Finance Administration (HCFA) rarely sanctioned the homes that harmed patients, and thus the reporting system did not have its intended effect of protecting patients from harm. In general, it appears difficult for the federal government to effectively monitor the quality of the data provided to them by states in the human services area where there is a lack of "self-correcting" mechanisms (e.g., a customer who protests an inaccurate bill). Also, this example shows that qualitative information such as face-to-face interviews and in-person visits to facilities is crucial to checking the validity of quantitative measures concerning important and sensitive measures of outcomes.

The implementation of statewide child welfare automation provides still another example of the difficulties of designing and implementing federal–state intergovernmental information systems. The development of these systems has taken well over a decade (U.S. GAO, 2003) and remains problematic and thus is instructive for our purposes. States have the option of developing their own systems or of receiving matching federal funds. If states took federal funds, it was expected that they would utilize models of other states that had already developed systems in order to save time and resources. The state systems were required to meet standards established by the federal government. As with the nursing home case, the states did not believe that they received clear guidance from the federal government on issues related to data quality. Some states such as Vermont did not join the federal matching effort because they viewed the federal requirements as too restrictive and not relevant to their efforts (U.S. GAO, 2003). Cuddy (2001) argues that the federal approach to intergovernmental systems is outdated because it assumes that system development is linear and sequential and imposes heavy paperwork and reporting requirements whenever changes need to be made to the original plan while new system development approaches are "fast-moving and flexible" and constantly changing to meet user needs.

The borrowing of other state systems proved to be problematic for some states such as New York and Colorado because their own systems and problems did not match up with the borrowed systems and system sharing led to more problems than would have been the case if they had developed systems on their own. The quality of the data, as with all systems, is dependent on the street-level "bureaucrats," in this case, the caseworkers who input the data. The states want the system to mirror their own processes but processes vary from state to state. For example, Iowa divides child welfare work between child abuse neglect investigations and ongoing case management processes. Thus, system development is a difficult task because it requires that the developers have a deep understanding of the work processes of the end users, but there was high turnover among the private vendor staff that developed many of the state systems. One lesson learned is that a relatively successful approach to the development of systems was the encouragement of user groups. These groups freely exchanged a great deal of information that facilitated success. The reporting needs of states differ from those of the federal government and these differences affect the reliability of the data (U.S. GAO, 2003: 24):

> ... 36 of the 50 states ... reported that technical challenges, such as matching their state data element definitions to HHS's data categories, affected the quality of the data that they report to the federal government ... . In cases where state policy differs from federal policy, state officials must carefully reformat their data in order to meet federal reporting requirements.

Agreement on basic definitions is also a problem. For example, how does one count the number of times a child moves while in foster care? This can be a crucial number because it is often assumed that a large number of moves is undesirable and reflects negatively on the agency. But there is variation in how states reported the number of movements. For example, the states claim that the federal government in some places instructs them to count as a move "anytime a child sleeps in a different place" and in other cases, the federal government excludes "runaways" and "trial home visits" from contributing to the number of movements (U.S. GAO, 2003: 29).

Another point raised by the federal–state intergovernmental systems is the crucial role played by software vendors and private agencies that deliver the services. Much of the software development at all levels of government is done by private vendors and their strengths and limitations affect the quality of the systems they develop and thus they must be considered, in effect, as part of the intergovernmental system. Likewise, many of the services delivered by federal and state programs are done by private service provider organizations (both nonprofit and for-profit) and they in effect become the end users of intergovernmental information systems and part of the information system even though they are not government employees.

F. Informal Sharing

There is a tremendous amount of informal sharing of information among IT professionals in governments. In the IT listservs that are aimed at governments such as that of the GMIS and the Innovations Group, members share their experiences with hardware, software, and a variety of issues. Request for proposals (RFPs) and other documents are also freely shared. Indeed, informal sharing may even include code of applications written by one government that another government can use.

This informal sharing may remain entirely informal and may exist among governments that are near to one another or face common problems. The informal sharing may be encouraged and even, to some extent, organized by the formation of formal groups whose purpose is, in effect, to share their expertise. Examples of attempts to build these *communities of practice* include special-interest groups formed by the Federal CIO Council. A community of practice refers to people who share an interest in a topic, issue, or problem. The community can be within a single organization or could exist across organizational boundaries. It could be based entirely on face-to-face or phone conversations, or both, but it is now customary to "digitize their exchanges" via listservs, online discussion boards, or other forms of digital communication (Newcombe, 2000b; Schwen and Noriko, 2003). It is difficult to overestimate the importance of informal sharing as IT professionals and others are able to obtain valuable information that would likely be expensive, time-consuming, and perhaps even impossible to get through formal channels or contracts with consultants.

V.   A FRAMEWORK FOR STUDYING SHARING RELATIONSHIPS

In attempting to define sharing relationships, I begin with two ideal-type situations to identify the extremes of sharing and lack of sharing among systems. In one case, let us imagine two organizations that are legally separate entities but that have completely merged their information systems so that hardware, software, and data are totally shared, including even informal information that is not available on the computerized systems. In the second case, let us conceive of two organizations that exist in the same environment but for whatever reasons do not share any hardware, software, or even swap information of any kind, whether formal or informal. We can use these two extremes to conceive of sharing as representing points on a continuum between total sharing and total nonsharing.

This is a useful mechanism because it allows us to study degrees of sharing as a variable — it is not an "all-or-nothing" kind of phenomenon. IT sharing can involve a number of different elements. First, organizations can share hardware, including computers, servers, networks, fiber, etc. We have pointed out a number of such cases, with hardware sharing being particularly common among local governments whose jurisdictions overlap or are geographically close. Second, they can share software applications. We saw examples of this where the sharing was voluntary and involuntary such as in child welfare development case where the federal government established requirements for sharing. Third, they may share IT personnel, as illustrated in the GIS Consortium in Illinois. Fourth, they may share funding. The sharing of funding can take on complexities as in the Illinois case where several small municipalities banded together to achieve a favorable contract with a private vendor for IT services, and thus their systems remained separate. Fifth, organizations can share the formal information that resides in their IT systems such as reports and databases. As we saw in several of the federal–state intergovernmental systems, it is impossible for there to be a single system and thus the approach of the federal government is to establish information requirements and standards (e.g., concerning data reliability and privacy) to which the states are supposed to adhere. Sixth, they can share informal information that is nondigitized, which can include information about matters such as values, procedures, and political and organizational issues that they may be reluctant to commit to print or digital form. We pointed to listservs aimed at government IT professionals such as GMIS and Innovations Group but informal sharing among governments is, I believe, hugely important but has been largely ignored as a research topic.

Sharing then is complex and can take many forms and can help to achieve a degree of integration among information systems. In order to assess the state of sharing or integration among two or more systems, I propose that the dimensions given in Figure 5.1 be studied:

When I first began this research, when I used the terms interorganizational and intergovernmental information sharing, I conceived of sharing as referring to cases

Hardware resources: _|_____|_
                    No sharing   Total integration of hardware

Software resources: _|_____|_
                    No sharing   Total integration of software

Personnel resources: _|_____|_
                    No sharing   Total integration of IT personnel

Formal information: _|_____|_
                    No sharing   Total sharing of formal information

Informal information: _|_____|_
                    No sharing   Total sharing of informal information

Figure 5.1   Sharing and integration of IT resources between organizations.

there were hardware or software systems involved. It seemed to me that such sharing was needed to constitute a true interorganizational information system. However, as I progressed in my research on sharing, I realized that much of the sharing that exists does not involve formal systems at all but that these other forms of sharing can nevertheless be extremely important to the organizations involved and in my view need to be incorporated into an overall model of sharing.

Three other dimensions that appears to me to be important is the extent to which sharing is voluntary, the degree to which power over sharing is equal among the organizations involved, and the sensitivity of the information to be shared (see Figure 5.2). To what extent does one organization dominate? If one organization dominates, it may speed formal integration and make sharing easier, though it also may create resentment and passive resistance among the other organizations. Much of the literature on interorganizational systems has focused on voluntary efforts where it is extremely important that each organization be given its due and treated equally. Agranoff and Lindsay (1983: 236) studied several successful intergovernmental bodies and conclude that it is important that the autonomy of each be respected, that each have a feeling of joint ownership and stake, and that the relationships be "non-hierarchic, non-systematic, and non-superior-subordinate in nature." In some of the cases above (e.g., the Illinois GIS case), it appears that such a nonhierarchical relationship is practiced. But in several of cases cited above, such as the federal–state and state–local examples, there is a clear dominance of one actor over others due to factors such as legal authority, control over funding, control over expertise, and other resources. The degree of symmetry in costs and benefits is a related issue and most likely overlaps the autonomy issue. In our review,

_|_____|_
One organization dominates   Organizations equal role in decision-making
_|_____|_
Asymmetric benefit to cost ratio perceived Symmetric benefit to cost ratio perceived
_|_____|_
Information is perceived as highly sensitive Information is perceived as nonthreatening
_|_____|_
Trust lacking between sharing organizations Strong trust exists between sharing organizations

Figure 5.2   Key factors that influence sharing relationships.

we saw the tendency of the dominant organization in sharing. Asymmetry of benefits may also engender active or passive resistance on the part of the weaker units if they believe they are not getting a worthwhile return for their efforts.

Another implication of our analysis is that some data are especially sensitive because they affect funding or may be perceived as reflecting on the quality, effectiveness, and efficiency of services rendered. The development of sharing concerning sensitive data will be especially difficult. Agranoff and Lindsay (1983) in their study of intergovernmental management noted that these organizations often "avoided the most sensitive issues" such as program evaluations and threats of elimination of services. It appears that successful sharing is much easier when it does not involve information that could be perceived to have a big impact on issues such as funding and evaluation. Many of the successful case studies described by Dawes et al. (1997) appear to be of a nonthreatening nature while the cases where sensitive data were involved (e.g., the CTG homeless case and the GAO studies of child welfare and nursing home abuse) concern very sensitive issues and thus the difficulties are much greater. Legal mandates and funding incentives may be needed to force sharing of sensitive information. For example, Sherrill (2001: 9) reports that most of the linkages established between TANF (the new welfare program) and other programs existed where there was either a federal mandate or funding incentives and that desirable linkages that did not have mandates or funding incentives had not been established. The movement to put performance data such as "organizational report cards" on the Internet for accountability purposes is becoming common and is required in some situations, such as those concerning school performance (Gormely and Weimer, 1999). Organizations are likely to want to exert more control over how such sensitive information is presented (Rocheleau, 2002).

The above case studies showed that the development of successful voluntary sharing relationships usually takes a long period of development and necessitates a good degree of trust among the sharing organizations. Often, the sharing develops incrementally from informal and limited types of sharing to more extensive efforts and formalized efforts. Trust appears to be strongly influenced by face-to-face contact and the opportunity for informal sharing prior to formal sharing. Undoubtedly, e-mail exchanges, even though they are digital, over time may now substitute for some of the old phone or face-to-face contact. Of course, many intergovernmental systems, such as those involved in human services, are necessary and mandated and thus tend to be developed without the time to develop the informal knowledge, trust, and recognition of the other actor's needs that characterizes voluntary sharing efforts. As a consequence, mandated intergovernmental systems have encountered many problems.

VI. CONCLUSION

Overall, the degree of sharing has greatly improved over the last decade due to the development of hardware and software standards as well as the development of the Internet and other forms of networking such as intranets. Moreover, organizations now view information as a strategic asset and are attempting to create enterprise-wide systems that make sharing easy. These same developments also create the possibility for easier sharing between organizations.

Nevertheless, our review shows that technological developments are not sufficient to assure successful sharing. Interorganizational and intergovernmental sharing of IT resources are important and complex phenomena that have received little attention by researchers. Successful sharing requires that each organization understand the other's organization, its culture, and its procedures. The system developers need to understand the processes of the system's end users and this takes deep knowledge that can only be obtained by open sharing by the end users or by participant observation. The importance of understanding processes is true whether system development is intraorganizational or interorganizational, and this point has been emphasized by organizations such as Wal-Mart according to a recent story (Schrage, 2003):

> He [Wal-Mart's then-CIO] told me that before Wal-Mart's people actually write and deploy an app, they make the developer's work in the job the app is being written to support. If Wal-Mart devices a new point-of-sale system, for example, software members have to spend time working the cash registers first.

The same need to achieve deep understanding of the processes exists in governmental interorganizational systems but the complexity is far greater given the fact that the developers are "outsiders" and will not be trusted to the same extent as organizational members. There are additional problems such as the fact that the vendor IT employees who actually develop the systems often have high turnover rates. Likewise, the end users at the bottom of the human services system are often private-sector employees, such as employees of nursing homes funded by the Medicaid program or child welfare workers in nonprofit human service organizations who minister to abused children. In short, both the designers and end users in today's so-called "intergovernmental information systems" in the human services area are often private-sector employees. The governmental role in human services is to provide funding and oversight, and to integrate the information in order to evaluate services and provide for accountability to the public.

Federal-state nursing home, child welfare, and work training cases suggest that in order to be effective in achieving its goals, an intergovernmental information system needs to have clear definitions of key concepts and measures understood by all parties. Second, the sharing must mesh well with the personnel and funding systems and rewards of the organization. Examples like the Chicago Police Department and WIA cases suggest that the personnel systems and funding of the organizations involved must reward sharing or, no matter how advanced the hardware and software involved, the system is likely to be ineffective due to overt or passive resistance (e.g., the provision of missing or poor quality data).

Most importantly, governments need to gather a variety of types of information and not rely on one source (particularly if this single source is likely to have a bias). In many of the examples cited above, it is clear that qualitative information such as through interviews with direct-service providers is key to detecting problems concerning sensitive issues such as harm to patients. Despite the tremendous growth in digitized information systems, qualitative data are absolutely essential to obtaining deep knowledge about important issues but the role of qualitative data has been largely neglected by information researchers whose enthusiasm for digital systems has blinded them to need for other types of information. In my view, the gathering and use of qualitative data should be an integral part of information management if it is to be effective.

In the last decade, sharing of IT resources among governments has become a common goal but there is little serious empirical research concerning this phenomenon in the public sector. In attempting to identify sources for this article, I relied heavily on a few sources, such as studies done by the CTG, the U.S. GAO, and news articles from *Governing Magazine*, and *Government Technology*. We need in-depth research that follows sharing relationships through time. We need to develop some common measures to determine the degree of sharing and integration. We also need in-depth comparative qualitative studies to examine the impact of variation in key aspects of sharing such as the degree of symmetry of costs and benefits. Much of the literature, such as that of the CTG (e.g., Dawes and Prefontaine, 2003), has focused on "collaborative efforts" that are voluntary in nature and often do not involve highly sensitive information. The most challenging and important sharing is often that which is mandatory and related to highly sensitive information such as performance evaluation. In short, the exploration of IT sharing needs a great deal of development.

REFERENCES

Agranoff, R., Lindsay, V.A., Intergovernmental management: perspectives from human services problem-solving at the local level, *Pub. Adm. Rev.*, 43, 227–237, 1983.

Bamberger, W.J., Sharing geographic information among local government agencies in the San Diego region, in *Sharing Geographic Information*, Onsrud, J.H. and Rushton, G., Eds., Center for Urban Policy Research, Rutgers University, New Brunswick, NJ, 1995, pp. 119–137.

Boddy, D., Implementing interorganizational IT systems: lessons from a call centre project, J. *Inf. Technol.*, 15, Part 1, 29–38, 2000.

Bozeman, B. and Bretschneider, S., Public management information systems: theory and prescription, *Pub. Adm. Rev.*, 46, 475–487, 1986.

Brown, M.M. and O'Toole, L.J., Implementing information technology in government: an empirical assessment of the role of local partnerships, J. *Pub. Adm. Res. Theo.*, 8, 499–525, 1998.

Buston, J.C., personal communication (e-mail), 9/9/2003.

Carr, N.G., It doesn't matter, *Harv. Bus. Rev.*, 81, 41–49, 2003.

Center for Technology in Government (CTG), Reconnaissance Study: Developing a Business Case for the Integration of Criminal Justice Information, 1999
http://www.ctg.albany.edu/projects/doj
Retrieved on 1/6/2002.

Center for Technology in Government (CTG), *Building Trust before Building a System: The Making of the Homeless Information Systems*, Center for Technology in Government, Albany, NY, 2000
http://www.ctg.albany.edu/projects/hims
Retrieved on 12/7/2000.

Clemons, E.K. and Knez, M., Competition and cooperation in information systems innovation, *Inf. Manage.*, 15(1), 25–35, 1988.

Cox, B., Reengineering Business Process to Integrate the Delivery of Human Services in North Carolina, paper prepared for the Conference on Modernizing Information Systems for Human Services, Reston, VA, June 28–29, 2001.

Cuddy, J., Re-engineering the Approach by which the Federal Government Approves and Monitors the Creation of State Human Services Information Systems, paper prepared for the Conference on Modernizing Human Information Systems for Human Services, Reston, VA, June 28–29, 2001
http://www.gao.gov/special.pubs/GAO-02-121/ap4.pdf
Retrieved on 10/3/2003.

Daniels, A., The Child Support Computer Meltdown, *Governing Magazine*, September, 1997
http://www.governing.com/archive/1997/sep/child.txt
Retrieved on 8/7/2003.

Dawes, S.S., Pardo, T.A., Green, D.E., McInemey, C.R., Connelly, D.R., and DiCaterino, A., *Tying a Sensible Knot: A Practical Guide to State-Local Information Systems*, Center for Technology in Government, Albany, NY, 1997
http://www.ctg.albany.edu/publications/guides/tying
Retrieved on 8/12/2003.

Dawes, S.S. and Prefontaine, L., Undertanding new models of collaboration for delivering governments services, *Comm. ACM*, 46, 40–42, 2003.

Derthick, M., *Uncontrollable Spending for Social Services*, The Brookings Institution, Washington, D.C., 1975.

Douglass, M., One-Stop Shopping, *Government Technology*, August 2003
http://www.govtech.net/magazine/story.php?id = 62033
Retrieved on 8/6/2003.

Garris, M., personal communication (e-mail), September 9/19/2003.

Gormely, W.T., Jr. and Weimer, D.L., *Organizational Report Cards*, Harvard University Press, Cambridge, Massachusetts, 1999.

Government Without Boundaries, Government Without Boundaries: A Management Approach to Intergovernmental Programs, Executive Summary, 2003
http:www.gwob.gov/report/executivesummary.html
Retrieved on 9/7/2003.

Hahm, S.D., Szczypula, J., and Plein, L.C., Barriers to information sharing in state agencies: the case of the Texas General Land Office, *Int. J. Pub. Adm.*, 18, 1243–1267, 1995.

Hall, K.A., Intergovernmental cooperation on ERP systems, *Gov. Fin. Rev.*, December, 17, 6–13, 2001.

Hall, K.A., personal communication (via e-mail) 9/5/2003.

Hibbard, J., Pull technology fights back, *Computerworld*, 31, 25–35, 1997
Retrieved from ABI_Inform on 11/3/2003.

Institute of Electrical and Electronics Engineers, *IEEE Standard Computer Dictionary: A compilation of IEEE Standard Computer Glossaries*, New York: N.Y., 1990.

Kumar, K. and Dissel, H.G., Sustainable collaboration: managing conflict and cooperation in interorganizational systems, *Manage. Inf. Syst. Q.*, 20, 279–300, 1996.

Landkamer, J., Minneapolis–St. Paul's Metro GIS: a collaborative effort overcomes obstacles to data sharing, *GeoWorld*, 16, 2003
http://www.geoplace.com/gw/2003/0303/0303.mnn.asp
Retrieved on 8/1/2003.

Landsbergen, D., Jr. and Woken, G., Jr., Realizing the promise: government information systems and the fourth generation of information technology, *Pub. Adm. Rev.*, 61, 206–220, 2001.

Laudon, K.C., *Computers and Bureaucratic Reform: The Political Functions of Urban Information Systems*, John Wiley & Sons, New York, 1974.

Laudon, K.C., *Dossier Society*, Columbia University Press, New York, 1986a.

Laudon, K.C., Data quality and due process in large interorganizational record systems, *Comm. ACM*, 29, 4–11, 1986b.

Meier, J. and Sprague, R.H., Jr., The evolution of interorganizational systems, *J. Inf. Tech.*, 6, 184–191, 1991.

NASCIO (National Association of State Chief Information Officers), Concepts for Integrated Justice Information Sharing, July, 2003, Version 1.0
https://www.nascio.org/hotIssues/EA/Con Ops2003.pdf
Retrieved on 10/28/2003.

Nathan, R., and Ragan, M., Federalism and Its Challenges, The Nelson A. Rockefeller Institute of Government, Albany, prepared for the Conference on Modernizing Information Systems for Human Services, Reston, VA, June 28–29, 2001. Revised on 10/9/2001
http://www.rockinst.org/publications/general_institute/NathanRaganInfSys.pdf
Retrieved on 8/19/03

Newcombe, T., Technology Helps States Transform Welfare, *Government Technology*, April, 2000a
http://www.govtech.net/magazine/gt/2000/apr/feature/feature.phtml
Retrieved on 10/1/2003.

Newcombe, T., The Art of Knowledge Sharing, *Government Technology*, June, 2000b, pp. 19–20 and 49.

Norton, P., A Minnesota consortium finds benefits in sharing, *Gov. Fin. Rev.*, June, 11, 43–45, 1995.

Onsrud, H.J. and Rushton, G., *Sharing Geographic Information*, Center for Urban Policy Research, Rutgers University, New Brunswick, NJ, 1995.

O'Shea, T.C., Analyzing police department data: how and how well police officers and police departments manage the data they collect, in *Criminal Justice in the 21st Century*, Moriarty, L.J. and Carter, D.L., Eds., Charles C. Thomas, Springfield, IL, 1998, Chap. 6, pp. 83–98.

Payton, F.C., Lessons learned from three interorganizational health care information system. *Inf. & Manag.*, 37, 311–321, 2000.

Perlman, E., TechnoTrouble, *Governing Magazine*, September, 1998
http://www.governing.com/archive/1998/sep/tech.txt
Retrieved on 9/23/2003.

Perlman, E., Playing Together, *Governing Magazine*, August, 2001
http://www.governing.com/archive/2001/aug/egshare.txt
Retrieved on 10/1/2003.

Perlman, E., The Anti-Silo Solution, *Governing Magazine*, January, 2003
http://www.governing.com/archive/2003/jan/it.txt
Retrieved on 10/28/2003.

Peterson, S., The XML Factor, *Government Technology*, April, 2003
http://www.govtech.net/magazine/sup_story.php?magid=8&id=42782&issue=4:2003
Retrieved on 10/20/03.

Pinkard, J., Director of Information Technology, Mecklenberg County, North Carolina, e-mail communication, 9/5/2003.

Porter, M. and Millar, V.E., How information gives you competitive advantage, *Harv. Bus. Rev.*, 63, 149–160, 1985.

Poulakos, J., Giving communication a push, *Am. City Cty.*, 117, 12, 2002.

Ragan, M., Building comprehensive human service systems, *Focus*, 22, 58–60, 2003a.

Ragan, M., *Managing Medicaid Take-up*, Federalism Research Group, State University of New York, January, 2003b.

Robinson, B., Mapping users plot new ways to share, *Fed. Com. Week.*, 11, 34–36, 2003.

Rocheleau, B., Computers and horizontal information sharing in the public sector, in *Sharing Geographic Information*, Onsrud, H.J., Rushton, G., Eds., Center for Urban Policy Research, Rutgers University, New Brunswick, NJ, 1995, pp. 207–229.

Rocheleau, B., Interorganizational and interdepartmental information sharing, in *Advances in Social Science and Computers*, Nagel, S.S., Garson, D.G., Eds.,Vol. 4, JAI Press, Greenwich, CT, 1996, pp. 183–203.

Rocheleau, B., Information Systems and Accountability, paper presented at the 2002 Conference of the American Society for Public Administration, Phoenix, AZ, March 25, 2002.

Rocheleau, B. and Wu, L., Public vs. private information systems: do they differ in important ways: a review and empirical test, *Am. Rev. Pub. Adm.*, 32, 379–397, 2002.

Schrage, M,. Don't trust your code to strangers, *CIO Magazine*, September 15, 2003
http://www.cio. com/archive/091503/work.html
Retrieved on 9/24/2003.

Schwen, T.M. and Noriko, H., Community of practice: a metaphor for online design, *Inf. Soc.*, 19, 257–270, 2003.

Sherrill, A., The Capabilities of State Automated Systems to Meet Information Needs in the Changing Landscape of Human services, paper prepared for the Conference on Modernizing Information Systems for Human Services, Reston, VA, June 28–29, 2001.

Swope, C., Common code, *Governing*, August, 18, 36–38, 2003.

Thomey, T., Senior Manager with Municipal GIS Partners, Inc., Interview (via telephone), August 14, 2003.

U.S. GAO (United States General Accounting Office), *Welfare Reform: Improving State Automated Systems Requires Coordinated Effort*, Government Printing Office, Washington, D.C., April 2000 (GAO/HEHS-00-48).

U.S. GAO (United States General Accounting Office), *Human Services Integration: Results of a GAO Cosponsored Conference on Modernizing Information Systems*, Government Printing Office, Washington, D.C., January 2002a (GAO-02-121).

U.S. GAO (United States General Accounting Office), *Nursing Homes: Federal Efforts to Monitor Resident Assessment Data Should Complement State Activities*, Government Printing Office, Washington, D.C., February 2002b (GAO-02-279).

U.S. GAO (United States General Accounting Office), *Workforce Investment Act: Improvements Needed in Performance Measure to Provide a More Accurate Picture of WIA's Effectiveness*, Government Printing Office, Washington, D.C., February 2002c (GAO-02-275).

U.S. GAO (United States General Accounting Office), *Child Welfare: Most States Are Developing Information Systems but the Reliability of the Data Could Be Improved*, Government Printing Office, Washington, D.C., July 2003 (GAO-03-089).

U.S. GAO (United States General Accounting Office), *Geographic Information Systems: Challenges to Effective Data Sharing*, Government Printing Office, Washington, D.C., 2003b, (GAO-03-874T).

Vandenberg, R., Director of Communications Technology, City of Reno, Nevada, personal communication (e-mail), September 5, 2003.

Weinman, L., *Dreamweaver 4: Hands-On Training*, Peachpit Press, Berkeley, CA, 2002.

6

IMPLEMENTING E-GOVERNMENT PROJECTS: ORGANIZATIONAL IMPACT AND RESILIENCE TO CHANGE

Mila Gascó

International Institute on Governance of Catalonia

CONTENTS

I.   Introduction 84
II. Toward a new public management 84
III. Electronic government programs 86
IV. Digital government initiatives and change processes 87
V.   Conclusions: implications for public managers 90

ABSTRACT

The need for efficacy and efficiency has given rise to multiple attempts to reform public administrations and to modernize the states. During the last few years, a new tool has become available: information and communication technology (ICT). This technological innovation in the public sector has resulted in digital administration and government programs that have not always been successful. To understand why requires analyzing the organizational and institutional setting where the transformations that are related to the adoption of ICTs in the public sector occur. Therefore, this chapter will explain how the adoption of new technologies has given rise to important organizational change processes but has not necessarily provoked cultural alterations or institutional changes. Also, it will show that those factors that produce resilience to technological change are not different from those related to other public administration transformations since all of them are rooted in one particular type of institution defined by the attributes of the bureaucratic model.

I. INTRODUCTION

The technological gains achieved during the last decades are one of the most important elements that have given rise to the astonishing wave of wealth and welfare in the most developed countries. Electronic commerce and information and communication technologies (ICTs) have become powerful economic growth motors. They are producing important productivity increases and are transforming the world's structure. However, these developments are unequal, depending on the field where they take place. Thus, while the entrepreneurial spheres can be considered ICT experts, public administrations advance slowly. What is going on? What are the obstacles encountered by public managers? How can ICTs help governments become more productive?

To give an answer to this and other similar questions requires an analysis of the organizational and institutional setting where the transformations that are related to the adoption of ICTs in the public sector occur. Therefore, it is the purpose of this text to approach this issue from an analytical perspective, considering the e-government initiatives as a fundamental part of state reform processes and studying, given this context, their impact. In order to do so, the following aspects must be taken into account:

1. The reformist trends and the state modernization
2. The adoption of ICTs in the public sector
3. The organizational and institutional impacts of e-government projects

II. TOWARD A NEW PUBLIC MANAGEMENT

"Government reinvention" is largely a new terminology and repackaging of longer-term processes of public sector reform. Such processes have been particularly prevalent since the 1970s when three factors ... began to combine: a sense of crisis in the public sector, a renewed ideology that provided a response to crisis and, at times, political will and power to enact those responses. Typically those responses did and do consist of five main components: increased efficiency, decentralization, increased accountability, improved resource management, and marketization (Heeks, 1999: 9).[1]

The term *management* has not always been used when describing the work of public administrations. As Heeks (1999) points out, it has been in the late 1980s and early 1990s that a new terminology has emerged in the public sector as a consequence of the new structures, processes, and tools that the longer tradition of public-sector reform gave rise to.

---

[1] According to Heeks (1999), the perceived problems focused on inputs (in a number of countries, the public sector was seen to require unsustainable large or increasing public expenditure), processes (there was concern about examples of waste, delay, mismanagement, and corruption within the public sector, all of which contributed to inefficiency in the conversion of public expenditure into public services), and outputs (there was a feeling that the public sector was not delivering what it should from adequate defense and policing through support for agriculture and industry to education, housing, and health or social welfare). In sum, "the sense of difficulties came to cover *what* the public sector was doing (the public sector's role) and also *how* it was doing it (public sector organization and management)."

Before the need to change was obvious, public administrations were structured according to the bureaucratic organization. For some time, this model was successful due to its focus on hierarchy, predictability, specific work division, and merits-based performance. Siegel (1996) states that in the U.S., the bureaucratic paradigm worked because it solved the basic problems that people wanted to see solved. It gave the unemployed security; it produced stability, and a strong feeling of justice and equity; it provided all the expected goods and services during the industrial age (such as roads, schools, highways, or health to name a few examples). Osborne and Gaebler (1993) add that this was particularly true in crisis times such as the Great Depression and the two world wars.

However, the exigencies of an increasingly complex and changing society made the bureaucratic model obsolete, unsuitable, and inappropriate. According to Siegel (1996) the surviving of bureaucratic organizations has given rise to several dysfunctions because:

1. They condition the legitimacy of political decisions and refer them to the law
2. Their organizational capacity stresses a culture of legality instead of emphasizing other values
3. Only senior public managers are in control of their extremely predictable and rational processes, their focus on quantity, and their strong hierarchical structures
4. Their slow nature has impeded adaptation to new times
5. They have not been quality-oriented structures

The existence of all these problems has stimulated public servants' and politicians' interest in the definition of a new innovative framework that overcomes the bureaucratic paradigm and that is usually rooted in the neoliberalism ideology. Therefore public administrations have gradually become big companies that offer a wide range of services and that focus on providing them correctly and efficiently. Allison (1983) explains the main tasks of the new public management model, which are:

1. Strategic management (i.e., to set flexible goals and priorities and to design operative plans to achieve them)
2. Internal components management (i.e., to organize and manage human and financial resources and to control the results obtained)
3. External components management (i.e., to deal with public external units, with independent organizations, with media, and with the citizens)

In doing so, public administrations emphasize:

1. The new organizational culture, which is more accountable and citizen-oriented (it pursues efficiency, innovation, and continuous improvement)
2. The need to have professional public servants
3. The inclusion of evaluation measures to control how the public sector operates
4. The new management tools that stress the use of private-sector managerial techniques, such as process management, management by objectives, or the total quality models

Several initiatives based on the above aspects are being almost universally undertaken or imposed.

> For the majority of public servants the issue is not the rights and wrongs of reform, but how best to implement reform initiatives in which they find themselves involved (Heeks, 1999: 14).

III.   ELECTRONIC GOVERNMENT PROGRAMS

More and more governments and public administrations are getting used to the new tools brought about by the new information society. As Fountain (2001) states, the Internet and a growing array of ICTs not only modify possibilities for organizing communication, work or business but also government and the state. Thus, ICTs, and particularly, e-government projects, become a powerful way to contribute to the public administration reform and modernization processes.

According to Gascó (2003), governments and the different public administration levels can simultaneously be subjects and objects of the embeddedness of new ICTs. As subjects, the government's role is key to influencing the design of a telecommunications regulatory framework that promotes competition and facilitates citizen access, the formulation of measures that increase confidence in electronic transactions, or the establishment of minimum services in order to satisfy the demands of the less favored groups.

As objects, governments and public administrations share the new opportunities offered by ICT's adapting them and using them, either internally (within the administration or among administrations) or externally (affecting the citizen–government or administration relationships), in order to increase their efficiency, effectiveness, and political legitimacy. When this happens, electronic or digital government initiatives are taking place.

Although several authors have helped clarify the meaning of the e-government concept, for the purpose of this chapter, this term is related to all those activities based on the modern ICTs (and particularly on the Internet) that the state carries out in order to increase public management efficiency, to improve citizen-oriented public services, and to provide a more transparent performance framework.

As a result, going digital does not mean buying some computers or designing a website to display information. On the contrary, it has to do with transforming the fundamental relationship that exists between the government and the general public. As the InfoDev and the Center for Democracy & Technology (2002: 5) declare, "e-government is not just about the automation of existing process and inefficiencies. Rather, it is about the creation of new processes and new relationships between governed and governor." Accepting this notion, and therefore that of the Garnert Group (2000), implies admitting the existence of two components:

1. Electronic governance, which emphasizes citizens', stakeholders', and elected representatives' unity in order to take part in the governance of communities with electronic equipment
2. Electronic service delivery, which guarantees the provision of government services through the use of electronic tools

Several initiatives can therefore take place when considering electronic government actions. Indeed, generally speaking, two types can be distinguished: all those programs related to the use of ICTs in internal processes and structures and all those that use ICTs when governments and administrations consider their relationships with other actors (citizens, civil organizations, and firms). The first group gathers initiatives under the name of electronic or digital public administration or back-office adjustments whereas the second one is known as electronic, digital, or online government or front-office adjustments.

At the same time, when considering the relationships between the government and other parties, there are several types of programs that may be designed. Given the objective of this chapter, it is interesting to refer to:

1. *Citizen access to different types of information*: The government is the greatest gatherer, processor, and keeper of any kind of information. Besides using information for its own goals, government can share information with interested citizens and organizations. Therefore when talking about an information provision initiative, the following must be considered: (a) information that the government wants to disseminate (news, regulations, policies, or laws), (b) information that the government gathers for its own use but that can be given to other users (geographical, economic, or demographic data), and (c) information that the government is required to provide as a result of citizen demands (performance indicators, personal data, or management and budget reports).

2. *Online transactions*: When electronic transactions become a possibility, citizens and firms are able to fulfil requirements and formalities 24 hours a day, 7 days a week, and 365 days a year from any part of the country by means of a computer at home, at the school, or at a public telecenter.

3. *Public services provision*: Offering public services through the Internet is one of the most interesting experiences when digitizing the state. The so-called online services are better adjusted to the users and therefore fully satisfy their expectations because they get rid of distances, inequalities, and physical obstacles. Many of the most successful initiatives in this sense have to do with medicine or education.

4. *Democratic process and citizen participation*: Undoubtedly, ICTs adoption gives rise to important changes between the citizen and the state that affect the democratic process and the government structures. Particularly, the Internet potential rests on its nonhierarchical and cybernetic character that favors interactivity. In this sense, electronic government initiatives do also include electronic democracy experiences, that is actions that require the use of the information, knowledge and communications technologies in order to promote democracy (Hacker and Van Dijk, 2000).

IV. DIGITAL GOVERNMENT INITIATIVES AND CHANGE PROCESSES

Much has been written about the potential benefits of developing and implementing an e-government strategy.In the first place, digitization has cut transaction costs all the way to zero in some cases.One of the more important examples lies in costs savings generated by online bill payment and document download. Fountain (2001: 5) states, "movement from paper-based to web-based processing of documents and payments typically generates administrative costs savings of roughly 50 per cent." Governments as well as intermediate institutions (such as banks) and users benefit from using the Internet in this sense.

The possibility of lowering costs gives rise to efficiency gains because now governments have the chance to achieve their objectives using fewer resources, such as time, money, and physical inputs. "Public organizations are rapidly becoming networked, and they are using these networks to produce and deliver services. This will ultimately lead to efficiency improvements, much as has happened with the private sector," explains Mechling (2002: 155).

Finally, from a strategic point of view, the new ICTs, and specifically the Internet, may change the way governments pursue their goals. On one hand, new opportunities arise when governments use networks. Electronic procurement, for instance, permits the creation of "wider, deeper, and more transparent markets that allow government agencies to reduce administrative costs and to obtain lower prices in markets" (Fountain and

Osorio-Urzua, 2001: 239). On the other hand, at the organizational level, important transformations occur because information technologies (ITs) affect the chief characteristics of the Weberian bureaucracy, and therefore, they reshape the production, coordination, control, and direction processes that take place within the public sector (Fountain, 2002).

Because of these major changes, e-government, in sum, may lead to a more citizen-oriented government that offers an improved range of services. This, in return, increases the level of satisfaction among the population as well as the acceptance of the public sector (Bertelsmann Foundation, 2002).

If organizational change is understood as the design and implementation, in a deliberate way, of a structure innovation, a policy, a new goal, or an operational transformation (Thomas and Bennis, 1972), there is no doubt about the implications of the electronic government initiatives in terms of organizational change.

What is not clear, though, is that ICT applications within the public sector result in institutional alterations (formal or informal); or as the economist North (1990) says, "in game rules reforms; or strictly speaking, in constrains that men impose on the economic, political, or social interaction."

This is a fundamental element since this chapter considers new ICTs to be efficient tools for pursuing state modernization, a process that gives rise to new public rules and ways of operating that condition the incentive systems that determine administrative and political behavior.

Therefore, why do organizational changes originating from the adoption of new technologies by the public sector not turn into institutional transformations? To give an answer to this question one must analyze the institutional change process.

In the first place, it is important to admit that the existence of institutional change factors does not necessarily produce such change. Due to the close link between institutions and the mental maps of the involved actors, the alteration of rules and games will only take place when these actors perceive that the new institutional arrangements will give rise to a situation better than the current one (North, 1994). According to Gascó (2003: 10), "institutional change occurs whenever an alteration of relative prices is perceived by one of the parties taking part from a transaction as a win–win situation for that party or for all the participants involved. Therefore, institutional change depends on the actors' perceptions with respect to the gains (the pay-offs indeed) to be obtained."

If this is so, and that is what this chapter is assuming, a second conclusion can be drawn: technology transformations do not necessarily alter the status quo of public organizations. Also, different e-government initiatives do not necessarily modify the type of institution where they are implemented because achieving efficiency and transparency in public administration operations does not obligatorily lead to the cultural change that motivates the transformation of actors' mental models.

Although it may seem contradictory, this argument can be explained by taking into account the rules of the game that nowadays guide how public administrations work, because ICT applications are being implemented considering the type of institution. As Fountain (2001: 3) declares, "The choices we face in the present regarding the use of digital tools and the institutional arrangements in which they are embedded will influence the way governments work around the globe during the next century and beyond." Indeed, technological innovations, and particularly e-government programs, are implemented in bureaucratic organizational structures and therefore they are conditioned by the obstacles and problems (see the above section) this type of structure gives rise to.

One of these restrictions is the strong resilience to change that public servants and politicians (two of the groups of actors involved in the transformations) experiment.

What are the bureaucracy's attributes that motivate reluctance to the paradigm change to the institutional transformation?

Many authors have already tried to answer this question. Generally speaking, the same components of the model that made it successful for a period of time have resulted in its malfunctioning as well. Thus, job definition and task precision, the uniformity in routines and procedures, organizational continuity, the aversion to risk,[2] and reliability are some of the bureaucratic structure characteristics that give rise to a closed system based on certainty and exact precision. Given these attributes, the bureaucratic system is perceived by its members as stable and secure (Chiavenato, 1986).

As a consequence, a new situation, such as the one originating because of the introduction of technologies in the public sector, can give rise to uncertainty and distrust, stop routine, cause menace to acquired status, and become a future source of insecurity. Thus, the new arrangements may be perceived as being worse than the preceding ones (because they produce less profit or give rise to losses). According to Heeks and Davies (1999: 32), "Public sector managers may rationally choose to ignore IT, as they perceive a lack of clear evidence about its positive impact." Wirszycz (1997: 12) adds that there is also continuing evidence of "a fear among … employees that the introduction of computer will lead to a loss of jobs. Along with the added stress from being asked to master the technology, this fear is a significant force hindering the move towards improved public service delivery." The Working Group on e-Government in the Developing World (2002) completes this statement when it points out that civil servants may resist e-government projects due to several reasons: fear that they will lose power, unfamiliarity with technology, or the fear that technology will mean more work for them. Last, Fountain and Osorio-Urzua (2001) refer to the political variables that will influence whether an e-government initiative will be undertaken at all or, what is more important, whether it will be accepted at all by the parties involved, therefore giving rise to their perception alterations. Thus, they name the perceptions of public servants about the potential labor cuts, administrative turnover, or changes in executive direction generated by e-government development as some of the political variables.

Resilience to change becomes a stronger attitude in those odd situations where formal bureaucracies coexist with prebureaucratic structures that have given rise to patronage practices and patterns that are difficult to eradicate. That is the case in many Latin countries, particularly South American ones (Ramió, 2001). There, public servants may have a "strong concern that new, automated processes will mean fewer opportunities to receive unofficial payments or bribes in return for using their discretion to help certain parties" (Working Group on e-Government in the Developing World, 2002: 18).

Finally, the public sector has had more than its fair share of failed reform projects. Past experience has also conditioned the perceived value of benefits and has therefore promoted a resistance to change. In this sense, Isaac-Henry (1997: 141) declares that in the public sector "a common concern was that in a large number of cases IT systems did not deliver the anticipated benefits." Thus, past heritage conditions new projects of change.

---

[2] "Like all reform initiatives, those involving IT require political support and personal motivation from key stakeholders in order to proceed. Yet IT is often seen as risky in a public sector that typically has risk-aversion as one of its cultural mainstays. In this situation, stakeholders will not be motivated to support or to contribute to IT projects" (Heeks and Davies, 1999: 32).

To sum up, the real problem when implementing e-administration and e-government initiatives is not the organizational change that they provoke but the norms, processes, and values transformations assumed by the actors in order to interpret the new situation.

V. CONCLUSIONS: IMPLICATIONS FOR PUBLIC MANAGERS

The need for efficacy and efficiency has given rise to multiple attempts to reform public administrations and to modernize the states. During the last few years, a new tool has become available: ICT. This technological innovation in the public sector has resulted in digital administration and government programs.

The adoption of new technologies has given rise to important organizational change processes but it has not necessarily provoked cultural alterations or, as explained previously, institutional changes. It has been the purpose of this chapter to show that, indeed, those factors that produce resilience to technological change are not different from those related to other public administration transformations. That is so because all of them are rooted in one particular type of institution defined by the attributes of the bureaucratic model.

In this sense, the classic organization theory suggestions about how to manage a change within an organization are also valid in the public context. Education and communication strategies, support, negotiation, and participation must accompany the technological innovation transformations, considering that longtime bureaucratic behaviors cannot be eradicated with isolated short-run policies brought about by the implementation of e-government initiatives. The Working Group on e-Government in the Developing World (2002: 18) states that "e-government leaders must identify the most likely sources of resistance and devise a plan to overcome them." This plan can include several effective actions such as seeking "buy-in" (it is better to involve civil servants from the beginning instead of imposing them with what to do and how to do it), explaining to workers the goals of the program as well as its benefits, training,[3] assigning clear responsibilities, and evaluating progress on e-government projects.

> The most perplexing problems ... are almost always the ones created as a result of the politics of organizational change. If change-related issues get the kind of consideration they warrant, then implementing e-government programs will be a much less complicated exercise (Ronaghan, 2002: 49).

Nevertheless, to assess technological change is not the only challenge that public managers face. E-government projects will result in an efficient, citizen-oriented, transparent, and accountable culture only if this type of culture is truly assumed by public servants, that is, if an institutional change is achieved.

REFERENCES

Allison, G., Public and private management: are they fundamentally alike in all unimportant respects? in *Public Management: Public and Private Perspectives*, Perry, J. and Kraemer, K., Eds., Mayfield Publishing, California, 1983, pp. 72–91.

---

[3] "Senior public officials — both managers and politicians — often lack IT skills and even IT awareness (...). They are therefore reluctant to support, or even to discuss, reforms that involve information technology" (Heeks and Davies, 1999: 32).

Bertelsmann Foundation, *Balanced e-Government: Connecting Efficient Administration and Responsive Democracy*, 2002
http://www.begix.de/en/ (accessed January 3, 2003).

Chiavenato, I., *Introducción general a la teoría de la administración*, McGraw-Hill, Mexico D.F., Mexico, 1986.

Fountain, J.E., *Building the Virtual State. Information Technology and Institutional Change*, Brookings Institution Press, Washington, D.C., 2001.

Fountain, J.E., A theory of federal bureaucracy, in *Governance.com. Democracy in the Information Age*, Nye, J. and Kamarck, E., Eds., Brookings Institution, Washington, D.C., 2002, pp. 117–140.

Fountain, J.E. and Osorio-Urzua, C.A., Public sector: early stage of a deep transformation, in *The Economic Payoff from the Internet Revolution*, Litan, R. and Rivlin, A., Eds., Brookings Institution and Internet Policy Institute, Washington, D.C., 2001, pp. 235–268.

Gartner Group, *Singapore's e-Government Initiative*, Gartner First Take, Standford, 2000.

Gascó, M., New technologies and institutional change in public administrations, *Social Science Computer Review*, 21, 6–14, 2003.

Hacker, K. and Van Dijk, J., *Digital Democracy: Issues of Theory and Practice*, Sage, London, 2000.

Heeks, R., Reinventing government in the information age, in *Reinventing Government in the Information Age. International Practice in IT-Enabled Public Sector Reform*, Heeks, R., Ed., Routledge, London, 1999, pp. 9–21.

Heeks, R. and Davies, A., Different approaches to information age reform, in *Reinventing Government in the Information Age. International Practice in IT-Enabled Public Sector Reform*, Heeks, R., Ed., Routledge, London, 1999, pp. 22–48.

Infodev and Center For Democracy & Technology, *The e-Government Handbook for Developing Countries*, InfoDev–World Bank, Washington, D.C., 2002.

Isaac-Henry, K., Management of information technology in the public sector, in *Management in the Public Sector*, Isaac-Henry, K., Painter, C. and Barnes, C., Eds., International Thomson Business Press, London, 1997.

Mechling, J., Information age governance, in *Governance.com. Democracy in the Information Age*, Nye, J. and Kamarck, E., Eds., Brookings Institution, Washington, D.C., 2002, pp. 141–160.

North, D., *Institutions, Institutional Change and Economic Performance*, Cambridge University Press, Cambridge, U.K., 1990.

North, D., Institutional Change: A Framework of Analysis, *Working Papers in Economics*, 1994
http://netec.mcc.ac.uk/adnetec-cgi-bin/get_doc.pl?urn = RePEc:wpa:wuwpeh:9412001&url = http%3A%2F%2Feconwpa.wustl.edu%3A8089%2Feps%2Feh%2FPapepers%2F9412%2F9412001.pdf (accessed August 10, 2002).

Osborne, D. and Gaebler, T., *Reinventing Government: How the Entrepreneurial Spirit Is Transforming the Public Sector*, Plume/Penguin Books, New York, 1993.

Ramió, C., Los problemas de la implantación de la nueva gestión pública en las Administraciones públicas latinas: Modelo de Estado y cultura institucional, *Reforma y Democracia*, 21, 2001
http://www.clad.org.ve/rev21/ramio.pdf (accessed August 12, 2002).

Ronaghan, S., *Benchmarking e-Government: A Global Perspective*, United Nations Division for Public Economics and Public Administration and American Society for Public Administration, New York, 2002.

Siegel, M., Reinventing management in the public sector, *Federal Probation*, 60, 30–36, 1996.

Thomas, J.M. and Bennis, W.G., Eds., *The Management of Change and Conflict*, Penguin, Baltimore, MD, 1972.

Wirszycz, R., Smashing the glass hurdles of human fear, *Government Computing*, 11, 12, 1997.

Working Group on e-Government in the Developing World, *Roadmap for e-Government in the Developing World. 10 Questions e-Government Leaders Should Ask Themselves*, Pacific Council on International Policy — The Western Partner of the Council on Foreign Relations, Los Angeles, 2002
http://www.pacificcouncil.org/pdfs/e-gov.paper.f.pdf (Accessed December 15, 2000).

7

UNDERSTANDING LARGE-SCALE IT PROJECT FAILURE: ESCALATING AND DE-ESCALATING COMMITMENT

Mark R. Nelson
Rensselaer Polytechnic Institute

CONTENTS

I. Introduction 94
II. Escalating and de-escalating commitment to failure 94
    A. Escalation of commitment 95
    B. De-escalation of commitment 98
III. The threat of reescalating commitment in a large-scale context 99
IV. Reescalating commitment and repeated failure — an example 100
V. Practical implications of escalating and de-escalating commitment 102
VI. Conclusion 103
Acknowledgments 104
References 104

ABSTRACT

The number and size of information technology (IT) projects in government agencies is on the rise. This trend is motivated by a desire to integrate and modernize various existing systems in order to improve the efficiency and effectiveness of government operations and service to the public. However, these large-scale IT projects are particularly prone to failure. Unfortunately, for large-scale IT projects in a public-sector context, failure is unlikely to be a one-time event. Instead, once one attempt fails another will begin. Increasing commitment to success yields subsequent project iterations that are both increasingly costly and increasingly less likely to succeed. This chapter looks at how commitment to large-scale IT projects in the public sector escalates and de-escalates repeatedly over time. The consequences of such cycles are discussed, including specific concerns and recommendations for public-sector managers of large-scale IT projects.

I. INTRODUCTION

Each year organizations around the world, both public and private, spend a combined total of billions to trillions of dollars implementing information systems (ISs). Many of these information technology (IT) projects fail to reach their intended goals or are abandoned before completion (Cats-Baril and Thompson, 1996). Failure rates are highest among large-scale IT projects, where estimated failure rates exceed 50 to 75% (Gibbs, 1994; Standish Group, 1994; CSTB, 2000). Between 1985 and 1995 alone the U.S. federal government spent over $200 billion on large-scale IT projects that failed to produce desired results (GAO, 1995a, 1995b). We define large-scale systems by the amount of information management resources required to implement the system. Specifically, a project is large-scale if it requires multiple levels of management to coordinate, costs over $10 million, or requires more than 6 months to develop (Zmud, 1980; Standish Group, 1994). Consistent with the increasing investment patterns oriented toward implementing large-scale systems, such as enterprise resource planning (ERP) and global supply-chain integration systems, IS researchers are beginning to recognize the need for more research into the processes that lead to the success or failure of these projects.

It would not be a surprise to most managers to hear a round of laughter following a claim that a planned IT project will be completed on time and on budget. It is common knowledge that IT projects often exceed budget and schedule expectations. In fact, IT projects, and especially large-scale IT projects, are more prone to fail on these criteria than non-IT projects (Zmud, 1980; Keil and Mann, 1997). Given what we know about how to make system implementation successful, why do we see such high failure rates and overruns among large-scale IT projects? The answer is that there are gaps in our knowledge of the *processes* that surround the implementation process (Montealegre, 1996). What is particularly important is the process by which large-scale IT projects tend to become "runaway" events — growing far beyond their planned budgets and schedules. Of equal interest and importance are the processes or actions required to bring such runaway projects back under control. Typically, we describe these countervailing forces as escalating and de-escalating commitment and we have great interest in understanding the processes by which commitment to failing courses of action escalate and de-escalate over time.

This chapter provides an overview of our current understanding of the factors and processes that drive the escalation and de-escalation of commitment to failing IT projects. Factors and process dimensions unique to public-sector IS projects are described in context. They are also linked together to show how, particularly in large-scale public-sector IT projects, failure is unlikely to occur only once, resulting in multiple cycles of escalation in de-escalation. The chapter culminates in a brief case study discussion of the modernization efforts at the Internal Revenue Service (IRS) to demonstrate the underlying processes and concerns that may drive repeated failure of IT projects in a public-sector context. The chapter concludes with a discussion of practical implications for public-sector organizations.

II. ESCALATING AND DE-ESCALATING COMMITMENT TO FAILURE

Over last decade we see a growing body of evidence in the research literature attempting to explain IT project escalation and de-escalation. Traditionally, escalation theory concentrates on the nature of continued or increasing commitment to a course of action, despite indications that the course of action may be leading to project failure (Keil et al., 2000). De-escalation theory, in contrast, is concerned with how such commitment is reduced (Keil and Robey, 1999). The literature includes both factor-based (variance theory) models and process-based (process theory) models to explain these phenomena. A variety of theoretical viewpoints have been used, including escalation of conflict (Teger, 1980), entrapment (Brockner and Rubin, 1985), escalation of commitment (Staw, 1981; Brockner, 1992; Keil et al., 2000), abandonment theory (Ewusi-Mensah and Przasnyski, 1991, 1995), and project redirection (Keil and Robey, 1999; Montealegre and Keil, 2000). The existing literature also provides sufficient evidence to demonstrate that escalating and de-escalating commitment to failing IT projects exist in a variety of settings independent of whether we examine the phenomena in a government agency or in a private-sector business (Staw, 1981; Keil et al., 1994–1995; Keil et al., 2000). Despite the existing literature, there is still much we do not know about how these phenomena play out in large-scale IT projects.

While we have few studies that examine escalation and de-escalation of commitment in large-scale IT projects, we can expect that they will be more prone to experience these phenomena. As previously noted, IT projects are more likely to escalate than other types of projects (Keil and Mann, 1997), and over half of large-scale IT projects fail (Gibbs, 1994; Standish Group, 1994; CSTB, 2000). Large-scale IT projects require significant resource commitment, are driven by strategic imperatives, and are less likely to end on time and on budget. Furthermore, as we see in cases like the modernization of the IRS, these large-scale IT efforts may escalate in cost and timeline until they are terminated. However, the strategic imperatives that initiate the projects persist, resulting in the project "rising from the ashes" like the mythical phoenix. With each rebirth we see that the likelihood of escalation becomes greater and the cycle of escalation and de-escalation continues. Building a better understanding of the processes involved in this cycle is critical for furthering our understanding of these phenomena from both theoretical and applied perspectives. Through better understanding of these phenomena we may be able to gain better control over large-scale IT projects and either increase their chance of success or decrease the cost of failure.

The remaining part of this section will provide enhanced detail on the nature of escalation and de-escalation. An effort will also be made to link these concepts to explain when and how a project that terminates is likely to be reborn.

A. Escalation of Commitment

While there are different degrees of failure, we have particular concern for "runaway" IT projects that continue to consume valuable resources without ever reaching their objectives (Keil et al., 1994–1995). These projects may eventually be abandoned or redirected, but before that happens we may expend significant organizational and societal resources. These runaway IT projects or other IT projects that fail exhibit many of the factors we associate with escalating commitment, thus making escalation theory a useful mechanism to study and explain IT failure (Keil et al., 2000). While there are numerous approaches to studying escalation, most of the literature concentrates on escalation as a function of commitment and its determinants (Staw 1976; Staw 1981; Brockner 1992). Today, most of these determinants are divided into one of four categories: project, psychological, social, and structural (Staw and Ross, 1987; Newman and Sabherwal, 1996).

Project determinants capture objective characteristics of a specific project. Project determinants set up the initial conditions for escalation by influencing the initial decision to commit to a project. For large-scale projects, this includes aspects like the strategic imperatives that require a project be done — such as a failing infrastructure, limited functionality, data problems, and so forth. Other project determinants may include the size or complexity of the project and its anticipated duration. Size may be determined by anticipated lines of code, volume of information to be stored, size of the development team, number of levels of management, or overall anticipated development cost. Project determinants also include economic determinants, such as the amount of expected payback vs. the costs required to continue or terminate the project. Project management variables, such as how cost and schedule estimates are created, how systems analysis and design activities are performed, or how information is communicated, may also be considered project determinants, especially if such practices are not standardized across projects. The more standardized or embedded project management techniques are within an organization, the more these variables become structural determinants of escalation because the determinants are no longer unique characteristics of an individual project. It is the magnitude and strategic importance of the project determinants early in a project that help set the stage for escalation to occur as time advances.

Psychological determinants concentrate on the characteristics of the decision-maker's relationship with a project. This category looks at individual-level determinants and has been a primary focus of escalation research. A major stream in this viewpoint is self-justification theory, which essentially states that individuals responsible for making decisions to commit resources to a project are typically more committed to continuing a failing project than those not involved in making resource decisions. In this situation, the individual may be unwilling to acknowledge to himself or herself that a mistake was made. This leads to project escalation as committed decision-makers place more resources into a project in order to justify prior investments.

Social determinants are closely related to psychological determinants. The key difference is that social determinants consider how the commitment of individuals is influenced by their social environment. One explanation of the effect of social determinants is self-presentation theory. Self-presentation theory suggests that a decision-maker will persist in supporting a project in order to avoid losing credibility in front of peers or in the organization. Typically, the more social pressure there is to be successful and make "correct" decisions and no mistakes, the more likely a project will escalate. For example, a decision-maker whose promotion is dependent upon a project success is much more likely to continue increasing investment in a project despite indications that the project is likely to fail. The social determinants viewpoint also captures situations where individual decision-makers choose to act in patterns consistent with other decision-makers in an organization. Thus social determinants lead to escalation through attempts by the individual decision-maker to "look good" (or not look bad) or adhere to social norms within the organization.

Structural determinants differ from the prior categories in that they attempt to capture characteristics of the project environment that may cause escalation. Structural determinants tend to become more important to escalation over time and reflect changes that must occur to the organization for the project to continue or be terminated. For example, if over time a large investment is made in computer hardware and software, and new employees are hired and trained, the cost and change implications of canceling a project favor project continuation. Structural determinants also consider issues of project embeddedness characterized by the statement, "We've always done things this way." This is a particular risk in large-scale IT projects that span many years. During that time period the project itself becomes a day-to-day function of the organization and the prospect of terminating a failing project is often not seen as an option. To the extent that the project is tied to strategic imperatives or mission-based values of an organization, the likelihood of escalation also increases. Thus structural determinants influence escalation by creating organization-level drivers for a project to continue even in the face of almost certain failure.

These factors fit together to form an escalation process in a fashion similar to what is shown in Figure 7.1. With each decision to persist, the project factors have less of an effect and the psychological and social determinants increase. As time progresses, structural factors begin to supercede the effect of individual decision-makers as the project becomes an embedded process within the organization.

How does the escalation process evolve? Well, as the projects are long-term (project determinant), costly (project determinant), and by definition large-scale (project determinant), they are not undertaken lightly. The rationale is based on a strategic imperative (project/structural determinant) that is most likely tied to serving the public good (social determinant) or the agency's ability to fulfill its mission (structural determinant). If negative information does not pass upward to decision-makers (social determinant), as the project progresses a situation of information asymmetry emerges. Project decision-makers may make additional decisions to commit based on the incorrect information, on the amount of prior investments made (psychological determinant), or out of the desire to avoid negative public impressions of how the project is being managed (social determinant). As the project expenditures become larger relative to the payoff (project determinant), the need to be successful and justify prior expenditures and decisions becomes greater (psychological determinant). Also, as time progresses, the project becomes increasingly embedded in the organization (structural determinant) as people are hired, systems and processes are put in place, and operational mechanisms are adopted.

In the public sector, the likelihood of escalation is increased by a variety of specific factors. First, the inherent political nature of the environment may create support for continuing a project outside any individual decision-maker's influence (structural determinant). Second, changing legislative environments or project audits by agencies like the General Accounting Office may result in frequent changes to project requirements or

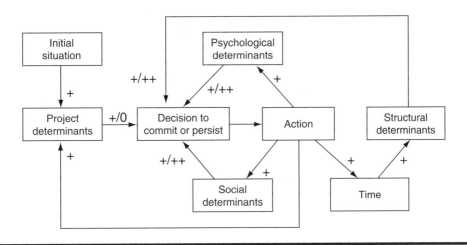

Figure 7.1 Simplified model of the escalation process.

other aspects of scope (project determinants). Third, the need to make responsible use of taxpayer dollars, particularly in light of past failures, creates a need for the project to be successful in order to preserve public trust (social determinant). Fourth, large-scale projects planned to take a decade or more (project factor) require operational infrastructures (structural determinant) that include employees, managers, equipment, and space that must be maintained over the lifetime of the project. These operational infrastructures can be difficult to remove in bureaucratic organizations as once established they are more easily embedded into the organization (structural determinant). Finally, the fairly widespread lack of standardized best practices, until recently, for IT project management and enterprise-wide projects (project/structural determinant), often due to lack of skills or social norms (structural determinants), resulted in projects prone to go wrong and few mechanisms to effectively identify that a project is off-course. The presence and persistence of these and other determinants of escalation make it critical that government agencies engaged in large-scale IT projects watch for signs that projects are escalating without likelihood of a successful completion.

B.   De-escalation of Commitment

De-escalation explores the factors and processes that reduce commitment to escalated projects. There has been far less research on de-escalation than there is on escalation. However, the concept of de-escalation and IT failure in the literature is sufficiently broad to capture two possible outcomes: complete project termination as defined by abandonment theory (Ewusi-Mensah and Przasnyski, 1991, 1995), and more recently project redirection (Montealegre and Keil, 2000). Due to the persistence of strategic imperatives in large-scale IT projects, redirection is an important alternative to abandonment as it is a likely outcome for large-scale IT projects that fail.

There are a variety of conditions that may initiate de-escalation of commitment to failing projects. Like escalation, these conditions or factors span a range of concepts, which include changes in top management, publicly stated limits, availability of alternatives, making negative outcomes less threatening, regular evaluation of projects, external pressure on the organization, unambiguously negative feedback, and several others (Montealegre and Keil, 2000). The presence of one or more of these conditions does not guarantee that a runaway project will de-escalate, nor do we know if there are conditions that promote de-escalation that are unique to public-sector organizations or to large-scale IT projects.

Montealegre and Keil (2000) presented a four-stage model of the de-escalation process to explain how de-escalation occurs in large-scale projects. Their model, developed by studying the IT baggage-handling system at Denver International Airport, captures the de-escalation process as it occurs through four phases: problem recognition, reexamination of the prior course of action, search for an alternative course of action, and implementation of an exit strategy. The crux of this model begins with the conclusion that a runaway project will not de-escalate until there is significant external pressure or other very unambiguous evidence that indicates a project is likely to fail. Once major problems that threaten success are identified, the next phase involves clarifying the magnitude of the problem and the likelihood that the risk of failure will be realized. As the size and nature of the problem become understandable, the project may begin to be redirected. As a new direction is identified, the change and redirection must be managed to ensure acceptance. As a final stage, the new direction is implemented and the old direction is abandoned. This model represents an important contribution to our understanding of how commitment to failed projects is curtailed as it is perhaps the only study to view this phenomenon from a process perspective.

III. THE THREAT OF REESCALATING COMMITMENT IN A LARGE-SCALE CONTEXT

One of the biggest concerns we have with the escalation and de-escalation of large-scale IT projects is that once they fail, they are likely to be reborn, only to escalate and fail once more. This potential for failed projects to be reborn and fail again can be seen in both private-sector contexts, such as the Taurus Project in the United Kingdom, and public-sector organizations, such as the modernization efforts of the Internal Revenue Service (Chanvarasuth et al., 2002). Furthermore, it is not only possible but likely that once a failed large-scale IT project begins again the pressures to escalate, and escalate more than the prior iteration, are even greater due to the historically accumulated escalation factors. Thus the potential for a large-scale IT project to repeatedly escalate and fail should create significant concern for public-sector IT project managers, particularly with the expectation that subsequent failures are likely to cost more than earlier failures.

Like escalation and de-escalation individually, there is an identifiable process that explains how failed large-scale IT projects are reborn and return to a state of escalation and eventual failure. A simplified version of this process is depicted in Figure 7.2. The process begins with the initiation of the project and the initial decision to commit. It is the rationale that supports this decision and the strategic imperatives that drive it that provide the groundwork to explain why a project must begin again after each failed attempt. As the project proceeds, it advances into its first escalation cycle, as described above. Eventually, an event will occur to trigger the de-escalation process. This process will likely play out as described in the prior section, with the project ending in a state of acknowledged failure. Up to this point the nature and process of escalation and de-escalation has occurred in a manner consistent with any type of project that goes through this process

For large-scale IT projects, the future path of escalation is different. Unlike smaller projects, which may be less mission-critical in nature, large-scale projects are bound by the original strategic imperatives that created them. In fact, following a potentially lengthy time period during which the initial escalation and de-escalation process occurred, the strategic imperatives may have become even more critical to the success or the survival of the organization. So, while smaller projects that fail or de-escalate may be permanently terminated after they de-escalate, large-scale projects are almost certain to be reinitiated.

Each time a project is reinitiated we notice that the factors that promoted escalation the first time are even greater the next time around. The estimated cost of the new project is higher and the need to be successful is greater. The increase in these factors can be explained in several ways. First, the perception of sunk cost is higher because the reinitiated project carries forth the costs incurred on prior attempts. Second, the social pressure to succeed is greater because having failed in prior iterations the organization does not want the negative publicity of failing again. This is probably even truer for public-sector organizations that are often driven by the need to be responsible stewards of taxpayer dollars. Repeated failure and negative publicity can erode the public trust in government services, which is a matter of critical concern to a number of federal agencies. Third, the social embeddedness of the project as an agency initiative continues to increase as even more staff and more resources are thrown into making the reinitiated

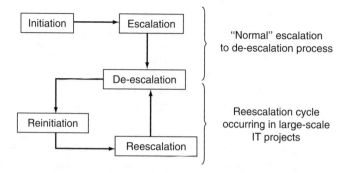

Figure 7.2   Simplified model of the reescalation cycle.

project successful where prior iterations failed. Fourth, belief that the reinitiated project will be successful even though prior iterations failed increases both the psychological and the social costs of withdrawal. This belief occurs because following each failed attempt some effort is made to understand why the project failed and attempts are made to resolve those issues. By increasing the belief in success however, the incentive to withhold negative information about project shortcomings also appears to increase. Finally, there is the problem that time and operating requirements do not stand still. Frequent changes to operating guidelines, legislation, or policy typically result in changes to the scope of the project. As the project scope changes it becomes more difficult to manage the project to a successful conclusion.

The result of these and other conditions is that the reinitiated project will escalate again. Because the stakes and the cost of failure are higher for the project, the incentive to withhold negative information on the project is also greater. This will allow the project to escalate further, before a critical point that returns the project to a new cycle of de-escalation and reinitiation is reached. In the private sector, this may ultimately lead to death of the organization. However, in a public-sector organization charged with fulfilling a public need, such as collecting tax revenues or defending the nation, it is most unlikely that complete failure of the system will result in termination of the agency. Thus large-scale public sector projects have the potential to continue the reescalation process for not only years, but decades. The next section of this chapter will briefly describe one such example that did just that.

IV.   REESCALATING COMMITMENT AND REPEATED FAILURE — AN EXAMPLE

The efforts to modernize the U.S. IRS span over three decades, hundreds of workers, and billions of dollars, quite arguably making it a very large-scale IT project. The magnitude of the modernization effort at the agency is perhaps best summarized by a quote from a relatively recent IRS (2000: 1) report:

> It is important to understand the kind of processes needed to modernize IRS'
> systems. This process has sometimes been compared to designing and build-
> ing a new airliner or a huge office building .... A better metaphor would be a
> project to redesign and rebuild a large, densely populated city, such as New
> York City, complete with rebuilding all the subways, utility lines, surface

transportation and tall buildings, all without delaying or injuring any residents or businesses while accommodating ongoing growth and changes in the daily pattern of living and working.

In testimonies before Congress, top members of the General Accounting Office testified that problems similar to those at the IRS can be found in almost all federal agencies in the U.S., noting that the U.S. federal government spent over $200 billion on large-scale IT projects that failed to produce desired results in the prior decade (GAO, 1995a, 1995b). The IRS is a particularly interesting example, however, because it is considered to be a well-managed agency. As Bozeman (2002: 11–12) described:

> Were the IRS case unique because the IRS is a uniquely mismanaged agency, then we would simply expect that well-managed agencies would not repeat the same mistakes. But the IRS is not uniquely mismanaged, having (now and in the past) competent top leaders, strong career public management traditions, solid training programs, and the respect of many of the people who work most closely with the IRS — vendors, contractors, and other government agencies ... . The IRS failures with IT modernization are of great interest *because* the IRS has talented managers and, in many respects, excellent resources. If the IRS IT modernization failures comprise a morality tale, its name should be "How Good Managers, Confronting a Critical Mission, with Great Dedication and Billions of Dollars, Can Nonetheless Fail."

So what went wrong? Well, one thing we can quickly notice when examining project data over the lifespan of modernization efforts is that the effort to modernize failed not once but several times. Each failure cost the agency more in terms of person-hours and money than the previous iteration, with recent past and projected future attempts costing *billions* more than earlier efforts. Indeed, the current modernization effort, the Business Systems Modernization Project, has an estimated cost in excess of $10 billion, which is more than three times the cost of the last effort (Varon, 2001). What we can learn from this case is something about why and how large-scale IT projects escalate and de-escalate over long periods of time.

For the IRS, the original modernization project began with a set of strategic imperatives that were based on the inefficiency and ineffectiveness of the existing system coupled with capacity concerns and access problems. These concerns and problems justified the initial expense of modernization over 30 years ago, and are still key drivers of the need to modernize. After the initial commitment to modernization, it was not long before the project began to escalate. The early project suffered from project management and other control problems that affected the perceived project economics (GAO, 1981: 2). As time progressed, the psychological and social costs of withdrawal increased even as the clarity that the project was not making progress became greater. The environmental events in particular resulted in changes to project scope or direction as operating policies changed or new data problems were uncovered. As subsequent project actions were taken and environmental events occurred, the commitment to the project increased. The project became more institutionally embedded, receiving increased political support within and outside the agency. All of these factors combined further escalate the modernization effort.

Failing projects cannot continue escalating forever, nor does that happen for the IRS. In each attempt to modernize the IRS, a point is reached where the project begins to de-escalate. In each iteration this happens in much the same way that the literature suggests. First, the agency reaches a state where the nature of the problem becomes unambiguous, typically through reports in the media. Once the negative media coverage begins, it appears to not be long before the full breadth and magnitude of the project problems become clear and public. This enables the agency and related oversight bodies, such as the GAO and the Congress, to identify various options and implement a termination strategy. A playing out of this process can be seen again and again throughout the history of agency modernization.

With the termination of each modernization effort, several things happened at the IRS. First, there is some analysis of what went wrong and why the project failed. Invariably, this uncovers problems with project management, some that will be corrected, and others that persist since the first attempt to modernize. The persistence of these project management issues over time provides the groundwork for future project problems. Second, what is clearer to the agency is that the need to modernize is greater after each project failure than in the prior attempt. As time passes, the strategic imperatives grow as the aging infrastructure becomes less efficient and less effective. Capacity and access concerns grow, and in the case of the IRS, an increasing number of data accuracy and consistency problems begin to emerge. Combined, these problems begin to have a greater impact on the successful functioning of the agency.

At this point, the original strategic imperatives are sufficient to justify committing to a new modernization project based on the economics alone. However, the intensified strategic imperatives stemming from the passage of time and prior failures produce more than just project reinitiation. They also fuel many of the psychological and social factors of escalation. Indeed, while early iterations of IT project escalation may begin with project factors, later iterations are more likely to begin with significant psychological and social factors of escalation well developed. Combined with the impact of past failures, agency desires to spend taxpayer dollars responsibly and to serve the public well create additional incentives for project escalation in the form of "success at any price." With each iteration, the need to be successful and the belief that success will occur is greater. These needs and beliefs significantly increase the psychological and social costs of withdrawal when there is evidence that the project may not be going well (Kaplan, 1999: 1). In the IRS this surfaces as fear among project personnel to report mistakes or problems, even when it is abundantly clear that problems cannot be resolved with available timelines and budget (Bozeman, 2002).

Thus within the lifetime of modernization efforts at the IRS we see a reemerging pattern of escalating commitment to project success, followed by public failure and eventually reinitiation and reescalation. In each cycle the project's motivation to escalate is greater, if for no other reason than the fact that the stakes of failure have increased both in terms of pure project economics and in terms of psychological and social pressures. Interestingly, we see similar storylines being played out in large-scale projects throughout a variety of public-sector organizations. This leads us to a series of issues managers of large-scale IT projects should consider in order to gain control over the escalation process.

V. PRACTICAL IMPLICATIONS OF ESCALATING AND DE-ESCALATING COMMITMENT

The concepts presented in this chapter highlight how important it is for managers of large-scale IT projects to be aware of the persistence of environmental, strategic/organizational, group/project, and individual factors that may increase the chance of IT project escalation. The high rate of failure among large-scale IT projects results in significant financial losses and public relations concerns. Large-scale IT projects are more complex than smaller projects, and it is possible that warning signs or problems that a project is escalating or is in trouble can get lost in a mass of recommendations and suggestions, particularly in a public-sector context. This suggests that better knowledge management techniques may help project managers focus on recognizing the "real problem" before a project escalates out of control. Because of the size of the prior lost investment and the increasing importance of strategic imperatives over time, managers of large-scale IT projects must be more aware of the psychological and social sources of escalation (e.g., sunk cost effects, self-justification, and self-presentation) in subsequent iterations of a project. Awareness will enable these issues to be managed and for project managers to employ de-escalation strategies and techniques at signs of trouble.

The importance of using good project management techniques and software development practices cannot be understated. In early attempts at managing large-scale projects, organizations should focus on developing strong project management and systems development skills and experience to minimize their effect on escalation. Many of the problems and the degree of escalation encountered in large-scale IT projects might be overcome if project management problems are resolved early in the project cycle. Problems with project management or systems development techniques quickly lead a project to run behind schedule and over budget. Once that happens, psychological and social factors of escalation are triggered at which point it becomes more difficult to control the escalation process.

Finally, within a public-sector context, managers of large-scale IT projects and external project stakeholders should be more aware of the effect that legislative changes or other environmental factors may have on project escalation. For example, in the case of the IRS, legislation often resulted in changes to project scope. These could occur directly, as in situations where tax law is updated, or more indirectly, as occurred with the Chief Financial Officers (CFO) Act of 1990, which resulted in discovery of financial management problems in the agency that were a result of infrastructure problems. A better mechanism should be developed to incorporate scope changes, which are inevitable for large-scale IT projects in a dynamic political and legal environment.

VI. CONCLUSION

It is increasingly common and desirable for public-sector agencies to integrate data and systems within and between organizations. From an applied perspective, integrated systems hold the promise for improving service to citizens at a reduced cost. Thus we see a number of federal agencies in the U.S. engaged in large-scale IT modernization or integration efforts. However, the challenge for public-sector agencies lies in the fact that many agencies rely on aging legacy infrastructures that contain a wide variety of hardware platforms and software applications. Attempting to modernize and integrate these diverse systems leads to ever-larger and more complex IT projects. This is a concern because, as noted earlier in this chapter, large-scale IT projects are more prone to both failure and escalation. Improving our ability to successfully implement such large-scale projects is important as the number of large-scale projects continues to increase throughout the public sector.

There are a variety of factors that increase commitment to projects that are failing or in trouble. In addition to general factors that may occur in any type of project, there are some factors more specific to public-sector IT projects and to large-scale IT projects.

From a public-sector perspective, environmental factors such as changes in legislation and intervention by external oversight agencies may be important contributors to the escalation process. The presence of societal service concerns in public agencies is also likely to increase the likelihood that negative information on project progress is unlikely to surface, further contributing to project escalation. Similarly, large-scale IT projects, because of their size, are particularly motivated by the persistence of strategic imperatives. The size of these projects, particularly if they have already failed once, create conditions where psychological factors leading to escalation are likely to be stronger as a result of both the increased importance of persistent strategic imperatives and the perceptions of prior sunk-cost and failure issues. This means that managers of large-scale IT projects in the public sector must be particularly vigilant to signs of project escalation so that steps can be taken to control the escalation process. Actions that improve both project and knowledge management so that persistent problems are resolved before subsequent implementation cycles may help reduce the severity of IT project escalation in public-sector organizations.

Undoubtedly, IT project escalation and de-escalation are complex processes, which currently are not completely understood. More research needs to take place to better understand the aspects of these processes that are unique to large-scale IT projects and public-sector IT projects. This chapter presents an overview of escalation and de-escalation based on our current understanding of these phenomena. This overview provides some insight for IT project managers in terms of better understanding of why IT projects fail and how to recognize when and why large-scale IT projects may be in trouble. Future research on these processes in large-scale public-sector IT projects will improve our ability to develop techniques to help managers implement these projects successfully for the benefit of government organizations and the society they serve.

ACKNOWLEDGMENTS

I thank the Lally School of Management and Technology at Rensselaer Polytechnic Institute for seed funding to support this research. I also extend my appreciation to the doctoral students and undergraduate research program students for their varied contributions to different stages of this research.

REFERENCES

Bozeman, B., Government management of information mega-technology: lessons from the internal revenue service's tax systems modernization, *New Ways to Manage Series*, The Pricewaterhouse Coopers Endowment for the Business of Government, Arlington, VA, 2002.

Brockner, J., The escalation of commitment to a failing course of action: toward theoretical progress, *Academy of Management Review*, 17, 39–61, 1992.

Brockner, J. and Rubin, J.Z., *Entrapment in Escalating Conflicts: A Social Psychological Analysis*, Springer-Verlag, New York, 1985.

Cats-Baril, W.L. and Thompson, R.L., *Information Technology and Management*, Irwin, Boston, 1996.

Chanvarasuth, P., Nelson, M.R., and Ravichandran, T., Exploring re-escalation cycles in system implementation: extending project escalation and de-escalation theories, in *Proceedings of the Asian–Pacific Decision Sciences Institute (APDSI) 2002 Conference*, Bangkok, Thailand, July, 2002.

CSTB, *Making IT Better: Expanding Information Technology Research to Meet Society's Needs*, Committee on Information Technology Research in a Competitive World, Computer Science and Telecommunication Board, National Research Council, National Academy Press, Washington, D.C., 2000.

Ewusi-Mensah, K. and Przasnyski, Z.H., On information systems project abandonment: an exploratory study of organizational practices, *MIS Quarterly*, 15, 67–85, 1991.

Ewusi-Mensah, K. and Przasnyski, Z.H., Learning from abandoned information systems development projects, *Journal of Information Technology*, 10, 3–14, 1995.

GAO (General Accounting Office), *Government-wide Guidelines and Management Assistance Center Needed to Improve ADP Systems Development*, General Accounting Office, Washington, D.C., February, 1981 (GAO/AFMD-81-20).

GAO (General Accounting Office), *Tax Systems Modernization: Unmanaged Risks Threaten Success*, General Accounting Office, Washington, D.C., February 16, 1995a (GAO/T-AIMD-95-86).

GAO (General Accounting Office), *Government Reform: Using Reengineering and Technology to Improve Government Performance*, General Accounting Office, Washington, D.C., February 2, 1995b (GAO/T-OCG-95-2).

Gibbs, W.W., Software's chronic crisis, *Scientific American*, 271, 86–95, 1994.

IRS (Internal Revenue Service), *IRS Organization Blueprint 2000*, Document 11052, Internal Revenue Service, Washington, D.C, 2000.

Kaplan, K., Bringing the IRS into the 21st Century, *Los Angeles Times*, June 27, 1999, p. C1.

Keil, M. and Mann, J., The nature and extent of information technology project escalation: results from a survey of IS audit and control professionals, *IS Audit and Control Journal*, 1, 40–48, 1997.

Keil, M., Mann, J., and Rai, A., Why software projects escalate: an empirical analysis and test of four theoretical models, *MIS Quarterly*, 24, 631–664, 2000.

Keil, M., Mixon, R., Saarinen, T., and Tuunainen, V., Understanding runaway information technology projects: results from an international research program based on escalation theory, *Journal of Management Information Systems*, 11, 65–85, 1994–1995.

Keil, M. and Robey, D., Turning around troubled software projects: an exploratory study of the de-escalation of commitment to failing courses of action, *Journal of Management Information Systems*, 15, 63–87, 1999.

Montealegre, R., What Can We Learn from the Implementation of the Automated Baggage-Handling System at the Denver International Airport? 1996 Americas Conference, Association for Information Systems, Phoenix, AZ, August, 1996.

Montealegre, R. and Keil, M., De-escalating information technology projects: lessons from the Denver International Airport, *MIS Quarterly*, 24, 417–447, 2000.

Newman, M. and Sabherwal, R., Determinants of commitment to information systems development: a longitudinal investigation, *MIS Quarterly*, 20, 23–54, 1996.

Standish Group, *CHAOS: A Recipe for Success*, 1994
http://www.standishgroup.com/sample_research/chaos_1994_1.php
Accessed on September 1, 2003.

Staw, B.M., Knee-deep in the big muddy: a study of escalating commitment to a chosen course of action, *Organizational Behavior and Human Performance*, 16, 27–44, 1976.

Staw, B.M., The escalation of commitment to a course of action, *Academy of Management Review*, 6, 577–587, 1981.

Staw, B.M. and Ross, J., Behavior in escalation situations: antecedents, prototypes, and solutions, *Research in Organization Behavior*, 9, 39–78, 1987.

Teger, A., *Too Much Invested to Quit*, Pergamon Press, Elmsford, NY, 1980.

Varon, E., The taxman's burden, *CIO Magazine*, 14, 62–74, 2001.

Zmud, R., Management of large software development efforts, *MIS Quarterly*, 4, 45–55, 1980.

8

REVISITING VIRTUAL LOCALS AND COSMOPOLITANS "IN AND AS" ELECTRONIC GOVERNANCE: A COMPARATIVE ANALYSIS OF THE SOCIAL PRODUCTION OF AN ACADEMIC COMMUNITY

Lynn M. Mulkey
University of South Carolina

William L. Dougan
University of Wisconsin

Lala Carr Steelman
University of South Carolina

CONTENTS

I. Introduction 108
II. Background 109
    A. Literature review from baseline research on virtual locals and
       cosmopolitans 110
    B. Statement of the problem 113
III. Method 114
    A. Sample 114
    B. Selecting messages from the archives 115
    C. Analytic/observational approach 115
    D. Measures 116
IV. Results and discussion 117
    A. Virtual cosmopolitans 117
    B. Virtual locals 120

V. Summary and conclusion.. 123
References... 123

ABSTRACT

This investigation advances recent research on the relevance of Robert Merton's theory of "locals" and "cosmopolitans" for understanding the governance of virtual academic organizations. It addresses whether virtual communities have the same essential characteristics as those typically observed in face-to-face communities from which the local–cosmopolitan dichotomy was originally applied. Findings from past exploratory research suggest the significance of this traditional conceptualization of professional role/normative structure and orientation for describing and explaining the construction and achievement of an academic community in a virtual realm. This study extends what we know about the degree to which cosmopolitan and local norms have utility for making sense of virtual communities. It employs qualitative modes of observation, particularly a version of ethnomethodological technique, which presupposes that reality is socially constructed as opposed to being universally present *a priori* in an external world for us to observe. It explores how norm construction in public access data obtained for previous research — faculty at a large state university — compares with observations made on a sample of electronic communications among members of the American Society of Public Administration (ASPA). In our preliminary investigation, we predicted that the virtual context of discourse would blur the distinctions between locals and cosmopolitans; because of the medium, institutional, and local goals becoming aligned and clearly less discrepant. Across different types of virtual communities, however, electronic governance seems to discourage compromise in the approach to solving tasks. Rather normative orientations were palpable and pronounced and the localism and cosmopolitanism professional role orientation split persisted. Moreover, the segregation of orientations led us to test whether online interaction segregated as well. Virtual communities appear especially amenable to self-selection and exclusivity of these normative orientations for fulfilling the functions of academic institutions. Hence, we introduce the significance of "virtual locals and cosmopolitans." Implications are for public administration as it pertains to a virtual academic community.

I. INTRODUCTION

This chapter investigates the structure of relationships as it is constructed to achieve organizational functions in an academic context. It reasons, as have researchers studying the gamut of virtual environments (Kling, 2000), that virtual and face-to-face roles differ with respect to the social production of governance (Michalski, 1995; Babbie, 1996; Romm and Pliskin, 1996; Turkle, 1997, 1999; Walsh and Bayma, 1996; Wellman and Salaff, 1996; Etzioni and Etzioni, 1997; Haythornthwaite and Wellman, 1998; Komito, 1998; Franbel et al., 1999; Wellman, 1999, 2001; Baker and Ward, 2000; Etzioni, 2000; Kling and McKim, 2000; Williams, 2000; Hampton and Wellman, 2001; Kazmer and Haythornthwaite, 2001; Koku et al., 2001; Barab, 2003; Barab et al., 2003; De Cindio et al., 2003; Ferber et al., 2003; Foltz and Foltz, 2003; Kling et al., 2003; Lamb and Kling, 2003; Zucchermaglio and Talamo, 2003).

Former studies suggest that the transformation of a group into a community is a major accomplishment that requires special processes and practices (Kling and Courtright, 2003). A recent exploratory investigation of the values and the normative structure of a virtual academic community suggests that two classical orientations regarding the role structure of academic professionals continue to be relevant for characterizing virtual social relationships (Mulkey et al., in press). They are the local and cosmopolitan orientations first described by Merton (1959). Our previous investigation revisited Robert Merton's concepts, "locals" and "cosmopolitans," as they apply to academic organizations. On basis of Eichorn's (2001) successful use of ethnographic techniques to examine communities as no longer bound to geography or place, we conducted a semi-ethnographic exploration of electronic governance by analyzing the discourse of a virtual bulletin board. By predominantly employing archival data consisting of electronic mail communications among faculty in a midwestern university, the professional role structure of a virtual academic community was identified. Role orientations for airing concerns over compliance with professional role demands are compatible with the long-standing concepts, locals and cosmopolitans. The virtual context of discourse was expected to confound the distinctions between locals and cosmopolitans, because the virtual medium facilitates the alignment of interests. Counter to what we anticipated, electronic governance that seems to encourage coalition in the approach to solving tasks, in fact, makes the demarcation more pronounced and the localism and cosmopolitanism professional role structure resists chance. These findings corroborate the speculations of some about the dividing and the bridging and bonding role of online communities (Norris, 2002). Results also show that locals tend to self-subscribe to university faculty bulletin boards. Cosmopolitans may then self-select to other types of academic bulletin boards. On the basis of these preliminary findings, we consider how norms are produced in local and in cosmopolitan virtual communities, the former the previously investigated faculty bulletin board at a large state university and the latter a public access bulletin board of a large professional organization, the American Association of Public Administration. We conduct an exploratory analysis of whether the prescribed relations characterize the more political and informal associations characteristic of local constituencies or the apolitical and formal, universalistic associations characteristic of cosmopolitan constituencies for achieving the functions of the academic organization.

II. BACKGROUND

We lump together and set apart much of the previous literature on virtual communities in terms of its relevance to our present investigation. By this we mean that the behavioral norms that constitute virtual communities have not been analyzed, until very recently (Mulkey et al., in press), in terms of their "local" vs. "cosmopolitan" character. We paraphrase this previous work as it concerns the logic infusing and bolstering of the present study. These researchers argue, "before the widespread infusion of computer technology, social scientists amassed a fundamental knowledge of the values and professional role structure of academia." The electronic medium of communication provides another opportunity for further specification and respecification of the social "achievement" of academic community. The sociocultural mechanisms that create and sustain one community of higher education are documented by employing data from a network archive at a state-funded university. This exploratory study, by employing data from a public-access network archive at a state-funded university (a context for communication), investigated how the emergence of norms define and govern electronically the academic community. It documented the exchange of faculty members on the electronic (e-) bulletin board, and how these messages are as functionally imperative to higher education governance as a formal contest for exchange, such as faculty meetings. By employing ethnomethodological logic, the researchers (Mulkey et al., in press) state both modes of communication are interpreted as part of a broader social situation. They claim, if university governance consists of a set of practices that made sense in the context of disseminating and creating knowledge, both and all affirmations and disruptions to this activity make the academy recognizable as what we all know it to be. Talk "about" the academic community, "is" the academic community; it is not found outside the community, but is inseparable form, embedded in the social apparatus that makes it apparent as one. The bulletin board provides as much an opening for normalizing human relations as does the work of more formal modes of academic governance such as faculty meetings.

By continuing to follow the reasoning established in previous research on locals and cosmopolitans in a virtual academic community, in the same manner that science is more than a laboratory or experiment, Mulkey and Dougan (1996) found that the norms that constitute an academic community extend beyond the classroom or scholarly activities. Technology provides a new and virtual context for defining and sustaining community. It allows us to glean an understanding of the structure of community not typically available through routine observation. Of particular interest in the baseline investigations is how the effective functioning of the university as an organization is achieved through a bifurcated governance between faculty and administration, a term often used to mean the chasm between the administration and the faculty in terms of regulatory functions. The organizational structure can be conceptualized as consisting of a professional role structure of "locals" and "cosmopolitans." These concepts are useful for examining how contentions surrounding a bifurcated governance are resolved in a variety of formally and informally organized face-to-face contexts. Online chat was shown to provide a new context in which conversations and messages with respect to academic governance take place. The study investigated the utility of computers for constructing local and cosmopolitan orientations in and as the virtual academic community. The conceptual tools are a means for making sense of organizational problems, such as multiple career lines, differential incentive systems, needs for loyalty vs. expertise, and so forth.

No previous application of Merton's (1959) formulations to this form of discourse had been conducted. It was thought that electronic governance may facilitate an informal forum whereby participants are brought together to resolve conflicts before they evolve into broader ones or they may exacerbate conflict by making professional standards readily available in an informal context. With clues from prior investigation, locals were expected to use electronic formats for the exchange and institutionalization of ideas more than cosmopolitans, or cosmopolitans might subscribe to the use of selective virtual formats. Findings showed the orientations of cosmopolitans and locals persist in a virtual community and normalize the work of an academic community.

A. Literature Review from Baseline Research on Virtual Locals and Cosmopolitans

We present the literature review from the baseline study on virtual locals and cosmopolitans as generic to our present problem for study (Mulkey et al., in press). The normative/organizational structure of the academy is well documented in literature that extends well over the years (i.e., Neumann and Neumann, 1982; Zvekic, 1984; Hunt, 1987; Nederhof,

1992; Szerszynski and Urry, 2002). In particular, disputes concerning effective governance and operations emanate from the traditionally depicted bifurcated governance in higher education. Both faculty and administration are interdependent and play key roles in normalizing the role structure of the institution. This organizational model can lend itself to conflicts between faculty and administration constituencies. Mauksch (1986) notes, for example, as educational institutions move toward bureaucratic format, teaching and the control of teaching are slowly but persistently transferred from collegial to administrative structures. As teaching becomes increasingly judged by output and efficiency, the professor moves from an academic status to that of an employee.

Professional responsibilities of faculty are defined, monitored, and socially controlled by a dialogue between faculty and administration (Hill, 1974; Baker, 1984). As a body of experts, faculty informs administration of acceptable standards concerning teaching, scholarship, and service (Mauksch, 1986; Bevis and Kirchhoff, 1987). Responsiveness to these demands has led, on the part of faculty and other professions, to the production of two distinct normative structures — localism and comospolitanism (Cornwall, 1987; Wright and Larwood, 1997). Cosmopolitan–local, an attitudinal construct, is used to predict and explain variation in the manifest professional behavior of professionals in complex organizations. It is used to predict and explain variation in response to organizational and professional role prescriptives (Gouldner, 1957, 1958; Merton 1959; Goode, 1960; House, 1969; Delbecq, 1970; Grimes, 1970, 1980; Patterson, 1971; Berger, 1973; Dicker, 1974; Almy, 1975; Kirschenbaum, 1976; London and Cheney, 1977; Stahl, 1978; Fairweather, 2002). Cosmopolitan–local, an attitudinal construct, is used to predict and explain variation in professional behavior in complex organizations (Robertson, 1983). Some see the significance of this construct for understanding a "democratic" community; local elites use civic space less as a means to democratize local government than to consolidate power in the hands of the elite (Durrill, 2002). Differing professional role orientations create barriers and challenges for collaboration in delivering higher education programs (Stein, 2001). Factor analytic studies conducted by Grimes (1980) identified five dimensions of the more complex model: professional commitment, commitment to organizational goals, organizational immobility, concern for advancement, and reference group orientation. These dimensions are correlated to selected biographical, behavioral, and organizational variables. Baker (1984) addresses the complexities of local and cosmopolitan orientations of faculty in terms of primary and secondary commitments to teaching, research, and service. He observes various inner- and outer-reference group orientations that have the capacity to renew professional commitment and advance academic skills. Analysis of data from the 1993 National Survey of Postsecondary Faculty shows that faculty value teaching over research. At the same time, the explicit reward structure of academics favors research and publication, rewarding productivity in these arenas with money and status. Implications of this disconnect between values and rewards are for faculty careers, policy, and practice (Leslie, 2002). The concepts of localism–cosmopolitanism suggest the following.

Generally, locals have been described as responsive to immediate primary group pressures in contrast to the cosmopolitan's sensitivity to a broader range of impersonal demands (Merton, 1959). In a study of reading, intellectualism, and cosmopolitanism, Dicker (1974) corrobroated Merton's original idea of a positive association between orientations toward larger social structures, psychological detachment from the community, geographical mobility, and intellectualism. Gouldner (1957, 1958) shows that faculty committed to professional principles were least likely to express loyalty to a particular college community. Similarly, Blau and Scott (1962) report that persons strongly committed to a local welfare agency are least likely to question agency directives or to consider leaving their present position. These conceptual demarcations are also applicable to professionals such as judges who possess and experience a mixture of orientations classifiable as cosmopolitan or local. The professional–local orientation develops from the institutional adaptability of bureaucracy to professional requirements and vice versa (Zvekic, 1984). Professional orientation among social scientists affects the attitudes they hold toward their jobs (Neumann and Neumann, 1982; Bute, 1998).

Among engineers, both cosmopolitans and locals/cosmopolitans exhibit stronger orientations toward internal work groups and external professional groups than locals; among scientists, locals are more oriented toward their internal departments than are cosmopolitans (Morse, 1974; Rotondi, 1977; Stahl, 1979). In a study of Australian scientists, Hill (1974) finds that localism might be more important than cosmopolitan norms with respect to knowledge production. Relationships between cosmopolitan–local orientation and measures of job performance were examined for technical employees in architectural firms. A cosmopolitan orientation is characterized by participation in professional societies and contributions to professional journals, and a higher level of education than is the rule for a local orientation. The latter is characterized by reluctance to leave the firm, a belief in the importance of employee unity, and intellectual stimulation acquired from company colleagues. Cosmopolitan orientation is positively related to supervisor ratings of following prescribed work hours and supervisor and coworker ratings of impressing others. Local orientation is positively related to coworker ratings of task performance and negatively related to coworker ratings of impressing others (London and Cheney, 1977). Goldberg (1976) critiques the cosmopolitanism–localism contrast widely used by social scientists, namely the equating of cosmopolitanism with professionalism. He claims the uncertainty of how to categorize scholars can be eliminated by returning the concept to its original usage — that of designating outer- and inner-reference groups. This more restricted definition allows testing of the hypothesis that a mixed type called "cosmo–local," is optimally suited to the professional role. "Cosmo–local" types who score high on both cosmopolitanism and localism are more likely than others to hold professional values and to have attained the autonomy required of professionals.

Pure cosmopolitans are actually more reluctant to seek expertise while the cosmo–local type are more sensitive to changes favorable to professional behavior; this relation was conditioned by such variables as career stage, work environment, and primary occupational role. Among industrial and management engineers, not surprisingly, locals are less likely to move (Kirschenbaum, 1976). Almy (1975) investigated the local–cosmopolitan attitudes of U.S. city managers. Following the idea of the multidimensionality of the cosmopolitan–local distinction initially introduced by Gouldner (1957) and verified by Flango (1974) we found a third each of the subjects reflected local, intermediate, and cosmopolitan attitudes. Local and cosmopolitan city managers differ with respect to education, tenure of office, childhood experiences. Some research supports the main idea embodied in the cosmopolitan risk management theory that individuals who are highly cosmopolitan have multiple, permeable dossiers. Cosmopolitans are more inclusive in their risk management judgments, expressing equal concern for local and national issues, while pluralistic decision-makers express greater concern for local issues. Cosmopolitanism aids in the solution of social problems (Earle and Cvetkovich, 1997).

Since Merton's (1959) cosmopolitan–local dichotomy, a number of researchers (i.e., Grimes, 1970; Patterson, 1971; Berger, 1973; Lammers, 1974) have reanalyzed and evaluated whether the construct is unidimensional or multidimensional in nature. Accordingly, they argue for a reformulation of the unidimensional polar cosmopolitan local model of Gouldner (1958, 1959) in which latent role identity is focused on either the profession or the local work setting.

Inferences drawn from these studies are: (1) administrative influence on faculty may be negligible for persons maintaining a cosmopolitan orientation, and therefore, (2) ruptures in faculty relations with administration may cause perceptions of disagreement only for those sensitive to these relations, that is, persons maintaining a local orientation.

Electronic bulletin board communication has implications both theoretically and practically for the cosmopolitan–local organizational governance in higher education (Dean, 2001). Namely, distinctions between the reference groups of cosmopolitans and locals become blurred because it makes administration and faculty increasingly aware of informal discourse, with subsequent possibly greater eruptions of conflict than if faculty brought their issues to the table in faculty meetings. Hence, demands from reference groups external to the local context become incorporated into informal dialogue. Under such conditions, more conflicts might happen than if faculty settled their differences in direct dialogue. Theories of deliberative democracy call for cooperative dialogue in pursuit of mutual understanding that may foster democratic deliberation (Gatz and Hirt, 2000; Welsh, 2002). Electronic governance transcends space, time, and geography because it moves from the concrete and the particular toward the cosmopolitan, general, and the universal — what Entrikin (1999) refers to as academic and social intergration in cyberspace.

Organizational disputes happen when there is tension between organizational and institutional goals; moreover, the degree to which organizational and institutional goals coincide determines one of three orientations of individuals participating in "Fac Chat" — "locals," "cosmopolitans," and "intermediates" (Nelson and Tallman, 1969). Goals set for academic institutions for members of the academic community include research, teaching, and service components. The role structure for members of the academy is set up to encourage these functions. At the institutional level, professionalism requires scholarly publication and obtaining extramural funding for research. When within an organization, administrative goals are consistent with faculty organizational goals and faculty members assume a local–cosmopolitan structure; correspondingly when administration goals are incompatible with faculty goals, tension develops in the organization. Tensions are built reflexively and squarely around the comparability between institutional (administrative) and faculty goals and are expressed operationally by varied reactions to community events. Because of congruence of goals, a local orientation, for example, could help maintain the opportunity to meet research demands through grant collaboration, release-time agreements, sabbatical leaves, and so forth. Among professors, those who do not commit wholly to localism or cosmopolitanism may extract advantage from both. The bulletin board facilitates congruence between institutional and administrative goals with those of the faculty by providing knowledge.

B. Statement of the Problem

The present study builds on previous research showing that electronic governance in a virtual academic community can be understood by employing the concepts of "local" and "cosmopolitan" professional role orientations (Mulkey et al., in press). Electronic governance via bulletin board communication exaggerates the boundaries between locals and cosmopolitans, the traditional professional role division of academia. Locals also tend to self-select to university-based faculty bulletin boards. If traditional structures persist, then consistent with the conceptualization and results of this antecedent investigation, we expect that faculty with a local orientation will be more likely to express acceptance of their administrators' views than faculty having a cosmopolitan orientation. More conformity is expected mainly because individuals characterized as locals might perceive their work in terms of its personal relevance, link these perceptions to primary communities, and therefore constrain the number of reference groups available to them (De Cindio et al., 2003). Conversely, cosmopolitans are less attached to their immediate milieu and broaden their access to actual or potential reference groups. Their views should be grounded less on what significant others, especially their local administrators, opine. Cosmopolitan and local concerns do not seem to converge, resulting in an intermediate type of normative orientation; external demands posed in an informal setting may facilitate conflict and forge cosmopolitan vs. local allegiances. While we have no clear prediction, we will excavate the normative boundaries of a primarily cosmopolitan bulletin board and compare them with those of our previously researched local bulletin board. Our informed hunch is virtual environments provide easy access for cosmopolitans and locals who seek out bulletin boards exclusive to their own interests for defining and solving the problem of academic community.

III. METHOD

A. Sample

The observational process for our analysis consisted first of selecting two collections of electronic mail messages corresponding to different and distinct virtual communities, one likely to exemplify the participation of constituents with cosmopolitan agendas and roles and the other likely to exemplify the participation of constituents with local agendas and roles. The two virtual communities were thus chosen so as to emphasize the contrasts between local and cosmopolitan membership.

A number of considerations were involved in the choice of the two groups of messages. First, the virtual communities needed to consist of relatively high percentages of academic members. Second, the communities needed to be chosen so as to maximize the likelihood of observing cosmopolitan–local differences in the content of the messages. Third, an archive of messages corresponding to a significant length of time needed to be available for each of the virtual communities. Finally, the virtual communities needed to contain significant percentages of messages containing content pertaining to the duties or responsibilities of members both within the academic community and in relation to communities outside of the virtual community, thus enabling an exploration of content pertaining to the construction of norms.

One set of messages (the Local Virtual Community) consisted of contributions from the members of a midwestern state university classified as a Carnegie Doctoral II institution. The Local Virtual Community was initiated by individuals at the university "primarily to facilitate discussion about important XXX issues." (*The letters XXX were chosen so as to correspond to the initials of the university without revealing the identity of it.*) These issues consisted of problems, experiences, and circumstances common to the faculty at that particular academic institution. Analysis showed that the preponderance of messages consisted of individuals who posted from a single subdomain of the Internet (xxx.edu), corresponding to that particular university. The individuals who submitted the messages consisted entirely of faculty (and some academic staff) affiliated with the university.

The second set of messages (the Cosmopolitan Virtual Community) consisted of contributions submitted by members of an organization started "to professionalize the public service, to keep members on the cutting edge of good government, and to help answer the enduring question of how to make government work better." The society contains significant percentages of academic faculty, and analysis showed that individuals who were affiliated with educational organizations were responsible for a preponderance of the messages found in the archives.

B. Selecting Messages from the Archives

The process of selecting messages from the archives consisted of two stages. The first stage involved an examination of each of the messages of each archive (513 messages in the case of the Local Virtual Community and 601 messages in the case of the Cosmopolitan Virtual Community). Those messages that included content that could possibly be construed as an attempt by the person who submitted the message to define, direct, discuss, influence, or comment on the norms pertaining to readers or other members of the community with which they were affiliated were included in a selected group of messages for each virtual community. This process resulted in selection of 272 (of 513) messages for the Local Virtual Community and 107 (of 601) messages for the Cosmopolitan Virtual Community. The time periods corresponding to these selected messages were approximately 11 months for the messages from the Local Virtual Community and 3 years, 1 month for the messages from the Cosmopolitan Virtual Community.

Once selected in the first stage, messages were considered more closely to determine what they revealed about the underlying premises and rhetoric regarding the roles of members of the virtual communities from which they were extracted. Messages that contained content that was significant in revealing the processes by which the construction of the role structure took place were selected for the subsample for each virtual community. These messages became the means by which the arguments and insights regarding the construction of the roles of cosmopolitans and locals were generated for this study.

C. Analytic/Observational Approach

Making sense of virtual governance draws from an assortment of qualitative modes of observation that include ethnography, ethnomethodology, grounded theory, and case studies/content analysis. These approaches to study enable us to observe social life in its natural setting and to make observations not easily reduced to numbers. In a study that examined electronic mail communication exchanged in a period of 3 years by an interorganizational community of software developers using the notion of genre repertoire, Eichorn (2001) notes ethnography seeks to examine the field not only as a place where research is carried out, but also as a methodological construction. Ethnography typically differs from other modes of observation in that it seldom approaches the task with precisely defined hypotheses to be tested, rather it attempts to make sense out of an ongoing process that cannot easily be predicted in advance — developing tentative conclusions that suggest particular types of further observations, making those observations, and thereby revising conclusions. This method more aptly generates theory alternating from induction to deduction. Nuances of attitude and behavior that might escape researchers are captured using this approach. Organizations and the analysis of the positions people occupy and the behavior associated with those positions comprise several elements of social life appropriate for qualitative research. Ethnography focuses on detailed description rather than explanation in order to fully learn about social life. Drawing also from ethnomethodology, this study presupposes reality is socially constructed rather than being "out there" for us to observe. People describe their world not "as it is" but "as they make sense of it." Moreover, this technique focuses on the discovery of implicit, usually unspoken assumptions and agreements. Grounded theory seeks to derive theories from an analysis of the patterns, themes, and common categories discovered in observational data. Case studies focus on in-depth examination of a single instance of some social phenomenon and we treat the bulletin board as consisting of "content" to be studied in each in two cases. Elements of the variety of approaches guide our observations.

Originally, we were not sure if localism and cosmopolitanism, when studying higher education, applied to electronic (online) governance. We therefore were heavy-handed with qualitative assessment, by selecting exemplary cases consistent with local and cosmopolitan orientations toward faculty governance. The electronic venue is distinct because it lends itself to the construction of informal norms in contrast to the more formal ones ordinarily espoused in faculty meetings and other face-to-face encounters. While it is helpful to apply the logic of localism and cosmopolitanism when studying higher education, these distinctions may or may not apply to electronic (online) governance; this has yet to be determined. Our earlier research coded and quantified the degree of localism and cosmopolitanism in a virtual academic community, but further excavation of the relevance of these concepts in virtual academia is required (Mulkey et al., in press). In other words, before we can determine the frequency of an item, we must make sure of what that item is and what is its nature. In the present study, we are therefore atuned to a qualitative inquiry. Such an approach not only allows us to identify and select exemplary cases of local and cosmopolitan orientations toward faculty governance but also permits the detection of nonfit or departure from this conceptualization.

The present study peruses two cases of a virtual academic community, one constituted predominantly by local subscribers (Mulkey et al., in press) and the other by cosmopolitan subscribers. Discourse is considered in terms of whether its features can be characterized as local or cosmopolitan, respectively. This approach intentionally foregoes aims at generalization and random sampling, in place of taking each communication as itself as an example of norm construction. Text is selected to show how locals and cosmopolitans use discreet bulletin board venues to construct the norms specific to their interests.

D. Measures

Following Mulkey et al. (in press), local and cosmopolitan classification schemes were developed from the general literature on cosmopolitans and locals, including a scale devised by Thielbar (1966) and Nelson and Tallman (1969). Locals and cosmopolitans participate in insuring the functions of higher education by negotiating between the various responsibilities they advocate. Locals have an orientation that personalizes the environment by projecting individualistic and personal conceptions on to complex current events and by underscoring the virtues of their local, collegial group; they exhibit broad affinity for primary group perspectives and relations. Thielbar (1966) refers to this tendency as "primary centrism." Respondents' attachment to local vs. cosmopolitan interests are coded by using one or more of the following criteria.

Locals react to local issues dependent on the degree of congruence between institutional and administrative goals. (The electronic outlet many minimize disputes by encouraging convergence of local and institutional goals.) Locals are identifiable by their conformity to administration (a local reference group). Cosmopolitans will be recognized as having less concern for local administrative mandates due to a broad range of reference groups and more concern with external and impersonal demands, such as writing grants and getting published. Locals extol the virtues of the communities in which they live. They show loyalty and organizational immobility. They stress the virtues of the friendly community and the belief in the importance of employee unity. They are less likely to question directives from university or state agencies. Cosmopolitans demonstrate organizational mobility, autonomy, and concern for outer-reference groups and academic advancement (scholarship). Locals react to well-established norms when there is little congruence between administrative and institutional goals.

We supplement our previously stated theoretically driven speculations with some theory-generating investigation concerning electronic patterns of communication — the general nature of responses, their frequency and number of referrals, and their time dependence. We also include whether differences in cosmopolitan and local response relate to gender.

IV. RESULTS AND DISCUSSION

This investigation explores the nature of virtual academic governance. Prior scholarship has identified two professional role structures that emerge with respect to the demands of teaching, scholarship, and service — localism and cosmopolitanism. Generally, locals develop ties to the particular concerns of the immediate and primary community whereas cosmopolitans tie themselves to a broader range of impersonal expectations. In our preliminary research, we had surmised that the opportunity for "virtual" interaction might elevate or lessen the typical separation between locals and cosmopolitans in achieving educational goals. We thought expectations of external professional reference groups that are brought to bear in such informal settings making if difficult, if not impossible, to retain a "local" view. The boundaries of interest become blurred. On the other hand, we thought the immediacy of internal and external concerns quickly communicated via the computer may intensify and expose conflicts that are seething. The results that are reported below suggest that the separate norms of locals and cosmopolitans are expressed by their allegiance to separate electronic bulletin boards; the virtual medium inclines members of academic community to segregate their normative structures. Virtual communication is conducive to exclusive forums for norm construction.

Results from our analyses are presented as qualitative excerpts. They are divided into responses from the local bulletin board and then from the cosmopolitan bulletin board.

A. Virtual Cosmopolitans

As an Association or Non-profit professional I'd like to invite you to subscribe to the FREE "Associations and the Web Electronic Newsletter." This newsletter is extremely useful and has articles about Association-related marketing, technology, web resources, RFPs, iMIS, TIMSS and what's hot/what's not.

This response shows a degree of diffidence and less concern with the host university and defines external and nationally grounded standards of interest pertaining to research, and other academic responsibilities for evaluating local decisions.

My statement did not imply that technology could not be mobilized or that it would not be mobilized for a variety of agendas. What I said is it is neutral — not passive — philosophically and that allows it to be harnessed to a variety of purposes ... elected officials use the technology for their purposes while administrators do theirs.

This cosmopolitan response constructs the norm of segregated and exclusive venues for competing agendas.

"Does the government want as much accountability as it is possible to achieve with the available resources, or does the government want their accountability to remain at the minimum of what is politically acceptable? ... We are maximizing accountability, openness, and participation — and our technological initiatives are making this possible. The "In Touch" feature of our website allows for documents, agendas, minutes, notices, etc. to be made available to citizens automatically by signing up to the feature.

The above message indicates responsiveness to a broad range of impersonal goals. Also demonstrated is a lack of adherence to primary reference group pressures.

We have rooted Public Administration in notions of efficient management, not just equitable governance ... . This requires considerable education of the public and a large dose of political philosophy in universities. Universities have been dominated by researchers whose notions of neutrality and a focus on policy has let elected officials control politics.

This response defines constructs a cosmopolitan norm of little reaction to local concerns and disagreement with local authority.

Otherwise, eGovernment will just mean less direct contact with real humans who work in the administration.

This response constructs impersonal norms for interaction, therefore it is cosmopolitan in character.

We need to change the system so that selecting "reply" option in E-Mail does not just send the response to the person who wrote the message. It should send the response back to the list serve itself.

This electronic communication illustrates norm construction that applies to a large, external, and universal system.

Technology is a means and by its use in a system, will tend to promote the ends currently pursued by the system unless decisions are made otherwise.

The broad, as opposed to limited, nature of the reference group expressed in this communication identifies it as an example of generic cosmopolitan norm definition.

Public Web Sites are assets for a community and are very beneficial. However, they are part of a system and will not by themselves alter that system.

This communication shows a class cosmopolitan component by defining the significance of a remote reference group.

"Collective decisions to deploy e-gov through the Web creates an ideological paradigm. ... The Web and therefore, e-everything has become a cyber-movement that defines the way whole societies will interact with each other. The Web is a driving component of the technological revolution that is globally transforming political cultures into an absolute reliance on electronic communications as a fundamental medium for human interaction. Without specific laws to safeguard its use, the Web has the potential to create a Cyber-Reich ...

Another cosmopolitan-norm-generating response is indicated by the respondent's concern over "whole" rather than "particular" communities.

I for one would appreciate our list members not sending messages with political references ... . I distinguish between political information and partisan assertions ...

The apolitical and nonparticularistic quality of cosmopolitan norms are illustrated here.

Can't we all just get along? I am establishing a cooling off period on the ASPA listserv. Any messages that are posted to the listserv now require my approval before they are distributed to each of you. I hope you trust me to determine what is and is not appropriate material.

Cosmopolitan norms construct and sustain a top-down management of

It is also high time we reconsider the basic question of what is the purpose of the national council and council members.

Cosmopolitan norms encourage attention to external reference groups.

I agree with you on all counts. I, too, prefer client as a term. I see clients and citizens as very different than consumers. Clients have special claims upon the services of institutions, such as students at a university. Clients also have duties and responsibilities to the institution and enjoy a privileged relationship with the particular professionals responsible for their welfare. In the cases of law and medicine, these relationships have been formalized and even protected from other public authorities. And as a public university, we professors have many duties, often indirect and subtle, to citizens. These transcend profit for sure. Competition is not functional in many cases, even in the private sector. . . . the main issue is less economics than it is political. The concern is how do we serve clients faithfully and in the larger public interest.

Cosmopolitan norms are set forth in these comments as they construct virtual academic community and public administration, namely through advocacy of apolitical behaviors.

B.   Virtual Locals

I agree with Will. You should have invited people to join this list if they wanted to, but you should not have forced all employees onto the list. This is an intrusion into our privacy.

A local orientation is illustrated by this respondent's assertion against generalized interactions in favor of individual and personalized allegiances.

My suggestion, then, is that there should be departments of computer science, English, math, history, anthropology, space studies, etc. Some of these departments will have a presence on all eleven campuses in the state, others might be represented on a proper subset of those campuses. There needs to be a procedure for selecting a department chair; we can argue about how it should be implemented.

Promulgated here is a local sentiment having no reference to external reference groups.

At last, the kind of message [this bulletin board] was supposed to induce. To all I would simply say the folks who originated this idea had (and have) high motives: to provide an opportunity for faculty exchange on serious subjects . . . perhaps this mechanism is not quite right, but I'm sure colleagues will continue to refine it.

Local norms are exemplified in this communication through reference to its support of local faculty concerns.

If everyone uses titles to their postings that are very explicit, it will help those staying on the list to pick and choose what they read, and to prioritize.

This comment displays its local character by its internally generated recommendations without reference to external reference groups.

I agree with those who say that it ought to be possible to cooperate between campuses . . . , but "ought to" and "doing" are different things. After all, we haven't done much of anything in the way of substantial restructuring here . . . — how can we expect to do it across the system?

Emphasis on the maintenance of immediate ties and concerns characterizes this comment.

> The question then becomes, how should the "impulse" to duplicate programs in times of fiscal pressure be redirected in more productive ways?

This excerpt of discourse constructs a norm of localism by indicating a resistance for external and universal standards.

> There are a "ton" of verify difficult governance problems which he avoids. I am reminded of Will Roger's remarks about solving the U-Boat problem in WW I. He indicated the solution was easy — just boil the oceans. When asked how he would do that he commented that the implementation of the idea was a technical problem that was beneath his level.

As in the previous response, a resistance to standardization and external reference groups is the tenor of localism norms.

> I'm enthusiastic about electronic publication developments, but I'm not optimistic that it will help much for some time.

This comment implies localism because of the respondent's adherence to local norms and objection to external professional criteria.

> ... In a less clumsy sentence let me say that the relationships between faculty priorities and the priorities of other interested parties are (or should be) subject to a protracted series of negotiations. Let me also say that such negotiations can only proceed, productively that is, if we acknowledge that there are times when university professors know more about the mission of the university than administrators, students, parents, business-people.

The respondent acknowledges administrative goals, but in fact exhibits the demeanor of a local by extolling local virtues and the belief in employee unity.

> B's e-mail raises some interesting and valid points, particularly about faculty viewpoints not being heard enough. However, I still vote for restricting access. The media monitoring factalk still is more like eavesdropping. Reporting information based on eavesdropping doesn't necessarily result in complete or quality reporting, either. Also, I am very concerned about the amount of information exchanged among faculty and administrators if someone is "monitoring" our conversations all the time. I find it a challenge (believe it or not) to share my views with a wide audience — many of whom I've never met — over electronic mail. My understanding is that I'm not alone in this. Then, if the media were involved, I think it would make the situation worse. Add to that the complication of not knowing with certainty the source of the information/opinions contained in the email. Even without the technological possibilities — and flaws — of electronic forms of communication, accurate reporting of information and its sources is difficult enough ... . To top it all off, restricting factalk affords the listserv participants a certain level of respect — respect of their communication with colleagues and respect for their honest and open opinions (which we don't get one hundred percent, of course, but the situation would be worse with media monitoring).

This excerpt depicts the local professional orientation; the staunch dismissal of an open dialogue with administrators shows adherence and responsiveness to primary reference group pressures.

> National surveys including our faculty as well as our campus surveys over time have indicated that many faculty on this campus are concerned that juried research is given too much weight in promotion and tenure decisions compared to the importance of teaching and service; that they wish teaching and service were valued more here; and that they would appreciate more flexibility in crafting careers or in altering priorities during mid-career.

The norm of localism is evident in the above comment because of a rejection of externally defined mandates for performance.

> I worked with a number of faculty and staff who actually spent more time in a given year on union related activities than they did teaching or engaging in scholarship or service. It also seemed that the institutions hired proportionately more administrators and attorneys than the two non-union institutions with which I've been affiliated.

The above response attests to a local response to the bifurcated structure of governance in academia, whereby faculty are less concerned with external professional standards than they are with peer-group solidarity.

> Regrettably until faculty members and faculty unions take this denial of due process into the courtrooms, administrators will not give up SET voluntarily.

Unionization interests reflect local normative orientation in the above response.

> The idea for a Scholars' Fair when the Board meets here is excellent! Showing the Board and public what we do is important.

Localism tends to focus a person's interests internally rather than externally; this is the case with the above response.

> I need not tell you of the importance of maintaining a good library, with up to date collections of books and journals. It is so fundamental — any half decent university knows that. Yet, our library resources continue to decline and have been doing so for so long that catching up will be very difficult.

The above comment suggests an adherence to local and provincial standards for assessing the university; new information management systems have outdated the notions of "traditional" library.

> I'm enthusiastic about electronic publication developments, but I'm not optimistic that it will help much for some time.

Here again, reservation, reluctance, and reticence attest to localism. It surfaces pertaining to an immediate commitment to broad-based technologies and standards for operation.

I have often wondered why there has not been a faculty uprising in my 7+ years here. I think I know why, at least partly: crummy salaries only apply to a certain percentage of the faculty … . Another reason is that in this area, the perception is that 30K is a good salary for anyone.

The idea of faculty uprising is indicative of a local normative orientation in approaches to governance.

Numerous other comments can be classified as local or cosmopolitan showing the utility of this framework for examining how the electronic medium is associated with virtual academic governance and public administration. The bottom line is that the ease of access to communication coupled with polarized interests fosters a new form of community. In a sense the landscape is one analogous to gated communities where the e-venue promotes the emergence of private and exclusive groups.

V. SUMMARY AND CONCLUSION

This study extends the work of previous exploratory investigation of the normative structure of electronic governance by analyzing the discourse of a virtual bulletin board (Mulkey et al., in press). As in the previous research, we contend that virtual bulletin board communication constitutes academic community by defining and solving the problem of professional responsibility. Institutional goals and local administration goals are traditionally divergent and forge local and cosmopolitan responses to the demands of academic mandates for scholarship, teaching, and service. Electronic governance brings external demands to bear in an informal setting to create conflict and reinforce cosmopolitan and local orientations. While e-governance has the potential to facilitate coalition in the approach to solving tasks, the "lions work together and can get larger prey," localism and cosmopolitanism prevail. Given the discreet nature of the normative structure of electronic governance, we were inclined to further explore how the medium might lend itself to exclusivity of participation. Hence, the online medium can facilitate the development of local and cosmopolitan bulletin boards, two separate spheres that segregate and contain the circulation of information. The analyses of excerpts from two electronic venues reveals indeed that local and cosmopolitan subscribers alike create environments that define and maintain their norms for achieving institutional goals. Voluntary electronic communication may select only locals because locals tend to be reactive to concerns of academia whereas cosmopolitans are too busy living up to meeting with the criteria of external reference groups to be bothered with local considerations. Yet, cosmopolitans exploit the online medium as a place to define and maintain their norms for fulfilling the mandates of academia. Virtual communities seem conducive to self-selection and exclusivity of these normative orientations for fulfilling the functions of academic institutions. Hence, we introduce the significance of "virtual locals and cosmopolitans." Further research on electronic governance in virtual academic communities can continue to document the local and cosmopolitan normative environment as exclusive and segregated.

REFERENCES

Almy, T.A., Local–cosmopolitanism and U.S. city managers, *Urban Affairs Quarterly*, 10, 243–272, 1975.

Babbie, E., We am a virtual community, *American Sociologist*, 27, 65–71, 1996.

Baker, P.J., Local and cosmopolitan orientations of faculty: implications for teaching, *Teaching Sociology*, 12, 82–106, 1984.

Baker, P. and Ward, A., Community formation and dynamics in the virtual metropolis, *National Civic Review*, 89, 203–221, 2000.

Barab, S.A., An introduction to the special issue: designing for virtual communities in the service of learning, *Information Society*, 19, 197–202, 2003.

Barab, S.A., MKinste, J.G., and Scheckler, R., Designing system dualities: characterizing a web-supported professional development community, *Information Society*, 19, 237–257, 2003.

Berger, P.K., Cosmopolitan–local: a factor analysis of the construct, *Administrative Science Quarterly*, 18, 223–235, 1973.

Bevis, M.E. and Kirchhoff, K., Role development in an applied discipline: clinical nurse researchers, *Current Research on Occupations and Professions*, 4, 69–86, 1987.

Bute, M., Cosmopolitan sociology and the well-informed citizen: an introductory essay, *Sociological Imagination*, 35, 219–225, 1998.

Cornwall, J.R., Cosmopolitan–local: a cross-lagged correlation of the relationship between professional role orientations and behaviors in an academic organization, *Human Relations*, 40, 281–297, 1987.

Dean, J., Cybersalons and civil society: rethinking the public sphere in transnational technoculture, *Public Culture*, 13, 2001.

De Cindio, F., Gentile, O., Grew, P., and Redolfi, D., Community networks: rules of behavior and social structure, *Information Society*, 19, 395–407, 2003.

Delbecq, A.K., Local–cosmopolitan orientations and career strategies of specialists, *Academy of Management Journal*, 13, 373–388, 1970.

Dicker, M., Reading, intellectualism and cosmopolitanism: a study of community orientations, *Journal of Political and Military Sociology*, 2, 221–236, 1974.

Durrill, W.K., A tale of two courthouses: civic space, political power, and development in a new South Community, 1843–1940, *Journal of Social History*, 35, 659–681, 2002.

Earle, T.C. and Cvetkovich, G., Culture, cosmopolitanism, and risk management. Risk analysis, *International Sociology*, 14, 269–282, 1997.

Eichorn, K., Sites unseen: ethnographic research in a textual community, *International Journal of Qualitative Studies in Education*, 14, 565–578, 2001.

Entrikin, K.N., Political community, identity and cosmopolitan place, *International Sociology*, 14, 269–282, 1999.

Etzioni, A., E-Communities Build New Ties, but Ties that Bind, *The New York Times*, Feb. 10, 2000, p. 7.

Etzioni, A. and Etzioni, O., Communities: virtual versus real, *Science*, 277, 295–298, 1997.

Etzioni, A. and Etzioni, O., Face-to-face and computer-mediated communities: a comparative analysis, *Information Society*, 15, 241–249, 1999.

Fairweather, J.S., The mythologies of faculty productivity: implications for institutional policy and decision making, *The Journal of Higher Education*, 73, 26–48, 2002.

Ferber, P., Foltx, F., and Pugilese, R., The politics of state legislature web sites: making e-government more participatory, *Bulletin of Science, Technology, and Society*, 23, 157–168, 2003.

Flango, V., The dimensionality of the cosmopolitan–local construct, *Administrative Science Quarterly*, 19, 198–210, 1974.

Foltz, F. and Foltz, F., Religion on the Internet: community and virtual existence, *Bulletin of Science, Technology and Society*, 23, 321–331, 2003.

Frankel, M.S., Kling, R., Lee, Y.-C., and Teich, A.L., Anonymous communication policies for the Internet: results and recommendations of the AAAS Conference, *Information Society*, 15, 71–78, 1999.

Gatz, L.B., and Hirt, J.B., Academic and social integration in cyberspace: students and e-mail, *The Review of Higher Education*, 23, 299–318, 2000.

Goode, W.J., A theory of role strain, *American Sociological Review*, 25, 483–496, 1960.

Goldberg, A.I., The relevance of cosmopolitan/local orientations to professional values and behaviour, *Sociology of Work and Occupations*, 3, 332–356, 1976.

Gouldner, A., Cosmopolitans and locals: toward an analysis of latent social roles — I, *Administrative Science Quarterly*, 2, 281–306, 1957.

Gouldner, A., Cosmopolitans and locals: toward an analysis of latent social roles — II, *Administrative Science Quarterly*, 2, 444–480, 1958.

Grimes, A.J., Cosmopolitan–local: evaluation of the construct, *Administrative Science Quarterly*, 15, 407–416, 1970.

Grimes, A.J., Cosmopolitan–local: a multidimensional construct, *Research in Higher Education*, 13, 195–211, 1980.

Hampton, K. and Wellman, B., Long distance in the network society: contact and support beyond Netville, *American Behavioral Scientist*, 45, 476–496, 2001.

Haythornthwaite, C. and Wellman, B., Work, friendship and media use for information exchange in a networked organization, *Journal of the American Society for Information Science*, 12, 1101–1115, 1998.

Hill, S.C., Questioning the influence of a social system of science: a study of Australian scientists, *Science Studies*, 4, 135–163, 1974.

House, R.J., Cosmopolitans and locals: some differential correlations between leader behavior, organizational practices, and employee satisfaction and performance, *Academy of Management Journal*, 12, 135–138, 1969.

Hunt, J.G., Content, process, and the Matthew effect among management academics, *Journal of Management*, 13, 191–211, 1987.

Kaymer, M.M. and Haythornwaite, C., Judging multiple social worlds: distance students online and offline, *American Behavioral Scientist*, 45, 510–530, 2001.

Kirschenbaum, A., Organizational behavior, career orientation, and the propensity to move among professionals, *Sociology of Work and Occupations*, 3, 357–372, 1976.

Kling, R., Special informatics: a new perspective on social research about information and communication technologies, *Prometheus*, 18, 245–264, 2000.

Kling, R. and Courtright, C., Group behavior and learning in electronic forums: a sociotechnological approach, *Information Society*, 19, 136–221, 2003.

Kling, R. and McKim, G., Not just a matter of time: field differences and the shaping of electronic media in supporting . . . , *Journal for the American Society for Information Science*, 51, 1306–1321, 2000.

Kling, R., McKim, G., and King, A., A bit more to it: scholarly communication forums as socio-technical interaction networks, *Journal for the American Society for Information Science and Technology*, 54, 47–68, 2003.

Kling, R., Teich, Al., Lee, Y.-C., and Frankel, M.S., Assessing anonymous communication on the Internet: policy deliberations, *Information Society*, 15, 79–93, 1999.

Koku, E., Nazer, N., and Wellman, B., Netting scholars: online and offline, *American Behavioral Scientist*, 44, 1752–1775, 2001.

Komito, L., The Net as a foraging society: flexible communities, *Information Society*, 14, 97–107, 1998.

Lamb, R. and Kling, R., Reconceptualizing users as social actors in information systems research, *MIS Quarterly*, 27, 197–226, 2003.

Lammers, C.J., Localism, cosmopolitanism, and faculty response, *Sociology of Education*, 47, 129–158, 1974.

Leslie, D.W., Resolving the dispute: teaching is academe's core value, *The Journal of Higher Education*, 73, 49–73, 2002.

London, M. and Cheney, L., The relationship between cosmopolitan local orientation and job performance, *Journal of Vocational Behavior*, 11, 182–195, 1977.

Mauksch, H.O., Teaching within institutional values and structures, *Teaching Sociology*, 14, 40–49, 1986.

Merton, R.K., *Social Theory and Social Structure*, Free Press, Glencoe, IL, 1959.

Michalski, J., What is virtual community?, *New Perspectives Quarterly*, 12, 44–47, 1995.

Morse, E.V., Cognitive skills: a determinant of scientists local–cosmopolitan orientation, *Academy of Management Journal*, 17, 709–724, 1974.

Mulkey, L.M. and Dougan, W.L., Science as it consists of normalized practices, *The American Sociologist*, 27, 56–61, 1996.

Mulkey, L.D.W. and Steelman, L., Cosmopolitans and locals in and as a virtual academic community, *International Journal of Public Administration*, 28, in press.

Nederhof, A.J., International comparison of department's research performance in the humanities, *Journal of the American Society for Information Science*, 43, 249–257, 1992.

Nelson, J.I. and Tallman, I., Local–cosmopolitan perceptions of political conformity: a specification of parental influence, *American Journal of Sociology*, 75,193–207, 1969.

Neumann, Y. and Neumann, L., Faculty work orientations as predictors of work attitudes in the physical and social sciences, *Journal of Vocational Behavior*, 21, 359–365, 1982.

Norris, P., The bridging and bonding of on-line communities, *Harvard International Journal of Press/Politics*, 7, 3–14, 2002.

Patterson, J., The cosmopolitan local: a reanalysis of the construct, *The Kansas Journal of Sociology*, 7, 70–79, 1971.

Robertson, T.S., Organizational cosmopolitanism and innovativeness, *Academy of Management Journal*, 26, 332–339, 1983.

Romm, C.T. and Pliskin, N., Diffusion of e-mail: an organizational learning perspective, *Information and Management*, 31, 37–47, 1996.

Rotondi, T., Jr., Reference groups and local cosmopolitanism, *Social Behavior and Personality*, 5, 257–262, 1977.

Stahl, M.J., Operationalizing the moskos institution-occupation model: an application of Gouldner's cosmopolitan–local research, *Journal of Applied Psychology*, 63, 415–422, 1978.

Stahl, M.J., Cosmopolitan–local orientations as predictors of scientific productivity, organizational productivity, and job satisfaction for scientists and engineers, *EE Transactions on Engineering Management*, 26, 39, 1979.

Stein, R.B., Collaboration in delivering higher education programs: barriers and challenges, *The Review of Higher Education*, 24, 4, 2001.

Szerszynski, B. and Urry, J., Cultures of cosmopolitanism, *Sociological Review*, 50, 461–482, 2002.

Thielbar, G.W., Localism-cosmopolitanism; social differentiation in mass society, thesis, Minnesota, 1966.

Turkle, S., Multiple subjectivity and virtual community at the end of the Freudian century, *Sociological Inquiry*, 67, 72–84, 1997.

Turkle, S., Looking beyond cyberspace: beyond grounded sociology, *Contemporary Sociology*, 28, 643–649, 1999.

Walsh, J.P. and Bayma, T.,Computer networks and scientific work, *Social Studies of Science*, 26, 661–703, 1996.

Wellman, B., Living networked in a wired world, *EE Expert Intelligent Systems and their Applications*, 14, 15–18, 1999.

Wellman, B., Physical place and cyberspace: the rise of personalized networking, *International Journal of Urban and Regional Research*, 2, 227–252, 2001.

Wellman, B. and Salaff, J., Computer networks as social networks: collaborative work, telework and virtual community, *Annual Review of Sociology*, 22, 213–238, 1996.

Welsh, S., Deliberative democracy and the rhetorical production of political culture, *Rhetoric and Public Affairs*, 5, 2002.

Williams, M., Virtually criminal: discourse, deviance and anxiety within virtual communities, *International Review of Law, Computers, and Technology*, 14, 95–105, 2000.

Wright, T.A. and Larwood, L., Further examination of the cosmopolitan–local latent role construct, *Psychological Reports*, 81, 897–899, 1997.

Zucchermaglio, C. and Talamo, A., The development of a virtual community of practices using electronic mail and communicative genres, *Journal of Business and Technical Communication*, 17, 259–285, 2003.

Zvekic, U., Cosmopolitan and local orientation in the judicial profession, *Sociologija*, 26, 139–157, 1984.

9

INFORMATION TECHNOLOGY INVESTMENT AND ORGANIZATIONAL PERFORMANCE IN THE PUBLIC SECTOR

Pamela Hammers Specht
University of Nebraska

Gregory Hoff
University of Nebraska

CONTENTS

I.   Introduction 128
II. Review of literature 129
III. Framework 135
IV. Conclusion 139
Acknowledgments 140
References 140

ABSTRACT

This chapter addresses how an organization can tie an information technology (IT) investment to the benefit of increased performance. A significant issue faced by managers is determining what will be measured or tracked to accurately represent investment and performance. The issue is explored through an extensive literature review. Because little literature covering these measurement topics in the public sector exists, applicable private-sector literature is included. A framework useful in developing appropriate measures is offered to public-sector managers. Finally, guidelines based on the literature are presented. The guidelines can assist the manager in decision-making and provide more tangible information in business cases connecting IT investment to organizational performance.

I. INTRODUCTION

The penetration of information technology (IT) into all aspects of organizations has continued in the private and public sectors. New channels for delivering services are being created with different expectations and risks that did not previously exist. New tools and techniques are continually emerging. In times of limited resources and increased accountability, persons in positions of responsibility have to know what investment is being made by their organization in IT. The critical question becomes, "Does this investment improve how the organization meets its goals and fulfills its mission?"

Investment in IT has increased exponentially in the public, as well as the private, sector. Managers know that acquiring the hardware and software, although costly, is only a fraction of the expense. Other costs can include training users and IT staff, hiring IT staff, establishing help desks, providing support for remote locations, and increasing the salaries of IT staff to be competitive with other organizations needing technology personnel. Because of the expense of IT, managers are having to address issues of IT investment linkage to organizational performance.

In many instances, managers are developing a business case to sell the significance of an IT investment. A well-developed business case explaining the return on the IT investment is becoming the best way to get support. A business case includes justifying the outlay by quantifying the value of IT. A business case also offers the benefit of building consensus, establishing priorities, managing project scope, and establishing measurements. Measuring IT investment is difficult because many of the benefits are qualitative and indirect. For example (Wena et al., 1998), a decision support system (DSS) can improve a manager's decision-making capability, but it is difficult to predict the extent to which the DSS will actually lead to better decisions.

The most significant issue in studying the relationship between IT investment and organizational performance is to determine what will be measured or tracked. IT investment should be made as a contribution to the accomplishment of some portion of the organization's strategic plan. Therefore, measures chosen by the public-sector manager to determine the impact of IT investment on organizational performance should be strategic-plan-driven. Most significant IT investments are actually a support for a business redesign effort connected to an organizational strategy, not an IT project for IT's sake (Stevens, 1998). Knowing this does not make the choice of measures an easy one. The impacts of IT investment may be due to "ripple effects," making the measurement process very complex. There have been attempts at identifying types of impacts. For example, Ammons (2001) offered four types of public-sector performance measures: "workload (output) measures; efficiency measures; effectiveness (outcome) measures; and productivity measures." Unfortunately, metrics for each category are not readily agreed upon.

There is a lack of consensus in the literature on the defining and measuring of IT and organizational performance. IT can include information systems, data communications, personnel, hardware, software, and infrastructure investment such as wiring. Organizational performance can involve financial or productivity measures. IT can possibly impact one type of organizational performance, but not another. Also, the type of impact (negative, none, or positive) can depend on the measure chosen for IT.

Management will want to decide what benefits an IT investment will provide and to whom, determine the criteria for a successful result, and then measure those criteria. For example, management can develop criteria for the efficiency or the effectiveness of users of a specific application that IT might impact.

Figure 9.1 Measurement of the impact of IT investment on organizational performance over time.

Unaddressable complexity and confusion can arise from attempting to measure directly the impact of IT investment on organizational performance. There are steps between the actual investment and a change in organizational performance occurring. Benefits cannot be seen, sometimes for several years. Data collection needs to be over time, with intermediate measures taken. Figure 9.1 addresses the significant issue of what to measure and emphasizes the need to collect information or data over time. IT pays off usually only in the long term because of the long learning and development period necessary to take advantage of IT.

This chapter contains a thorough literature review followed by an example of a framework that managers can use in determining the impact of IT investment on organizational performance. The literature review covers articles related to private- as well as public-sector organizations. The review emphasizes examples of measures of IT investment and performance and business unit and organizational performance.

II. REVIEW OF LITERATURE

Table 9.1 presents an overview of the literature covering research studies appropriate to the linking of IT investment and organizational performance in the private sector. The majority of studies have been conducted in the private sector. Table 9.2 presents a literature overview of studies of the impact of IT investment in the public sector.

Although not a research study, an article by Halachmi and Bouckaert (1994) reviewed performance measurement, organizational IT, and organizational design. The review covered factors pertinent to this discussion. The main users of high-level IT are white-collar workers. Demonstrating increased productivity with these users is more difficult because inputs and outputs are not easily defined. Public-sector organizations, especially governments, also experience difficulty measuring IT significance because of the problems inherent in defining inputs and outputs. The public sector also uses more than just efficiency and effectiveness as measures of performance. Private-sector organizations can use Return on Investment (ROI), Return on Equity (ROE), market share, cash flow, and so forth, but these measures are not applicable, for example, to governments. The authors call for the development of performance measures linking IT performance and organizational performance to enhance the control over IT expenditures.

Most of the studies indicate that measuring IT investment is difficult because there is a lack of information on how to define and measure IT. There seems to be a need to get down to the application level to decrease complexity. But complexity still exists because deciding what to measure is still difficult. The manager may want to look at non-IT staff costs (such as training), cost of support of application over time, cost of maintenance, cost of the roll-out in terms of man-hours — all of these measures have direct and indirect aspects, causing complexity. Chosen measures for the IT investment also depend on how IT performance and business unit/organizational performance are defined. For example,

Table 9.1 Overview of Literature Linking IT Investment and Organizational Performance (Examples of Measures from the Private Sector)

Author	Year	Measures of IT Investment and Performance	Measures of Business Unit and Organizational Performance
Miron	1988	Performance: IT fit to strategy	
Weill	1990	Performance: IT fit to strategy	
Alpar and Kim	1990	Investment: ratio of IT expenses to number of computerized applications	Ratio of profit to equity
Banker et al.	1990	Investment: cost of system materials for a specific application	Sales, efficiency
Harris and Katz	1991	Investment: ratio of IT expenses to total operating expenses	Ratio of total operating costs to income
Barua and Kriebel	1991	IT efficiency: economic benefits, quality, fixed and variable IT costs	
Morishima	1991	Performance: usage	Employee productivity, labor cost, profitability
Weill	1992	Investment: ratio of IT expenses to sales Performance: management commitment, user information satisfaction	
Mahmood and Mann	1993	Investment: IT budget as a percent of revenue, value of IT as a percent of revenue, percent of IT budget spent on staff, percent of IT budget spent on training IT staff, number of PCs as percent of total employees	
Dos Santos et al.	1993	Performance: innovativeness of IT	
Sethi et al.	1993	Investment: annual IS budget as a percent of revenue, currentness of IS equipment as a percent of revenue, IS staff cost as a percent of IS budget, number of computers to number of employees	
Smith and McKeen	1993	Performance: IT *effectiveness* — IT usage	Revenue due to IT investment
Glazer	1993	Performance: determine value of information generated (gives examples)	
Kettinger and Grover	1994	Performance: provision of sustained competitive advantage (gives measurement examples)	Market share
Hagedoorn and Schakenraad	1994	Investment: number of strategic linkages for IT	

Table 9.1 Overview of Literature Linking IT Investment and Organizational Performance (Examples of Measures from the Private Sector) — continued

Author	Year	Measures of IT Investment and Performance	Measures of Business Unit and Organizational Performance
Farbey et al.	1994	Performance: impact on reputation, computing, informing, communications, and learning	
Brynjolfsson	1994	Performance: timeliness, quality, flexibility of information	Productivity: quality and quantity of customer service, product variety
Pastore	1993	Performance: user satisfaction with IS deliverables	Customer satisfaction
Lunsford and Simpson	1995	Performance: IT fit with strategy	
Computerworld	*1995*	Performance: IT fit with strategy	
Fielder and Gatian	1995		Long-term financial success due to IT usage (examples given)
Saarinen and Kivijarvi	1995	Investment: ratio of IT expenses to number of employees	Changes in decision-making, communication, and work processes
Barua et al.	1995	Performance: impact on operations such as capacity utilization, inventory turnover	
Mukhopadhyay and Kekre	1995	Performance: cost savings	
Dos Santos and Peffers	1995	Investment in a specific IT	
Yuthas and Eining	1995	Performance: usage and satisfaction with IT, decision effectiveness (user accuracy and quality)	
Rao et al.	1995	Implementation success (acceptance, usage, integration)	
Duncan	1995	Performance: infrastructure flexibility (e.g., configuration rules, access and connectivity standards, excess capacity)	
Mitra and Chayam	1996	Performance: increase in control for managers	Labor costs
Nelson and Cooprider	1996	Performance: IS department's relationship with other departments, amount of shared knowledge due to IT	

continued

Table 9.1 Overview of Literature Linking IT Investment and Organizational Performance (Examples of Measures from the Private Sector) — continued

Author	Year	Measures of IT Investment and Performance	Measures of Business Unit and Organizational Performance
Karimi and Gupta	1996	Performance: IT maturity (ability to integrate IT aspects), technology penetration in the organization, top management knowledge of IT, extent of following IT plan	
Rai et al.	1996		Labor efficiency
Brynjolfsson and Hitt	1996		Rate of return on computers
Hitt and Brynjolfsson	1996	Investment computer capital, IS labor	Value created for customers, organization output impacted by IT
Husein and Moreton	1996		Productivity
Neunaha	1996		IT has a productive, coordinative, and informative impact
Dos Santos et al.	1996	Investment: processor value as percent of revenue, IS budget as percent of revenue, IS staff and training as percent of IS budget, number of PCs per employee	
Mukhopadhyay et al.	1997		Quality, timeliness, output
Raj et al.	1997	Performance: link to strategy Investment: hardware, software, telecommunications, IS staff	Labor and administrative productivity
Byrd and Marshall	1997	Investment: number of PCs as percent of employees, percent of IT budget spent on training and on IT staff	
Dewan and Min	1997	Investment: value of central processors + value of desktops + MIS budget dedicated to IS staff	IT investment provides better return for organization than investment in labor although not as dramatic for service-sector organizations
Wena et al.	1998	Performance: methods for risks and benefits explained (e.g., vulnerability of hardware, costs of implementation, automate tasks)	

Table 9.1 Overview of Literature Linking IT Investment and Organizational Performance (Examples of Measures from the Private Sector) — continued

Author	Year	Measures of IT Investment and Performance	Measures of Business Unit and Organizational Performance
Brynjolfsson and Hitt	1998		IT enables organizational change but investment and performance of IT is minimal compared with investment and performance gains of organizational change
Brynjolfsson et al.	1998	Investment: computer capital, organizational adjustment costs (training, organizational change, relationship building)	"Computer-intensive firms have distinctly different organizational characteristics: involving teams, broader jobs, greater decentralization of decision-making"
Dewan and Kraemer	1998	Investment: hardware, data communications, software, and services	
Francalanci and Galal	1998	Investment: IT expenses, worker compensation	Decentralization of decision-making leading to heavier reliance on managers, less reliance on clericals and professionals
Devaraj and Kohli	2000	Investment: IT labor, capital, and support; business process redesign Performance: revenue, customer satisfaction	"Changes in patient care; better financial & quality outcomes"
Tallon et al.	2000	Investment goals: *operational effectiveness* — "cost reduction, improving quality and speed, and enhancing overall firm effectiveness;" *strategic positioning* — "extending geographic reach, changing industry and market practices" Performance: process planning and support, supplier relations, production and operations, product and service enhancement, sales and marketing support, customer relations	IT closely aligned with business strategy and executive ability to express provided higher perceived performance from IT investment

continued

Table 9.1 Overview of Literature Linking IT Investment and Organizational Performance (Examples of Measures from the Private Sector) — continued

Author	Year	Measures of IT Investment and Performance	Measures of Business Unit and Organizational Performance
Greenan and Mairesse	2000	Performance: labor productivity increases	
Bresnahan et al.	2002		IT decreases number of low-skill workers and increases number of high-skill workers
Brynjolfsson et al.	2002	Investment: computer assets + intangible assets (implementing new processes, training, and incentive systems)	IT is catalyst for organizational improvements in business processes, worker knowledge, monitoring and reporting, and incentive systems
Dedrick et al.	2003	Performance: automation of processes, enabler of organizational change	Productivity
Lanham	2003	Performance: "responsiveness to the comments and inquires of both politicians and citizens, risk management efforts undertaken to protect the public trust and property and means to gauge how faithfully the system addresses principles of democratic governance"	
Rau and Bye	2003	Performance: "expense containment, process improvement, customer advantage, talent leverage"	

if the goal is to increase organizational productivity, the measure of IT performance may be the number of clients served, rather than user satisfaction.

As can be seen from Table 9.1 and Table 9.2, measures of IT investment and performance include determining fit to organizational strategy, using financial ratios, identifying quantity of IT (e.g., number of computerized applications), IT usage, satisfaction with IT, commitment of management, and quality and quantity of information provided. Business unit and organizational performance measures in the studies included financial ratios, employee productivity, labor cost, profitability, customer satisfaction, and efficiency. Some of the studies also used measures such as ROI, ROE, and sales growth. These measures are not included in Table 9.1 because they are not useful to most public-sector organizations. Public-sector studies (Table 9.2) identified service delivery characteristics, positive organizational change, and integration with other state systems as possible measures of unit and organizational performance.

Other authors who have reviewed the research (e.g., Kauffman and Weill, 1989; Wena et al., 1998) suggest that the benefits and the risks of the IT investment need to be considered because the impact on the organization is affected by the extent to which IT benefits are maximized and the risks are minimized. IT investment benefits fall into four categories: increase in productivity, facilitating management, gaining competitive advantage, and providing a solid base for business redesign. Productivity gains can include decreases in communication time; increases in quality service, timeliness and accessibility of information; and operating improvements. Benefits for management can include decreased time to decision, better control, and improvement of employee work life. Competitive advantage can be impacted by IT through a decrease in supplier costs, ability to offer better services, and improving operating margins relative to competitors.

IT risks are physical and managerial (Wena et al., 1998). Physical risks include hardware security (need for protection from theft and viruses), and software security (privacy concerns, piracy, and alteration). Loss of data is a physical risk. Managerial risks include exceeding cost of implementation or time for implementation and employee resistance leading to low usage.

III. FRAMEWORK

A framework is presented in Figure 9.2 (adapted from Kinsella, 1997). The framework is an example of an approach public-sector managers can use to determine how IT impacts organizational performance. By understanding what the desired impact of the IT investment is, a manager should be able to better determine what measures to use to ascertain success of the investment. The basic assumption used with the framework is that the IT investments are being considered for the purpose of increasing organizational efficiency and effectiveness. Neunaha (1996) also used a framework, adding innovation to efficiency and effectiveness to assess the business value of IT investment.

An efficient IT investment works to reduce waste or redundancy. An efficient IT investment is typically implemented with the goal of increased productivity through lowering costs, reducing errors, and maintaining costs with a higher level of output. An IT investment aimed at increased effectiveness attempts to impact performance by making it better or different. Increased capability, improved information access, and new services are a few goals for an effective IT investment.

Each IT investment can be strategic, informative, or transactional (Weill, 1992). A strategic IT investment is connected to the general goals of the business, with the aim of positively changing the business of the organization to provide a competitive advantage. Strategic IT attempts to place an organization ahead of its competition. Although public-sector organizations sometimes do not have competitors as normally envisioned, most still have the strategy of "staying in business." This strategy can involve establishing a niche to insure not having competition or not having successful competition.

An informative use of IT provides management with better decision-making information. An example of an informative IT is an information system that provides management with custom reports, such as a state health department system that provides

Table 9.2 Overview of Literature Linking IT Investment and Organizational Performance (Examples of Measures from the Public Sector)

Author	Year	Measures of IT Investment and Performance	Measures of Business Unit and Organizational Performance
Kraemer et al.	1995		"Flexibility in delivery of services, closer linkage of city government with citizen and corporate clients, improved decision making processes, bureaucratic innovation with regard to computer use"
Pinsonneault and Kraemer	1997	Investment: extent of IT penetration (gives examples) Performance: degree of centralized decision making	
U.S. GAO (GAO/ AMID-98-89)	1998	Performance: *strategic* — enterprise mission goals, portfolio analysis and management, financial and investment performance, IT resource usage; *customer* — partnership and involvement, satisfaction, business process support; *internal business* — applications development and maintenance, project performance, infrastructure availability, enterprise architecture standards compliance; *innovation and learning* — workforce competency and development, advanced technology use, methodology currency, employee satisfaction and retention	The organization will mature in stages as performance management culture develops
Schorr and Stolfo	1998	Performance: maintenance of individual rights and privacy, direct access to government information and services, data mining for government research topics, research grants	
RPPI	2000	Investment: "share-in-savings" contracts, retention of IT staff Performance: meeting citizen expectations, security and privacy	Integration with other state systems, operation transformation

Table 9.2 Overview of Literature Linking IT Investment and Organizational Performance (Examples of Measures from the Public Sector) — continued

Author	Year	Measures of IT Investment and Performance	Measures of Business Unit and Organizational Performance
Performance Institute	2002	Performance: *cost efficiency* — cost per unit output, cost per unit activity, average transaction processing time, transactions per employee, decrease in management layers, prevention of business disruptions; *transactions* — channel comparison measures, percentage of aborted or incomplete transactions, customer traffic; *improved accessibility* — market share, cycle-time-to-client, customer satisfaction with ease of access and use, service availability, reduced constituent cost, depth of online service, number of entry points, service reliability, special need accessibility, service/product integration, reduction in security/privacy breaches, client loyalty; *enhanced capability* — use/adoption rate, improved capacity, customer satisfaction with utility or benefit of product/service, accuracy of service/product provision	Improved mission result as defined by individual agency
Gresham and Andrulis	2003	Performance: reduce operational expenses, improve data accuracy, improve information distribution, improve information analysis, reduce services costs, improve services delivery, efficient/effective customer services, improve employee skills	
O'Connell	2003	Performance: communication improvement, information availability during crisis, availability to services, customer satisfaction, adherence to regulations, reduction of printed reports, reduction in tax assessment errors	

continued

Table 9.2 Overview of Literature Linking IT Investment and Organizational Performance (Examples of Measures from the Public Sector) — continued

Author	Year	Measures of IT Investment and Performance	Measures of Business Unit and Organizational Performance
Scherlis and Eisenberg	2003	Performance: ubiquity of service, trustworthiness, information access, and confidentiality, use of research programs	Crisis management, federal statistic collection

county-by-county immunization by age group information. Immunization education programs can be developed or refined based on information from such a report.

A transactional IT is the automation of a process. For example, a transactional IT might automate the appointment scheduling for a local community mental health center.

The framework then consists of cells representing the desired impact of an IT investment. An investment could be represented in more than one cell.

On the basis of cell location, measures can be developed to determine the IT investment's impact. These measures are very specific to the situation. For example, if an organization implements a strategic use of IT, then cost per employee should not be used as a measure. Likewise, if an informative use of IT is the goal, determining increased productivity per employee is not an appropriate measure for impact on performance.

The framework also shows the importance of flexibility, quality, and "customer" service. IT investments should include ways of assessing impact on organizational flexibility, on service or product quality, and on customer service. Research has shown these three items are applicable to every IT investment. Therefore, flexibility, quality, and

Type of IT [a]	Business Purpose of IT [b]	
	Efficiency	Effectiveness
Strategic	Establish direct contact with customer to make quick changes to meet needs	Create a new service
Informative	Automate middle-management routine decision-making	Track changes in supplier prices
Transactional	Accelerate business processes and decrease costs	Add new customers because partial automation of service delivery is more flexible

Flexibility, Quality, and Customer Service Measures (vertical)

Flexibility, Quality, and Customer Service Measures (horizontal)

Figure 9.2 Framework example for measuring impact of IT investment on organizational performance. ([a]From Weill, 1992. [b]Adapted from Kinsella, 1997.)

customer service span the entire framework. For example, does IT allow for organizational changes? Changes will occur and assessing IT's ability to adapt gives management a perspective on the potential life of the IT. Quality must be maintained or increased for every form of IT investment. Research has shown that quality is of paramount importance no matter what service or product is offered. Looking at quality before and after IT implementation can give management a feel for IT's effect on quality. Customer service must be maintained not only externally, but internally as well.

The framework is not the complete answer to the complex problem of measuring the impact of IT investment on organizational performance. However, it does give a starting point for managers to develop organizational performance criteria for an IT investment.

IV. CONCLUSION

Additional guidelines for measuring the impact of IT investment on organizational performance are the following:

1. Measures need to evaluate an IT project in relation to current business strategies, goals, and objectives.
2. Measures need to be taken at several points in time. The benefits of IT investment may not be uncovered for several years or may increase (or decrease) over time. To uncover any changes over time in performance due to IT investment, measures over time are necessary.
3. Measures need to address several levels of organizational performance. For example, a productivity change at an individual level could lead to the restructuring of a task at a departmental level, and then to a change in the services offered to customers/clients at a strategic business unit level (Huff, 1990).
4. Intangible measures of value in the use of IT need to be considered. It is not necessary to translate intangible benefits into dollars or some other quantitative measure (Huff, 1990). For example, public-sector managers are interested in the value of IT to customer or client relations. A good web page answering most frequently asked questions about the services the agency offers generates good will and saves labor costs.
5. Investigation at the application level needs to determine whether the deployment of a specific IT resulted in a performance gain, making the analysis much simpler (Banker et al., 1990).
6. Multiple measures need to determine the linkage between IT investments and organizational performance, which is complex, requiring, for example, multiple measures of performance at one organizational level or one measure used at several organizational levels (such as the individual, the team, or the department).
7. More recent IT investments have been accompanied by business process redesign or business reengineering, which can also improve performance. In these situations, the manager has to be mindful of separating IT impact from the redesign impact on performance.
8. IT investment success is the responsibility not only of the IT department, but also of all the management. IT supports business projects. When the business case for an IT investment is established, the responsibilities of management should be clearly outlined. Ownership of each business benefit of an IT investment must be identified.

ACKNOWLEDGMENTS

The authors would like to thank Mary Dillon and Dan Kinsella, graduate students at the University of Nebraska at Omaha, for their assistance in writing this chapter.

REFERENCES

Alpar, P. and Kim, M., A microeconomic approach to the measurement of information technology value, *J. Manage. Inf. Syst.*, 7, 55–69, 1990.

Ammons, D.N., *Municipal Benchmarks: Assessing Local Performance and Establishing Community Standards*, Sage, Thousand Oaks, CA, 2001.

Banker, R.D., Kauffman, R.J., and Morey, R.C., Measuring gains in operational efficiency from information technology: a study of the positran deployment at Hardee's Inc., *J. Manage. Inf. Syst.*, 7, 29, 1990.

Barua, A. and Kriebel, C.H., An economic analysis of strategic information technology investments, *MIS Q.*, 15, 313–333, 1991.

Barua, A., Kriebel, C.H., and Mukhopadhyay, T., Information technologies and business value: an analytical and empirical investigation, *Inf. Syst. Res.*, 6, 3–23, 1995.

Bresnahan, T.F., Brynjolfsson, E., and Hitt, L.M., Information technology, workplace organization and the demand for skilled labor: firm level evidence, *Q. J. Econ.*, 117, 339–376, 2002.

Brynjolfsson, E., Technology's true payoff, *Informationweek*, 496, 34–36, 1994.

Brynjolfsson, E. and Hitt, L., Paradox lost? Firm-level evidence on returns to information systems spending, *Manage. Sci.*, 42, 541–558, 1996.

Brynjolfsson, E. and Hitt, L.M., Beyond the productivity paradox: computers are the catalyst for bigger changes. *Communications of the ACM*, 41, 49–55. August 1998.

Brynjolfsson, E., Hitt, L.M., and Yang, S., Intangible assets: how the interaction of information systems and organizational structure affects stock market valuation, Proceedings of the International Conference on Information Systems, Helsinki, Finland, Aug., 1998.

Brynjolfsson, E., Hitt, L.M., and Yang, S., Intangible assets: computers and organizational capital, *Brookings Pap. Econ. Act.*, 1, 137–181, 2002.

Byrd, T. and Marshall, T.E., Relating information technology investment to organizational performance: a causal model analysis, *Omega*, 25, 43–56, 1997.

Damned if you do, damned if you don't, *Computerworld*, 29, 98, 1995.

Dedrick, J., Gurbaxani, V., and Kraemer, K. Information technology and economic performance: a critical review of the empirical evidence, *ACM Computing Surveys*, 35, 1–28, 2003.

Devaraj, S. and Kohli, R., Information technology payoff in the health care industry: a longitudinal study, *J. Manage. Inf. Syst.*, 16, 41–68, 2002.

Dewan, S. and Kraemer, K.L., International dimensions of the productivity paradox, *Commun. ACM*, 41, 56–62, 1998.

Dewan, S. and Min, C.K., Substitution of information technology for other factors of production: a firm level analysis, *Manage. Sci.*, 43, 1660–1675, 1997.

Dos Santos, B.L. and Peffers, K., Rewards to investors in innovative information technology applications: first movers and early followers in ATMs, *Organ. Sci.*, 6, 241–259, 1995.

Dos Santos, B.L., Peffers, K., and Mauer, D.C., The impact of information technology investment announcements on the market value of the firm, *Inf. Syst. Res.*, 4, 1–23, 1993.

Dos Santos, B.L., Rajagopalan, S., and Rao, R.H., Technology investments and firm performance, *Baylor Univ. WWW*, 4, 4, 1996.

Duncan, N.B., Capturing flexibility of information technology infrastructure: a study of resource, *J. Manage. Inf. Syst.*, 12, 37–58, 1995.

Farbey, B., Targett, D., and Land, F., The great IT benefit hunt, *Eur. Manage. J.*, 12, 270–279, 1994.

Fielder, T. and Gatian, A.W., Strategic information systems and financial performance, *J. Manage. Inf. Syst.*, 14, 215–249, 1995.

Francalanci, C. and Galal, H., Information technology and worker composition: determinants of productivity in the life insurance industry, *MIS Q.*, 22, 227–241, 1998.

Glazer, R., Measuring the value of information: the information-intensive organization, *IBM Syst. J.*, 32, 99–110, 1993.

Greenan, N. and Mairesse, J., Computers and productivity in France: some evidence, *Econ. Innovation New Tech.*, 9, 275–315, 2000.

Gresham, M. and Andrulis, J., Operational Efficiency and Organizational Effectiveness: How Do State and Local Government Initiatives Measure Up? 2003. http://www-1.ibm.com/services/files/ibv_maryland.pdf

Hagedoorn, J. and Schakenraad, J., The effect of strategic technology alliances on company performance, *Strateg. Manage. J.*, 15, 291–310, 1994.

Halachmi, A. and Bouckaert, G., Performance measurement, organizational technology and organizational design, *Work Stud.*, 43, 19–25, 1994.

Harris, S.E. and Katz, J.L., Organizational performance and information technology. Investment intensity in the insurance industry, *Organ. Sci.*, 2, 263–296, 1991.

Hitt, L.M. and Brynjolfsson, E., Productivity, business profitability, and consumer surplus: three different measures of information technology value, *MIS Q.*, 20, 121–143, 1996.

Huff, S., Evaluating investments in information technology, *Bus. Q.*, 54, 42–45, 1990.

Husein, T. and Moreton, R., Electronic commerce: a consideration of implementation, *J. Appl. Manage. Stud.*, 5, 77–85, 1996.

IT's feet are held to flame, *InternetWeek*, Issue 687, October 27, 1, 1997.

Karimi, J. and Gupta, Y.P., Impact of competitive strategy and information technology maturity on firms' strategic response, *J. Manage. Inf. Syst.*, 12, 55–89, 1996.

Kauffman, R.J. and Weill, P., An Evaluative Framework for Research on the Performance Effects of Information Technology Investment, Proceedings of the Tenth International Conference on Information Systems, Boston, 1989.

Kettinger, W.J. and Grover, V., Strategic information systems revisited: a study in sustainability and performance, *MIS Q.*, 18, 31–59, 1994.

Kinsella, D., Electronic Commerce and Business Performance, Course Project, University of Nebraska at Omaha, Omaha, NE, 1997.

Kraemer, K.L., Dedrick, J., and King, J.L., The Impact of Information Technology on City Government in the United States, Center for Research on Information Technology and Organizations, IT in Government, Paper 77, 1995. http://repositories.cdlib.org/crito/government/77

Lanham, R., Better Scorecards for Government IT Project Performance, *PA Times*, 26, 6, 2003.

Lunsford, J. and Simpson, S., TIB/Brintech Technology Management Service: high performance technology utilization; core competencies for survival and success, *Tex. Banking*, 84, 8–11, 1995.

Mahmood, M.A. and Mann, G.J., Measuring the organizational impact of information technology investment: an exploratory study, *J. Manage. Inf. Syst.*, 10, 97–123, 1993.

Miron, M., The myths and realities of competitive advantage, *Datamation*, 34, 71, 1988.

Mitra, S. and Chayam, A.K., Analyzing cost-effectiveness of organizations: the impact of information technology spending, *J. Manage. Inf. Syst.*, 13, 29–58, 1996.

Morishma, M., Information sharing and firm performance in Japan, *Ind. Relat.*, 30, 37, 1991.

Mukopadhyay, T. and Kekre, S., Business value of information technology: a study of electronic data interchange, *MIS Q.*, 19, 137–157, 1995.

Mukopadhyay, T. and Rajiv, S.S., IT impact on process output and quality, *Manage. Sci.*, 43, 1645–1659, 1997.

Nelson, K.M. and Cooprider, J.G., The contribution of shared knowledge to IS group performance (IS organizations), *MIS Q.*, 20, 409–433, 1996.

Neunaha, R.R., IT: nature of impact on potential value to business operations, *South. Ill. Univ. WWW*, 3, 1996.

O'Connell, K.A., Computerizing government: the next generation, *Am. City Cty.*, 118, 36–45, 2003.

Pastore, R., A measured success, *CIO*, 7, 40–46, 1993.

Performance Institute, Creating a Performance-Based Electronic Government, 2002. http://www.performanceweb.org/research/egovernmentreport.pdf

Pinsonneault, A. and Kraemer, K.L., Middle management downsizing: an empirical investigation of the impact of IT, *Manage. Sci.*, 43, 659–679, 1997.

Rai, A., Patnayakuni, R., and Patnayakuni, N., Refocusing where and how IT value is realized: an empirical investigation, *Omega*, 24, 399–413, 1996.

Rai, A., Patnayakuni, R., and Patnayakuni, N., Technology investment and firm performance, *Commun. ACM*, 40, 89–97, 1997.

Rao, H.R., Pegels, C.C., and Hwang, K.T., The impact of EDI implementation commitment and implementation success on competitive advantage and firm performance, *Inf. Syst. J.*, 5, 185, 1995.

Rau, S.E. and Bye, B.S. Are you getting value from your IT?, *J. Bus. Stra.*, 24, 16–20, 2003.

RPPI, A Report to the 43rd President and 107th Congress: Transitioning to Performance-based Government, 2000.
http://www.rppi.org/transition2000.html

Saarinen, T. and Kivijarvi, H., Investment in information technology and the financial performance of the firm, *Inf. Manage.*, 28, 143, 1995.

Scherlis, W.L. and Eisenberg, J., IT research, innovation, and e-government, *Commun. ACM*, 46, 67–68, 2003.

Schorr, H. and Stolfo, S.J., A digital government for the 21st century, *Commun. ACM*, 41, 15–19, 1998.

Sethi, V., Hwang, K.T., and Pegels, C., Information technology and organizational performance: a critical evaluation of Computerworld's index of information systems effectiveness, *Inf. Manage.*, 25, 193–206, 1993.

Smith, H.A. and McKeen, J.D., How does information technology affect business value? A reassessment and research propositions, *Can. J. Admin. Sci.*, 10, 229–240, 1993.

Stevens, T., The best way to get support for a significant IT investment — and manage the project downstream — is with a sound, tangible business case of return on that investment, *Ind. Week.*, 24, 22–26, 1998.

Tallon, P., Kraemer, K.L., and Gurbaxani, V., Executives perspectives on the business value of information technology, *J. Manage. Inf. Syst.*, 16, 145–173, 2000.

U.S. GAO (U.S. General Accounting Office), Executive Guide: Measuring Performance and Demonstrating Results of Information Technology Investments, Washington, D.C. (GAO/AIMD-98-89, 1998).

Weill, P., Strategic investment in information technology: an empirical study, *Inf. Age*, 12, 140–147, 1990.

Weill, P., The relationship between investment in information technology and firm performance: a study of the valve manufacturing sector, *Inf. Syst. Res.*, 3, 307, 1992.

Wena, H.J., Yen, D.C., and Lin, B., Methods for measuring information technology investment payoff, *Hum. Syst. Manage.*, 17, 145–153, 1998.

Yuthas, K. and Eining, M.M., An experimental evaluation of measurements of information system effectiveness, *J. Inf. Syst.*, 9, 69–85, 1995.

10

ELECTRONIC DATA SHARING IN PUBLIC-SECTOR AGENCIES

Irvin B. Vann
North Carolina State University

CONTENTS

I.   Introduction 143
II. Paperwork reduction 144
III. Public vs. private information systems 145
IV. Data-sharing research 147
V.   Data-sharing initiatives 149
    A.   E–government 149
    B.   Homeland security 150
VI. Conclusion 151
References 152

ABSTRACT

Information technology (IT) is viewed as one of the solutions for reducing the information "collection burden" on citizens and businesses. Using technology, information sharing between government agencies is frequently proposed as the method to efficiently use the vast amounts of information collected by government. The terms information sharing and data sharing are frequently used synonymously despite being separate concepts. This chapter examines both concepts as found in public administration literature and proposes some clarifications between them.

I. INTRODUCTION

In the past 2 years information sharing between public-sector agencies has gained new prominence. After the September 11, 2001 terrorist attacks, the lack of information sharing between agencies was perceived as limiting a preemptive response by the various federal government agencies. Popular media criticized a number of agencies for having small pieces of a bigger picture and failing to cooperate in "seeing" the whole.

The Government Accounting Office (GAO, 2001) noted that before September 11, 2001, over 40 different agencies had some responsibility for combating terrorism without any formal structure for sharing information between them.

All levels of government collect, store, analyze, and disseminate a vast amount of information as well as data. Much of this activity occurs within three types of interactions: government-to-government, government-to-citizen, and government-to-business (e-government initiative). Today, the term "information" is often synonymous with digital information, computers, and the Internet. However, before personal computers and the Internet, government information was paper based, with special computing centers dedicated to statistically analyzing selected data sets (Penn, 1997). Collecting information became known as the collection burden and the term "government paperwork" became synonymous with redundant inefficiency.

II. PAPERWORK REDUCTION

In an effort to reduce costs and the information collection burdens, Congress passed the Paperwork Reduction Act of 1980 (PRA, 1980). The PRA of 1980 built upon previous efforts to reduce government paperwork. It was the first major legislation to manage government information as a resource and assign one agency to establish guidance and monitor its use.

As part of the act, Congress designated the Office of Management and Budget (OMB) to oversee information policy and created within it the Office of Information and Regulatory Affairs (ORIA) to assist in implementing the policies. The oversight areas assigned to OMB were general information policy, information collection, records management, privacy information, and automated data processing (ADP) (PRA, 1980).

The PRA of 1980 also assigned general responsibilities to agencies. First, each federal agency was required to conduct its information management activities efficiently and economically. Second, federal agencies were not to collect information that was available through other government resources and they were required to "tabulate" their information so it could be made available to other agencies (PRA, 1980). One of the measurable tasks in the PRA was to reduce the paperwork burden 25% by October 1, 1983.

In 1995 Congress passed a new PRA. In the years between 1980 and 1995 information technology (IT) changed from centralized automated data processing to decentralized networks. The PRA of 1995 moved IT from a supporting to a central role in providing government services by insisting on its use to improve mission performance in agencies (GAO, 1994).

Since 1980, the paperwork reduction concept has rippled from federal to state government levels. Many state governments adopted similar paperwork reduction initiatives, also attempting to reduce the information collection burden on citizens. And like the federal government, the states also looked to IT for reducing the information collection burden by reducing collection redundancy.

Both federal and state governments invested heavily in IT in the 1980s and the 1990s. The increasing federal budget for IT is one indicator of explosive expansion during the 1990s. From 1982 to 1994 the federal government had spent over $200 billion on IT systems or an average of $16.6 billion per year (GAO, 1994). In 1996 the federal government allocated about $24 billion for IT products and services (GAO, 1996). In fiscal year 2002, the Bush administration allocated approximately $44 billion for IT services and systems (OMB, 2002).

The Clinger–Cohen Act of 1996 was also instrumental in government IT expansion. It strengthened the PRA by elevating the senior information managers in all federal agencies to chief information officers (CIOs) at the executive level. It also established the interagency CIO council and streamlined purchasing rules for new IT systems. IT has now become a core element of managerial reform in public agencies and is seen as a critical element in improving both managerial efficiency and the quality of service delivery to citizens (Ho, 2002).

However, large investments in IT have not equaled improved delivery of government services (GAO, 1997). Some of the noted failures in 1990s included (GAO, 1994, 1996):

■ Millions in unauthorized student loans due to poor information tracking
■ $1 billion of mistaken Medicare payments
■ FAA air traffic control modernization
■ IRS tax system modernization

Despite both the PRA and the investments in technology, the GAO (2002a) observed that the paperwork burdens on citizens by the federal government were increasing rather than decreasing.

One issue limiting the effectiveness of IT is the "stand alone" nature of systems agencies developed in their acquisition phases. The OMB's associate director for IT and e-government has noted that 20% of federal IT investment would be spent on redundant technology and services (Chabrow, 2003). Scholars and practitioners have noted that data collected by public agencies often ends up in data "silos," isolated from other organizations and sometimes isolated from other departments within an agency (Industry Advisory Council, 2002).

The Bush administration contends that agency-centered IT initiatives have limited the federal government's productivity gains and level of citizen service (OMB, 2002). One of the major objectives of the Bush administration's e-government strategy is to overcome the silo approach to implementing IT (OMB, 2002). Landsbergen and Wolken (2001) noted that sharing data among public agencies generally improves effectiveness, efficiency, and responsiveness.

Despite significant expenditures in IT, empirical research on its effect in public-sector agencies has been limited (Kraemer and Dedrick, 1997; Rocheleau, 2000; Lee and Perry, 2002). Early in the public-sector technology expansion, Caudle (1990) proposed shifting from studying the impact of acquiring technology to studying information as a manageable resource. Kraemer and Dedrick (1997) noted that research about computers and public organizations was slanted toward promoting computing rather than studying its impacts. As Caudle (1990) proposed, studying information management across functional areas should become a major dimension of policy studies. Given today's even larger-scale investments in IT; data sharing becomes all the more important.

III. PUBLIC VS. PRIVATE INFORMATION SYSTEMS

In public-sector literature, a distinction has been made between the management of public- and private-sector information systems. The difference does not exist in the technology per se but in the application of it. Information systems in private-sector companies exist to create a competitive advantage for the company. Competitive advantage means finding customers first and creating demands for products or services.

Additionally, competitive advantage includes enticing customers away from other companies and maximizing company profit.

In public agencies, information systems are designed to support service delivery to the broadest spectrum of customers. All citizens are potential customers of the public agency and the service must be available, sometimes independently of the demand. Other differences for public agencies include greater transparency, greater political accountability, and the need to consider a diffuse range of public objectives rather than an empirically measurable "bottom line" of profits.

Early research exploring the differences between private- and public-sector organizations proposed different performance models for each type of information system. Mansour and Watson (1980) defined computer-based information system (CBIS) performance as a function of five groups of variables: hardware, software, organizational behavior, structure, and the environment. The environmental variables measured the products, customers, competition, and regulations. Their model explained information system performance in private-sector companies very well (Mansour and Watson, 1980).

However, the model was not applied to the government agencies in the study. Mansour and Watson (1980) hypothesized the environmental variables as they had defined them were not applicable to government agencies and excluded them in their model analysis. When the environmental variables were excluded, the remaining variables in the model were not significant in explaining the performance of government information systems (Mansour and Watson, 1980).

Differences in public and private information systems motivated Bozeman and Bretschneider (1986) to develop a new theoretical framework from existing management information system (MIS) literature. Rather than MIS, the new framework became public management information systems (PMISs). In the PMIS framework the external variables excluded by Mansour and Watson (1980) are redefined to address the differences between public and private organizations.

Bozeman and Bretschneider (1986) proposed that the environmental factors differentiating PMIS and MIS would extend from economic and political models of "publicness." Politically, public-sector managers are open to the scrutiny of the citizens they serve as well as the influence of interest groups. Moreover, they operate in the absence of free market incentives for developing and implementing new information systems (Bozeman and Bretschneider, 1986).

Later Bretschneider (1990) empirically tested the hypothesis of a distinction between the management of information systems in the public and the private sector. Bretschneider (1990) determined that public- and private-sector information systems differed at the organizational level in their interdependence, level of "red tape," evaluation of hardware and software, planning, and finally the positioning of the MIS director within the organization.

Bretschneider (1990) found that public agencies were more interdependent and bound by more regulations or "red tape" in their business operations than their private-sector counterparts. Regarding the evaluation of hardware and software, public agencies were more focused on the "state of the art" than private-sector companies. This is due in part to the longer budget cycles found in the public sector. Public-sector agencies also had more formal planning processes than private agencies. Finally, the director of MIS in public-sector agencies was likely to be in a lower organizational position than in private-sector organizations (Bretschneider, 1990).

The Clinger–Cohen Act of 1996 addresses two of the differences Bretschneider (1990) discovered in the management of public and private information systems. First, the

Clinger–Cohen Act changed the procurement of IT from centralized to decentralized, although funding to purchase new IT may be an issue for an agency. Second, the MIS directors at the agency level were elevated to CIOs and made part of the executive staff (Clinger–Cohen Act, 1996). Even though it incorporates some private-sector practices, information systems management in public agencies remains functionally distinct from management in public companies.

IV. DATA-SHARING RESEARCH

Public- and private-sector information systems have evolved through four generations, the experimental, the mainframe, microcomputer, and now the networking generation (Anderson and Dawes, 1991; Landsbergen and Wolken, 2001). Each new generation in computing provides greater technical opportunity to work more efficiently by electronic data sharing.

Early in the technology expansion, the GAO (1992) highlighted how the lack of strategic vision, stand-alone systems, and scattered information limited the productivity of federal agencies. Ten years later the GAO (2002a) still notes that the federal government does not have a strategic vision for IT, builds stand-alone systems, and scatters information between agencies. In a recent annual survey of CIOs, unifying automation islands across agencies was number 5 in a "top ten" list of technology challenges (*Government Technology News*, 2003).

Weiss (1987) observed that public agencies are frequently scolded for inefficiency, redundancy, and failure to cooperate in their operations. Sharing information is often recommended to agencies as a method to mitigate these problems. As computerized IT became more prominent, electronic information sharing was proposed as a method to increase productivity, improve policymaking, and integrate public services (Center for Technology in Government, 1999).

Just as information systems management is different between the public and private sector, data sharing has a different purpose too. Barrett and Konsynski (1982) proposed that interorganizational information systems developed for three economic reasons:

- ■ Cost reductions
- ■ Productivity improvements
- ■ Product/market strategy

Public- and private-sector agencies are somewhat alike regarding the first two proposals, cost reductions and productivity improvements. As IT spread in government, cost reductions and productivity improvements have been frequently cited as the primary reason for the expansion. However, public and private sectors differ in their approach to the third proposal. The objectives for product/market strategy are not traditionally associated with government agencies. Although government may enter a new product/market area, it is usually the only or most able provider for that product or market area.

Often the terms "data" and "information" are used synonymously. However, data and information are more formally defined as different concepts. Miller et al. (2001) noted that data are observable facts arranged and interpreted by a set of rules. A record in a database file is composed of observable facts or data arranged and interpreted by a set of rules. For example, a record might identify an individual as a white male, college educated, and making a certain income. Information, however, is the result of aggregating and interpreting a collection of data. In the previous example the average or median salary of a collection of the white males is information as opposed to data.

Many of the suggestions for improving government efficiency use the term "information sharing." However, when the suggestion is studied in its context, it is actually data and not information that should be shared between agencies. Due to the fuzziness of the definitions, empirical research on electronic data sharing has been limited and constitutes a significant gap in the literature. In spite of its importance, little is known about the factors underlying the propensity of an agency to share electronic data.

Some authors define data sharing broadly. Dawes (1996), for instance, defined data as program information documenting the nature, content, and operation of public programs. Her definition is not restricted to computerized data but includes paper and machine-readable data also. Data sharing for Dawes means exchanging or otherwise giving other executive agencies access to program information (Dawes, 1996).

Rocheleau (1996), in contrast, defined data sharing in more narrow terms as the exchange of an organization's information residing in its MIS. These data could include budgetary, personnel, information on clients, organizational activities, and other types of data that organizations maintain in their files. Sharing could range from the selective release of part of a database (extract) to total sharing of the database. Sharing files owned by an organization is different from sharing personal communications where individuals own the information being communicated (Rocheleau, 1996).

Rocheleau (1995), one of the few researchers who have investigated the correlates of data sharing, studied the rate of information sharing between police and other city departments in central Illinois. The highest rate of sharing was with the administrative and budget departments. His qualitative data suggest that a large proportion of sharing is due to factors such as hierarchical authority and accountability requirements rather than the task-oriented reasons one would expect. Statistical analysis showed the use of electronic data exchange did encourage a higher overall rate of sharing between departments. Other variables, including hardware configurations, departmental size and autonomy, and crime-related variables, were not found to be significant (Rocheleau, 1995).

By reviewing the available literature, Rocheleau (1996) noted that much of the research on electronic communication focused on interpersonal communication rather than organizational communication. He identified factors easing information exchange between organizations as well as factors inhibiting information exchange. The factors easing the exchange were: common goals, technological compatibility, legal mandates, organizational survival needs, external incentives, symmetry of benefits, individual incentives, and top management interests. The factors impeding data sharing were: need for autonomy, database incompatibilities, privacy restrictions, limitations of computerized information, and asymmetry of benefits (Rocheleau, 1996). Although Rocheleau (1996) identified nine hypotheses about public-sector information sharing, they were developed from existing literature and have not been empirically confirmed.

Dawes (1996: 391) studied the *attitudes* of public managers regarding data sharing in New York State. In her results she noted, "Though representing different agencies eight in ten respondents judged information sharing to be moderately to highly beneficial." Dawes (1996) found that more experienced respondents were likely to recognize and endorse these benefits. Public managers in the study wanted a legal framework and formal policies to guide information-sharing decisions and activities. They also wanted effective tools for "managing public data and for sharing it effectively (Dawes, 1996: 391)."

Dawes (1996) developed a data-sharing model, incorporating an agency's experience in conjunction with the actual benefits and risks of a project. Public agencies begin data-sharing projects in response to a pressing problem. In a mutual project, each agency has preconceived expectations of the data-sharing experience. During a data-sharing project, agencies will add to their experience as well as create a set of expectations for similar projects in the future. If the benefits outweigh the risks, the participating agencies will use the data-sharing solution again. If the risks outweigh the benefits, the agencies will infrequently choose a data-sharing solution again (Dawes, 1996).

Building on research by Dawes (1996), Landsbergen and Wolken (2001) used case study methodology to conclude that the purely technical issues of computer hardware and software compatibility were receding in importance as impeding factors to data sharing. With many technical issues resolved, the focus should shift to issues of inter-operability. Moving beyond the technical issues, "data sharing implies a richer set of political, organizational, and economic issues" (Landsbergen and Wolken, 2001: 212). Fundamentally, interoperability now means data sharing, not technical compatibility (Landsbergen and Wolken, 2001).

V.   DATA-SHARING INITIATIVES

A.   E–Government

The "e-government" paradigm is a recent development in PMIS. Conceptually, e-government centers on government-to-citizen service delivery, using Internet technology with the ultimate goal to provide a selection of services to citizens via one Internet portal or access point (OMB, 2002). The technical aspects of accessing the service or conducting business across agency boundaries and databases remain invisible to the citizen. E-government also incorporates data exchanges between different levels of government as well as between government and business.

Layne and Lee (2001) proposed that e-government develops in four recognizable and progressively complex stages: (1) cataloging, (2) transaction, (3) vertical integration, and (4) horizontal integration. Stages 1 and 2 are essentially data silos where citizens must access each agency website to transact business with government. Stage 3 is the start of access at different levels but among functional lines. Stage 4 is achieved when the citizen uses one entry to access data and services across organizational boundaries.

Stage 1 is the easiest to implement in terms of complexity and organizational commitment (Layne and Lee, 2001). It consists of creating a web presence and providing simple services like downloadable forms. Many government agencies have already achieved this stage of e-government and the informational website is now practically ubiquitous.

In stage 2 citizens are able to interact with one agency at a particular level of government (Layne and Lee, 2001). Examples of this stage include renewing drivers' licenses online or filling out online forms and then submitting the data to the agency. Electronic transactions between citizens and government agencies are now very common.

Lane and Lee (2001) describe stage 3 as working at different levels within common functions. For example, a health and human services department at the state level is more likely to share data with its federal counterpart or even the health and human services in another state before it shares data with another function within its home state. Consequently, citizens may benefit from this vertical relationship by going to one website to interact with more than one level of government. Rocheleau (1996) hypothesized that data sharing is more likely when agencies share common functions.

Stage 4 of e-government is horizontal integration across the different functions of government. In this stage citizens use one portal to access all services. Layne and Lee (2001) noted that stage 4 has not been achieved yet; however, they cite two websites that incorporate some of the aspects of this stage. The two sites were developed under the "Access America" initiative. One is now called FirstGov for seniors and found at http://www.seniors.gov. The other is for students and is located at http://www.students.gov. Each of the websites provides the capability to search a variety of databases at different levels of government for information.

At the organizational level, e-government changes the traditional bureaucratic paradigm from an agency-centric to a more citizen-centric focus (Ho, 2002). Achieving transparency, one of the goals of e-government, involves abandoning bureaucratic command and control and embracing the concepts of facilitation and coordination (Ho, 2002). Without data sharing, transparency between agencies will not be achieved. For citizens, this means continuation of the status quo where communication is essentially with one agency at a time and the Internet and e-mail replace the telephone as a method of communication.

In February 2002 the Bush administration published a strategic e-government document for federal agencies. The e-government task force identified 24 initiatives for integration across agency boundaries with the potential of saving at least $1 billion. E-government is envisioned as a one-stop, citizen-centric, result-oriented, and market-based approach. The architecture proposed for implementing this strategy requires an unparalleled effort of data sharing (OMB, 2002). Implementing e-government depends on the extent that factors promoting and impeding data sharing are well understood.

B. Homeland Security

The benefits of data sharing for government processes have been emphasized as long as agencies have been using ADP equipment. Since September 11, 2001, the federal government has refocused on the issues of information sharing within law enforcement and national security channels. In its review of national preparedness, the GAO (2002b) noted that intelligence, law enforcement, and response information are not effectively shared. The GAO (2002a) also noted, like Dawes (1996), that the reasons for not sharing information include stovepiped organizational structures and "turf" issues.

Solutions to improving information sharing among law enforcement, emergency management, and national intelligence encompass two general areas, managerial and technical. One management-based approach that is showing promise to promote information sharing stems from Presidential Decision Directive (PDD) 63 issued by the Clinton administration in 1998. This directive outlined the critical infrastructure protection (CIP) program. The program establishes two different information-sharing entities, the National Infrastructure Protection Center (NIPC) and Information Sharing and Analysis Centers (ISACs).

The NIPC is the federal government's focal point and coordinating body in a crisis. In theory it is linked electronically to both the federal government and the ISACs. It is the only center the government has solely dedicated to sharing information between agencies as well as the private sector.

The ISACs are aligned with the critical infrastructures areas and serve as an information conduit. The critical infrastructure areas are: information and communication, banking and finance, water supply, transportation, emergency law enforcement, disaster services, public health, and power. The centers receive "sanitized" information as opposed to data from the NIPC. They also submit information to the NIPC for analysis.

One technical solution with the capability to facilitate data sharing between different agencies is extensible markup language (XML). It is a set of standards that facilitates data exchanges between different computer applications using the Internet or another digital communication channel (GAO, 2002a). XML uses standard "tags" that identify types of data. The "tags" function as a translator between different databases. For example, a standard tag such as <Name> could be used to link an individual's name across databases. Each agency would ensure that database fields corresponding to an individual name would be matched against the <Name> tag (GAO, 2002a).

VI. CONCLUSION

As previously noted, governments collect vast amounts of data and create an equally vast amount of information. During the 1990s, all levels of government expanded their use of IT. Because managing public information systems is different, the expansion in technology was an effort for government to reduce the information collection burden, streamline operations, and become more citizen focused (Dawes, 1996; Ho, 2002). One method of achieving these goals is to use IT to share data among agencies. Sharing allows agencies to take advantage of the vast amount of data collected by government and avoids the creation of redundant information systems.

Computing is now in its fourth generation and the possibilities for data sharing between agencies using networks and the Internet has never been greater. As a consequence of new technologies, the federal government is attempting to implement electronic data sharing in two large initiatives, e-government and homeland security.

E-government encompasses efforts to establish citizen centric two-way services by using data sharing as well as Internet technologies. The e-government paradigm is the capstone in the movement to use information resources more efficiently. When it is fully established, citizens will be able to access a variety of government services through one electronic portal.

Establishing the Department of Homeland Security (DHS) represents one of the largest and most urgent efforts in government data sharing. The department encompasses 22 different agencies with varied requirements for interagency data sharing. Although the urgency is clear, the GAO (2002b) noted there are still considerable barriers to effectively collecting and sharing data.

Despite these initiatives, data as well as information sharing are difficult to initiate as well as sustain. Discussions of either invoke issues of "turf," "bureaucracy," and "power" to justify why agencies do not share information (Dawes, 1996; GAO, 2002a). The definition of data sharing is also an issue in understanding and implementing it. Data sharing and information sharing are often discussed synonymously although they are different concepts. As agencies improve electronic sharing, research on the correlates of data sharing will enable government to achieve the goals first proposed over 20 years ago.

REFERENCES

Andersen, D.F. and Dawes, S.S., *Government Information Management*, Prentice-Hall, Englewood Cliffs, NJ, 1991.

Barrett, S. and Konsynski, B., Interorganizational information sharing systems, *MIS Quarterly*, 6 (Special Issue), 93–105, 1982.

Bozeman, B. and Bretschneider, S., Public management information systems: theory and prescription, *Public Administration Review*, 46, 475–487, 1986.

Bretschneider, S., Management information systems in public and private organizations: an empirical test, *Public Administration Review*, 50, 536–545, 1990.

Caudle, S.L., Managing information resources an state government, *Public Administration Review*, 50, 515–524, 1989.

Caudle, S.L., Marchard, D.A., Bretschneider, S.I., Fletcher, P.T., and Thurmaier, K.M., *Managing Information Resources: New Directions in State Government — A National Study of State Government Information Resources Management*, School of Information Studies, Syracuse University, Syracuse, NY, 1989.

Center for Technology in Government, *Research and Practical Experiences in the Use of Multiple Data Sources for Enterprise Level Planning and Decision Making: A Literature Review*, University at Albany/SUNY, Albany, NY, 1999.

Chabrow, E., Government Agencies Struggle to overcome the many barriers to collaboration. *Information Week*, Pg 6, Sep. 1, 2003.

Dawes, S.S., Interagency information sharing: expected benefits, manageable risks, *Journal of Policy Analysis & Management*, 15, 377–394, 1996.

GAO (Government Accounting Office), *Information Management and Technology Issues*, U.S. Government Printing Office, Washington, D.C., 1992 (GAO/OCG-93-5TR).

GAO (Government Accounting Office), *Executive Guide: Improving Mission Performance through Strategic Information Management and Technology: Learning from Leading Organizations*, U.S. Government Printing Office, Washington, D.C., 1994.

GAO (Government Accounting Office), *Information Management Reform: Effective Implementation Is Essential for Improving Federal Performance*, U.S. Government Printing Office, Washington, D.C, 1996 (GAO/T-AIMD-96–132).

GAO (Government Accounting Office), *Information Management and Technology*, U.S. Government Printing Office, Washington, D.C., 1997 (GAO/HR-97-7).

GAO (Government Accounting Office), *Combating Terrorism: Selected Challenges and Related Recommendations*, U.S. Government Printing Office, Washington, D.C., 2001 (GAO-01-822).

GAO (Government Accounting Office), *Information Resources Management: Comprehensive Strategic Plan Needed to Address Mounting Changes*, U.S. Government Printing Office, Washington, D.C., 2002a (GAO-02–292).

GAO (Government Accounting Office), *National Preparedness: Integrating New and Existing Technology and Information Sharing into an Effective Homeland Security Strategy*, U.S. Government Printing Office, Washington, D.C., 2002b (GAO-02-218-811T).

Ho, A.T.-K., Reinventing local government and the e-government initiative, *Public Administration Review*, 62, 434–443, 2002.

Industry Advisory Council, Cross-Jurisdictional e-Government Implementations, 2002
Available at http://www.iaconline.org/
Accessed on 10/12/2002.

Kraemer, K.L. and Dedrick J., Computing and public organizations, *Journal of Public Administration and Theory*, 7, 89–112, 1997.

Landsbergen, D., Jr. and Wolken, G., Jr., Realizing the promise: government information systems and the fourth generation of information technology, *Public Administration Review*, 61, 206–220, 2001.

Layne, K. and Lee, J., Developing fully functional e-government: a four-stage model, *Government Information Quarterly*, 18, 122–136, 2001.

Lee, G. and Perry, J.L., Are computers boosting productivity: a test of the paradox in state governments, *Journal of Public Administration and Theory*, 12, 77–102, 2002.

Mansour, A. and Watson, H.J., The determinants of computer-based information systems performance, *Academy of Management Review*, 23, 521–533, 1980.

Miller, B., Malloy, M.A., Masek, E., and Wild, C., Towards a framework for managing the information environment, *Information, Knowledge, and Systems Management*, 2, 359–384, 2001.

OMB (Office of Management and Budget) IT Spending.
http://www.whitehouse.gov/omb/infoorg/infopoltech.html
Retrieved 10/16/2002.

Penn, I.A., Information management legislation in the last quarter century: a records management disaster, *Records Management Quarterly*, January, 31(1), 3–9, 1997.

PRA (Paperwork Reduction Act of 1980), P.L. 96–511, 94 Stat 2812, *US Statues at Large*, Part III, Vol. 94, U.S. Government Printing Office, Washington, D.C., 1981.

Rocheleau, B., Computers and horizontal information sharing in the public sector. In Harlan J., and Gerard R., Eds., *Sharing Geographic Information*, Center for Urban Policy Research, New Brunswick, New Jersey, 207–230, 1995.

Rocheleau, B., Interorganizational and interdepartmental information sharing, in *Advances in Social Science and Computers*, Garson, G.D. and Stuart S.N., Eds., JAI Press, Grenwich, CT, Vol. 4, 1996, pp. 183–204.

Rocheleau, B., Prescriptions for public sector management: a review, analysis, and critique, *American Review of Public Administration*, 30, 414–435, 2000.

Weiss, J.A., Pathways to cooperation among public agencies, *Journal of Policy Analysis and Management*, 1, 94–117, 1987.

What keeps federal CIOs up at night?, *Government Technology News*, Nov. 21, 2003
http://www.govtech.net/?page=news/news&ID=78488
Accessed on 11/30/2003.

11

GOVERNANCE IN THE ERA OF THE WORLD WIDE WEB: AN ASSESSMENT OF ORGANIZATIONAL OPENNESS AND GOVERNMENT EFFECTIVENESS, 1997 TO 2001

Todd M. La Porte
George Mason University

Chris C. Demchak
University of Arizona

Christopher Weare
University of Southern California

CONTENTS

I.	Introduction	156
II.	Openness as an administrative attribute	157
III.	Cross-national comparison of website diffusion and website openness	158
IV.	Measuring openness: the WAES methodology	158
	A. Transparency	159
	B. Interactivity	160
V.	Diffusion of the Web in ministries	162
VI.	Transparency, interactivity, and openness trends worldwide	162
VII.	Openness and government performance	163
	A. Government performance indicators	164
VIII.	Model estimation	167
IX.	Conclusion	169
	Acknowledgments	169

ABSTRACT

Important attributes of governance may be captured by tracking and evaluating the use of networked information systems in public organizations, both internally, in terms of bureaucratic structure and functioning, and externally, in terms of service delivery and citizen contact. Concepts that can bridge the various converging domains of information technologies (ITs), public administration and public-sector management, comparative political studies, and democratic theory are needed. We contend that bureaucratic openness, administrative efficiency, and increased public participation are separate but potentially linked aspects of increasing reliance on electronic networked information systems, principally the Internet. This chapter updates our earlier report on a systematic long-running research program, supported by the National Science Foundation, to survey and analyze these trends. We will also analyze the effects of these digital government efforts, and relate them to several government performance measures, including standard economic growth rates, government performance data, and data on democratic institutions. In so doing, we test propositions developed at the beginning of this project on the relationship of networked information systems to organizational and administrative effectiveness.

I. INTRODUCTION

Popular and scholarly writing about contemporary governance suggests that its future increasingly depends on new bureaucratic and political arrangements, often, though not always, with a technological assist from networked electronic information systems (e.g., Osborne and Gaebler, 1992; Pierre, 1995; Peters and Pierre, 1998; Thomas, 1998). E-government has considerable promise to improve a wide range of government functions, it is argued, and many countries, both in the developed and in the developing world, are currently grappling with how best to realize that promise.

New ideas about governance have also emerged, stressing collaborative relationships, network-like arrangements, and hybrid public–private partnerships between various agencies and organizations, which enable more effective problem solving and greater citizen participation in public affairs than in the past (e.g., Mechling, 1994; O'Toole, 1997; Mayntz, 1998; Koppel, 1999).

Students of political science and public administration have increasingly focused on the subject of IT in government and its implications for democracy, for governance, and for public administration (e.g., Danziger et al., 1982; Frissen et al., 1992; Snellen and van de Donk, 1998; Weare et al., 1999; Garson, 2000).

Nevertheless, as we have argued in our contribution to the earlier edition of this volume, more empirically grounded large-scale research is needed in this fast-moving domain. After nearly a decade of use of the Web in governments around the world, we believe we now have sufficient data to evaluate the effect of these systems on government's effectiveness and contribution to more public participation.

In particular, we believe that important attributes of governance may be captured by tracking and evaluating the use of networked information systems in public organizations, both internally, in terms of bureaucratic structure and functioning, and externally, in terms of service delivery and citizen contact. Concepts that can bridge the various converging domains of ITs, public administration and public-sector management, comparative political studies, and democratic theory are needed to begin to bridge the conceptual divide between democracy and bureaucracy that has bedeviled public administrationists and political scientists for decades (Appleby, 1952; Waldo, 1980; Woller, 1998).

In nearly all countries, to some degree, there are three principle threads of e-government reform: (1) development of bureaucratic processes to provide greater administrative convenience, transparency, interactivity, and openness, (2) efforts to improve management processes to achieve cost savings and efficiencies, and (3) development of means to increase public participation in both electoral and the regulatory processes to respond better to expressions of popular will and increase government legitimacy and support. We contend that bureaucratic openness, administrative efficiency, and increased public participation are separate but potentially linked aspects of increasing reliance on electronic networked information systems, principally the Internet.

This chapter updates our earlier report (Demchak et al., 2000) on a systematic long-running research program, supported by the National Science Foundation, to survey and analyze these trends, focusing (1) on the diffusion of networked ITs around the world in national-level governments, (2) on bureaucratic developments to increase administrative transparency, interactivity, and openness, and (3) on the later-starting efforts to boost public participation in deliberative processes.

We will also analyze the effects of these digital government efforts, and relate them to several government performance measures, including (1) standard economic growth rates, (2) recently published data from the World Bank's Government Performance Project (Kaufmann et al., 1999, 2002), and data collected by the Integrated Network for Societal Conflict Research Program (INSCR) on the development of democratic institutions, the degree of political competition, and the stability of regimes (Marshall and Jaggers, 2002). These include constructed indicators measuring government effectiveness, political stability, voice and accountability, regulatory quality, rule of law, and control of corruption. In so doing, we will test propositions we developed at the beginning of this project on the relationship of networked information systems to organizational and administrative effectiveness (Friis et al., 1998; Demchak et al., 2000; La Porte and Demchak, 2001; La Porte et al., 2002).

II. OPENNESS AS AN ADMINISTRATIVE ATTRIBUTE

In introducing the concept of openness, we propose to contribute to the debate about the proper relationship between democracy and bureaucracy. Accountability is the authoritative exercise of oversight, either by elected officials of the activities of the bureaucracy, or by the citizenry, through regular elections, exercising oversight of the legislature. In our view, openness may be considered an allied but conceptually distinct element of accountability in that an open government agency can be continuously assessed by citizens through their everyday interactions.

Openness is an important enabling condition for the exercise of oversight. As the political role of bureaucracies becomes more widely recognized, the classic distinction between political decisions taken by elected officials in a deliberative process and administrative execution of those decisions by a disinterested civil service has become less descriptive. This new reality is in many respects the underlying cause of the embrace of the notion of *governance*, as a separate phenomenon from *government* (Pierre, 1995; Peters and Pierre, 1998; Peters, 2001). We argue that empirical measures of organizational openness permit the assessment of aspects of this phenomenon in politically and administratively useful ways.

In an earlier work we have argued that the World Wide Web is a useful vehicle to evaluate public organizations' openness (Demchak et al., 2000; La Porte and Demchak, 2001; La Porte et al., 2002). This is now even more the case than in the past. The Web is a growing facet of the public face of government, and it increasingly instigates and reflects internal structural and procedural dimensions of organizations' nonelectronic existence. Websites are increasingly the authoritative organs of information dissemination in both the public and the private spheres. It is not the only modality by which public and quasipublic institutions reach their stakeholders, but it is increasingly the preferred option for reasons of relatively low cost and rapid turnaround.

III. CROSS-NATIONAL COMPARISON OF WEBSITE DIFFUSION AND WEBSITE OPENNESS

Annually since 1995, the Cyberspace Policy Research Group (CyPRG), based at George Mason University and the University of Arizona, has surveyed all national-level government web operations, worldwide, to assess how extensively the Web has been adopted by government organizations. Since 1997, CyPRG has also assessed how the web technologies have been implemented in each organization and country. In order to do this, the research team has measured the degree of website *transparency* and website *interactivity*, two main components of organizational openness (Demchak et al., 2000). The third main component of openness, used in performing international comparisons, is website *density*, the percentage of a government's ministries that have a web presence.

Our measurement method, dubbed the Website Attribute Evaluation System (WAES) is based theoretically on suggestions from Deutsch (1966: 21) and Wilson (1989: 377) that openness is the extent to which an organization provides comprehensive information about its attributes and maintains timely communications with its various public (Demchak et al., 2000). The operationalization of transparency and interactivity puts citizen concerns at the center: what would a citizen want to know about a government agency's activities or services, and what would a citizen want to do with an agency to respond or initiate actions desired or required under the law.

IV. MEASURING OPENNESS: THE WAES METHODOLOGY

Earlier work described the WAES methodology, data, and preliminary findings (Demchak et al., 2000), which will be briefly summarized here. WAES permits the evaluation of any website by coding a dichotomous variable that records the presence or absence of a number of specific attributes, described below. There are 31 to 45 criteria in all, depending on the year; updates to the measurement instrument have been made to keep up with rapid Web developments. Assessments are generally performed from the spring to fall of each year.[1]

Table 11.1 Web Operations and Organizational Transparency

Ownership	Tests how involved the agency is with the site: is the agency taking charge of the site itself, indicating involvement and resource expenditure, or is the site the creature of some other entity?
Contact information	Tests whether individuals or positions inside the organization can be reached by outsiders: is address or position information available for people beyond the webmaster?
Organizational or operational information	Tests for information about the organization's operations or its role in a wider issue network: can users get information about (1) the agency's own goals and structure and (2) about other groups, in or outside the government, that play roles in the policy arena?
Issue information	Tests for information about the policy niche of the organization: can users get information about the issues that the organization is principally concerned with?
Citizen consequences	Tests the extent to which the organization indicates what citizens are required to do to comply with laws or regulations, and helps them to do so: can users get texts of laws, rules or other requirements, instructions, forms, or apply to appeals processes?

Table 11.2 Web Operations and Organizational Interactivity

Privacy and security	Tests whether the agency has provided clickable e-mail addresses: can a user simply click on a link or a button on a web page and compose an e-mail message to the people most closely associated with the web operation or other officials?
Reachability	Tests the extent to which the organization permits users to reach deeply inside the agency to a variety of staff: can users click on links to a number of different staff members, or participate in chat rooms or discussion lists?
Organizational or operational information	Tests how smoothly users can find their way around the organization's structure or the wider issue area: can users click on and download mission statements, or easily find archived information?
Issue information	Tests for interactive means to access information about issues in other organizations: can a user find information about a policy issue outside the agency, both in and outside of government?
Citizen consequences/ responsiveness	Tests for interactive capacity to provide responsive service to citizens, including those with language differences or access disabilities: can a user seek dispute resolution, access and submit forms, navigate site easily, regardless of disability?

A. Transparency

Transparency refers to the availability of information for navigating a large-scale social system. It constitutes a layman's basic map of the organization as depicted in the information on the site. The five elements of web-based transparency are outlined in Table 11.1 and Table 11.2 and are listed in order of increasing difficulty for an organization to provide. These five subelements of WAES reveal essential information about the web activities of the organization, the depth of access it allows, the depth of knowledge about processes it is willing to reveal, and the level of attention to citizen response it provides.

Ownership tests for evidence of how involved the agency is with the site. The aim is to ascertain whether the agency itself is tailoring the material for the site or has shunted these content decisions to someone else, such as a central government bureau. Agencies that own their own web operations are more likely to consider it a key part of their organization compared with those that leave the development of their website to others.[2]

Contacts and reachability assesses the website visitor's ability to contact individuals or positions inside the organization. This attribute indicates the agency's willingness to permit outsiders to reach inside the organization beyond the webmaster gateway, and thereby to see inside the organization in a more detailed way. Agencies vary greatly in their approaches to contact with outsiders, with some willing to provide detailed contact information and others preferring to centralize it by providing a one-stop-shop point of contract.

Organizational information assesses how well information is provided about an organization's operations and its connection with related organizations or information. The criteria test for indications of where an organization is headed and how it is structured. This is in part revealed by use of vision and mission statements and organizational charts.

Issue information assesses how well an organization informs users about the issues for which it is responsible, and measures the ease of access to reports, government data, archives, and government information policies. Here the agency also indicates its understanding of the scope of its operating and policy environment by including links to other agencies or nongovernmental organizations relevant to its own work and therefore to the public at large. By charting this subset of attributes, we can study the evolution of governmental web-based networks.

Citizen consequences and responses assesses what an organization requires of a citizen to comply with regulations or laws, to take advantage of programs or to use government services, and to provide recourse when disagreements arise. For example, putting official forms on the site, or explaining how to initiate a dispute resolution process or contact an ombudsman, demonstrates that an agency is anticipating citizens' needs and is willing to respond to problems. This set of criteria relates to the effort that an agency makes to present information and services to citizens most directly. Doing so generally takes considerable organizational resources.

B. Interactivity

Interactivity is a measure of the level of convenience or degree of immediate feedback, which is the second component of openness. The more interactive the site is across the first four transparency attributes, the greater is the demonstrated level of agency concern

---

[2] Earlier versions of the major evaluation criteria included *Freshness* as a separate measure. In late 2000, the project team revised the criteria to reflect current practice, and included *Freshness* in the *Ownership* category. The logic of measuring organizational attentiveness remains: keeping a site up to date is costly, and the more frequently it is updated, the more likely it is that an agency's managers regard the site and its services as essential parts of the agency's activities.

for the convenience of the citizen and the speed of communications between the agency and its clients. Interactivity assesses the extent to which elements of transparency are "clickable" for a site visitor. The greater the "click value" the more convenient it is to acquire data or interact with the agency and thus the more the agency encourages the client to make use of the site and the agency. Interactivity questions roughly parallel those for transparency.

Security and privacy checks the extent to which a site ensures that users' personal information is not compromised while using the website (use of secure servers, passwords, especially for transactions) and that citizens can use the site without providing too much personal information *as a condition of use* (use of "cookies," or requiring extensive identifying information).

Contacts and reachability focuses on the extent to which the organization permits the client to electronically reach inside the agency with clickable dialog boxes or hotlinks, for example, whether senior officials are listed with active hotlinked e-mail addresses. It also tests the extent to which the agency prescribes the form of contact through use of structured dialog boxes and the like, rather than simple e-mail.

Organizational information measures how easily a user can navigate inside the organizational structure or wider issue community via the site. This criterion tests the extent to which the agency begins to demonstrate sophistication in both its concept of citizen involvement in the agency's operations and in the scale of investment in technical sophistication to achieve openness.

Issue information is the clickable correlate to transparency's "issue information" element. It assesses the ease with which citizens can contact other policy-domain organizations via hypertext links on the site.

Citizen consequences and responses is the clickable correlate to transparency's "citizen consequences" element. It assesses the extent to which citizens can easily review and input or receive responses to these consequences, and tests for efforts to accommodate users with disabilities and who may not read or speak the national or dominant language of the country. This section is the most challenging in terms of technical sophistication and in willingness of the agency to accept input from external sources. One criterion tests for a particularly courageous level of openness. It asks if the agency has made a citizen's appeal process open to online submission. A relatively unconstrained online appeal process with automatic agency-reply deadlines requires substantial changes to internal processes and budgets to accommodate these demands. This feature indicates unprecedented agency support for both openness and for the new technology. Table 11.1 and Table 11.2 summarize these criteria.

Transparency and interactivity scores are calculated from the raw data by adding individual criteria numbers. Where scores are not binary, for example, in the number of forms available, or the depth of detail provided in organizational charts or other graphical representations of organization structure, a top limit of no more than two is imposed. These raw sums are prorated to adjust for the number of criteria, which differs between transparency and interactivity, and from year to year. The maximum score for each variable is 1.0. Thus, scores are reasonably comparable over time.

The *level of openness* of a government is computed by taking the average of transparency and interactivity scores for all evaluated organizations, adding them, and multiplying this result by the percentage of ministries in the government with a website. This yields a single numerical country score that captures all three dimensions: transparency, interactivity, and web density.

It is apparent that CyPRG data can be used to examine the characteristics of individual organizations, to make comparisons with other organizations or aggregates, and to make more systematic assessments or benchmarks of national digital government performance. Because the data are based on small details of web-based information that are grouped into coherent categories, it is possible to depict an organization conceptually, and in a way that facilitates comparison and contrasts.

V.   DIFFUSION OF THE WEB IN MINISTRIES

Since its introduction in 1992, the Web has been expanding rapidly throughout governments around the world. By 2003, virtually all governments had at least one website, whether it be a full range of websites at all levels of national, provincial, and local levels, or a single embassy website. To ensure consistent measurements cross-nationally, CyPRG has focused its research on governmental units at the ministry level, defined as organizations whose leader is the head of state, the chief executive, a member of the national government cabinet, houses of the national legislature, and the central bank. Subsidiary sites are not included in our main data analysis, though they often are the first organizations to acquire a web capability; a more detailed study would undoubtedly find much activity at the subnational level.

In the 2001 census, CyPRG found that there were 171 countries with at least one national ministry level website, of a total of 193 countries worldwide.[3] Table 11.3 shows the diffusion of the Web into countries and ministries worldwide: at the conclusion of the 2001 CyPRG census of national-level web presence, 51% of all ministries had a website. Table 11.4 shows the countries that did not have a website at the national level at that time.

VI.   TRANSPARENCY, INTERACTIVITY, AND OPENNESS TRENDS WORLDWIDE

As the Web has spread, governments have become more adept at using its features to provide information and services. This can be seen in global median transparency and interactivity levels, which have steadily increased from 1997 to 2001, though individual countries' trajectories vary. Table 11.5 shows these overall trends. Note that transparency levels (0.51) are almost double of interactivity levels (0.31); this reflects the much greater organizational effort associated with enabling transactions as opposed to static information presentation. Organizations find that it is easier to make information available than to make it convenient for external stakeholders to acquire. Electronic interactivity is likely to be much more difficult to organize, in terms of back-office operations, reorganized workflows, and sharing needs than simply providing for basic electronic access (Turban et al., 1999; Sproul and Kiesler, 1991).

These results are largely supportive of other work that finds that existing government implementation of network technologies focuses on information dissemination and simple transactions and has yet to address issues of organizational redesign and citizen

---

[3] Numbers of countries vary, depending on the standards of the recognizing agency. For example, the U.S. Central Intelligence Agency maintains records on 270 countries, dependencies, and areas, and has cabinet lists for 195; the World Bank notes 148 countries.

Table 11.3   Diffusion of the Web in National-Level Ministries, 1997–2001

	Countries with Ministry Websites	Ministries with Websites, Worldwide	Percentage of Ministries with Websites, Worldwide
1997	63	468	0.14
1998	96	748	0.22
1999	103	856	0.25
2000	154	1411	0.42
2001	173	1731	0.51
Total possible	193	3384	100

Table 11.4   Countries with No Ministry Websites, 2001

Afghanistan	Bhutan	Central African Republic
Chad	Comoros	Congo
Equatorial Guinea	Eritrea	Guinea-Bissau
Haiti	Kiribati	Laos
Libya	Nauru	Palau
St. Vincent and the Grenadines	Seychelles	Somali Republic
Suriname	Tajikistan	Tonga
Tuvalu		

Table 11.5   Transparency, Interactivity, Openness, Worldwide, 1997–2001

	Median Transparency	Median Interactivity	Median Openness
1997	0.38	0.12	0.11
1998	0.42	0.15	0.19
1999	0.52	0.18	0.26
2000	0.53	0.24	0.30
2001	0.51	0.31	0.35

participation (West, 2002; Ho, 2002; Moon, 2002). Openness has also steadily increased, from 0.11 in 1997 to 0.35 in 2001.

VII.   OPENNESS AND GOVERNMENT PERFORMANCE

Earlier CyPRG efforts to isolate the correlates of openness yielded meager results (La Porte and Demchak, 2001; La Porte et al., 2002). Openness data were tested against a number of economic, social, and cultural indicators:

- National income per capita
- Level of central government expenditures
- Degree of integration with the world economy through trade or capital flows
- Levels of staffing and spending on scientific research and education
- Penetration of computers and the Internet
- Presence of cultural values, specifically the degree of individualistic, masculine, postmaterialist behaviors and levels of interpersonal trust

- ■ Types and levels of democracy, political rights and civil liberties, and national election turnout rates
- ■ Type of legal system (common law, civil law, Islamic law, etc.)

The analyses found that national income was only weakly related to openness. Other hypotheses were found not to be significant in explaining openness levels in either the OECD or the non-OECD countries.

Therefore, we concluded that openness was an independent variable in its own right, tapping an aspect of administrative behavior that was important yet undercharacterized. Our hypothesis that openness is a unique aspect of organizational behavior, not derivative of other cultural, political, or economic factors, is strengthened by analysis of more recent data covering a larger number of countries. The comparative data and the statistical analyses showed that openness is a novel, interesting, and useful indicator for social science analysis of administrative behavior and governance. Our earlier work led us to conclude that openness measures are a distinct and simple measure of administrative arrangements that underpin emerging notions of governance, one that allows us to consider a range of questions about the nature of political order in the age of networked information systems.

While openness may be an interesting phenomenon in and of itself, it bears little more than passing academic interest if it is unrelated to any outcomes we care about. However, we propose that openness has direct implications for the quality of governance, both on democratic theory grounds, as suggested above, and on the pragmatic grounds that greater openness may lead to improved government performance.

In this connection, we rely on the notion of *enactment* in the work of Weick (1979), whose research in organizational learning led him to assert that organizations interact with their environments, learn from them, and then seek to shape their environments to their own objectives.

Specifically, we believe that organizations with well-developed web operations and experience with web techniques and systems are likely to be seen as more effective administratively than organizations with relatively weak Web operations. This increased effectiveness is due, we argue, to greater organizational transparency and interactivity that webbed organizations have with their environments, which in turn is due to increased sophistication of the technical features incorporated into websites, which are reflected in their transparency, interactivity, and openness scores.

Thus, we hypothesize that the more open an organization is, the more effective administratively it is likely to be, all other things being equal. Additionally, we hypothesize that adoption of networked ITs is likely over time to stimulate organizational openness.

A. Government Performance Indicators

Since our earlier analyses on the correlates of openness were performed, we have become aware of new data on government performance published by a team of researchers at the World Bank (Kaufmann et al., 2002). Having data that systematically describe government performance in other than gross economic terms helps enormously in testing the contribution to governance of openness and networked information systems. The following sections analyze these relationships.

World Bank governance data consist of six indicators that capture various aspects of government performance:

- Voice and accountability
- Political stability
- Government effectiveness
- Regulatory quality
- Rule of law
- Control of corruption

These indicators were constructed from nearly 200 measures developed and published by 15 different organizations. While some measures include objective criteria, such as voter turnout, many others are based either on polls or on surveys, and therefore tap perceptions by citizens and business leaders about conditions in each country. The authors are careful to emphasize the inherent difficulties in producing comparable measures across nations with very different cultural and sociopolitical conditions. The data have been rigorously tested to produce more-or-less consistent country-to-country comparisons for all countries, for 1996, 1998, 2000, and 2002. Governance is defined by the World Bank team:

as the traditions and institutions by which authority in a country is exercised. This includes (1) the process by which governments are selected, monitored and replaced, (2) the capacity of the government to effectively formulate and implement sound policies, and (3) the respect of citizens and the state for the institutions that govern economic and social interactions among them (Kaufmann et al., 2002).

Each principal component is summarized briefly in Table 11.6.

The World Bank's government effectiveness measure is of particular interest because it focuses on the administrative apparatus of the state most closely tied to web operations. To be sure that openness and government effectiveness measure different things, we inspected the variables used to build the indicator; they are listed in Table 11.7 below. We believe that openness as we have defined and measured it, and government effectiveness

Table 11.6   World Bank Governance Indicators

Voice and accountability	Extent to which citizens can participate in the choosing of governments, measures of media independence
Political stability	Perceptions of likelihood that the government will be destabilized, insecurity will affect citizens' selection of governments
Government effectiveness	Perceptions of the quality of public service provision, bureaucracy, competence, independence from political pressure, and credibility of government commitments: inputs to policy process
Regulatory quality	Incidence of market-unfriendly policies, controls or supervision, perception of regulatory burden
Rule of law	Extent to which citizens have confidence in and abide by societal rules, perceptions of crime, effectiveness of judiciary, enforceability of contracts
Control of corruption	Perceptions of corruption, measured in a variety of ways: payments to get things done, corruption of political leaders, state capture

Source: From Kaufmann et al., 5–6, 2002.

Table 11.7 Data Categories for World Bank Government Effectiveness Indicators

Representative Sources	Nonrepresentative Sources
Government policy (probusiness)	Red tape/bureaucracy
Government/institutional efficacy	Institutional failure: institutional rigidities that hinder bureaucratic efficiency
Government ineffectiveness: quality of the government's personnel	Bureaucratic delays
Government instability: high turnover that lowers the quality of the government's personnel	Government and administration: decentralization and transparency
Government stability: its ability to carry out programs	Competence of public-sector personnel relative to the private sector
Bureaucratic quality: civil service's institutional strength, free from political influences	Wasteful government expenditure
Likelihood that when a government official acts against the rules, one can go to another official or a superior and get correct treatment	Government commitments are honored by new governments
Management time spent with bureaucrats	Management time spent with bureaucracy
Efficiency customs	Public service vulnerability to political pressure
General condition of roads you use	Competence of public-sector personnel relative to the private sector
Efficiency of mail delivery	Wasteful government expenditure
Quality of public health care provision	Strength and expertise of the civil service to avoid drastic interruptions in government services in times of political instability
Government efficiency in delivering services	Effective implementation of government decisions
Predictability of changes in rules and laws	Bureaucracy as an obstacle to business development
Credibility of government's commitment to policies	Exposure of public service to political interference

Source: From Kaufmann et al., The World Bank, 55, 1999, http://econ.worldbank.org/docs/ 919.pdf

as operationalized by the World Bank team are distinct concepts, capturing different dimensions of bureaucratic behavior. We have chosen the term *administrative effectiveness* rather than government effectiveness as we feel a more restricted meaning more accurately captures the underlying behavior the indicator embodies.

Box 11.1: Structural Equation Model

$$\text{Effectiveness} = \text{openness} + \text{PCGDP} + \text{democracy} + \text{durability} + \text{law} \quad (11.1)$$

$$\text{Openness} = \text{effectiveness} + \text{PCGDP} + \text{democracy} + \text{school} + \text{Internet} + \text{Web}_{1998} \quad (11.2)$$

Where:

Effectiveness	= World Bank index of administrative effectiveness
Openness	= CyPRG index of website transparency and interactivity
PCGDP	= Purchasing parity per capita gross domestic product
Democracy	= Polity IV project index of democratic governance
Durability	= Polity IV measure of durability of existing regime
Law	= World Bank index of the rule of law
School	= Average secondary school enrollment, percent
Internet	= Internet users per 1000 people
Web_{1998}	= Percent of ministries with functioning websites in 1998

VIII.   MODEL ESTIMATION

To examine the relationship between openness and administrative effectiveness, we develop a structural model, depicted in Box 11.1. A structural model is necessary to account for the reciprocal causality between openness and administrative effectiveness resulting from our hypotheses that openness both reflects administrative effectiveness and leads to improved effectiveness.

In Equation 11.1, administrative effectiveness is modeled as a function of web openness, economic performance, the development and durability of competitive democratic institutions, and the rule of law. We hypothesize that administrative effectiveness increases with economic capacity and the competitiveness of democratic institutions. Social consensus supporting the rule of law is an important precursor variable in that it creates an environment in which ministries can develop, implement, and administer rules. Finally, we hypothesize that administrative effectiveness is developed over time. Thus, regime durability is important for providing sufficient political stability to enable agencies to develop their capacities.

In Equation 11.2, openness is modeled as a function of administrative effectiveness based on the notions that openness reflects effectiveness and that better-managed agencies have greater capacity to invest in a higher-quality web presence. We include economic capacity and the competitiveness of democratic institutions for similar reasons as in the effectiveness equation.

In addition, we hypothesize that openness is also influenced by societal levels of Internet capacity, resulting from familiarity with the technology and how it has been operationalized by public agencies. Consequently, we include variables measuring education levels of the population, rates of Internet access in homes, and a measure of ministry experience with Internet technologies, measured in number of years the ministry has had a presence on the Web.

We estimate these equations employing two-stage least square procedures to account for the endogeneity of effectiveness and openness in these two equations.[4] Each of the

Table 11.8 Structural Model Estimation Results

Explanatory Variables	Dependent Variable	
	Effectiveness	Openness
Constant	$-.245^{***}$	$.161^*$
	(.001)	(.094)
Effectiveness	—	.052
		(.775)
Openness	$.135^{**}$	—
	(.026)	
PCGDP	.091	.025
	(.158)	(.890)
Democracy	.017	$.133^*$
	(.561)	(.082)
Durability	.036	—
	(.297)	
Law	$.782^{***}$	—
	(.000)	
School	—	$.234^{**}$
		(.031)
Internet		$-.147^{**}$
		(.041)
Web_{1998}	—	$.495^{***}$
		(.000)
Adjusted R^2	.94	.59
N	97	97

Note: Reported coefficients are standardized coefficients expect for the intercept term. Significance tests are reported in parentheses.

$***p < .01; **p < .05; *p < .10.$

equations is identified because each equation includes sufficient exogenous variables unique to that equation. Thus we are able to construct instruments for the endogenous variables (e.g., openness in Equation 11.1 and effectiveness in Equation 11.2) and employ them to estimate each equation. The results are presented in Table 11.8.

The first model, which focuses on the effects of web openness, supports the hypothesis that web openness has an independent effect on administrative performance. By far the most important determinants of administrative effectiveness are the social norms that support the rule of law.

Nevertheless, controlling for economic and political conditions, the coefficient for openness is still positive and statistically significant. The coefficients for economic and political performance are in the expected direction, but interestingly, none of them are statistically significant once one controls for the rule of law and web openness.

The second model, which focuses on the determinants of openness, also accords with expectations, though there are some important anomalies. All of the variables measuring the social capacity for Internet use are statistically significant. The coefficient for Internet access, contrary to expectations, however, is negative. This may be because there is a slight negative correlation between education and Internet access in our data.

As expected, schooling and ministry experience with websites are positively and strongly related to increased levels of web openness. These two variables account for the lion's share of the variation in the dependent variable.

Competitiveness of democratic institutions is also positively related to openness, though this coefficient does not quite attain standard levels of statistical significance. Interestingly, when controlling for political environment and Internet capacity, neither administrative effectiveness nor economic output are statistically significant.

IX. CONCLUSION

These results suggest that openness has a direct effect on administrative effectiveness; the number of agencies online in 1998, Internet penetration, and schooling are all significant (democratic governance is significant at the 10% level). But, significantly, the reverse relationship is not supported: it appears that administrative effectiveness does not affect openness.

Thus, our earlier contention, that the Internet may be a powerful mechanism promoting administrative effectiveness (Friis et al., 1998; Demchak et al., 2000) is strongly supported by these results. Even a poorly run agency can develop a high-quality online presence once it has experience with the Internet.

Subsequently, web presence appears to motivate the agency, possibly through increased expectations on the part of its constituents or by identification of new modes of operation, to operate more effectively. Organizational web operations appear to be creating a virtuous cycle of opportunities, demands and expectations, and administrative responses.

ACKNOWLEDGMENTS

This work was supported by the National Science Foundation grant no. SES9907996.

REFERENCES

Appleby, P.H., *Morality and Administration in Democratic Government*, Louisiana State University Press, Baton Rouge, LA, 1952.

Danziger, J.N. et al., *Computers and Politics: High Technology in American Local Governments*, Columbia University Press, New York, 1982.

Demchak, C.C., Friis, C., and La Porte, T.M., Webbing governance: national differences in constructing the public face, in *Handbook of Public Information Systems*, Garson, G.D., Ed., Marcel Dekker, New York, 2000.

Deutsch, K.W., *The Nerves of Government*, Free Press, New York, 1966.

Friis, C., Demchak, C.C., and La Porte, T.M., Configuring public agencies in cyberspace: a conceptual investigation, in *Public Administration in an Information Age: A Handbook*, Snellen, I.Th.M. and van de Donk, W.B.H.J., Eds., IOS Press, Amsterdam, 1998.

Frissen, P.H.A. et al., Eds., *European Public Administration and Informatization,* IOS Press, Amsterdam, 1992.

Garson, G.D., Ed., *Handbook of Public Information Systems,* Marcel Dekker, New York, 2000.

Ho, A.T.-K., Reinventing local governments and the e-government initiative, *Public Administration Review*, 62, 434, 2002.

Kaufmann, D., Kraay, A., and Zoido-Lobatón, P., Governance Matters, The World Bank, 1999 http://econ.worldbank.org/docs/919.pdf

Kaufmann, D., Kraay, A., and Zoido-Lobatón, P., Governance Matters II: Updated Indicators for 2000/01, The World Bank, 2002
http://econ.worldbank.org/files/11783_wps2772.pdf

Koppel, J.G.S., The challenge of administration by regulation: preliminary findings regarding the U.S. government's venture capital funds, *Journal of Public Administration Research and Theory*, 9, 641–666, 1999.

Kraemer, K.L. and King, J., Computers and the constitution, in *The American Constitution and the Administrative State: Constitutionalism in the Late 20th Century*, Stillman, R.J., Ed., (262-ff), University Press of America, Lanham, 1989.

La Porte, T.M. and Demchak, C.C., Hotlinked Governance: A Worldwide Assessment, 1997–2000, paper presented at 6th National Conference on Research in Public Management, Bloomington, IN, 2001.

La Porte, T.M., Demchak, C.C., and de Jong, M., Democracy and bureaucracy in the age of the web: empirical findings and theoretical speculations, *Administration & Society*, 34(3), 411–446, 2002.

Marshall, M.G. and Jaggers, K., *Political Regime Characteristics and Transitions, 1800–2002*, Dataset Users' Manual, Center for International Development and Conflict Management, University of Maryland, College Park, 2002.

Mayntz, R., New Challenges to Governance Theory, Jean Monnet Chair Paper RSC 98/50, European University Press, Florence, 1998.

Mechling, J., A customer service manifesto: using IT to improve government services, *Government Technology*, January, S27–S33, 1994.

Moon, M.J., The evolution of e-government among municipalities: rhetoric or reality?, *Public Administration Review*, 62, 424, 2002.

Osborne, D. and Gaebler, T., *Reinventing Government*, Plume, New York, 1992.

O'Toole, L.J., Treating networks seriously: practical and research-based agendas in public administration, *Public Administration Review*, 57, 45–52, 1997.

Peters, G., *The Future of Governing*, 2nd ed., University of Kansas Press, Lawrence, KS, 2001.

Peters, G. and Pierre, J., Governance without government? Rethinking public administration, *Journal of Public Administration Research and Theory*, 8, 223–243, 1998.

Pierre, J., Ed., *Bureaucracy in the Modern State : An Introduction to Comparative Public Administration*, E. Elgar, Aldershot, U.K., 1995.

Snellen, I.Th.M. and van de Donk, W.B.H.J., Eds., *Public Administration in an Information Age: A Handbook*, IOS Press, Amsterdam, 1998.

Sproul, L. and Kiesler, S., Connections: New Ways of Working in the Networked Organization, MIT Press, Cambridge, MA, 1991.

Thomas, C., Maintaining and restoring public trust in government agencies and their employees, *Administration & Society*, 30, 166–193, 1998.

Turban, E., McLean, E., and Wetherbe, J., *Information Technology for Management: Making Strategic Connections for Strategic Advantage*, 2nd ed., John Wiley & Sons, New York, 1999.

Waldo, D., *The Enterprise of Public Administration*, Chandler and Sharp, Novato, CA, 1980.

Weare, C., Musso, J., and Hale, M.L., Electronic democracy and the diffusion of municipal web pages in California, *Administration & Society*, 31, 1, 3–27, 1999.

Weick, K.E., *The Social Psychology of Organizing*, 2nd ed., Random House, New York, 1979. Originally published in 1969.

West, D.M., State and Federal e-Government in the United States, 2002, Taubman Center for Public Policy, Brown University, Providence, RI, 2002.

Wilson, J.Q., *Bureaucracy*, Basic Books, New York, 1989.

Woller, G.M., Toward a reconciliation of the bureaucratic and democratic ethos, *Administration & Society*, 30, 1, 85–109, 1998.

PART III

POLICY ISSUES

12

SOCIAL STRATIFICATION AND THE DIGITAL DIVIDE*

Kenneth R. Wilson
East Carolina University

Jennifer S. Wallin
RTI International

Christa Reiser
East Carolina University

CONTENTS

I.	Introduction	174
II.	Access to information technology	174
III.	The digital divide	175
	A. Race	175
	B. Geographic location	176
	C. Gender	176
	D. Control variables	177
IV.	Research design	177
	A. Dependent variables	178
	B. Independent variables	178
	C. Control variables	178
V.	Results	179
VI.	Conclusion	182
	References	183

* This chapter is adapted from Social Stratification and the Digital Divide originally published in *Social Science Computer Review*, May 2003. The North Carolina Vision 2030 Project and the North Carolina Board of Science and Technology funded this project. The authors would like to thank Jane Patterson, Margic Boccieri, and Deborah Watts for their support and insights in developing this project and for their concern with the people in eastern North Carolina.

ABSTRACT

The "digital divide" is the concept developed to describe the gap between those who are reaping the advantages of new information technology (IT) and those who are not. Rural residence, race, and gender have been linked to the digital divide. While recent studies show that the size of the divide has been shrinking for many groups, this chapter explores whether socioeconomic factors explain the racial, geographic, and gender divides. Rural, minority, and female respondents were less likely to have home computers or be connected to the Internet. Controlling for socioeconomic variables, the effects of rural residence and gender disappeared but African Americans were still less likely to have home computers or Internet access. When public Internet access was examined, rural residence and gender had no effect but African Americans were more likely to know of public facilities in their community even when socioeconomic variables were controlled. Race and gender did not affect willingness to participate in Internet training programs but rural residents were less willing than urban residents. The effect of rural residence disappeared when socioeconomic controls were introduced. Future research needs to better understand the implications of different ways of using new technology (i.e., public vs. private access) and determine if digital technology deepens socioeconomic chasms or provides new opportunities.

I. INTRODUCTION

A "digital infrastructure" is rapidly spreading throughout most corners of our society. In the process, many aspects of American society, from the way we educate our children, to how we interact with elected officials, to how we meet the people we date and marry, are being transformed (Bucy, 2000; Lauman, 2000; Attewell, 2001; Seccombe and Warner, 2004). According to Lebo (2000), the Internet is the fastest-growing technology in human history. While many are touting the arrival of computers and the Internet, it is clear that all do not and will not have access to this new technology. The "digital divide" is a concept developed to describe the gap between those who are reaping the advantages of this new technology and those who are not. Issues related to computer use (rather than access) have been captured by the phrase, "the second digital divide" (Attewell, 2001). Among others, rural residence, race, and gender have been linked to the digital divide (Bimber, 2000; Green, 2002). Recent studies show that the size of the divide has been shrinking for many groups (Haythornthwaite, 2001; NTIA, 2002).

This chapter focuses on the "first digital divide" and explores whether the gaps in access to information technology (IT) associated with race, geography, and gender exist in North Carolina and if these gaps can be explained by other important social factors (e.g., income, education, age, employment, marital status, and children living in the household). A better understanding of the social and economic factors that produced these divides should help us understand why they are shrinking and the kinds of changes that may occur over the next decade.

II. ACCESS TO INFORMATION TECHNOLOGY

The digital divide has become an important focus of research because it involves more than simply documenting the characteristics of people who own computers. The increasing popularity and economic utility of computers and the Internet has brought changes in the way our society and its individuals interact — the way we shop, find employment, pay taxes, use the library, and even earn college degrees (Bertot and McClure, 1998; Bimber, 1999; Brodie et al., 2000; DiMaggio et al., 2001; Katz et al., 2001). The Internet has brought abrupt changes in our society within a very short period of time. The first personal computer was sold during the 1980s (Stewart, 1999). Research for the National Telecommunications and Information Administration (NTIA) documents rapid growth in the number of American households that have a home computer and home access to the Internet (NTIA, 1995a, 1995b, 1998, 1999, 2000, 2002). In 1993, only 33% of American households owned computers, and 10% had Internet access at home. The most recent research estimates that in September 2001, 56.5% of American households had home computers and 50.5% had home Internet access (NTIA, 2002). This study also showed that many more Americans were using the Internet outside the home (NTIA, 2002).

The new IT has become the backbone of the emerging knowledge economy. The ability to access and use this technology effectively will be the key to economic success for both individuals and communities. This new technology is being incorporated into the public school curriculum and is transforming the way information is being created and distributed. Communities that wish to keep or recruit new high-paying jobs need to provide businesses with high-speed access. Individuals must learn to use this new technology in order to have any chance of being successful in the emerging knowledge economy (Vision 2030, 2000; DiMaggio et al., 2001; Green, 2002).

III. THE DIGITAL DIVIDE

In October 1993, the U.S. Department of Commerce adopted the goal of providing universal telecommunication and Internet access (NTIA, 1993). In 1997, the president declared a goal of wiring every home by the year 2007 (NTIA, 1998). North Carolina has recognized the need for universal Internet access to spread the benefits of economic development and increase citizen access to the state government (Rural Prosperity Task Force, 2000; Vision 2030, 2000). Most North Carolina counties have public Internet access available in libraries or local community colleges. These facilities may provide an alternative to home Internet access (Lentz et al., 2000).

While there was a national commitment to universal access, some groups were falling through the cracks (Schement, 1998; Attewell, 2001). Research showed that many factors were associated with access to the new information society including three factors — race, gender, and geographic location — which have often been associated with social disadvantages. This chapter explores the differential access to home computers and the Internet associated with these factors in North Carolina and then tests whether these differences are due to other social and economic conditions.

A. Race

Computer and Internet users are divided along the lines of race. White households are far more likely to have computer access from their homes than Black or Hispanic households (NTIA, 1995a, 1995b, 1998, 1999, 2000; Attewell, 2001). NTIA reported that in 1997 White households were still more than twice as likely (40.8%) to own a computer than Black (19.3%) or Hispanic (19.4%) households and this relationship held across all income levels. They also reported that home Internet access was three times higher for

White households than for Black or Hispanic households (NTIA, 1998). During the late 1990s, all groups experienced tremendous increases in home computer ownership and home Internet access, although White households (55.7%) were still more likely than Black (32.6%) or Hispanic (33.7%) households to own computers. According to most, the size of the gap had not increased since 1998. However, according to U.S. Department of Commerce figures (2000), from 1994 to 2000, the technology gap between Blacks and Whites increased. This situation is expected to be remedied as the cost of computers goes down.

With regard to home Internet access, White households (46.1%) were still more likely than Black (23.5%) or Hispanic (23.6%) households to have home Internet access and the size of these gaps continued to grow (NTIA, 2000). The most recent research documented continued growth in computer and Internet usage for all racial groups. In 2001, White Americans were still more likely to use a computer or the Internet than Black or Hispanic Americans but the proportion of Black and Hispanic computer and Internet users was growing at a more rapid rate than the proportion of White users (NTIA, 2002).

B. Geographic Location

In addition to race, geographic location plays a major part in determining who owns a home computer and who has home access to the Internet (NTIA, 2000; Rural Prosperity Task Force, 2000; Lentz and Oden, 2001). While the size of the difference between urban and rural areas in home computers seems to have stabilized, in most areas of IT the gap between urban and rural areas is growing. Urban residents are far more likely to have access to computer services than their rural counterparts (e.g., DSL, cable modems, and digital television). This makes it more difficult for rural businesses to compete against businesses located in urban areas and prevents people who live in rural areas from benefiting from economic opportunities that urban areas have taken for granted (Strover, 1999; Hindman, 2000; Parker, 2000; Drabenstott, 2001; Lentz and Oden, 2001). Even among college students who have free Internet access on campus, students from families living in rural areas access the Internet less than students from urban areas. While these rural students clearly recognized the importance of the Internet to the future of their communities, they had less time to use it because they were more likely to commute to the university than the urban students (Crews and Feinberg, 2002).

C. Gender

Many studies have documented gender differences in computer and Internet usage (Bimber, 2000; NTIA, 2000; DiMaggio et al., 2001; Jackson et al., 2001; Volman and van Eck, 2001). Some researchers trace this gender gap to the idea that computers and the Internet (as well as technology in general) are "gendered" (Green, 2002). This is reflected in cultural stereotypes that indicate that computers and the Internet are more appropriate activities for men than for women (Fletcher-Flinn and Suddendorf, 1996; Reinen and Plomp, 1997). Male values may also be embedded in the design of advanced technology so that it becomes associated with a masculine identity. And when women decide to use computers and the Internet, they may find that the available software and websites do not reflect their needs or interests. Some of the differences between men and women in their Internet use and access can be explained by various socioeconomic factors (Bimber, 2000).

While there has been a gap between men and women in their computer and Internet usage, between 1998 and 2001 women raised their Internet use and closed this gap. Katz et al. (2001), using cohort data from national representative telephone surveys from 1992 to 2000, show that new Internet users are proportionally more likely to be female than is found in surveys that look at usage status in any given year. In 2001, 53.9% of men and 53.8% of women reported using the Internet (NTIA, 2002). However, though both women and men seem to be equally likely to use the Internet, once online, "Women remain less frequent and less intense users of the Internet" (Ono, 2003: 112).

D.   Control Variables

Income is a major determinant of whether an individual can afford to buy a home computer or pay for home Internet access (Lipke, 2000; NTIA, 2000, 2002; Warschauer, 2003). Computer ownership is more widespread for those with high incomes. According to the Benton Foundation, by late 2001, 80% of those with annual household incomes of $75,000 or more used a computer, compared with only 25% of the poorest American families (Warschauer, 2003). Lower levels of household income tend to be associated with the three social divides that are the focus of this study. Since computers and Internet access are expensive, the new digital disadvantages may simply reflect the lower level of economic resources available to rural, female, and minority households.

Education can prepare people to learn the new skills and procedures required to enter the new technological world. Americans with a college education are almost six times as likely to have a home computer (75.7% compared with 12.8%) or home Internet access (69.9% vs. 11.7%) as those with an elementary-school education (NTIA, 2000). NTIA estimates that income and education together account for half of the racial differences in Internet access (NTIA, 2000).

A number of other variables influence the level of digital inclusion in the year 2000. Young (18 to 24) adults had Internet usage rates very similar to adults between 25 and 49 (56.8% vs. 55.4%). Only 29.6% of older adults reported using the Internet (NTIA, 2000). Two-parent households are much more likely to have home Internet access than single-parent households (60.6% vs. 35.7% male-headed and 30.0% female-headed) (NTIA, 2000). Computer and Internet access may also augment a child's leaning experience in school (Lauman, 2000). Thus income, education, age, marital status, employment status, and the presence of children in the household may influence the relationship between the primary independent variables and the dependent variables and will be statistically controlled to determine the extent to which the independent variables still create digital divides.

IV.   RESEARCH DESIGN

As part of the Vision 2030 project, the North Carolina Board of Science and Technology asked the East Carolina University Survey Research Laboratory to develop a survey to measure public perceptions of the role and importance of science and technology in the North Carolina economy. A general population telephone survey employed random digit dialing using a sample purchased from Survey Sampling, Inc. There were 522 interviews completed statewide. The response rate was 52%. These data have been weighted to insure an accurate geographic distribution across the entire state of North Carolina.

A. Dependent Variables

Respondents were asked if they had a computer in their homes. Those who had a home computer were asked if it was connected to the Internet. Respondents were also asked if they had Internet access at a local library or community college. Finally, they were asked if they would be willing to complete a training program over the Internet if it would qualify them for a better position. For each of these variables, "No" was coded as zero and "Yes" was coded as one.

Over half of the households (58.0%) had a home computer and 38.9% of the households were connected to the Internet. This is higher than the NTIA (2000) estimate that 45.3% of North Carolina households had computers and 35.3% had Internet access. This probably reflects the fact that households without telephones were excluded from our survey. About twice as many respondents (75.2%) reported that they had public access to the Internet at a local library or community college. Roughly two out of three respondents (68.3%) said they would be willing to complete a training program over the Internet if it would qualify them for an improved position.

B. Independent Variables

Three independent variables were used in this study. The first classified the respondents' place of residence based on the county population. Counties with populations under 100,000 were classified as rural (1) and counties with populations of 100,000 or more were classified as urban (0). The sample contains 39.2% of respondents living in rural counties and 60.8% of respondents living in urban counties.

Respondents were also asked about their race. Because fewer than 20 respondents identified themselves as races other than African American or White, they were dropped from this analysis. The respondents were 80.4% White and 19.6% African American. The higher numerical value was assigned to African Americans. Respondents were also asked to indicate their gender. The respondents were 44.9% male and 55.1% female. The higher value was assigned to females.

C. Control Variables

Respondents were also asked a set of questions about their social and economic backgrounds. These variables included the respondent's family income, education, age, work status (not full-time or full-time), marital status (not married or married), and children living at home (no or yes). To assess family income, respondents were asked to select one of ten categories ranging from "under $5000 per year" to "over $100,000 per year" that best reflected the total earnings of everyone living in their household. The median family income for this sample was about $30,000 per year. To measure education, respondents were asked to indicate the highest degree that they had earned. Of the respondents, 12.5% had not graduated from high school and 43.1% had just earned a high school degree. Another 31.7% had earned one or more college degrees.

To measure age, respondents were asked the year they were born. Their age was then determined by subtracting this from the year in which the interview occurred. The median age was about 45 and 13.4% of the respondents were 65 or older. Respondents were asked about their current work and marital status. Of the respondents, 60.2% were employed full-time and 60.7% were currently married. Respondents were asked if there were children under 18 currently living in their household. Of the respondents, 42.6% reported that there were children living in their household and the remaining 57.1% did not have children living with them.

V. RESULTS

The results of the bivariate logistic regression between each independent variable and each dependent variable are presented in Table 12.1. Black, rural, and female respondents were significantly less likely to have home computers than White, urban, and male respondents. Respondents with higher incomes and more education were more likely to have home computers. Age did not significantly affect home computer ownership.

Respondents who were employed full-time, married, and had children living at home were more likely to have home computers. Black, rural, and female respondents were significantly less likely to have home Internet access than White, urban, and male respondents. Respondents with higher incomes and more education were more likely to have home Internet access. Older respondents were less likely to have home Internet access than younger respondents. Respondents who were employed full-time and had children living at home were more likely to have home Internet access. Marital status did not significantly influence the likelihood of home Internet access.

Over three fourths of the respondents were aware of public Internet access in their communities. Black respondents, younger respondents, and respondents with children living at home were more likely to know of public Internet access in their communities. None of the other independent or control variables significantly influenced awareness of public Internet access. Over two thirds of the respondents reported that they would be willing to complete a training program over the Internet. Race and gender did not significantly influence respondents' willingness to take a course over the Internet. Respondents who were older and lived in rural areas were less likely to be willing to take a course over the Internet. Respondents who had more education and income were more willing to complete an Internet course, as were respondents who were employed full-time and who had children living at home.

The results for the logistic regression analysis of home computers and home Internet access are presented in Table 12.2. The first model shows the effects of the three

Table 12.1 Bivariate Logistic Regression Analysis of Home Computers, Internet Access, Public Internet Access, and Internet Training

	Home Computer		Internet Access		Public Access		Internet Training	
	Exp (B)	Sig	Exp (B)	Sig	Exp (B)	Sig	Exp (B)	Sig
Race	0.249	0.000	0.260	0.000	2.064	0.033	0.953	0.860
Rural residence	0.643	0.034	0.498	0.001	0.795	0.331	0.605	0.022
Gender	0.651	0.039	0.635	0.029	1.373	0.175	0.865	0.505
Income	1.375	0.000	1.434	0.000	1.042	0.372	1.094	0.037
Education	1.927	0.000	1.869	0.000	1.170	0.112	1.298	0.005
Age	0.988	0.053	0.986	0.038	0.975	0.001	0.953	0.000
Full-time job	1.691	0.012	2.436	0.000	1.146	0.565	2.441	0.000
Married	2.058	0.001	1.485	0.065	0.814	0.395	0.838	0.428
Children at home	2.164	0.000	1.695	0.011	2.219	0.002	2.156	0.001

Table 12.2   Logistic Regression Analysis of Home Computers and Internet Access

	Home Computer				Home Internet Access			
	Exp (B)	Sig	Exp (B)	Sig	Exp (B)	Sig	Exp (B)	Sig
Income			1.168	0.009			1.237	0.001
Education			1.686	0.000			1.527	0.000
Age			0.984	0.051			0.985	0.091
Full-time job			1.293	0.344			0.773	0.336
Married			0.669	0.151			1.023	0.937
Children at home			1.842	0.019			1.342	0.253
Race	0.249	0.000	0.327	0.000	0.265	0.000	0.345	0.003
Rural residence	0.608	0.021	0.946	0.825	0.614	0.024	0.767	0.296
Gender	0.649	0.046	0.688	0.133	0.506	0.003	0.760	0.266
Constant	18.466	0.000	1.894	0.530	8.414	0.000	0.663	0.695
Model chi-square (df)	36.943 (3)	0.000	104.590 (9)	0.000	36.137 (3)		98.355 (9)	0.000
CV block chi-square (df)			89.364 (6)	0.000			86.138 (6)	0.000
IV block chi-square (df)	36.943 (3)	0.000	15.226 (3)	0.002	36.137 (3)		12.217 (3)	0.007
Correct predictions (%)	65.5		73.4		63.4		68.9	
Cox & Snell R^2	0.090		0.233		0.087		0.220	

independent variables when no other variables were included as controls. Rural respondents were significantly less likely to have a home computer than urban respondents. Only 51.6% of the respondents living in rural counties had a home computer compared with 62.5% of the respondents living in urban areas. African American respondents were significantly less likely to have a home computer than White respondents. Only 31.2% of the African Americans had a home computer compared with 64.8% of the White respondents. Female respondents were significantly less likely to have a home computer than were male respondents. Only 53.5% of the female respondents had a home computer compared with 63.8% of the male respondents.

When income, education, age, work status, marital status, and children living at home were entered into the equation, the effects of rural residence and gender were no longer statistically significant. However, African American respondents were still significantly less likely to have a home computer. Households where the respondents report higher levels of education and income were more likely to have a home computer. Households that include children under 18 were also more likely to have a home computer. Over two thirds (67.2%) of the households with children have a home computer. All the three independent variables also had significant effects on having home Internet access. Rural respondents were significantly less likely to have home Internet access than urban respondents. Only 29.2% of the respondents living in rural counties had home Internet access compared with 45.4% of the respondents living in urban areas. African American respondents were significantly less likely to have home Internet access than White respondents. Only 16.9% of the African Americans had home Internet access compared with 44.5% of the White respondents. Female respondents were significantly less likely to have home Internet access than were male respondents. Only 34.4% of the female respondents had home Internet access compared with 45.2% of the male respondents.

When income, education, age, work status, marital status, and children living at home were entered into the equation, the effects of rural residence and gender were no longer statistically significant. However, African American respondents were still significantly

Table 12.3 Logistic Regression Analysis of Public Internet Access and Internet Training

	Public Internet Access				Internet Training			
	Exp (B)	Sig	Exp (B)	Sig	Exp (B)	Sig	Exp (B)	Sig
Income			1.041	0.522			0.963	0.538
Education			1.162	0.201			1.268	0.036
Age			0.981	0.026			0.958	0.000
Full-time job			1.310	0.353			0.664	0.128
Married			1.067	0.824			0.895	0.704
Children at home			2.009	0.012			1.353	0.257
Race	2.023	0.037	2.193	0.033	0.976	0.930	0.795	0.462
Rural residence	0.758	0.245	0.971	0.911	0.602	0.021	0.858	0.540
Gender	1.365	0.185	1.377	0.209	0.852	0.466	1.023	0.928
Constant	0.864	0.791	0.464	0.481	3.507	0.012	26.251	0.003
Model chi-square (df)	8.045 (3)	0.045	28.222 (9)	0.001	5.770 (3)	0.123	57.587 (9)	0.000
CV block chi-square (df)			31.894 (6)	0.001			56.615 (6)	0.000
IV block chi-square (df)	8.045 (3)	0.045	6.328 (3)	0.097	5.770 (3)	0.123	0.972 (3)	0.808
Correct predictions (%)		75.2		76.4		68.3		72.3
Cox & Snell R^2		0.020		0.069		0.015		0.136

less likely to have home Internet access. Households where the respondents report higher levels of education and income were more likely to have home Internet access.

The results for the logistic regression analysis of public Internet access and of the respondents' willingness to complete an Internet training course are presented in Table 12.3. Rural residence and gender do not significantly influence the respondents' likelihood of knowing about a public Internet access in the area. Race significantly influences awareness of public Internet access, with 84.4% of the African American respondents and 72.9% of the White respondents reporting that they had public access to the Internet at a local library or community college. This racial difference does not disappear when income, education, age, work status, marital status, and children living at home are entered into the equation. Younger people and people with children living at home were more likely to be aware of local public access to the Internet. Most of the respondents (83.3%) who have children living in their homes were aware of public Internet access.

Race and gender did not significantly influence respondents' willingness to complete a training course over the Internet. Rural respondents were significantly less likely to be willing to complete an Internet training course than respondents living in urban counties, with 72.5% of the rural respondents reporting that they would be willing to complete a training course that prepared them for a better job over the Internet compared with 61.7% of the urban respondents. When the social and economic variables were controlled, the effect of rural residence disappeared. Age and education did significantly influence respondents' willingness to get training over the Internet. The younger, more educated respondents expressed more willingness to complete an Internet training course, as did respondents with children living at home.

VI. CONCLUSION

As in many other studies, rural residence, race, and gender significantly influenced whether or not respondents had a home computer and home Internet access. Using multivariate statistics to eliminate the effects of other important social and economic variables, this study has shown that the effects of gender and rural residence are primarily due to differences in income and education. In the case of having a home computer, the presence of children in the home also played an important role. These control variables did not explain the influence of race. Holding all the other variables constant, White respondents were still more likely to have a computer and be hooked up to the Internet at home than were African American respondents.

The analysis is consistent with more recent research that shows the digital divide to be closing more rapidly in some areas than in others. To the degree that the digital divides were created by the expenses associated with being an early adopter of a new technology, the divides should close as these expenses decrease. To the degree that the digital divides were created by the difficulty in learning to use new and unfamiliar technology, the divides should close as the procedures become more user-friendly and more commonplace. To the degree that the new technology is perceived as being important to successful careers, parents will devote more resources and effort to helping their children become comfortable with it.

The racial digital divide is the strongest and cannot be explained by social and economic variables. However, at least in North Carolina, the racial divide takes an interesting form. While African American households were less likely to have a home computer or home Internet access, they were more likely to be aware of free public access to computers and the Internet. This suggests that the public policy of creating public Internet access has been successful, at least in raising awareness levels. The finding that African American and White respondents were equally willing to learn new job skills over the Internet suggests that the differences in the material possessions (i.e., computers and Internet connections) should not be mistaken for differences in attitudes and beliefs. More research is clearly needed to understand how the different methods of accessing the Internet influence users' experiences, attitudes, skills, and the benefits that they derive from the Internet. As Warschauer (2003: 44) cautions, " . . . technology must be considered within a specific context that includes hardware, software, support resources, infrastructure, as well as people in various roles and relationships with one another and with other elements of the system."

These findings suggest that social and economic variables are not sufficient to understand the changing digital divide. North Carolina's public policy commitment to providing public Internet access across the state may have provided some groups with the ability to benefit from and develop their skills using new technology that they could not have afforded otherwise. The availability of public Internet access may have also fostered cultural beliefs and attitudes that make more rapid progress possible. On the other hand, the availability of public computers and Internet access may have slowed the acquisition of private technological resources in some groups. Further research is necessary to document how community resources and infrastructure interact with personal resources, skills, and attitudes to facilitate or hinder the adoption of new technologies. We must also remember that "Access to technology does not necessarily lead to its use, and information does not necessarily fuel self-empowering activity" (Green, 2002: 105). Snyder et al. (2002) studied families in Australia and found that having access to information and communication technologies at home did not allow them to overcome the digital divide. The authors warn that old inequities have not disappeared and are taking new forms congruent with our computer-mediated society. We agree with Snyder and coauthors that "access" to computers and the Internet must be reconceptualized and expanded to take into account "quality" and "quantity of access" as well as who gets the benefits that can come with computer-related resources.

REFERENCES

Attewell, P., The first and second digital divides, *Sociology of Education,* 74(3), 252–259, 2001.

Bertot, J.C. and McClure, C.R., *The 1998 National Survey of U.S. Public Library Outlet Internet Connectivity: Final Report,* American Library Association, Chicago, IL, 1998.
Online: http://www.ala.org/oitp/digitaldivide/survey.html
Revised on February 1999.

Bimber, B., The Internet and citizen communication with government: does the medium matter?, *Political Communication,* 16, 409–429, 1999.

Bimber, B., Measuring the gender gap on the Internet, *Social Science Quarterly,* 81, 868–876, 2000.

Brodie, M., Flournoy, R.E., Altman, D.E., Benson, J.M., and Rosenbaum, M., Health information, the Internet, and the digital divide, *Health Affairs,* 19, 255–265, 2000.

Bucy, E.P., Social access to the Internet, *Harvard International Journal of Press-Politics,* 5, 50–61, 2000.

Crews, M. and Feinberg, M., Perceptions of university students regarding the digital divide, *Social Science Computer Review,* 20, 116–123, 2002.

DiMaggio, P., Hargittai, E., Neuman, W.R., and Robinson, J.P., Social implications of the Internet, *Annual Review of Sociology,* 27, 307–336, 2001.

Drabenstott, M., New policies for a new rural America, *International Regional Science Review,* 24, 3–15, 2001.

Fletcher-Flinn, C.M. and Suddendorf, T., Computer attitudes, gender and exploratory behavior: a developmental study, *Journal of Educational Computing Research,* 15, 369–392, 1996.

Green, L., *Communication, Technology, and Society,* Sage, Thousand Oaks, CA, 2002.

Haythornthwaite, C., Introduction: the Internet in everyday life, *American Behavioral Scientists,* 45, 363–382, 2001.

Hindman, D.B., The rural–urban digital divide, *Journalism and Mass Communication Quarterly,* 77, 549–560, 2000.

Jackson, L., Ervin, K.S., Gardner, P.D., and Schmitt, N., Gender and the Internet: women communicating and men searching, *Sex Roles,* 44(5/6), 363–379, 2001.

Katz, J.E., Rice, R.E., and Aspden, P., The Internet, 1995–2000: access, civic involvement and social interaction, *American Behavioral Scientist,* 45, 405–419, 2001.

Lauman, D., Student home computer use: a review of the literature, *Journal of Research on Computing in Education,* 33, 196–203, 2000.

Lebo, H., *Surveying the Digital Future,* UCLA Center for Communication Policy, Los Angeles, CA, 2000.

Lentz, R.G. and Oden, M.D., Digital divide or digital opportunity in the Mississippi Delta region of the US, *Telecommunications Policy,* 25, 291–313, 2001.

Lentz, B., Straubhaar, J., LaPastina, A., Main, S., and Taylor, J., Structuring Access: the Role of Public Access Centers in the "Digital Divide", paper presented at the International Communication Association meetings in Acapulco, 2000.
Online: http://www.utexas.edu/research/tipi/

Lipke, D.J., Dead end ahead?, *American Demographics,* 22, 10–12, 2000.

NTIA (National Telecommunications and Information Administration), National Information Infrastructure: Agenda for Action, 1993.
Online: http://metalab.unc.edu/nii/toc.html

NTIA (National Telecommunications and Information Administration), Connecting The Nation: Classrooms, Libraries, and Health Care Organizations in the Information Age, 1995a.
Online: http://www.ntia.doc.gov/connect.html

NTIA (National Telecommunications and Information Administration), Falling through the Net: A Survey of Have Nots in Rural and Urban America, 1995b.
   Online: http://www.ntia.doc.gov/ntiahome/digitaldivide/
NTIA (National Telecommunications and Information Administration), Falling through the Net II: New Data on the Digital Divide, 1998.
   Online: http://www.ntia.doc.gov/ntiahome/digitaldivide/
NTIA (National Telecommunications and Information Administration), Falling through the Net: Defining the Digital Divide, 1999.
   Online: http://www.ntia.doc.gov/ntiahome/digitaldivide/
NTIA (National Telecommunications and Information Administration), Falling through the Net: Toward Digital Inclusion, 2000.
   Online: http://www.ntia.doc.gov/ntiahome/digitaldivide/
NTIA (National Telecommunications and Information Administration), A Nation Online: How Americans Are Expanding Their Use of the Internet, 2002.
   Online: http://www.ntia.doc.gov/ntiahome/dn/index.html
Ono, H., Gender and the Internet, *Social Science Quarterly*, 84(1), 111–121, 2003.
Parker, E.B., Closing the digital divide in rural America, *Telecommunications Policy*, 24, 281–290, 2000.
Reinen, I.J. and Plomp, T., Information technology and gender equality: a contradiction in terminis?, *Computers & Education*, 28, 65–78, 1997.
Rural Prosperity Task Force, Rural Prosperity Task Force Final Report, 2000.
   Online: http://ruraltaskforce.state.nc.us/finalreport/report.html
Schement, J.R., *The Persistent Gap in Telecommunications: Toward Hypotheses and Answers*, Benton Foundation, Washington, D.C., 1998.
   Online http://www.benton.org/Policy/Schement/TRPI98/home.html
Seccombe, K. and Warner, L.R., *Marriages and Families, Relationships in Social Context*, Wadsworth, Ontario, Canada, 2004.
Snyder, I., Angus, L., and Sutherland-Smith, W., Building equitable literature futures: home and school computer-mediated literary practices and disadvantage, *Cambridge Journal of Education*, 32(3), 367–383, 2002.
Stewart, T.A., A nation of Net have nots? No, *Fortune*, 1, 184–188, 1999.
Strover, S., Rural Internet Connectivity, paper presented at the Telecommunications Research and Policy Conference, Austin, TX, 1999.
   Online: http://www.utexas.edu/research/tipi/
Vision 2030, *Vision 2030: Mapping the Future*, North Carolina Board of Science and Technology, 2000.
   Online: http://www.governor.state.nc.us/govoffice/science/projects/nc2030.html
Volman, M. and van Eck, E., Gender equity and information technology in education: the second decade, *Review of Educational Research*, 71(4), 613–635, 2001.
Warschauer, M., Demystifying the digital divide, *Scientific American*, 289(2), 42–47, 2003.

13

INTELLECTUAL PROPERTY FOR PUBLIC MANAGERS

Roland J. Cole
Barnes & Thornburg

Eric F. Broucek
DHL Express

CONTENTS

I.	Importance of intellectual property	186
II.	A bit of history	186
	A. Competition among equals	187
	B. Permission from the king	187
	C. To stimulate progress in the arts and sciences	187
	D. The results of history	188
III.	Types of intellectual property	188
	A. Patents	188
	B. Trademarks, service marks, trade dress	189
	C. Copyrights	190
	D. Trade secrets	190
IV.	Federally purchased intellectual property	190
	A. Limited rights	191
	B. Unlimited rights	191
	C. Restricted rights	191
V.	Federally created intellectual property	192
VI.	Violations by federal employees	192
VII.	State-purchased IP	192
VIII.	State-created IP	193
IX.	Violations by state employees	193
X.	Violations by local government employees	194
XI.	Fair use and the bounds of protection generally	194
	A. Trade display properties	194
	B. Trade secrets	195

C. Patents.. 196
D. Copyrights 197
E. Websites ("home pages and more").. 199
XII. Further reading.. 200
A. Books... 200
B. Internet resources... 200
XIII. Summary chart 201

ABSTRACT

This chapter starts with a discussion of the importance of intellectual property (IP). It then sets forth a bit of its history. Next, it describes the four major types of IP. It then discusses the special rules surrounding the federal government's acquisition and creation of IP, then the role of the states (in this context, local governments are similar to states). Finally, it concludes with a table summarizing some of the major points made about each type of IP.

I.   IMPORTANCE OF INTELLECTUAL PROPERTY

Perhaps more than anything else, it is the incredible amount of competition that exists in virtually every marketplace that has been the driving force behind the rapid rise in the importance of intellectual property (IP). The tremendous amount of resources spent to develop new technologies or to launch an advertising campaign for a new product or service makes the protection of an invention or a trademark vital to eventually receiving a return on the initial, necessary investment. Otherwise, competitors can spring up almost overnight, claiming to offer your product or service to your marketplace with allegedly lower prices, better service, or superior quality.

This highly competitive environment has created a keen awareness of the value of IP and methods for its creation and protection. Companies in every field are filing increasing numbers of patent applications each year. There are well over 200,000 patent applications filed each year in the U.S. alone. Companies are also securing trademark protection for their trademarks and service marks before making any significant investment in marketing or advertising their products and services. Each year, there are more than $100 billion worth of goods and services sold by companies that had a license to sell IP owned by someone else.

Along with this increased rate of creation of IP comes an increase in disputes over infringement of IP rights. Whereas patent infringement cases used to be fairly rare, now there are several thousand filed every year, with the number increasing dramatically with each new year. This means that not only must one be vigilant about opportunities within their own organizations to create valuable IP but one must also beware of infringing upon the ever-increasing number of patents, trademarks, and other types of IP that are owned by others.

II.   A BIT OF HISTORY

We often favor a historical approach to help us understand some of the nuances of current public policies. We find the approach especially helpful in the area of IP, both because the subject has a much longer history than many at first think and because the various types of IP come from two very different traditions.

A.   Competition among Equals

Trademarks, trade dress, the "right of publicity," and trade secrets have been the subject of legal action for centuries, as both courts and legislatures have wrestled with what is "fair" competition and what is not. As one can imagine, various legal systems in various places have exerted more or less control over time. But the concept of what is "fair" among competitors and for the benefit of consumers has remained a central theme. These forms of IP still retain a strong flavor of "bottom-up," case-by-case determination, even when national legislatures have adopted statutes providing for national registration (at least for trademarks), as the U.S. has done with the Lanham Act.

B.   Permission from the King

Patents and copyrights have a very different history. The terms were first used to indicate permission from the king to carry on what were otherwise considered dangerous or subversive activities. To start a new business, whether or not based on a new technology, was often very disruptive to the social order, and the man (rarely woman) that wanted to do so often had to obtain "Letters Patent" for permission to do so.

The right to copy and distribute written material (or even pictures) was also considered dangerous and thus requiring careful regulation. Only certain printers were given that right, subject to careful attention to their loyalty to the king or queen granting such permission.

C.   To Stimulate Progress in the Arts and Sciences

Against this background, the policy in the U.S. Constitution that inventors and authors were to be rewarded with such rights, in order to promote science and the arts, was a dramatic change in the history of the terms patent and copyright. The U.S. was not the only country experimenting with such rights for creators rather than distributors, so it was not alone in this change, but it was a dramatic step nonetheless.

Thus the more modern theory is not limiting activity to loyal subjects of the crown, but encouraging creative activity. Inventors willing to share their invention with the world (a patent application becomes public once granted, and requires the inventor to describe the "best method" of practicing the invention) get the "reward" of a legal right to keep others from practicing their invention for a period of time. Note, by the way, that the inventor may not have the right to practice the invention, since it may require the use of other patented inventions, etc., that are not available to the inventor. But the inventor always has the right to prevent others in the U.S. from practicing and to prevent those who have used the invention to import the invention or the products of it into the U.S.

In the invention case, only named individuals can be inventors, and a patent application can be denied and a granted patent revoked if the application does not list all such individuals and only such individuals. In modern corporate America, individual inventors are usually employees under an employment agreement that requires them to assign their rights to their employer, but the system preserves the idea of individual inventors throughout the application.

Similarly, the creator of a written work (including a computer program), a musical composition, a statue, an audiovisual work, or some combination of one or more of those, gets five exclusive rights to his or her creation — to perform it, to display it, to reproduce it, to distribute it, and to prepare derivative works based on it. In return, the creator has to give up certain rights with regard to each copy that he or she sells, although under the doctrine of "moral rights," added to the U.S. system in 1989, the creator can prevent certain forms of display or alteration of the work that would cast aspersions on the work or the creator. If the creator wants the additional rights stemming from federal registration, he or she has to provide two copies of the work to the U.S. Library of Congress and pay a fee.

The copyright law does not have the same deference to the individual that the patent law does. The copyright law allows a corporation (or other body) to be considered the creator, with all (or almost all) of the rights accorded to an individual creator. In fact, the law deems certain acts of creation done by an employee whose job duties include such acts of creation to automatically become the property of the employer, even if there were no explicit employee agreement.

The copyright law does have some deference to the creator as opposed to assignees. However, in the absence of a specific agreement signed by the creator, the person who pays for a creator who is not an employee to make a creation gets to own a copy of the creation, but does *not* have any of the copyrights to that creation. If you buy a photographic portrait of yourself from a professional photographer, for instance, you own that copy, but ordinarily you do *not* get the negative and you have *no* right to make copies for your friends and family — you have to get permission from the photographer or, more likely, buy your copies from him or her.

D. The Results of History

The net result of this history is that patents and copyrights both have a flavor of top-down permission to individuals that is entirely different from the "bottom-up, trade competition" flavor of trademarks, trade secrets, and other similar IPs. These differences show up, in our view, in the way courts interpret statutes and decide cases. The differences are perhaps most dramatic in comparing technology protected by a patent vs. technology protected by a trade secret. However, we think they also underlie other differences, such as those between how the courts treat the concept of copyright "expression" vs. how the courts treat the concept of trademark "secondary meaning."

III. TYPES OF INTELLECTUAL PROPERTY

A. Patents

Congress has the power to enact laws relating to patents by a grant in the Constitution, Article I, Section 8. The current patent laws are codified in Title 35 of the U.S. Code.

A patent is a grant by the federal government giving the inventor or inventors of an "invention" the right to control the use, manufacture, and sale of the invention for a specified period of time. After the time period has expired, anyone is free to use, make, or sell the invention.

There are three types of patents: utility, design, and plant patents. A utility patent is by far the most common type of patent granted and is the type of patent most people are somewhat familiar with.

A utility patent can be obtained to cover machines, articles of manufacture, compositions of matter, and methods or processes of accomplishing something useful. The invention also must be novel (no one has previously invented it), useful (it has some utility), and nonobvious (it is not a simple, obvious change or modification to an existing invention). The term of a utility patent is typically 20 years from the date of filing of the application with the U.S. Patent and Trademark Office (USPTO).

In order to obtain a patent, the inventor must draft an application that discloses a wide variety of information concerning the invention. Typically, a patent attorney is used as the applications have strict requirements. In addition, the claims that are put into the application ultimately determine the scope of the patent granted and a patent attorney is usually needed to draft the claims for maximum coverage. The completed application is then filed with the USPTO. The invention now has "patent pending" status. Now the pending application must be "prosecuted" before the USPTO. This is usually done through the exchange of letters, amendments, etc., although sometimes it is done in person with the examiner assigned to your application. This process will typically take anywhere from 15 to 36 months, with an average time of 18 to 24 months to obtain a patent.

The holder of a patent is responsible for "policing" the patent. This means that the USPTO does not enforce your patent or even watch for infringers of your patent. You must be vigilant and if someone infringes your patent, you may have to sue them for patent infringement to stop the infringing activity and to receive any damages you might be entitled to receive.

B.   Trademarks, Service Marks, Trade Dress

Congress has the power to regulate interstate commerce by a grant in the Constitution, Article I, Section 8. Congress exercised this power by enacting the Lanham Act, which is the federal statute dealing with trademarks, codified at Title 15 of the U.S. Code.

A trademark is one or more words, designs, and/or colors used to identify the source or origin of goods or services. Even sounds, distinctive packaging, and building designs have become trademarks. The owner of a trademark has the exclusive right to use the trademark to identify his or her products or services. A trademark used to identify services rather than goods is often called a service mark. The term "trade dress" refers to the overall impression created in the marketplace by goods or services due to their packaging or design in the case of goods or to the interior or exterior design of a place of business in the case of services. The packaging of my product may be entitled to trademark protection as trade dress even though packaging cannot actually be registered as a trademark.

One creates certain common law rights in a trademark simply by starting to use the mark for a commercial purpose. These rights typically give you the right to the exclusive use of your mark for your particular class of goods or services within your existing marketplace, i.e., where you have already used the mark. Many people desire a broader scope of protection and decide to seek federal registration for their trademark. This involves filing, and prosecuting, a trademark application with the USPTO. If registration is granted, the registrant now has national rights to use the trademark, even in markets where the registrant has not done business. All of the existing trademark registrations are available in any one of a number of databases that are considered "notice" to the public that a particular trademark is owned by another and is not available for your use.

The owner of a trademark can keep his or her rights in the mark as long as he or she continues to use the mark. Currently, trademark registrations must be renewed every 10 years, at which time the owner must show evidence of current use of the mark in order to have it renewed.

As is the case for patents, the owner of a trademark is responsible for policing the use of the mark. If another party is using your trademark or a mark that you feel is confusingly similar to your mark, you may have to sue them for trademark infringement in order to stop their infringing activity.

C. Copyrights

Copyright protects works of original authorship from unauthorized copying, distribution, or display depending on the form of work involved. Copyright protection begins as soon as an idea is expressed in some tangible form, such as printing it on paper or recording it on film. It is said that copyright protects the expression of ideas, but not the ideas themselves. One will usually see either the word "copyright" or the symbol © (the letter "c" in a circle) on a work, which signifies that the author is claiming a copyright in the work. The use of the word or symbol is not mandatory but is strongly recommended. You do not have to register your work to receive copyright protection but there are additional damages that can be recovered in a lawsuit if the copyrighted work was registered. Works are registered by submitting copies to the U.S. Copyright Office with a small fee ($30 at the time of writing). There is some protection given to copyrighted works outside of the U.S. by virtue of a number of international treaties with foreign nations.

D. Trade Secrets

A trade secret is any valuable information that was created by the expenditure of money and time and that is kept confidential. The law of trade secrets exists solely at the state level in that each state has its own laws concerning the protection of trade secrets. There is no federal law regarding trade secrets. There is no filing or registration process available for trade secrets. Because the trade secret must be kept confidential, the protection given to the trade secret extends only to the misappropriation of the information by those to whom the information was disclosed in confidence, typically employees, consultants, contractors, etc. The formula for Coca-Cola is an example of a trade secret. The Coca-Cola Company goes to great lengths to keep the formula confidential and it only discloses it to those who need to know the formula in order to produce the product. If someone independently creates the formula for Coke, however, the law of trade secrets gives no protection to the Coca-Cola Company.

IV. FEDERALLY PURCHASED INTELLECTUAL PROPERTY

The government often obtains the use of IP by contracting with its creators. Often, through a research or development contract, it even pays for IP to be created. The general rules for government purchase of most types of IP are set forth in Part 27 of the Federal Acquisition Regulations, also known as 48 CFR 27. Of course, as with most federal issues, all sorts of exceptions and special cases exist, but here are the general ideas.

Part 27 addresses patents, copyrights, data, software, and "special works." Special works are usually audiovisual materials protected by copyright. Part 27 does not address trademarks. Data are more or less a catch-all term for trade secrets and other material not explicitly protected by a patent or a copyright.

A. Limited Rights

In general, the government wants to obtain what it calls "limited rights" to IP created at "private" (including nonfederal government) expense and what it calls "unlimited rights" to IP created at the expense of the federal government. The federal government generally allows the creator to retain a title in his or her own name, together with all the rights consistent with the grant the creator has made to the federal government. Sometimes, especially with projects that pay for IP to be created, the subject matter is so sensitive (nuclear weapons, etc.) that the federal government takes the title and all the rights. In addition to being created at nonfederal expense, the IP must be held by the private party in some protected fashion (trade secret, copyright, or patent).

Up until the first Clinton administration, the system was more likely to allow nonprofit organizations (mainly universities and scientific institutes) and small businesses to retain title. At that time, however, both the Republican Congress and the Democrat administration wanted more private use of government-sponsored IP and felt increased private ownership was more likely to produce such use. The government usually retains what it calls "march-in" rights, however, which would allow it to take the title and assign it to someone else if the original title holder was not using its ownership to make the IP available through manufacturing or licensing. Simply sitting on the title is not acceptable.

Limited rights basically give the federal government the right to use the property for government purposes. To use for government purposes, the government may be able to assign rights to one or more of its contractors (other than the titleholder) for the contractor to carry out some government purpose. Note, however, that if the IP obtained includes trade secrets, the government usually assumes the obligation to keep the IP secret from those not officially authorized to use it for permitted purposes.

B. Unlimited Rights

Unlimited rights basically give the federal government all the rights it would have if it were an owner, except that it cannot grant an exclusive license, since the owner also has unlimited rights. But the government could grant a nonexclusive license to one or more parties, or indeed to each and every citizen in the U.S. and elsewhere.

C. Restricted Rights

Computer software can be a special case. If the software is created at federal government expense, the government usually demands and receives unlimited rights. If the government funds a major development, but one based on previous software created at non-federal government expense, the government usually demands and receives limited rights. If the government simply wants to use software that has been created entirely at nonfederal expense (e.g., off-the-shelf commercial software), it demands and receives restricted rights, which are more or less the same rights that a nongovernment user would obtain. The difference is that the government usually demands and gets unlimited rights to what is calls "form, fit, and function" data, which generally refer to any special instructions for the use of the restricted rights software.

So both buyers and users need to keep unlimited rights, limited rights, and restricted rights in mind when dealing with IP created by a nonfederal party.

V. FEDERALLY CREATED INTELLECTUAL PROPERTY

Many federal government employees are in a position to create property that might be eligible for IP protection. Government scientists and engineers develop new technologies, many government workers write software, and almost all government employees author writings. Some government employees even create audiovisual works. Traditionally, works created by someone paid by the federal government were considered to be placed in the public domain. The government might register a patent on some of the sensitive technologies in order to have a precise description of what it was then going to classify and prohibit for use, but if the technology or writing were not controlled in that fashion, at least every U.S. party was presumed to have unlimited rights to its use.

Here again, starting in the 1980s through the writing of this material in 2004, the law has been changed to allow government technologies, writings, and other IP-type property, especially computer software, to be registered with the federal government (patent or copyright) and licensed to one or more private parties. The basic idea is that some of this IP is more apt to be used if a private party can turn it into a product or service while knowing that either no one else (an exclusive license) or very few others (a nonexclusive license) can use the same technology to compete with the party willing to make the development investment. In addition, to keep necessary skills from leaving the federal government, the law has allowed, indeed required, that revenue from the IP that the government licenses be shared with the individual government employees involved in its creation.

This is a relatively new concept for the federal government and actual policies and procedures are still being worked out. So far, the easiest cases have involved IP protected by one or more patents, where the individual inventors have always had to be identified. Copyright, which allows registration by a corporate author without even listing individuals, has been somewhat less clear. Trade secrets, which conflict directly with concepts of open government, freedom of information, and the like, have been even harder. It is one thing for the government to agree to keep the secrets of its contractors; it is another thing for it to keep secret contacts and means of doing business, except in traditional areas of national security.

VI. VIOLATIONS BY FEDERAL EMPLOYEES

Part 27 discusses the potential misuse of IP by the federal government. The aggrieved party can bring a case in the U.S. Court of Claims, where it can obtain both injunctive relief (stop the misuse) and damages, measured more or less as if the misuse had been by a private party.

VII. STATE-PURCHASED IP

The system governing the purchase of IP by a state government or agency is particular to each state. Typically, a state will have some laws that mirror the far in terms of government acquisition of property of all types. The purchase itself is done by a contract that will be governed by that particular state's contract law.

VIII.   STATE-CREATED IP

The rights of a state government or agency to own or use IP created either by state employees or by contractors at state expense is entirely dependent on that particular state's law. Even in the absence of a specific agreement with the employees or contractors to assign rights in any IP that is created, the agency will typically have "shop rights" in the case of patents, which allow the agency to continue using the invention or technology in question without paying royalties.

In the case of trademarks, a government agency can be the applicant in a trademark registration, which results in the agency owning the registration when it issues. There is no need to have an individual obtain the trademark registration and then assign it to the agency.

IX.   VIOLATIONS BY STATE EMPLOYEES

When one or more employees of a state agency are misusing IP, the situation is more complicated. If the aggrieved party is willing to sue the state in a state court, the case will be governed by whatever exceptions to sovereign immunity that state has granted. If the state has had a contract with the party and is misinterpreting the contract, the state generally allows disputes over contracts it has entered into to be settled in the state court. If the state has not entered into a contract, but is allegedly violating the rights granted by a federal patent or copyright law, the situation is less clear, especially if there is only economic loss, rather than damage to a person or physical property.

In many cases, however, the aggrieved party is from out of state, and the dispute involves the federal law on patents or copyrights. However, the 11th Amendment to the U.S. Constitution generally forbids use of the federal courts for a citizen of one state to sue the government of another state. This principle has been extended to prohibit use of the federal courts to sue a state, even if the person bringing the suit is a citizen of the state involved. The 14th Amendment allows Congress to create exceptions to the operation of the 11th Amendment, but the federal courts have allowed only some of the exceptions Congress has tried to create. The courts usually require that Congress have passed a very explicit and limited statute for something truly "federal."

The cases on whether a patent or copyright issue meet this test are mixed. The latest cases are *Florida Prepaid Postsecondary Education Expense Board v. College Savings Bank* (98–531), 527 U.S. 627 (1999), for patents and trademarks, and *Chavez v. Arte Publico Press*, 139F.3d 504 (5th Cir. 1998), for copyrights. Both held that Congress had *not* acted with enough specificity to allow states to be sued for IP violations, even though 17 USC 511 says that states "shall not be immune" to suits for copyright violations and 35 USC 271 (h) says that "Any State, and any such instrumentality, officer, or employee, shall be subject to the provisions of this title in the same manner and to the same extent as any nongovernmental entity." Several bills have been introduced in the Congress to meet the specificity requirements imposed by the Supreme Court, or requiring states to waive the 11th Amendment immunity in order to hold their own IP, but none have been passed as yet.

Nonetheless, most states, and state agencies, do not appear to rely on this "immunity" to violate IP with impunity. It is usually bad politics, if not bad law, to violate the rights of private parties, and often contractual provisions make the state liable under state contract law, without reaching federal IP law. Moreover, the immunity of the state's agencies, officers, and employees does not extend to contractors, so a printing shop asked by the state to make unauthorized copies is fully liable, even though the state might be immune.

X. VIOLATIONS BY LOCAL GOVERNMENT EMPLOYEES

Local governments do not have the same amount of protection from the 11th Amendment, since the law treats them in three different ways, depending on the subject matter involved. Sometimes they are considered divisions of state government; sometimes they are considered independent governments; sometimes they are considered a form of collective enterprise much like a corporation. The last distinction is usually made between a local government doing something "municipal" vs. doing some "proprietary." For example, providing police protection or levying taxes are usually deemed to be municipal, while operation of city power or water facilities are usually considered proprietary. The fact that either could be provided by a private organization is not dispositive; the fact that it is provided by many or few local governments seems more important.

Thus an alleged violation of an IP provision (outside a contract with the aggrieved party) might be in support of either a proprietary function or a municipal function. If the violation is in support of a proprietary function, the case would look much like that against a private corporation. If the violation is in support of a municipal function, the situation is less clear. Perhaps the deference accorded to states would apply. However, note that violations of software copyright in support of running a school system have been dealt with in a court, even though elementary and secondary education is almost always considered a municipal function, and indeed is a state function under most state constitutions. Nonetheless, the local government is held to be a "nonstate" contractor when performing this "state" function.

XI. FAIR USE AND THE BOUNDS OF PROTECTION GENERALLY

In addition to the special conditions surrounding IP and public managers, the general rules still apply. Here are some of the more often cited of those general rules.

One often hears about the "fair use" of IP owned by others. Indeed, since trademarks, trade secrets, trade dress, and right of publicity all stem from unfair trade practice rules, the concept of fairness is inherent in these forms of property. The legislatures and courts have established rules about what is fair regarding use of the IP in question, and how close one can come to the IP itself without being deemed to be using it.

A. Trade Display Properties

For trade display properties (trademark, trade dress, and right of publicity), the general standard is "likelihood of confusion." This applies both to your use of the trade display property and your use of close substitutes. Your use must either be authorized by the owner or make it clear that you are referring to the goods, services, establishment, or persona of the owner, not you. For instance, you can use the trademark IBM when referring to IBM computers, even when comparing them to yours, as long as you make it clear that your computers did not come from IBM.

The same standard applies to your use of close substitutes. In a court case, the judge or jury will try to determine how likely your use is to confuse the relevant audience. If your use pertains to another good or service in another trademark class (e.g., Apple computers vs. Apple records) it will probably be deemed lawful, unless the mark is so "famous" that everyone presumes the original owner has simply broadened its offerings. This famous mark standard has been used to prevent McBeds for a hotel chain, for instance, since McDonald's was such a famous mark.

The same principle has allowed the owners of a long and widely used trademark to prevent the use of that mark as a domain name by others, even if the others registered the domain name first, and even if they are using it in different trademark classes. The individual who registered mtv.com, for instance, had to give it up to MTV, the TV channel. The adult site that registered candyland.com had to give it up to the toy company that has been manufacturing the game Candyland for decades. On the other hand, if apple.com were in dispute between Apple Computer Inc. and Apple Records Inc., the outcome is not clear as of this writing.

Since there is one dominant set of domain names for commercial enterprises (those that end with ".com"), although others are being authorized, the competition is intense for memorable names. We suspect, however, that technology will provide a major lessening of this problem. One proposal already adopted is to add alternatives to ".com," such as ".firm," ".info," etc. Another is to expand the power of the browser so that entering a company name will find the domain registered to that company, regardless of how memorable the domain name itself is. This feature already works in some browsers — entering "America West Airlines" in place of an address like "www.americawest.com" into the latest versions of most browsers will find the website, even if the domain name looks nothing like "americawest."

Since government agencies are usually assigned ".gov" as the last part of their domain names (or ".mil" for military agencies, or ".edu" for educational institutions, or ".org" for nonprofit organizations and groups), they are usually not in conflict with commercial counterparts, although they may be in conflict with each other. However, the likelihood of confusion issue may still apply — for example, if someone has registered "harvard.com," "yale.com," "princeton.com," etc. with a view to offering a prestige address that has nothing to do with the famous institutions at "harvard.edu," "yale.edu," and "princeton.edu." If the domain harvard.com is used for a business in Harvard, Idaho, it may be okay; if it is used to trade on the prestige of Harvard University, it is likely to be deemed unlawful on traditional "likelihood of confusion" or "unfair trade" grounds.

Rights of publicity, which are protected by various state statutes, are a bit more variable, and may be protected, in states like Indiana and California, with strong publicity laws, even if there is no likelihood of confusion. On the other hand, even these strong statutes provide exemptions for news reporting and other similar situations, so unless the public manager is trying to use a "name, voice, or likeness" to advertise something, the use may be an exception to the rule.

B.   Trade Secrets

Trade secret is an easier case in many ways. First of all, the protection generally applies only to the exact information kept secret. Very close substitutes are acceptable, so long as they do not stem from unlawful access to the secret itself, or from an unacceptable use of lawful access to the secret, such as by a licensee of the secret or a former employee of the company holding the secret.

Since trade secrets may be licensed, but are otherwise unknown to the world (or they lose their "secret" status), the use provisions of the license generally set forth what can be done with the secret by those who know it lawfully.

Once secret status is lost, the entire world is free to use the information, except for those, if any, who unlawfully caused the secret to be lost, or who learned the secret from someone who was transferring it to them unlawfully. The traditional case is that neither the former employee of a company with a trade secret, nor his or her new employer, can use the secret, even if the company did not know the information was secret when the former employee passed it on.

Consider independent discovery of the information covered by a trade secret. No matter how much Example Cola's formula is identical to Coca-Cola's secret formula, if Example did not have any access to the Coca secret, Example can have its own IP rights in its own formula. In fact, as a dramatic example of the reward for disclosing to the world, if Example obtains a patent on its formula, in return for describing it in detail in its patent application, and thus releasing it to the world after the patent term expires, Example may even be able to stop Coca from using the same formula that it had also invented, but kept secret. There are some exceptions for people who have invented a technology and are using it but did not patent it that would allow them to keep using it, but any expansion of their use is likely to require permission of the patent holder.

C. Patents

Patents are the opposite extreme of trade secrets, since they are displayed to the public in detail through the granted patent document. The detailed description of the invention and how to practice it appears on paper at the USPTO and in U.S. Depository Libraries around the country. Now, all the patents back to 1971 are available at various sites through the Internet (see "Internet Resources") in full-text searchable form, and the USPTO has image-only versions of patents much further back than that.

However, the only concept of "fair use" is that someone may "practice the patent" in order to study the invention it presents. This does not mean to "use the patent for research purposes." Many universities and other research institutes have found to their dismay that the fact they are using the patent to do research in biology, anthropology, or whatever does *not* eliminate the need to get the permission of the patent holder. Only the study of the patented invention itself is covered — all other uses require permission.

Also, since the intimate details are on public display, the courts have been reluctant to allow outsiders to use very close substitutes. Under the "doctrine of equivalents," outsiders who try to accomplish the same purpose using the same means, but with insignificant differences in various steps along the way, will be required to obtain permission from the patent holder.

Since patents vary widely in how broad the language is by the time they are granted, the zone within which an alternative will be deemed insufficiently different varies sharply by patent. In fact, in cases where the invention has high commercial value, the cases will be litigated to the tune of more than $1,000,000 spent by each side in fees to attorneys and expert witnesses and appeals all the way to the Supreme Court.

D. Copyrights

These items present the most complex cases of fair use and bounds. Here again, the warring traditions of restricting sedition vs. encouraging creative activity interplay. The copyright statute itself sets out limitations on the exclusive rights one obtains through copyright, which are called fair use, plus other specific limitations that allow copying and distribution for face-to-face classroom teaching, developing access for the handicapped, and other similar situations. With regard to more general fair use, the statute (17 USC 107) says that copying a work "for purposes such as criticism, comment, news reporting, teaching, scholarship, or research, is not an infringement." Each use, however, will be examined to see if it qualifies as fair use by applying four factors that include:

1. The purpose of the use such as commercial or nonprofit, educational, etc.
2. The nature of copyrighted work — educational, entertainment, particular medium
3. The amount or percentage of the work copied
4. The damage to the market value of the work, if any

Each of these is considered a limited exception to the requirement that all exercise of the five statutory rights ordinarily requires permission from the copyright holder. Such permission may be implicit or oral, but it must be given if the use is to be lawful.

There are some confusing factors. Perhaps the primary confusing factor is the nature of the rights held by the copyright owner. Somewhat similar to a trade secret, the rights really speak very little to the item itself. If another creator produces an identical work, but did *not* copy, that second creator can have full copyrights to his or her work. In the early days of applying copyright to computer programs, many companies experimented with a "clean room" procedure, where programmers who had never seen the source code, object code, or the program in action were asked to produce a program with similar functions. The argument was that if the code turned out to be identical, it was still a separate act of creation, not based on copying.

A second confusing factor is that access to the original work, plus substantial similarity in the second work, is considered prima facie evidence of copying. The problem for the second creator is not the substantial similarity per se, but the fact that a court will consider it almost certain evidence that the second person was a copier, not a creator. In the absence of a "clean room" procedure such as that described above, the second person will have a hard time proving an independent creation.

A third confusing factor is the doctrine of "scenes a faire." The term stems from the use of traditional situations and traditional roles in many stage plays, but has obvious applications to novels and even software programs. If one creative work uses standard elements (the poor but beautiful girl, the rich but evil man, etc.), it can contain a copyright in the way it used them, but not in the standard items themselves. On the other hand, if the element is itself unique — a character such as Bugs Bunny, or Mickey Mouse, or Kermit the Frog — any use of that element is very likely to be subject to a copyright claim. (A further complication arises when the character, such as Snow White, is drawn from earlier works that are out of copyright. Theoretically, the protection should only cover the elements added by the author of that use, but it is often hard to define what has and has not been added by each user of an older character.)

The doctrine that allows a copyright holder to claim a violation for the use of a single element is that copying "any significant portion" of a copyrighted work is unlawful, and significance is measured by importance, not size. Some cases have even held copying a few seconds of a sound recording is enough to constitute a violation.

These factors combine when a commercial publisher republishes something whose basic content has entered the public domain long before — the Bible and other such religious works as well as the classic novels come immediately to mind. The publisher can still hold copyright in "elements" of his publication and prevent "pure copying" of its additions — such as headings, footnotes, explanatory material, pictures, and the like. This debate is raging as we write concerning formal judicial opinions — as the law of the land, perhaps the most inherently public domain acts of creative authorship. The publishers have long claimed copyright in their pagination, their correction of typographical and grammatical errors, etc. The net result has been that the "official" version is that published by usually one or both of two commercial publishers. Lately, however, the federal courts have issued rulings narrowing the scope of what the publishers can claim as their material, leaving competing publishers free to copy the public domain portions of such legal material.

A fourth confusing factor is that the copyright holder's rights include the right to prepare, and to prevent others from preparing, derivative works of the original work. Derivative work does not have a precise meaning, but has been held to include translations into another language or in the case of computer programs either into another language or for another operating system. Derivative work also includes adaptation to another media, as when a novel or a stage play becomes a screenplay; and revised editions of the original work. Some of these look very different from the original work, but all are deemed to be "copied" from it.

A fifth confusing factor is that the owner of a copyrighted work has, by statute and common law, certain rights to it, despite the desires of the copyright holder. An owner of a computer program is allowed by law to make archival or backup copies, and to make the copy that goes from the hard disk into the random access memory (RAM) of the computer in order to run the program. Computer program owners are even allowed to create derivative works to the extent needed to modify the program to make it run on a single computer. Note that the publishers of computer software usually try to cast the transaction as a license for use, and thus impose more restrictions than the "sale" of a "copy" would allow. At the same time, many software users challenge these restrictions in court, arguing that most transactions are much more like a sale than a license. As one might guess, the law is unsettled at this point.

All owners of copyrighted works are allowed to transfer ownership of the work to others, so long as the transferor retains no copies. All owners of a copyrighted work are allowed to display the work privately, but not publicly. Of course, what is private and what is public is not clear. Showing a video in a bar is obviously public, but what about in your home for a few friends? What about 50 friends? The distinction also comes up in cases where someone has received a letter from a famous person. The recipient clearly owns his or her copy, and can transfer it to another. However, some such transfers are so likely to violate the display or performance right that they are not allowed. So, I may be allowed to sell my (mythical) copy of my letter from Frank Sinatra to another person, but selling it to a museum or newspaper is extremely likely to get it either copied or publicly displayed, and I do not have the right to grant that permission. Only the estate of Sinatra has that right. It may be that I could sell the copy if the estate would grant the display permission, but the estate probably has to be involved.

Another such confusing factor is the operation of joint ownership. If a copyrighted work has joint creators (two authors of a book or a software program, for instance), each has almost unlimited rights to the work, including the right to transfer such rights to others. In the absence of an explicit agreement between the joint authors, one may be liable to the other for an accounting (to share any profits generated by the sole use of one author), but the exercise itself (such as a transfer of rights to a third party) remains valid.

Another confusing factor is that the right of transfer belongs to those that "own" a copy, but not to those "licensing" a copy. Most software is "licensed" not "sold" according to the publishers, although the courts treat a license that involves a one-time fee for a perpetual license as equal to a sale for transfer purposes. Also, Congress has intervened to explicitly prohibit rental of some items (such as computer programs) where copying while renting is likely.

A last (in this list at least) confusing factor is that copyright lasts for a very long time. We agree with the analyses that find copyright is most valuable if it is neither too short nor too long. (We think somewhere in the 14 to 40 years is about right.) However, the current state of the law in the U.S. (and by treaty throughout most of the world) is the life of the author (or last living author for joint works) plus 70 years if created by individuals, and 95 years from first publication or 120 years from first creation, whichever is shorter, if created by an organization. To us, this length of time is likely to cause all sorts of inadvertent misuse, especially since the rule used to be 28 years, with a renewal for another 28 years only if the copyright holder filed for renewal with the U.S. Copyright Office. A lawsuit that claimed that such long terms violated the "for limited times" provision of the U.S. Constitution reached the Supreme Court, but the Court held that even life plus 70 was "limited" enough to pass the constitutional test.

E. Websites ("Home Pages and More")

Many government agencies use websites (a "home page" plus many more pages) to distribute information, allow clients to provide feedback, and for other purposes. Although the law is evolving rapidly in this area, certain principles have already emerged that the public manager should keep in mind.

First, although a website may look like a single copy to its creator, both the law and the technology treat it like a stack of brochures (or a stack of books, depending on the size of the website). Each "view" of a web page actually requires the viewing computer to obtain a copy of that page on the viewing computer, and then for the viewing computer's browsers to read that copy into the video display of the viewing computer. Thus, every viewer makes a copy.

Ordinarily, these copies are kept in what the browser programs call a "cache directory" and are automatically deleted after so many days or when the cache directory reaches a certain size. If the viewer wants to keep a copy indefinitely, he or she explicitly directs the browser to print or save the page being viewed. Some browsers can even print or save the entire website in one command.

Thus pictures or wording obtained from others is subject to general copyright laws — you cannot display it on your site, where it will be copied each time it is viewed, unless you have the permission of the copyright holder.

In the web context, this concern about providing a stack of brochures has extended to the hyperlinks on the website. One of the original goals of web technology was to make clicking on footnotes in scientific papers immediately display the referenced section of the referenced paper. This is fine in a scientific community that wants everybody to see everything, but has run into strong opposition now that many websites are for commercial purposes and often supported by commercial advertising.

So far (as of December 2003), it appears that two principles usually apply. One, your link to a page or item (such as a picture) on another site should *not* be done in a way that makes it appear to the viewer that the item came from you. So, a link to a picture such as that of Mickey Mouse or other copyrighted picture that shows up as his picture on your site has usually been ruled unlawful. Similarly, if you put a "frame" of your content around a "page" of material from others, that is likely to be deemed unlawful.

The harder question is when your site links to an individual page deep within the website of another. Lawyers and others still presume it is safe to put a link to another site's home page and tell viewers to follow certain links from there, but to put a link to someplace other than the home page is subject to litigation, since it bypasses the advertisements, disclaimers, etc. that the website owner wants viewers to see on their way to the page in question.

Some government agencies may face a jurisdictional question that is analogous to the commercial one, even when no commercial websites are involved. When one agency refers to the website of another, it may appear to the viewer that the first agency has exceeded its legal authority, unless the linking process makes it clear that the linked material came from another agency.

The bottom line is that although websites came be a dramatic improvement in the communication between a government agency and its clients, the design and use of the website is still subject to laws governing the agency, including the IP laws.

XII.   FURTHER READING

A.   Books

One of the books both authors have found particularly helpful as a general, almost layperson overview is *Intellectual Property: Patents, Trademarks, and Copyrights — In a Nutshell* by Arthur R. Miller and Michael H. Davis (West Publishing Co, St. Paul, MN, 1983). The 4th Reprint, published in 1988, is the version used by one author; the other used a version published sometime in the 1990s. The West Nutshell series is uneven, but when it is good, it is very good, and we both really liked this view of IP. It may be just a bit detailed for a general audience, but a public manager that deals with IP on a frequent basis will appreciate the broad, nontechnical coverage.

B.   Internet Resources

What follows are several useful Internet sites. Each of these sites maintains updated links to additional useful sites.

The U.S. Patent and Trademark Office (http://www.uspto.gov)

This site is the best single source for patent and trademark information. The site offers searching of databases for both patents and trademarks as well as filing forms, fee information, statutes and rules, and contact information. Start here before going to other sites.

The U.S. Copyright Office http://www.copyright.gov

Again, like the USPTO site above, this site should be the starting point for copyright questions. There is a variety of general copyright information, filing forms, statutes, and links to additional sites.

XIII. SUMMARY CHART

The following chart summarizes many of the attributes of the four main types of IP we have been discussing.

Attribute	Patent	Copyright	Trademark	Trade Secret
Origin	U.S. Constitution	U.S. Constitution	Common law of unfair trade	Common law of unfair trade
Protects	Invention — process, machine, composition of matter, or article of manufacture	Expression in writing, music, arts	Mark on goods or services	Technical secrets (like Coke recipe) and business secrets (like customer list)
Key federal statute	35 USC 1001	17 USC 101	15 USC 1051	None
Federal treatment regulations	48 CFR 27	48 CFR 27	48 CFR 27	48 CFR 27
Federal registration	Required	Optional, but gives additional rights	Optional, but gives additional rights	None
State registration	None	None	Optional, but gives additional rights	None
Term	20 years from filing	Life of author plus 70 years if person; 95 from publication or 120 from creation if corporation	As long as in use	As long as kept secret
Power against independent creator	Can exclude other inventors	None unless other copied you	Depends on use — you have priority where you used first, but also varies by the 45 trademark classes, except greater power for "famous marks"	None unless the person stole your secret or got it from someone known to have stolen it
State statute	None	None	State trademark act	State trade secrets act (may be Uniform Trade Secrets Act)

continued

— continued

Attribute	Patent	Copyright	Trademark	Trade Secret
Useful websites	See text; the same site tends to discuss many forms of IP			
Historical origin	Royal permission	Royal permission	Fair trade	Fair trade
Protection standard	No equivalence	Fair use	No confusion	No stealing

14

CYBERSECURITY CONSIDERATIONS FOR INFORMATION SYSTEMS

Cynthia E. Irvine
Naval Postgraduate School

CONTENTS

I.	Introduction	204
II.	Computer misuse: threats and vulnerabilities	206
	A. Human error	206
	B. User abuse of authority	206
	C. Direct probing	206
	D. Probing with malicious software	207
	E. Direct penetration	207
	F. Subversion of security mechanism	207
III.	An alternative	208
IV.	Security policy	209
V.	Secure system construction	211
	A. Psychological acceptability	211
	B. Least privilege	211
	C. Fail-safe defaults	212
	D. Complete mediation	212
	E. Separation of privilege	212
	F. Economy of mechanism	212
	G. Least common mechanism	213
	H. Open design	213
VI.	Cost of security	215
	A. User training	215
	B. Decreased system performance	215
	C. Security administration	216
	D. Audit and intrusion detection administration	216
	E. Consultants	216
VII.	Conclusion	216
References		216

ABSTRACT

The significant efficiencies possible through the use of information technology (IT) in public systems are alluring; however, as the value of the information stored electronically increases, computer systems become targets for abuse and attack. To ensure continued public confidence in these systems, managers need to understand the impact of security shortcomings in their automated systems. A high-level taxonomy of threats to information systems is presented to provide a basis for security requirements. Fundamental concepts of computer security are reviewed. The costs and benefits of investment in cybersecurity will be introduced. The concept of organizational information policy, mechanisms for its enforcement, and the value of assurance and the notion of costs and benefits of investment in cybersecurity are presented.

I.   INTRODUCTION

Advances in information technology (IT) have resulted in a transformation of business processes. With automated support, it is possible to rapidly adapt production and distribution to changes in market demands, with resulting increases in enterprise productivity. Although organizations have embraced IT and have integrated it into their information management activities, they have done so with caution. For example, the Internet may be used to supplement public relations and marketing, and to provide an interface for customers or clients, but core business activities are isolated from and do not rely on the open Internet. Instead, organizations achieve widespread or global connectivity by combining corporate local area networks (LANs) with leased wide area systems or virtual private networking solutions. These network architectures are complicated and usually expensive. Organizational networks, although key to the growth and effectiveness of many businesses, have yet to fully utilize the Internet, and, for many enterprises, the promise of the Internet remains a chimera. This situation has arisen because a key enabling technology has not been adequately addressed. That technology is security.

Constructing systems with more than a superficial assurance that security will be correctly enforced is difficult. Historically, the desire for rapid advances in functionality and performance have resulted in little attention to security on the part of commodity IT product vendors. Many fundamental security concepts have been known for decades, yet the extra effort required to construct secure systems has precluded their development for environments where security did not "appear" to be critical. Unfortunately, we have arrived at a point where lack of security is overwhelming many organizations. Spam is becoming an increasing drag on worker productivity: employees are bombarded with distracting missives and must sort through dozens of irrelevant messages to find work-related e-mail. Rampant and rapidly propagating worms and viruses can cause unpredictable discontinuities in business processes at critical junctures. Popular operating systems, applications, and their respective updates are of low integrity: opportunities for the insertion of malicious code into the heart of one's systems abound.

Organizations are increasingly moving toward the use of computers as not only repositories for public records but as a distributed interface for update and maintenance. For example, in California, county recorders are actively pursing electronic recordation of real estate transactions (Bernhard, 1999). Clearly, this results in significant cost savings in terms of handling and paperwork, yet such systems, despite claims that the use of cryptography makes them "secure," create new opportunities for fraud and malice, the consequences of which, especially in the case of real estate transactions, are dire and difficult to undo. It is imperative that those responsible for the public trust understand the repercussions of these changes. Even though records might be maintained in a relatively secure repository, a questionable assumption at best considering the numerous flaws found in typical commercial systems, the many systems that might provide input to these records and the networks that connect them are patently insecure.

The vulnerabilities of current IT systems have become regular fare in the press. Hardly a day passes without several news items or articles about some security bug or exploit. So managers have been forced into a procrustean bed: they must use IT to be competitive but in doing so appear to be doomed to languish in an unending purgatory of system attack and repair. To meet due diligence requirements, corporate information officers in all sectors must take measures to protect their networks and to create better security architectures. With no assurance regarding the security qualities or even the provenance of software and systems, system owners have few components from which to construct sound security architectures. Consequently, we have entered a period of cybersecurity uncertainty.

Today, software and systems are created with disclaimers telling the public to use these technologies at their own risk. This state cannot exist indefinitely, and litigation is inevitable. Within cyberspace, disputes will arise regarding the ownership of information, protection of information from theft and trespass, and liability from system or software malfunction. Security measures will be subject to legal scrutiny. For computer systems to be operated within a litigious context, organizations will be required to articulate corporate information policies so that computer system implementations are consistent with organizational rules and directives. In addition, accountability mechanisms for automated systems will be required so that disputes can be resolved. Computer security involves the design, implementation, and operation of computers to permit only authorized disclosure or modification of information. Often included under the rubric of computer security is the subjective notion of availability, i.e., providing some guarantee that when computing resources are needed they will be present. Gligor (1983) argues that there is no mechanism or model that is able to provide necessary and sufficient solutions to this problem. Computer owners should keep this in mind when making legally binding promises regarding availability.

It is also important to carefully distinguish between software safety (Levenson, 1995) and computer security. Safety provides the assurance that a computer program does what its owners intend it to do. Security requires that systems exhibit no unintended functionality. In a sense, the problem of security is to demonstrate that the system does not do (or permit) anything that is not in the specification. It is a negative requirement. Of course, since we would like the security mechanisms to work correctly, computer security engineers use many of the concepts of safety and software engineering to design and construct secure systems (Denning, 1982; Gasser, 1988; Pfleeger, 1996; Summers, 1997).

Computer and network security can be divided into three synergistic areas: security within computers, security for communications between computers, and secure management of systems. These elements overlap and must be in place in order to achieve a secure operational system (National Computer Security Center, 1994). To assess the security of an IT system all elements must be reviewed. The weakest component of the overall security posture is likely to be the avenue for attack. This chapter will focus on technical aspects of security in computers and will touch upon emerging concerns and costs associated with computer security. First, we must understand the computer security problem.

II.   COMPUTER MISUSE: THREATS AND VULNERABILITIES

Misuse of computers can include theft of machine cycles, unauthorized use of peripherals, modification of critical data, or capture of sensitive or proprietary information. Computer misuse results from the existence of one or more system vulnerabilities that can be exploited by a threat, where a threat is an active entity that exploits a vulnerability to gain unauthorized access to system resources.

Brinkley and Schell (1995a) describe several forms of computer abuse. All result in the unauthorized modification or disclosure of information and are briefly presented here.

A.   Human Error

Mistakes in system usage are unavoidable but may open a window of opportunity, allowing an attacker to exploit an error-caused vulnerability. The attacker will have to wait until the vulnerability appears, so the probabilistic nature of vulnerabilities resulting from human error may render them less attractive than more deterministic approaches. A combination of user training, appropriate user interfaces, and security controls can help minimize user errors.

B.   User Abuse of Authority

Here an authorized user misuses permissions, "cooking" financial records or other information. Intricate schemes may be developed involving several accomplices. Security controls can restrict privileges and provide an automated audit of the activities of authorized users.

There is an even darker side to insider activities (Winkler, 1997; Denning, 1999). Sensitive or proprietary information is highly vulnerable to individuals who have been compromised by an adversary. Treason, whether to the state or to a business, can be deterred by background checks and various technical mechanisms and procedures; however, if the traitor has access to a particular piece of sensitive information and is willing to steal it at any cost — an information kamikaze — then, although subsequent capture may be guaranteed, complete protection against compromise cannot be provided: an insider can memorize the information and sell it on a street corner.

C.   Direct Probing

This form of abuse involves the manipulation of permitted functions presented at the system interface in unintended ways. Stories of careless or inadequate system administration abound. Systems installed with default or no passwords are unfortunately common. The assumption that the computer systems will be operated in a benign environment renders them vulnerable to probing attacks, sometimes from across distant networks (Stoll, 1989; Denning, 1990). Often, one or more hackers issue inappropriate commands to the target system in order to gain control over selected system assets. Both careless administration and the inability to impose fine-grained security controls, i.e., management of permissions on a per user basis rather than on broad groupings of users, create an environment that invites direct probing.

D. Probing with Malicious Software

As in the previous case, the computer is probed in ways that are permitted, but not intended. However, in this instance a well-intentioned user of the target system becomes an unknowing accomplice. This is accomplished using Trojan Horse software, i.e., software that provides some "normal" function that serves as a cover for its clandestine, malicious function. The unsuspecting user executes the "normal" function and, in the background, the clandestine function executes with the user's current permissions, all within the context of the user's authorized activities. Such software can consume machine resources, copy, or modify sensitive information. If auditing is turned on, the victim may be blamed for espionage or sabotage, yet the victim has no idea that the Trojan Horse was hidden within the "normal" software. Clearly, issues of accountability are muddied when Trojan Horses can execute behind the scenes.

There are many breeds of Trojan Horses: viruses, worms, and logic bombs. Denning (1990) and Hoffman (1990) provide many examples of malicious software that are Trojan Horses. The increased use of downloadable software and mobile code without commensurate mechanisms to assure its origin or integrity pose serious threats to typical user systems.

E. Direct Penetration

This form of misuse involves the exploitation of a flaw in the system's security mechanisms. Here administration of the system may be perfect, but an error in design or in implementation makes the system vulnerable to attack through exploitation of that flaw. Starting in the 1960s, tiger teams conducted successful penetrations by exploiting software and hardware flaws (Anderson, 1972). System programmers would patch the flaws, but these activities invariably resulted in the creation of new flaws that were subsequently attacked. The result was a game of "penetrate and patch," always won by the penetrators who only had to find one exploitable flaw, and lost by system owners who needed to find and repair all flaws. The Multics vulnerability analysis (Karger and Schell, 1974, Karger and Schell, 2002) and Landwehr et al.'s (1994) software flaw taxonomy provide background material illustrating the problem.

F. Subversion of Security Mechanism

This is the insertion by an adversary of a *trapdoor* within the system that will provide a toehold for subsequent system exploitation. In a now classic analysis, Myers (1980) describes the many ways that a system can be subverted throughout its life cycle. The ease with which a highly effective artifice, undetectable through system usage monitoring, can be inserted into a system has been demonstrated (Anderson, 2002; Lack 2003, Murray, 2003, Rogers, 2003).

Once an artifice is inserted, it can be virtually impossible for system security personnel (or even system designers) to locate. A common artifice is a trapdoor that permits an adversary undetected access to the computer system. Karger and Schell (1974) suggested a particularly insidious trapdoor, which was made famous by Thompson (1984). The trapdoor replicated itself, but could only be found by inspecting the executable code for the Unix operating system and its compiler. Other artifices may activate as a result of triggering events to cause system malfunction, information corruption, or exfiltration. Modern commercial operating systems consist of tens of millions of lines of code and provide ample hiding places for subversive code. In fact, many vendors willingly permit their system developers to put artifices into commercial products. Many operating systems and applications are already known to contain large unexpected code modules that have been nicknamed "Easter Eggs" (Wolf and Wolf, 2003).

III. AN ALTERNATIVE

The examples of computer misuse and the experience of the penetrators and tiger teams lead us to conclude that building a flawed system with the hope of later securing it will fail. Instead, a constructive approach to secure system design and development is recommended. A notion that has been subjected to scrutiny and continues to be found valid is that of a security mechanism that enforces a policy relating to the access of active system entities, which we can loosely think of as processes or programs in execution, to passive system resources (objects) based on authorizations. The reference monitor concept (Anderson, 1972) is an abstract notion that articulates the ideal characteristics of a reference validation mechanism:

- It is tamperproof.
- It is always invoked to check access requests.
- It is small enough to be subjected to analysis and tests, the completeness of which can be assured, thus providing confidence in its correct enforcement of policy.

The objective of the secure system designer is to use the reference monitor concept as an ideal to which actual system implementations strive. The degree of success in realizing the objectives of the reference monitor concept becomes a measure of confidence in a systems' ability to enforce organizational security policy.

There are several stages in the development of a secure system. First, the organization's security policy for people's access to information must be articulated and translated to a computing context. Second, a system must be constructed to enforce the security policy. To address the threats of direct penetration and subversion, system builders will need to provide some level of confidence that security mechanisms actually enforce the policy and that the system developers have limited the possibility of flaws and artifices. This construction process is analogous to those that students create in geometry. Their proofs are by a constructive demonstration rather than by induction. To demonstrate that a system is secure, it is necessary to demonstrate that all of the code in the system is supposed to be there and is needed to do the job, and that there is nothing extra. Extra code equates to unspecified functionality, which might include trapdoors or intentional flaws built into the system. Third, the system must be maintained and managed so that the possibility of accidents or subversion is minimized and personnel understand how to use the system properly. Finally, the system should be subjected to third-party review. For many, computer systems are black boxes. We cannot examine proprietary source code to ensure that the vendor has built the system as claimed. Fortunately, an evaluation process is in place that gives those acquiring systems a measure of its security functionality and assurance.

IV. SECURITY POLICY

Articulation of a security policy reflecting the way an organization actually treats its information is essential to computer security. Only when the policy has been clearly expressed can systems be designed and implemented to enforce it.

Understanding organizational policy is not easy. Sometimes it is unwritten, but often the documented policy lies at the bottom of a desk drawer, untouched since its formulation. Policies should be stable (policies that permit frequent changes in permissions to access to information will be described later), but they may gradually evolve. For example, when a start-up business is small, access to personnel and accounting records may be authorized for a single administrator. Two years later, when the business has hundreds of employees, different departments may manage personnel and accounting and access restrictions between departments are probably appropriate.

Sterne (1991) notes that organizations must state security policy objectives, an organizational security policy, and an automated security policy. These move from high-level statements to specific rules and restrictions pertaining to automated systems and are reviewed below.

A few of the more obvious questions to be answered when attempting to articulate security policy include: What information is to be protected? Who is to be allowed access to a particular item or set of information and what will the user be permitted to do to it? What rules or regulations will be invoked to decide who has access to specific information? Does the policy that has been described on paper actually reflect what the organization is really doing (or should be doing)? If an organization does not engage in secure information management in the physical world, then it is unlikely that a translation of these practices to cyberspace will result in any improvement. Sometimes management will state requirements for its computer systems that are not part of the organization's business practice. For example, suppose high-level policy states that no information is to be exchanged between the human resources and the public affairs departments. Also suppose that actual practice involves regular movement of information between the two departments. Then a new computer security policy prohibiting this flow of information across the network will be ignored and useless, or it will render daily operations cumbersome and infeasible. A review of security policy may offer an opportunity to effect improvements in the way business is conducted, but the computer should not be viewed as a panacea for ingrained, sloppy information management practice.

There are two fundamentally different types of security policies, nondiscretionary and discretionary, and the mechanisms for their enforcement differ.

Nondiscretionary security policies are global and persistent policies relating the access by individuals to information. Information is organized into broad equivalence classes, such as *secret* and *unclassified* or *proprietary* and *public*. The intent of mandatory policies is to describe the permitted information flows between these classes.

As an example, consider an organization that has partitioned its information into two integrity-related closed user groups: Trustworthy and Pond-Scum. The integrity attributes of information are maintained throughout the organization and do not vary by time of day, or by the day of the week. In the paper world, specific users are given authorization to view and modify information. Only those who are highly trusted are able to change Trustworthy documents. Since these trusted users exercise judgment, they can be relied upon not to enter information of Pond-Scum integrity into Trustworthy documents. Similarly, within a computer a trustworthy authorization level can be assigned to an active entity, permitting it access to certain trustworthy documents. Unfortunately, software does not possess judgment and could even contain a malicious Trojan Horse intent on corruption of Trustworthy documents. Thus, in a technical expression of the policy, Trustworthy processes are not permitted to read Pond-Scum (Biba, 1977). The Trustworthy processes can, of course, read information of even higher integrity and they can "improve" Pond-Scum by writing Trustworthy information into the Pond-Scum domain. In addition, Pond-Scum entities can always improve themselves by reading from Trustworthy objects and modifying Pond-Scum information accordingly. Our rules will also confine trustworthy processes to read and execute only trustworthy code. So if code certification and authentication methods were available, trustworthy code could be identified.

Similar policies can be constructed for confidentiality. The most familiar is the military classification system with *top secret, secret, confidential,* and *unclassified* labels. Equally useful labels can be applied in the commercial setting by changing the names to *proprietary, company sensitive,* and *public* (Lipner, 1982). For confidentiality, the read/write situation is turned upside-down (Bell and LaPadula, 1973). Entities having low-secrecy labels cannot read information with high-secrecy labels, but high-secrecy entities can read low-secrecy information. Trojan Horses are thwarted by barring active entities at high-secrecy levels from writing to objects at lower-secrecy levels; however, it is permissible for low-secrecy entities to write to high-secrecy objects. In all cases, both active and passive entities are assigned immutable labels that are compared when accesses are attempted.

A mandatory security policy can often be recognized by the degree of damage its violation would cause the organization and the punishments associated with policy violation. Policy violations that would result in the financial ruin of the organization and imprisonment or dismissal of personnel are likely to be mandatory. Less severe punishments are meted out for violations of the second general type of policies: discretionary policies.

Discretionary security policies are neither global nor persistent. Access to information can be granted or denied by an individual or a process acting on behalf of an individual. This ability to change access rights "on the fly" makes discretionary mechanisms very flexible, but vulnerable to attacks by Trojan Horses. Malicious software can act in a manner dramatically opposed to the user's intent.

A real example illustrates this point. Today websites provide active code modules, or applets, that are automatically downloaded to the user's web browser and executed by browser-enabled software packages. A group of hackers constructed a website that contained executable content. When victims accessed the site, not only did the executables provide them with the expected service, but, behind the scenes, a Trojan Horse with the potential to change permissions installed an artifice in each victim's financial package. When the financial system was activated, funds were transferred from the victims' bank accounts to that of the hackers. Although the victims may have had discretionary controls on their financial programs and files, the Trojan Horse was executing with the victim's authorizations. So, the Trojan Horse was able to manipulate the access controls and insert its artifice. This example also illustrates the powerful benefits of nondiscretionary controls. Had mandatory integrity controls been in place, the malicious software (Pond-Scum) could have been contained. With the victim's active entity for web browsing running with Pond-Scum integrity, the Trojan Horse would not have be able to write to Trustworthy.

An examination of organizational risk with respect to policy enforcement in an information system will permit management to understand how measures can be taken to improve the overall security posture. Jelen and Williams (1998) provide insights into understanding risk and assurance. Of course, mechanisms must be accompanied by management strategies to insure that external aspects of security complement those within the system.

Once the security policy has been articulated by management, a technical interpretation of policy must be formulated. Technical policies relate the access of active entities to passive containers of information such as files, directories, programs, pages, records, etc. When access to information is requested, there are only two fundamental access requests: read and write. There is no notion of maybe in a computer: a yes or no answer must be returned — access is either granted or denied. Equivocation can appear to be provided by elaborate software systems built using read and write controls, but fundamentally, the choices are zero or one, read or write, yes or no.

Careful analysis of security policy expressed in terms of a mathematical model can be beneficial. First, if the policy is inconsistent, the mathematical proof of the policy will fail. Thus the expense of building a flawed system can be avoided. Second, the mathematical expression of policy provides system developers with a starting point for mapping system design and implementation to policy. This mapping provides assurance that the organization's policy has been correctly implemented.

V. SECURE SYSTEM CONSTRUCTION

Once a formal or an informal model has been developed, system designers apply an arsenal of software engineering techniques to construct the hardware and software mechanisms that provide trustworthy security policy enforcement (Gasser, 1988; Brinkley and Schell, 1995b). In their seminal paper on system security, Saltzer and Schroeder (1975) identified design principles for the construction of secure systems. We will start with these.

A. Psychological Acceptability

The human interface provided by the system should be easy for users to understand and use. Complex interfaces that do not match the user's mental image of protection objectives are likely to be unsuccessful. Instead, protection should seem natural, simple, and efficient, otherwise users will bypass them or avoid the system altogether.

A simple example of a psychological acceptability problem is that of user passwords. A recommended password is eight characters long and consists of upper- and lower-case characters, numbers, and punctuation characters. If each user is required to memorize several such passwords, it is likely that the passwords will be manually recorded somewhere in the individual's workspace. Thus corporate systems are vulnerable to break-in by anyone with access to the office: repairmen, janitors, etc. A single sign-on mechanism for users would be preferable.

Another area where psychological acceptability plays a role is that of interfaces for discretionary access control management. Current interfaces are difficult to manage and understand. Easy-to-use interfaces are needed to encourage appropriate use of discretionary controls.

B. Least Privilege

No individual should be provided with greater access to information than needed to do his or her job. With access limited to the information domain of the job at hand, the potential for widespread damage is limited. Auditing of activities within a particular domain permits system owners to narrow the scope of potential misuse.

Least privilege is essential for circumscribing the effects of malicious software and Trojan Horses. In our website example, if the system allows users to enter a circumscribed Pond-Scum domain before downloading and executing Pond-Scum material, then the effects of the malicious software can be limited and trustworthy domains can be protected from corruption. When applied to confidentiality, least privilege can prevent malicious software from reaching into other domains to grab information for exfiltration to hostile entities.

Systems can be internally structured to enforce least privilege. Such mechanisms can be used, for example, to prevent applications from corrupting libraries and the operating system.

C. Fail-Safe Defaults

Two approaches to granting permission to information are possible taken. In the first case, everyone has access unless explicitly denied. The second, and more conservative, approach assumes that initially all access is denied and that permission is subsequently granted. Lunt (1989) provides a detailed discussion of these concepts as they apply to discretionary security policies.

The notion of fail-safe defaults applies not only to files and databases, but to entire systems. For example, the concept of trusted recovery implies that, should a system crash, then, when operation is restored, security controls are in place and unauthorized users do not suddenly have unexpected access to system resources.

D. Complete Mediation

Authorization must be checked for every access to every information object. This notion clearly parallels the reference monitor concept. In a networked system, it implies consideration of a systemwide view of authorization, delegation, and access control. From the enterprise perspective, this view permits a chain of accountability to be established. It also requires careful examination of users' authorizations during the course of a task. If authorizations may change, then access rights should be changed as well. For example, if a user is authorized to access trustworthy information and then wishes to change to the Pond-Scum domain, then before changing user authorizations, all write access to trustworthy information should be terminated.

E. Separation of Privilege

A protocol requiring satisfaction of two or more conditions before certain actions provides a more robust security mechanism. For example, a rocket launching system may require two or more persons to agree to its start-up. Banking systems may require authorization from both a teller and a supervisor before the execution of transactions over a certain amount.

F. Economy of Mechanism

This principle is associated with the confidence one may have that a protection mechanism correctly reflects policy in both its design and its implementation. If the security mechanism is large and spread throughout chunks of a huge system, the majority of which provides business functionality and has no relevance to protection, then it will be difficult, if not impossible, to locate all of the security-relevant components. This will make analysis of the security mechanism problematic. In addition, side effects from non-security-relevant components could render the protection mechanism ineffective. Traditionally, it has been argued that security mechanisms should be implemented in small, complete components at the lowest levels of system hardware and software. Any components upon which the security mechanism depends must have assurance of correctness and tamper resistance at least commensurate with that of the security mechanism itself. Today, the complex mechanisms of application- and sockets-based security share all of the vulnerabilities of the underlying system.

G. Least Common Mechanism

Physical and logical separation of mechanisms provide isolation of users and their domains from those of others. Variables and resources shared among users can become vehicles for information channels, including covert channels.

Covert channels (Lampson, 1973) involve the manipulation of system resources in a manner unintended by system designers to signal information from a sensitive domain to a less sensitive one. For example, a process running at proprietary could consume all available disk space so that when a public process attempts to write to disk it will receive an error message. By consuming and releasing disk space, the proprietary process can cause the public process to receive a sequence of success or error messages when it attempts to allocate disk space. This sequence of messages can be used as a signal composed of zeros and ones to smuggle information from proprietary to public. Thus highly sensitive information such as encryption keys could be leaked. Considerable effort to eliminate or limit the bandwidth of covert channels is part of the development process of high-assurance computer systems; however, there are open research issues in the area of covert channels, so they remain an area of concern for systems containing very sensitive information.

Least common mechanism can also be applied in the context of granting privileges. Mechanisms that permit users to assume privileged status in order to accomplish an ordinary function are, from a security perspective, inferior to those that restrict privileges. The Unix operating system (Ritchie and Thompson, 1974) contains the infamous *setuid* mechanism that permits user's privileges to be amplified to those of the system administrator for certain functions (Levin et al., 1989). Flaws in the design and implementation of such privileged modules allow users to break out of the program and have unrestricted access to system resources.

H. Open Design

If the security of a system depends on the secrecy of its design, this will be an invitation for espionage on the part of adversaries. By submitting the security mechanism to scrutiny by unbiased third parties, its effectiveness can be assessed and potential flaws identified in advance.

An example from history shows that a closed design is no guarantee of security. Before 1949 (Shannon, 1949), cryptographic systems were based on complex, but secret algorithms. During World War II, careful analysis by the Allies combined with a failure on the part of the Germans to recognize weaknesses in their secret cryptographic mechanisms resulted in a decisive advantage for the Allied forces (Kahn, 1996). Information theory (Shannon, 1948) provides a basis for analyzing cryptographic algorithms and, today, most are available for open review. Today, the secrecy of communications depends on a mathematical understanding of the strength of the algorithms used, protection of the cryptographic keys, and systems designed so that invocation of cryptographic mechanisms will not be bypassed or subverted.

Organizations obtaining security equipment and mechanisms need to validate vendors' claims. Independent evaluations by unbiased parties are needed. In the absence of independent evaluations, a vendor can claim that a security mechanism solves all problems, while, in fact, the mechanism may do little or might even diminish an organization's system security. In addition, a rating scale is needed so that vendors know when they have done enough to satisfy a specific set of standardized criteria. Using these, the functional mechanisms for security policy enforcement and the constructive security techniques applied during system design and development can be assessed. The latter provide confidence that the mechanisms meet security objectives and embody the philosophy of the reference monitor concept.

It would seem that open design is an anathema for the vendors of proprietary systems. Fortunately, there is an alternative to making all proprietary systems open source. A framework for the evaluation of proprietary systems has been developed that allows security assessments to be conducted at designated laboratories. The common criteria (National Institute of Standards and Technology, 1999) provide a framework for standards against which secure systems and subsystems can be constructed and evaluated.

Although not principles for secure system design, Saltzer and Schroeder described two notions that merit discussion.

The first is *work factor*. This is often applied in cryptography, where it might measure the number of machine cycles necessary to mount a brute force attack against a cryptosystem. The work factor may cause an adversary to seek a more subtle, but ultimately faster, cryptanalytic attack on the system through the science of cryptanalysis (Schneier, 1996). A secure system's ability to control users' access to information and maintain logs for accountability is not based on secret keys, but rather on sound engineering principles used to build a trustworthy mechanism enforcing security policy. A well-constructed system may force the adversary to choose alternative, less costly attacks such as social engineering.

The second is *compromise recording*. This is related to auditing, which records or detects when information has been compromised, but fails to prevent it. Bonyun (1981) discusses issues related to the creation of a coherent, traditional logging process where selected events are recorded for subsequent analysis. In the last section of his paper, he introduces the notion of active auditing, an idea that has evolved into the many intrusion detection systems currently available today. Porras (1992), Lunt (1993), and Amoroso (1998) provide useful surveys of intrusion detection techniques.

A mechanism for compromise recording will depend on a system that provides protection for its essential elements, e.g., the audit log and the logging mechanisms. An accountability mechanism that lacks integrity may be worse than none. Compromise recording mechanisms must have sufficient assurance to be admissible as evidence in litigation. As an example, suppose that we have an authenticator mechanism (digital signatures and or cryptographic checksums) to set an alarm when information is modified without authorization. Recalculation of the signature or checksum is required to detect the change. Here we must have assurance of the correctness and penetration resistance of the mechanisms used to protect the checksum computations, the cryptographic keys, the rule-based system to flag any modifications, and the logs used to store flagged events.

Authentication is a fundamental requirement for secure systems. There must be mechanisms in place to permit users to be authenticated to systems so that a binding can be established between a user's identity and the processes established to act on behalf of that user. This notion extends from the desktop to those in client–server relationships that may be established during the user's session. To avoid spoofing by malicious software, users need a "trusted path" to their systems so that the systems can be authenticated to the user. Again, this notion extends to client–server relationships. The trusted path may also be invoked during security-critical activities for which clients and servers need to reauthenticate themselves. Reauthentication across network connections remains an area for research and development.

Creation of network connections should be based on some mutual understanding of the trustworthiness of the remote system. In a heterogeneous environment, some standard attributes that can be used to characterize end-system security properties are needed. Frameworks for trust relationships (Blaze et al., 1996) are still emerging and will require an infrastructure of registration and verification authorities for system identifications and trust attributes. The evolving public key infrastructure is likely to provide a context for these frameworks. Kaufman et al. (1995), Smith (1997), and Stallings (1998) give useful surveys of cryptographic techniques and protocols for networked and internetworked systems. Vehicles to insure that cryptographic keys are recoverable for both operational and legal purposes, while insure privacy for individuals and organizations, are needed.

VI. COST OF SECURITY

Management must be sensitive to the total cost of ownership associated with security mechanisms and procedures. Because many organizations do not want to reduce user confidence by openly discussing security problems, there are few case studies and the true cost of system insecurity and the cost of installing and maintaining security features are difficult to determine. Acquisition and installation is only a portion of the cost of a security measure. Other costs include the following:

A. User Training

If the mechanism is not transparent to users, they must be trained to use it, and management must make periodic checks to insure that users have integrated the mechanism into their routine activities. Part of training will include helping users take responsibility for the security of their systems and information.

B. Decreased System Performance

Many add-on security mechanisms, such as host-based intrusion detection, take machine cycles from productive activities. These must be considered and sufficient resources acquired to support both add-on security mechanisms and processing required for organizational business.

C. Security Administration

System administrators must be trained to configure and manage security mechanisms. Depending on the security mechanisms chosen, network connections must be scanned, password systems maintained, encryption keys and devices managed, firewall configurations maintained, virus scanners updated, flawed systems patched, etc. The administration of security controls can be quite time consuming and, if the computer system is a large network, additional personnel may be required. When the network is under attack, security administrators can be overwhelmed.

D. Audit and Intrusion Detection Administration

If audit logging or intrusion detection systems are deployed, these will require configuration and maintenance. Rules and triggers will have to be set as the security posture of the organization evolves. Audit logs must be reduced and analyzed. Special skills are required to support these often time-consuming activities.

E. Consultants

Where in-house expertise is insufficient, consultants may be needed to conduct risk assessments, devise network security architectures, and assist in handling security incidents or attacks. Both government-supported and private computer emergency response teams are available to help with incident handling.

VII. CONCLUSION

A million happy users may be oblivious to exploitable flaws in their systems. The absence of a discovered security bug does not mean that a system is secure. Despite our understanding of the principles of design and implementation of secure systems, commodity products provide mostly superficial security. Thus, system designers often resort to *ad hoc* solutions. These are intended to lower security risks by creating layers of protection. Unfortunately, if each of these layers is not truly trustworthy, then it is not too difficult for the layers to be penetrated and the systems overthrown. Managers need confidence that their security policies will be enforced, but they must play a role by carefully describing the policy and insuring that, once systems are in place, the organization embraces the day-to-day challenges of administering and maintaining their secure systems.

REFERENCES

Amoroso, E.G., *Intrusion Detection: An Introduction to Internet Surveillance, Correlation, Traps, Trace Back and Response*, Intrusion, Net Books, 1999.

Anderson, J.P., *Computer Security Technology Planning Study*, ESD-TR-73-51, Air Force Electronic Systems Division, Hanscom AFB, Bedford, MA, 1972 (Also available as Vol. I, DITCAD-758206; Vol. II, DITCAD-772806).

Anderson, E.A., A Demonstration of the Subversion Threat: Facing a Critical Responsibility in the Defense of Cyberspace, Masters thesis, Naval Postgraduate School, Monterey, CA, March, 2002.

Bell, D.E. and LaPadula, L., *Secure Computer Systems: Mathematical Foundations and Model*, M74-244, MITRE Corp., Bedford, MA, 1973.

Bernhard, T., *An Electrifying Image*, California County, California State Association of Counties, Sacramento, CA, January/February, 1999
  Also available at http://www.csac.counties.org/counties_close_up/issues_and_trends/electronic_ recordation.html
  Accessed on December 2003.

Biba, K.J., *Integrity Considerations for Secure Computer Systems*, ESD-TR-76-372, MITRE Corp., Bedford, MA, 1977.

Blaze, M., Feigenbaum, J., and Lacy, J., Decentralized Trust Management, Proceedings of the 1996 IEEE Symposium on Security and Privacy, Oakland, CA, May, 1996, pp. 164–173.

Bonyun, D., The Role of a Well Defined Auditing Process in the Enforcement of Privacy Policy and Data Security, Proceedings of the 1981 IEEE Symposium on Security and Privacy, Oakland, CA, Apr., 1981, pp. 19–25.

Brinkley, D.L. and Schell, R.R., What is there to worry about? An introduction to the computer security problem, in *Information Security: An Integrated Collection of Essays*, M. Abrams, S. Jajodia, and H. Podell, Eds., IEEE Computer Society Press, Los Alamitos, CA, 1995a, pp. 11–39.

Brinkley, D.L. and Schell, R.R., Concepts and terminology for computer security, in *Information Security: An Integrated Collection of Essays*, M. Abrams, S. Jajodia, and H. Podell, Eds., IEEE Computer Society Press, Los Alamitos, CA, 1995b, pp. 40–97.

Denning, D.E., *Cryptography and Data Security*, Addison-Wesley, Reading, MA, 1982.

Denning, P.J., Ed., *Computers under Attack: Intruders, Works and Viruses*, ACM Press, New York, 1990.

Denning, D.E., *Information Warfare and Security*, Addison-Wesley, Reading, MA; 1999, pp. 131–161.

Gasser, M., *Building a Secure Computer System*, Van Nostrand Reinhold, New York, 1988.

Gligor, V., A Note on the Denial of Service Problem, Proceedings of the IEEE Symposium on Security and Privacy, Oakland, CA, May, 1983, pp 139–149.

Hoffman, L., Ed., *Rogue Programs: Viruses, Worms and Trojan Horses*, Van Nostrand Reinhold, New York, 1990.

Jelen, G.F. and Williams, J.R., A Practical Approach to Measuring Assurance, Proceedings of the Fourteenth Computer Security Applications Conference, Phoenix, AZ, Dec., 1998, pp. 333–343.

Kahn, D. *The Codebreakers: The Comprehensive History of Secret Communications from Ancient Times to the Internet*, 2nd ed., Scribner, NY, 1996.

Karger, P.A. and Schell, R.R., *Multics Security Evaluation: Vulnerability Analysis, ESD-TR-74-193*, Vol. II, Information Systems Technology Application Office, Deputy for Command and Management Systems, Electronic Systems Division (AFSC), Hanscom AFB, MA, 1974.

Karger, P.A. and Schell, R.R., Thirty Years Later: The Lessons from the Multics Security Evaluation, Proceedings of the Annual Computer Security Applications Conference, Las Vegas, NV, Dec., 2002, pp. 119–126.

Kaufman, C., Perlman, R., and Speciner, M., *Network Security, Private Communication in a Public World*, Prentice-Hall, Englewood Cliffs, NJ, 1995.

Lack, L., Using the Bootstrap Concept to Build an Adaptable and Compact Subversion Artifice, Masters thesis, Naval Postgraduate School, Monterey, CA, 2003.

Lampson, B.A., Note on the confinement problem, *Comm. ACM*, 16, 613–615, 1973.

Landwehr, C.E., Bull, A.R., McDermott, J.P., and Choi, W.S., A taxonomy of computer program security flaws, *ACM Comput. Surv.*, 26, 211–254, 1994.

Levenson, N., *Safeware*, Addison-Wesley, Reading, MA, 1995.

Levin, T., Padilla, S., and Irvine, C., A Formal Model for UNIX SETUID, Proceedings of the 1989 IEEE Symposium on Security and Privacy, Oakland, CA, May, 1989, pp. 73–83.

Lipner, S., Non-discretionary Controls for Commercial Applications, Proceedings of the 1982 IEEE Symposium on Security and Privacy, Oakland, CA, Apr., 1982, pp. 2–10.

Lunt, T.F., Access Control Policies: Some Unanswered Questions, *Comput. Security*, 8, 43–54, 1989.

Lunt, T.F., A survey of intrusion detection techniques, *Computers and Security*, 12, 405–418, 1993.

Murray, J., An Exfiltration Subversion Demonstration, Masters thesis, Naval Postgraduate School, Monterey, CA, 2003.

Myers, P., Subversion: The Neglected Aspect of Computer Security, Masters thesis, Naval Postgraduate School, Monterey, CA, 1980.

National Computer Security Center, Introduction to Certification and Accreditation, NCSC-TG-029, National Computer Security Center, 9800 Savage Road, Fort George G. Meade, MD, 1994.

National Institute of Standards and Technology, Common Criteria for Information Technology Security Evaluation, Version 2.1, CCIMB-99-031, August, 1999
http://csrc.nist.gov/cc/
Accessed on December 2003.

Neumann, P.G., *Computer Related Risks*, ACM Press, New York, 1973.

Pfleeger, C.P., *Security in Computing*, 2nd ed., Prentice-Hall, Englewood Cliffs, NJ, 1996.

Porras, P.A., STAT a State Transition Analysis Tool for Intrusion Detection, Masters thesis, University of California, Santa Barbara, CA, 1992.

Ritchie, D.M. and Thompson, K., The Unix Time-Sharing System, *Comm. ACM*, 17, 365–376, 1974.

Rogers, D.A., Framework for Dynamic Subversion, Masters thesis, Naval Postgraduate School, Monterey, CA, 2003.

Saltzer, J.H. and Schroeder, M.D., The Protection of Information in Computer Systems, Proceedings of the IEEE 63, 1278–1308, 1975.

Schneier, B., *Applied Cryptography*, 2nd ed., John Wiley & Sons, New York, 1996.

Shannon, C.E., Mathematical theory of communication, *Bell Syst. Tech. J.*, 27, 379–423, 623–656, 1948.

Shannon, C.E., Communication theory of secrecy systems, *Bell Syst. Tech. J.*, 28, 656–715, 1949.

Smith, R.E., *Internet Cryptography*, Addison-Wesley, Reading, MA, 1997.

Stallings, W., *Cryptography and Network Security Principals and Practice*, 2nd ed., Prentice-Hall, Englewood Cliffs, NJ, 1998.

Sterne, D., On the Buzzword Security Policy, Proceedings of the IEEE Symposium on Research in Security and Privacy, Oakland, CA, May, 1991, pp. 219–230.

Stoll, C., *The Cuckoo's Egg*, Doubleday, New York, 1989.

Summers, R., *Secure Computing*, McGraw-Hill, New York, 1997.

Thompson, K., Reflections on trusting trust, *Comm. ACM*, 27, 761–763, 1984.

Winkler, I., *Corporate Espionage*, Prima, Rocklin, CA, 1997.

Wolf, D. and Wolf, A., The Easter Egg Archive, 2003
http://www.eeggs.com/
Accessed on December 2003.

15

INFORMATION AND TERRORISM AGE MILITARIES

Chris C. Demchak
University of Arizona

CONTENTS

I.   War, surprise, and militaries... 219
II. Twenty years of transition to the information and terrorism age 221
III. Global diffusion of the U.S. model of IT-enabled military................................ 226
IV. The gold standard military aims higher 229
V.   IT and the U.S. army's future plans 230
VI. A new kind of military in the webbed world 231

The common theme in firepower case studies [of limited wars — First Indochina War, Second Indochina War, Afghanistan Intervention, Falklands War, Gulf War [1991]. . . . is the recurring inability of the side with the firepower advantage to find the enemy with sufficient timeliness/speed and accuracy to exploit that advantage fully and efficiently (Scales, 1995: 292).

I. WAR, SURPRISE, AND MILITARIES

Organizations fight wars. Militaries are public organizations with a peculiarly onerous brief. If they fail at war, the community is destroyed or overrun. Modern states have grown up around this urge to obtain capital to pay for the tools deemed necessary to avoid losing a war.[1] This burden underlies all the choices militaries make, even in the pursuit, selection, and use of information technologies (ITs). This apocalyptic social construction of their mission is so ingrained that even when the national military is little

---

[1] For an excellent discussion of the interwoven history of war and the development of the modern state, see Tilly (1992). For larger review of urbanization and warfare, and its consequences today, which influence military choices directly, see O'Connell (1995).

more than an abusive political party, it is given legitimacy and associated resources no other organization could command.[2]

Organizations can, nonetheless, lose wars. Historically, wars are lost for three main reasons: overwhelming resource imbalances, lack of will (variously defined), and the endemic surprise of complex systems.[3] All the three main categories involve timely knowledge shortfalls, and hence some military leaders are generally fixated on knowing more. The French military "general staff" from the late 1800s and later the Americans innovatively installed an intelligence officer and staff as coequal to the operations, logistics, and personnel officers who control the commander's staff. It was later hallowed in the Western version of a corporate staff as U.S. corporations copied the military in the 1920s.[4] The information needed is holistic, answering questions ranging from what it will really take to win and how to get that amount (resources), to what losing will really do to the community (will), and to what unknowns are critical to the circumstances (surprise). Not having acquired enough knowledge at a critical juncture consistently tips the balance toward defeat in key conflicts noted by history.[5] Thus, military organizations routinely prepare for the worst case, reasoning that being able to survive those circumstances greatly decreases the overall chance of any shortfall being able to cripple the forces and produce a defeat.

ITs play an ever-widening role in the modern military's compulsive desire to never face a knowledge shortfall in any of these three critical categories. From creative budgeting, to "embedded journalists," to spy satellites, if an information system offers a reliable way to provide potentially devastating information in advance of need, then military leaders are interested, even if their budget cannot currently afford it.[6] Similarly, what a military does not know about itself has also proven devastating at times. The internal surprise is more often than not a failure in logistics. Historically, beans, bullets, tents, and fuel are not sexy issues for fighting leaders who have often enough been too optimistic about the preparedness of their forces for surprise.[7] Modern militaries, therefore, fixate on "knowing" in order to reduce the uncertainties of their operations and the likelihood of losing.

Of the three main reasons to lose (resources, will, and surprise), the role of the unexpected is one of the most enduring themes of military history, embedded stories,

---

[2] The history of African and Latin American militaries is replete with this situation. See Arlinghaus (1984) and Reno and Klock (1999) for a review of African militaries. For a different view sustaining this assertion that this fear of failure can command legitimacy out of proportion to the threat, see also Hansen.

[3] Though an oversimplification, it is possible to group the military history of wars into these three categories with few outliers. See O'Connell (1989) and Keegan (1993).

[4] See Chandler (1961) and Weigley (1984).

[5] The military history literature making this point is vast. For the reasons noted, military history tends to highlight the surprising defeats. For a highly readable review, see Seymour (1988).

[6] Shortly after the fall of the Berlin Wall, the Chief of the General Staff of Hungary said in a small group interview that he was entertaining offers for a brand-new Western aircraft identification system. He noted that he did not have enough money to pay his third-quarter heating bills in the army barracks but, as a sovereign nation, Hungary needed to have this technology nonetheless. See Interviews, personal (1990–1).

[7] This work would be remiss if it did not note the seminal contributions of Sun (1963), Jomini (1971), and Clausewitz (1976) here. The essence of these authors' popularity in modern military studies is their acknowledgement of, and solutions for, the problem of complexity and the consequent surprises in battle.

and professional study. In this category are such things as unforeseen emergence of a great leader, the covert theft of otherwise unbeatable battle plans, the novel use of new or adapted technologies, and the unnoticed aspects of complicated environments like hidden ravines, buried water wells, or cloaked straits, and even winter weather in summer.

The implications of this underlying fear of being surprised cannot be overstated. It influences everything from chasing bigger weapons to sizes of divisions to choices in R&D. It is in this context that ITs have been increasingly interwoven into the general concept of what constitutes a modern military across the global military community. In the Westernized world, tenets and roles of the national militaries have changed to embrace the knowledge expectations of these technologies. In the developing world, the goals of many militaries not much more than constabulary forces have veered toward modernizing electronically. IT offers a prospect long sought by militaries, the ability to know in advance such that one can possibly never be surprised. It is an extraordinary and overly optimistic expectation but it fuels the current pell-mell conceptual and real integration of IT and defense forces around the globe.

This chapter will review this evolution and its implications in three sections.[8] The first section will discuss the changes in the tenets of modern militaries in the last 20 years in parallel to the developments of ITs. The second section will briefly review how these tenets have diffused globally to influence the modernizing preferences of military organizations outside of the Westernized world. The third and final section will address the organization conceivably the most profoundly committed to integrating ITs in all aspects of its operations, the U.S. Army, and recommend an alternative model of a modern IT-based military organization for consideration and future research.

II.   TWENTY YEARS OF TRANSITION TO THE INFORMATION AND TERRORISM AGE

Now at the true dawn of the information-enabled age, militaries have progressed from seeking bigger, heavier, and more deadly to wanting faster, further, and smarter capabilities. At the end of a historically short day, the older modern technology triad of guns, bombs, and nukes has widened to include "information" as a destructive, or at least disruptive, weapon. As leaders of the global military community increasingly seek defense modernization, the traditional emphasis on lethality, reach, and resupply has widened to give more equal weight to historically less emphasized needs for accuracy, legitimacy, and speed/timeliness.

Moving from a dominating superpower competition to the fractiousness of multistate conflicts, the past 20 years for the global community have provided a watershed for the development and the global perception of the implications of new military technologies. In the middle of the period, one superpower imploded politically without nuclear or conventional war while an undeclared war in a periphery state (Iraq, 1991) provided at first blush an early exemplar of new warfare based on computerized knowledge. Several small wars later, the remaining superpower has irreversibly changed the expectations of warfare from long society-devastating slogs to short, violent engagements in which regimes but not whole societies are brutalized.

---

[8] The empirical bases on which these sections are drawn have been previously published in Demchak (2000, 2003a, 2003b).

This transformation emerged as a by-product of the almost evenly matched Cold War competition of superpowers. Force on force comparisons did not give either Western or Soviet military organizations the confidence that they had the overwhelming resources to force a defeat. Both sides also knew that, in such an engagement, the differences in ideology would ensure no lack of leader or societal wills in pursuing survival. Hence, the outcomes would hinge on the ability to surprise the other and survive one's own internal failings. This recognition reinforced the normal military tendency to seek advanced knowledge about the enemy's abilities and about likely outcomes.

The IT evolution began with U.S. Army efforts in World War II to find pivotal bomb targets to force Germany to capitulate. Later, the nuclear race required extensive computing power to determine the best targets for a U.S. counterattack should the Soviet Union attack first. Once the knowledge pursuit was channeled into electrons and vacuum tubes, the normal organizational logic to improve the tool stimulated funding to universities to make a better tool, leading eventually to integrated circuit boards and the Internet.[9] The initial goal was never to transform society, or even affect it, but rather to solve a military uncertainty, avoid surprise (or impose it), and make sure the fighting organization could not be defeated.[10]

One may categorize threats in the same way that natural disasters are assessed in risk analysis.[11] From the mid-1970s to the mid-1980s, war among the major powers — the Soviet Union, the U.S., and (in geostrategic terms) China — was a low-probability, high-consequence limited-source event for all parties. In response, technological choices tended to be relatively focused on the threats of specific nations or alliances. In technological developments, the U.S. took the lead in meeting the conventional and nuclear threats with renewed nuclear deterrence. Major scientific and engineering advances were justified in the U.S. in the name of meeting Cold War nuclear force on force, targeting requirements, and Star Wars defense plans during this period. The beneficiaries were the rising field of precision-guided munitions and rapid telemetry and communications, all needed if an overwhelming convention army was to be stopped in its tracks en route to Bonn or Seoul.[12]

In the process, however, the groundwork was laid for new paths in technologies that were induced from, and shared with, the wider commercial community. Historically, the

---

[9] For a review of the technological developments resulting in the integration of the printed circuit board into military tools, see Friedman and Friedman (1996).

[10] This organizational logic is often missed by critics of the U.S. military and its industrial connections. However strong the iron triangles of the Pentagon, Congress, and military manufacturers may seem from the outside, the military rationale is not to make profits or votes, but reduce uncertainty in war in order to never fail. This powerful incentive has no metric indicating good-enough security, hence, it is always pushing the services to try to get more and better assurances in equipment, processes, and resources. For a good review of this process, see McNaugher (1989).

[11] Risk analysis is a largely U.S.-dominated literature. The techniques were first developed as mathematical exercises in nuclear exchanges studied largely within the nuclear defense industry for many years. With the spread of systems analysis beyond defense in the 1960s, mathematical risk analysis became required in environmental impact statements and from thence, a major subfield was developed. A good discussion of this kind of analysis is found in the literature on large-scale technical systems as presented in Mayntz and Thomas (1988).

[12] The situation was worse on the Soviet side. In 1983 to 1984, the aging leadership became convinced of an imminent U.S. attack during the NATO annual exercise "Able Archer." Their mobilization actions puzzled and frightened U.S. analysts. See O'Connell (1995). For standard perspectives of the era, see Alford (1983), see also Deitchman (1983).

key characteristic of military innovations was their demonstrated ability to "decisively erode the war-making ability of the enemy."[13] By the beginning of the 1980s, lethality was still uppermost in a standard military hierarchy of needs but few were willing to rest everything on nuclear levels of lethality. Given the Soviet quantitative edge, which for budgetary reasons the Western nations were unwilling to match quantitatively in conventional standing forces, military leaders knew a smaller NATO force would have trouble stopping the momentum of a massive Warsaw Pact attack without equally credible lethality. Even the compensating mechanisms of long-range reach and resupply were increasingly seen to be insufficient to meet the 1970s to early 1980s Soviet buildup.[14]

Organizational logic began to operate in facing this conundrum. If the West was unwilling to match the Soviets in raw numbers, then it had to not only reach well into Pact forces to head off such an exchange but also to do it extremely accurately. Smaller forces cannot afford to be wrong in their targeting. That kind of accuracy actually required exceptional speed in second strike or, more practically, first use of nukes. Using nuclear weapons, however, was a major sticking point for NATO allies and increasingly unusuable.[15]

This period of Western unwillingness to expand the traditional lethality with quantity forced an openness to new ideas. Unable to rely on simply overwhelming blast capabilities, the U.S. in particular had already turned segments of its defense research communities to seeking nonnuclear alternatives to large conventional standing forces, laying the groundwork for the emergence of integrated IT-enabled systems.[16] The new ideas were originally intended to alert NATO to, and facilitate the destruction of, a massive conventional force led by the Soviet Union and operating on the North German plain, or, at worst, in the hills of Korea. The new technologies focused in budgetary terms on improving the accuracy of lethal power application, i.e., satellite improvements in targeting and communicating guidance to/from/about munitions and longer-range missiles. The beneficiaries of these intense research programs, however, went well beyond missiles to include a wide variety of blast technology delivery systems (i.e., tanks, ships, and aircraft).

By the end of the 1980s, the push to make everything faster and more accurate had developed a life of its own in the massive U.S. defense industry, with proposed applications well beyond merely blasting the Soviet forces harder.[17] Although the inventories of major militaries ended the decade much like they had begun — heavy units focused on blast technologies, the U.S.'s vigorous defense and planning community's search for accurate and timely as well as legitimate (few casualties) means of warfare had produced both conceptual and real products.[18] Possible developments in one area of the defense community slowly trickled around to other elements, though not consistently resourced or implemented. The visions of a modern military began to include seamless communi-

---

[13] See Friedman and Friedman (1996: 25).

[14] See the volume on NATO–Warsaw Pact mobilization disparities by Simon (1988) and an earlier similar analysis by Gordon (1984). The concept of "senility" in weapon systems was first presented by Kaldor (1981). A later more refined discussion is provided by Gray (1993). The term "senility" is authored by Friedman and Friedman (1996). For assessments of the U.S. nuclear weapon system in particular, see Bracken (1983). See also Sagan (1989).

[15] See Gray (1993: 85) and O'Connell (1995: 237).

[16] For a contemporaneous and enthusiastic presentation of this view, see Barnaby and Borg (1986).

[17] Gray (1993: 73) argues persuasively that this is a typical American approach to military technology. See also McNaugher (1989) for an equivalent argument about the U.S. weapon acquisition system.

[18] See Libicki (1997) and Alberts et al. (1999).

cations for reasons other than just directly hitting a target harder. Basic ground vehicles could be fitted with secure burst communications technologies and even individual soldiers could access satellite data. Aircraft heads-up displays could be holographic and ships' tracking skills could exceed the abilities of the humans in using the technology.[19]

Historically, militaries need a test case to be persuaded that the great new ideas will work. Only the U.S. had the full array of the new advances, though not fully integrated across its forces. The new systems were by and large individually low-payload, "smart" (accurate), flying (speed) standoff systems such as upgraded Tomahawk missiles. They required extensive organizational resources such as the ability to acquire, refine, and distribute satellite imagery via advanced communications systems to make them all perform effectively together. With no military peer competitor, the IT developments in the U.S. military should have gone into stasis in a well-known historical pattern in which legislatures refuse to fund systems not responding to a clear peer-level threat. So it is with remarkably good timing that the Gulf War of 1991 occurred just when military leaders needed to show increasingly skeptical legislatures of a continuing need for their services. This need was especially true among always cost-conscious NATO allies in Europe where the loss of a clear-cut low-probability, high-consequence threat in favor of many high-probability — individually low consequence — multiple-source threats encouraged withdrawal from expensive modernization plans.

Although a largely traditional exercise, with heavy bombing reducing the enemy to near paralysis, the military-dominated Gulf War of 1991 news coverage deliberately emphasized a new age of warfare both to reassure the U.S. public and to deceive and deter potential enemies. This new age would be led by the precision that only computers could provide. This precise knowledge would be evident in what one side could know about another, in how fast one side could simultaneously attack another, in how accurately one side could sidle into the crevices of another side's less advanced defenses, and in how few casualties the winning side could experience.[20]

Acceptance and possible assimilation of new technologies using speed and accuracy enhancements required just such a persuasive and public test of their capabilities to ensure continued funding for NATO, let alone for advanced technologies. Previous tests, such as U.S.'s use of the F117A Stealth Fighters in Operation Just Cause in Panama in 1989 or simple communications in Grenada several years earlier, had been turned into jokes internationally.[21] Neither example encouraged public support for the "modern" costly military. With Gulf War I, the opportunity to show what the technology could do was irresistible and was exploited.

This early conflict became a technology showcase as the first "information age war" equally because of the fear of friendly casualties and of the subsequent need for deception. As the Western world grew both more prosperous and more democratic,

---

[19] The literature on military technological advances is simply overwhelming and summary pieces are usually out of date by the time of publication. Nonetheless, Friedman and Friedman (1996) is an excellent first stop with an impressive bibliography to use for further research.

[20] For discussions of how the Gulf War's military lessons were distorted, see Watson (1993) and Rochlin and Demchak (1991) and Tsouras (1993). For later discussions, see Adams (1998) and Friedman and Friedman (1996).

[21] The stealth aircraft hit apartment complexes in Panama while soldiers landing in Grenada in Operation Urgent Fury (1983) had had to use public phones and personal calling cards to communicate effectively with senior leaders in the U.S. See Adkin (1989).

across democratizing states, it has become a "prerogative not to be killed capriciously.[22] Weapons of indiscriminate destruction — the classic blast technologies — had lost legitimacy. A type of warfare that seemed more sanitary, more like to hit only the guilty, not the innocent, was naturally going to be popular, if one had to have military deaths at all. This perception of war was growing throughout the Westernized nations, constraining the military organizations in even a nation as practiced in war as Israel.[23] A key consideration for the conduct of modern war was inaugurated — the requirement to be seen to be avoiding both friendly and innocent casualties alike. This ability depended even more than any previous military requirement on the accuracy, speed, and employment of knowledge, specifically by using computers.

Second, making tactical decisions with an eye to the evening's instantaneous coverage also became hallowed as part of the information operations of a modern military. For example, knowing that Iraqi intelligence would be getting most of their information from international TV and print media, Allied force planners in Gulf War I deliberately created the perception of a old school warplan led by a massive Marine amphibious assault near Kuwait City.[24] Similar steps were taken in the Bosnia, Kosovo, and recent Gulf War II conflicts, all integrated in the information operations part of overall tactical operations.[25]

Moreover, unfortunately for the Iraqis, some critical systems developed for possible global battles with Soviet forces proved quite adaptable to the desert. The performance of the satellite communications nets and the ever more accessible widening satellite-based global positioning system (GPS) were sufficient to keep strong military interest in improvements throughout the 1990s. As a result, although an objective assessment of the fielded forces would not have justified characterizing this 1991 conflict as the first new age war,[26] later promoters of information warfare — a very different kind of conflict — routinely used and still use the Gulf War I as an example of the first foray into this new battle technology.

The decade of the 1990s was, thus, novel for the continuing vigor of the dominant military's search for new technologies and expected certainties in relative peacetime. The exceptionally rapid development of civilian IT intended for business, not military, competition, enhanced this symbolic acceptance of military technologies as the answer to the age-old hunt for knowledge to avoid surprise. By the onset of Gulf War II, the key symbol of a "modern" military had become its relative ability to use ITs to ensure effectiveness,

---

[22] See O'Connell, (1995: 233).

[23] See Adams (1998: 296) for a good discussion of the dominance of the idea that information warfare can produce a "sanitary war" where no friendlies and few innocent enemies die. See also Howard et al. (1994). For a discussion of this process in Israel, see Cohen (1995).

[24] As an axiom, it has little in recent times to justify it. In the 1920s, the House of Saud attacked through a trackless desert to take Mecca and in 1967 Israelis attacked through the Negev desert. See Adams (1998: 48–49).

[25] Militaries have always written the stories of their battles but generally the battles were over and the victor wrote the final recount. It is the instantaneous transfer of interpretations of events by the world's journalists with incomplete knowledge — and the use of those data by opponents to stiffen resistance — that has forced the public affairs aspects of IT inside military planning. See Lambeth (2000: 173–232) and Cohen (2001).

[26] This point has become unquestioned by most security studies scholars. While elements of advanced technologies were present, as were some impressive video releases for the press, the bulk of the war was conducted by conventional 1970s to 1980s forces. See Adams (1998) and Pagonis (op cit.) among many others who have made this point.

cost savings, and international legitimacy in targeting away from "innocents."[27] In the process, traditional military needs of lethality, reach, and resupply have had to share billing, even concede status, with needs for accuracy, speed, and legitimacy.

The implications for the operations of military organizations are unprecedented. Critical to this image of future operations are the rapidity and the near-instantaneous character of deployment actions, and the lack of need for force structure called "mass" given the potential for pinpoint accuracy of information systems throughout the organization. By the end of the 1990s, these newer notions of the power of speed and integration have become so powerfully embedded that, before Gulf War II in 2003, senior army officers agreed to field troop levels roughly half of their initial estimates of 500,000 needed to defeat of Iraqi forces.[28] These notions have become similar to what Fountain has called "deep institutions" — those deeply embedded expectations about reality that strongly alter what institutional actors will attempt to accomplish with, or around, emerging information tools.[29] ITs have become profoundly synonymous with military organizations in this emerging information and terrorism age.

III. GLOBAL DIFFUSION OF THE U.S. MODEL OF IT-ENABLED MILITARY

Beyond the Westernized nations and the Cold War era, the intertwining of ITs and modern military organizations has proceeded through the 1990s to involve the global military community both symbolically and operationally. As early as 1997, the GAO estimated that at least one half of the countries of the world were planning on electronically modernizing their military forces. My contemporaneous research looked at the period 1992 to 1997 for evidence that globally, defense leaders were declaring an intent to become more electronic in the national military, signing contracts for advanced computers for military platforms, and finally attempting to acquire networked battle

---

[27] The evidence is widespread in the statements of leaders and in the material they contract to buy. See almost any issue of Jane's Defense Weekly over the past 5 to 7 years. See Binnendijk (1998). For a more European view, see IISS (1998). For a more quantitative assessment of this global spread, see Maze and Demchak (2003a).

[28] It is instructive that Defense Secretary Rumsfeld, out of the government for 25 years, was the prime believer in the efficacy of much smaller forces equipped with modern technologies. According to many reports, he initially wanted less than 70,000 forces in total because of the value added by information technologies. See Shankar (2003). As it happened, that optimism was and was not supported. The war was "won" as the enemy units melted away in front of the onslaught. However, too few troops were deployed to perform the nonadvanced logistics tasks such as guarding the long lines of supply as the forward troops moved very rapidly through enemy territory. At the most senior defense levels, it was thought the enemy would be so cowed by demonstration of modern accuracy and might that counterattacks would not be attempted or be effective once the efficient advancing troops had passed on through. Furthermore, the current technological choices in the military are not well suited for what has developed — spontaneous and incited insurgency. The visions of a modern military have not fully absorbed the implications of no longer having the convenience of a Soviet era main enemy organization against whom to target large units.

[29] For a profoundly thought-provoking work combining theory and empirical work on the topic of integrating information technologies into public organizations, see Fountain (2002).

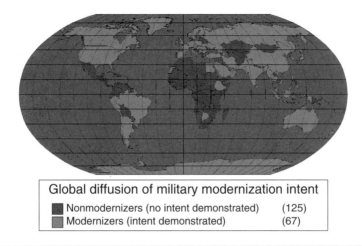

Global diffusion of military modernization intent

■ Nonmodernizers (no intent demonstrated)   (125)
▨ Modernizers (intent demonstrated)   (67)

Figure 15.1   Massive natural experiments — global modernization.

management systems. At that time, 30% of the world's countries met at least one of these criteria (Figure 15.1). A recent review suggests this number has risen sharply.[30]

The most plausible explanation is the catalyzing power of a demonstration case. Gulf War served not only to justify domestic military spending for the U.S. but it also proved a watershed conflict in symbolic terms across the world's military communities. The U.S.-defined vision of a modern accurate and fast military organization tied to electronic networks has become defining globally. Emerging loosely from a widespread U.S. defense community debate about a "Revolution in Military Affairs" (RMA),[31] the image of a 21st century military has been captured formally in U.S. government documents. It is a small, rapidly deployable, highly accurate, stealthy, highly lethal, extremely well skilled, and less costly force.

In 1996 and in 1997, the U.S. Joint Chiefs of Staff published two seminal documents capturing their consensual image of information warfare and what kind of organizational functions will be available with the move to this new kind of warfare: "Joint Vision 2010" and "Concept for Future Joint Operations."[32] Together these captured the imagery of the future structure, capabilities, operations, and potentials for success that the senior leaders want to guide the evolution of the current force into an information era military. Current documents such as a recent Quadrennial Defense Review (QDR) and updates to the various service mission statements such as "Joint Vision 2020" continue this imagery, adding network and other complexities as technical possibilities have widened commercially as well as militarily.[33]

---

[30] I do not have the fully updated figures and base this estimate on a shallow review of the leader statements from nations who were nonmodernizers in 1997. For the method and original numbers, see Demchak (2003a).

[31] The U.S. Department of Defense's Office of Net Assessments defines RMA as "a major change in the nature of warfare brought about by the innovative application of technologies which, combined with dramatic changes in military doctrine and operational concepts, fundamentally alters the character and conduct of operations". This quote is from Tilford (1995).

[32] See CFJO (1997) and JV2010 (1997). See also Kline (1999).

[33] See Adams (1998) and QDR (2001).

This diffusion of the U.S. RMA model has two major implications. First, the capabilities of possible future state-level enemies changes dramatically. Second, through legitimate avenues of global military defense acquisition, the modern tools of intelligent warfare pass into the hands of political leaders of otherwise not widely electronic nations and, in some, into the hands of intelligent terrorists. The highly electronic military is knowledge-focused but less redundant or robust if caught off guard. As a result, there is a logical tendency to accelerate operations, even preemptively, in order to not be caught with too little information.

If the globe's militaries are increasingly similarly equipped with opaque technologically complex capabilities, actors in neighboring countries will find it increasingly difficult to accurately gauge intentions or capabilities of states physically adjacent or reachable by long-range weapons and forces. It is much easier to count tanks and jets in order to know what one's neighbor is capable of doing. In addition, the movement of tanks and jets suggests intentions as well as capabilities. Since desired features of modern electronic equipment are their small size and very rapid operations, it will be more difficult for external observers to know if a modernized military is preparing for hostilities.

Furthermore, senior political and military leaders may not understand the consequences of decisions involving their forces.[34] In an increasingly anarchic international structure, the creation of an international community of militaries reputed to have great speed and lethality is not likely to enhance peaceful longer-term relations. For example, no matter how much Argentina's leaders feel Chile is currently not a threat, they will find it more difficult to ignore the possibility when the Chileans succeed in creating functional highly technologically enhanced, rapid-reaction air mobile brigades. These units will change from being perceived as sluggish and predictable to being promoted domestically and with pride as quickly transportable assault elements with small but highly lethal weapon systems. Chile's neighbors will find it necessary to focus once again on their local environment and respond not to Chile what does (actions/intentions), but more suspiciously to what Chile is capable of doing.

For another example, Middle Eastern militaries developed a penchant for the latest equipment of modern militaries during the heyday of oil revenues. That equipment, however, tended to be isolated, nonnetworked platforms such as fighter jets that required consistent technological support from the selling Westernized nation. These large pieces were obvious, unlike the small packages of highly networked, electronic assault or disrupt equipment being developed today for the uses of advanced military forces. While the latter tools require more organizational skill for them to be used as intended, they are able to be diverted more easily to other uses against populations or communities than the larger more impressive looking fighter jets.

The widespread integration of IT into military equipment has also worsened the problem of the spread of technologies that have both civilian and military uses into nations with loose controls over their organizations. Unfortunately, the world's major defense manufacturers are inadvertently fueling this proliferation in their cut-throat competition for new government markets. Their representatives widely promote the modern military image as the best and most secure alternative for any nation. Their

---

[34] History is replete with sad consequences when senior leaders do not fully understand their military organization's capabilities. See Bracken (1983); Strachan (1983); Art and Jervis (1986); Sagan (1989, 1993); Van Creveld (1989); Demchak (1991).

financial arrangements promote acquisition by nations whose security situation by no means requires such equipment.[35] Even nations whose history suggests they are more likely to use their military to quell national dissent than repel an invading foreigner succumb to the prestige need to be included among the modernizing militaries. For example, Thailand with its turbulent history of military coups has declared a plan to acquire deepwater submarines and tiny Botswana was among the declared modernizer nations early on.[36]

At the other end of the spectrum, IT systems are often critical to technologies that have both military and civilian uses (called "dual use"), and the spread of these capabilities encourages misunderstandings. For example, one large nation became concerned that another nation's seemingly innocent economic activity was being also used to produce chemical weapons. As a result, the U.S. launched cruise missiles against a suspicious facility, said to be producing for terrorists, in Sudan in 1998. The owners claimed it was merely a pharmaceutical factory. Reports claiming both interpretations of what that factory was producing have been widely published, without clear resolution.[37]

The flexibility of IT-enabled military capabilities, as they spread globally in operational capabilities, will also make organizations opposing the Westernized nations more difficult to disrupt when conflict erupts. Small, resilient, locally networked systems are often difficult to penetrate from a distance and their size makes them hard to identify from the outset. Long before hostilities are imminent, however, as the model spreads symbolically and professionally, more nations will seek to acquire the image of a military with these modern, difficult to defeat capabilities, even if the operational reality is quite different. As these global conditions develop, misperception and crises are more likely. Preemption is a highly likely outcome of misperception in global politics.

IV. THE GOLD STANDARD MILITARY AIMS HIGHER

Among the U.S. military services leading the development of the RMA military and its model, the U.S. Army is arguably already the most networked military in the world. At last count in mid-2003, the service had more than 925 logistics systems and 330 personnel systems.[38] In September 2003, the U.S. Army announced the start of a number of contracts to make the service one of the most integrated militaries of the world, combining seamlessly not only these logistics and personnel systems, but all such systems used by the service. The first tranche of these contracts in September 2003 alone totaled $500 million, with more contracts imminent.[39]

Since most military organizations of the world are first and foremost ground organizations, what the U.S. Army — with its size, budget, global presence, and recent successes – chooses to pursue has effectively percolated through the global defense community as the gold standard for success in modernizing. This section will focus on the current plans of the U.S. Army and some of its shortcomings currently and over the likely long run. The section will conclude with an alternative proposal about an organizational

---

[35] There is a large literature on technology transfer across militaries to the developing world. For a useful review of the origins of this exchange, see Brzoska and Ohlson (1991).

[36] See Demchak (2003a).

[37] See Zill (1999).

[38] See Hsu (2003).

[39] See Hsu (2003).

model for the U.S. and other armies called the Atrium. This model is built on the successes in IT integration and knowledge management in several Japanese corporations.

V.   IT AND THE U.S. ARMY'S FUTURE PLANS

In 2001 to 2002, the U.S. Army began its "Army Enterprise Infostructure Transformation" (AEIT) program involving hundreds of millions of dollars intended to reform disparate army information systems globally into a network-centric, knowledge-based environment. The program is unique among the U.S. services in planning to integrate legacy and newer systems across a flexible architecture rather than one single infrastructure. The overall plan is managed by dividing the capabilities desired in commodities-based functional areas (servers, software, etc.) and services to the users (site surveys, onsite systems integration, etc.).[40]

To increase the likelihood of success in integrating all these legacy systems, the transformation plan is in stages. The first stage — itself a massive endeavor — consolidates centrally the e-mail systems and network management.[41] This part of the transformation alone involves integrating 1.5 million users into a secure MS Active Directory installation. The application allows administrators to remotely manage and control access centrally to tens of thousands of servers and machines.[42] The army has gone so far as to reorient and rename its traditional Signal Command as Network Enterprise Technology Command (Netcom).[43] Consolidation of all the army's systems began in November 2002 and is slowly progressing as funding becomes available to move prototype systems beyond pilot programs into integration.[44]

These ambitious plans to flexibly integrate existing systems, however, are currently foundering. One difficulty is the compartmentalized data and the data needed to build confidence in a new application. Not only does the transformed military need to provide data to a wide array of users but it also needs to simultaneously curb the distribution of information that is classified. In Iraq, operators were unable to send logistics system data to unit leaders because the unclassified logistics data could not be mingled with classified data. Furthermore, U.S. forces in Iraq complained about having too little material in stock in the country although the material was in the pipeline back to the U.S.

One case in point is the army's logistics system recently designed to be a "pull" rather than a push system. In the former, the central distributor looks at what has been used by a unit in the last few months and resupplies according to that usage. This system was a replacement for the old push systems developed during World War II and the inability to communicate readily. A push system literally pushes resupplies as close as possible to units and stocks items that may or may not have been used in the last few months. But, as has happened in Iraq War II, the pull system is so lean that few units under a surge in battle or policing get all that they need. The new crisis is so different from previous patterns that the computer at the depot was not programmed to think ahead sufficiently.

---

[40] See Hsu (2003).
[41] See Caterinicchia (2002c).
[42] See Caterinicchia (2002a).
[43] As of October 1, 2002. See Caterinicchia (2002b).
[44] See Caterinicchia (2001a).

Furthermore, the integration plan itself seems to have no set format and unrealistic expectations about technologies and funding, at least from the perspective of the U.S. General Accounting Office. The most challenging areas identified by this report are telling: technology, staying on schedule, acquisitions, operations, human capital and funding.[45] It is going to be more difficult to actually implement this transformation than to spread it as a globally accepted future for all militaries. A large part of this difficulty is the impreciseness of the overarching vision of what will emerge as the military transforms with its information systems. The final section proposes an alternative.

VI. A NEW KIND OF MILITARY IN THE WEBBED WORLD

It is necessary to round the circle and speculate on what security forces might look like in the future. As the global community learns, the challenge with terrorists loose in the information age is to gain strategic depth by making attacks very hard and perceived to be rarely successful. The forces must be able to operate globally and to reinsert, restructure, or reinforce elements of personal risk, organizational expense, or bad publicity back into the calculus of would-be attackers in order to preemptively deter, disrupt, or destroy their operations.

How does one organize an IT-enabled military successfully for today's security challenges, especially when more and more hostile organizations will be digitized? From the outset, there are scale and tempo difficulties. First, the routine actor scale on the Internet is at a constabulary level while the potential consequences are at the military level. Military organizations fight other organizations in wars while small groups more typically are pursued by police forces.[46] This means a large adjustment in military unit knowledge acquisition abilities toward more comprehensive collection and then data mining rather than targeting collection closely and narrowly just before operations.

Second, strategic depth in Internet terms is best defined in time either before an attack to prepare against it, deter it, or configure a mitigation, or during the attack to tag the avenues of approach for pursuit, termination, mitigation, future defense, or retaliation. After the attack, attackers melt so quickly into the turbulence that only in highly unusual cases will the resources be available to carefully track individual perpetrators down. In one well-documented electronic case, the hacker took half an hour to crack into the university's computer and spent only an hour inside but it took over 36 hours to track the hack.[47] Hence, preemptive knowledge of methods, likely targets, source scripts, and likely settings for assaults becomes essential for reestablishing strategic depth.

Third, the balance of security and civil liberties will have to emerge dynamically in political and legal arenas. The dispute about the FBI's Carnivore program is only the first salvo in this process. It seems clear now that anonymity will be profoundly dead and

---

[45] See Caterinicchia (2001c, b) and GAO (2002).

[46] The potential for damage with sufficiently motivated hackers is impressive. Hackers called the "Phonemasters" hacked into the electric power grid and the U.S. air traffic control system, along with stealing credit card numbers. While they did nothing with that access then, there were fewer hacktivists around at the time who might have been interested in exploiting that avenue. Today this opportunity is less likely to be missed if available; the threat is clearly national in scope. See Manjoo (2001).

[47] Lemos (2001).

profiling by Internet behavior will be a key data-mining goal. This process, however, will require something short of a war but more than peace in operational tempo.

Rather than discuss brigades, squadrons, and carrier groups in these final paragraphs, I want to suggest what the physical reality of a military primarily self-perceived as "I-fighters" would look like. It would be knowledge-oriented with organizational structure, processes, and focus that reflect the medium's focus on information flows, use, and decisions. The organization needs to be socially constructed with an initial understanding of how to obtain, refine, and use knowledge while surrounded by interrelated complex systems, rogue surprises, knowledge burdens, and dependence on initial conditions. It would conduct 24 hours, 7 days a week ("24/7") collection and refinement operations in order to create the profiles necessary to ensure safety. It would act as needed in the form of task forces created for these kinds of missions.

One possible model of such a military is the "Atrium" model[48] adapted for militaries from the Nonaka and Takeuchi "hyperlinked" organization model.[49] The Atrium military has three main organizational elements. First, there is the main "core" of operations functionally divided as most militaries are today but with fewer subdivisions. Here are the finance, personnel, transportation, operations, logistics, and recruitment elements that keep main systems functioning. Then there is the Atrium — a massive and constantly growing coexisting and global computerized database that is graphically accessible much like a 3D website. The name is chosen because of the character of this database as a conceptual space with which one interacts much like a trusted colleague. Military members would formally interact with the Atrium in three ways: as consumers of knowledge from queries they inputted, as contributors providing explicit and implicit data to the underlying matrix, and as knowledge producers refining the information into knowledge that is then available through various recall and query techniques to the consumers. Finally, there are the task forces. Unlike the original Nonaka and Takeuchi model, the task forces are not corporate sources of innovation but the deployed action elements of the military (Figure 15.2).

The Atrium collects and uses implicit knowledge in its efforts to act proactively. Individuals rotate in this military through acting in a task force in an "eye-fighting" team, a peace-keeping capacity, or a deployed warfighting operation, then as a functional member of an operation in the core, and then, after each of the previous assignments, as a producer or contributor of data in the Atrium. During each core or task force assignment, the individual is also a consumer of Atrium's extensive data-mining products. In fact, in this military, all members from career soldiers, short-termers, conscripts (if any), and reservists interact daily with the Atrium. The goal is to globally collect explicit and implicit knowledge in order to innovate screening functions and then deterrent, disruptive, or punitive responses in the process of maintaining electronic as well as physical national security. As a side benefit, it is likely police forces will be linked to the Atrium to free ride on the knowledge wealth being created.

At the end of the day, something like this kind of knowledge-focused military will be necessary because of the 24/7 need for sophisticated and innovative screening of web activities to stay ahead of the evolution in assault avenues. The continuous mission to deter, divert, derail, deceive, disrupt, or destroy the national security threats coming over a relatively open Internet will also blur historical notions of peace and war. This is new

---

[48] Demchak (2001).

[49] Nonaka and Hirotaka Takeuchi (1997).

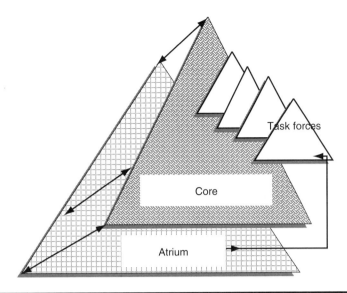

Figure 15.2   The Atrium model graphic.

legal and social territory indeed. On the other hand, as these operations are nonlethal in the main, this outcome is not clearly curtailed by international conventions, nor is it likely to be strongly resisted by populations interested in surfing safely on the Web. Certainly, if it provides security for business enterprises at a cost of a fraction of the currently growing security costs, the development of such a military is likely to be encouraged by these stakeholders.

If there is political and corporate consensus that the Internet is to remain freely available, this kind of military then becomes possible despite current military reservations. Indeed, other nations do acquire means of threatening Westernized nations electronically, then Western militaries would feel the pressure to balance in electronic capabilities to proactively predict attacks and protect military forces. In that case, an Atrium-like military could emerge, providing skills that could later be co-opted into saving or resurrecting a free and safer wider society.

REFERENCES

Adams, J., *The Next World War: Computers Are the Weapons and the Front Line Is Everywhere*, Simon & Schuster, New York, 1998.

Adkin, M., *Urgent Fury: The Battle for Grenada*, DC Heath and Company, Lexington, MA, 1989.

Alberts, D.S., John, J.G., and Stein, F.P., *Network Centric Warfare: Developing and Leveraging Information Superiority*, Department of Defense C4ISR Cooperative Research Program, DoDCCRP Publications, Washington, D.C., 1999.

Alford, J., Perspectives on strategy, in *Alliance Security: NATO and the No-First-Use Question*, Steinbruner, J.D., and Leon, V.S., Eds., The Brookings Institution, Washington, D.C., 1983.

Arlinghaus, B.E., *Military Development in Africa: The Political and Economic Risks of Arms Transfers*, Westview Press, Boulder, CO, 1984.

Art, R., Robert, J., *International Politics: Anarchy, Force, Political Economy and Decision-making*, Little, Brown and Company, Boston, 1985.

Barnaby, F. and Borg, M.T., Eds., *Emerging Technologies and Military Doctrine*, St. Martin's Press, New York, 1986.

Binnendijk, H., Ed., *Strategic Assessment: Engaging Power for Peace*, National Defense University Press, Washington, D.C., 1998.

Bracken, P., *The Command and Control of Nuclear Forces*, Yale University Press, New Haven, CT, 1983.

Brzoska, M. and Thomas, O., *Arms Transfers to the Third World, 1971–85*, Oxford University Press, New York, 1991.

Caterinicchia, D., Army HQ Changes Affect IT Buys, *Federal Computer Week*, Nov. 21, 2001a, Online.

Caterinicchia, D., Army HQ Changes Affect IT, *Federal Computer Week*, Dec. 19, 2001b, Online.

Caterinicchia, D., Army Transformation Faces Uphill Battle, *Federal Computer Week*, Nov. 30, 2001c, Online.

Caterinicchia, D., Army Closes in on Transformation, *Federal Computer Week*, Apr. 1, 2002a.

Caterinicchia, D., Army Poised for Mannheim Project, *Federal Computer Week*, Apr. 11, 2002b, Online.

Caterinicchia, D., Army Tech Plan Drafted, *Federal Computer Week*, Apr. 29, 2002c, Online.

CFJO, Concept for Future Joint Operations, Joint Chiefs of Staff, Department of Defense, United States Government, U.S. Government Printing Office, Washington, D.C., 1997.

Chandler, A., *Strategy and Structure*, MIT Press, Cambridge, MA, 1961.

Clausewitz, C. von., *On War*, Howard, Michael, and Paret, P., Eds. and trans., Princeton University Press, Princeton, NJ, 1976.

Cohen, S., The Israel defense forces from a people's army to a professional military — causes and implications, *Armed Forces and Society*, 21, 237–254, 1995.

Cohen, E.A., *War Over Kosovo: Politics and Strategy in a Global Age*, Columbia University Press, New York, 2001.

Deitchman, S., *Military Power and the Advance of Technology: General Purpose Military Forces for the 1980s*, Westview Press, Boulder, CO, 1983.

Demchak, C.C., *Military Organizations, Complex Machines: Modernization in the U.S. Armed Services*, Cornell University Press, Ithaca, NY, 1991.

Demchak, C.C., Watersheds in perception and knowledge: security and technology in the past twenty years, in *Critical Reflections on Security and Change*, Croft, S. and Terriff, T., Eds., Frank Cass, London, 2000.

Demchak, C.C., Knowledge burden management and a networked Israeli defense force: partial RMA in "Hyper Text Organization"?, *Journal of Strategic Studies*, Special Issue, Israel's National Security Conception on a Crossroad, volume 24, number 2, 2001.

Demchak, C.C., Creating the enemy: worldwide diffusion of an electronic military, in *The Diffusion of Military Knowledge from the Napoleonic Era to the Information Age*, Goldman, E. and Leslie, C.E., Eds., Stanford University Press, Stanford, CA, 2003a.

Demchak, C.C., Wars of disruption: international competition and information technology-driven military organizations, *Contemporary Security Policy*, 24, 75–112, 2003b.

Fountain, J., *Building the Virtual State*, Brookings, Washington, D.C., 2002.

Friedman, G. and Friedman, M., *The Future of War: Power, Technology and American World Dominance in the Twenty-First Century*, St. Martin's Griffin Press, New York, 1996.

GAO (General Accounting Office), *Military Transformation: Army Has a Comprehensive Plan for Managing Its Transformation but Faces Major Challenges*, U.S. Government Printing Office, November 21, Washington, D.C. (2001GAO-02-96).

Gordon, M.R., Technology and NATO defense: weighing the options, in *Conventional Deterrence: Alternatives for European Defense*, Golden, J.R., Asa, A.C., and Bruce, E.A., Eds., Lexington Books, Lexington, MA, 1984, pp. 149–162.

Gray, C.S., *Weapons Don't Make War: Policy, Strategy, and Military Technology*, University Press of Kansas, Lawrence, KS, 1993, p. 77.

Hanson, V.D., *Carnage and Culture: Landmark Battles in the Rise of Western Power*, Doubleday, New York, 2001.

Howard, M., Andreopoulos, G.J., and Shulman, M.R., Eds., *The Laws of War: Constraints on Warfare in the Western World*, Yale University Press, New Haven, CT, 1994.

Hsu, E., Army awards four contracts to transform information technology, *Inside the Army*, 15, 38, 2003.

IISS, *Strategic Survey, 1997–1998*, International Institute for Strategic Studies, Brassey's, London, 1998.

Interviews, personal, Grant 1990 US Army Research Institute and 1991 MacArthur Foundation, Budapest, Hungary, 1990–1991.

Jomini, Baron de., *The Art of War*, Mendell, G.H. and Churchill, W.P, Trans., Greenwood Press, Westport, CT, 1971.

JV (Joint Vision) 2010, Joint Vision 2010, Joint Chiefs of Staff, Department of Defense, United States Government, U.S. Government Printing Office, Washington, D.C., 1997.

Kaldor, M., *The Baroque Arsenal*, Andre Deutsch, London, 1981.

Keegan, J., *A History of Warfare*, Vintage Books, New York, 1993.

Kline, J., Joint Vision 2010: accelerated cumulative warfare, in *Essays on Strategy XV*, Sommerville, M.A., Ed., Institute for National Strategic Studies, National Defense University, Washington, D.C., 1999, pp. 3–26.

Krepinevich, A.R., Cavalry to computer: the pattern of military revolutions, *The National Interest*, 37, 30–42, 1994.

Lambeth, B.S., *The Transformation of American Air Power*, Cornell University Press, Ithaca, NY, 2000.

Lemos, R., How Much Does It Cost to Track a Hack?, *ZD Net News*, Mar. 22, 2001, Online.

Libicki, M.C., *Defending Cyberspace and Other Metaphors*, National Defense University Press, Washington, D.C., 1997.

Manjoo, F., So Many Worms, So Little Information, *Wired News*, Apr. 10, 2001, Online.

Mayntz, R. and Thomas P.H., Eds., *The Development of Large Technical Systems*, Westview Press, Boulder, CO, 1988.

Maze, R., The war that will never be won, *Army Times* (5 August) 26, 1996.

McNaugher, T.L., *New Weapons, Old Politics: America's Military Procurement Muddle*, The Brookings Institution, Washington, D.C., 1989.

Nonaka, I. and Hirotaka Takeuchi, A new organizational structure (HyperText Organization), in *Knowledge in Organizations*, Prusak, L., Ed., Butterworth-Heinemann, Boston, 1997, pp. 99–133. Originally, A dynamic theory of organizational knowledge creation, *Organization Science*, 5, 1, 1994.

O'Connell, R.L., *Of Arms and Men: A History of War, Weapons and Aggression*, Oxford University Press, New York, 1989.

O'Connell, R.L., *Ride of the Second Horseman: Birth and Death of War*, Oxford University Press, New York, 1995, pp. 224–225.

Pagonis, W.G., *Moving Mountains: Lessons in Leadership,* Harvard Business School Press, Boston, MA, 1992.

QDR, Report of the Quadrennial Defense Review to Donald Rumsfeld Secretary of Defense, US Government Department of Defense, U.S. Government Printing Office, Washington, D.C., September 30, 2001.

Reno, W. and Klock, S., *Warlord Politics and African States*, Lynne Rienner, New York, 1999.

Rochlin, G.I. and Demchak, C.C., The Gulf War: ascendant technology and declining rapability, *Survival, Journal of the International Instutute of Strategic Studies*, 33, 260–273, 1991.

Sagan, S.D., *Moving Targets: Nuclear Strategy and National Security*, Princeton University Press, Princeton, NJ, 1989.

Sagan, S.D., *The Limits of Safety: Organizations, Accidents and Nuclear Weapons,* The Princeton University Press, Princeton, NJ, 1993.

Scales, R.H.J, *Firepower in a Limited War*, Revised, Presidio Press, Novato, CA, 1995, p. 292.

Seymour, W., *Decisive Factors in Twenty Great Battles of the World*, Sidgwick & Jackson, London, 1988.

Shankar, T., Calling Troop Levels Adequate, Rumsfeld Defends War Planning, *Los Angeles Times*, Mar. 31, 2003, Online.

Simon, J., Ed., *NATO–Warsaw Pact Force Mobilization*, National Defense University Press, Washington, D.C., 1988.

Strachan, H., *European Armies and the Conduct of War*, Unwin Hyman, London, 1983.

Sun Tzu, *The Art of War*, Griffith, S.B., Trans., Oxford University Press, London, 1963.

Tilford, E.H., The Revolution in Military Affairs: Prospects and Cautions, published papers, U.S. Army War College, Carlisle, PA, May 1, 1995.

Tilly, C., *Coercion, Capital, and European States, Ad 990–1992 (Studies in Social Discontinuity)*, Blackwell, London, 1992.

Van Creveld, M., *Technology in War*. The Free Press, New York, 1989.

Watson, B.W. and Tsouras, P.G., Eds., *Military Lessons of the Gulf War*, Presidio Press, Novato, CA, 1993.

Weigley, R.F., History of the United States Army, 2nd ed., Indiana University Press, Bloomington, IN, 1984.

Zill, O., The Controversial US Retaliatory Missile Strikes, *PBS Frontline*, Apr., 1999, Online.

16

E-RULEMAKING

Stuart W. Shulman
Drake University

Lisa E. Thrane
Iowa State University

Mark C. Shelley
Iowa State University

CONTENTS

I.	Introduction	238
II.	The institutional context	239
III.	Data collection and analysis	240
IV.	Agency perspectives on the rulemaking process	240
	A. Challenges	240
	B. Shift to e-rulemaking	242
	C. Better IT tools	242
V.	Interest group perspectives on the rulemaking process	243
	A. Challenges	243
	B. Shift to e-rulemaking	244
	C. Better IT tools	245
VI.	Comparative analysis	245
VII.	Conclusions and some extensions	247
	A. Innovation and diffusion	248
	B. Democratic theory	249
References		250

ABSTRACT

In the context of wider e-government assumptions, this chapter presents and assesses the debate about the future of e-rulemaking. We examine the impact of electronic enhancements to the collection and synthesis of public commentary. Focus group data are presented to highlight a number of competing values that are at stake as public managers implement e-government. We speculate about the next steps that might culminate in a public information system for e-rulemaking that is technologically robust, applied in the most appropriate ways possible, and a genuine enhancement to both regulatory and democratic processes.

I. INTRODUCTION

A consensus appears to be emerging about the general purpose of e-government initiatives in the U.S. It is now commonly argued that well-designed e-government is capable of providing faster, cheaper, and better-quality government services (Comedy, 2002; Schelin, 2003; Swiss, 2003). Once thought by many to be elusive public goods dispensed rather unevenly by an impenetrable phalanx of oddly named agencies, those same government services now, as a matter of policy and practice, often reside no further than "three clicks" away from a digital citizen entering a web-based federal portal (Fletcher, 2004). Thus, e-government is presumed to be intuitive and effective, even if the metrics for demonstrating this (e.g., page hits) are crude and tell us little (Franzel and Coursey, 2004).

Insofar as it facilitates citizen–government interaction, the operating assumption is that "best practices" in e-government enhance the democratic process (Holzer et al., 2004). Advocates seem to be saying that democracy can be "new and improved," and that information technology (IT) is the linchpin that will make it possible. Forget, for now, that "efficient deliberation" well may be an oxymoron. Clearly, there are fears in and out of government about the effect of unleashing vast quantities of electronically produced public input (Rocheleau, 2003). Proponents of the digital government revolution nonetheless wish us to believe that all the values important to building the e-government consensus can be maximized simultaneously through the development of appropriate software applications, user-friendly human–computer interfaces, and a federal enterprise architecture running on sound business principles. Whether all public-sector functions can operate well based on the successful application of an e-business model remains to be seen (Garson, 2004).

In the case of federal rulemaking, only a few observers will object to ongoing efforts aimed at better informing and engaging the citizenry, while making government more efficient, responsive, and accountable. Disagreements tend to occur, however, when the means to these ends are sought through unreflective and indiscriminate applications of IT to existing bureaucratic practices. An important debate now unfolding concerns how best to build electronic citizen–government architectures that remain true to the principles underlying e-government consensus.

This chapter presents only a snapshot of the debate about the future of e-rulemaking. We argue that simply speeding up, streamlining, or otherwise enhancing the collection and synthesis of public commentary inherent in the rulemaking process runs the risk of undermining the role of public mediators, such as interest groups and of government experts, whose job it is to exercise discretion bounded by a mandate from Congress, and oversight from the Office of Management and Budget (OMB). What is most needed at this stage in the development of the e-rulemaking enterprise is to articulate the trade-offs inherent in certain IT-driven e-government innovations.

In what follows, we set out the context in which key decisions about the new federal e-rulemaking architecture are being considered. First, we provide an overview of recent literature on political and IT-management issues in e-rulemaking. Second, we present a comparative analysis based on the findings from a pair of e-rulemaking focus group sessions with agency personnel and representatives of interest groups during a workshop held at the National Science Foundation (NSF) during the fall of 2003. Finally, we speculate about the next steps that might be taken to allow the dialogue that is underway to culminate in a public information system for e-rulemaking that is technologically robust, applied in the most appropriate ways possible, and a genuine enhancement to both the regulatory and the democratic processes.

II. THE INSTITUTIONAL CONTEXT

In regulatory rulemaking, the stakes are often high. Rulemaking scholars note that the writing of regulations requires delicate decision-making to be made in a politically charged, information-intensive environment (Kerwin, 2003; Lubbers, 2003). One study presented to the House Government Reform Committee estimated that regulations "aimed at protecting health, safety, and the environment alone cost over $200 billion annually or about 2% of GDP" (Hahn and Litan, 2003: 2). While creating significant costs, the thousands of rules promulgated yearly "collectively deliver enormous benefits to society" (Coglianese, 2004). Critics of the role played by federal agency personnel suggest that these high-stake decisions are often made without adequate data, transparency, or accountability, and too often reflect the dominance of well-organized interests in Washington, D.C. (Skrzycki, 2003a). For some, e-rulemaking presents a chance to open the process to greater scrutiny and more balanced access to decision-making.

In 1998, Professor Stephen Johnson published a pathbreaking analysis of the potential impact of the Internet on rulemaking. His basic question — does the Internet change everything? — has remained pertinent and for the most part unanswerable to this day (Johnson, 1998). Intuitively, we are tempted to agree with scholars who speculate that IT-enhanced rulemaking may result in better rules, based on sound data, and arising from transparent, deliberative, inclusive, and accountable processes (Brandon and Carlitz, 2002; Carlitz and Gunn, 2002). Yet, in the absence of compelling studies demonstrating this is a general trend observable across a variety of rulemaking agencies, it is perhaps more prudent to be skeptical of the prospect for IT-driven change to transform the entrenched politics of rulemaking (Schlosberg and Dryzek, 2002; Tesh, 2002).

The task of improving regulatory functions is highly complex, with sharp disagreements about what actually constitutes better regulation (Fischbeck et al., 2001). It is clear, however, that it will take several years of research to establish new baseline data to begin to be able to generalize about the impact of IT enhancements on idiosyncratic elements of rulemaking, such as the role for public participation in the notice and comment process (Beierle, 2003; Shulman et al., 2003). New theories of bureaucratic change are needed to understand better the diffusion of technology and its impact on business process reengineering (Fountain, 2002a; Holden, 2003). While the e-rulemaking research agenda is crystallizing a new community of scholars interested in public administration issues (Garson, 2003; Shulman, 2005), there are a number of professional hurdles that keep studies of the impact of IT on agency practices somewhat marginalized, particularly within the discipline of political science (Fountain, 2001, 2002b).

Whether or not the Internet changes anything that actually matters, the technical development of a unified federal system e-rulemaking is ongoing (EPA, 2003). As is the case with many large-scale IT rollouts, the only certainty at this point is the emergence of unintended consequences (Fountain, 2003; NRC, 2000, 2002). The e-rulemaking initiative is part of the 24-point e-government element of the president's management agenda (OMB, 2002, 2003a). Many of the imperatives emphasized by the OMB are supported by legislation, including the e-Government Act of 2002 (OMB, 2003b). In addition, a number of General Accounting Office reports have trumpeted the possibilities for seamless electronic access to rulemaking documents and officials (GAO, 2000, 2001, 2003).

As of January 23, 2003, a new federal portal is open at www.regulations.gov (Skrzycki, 2003b). This relatively simple interface (known as Module 1) allows access to all federal rules open for public comment and provides a web-based form for submitting comments to the appropriate federal agency. Later iterations will allow for the migration of all federal e-rulemaking to a single, unified docket system (Module 2), and will unveil an optional set of tools (a "Reg-Writers Workbench") for the rule writers charged with the task of analyzing the significance of public comments (Module 3). It is against this backdrop that our eRulemaking Research Group convened a 2-day workshop at the NSF in Arlington, Virginia.

III. DATA COLLECTION AND ANALYSIS

The data were collected in the fall of 2003. Four focus groups were conducted: 2 for 14 government agency representatives and 2 for 13 interest group representatives who attended an e-rulemaking workshop sponsored by the NSF. In addition, the four principal investigators and the four additional academics facilitated and participated in the focus group discussions. The participants signed informed consent forms. They were instructed that their participation was strictly voluntary and that they may choose not to respond to a question or to withdraw from the group at any time. Permission to tape record the focus group was granted by the participants for the exclusive purpose of accurately capturing and retaining their comments for analysis. The participants were assured that their comments would be kept confidential. In addition, the participants were assured that their comments would not be attributed to them in any way, nor would the analysis identify any participant by name or title/role (unless they specified otherwise). The discussion within each group lasted approximately $1\frac{1}{2}$ to 2 hours.

Participants provided feedback at the end of the focus group session, when a brief summary was presented that outlined the critical points of discussion. The focus groups were later transcribed and analyzed. Upon analysis of the participants' feedback, themes emerged and illustrative quotes were sorted by thematic categories. Then, the researchers sought clarification from participants about the draft focus group reports. It is evident that there were shared themes that demonstrated an overlap between the groups, as well as competing conceptualizations of the e-rulemaking environment. The focus groups were guided by a set of questions exploring the impact of IT on rulemaking, barriers to effective participation, and methods to enhance the rulemaking process for interest groups and agency personnel. In addition, group commonalities and differences were examined, which highlighted divisions and possible technological and informational bridges that may encourage a spirit of cooperation between the two groups.

IV. AGENCY PERSPECTIVES ON THE RULEMAKING PROCESS

A. Challenges

Participants first were asked to discuss the rulemaking challenges faced by their agencies. Several agency representatives expressed the sentiment that the rulemaking process is adding to their workload when budgets have declined. One person indicated that the "high volume of comments" has created a "crisis of getting all these form letters and having to parse things out." Another participant said, "We're getting many more and more comments at a time of having diminished resources to respond to them." Even with the volume of comments, six participants suggested "including comments on the preamble discussion." It was argued that these ideas might not be captured otherwise. Two agency representatives indicated that general paper comments tend to be lengthier, research-intensive documents that "cover the whole spectrum of issues." On the other hand, electronic comments tend to be more opinion-based and focus "on a particular issue or a bone they want to pick with the agency." A participant indicated that written comments submitted by "Joe Public" are "brief and to the point." It was suggested that regardless of the method of submission, a commenter who has vested interest in the outcome will write a more persuasive document.

One individual shared how mass-form letters were counted. The participant said, "This would be the exact same letter ... . Different people signed it; the wording was exactly the same. That counts as one entry of the docket." One participant said, "We oftentimes end up noting the volume of the response, but have to say 'though a number of people raised this issue, there were no substantive data submitted ... . And so, you note it, and there's nothing you can do." Several agency representatives noted that sorting documents by support/opposition to a particular rulemaking could have the unintended consequence of transforming the process into a referendum. It was suggested by some that since the opposition tended to comment more often, rulemaking could be driven by this bias. In addition, it also could generate an onslaught of nonsubstantive comments from both camps designed to tip the scales in their own favor.

Some participants noted that data compilation and management created challenges at various stages of the process. One participant mentioned that it was difficult to gather data from "diverse and small sources" like small businesses "to develop technical analyses...which we use to propose and ultimately promulgate a rule." After obtaining valid data, another individual said, "Being able to access it and present it in a way that is palatable and understandable by the decision-makers" is a primary goal.

Several agency representatives reported that the political climate, congressional mandates, and court requirements presented barriers to effective rulemaking. Five people suggested that the political climate was a significant factor. There was a sentiment among some agency representatives that the current regulatory climate made their jobs difficult. On the other hand, not all participants agreed that their agencies were "subject to the same political whims."

A participant said, "All the congressional mandates and the legislative challenges and the endless stream of supporting analyses that have to be written just this way or just that way" compound the problem. Two individuals commented that Congress has mandated "yet another layer in our regulations, whereby we have to do a concept paper that needs to go up in the chain before we can even start to do a proposed rule." Three participants emphasized the challenges associated with court requirements. One person said, "The courts have this process of judicial review. Questioning about what the arbitrary and capricious test means has added a lot of requirements to the rulemaking process." Two persons noted the incongruity between accessible language and legal jargon. One person said, "We do have attorneys that review all our rules before they get published." Attorneys review the language that was "hopefully in plain English, and then if they see legal problems with it; they correct them," the participant added. However, not all participants reported legal challenges as a significant obstacle.

B. Shift to e-Rulemaking

Most agencies reported an electronic shift. One agency representative commented that "we've done a lot to change the way we disseminate information, and we've used the Web effectively." The person reported that the *Federal Register* was concerned that their documents were first published on the Web. On the other hand, stakeholders had more time to review "rules and comment." One participant indicated, "In the last 5 years or so, we've become … more proactive … about trying to go out and notify people about the availability of a rule for comment." In addition, one agency held "on-line public meetings on the Web" and gathered information via "consumer complaint hotlines." One participant related the success of requesting e-mail submissions. The person said, "Just a year, year and a half ago, my agency established one e-mail address that's in every *Federal Register* notice … . Now that gives us an on-line searchable database of almost everything." One participant discussed the challenges of being a contact for a major rule. The participant stated, "His voicemail box fills up every 15 minutes. And his e-mail, he got between 2 and 2000 a day." An individual suggested that there are occasions when a high volume of comments is useful but need to be separated from substantive comments.

The transition to e-rulemaking has not been a seamless process. Although most representatives reported their agencies had adapted successfully to e-rulemaking, two participants noted cultural snags. One person shared that with higher comment volume, the agency would need to become automated, but this would go against the grain of the agency's culture. If there were a discrepancy between ease of submission and system or data security, "Then it just won't happen," a participant commented. A few agency representatives discussed concerns about comment deadlines, file formats, attachments, and demographic data collection in an e-rulemaking environment. One person asked, "If we go to an EDOCKET system, are we now going to formally abide by the cutoff period for the comments?" In reference to unzipping comment files, it was problematic for three participants. Another person recommended not underlining words because "that was fine in the hard copy; but when the PDF was read, it's blank." The inclusion of copyrighted articles in comments and confidential business information (CBI) generated discussion among six participants. One participant requested a box that could be checked if an electronic document had an attachment. In regard to EPA's EDOCKET, another person indicated it would be convenient to have the option of remaining anonymous or providing one's name, location, and organization.

C. Better IT Tools

Agency representatives reported a need for technological innovations to smooth the transition to e-rulemaking. Many agency representatives defined various electronic tools that would be useful. These included guided commenting, section analysis, duplicate detection, text clustering and summarization, ready access to the comment database, and sorting capabilities. Many participants shared that IT could help citizens write better comments by guiding their responses or by offering specific guidelines. One person stated, "We could use technology to focus the commenters into the areas that are useful." Another participant added, "You could link to a certain part of the rule. What you would be doing is making people structure their comments in a manner that would be easier for you to do the analysis later." Six individuals recommended a "section-by-section analysis" tool. One person indicated, "If there was any way to encourage commenters to follow that sort of format, I think that would be a great service." A participant suggested that users could be educated about a particular site by adding links about "how to write a good comment or how to search easier."

Seven participants noted the importance of tools that would detect copies, duplicates, and near-duplicates. One person stated, "We have these long form comments; and at the end, there's this one nugget that actually is something we need to address, or we are going to end up in litigation." Two people specifically mentioned a clustering tool. One participant stated that an automated method to cluster "a particular category" would save the time of going "through every single comment."

Two participants desired an electronic tool that "could generate essentially a list of commenters, or an index of material in the docket." It would allow agencies to respond to questions about commenters and reference the edocket number. In addition, "When we are defending the rule, we bring the whole docket into evidence by submitting the index," suggested a participant. One individual pointed out that "a quick transmittal of the body of comments received" was needed. Three participants viewed the summary tool with enthusiasm. However, two people disagreed. One person said, "I didn't think that the technology had advanced enough to really make that useful."

V. INTEREST GROUP PERSPECTIVES ON THE RULEMAKING PROCESS

A. Challenges

Limited financial resources posed constraints for most interest groups. One participant pointed out that interest groups have limited resources and choose only a few "hot topics ... a year ... to be effective." A participant noted that the "pre-proposal stage" was critical, but dependent on resources, which precluded many interest groups from effective participation. In addition, this individual added, "There's not a lot of impact of all those comments in the actual final outcome of the rule." One person suggested that, comparatively speaking, there was a better opportunity to influence the "governing process" because of the "politicized" nature of rulemaking.

Many interest group representatives reported that their participation in rulemaking was motivated by several goals: to influence the outcome of a rulemaking; to be an advocate; to mobilize and educate their members; to conduct outreach by ensuring "that more people get involved in the whole process"; or to hold agencies and Congress accountable. A participant indicated that comments provide a public record so that agencies are held accountable and can be kept in check by the legislative branch. Four participants noted that they were hired to "advance the interests of our members." Six participants indicated that they intended to shape the outcome of the rule, while two others were more skeptical. Two participants specifically suggested that they were motivated to influence the rule by offering substantive "high-quality comments."

The point also was made by three participants that ranking the type of comments into categories such as "qualitative vs. quantitative," "substantive vs. non-substantive," and "mass form letter vs. non [form letter]" was a cause for concern. One individual agreed that there is "a distinction in sorting and reading mass comments versus other comments." However, it was suggested that mass communications should not be labeled nonsubstantive, because they would be marginalized "instantly." One participant raised the issue that e-rulemaking must guard against the tendency to silence the "non-electronic voice." Most participants indicated that the digital divide precludes certain groups of people and communities from public participation. An individual stated, "We've always got to deal with those who do not and will not have it [information technology]."

The lack of standardization in comment submission requirements (i.e., triplicate, hard copy, etc.), mandatory demographic characteristics, and short comment periods increased the burden on many interest groups. In reference to submission requirements for a specific rulemaking, one participant said, "All comments were to be filed in triplicate and hard copy. The agency required the three copies be together, and we had to collate separate piles of three for each person." In addition, many participants indicated that it would be helpful to have access to submitted comments and summary statistics as well as agency staff to "answer questions." One person added that agencies "that are not responsive are probably the most frustrating."

An individual argued that the burden to collect and analyze data should not fall on interest groups. The participant stated, "The federal government should have that research completed as a basis before they even begin these rulemakings. We should be supplementing good information they already have" instead of compiling it. It was suggested that rulemaking is an inherently adversarial process punctuated by amiable relations with agencies. A participant stated, "So at one level, we are viewed as a resource. At the same time, we fight with agencies about a lot of things ... . It's not personal. It is just the way the process works."

B. Shift to e-Rulemaking

Overall, most participants suggested that making the commenting process easier would facilitate the e-rulemaking process. One person stated that outreach is desired specifically when regulations impact their group or their members. Two participants mentioned the importance of agency outreach to a cross-section of interest groups. A person stated that the organizational culture "is very much pushing e-activism," but concerns were voiced about IT-illiterate interest group members and citizens. A participant shared that "income, age, and ethnicity impact the access to tools used to comment on the Internet." One individual said, "In order for our communities to access eGov efficiently and easily is going to take a significant investment in technology."

However, several participants pointed out that limiting methods of submission, particularly e-mail, and creating barriers to e-submission hindered a democratic process. Another individual suggested that the "infrastructure of these agencies sometimes is inadequate to receive mass comments from citizens." One participant mentioned how "Spam filtering" and "randomly generated images with numbers on them ... which require an authentication code" thwart the commenting process. Although it was recognized that Spam filters were needed, there was a concern about additional barriers for citizen participation.

Other discussion points involved web forms, interfaces, and usability. There was an observation by some participants that members should not be forced to "use a government-run Web form." Some participants noted a concern about the capability of online forms to receive attachments. A person said, "An automated receipt that provides confirmation of your comment doesn't necessarily indicate your attachments came through." Four participants recommended a "standard that allows advocacy groups to submit comments that directly interfaces with any databases that are being developed." In response to a question on whether interfaces should differ for first-time users and professional users, there was general agreement that standardization and usability were important. Generally, participants desired options within a standardized process. One person said, "Regular users will know what the standards are when they go to each different place, but also, there are many options for the new user to choose from so that they can submit in a way that is easy for them."

C. Better IT Tools

According to interest group representatives, IT tools must enhance a democratic process. Interest group representatives discussed how agencies should use IT tools in rulemaking. The emphasis was on promotion of citizen participation, examination of substantive comments, rational decision-making, consensus building, and compilation of data. Overall, many participants wanted more transparency in how agencies made decisions. The process should be giving ordinary people opportunities to put comments in. A few participants recommended a timeline on rulemakings because it would educate the public by "having descriptions of the different steps in the process" and inform interest groups if "an agency decides they will never issue a final ruling on something after receiving the public comments." There was recognition that IT tools need to be tailored to a "number of users."

One participant indicated that IT tools could help interest groups view, search, and sort the database of comments. Two people mentioned that it would be helpful when viewing comments online if there were a "view all page." Regarding regulations.gov, two persons indicated that it would be beneficial to analyze the differences and similarities between their comments and those from other groups. Also, a participant shared that it was cumbersome to find the "comments from a couple of particular groups .... There were five or six groups working on it together, and each of us only found a few of them." One individual was concerned that citizens would make erroneous assumptions because they would be unaware that other stakeholders had not weighed in on the matter. In addition, two individuals wanted a tool that would distinguish which regions of the country were less responsive to their outreach, so they could alter their approach.

It was suggested that future IT tools must be "incredibly user-friendly," so interest group representatives could run frequencies and use search and sort functions to understand "how specific comments differ from canned letters with duplicates and duplicates plus." In addition, an individual suggested that it would helpful to separate the duplicate comments from the other unique comments. This person stated, "This would make it a more easily searchable database for the agency as well as for us. These two kinds of comments serve two different purposes." One participant commented that assessing near-duplicates would be a great benefit for interest groups. The individual stated, "If, for instance, half the people have changed the letter to add this one position," it is worth knowing. Another person was interested in the "keyword tools" to search for "phrases," "to get a sense of the range of ideas in comments and keywords that were there."

VI.   COMPARATIVE ANALYSIS

The interrelationship between technology, social relations, and public values is key to designing a system that serves the needs of all stakeholders. The transition to electronic rulemaking creates immediate IT needs for agencies and interest groups alike. It increases the burden on agencies to sort through and synthesize enormous amounts of information generated from mandated public participation. Several agency representatives remarked on the need for IT tools to reduce the burden of searching for "nuggets" of information in mass-form letters. Many noted numerous tools that would help them collect, manage, and slice up a comment database, so they could meet the dual objectives of writing good rules and providing interest groups with requested information.

IT places financial strains on interest groups as they adapt to agencies' comment submission requirements, rally their constituents, and provide outreach to IT-disenfranchised citizens. Many participants suggested that e-rulemaking is an additional cost and increases digital inequality. Interest groups seek IT tools that will make the rulemaking process more transparent and ensure that their positions are heard. Cross-agency standardization of comment submission, web interfaces, and e-mail submissions with confirmation that all files are received would be valuable to many interest groups. Many participants were interested in data management tools, such as duplicate detection, and search and sort functions.

Nevertheless, to apply an "IT fix" to streamline public commentary in the absence of reflection may have the unintended consequence of undercutting the symbiotic relationship between agency experts and interest groups. For the most part, IT tools that were desired by stakeholders did not radically reassess the rulemaking process, but addressed their most pressing needs. It seems that, to have a meaningful impact on the democratic and regulatory processes, technological innovation cannot operate in isolation from the values that infuse a collaborative exchange. Discourse, reflection, and inclusion of difference would expand e-rulemaking and dramatically change the types of technology that would have currency.

It is apparent from the perspectives of agency personnel and representatives of interest groups that there is a mutually shared interest in improving regulation. Some agency representatives reported that their aim was to write quality regulations, but that they were hampered by legislative and legal challenges, which have added layers of requirements to the rulemaking process. However, skepticism and distrust between the two entities cloud these points of commonality. Many interest group representatives report their efforts are devalued in the process, their writing campaigns are "pigeonholed as "nonsubstantive," and agencies are nonresponsive to their concerns. On the other hand, several agency representatives questioned the authenticity of interest groups' commitment to the process. With regard to mass communication, an agency representative hypothesized that their "motivation might be fundraising, or increasing their profile, or simply winning the issue." Another agency participant questioned whether interest groups were motivated to "make a political point" or a rational argument supported by data. As these focus groups have highlighted, the success of IT-driven e-government innovations rests on a solid foundation of group relations. Informational and technological bridges are thus built on a foundational equivalent of trust that is reinforced through continued dialogue and an open exchange of stakeholder ideas. In an e-rulemaking environment, trust is demonstrated through authenticity and security of information and technological integrity. Otherwise, "people aren't going to buy into it," one agency representative added.

Agency personnel and interest group representatives share a belief that e-rulemaking should promote a democratic process. However, this shared belief structure does not translate into attributing the same value to certain forms of civic participation. It was evident that many interest group representatives are concerned that e-rulemaking may have the net effect of cutting them out of the democratic process. Furthermore, there was a palpable concern among several interest groups that IT would silence the "nonelectronic voice," and amplify long-standing social and economic inequities. In addition, most interest groups sought open access to the comment database, so that agencies and Congress were held accountable to the public.

Some interest group representatives were suspicious of structured commenting. An interest group participant stated, "We don't think the scope of their questioning related to the rulemaking is sufficient; so often times, we are providing answers to questions they didn't ask." This individual was concerned that if comments not directly relevant to a specific section were placed in the "other category," they would be "marginalized." An agency representative also was concerned about guided commenting, because some of "the best data to help guide my rule" may crosscut several issues.

Several interest group representatives suggested that agencies should support political participation through the solicitation of substantive comments while not devaluing citizen involvement in the form of mass mailings. For the most part, agencies acknowledge that mailing campaigns do not carry the same weight as substantive comments. From an agency perspective, it is not any more conducive to a democratic process if rulemaking turns into a referendum and the oppositional voices drive the outcome.

But, agencies also are faced with the responsibility of building consensus from conflicting viewpoints. An interest group representative reflects on agencies' use of IT to build "a comprehensive objective record." This individual argues that "if we can use the technology to really get to the quality of the information upon which these decisions are based, I think we could get both sides to agree a little bit more." This would seem to suggest that the quality of information influences the nature of the discourse among stakeholders. Therefore, electronic participation in rulemaking should not be justified solely on economic grounds, but also by its impact on the democratic process. It seems fundamental to a public information system for e-rulemaking to construct places for deliberation. If IT provides a place for discussion, reasoning, and engagement across lines of difference, stakeholders indeed may make proposals, attempt to persuade others, listen to the responses of those others, and determine the best outcomes and policies based on the arguments and reasons fleshed out in public discourse.

The ideal of deliberation is that of communication that actually changes the preferences of participants in the face of the arguments and positions of others. In this way, a process of democratic rulemaking cannot be one-way, with an agency either positing a position for citizens to accept or simply taking note of objections to proposed rules. There must be room in the design of the online procedure for individuals not only to deliberate with others, but also to note changes in their own position. Authenticity within deliberative democracy depends on participants affecting the outcome of the process; this, of course, includes the possibility of changes to proposed agency policy.

VII. CONCLUSIONS AND SOME EXTENSIONS

The comments provided by the participants in these focus groups provide an emergent perspective on the dominant themes related to federal e-rulemaking in contemporary political discourse. Their comments addressed the impact of IT on rulemaking, barriers to effective participation, and how to enhance the rulemaking process both for groups interested in providing input and for the agency personnel who must receive and process that input and respond with policy outputs. In all respects, the emergent federal e-rulemaking system must find ways to provide more equitable access and fair treatment of the viewpoints that are expressed. Two main themes are of particular relevance to this study: (1) the innovation and diffusion of electronic methods for federal rulemaking, and (2) implications for democratic governance and democratic theory.

A. Innovation and Diffusion

One of the dominant themes we see emerging from these focus group data is the need to provide for electronic-based innovation in federal rulemaking and for the diffusion of that innovation throughout the federal rulemaking regime. Diffusion of innovations theory offers demand-side explanations of what is involved in facilitating broadly based, if not universal, participation in federal e-rulemaking. Rogers' (2003) model of adoption explains the process by which an innovation is implemented. Adoption occurs over time and through a series of stages. First, an individual, or, by extension, a government agency or an interest group, must learn about a new idea or approach before forming an attitude about it. This model posits that an attitude must be formed before behavior can follow that either supports or rejects the new technology. In Rogers' persuasion stage, an individual forms attitudes about a particular innovation. One can be persuaded to adopt an innovation if it has obvious advantages and is relevant to one's life. One's behavioral intention is manifested in the decision to accept or reject the new idea. Individuals put the innovation to use, and over time it becomes routinized in everyday life (Rogers, 2003). This entire process of adoption and diffusion of innovation is influenced by social relationships and individuals' knowledge base. Personal, agency, and group characteristics carry great weight in shaping both access to an innovation and receptivity to exploring technological advances.

The ongoing public debate about disparate levels of access to the Internet and functional knowledge about how to use it most effectively for federal e-rulemaking reflects competing conceptualizations of governance and citizenship. A focus on IT literacy (ITL) reveals a problem that is far more complicated than debates about the various pathways to universal IT access. However, less data-based information exists regarding the effectiveness of interventions that seek to identify and remove barriers to group or individual equity in citizenship in a comprehensive and systematic manner. Improving ITL "is not simply a matter of running wire and providing public computers — it is also a matter of ensuring that people have the requisite skills to use the technology and that they see the relevance of technology in their lives" (Organization for Economic Cooperation and Development Secretariat, 2000; Seiden, 2000). We are more skeptical than the National Research Council that the full array of capabilities, concepts, and skills can be made universal, but agree with those authors that implementation needs will vary across population groups (National Research Council, 1999).

Citizen groups with lesser resource bases and underdeveloped technological infrastructures, like educationally and economically disenfranchised citizens, may face unique challenges that influence their desire to become more IT-fluent. Becoming a digital citizen, either as an individual or as a group, is a process influenced by technological attitudes that may have the effect of widening the digital gap between those groups that already know how to use IT to maximize their impact on federal rulemaking and those that as yet are relatively clueless how to go about achieving that aim. Future research may seek to identify the attitudinal and organizational elements that influence ITL and thus are most likely to foster digital citizenship and interest group effectiveness in e-rulemaking. Similarly, future studies could focus on the different strategies pursued by federal agencies for the adoption and diffusion of IT to promote linkages between citizenship and ITL.

Citizenship is increasingly mediated by digital communication (Hernon, 1998; Larsen and Rainie, 2002; Temin, 1997). Political parties interact with members online; interest groups use websites and e-mail to woo the public; media organizations perpetually update the news on their information-rich sites; government makes vital information and documents available and collects it from citizens via the World Wide Web (Fountain, 2001). Online information can provide the basis for environmental or personal health protection (Beierle and Cahill, 2000; Fox and Rainie, 2002). These and other communicative functions are all aspects of the emerging digital citizenship (Black, 1998; Davis, 1999). The rise of the "virtual" individual and of cyberspace community substantively changes both the manner in which citizens can engage democracy and the prerequisites for equitable participation (Baddeley, 1997; Jordan, 1999; Moore, 1999). Though IT should make it easier for all citizens and groups to conduct their routine business with the government, in fact, it appears to be widening the gap between the IT literate and those without basic navigational skills.

Most research on digital divide issues has focused on how individual and family characteristics, and differential education opportunities, impinge on the ability to master technological fluency. It is as yet unclear whether similar delimiters of group and institutional ITL can be determined, and, if they can be determined, how their inequitable consequences may be ameliorated. Debates about establishing criteria for an ITL baseline are complex and controversial. The rapid pace of technological change makes it problematic to state definitively that certain IT skills are essential to underpin universal digital citizenship (McNair, 2000). Nonetheless, the presence of a moving target does not justify inaction, whether one believes in the existence of a digital gap or not (Walsh et al., 2001). The ability of citizens and groups to make use of electronic means to impact federal rulemaking must be considered against the backdrop of findings by the National Center for Education Statistics (1992) that about 8 million adults could not perform simple literacy tasks and over 20% had only the most rudimentary reading and writing skills. Nearly half of the adult population "were apt to experience considerable difficulty in performing tasks that require them to integrate or synthesize information from complex or lengthy texts." Patterns of institutional technological learning and how the playing field for technological access to government policymakers could be leveled among competing interests remain to be ascertained, although analyses of individual ITL such as that provided by the Web-Based Education Commission (2000) may provide fruitful clues to guide that research agenda. The structure and limitations of government-provided portals for more equitable access likely will lead to future policy debates echoing those regarding market-based IT diffusion regarding organizations that are ITL "have-nows" vs. the "have-laters" (Symposium, 2000; Mueller, 2001).

B. Democratic Theory

Studies of the federal rulemaking process (e.g., Kerwin, 2003; West, 1985; Woll, 1977) have established the link between agency activities and democratic theory. Other research has elaborated the link between democratic theory and societal change. For example, Shapiro (2003) argues that democracy should be geared toward minimizing domination throughout society, to redress the challenge posed by ethnic differences and claims for group rights, and inequities related to the unequal distribution of income and wealth.

Folbre (2001) embodies her discussion of democratic theory in economics and family values, focused on the moral and ethical aspects of governance in conjunction with feminist economics and social justice. Dahl (1985) similarly connects democracy to developments toward economic equality manifested in employee ownership and worker participation in management decision-making. They and others (e.g., Barber, 1984, 1992; Dryzek, 1990, 2000; Held, 1987; Pateman, 1970) provide different perspectives on the nature of democratic government and establish a framework to consider the nimbleness with which governments must be able to adapt to new circumstances such as technological innovations. The adoption of innovations by local governments has been a subject of previous studies (Bingham, 1976; Larsen and McGuire, 1998). Kautz and Pries-Heje (1996) have addressed the diffusion and adoption of IT, and Stoneman (2002) has studied the economics of technological diffusion. Kirkman (2002) questioned the global readiness for IT, and McMeekin (2002) sees innovation as dependent on demand for the fruits of the innovation. The Organization for Economic Cooperation and Development (1999, 2001a, 2001b) has investigated various cross-national dimensions of innovation, through cooperation in national innovation systems, the mobility of skilled personnel in national innovation systems, and the management of national innovation systems. Shulman (1999) and Chesbrough (2003) provide arguments for open innovation, to create and profit from technology, and for "owning the future." These are among the issues — at the interface between technological innovation and democratic theory — that will need to be dealt with successfully by current and future leaders in e-rulemaking.

We find echoes of these issues, as well as at least hints of some possible resolutions, in the comments provided by these interest group and federal agency focus group participants. The future configuration of federal e-rulemaking structures and procedures will depend on how these potential resolutions play out, and that configuration in turn will shape both the technological future of citizen-group–government interaction and the nature of governance.

REFERENCES

Baddeley, S., Governmentality, in *The Governance of Cyberspace*, Loader, B.D., Ed., Routledge, New York, 1997, pp. 64–96.

Barber, B.R., *Strong Democracy: Participatory Politics for a New Age*, University of California Press, Berkeley, 1984.

Barber, B.R., *An Aristocracy of Everyone: The Politics of Education and the Future of America*, Ballantine, New York, 1992.

Beierle, T.C., Discussing the Rules: Electronic Rulemaking and Democratic Deliberation, Resources for the Future Discussion Paper 03–22, 2003
   Available at: http://www.rff.org/disc_papers/PDF_files/0322.pdf
Last accessed on 06/02/2003.

Beierle, T. and Cahill, S., *Electronic Democracy and Environmental Governance: A Survey of the States*, Resources for the Future, Washington, D.C., 2000
   Available at: http://www.rff.org/CFDOCS/disc_papers/PDF-files/0042.pdf
Last accessed on 12/15/2000.

Bingham, R.D., *The Adoption of Innovation by Local Government*, Lexington, Lexington, MA, 1976.

Black, E.R., Digital democracy or politics on a microchip, in *Digital Democracy: Policy and Politics in the Wired World*, Alexander, C.J., and Pal, L.A., Eds., Oxford University Press, Ontario, 1998, pp. xii–xv.

Brandon, B.H. and Carlitz, R.D., Online rulemaking and other tools for strengthening civic infrastructure, *Administrative Law Review*, 54, 1421–1478, 2002.

Carlitz, R.D. and Gunn, R.W., Online rulemaking: a step toward e-governance, *Government Information Quarterly*, 19, 389–405, 2002.

Chesbrough, H.W., *Open Innovation: The New Imperative for Creating and Profiting from Technology*, Harvard Business School Press, Boston, 2003.

Coglianese, C., Information technology and regulatory policy: new directions for digital government research, in *Social Science Computer Review*, 22, 85–91, 2004.

Comedy, Y.L., The federal government: meeting the needs of society in the information age, in *Advances in Digital Government: Technology, Human Factors, and Policy*, McIver, W.J., Jr. and Elmagamid, A.K., Eds., Kluwer, Boston, 2002, pp. 215–229.

Dahl, R.A., *A Preface to Economic Democracy*, University of California Press, Berkeley, 1985.

Davis, R., *The Web of Politics: The Internet's Impact on the American Political System*, Oxford University Press, New York, 1999.

Dryzek, J.S., *Discursive Democracy: Politics, Policy, and Political Science*, Cambridge University Press, New York, 1990.

Dryzek, J.S., *Deliberative Democracy and Beyond: Liberals, Critics, Contestations*, Oxford University Press, New York, 2000.

Environmental Protection Agency (EPA), eRulemaking Fact Sheet, 2003
Available at: http://www.regulations.gov/images/eRuleFactSheet.pdf
Accessed on 12/07/2003.

Fischbeck, P.S., Farrow, R.S., and Morgan, M.G., Introduction: the challenge of improving regulation, in *Improving Regulation: Cases in Environment, Health, and Safety*, Fischbeck, P.S. and Farrow, R.S., Eds., Resources for the Future, Washington, D.C., 2001, pp. 1–13.

Fletcher, P.D., Portals and policy: implications for electronic access to U.S. Federal Government Information and Services, in *Digital Government: Principles and Best Practices*, Pavlichev, A. and Garson, G.D., Eds., Idea Group, Hershey, PA, 2004, pp. 52–62.

Folbre, N., *The Invisible Heart: Economics and Family Values*, New Press, New York, 2001.

Fountain, J., *Building the Virtual State: Information Technology and Institutional Change*, Brookings, Washington, D.C., 2001.

Fountain, J., *Information, Institutions, and Governance: Advancing a Basic Social Science Research Program for Digital Government*, Harvard University, Cambridge, MA, 2002a.

Fountain, J., A theory of federal bureaucracy, in *Governance.com: Democracy in the Information Age*, Kamarck, E.C. and Nye, J.S., Jr., Eds., Brookings Institution Press, Washington, D.C., 2002b, pp. 117–140.

Fountain, J., Prospects for improving the regulatory process using e-rulemaking, *Communications of the ACM*, 46, 63–64, 2003.

Fox, S. and Rainie, L., Vital Decisions: How Internet Users Decide What Information to Trust When They or Their Loved Ones Are Sick, 2002
Available at: http://www.pewinternet.org/reports/pdfs/PIP_Vital_Decisions_May2002.pdf
Last accessed on 05/01/2002.

Franzel, J.M. and Coursey, D.H., Government web portals: management issues and the approaches of five states, in *Digital Government: Principles and Best Practices*, Pavlichev, A. and Garson, G.D., Eds., Idea Group, Hershey, PA, 2004, pp. 63–77.

Garson, G.D., Toward an information technology research agenda for public administration, in *Public Information Technology: Policy and Management Issues*, Garson, G.D., Ed., Idea Group, Hershey, PA, 2003, pp. 331–357.

Garson, G.D., The promise of digital government, in *Digital Government: Principles and Best Practices*, Pavlichev, A. and Garson, G.D., Eds., Idea Group, Hershey, PA, 2004, pp. 2–15.

GAO (General Accounting Office), *Federal Rulemaking: Agencies' Use of Information Technology to Facilitate Public Participation*, Government Printing Office, Washington, D.C., 2000 (GAO-00-135R).

GAO (General Accounting Office), *Regulatory Management: Communication about Technology-Based Innovations Can Be Improved*, Government Printing Office, Washington, D.C., 2001 (GAO-01-232).

GAO (General Accounting Office), *Electronic Rulemaking: Efforts to Facilitate Public Participation Can Be Improved*, Government Printing Office, Washington, D.C., 2003 (GAO-03-901).

Hahn, R.W. and Litan, R.E., Recommendations for Improving Regulatory Accountability and Transparency, Testimony before the House Government Reform Committee, 2003
http://aei-brookings.org/admin/pdffiles/phpk0.pdf
Accessed on 12/07/2003.

Held, D., *Models of Democracy*, Stanford University Press, Stanford, 1987.

Hernon, P., Government on the web: a comparison between the United States and New Zealand, *Government Information Quarterly*, 15, 419–443, 1998.

Holden, S.H., The evolution of information techology management at the federal level: implications for public administration, in *Public Information Technology: Policy and Management Issues*, Garson, G.D., Ed., Idea Group, Hershey, PA, 2003, pp. 53–73.

Holzer, M., Hu, L.T., and Song, S.H., Digital government and citizen participation in the United States, in *Digital Government: Principles and Best Practices*, Pavlichev, A. and Garson, G.D., Eds., Idea Group, Hershey, PA, 2004, pp. 306–319.

Johnson, S.M., The Internet changes everything: revolutionizing public participation and access to government information through the Internet, *Administrative Law Review*, 50, 277–337, 1998.

Jordan, T., *Cyberpower: The Culture and Politics of Cyberspace and the Internet*, Routledge, New York, 1999.

Kautz, K. and Pries-Heje, J., Eds., *Diffusion and Adoption of Information Technology: Proceedings of the First IFIP WG 8.6 Working Conference on the Diffusion and Adoption of Information Technology*, Oslo, Norway, Oct. 1995, by IFIP WG 8.6 Working Conference on the Diffusion and Adoption of Information Technology, Chapman & Hall, New York, 1996.

Kerwin, C.M., *Rulemaking: How Government Agencies Write Law and Make Policy*, 3rd ed., CQ Press, Washington, D.C., 2003.

Kirkman, G.S., Ed., *Global Information Technology Report, 2001–2002: Readiness for the Networked World*, Oxford University Press, New York, 2002.

Larsen, T.J. and McGuire, E., Eds., *Information Systems Innovation and Diffusion: Issues and Directions*, Idea Group, Hershey, PA, 1998.

Larsen, E. and Rainie, L., The Rise of the e-Citizen: How People Use Government Agencies' Web Sites, 2002
Available at: http://www.pewinternet.org/reports/pdfs/PIP_Govt_Website_Rpt.pdf
Last accessed on 07/09/2002.

Lubbers, J.S., *A Guide to Federal Agency Rulemaking*, 3rd ed., ABA Publishing, Chicago, 2003.

McMeekin, A., Ed., *Innovation by Demand: An Interdisciplinary Approach to the Study of Demand and Its Role in Innovation*, Manchester University Press, Manchester, NY, 2002.

McNair, S., The emerging policy agenda, in *Learning to Bridge the Digital Divide*, 2000
Available at: http://www.oecd.org/publications/e-book/9600081e.pdf
Last accessed on 12/18/2000.

Moore, R.K., Democracy and cyberspace, in *Digital Democracy: Discourse and Decision Making in the Information Age*, Hague, B.N. and Loader, B.D., Eds., Routledge, New York, 1999, pp. 39–59.

Mueller, M.L., Universal service policies as wealth redistribution, in *The Digital Divide: Facing a Crisis or Creating a Myth?*, Compaine, B.M., Ed., MIT Press, Cambridge, MA, 2001, pp. 179–187.

National Center for Education Statistics, 1992 Adult Literacy Survey, 1992
Available at: http://nces.ed.gov/naal/naal92/overview.html
Last accessed on 12/19/2000.

National Research Council, *Being Fluent with Information Technology*, National Academy Press, Washington, D.C., 1999.

National Research Council, *Making IT Better: Expanding Information Technology Research to Meet Society's Needs*, National Academy Press, Washington, D.C., 2000.

National Research Council, *Information Technology Research, Innovation, and e-Government*, National Academy Press, Washington, D.C., 2002.

OMB (Office of Management and Budget), The President's Management Agenda, 2000
   Available at: http://www.whitehouse.gov/omb/budget/fy2002/mgmt.pdf
   Last accessed on 12/07/2003.

OMB (Office of Management and Budget), E-Government Strategy, Implementing the President's Management Agenda, 2003a
   www.whitehouse.gov/omb/egov/2003egov_strat.pdf
   Accessed on 12/07/2003.

OMB (Office of Management and Budget), Implementation Guidance for the e-Government Act of 2002, 2003b
   Available at: http://www.regulations.gov/images/eGovinterpretation-mo-03-18.pdf
   Last accessed on 12/07/2003.

Organization for Economic Cooperation and Development Secretariat, Emerging trends and issues: the nature of the digital divide in learning, in *Learning to Bridge the Digital Divide*, 2000
   Available at: http://www.oecd.org/publications/e-book/9600081e.pdf
   Last accessed on 12/18/2000.

Organization for Economic Cooperation and Development, *Managing National Innovation Systems*, Organization for Economic Cooperation and Development, Paris, 1999.

Organization for Economic Cooperation and Development, *Innovative Networks: Co-operation in National Innovation Systems*, Organization for Economic Cooperation and Development, Paris, 2001a.

Organization for Economic Cooperation and Development, *Innovative People: Mobility of Skilled Personnel in National Innovation Systems*, Organization for Economic Cooperation and Development, Paris, 2001b.

Pateman, C., *Participation and Democratic Theory*, Cambridge University Press, Cambridge, U.K., 1970.

Rocheleau, B., Politics, accountability, and governmental information systems, in *Public Information Technology: Policy and Management Issues*, Garson, G.D., Ed., Idea Group, Hershey, PA, 2003, pp. 20–52.

Rogers, E.M., *Diffusion of Innovations*, 5th ed., Free Press, New York, 2003.

Schelin, S.H., E-government: an overview, in *Public Information Technology: Policy and Management Issues*, Garson, G.D., Ed., Idea Group, Hershey, PA, 2003, pp. 120–137.

Schlosberg, D. and Dryzek, J.S., Digital democracy: authentic or virtual?, *Organization & Environment*, 15, 332–335, 2002.

Seiden, P.A., Bridging the digital divide, *Reference and User Services Quarterly*, 39, 2000
Accessed via "Infotrac" Expanded Academic Index Copyright (c) 2000, Gale.

Shapiro, I., *The State of Democratic Theory*, Princeton University Press, Princeton, NJ, 2003.

Shulman, S.W., *Owning the Future*, Houghton Mifflin, Boston, 1999.

Shulman, S.W., Schlosberg, D., Zavestoski, S., and Courard-Hauri, D., Electronic rulemaking: new frontiers in public participation, *Social Science Computer Review*, 21, 162–178, 2003.

Shulman, S.W., eRulemaking: issues in current research and practice, forthcoming in the *International Journal of Public Administration*, 2005.

Skrzycki, C., *The Regulators: Anonymous Power Brokers in American Politics*, Rowman & Littlefield, Lanham, MD, 2003a.

Skrzycki, C., US opens online portal to rulemaking, *Washington Post*, Jan. 23, 2003b, p. E01.

Stoneman, P., *The Economics of Technological Diffusion*, Blackwell, Malden, MA, 2002.

Swiss, J.E., Information technology as a facilitator of results-based management in government, in *Public Information Technology: Policy and Management Issues*, Garson, G.D., Ed., Idea Group, Hershey, PA, 2003, pp. 170–189.

Symposium, *Insight on the News*, 16, 2000
   Accessed via "Infotrac" Expanded Academic Index Copyright (c) 2000, Gale.

Temin, T.T., Fed services coming to a store near you, *Government Computer News*, 16, 70, 1997.

Tesh, S.,The Internet and the grassroots, *Organization & Environment*, 15, 336–339, 2002.

Walsh, E.O., Gazala, M.E., and Ham, C., The truth about the digital divide, in *The Digital Divide: Facing a Crisis or Creating a Myth?*, Compaine, B.M., Ed., MIT Press, Cambridge, MA, 2001, pp. 279–284.

Web-Based Education Commission, The Power of the Internet for Learning: Moving from Promise to Practice, 2000
    Available at: http://www.schooltone.com/WBECReport.pdf
    Last accessed on 12/20/2000.

West, W.F., *Administrative Rulemaking: Politics and Processes*, Greenwood, Westport, CT, 1985.

Woll, P., *American Bureaucracy*, Norton, New York, 1977.

17

CITIZEN PARTICIPATION AND DIRECT DEMOCRACY THROUGH COMPUTER NETWORKING: POSSIBILITIES AND EXPERIENCE

Carmine Scavo

East Carolina University

CONTENTS

I.	Introduction	256
II.	Information, communication, and participation	257
	A. Information Acquisition	258
	B. Political Communication	262
	C. Citizen Participation	265
III.	Components of an electronic democracy	269
	A. Network Functionality	269
	B. Fair and Equitable Access	271
	C. The Spirit of Community	273
	D. Closeness vs. Deliberativeness	275
IV.	Conclusion	276
References		278

ABSTRACT

The use of computer networking technology by government has increased dramatically in the last few years. What we originally saw as promising experiments just a few years ago have now become institutionalized. Larger numbers of Americans are going online to access government information, register their views with government, share political information and opinions with other citizens, and so forth. One major question continues to nag much of the analysis of online political participation — will computer networking bring increased democracy to the U.S.? This chapter examines this question by citing the computer networking experience of various levels of government in the U.S., the work of various nongovernmental organizations, and the theoretical formulations of various analysts and researchers. The chapter concludes on a promising note — while computer networking has not remade American democracy, the growing presence of computer networking in government is having some influence in several different areas of government involvement.

I. INTRODUCTION[1]

There is no doubt that computer networking technology has created a new medium of political communication that, like other innovations in communication, can generate new relationships between the mass public, the government, and the political organizations that link the two. In the 21st century U.S., government is using computer networking to deliver information and services to the public and to obtain feedback on these services and information. Political organizations and candidates have embraced computer technology and are relying on it for the practice of politics — voter mobilization, volunteer recruitment, fundraising, and the organization of collective action. More and more citizens are going online to register their views with governments, link with like-minded fellow citizens, share political information, and participate (at least, virtually) in politics. And yet questions still loom: will computer networking bring increased democracy to the U.S., and if so, how?

This chapter looks at some of the current government and political uses of computer networking and the Internet. It subscribes to the view that public managers, who are under constant pressure to increase public trust and engagement in government, should take advantage of advanced computer networking to improve their communications with citizens and to create more opportunities for citizen participation in government. The main goal of this chapter is to shed some light on how the functioning of democracy is possibly being strengthened through computer networks, particularly at the local level. The chapter begins with a discussion of how computer technologies can enhance the function of the U.S. democratic system, with an emphasis on three areas: increasing voter information, improving the quality of political communications, and promoting a high level of citizen participation. The chapter then moves on to describe some major innovations in the use of computer networking in political and governmental affairs and examines the impacts of these innovations on public management.

The first version of this chapter appeared in 2000 and was researched and written in 1999. The mid-1990s was a time of tremendous growth of the Internet and of computer networks in the U.S., but as the decade ended, growth in the number of new Internet users was beginning to level off. Growth did not accelerate again (but at nowhere like the rates of the mid-1990s) until 2002, when it was reported that some 66% of U.S. adults were using the Internet (Greenspan, 2002). From the last decade of the 20th century to the first decade of the 21st, the Internet went from a novelty to a virtual necessity for many in the U.S. In the process, the Internet also became much more institutionalized. As the ".com bubble" of the late 1990s burst, many questionable uses of the Internet were abandoned and the mood of Internet use became more skeptical. Many users became

---

[1] I wish to thank Yuhang Shi for his coauthorship of the first version of this chapter. The current version is a thorough update and rewriting of that version.

more appreciative of security and cost issues in the use of computer networks while also seeking to discover whether virtual methods of conducting their affairs actually were superior to their more traditional alternatives. Thus, this chapter has a more questioning tone than did its first version — it is not as optimistic about the promises of computer networks in remaking American democracy. Part of that is the result of national experience with some of the techniques and processes whose potential we could only describe some 4 years ago. The chapter still concludes on a positive note. While we do not think that the U.S. has reached a point where representative democracy can be replaced with direct democracy through computer networking, and we are uncertain about whether the problems associated with security and representation can ever be completely solved, we nevertheless think that a well-designed online public information system can significantly improve democracy in the U.S.

II. INFORMATION, COMMUNICATION, AND PARTICIPATION

Like all other innovations in communications technology, the rapid growth of computer networks has rekindled our long-cherished dream for greater citizen involvement in the political process. This is because, compared with other methods we have used in communicating about politics, computer networks provide a much less expensive alternative and allow individuals to do many things that were formerly impossible to do.[2] With the technologies currently available, democratic life can be improved in at least three different areas. First, computer networks can be used to make political information more accessible and therefore help citizens become better informed about current political and policy issues. Second, computer networks can facilitate a direct dialogue between public officials and citizens. At the barest minimum, this will help make government more open, responsive, and accountable and therefore more worthy of citizens' trust. Political debate and interest can be stimulated in formerly apathetic citizens by making it less costly for them to engage in political discourse. Third, the first two items can lead to an increase in citizens' likelihood of voting and becoming involved in policymaking. In sum, computer networks have the potential to reduce the distance between citizens and their government, thus making government more responsive to the wishes of the population.

The specific technologies of the Internet and the Web discussed in this chapter include advanced website design, applications of e-commerce, e-mail, bulletin boards, web logs (blogs), etc. While it is tempting to state that increased use of these technologies by government and the public will result in a remaking of the relationship between government and the public, such a position is more of an assumption than an empirical reality. As Garson (2000) has observed, the idea that information technology (IT) contributes to making government more progressive is only one of four possible theories of the effects of IT on government operations. While this theory (the decentralization/democratization theory) is "the leading theoretical perspective on the impact of information technology on organizational life," another theoretical formulation — dystopian theory — can lead to exactly the opposite conclusions — that government (or large

---

[2] The idea that political activism is determined in part by considerations of costs — whether they be financial or nonfinancial in nature — involved in the acquisition and communication of information has a long tradition in research on political behavior. A pioneering work is *An Economic Theory of Democracy* by Downs (1957).

corporations) can use advanced IT to manipulate the public and control mass behavior (Garson, 2000: 592).

The experience of the 4 years since the original version of this chapter appeared demonstrates that the dramatic increase in the use of computer networking by political and governmental bodies has not remade democracy in the U.S. or unmade it. Instead, the technologies have become incorporated into a framework of U.S. democracy and have caused incremental changes — a position that Garson (2000) terms sociotechnical systems theory. Some of these incremental changes have been in normatively positive directions, others in normatively negative directions.

A. Information Acquisition

The bulk of political information in the modern world comes from television, radio, newspapers, and magazines. These media require varying degrees of effort or "invest-ment" on the part of those who view or listen to the source. They have all, however, been accepted to various degrees by the public and have played a critical role in the evolution of political communication — newspapers in the 19th century, radio in the 1930s, and television since the 1960s. In public opinion polls, when respondents are asked questions about the importance of various media as sources of information on political campaigns and candidates, television, on the one hand, and newspapers and magazines, on the other, vie consistently with each other for the topmost spot.[3] Radio plays somewhat of a lesser, although important, role as a source of information. However, all of these media have several constraints that have caused them to be questioned by various parts of the American public. First, these media are constrained by space and time considerations. The typical television news show only runs for 30 minutes, of which only 20 minutes actually carry news (the other 10 minutes carry advertising). Of these 20 minutes, perhaps only 5 or 10 minutes are devoted to political news. The front pages of newspapers have similar constraints and so have difficulties devoting space to in-depth coverage of candidates' policy positions. Second, there has been a great centralizing tendency in the ownership of media outlets in the U.S. over the last 10 years or so. Many local radio stations have been bought by national chains (i.e., Clear Channel Broadcasting); several of the major television networks have been taken over by large commercial enterprises (Disney, General Electric, etc.); newspapers also show some degree of centralization — one need only look at the front page of any local newspaper in the U.S. on any given day to see the predominance of Associate Press or Reuters news articles. Third, portions of the U.S. public have lost trust in the media as an unbiased source of news on politics. A 2003 *USA Today*/ CNN/Gallup poll found that only 36% of respondents trusted the media to get the facts straight, down from some 54% in 1989 (Johnson, 2003). To many, the Internet represents a much less mediated source of information. As one observer put it:

---

[3] For example, The Center for Congressional and Presidential Studies (2000) found that the percentage of respondents citing newspapers and magazines as a very important source ranged from 42 to 49% (in studies in March and October 2000) while those citing television as a very important source ranged from 46 to 47% (19 to 20% said the Internet was a very important source). The Pew Research Center (2003) found that 66% of respondents cited television as their principal source of campaign news (half of these specifically cited *local* television, and another one third cited cable television, leaving only 7% citing network television), 33% said newspapers, 13% said radio, and 7% said the Internet.

There is a feeling that the Internet is full of junk and it is, but it is also full of free-thinking and spirited debate about the issues that affect us all. Even though much of the Internet has come under the watchful eye of the dominant corporate media empires, that free-wheeling and vigorous exchange of ideas and values is ongoing; the media magnates have not figured out yet how to stifle the obvious groundswell of people who are just plain angry about watching our world sliding into a toilet and who are increasingly convinced that everyone is lying to us about it (Harris, 2003).

The typical American seeking to be well informed on political or policy matters thus faces a rather daunting task. How, for example, does one find out what is in a bill pending in the city council and how a council member stands on that bill? How does one find out provisions of analogous bills being debated before a state legislature or even before the U.S. Congress? Computer networks, with an almost limitless carrying capacity and flexibility, open up the possibility of a better-informed citizenry. An online visit to the U.S. House of Representatives website (www.house.gov), the North Carolina General Assembly website (www.ncga.state.nc.us), or the Raleigh city council's website (www.raleigh-nc.org/main/council.htm) would provide a person with detailed information on the contents of a bill and its current status in the legislative process, committee jurisdictions, hearing, weekly and annual schedules, members' backgrounds and vote records, and a great deal of additional information.

Political campaigns have made great headway in adapting computer networks as tools to provide information to those who might be interested in voting for candidates. By the 1996 presidential election, all the major presidential candidates had a web presence and they were using these sites to deliver campaign literature, recruit volunteers, and solicit donations. In the 1998 election cycle, the Internet gained even broader use. Nearly two thirds of races were fought virtually as well as physically, with challengers outnumbering incumbents and Republicans outnumbering Democrats on the Web (Martin, 1998). Across all competitive races — U.S. Senate, U.S. House of Representatives, and governorships — candidates' web presence was greater than in noncompetitive races. At least 18 candidates — 7 for governorships and 11 for U.S. Senate seats — equipped their websites with the ability to receive online credit-card donations directly from supporters (Kamarck, 1999). In the 2000 presidential elections, the campaigns of both the major party candidates — Al Gore and George W. Bush — developed sophisticated websites and made heavy use of the Internet to provide information to their supporters and to solicit donations from them. The trend continued and accelerated into the 2002 elections. E-voter (2002) reported that eight Republican U.S. Senate candidates, running in tightly contested elections, purchased banner advertisements on AOL websites. Six of the eight won their elections. Various authors have noted that the provisions of the McCain-Feingold campaign finance reform bill do not regulate candidate use of the Internet. Thus, expenditures on independent websites do not come under the bill's spending limitations, an omission that many see as causing a huge upsurge in Internet interest by political campaigns in the future (E-voter Institute, 2002; Institute for Politics, Democracy, and the Internet [IPDI], 2002). In addition, using the Web to solicit donations may result in more small donations, all of which count as "hard money." Many of the candidate websites in the 2002 elections were not, however, particularly well developed, and a number of commentators were rather critical of the lack of imagination candidates showed in their use of the Web (IPDI, 2002; Bowman, 2002).

As the 2004 presidential election season begins, the campaign of Democratic presidential contender, and former Vermont Governor, Howard Dean has made the greatest use of the Internet. Research by Schneider and Foot (2003) shows that of 39 website features coded, Dean's website[4] (www.deanforamerica.com) contains 30 such features, more than any other Democrat and also more than President Bush's re-election website (www.georgewbush.com). Dean's website features the ability to donate money and to volunteer for campaign activities; there is a Dean shop that sells campaign-related material (shirts, hats, etc.) as well as a web-log (blog) website that compiles the personal stories of Dean volunteers around the U.S. The fundraising successes of the Dean campaign have been widely noted (Bruner, 2003; Drinkard and Lawrence, 2003; Mariantes, 2003; Tull, 2003) and apparently have generated enough funding that he, after conducting an online vote of his supporters, declined federal matching funds. This made him the first Democratic presidential candidate to do so.

By the beginning of the 2004 elections, web management companies became a fixture in political campaigns. Companies specializing in developing effective websites for those running for office include TheCampaignHQ.com, votenetsolutions.com, and Convio.com.[5] Early on in its decision to develop a prominent web presence, the Dean campaign decided to contract its web resources out to Convio rather than to develop those resources in house. Convio, which describes itself as "the leading online constituent relationship management (eCRM) company for the nonprofit sector" (Tull, 2003), lists the American Society for the Prevention of Cruelty to Animals (ASPCA), the Chesapeake Bay Foundation, Mothers Against Drunk Driving (MADD), and the National Trust for Historic Preservation as some of its other clients. The Dean campaign attributes some of its record-setting success in fundraising via the Internet — $3.6 million in the second quarter and $7.4 million in the third quarter of 2003 — to the work of Convio. Tricia Enright, Communications Director for the Dean campaign, commented, "The results we're getting with Convio truly show what the Internet can mean to an organization that needs to build support in all forms, including but not limited to fundraising" (Tull, 2003).

It is clear that there is a major distinction in the use of the Web between those sources of information that are simply transposed from other media (print, broadcast, etc.) and those that are designed to take advantage of the Web's unique resources. For example, placing verbatim articles from print newspapers on the newspaper's website may increase readers' numbers and geographical dispersion, but it is difficult to argue that this increase in readership is dramatically changing U.S. democracy. On the other hand, soliciting donations for a political candidate via a secure website *has* contributed to a shift in the political fortunes of Howard Dean and, potentially, the Democratic Party. And Dean's use of the online voting features of his website to poll his supporters on the issue of accepting or declining federal matching funds is unique in electoral history. When readers

---

[4] Actually, this should be called Dean's *family* of websites since the website that solicits volunteers (action.deanforamerica.com/meet/), the young person's website (www.generationdean.com), the fundraising website (https://secure2.convio.net/dfa/site/Donation) are all isolated from the main campaign website.

[5] A constantly updated listing of Internet-based companies that develop and maintain websites for political campaigns, interest groups, and nonprofit organizations can be found at the Open Directory Project's website: dmoz.org/society/politics/Campaigns_and_Elections/Products_and_Services/ Internet/. The site now lists some 50 of these companies.

go to an online archive to retrieve newspaper and magazine articles to send via e-mail to friends, they are repeating the same activities as their parents did when they cut those articles out of the print version of the newspaper or magazine and sent them via land mail to their friends. Sending the article electronically to a large number of friends simultaneously can be done at much reduced cost than photocopying the print version of the articles and sending them out via land mail, even though such simultaneous transmission is most likely a violation of the newspaper or magazine's copyright on the original article.

Computer networks are especially good for exposing citizens to the views or information that may be truncated or ignored in other media where a few big players tend to dominate the scene. The lower costs involved with the publication of material on the Web results in longer and more pieces being published on a variety of topics — some of which might not be commercially viable in a print environment — by a large number of entrepreneurial publishers. The result has been a tremendous outpouring of information in an anarchic environment, allowing the knowledgeable user to be able to gather virtually all shades of opinion (or to tailor the opinions gathered to be in exact agreement with his or her own) but providing a perplexing series of obstacles to the inexperienced user or the user looking for a single definitive source. One need only do a search in any major search engine (Google, Yahoo!, Metacrawler, Dogpile, etc.) on a simple concept to see the wide variety (and lack of consensus) that the Web contains on the topic in question. Differentiating between the mainstream sources and the fringe, between the credible and incredible sources, between the straightforward and satire sites, etc. can be difficult for the novice and has resulted in a number of embarrassing and humorous episodes.

The experienced user or the user who has been directed by online or off-line instructions can identify a variety of useful policy or political websites that provide a treasure trove of information:

■ Project Vote Smart, a website maintained by volunteers since 1990 (www.vote-smart.org), disseminates information about political candidates via the Web. Project Vote Smart's nonprofit, nonpartisan site allows a visitor to view the facts on tens of thousands of incumbents and challengers at the federal and state levels. Information on the site is organized around five major themes: backgrounds, issue positions, voting records, campaign finances, and performance evaluations. The site also tracks congressional legislative actions and a diversity of perspectives on various ballot issues. As the site owners claim, the project is intended to offer a comprehensive information service that would enable citizens to monitor and supervise elected officials and to compare their campaign promises with their actual job performance once in office.

■ The American Enterprise Institute (AEI) provides policy analysis from a somewhat conservative perspective. The AEI website (www.aei.org) maintains an archive of policy-relevant literature on recent public policy issues and also lists AEI fellows, including such prominent former government officials as Robert Bork (Federal Court judge nominated by President George H. W. Bush to the U.S. Supreme Court), Newt Gingrich (former Speaker of the U.S. House of Representatives), Lynn Cheney (former Chair of the National Endowment for the Humanities and wife of the Vice President of the U.S.), and Jeanne Kirkpatrick (former U.S. Ambassador to the United Nations). By clicking on the individual fellow's icon, the user can send the fellow an e-mail and possibly engage in a policy discussion with that fellow.

■ The Center for Responsive Politics maintains the website www.opensecrets.org, which tracks campaign contributions to political candidates. Financial reports filed with the Federal Elections Commission (FEC) by announced presidential candidates are listed on the site virtually as soon as they are filed by the campaign. Actions by the FEC are also tracked, as are court cases and analyses of congressional votes. (One recent analysis found that vote on the November 2003 Medicare reform bill moving through Congress was tracking with the amount of contributions representatives had received from political action committees associated with health maintenance organizations, health insurers, and pharmaceutical companies. Representatives voting in favor of the bill received approximately twice the amount of funding from these lobby groups as did those voting against the legislation.) The names of individual donors to political campaigns and the amount of money they gave to the campaign can be listed back to 1990. And the site maintains the latest information on legislation regulating campaign finance.

■ The California Voter Foundation (www.calvoter.org) describes itself as a "nonprofit, non-partisan organization promoting and applying the responsible use of technology to improve the democratic process." The website provides information on issues associated with technology and voting (security, online archiving of candidate information, etc.). The California Voter Foundation states its mission:
    Information is power, and improving access to information helps level the playing field between those who have money and those who don't. Exposing campaign contributions on the Internet — what CVF calls 'digital sunlight' — also helps reduce the influence of money by making its role in politics more transparent. Through our work on the Internet, CVF is helping to shape a political culture that is more responsive, accountable and accessible to everyone (California Voter Foundation, 2003).

Other websites with policy information include those of the Center for Public Integrity (www.publicintegrity.org), the Economic Policy Institute (http://epinet.org), and many others.[6]

B. Political Communication

Before the advent of computer-mediated political communication, a citizen could register his or her opinions with the government and communicate with fellow citizens through personal visits, mail, or by telephone. But each of these one-to-one means of communication has costs associated with them — costs that often have a deterrent effect on many potential users. U.S. public officials often complain about how difficult it is for them to ascertain how "average citizens" feel about various issues and how they fear that much of the communication they receive from their constituents is stimulated by interest groups, who represent organized or resource-rich interests much better than they do disorganized or resource-poor interests and who are attempting to replace one-to-one communications with many-to-one communications. To compensate for the bias that is apparent in interest group communications, officials often rely on media reports or the work of pollsters to provide them with information from the "silent majority." But journalists are not account-

---

[6] A full listing of policy "think tanks," their areas of expertise, and their websites can be found at the website of the University of Michigan library — http://www.lib.umich.edu/govdocs/psthink.html.

able to anyone except their employers and can therefore substitute their own professional or personal tastes (or those of their employers) for what the public actually thinks and feels. Pollsters are in a similar situation. Also, the number of polls being conducted in the U.S. today, along with the different findings one can generate in polls as a result of differing methodologies, question wordings, etc. make it difficult for a public official to "govern by the polls," although many officials have recently been accused of attempting to do so.

In the current age, one-to-one communication has added e-mail and text messaging to this mix, making direct communication easier and less costly than it was. E-mail is perhaps the most familiar tool one can use for one-to-one correspondence between government and citizens and among citizens. In the late 1990s, the Clinton administration made it extremely easy for average citizens to send e-mails to the president. All that was necessary was for an e-mail user to send a message to president@whitehouse.gov. Messages were read by one of a large number of volunteers, whose job it was to read incoming e-mail and respond to the mail. Messages were routed to officials in the White House, as volunteers apparently saw fit, and at least some e-mails received official responses. A system like this can work properly, however, only if the incoming e-mails do not reach the point of overloading the system's capacity — electronic or human. By the first few years of the Bush administration, the number of e-mails being received by the White House was reaching 15,000 per day (Markoff, 2003) and, for a variety of reasons, the White House decided to reconfigure how e-mails reach the president. In its current form, begun in the summer of 2003, those who send e-mails to the president are sent to a series of web pages where they must input additional information before the message actually goes to a human reader. While it is still possible to send an e-mail directly, as it was earlier, the sender may only receive an automated response (Markoff, 2003).

For one-to-many communications, both mailing lists and bulletin boards can be used to exchange information and ideas. Abramson et al. (1988) describes an early use of a bulletin board by Michigan State Senator William Sederburg. In 1985, over 4000 people accessed the senator's two bulletin boards and left some 12,000 messages. One needs to remember that these messages were not responses to questions in a public opinion poll but were unsolicited opinions organized around two broad topics — politics and higher education. In the early 2000s, bulletin boards have become widely used in a variety of ways — most online versions of newspapers, for example, have several bulletin boards where readers can discuss sports, current events, local politics, and many other topics. And the use of mailing lists has become even more widespread. In a more innocent time, mailing lists were developed by users by either identifying like-minded fellow e-mail users or by requesting users to register for the mailing list, whereas now mailing lists can be developed by programming computers to look for active e-mail addresses. Spammers can program their computers to search the Web, looking for websites, chat rooms, or other sites, where individuals may have entered their e-mail addresses. It is then a simple task to copy the e-mail address to a database and to use it to develop mailing lists. Spammers have also devised programs to send e-mail "probes" (blank messages that test whether an e-mail address is active or not) to all possible variations of popular e-mail domains. So a probe can be sent to all likely combinations of e-mail addresses at a popular domain — from AAA@earthlink.net to ZZZ@earthlink.net, for example. The addresses of the e-mails that are actually delivered are catalogued and the addresses of those that are not delivered are simply discarded. Since e-mail is free for most users, this process is inherently cost effective, especially since the list of active e-mail addresses can be sold to other spammers who use them to send broadcast advertising for a variety of their products and services. In 2002, the first use of spam in a political campaign appeared. California's Secretary of State Bill Jones, running for the Republican nomination for governor, sent out more than a million e-mail pleas for votes and donations, spurring protests from a large number of Californian Internet users (Nissenbaum, 2002).

One promising use of many-to-many communications is exemplified by the Minnesota e-Democracy project (www.e-democracy.org). Minnesota e-democracy describes itself as "a non-profit, non-partisan citizen-based project, whose mission is to improve participation in democracy in Minnesota through the use of information networks." It hosts a number of online-managed[7] listings where members can discuss current political issues. E-mail format was chosen by the organizers over more anarchic discussion forum formats for a variety of reasons — e-mail is easy to use and it is the most popular of all online tools. But more than this, e-mail also does not require participants to "join" a forum each time they go online and e-mail also has its own evolving rules of etiquette. The self-developed rules of Minnesota e-Democracy call for a 6-month suspension from the forum for a breach of a rule after one warning. "However, members are encouraged to take responsibility for guiding each other ... via private e-mail, as to what is deemed suitable posting content and style" (Dahlberg, 2001: 5).

The Minnesota e-Democracy website displays a listing of e-mail discussion lists — oriented toward statewide Minnesota issues and politics, local Minnesota issues and politics, Iowa issues and politics, U.S. elections, other issues. A user can register for any of the lists he or she wishes and then begin receiving and sending e-mail within a short period of time. Recent topics discussed on the state political list include gay marriage, the possibility of electronic voting, and the death penalty in Minnesota.

The topical lists have somewhere between 100 and 500 registered members and the number of postings each day is rather large. However, participation is not evenly distributed. In 1999, for example, 28 of the 276 Minnesota Politics Discuss (MPD) participants posted over 75% of all messages (posting over 50 times each). Only about 50% or 276 of approximately 450 subscribers ... posted at all" (Dahlberg, 2001: 11). To increase the number of participants and to keep the list from being monopolized by a small number of participants, Minnesota e-Democracy instituted a two-message-per-day rule, which has apparently increased the number of participating users. The list is also not representative of the demographic structure of the state of Minnesota; in a summer of 1998 analysis of 122 participants' postings, 61% were male, 15% were female, and 24% were unidentifiable. Other analyses showed that over 70% of all postings were from males. Participants also tend to have above-average educational backgrounds and ethnic minorities tend to be poorly represented (Dahlberg, 2001).

Another area for the use of computer networks is grassroots mobilization and organization. Through mailing lists and bulletin boards, one can find hundreds or thousands of like-minded fellow citizens in or outside a community, who one may never meet personally. This has made it more possible for citizens to form spontaneous groups of wide ideological hues and to sustain, expand, and organize political actions to influence public policies. The recent protests against globalization, which occur at nearly every meeting of the World Trade Organization or other international economic or financial

---

[7] Online lists can be moderated — in which the list manager receives and approves all posting before they are put on the list; managed — in which the manager only has "housekeeping" functions (keeping the list on topic, warning about inflammatory postings, etc.); or unmoderated, in which all postings are sent directly to the list without any intervening authority.

groups, were organized through e-mail lists and bulletin boards. One need only access the website www.protest.net to find a calendar listing almost every international meeting of any potential target group, and the protests that are planned to take place at the meeting of that group. The new phenomenon of the "flash mob" — people gathering at a given location to engage in some purpose that is revealed when they arrive, and then disappearing quickly — is almost wholly an Internet-inspired creation. E-mail is used to distribute the instructions as to where to gather and as to whom to look for further instructions.[8] Whether flash mobs are protests or performance art cannot currently be ascertained, but the phenomenon is heavily Internet oriented.

C. Citizen Participation

Two hundred years ago, the framers of the U.S. Constitution designed a republican form of government. Since then numerous changes have been made in an attempt to expand the scope of political participation. The most prominent of these are the expansion of the universe of eligible voters to, first, men who did not own property, and later to former slaves, women, and 18-year olds. In most states, the choice of who is listed on an election ballot is determined in a primary election, a device designed to increase citizen participation. In New England, the tradition of the town meeting exists to the current day. Issues of importance to the community are decided in meetings of all adults who care to take part. In some areas of New England, local government budgets are established in a similar way. In other parts of the U.S., citywide or statewide elections determine tax rates, term limits, and a variety of policy issues. Recall elections can be used to turn unpopular officeholders out and replace them with challengers, as Governor Gray Davis of California learned to his dismay in October 2003 when he was voted out of office in a recall election and replaced by Arnold Schwarzenegger.

Whether we are interested in participating in elections, town hall meetings, or referenda, participation has dropped over the last 50 years or so. Only about half the eligible voters cast their ballots in presidential elections and only some 39% of eligible voters bothered to vote in the 2002 midterm elections. Local elections draw far fewer voters, with percentages of eligible voters dropping into the twenties or even teens in city council, county commission, judicial, and other races. The precise reasons for such abysmal voter turnout in the U.S. are still subject to debate but one widely recognized factor is voter registration. Voter registration became increasingly simple in every state in the U.S. over the course of the 20th century, but the fact that voters must register (at least) 30 days before an election is a deterrence to their probability of voting. Brians and Grofman (2001) show that allowing election day registration would result in approximately a seven-percentage-point increase in voter turnout in a typical U.S. state. Registration is a barrier to voting for two reasons: first, registration requires one to expend some resources over and above the resources expended in voting. In many states, one must travel to a specific location to register (and also later to vote). Some people need to leave work or school. Second, requiring voters to register (typically) 30 days before an election forces them to do so at a time that they might not be particularly interested in the election campaign or, for some campaigns, at a time when the campaign has not yet even

---

[8] In one recent flash mob event in New York, e-mailed instruction told participants to look for people carrying a copy of the *New York Review of Books*. These people distributed printed instructions as to what the mob was to do next (Ryan, 2003).

begun. While the Motor Voter Registration Act eased the difficulties of registering some-what, registration still continues to be a substantial barrier to voting.

Recently, several states and localities have experimented with alternative voting techniques in order to redress dropping voter participation rates. In North Carolina, for example, "no excuse" absentee balloting has been allowed for the last few election cycles. This allows voters to request, either by mail or in person, an absentee ballot up to several weeks before the election. If the ballot is requested in person, it can be completed and submitted at the time it is requested. Texas uses a similar system that allows voters to cast their ballots up to 17 days before an election. Beginning in 1998, Oregon began experimenting with mail-in ballots. Ballots are mailed to eligible voters some 3 weeks before election day and the ballots can either be mailed in or returned in person to the Board of Elections. Washington has followed Oregon's example and the number of people in that state receiving their ballots through the mail for every election may soon become a majority (Elliot, 2001). Traditional voting on election day is, of course, allowed in all of these states. Vote-by-telephone experiments have been tried in a variety of Canadian municipal elections but have not been widely used in the U.S.

Computer networks can do better than this. A wide variety of businesses have equipped their websites with a function that allows a customer to register with a merchant and send feedback to the manufacturer of a product. All the major news organizations use the Web to poll the public on a wide variety of issues. While governments have generally lagged behind business in the adoption of web technology, several recent cases provide some encourage-ment. Voter registration information is available online in a number of states. In some states (South Carolina, for example) voters can download a registration form from the state website. Beyond this, several states have begun to experiment with online voting. For example, in the 2000 presidential primary season, the Arizona Democratic Party held its statewide presidential primary partially online. Voters could vote from home using a secure website, they could go to a large number of computer kiosks that took the place of precinct voting places, or they could cast their votes either by telephone or in more traditional ways (some 42% voted online). While there were several court challenges to this election (notably by the Voter Integrity Project), the results were certified by the State Board of Elections. As described by Booker et al. (2000), "voting online in this primary was anything but a simple task, and certainly no less costly than voting in person." Voters needed to apply for an online ballot some 6 weeks before election day, obtain a personal identification number (PIN), read an online statement by the Chair of the Arizona Democratic Party, agree with the voting statement, enter the PIN, enter the voter's e-mail address, respond to several questions (to confirm the voter's identity), verify the voter's address, and then vote. A successful vote resulted in the appearance of a certificate screen, which the voter could print out and save as a souvenir. Even though the process of voting was complicated, some 50% of those eligible to vote in this primary election did so, a much higher turnout rate than that in other primary elections in 2000.[9]

The 2000 U.S. presidential election, culminating with George Bush's razor-thin victory in Florida — amidst claims of lost ballots, wrongly designed ballots, and the problems

---

[9] It is somewhat difficult to disentangle the increase in voter turnout owing to use of the Internet from the increase in voter turnout as a result of the other reforms the Arizona Democratic Party instituted in this primary election. While "[t]he scheme as a whole increased significantly the convenience of voting for those with ready access to the Internet and familiarity with its use …," it also "somewhat, but not as greatly, increased the convenience of voting by traditional means when compared with the 1996 Arizona Democratic presidential primary" (Pershing, 2001: 1174).

associated with punch card voting — brought attention once again to the technology of voting in the U.S. Beginning in 2001, the U.S. Congress and several states examined the possibility of moving toward online voting, completely replacing the hodge-podge of voting techniques (paper ballots, lever-operated voting machines, punch card ballots, optical scanning devices, etc.). Several major issues arise in the discussion of online voting. First are issues related to security — both ballot security and verification that only registered voters are voting and that each voter casts only one vote. Ballot security involves the possibility of a stolen election — that somehow a corrupt candidate or political party can change the votes stored electronically — the online analogue of stuffing the ballot box. More sinister than this is the possibility that computer hackers can make their way into the system to disrupt the election, either through a denial of service type attack that would shut down the server that was collecting votes or through the introduction of a computer virus or Trojan horse into the election software system. Even worse than this is the scenario painted by the Voter Integrity Project in its suit against the Arizona Democratic Party's 2000 online presidential primary. The Voter Integrity Project described the possibility that a foreign terrorist group could alter the results of an election in the U.S. in such a way that the alteration would be undetectable or that the administration of the election could fall into the hands of a foreign-owned company (Burke, 2000).

A second set of issues concerns access to the Internet. There is disagreement on the issue of whether online voting might exacerbate the problem of differential voting rates for wealthier and poorer individuals. While Alvarez and Nagler (2001: 1152) conclude, "Internet voting is likely to exacerbate the current problem of class-bias in American elections if it is introduced any time in the near future," Morris (2001: 1051) responds, "The heralded digital divide, in which minorities and poor people are shut out of participation over the Internet will fade into the past as soon as Internet access is divorced from personal computers ... . When the average family can access the Internet through their TV sets, even the poorest communities will enjoy a very high level of Internet participation." While "the digital divide" (differential Internet usage by some classes as compared with others) has declined in recent years, there are still some differences in Internet usage between some groups of Americans and others. This is particularly the case when we compare urban, suburban, and rural areas. Large areas of rural America currently do not have ready access to the Internet except by long-distance telephone connections to remote Internet service providers (ISPs), or satellite connections.

At least two major studies of the possibility of online voting took place in the past few years — one by the California Internet Voting Task Force (2000) and the second by the Internet Policy Institute (IPI, 2001). Both delivered massive reports on the feasibility of moving toward Internet-based voting.

The California task force studied security and access issues surrounding Internet voting and also examined the potential implementation of Internet voting in that state. They concluded:

> [I]t is technologically possible to utilize the Internet to develop an additional method of voting that would be at least as secure from vote-tampering as the current absentee ballot process in California. At this time, it would not be legally, practically, or fiscally feasible to develop a comprehensive remote Internet voting system that would completely replace the current paper process used

for voter registration, voting, and the collection of initiative, referendum, and recall petition signatures (California Internet Voting Task Force, 2000: 1).

In order to implement even a limited form of Internet voting, however, election officials would need the investment of significant fiscal and human resources. In the time that a transition from paper ballots (or their analogues) to an Internet voting system will occur, county election officials would be required to ensure the security of both systems of voting, at least doubling the amount of effort now required. New security routines would need to be developed to ensure that individual votes were secure from tampering or invasions of privacy, that the voting database was not altered, and that the voting system was not infected by computer viruses or worms. One can only imagine the target that a statewide or national election would present to a talented, mischievous computer hacker. And questions concerning equal access to the system would also need to be answered.[10]

IPI (2001) arrived at similar conclusions concerning the security, access, and implementation of Internet voting on a national scale. If anything, IPI took an even more incremental approach to the topic than did the California task force. IPI looked first at Internet voting at current polling places, then at Internet voting at kiosks, and finally at home- or office-based Internet voting. They found that, "Poll site Internet voting systems offer some benefits and could be responsibly fielded within the next several election cycles .... [However] remote Internet voting systems pose significant risk to the integrity of the voting process, and should not be fielded for use in public elections until substantial technical and social science issues are addressed" (IPI, 2001: 2).

One of the questions that according to IPI needed further research is the actual benefits Internet voting might yield, in particular, its effect on turnout. Internet voting promises greater convenience to the voter, lowering the costs of voting as compared with traditional ways, and thus making it somewhat more rational to vote. However, previous research has shown that, "information, motivation, and mobilization are much more powerful forces shaping voter turnout than convenience" (IPI, 2001: 24). Convenience may not be the only factor; in fact, the complexity of this relationship can best be demonstrated by citing the paragraph verbatim from the IPI report:

> A number of possibilities associated with the Internet's impacts on voting have been advanced. One possibility is that the convenience, attraction, and familiarity of the Internet, especially among young voters, would lead to a sustained increase in turnout. Another possibility is that Internet voting may initially attract voters due to the popularity of the medium and the publicity surrounding the election. However, this affinity may diminish over time if the motivation for voting is primarily novelty. Another possibility is that Internet voting could actually depress voter participation in the long run if it is perceived to undermine the legitimacy of the balloting process or feeling of civic participation ... . It is also possible that remote Internet voting would be such a

---

[10] The federal Voting Rights Act of 1965 assures equal access to the polls for all U.S. citizens and lays out special precautions that need to be addressed so that the voting rights of historically underrepresented minorities are not adversely affected by changes in the procedures used in voting. A system of Internet-based voting might discriminate against minority or rural voters (if implemented at the current time) or to others who do not own a personal computer *unless* such a system also included increased avenues for non-Internet-based voting (as did the 2000 Arizona Democratic Party primary election). See Pershing (2001).

significant departure from previous forms of voting that a new body of research on what motivates voters will be needed (IPI, 2001: 24–25).

Perhaps the simplest form of Internet-based voting is an electronic variation of absentee balloting (Elliott, 2001). Currently, when an individual casts an absentee ballot by mail, the voter completes a paper ballot and puts this into some sort of security envelope that has no identifying characters on it. This security envelope is either handed directly to an election official or put into another mailing envelope that has a space for the voter's signature, and sent via U.S. mail to the elections office. When the envelope is received, the voter's signature is checked, the outside envelope discarded, the inside envelope opened, and the vote counted. E-mail could be used as an electronic analogue to this process. The ballot could be sent to the individual through a secure e-mail message. The voter could then either print out the ballot and return the hard copy to the elections office or fill out the online ballot, save it, and send it back as a file attachment. The e-mail to which the ballot is attached would, of course, have identifying characteristics on it but the file attachment (the ballot) would not. Procedures would need to be developed so that the election official who stripped the attachment off the e-mail would not be able to link the two and thus determine for whom the voter had actually voted. This could be done either through the use of software or through the use of a second file attachment so that the ballot is actually an anonymous file attached to an anonymous file that is attached to an e-mail message.

III. COMPONENTS OF AN ELECTRONIC DEMOCRACY

With their distinct superiority in transmission capability, flexibility, interactivity, and low cost, computer networks have found niches in government and have thus made government more open and accessible. The predictions that progress in telecommunications could eventually turn the U.S. representative system into a direct democracy, made by futurist John Naisbitt in his book *Megatrends*, seem somewhat quaint from our perspective of an age in which the first computer networks to put government online have already been implemented. But a baby's crawling stage also seems quaint after that baby has taken his or her first steps. By focusing on this quaintness, we are, however, focusing on past performance rather than future promise and ignoring the possibility that those first steps could lead to long-distance hiking, climbing ladders, or running the marathon.

When a government puts itself online to encourage more political involvement, public managers face a series of challenges. Needless to say, they must learn many new skills to become technically more competent. They may also have to adapt themselves to a new environment in which they may not feel as comfortable as they did in the past. This is because the openness emanating from the use of computer networks may subject them to more public scrutiny and pressure. The following sections address some major issues involved in designing and operating an electronic democracy and the implications these have for public managers using the lessons gleaned from the descriptions in the sections above.

A. Network Functionality

The barest minimum form of a public information system that might serve as a reliable source for public information and an effective means for political communication and participation would comprise five network functions, each having a unique application. Such a local government system is sketched in Table 17.1. The most important element in

Table 17.1 Application Components of an Online Public Information System

Function	Application	Examples of Use
Read-only web pages	Information dissemination	Information on policies and operation of government accessible by the general public; links to other relevant information on the Internet
E-mail or web form	Communication	Communication with key officials
Mailing list	Communication and information dissemination	Discussion groups accessible by subscribed citizens; information on policies and operation of government disseminated to target groups of citizens
Bulletin board	Communication	Discussion groups accessible by the general public
Interactive web page	Citizen participation	Referendum issues; name and background of candidates and their positions on issues; election time and places; voter registration; balloting; links to other relevant information on the Internet

this system is the Web, which provides the means for information dissemination, citizen–government communication, and citizen participation. E-mail is for one-to-one communication between citizens and public managers. Mailing lists and bulletin boards serve as public forums where citizens and public managers can come together to discuss local issues. The building of such a system has not been easy; the most common constraint is the lack of financial resources and technical expertise (Scavo and Shi, 1999). A second roadblock has been the lack of a sound infrastructure for fast transmission of digital data in some communities, but this has been relegated to fewer and fewer communities in the last 5 years. Even though federal funds in the 1990s were committed to assisting communities eager to get wired and to lowering the costs of telecommunications access, local governments still needed to assemble resources to pay their share of the development efforts. Public managers were thus in the position of attempting to build a consensus to commit more community resources to the effort if an online public information system was indeed to be built.

In addition to the need to find necessary resources and expertise, public managers must make several other decisions. The first concerns what information is to be posted on the system. This is a difficult question and will certainly vary from case to case. We suggest two common rules. First, all the information that can be made public and that is of importance to the public should be put online, as far as security concerns will allow.[11] Information on the agency's services; programs; policies or regulations, names, telephone numbers, and e-mail addresses of its key personnel; job opportunities; important

---

[11] The original version of this chapter was more sanguine about the openness of computer networks. The September 11 terrorist attacks on the U.S. and the resulting war on terrorism have changed our thinking on this and we now put a higher premium on security considerations. One can see this evolution by comparing Scavo and Shi (1999) with Scavo (2003).

events associated with the organization; and so forth can be made online. As a tool of citizen participation, a public information system should also provide information on elections, candidates, balloting issues, and links to other Internet sites that provide different views on a particular policy matter.

The second decision concerns the organization of information. There is a temptation to use an online public information system as a broadcasting medium, where information is delivered in an unorganized manner. When a user comes to visit the system, he or she seeks something special. For this reason, the information provided on the system must be organized and archived in a way that the information can be retrieved through some structured menu or search mechanism. Otherwise, anybody can be overwhelmed by an overabundance of information. An informative public information system depends on a well-designed and well-kept database. The same rule can be applied to bulletin boards, where conversations or exchanges should be separated along topic lines.

The third decision concerns network security — a growing concern in the 21st century. Because the technologies used in computer networks are not perfect, there is a widespread concern about the integrity of the political process once the government moves online. Specifically, for an online public information system, there are several aspects to the goal of security. First, the system must be able to protect itself from hackers who may break into the system, steal confidential data, or seek to slow down or paralyze the system. Second, the system must be able to detect viruses or worms that might alter or destroy the information posted on the system or disable or destroy the system itself. Third, the system must be able to maintain the confidentiality of communications between citizens and government officials. Fourth, the system must be able to verify the identity of a citizen when he or she uses it to register to vote or to cast a ballot. And finally, the transmission from and to the system must be shielded from interception or eavesdropping. Great progress has been made toward achieving these goals and yet their final accomplishment has not yet been attained. What is most important is that public managers should not leave the job of security to technicians alone. Technicians often want to design a system that is technically secure but can be fooled in simple "human" ways — one person using another's personal identification number, for example. After all, the most securely locked door can be opened by a talented locksmith, but it would require far more expertise to fool an alert human guard stationed at the same door. One need only recall the levels of security designed into the 2000 Arizona Democratic primary, some of which were technical in nature (e.g., encryption of online submitted ballots) while others were more "human" in nature (e.g., properly answering a series of personal questions).

B. Fair and Equitable Access

Electronic democracy must be universally accessible, something that is not yet attainable even in the most technologically advanced countries on Earth. Internet access in the U.S. still tends to be unequally distributed, although the severity of that inequality has been dropping in recent years. Minorities, people living in rural areas, low-income individuals, and people with disabilities still have less access to personal computers and the Internet than do whites, suburbanites, and wealthier individuals. Across these groups, people with disabilities (21.6%), African Americans (23.5%), and Hispanics (23.6%) show the greatest disparities in comparison with the general population (42.1%) of U.S. Internet users (NTIA, 2000). The gap between male and female use of the Internet had largely disappeared by 2000, although the NTIA study could not identify the degree of similarity in the pattern of Internet usage — what websites people access, etc. — for males and females.

While the digital divide was a very popular topic for research in the late 1990s, its usefulness as a description of current domestic Internet usage has recently been challenged by empirical reports like that noted above and by analysts of Internet trends. For example, Warschauer (2003: 2) is critical of the term, itself. "[T]he simple binary description of a divide fails to do justice to the complex reality of various people's differing access and usage of digital technology." Later, Warschauer notes that the key is not simply accessibility to computers and the Internet as many have focused on, but actual use of them, a wholly different matter:

> The key issue is not unequal access to computers but rather the unequal ways that computers are used. Out studies note that kindergarten through 12th grade students who enjoy a high socioeconomic status more frequently use computers for experimentation, research and critical inquiry, whereas poor students engage in less challenging drills and exercises that do not take full advantage of computer technology. In mathematics and English classes, where drills are common, poor students actually have more access to computers than do more affluent ones. Only in science classes, which rely on experiment and simulations, do wealthy students use computers more. Once again, the 'digital divide' framework that focuses on access issues alone fails to face these broader issues in technology use and learning (Warschauer, 2003: 7).

From the perspective of government, the focus on access is barrier enough. Local governments in particular have been dealing with Internet access issues since the mid-1980s and various communities have tried to reduce barriers to access. Some are attempting to tackle the problem of differential use in addition to differential access. One local government — Oakland County, Michigan — can serve as an example. Oakland County began implementation of its own fiber optics network — OAKNet — in 2002. OAKNet connects all local government agencies with county agencies and the county's IT building. Local governments — cities, villages, townships — can connect to the network at minimal cost, reducing their own expenditure of resources in developing stand-alone sites while increasing network functionality and coordination. The designers of the Oakland County system are committed to reducing the traditional social and economic barriers to access and to reducing other barriers — "varying literacy levels, relevant online content, and institutional constraints on computer access and use" (Oakland County, 2002).

It is clear that the easy questions of access have almost been answered through the lowered costs and increased availability of technology along with the delinking of Internet usage from personal computers. The decline in the price of personal computers and Internet connections has put both in the reach of lower-income families. The emphasis that schools are putting on Internet usage and computer literacy has increased the necessity to have Internet connections at home for all families with children. For those families who cannot have such connections, public libraries, Internet cafes, public kiosks, etc. all provide free or low-cost Internet usage. The Internet becoming independent of the personal computer is no longer simply a promise; Internet connections via television are possible in many areas, and individuals around the country access e-mail and other Internet services via personal digital assistants (PDAs) or cellular telephones.

And various software programs and hardware components are being engineered to allow individuals using computers to interact with those who do not have computer access.[12] So the issues associated with differential access because of socioeconomic status are on the verge of being solved. But the more difficult access questions — how the Internet is actually used by different socioeconomic groups; how hardware can be made accessible to the disabled; how illiterate people can attain a level of literacy necessary to make use of the Internet, differences between relatively slow dial-up access, and quicker broadband access, etc. — are far from being solved. Some, in fact, are only beginning to be addressed.

To investigate some of these issues, Brown University's Center for Public Policy has conducted a survey of government websites each year since 2000. Its most recent report has been published as West (2003). This report shows that while both federal and state government websites have improved their accessibility to the disabled, to those with low literacy, and to those who speak foreign languages over the last 4 years, there is still great room for improvement. For example, at a time when the typical American is reading at the 8th-grade level, only 12% of the 1663 state and federal government websites examined read at this level or below, as measured by the Fleisch-Kincaid test used by the U.S. Department of Defense as a rest of readability. The vast majority of sites (67%) read at the 12th-grade level. Even agencies that were potentially geared toward users with low levels of education (corrections, for example) did not have websites that were readable by people with less than a 12th-grade education. Disability access was measured using the "Bobby" test (www.bobby.watchfire.com). Each website was evaluated against Priority Level one standards developed by the World Wide Web Consortium (W3C) standard (less strict) and the legal requirements of Section 508 of the U.S. Rehabilitation Act of 1973 (more strict). In 2003, some 47% of federal government websites passed the W3C standard while 22% passed the 508 standard. Some 33% of state government websites passed the W3C standard and 24% passed the 508 standard. As for foreign language access to websites, some 13% of all state and federal websites made some accommodation for non-English speakers (from providing a text translation to free translation software). This was up from some 4% in 2000. States varied tremendously on this standard from a high of 55% of official state websites in Texas down to 0% in Alaska, Hawaii, Montana, and West Virginia (West, 2003).

C. The Spirit of Community

In its most rudimentary form, the phrase "spirit of community" means the degree to which members of a community are concerned about one another, even though they differ in every conceivable way, and the degree to which they respect different opinions. In certain ways, the way we use this phrase compares with Putnam's (2000) use of the phrase "social capital." This may be an attitude or it may be an affection, but it is clear that people sharing a strong spirit of community will have more social interaction and mutual understanding, two critical conditions for any democracy to work well. This concept becomes relevant here because it is unclear how computer networks interact with the spirit of community. It is clear, from the case of Minnesota e-Democracy cited above, that

---

[12] For example, software that allows computers to send faxes directly to fax machines has been available for many years. Recently, however several vendors have introduced the reverse — fax machines that will scan pages and send the file as an e-mail to a recipient.

the spirit of community exists in the e-mail lists in that venue. Is this because the computer interaction has heightened participants' feelings of the spirit of community? Is it because the spirit of community in Minnesota — a state that political culture theorists would call an exemplar of moralistic political culture — preexisted the establishment of Minnesota e-Democracy and so an experiment of this type would show less success elsewhere? Or has the Minnesota e-Democracy experiment actually eroded a preexisting high sense of the spirit of community? These are questions that are unanswerable at the current time. What we can say about these questions is that there is no guarantee that computer networks will increase the spirit of community and that there is at least the possibility that computer networks may actually erode that spirit (Levine, 2002). When people go online, they have certain predispositions or needs — not everybody is interested in politics or views opposing their own. So while computer networks have done a wonderful job in bringing together a wealth of information and a wide range of perspectives, many people surfing the Internet seek to interact only with those who share their own passions, ideologies, or points of view (Corrado and Firestone, 1996; Hill and Hughes, 1998). The danger in this is the deterioration in concurrence across different sections of a community. As Thompson (1998) writes, "If citizens communicate with the like-minded more than before, what their minds like is more circumscribed than before."

Networks may also encourage incivility in political discourse. Internet communications tend to be more anonymous than face-to-face communications (Bellamy and Hanewicz, 2001; Levine, 2002) and this can lead to inattention to social norms in Internet interactions. In Santa Monica, California, a small group of 30 to 40 heavy Internet users dominated the city's public information system and engaged in personal attacks and abusive behavior toward other users. In response to this, usage of the system declined (Docter and Dutton, 1998). And yet the practise of policing Internet conversation raises serious First Amendment questions and also violates the spirit of the Internet as an anarchic environment. It is for this reason that systemwide informal norms such as those developed in the Minnesota e-Democracy project become so important. Rather than relying on external enforcement to ensure good behavior, the users themselves police the system, encouraging good behavior and disapproving of bad behavior. But, again, this raises questions about whether this form of enforcement would work anyplace else than in the moralistic political culture of Minnesota. As Cain (2001: 1005) writes, "Whether the Internet eventually serves either democratic or anti-democratic purposes will depend on the institutions and norms that govern and protect Internet users and communities."

For public managers, regulation — whether external or internal — is only part of the solution. A more critical challenge is how to promote the spirit of community in their jurisdictions as electronic democracy begins to spread. For the technologies to perform positively, public managers may have to find ways to encourage more citizens to socialize with one another, to better understand one another, and to engage in a broader, more informed dialogue in a constructive manner. This task is more difficult than it appears, for such an effort will require public managers to assume the role of civic leaders, which is hardly compatible with the typical job description for their profession and the preoccupation with economic and organizational efficiency in their training. Yet, since we cannot find a local government agency that is willing to fund the position of civic leader, public managers may have to be convinced to expand or redefine their roles.

D. Closeness vs. Deliberativeness

Computer networks bring people closer to government, thus giving them more influence on public policymaking. The irony is that this closeness may also undermine the quality of decisions and pose threats to civil liberties. In electronic democracy, public managers may find more confusing voices in the public forums, less time for genuine and thoughtful deliberation in the decision-making process, and more pressure to respond to instantaneous public sentiment. Factions may find it easier to form a dominant coalition, for now they have fewer logistical difficulties in coalition making (Thompson, 1998). Presumably, all these changes may lead to more hasty decisions and less protection of minority interests, a scenario that not only scared the framers of the U.S. Constitution 200 years ago but also currently prompts many objections to electronic democracy.

The instantaneous nature of communications linked together via computer networks can lead to both good and ill. One need only remember the flood of rumors that filled the Internet in the immediate aftermath of the terrorist attacks on the U.S. on September 11, 2001. Network and cable television news played into the frenzied atmosphere by citing some of the rumors — that a bomb had gone off in the U.S. Capitol; that President Bush had been attacked, etc. — as evidence that the attacks were part of a much larger plan. But the reduction in the delay from the time that news is generated and the time that it is received by the mass of the public is not intrinsically a bad thing nor are the "good old days" of long delays worth resurrecting. It is only necessary to recall that the final battle of the War of 1812 — the Battle of New Orleans, a decisive victory by U.S. forces under the command of General Andrew Jackson — was fought several months after the Treaty of Ghent ending that war was actually signed by U.S. and British negotiators. General Jackson and his British counterpart had not yet heard that the war was over.

There are several points to be made here. First, increasing the closeness of citizens to government officials has been a goal of many of the government reforms instituted in the U.S. since our foundation. Democratization and political equality are two prime values of our society and it is difficult for one to argue that effective government in the U.S. might require less democracy and more political inequality. Civil liberties and minority rights can be protected in an electronic democracy to the same degree that they have been protected throughout U.S. history. The key to much of this is our conception of human nature. The framers of the U.S. Constitution did not view humans very optimistically and so concluded that barring external checks, one person or small group of people would seek to tyrannize others. A modern society of mature, educated, networked individuals may not need the same degree of external checks or may exist quite nicely using internal checks (self-policing) rather than external checks. A technology as powerful as computer networking carries with it some responsibility for mature use. If immature, unethical, or inappropriate use of the Internet becomes rampant, calls for government regulation will increase and external checks may become necessary. At the current time, legislation regarding the regulation of spam, for example, is being considered by the U.S. Congress, and legislation attempting to regulate sexually explicit websites has already been passed (and found unconstitutional by the U.S. Supreme Court). The many-voiced anarchic nature of the Internet is threatened by these seemingly innocent efforts. One can imagine a future scenario of a heavily government regulated Internet resembling a "vast wasteland," the famous phrase that Federal Communications Commission head, Newton Minnow, used to describe 1960s-era television.

A second practical point is that the role of a public manager does not get any easier if electronic democracy succeeds in increasing the number of citizens who participate in government. Quite conversely, this would put more pressure on them, and their role in the policymaking process would become more critical. Public managers would become more involved in defining a meaningful public agenda, engaging in an informed dialogue with interested citizens, seeking to build understanding of complex public policy issues, and building increased respect for minorities. In recent years, there have been many calls for insulating public officials from public pressure — making the Burkean claim that public officials need to exercise their best judgment over public policy, only possibly being guided by the wishes of constituents. While some separation between public officials and the mass of the public is perhaps necessary and may even be laudable, would it not be better if the sentiments conveyed to public officials by the mass were more informed rather than less, more deliberate rather than spontaneous, and more rational rather than emotional? All of this is possible with the use of online discussion groups, perhaps even organized by elected officials who truly care about the sentiments of their constituents. Public officials need to rethink the roles that they play in the public sphere, and one of their new tasks may be ensuring the quality of public discourse carried out on a public information system.

IV. CONCLUSION

By discussing the possibilities of the establishment of electronic democracy in the U.S. and by describing the first teetering baby steps actually taken to implement e-democracy, this chapter has raised fundamental questions of democratic theory. The thorniest question raised is: if governments in the U.S. and elsewhere can seek to increase citizen participation through the use of computer networks, *should* they do so? Some public officials consider citizen participation to be on the "costs" side of any cost–benefit analysis — seeking public input only complicates the process of making decisions, falsely increases public expectations of what may result, and results in decisions that are delayed and often not as "good" as when the public were not consulted in the first place. We find this perspective to be completely short-sighted. Involving the public in decision-making increases the possibility that the outcome of the decision-making process will be what the public wants, certainly a different but no less accurate definition of "good" than used previously.

It is clear that where government has experimented with computer networking as a way to increase citizen participation, citizens have taken advantage of the outlets. Large numbers of citizens utilize Minnesota e-Democracy or the Seattle Community Network (www.scn.org) or their analogues in a number of cities and states around the U.S. and in many foreign countries. Bulletin boards, electronic town meetings, chat rooms, e-mail lists, threaded discussions, and so forth have all become popular ways for citizens to communicate among themselves and with government officials, wherever they have been organized. It is also clear that there is no long line of citizens demanding that government go online; it is typically government itself that has initiated the process and citizens who have enjoyed the benefits. Former Speaker of the U.S. House of Representatives Newt Gingrich was the driving force behind Thomas — the online website and database that put much of the U.S. House of Representatives online in the mid-1990s. Once Thomas was organized and running, members of Congress, lobbyists, congressional researchers, and ordinary citizens took advantage of the technology and the information that the technology made available. But it was a policy entrepreneur — here a government official — who opened the system up to the citizenry, not the citizenry who demanded that it be opened.

It is also clear that problems of security and verification will plague any online public information system for many years. While it is possible to use technology to provide some safeguards for individuals using the systems, and to enforce some basic rules embedded into the system, all of these safeguards fail if individuals do not take sufficient precautions with their personal information. Even the most sophisticated passworded websites fail when individual users share their own passwords with others or make it easy for their passwords to be stolen by using the same one for several different websites — secure or not. It is simply impossible at the current time, and for the foreseeable future, for a computer system to guarantee that the person behind the mouse or keyboard is actually you and not somebody masquerading as you. If, for example, a local government institutionalized citizen feedback into its policymaking system (such that citizen comments on a bulletin board were used in the budgeting cycle), how could that government be sure that it was not simply one interest group who was sending messages to the bulletin board from a variety of e-mail addresses? How could that government be sure that the interest group was not providing incentives for citizens to messages from their own e-mail addresses? At the present time, most systems of verification are simply sophisticated versions of the honor system. What these systems do well, however, is to accomplish several precursors to complete verification — limiting individuals to one session in a discussion forum or one vote in a feedback session (or at least one vote from each e-mail address for which the individual is registered), requiring that all discussants sign in with a real name, phone number, or other identifying information, etc. Beyond this, computer networks, like all other forms of political participation, virtual or physical, cannot guarantee that vote trading is not taking place. Often, however, critics of computer networks want to hold them to a higher standard, one that would make the designers guarantee that the system is more secure than what it would replace. This is virtually impossible.

Our current experience with the Internet and computer networking is not nearly as innovative and positive as what some writers of just ten or so years ago would have predicted. But it is also not nearly as apocalyptic as other writers warned. Government institutions and U.S. populations are both just beginning to come to grips with the changes that the Internet is making in society, government, and the relationship between the two. Predicting the future possibilities of establishing direct democracy through computer networking on the basis of current usage puts us in the same situation that Galston (1999) describes in predicting the future of television by examining television usage in 1952. "Scholars in 1952 studying (say) the social effects of television might have noted how neighbors crowded into a living room to watch the only set on the block, and they might have drawn conclusions about the medium's community-reinforcing tendencies that would have seemed antique only a few years later" (Galston, 1999: 45). How can one confidently predict that voting online might therefore lead to more individualism and help destroy the "vital public ritual that increases social solidarity and binds citizens together" (Valelly, 1999: 20)?

Our abilities to predict the future are often hampered by our imagination — on the one hand, we want to see the future as only incrementally different from the present; on the other hand, we want to see the future as a complete break with the present. In reality, the future is most likely a combination of both. Often, periods of incremental change lead to sudden discontinuous change in a system (Baumgartner and Jones, 1993; John, 2003). One relevant example may be the incorporation of distance education (DE) techniques into the university classroom. While one might conceive DE to be a wholly different method of delivering university course content, one might also think of DE techniques (posting lecture notes and syllabi online, e-mail discussion topics, etc.) as add-ons to the more traditional methods of delivery. As university professors experiment with DE techniques by adding them to their classroom courses (incremental change), they may also become more open to the idea of moving their courses wholly online (discontinuous change). And when courses move completely online, university education changes dramatically.

One can foresee a similar movement in the use of computer networks and online techniques in the service of U.S. democracy. At first, the technology is merged into current systems and the uses found for it resemble those for more traditional technologies. As the new technology becomes more accepted, new uses are found for it. Eventually the system can reach a "tipping point" (Gladwell, 2002), where the system turns over into a new state. As we have discussed in this chapter, there are numerous problems with various aspects of that new state of the system, but those problems are not unsolvable and their mere presence, while possibly delaying the implementation of new technologies, cannot completely deter them. Just as major retailers have learned to cope with the fact that an increasing number of shoppers are going online to make their purchases, and just as those individual shopper preferences are remaking the retail universe in the U.S., government must adapt to the changing behavior of citizens. As more and more citizens go online to conduct their daily business — paying bills, shopping, reading the news, chatting with friends and family, reading and sending e-mail, etc. — they will simply expect similar services to be offered by their governments. If government does not accommodate to these changing expectations, it risks being seen as irrelevant or obsolete in the modern world.

REFERENCES

Abramson, J.B., Arterton, J.C., and Orren, G.R., *The Electronic Commonwealth: The Impact of New Media Technologies on Democratic Politics*, Basic Books, New York, 1988.

Alvarez, R. and Nagler, J., The likely consequences of Internet voting for political representation, *Loyola of Los Angeles Law Review*, 34, 1115–1152, 2001.

Baumgartner, F. and Jones, B., *Agendas and Instability in American Politics*, University of Chicago Press, Chicago, 1993.

Bellamy, A. and Hanewicz, C., An exploratory analysis of the social nature of Internet addiction, *Electronic Journal of Sociology*, 5, 2001
http://www.sociology.org/content/vol005.003/ia.html

Booker, K., French, C.T., Martin, A., and Weinstock, J., Voter Turnout and Online Voting, 2000
http://www.reed.edu/gronkep/webofpolitics/projects/onlinevoting/contents.html

Bowman, L., Campaign Sites Miss Web Boat, 2002 news.com.com/2100-1023-964629.html

Brians, C.L. and Grofman, B., Election day registration's effect on U.S. voter turnout, *Social Science Quarterly*, 82, 170–182, 2001.

Bruner, R., Fundraising Expert Says Dean's Success an Anomaly, 2003
www.uptospeed.com/archives/2003/07/22/fundraising_expert_says_Dean's_success_an_anomaly.html

Burke, L., No Voting Opportunity for All, *Wired News*, March 13, 2000
www.wired.com/news/politics/0,1283,34914,00.html

Cain, B., The Internet in the (dis)service of democracy?, *Loyola of Los Angeles Law Review*, 34, 1005–1021, 2001.

California Internet Voting Task Force, A Report on the Feasibility of Internet Voting, 2000
www.ss.ca.gov/executive/ivote/final_report.htm

California Voter Foundation, 2003 Program Goals
http://www.calvoter.org/aboutcvf.html

CampaignHQ.com, Give Your Campaign an Extra Edge, 2002
www.thecampaignhq.com/index.htm

Center for Congressional and Presidential Studies, Public Attitudes Toward Campaigns and Campaign Practices, 2000
http://www.american.edu/spa/ccps/pdffiles/publicattitudes.pdf

Corrado, A. and Firestone, C., Eds., *Elections in Cybersapce: Toward a New Era in American Politics*, Aspen Institute, Washington, D.C., 1996.

Dahlberg, L., Extending the Public Sphere through Cyberspace: The Case of Minnesota E-Democracy, *First Monday*, 2001, 6(3) (March, 2001)
http://firstmonday.org/issues/issue6_3/dahlberg/index.html

Docter, S. and Dutton, W., The First Amendment online: Santa Monica's public electronic network, in *Cyberdemocracy: Technology, Cities and Civic Networks*, Tsagarousianou, R., Tambini, D., and Bryan, C., Eds., Routledge, New York, 1998, pp. 125–151.

Downs, A., *An Economic Theory of Democracy*, Harper & Brothers, New York, 1957.

Drinkard, J. and Lawrence, J., Online, Off and Running: Web a New Campaign Front, *USA Today*, July 14, 2003
usatoday.printthis.clickability.com/pt/cpt/action = cpt&expire = &urlID = 6911704

Elliot, D., Examining Internet Voting in Washington, 2001
www.electioncenter.org/Voting/InetVotingWhitePaper.html

E-Voter Institute, E-Voter 2002 Study Reveals Internet Use in Senate Races Campaign Finance Reform Will Place Premium on Internet Access to Voters, 2002
www.e-voterinstitute.com

Gladwell, M., *The Tipping Point: How Little Things Can Make a Big Difference*, Little, Brown, Boston, 2002.

Galston, E., (How) does the Internet affect community? Some speculation in search of evidence, in *Democracy.com? Governance in a Networked World*, Kamarck, D. and Nye, J., Eds., Hollis Publishing Company, Hollis, NH, 1999, pp. 45–61.

Garson, D., Information systems, politics, and government: leading theoretical perspectives, in *Handbook of Public Information Systems*, Garson, D., Ed., Marcel Dekker, New York, 2000, pp. 591–609.

Greenspan, R., Two-Thirds Hit the Net, *CyberAtlas*, April 17, 2002
http://cyberatlas.internet.com/big_picture/geographics/print/0,,5911_1011490,00.html

Harris, P., You'll Never See This on CNN, 2003 http://www.yellowtimes.org/article.php?sid = 1627

Hill, K.A. and Hughes, J.E., *Cyberpolitics: Citizen Activism in the Age of the Internet*, Rowan & Littlefield, Lanham, MD, 1998.

Institute for Politics, Democracy, and the Internet (IPDI), Online Campaigning 2002: A Primer, 2002
http://www.ipdi.org/primer2002.pdf

IPI (Internet Policy Institute), Report of the National Workshop on Internet Voting: Issues and Research Agenda, 2001 www.digitalgovernment.org/archive/library/doc/ipi_onlinevoting.jsp

John, P., Is there life after policy streams, advocacy coalitions, and punctuations: using evolutionary theory to explain policy change?, *Policy Studies Journal*, 31, 481–498, 2003.

Johnson, P., Trust in Media Keeps on Slipping, *USA Today*, May 27, 2003
http://www.usatoday.com/life/2003–05–27-media-trust_x.htm

Kamarck, E., Campaigning on the Internet in the elections of 1998, in *Democracy.com? Governance in a Networked World*, Kamarck, D. and Nye, J., Eds., Hollis Publishing Company, Hollis, NH, 1999, pp. 99–124.

Levine, P., The Internet and Civil Society, The International Media and Democracy Project, July 11, 2002
http://www.imdp.org/artman/publish/article_29.shtml

Mariantes, L., Web May Revolutionize Fundraising, *Christian Science Monitor*, July 31, 2003
    www.csmonitor. com/2003/p02s01-uspo.html

Markoff, J., To eMail the President, Download Some Patience, *Mercury News*, July 17, 2003
    http://www.siliconvalley.com/mld/siliconvalley/6330165.htm

Martin, R., Get Wired, Get Votes, Get Cash, *CNN News Report*, Nov. 3, 1998
    Cnnfn.com/hotstories/washun/9811/03/election

Morris, D., Direct democracy and the Internet, *Loyola of Los Angeles Law Review*, 34, 1033–1053, 2001.

Naisbitt, J., *Megatrends: Ten New Directions Transforming Our Lives*, Warner Books, New York, 1982.

Nissenbaum, D., Use of Spam in Political Campaign Spurs Debate, *Mercury News*, April 3, 2002 www.
    siliconvalley.com

NTIA (National Telecommunications and Information Administration), Americans in the Information
    Age Falling through the Net, October 16, 2000
    www.ntia.doc.gov/ntiahome/digitaldivide/

Oakland County, Providing All County Residents with Access to eGovernment Services, 2002
    www.co.oakland.mi.us/anout/access.html

Pershing, S., The Voting Rights Act in the Internet Age: an equal access theory for interesting times,
    Loyola of Los Angeles Law Review, 34, 1171–1212, 2001.

Pew Research Center, Modest Increase in Internet Use for Campaign 2002: Political Sites Gain, but Major
    News Sites Still Dominant, 2003
    http://people-press.org/reports/display.php3/ReportID = 169.

Putnam, R., *Bowling Alone: The Collapse and Revival of American Community*, Simon & Schuster, New
    York, 2000.

Ryan, M., All in a Flash: Meet, Mob, and Move on, *Chicago Tribune*, July 11, 2003, p. 1.

Scavo, C., World Wide Web site design and use in public management, in *Public Information Technol-
    ogy: Policy and Management Issues*, Garson, G.D., Ed., Idea Group, Hershey, PA, 2003,
    pp. 299–330.

Scavo, C. and Shi, Y., World Wide Web site design and use in public management, in *Information
    Technology and Computer Applications in Public Administration: Issues and Trends*, Garson,
    G.D., Ed., Idea Group, Hershey, PA, 1999, pp. 246–266.

Schneider, S. and Foot, K., The 2004 US Presidential Election: A View from the Web, 2003
    www.politicalweb.info/2004/2004.html

Thompson, D., James Madison on cyberdemocracy, in *Democracy.com? Governance in a Networked
    World*, Kamarck, D. and Nye, J., Eds., Hollis Publishing Company, Hollis, NH, 1998, pp. 35–42.

Tull, S., Howard Dean's Presidential Campaign Raises $3.6 Million Online in First 90 Days Using
    Convio's Internet Software and Services, 2003
    charitychannel.com/printer_6419.shtml

Valelly, R., Voting alone: the case against virtual ballot boxes, *The New Republic*, 221, 20–22, 1999.

Warschauer, M., Demystifying the digital divide: the simple binary notion of haves and have-nots does
    not compute, *Scientific American*, 289, 42–47, 2003.

West, D., State and Federal E-Government in the United States, 2003
    http://www.insidepolitics.org/egovt03us.html

18

INTERNET TAX POLICY: AN INTERNATIONAL PERSPECTIVE

Dale Nesbary
Oakland University

Luis Garcia
Suffolk University

CONTENTS

  I. Introduction 282
 II. Methods 282
III. Literature 283
    A. International Internet tax policy — Europe 284
    B. Australia 285
       1. Income tax 286
       2. Goods and service tax (GST) 286
    C. Canada 287
       1. Canadian GST/sales tax 287
    D. U.S. Internet tax policy 287
 IV. Findings and discussion 289
    A. Factors associated with the application of Internet taxes 289
    B. Data reduction and regression output 290
  V. Summary and recommendations 294
    A. Inconsistency in Internet tax policy 296
    B. Double taxation 296
    C. Overreaching 296
References 297

ABSTRACT

The sale of goods and services over the Internet is approaching $50 billion (U.S.) annually in the U.S. and many times that amount internationally (Business Wire 1). This relatively new form of commerce has led to concern and interest on the part of governments, businesses, and individuals about the collectivity of taxes on Internet transactions, downloads, and access. This chapter examines Internet tax policies of U.S., Canada, Australia, U.K., and the European Union nations. It is intended to serve as a state-of-the-art paper on international Internet tax policy and to offer recommendations for model Internet tax policy.

I. INTRODUCTION

It is particularly important for Congress to be on record now in support of a permanent moratorium on e-commerce tariffs because of the pending meeting of the World Trade Organization in Seattle on November 30. Presently, none of the WTO's more than 130 members has such a tariff. But several are thinking about it. Now is the time to act — before bad things happen.

So spoke U.S. Representative Christopher Cox (Republican, California) in 1999 regarding his proposed "Global Internet Tax Freedom Act." Cox and cosponsor Senator Ron Wyden (Democrat, Oregon) hoped that their bill would send a strong message to nations wishing to collect new tax revenue from Internet activity. The Internet Tax Freedom Act (ITFA), also sponsored by Cox and Wyden, was enacted into U.S. law in 1998 and reauthorized in 2001, and imposed similar restrictions on state governments in the U.S. Inasmuch as Internet commerce is growing exponentially in the U.S. and internationally (BizRate.com), governments, businesses, and individuals are interested in the collectivity of Internet taxes. Many in government see Internet taxes as a panacea for the fiscal problems in which they find themselves, while business often views Internet taxes as an unnecessary and perhaps improper government intrusion on their ability to do business (Biggart et al., 2002: 17). Individuals are often confused about their personal tax liability (Nesbary, 2003). Almost everyone agrees, however, that electronic commerce, particularly Internet commerce, has led to an erosion of the tax base, an issue that must be addressed quickly (Jones et al., 2002: 41).

This chapter examines Internet tax policies of U.S., Canada, Australia, U.K., and the European Union nations. Specifically, Internet sales, download (bit), and access taxes will be examined. Both quantitative and qualitative data will be reviewed, including national population, national budget policy, and national tax policy. This chapter is intended to serve as a state-of-the-art paper regarding international Internet tax policy and to offer recommendations for model Internet tax legislation.

Finally, analyses of taxes on electronic commerce most often refer to either "Internet taxes" or "e-commerce taxes." This is because the terms Internet and e-commerce may be seen as interchangeable. For example, the Web, e-mail, instant messaging, or other common Internet applications use electronic devices, while electronic devices (computers, cell phones, PDAs, Blackberry, and others) often utilize Internet protocols. Accordingly, I use both terms interchangeably.

II. METHODS

This investigation uses two methods:

1. A state-of-the-art review of the Internet taxation literature
2. An examination of Internet tax policies of the nations being investigated

A number of primary sources were used, including Vertex TaxCybrary (www.vertexinc. com). Vertex TaxCybrary focuses specifically on the implications of the Internet on state and federal tax law in the U.S. Second, a web survey of the other nations that were part of the investigation was conducted. These phone and e-mail inquiries helped complete and validate data not obvious from web searches. From these sources, tables were constructed regarding the nations investigated, including data on population, fiscal factors, technology, and tax policy. Additionally, an extensive literature review was conducted. In earlier research, I found limited scholarly research on Internet tax policy in the U.S. and nearly none on international Internet tax policy (Nesbary, 2000: 23). Today, there exists a growing body of literature on Internet tax policy, both internationally and in the U.S.

Data were analyzed using Microsoft Excel. A standardized Ordinary Least Squares (OLS) regression was run to determine if demographic, fiscal, and technology organization factors influence the existence of Internet taxes.

III. LITERATURE

An increasing body of literature reveals that the Internet is having a growing effect on commerce and revenue systems. This effect is manifested in decreasing revenues to brick-and-mortar business and increasing revenues to businesses able to take advantage of Internet technologies (Lewandowski, 2001: 19). It also manifests itself in a slow, but inexorable, drain of tax revenues, particularly consumption taxes, on brick-and-mortar businesses. It is currently estimated that if states maximize the collection of Internet revenue, they would be adding a significant amount to their sales tax base (Frieden and Porter, 1996). In addition, some argue that both Internet and other interstate/ international commerce should be examined more closely. Joe Morrow, Managing Director of Morningstar Consulting Group, articulates this position well:

> ... Tax mechanisms created for a physical world do not, and should not be expected to, work in a virtual world. We have seen that with catalog sales for 25 or more years and catalog sales have been a bigger drain on annual state sales tax revenues than every cumulative Internet sale combined. The hype around the Internet, and the reasonable growth projections, has just heightened our awareness to the issue.... Reformulating the tax mechanism and standardizing the scope of sales taxes across the states will capture more sales tax revenue, decrease administrative burdens, and level the playing field for local, Internet, and catalog merchants (Morrow Interview).

This is important since tax collection in a networked environment can be problematic. Given the lack of law or of software or the unwillingness of the consumer to self-assess, nations and states have a particularly difficult time with collection (Cockfield, 2002: 5).

Boccaccio and De Bonis (2001) argue that even the catalog sales analogy has problems to the extent that mail order traditionally requires a person to contact a person at a physical location. This may be fundamentally different than Internet orders. An Internet order may be placed by a person, through a router, to a server, in another location, to a router in another location, to a warehouse in yet another location. Given these manifold issues, it is important to examine in detail actions taken by nations and the U.S. states with respect to managing Internet tax and collection mechanisms and in determining location (nexus).

Additionally, some countries choose to apply a specific value-added tax (VAT) on software. The "Spanish VAT on software products and related assistance to Spanish client through the Internet by an enterprise that is not established in Spain" applies to standard software when that software is delivered to the Spanish VAT territory and the software is physically imported into Spain (Gomez-Arnau, 2000: 72). Still other nations see Internet commerce as a potential drain on their revenue because of the way they have defined taxability historically. Hong Kong has been a source-based taxing entity for some time. Many government officials there fear that the inherent difficulty in defining source in an Internet-based economy will cause significant difficulty in keeping tax revenues at a reasonable level (Ho et al., 2001: 343). Indeed, some argue that the current framework for international, national, and state taxation, based generally on physical presence and physical delivery of goods and services, may not be appropriate for dealing with global e-commerce and cyberspace transactions (Irion, 2000: 18).

On July 1, 2003, the aforementioned EU VAT was instituted and applied to goods downloaded over the Internet, including software, music, and videos from U.S.-based companies. This new tax is not in concert with current U.S. policy in that Congress and the president authorized a moratorium on new e-taxes during the Clinton administration. The moratorium expired on November 1, 2003. On Wednesday, November 28th, the President signed legislation extending the moratorium to November 1, 2007 (Garretson 2004).[1] The Bush administration is displeased with the EU move and will address the issue with both the Organization for Economic Co-operation and Development and the World Trade Organization (Moschella, 2002: 21). In Europe, national VATs tend to add 15 to 25% to the prices of goods and services (Moschella, 2002: 22). The differing approaches of U.S. and EU Internet tax policy may already be having an effect. Lewis (2001: 15) notes that through 2001, European business to consumer (B2C) e-commerce totaled only $650 million in 1998 and lagged U.S. B2C e-commerce by 18 months as late as 2001. Lewis notes that, in 1998, U.S. B2C Internet commerce totaled $11.5 billion and is expected to grow to $126 billion by the end of this year.

A. International Internet Tax Policy — Europe

As the Internet and the World Wide Web become a primary medium of commerce, tax and policy analysts are taking note. The World Trade Organization, the Organization for Economic Cooperation and Development (OECD), the European Commission, the Japanese Ministry of International Trade and Industry, the Australian Tax Office, the French Ministry of Finance, the Irish Revenue Commissioners, and the Netherlands Ministry of Finance have all issued papers or held conferences between 1998 and 2002 discussing the effects of e-commerce on the tax world (Desimone, 2002: 2). At the same time, governments around the world faced severe fiscal problems and viewed the Internet as a potential pot of gold with respect to obviating the need to raise general revenues (Bryan, 2003: 34; Geewax, 2003: 1).

The OECD (http://www.oecd.org) has been a leading international organization in researching taxation issues arising from e-commerce. Understanding the significant changes in tax policy and business development occurring as a result of e-commerce, the

---

[1] Garretson, C. Net still a tax fee zone. PC World, November 29, 2004. Available at: http://www.pcworld.com/news/article/0,aid,73666,00.asp (Retrieved December 14, 2004).

OECD took a number of proactive steps. Most importantly, the OECD sponsored a number of conferences on the subject and provided direction to nations with respect to international commerce generally and e-commerce in particular. The OECD published a report entitled *Electronic Commerce: Taxation Framework Conditions* in October 1998, outlining the following five guiding taxation principles that should apply to e-commerce:

- ■ Neutrality
- ■ Efficiency
- ■ Certainty and simplicity
- ■ Effectiveness and fairness
- ■ Flexibility

The OECD recommendations were not lost on tax administrators. The Australian Taxation Office (ATO) understood the various dimensions of Internet commerce and prepared a strategy to address potential shortfalls in existing revenue and likely lost revenue due to new Internet technologies. In a 2002 report, they argued that:

- ■ The economics of the Internet makes international trading operations viable for much larger numbers of businesses. In addition, new kinds of profitable businesses are emerging. These factors will be beneficial to the economy, but present issues for the ATO to manage.
- ■ The need to clarify the law relating to taxation for businesses operating on the Internet is crucial, as lack of clarity in the law in this area could give rise to serious problems for taxpayers. Tax law relating to commercial transactions on websites is of particular concern.
- ■ The need to examine tax compliance strategies in an environment very different from the "real" world is essential (Electronic commerce project 5).

The ATO had been examining the implications of Internet commerce on provincial and federal revenues for some time and had released a detailed analysis of the issue in 1999 (Australian Tax Office). The report, entitled "Tax and The Internet Second Report," is available at http://www.ato.gov.au/content.asp?doc=/content/Businesses/ecommerce_Tati2.htm.

What can be culled from these reports? The European Union's tax system imposes tax on digital purchases based on the location of the supplier. Therefore, all products digitally delivered by companies in the EU carry an added tax — no matter where in the world their customer is located. Many European companies believe the change will be for the better, since the current system puts companies based in Europe at a disadvantage in the digital marketplace. Europeans buying from the U.S. or other non-EU countries can avoid paying high VAT, while European companies have to charge VAT, which ranges from 15 to 25%, depending on the country in which the company operates.

B. Australia

Following is a brief examination of taxes imposed in Australia in regard to e-commerce. This examination includes the Australian Income and Goods and Services taxes.

1. Income tax

Australia uses a residence-source-business basis model in determining who pays personal income tax with respect to Internet-related income:

1. Residence of the taxpayer.
2. Source of income.
3. The presence or absence of a permanent business establishment (PE)

Even though these income tax rules are in effect, applying tax to e-commerce is not clear-cut because Internet transactions can be unlimited and are often intangible, an enterprise may be able to change its place of business to a low-tax jurisdiction merely by changing the location of a server, and the residence or PE status of a company may be difficult to ascertain where it carries on business in cyberspace or is managed and controlled in cyberspace (Tax Law 1).

2. Goods and service tax (GST)

GST is charged at the rate of 10% on the supply of goods and services in Australia and on goods imported into Australia under the tax system (Goods and Services Tax Act, 1999). The GST is applicable if the goods or services are provided or supplied in Australia. A supply of anything other than goods or real property is subject to GST if the supply is provided in Australia or the supplier functions as an enterprise that the supplier carries on in Australia (Fitzgerald, 1999). Several issues arise in relation to supplies on the Internet and the GST. Moreover, supplies of software and intangible products online and Internet sales are generally taxable under the GST. Although geographical boundaries disappear, Internet sales do not escape GST. A registered supplier must charge GST on transactions that would be classified as "taxable" under the GST Act. Additionally, where reciprocal advertising agreements exist between websites, revenue produced may be taxable. Royalties received for sales made through linked-partner websites may trigger a GST liability depending on the location of the revenue recipient. Interestingly, the supplier has no legal obligation to issue a "tax invoice" unless the recipient requests one.

These are some examples involving the GST levied by Australia. By examining Australia's tax system, or the tax system of any other country for that matter, it is clear why developing an e-commerce taxation system is not going to be a quick process. Countries must take into account how their own tax structure and the tax structure of other countries will endure Internet commerce. If Internet taxation is imposed, it is important that countries work together to ensure a fair solution for all the stakeholders involved.

Australia is not alone in its attempts to address these issues. On February 12, 2002, member nations of the European Union agreed to rules under which their VAT would be levied. The new rule provides that "EU suppliers will no longer be obliged to levy VAT when selling in markets outside the EU," thereby removing a significant competitive handicap (Europa Website, June 12, 2003).

Moreover, the GST Act passed by the federal parliament does not contain the same place of taxation rules as the European Union countries. This could mean that consumers purchasing services from an international service provider may be subject to double taxation (Fitzgerald, 1999).

C. Canada

Canada has also taken action with respect to the taxation of Internet commerce. The Canadian Constitution Act of 1867 allocates taxing power in Canada between the federal and provincial governments. The parliament of Canada has legislative authority to raise money "by any mode or system of taxation." Therefore, it can raise money through direct or indirect taxation. On the other hand, provinces are limited to "direct taxation within the province in order to the raising of revenue for provincial purposes" (Borraccia, 1998: 2).

1. Canadian GST/sales tax

When exploring the topic of Internet taxation in relation to Canada, it is important to examine the Excise Tax Act (http://laws.justice.gc.ca/en/E-15/) and the Customs Act (Canadian Customs and Revenue Agency website). The Excise Tax Act imposes a value-added-type tax known as the Goods and Services Tax (GST). The Customs Act imposes duties on the importation of various goods into Canada.

Each Canadian province imposes income taxes and, other than Alberta, each imposes a retail sales tax. Three of the provinces have entered into an agreement with the federal government to combine their sales taxes with the GST in the form of a harmonized sales tax or "HST" (Borraccio, 1998: 2).

Currently, Canada is examining ways to collect taxes on Internet gaming, specifically focusing on online Bingo (Raizel, 2001: 20). This follows the U.K. approving online Bingo in March 2002. Canada's online Bingo proceeds are predicted to earn 90% net income, much more than the 50% earned by other online gaming in the country.

D. U.S. Internet Tax Policy

In the late 1990s, many states in the U.S. were taking full advantage of the revenue possibilities of Internet commerce. By 1998, many states had imposed taxes on Internet sales, access, or downloads (Nesbary, 2000: 18). Notwithstanding these efforts to capture Internet revenue, some argued " ... that the ever-increasing volume of purchases over the Internet and by mail order is seriously eroding sales and use tax revenue, and that this erosion will grow dramatically over time" (Towne, 2002: 2).

Several models of taxing Internet commerce have emerged at the state level in the U.S. My 2000 analysis revealed that some states tax downloaded information and software, while others tax goods and services sold via the Internet in the same manner as catalog sales. Still others tax installation and connection fees of online services (such as America Online, the Microsoft Network, Net Zero). Whatever the taxing mechanism, any blanket tax levied on Internet commerce may ultimately be found to be in violation of the Commerce Clause of the U.S. Constitution (Article 1, Section 8, Clause 3). As interpreted in case law, Article 1, Section 8, Clause 3 provides that Congress may "regulate Commerce with foreign nations, and among the several states and with the Indian tribes." As a result, the states have no significant role in interstate commerce. The federal courts have occasionally given the states some leeway, however, generally they have come down on the side of congressional control of interstate commerce and against the states (Nesbary, 2000: 20).

A primary issue with respect to the taxation of Internet commerce in the U.S. is the location where the transaction takes place. This concept, known as nexus, has a long tradition in the U.S., based most fundamentally on the Commerce Clause.

There are generally two categories of income from which a country derives its taxing authority:

1. On income of its residents regardless of the place where the income is produced
2. On income produced within a country regardless of the residency of the income producing entity

Thus, in the first instance, taxes are collected based on where the product is produced, while in the second instance, taxes are collected regardless of the residency of taxpayers.

With respect to interstate commerce in the U.S. this two-dimensional construct has developed into a three-dimensional construct over time. Destination, residence, and source-based taxes are these three dimensions (Fox and Murray, 1997: 573). Destination-based taxes tax goods at the site of consumption, while residence taxes are imposed where the taxpayer's headquarters are located. Source-based taxes tax goods where production takes place. For purposes of illustration we will use personal computer production and sales. Let us assume that the computer company is headquartered in Texas, the computer is produced in California, and is purchased in Rhode Island. In a destination-based tax system, sales taxes would be collected in Rhode Island; while in a residence-based system sales taxes would be collected in Texas. Given a source-based system, sales taxes would be collected in California.

The states are taking additional measures to ensure that tax administration is conducted in an efficient and as effective a manner as possible. The collection of sales or use taxes has always been an issue in the relationship with remote vendors. With so many different regulations on sales taxes, efforts are being made to simplify the process. The Streamlined Sales Tax Project was established in 1990 to improve sales-and-use-tax administrative systems for government tax administrators as well as large and small businesses. As of May 15, 2003, ten states had enacted legislation providing for full compliance with the SST (its Model Uniform Sales and Use Tax Act) and another 18 have legislation in process to fully or partially comply (NCSL, 2003). The project began as an outgrowth of the Advisory Commission on Electronic Commerce (ACEC). The ACEC was established under the federal ITFA and was charged with conducting a thorough study of federal, state, local, and international taxation and tariff treatment of Internet transactions (Gates and Hogroian, 2001: 858). The states are hoping that by solving problems currently associated with collecting sales tax revenue from remote sellers, it will be easier to collect sales tax from Internet purchases.

In response to the myriad issues impacting Internet commerce and taxation in the U.S., ITFA, a 1998 federal statute imposing a 3-year moratorium on new Internet taxes, was signed into law. IFTA did not change the sales tax collection or application process, but it did provide for the appointment of an advisory commission to create recommendations about how taxes should be treated in respect to online commerce. The mission of the Advisory Commission of Electronic Commerce Committee established by Congress is to examine the following:

1. Foreign barriers to Internet commerce
2. The collection and administration of consumption taxes on electronic commerce in and outside of the U.S.
3. The impact of the Internet and Internet access on the federal revenue base

4. The development of model state legislation providing for uniform tax treatment of Internet commerce
5. The effects of taxation (or lack of taxation) on Internet commerce, both at state and federal levels
6. Ways to simplify federal and state taxation of telecommunication services

In October 2001, IFTA was extended by 2 years, giving U.S. state and local governments more time to devise a scheme to address tax and policy implications of this new medium and consider appropriate mechanisms for taxing Internet activity (Desimone, 2002).

IV.   FINDINGS AND DISCUSSION

This chapter examines the application of Internet taxes in a number of areas, including qualitative information collected from websites, interviews, and a review of the literature. Other areas to be explored include the frequency and level of Internet taxes and factors associated with the application of Internet taxes. These analyses allow for a more thoughtful examination of Internet tax policy.

A.   Factors Associated with the Application of Internet Taxes

This chapter employs a standardized OLS regression to identify factors associated with the application of taxes on Internet commerce. Dependent variables include:

■ Taxation of goods and services sold over the Internet (sales and VAT taxes)
■ Taxation of Internet access fees
■ Taxation of data downloaded from the Internet (bit tax)

Two independent variables were selected, including national population and national budget. The following nations were included in the regression:

■ Australia
■ Austria
■ Belgium
■ Canada
■ Denmark
■ U.K.
■ Finland
■ France
■ Germany
■ Italy
■ Netherlands
■ Portugal
■ Spain
■ Sweden
■ Switzerland
■ United States

Australia, Canada, and the U.S. were also examined in detail at the provincial or state level. The intent was to get a sense of both national and provincial policy with respect to Internet taxation.

In my 2000 investigation of Internet taxation in the U.S., there was a significant relationship between the existence of a general sales tax and an Internet sales tax. Population and budget also revealed some interesting results. Other relationships, such as the relationship between administrative structures and the application of Internet taxes, were not included.

B. Data Reduction and Regression Output

Table 18.1 outlines the frequency of Internet taxes among the nations investigated. It also includes national budgetary and population data. Internet taxes are defined in this chapter as being applied nationally when either of the following two criteria is met: (1) federal law applies an Internet tax or (2) a majority of the provinces or states apply an Internet tax. The U.S., for example, does not apply a national consumption tax on Internet sales, download, or access; however a great majority of the states do (Nesbary, 2000: 24). Thus, the U.S. is listed as applying Internet taxes on a national basis.

At least ten countries (62.5%) apply some sort of standard Internet tax. Ten countries apply an Internet access or download tax, while 13 countries apply an Internet sales tax. Portugal and Denmark apply no Internet taxes at the national level, while the remainder do apply Internet taxes at the national level or the majority of their provinces or states do. Of the 16 nations investigated, only Finland, Italy, Spain, and Sweden do not apply all the Internet taxes at some level. Only Netherlands does not report any Internet taxation at the national level.

Table 18.1   Frequency of Internet Taxes (Country, Province, and State Data)

Country	Number of States	Internet Access Charges Tax (%)	Internet Sales Tax (%)	Download Tax (%)
Australia	8	8 (100)	8 (100)	8 (100)
Canada	14	5 (35.7)	13 (92.9)	1 (7.1)
U.S.	50	7 (14)	44 (88)	25 (50)
Australia		Y	Y	Y
Austria		Y	Y	Y
Belgium		Y	Y	Y
Canada		Y	Y	Y
Denmark		N	N	N
U.K.		Y	Y	Y
Finland		N	Y	N
France		Y	Y	Y
Germany		Y	Y	Y
Italy		N	Y	Y
Netherlands		Y	Y	Y
Portugal		N	N	N
Spain		Y	Y	N
Sweden		N	Y	N
Switzerland		N	N	N
U.S.		Y	Y	Y
Totals		10	13	10
N		16	16	16
Percent totals		62.5	81.3	62.5

Table 18.2, Table 18.3, and Table 18.4 outline the results of the standardized OLS regression. Of note, national budget rather than national population has the stronger relationship with the application of all Internet taxes, including access, sales/VAT, and download. However, the apparent strength in relationships may not be explained by the independent variables used in this investigation. *P* scores were .598, .972, and .567, respectively. These are all strong positive relationships. Conversely, Beta scores were

Table 18.2 Internet Access Tax

						Regression Statistics
Multiple *R*						0.351
R^2						0.123
Adjusted R^2						−0.012
Standard error						0.503
Observations						16

			ANOVA		
	df	SS	MS	F	Significant F
Regression	2	0.462	0.231	0.913	0.426
Residual	13	3.288	0.253		
Total	15	3.750			

	Coefficients	Standard Error	t	P	Lower 95%	Upper 95%	Lower 95%	Upper 95%
Intercept	1.487	0.151	9.820	.000	1.159	1.814	1.159	1.814
Budget	0.001	0.001	0.541	.598	−0.002	0.003	−0.002	0.003
Population	−0.007	0.009	−0.793	.442	−0.027	0.012	−0.027	0.012

	Residual Output		
Observation	Predicted Internet Access Charges Tax	Residuals	Standard Residuals
Australia	1.44991157	−0.449911573	−0.96092824
Austria	1.46232541	−0.462325412	−0.98744191
Belgium	1.46117436	−0.461174362	−0.98498348
Canada	1.38098874	−0.380988739	−0.81372176
Denmark	1.47967258	0.520327425	1.11132353
U.K.	1.32247022	−0.322470224	−0.688737
Finland	1.47096993	0.529030068	1.12991077
France	1.21643931	−0.216439313	−0.4622745
Germany	1.47775507	−0.477755073	−1.02039683
Italy	1.37378628	0.626213723	1.33747715
Netherlands	1.46089509	−0.460895089	−0.98438701
Portugal	1.44124551	0.558754494	1.19339667
Spain	1.26260695	−0.262606945	−0.56088006
Sweden	1.49389132	0.50610868	1.08095491
Switzerland	1.45219313	0.547806872	1.17001457
U.S.	0.79367453	0.206325468	0.44067319

Table 18.3 Internet Sales Tax

	Regression Statistics
Multiple R	0.260
R^2	0.067
Adjusted R^2	−0.076
Standard error	0.418
Observations	16

ANOVA

	df	SS	MS	F	Significant F
Regression	2	0.164	0.082	0.470	0.635
Residual	13	2.273	0.175		
Total	15	2.438			

	Coefficients	Standard Error	t	P	Lower 95%	Upper 95%	Lower 95%	Upper 95%
Intercept	1.253	0.126	9.959	.000	0.982	1.525	0.982	1.525
Budget	0.000	0.001	−0.036	.972	−0.002	0.002	−0.002	0.002
Population	−0.001	0.007	−0.171	.867	−0.017	0.015	−0.017	0.015

Residual Output

Observation	Predicted Internet Sales Tax	Residuals	Standard Residuals
Australia	1.222	−0.222	−0.570
Austria	1.242	−0.242	−0.621
Belgium	1.238	−0.238	−0.612
Canada	1.206	−0.206	−0.530
Denmark	1.245	0.755	1.940
U.K.	1.185	−0.185	−0.475
Finland	1.246	−0.246	−0.631
France	1.170	−0.170	−0.437
Germany	1.116	−0.116	−0.297
Italy	1.163	−0.163	−0.418
Netherlands	1.229	−0.229	−0.588
Portugal	1.239	0.761	1.955
Spain	1.198	−0.198	−0.510
Sweden	1.238	−0.238	−0.612
Switzerland	1.243	0.757	1.944
U.S.	0.821	0.179	0.460

less significant, with at or near-zero scores for both national budget and population. This indicates a lack of causality and a lack of direction with respect to causality that may exist. Adjusted R^2 was also low in all cases, meaning that very little of the variance of incidence of Internet taxation may be attributed to the population or to the budget. In summary, these data reveal that strong relationships exist among the data; however, causality and direction are both unclear.

Table 18.5, Table 18.6, and Table 18.7 outline Internet tax activity in the provinces and states of Australia, Canada, and the U.S. While none of the eight Australian provinces have enacted legislation to tax Internet commerce specifically, all collect Internet sales taxes via the national GST. Of the fourteen Canadian provinces, five assess an Internet access tax, thirteen assess an Internet sales tax, and one assesses a download tax. In the U.S., seven states assess an Internet access tax, forty-four assess an Internet sales tax, while twenty-five assess a download tax. With the impending expiration of the ITFA, four

Table 18.4 Download Tax

					Regression Statistics
Multiple R					0.387
R^2					0.150
Adjusted R^2					0.019
Standard error					0.495
Observations					16

			ANOVA		
	df	SS	MS	F	Significant F
Regression	2	0.561	0.280	1.143	0.349
Residual	13	3.189	0.245		
Total	15	3.750			

	Coefficients	Standard Error	t	P	Lower 95%	Upper 95%	Lower 95%	Upper 95%
Intercept	1.478	0.149	9.915	.000	1.156	1.800	1.156	1.800
Budget	−0.001	0.001	−0.587	.567	−0.003	0.002	−0.003	0.002
Population	0.002	0.009	0.276	.787	−0.017	0.022	−0.017	0.022

	Residual Output		
Observation	Predicted Download Tax	Residuals	Standard Residuals
Australia	1.414	−0.414	−0.898
Austria	1.464	−0.464	−1.005
Belgium	1.454	−0.454	−0.984
Canada	1.428	−0.428	−0.927
Denmark	1.458	0.542	1.176
U.K.	1.414	−0.414	−0.898
Finland	1.468	0.532	1.154
France	1.463	−0.463	−1.005
Germany	1.062	−0.062	−0.134
Italy	1.299	−0.299	−0.649
Netherlands	1.426	−0.426	−0.923
Portugal	1.474	0.526	1.140
Spain	1.510	0.490	1.064
Sweden	1.424	0.576	1.249
Switzerland	1.477	0.523	1.134
U.S.	0.766	0.234	0.507

Table 18.5   Internet Tax Activity in the Australian Provinces

Province	Internet Access Charges Tax	Internet Sales Tax	Download Tax	Pending Legislation	Province Budget (in Billions)	Province Population (in Millions)	Sales Tax Levied
Australian Capital Territory	N	N	N	N	2.197	0.322	Y, GST
New South Wales	N	N	N	N	31.102	6.657	Y, GST
Northern Territory	N	N	N	N	3.184	0.197	Y, GST
Queensland	N	N	N	N	20.181	3.729	Y, GST
South Australia	N	N	N	N	7.205	1.522	Y, GST
Tasmania	N	N	N	N	2.389	0.473	Y, GST
Victoria	N	N	N	N	24.76	4.888	Y, GST
Western Australia	N	N	N	N	11	1.934	Y, GST

Table 18.6   Internet Tax Activity in the Canadian Provinces

Province	Region	Internet Access Charges Tax	Internet Sales Tax	Download Tax	Pending Legislation	Province Budget (in Billions)	Province Population (in Millions)	Sales Tax Levied
Alberta	Praire	N	Y	N	Y	19.200	2.9748	N
British Columbia	Pacific	Y	Y	N	Y	12.594	3.9077	Y
Manitoba	Atlantic	Y	Y	N	Y	6.600	1.1196	Y
New Brunswick	Atlantic	N	Y	N	Y	4.949	0.5666	N
Newfoundland	Atlantic	N	Y	N	Y	4.000	0.5281	N
Northwest Territory	Territories	N	Y	N	Y	1.055	0.0373	Y
Nova Scotia	Atlantic	N	Y	N	Y	4.460	0.9416	N
Nunavut	Territories	N	Y	N	Y	0.754	0.0267	N
Ontario	Ontario	Y	Y	Y	Y	63.270	11.4101	Y
Prince Edward Island	Atlantic	N	Y	N	Y	0.9798	0.1389	Y
Quebec	Quebec	Y	Y	N	Y	6.320	7.2375	Y
Saskatchewan	Prairies	Y	Y	N	Y	48.253	0.9780	Y
Yukon	Territories	N	Y	N	Y	0.550	0.0287	N

U.S. states have introduced legislation during the current year to modify Internet tax laws. Thirteen of 14 Canadian provinces have introduced legislation, while no Australian provinces have pending Internet tax legislation.

V.   SUMMARY AND RECOMMENDATIONS

Many countries are making moves to modify their tax laws to take Internet commerce into account. Much of what has been done so far attempts to treat Internet taxation in a

Table 18.7 Internet Tax Activity in the U.S. States

State	Demographic Factors		Fiscal Factors			
	State Budget (in Millions)	State Population (in Millions)	Sales Tax Levied	Internet Access Charges Tax	Internet Sales Tax	Download Tax
Alabama	5,362	4.45	Y	N	Y	Y
Alaska	2,373	0.63	N	N	N	N
Arizona	6,337	5.13	Y	N	Y	Y
Arkansas	3,182	2.67	Y	N	Y	N
California	76,863	33.87	Y	N	Y	N
Colorado	6,694	4.30	Y	N	Y	Y
Connecticut	11,664	3.40	Y	N	Y	Y
Delaware	2,454	0.78	N	N	N	N
Florida	16,643	15.98	Y	N	Y	N
Georgia	15,486	8.19	Y	N	Y	N
Hawaii	3,656	1.21	Y	N	N	N
Idaho	1,980	1.29	Y	N	Y	Y
Illinois	24,248	12.42	Y	N	Y	Y
Indiana	9,643	6.08	Y	N	Y	Y
Iowa	4,600	2.93	Y	N	Y	N
Kansas	4,466	2.69	Y	N	Y	Y
Kentucky	7,082	4.04	Y	N	Y	Y
Louisiana	6,538	4.47	Y	N	Y	Y
Maine	2,584	1.27	Y	N	Y	Y
Maryland	10,947	5.30	Y	N	Y	N
Massachusetts	22,822	6.35	Y	N	Y	N
Michigan	9,170	9.94	Y	N	Y	N
Minnesota	13,059	4.92	Y	N	Y	Y
Mississippi	3,538	2.84	Y	N	Y	Y
Missouri	7,643	5.60	Y	N	Y	N
Montana	1,356	0.90	Y	N	N	N
Nebraska	2,599	1.71	Y	Y	Y	Y
Nevada	1,890	2.00	Y	N	Y	N
New Hampshire	1,167	1.24	N	N	N	N
New Jersey	21,101	8.41	Y	N	Y	N
New Mexico	4,049	1.80	Y	Y	Y	Y
New York	41,222	18.98	Y	N	Y	Y
North Carolina	13,741	8.05	Y	N	Y	N
North Dakota	812	0.64	Y	Y	Y	Y
Ohio	21,627	11.35	Y	Y	Y	Y
Oklahoma	5,016	3.45	Y	N	Y	N
Oregon	4,665	3.42	N	N	N	N
Pennsylvania	20,782	12.28	Y	N	Y	N
Rhode Island	2,650	1.05	Y	N	Y	N
South Carolina	5,162	4.01	Y	N	Y	N
South Dakota	850	0.75	Y	Y	Y	Y
Tennessee	7,547	5.69	Y	Y	Y	N

continued

Table 18.7   Internet Tax Activity in the U.S. States — continued

	Demographic Factors		Fiscal Factors			
State	State Budget (in Millions)	State Population (in Millions)	Sales Tax Levied	Internet Access Charges Tax	Internet Sales Tax	Download Tax
Texas	30,572	20.85	Y	Y	Y	Y
Utah	3,731	2.23	Y	N	Y	Y
Vermont	872	0.61	Y	N	Y	N
Virginia	12,043	7.08	Y	N	Y	N
Washington	11,226	5.89	Y	N	Y	Y
West Virginia	2,817	1.81	Y	N	Y	Y
Wisconsin	11,259	5.36	Y	Y	Y	Y
Wyoming	630	0.49	Y	N	Y	Y

manner similar to other international and interstate commerce. There exist some issues that must be addressed.

A.   Inconsistency in Internet Tax Policy

While policymakers understand the need to address the issue of how to handle Internet taxation, methods are somewhat lacking. This chapter has demonstrated that there is inconsistency in Internet tax treatment among countries, as well as among states and provinces. In some instances, downloads are taxed and in others they are not. While Internet sales are generally taxed, they are taxed at different rates (EU) or not taxed at all. The ITFA and the Simplified Sales Tax Project are examples of initiatives designed to provide some coherence and consistency to Internet taxation. Countries and their states and provinces must subscribe to initiatives designed to apply consistency to Internet taxation.

B.   Double Taxation

Because of differing definitions of location (nexus), there exists the potential that certain goods or services may be double-taxed. For example, if a company in a country with source-based Internet taxation sells to a customer with destination-based Internet taxation, the possibility exists that the customer may pay taxes twice on the goods or services purchased. Countries, states, and provinces must endeavor to define nexus in the same manner.

C.   Overreaching

Before the passage of ITFA in the U.S., states attempted to apply many kinds of taxes to goods and services that were otherwise untaxable under existing Internet commerce law. ITFA barred the states from enacting new Internet taxes until Congress reviewed Internet tax policies in a comprehensive manner. As described earlier, conferences were held worldwide to address these and similar issues. Particularly in times of fiscal distress, Internet commence must not be used as a "cash cow" to bail out states and provinces when other more traditional revenue enhancement mechanisms exist.

It is hoped that these recommendations specifically and this chapter generally will provide guidance to those interested in addressing issues regarding taxation of Internet commerce. Clearly, many countries are concerned with both the loss of tax revenue and the likelihood that Internet taxes have the potential to become a significant income source. More research is obviously needed. However, given the wide variety of ongoing research in the field of Internet taxation and electronic commerce, states, provinces, and countries will have an advantage over Internet tax researchers of just a few years ago.

REFERENCES

Biggart, T.B., Harden, J.W., and Flanagan, R.L., Taxation of electronic retailers, *Strategic Finance Magazine*, 83, 17–18, 2002.

Boccaccio, M. and De Bonis, V., Electronic commerce and taxation, *Economia Internazionale*, 54, 435–458, 2001.

Borracia, S.M, Taxation of Electronic Commerce in Canada, 1998
Available at: http://articles.corporate.findlaw.com/articles/file/00001/003033/title/Subject/topic/Tax%20Law_Int/filename/taxlaw_1_ 298
Retrieved on 6/5/2003.

Bryan, M., ATO moves on e-commerce loss, *Australian Financial Review*, Small Business Section P. 34, February 25, 2003
lexis nexis search keywords "internet tax revenue"
Retrieved on 5/24/2003.

Cockfield, A., The Law and economics of digital taxation: challenges to traditional tax laws and principles, *International Burueau of Fiscal Documentation*, Working Paper, 2002
Available at: www.innovationlaw.org/pages/cockfiled_InformationEconomics5.0.pdf
Retrieved on 5/29/2003.

Desimone, D.C., From Florida to Kabul: 2001 in review, *Government Finance Review*, 18, 50–53, 2002.

Fitzgerald, G., The GST and electronic commerce in Australia e law, *Murdoch University Electronic Journal of Law*, 6(3), 1999
Available at: http://www.murdoch.edu.au/elaw/issues/v6n3/fitzgerald 63.html
Retrieved on 11/17/2004.

Fox, W. and Murray, M., The sales tax and electronic commerce: so what's new?, *National Tax Journal*, 50, 573–592, 1997.

Frieden, K.A. and Porter, M.E., The Taxation of Cyberspace: State Tax Issues Related to the Internet and Electronic Commerce — Part II. The Future State Taxation of Electronic Commerce, 1996
Caltax: http://www.caltax.org/andersen/contents.htm

Gates, V.A. and Hogroian, F., The streamlined sales tax project, *The Tax Adviser*, 32, 857–859, 2001.

Geewax, M., States Look to Internet for Tax Revenue, *Cox News Service*, Press Release, Sunday, Mar. 9, 2003
Available at: http://www.hartfordinformer.com/main.cfm/include/smdetail/synid/81776.html
lexis nexis search keywords "internet tax revenue"
Retrieved on 5/24/2003.

Gomez-Arnau, P.M., The taxation of Internet commerce in Spain, *International Tax Journal*, 26, 70–78, 2000.

Ho, D., Mak, A., and Wong, B., Assurance of functionality of tax in the e-business world: the Hong Kong experience, *Managerial Auditing Journal*, 16, 339–346, 2001.

Interview with Joe Morrow, Managing Director, Morningstar Consulting Group dated May 28, 2003.

Irion, J.K., Tax risks every e-commerce executive should know, *Information Strategy*, 16, 18–29, 2000.

Jones, R. and Basu, S., Taxation of electronic commerce: a developing problem, *International Review of Law, Computers and Technology*, 16, 35–52, 2002.

Lewandowski, R., The Net tax nightmare, *CA Magazine*, 134, 18–24, 2001.

Lewis, J., Weaving electronic commerce into global business and financial management, *Afp Exchange*, 21, 14–17, 2001.

Moschella, D., U.S.–Europe rifts may spill into IT, *Computerworld* (Framingham, Mass), 36, 21, 2002.

NCSL (National Conference of State Legislatures), 2003–2004 State Action on Legislation to Comply with the Streamlined Sales and Use Tax Interstate Agreement. National Conference of State Legislatures, November 12, 2004
Available at: http://www.ncsl.org/programs/fiscal/ssutachart1.htm.
Retrieved on November 18, 2004.

Nesbary, D., The taxation of Internet commerce, *Social Science Computer Review*, 18, 17–39, 2000.

Nesbary, D., Survey of Students Enrolled in Government Information Systems Course, Public Administration, 621 at Oakland University, Spring Semester, 2003.

Raizel, R., Tax and the Internet: Second Report, Australian Taxation Office, 1999
Available at: http://www.ato.gov.au/content/Businesses/Downloads/ecommerce_tati2.pdf
Retrieved on 5/26/2003.

Raizel, R., Beach blanket bingo, *Canadian Business*, 74, 20, 2001.

Towne, G., VAT on Electronic Commerce: The New Legislation, The European Commission: Tax and Customs Union, 2002
Available at: http://europa.eu.int/comm/taxation_customs/taxation/ecommerce/vat_en.htm
Retrieved on 5/26/2003.

19

TAKING ADVANTAGE OF THE INFORMATION AGE: WHICH COUNTRIES BENEFIT?*

Shelly Arsneault
California State University

Alana Northrop
California State University

Kenneth L. Kraemer
University of California

CONTENTS

I.	Introduction	300
II.	Data	303
III.	Computerization in 1993: hypotheses and findings	303
	A. Economically advanced nations are more likely to have adopted computers	305
	B. Nation-states with more educated populations and ones with more open access to information are more likely to have adopted computers	306
	C. Nation-states that have a higher saturation of information medias are more likely to adopt computers	308
IV.	Internet use in 2001: hypotheses and findings	309
	A. Economically advanced nations will make more extensive use of internet technology	309
	B. Nations with more educated citizens and ones with more open access to information are more likely to use internet technology	310
	C. Nation-states that have a higher saturation of information media are more likely to use internet technology extensively	311
V.	A note on causal order	312

---

* Data collection for this research has been supported by the U.S. National Science Foundation (CISE/IIS/ITR #0085852). Any opinions, findings, and conclusions or recommendations expressed in this material are those of the authors and do not necessarily reflect the views of the National Science Foundation.

VI. Conclusions 313
References 315

ABSTRACT

This study addresses the issue of technological advance by reviewing the factors that led countries to computerize at high rates during the 1990s and asking which countries have been most likely to take advantage of the Internet as it gains wide popularity at the start of the 21st century. We find that the profusion of information infrastructure is a key mediating force determining the likelihood of a nation-state making use of computers in the early 1990s, and the Internet early in the 21st century. To fully participate and gain the economic, political, and social benefits of computers and the Internet, nations are advised to expose their citizens to earlier generations of mass information media and to provide them an extensive information infrastructure.

I. INTRODUCTION

For years it has been debated to what extent computer technology leads to payoffs for government and business, ranging from time and personnel savings to better service delivery and new services (Blauner, 1964; Simon, 1965; Downs, 1967; Kraemer et al., 1981; Danziger et al., 1982; Atwell and Rule, 1984; Leavitt and Whisler, 1985; Northrop et al., 1990; Taylor et al., 1996). The literature offers evidence that there are some costs and many benefits. Overall, political leaders assume that computers and related technologies lead to economic and social progress. Estimates are that two thirds of new jobs in the U.S. demand some experience with computers. It has also been pointed out that computer experience brings higher wages (Krueger, 1993; Bresnahan et al., 2002). Government officials recognize these trends and have acted accordingly. For example, the policy prescription from the Clinton/Gore administration was to give priority to computer and Internet usage in classrooms, and by 2001, 99% of public schools had Internet access, compared with only 35% in 1994 (NCES, 2002). The presumption is that one will be left behind in job skills and social avenues if one does not have access to the latest technology. This presumption is also made on the nation-state level; i.e., nations with little or no computer access will be left behind economically and socially (Lall, 1985; Dahlman and Frischtak, 1990; Inman and Burton, 1990; Mody and Dahlman, 1992; Kraemer and Dedrick, 1994).

As Bill Gates states in a January 1997 interview in *George*, "Every politician wants to be associated with the future. There's no country where I've gone where there hasn't been interest among the top political leaders in sitting down and talking with me. Part of it is the legitimate issue of talking about how their country can exploit technological advances, and part of it is just trying to associate themselves with technology and the bright future that comes with that" (Kennedy, 1997).

Political leaders and their policy staff could address their national information policy needs better if they had a clearer knowledge of which nations currently have the edge in the information age and why. For example, we know that nations with strong economies, education systems, and communications infrastructures have been leaders in computer usage (Northrop and Kraemer, 2000), but what about the Internet? It is increasingly important for policymakers to understand which countries are also successfully managing the Internet and the World Wide Web, and what potential benefits will accrue from this success. Just as the Industrial Revolution changed the face of economic and political power, so too may the Information Revolution. The Industrial Revolution was machine-driven by the invention of the steam engine and the cotton gin. The Information Revolution is also machine-driven with the invention of the mainframe computer and, more recently, the personal computer and the means to connect computers, specifically the Internet and the communication networks on which the Internet rides.

One source of advice and insight for political administrators is the community of scholars who are often called upon to shape policy. Yet political scientists have largely ignored the study of computers. While the field of public administration has clearly recognized the important role of computers (NASPAA Ad Hoc Committee on Computers in Public Management Education, 1986; Ronaghan, 2002), it has largely ignored the impacts of computers in its journals and textbooks (Northrop, 1997, 2003). Moreover, those articles that do deal with computers talk almost exclusively about the experiences of U.S. cities and the federal government or curricula issues for universities. Fortunately, because computer technology is thought to be intimately related with economic development (Kraemer and Dederick, 1994; Dederick et al., 2003) and even perhaps with democratization (Kedzie, 1995; Allison, 2002a), political scientists have begun to catch up with political leaders and focus on computerization so they can better advise policy-makers and assess policy outcomes.

In particular, people in the field of comparative politics have become interested in the impacts of computerization as they relate to theories of modernization and development (Al-Abdul-Gader, 1999; Tan et al., 1999a), while people in the field of international relations are beginning to examine the impacts of computerization as they relate to changing political power (Nye and Owens, 1996; Allison, 2002a; Kalathil and Boas, 2003) and perhaps even the decline of the nation-state (Blumenthal, 1988; Mathews, 1997). For instance, it has been argued that computers can bring people to distant or unknown places, enabling them to identify with regional, national, and even trans-national groups (Giddens, 1981; Sassen, 1996). Huntington (1996) takes the opposite position that as countries modernize, and computers are certainly modern symbols and media, they actually become more parochial as they seek solace in cultural traditions. Nonetheless, computers are thought to have consequences for people's senses of community; as Putnam (2000: 171) explains, "Telecommunications in general and the Internet in particular substantially enhance our ability to communicate; thus it seems reasonable to assume that their net effect will be to enhance community, perhaps even dramatically". These impacts have enormous political relevance for political leaders and their policy staff. In 2002, for example, the American Society for Public Administration and the United Nations (UN) collaborated on a study which found that the Internet has increasingly become a tool used by governments on a daily basis (Ronaghan, 2002).

The present study addresses the issue of technological advance by reviewing the factors that led countries to computerize at high rates during the 1990s and asking which countries have been most likely to take advantage of the Internet as it gains wide popularity at the start of the 21st century. This study uses two databases, one from 1993, when computers had just attained mass appeal, and a second from 2001, when the use of the Internet had taken off worldwide. The first database consists of 41 nations and the former colony of Hong Kong, the second consists of 43 nations and Hong Kong (Table 19.1).[1] The study

---

[1] The two additional nations in the 2001 data set are Egypt and Malaysia. While neither nation is at the highest extreme on any of our measures, nor is it at the extreme bottom. Thus, Egypt and Malaysia were included in the 2001 analysis to add predictability and generalizability of the conclusions internationally.

Table 19.1 Database of 44 Countries

Argentina	Hong Kong	Poland
Australia	Hungary	Portugal
Austria	India	Russia
Belgium	Indonesia	Singapore
Brazil	Ireland	South Africa
Canada	Israel	Spain
Chile	Italy	Sweden
China	Japan	Switzerland
Czech Republic	Republic of South Korea	Taiwan
Denmark	Malaysia	Thailand
Egypt	Mexico	Turkey
Finland	Netherlands	United Kingdom
France	New Zealand	United States
Germany	Norway	Venezuela
Greece	Philippines	

hypothesizes that the profusion of information infrastructure (e.g., televisions and, in particular telephones) is a key mediating force determining the likelihood of a nation-state making use of computers in the early 1990s, and the Internet early in the 21st century. After discussing the 1993 results, which show the progress of computerization across nations, we examine the latest in information technology (IT), asking what factors explain Internet adoption around the world? Are the economic, social, and information infrastructure factors that lead to computer use the same factors that explain Internet use, or are there other phenomena at work? Comparing these two waves of IT use allows for a broader picture of technology change and adaptation across the globe.

The data tell the unsurprising tale of the rich getting richer, and, therefore, the poor getting poorer. Past studies have also found rich nations benefiting but focus on debating whether the economy drives computer adoption or whether computer adoption also can "turn on" the economy (Rahim and Pennings, 1987; Mody and Dahlman, 1992; Kraemer and Dedrick, 1994, 1996; Freeman, 1996). There is evidence to support both positions. Past studies have also addressed the role that education and free access to information plays in computer adoption and the role of computers in expanding education and free information access. This study argues that prior studies, by focusing on directionality of economic causality or the role of social vs. economic factors (Weingart, 1984; Mackenzie, 1992; Laporte et al., 2001), have missed key mediating forces to Internet and web usage, i.e., the dominant and critical role of earlier information media. Of great importance is the fact that access to one information medium supports access to another. Nations cannot simply concentrate on national computer policy to bring their nations into the information age. As an integral part of such a national policy they need to concentrate on building, on a mass level, earlier information media so that their work force can readily adapt to the use of computers and expand the potential benefits of the Internet. The key to wide use of technology is not simply wealth of a nation or a highly educated population with free access to information, but a mature information infrastructure. This study hypothesizes that use of the Internet is especially fostered in nations with wide access to various forms of communication technology, in particular, telephones and cell phones.

The importance of an information infrastructure for technology use points to the key benefit to be garnered from the Internet: providing communication links between governments, between the citizen and the government, and between citizen and citizen. From e-mail exchanges between citizens during times of war, to facilitation of more representative policymaking, to fostering peace between nations, Internet use offers the prospect of advancing communication in the public sphere in nations across the globe (Allison, 2002b). The "information age" is no misnomer; information is precisely the issue, and, therefore, governments that fear and restrict access to information will find it difficult to accrue the benefits of the Internet and of other ITs, regardless of the status of their information infrastructures.

II. DATA

The data for this study have been developed and maintained by the Center for Research on Information Technology and Organizations at the University of California, Irvine. The data come from many different sources, ranging from UN statistics to those kept by the computer industry. Table 19.2 lists the sources of all variables in this study.

The countries in the database (Table 19.1) are those commonly tracked by industry analysts such as International Data Corporation and Dataquest because they represent important computer markets for which other secondary data also were available for the time periods in the study (Table 19.2). There is no country with no computers per 1000 in the data set, and thus such countries are not able to suppress correlations by their sheer dominance of cases. In 2001, among the 44 countries studied, the lowest number of computers per 1000 citizens is 5.84 (India).[2] The highest is 625 (U.S.). The mean is 220, and the median is 157 per 1000.

The sample is heavily weighted toward Europe and North America with twenty-three countries, one country is in Africa, two are in the Middle East, five in Latin America, eleven in Asia, and then there are the countries of Australia and New Zealand. While there is a decided overweighting of advanced industrialized countries in the sample, there is also extreme variation, as one will see, on all variables starting from gross domestic product (GDP), education, and newspaper circulation to computer and Internet use.

While longitudinal data would be better, earlier data reduce the sample, making statistical analysis very distorted and near impossible in terms of statistical significance. In addition, several of the indices used in the analyses have not been collected over time. Thus, all variables in the original study come from 1993; the variables in the current analysis of Internet use are as close to 2001 as possible (ranging between the years 1999 and 2001).

III. COMPUTERIZATION IN 1993: HYPOTHESES AND FINDINGS

This section looks at the first wave of IT to cross the globe, as measured by computer use in 1993.[3] It addresses whether a nation's economic, social, or information infrastructure

---

[2] For 2001, there are four nations with missing data. The four missing nations and the corresponding numbers of personal computers per 1000 population for 2000 are: Austria (280), Canada (403), Denmark (431), and Switzerland (500).

[3] This period refers mainly to mainframe and minicomputer use. The personal computer was first introduced in 1979 but did not begin to take off until IBM entered the market in 1993, so our break point is particularly appropriate.

Table 19.2   Sources of All Variables for the 44 Countries

Variable	Source
Computers per person (1993)	Juliussen, Egil, and Karen Petska-Juliussen. *The 7th Annual Computer Industry Almanac*, 1994–95. Dallas, TX: Computer Industry Almanac, Inc., 1994
Internet users per 1000 (2001)	International Telecommunication Union, *World Telecommunication Indicators Database*, ITU, Geneva, 2002
Televisions per person (1993)	*The 7th Annual Computer Industry Almanac*, Computer Industry, Almanac, Inc., Dallas, TX, 1994–1995
Televisions per person (2001)	International Telecommunication Union, *World Telecommunication Indicators Database*, ITU, Geneva, 2002
GDP per capita ($, 1993)	International Telecommunication Union, 1995
GDP per capita ($, 2001)	*World Development Indicators Database Online*, The World Bank, Washington, D.C., 2003
Main telephone lines per 100 inhabitants (1994); cellular mobile phone subscribers per 100 inhabitants (1994)	International Telecommunication Union, Switzerland; *World Telecommunication Development Report*, Geneva
Main telephone lines per 100 inhabitants (1999); cellular mobile phone subscribers per 100 inhabitants (1999)	International Telecommunication Union, *World Telecommunication Indicators Database*, ITU, Geneva, 2001
Population (%) with some tertiary education (1992) Population (%) with some secondary education (1992) Newspaper circulation per 1000 inhabitants	United Nations, *Statistical Yearbook*, United Nations, New York, 1995
Population (%) with some tertiary education (2000) Population (%) with some secondary education (2000) Newspaper circulation per 1000 inhabitants	*World Development Indicators Database Online*, The World Bank, Washington, D.C., 2003
Literacy	*The Grolier Multimedia Encyclopedia* (*interactive multimedia*), Grolier Electronic Publishing, Danbury, CT, 1996
Productivity in manufacturing ($, 1992)	EMF Foundation, *World Competitiveness Report* 1995, The Foundation, Cologny/Geneva, Switzerland, 1995
Social infrastructure (1993 data set)	*The Dorling Kindersley World Reference Atlas*, Dorling Kindersley, New York, 1994 *Freedom Review*, Freedom House, New York, 1995 United Nations Development Programme (UNDP), *UNDP Annual Report/UNDP*, UNDP Division of Public Affairs, New York, 1992–1995

Table 19.2   Sources of All Variables for the 44 Countries — continued

Variable	Source
Social infrastructure (2001 data set)	Sub-index of the IDC Information Society Index, *The 2001 Worldwide Black Book*, International Data Corporation, Framingham, MA
Information infrastructure (1993 data set)	International Telecommunication Union 1994, *Annuaire Statistique de l'UIT/Union Internationale des Telecommunications*, Geneva; L'Union, Switzerland *The Dorling Kindersley World Reference Atlas*, Dorling Kindersley, New York, 1994 United Nations Development Programme, *UNDP Annual Report/UNDP*, UNDP Division of Public Affairs, New York, 1992–1995
Information infrastructure (2001 data set)	Sub-index of the IDC Information Society Index, *The 2001 Worldwide Black Book*, International Data Corporation, Framingham, MA

Table 19.3   Pearson Correlations between Economic, Social, and Information Infrastructure Variables and Computers per Person

	Computer Use per Person (1993)	Controlling on GDP	Controlling on Social Infrastructure	Controlling on Information Infrastructure
Per capita GDP (1993)[a]	.78*	—	.52*	.07
Social infrastructure[b]	.89*	.53*	—	.07
Information infrastructure[c]	.93*	.81*	.80*	—

*Significant at .05 level.
**Significant at .01 level.
[a]Curve fit is power based.
[b]Curve fit is growth based.
[c]Curve fit is linear based.

plays a role in computer adoption. Each hypothesis will be considered in the order of its causal ability to influence computerization, starting with the economy.

A.   Economically Advanced Nations Are More Likely to Have Adopted Computers

The assumption is that economically advanced nations have the financial conditions for individuals, companies, and government to take advantage of computers as productivity boosters. The economic state of a nation is measured by per capita GDP in U.S. dollars in 1993; at the time the average GDP was $11,577.

This hypothesis is strongly supported (.78) and significantly so, as such the higher the GDP is per person, the higher the number of computers in that nation per person (Table 19.3). GDP is not, though, a linear predictor of computers per person. In other words, it is not simply the case that for each unit increase in GDP, a constant unit increase in computers per person will result. The relationship between the two is curvilinear: as the GDP of a nation-state increases, computers increasingly become more common. Using SPSS's curve fit function, the relationship between GDP and computers per person was found to best be described as a power base relationship. Thus, the GDP–computers relationship was converted to a power base in order to perform statistical analysis, which assumes linearity, with which the power base conversion is consistent.

GDP is a broad measure of the level of economic development in a nation. Obviously, it takes financial resources for a government or corporation or individual to purchase and maintain a computer. So it is not surprising that a strong association exists between GDP and computer penetration in a nation.

Because the data indicated that the relationship between a country's GDP and its computer adoption had grown in recent years, the relationship was further specified. Since the last machine-driven revolution changed the face of economic power among nation-states by elevating the manufacturing base over the agricultural, the role of manufacturing was explored. In other words, the relationship between GDP and computers was examined to see if it stood up after factoring out the major economic influence of manufacturing operations. About one third of the association between GDP and computerization can be attributed to the nation's productivity in manufacturing (Table 19.4). This finding attests to the important role computers play in this economic sector. Computers are used not only in the administrative side of manufacturing but also in the design, assembly, and delivery of products. Still, a strong relationship between GDP and computers exists (.49) after the key role that manufacturing plays in GDP and computer adoption is eliminated. Thus, sectors beyond the important manufacturing one lay a base for a country's computerization.

B. Nation-States with More Educated Populations and Ones with More Open Access to Information Are More Likely to Have Adopted Computers

The assumption is that a nation-state cannot leap into the information age if it does not have a base of educated, literate citizens who are also free to access information and the said information is not limited. Use of the computer requires the ability to read and write at a level far beyond basic literacy. Literacy typically refers to a mere ability to read and write enough to get around in daily life; a third-grade education in the U.S. represents this level. In contrast, computer use requires higher levels of literacy and some basic level of computer literacy.

But having an educated population may not be sufficient to open the nation to computers. It is very important that the nation-state be characterized by a free press

Table 19.4 Pearson Correlations between GDP and Computers per Person Controlling on Economic components

GDP	Controlling on Productivity in Manufacturing
.78*	.49*

*Significant at .05 level.

and a greater tolerance of civil liberties. The issue is that computers increase citizens' ability to access information both within and outside the country. Therefore, countries that want to limit citizen access to information as well as limit citizen ability to convey information to media and international sources may face a dilemma with computer adoption. In sum, nation-states may need a certain social infrastructure to be able to move into the information age.

The measure of social infrastructure is an index composed of percent secondary school enrollment, percent tertiary school enrollment, newspaper readership per 1000, and measures of press freedom and civil liberties (see Table 19.2). China had the lowest score on this index (91) and Canada the highest (496), with the average being 356.

This hypothesis is as strongly supported as the first one (Table 19.3). It too is not linear. The greater the social infrastructure of a nation, the greater the nation's adoption of computers. This curvilinear relationship was converted to a growth base for analysis purposes, again using SPSS's curve fit function to find the best curvilinear base to describe the relationship between the social infrastructure and computers per person. The resulting correlation is .79.

All the countries fit this curve except one, Singapore, which has far more computers per person (.13) than it should, given its low value on the social infrastructure measure (233). Singapore has overcome its social constraints to computerization because of the very active role of the government. The strong centralized government in Singapore has made a concerted effort to leap into the information age by developing national plans to computerize the government sector and the country in general (Gurbaxani et al., 1990; Koon Wong, 1999; Palvia and Tung, 1999; Wong, 1999; Kalathil and Boas, 2003).

Table 19.5 presents the results of a component analysis of the social infrastructure index. Education at the university level appears to be one key to computer diffusion in a nation, while the percent of a nation's population with some secondary education has no effect on the relationship between a nation's social infrastructure and computer penetration. Still, university education, while important, only has a small effect on the relationship (.16 in Table 19.5). Newspaper circulation has a negligible effect (.06). What is interesting is that when one controls on tertiary- or university-level education and newspaper circulation together, one sees a large cumulative effect (.37). This effect is almost twice as great as the individual effects (.16 and .06). In other words, the more the number of people who have attended a university and the higher the newspaper

Table 19.5 Pearson Correlations between Social Infrastructure Index and Computers per Person Controlling on Index Components

Social Infrastructure Index	Controlling on			
	Percent Secondary School	Percent Tertiary School	Newspaper Circulation per 1000	All Three
.79*	.79*	.63*	.73*	.42*
	(.00)[a]	(.16)	(.06)	(.37)

*Significant at .05 level.

[a]Number in parentheses represents the portion of the zero-order correlation that is attributable to the components controlled on.

circulation in a nation, the much higher likelihood that computers have penetrated into that society.

What could explain this heightened effect? A hint is provided by the fact that about half of the association between social infrastructure and computer diffusion is attributable to press freedom and civil liberties, the other components of the index. (These are not controlled for in Table 19.5, but because they are the other components of the index, press freedom and civil liberties have to explain what education and newspaper circulation cannot, which is .37 association.) As was suggested earlier, the education level of its citizens is only one ingredient in a nation's ability to utilize computers. The more highly educated a population is, the more likely that the nation can utilize computers for sophisticated tasks, from graphic design, inventory and budgetary control to scientific and military research. But it appears also to be important that press freedom and tolerance of civil liberties be present for truly high computer adoption. Countries that want to limit citizen access to information and their ability to convey information face a dilemma, then, when they wish to encourage computer use to get economic benefits.

In sum, taken together, education and newspaper circulation expand the possibility of information flow. To these add uncensored information in the media and a tolerance for citizen expression, and a nation has an exponential ability to use and grow from information. Computers are just one of the medias for realizing this ability.

C. Nation-States that Have a Higher Saturation of Information Medias Are More Likely to Adopt Computers

The assumption is that access to one medium supports access to another. For example, families used to sit around the living room listening to the radio; then they did the same thing with the advent of television. And the seeds for the personal computer revolution may have been sown in countries where children grew up with television. Children can view computers as an interactive television. Then there are the direct links between medias: phones make fax machines possible, satellites make cell phones possible, and telephones make Internet access possible.

The measure of saturation of information media is an index composed of number of telephone lines per 100 households, radio ownership per 1000 inhabitants, television ownership per 1000 inhabitants, fax ownership per 100 inhabitants, cellular phones per 100 inhabitants, and cable/satellite television coverage. This composite measure is referred to as the information infrastructure. Indonesia had the lowest score on the measure (145) and the U.S. the highest (2810), with the average being 983.

This hypothesis is the most strongly (.93) and significantly supported (Table 19.3). The data indicate an almost perfect linear relationship between a nation's information infrastructure and its adoption of computers. As Table 19.6 indicates, about one fourth of the relationship between the information infrastructure of a nation and its adoption of computers can be attributed to how common televisions are and another one fourth to how common telephones are. Cellular phones contribute half as much, or one eighth. Note that these three devices are independent of each other and thus have an additive role in explaining what parts of the information infrastructure are associated with computer adoption. The overlap among the three measures is a negligible .06.

To illustrate, the U.S. has 0.97 telephones, 0.90 televisions, and 0.29 computers per person. Great Britain has 0.62 telephones, 0.45 televisions, and 0.16 computers

Table 19.6   Pearson Correlations between Information Infrastructure Index and Computers per Person Controlling on Index Components

Information Infrastructure Index	Controlling on			
	TVs	Phones	Cellular Phones	All Three
.93*	.69*	.70*	.81*	.28*
	(.24)[a]	(.23)	(.12)	(.65)

*Significant at .05 level.
[a]Number in parentheses represents the portion of the zero-order correlation that is attributable to the components controlled on.

per person. Taiwan has 0.42 telephones, 0.27 televisions, and 0.007 computers per person. India has 0.01 telephones, 0.05 televisions, and 0.00 computers per person.

These data suggest that information medias support each other. For example, telephones can enhance the power of computers by connecting one computer to another and by expanding data retrieval possibilities, such as through the Internet. While it is hard to imagine how televisions directly enhance the power of computers, a society used to looking at a television screen can more easily adapt to looking at a computer screen. And a society saturated with information media likely will be more aware of, interested in, and willing to learn about and own new information medias such as computers. In sum, the data suggest that nations with a strong information infrastructure will expand that infrastructure by a dramatically higher adoption of computers.

IV.   INTERNET USE IN 2001: HYPOTHESES AND FINDINGS

The following analysis looks beyond computerization to the latest wave in IT, the Internet. Using the same hypotheses from computerization in 1993, we examine the factors contributing to the varying uses of Internet across nations nearly a decade later. It is important to know whether or not nations will follow the same pattern in the use of Internet as was noted with computerization. The dependent variable is the number of Internet users per 1000 in 2001. The lowest level of Internet usage occurs in India, with only 6.8 users per 1000, the highest level of usage is in Norway, where over half of the citizens are Internet users (596.29 per 1000). Noteworthy in its own right is the fact that, on average, nearly one quarter of the citizens of these 44 nations are Internet users (246.81 individuals per 1000).

A.   Economically Advanced Nations Will Make More Extensive Use of Internet Technology

Again, the assumption is that economically advanced nations have the financial conditions for individuals, companies, and government to take advantage of the Internet. The economic state of a nation is measured by 2001 per capita GDP in constant U.S. dollars in 1995. India had the lowest GDP ($477) and Switzerland the highest ($47,064), with the average being $17,423.

All three independent variables, economic, social, and information infrastructure, have a very strong, statistically significant zero-order relationship with Internet users

Table 19.7 Pearson Correlations between Economic, Social, and Information Infrastructure Variables and Internet Use per 1000 People

	Internet Use per 1000 (2001)	Controlling on GDP	Controlling on Social Infrastructure	Controlling on Information Infrastructure
GDP 2001/per capita[a]	.85**	—	.47**	.38*
Social infrastructure[b]	.88**	.61**	—	.53**
Information infrastructure[c]	.85**	.51**	.47**	—

*Significant at .05 level.
**Significant at .01 level.
[a]Curve fit is power based.
[b]Curve fit is cubic based.
[c]Curve fit is power based.

and equally so (Table 19.7). As with the original analyses, the relationship between GDP and Internet use is not linear, thus the SPSS curve fit function was used to convert the relationship to a power base. The result indicated a correlation of .85 between Internet users and GDP. When controlling for GDP, the relationships between social infrastructure and information infrastructure remain strong and statistically significant, although they are weaker than when not controlling for GDP (.61 and .51, respectively, Table 19.7). Thus GDP is important, but certainly not singularly key.

B. Nations with More Educated Citizens and Ones with More Open Access to Information Are More Likely to Use Internet Technology

The assumption remains that a nation-state cannot take full advantage of the information age if it does not have a base of educated, literate citizens with wide and open access to information. Because the Internet increases citizens' ability to access information both within and outside the country, nations that seek limits on citizen access to information may face a challenge with the growing use of Internet technology. Again, social infrastructure is measured by education enrollment, newspaper readership, press freedom, and civil liberties. In 2001, China had the lowest score on this index (385) and Norway the highest (1542), the average score being 967.

All three independent variables, economic, social, and information infrastructure, have a very strong, statistically significant relationship with Internet users, but the relationship with social infrastructure is the strongest (.88, see Table 19.7). Again, the relationship is not linear so that the SPSS curve fit function was used to convert the relationship to a cubic base. We can see in Table 19.7, that when the influence of social infrastructure is controlled, the relationships between Internet use and both GDP and information infrastructure are much lower (.47 and .47). Thus, social infrastructure is important, and more so than GDP.

Table 19.8 controls on the social infrastructure components, political rights and civil rights, in addition to the education and newspaper controls used in the 1993 study. As we can see, advanced education and the civil rights index contribute the most to the relationship between Internet use and social infrastructure (.14 and .11, respectively).

Table 19.8 Pearson Correlations between Social Infrastructure Index and Internet Use per 1000 People Controlling on Index Components

Social Infrastructure Index	Controlling on				
	Percent Secondary School	Percent Tertiary School	Newspaper Circulation per 1000	Political Rights Index	Civil Rights Index
.88**	.83**	.74**	.81*	.86**	.77**
	(.07)[a]	(.14)	(.07)	(.02)	(.11)

*Significant at .05 level.

**Significant at .01 level.

[a]Number in parentheses represents the portion of the zero-order correlation that is attributable to the components controlled on.

Secondary education and newspaper circulation each add .07 to the relationship, while political rights add very little (.02). All controls have statistically significant relationships with Internet use. The important point is really that the combination of education, newspaper readership, and political rights are what drive Internet use, rather than the singular importance of any component of the social infrastructure alone.

C. Nation-States that Have a Higher Saturation of Information Media Are More Likely to Use Internet Technology Extensively

The final assumption is also the same as in the study on computerization: access to one information medium supports access to another. The measure of saturation of information media is the information infrastructure index, which consists of data on the number of telephone lines, radio, television and fax ownership, cellular phones, and cable/satellite television coverage. In 2001, Indonesia had the lowest score on the measure (145) and the U.S. the highest (2810), with the average being 983.

Again, the relationship is not linear but was converted to a power base using the SPSS curve fit function. The resulting analysis indicates that a strong (.85), statistically significant relationship exists between Internet use and information infrastructure (Table 19.7). When controlling on GDP, the relationship between Internet use and social infrastructure declines but is still strong, at .53. Echoing the conclusions about computer use in 1993, controlling on the information infrastructure index reduces the correlation between GDP and Internet use from a very strong .85 to a moderate .38.

Finally, when controlling on the index components of television, telephone, and cellular phone saturation, we find that cellular phone usage contributes the greatest amount to the relationship with Internet use (.21) (see Table 19.8 and Table 19.9). Televisions continue to contribute a fair amount to the relationship (.16). The variable that would be expected to contribute the greatest portion of the information infrastructure index to its relationship with Internet users is telephone lines; although the contribution appears to be quite high (.60), curiously the relationship is statistically significant at only the .10 level.

Table 19.9   Pearson Correlations between Information Infrastructure Index and Internet per 1000 People Controlling on Index Components

Information Infrastructure Index	Controlling on			
	TVs	Phones	Cellular Phones	All Three
.85**	.69**	.25	.64**	.40*
	(.16)[a]	(.60)	(.21)	(.45)

*Significant at .05 level.

**Significant at .01 level.

[a]Number in parentheses represents the portion of the zero-order correlation that is attributable to the components controlled on.

V.   A NOTE ON CAUSAL ORDER

As was stated in the introduction, political leaders presume computerization will lead to economic and social benefits. This presumption implies a feedback route from computerization to the economy. And, in fact, a study of 12 Asia Pacific countries for the period from 1984 to 1990 did find such a link to economic growth when considering the wider variable of ITs, which would also include semiconductors and software (Kraemer and Dedrick, 1994). There is also the weight of historical evidence that supports a feedback route for technology in general (Rosenberg, 1982). An excellent literature review of studies investigating the feedback route is Dedrick et al. (2003), which clearly shows that there are positive and consistent IT impacts on productivity at the firm, industry, and national levels. These impacts can vary by time period, and statistical measures used, but in general they are positive.

The causal relationship between GDP per capita and computer or Internet usage in this study is likely not compromised by a measurable feedback route, given the time frame of the study's computer data (1993) and given that the key output measurements are computer and Internet usage. Aside from the fact that this study did not measure GDP growth, there are sound reasons to believe that the economic and social benefits from computerization and the Internet have a long time lag and, therefore, cannot be significantly and measurably contributing to GDP per capita at this time. While computers have been around for over 50 years, their diffusion into society beyond government and beyond Western industrial countries is very recent and just becoming measurable. New technologies require time not only for widespread adoption but also for organizational and personnel adjustments to be made to use the technologies so that benefits are realized (David, 1989). Furthermore, the levels of GDP per capita of the countries, whether high or low, have been that way for years before the advent of computers. Hence, this study's use of GDP per capita as an independent variable and computers and Internet use per person as dependent variables seems reasonable. Similar arguments can be made for the social infrastructure and information infrastructure variables being independent variables, as of yet not discernibly affected by feedback from computerization and Internet use.

Finally, without the ability to do an experiment, one can only use accepted criteria to establish causation (Moore, 1997). The five criteria apply in the case of each of this study's independent variables: (1) the associations are strong, (2) the associations are consistent,

(3) higher "doses" are associated with stronger responses, (4) the alleged causes precede the effect in time, and (5) the alleged causes are plausible.

VI. CONCLUSIONS

There are benefits to be accrued when computers are used alone; however, they are nowhere near as great as when computers are connected in networks, whether local, intranet, or Internet. Moreover, the greater the number of connections with the Internet, the greater the benefits, because an individual is able to communicate with more people and access more information. In other words, computers and telecommunication networks offer network economies in which benefits increase exponentially as the number of people and amount of information on a network increases. This is one of the reasons why liberalization of telecommunication networks is important. Control of information or access to networks limits the benefits of the technology.

This study attempts to explain which nations have taken the lead in the information age. Economic, social, and information infrastructure factors were each explored and found to have a significant and strong association with the likelihood of a nation being "online." In essence, the economic and social levels of a nation shape the spread of information medias, such as televisions, telephones, and fax machines, which in turn fuel the use of IT.

Does this mean the rich get richer? It appears that well-off nation-states have the decided edge in utilizing computers and the Internet for economic and social gain. But the story is a bit more complicated. Being rich is only one determinant. A country also needs a very highly educated population; but also important, the society needs to be open to the sharing of information as indicated by its newspaper readership, tolerance of civil rights, and press freedoms. These economic and social factors set the stage for the building of a massive information infrastructure, and the economic and social infrastructures may gain from the building of that information infrastructure. The information infrastructure, in particular, has been found to be key to a nation's ability to use and gain from IT in business and government. Therefore, some countries, such as Singapore, can successfully skip the expansion of civil rights and press freedoms and still leap into the information age (Kalathil and Boas, 2003).

These findings bode well for countries with strong information infrastructures and citizens adept with technology. In the U.S. and Japan, for example, children are well known for their addiction to television and other information medias, from radios to cell phones, to DVDs. In Singapore, school-aged children make much use of pagers, an indication of their assimilation to technology usage (Corbett et al., 1999b). It is this affinity that may make children quick learners and frequent users of computers and the Internet. We expect the drive to adopt the Internet to continue with the U.S. and Japan on the forefront. Countries that lack such a high level of information medias or the open access to information allowed in these countries will be the losers in terms of Internet use and, therefore, potential payoffs.

The government actions taken by countries in the early 1990s reflected and were limited by their economic and political environments (Kahin and Wilson, 1997: ix). For example, India responded to its slow economic growth with economic reforms in the 1990s. These reforms, shaped by internal political struggles, play a role in an inconsistent national information policy that on the one hand has encouraged computer adoption and on the other limited the benefits and production of computers by extremely high licensing fees for electronic mail providers, $80,000, and low computer production and high cost due to fragmented licensed production capacities (Petrazzini and Harindranath, 1997). The internal struggles over privatization, national self-reliance, and high tariffs in general have major consequences for the future computerization of India.

However, while many countries of the world are behind advanced nations like the U.S., Canada, and Japan in Internet use and telecommunication networks, Kahin and Wilson (1997) noted that governments have been quite active in constructing and managing national information infrastructures. For example, Ronaghan (2002: 4) reports that the Internet has been an important driver of change and that, "For a large majority of countries, national e-government program development is occurring in a swift and dynamic manner and for now change is the only constant."

Will the Internet change the face of economic and political power? The data make one lean toward saying no. Economically advanced nations and nations with greater social freedoms are the most likely to have computers and use the Internet and thus are most likely to benefit from both. Nations that attempt to limit access or free flow of information, therefore, face a dilemma. While some, including China, Singapore, and many Middle Eastern nations, might limit Internet access to ensure political stability, by doing so, they reduce the potential benefits to be gained through the information age.

This is not a serious problem in the short term for a country like Singapore, which is already developed, but it is a problem for a country like China, which seeks accelerated long-term economic development. Such development is likely to be much slower if access and information flows are constrained, even with the growth of telecommunication networks. Economic choices are known to have repercussions for authoritarian regimes and movements to democracy (Diamond and Plattner, 1995; Haggard and Kaufman, 1995).

One example of this comes from the People's Republic of China (PRC) which hosts at least five Internet chat rooms in which members are not allowed to use profanity or discuss politics. These restrictions lead Corbett et al. (1999b) to conclude that chat rooms are not intended for information exchange in China but are simply status symbols for a burgeoning Chinese upper class. In addition, China has had difficulty implementing its "one country, two systems" concept with Hong Kong because Hong Kong, with one of the most advanced telecommunication networks in the world, stands in sharp contrast to mainland China. The government of the PRC has attempted to restrict and manage Internet access because, "[t]he paramount goal of many Chinese leaders is to maintain social stability and political control" (Burn and Martinsons, 1999: 32). This strategy could have negative consequences over the long term if these decisions "hinder the development of an information highway into the PRC and thereby inhibit the modernization of China" (Burn and Martinsons, 1999: 32). There is mounting evidence, however, that because authoritarian regimes drive their national technology agendas, compliance with state norms has been reinforced through self-censorship by individual and business Internet users. Even Western companies have acquiesced to regime standards when doing business in nations like Singapore and China (Kalathil and Boas, 2003).

Our findings highlight the connection between earlier home and business technology and current IT use. For example, the spread of television as a consumer product has served as a stimulus to the drive toward computerization, opening up its economic and political potential. Importantly, a society may not be able to advance into the information age without its future work force being used to other information medias such as televisions, fax machines, and cell phones. For instance, if the general population of developing countries does not watch television, they may be unable to understand or automatically relate to sounds and images on computer screens. Being used to hearing a door close off camera or being able to recognize how certain music sets the stage for "scary events," for example, allows people in developed vs. developing countries to follow movies (Greenfield, 1984). The same can be said about computer CD-ROMs. To illustrate at the most simple level, consider an individual not used to watching television. How would he or she be able to understand what the "ta da" sound that a computer makes when it opens up a program means? In sum, not being exposed to television or telephones makes using computers a much harder and maybe even an incomprehensible task for average workers.

In conclusion, as the UN study (Ronaghan, 2002) and this project indicate nations are increasingly taking advantage of the information age. To fully participate and gain the economic, political, and social benefits of computers and the Internet, nations would be well advised to expose their citizens to earlier generations of mass information medias and to provide them an extensive information infrastructure. As we found, nearly one quarter of people in our study nations are already online; because the Internet is spreading now, governments must act now to benefit from the information age.

REFERENCES

Atwell, P. and Rule, J., Computing and organizations: what we know and what we don't know, *Communications of the ACM*, 27, 1184–1192, 1984.

Al-Abdul-Gader, A., *Managing Computer Based Information Systems in Developing Countries: A Cultural Perspective*, Idea Group, Hershey, PA, 1999.

Allison, J.E., Ed., *Technology, Development and Democracy: International Conflict and Cooperation in the Information Age*, State University of New York Press, New York, 2002a.

Allison, J.E., Ed., Information and international politics: an overview, in *Technology, Development and Democracy: International Conflict and Cooperation in the Information Age*, State University of New York Press, New York, 2002b.

Blauner, R., *Alienation and Freedom: The Factory Worker and His Industry*, University of Chicago Press, Chicago, 1964.

Blumenthal, W.M., The world economy and technological change, *Foreign Affairs*, 66, 529–550, 1988.

Bresnahan, T.F., Brynjolfsson, E., and Hitt, L.M., Information technology, workplace organization, and the demand for skilled labor: firm level evidence, *The Quarterly Journal of Economics*, 117, 339, 2002.

Burn, J.M. and Martinsons, M., Information technology production and application in Hong Kong and China: progress, policies and prospects, in *Information Technology Diffusion in the Asia Pacific: Perspectives on Policy, Electronic Commerce and Education*, Corbett, P.S., Tan, F.B., and Wong, Y., Eds., Idea Group, Hershey, PA, 1999.

Corbett, P.S., Tan, F.B., and Wong, Y., Eds., *Information Technology Diffusion in the Asia Pacific: Perspectives on Policy, Electronic Commerce and Education*, Idea Group, Hershey, PA, 1999a.

Corbett, P.S., Tan, F.B., and Wong, Y., Eds., Placing the contributions in context, in *Information Technology Diffusion in the Asia Pacific: Perspectives on Policy, Electronic Commerce and Education*, Idea Group, Hershey, PA, 1999b.

Dahlman, C.J. and Frischtak, C.R., *National System Supporting Technical Advance in Industry; the Brazilian Experience*, Industry Series Paper No. 32, Industry and Energy Department, The World Bank, Washington, D.C., 1990.

Danziger, J.N., Dutton, W.H., Kling, R., and Kraemer, K.L., *Computers and Politics*, Columbia University Press, New York, 1982.

David, P., Computer and Dynamo: The Modern Productivity Paradox in a Not-Too-Distant Mirror, Working Paper, Center for Economic Policy Research, Stanford University, Palo Alto, CA, 1989.

Dederick, J., Gurbaxani, V., and Kraemer, K., Information technology and economic performance: a critical review of the empirical evidence, *ACM Computing Surveys*, 35, 1–28, 2003.

Diamond, L. and Plattner, M.F., *Economic Reform and Democracy*, Johns Hopkins University Press, Baltimore, 1995.

Downs, A., A realistic look at the final payoffs from urban data systems, *Public Administration Review*, 27, 204–210, 1967.

Freeman, C., The two-edged nature of technological change: employment and unemployment, in *Information and Communication Technologies*, Dutton, S.H., Ed., Oxford University Press, Oxford, 1996.

Giddens, A.A., *Contemporary Critique of Historical Materialism*, Macmillan, U.K., 1981.

Greenfield, P.M., *Mind and Media*, Harvard University Press, Cambridge, MA, 1984.

Gurbaxani, V., Kraemer, K.L., King, J.L., Jarman, S., and Dedrick, J., Government as the driving force toward the information society: national computer policy in Singapore, *Information Society*, 7, 155–185, 1990.

Haggard, S. and Kaufman, R.R., *The Political Economy of Democratic Transition*, Princeton University Press, Princeton, NJ, 1995.

Huntington, S.P., The West: unique, not universal, *Foreign Affairs*, 75, 28–46, 1996.

Inman, B.R. and Burton, D.F., Jr., Technology and competitiveness: the new policy frontier, *Foreign Affairs*, 69, 116–134, 1990.

Kahin, B., and Wilson, E.J., III, Eds., *National Information Infrastructure Initiatives*, MIT Press, Cambridge, MA, 1997.

Kalathil, S. and Boas, T.C., *Open Networks, Closed Regimes: The Impact of the Internet on Authoritarian Rule*, Carnegie Endowment for International Peace, Washington, D.C., 2003.

Kedzie, C.R., *Democracy and Network Interconnectivity*, RAND, Santa Monica, CA, 1995.

Kennedy, J., Interview with Bill Gates, George, January, 1997.

Kraemer, K.L. and Dedrick, J., Payoffs from investment in information technology: lessons from the Asia-Pacific region, *World Development*, 22, 1921–1931, 1994.

Kraemer, K.L. and Dedrick, J., IT and economic development: international competitiveness, in *Information and Communication Technologies*, Dutton, W.H., Ed., Oxford University Press, Oxford, 1996.

Kraemer, K.L., Dutton, W., and Northrop, A., *The Management of Information Systems*, Columbia University Press, New York, 1981.

Krueger, A.B., How computers have changed the wage structure: evidence from microdata, 1984–1989, *The Quarterly Journal of Economics*, 108, 33–60, 1993.

Lall, S., Trade in technology by a slowly industrializing country: India, in *International Technology Transfer: Concepts, Measures and Comparisons*, Rosenberg, N. and Fischtak, C.R., Eds., Praeger, New York, 1985.

La Porte, T.M., Demchak, C.C., and Friis, C., Webbing governance: global trends across national-level public agencies, *Communications of the ACM*, 44, 63–67, 2001.

Leavitt, H.J. and Whisler, T.L., Management in the 1980s, *Harvard Business Review*, 36, 41–48, 1985.

Mackenzie, D., Economic and sociological explanation of technical change, in *Technical Change and Company Strategies*, Coombs, R., Saviotti, P., and Walsh, V., Eds., Academic Press, U.K., 1992.

Mathews, J.T., Power shift, *Foreign Affairs*, 76, 50–66, 1997.

Mody, A. and Dahlman, C., Performance and potential information technology: an international perspective, *World Development*, 20, 1703–1719, 1992.

Moore, D.S., *Statistics: Concepts and Controversies*, W.H. Freeman, San Francisco, 1997.

NASPAA, Ad hoc committee on computers in public management education. Curriculum recommendations for public management education in computing, *Public Administration Review*, 46, 595–602, 1986.

NCES (National Center for Education Statistics), Internet Access in U.S. Public Schools and Classrooms: 1994–2001, United States Department of Education, Washington, D.C., 2002.

Northrop, A., Computing education in public administration journals and textbooks, *Social Science Computing Review*, 15, 40–47, 1997.

Northrop, A., Information technology and public administration: the view from the profession, in *Public Information Technology and Management Issues*, Garson, G.D., Ed., Idea Group, Hershey, PA, 2003.

Northrop, A. and Kraemer, K., The information age: which countries will benefit?, in *Handbook of Public Information Systems*, Garson, G.D., Ed., Marcel Dekker, New York, 2000.

Northrop, A., Kraemer, K.L., Dunkle, D., and King, J.L., The payoffs from computerization: lessons over time, *Public Administration Review*, 51, 505–514, 1990.

Nye, J.S., Jr. and Owens, W.A., America's information edge, *Foreign Affairs*, 75, 20–34, 1996.

Palvia, S.C. and Tung, L.L., Internet use and issues in Singapore and USA: a comparative study, in *Information Technology Diffusion in the Asia Pacific: Perspectives on Policy, Electronic Commerce and Education*, Corbett, P.S., Tan, F.B., and Wong, Y., Eds., Idea Group, Hershey, PA, 1999.

Petrazzini, B.A. and Harindranath, G., *Information Infrastructure Initiatives in Emerging Economies: The Case of India*, Kahin, B. and Wilson, E.J., III, Eds., MIT Press, Cambridge, MA, 1997.

Putnam, R.D., *Bowling Alone: The Collapse and Revival of American Community*, Simon and Schuster, New York, 2000.

Rahim, S.A. and Pennings, A.J., Computerization and Development in Southeast Asia, Asian Mass Communication Research and Information Center, Singapore, 1987.

Ronaghan, S.A., *Benchmarking E-Government: A Global Perspective — Assessing the UN Member States*, United Nations, New York, 2002.

Rosenberg, N., *Inside the Black Box: Technology and Economics*, Cambridge University Press, New York, 1982.

Sassen, S., *Losing Control? Sovereignty in an Age of Globalization*, Columbia University Press, New York, 1996.

Simon, H.A., *The Shape of Automation for Man and Management*, Harper & Row, New York, 1965.

Taylor, J., Ballany, C., Raas, C., Dutton, W.H., and Peltu, M., Innovation in public service delivery, in *Information and Communication Technologies*, Dutton, W.H., Ed., Oxford University Press, Oxford, 1996.

Weingart, P., The structure of technological change, in *The Nature of Technological Knowledge*, Laudon, R., Ed., Reidel, Dordrecht, Netherlands, 1984.

Wong, T., Information technology development in Singapore and its geographical effects, in *Information Technology Diffusion in the Asia Pacific: Perspectives on Policy, Electronic Commerce and Education*, Corbett, P.S., Tan, F.B., and Wong, Y., Eds., Idea Group, Hershey, PA, 1999.

PART IV

CASE STUDIES

20

THE ROLE OF INFORMATION TECHNOLOGY AND THE NEW YORK STATE LEGISLATURE

Antoinette J. Pole
The City University of New York

CONTENTS

I. Introduction 321
II. Literature review 322
III. Research objective and hypotheses 323
IV. Case selection, data collection, and operationalization 324
V. Analysis 325
    A. Historical evolution of IT in the New York State legislature 325
    B. IT and casework 327
    C. IT and policy formulation 329
VI. Conclusion 332
References 333

ABSTRACT

This chapter explores the role of computing technology in the New York State legislature from 1980 through 2003. It examines how information technology (IT) has affected casework and policy formulation. I assess the level of collaboration, efficiency, and acceptance toward new technologies in these areas. Overall, there is increased collaboration on casework and policy formulation as a result of e-mail and the Internet. I also find that there is a greater degree of efficiency, but the acceptance of new technologies is not universal.

I. INTRODUCTION

A revolution in information technology (IT) occurred in the 1960s that promised to make daily tasks in the workplace both quicker and easier. Introduced in the late 1950s, the first computers relied on "punched cards" to store information. The creation of transistors and circuits in the 1960s led shortly thereafter to the widespread proliferation of computers. Transistors and circuits increased the speed and storage capacity of computers. The introduction of chip technologies and the subsequent integration of circuit technology in the 1970s again dramatically improved the capacity and capability of computers (Danziger et al. 1982). It was during this period that personal computers first appeared in the workplace. While significant advances in IT were quickly introduced in the private sector in the U.S., this was not the case in the public sector. Apart from universities, the implementation of new technology in the public sector — government and nonprofit organizations — unlike in the private sector, has proceeded gradually and cautiously over the last 35 years.

This chapter examines the role of IT in the New York State legislature from the latter part of the twentieth century through 2003. Largely qualitative, this research is both descriptive and exploratory, providing the reader with an overview of the evolution of IT in the legislature and how IT is employed for casework and policy formulation. In addition, this research is a test case for subsequent comparative state studies. I assess the degree to which IT has fostered or hindered collaboration, the level of efficiency, and whether members and their staff embrace technological changes in the New York State legislature. In general, I find that there has been increased collaboration and efficiency as a result of technological advancements. In general, staff and younger individuals have embraced technological advances, while a minority of state legislators and older individuals have been resistant to advances in IT.

Studying the nexus between IT and government is important for several reasons. First, while investigations of the influence of IT on urban, other local governments, and the federal government have been conducted, research on state-level government is largely absent. I suspect that this area has been neglected because studying state governments in the U.S. is cumbersome and costly. States are numerous and collectively are an enormous geographic entity. Second, e-mail and the Internet have arguably influenced the way we live and work more than anything else in the last 20 years. It is important to know how these technologies have influenced representative governments. Are state legislators responding to constituent concerns more quickly because of IT? Is there more collaboration between and among state legislators as a result of IT? This research informs both state legislators and scholars about the practical and theoretical implications of e-mail and the Internet. Finally, this research is also valuable because it contributes to our understanding of whether technology has fostered or hindered collaboration and efficiency, in addition to assessing whether members and their staff embrace technological changes. Although this chapter examines a state legislature, these issues extend to all levels of government.

II. LITERATURE REVIEW

As characterized by Bimber (2003), recent accounts of IT and government can be divided into two camps, the optimists and the pessimists. Authors in the former camp, Dahl (1989), Grossman (1995), Browning (1996), Rosenthal (1998), Bennett and Fielding (1999), assert that IT is beneficial. They maintain that IT will increase political participation and democratization and ultimately lead to better representation. The latter camp, Abramson et al. (1988), Barber (1998), Davis (1999), and Bimber (2003), argues that technology will not necessarily improve the prospects for political participation and democratization. Instead, the pessimists state that e-mail and the Internet may result in less deliberation and government by opinion polls. They suggest that those who already wield media power will also monopolize new technologies, minimizing any perceived benefits that e-mail and the Internet may have yielded. Although these debates outline the merits and dangers concerning the nexus between IT and government, none examine whether there is increased collaboration and efficiency, due to IT, or resistance to technology.

In contrast, Caudle et al. (1989) conduct an extensive cross-sectional study of IT in state governments, evaluating how technology facilitated coordination between the executive and state agencies, and between the executive branch and the legislative branches. The authors record and analyze management policies and practices that apply to IT in state governments, focusing on data processing, telecommunications, and office systems. The "frequent sharing of data from a program within an agency and the state legislature," in addition to budget requests and routine oversight from state legislatures, are specific areas where IT has facilitated coordination. While their study focuses on the role of management from the perspective of the state as a whole, the authors maintain that state legislatures need cooperation and support from individuals at all levels of government if the management of information resources is to succeed. This analysis acts as a basis for studying whether technology has fostered endogenous and exogenous collaboration in the New York State legislature.

Kraemer et al. (1981) examine the reform and postreform approaches to implementing technology in organizations paying close attention to efficiency. The reform approach, rooted in the Reform Movement of the early 1900s, favors the implementation of scientific management and business principles in government, with an emphasis on efficiency. Conversely, the postreform approach focuses on the quality of life within an organization and the responsiveness of organizations to clientele. The authors illustrate how technological developments, structural arrangements, sociotechnical designs, and organizational contexts in local governments differ under each approach. They find that exclusive reliance on either the reform or the postreform approach is problematic. Instead, Kraemer and Dutton favor mixing the two approaches, while incorporating a third approach, which posits that organizational performance is related to the community and surrounding socioeconomic factors. Proponents of advances in IT typically claim that new technologies will lead to increased efficiency. Kraemer and Dutton's analysis addresses the importance of efficiency, which is important to my research.

Frantzich (1982) investigates the role of computers in Congress, assessing whether individuals resist innovation or embrace it. He seeks to determine whether theories of innovation apply to political institutions and members or whether theories are institution-specific. Focusing on political precursors, strategies, and consequences of technical innovation, Frantzich conducts a microlevel study of the House of Representatives and the Senate, noting how computers have resulted in internal changes in addition to assessing differences among individuals. He finds that computerization has resulted in increased efficiency in correspondence, mailings, and the tabulation of roll call votes. While Frantzich's study focuses on the role of computers at the national level, I apply the notion of resistance or acceptance toward technological innovations to the New York State legislature.

III. RESEARCH OBJECTIVE AND HYPOTHESES

This research traces the chronological evolution of IT in the New York State legislature from the mid-1980s to the present. Specifically, I study how technology affects casework and the formulation of legislation. In addition, I assess the degree to which technological advances foster or hinder collaboration and efficiency, and whether members and their staff embrace IT.

Upon examining the New York State legislature I find that legislators have ample access to personal computers and that these computers are fairly new, having been purchased within the last 3 to 5 years. In addition, I expect that e-mail and the Internet are used extensively for casework and the formulation of legislation. In addition, I expect to find increased collaboration and efficiency in the state legislature, both internally and externally. I also posit that legislators and staff are receptive to new technology, and that it makes them more efficient and it makes it easier to accomplish day-to-day tasks.

IV. CASE SELECTION, DATA COLLECTION, AND OPERATIONALIZATION

Since this research is largely exploratory and descriptive, I conducted a case study. I selected the New York State legislature, a bicameral body comprising the Assembly (commonly known as the House in other states) and the Senate. The Assembly comprises 150 members and the Senate comprises 61 members, each legislator representing a single Assembly or Senate district within the state. At present, the legislature is divided, with a Democrat majority in the Assembly and a Republican majority in the Senate. State legislators in New York have two offices, one in the district they represent called the district office and a second office in Albany, the state capitol. These offices are staffed with two or more individuals depending on whether a member is in the minority or the majority party and whether a member chairs a committee or holds a leadership position.

Nicholson-Crotty and Meier (2002) defend the study of single states or smaller comparative state studies, asserting that important theoretical propositions have grown out of smaller studies, pointing to exploratory and subsequently seminal works by Dahl and Hunter. My research is largely exploratory since there have been few empirical studies that examine the impact of IT on state legislatures. The authors argue that the theory, the validity of the indicators, and the rigor of the measurement should be used to judge the quality of research rather than the number of states employed.

To measure collaboration, efficiency, and resistance toward new technologies I generated a survey in October 2002 that was sent to all New York State legislators. With 50 state legislators responding, the survey yielded a 24% response rate. In my experience as a researcher and staff, I have found that legislators in New York are reluctant to respond to surveys. They are extremely cautious about having their opinions recorded even though their responses are anonymous. Insight regarding how advances in IT have influenced the state legislature may still be gleaned despite the somewhat low response rate. In addition to the survey, I conducted 18 in-depth open-ended interviews between February and March 2003. Finally, I also used primary documents, including manuals and memoranda, to research the evolution of IT in the New York State legislature.

Several terms must be defined before proceeding further. First, constituent services and casework are services or assistance that legislators provide to their constituents, usually unrelated to formulating legislation. The terms constituent services and casework are used interchangeably. Casework is communication between a legislator and his constituent and it ranges from a simple request for phone numbers of state agencies or departments to more complex problems associated with social security benefits or the impending loss of one's home. According to Mayhew (1974) responding to constituent correspondence is important if legislators wish to be reelected.

Collaboration, efficiency, and resistance also need to be defined. Collaboration is defined as cooperation, teamwork, partnership, or assistance. It is the joining of individuals, or technology, or both that would normally not have an opportunity to be brought together. Efficiency is the reduction in the time or the ease with which a task may be accomplished. Finally, resistance to technology is an unwillingness or opposition to new technology, while acceptance is the opposite. Quantifying these variables is exceedingly difficult, but the survey and the in-depth interviews ask respondents to characterize collaboration, efficiency, and acceptance verbally and on the basis of scales.

V. ANALYSIS

A. Historical Evolution of IT in the New York State Legislature

Before the 1980s, few state legislatures had personal computers. In New York some state legislators had personal computers, but the hardware and software were neither standardized nor networked. The use of personal computers in state legislative politics was fragmented and disparate. By the early 1980s, however, the New York State Assembly and Senate had acquired personal computers for state legislative offices in the capitol and the district through a contract with IBM. Personal computers notably aided correspondence — mail merges in particular, while computers also facilitated drafting bills, developing memorandums in support of or in opposition to legislation and preparing press releases. General clerical duties were more efficiently undertaken with the advent of the personal computer, though many individuals in the state legislature resisted advances in technology.

The New York State Legislature established two separately networked disk operating systems (DOS) in each chamber *circa* 1983, thereby centralizing and standardizing hardware and software within each house. This was accomplished by connecting individual personal computers, through telephone lines, to a mainframe computer. The mainframe computer, physically located in Menands, New York, is a large computer that speaks to other mainframes. It connects individual personal computers, and all users have access to the same programs or applications.[1] When booting-up their computers users receive a prompt, which asks them to "log on with a user id and a password." To connect to the mainframe Assembly users access the Assembly Communications (ACOM) program and Senate users access the Senate Operations Automated Program (SOAP). Users are then connected to the mainframe's OfficeVision program, which stores several applications.

Initially, the Assembly and Senate primarily relied on three programs: WordPerfect or Microsoft Word, OfficeVision, and DOS or OS/2. Both WordPerfect and Microsoft Word offer basic word-processing features, enabling users to accomplish tasks associated with casework and formulating legislation. Once users have logged on to the mainframe through ACOM they are connected to OfficeVision, the second program, which provides users with a variety of services or additional applications. The services under OfficeVision include e-mail, the Associated Press News Wire (AP), the calendar, phone directories, administrative notices, and the Legislative Retrieval System (LRS). The third program, DOS or OS/2, allows the user to make changes to the computer. For example, programs can be added or deleted, changes to the date and time can be performed, and diskettes can be formatted.

---

[1] Applications and programs are used interchangeably in reference to software.

Despite the centralization and standardization of hardware and software, the number of personal computers allocated to each state legislator remain disparate. These disparities can be attributed to the differences between the two chambers and the parties in power. For example, members of the majority party receive more computers than members of the minority party, though individuals who hold leadership positions are allocated more computers than nonleaders, regardless of party affiliation. Disparities in the quantity and type of personal computers in the Assembly are minimal compared to its Senate counterpart. One interviewee said, "Equipment in the Assembly is similar to the Supreme Court ruling of *Plessy v. Ferguson* doctrine of 'separate but equal'." Each office has its own separate equipment, but every office has the same or equal equipment (model and number). In contrast, the number of personal computers was never standardized in the Senate. As a result, party affiliation and leadership positions, including chairing committees, determine how many personal computers are allotted to a member's office. In the Senate the number of computers in each office typically ranges from 3 to 14.

A clunky, albeit usable, e-mail program was in place with the advent of the networked system in the mid-1980s. While sending e-mail internally was simple, sending messages externally was exceedingly difficult because users needed to include a "gateway number" in addition to an e-mail address to communicate with other users. The gateway number permitted the mainframe to locate and to speak to other systems. Oddly, few systems required gateway numbers since most systems were sophisticated enough to locate an e-mail address without it. While e-mail was in place, few individuals e-mailed with any regularity due to the complexities associated with using it. As a result, it was not used widely for communication or for information dissemination.

Advances in the early 1990s helped make the existing cumbersome system more user-friendly. In the Assembly, a graphics-based operating system, called Windows 3.0,[2] replaced DOS in 1991, eliminating the need for the command-line interface. Users could simply click on an icon, using a mouse, to access programs instead of typing commands. Following the installation of Windows 3.0, all computers in the Assembly were upgraded to Windows 3.1. In contrast, the Senate did not alter its operating environment, instead relying on the OS/2 system, a command-based interface system. Despite the antiquated operating system, the New York Senate was connected to the Internet in 1995. The Assembly lagged behind the upper house, not obtaining Internet access until June 1997, when it also simultaneously installed Windows 95. The Internet, accompanied by upgraded, user-friendly e-mail programs, significantly enhanced the prospects for communication and information dissemination. Before obtaining Internet access, technology only moderately improved administrative conditions for state legislators and staff. Although all state legislative offices in Albany were connected to the Internet by 1997, many district offices were not connected to the Internet until after 2000.

In the late 1990s state legislative sites, with separate URLs for each chamber, and individual member websites were developed. A plethora of information can be found on the state legislature's website, ranging from individual member biographies to the text of bills. The majority party in the Assembly limits the amount and type of information that appears on minority members' websites, while giving members of the majority party almost unlimited access to post to their sites. Finally, sessions are now broadcast via the

---

[2] Windows 1.0 and 2.0 preceded Windows 3.0 in the fall of 1985 and 1987 respectively, yet neither was widely received by the public, unlike their successor, Windows 3.0.

Internet with the advent of audio and video in the Assembly and SenNet TV in the Senate in 2002. Anyone who accesses the Assembly or Senate websites can watch and listen to sessions, thereby expanding access to the state legislature.

B.   IT and Casework

According to Jewell (1982), communicating and informing constituents, responding to policy, and attending to individual and group needs are key components of representation. Addressing and responding to constituent requests and inquiries, also known as casework, is central to the jobs of legislators. Requests and inquiries take many forms including phone, fax, U.S. Post, e-mail, courier service, or an office visit. According to the data, state legislators did not rank e-mail as one of the top two ways constituents contact their offices. Instead, 47% of state legislators (21 out of 45) ranked e-mail third, despite the volume of constituent e-mails and the frequency with which e-mail is checked. In addition, the data show that e-mail is employed less frequently than phone or the U.S. Post but more frequently than fax, office visits, or courier service.

The data show that on average New York State Assembly members receive 1196 e-mails from constituents and 1404 pieces of U.S. Post on a yearly basis. In the New York State Senate members received on average 2600 e-mails and 4732 pieces of U.S. Post on a yearly basis. New York State Assembly and Senate members received 0.009 and 0.008 e-mails, respectively, per capita on a yearly basis.[3] It is important to note that the levels of constituent correspondence vary depending on whether the legislature is in session. During session, which typically begins in mid-January and ends in June, members typically receive more inquiries.

While features associated with word processing such as cutting and pasting, checking grammar and spelling, and performing large mail merges have significantly improved the quality and speed with which offices can attend to casework, e-mail and the Internet have dramatically transformed casework and constituent communication and correspondence. The proliferation of Internet access has aided this transformation. Just under half of all adults reported using the Internet in 2000 and almost 59% of adults indicated using the Internet by the end of 2002 (Spooner, 2003). E-mail and the Internet appear to be especially beneficial for constituents. Constituents have access to their representatives through e-mail, the state legislature's website, and individual member websites. Contacting legislators through e-mail is often easier and more convenient than sending a letter via U.S. Post. State legislative websites provide visitors with a plethora of information, including contact and biographical information for legislative members, information on bills, press releases, links to other state agencies and departments, etc. For example, constituents use the zip code finder on the state site to locate their member or to obtain a state legislator's phone number to call about a problem or a bill. One member said, "They [individuals] call us even if it isn't our bill. We are getting a lot of hits as a result of the New York State website." Finally, individual member sites provide constituents with information pertinent to their district, in addition to providing more general information.

State legislators and staff rely on both e-mail and the Internet to address casework and to communicate with constituents. According to the data, 27 state legislators in New York (55%) indicated that they use e-mail for legislative business and casework. Of the 20 New

---

[3] The population of a New York Assembly district is 126,510 people and a New York Senate district contains 306,072 people.

York State legislators (41%) who do not use e-mail, 17 have staff (85%) that use e-mail for legislative business and casework, creating an environment where over 95% of state legislative offices (85 out of 88) access e-mail. Similarly, 23 out of 48 of New York State legislators (48%) use the Internet and 48 out of 49 staff (98%) indicated that they use the Internet for casework and legislation. When asked how e-mail has transformed their offices, a majority of staff reported that e-mail has increased their workload because it created another avenue for participation. A minority of respondents claimed that e-mail had little value or they did not use e-mail. While the data show that 39 out of 50 New York State legislators (53%) e-mail constituents, almost 95% of state legislators (47 out of 50) reported that they responded to e-mail that they received from constituents. In contrast, only 36 out of 50 respondents indicate that they use the Internet to respond to constituents' requests or concerns. Evidence of communicating and responding to constituents and attending to individual needs through e-mail is particularly strong, while there is some evidence of the Internet being used. Unfortunately, it is more difficult to gauge the impact of the Internet on casework since constituents can bypass legislators and directly access information on their own by going to the state legislature's website or to individual websites.

Both e-mail and the Internet facilitate collaboration on casework. In dealing with casework, e-mail is used to collaborate between the Albany and district office, be it forwarding a constituent e-mail from one office to another or discussing via e-mail how to deal with a particular constituent problem or request. The degree to which collaboration exists depends somewhat on the uniformity of software programs and the knowledge possessed by the individual user. For example, collaboration between the Albany and district office is frequently stymied when staff in the district office are unfamiliar with new programs. Their Albany counterparts typically gain knowledge of new programs more quickly because staff members take training classes that are offered on-site by the Office of Automated Data Processing and the Senate Office Automation Project, in the Assembly and the Senate, respectively. Information uploaded to the state legislature's website and individual websites can directly aid and assist constituents. Staff also use the Internet as a resource that aids in the provision of constituent services.

State legislators were asked whether they were more efficient as a result of e-mail. The data show that 41% (20 out of 49) of state legislators in New York feel they are *somewhat more* efficient and 20% (10 out of 49) reported feeling *much more* efficient due to e-mail. The survey also asked state legislators how quickly they respond to letters sent by U.S. Post compared to how quickly they respond to e-mail. This variable was recoded as an ordinal-level variable, with four discrete categories to produce meaningful categories. Only 35% of state legislators reported that they respond in less than 4 days, while almost half of all respondents said they average between 4 and 10 days to respond to letters sent by U.S. Post. Fifty percent of respondents answer e-mails in less than 4 days. The response time to e-mail is considerably shorter. Many staffers noted in interviews that they did not respond to constituent e-mail via e-mail, instead replying to e-mail through U.S. Post. Furthermore, they reported using e-mail when the responses were short and did not require a lengthy explanation, stating that they exercised caution when replying via e-mail because the member's signature does not appear at the end of an e-mail, unlike correspondence sent through U.S. Post. Many feared that e-mail responses could be unfavorably manipulated. Although e-mail was for the most part viewed favorably, there were some drawbacks associated with e-mail that hindered efficiency. During in-depth interviews, state legislators were asked to identify any challenges e-mail presented. Respondents noted that the sheer volume of e-mail that they receive often prevents or makes it difficult for them to respond to all e-mails. Another drawback, associated with the volume of e-mail, is the difficulty legislators have locating a particular e-mail message, which requires them to sift through large quantities of e-mail. Some also said that without any type of filtering software the volume of nonconstituent e-mail, spam, and viruses presents problems.

State legislators were also asked whether they were more efficient as a result of the Internet. Forty-two percent (17 out of 41) of respondents in New York said they are *much more* efficient and 39% (16 out of 41) reported that they are *somewhat more* efficient as a result of the Internet. Respondents asserted that the Internet provides abundant and instantaneous information, whenever one chooses to access the information. The Internet produces more background information and facilitates research, which resulted in fewer phone calls and faxes, in addition to providing some information that would have been nearly impossible to obtain without the Internet. Repeatedly, respondents echoed sentiments like this one, when asked whether the Internet helped state legislators to do a better job, "Definitely . . . it took forever to get Internet access. Within the past five years, we now all have Internet access. The legislature has finally embraced modern technology. It's made my job a heck of a lot easier. It's definitely made my job easier."

Assessing whether members and their staff embraced or resisted technological change as it relates to constituent services is more difficult. As mentioned, not all offices have embraced e-mail even though over half of the survey respondents indicated that they use e-mail for legislative business or casework. While a sizable number of state legislators have resisted e-mail, 95% reported using it. Some staffers commented that their member has actively decided not to use e-mail or staffers said that they do not check e-mail with any frequency. Despite the fact that few state legislators in New York use e-mail, 95% of constituent inquiries and requests sent via e-mail receive replies. This illustrates that state legislative offices have accepted that they must reply to e-mail from constituents. Interestingly, only 37 state legislators (100%) respond to e-mail via e-mail. Responding to e-mail via e-mail may seem routine and ordinary in most industries, yet many state legislators have resisted responding to e-mail via e-mail. In New York for example, many staffers told me that there is a perception that a reply sent by e-mail is somehow "less official" than a reply sent via U.S. Post, which appears on a letterhead and contains the state legislator's signature. Many state legislators and staffers said that when they do respond to e-mail via e-mail it is in instances when the reply requires a simple answer, when the reply contains a link to a website, or when the state legislator or staff are unable to respond to the constituent during normal business hours. Resistance to the Internet was more difficult to gauge though fewer state legislators reported using the Internet and almost all staff indicated using it. In terms of using the Internet for tasks related to casework, 36 out of 50 state legislators said they used the Internet to respond to constituent requests or concerns. During in-depth interviews, many staffers explained that they often used the telephone rather than the Internet in dealing with casework, be it calling the constituent directly or contacting the commissioner of a department.

C. IT and Policy Formulation

IT also affects policy formulation. Jewell (1982) underscores the importance of not only meeting constituent needs, but also responding to policy demands. The development of the Legislative Retrieval System (LRS), which tracks the life span of a bill from its introduction to its enactment into law, available through a networked database, significantly altered the performance of tasks related to legislation. E-mail and the Internet have also impacted policy formulation, though arguably the latter is used more extensively for tasks related to legislation. For example, 95% of respondents indicated that they use the Internet *to perform research* or *to check pending* legislation, yet only 17 out of 50 respondents said they used the Internet to draft legislation.

The creation of the LRS resulted in centralized and accessible information about bills through a networked database. Before establishing a networked system, a paper method of tracking legislation was employed. This practice is still in place even though most state legislators and staff rely on the electronic version. Sheets known as the *dailies* are distributed to each legislative office on a daily basis, apprising members and staff of the status of bills. After the dailies accumulate, they are consolidated and bound into books called the *Legislative Digest*, in which bills are organized and indexed by subject and sponsor, as well as numerically. Once a bill is enacted and signed into law, it is published in McKinney's, which is a series of books in which New York State statutes are consolidated.

With the advent of the LRS, tracking legislation improved markedly, especially from an efficiency standpoint. Offices reported that the LRS enables them to quickly access information on a bill since up-to-date information is available from a centralized location. Not all staff use the online version of the LRS and from time to time information is not available, either because of network problems or because the information has not been updated. For example, some staffers reported using the dailies rather than the LRS when searching for a bill numerically, because it is easier, quicker, or habitual. What information legislators or staff members have about a bill often determines whether they will access the dailies or the LRS. Three things, however, impede the efficiency of the LRS. First, information is not always updated in a very timely fashion. In some instances information appears in the dailies before it appears on the LRS. Second, keyword searches are often difficult to perform and do not yield good results. Third, the print feature on the LRS allows users to print only one screen at a time rather than printing an entire document. Despite these minor impediments, the LRS has significantly improved efficiency with respect to the tracking of legislation.

Determining if the LRS fosters collaboration and measuring the level of resistance to the LRS is difficult. The Legislative Retrieval System has contributed to collaboration as it enables members to develop a companion bill where one does not exist. Additionally, it supplies memoranda and the text of the bill, which are not available through the dailies or the *Legislative Digest*. Resistance to the LRS is minimal, even though some staff members refer to the dailies or the *Legislative Digest* rather than the electronic database. In these instances, staff said that referring to paper was sometimes more convenient or it was closer in proximity. Overall, members and staff have embraced the LRS as it facilitates rapid and comprehensive searches.

State legislators and staff rely not only on the LRS for policy formulation, but also on e-mail and the Internet. The survey asked state legislators to indicate whether e-mail and the Internet helped them to gauge what issues were important to constituents. The data show that over half of all state legislators, 25% (12 out of 48), find e-mail to be *very helpful* in gauging the policy preferences of constituents and 48% of individuals (23 our of 48) indicated that e-mail is *somewhat helpful*. E-mail is fairly helpful in terms of gauging policy preferences. This is arguably significant especially if it aids in policy formulation. In interviews, state legislators said they frequently receive constituent e-mail indicating that constituents favored or opposed a particular policy. New York State legislators reported in interviews that they track constituents' policy preferences that they receive via e-mail, often converting the e-mail to a hard copy and filing the printed version in the appropriate policy folder and showing the state legislators how many e-mails they receive on a given issue. The Internet has also been used as a conduit for communication and information dissemination in policy formulation. According to data, 8% of state legislators (4 out of 48) reported that the Internet was *very helpful*, while 40% of New York State legislators (19 out of 48) indicated that the Internet is *somewhat helpful* in terms of helping them to gauge the policy preferences of constituents. A sizable percent of state legislators however, 33% (16 out of 48), reported that the Internet has a *neutral* impact on helping them to gauge the policy preferences of constituents. One staff member in New York expanded on this in an interview explaining that,

> ... a lot of the e-mail that we get, you can see that people have visited the Assembly website because they are very specific about a bill. Prior to the development of the state legislature's website, only staff knew about bill numbers. This has enabled these people to have information so that they can better communicate their concerns to us.

As highlighted in the above quote, the state legislature's website and individual member sites provide detailed information on bills. In interviews, legislators asserted that not only does the state legislature's site serve constituents and various organizations but it also allows them to obtain information on bills.

It appears that the LRS, e-mail, and the Internet have led to increased collaboration. Legislators and staff can easily develop companion bills or draft new bills with the LRS. Memoranda and text of bills available through the LRS, which are not supplied through the dailies or the *Legislative Digest*, further aid state legislators and staff. The Internet, potentially, provides state legislators, staff, and constituents with the most assistance on policy formulation. A variety of websites can be accessed to gather information on a given policy area and individuals can access the state legislature's website to obtain information on bills. The Internet links individuals with information that they might not have had. Despite these benefits, the data show that the Internet is not useful for understanding the policy preferences of constituents. In contrast, e-mail appears to have significantly aided legislators in determining the policy preferences of constituents.

Increased efficiency in policy formulation emerges with the advent of e-mail and the Internet. From the perspective of constituents, a letter sent via U.S. Post may take several days to reach, a legislator whereas receiving an e-mail takes considerably less time. This is especially important when bills are being reviewed in committees or when they are being considered on the floor. E-mail can be sent in a timely manner. The only drawback is when constituents underestimate how much time legislators need to read and review their e-mail. For example, constituents who e-mail legislators 1 or 2 days before a bill is being considered may run the risk that their e-mail is not read and their opinion goes unnoted. From the perspective of state legislators and staff, e-mail and the Internet have improved efficiency in policy formulation. Becoming a cosponsor to a bill or drafting a companion bill is easier with the advent of e-mail and the Internet. Legislators can use e-mail to sign on as cosponsors, whereas previously this was done via paper. The development of a companion bill is also easier since prospective drafts of a bill maybe circulated between staff. It is markedly easier to amend electronic version of bills. In addition, searches for a bill that has already been drafted can be easily preformed through the Internet.

Few individuals have resisted using technology in the area of policy formulation. In some instances individuals used the dailies and the *Legislative Digest* rather than the LRS. However, most individuals do not consistently use the paper copies rather than the electronic version. Finally, resistance to e-mail and the Internet also appear to be quite low. State legislators and staff indicated using e-mail when they drafted bills, sending drafts both intraoffice and interoffice. Although used to a lesser degree by state legislators the Internet is used frequently by staff to develop policy.

VI. CONCLUSION

Until the introduction of Internet access in 1995 and 1997, technological advances in the New York State legislature had proceeded relatively slowly. While e-mail and the LRS were established before Internet access, the former was essentially unusable because it was not user-friendly. With access to the Internet came changes to the operating environment in the Assembly and new hardware in both chambers that led to transformations of the capacities and capabilities of state legislators and staff. Clearly, e-mail and the Internet have significantly enhanced communication and information dissemination for state legislators, staff, and constituents.

Collaboration via e-mail and the Internet have enhanced casework and policy formulation. E-mail bridges constituents and state legislators and provides another mode for communicating and disseminating information. Greater collaboration between the Albany and district offices has resulted from e-mail. Forwarding constituent e-mail from Albany to the district office and discussing how to deal with a particular problem via e-mail fosters cooperation. The Internet provides constituents with access to information ranging from phone numbers of legislators to the text of a bill. Before the advent of the Internet, few individuals would have specific knowledge about bills. Now, individuals can glean information on a bill number and are also privy to the status of the bill. This is an instance where individuals and technology are joined together when they otherwise might not have been. The Legislative Retrieval System also fosters a high degree of internal collaboration as it allows members of both houses — regardless of party — to access information simultaneously, in a centralized location.

Overall, efficiency in constituent services and the tracking of legislation have improved tremendously. Constituent services are more efficient because of word processing and e-mail. Responding to constituent correspondence may be performed more quickly and with fewer errors as a result of word-processing programs. While only slightly different, the response time to e-mails is less than the response time to letters sent via U.S. Post. The Internet has moderately improved the provision of constituent services. State legislators and staff can quickly and easily access information through a variety of websites ranging from the state legislature's website to state agency sites. The tracking of legislation through the LRS helps in almost instantaneously apprising members and their staff of the status of pending legislation. In addition, the LRS centralizes legislative information for both houses, providing text and memoranda, a schedule of committee meetings and hearings, and other information not available in the dailies or the *Legislative Digest*. Furthermore, searching for legislative information is easier and quicker with the addition of the keyword feature. The Internet allows research to be performed more quickly with the centralization of a wide variety of information that can be accessed via a computer.

Finally, the amount of resistance to technology varies, depending on the user and the technology employed. The skill possessed by the user clearly affects the level of comfort with and acceptance of new technology. In general, younger staff members have enthusiastically embraced new technology, while older staff and longtime employees are not as quick to embrace new technologies. Depending on the type of technology, acceptance or resistance was greater or lesser. For example, the Internet was embraced almost universally, while e-mail was resisted by a small percentage.

Technology is profoundly shaping the business of legislating. Both casework and policy formulation have been affected by new technology. The Internet is perhaps the most significant agent of transformation. Legislators and their staff have gradually become acclimated and accustomed to the changes in technology. The New York State Legislature can afford to ignore the sweeping technological advancements that are surrounding it, and members and staff should embrace technology and use it to craft legislation and to inform their constituents.

REFERENCES

Abramson, J.B., Arterton, F.C., and Orren, G.R., *The Electronic Commonwealth:The Impact of New Media Technologies on Democratic Politics*, Basic Books, New York, 1988.

Barber, B.R., The New Telecommunications Technology: Endless Frontier or the End of Democracy. (Chapter 3) Roger 6. Noll and Monroe E. Price. 1998. A Communications Cornucopia. Markle Foundation Essays on Information Policy.

Bennett, D. and Fielding, P. *The Net Effect: How Cyberadvocacy is Changing the Political Landscape*, 1999.

Bimber, B.A., *Information and American Democracy: Technology in the Evolution of Political Power, Communication, Society, and Politics*, Cambridge University Press, Cambridge, U.K., 2003.

Browning, G., *Electronic Democracy: Using the Internet to Influence American Politics*, Information Today Inc., 1996.

Caudle, S. and Marchand, D. et al., *Managing Information Resources: New Directions in State Governments*, A National Study of State Government Information Resources Management, School of Information Studies, Center for Science and Technology, Syracuse University, Syracuse, NY, 1989.

Dahl, R., *Democracy and Its Critics*, Yale University, New Haven, CT, 1989.

Danziger, J. and Dutton, W. et al., *Computers and Politics: High Technology in American Local Governments*, Columbia University, New York, 1982.

Davis, R., *The Web of Politics: The Internet's Impact on the American Political System*, Oxford University Press, Oxford, 1999.

Frantzich, S.E., *Computers in Congress*, Sage, Beverly Hills, CA, 1982.

Grossman, L., *The Electronic Republic*, Viking, New York, 1995.

Jewell, M.E., *Representatives in State Legislatures*, University of Kentucky Press, Lexington, KY, 1982.

Kraemer, K.L. and Dutton, W. et al., *The Management of Information Systems*, Columbia University, New York, 1981.

Mayhew, D., *Congress the Electoral Connection*, Yale University Press, New Haven, CT, 1974.

Nicholson-Crotty, S. and Meier, K.J., The practical research size doesn't matter in defense of single-state studies, *State Politics and Policy Quarterly*, 2, 411–422, 2002.

Rosenthal, A.L., *The Decline of Representative Democracy*, CQ Press, Washington, D.C., 1998.

Spooner, T., Internet Use by Region in the United States, August 27, 2003
http://www.pewinternet.org

21

MANAGING E-GOVERNMENT IN FLORIDA: FURTHER LESSONS FROM TRANSITION AND MATURITY

David H. Coursey
Florida State University

Jennifer Killingsworth
Florida State University

CONTENTS

I.   Introduction 336
II. The state of Florida: a fallen leader through political transition 336
III. Florida's e-government management history 337
IV. Reflections on e-government management: same old issues with a new
     technology 344
     A. Political influences 344
     B. Personnel issues 346
     C. Innovation 347
V.   Lessons learned from Florida: summary and conclusions 349
References 350

ABSTRACT

The state of Florida was clearly the leading state government in e-government in the mid-1990s. Explanations include political leadership and competition, innovative personnel practices, and entrepreneurial leadership. With a change in the governor's office in the 1998 election from a moderate Democrat to a firmly antigovernment conservative Republican, the state became one of the first to experience the influence of a dramatic government transition in e-government management philosophy. This chapter primarily reflects on the state's experience under Jeb Bush and whether commonly asserted public information management ideas are supported. Experiences, as in the pre-1998 period covered in the last edition of this volume, tend to support the importance of political leadership, personnel arrangements, and institutional structures on innovation.

I. INTRODUCTION

In just over a decade since the first graphical web browser, the World Wide Web (WWW) has become the central component of most governments' information technology (IT) efforts. Virtually every sizable government has some form of web presence, with significant online applications. Since the previous edition of this book, the focus on web services has changed. In the late 1990s, even the more advanced governments were just beginning to denote and implement applications. Reviews, like the previous version of this chapter, centered on innovation diffusion and implementation. E-government was, frankly, novel and poorly integrated into existing IT management and planning. That has changed. Governments now find an environment where e-government is arguably the underlying infrastructure for all of IT and face significant pressure to reorganize management functions, primarily toward centralized structures.

What has not changed is the fundamental question posed in the last edition: how is e-government management different from traditional IT and why? One of the greatest fallacies of public IT research has been the presumption that any new technology requires a virtual rewriting of all existing IT research. Partly, this problem derives from researchers brought into the area by the technology itself with little traditional background in the IT literature or its practice, and the tendency toward advocacy: positive, glowing stories of productivity gains, with few stories of failed projects or the reasons behind their demise. For example, the common push to centralize e-government functions toward eliminating service duplication and reducing costs is often touted as somehow new. It is not. The debate between the pros and cons of centralized vs. decentralized IT management has raged for decades. Even in Florida, the state had a well-touted centralized planning unit — the Information Resource Commission (IRC) in the 1980s, which was dismantled, primarily as it was seen as too centralized. Researchers should ask "what is different, if anything" first.

With the maturity of e-government, management concerns have become more pressing than in the early days centered on application development (and usually just conversion of an existing "paper process" with no real system reengineering first). Here, we revisit the state of Florida's web efforts. In the last edition, Florida was transitioning to a new Republican governor, Jeb Bush, and much of the existing infrastructure for web services was expected to be dismantled. We begin by reviewing why Florida is a good case study for e-government management issues, followed by a history of the state's efforts, including descriptions and roles of the major organizational players, and finally revisit the common public IT management issues from the last edition in the context of the Bush administration's efforts.

II. THE STATE OF FLORIDA: A FALLEN LEADER THROUGH POLITICAL TRANSITION

Florida may seem an unlikely candidate as a major player in web applications among state governments. After all, while the third largest state, it has a relatively small government operation compared with sister states. Also, Florida does not possess the computing, high-tech industry infrastructure so critical to efforts in Texas, North Carolina, and Washington (though the Bush administration is pushing high-tech company growth in Florida partly for this very reason).

Yet Florida, by many measures, was the leading state government in web services under the Bush administration in 1998. It was chosen as the best state government operation by *Government Technology* magazine in 1996 and 1997 and it was so dominant that it was excluded from the competition in 1998. In the previous edition, we argued that much of this success was due to very entrepreneurial management, high-level political resource support but without trying to detail plans and direction, perceived political gains having nothing to do with truly improved government service, and a strong emphasis on internal and state universities for development (Coursey and Killingsworth, 2000).

Since 1998, Florida is no longer the dominant leader and usually not ranked in the top ten by *Government Technology*. Partly, this was inevitable as other states begin to seriously address e-government. This is not to say overall e-government is not better in Florida today than in 1998. Just, relatively, Florida has clearly fallen.

The story behind Florida's drop from a clear leader to arguably just another state with reasonable efforts makes the state an important, unique case. Florida's experience rests on something most states have yet to really experience: a major political transition in established e-government management. Jeb Bush, a very conservative, proudly antigovernment Republican, is a stark change from the previous moderate, Democrat Governor Chiles. One of the traditional concerns of public IT is the danger of management instability associated with too much political visibility. E-government has been different from much of traditional IT in that it draws the attention, for good or bad, of top political officials. Bush, in fact, likes to be called "e-governor." Florida's experience is critical to understanding how much political transition can help, or hurt, e-government management and practice and begs the question as to how to properly instill necessary stability in what is now vital infrastructure to government operations.

III. FLORIDA'S E-GOVERNMENT MANAGEMENT HISTORY

Florida's web presence began as a very political battle between three agencies: the Department of Management Services (DMS), the Department of State (DOS), and the Department of Education (DOE). The Web was perceived, to varying degrees, by agency heads as a new area of organizational power and turf wars developed as to who would direct the state's web presence. Early development (before 1996) was primarily due to political considerations far more than due to any analysis of business problems or opportunities. For example, DMS' entry can be traced to Governor Chiles' concern over a cover story in the influential *Florida Trend* magazine in November 1994 blasting the state's lack of web progress.

The struggle for control and leadership reflected the decentralized nature of Florida's government. At the time, Florida had a clearly weak governor, with much of the executive branch headed by independently elected officials. DOS and DOE, but not DMS, were led by elected Republicans. The competition, particularly between DMS and DOS, was actually healthy in that each tried to outdo the other in applications. Both DMS and DOS primarily relied on internal personnel and relationships with the Askew School of Public Administration and Policy's (Florida State University) IT students and centered on application development. One major difference was DMS typically followed a cost recovery model while DOS felt services were already paid via tax dollars and even converted existing online applications that were fee-based into free applications.

While both DMS and DOS made significant contributions, by the end of Chiles' administration in 1998, DMS was the clear, almost default leader of the state's web presence. However, management structure was very weak. There was no clear authority over any IT planning in the overall executive branch, primarily due to the weak governor constitutional structure, and even agencies under the governor resisted any form of centralized control, partly due to the still existing dislike of the experience under the old IRC. DMS' service provision for various hosting and web assistance provided, at best, informal coordination. Most agencies had their own web operations, some quite disconnected from their normal IT management. Applications were typically agency specific, with few really cutting across agency bounds or restructuring services as activities independent of the existing agency management structures.

The lack of management structure was compounded by DMS' reliance on highly entrepreneurial management under Secretary Lindner. Lindner was a very aggressive advocate for e-government services. He created a very unique environment tolerant of risk, supportive of government employees, and quite aggressive about creating novel opportunities for young workers on projects featuring cutting-edge technology and scale, regardless of sector. Obviously, Lindner would not be around in a Bush administration simply for political reasons. The concern would be what would happen without such a central, politically supportive advocate.

The Bush administration had two clear differences in 1999. First, there was little belief in the ability of government workers to handle e-government services. Partly, this was due to the youthful, very inexperienced Bush team's ignorance about Florida's existing stature. It also reflected a core political philosophy that trusted private-sector innovation and believed private companies were more astute on web applications.

Politics was also at play. Bush wanted to be known as the "e-goveror," clearly an example of the use of the Web for political reasons, and needed to disassociate his efforts with those under Chiles as much as possible. Indeed, such highly touted innovative services like "Leasing Direct" and "Training Direct" were strongly de-emphasized and even dismantled. Unlike Chiles, Bush took a very personal interest in e-government and dabbled far more in the details. Chiles deferred to Linder. Bush was going to be far more proactive. Additionally, DOE and DOS were still under Republican control and quite loyal to Bush. Hence, Bush became the central IT political player, a major change from an era with competing agencies.

The transition to a private-sector model, lack of experience, and political power change had significant implications in Bush's early efforts. The first 2 years (1999 to 2000) are best characterized as a series of often well-intentioned, but mostly unsuccessful efforts. It is in this period that Florida lost its clear national leadership role.

Bush's advisors came into DMS presuming the state was backward in e-governance and with thinly veiled distrust of any existing e-government personnel. Many of the best DMS web staff had already left with Lindner, expecting just such a result. Most Bush staff had little, if any, real experience. Most glaring was Bush's choice of his e-government leader, Roy Cales. Lacking any college degree, much less in IT, and virtually no significant IT business experience and none in government, Cales' primary qualification was a political one: he developed the governor's campaign website (cf., Lauer, 2001). The idea that a basic website designer could tackle a state's e-government efforts was at best questionable and more realistically, tragically wrong. It also sent a very demoralizing signal to the many state IT employees who were far more qualified than Cales. But, qualifications were not Cales' only problem. His ethical suitability was questionable as he admitted to felony grand theft charges from 1985, though the charges were dropped after he paid back the money (Lauer and Bridges, 2001). Both problems would prove to be his undoing 2 years later.

However, to begin, Bush stressed the redesign of the state's web page, referring to it as the state's first web portal, www.myflorida.com. The claim was partly political and partly out of simple ignorance, as the state had long had a leading central site (the Florida Communities Network under DMS); it just did not have the sexy, popular new term from the private sector. Bush desired to spin the state's presence as his alone. Information Builders, a small firm with no significant government experience, was contracted to lead the effort.

Like many other efforts headed by governors, it was clear www.myflorida.com was going to be just as much a publicity page for the governor as a general site for state government. This lead to resistance among many state web workers within agencies who found the approach inappropriate. Furthermore, even with major agencies under the same party control, resistance toward a common portal still existed as agencies wanted to protect their turf.

The Bush administration, via Information Builders, attempted to dictate look and feel to all agencies, even those outside the governor's control, and even to go so far as to require all agencies to house their web operations at DMS. Such changes were not considered after any consultation with existing state web personnel, who were used to a rather free exchange of ideas. Rather, the Bush administration's initial approach was to tell agencies what to do, with virtually no feedback or state employee involvement. The governor was seen as trying to centralize control for its own sake and with a noticeably lower emphasis on application development. DMS web staff, after they had built the nation's leading web presence, were extremely demoralized when told a private company was taking over design and management efforts. They were reduced to simply communicating the governor's intentions and then handling the flack from the agencies. A lot of this communication came via the established DMS and state web worker user group meetings. Roy Cales constantly missed these events, despite assurance of attendance, which further damaged morale and encouraged an adversarial relationship.

The web portal, while developed and launched with much fanfare, found significant resistance. The Bush administration's failure to capitalize on existing state employee expertise severely hampered development and overall quality. The Bush administration failed to recognize the importance of the decentralized personnel and did nothing but exacerbate their distrust.

The web portal development's greatest problem was simply inexperienced leadership, with a dash of just way too much political involvement. New directives on look and feel, and how much they were to be enforced, were constant and confusing. Many state web workers developed a pattern of just ignoring requests from the governor's office as they came to expect almost immediate reversals or conflicting requests.

A simple, but notable example of the confusion caused by inexperience and political motivation was the governor's pronouncement that his personal e-mail address be placed at the top of every page. State web workers warned this would generate huge volumes of e-mail, and worse, the possibility of e-mail that likely concerned agency business being misdirected. Other state web workers saw it as rather shameless political publicity. About 6 months after many agencies had added the e-mail address, a simple memo asked for its removal and handed literally thousands of unanswered e-mails to the agencies for processing. As expected, volumes were about agency business, and the lack of response made the agencies look bad and angered not only state web personnel, but also general agency management.

However, Bush's online permitting effort is by far the best example of government IT management inexperience. Bush, strongly influenced by private e-commerce innovations, envisioned a one-stop web portal for all state permit processes. Citizens would not have to know what agency to go to for what permit and could actually complete entire permits online. Such a project was far more encompassing than anything under Chiles and, at the time, would have been a clearly unique application among state governments.

However, the lack of government experience and willingness to consult state experts, who warned of the potential project problems, directly led to a miserably failed project, at least in intended scope. First, Bush incorrectly assumed agencies could define all their permit processes. They could not, and even agencies very dependent on such work, like the Department of Environmental Protection, were plagued by the lack of permit documentation. Out-of-date forms were common. Historical knowledge and expertise on the purpose of various permit items was often long gone with employee turnover. Even simple listings of all permits and associated forms were scant. Second, Bush naively assumed permits are relatively simple forms like shopping carts on e-business sites. Hunting licenses and driver license renewals may be doable but environmental permits are hardly single-session, fast completion forms. Environmental permits can involve lots of forms and require tremendous technical expertise to complete, and, even more daunting, cut across not only state but also local and federal agencies. Hence, the state could not do such forms alone.

The failure to understand the true project scale produced the real killer: a totally insufficient resource plan. Agencies were expected to get all their permits up in 1 year, without any additional resources. Even worse, Bush and the Republican-controlled legislature felt citizens and businesses needed to be encouraged to use the new online permits and thus required agencies to waive permit fees for a period after development. Agencies privately howled. Knowing such applications would likely produce huge budget losses, especially as permit fees often supported other programs and not just the administrative processing costs, agencies stonewalled.

This period, 1999 to 2000, is when Florida virtually stopped developing new, major applications and clearly lost its leadership edge. Permit processes that were rolled out as part of a special permitting site (permitting.state.fl.us, now abandoned) were, in the end, just downloadable forms (e.g., Tallahassee Democrat, 2000). While the online permit project failure is not completely at fault, it is hard to ignore as a major factor. Information Builders was fired as well, as Bush became increasingly disenchanted with progress, both with the myflorida.com portal and the permit project.

Bush's first 2 years were at best unsuccessful. Existing personnel capacity was lost in favor of very inexperienced private-sector firms or appointments. Attempts to develop the better coordination needed were largely unsuccessful given the top-down approach attempted, with little consultation with a distrustful state web workforce. Moreover, even though controlled by the same party, many major executive agencies remained outside the governor's control, with separately elected heads. Many claims of innovative new projects and accomplishments, or even "firsts," were dubious examples of political spin. The state web portal already existed under Chiles, and online job bank and bidding processes (cf., Lauer, 2001), also claimed as major accomplishments, existed under the previous governor as well. Quite telling is the Bush administration's often cited increases in Florida's relative e-government ranking in 2001 by sources, such as the Center for Digital Government (cf., Lauer, 2001), which refer to changes since late 1999, the nadir of the Bush-created problems and hardly a comparison to the Chiles years.

Bush, and his staff, came in green. The question would be how they would learn. In 2000, the Bush administration decided the problem was decentralized IT management:

too many agencies under a "silo" mentality, no real coordination or control across agencies. Certainly, Florida did not have good e-government management structures in place. Some need for more centralized coordination was necessary.

That year, the State Technology Office (STO), under DMS, was formed (www.sto. state.fl.us). The STO, with Roy Cales in command, was to coordinate and assist agencies in e-government development and operations and reduce duplication. Hailed as the state's first chief information officer (CIO) (another dubious claim as the IRC head in the 1980s was essentially in the same role), Cales became the state's clear, central e-government figure. The ideal primary plan was to centralize all state IT staff and budget under STO control, a massive centralization and one that would be unprecedented in state government. It was also one carefully watched by other states. Agencies feared lost control over IT support. Many legislators, particularly Democrats, feared that too much control over hefty contracts and planning would be vested in one person, especially given Cales' personal history.

The model was definitely based on such reported efforts in the private-sector trade press, and questionably based on companies with far less work complexity and even size than the state government. No doubt, some of the benefits of centralization could accrue, like reduced operational costs and better cross-agency application planning.

However, centralization also has possible negative consequences, not realized partly due to the Bush administration's general government IT inexperience. Agencies develop strong relationships with vendors, which could be put at risk by centralized decision-making. Decentralization can also encourage innovation, as agencies compete for political visibility of quality applications and are free to experiment with varying approaches. Indeed, the very decentralized political scuffle between DMS and DOS was partly responsible for the state's leadership in the mid-1990s.

Laws passed by the 2000 and the 2001 legislature established and expanded Cales' power base, via the STO, over agencies. Concurrently, 2002 was to see a dramatic change in Florida's executive branch, with traditionally elected cabinet posts, such as DOS, becoming appointments giving the governor far greater power to centralize IT control. With a Republican-controlled Legislature having little concern over proposed plans, it seemed Cales was set to become a virtual king of Florida's e-government and IT.

During 2000 and 2001, problems began to emerge regarding Cales' past as well as quite questionable contracting. Supporters claimed such charges were personal attacks, especially from vendors not receiving awards or agencies upset over lost control. Perhaps this was true at a modest level, but it is hard to dismiss the events as just politics.

In 2000, Cales blocked a $15 million contract for laptop computers for state troopers. The intervention came only after a Congressman wrote the governor asking him to dismiss the bids and award the project to a politically connected new company (Lauer, 2001). Such actions were latched on to as proof positive of the dangerous political control over state IT dollars, at the possible expense of quality. It also created a poor vendor environment as many longtime state vendors became distrustful, as many began to assume, fairly or not, that political connections were the sole basis for awards. The incident encouraged the legislature to keep IT money in agency budgets, though the Bush administration originally wanted all budget authority transferred to the STO. Critics were open and harsh. For example, Doug Martin, a spokesman for the American Federation of State County and Municipal Employees stated, "[Cales] is still a despot...if you invest that much power in one man, the citizens of Florida are taking a big gamble. Is he going to use that power for taxpayers' benefit or the benefit of politically connected companies?" (Lauer, 2001: A1).

Meanwhile, further details of Cales' past began to surface. The 1985 felony grand theft charges were well known at appointment. But, it was discovered Cales' state job application was a bit short of honest. First, there was the claim that he supervised 20 employees in his company before working for the state. Cales claimed he was including contracted workers. The reality was his company, Gencom, had only two, including Cales. Second, he failed to mention the felony grand theft charges on his application, with the excuse that the form asks if you were ever convicted of a felony.

Just after Cales took highly publicized new powers via the STO in July 2001, with even more proposed centralization in the 2001 session, the bubble burst. In August, Cales was charged with grand theft for forging a document (claiming a contract with a local media outlet) to secure a bank loan in 1996, 3 years before his state job. He resigned, claiming he did not forge the document though it was clear the document included a forged signature as even the company representative's name was misspelled. Cales was forced to resign and the Bush administration was left with a serious public relations nightmare and threat to its consolidation plans (Lauer and Bridges, 2001). Cales would be acquitted in 2003, after the state prosecutors and law enforcement lost the crucial evidence, the forged document, which was just too fortunate for many Bush critics (Rosica, 2003).

The centralized contracting function was perhaps critics' greatest concern with the new STO and its powers. In 2002, a scathing report from the auditor general cited 28 allegations of mismanagement, conflicts of interest, and legal violations in purchasing. Included were severe allegations of soliciting money from businesses with state contracts, paying for services never received, and large contracts awarded to firms providing significant campaign donations without proper procedures or controls (Lauer, 2002a; Morgan, 2002). In 2003, a less critical report focused more on internal problems, including the lack of written work agreements with state agencies, no designated state privacy or security manager, and no security or recovery plans (State of Florida Office of the Comptroller, 2003; Cotterell, 2003c). All of these were requirements under the new Florida IT laws specific to the STO's role.

Much of the criticism related to the Cales administration and arguably the disorganization in its wake. After Cales' resignation, Kimberly Bahrami became acting director and, then in 2002, was officially appointed. Bahrami's background is significantly better than Cales, with solid government IT experience with the Department of Defense and a graduate education, though not directly in IT (Lauer, 2002b). Under her leadership, STO has addressed many of the audit criticisms, created a much-needed information security office (which was recently recognized by the Center for Digital Government as one of the country's best), and made good progress toward data center consolidation. Even Democrats have voiced support for Bahrami, and in general, there was far greater confidence in her professionalism than in Cales.

Another of Bahrami's challenges was arranging the privatization of much of the STO core functions. The ambitious privatization, called "MyFlorida Alliance," will turn over most services to two companies, Accenture and BearingPoint (though around 30 companies are involved in the venture), and transfer about 30% of its employees as well. While detailed tasks are not yet settled, Accenture will handle application management, including the state portal and e-government services while data center operation and desktop assistance go to BearingPoint. STO will retain its core management and planning functions and the company roles are seen as "day-to-day" activities.

The contract terms pay the companies mostly on a guaranteed minimum plus service fees to agencies and users. For example, someone renewing their state driver's license would see the fee goes toward Accenture. Up to 3% (the exact percentage will depend on service use) of revenues will be paid back to the state.

The change is not without concerns. One of the most controversial aspects is free use of the state's multimillion dollar Shared Resource Center, the state's key data center, among other state offices and equipment within STO. The companies will even be allowed to work on their own client's jobs at the state location. Even worse, there was a concern that the Bush administration originally planned to just give the center away, or sell it grossly undervalued, a plan that even had the powerful Republican legislative leadership troubled (Lauer, 2003a).

There is little doubt the Bush administration is taking a huge risk with the STO privatization as its enterprise model. The 7-year deal has no firm cost and by its nature actually encourages more work to be found, for good or bad, for greater profit. The security concerns and the appropriateness of a private firm using a state facility for its own work are troubling as well. There is questionable contract control as STO shares supervision of the work with the companies via the MyFlorida Alliance governing board. There is distrust of the two companies given their recent noted business ethics problems (Accenture is a spin-off of the former Andersen Consulting, based in Bermuda, and BearingPoint was formerly KPMG Consulting). The unsettled contract terms also spell potential trouble considering STO's questionable contracting legacy.

From a management perspective, the approach may be too focused on costs. One of the traditional IT costing debates has been regarding treating IT as an overhead or as an investment. The former tends toward user fee approaches and the latter disdains fees as they tend to squelch innovation where the benefits are distal or hard to quantify. The Bush administration is quite clear the new arrangement is primarily aimed at cost reduction. To quote the MyFlorida Alliance brochure, the alliance "will reduce the cost of government through the consolidation and sharing of resources . . . " (STO, 2003). STO claims a potential 30% cost savings, though evaluating that given the fee structure will be challenging. Bahrami even backs off the costs savings a bit, "I'm hesitant to use the word 'cost-savings' because some of those savings will be need to be reinvested to build out some of the portal infrastructure . . . " (Cotterell, 2003b: A1).

The fees from new services, and the greater returns associated with greater usage, does encourage innovative applications, at least to the companies and the STO, which gets the share of the state proceeds. The agencies, however, will likely not receive any direct payments. Agencies will perhaps see such user fees as just a cost reduction device to the discouragement of innovations at the agency level.

Yet, the Bush administration should be commended for trying a novel public/private approach. Certainly, it is far different from the massive government-based centralization planned under Cales. It also reflects a lesson learned from the failure of smaller, inexperienced firms in Bush's first term: work with large-scale companies with significant government experience.

A spin-off problem developing from MyFlorida Alliance is the new vendor registration system, www.myfloridamarketplace. DMS requires vendors to register with this system to receive any state contracts and, most controversially, pay the state a 1% surcharge for any state contract, with the money going to Accenture as well as to the state. Vendor registration is already mandated by the state, but is actually maintained by each agency. The charge would apply to most state contracts, even if not obtained via the system, and include school boards, courts, and universities typically not under the STO's authority. The Florida Legislature's Joint Administrative Procedures Committee has ruled the policy is outside

DMS' statutory authority and informed DMS/STO that it needs legislative approval. DMS disagrees and the system is sure to be a major IT issue in the next session (Lauer, 2003c). Such fees will likely not cost vendors, but instead raise contract prices as the 1% will probably just be factored into bids and negotiated pricing.

Outside of these programs, there have been some major upheavals in Florida IT in early 2004. First, Bahrami resigned in late February, citing the pursuit of other professional opportunities (St. Petersburg Times, 2004). Rumors among state IT staff circulated that the resignation related to continuing contract problems. Just a few weeks later, the Convergys payroll and benefit system difficulties became major news. Even the centralization strategy, so dominant in Bush's efforts, is questionable now as Bush has proposed legislation in the current legislative session, moving STO back under DMS, also likely due to dissatisfaction with contract management.

Bahrami headed STO over the Bush administration's landmark personnel management privatization with Convergys. Dubbed "People First," the project began moving virtually all state human resources tasks to the company in 2003, with significant web-based portions, including state employee insurance enrollment launched in September (Cotterell, 2003a; Cotterell, 2003d). Expecting it to go live on January 1, 2004, the Bush administration requested a 6-month delay in the Convergys contract due to problems in handling state workers' payroll (Williams, 2004). As a result, the state of Florida had to allocate emergency funding of $3.7 million to keep the old system operational (Bousquet, 2004). As a result, lawmakers have criticized the contract as being a "disaster" since it is costing more and taking longer than they were initially told (Bousquet, 2004). Even other states considering such personnel systems, like Ohio, are viewing the Convergys project as evidence that large-scale privatizations are, at best, extraordinarily difficult (Williams, 2004).

IV. REFLECTIONS ON E-GOVERNMENT MANAGEMENT: SAME OLD ISSUES WITH A NEW TECHNOLOGY

One of the primary historical tenets of public information management is there is some difference in managing information systems in the public sector (cf., Bozeman and Bretschneider, 1986). Fundamental issues in political involvement, personnel, and innovation have carried across various IT management efforts (cf., Bozeman and Bretschneider, 1986; Caudle, 1990; Kraemer and Dedrick, 1997). In the previous edition, these were discussed in relation to Florida's early efforts. Now, with the experience of the political transition, the movement toward a private-sector provision and enterprise model, and general maturity of the technology and its integration, are the early lessons from Florida any different, or do they perhaps further support previous conclusions?

A. Political Influences

Bozeman (1987) in his model of "publicness" discusses the concept of political authority flowing from the basic nature of a constitutional system where agencies' actions are controlled far more by legal factors and political cycles. The importance of politics at its many levels is a central theme in the public information management literature. The classic URBIS studies by Kraemer and colleagues (e.g., Kraemer and King, 1986; Kraemer et al., 1989) developed the concept of reinforcement politics where computing does not change the organizational power structure. Rather, the existing power structure tends to mold the use of information systems. These classic studies have been challenged in recent years, however, as changes in technology may create more decentralizing forces (e.g., Innes, 1988). Fountain (2001), via an institutionalism lens, finds e-government is associated with dramatic structural changes, yet such changes are clearly part of the political game.

Florida's pre-Bush web experience (1993–1998) strongly denotes the role of politics, especially with the rather public fight between DMS and DOS over e-government control. From an institutional perspective, the very nature of the state's divided executive branch formed the basis of divisions and competition. The perception of political gain from a web presence was a significant, if not the primary, factor in development.

Such top political involvement in web operations is at odds with much of the public information management literature where elected political leaders are rarely engaged (cf., Danziger et al., 1982). Why the difference? A likely explanation is the technology itself. The old URBIS studies centered on highly invisible core applications like financial management. The Web, however, is far more "sexy" politically.

There is little doubt that high-level political involvement continued under Bush. Witness Jeb Bush's desire to be known as the "e-governor." But, unlike Chiles, Bush was quite personally involved. Quite arguably, much of the confusion and disjointed policy in his first 2 years was created by a poor understanding and willingness to use Florida's existing capacities, far too much borrowing from private-sector e-commerce models, and staff not willing to confront and disagree with the governor, especially concerning the largely failed online permit project, and simply poor appointments (e.g., Cales). Also noticeably absent was competition. The competition between DOS and DMS did produce some healthy results. Under Bush, central leadership was clear.

One of the pitfalls of heavy political involvement in management control is too much dependency on election cycles and other political factors. As Bozeman and Bretschneider (1986: 484) warned in their prescriptions for public information management, "political executives' understandable concern with political cycles and quick results can undermine the long-term managerial objectives".

Florida's transition to Bush is a classic example of this problem. The state had run its e-government operation primarily via the personality of DMS Secretary Lindner, the political interest of the DOS Secretary Mortham, a small university unit for development assistance, and a loose association of state web developers, many not actually in IT units. Bush virtually ignored all previous work and what structure the state had was largely decimated in his first year. Projects like online permits were no doubt politically conceived but unrealistic in scope, poorly funded, and badly timed.

Chiles was just as politically motivated as Bush. The difference for Bush was that the Web was maturing. Leading applications were no longer simple sites. Chiles left little in professional structure. The Bush administration tried institutionalizing e-government, starting with the formation of the STO and now the MyFlorida Alliance. The preferred, very private-sector, centralized structures do reflect Bush's political views. Bush has also learned to leave e-government more to the professionals. In his first few years of office, the governor was characteristically very involved in application decisions. Today, while he maintains a central vision of e-government services for the state, the tactical decisions appear to be left to the STO. This better matches Chiles' approach of general support, but stays out of the details. But, how much the centralized model will prevail is very debatable at the time this chapter was written as current legislation calls for moving STO under DMS and presumably, some retraction of its approval and policy powers.

Have Bush's efforts produced a stable e-government structure that, unlike Chiles', can survive political transition? The MyFlorida Alliance contract noticeably extends beyond his elected term. Bush cannot succeed himself but it is likely a new Republican governor would maintain the relationship. A Democrat, however, is not as likely to support the heavily private sector model but the contractual arrangement limits policy flexibility. More centralized policy control, as it helps a governor regardless of party, is not likely to change. The question for Florida, given the vague STO status, is how much?

Perhaps the greatest lesson from Florida under both administrations is that top political involvement does matter. When involvement is quite general and highly strategic, leaving tactical decisions to capable professionals, political input is conducive. However, when top political leadership insists on detailed personal direction without reasonable resources or planning, failure is the norm. Transitions, as Bozeman and Bretschneider (1986) note, are extremely difficult, especially with major differences in political philosophy.

Florida also demonstrates that political involvement appears to influence institutions, far more than the reverse. Chiles, a Democrat, preferred in-house, mostly government-based solutions. Bush prefers the private sector with centralized policy control. E-government is quite malleable. However, the development of strong institutions, as e-government matures and melds into existing IT operations, may lessen the political maneuvers (cf., Fountain, 2001). Established e-government institutions could well shape political discourse. Politics affects IT choices, but IT possibilities influence policymaking. One vital research question is how this relationship varies over technological maturity. As e-government matures, and stable structures develop, will the dualism diminish?

B. Personnel Issues

One of the greatest alleged differences between public and private information management is the ability to attract and retain top personnel due to often dramatic salary differences and inflexible hiring procedures of civil service systems (e.g., Bozeman and Bretschneider, 1986; Bretschneider, 1990). Public agencies often develop IT workers from other professions and job lines in their agencies rather than directly hiring computing professionals. Supplementing information systems expertise with outside vendors is also common but the issue of outsourcing is fraught with management problems (Globerman and Vining, 1996) and even some evidence that it discourages the much-needed development of internal capacity (e.g., Norris and Kraemer, 1996).

Florida, under Chiles, avoided the usual personnel problems. DMS certainly had little problem attracting top web staff despite salary difficulties. Of course, DMS Secretary Linder made such staff a budgetary priority but the DMS case is instructive beyond executive leadership. Linder targeted younger employees where disparity in salaries was lower and offered them much greater work challenges and freedom than they would likely have found in a lower-level business operation. DMS turnover, despite the qualification and uniqueness of its web team, was surprisingly low owing to the often expressed high levels of job satisfaction and outright loyalty to Lindner (cf., Perez, 1997). Such loyalty, however, has its costs as the defection of many of Lindner's primary team with his departure from office attests.

Unlike Chiles, Bush does not believe in a government-centered model. His initial decisions to outsource the state web portal away from DMS and virtually ignore input from state web workers were highly demoralizing. Bush's major mistake was not to address the perception from staff that he was rather naive about e-government. He did not acknowledge previous work, he did not seek input, and he selected highly unqualified management and companies, at least in the view of many state web personnel.

Currently, many STO positions are being privatized via such arrangements as MyFlorida Alliance. Major support applications, like personnel, are also undergoing privatization with systems like "People First." Simply put, state workers are not involved in major application development and planning. Bush views the private sector as far more innovative and likely to have better ideas than the state government.

The personnel problem for Bush is that, especially at the agency level, there is not much incentive to work in IT. Under Chiles, e-government was seen by employees as a valuable career strategy and agencies were encouraged to develop applications. Such opportunities helped mitigate pay differences. Though pay differences between the state and the private sector have diminished with a poor economy, such a temporary reprieve from financial pressures will not last.

It could be argued that transitioning state workers, and those likely to work on state applications as new hires, will be better paid and treated in the private companies. MyFlorida Alliance potentially allows public workers to tackle government and private work within the same organization. The advantage could be greater personnel stability as the private-sector work will help support salaries. Larger companies, like Accenture and BearingPoint, probably have better potential career paths and mobility. Certainly, personnel will enjoy a much greater menu of projects. Such benefits are possible but IT privatization efforts can also reduce pay as technology substitutes for professional personnel, a common problem in help desk type conversions.

It is likely, however, that new employees (outside of those transferred from government) will not have a good public-sector background. Unlike agencies, the private companies may be far less likely to hire employees with government training. Traditionally, many government IT people start in government and then learn IT. In the private sector, the reverse is far more likely. Does this mean that private-sector companies will be staffed with employees with little ability to understand the complexities of government and perhaps incorrectly assume business school models? Or, will companies recognize this and seek employees with government backgrounds? Large companies accustomed to government work may be more understanding.

Bush's strategy is to have such companies do "day-to-day" operations and leave more policy control within his administration. Arguably, this diminishes the potential problems. Bush believes staff and support functions are privatization targets, leaving government agencies to their core mission, an almost politics–administration dichotomy. But, even routine operations can involve government complexity, and implementation is hardly removed from policy.

C. Innovation

There is a sizable debate over the causes of information systems innovation, whether demand push or technology pull is the greatest factor, and indeed, how innovative public agencies are in relation to the private sector (e.g., Caudle, 1990; Stevens et al., 1990; Bugler and Bretschneider, 1993; Pandey and Bretschneider, 1997). The general perception is that the public sector should be less innovative than business for reasons mostly related to expectations of public-sector red tape, fewer resources, and economic factors. However, Bretschneider (1990) has found that public managers tend to rely more on the proximity to "state of the art" in evaluating adoption of new technology than on such factors as economic criteria, like return on investment, more favored by private managers.

Florida's early web presence defies the usual presumption of public-sector tardiness in adopting new technologies. The Florida government clearly developed strong web capabilities long before many comparable Florida businesses (at least in terms of size). Florida's experience has been mirrored at other government levels as the earliest websites were predominately government. Why? Bretschneider's study offers an important, plausible explanation.

The perceived political value associated with demonstrating cutting-edge web technology became a critical factor in early adoption in Florida. Few novel technologies required such high political payout for such a low investment. Meanwhile, businesses waited until a larger user community developed to support e-commerce. Private web development hinged more on return on investment, while government focused on political return. Bretschneider's (1990) explanation for why state of the art is so important to public managers does not, however, consider the importance of such political motivations.

Florida's innovation lead dramatically dropped under Bush's first 2 years. Why? The necessary investment and professional expertise to remain state of the art began to drastically rise with e-government maturity about the time Bush took office. Launching a simple website was no longer front page news. Bush tackled very ambitious ideas, like the permit project, without the necessary supporting infrastructure. His private-sector strategy was poorly timed as in 1999 there still were not many firms with good e-government backgrounds to employ.

Today, it is far easier to find qualified private firms for e-government assistance. Arguably, it is almost a necessity at some level as the needed expertise, personnel, and other capacity is difficult for many governments to permanently staff. Managing and operating e-government is far different today than in the mid-1990s.

But, is the Bush model likely to foster innovation? Two of the potential weaknesses are far too much dependence on the private sector and on centralization. The Bush administration stresses both out of cost concerns, the goal to make government more efficient being overriding. Yet, such centralized policy control, and external operations, may hinder innovation. A lot of Florida's initial ideas came from the agency level. Such agency applications are far less likely under Bush's arrangements. Separating mission from support work (with such IT support going to the private sector) presumes innovation has little, if any, relation to daily experience.

What if ideas come from the MyFlorida Alliance employees who are now in the private sector? Who owns such intellectual property? The funding model does encourage the companies to develop new, successful applications but the ownership is unclear. Conversely, however, since the model tends to pay on the basis of use, there is little incentive toward innovations that reduce the need to use facilities and applications. Despite the cost control emphasis, the funding model actually encourages more applications, and greater use from the company perspective. One questionable assumption may be that every additional use is a substitute for a traditional paper- or person-based more expensive transaction.

Agencies, however, paying the companies have the opposite incentive. Fewer applications and requests for services via MyFlorida Alliance reduce cost. Benefits remain unclear or, in the case of fee-for-service applications, would likely not accrue to the agency.

Finally, the choice of when to favor standardization over creativity is always difficult in IT. E-government is no exception. Is e-government mature enough, and yet the best solutions and strategies are relatively known? Bush's philosophy could reduce costs but the likely trade-off is reduced variety and innovation.

V. LESSONS LEARNED FROM FLORIDA: SUMMARY AND CONCLUSIONS

Florida's web development is an interesting story in political competition, dramatic transitions and varied government/private-sector models, and entrepreneurial leadership. While part of the Florida story invokes common assertions about the deployment of new IT, the case also challenges many traditional beliefs.

One of these is the assumption that political leadership is not very conducive to generating capacity. Most of the literature espouses the importance of system direction from more permanent, lower-level staff (e.g., Caudle et al., 1991). In this case, top political leadership is highly involved, with mixed results. Is political leadership more important than we often expect?

In the previous edition, we cautioned against a resounding "yes" despite the success under Chiles out of fear of the coming Bush transition and the lack of real permanent management: "failure by DMS and DOS to enhance, even maintain, their present web capabilities would actually support the very fears and concerns of authors stressing the importance of middle, more permanent management . . . " (Coursey and Killingsworth, 2000: 342).

The Florida experience under Bush dramatically underscores this warning. No doubt Bush strongly supported e-government but the lack of a strong structural base, his flat refusal to utilize what did exist, and steadfast insistence on private-sector perspectives and companies that simply were not well developed at the time lead to a significant drop in the state's relative standing. However, like many states, Florida has made significant progress in establishing solid e-government infrastructure, admittedly with a lot of growing pains.

While Florida has established a good infrastructure, one pressing concern is lack of supervision. MyFlorida Alliance has questionable government control. Moreover, Florida will become quite dependent on outside companies for traditional internal staff operations. The Florida Legislature has no clear permanent committee anymore to evaluate IT policies. Massive turnover in IT qualified legislative staff give even the existing committees little ability to seriously evaluate the governor's policies. Related policy analysis organizations, often critical of Bush, have been targets for elimination as well. Only the auditor general remains as a credible supervisory check and the focus of such oversight is primarily legal and not managerial. Bush is arguably Florida's strongest governor, given the combination of reduced elected cabinet posts and Republican legislative control that questions very few of his policies.

This may be conducive to policy change but seriously undermines the ability to evaluate claims, such as cost savings. Insuring accountability is a major problem, especially after the auditor general reports of past questionable political dealings with contracts. Regardless of political party, it is all too easy for companies to compete via political favors than via quality or efficient service. MyFlorida Alliance will likely seek expansion to local government. Gaining control over state-level activities can help companies create a virtual monopoly over the state as local governments either rely on state-level expertise and resources, or conform their applications where data are shared. Barriers to entry and exit are significant and as such, the expected efficiency gains from market competition are likely illusory.

Personnel matters are dramatically different between Chiles and Bush. Florida enjoyed great success in securing and motivating public IT staff during the early e-government years, especially as operations were predominately in-house. A variety of approaches independent of pay created a strong internal staff. But, Bush is a radical departure toward private-sector control and transferring IT workers to private jobs. Will state employees be better off in private companies? Will private companies consider the importance of government background in new hires? These are critical questions.

Finally, Florida attests to the importance of political demand in innovation, tempered by the necessity of strong supporting infrastructure, and perhaps political leadership, leaving the tactical details to professionals. Much of Florida's early experience was political demand-pull fostered by significant interagency competition. Bush sees such agency competition as inefficient and prefers a centralized control and development environment. No doubt, Florida needed some more formal, centralized structure, particularly for applications and technologies cutting across agencies. The question remains: will presumed cost savings and better coordination via centralization and input of private-sector ideas improve innovation? Or, will the lack of agency involvement and incentives, state employee involvement, and disconnect between mission and staff lessen positive change?

These questions are critical. They involve serious academic study of complex relationships between policies, institutions and politics, and outcomes. All too often, e-government literature has been descriptive, reporting who is doing what and how well. It is time scholars focus more on how governments implement e-government and determine why projects fail and succeed, as well as the implications of various management strategies.

REFERENCES

Bousquet, S., Politicians Spar with State Over Contract, *St. Petersburg Times*, Feb. 20, 2004, p. B6.

Bozeman, B., *All Organizations Are Public*, Jossey-Bass, San Francisco, 1987.

Bozeman, B. and Bretschneider, S., Public management information systems: theory and prescription, *Public Adm. Rev.*, 46, 475–487, 1986.

Bretschneider, S., Management information systems in public and private organizations: an empirical test, *Public Adm. Rev.*, 50, 536–545, 1990.

Bugler, D. and Bretschneider, S., Technology push or program pull: interest in new information technologies within public organizations, in *Public Management: The State of the Art*, Bozeman, B., Ed., Jossey-Bass, San Francisco, 1993.

Caudle, S., Managing information resources in state government, *Public Adm. Rev.* 50, 515–524, 1990.

Caudle, S.L., Gorr, W.L., and Newcomer, K.E., Key information management issues for the public sector, *MIS Quarterly*, 15, 171–188, 1991.

Cotterell, B., 'People First' Outsourcing Is Underway, *Tallahassee Democrat*, May 5, 2003a, p. B1.

Cotterell, B., State's Tech Office to Be Privatized: Information Technology to Cost 30-Percent Less, *Tallahassee Democrat*, June 4, 2003b, p. A1.

Cotterell, B., Audit Criticizes State High-Tech Office, *Tallahassee Democrat*, Sept. 20, 2003c, p. A1.

Cotterell, B., People First's Time to Put Up or Shut Up, *Tallahassee Democrat*, Sept. 29, 2003d, p. B1.

Coursey, D. and Killingsworth, J., Managing government web services in Florida: issues and lessons, in *Handbook of Public Information Systems*, Garson, D., Ed., Marcel Dekker, New York, 2000, pp. 331–343.

Danziger, J., Dutton, W., Kling, R., and Kraemer, K., *Computers and Politics: High Technology in American Local Government*, Columbia University Press, New York, 1982.

Fountain, J., *Building the Virtual State: Information Technology and Institutional Change*, Brookings Institution Press, Washington, D.C., 2001.

Globerman, S. and Vining, A., A framework for evaluating the government contracting out decision with an application to information technology, *Public Adm. Rev.*, 56, 577–586, 1996.

Innes, J., Effects of data requirements on planning: case studies of environmental impact assessment and community development bloc grants, *Comput. Environ. Urban Syst.*, 12, 77–88, 1988.

Kraemer, K. and Dedrick, J., Computing and public organizations, *J. Public Adm. Res. Theor.*, 7, 89–112, 1997.

Kraemer, K. and King, J., Computing and public organizations, *Public Adm. Rev.* 46, 488–496, 1986.

Kraemer, K., King, J., Dunkle, D., and Lane, J., *Managing Information Systems: Change and Control in Organizational Computing*, Jossey-Bass, San Francisco, 1989.

Lauer, N., First Tech Chief Faces Tough Task: Roy Cales Will Oversee State's Technology Plans, *Tallahassee Democrat*, July 1, 2001a, p. A1.

Lauer, N. and Bridges, T. State's Tech Guru Resigns amid Controversy: Roy Cales Arrested as Plans Founder (sic) for Consolidated Technology Office, *Tallahassee Democrat*, Aug. 31, 2001b, p. A1.

Lauer, N., Tech Companies Face Contribution Analysis, *Tallahassee Democrat*, May 28, 2002a, p. A1.

Lauer, N., CIO for State's Tech Office Named: Acting Head Takes on Agency Under Fire, *Tallahassee Democrat*, June 29, 2002b, p. B1.

Lauer, N., Tech Office Up for Grabs: Company May Take Over State Facility, *Tallahassee Democrat*, Mar. 16, 2003a, p. A1.

Lauer, N., Workers in Tech Office to Be Axed but a Private Company May Hire Some of Them, *Tallahassee Democrat*, Oct. 19, 2003b, p. A1.

Lauer, N., Panel: Forced Vendor Listing Not Authorized, *Tallahassee Democrat*, Dec. 9, 2003c, p. B1.

Morgan, L., State Technology Office Broke Law, Audit Finds, *Tallahassee Democrat*, May 14, 2002, pp. 4B–5B.

Norris, D. and Kraemer, K., Mainframe and PC computing in American cities: myths and realities, *Public Adm. Rev.*, 56, 568–576, 1996.

Pandey, S. and Bretschneider, S., The impact of red tape's administrative delay on public organizations: interest in new information technologies, *J. Public Adm. Res. Theor.*, 7, 113–130, 1997.

Perez, J., Information Technology Innovation in the Public Sector: An Interpretive Investigation of World Wide Web Initiatives in State Agencies in Florida, Unpublished Doctoral dissertation, Florida State University, Tallahassee, FL, 1997.

Rosica, J., Cales Not Guilty of Theft: Case Went Forward Despite Lost Evidence, *Tallahassee Democrat*, Mar. 12, 2003, p. A1.

STO (State Technology Office), State of Florida, *My Florida Alliance* (brochure), State Technology Office, Tallahassee, FL, 2003.

State of Florida Office of the Comptroller, Audit of the State Technology Office, January 3, 2003 Available at: http://www.dbf.state.fl.us/aadir/sto_audit/sto_report_contents.html

Stevens, J., Cahill, A., and Overman, S., The transfer of information systems technology in state governments, *Comput. Environ. Urban Syst.*, 14, 11–23, 1990.

St. Petersburg Times, Technology Officer Quits Job, *St. Petersburg Times*, Feb. 5, 2004, p.B3.

Tallahassee Democrat, Permit Information Goes Online at Environmental Department, *Tallahassee Democrat*, Mar. 14, 2000, p. A4.

Williams, L., Critics Assail Convergys for Delays in Florida Deal, March 12, 2004 Available at: http://cincinnati.bizjournals.com/cincinnati/stories/2003/03/15/story3.html

22

EXPLORING INTERNET OPTIONS: THE CASE OF GEORGIA'S CONSUMER SERVICES

Gregory Streib
Georgia State University

Katherine G. Willoughby
Georgia State University

CONTENTS

I.   Introduction 354
     A.   Georgia's Office of Consumer Affairs 355
II. Theoretical framework 356
     A.   Effective online interactions may not be possible 357
III. Hypotheses 358
IV. Methodology 359
V.   Findings 360
     A.   Explaining contact preferences 362
     B.   The role of OCA support 362
     C.   The role of consumer problems 363
     D.   The role of demographic differences 364
VI. Conclusion 365
References 367

ABSTRACT

The e-government age has brought forth all sorts of expectations from citizens, elected officials, and public administrators regarding public service delivery. Many feel that advanced technologies and electronic communication formats can easily displace traditional methods of interaction between government agencies and citizens and subsequently produce greater efficiency of operation. On the other hand, much of the expectation about the possibilities of e-government ignores important externalities related to this service delivery method — in particular, differential access among citizens. In addition, these expectations assume that most citizens would prefer electronic over personal interaction (for the convenience) or at the very least would not indicate strong preference for the maintenance of traditional means of interacting with government agencies. This research examines citizens' perspectives about service delivery options of a state agency that specifically compares traditional means of delivery (like in-person office visits) with web-based ones. We present data from a yearlong series of four statewide polls that examined attitudes toward the services provided by Georgia's Office of Consumer Affairs and the citizen assessment of different service delivery options, including electronic communication methods. Our findings show a strong preference for in-person communication. We then extend the research to identify the factors associated with this preference. Our work is exploratory, but the findings do help to enhance our understanding of the hurdles that public administrators face as they seek to find ways to benefit from new communication technologies.

I. INTRODUCTION

The revolutionary aspects of using the Web to provide public services are exciting to contemplate. Currently, there is tremendous opportunity to transform the traditional closed bureaucratic paradigm into something more dynamic, flexible, and transparent. According to Ho (2002: 437), web-based service delivery emphasizes "teamwork, multi-directional networking, direct communication between parties, and a fast feedback loop." In addition to contributing to greater efficiency of operations and transactions, use of the Web by governments can empower citizens by facilitating their information gathering, offering flexible transaction choices, and improving their ability to communicate with policymakers and program managers. Such tools can be tailor-made to meet the needs of individual citizens through the creation of user-oriented portals (Ho, 2002).

This research examines the options available to a state government agency that could benefit from using web-based technologies. The governor's Office of Consumer Affairs (OCA) in the state of Georgia is involved in activities of a regulatory and distributive nature. Some of their work involves behind-the-scenes legal action, but much of what they do involves direct communication with citizens and information dissemination. In the long run, shifting their communication activities to the Internet could improve the quality of the services they provide to the public.

The growing information needs of U.S. citizens today certainly warrant that governments and agencies like the Georgia OCA consider web-based service enhancements. Indeed, Fors and Moreno (2002: 201) conclude, " . . . access to information and knowledge could be regarded as a basic need nowadays." Access to information and information technology is now "a part of the fabric of daily life" (National Science Board, 2002: 8–14). Of course, consumer transactions are an example of a situation where information is of vital importance. Threats to private consumers are more complex and less obvious than in the past. Being an educated consumer is now a basic life skill.

For example, the threat of old-fashioned robbery was obvious and easy to comprehend, but crimes such as identity theft are remote and ambiguous. The victim may not perceive harm for weeks, months, or even years after the initial theft. The threat of a physical attack arouses our instincts for self-protection, but only the very informed consumer will perceive the threat posed by identity theft. Furthermore, concepts such as truth in advertising take on new meaning when the products sold include child care, retirement plans, legal services, health care, and even cosmetic surgery. We now make life-altering decisions on a daily basis, and only some sort of a centralized agency can compile the data needed to identify the many different threats to the modern consumer and mobilize a response.

Another threat to consumers today is the growing sophistication of marketers who use new technologies to influence their shopping choices. They use knowledge of consumer demographics (Variyam et al., 1999) to flood consumers with focused advertisements online, via e-mail, and through traditional mail, and they track buying habits with ever-greater precision. Customer relationship strategies and software are blossoming, as are location-based systems that can even physically track customers to tap into individual preferences at the most opportune time (Variyam et al., 1999).

In this study, we use data from a series of four statewide polls to examine the interest of Georgian residents in new web-based service delivery options, as opposed to the traditional methods of contact between citizens and government, which include telephone and in-person office visits. The findings from this study raise interesting questions about the role of the Internet in the provision of public services. While the Internet presents some fantastic new opportunities, it may also pose some difficult challenges to public officials. The ideal scenario is that online capabilities can provide an entirely new way for governments to interact with citizens; in this case, empowering consumers with the information that they need to carry out transactions knowledgeably and efficiently. In darker scenarios, Internet services become just another unfunded mandate, provided side by side with existing services and generating additional costs to the agency.

A.   Georgia's Office of Consumer Affairs

Georgia, like many states, has made a visible commitment to consumer protection and education. The state created an Office of Consumer Affairs (OCA) in 1975 and it has grown into a consumer powerhouse offering a variety of services. It offers personalized case management, consumer information, and a wide array of possible actions, including investigation, mediation, criminal action, and the assessment of a number of different types of fees and fines (see Georgia's Office of Consumer Affairs, 2003).

The enforcement capacity of Georgia's OCA flows from existing laws. State statutes give the OCA great power to stop unfair or illegal business practices. The office enforces the state's fair business practices act, the lemon law (related to automobile sales), laws regarding tiered business opportunity sales, buying services, charitable solicitations, targeted unfair and deceptive practices, and Georgia's no-call law, among others.

Individual consumers can contact the OCA to request information "24 hours a day" by calling a local or a toll-free (in Georgia) number. The office staffs counselors by telephone and for walk-ins on weekdays from 9:00 a.m. to 4:00 p.m. (see "Frequently Asked Questions" accessible from Georgia's Office of Consumer Affairs, 2003). Currently, the OCA uses a number of methods to help educate Georgian consumers. The office staffs the telephone helpline, produces brochures, uses media outlets, such as newspapers, radio, and television, and frequently provides speakers for schools, professional associations, and community groups.

The office's web presence is basic and quite limited, however. The OCA home page provides access to general agency information and forms in Acrobat format for filing complaints. While brochures are available online in both English and Spanish, the website itself is not bilingual. The office website does offer links to consumer protection support entities both in the state and nationally, as well as links to other Georgian agencies that can help consumers when they have complaints or problems.

All consumer complaints must be in written form, and they can be completed in person or sent by traditional mail to the downtown Atlanta office. Consumers may fax written complaints of no more than five pages in length to OCA offices. While consumers can download the complaint form from the OCA website, there is no avenue for submitting complaints online at this time. Using Ho's (2002) government website characterization, the OCA web presence fits the category of information and is not user-oriented. Their website offers information, or links, or both to Georgian law and other materials that might be useful to consumers, but it does not facilitate individual citizen–agency transactions.

Although the OCA's efforts to reach citizens have been appropriate and helpful thus far, they have not greatly expanded the ability of the agency to keep up with demand. Clients of the OCA are generally first-time callers who contact the office to get help with a specific one-time problem. Therefore, most of the OCA staff time is now focused on counseling citizens with existing consumer problems either over the telephone or in person. Given the limits in fiscal, personnel, and other resources for servicing the victims of business fraud, the agency is seeking to enhance its consumer education services to prevent problems before they occur. Increased application of online resources via the World Wide Web and related information technologies appear to offer a way to get this done on a stagnant budget.

By all appearances, the OCA could benefit greatly from some advanced web-based technologies that aid in providing better services to citizens. As things stand now, the vast knowledge and experience of the OCA staff is shared only in an idiosyncratic way with those citizens who call on the telephone and ask the right questions. Of course, the office certainly does recognize the inefficiencies related to telephone communication. Staff members answer the same questions many times. The state population is growing far faster than the OCA budget, and presently the office is unable to expand services beyond its current capacity.

II. THEORETICAL FRAMEWORK

The OCA would like to enhance its information exchange with citizens for both management and fiscal reasons. This could be achieved by getting citizens to use their online information both before a transaction and when and if they encounter a problem. Before making a purchasing decision, appropriate information can help consumers to formulate reasonable expectations and this will help assure a satisfactory transaction. Research on consumers demonstrates that they possess "bounded rationality" and are generally unable to completely assimilate the total complexity of any given transaction process (Simon, 1957; Swait and Adamowicz, 2001). Expectations play a vital role in how satisfied consumers are with their decisions. Kopalle and Lehmann (2001) reviewed the factors traditionally related to a satisfactory consumer transaction. They found that actual experience and information from advertisements "and other sources" do affect expectations.

The Internet offers the perfect vehicle for helping consumers make better decisions. A well-designed site could guide and educate consumers, and if used, would ultimately lead to a reduction in the number of claims that OCA must investigate. Many citizens who experience a problem will certainly require personal attention, but few calls to OCA are unique. Whatever the problem, a large part of the call involves an explanation of OCA procedures and possible remedies. Every call is important, but few of them lead to legal action. Whether an expansion of online services would produce cost savings is unclear, but such an expansion would give the agency a better chance to meet the rapidly escalating information needs of Georgia's growing population. Serving citizens via personal one-on-one contact is not going to get the job done in the absence of a dramatic growth in the OCA budget. There is no evidence that this will happen in the near future. Like many state agencies at this time, the OCA is an agency expected to do a lot with very little.

There are certain costs associated with both parties here. That is, we recognize that the reliance on in-person communication places an extra burden on the caller. In most cases, callers would save time by visiting a well-designed website. Indeed, many citizens may hesitate to act on a consumer complaint out of concern for the personal costs involved. Alternatively, the upfront costs for site development must be borne by OCA, even though many benefits could result from a substantial reduction in the personal one-on-one assistance provided by staff.

A.   Effective Online Interactions May Not be Possible

OCA would likely succeed as an information provider using such venue, as this use of the Web appears to be most in line with citizen expectations. The U.S. Bureau of Commerce finds that searching for information is second only to accessing and sending e-mail when Americans' online activities are tabulated (National Science Board, 2002: 8–20). Most citizens now have high expectations for the online information and transaction capacities of public and private organizations. Horrigan and Rainie (2002) find that "84 percent of all Americans have an expectation of finding information online regarding health care, government services, news and business. That translates into nearly all Internet users (97 percent) and most non-Internet users (64 percent). For information or services from a government agency, 65 percent of all Americans expect the Web to have that information; 82 percent of Internet users say this and 39 percent of non-users say this." In addition, research by Thomas and Streib (2003) shows that citizens are highly satisfied with government websites.

Online services are a more questionable venture, however. The evidence shows that the Web has not yet lead to the development of better relationships between citizens and governments. While numerous initiatives have strongly promoted online capacity for government–government, government–business, and government–citizen transactions, there has been little progress in what we might call e-governance or e-democracy (the participation of citizens in policy development and deliberation). One obvious failure along these lines has been Internet voting, which is fundamentally an e-governance issue. This has failed to take hold in the U.S., despite our leadership in Internet access and server capacity (National Science Board, 2002).

Research on web use by local governments (Kaylor et al., 2001) and the states (Stowers, 1999) has also illustrated the limits of Internet technology. These studies leave one to conclude that the primary government web service available today is still the telephone book. There is also a recent study by Holden et al. (2003) indicating that local government managers may be somewhat ambivalent about the value of web services — viewing them as "a mixed blessing."

Thomas and Streib (2003) find that the so-called digital divide might even be greater for visits to government websites than for general use of the Internet. Differential access to the Internet remains a serious barrier. According to Milliron and Miles (2000):

> Data from the U.S. Education Department, the Federal Computer Weekly, and the National Center for Educational Statistics find great disparities in information

access across populations — White Americans are twice as likely as Blacks or Hispanics to have an Internet connection. Households with incomes of more than $75,000 per year are twenty times more likely to have access to the Internet than those with incomes in the $50,000-or-lower bracket. In addition, fewer than 39 percent of low-income schools have a classroom with an Internet connection.

Finally, there is also research from the private sector showing that Internet customer service is not always appreciated (Nigro, 2002) and that nearly half of online service questions cannot be resolved without a telephone call (Faloon, 2000). At the very least, these disparate perspectives on the value of the Web and web services recommend a cautious approach. While it seems likely that there are citizens who very much want to conduct their business online, and that such interaction could be beneficial, there is also reason to suspect that many will not be eager to break away from more traditional communication methods.

III.   HYPOTHESES

Given the exploratory nature of this study and our consideration of the literature related to consumer behavior and information needs, Internet service delivery, and the characteristics of the OCA, we present the following hypotheses:

1.   We expect Georgians to express strong support for the consumer education services provided by Georgia's OCA. Subgroup variations are expected to be minor. We believe that most Georgian citizens will realize that consumers need different types of assistance.
2.   We expect support to be strongest for OCA activities related to the provision of information and direct consumer assistance. These activities provide citizens with the greatest direct benefit.
3.   Overall, we expect to see stronger support for in-person contact than for web-based methods. However, we do expect to see a substantial interest in Internet communication options.
4.   We expect to find variability in support for different contact methods with the OCA. Three factors for which we expect to influence attitudes about service delivery options include: support of OCA activities, a recent consumer problem (or recent problems), and population demographics. We anticipate the following:
     (a)   We expect that support for OCA will translate into some type of increased support for e-government services. Respondents who indicate the most support for OCA might know more about the services already provided online and believe that electronic communications could produce good results.
     (b)   We expect that experiencing a recent consumer problem will increase support for in-person contact. Remembering a consumer problem well enough to mention it in an interview suggests a significant event. Such an experience would amplify any concerns the respondents might have about getting personal attention.
     (c)   There is ample evidence that population demographics have an impact on Internet access. We expect our findings to be most similar to those for overall Internet access, as described above, given that we are polling a general population.

IV. METHODOLOGY

Our methodology involved the use of the Georgia Poll, which is a statewide telephone poll conducted in each quarter of the year. These polls frequently examine public policy issues and the need for specific types of government services. Each poll successfully contacts roughly 800 Georgian residents.

All adults living in Georgia, with a working telephone (including new and unlisted numbers but excluding cellular telephone numbers), were eligible to be included in the poll. Interviewers made calls throughout the day, 7 days a week. Interviewers often made return calls by appointment. Research staff developed weights for the poll responses using the 2000 U.S. census data for the state of Georgia. As is the case with any poll, our results are likely to contain some error. Ninety-five percent of the time, error due to the random selection process will be no more than 3.5 percentage points plus or minus the reported percentage for 800 respondents. Other types of error occur when selected participants refuse to participate in the interview or cannot be contacted. Our polling staff made every possible effort to reduce these types of errors.

This study uses data from four polls. The first poll in the series was conducted in August 2001. Polling ended in June 2002. Georgia's Office of Consumer Affairs was involved in the development of the poll questions.

We compare the poll responses with data from the 2000 U.S. census in Table 22.1. The poll results generally conform to the population data on the critical variables of sex, race, and age. However, responses on the income variable diverge noticeably from the census data. Real differences in income levels could explain this; however, we also know that the poll respondents often did not want to provide information on their income. This variable does have a high number of missing values. Based on the comparison to the Census data, it appears that respondents with lower incomes were less likely to respond to this

Table 22.1   Poll Response Rates Compared with U.S. Census Data (2000)

	Comparisons	
Key Demographic Groupings	Georgia	Poll Data
Totals	8,186,453	3207
Sex		
Male	49.2	49.0
Female	50.8	51.0
Race		
Black	28.7	27.6
White	65.1	64.6
Other	6.2	7.8
Age		
18–29	24.5	31.3
30–44	33.4	34.3
44–65	29.0	24.7
65 and above	13.1	9.7
Income		
Below $25,000	24.0	22.9
Above $25,000	66.0	77.1

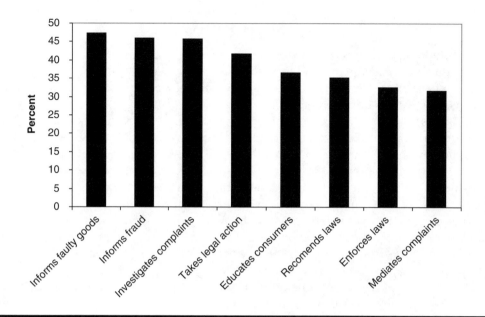

Figure 22.1 Respondents rating OCA services as very important (average *n* = 2875).

question. We will use extra caution in our interpretation of any analyses involving the income variable.

V. FINDINGS

Figure 22.1 displays the respondents' ratings of different OCA services. The possible responses were "very important," "important," "uncertain," and "not important." The figure displays the percentage of respondents choosing the "very important" category. Overall, these findings show that the poll respondents understood and supported the work done by OCA. Over half of the respondents gave most services the highest possible rating. The item with the highest percentage of "very important" ratings asked about OCA's efforts to inform consumers about fraudulent products and services. Other items with very high percentages include the investigation of consumer complaints and informing consumers about fraudulent business practices. Informing citizens and investigating complaints were the OCA activities that resonated most strongly with Georgian citizens.

The variations in the level of support were examined using an OCA support index that was created from the eight items displayed in Figure 22.1. These items produced an Alpha value of .97, and values for the index ranged from 8 to 32. A value of eight required giving the most positive possible response (very important) on each of the OCA service items, and a 32 required giving all the most negative responses. While 12% of the respondents had scores of eight on the index, less than 1% of the respondents had scores of 32. Indeed, 87% of the respondents received scores of 18 or higher, which required an average response of at least somewhat important on each of the eight items.

The poll respondents clearly appreciated the fact that Georgia's OCA was available to investigate consumer complaints and provide consumer information. This squares with our first and second hypotheses concerning the overall interest in OCA activities and the support for information provision and direct consumer help. We next examined service delivery preferences. The poll items asked about a variety of contact methods, ranging from in-person meetings and telephone calls to use of the Internet and regular mail. The respondents were asked to rate the effectiveness of each method, "if they had a consumer problem, such as a dispute with a business or a faulty product." Figure 22.2 displays the percentage of respondents indicating that each contact method is very effective.

Our findings indicate that in-person contact is most preferred. There is essentially a tie for second place, between a toll-free number and forms available in public places. Different types of Internet access follow in third place. The possible forms of Internet contact included an online form, e-mail access to OCA staff, and having downloadable forms available on the Internet. While we expected to find a preference for in-person contact, the strength of the preference is surprising, especially given that the poll questions specified that in-person consultations would take place in Atlanta at the home office of OCA. Internet communication appears to offer many advantages compared with this method of contact.

We constructed a variable from the items asking about Internet contact methods in an effort to learn more about the preferences for what we term P-government (people-oriented government requiring in-person or telephone contact) and e-government (online-oriented government). This variable divides the respondents into those that ranked both P- and e-government as effective, those ranking e-government as effective and not P-government, those ranking P-government as effective and not e-government, and those respondents who did not give an effective rating to either method of transacting with OCA. We assessed attitudes toward P-government using the in-person contact variable shown in Figure 22.1. The e-government rankings are derived from responses to an index that combined the three Internet-related items displayed in Figure 22.2. These

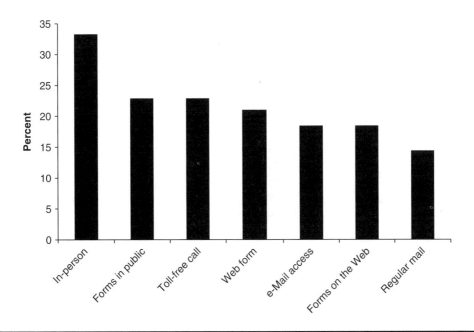

Figure 22.2   Respondents rating different contact methods as very effective (average _n_ = 2850).

items produce an Alpha value of .95. Figure 22.3 displays the responses to this new P-government and e-government variable.

As Figure 22.3 shows, the new variable gives us a much better view of how the poll respondents viewed these two different approaches for contacting OCA. For example, it shows that half of the respondents indicated that they liked both forms of interaction. While this grouping does hide the fact that some respondents gave a slightly higher rating for P-government items, it does show that many poll respondents were receptive to e-government access. The stronger support for P-government is also apparent in this figure. Nineteen percent of the poll respondents liked personal contact and had no interest in electronic contact. In contrast, only 6% of the respondents liked e-government and did not like P-government. Nine percent of the poll respondents doubted the effectiveness of both forms of interaction with OCA.

A. Explaining Contact Preferences

The descriptive findings are interesting, and they clearly show stronger support for personal contact with OCA. Yet, many questions remain about the variations in support for P- and e-government, as defined here. We explore this issue further by examining the impact of support for OCA activities, experiencing a recent consumer problem (or problems), and demographic variations.

B. The Role of OCA Support

As we noted above, the service provided by OCA goes beyond commerce, there is also an effort to build some type of relationship with citizen customers in need of assistance. Given this, support for P-Government may reflect a negative judgment about OCA, rather

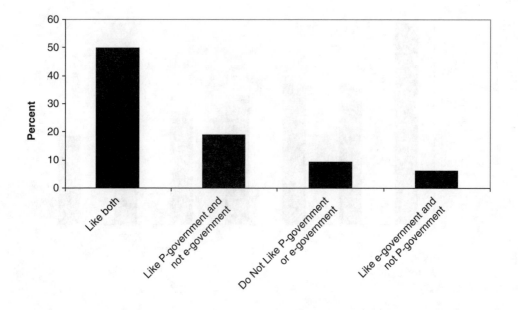

Figure 22.3   Respondent preferences for P-government and e-government (*n* = 2678).

Table 22.2 Respondent Contact Preferences by OCA Support

	n	Like Both	Like P-Government and Not e-Government	Do Not Like Either One	Like e-Government and Not P-Government
High support for OCA services	900	66.1	20.4	6.2	7.2
Moderate support for OCA	1023	62.1	21.7	9.4	6.8
Low support for OCA	559	45.6	24.3	21.1	8.9

Note: Findings are statistically significant.

than a dislike for Internet communication. Respondents may prefer personal contact as a way to spur OCA bureaucrats into action. One way we can explore this issue further is to examine the relationship between support for OCA and the variable we created showing different levels of support for P- or e-government. In this analysis, we use a recoded version of our support index. Table 22.2 displays our findings.

As Table 22.2 shows, we did find a relationship between support for OCA and attitudes toward different service delivery options. While there is little variation in the number of respondents who like electronic and not personal communication, the percentage of respondents approving both methods increases with OCA support. This table also shows that the percentage of respondents who like personal and not electronic contact peaks among those respondents with the lowest support for OCA. These findings are along the lines of what we expected. That is, that increased support for OCA would translate into a greater acceptance of alternative contact methods.

C. The Role of Consumer Problems

One of the interesting findings of this study was that only a small percentage of Georgian citizens indicated that they had experienced a problem with a consumer transaction in the last 6 months. Indeed, the incidence of reported problems is so low that we could not study them effectively without aggregating the findings from a number of different polls. With four separate polls, we had 355 respondents who reported one or more problems. The poll also asked about the type of problem experienced, presenting the respondents with five separate items asking about possible problem areas, including automobile sales and repairs; a grocery store purchase; home buying, construction, or remodeling; health care services and products; and general merchandise.

Experiencing a consumer problem may be important because it may heighten interest in OCA services. With so few respondents reporting consumer problems, the different delivery options might be so remote that the respondents did not give them much thought. It would seem likely that respondents who had experienced a problem would have an increased interest in the types of contact methods available, and that this might lead to a different set of responses. Table 22.3 presents the relationship between consumer problems and attitudes toward the different service delivery options. The table uses a variable we constructed that divides the respondents into three groups: those reporting no problems, those reporting one problem, and those reporting multiple problems.

Table 22.3   Respondent Contact Preferences by Consumer Problems

	n	Like Both	Like P-Government, and Not e-Government	Do Not Like Either One	Like e-Government and Not P-Government
Did not report a consumer problem in the last 6 months	2344	59.0	21.9	11.6	7.4
Reported a consumer problem in the last 6 months	75	57.3	25.3	9.3	8.0
Reported multiple consumer problems in the last 6 months	249	59.0	28.5	6.0	6.4

Note: These findings are statistically significant.

As Table 22.3 shows, we did not find that experiencing a consumer problem had a major impact on attitudes concerning service delivery options. There is a notable exception to this rule, however, and this is for respondents liking P-government and not e-government. There was a modest increase in the percentage of respondents in this column as consumer difficulties grew, peaking with those respondents who reported multiple consumer problems. This finding is roughly consistent with hypothesis that consumer difficulties would increase interest in in-person, one-on-one attention.

D.   The Role of Demographic Differences

It seems likely that attitudes about the different service delivery options covered in this study would have their roots in the digital divide. It is an accepted fact that access to Internet technologies is not evenly distributed. Given this, we expect to find support for e-government to be higher among those respondents likely to have access to Internet technologies. Such respondents would have the ability to communicate with OCA electronically, and they may be more comfortable with this type of technology. For this analysis, we looked at a large number of demographic variables, essentially identical to those used by Thomas and Streib (2003). As noted above, this study showed that the digital divide was even greater for visiting government sites than it was for general Internet use, so we do expect that these demographic variables will affect attitudes concerning e-government and P-government. Table 22.4 displays these findings.

Findings here indicate no striking relationships between the demographic variables and attitudes toward the different service delivery options. There are some statistically significant relationships, but these are more reflective of the sample size than the magnitude of the affects. These results do shed some light on the role that demographics play in helping to determine respondent attitudes. For example, it is interesting that support for P-government rises with income — just as Internet access rises. Older respondents also show greater support for P-government and a relatively striking dislike of e-government. This finding directly matches the Thomas and Streib (2003) study that found Georgians under 50 were more likely to access the Internet. Those respondents without children under 18 show less support for personal communication with the OCA, but we attribute this finding to the age variable.

Table 22.4   Respondent Contact Preferences by Demographic Characteristics

	n	Like Both	Like P-Government, and Not e-Government	Do Not Like Either One	Like e-Government and Not P-Government
Race					
African Americans	719	63.6	21.5	9.7	5.1
Whites	1686	57.9	22.8	11.2	8.0
Other	204	56.9	23.5	12.7	6.8
Sex					
Males	1306	58.7	22.2	11.6	7.4
Females	1362	59.1	23.1	10.5	7.2
Income*					
Below $25,000	377	61.0	20.1	14.3	4.5
$25,000 to $50,000	618	56.5	22.5	13.9	7.1
Above $50,000	649	60.9	24.8	6.8	7.6
Age*					
18–29	794	63.2	22.7	8.7	5.4
30–44	870	61.7	21.0	9.3	7.9
44–65	626	57.3	23.0	11.2	8.5
65 and above	246	46.7	30.1	15.8	7.3
Political affiliation*					
Democrat	901	63.3	19.4	11.9	5.3
Republican	685	59.3	22.8	9.9	8.0
Independent	612	55.4	25.3	10.6	8.7
None of the above	339	53.4	27.4	11.2	7.9
Education					
High school graduate or less	1011	60.5	22.4	11.6	5.4
Some college	719	58.5	23.4	10.8	7.2
College and above	893	58.4	22.3	10.0	9.3
Metro status					
Nonmetro	1744	58.8	22.5	11.1	7.6
Metro	936	59.3	22.8	11.0	6.9
Children under 18*					
No	1438	56.1	24.0	11.6	8.2
Yes	1214	62.3	21.0	10.3	6.2
Own residence					
No	646	59.6	25.2	8.9	6.2
Yes	1999	58.8	21.9	11.6	7.7

VI.   CONCLUSION

At this point, we are well into our first e-everything decade and the dust is starting to settle. Until recently, the Internet has been something of a phenomenon, and it has not been easy to tell fact from fiction. We are now beginning to get a better sense regarding the usefulness of Internet. In the realm of public administration, the first take on the Internet was that it would be an important productivity tool. Interest in these kinds of applications remains strong, but there is also a broader interest developing in digital governance — in finding ways to strengthen the linkages between citizens and governments. Our findings show that achieving these broader goals will be a great challenge.

We found that Georgian citizens appreciate OCA services; however, there is less agreement about the best way to deliver them. We did not focus as much on the delivery of information in this analysis but this is clearly an area where the agency can contribute. Our poll respondents do value specific consumer information like that about faulty goods and fraud. However, we also know that most consumers are comfortable making important decisions with only limited information. For most of us, consumer fraud, or suspicions about potential fraud, come as an unpleasant surprise. OCA can certainly help to encourage better consumer behavior, but they will never fully escape the need to help those who failed to think ahead.

The bulk of our analysis was about the treatment citizens preferred if they experienced a consumer problem, "such as a dispute with a business or a faulty product." This is not a classic e-government scenario. The provision of consumer services is not like renewing a driver's license or paying a bill. Georgia's Office of Consumer Affairs offers a far more extensive service when helping citizens who have experienced a consumer problem. They develop relationships of a sort with concerned citizens who are seeking government help. This is a democratic process to some extent, and similar to the work of local government planning and code enforcement offices, social service departments, state and federal regulatory agencies that work with business and governments, and citizen help desks.

Overall, what we find is a strong preference for in-person contact. A large proportion of the respondents viewed both P-government and e-government to be effective, but there was a clear preference for in-person communication. As we noted above, interviewers told the poll respondents that in-person meetings would take place in Atlanta, and responses given to the item about in-person meetings formed our P-government measure. To some extent, the appeal of in-person contact appears to defy logic. There are obvious benefits to other forms of communication.

Furthermore, we also know that the preference for in-person contact is relatively constant across a wide range of demographic variables. Our findings do show the affects of the digital divide only in a muted way. Those respondents that we know are the beneficiaries of the digital divide do not embrace Internet communication. We also found that respondents experiencing consumer problems are more likely to prefer in-person contact, and this is a very important finding. There is some reason to believe that these respondents are more typical of OCA clients than the poll respondents who had not experienced a problem.

Our findings certainly do not rule out the use of Internet communication. An effectively managed website may win over doubters. It would be up to OCA to prove that the concept can work, however, and this would present a substantial risk. They are in a difficult position. Financially, the most prudent course is for OCA to begin shifting a substantial portion of their operation to the Internet; however, the findings of this study do not indicate that this strategy is sure to succeed — at least not without substantial and sustained marketing to consumers. Citizens unable to call or visit the office efficiently may become dissatisfied, venting to elected officials or failing to benefit from the valuable service that the OCA is able to provide.

We have no way of knowing just how many government agencies find themselves in a situation similar to the OCA, but this situation cannot be unique. The fast growth of Atlanta and the state of Georgia coupled with the depressed economy make this dilemma starker — there has never been a worse time for governments to attempt to provide multiple means of carrying out the same activity. This is what is required to allow citizens to choose from either a well-designed website or an in-person visit.

Another insight offered by this research concerns the apparent way higher levels of support for the OCA increased acceptance of alternative service delivery methods. We need to know more about this relationship, but it does suggest that highly respected agencies may have an easier time building support for Internet-based communication methods. This offers some hope that the stalemate we identify in this chapter is not permanent. It is also possible that time will bring greater support for Internet services and so will make it easier for governments to promote them.

Overall, it is easy to be enthusiastic about Internet-based communication tools, even if they do not dramatically transform the way all types of organizations operate. The changes are going to come more slowly than some would like, however. Governments and government agencies seeking to benefit from using Internet tools must understand that successful implementation is likely to require aggressive promotion. Citizens do not appear eager to abandon the more traditional ways of communicating with government officials.

REFERENCES

Faloon, K., Internet Customer Service Falls Short, Supply House Times Newton, October 2000.

Fors, M. and Moreno, A.,The benefits and obstacles of implementing ICTs strategies for development from a bottom-up approach, *Aslib Proceedings*, 3, 198–206, 2002.

Georgia's Office of Consumer Affairs, 2003
   http://www2.state.ga.us/GaOCA/

Ho, A.T.-K., Reinventing local governments and the e-government initiative, *Public Administration Review*, 62, 434–444, 2002.

Holden, S.H., Norris, D.F., and Fletcher, P.D., Electronic government at the local level: progress to date and future issues, *Public Performance & Management Review*, 26, 325–344, 2003.

Horrigan, J.B. and Rainie, L., Counting on the Internet: Most Expect to Find Key Information Online, Pew Internet and American Life Project, December 29, 2002
   http://www.pewinternet.org/reports/ index.asp
   Accessed on 10/28/2003.

Kaylor, C.H., Deshazo, R., and Van Eck, D., Gauging e-government: a report on implementing services among American cities, *Government Information Quarterly*, 18, 293–307, 2001.

Kopalle, P.K. and Lehmann, D.R., Strategic management of expectations: the role of disconfirmation sensitivity and perfectionism, *Journal of Marketing Research*, 38, 386–394, 2001.

Milliron, M.D. and Miles, C.L., Education in a digital democracy, *Education Review*, 35, 50–62, 2000.

National Science Board, *Science and Engineering Indicators*, National Science Foundation (NSB-02-1), Arlington, VA, 2002.

Nigro, F., From the Outside: Mastering E-Customer Loyalty, *Bank Technology News*, January 1, 2002. Available at: http://static.highbeam.com/b/banktechnologynews/january012002/fromtheout sidemasteringecustomerloyalty/
   Accessed on 8/22/04.

Simon, H.A., *Administrative Behavior: A Study of Decision-Making Process in Administrative Organizations*, 2nd ed., The Free Press, New York, 1957.

Stowers, G.D.L., Becoming cyberactive: state and local governments on the World Wide Web, *Government Information Quarterly*, 16, 111–127, 1999.

Swait, J. and Adamowicz, W., The influence of task complexity on consumer choice: a latent class model of decision strategy switching, *Journal of Consumer Research*, 28, 135–148, 2001.

Thomas, J.C. and Streib, G., The new face of government: citizen-initiated contacts in the era of e-government, *Journal of Public Administration Research and Theory*, 13, 83–102, 2003.

Variyam, J.N., Blaylock, J., and Smallwood, D., Information, endogeneity, and consumer health behaviour, *Applied Economics*, 31, 217–226, 1999.

23

THE VIRTUAL VALUE CHAIN AND E-GOVERNMENT PARTNERSHIP: NONMONETARY AGREEMENTS IN THE IRS E-FILE PROGRAM

Stephen H. Holden
University of Maryland

Patricia D. Fletcher
University of Maryland

CONTENTS

I.	Introduction	370
II.	Virtual value chain literature	371
	A. Government information in the virtual value chain	373
III.	E-government literature	374
IV.	Study methodology	375
V.	Dimensions of public–private partnership in the IRS e-file program	375
	A. Institutional, business, and technical environment	375
	B. Political, social, economic, and cultural environment	377
	C. Public partners' characteristics and objectives	378
	D. Private partners' characteristics and objectives	380
VI.	A new model for collaboration	380
	A. Critical success enablers and barriers	381
	1. Public partners' characteristics and objectives	382
	2. Private partners' characteristics and objectives	382
	3. Barriers	383
VII.	The value chain revisited	384
VIII.	Conclusion	385
	References	385

ABSTRACT

Electric government (e-government) models generally espouse the principle of partnership with the private sector. What is not always clear is what is meant by partnership, though, and how public organizations should organize and manage such relationships to support e-government initiatives. This chapter relies on a conceptual framework of the virtual value chain to understand how a new form of collaboration emerged in the Internal Revenue Service (IRS) e-file program in 1999 and what dimensions helped to make it a success. As part of a larger, multi-nation study of public–private partnerships in e-government, this chapter examines the IRS e-file program, one of the largest, longest-standing (dating back to 1986) and most successful U.S. e-government programs with tens of millions of users each year. The IRS e-file program experienced dramatic changes in its long-standing partnership with the tax preparation and related software development industries in 1999 and 2000. It is possible, using the concept of the virtual value chain, to understand how the IRS rethought its relationship with its private-sector partners. A combination of conditions in the marketplace, in U.S. society, within the IRS, and among the private-sector partners helped to make this new model of collaboration quite successful. The chapter concludes by examining how the dimensions of partnership in the IRS e-file case and the concept of the virtual value chain might enable other public organizations to reconceptualize their e-government partnership arrangements with the private sector with a new model of collaboration.

I. INTRODUCTION

Many models of electronic government (e-government), both academic and commercial, stress the need for public–private partnership. Some of these models are descriptive and some are normative so it is not clear what the basis is for asserting the role of partnership in e-government implementations. More broadly, though, the term partnership is potentially problematic. Its meaning and significance varies greatly on the context in which it used as partnerships may involve contractual relationships, but may also involve less formal arrangements. The variability of these arrangements and the lack of an agreed-upon definition for the term raise potentially troubling questions for implementation and evaluation of e-government partnership initiatives. Despite this ambiguity around definitions, the "win–win" model of value implicit in the value chain, and more specifically the virtual value chain, may well help provide valuable insights into the worth of e-government partnerships.

As an idea and a term, e-government already suffers from a fair amount of ambiguity. In part because e-government has its roots in the literatures of public administration (PA), business administration, and information systems (IS), the term and concept of e-government is subject to continuing debate. This leaves us with the possibility of public managers trying to understand and employ two concepts, e-government and partnership, for which there is little agreement on basic meaning. How is it then that the public, potential private-sector partners, oversight organizations, or even sponsoring organizations can assess the results of e-government partnerships?

One plausible answer is relying on the management information system concept of the value chain, and in particular, the virtual value chain, as a way to both describe and evaluate e-government partnerships. While there are some professional and commercial publications that describe the role of the virtual value chain in e-government, the issue has not been the subject of systematic research. This chapter intends to address this gap in the existing literatures of IS, business administration, and PA. A value chain analysis of a specific e-government initiative will illustrate how this concept can fit into e-government models for public administrators.

An outline of the chapter follows. First, the chapter provides a brief review of the virtual value chain literature, with the goal of describing the concept and terminology as used in the private sector. Then, a review of selected pieces of e-government research seeks to make more explicit the implied role of the virtual value chain in e-government information and service delivery. Having laid this groundwork, the chapter then explores an endeavor by the Internal Revenue Service (IRS) to leverage its virtual value chain through nonmonetary agreements with various for- and not-for-profit partners as part of its electronic filing program, IRS e-file. A case study analysis of partnership in the IRS e-file program explores some of the management and policy issues the IRS encountered when it sought to manage its virtual value chain more explicitly like a private-sector firm. The chapter concludes with observations for organizations seeking to manage their virtual value chains effectively to enable or enhance their e-government offerings based on a new model for collaboration grounded the virtual value chain literature and the IRS e-file case study.

II.   VIRTUAL VALUE CHAIN LITERATURE

One only has to go as far as a recent edition of a leading IS journal to see both the promise, and to some extent, the confusion around the virtual value chain in e-government. Stafford (2003) extolled the virtues of filing his taxes electronically through a third party in an introduction to a special edition on "e-services." His brief introduction to a series of articles on e-services admitted the term was yet to be defined and he neglected to mention that his example involved e-government or a virtual value chain. Nonetheless, his story of preparing and filing his taxes online served as a great example of a consumer taking advantage of the virtual value chain that included a government agency and a private-sector intermediary. To explain why this is so requires a short explanation of value chains in general and the virtual value chain in particular.

The notion of value chains in organizations, primarily businesses, is certainly not new. It has existed for nearly two decades now as a powerful concept for businesses to identify and evaluate those "value" activities that create a product and deliver it to the customers. As introduced by Porter (1985), the value chain framework looks at inbound and outbound activities that both incur cost and create value for businesses. Players in most value chains include suppliers, producers, distributors, and customers. For instance, in Stafford's example, he was the customer, a commercial web-based tax preparation service was the distributor and producer, and a federal government agency, the IRS, was the supplier. The IRS supplies the rules for filing tax returns, the private-sector firm develops the software and distributes it as a service over the Web so that customers can prepare and file their taxes electronically.

It is the interactions among information, core operational activities, and the business infrastructure where value is determined. As in the example above, an organization's value chain consists of the network of suppliers, producers, distributors, and retailers that work together to create a product and bring it to the market. Porter and Millar (1985) originally called this the "value system" for a company. Organizations, therefore, have to decide which activities in their value chains they will keep in-house, contract for, or partner for. For instance, a company might decide to outsource customer support so it could focus its resources on product development.

Automobile manufacturers are often cited as an example of companies in a huge value chain, with the many parts and services suppliers providing inputs, the manufacturers adding value through the assembly process, and then the dealers (i.e., distributors) providing sales and service support. Each participant in the value chain provides a distinct and specialized service and, through its activities, makes the product more valuable. In early discussions of the value chain and in the automobile example above, information technology and information play a support role for firms in creating and extracting value from its core business processes.

The role of information and supporting technology becomes more prominent in maturing notions of the value chain. The emergence of the Internet and World Wide Web (aka the Web) as channels for conducting business opened up new opportunities to run companies more efficiently and effectively and possibly even open up new kinds of business. Rayport and Sviokla (1994) draw the distinction between value chains in the physical world of marketplace and the virtual world of "marketspace." Recognizing this important difference, Rayport and Sviokla (1995) coined the term "virtual value chain," which is defined as a set of value-adding activities connecting an organization's supply and demand sides in a virtual environment. They make the case that organizations that leverage the power of the Internet successfully in both the marketplace (i.e., traditional brick-and-mortar sales channels) and the marketspace (i.e., e-commerce websites or so-called "click-and-mortar" sales channels) go through a three-step process.

In this three-step process of exploiting the virtual value chain, companies still leverage information and technology, but in different and more strategic ways. First, consistent with a historic view of technology in the value chain, companies use information systems to gain greater "visibility" in business processes to ensure efficiency and effectiveness. As an example, the authors cite companies using information *about* their value chain more effectively to change strategy and tactics in the marketplace. Second, companies move beyond just monitoring the value chain to "mirror" some of their marketplace capabilities in the marketspace. This results in a strategic increase in scope. For instance, an auto manufacturer and an aircraft manufacturer both used virtual teams to speed up the product development process by orders of magnitude, yielding innovative new features unlikely to have been developed using a more traditional team approach. Third, companies leverage information beyond gaining visibility and mirroring capabilities to create new information products and forge new customer relationships. Many organizations have created virtual channels in marketspace as a complement to traditional retail and wholesale channels in the marketplace. These virtual channels maximize the information gathered and analyzed through the value chain and may spur the development of new and unique products and services not possible in the marketplace (Rayport and Sviokla, 1995).

While business literature discusses value chain analysis quite widely, neither the IS or PA literatures document its application to the public sector. One of the primary differences between the two sectors is the locus of control maintained over some of the value-adding processes, such as distribution. In the private sector, a company maintains active control over its distribution channels, meaning that it will decide who distributes its products (often through franchise arrangements) and how it is done (through licensing requirements). Value is added through business relationships that are managed actively. A government agency, on the other hand, may or may not have any control over distribution channels and likely has not considered managing those relationships explicitly.

A. Government Information in the Virtual Value Chain

Government information products are in the public domain, thus a formal agreement among the players need not exist in order to provide added value to the public. Schwartz (2000) points out that it is not only possible but also desirable for third parties to mirror the contents of government websites to promote wider access and dissemination of government information products. Thus, any third party may decide of its own accord to add value to a government information product and resell it, thereby making itself a distributor and hence part of the virtual value chain. The government agency in question may not even be aware of the relationship or of the enhanced product that is made available to the public.

One way that the private sector may add value to a government product is through a public–private partnership, which is a formal cooperative arrangement between public, private, and not-for-profit organizations, enabling the public organization to meet its policy goals (Linder and Rosenau, 2000). These partnerships tend to be complex and fluid structures, with multiple and sometimes competing goals among the partners. Public–private partnerships are often seen to be a way to overcome budgetary constraints and still provide better value to the public (Di Maio, 2002).

The potential for adding value to government information is vast. "The federal government is the single largest producer, collector, and disseminator of information in the United States" (Office of Management and Budget [OMB], 2000). The private sector adds value to government information in many ways. These include organizing and assembling the data in more useful formats, combining it with data from other sources, indexing and cross-referencing government data, updating government databases to ensure they are current and accurate, and expanding databases to make them more comprehensive. These enhanced products are then distributed in formats that are easy to use, convenient and useful to the public — often with a fee attached. Many such products are now available on the Internet, potentially increasing their ability to be accessed and used on a 24-hour-a-day basis by interested consumers.

This represents a rapidly changing and enormous shift in the way that the public interacts with the government. Historically, government information distribution has been very structured. Until recently the U.S. Government Printing Office (GPO) was the required printer for all federal government agency publications. A distribution system was created through the Federal Depository Library Program, a partnership between the GPO and state, private, and federal libraries in the U.S. and its territories. Agencies paid the GPO for the printing of their publications; however, over time they grew increasingly discontented with the GPO requirements, believing they could publish cheaper and more quickly using other means.

The close of the 20th century marks a significant shift in how such government information is disseminated. More agencies have been moving toward the electronic arena, placing information on their websites, which allows both cheaper dissemination and the ability to reach a larger user base. Information can be obtained directly, without going through conventional intermediaries, such as libraries and clearinghouses. Furthermore, information is available in multiple and more sophisticated formats, corresponding to increased user needs and expectations (Coalition for Networked Information, 1997).

III.   E-GOVERNMENT LITERATURE

E-government is a relatively new phenomenon and it has the potential to shift existing public-sector value chains. At the heart of the e-government movement is the aim of using technology to transform government service delivery (Pardo, 2000). More information has become available online as governments met the Government Paperwork Elimination Act (GPEA) requirement for all federal agencies to be online by October 2003 (Software Information Industry Association, 2001; Fletcher, 2002). E-government initiatives are launched daily, and the public is increasingly using the new electronic capabilities available. For instance, West (2003) reports that the number of online services found on federal and state websites nearly doubled between 2002 and 2003.

One estimate of online usage of government information is at 43% of the U.S. population (Quick, 2003). Another study (Council for Excellence in Government, 2003) suggests that almost seven out of ten Americans now have Internet access at school, at home, or at work; 75% of these American Internet users have accessed a government website at least once. Online access of government information and publications is a primary way that the public uses electronic government and it is growing quickly. Neilsen/NetRatings (2003) reports that the audience for federal e-government websites is growing rapidly, increasing 26% between December 2002 and February 2003.

Clearly, e-government is changing the dynamics of government information product and service distribution. By beginning to provide similar or duplicate services as existing third-party vendors provide, government agencies are clearly disrupting existing value chains (whether recognized or managed as such). For instance, when a federal agency enables an e-government capability that allows a user to avoid using and paying for a private-sector product or service, the agency has disrupted an existing value chain that included the private sector between the user and the government agency. As an example, some commercial tax preparation services and software developers considered IRS's implementation of the Telefile system, which allows selected taxpayers to prepare and file their 1040EZ using a touchtone phone, as an intrusion into markets created and nurtured by the private sector.

The question of what a government should or should not provide, and what should be left for outside vendors to develop, market, and sell becomes an increasingly important question for public policy debate. This becomes even more important as e-government offerings become more sophisticated, moving from posting information, to exchanging information interactively, to offering transactions electronically. Based on most models of e-government maturity, public users and government organizations derive the greatest benefits from e-government transactions compared with those obtained with more basic interactions (Hiller and Bélanger, 2001; Layne and Lee, 2001; United Nations, 2002).

Additionally, many governments have or plan to make significant investments in e-government in the upcoming years and want to ensure that the maximum number of users realize the advantages of accessing government information and services electronically. The governments also have a stake in users avoiding paper and phone interactions, as these channels for user interaction are both expensive and error-prone compared with electronic means.

These potentially conflicting interests in increasing e-government adoption need to be addressed in a myriad of settings. Value chain analysis is one way to evaluate how to increase product adoption and also understand supplier/distributor roles and responsibilities in the marketspace for e-government. The following case illustrates how one federal agency's e-government partnership can be understood better using virtual value chain analysis.

IV. STUDY METHODOLOGY

The IRS e-file program was selected as a case study participant in a multinational grant to research new models of partnership in public–private sector e-government initiatives.[1] There were four U.S. case studies, each chosen because they represented unique partnership models that were carried out in marketspace contexts, using an e-government information or service activity as the main product. The research team developed a conceptual framework comprising six dimensions to guide the study. The dimensions included:

- ■ Political, social, economic, and cultural environment
- ■ Institutional, business, and technical environment
- ■ Characteristics and objectives of public and private partners
- ■ Collaboration processes
- ■ Modes of collaboration
- ■ Project and collaboration performance measures

The project team developed an interview protocol and pretested it, and then standardized the questionnaire, which was used in all case interviews. A subset of these dimensions will be used for illustration in the IRS e-file case. The research team chose the IRS e-file program for one of its cases because it represented a long-term partnership arrangement that is still unfolding, thus presenting a more longitudinal picture of the evolution of public–private partnerships. A total of 12 respondents participated in the case study interview process. These respondents represented IRS employees working on e-file, IRS leadership, private-sector partners, stakeholders, and advisors. Secondary data analysis included examining relevant legislation, planning documents, evaluations of the IRS e-file program, and press coverage on this highly visible project. What follows is a presentation of the IRS e-file partnership case study, organized around the dimensions of the conceptual framework used in the multinational research grant.

V. DIMENSIONS OF PUBLIC–PRIVATE PARTNERSHIP IN THE IRS E-FILE PROGRAM

A. Institutional, Business, and Technical Environment

The electronic filing of income tax returns, now called the IRS e-file program, began with a partnership between the IRS and H&R Block in 1985 and has since grown to include a large portion of the tax preparation industry and individual taxpayers. Electronic filing, a method for sending tax returns prepared on a computer electronically instead of in paper form, began as a pilot project in 1986, processing about 25,000 returns (Venkatraman and

---

[1] This study was funded in the U.S. by the National Science Foundation and administered by the Center for Technology in Government for Fletcher's involvement and by the IBM Endowment for the Business of Government for Holden's involvement.

Table 23.1   Individual IRS e-File Volumes by Product (in Thousands)

Filing Season	Third Party	Telefile	Online	Total e-File Returns	Total Paper Returns	Electronic Share (Percent)
1986	25			25	103,030	<1
1987	78			78	107,000	<1
1988	583			583	109,700	1
1989	1,161			1,161	112,100	1
1990	4,204			4,204	113,700	4
1991	7,567			7,567	114,700	7
1992	10,919	125		11,044	113,600	10
1993	12,334	149		12,483	114,600	11
1994	13,502	519		14,021	115,900	12
1995	11,126	680	1	11,807	118,200	10
1996	11,971	2,839	158	14,968	120,400	12
1997	14,083	4,686	367	19,136	120,332	16
1998	17,668	5,955	942	24,565	122,967	20
1999	21,223	5,664	2,458	29,345	125,547	23
2000	25,201	5,161	5,019	35,381	127,474	28
2001	28,989	4,419	6,836	40,244	129,783	31
2002	33,288	4,176	9,428	46,892	130,625	36
2003	36,344	4,023	11,827	52,194	131,687	40

Kambril, 1991; Lacijan and Crockett, 2000). Since that time, the number of electronic returns has grown into millions per year. Last year (2003), Americans filed 51.7 million tax returns electronically out of total 132.3 million individual tax returns filed. This represents over one third (39.1%) market penetration for electronic filing (Internal Revenue Service, 2003). Table 23.1 illustrates the substantial growth in electronic filing between its inception in 1986 through the end of the 2003 filing season (June 27, 2003) (Internal Revenue Service, 2000, 2003). The IRS has achieved this level of success in its electronic filing program in the midst of significant technology and organizational change, as described below and in subsequent sections.

Electronic filing at the IRS relied, and continues to rely, on a combination of technologies that many commercial organizations might consider out of date. Until the year 2000, the IRS accepted much of its electronic filing in batches in selected IRS Service Centers on IBM Series 1 computers. By 2001, the IRS had finally retired the Series 1, which IBM did not even support any more, to move to somewhat more up-to-date Unix platforms, but transmitters still batched filings to the IRS over dial-up connections, dedicated leased lines, and in some cases using FTP over the Internet. While posted publicly, the standard for transferring electronically filed returns to the IRS is not considered an "open standard" in Internet terms (Internal Revenue Service, 2001). The IRS also maintained an extensive telephony infrastructure for its Telefile component, which allowed selected taxpayers to use a touchtone phone to file their simple 1040EZ return electronically.

Once the IRS accepts a return electronically, it goes through the same automated processing "pipeline" as returns that have been filed on paper. The primary difference is that electronically filed returns are subject to more error correction and edit tests before they get to the pipeline, resulting in error rates of less than 1% compared with the initial error rate on individual paper returns of approximately 20% (Internal Revenue Service, 2000). The IRS continues to perform weekly batch process on tax returns, using primarily Cobol software, which takes nearly a week to post new return data to the "Master File."

At the outset of the collaboration process, there were some technical and business capabilities the IRS lacked. It is worth noting that the IRS did not and does not have a user-friendly web interface for taxpayers who would like to file directly to the IRS. Other than through Telefile, all Internet filings are intermediated by third-party software providers. Before the new collaboration between the IRS and its private-sector partners, most electronically filed returns required a paper signature document, a paper payment, and payment by credit cards was not possible.

Even though the IRS did not accept returns electronically on its website, it nonetheless has a very popular website called the *Digital Daily* (launched in December 1997 and relaunched January 2002). This is a very robust gateway to services and information from the IRS to individuals, businesses, tax professionals, and nonprofit, and other public organizations. Special features of the website include electronic newsletters, the ability to download forms and news alerts from tax law updates to tax scam information.

B.   Political, Social, Economic, and Cultural Environment

There is one major piece of tax reform legislation that dominates the political and legal environment for the IRS e-file program. President Clinton signed the IRS Restructuring and Reform Act of 1998 (RRA 98) into law on July 22, 1998. It represents a major piece of legislation affecting the management and processes of the IRS in its interactions with taxpayers. A major objective of RRA 98 is to promote e-file usage. Additionally, it directs the IRS to reorganize from its current structure into one that is more customer-focused, serving groups of taxpayers with similar needs. Congress believed that increasing public adoption of IRS e-file was an important facet of that transformation (National Commission on the Restructuring the Internal Revenue Service, 1997). Congress clearly wanted more members of the public to experience the benefits of e-filing, such as reducing cycle times for refund processing from as long as 6 weeks to 10 days, reducing error rates from 20% to less than 1%, and providing an electronic acknowledgment of the IRS receiving and accepting an e-file return (Internal Revenue Service, 2000). These consumer benefits explain the customer satisfaction rates for e-file that rival those of private-sector financial services organizations (University of Michigan, 2002).

A key component of RRA 98 was the objective of making e-file a routine business process. Congress devoted a major section of the law to the promotion of e-file after considerable study and consultation with both the IRS and industry groups. More than just promoting IRS e-file, the law provided significant impetus to the program by setting a target that by 2007, 80% of returns be filed electronically. RRA 98 also provided significant support for the work of the Electronic Tax Administration (ETA) organization, a staff unit seen as critical to the modernized mission of the IRS. The ETA organization represents an institutional commitment and focus to the two-way electronic exchange of information the IRS has with all taxpayers (individual or business), taxpayer representatives, tax practitioners, and other government entities. As outlined in the first strategic plan for the ETA, the organization's agenda is a clear one — revolutionize how taxpayers transact and communicate with the IRS (Internal Revenue Service, 2000).

RRA 98 places Congress more directly in an oversight role to the IRS than for other e-government programs, requiring the IRS to report annually to Congress on their progress toward developing a paper-free tax system for appropriate taxpayers. As part of the governance structure overseeing the results of e-file, RRA 98 also created an oversight board to monitor the IRS e-file program and make sure it is organized and operates in a manner that facilitates meeting the missions of the IRS and the ETA. The ETA Advisory Council (ETAAC) both advises the IRS Commissioner and reports annually to Congress on its assessment of the IRS's progress and plans in implementing the electronic filing portion of the law. This Congressionally chartered group joined an already crowded field of organizations providing oversight to the IRS e-file program, including, taxpayers, the U.S. Congress, the General Accounting Office (GAO), the Department of Treasury, and the OMB.

Legislative- and executive-branch oversight organizations espoused support for electronic filing, but questions remain whether there was sufficient financial or policy support for changes needed to make electronic filing truly attractive compared with the paper alternative. The IRS e-file program had been under intense Congressional scrutiny and is the subject of many U.S. GAO audits. GAO (1996) had also placed the IRS's technology modernization program on a "high risk" list of federal agencies' efforts that require extraordinary management attention and oversight to ensure success (GAO, 1999). An important note here regarding the technology environment of the IRS is that its history was troubled and there were few IT implementation successes. Congress and GAO had little confidence that the IRS could modernize its general IT infrastructure, including electronic filing.

The economic and social environments for electronic government have created conditions in the recent years to make the implementation and success of electronic government applications such as e-file more realistic. The major factor is tied to Internet technology and the rapid diffusion of and access to the Web in the U.S. population (Department of Commerce, 2002). As the public becomes more comfortable with using the Internet, it is expected that they will move to transacting business with the government on the Internet. The recent survey by the Council for Excellence in Government (2003) bears this out in its finding that 75% of Americans who have used an electronic government website note that it makes interactions with government more convenient and much easier (than traditional interactions). This climate was and continues to be favorable to the IRS e-file program.

C. Public Partners' Characteristics and Objectives

Under former IRS Commissioner, Charles O. Rossotti, the IRS initiated its largest and most complex modernization effort in the past 50 years. The organizational modernization is a direct result of RRA 98, as mentioned above. At the same time, the IRS is also continuing is the Business Systems Modernization (BSM) program, a multiyear, multimillion dollar systems modernization effort. Both the organizational and systems modernization efforts reflect the IRS's goal to increase the satisfaction of their customers and to provide the American taxpayer with top quality service and information.

This is no small chore in light of the IRS's customer base and complex transaction levels. The IRS deals with more Americans than any other organization, public or private. The IRS is likely the largest information processor in the U.S. government and possibly the world, based on the information gathered annually through tax filings. OMB's (2003)

Information Collection Budget cites the IRS as accounting for 80% of the total of paperwork burden imposed by federal agencies on the U.S. public — approximately 6.7 billion hours per year. In tax year 2002, the IRS collected more than $2 trillion in revenue and processed 226,609,232 tax returns (all types) (Internal Revenue Service, 2002). By almost any measure, these data demonstrate IRS is one of the largest financial services organizations in the world. Beyond the complexity resulting from the sheer magnitude of the processing workload, the IRS manages the program in a very public and open environment, as mentioned earlier.

As noted above, the IRS e-file program is not a new project for the IRS. It is one that has been evolving over the past 15 years, responding to advances in technology and social acceptance of both computing and the Internet as a tool for business. This is consistent with the general nature of the IRS, which is considered to be deliberately slow and cautious. The IRS, in dealing with public tax dollars, was not eager to appear too revolutionary or hasty as it migrated to the Internet. Public scrutiny of this highly visible agency demanded that the agency fully think through issues around technology platforms, public acceptance, and Congressional attention.

As documented in the ETA's strategic planning document, *A Strategy for Growth*, the IRS recognized that its relationship with the authorized e-file providers needed to change to meet the legislative targets set out in RRA 98 (Internal Revenue Service, 2000). While not abandoning its regulatory and oversight responsibilities vis-à-vis the tax preparation industry, the IRS recognized that, in effect, it was a supplier of e-file products and services and that a variety of private-sector players were much like distributors to the public. Before the creation of the ETA organization, IRS and the tax industry had what both would call an indifferent to stormy series of interactions. The recognition that such an unproductive relationship would not support the needed growth in e-file and the invocation of the traditionally private sector model of supplier–distributor relationship enabled a relatively rapid change in the form and content of public–private partnerships in the e-file program.

Although the IRS as an institution is known to be cautious and resistant to change, as noted earlier, the IRS employees working on the IRS e-file program described themselves, and each other, to be organized and methodical, legalistic, and willing and insistent on thinking "out-of-the-box." This last characteristic is especially noteworthy given that the IRS is a "risk-averse organization" (Bozeman, 2002). Yet, without the ability and the freedom to think in an unconstrained manner, partners in the IRS e-file program believed that the collaboration would not have been successful. In the words of one of the ETA executives, the staff were encouraged to ask for "forgiveness rather than permission" throughout the collaboration process. Another asset of the IRS side of the partnership was their commitment to the success of the e-file program. Since they were allowed and encouraged to work "outside of the more bureaucratic" structure of the IRS, they could convert their commitment and enthusiasm to being entrepreneurial and innovative.

What the IRS brought to the partnership was a tremendous market opportunity for the tax preparation and filing community. The data on the Internet traffic to the IRS website, *The Digital Daily*, presented earlier bears this out. This was an untapped source of potential customers for future partners with the IRS. This also created tension throughout the project, however, as many perceived (incorrectly) that the IRS was itself going into the tax preparation and filing business. The major largest private-sector partners, H&R Block and Intuit, were very careful to make sure that the IRS was not going to take over their market. It is important to mention that these tax preparation businesses account for 55% of all individual tax returns filed.

D. Private Partners' Characteristics and Objectives

There is a distinction to be made between the long-standing IRS e-file partners and the subsequent collaboration model discussed below. As mentioned earlier, the IRS had been regulating tax preparers, transmitters (firms that translate completed IRS forms into the IRS-acceptable format), and software developers (firms that provide software to both taxpayers and tax preparers) participating in the IRS e-file value chain for some time. By far, the largest group was the tax preparers, which included commercial tax preparation businesses, independent tax preparers, certified public accountants, and enrolled agents. Under IRS rules governing the program, preparers and other providers approved to file returns electronically to the IRS have been called "Electronic Return Originators" (EROs). More recently, as part of the IRS e-file marketing campaign, EROs and other firms in the IRS value chain that the IRS regulates were recast as "Authorized e-file Providers." There are currently some 90,000 authorized e-file providers and 50 to 60 authorized e-file tax transmitters.

While the initial partnership was primarily between the IRS and the tax preparation industry, as the program has matured, the scope of partners and partnerships has broadened considerably. Currently, partnerships include not only a variety of tax preparation businesses, but software developers, third-party transmitters, credit card processors, and not-for-profit and professional groups that represent a variety of these same interests. The expanded breadth and scope of the partnerships are explained in more detail in the section on the new collaboration model.

A characteristic of the private-sector partners was that they were "itching for a change" in the tax preparation and filing process. It was cumbersome, complex, and paper-intensive. They saw e-file as an opportunity to reengineer the process, making it simpler, faster, and error-free. Other characteristics that the partners brought to the partnership were their knowledge in product development, their ability to promote the service, their ability to know who the right business partners would be for e-file and then put together coalitions that served everyone's needs. They brought to the table a very keen understanding of IRS policies and the tax environment. Additionally, they had experience and skills to enable electronic services and transactions on the Web, which the IRS did not have at that time.

To implement the e-file program successfully, IRS had to enlist and engage a complex group of stakeholders. Many professional and industry groups such as the Council for Electronic Revenue Communication Advancement, the National Association of Computerized Tax Processors, the American Institute of Certified Public Accountants, and the National Association of Enrolled Agents were also important stakeholders in this venture. Throughout the history of e-file, these stakeholder groups were more or less supportive of the program, depending on a range of external factors. During the early years of the electronic filing program, IRS's view of industry stakeholders was to see them as entities to be regulated. This was particularly true after the refund fraud problems of the early 1990s.

VI. A NEW MODEL FOR COLLABORATION

One of the most telling shifts in the partnership relationship between the IRS and the e-file industry came about through the Request for Agreements (RFAs) the IRS released on November 27, 1998. To help provide some focus to these requests for agreements, the

IRS identified several known impediments to e-file adoption based on informal discussions with stakeholders and distributors. Some of the known impediments included enabling electronic payments (including credit cards), eliminating paper signature documents, expanding marketing opportunities for the IRS e-file, and making electronic filing services available to low-income filers for little or no cost. The IRS sought private-sector suggestions and proposed solutions to help the IRS overcome all the identified challenges and any others the respondents might want to bring the IRS's attention.

With the advent of new e-commerce business models, the IRS used the RFA to establish whether it was possible to add products to the e-file program through private-sector initiative at little or no cost to the IRS. The RFA tested the notion that the IRS and commercial partners could establish a mutually beneficial exchange of value without using a traditional procurement vehicle that resulted in a contract where the IRS paid for goods and services. Instead of contracts, nonmonetary agreements became the mechanisms for the tax preparation industry to request either privileges or relief from IRS e-file regulations. This was contingent on the industry partners' ability to describe a new product feature they could offer that they believed would increase e-file filing volumes.

This collaboration represented all-new territory for the IRS, and as mentioned earlier, territory that was a big market opportunity for the private-sector partners. For the IRS, it represented an opportunity to add product features that customers (taxpayers) and distributors (EROs) wanted if the IRS was going to put a meaningful dent in the pile of paper returns being filed each April. The two sets of partners, therefore, shared one overriding common interest — they both wanted to increase the volume of electronic filing, albeit for different reasons. The new collaboration resulted in several new product features that arguably did help to increase IRS e-file volumes over the last several years. Most notably, the IRS signed nonmonetary agreements with private-sector and not-for-profit partners to eliminate paper signature documents, enable credit card payments, and create cooperative marketing opportunities.

While the above is not an exhaustive list of the nonmonetary agreements that the IRS struck with its external partners, they represent the most significant in terms of complexity to work through and the benefits to taxpayers, the IRS, and the partners. The IRS asked their value chain partners for help in addressing some long-standing, but agreed-upon problems. The IRS saw it as a benefit that the tax preparers teamed together to bring propositions to the IRS to solve these problems. This type of collaboration was seen as successful by the IRS staff. The tax preparers were able to make a number of recommendations to enhance the program as well, giving them input into program and product design they had requested for years.

A. Critical Success Enablers and Barriers

As the case study points out, there were a variety of factors that led to what many perceive to be a successful collaboration between the IRS and its e-file value chain partners. The dimensions of the conceptual framework for public–private partnership help to bring some structure to the enablers and barriers to the new collaboration. The following discussion highlights several of those dimensions that seemed most crucial in the success of the IRS e-file collaboration process.

1. Public partners' characteristics and objectives

In talking with the collaboration participants, it was clear that strong championship, leadership, and willingness to take risks were major factors in the success of the IRS e-file collaboration. Respondents consistently pointed to the risk-taking behaviors of the IRS/ETA executives and staff. This also did not go without notice in the federal IT community. The Assistant Commissioner for the ETA was awarded a 2000 "Federal 100" for his pioneering work on e-file (Federal Computer Week, 2000). Other behaviors helped urge the collaboration process on, including an ETA staff that was not reluctant to use intimidation, begging, or cajoling to move the project along. Another characteristic was that they never took "no" for an answer; if they received a no, they asked "why?"

An interesting and novel success factor for e-file was the ability of the IRS to actually go out and market its product — a critical value chain activity. This is not a common activity or budget line for federal agencies. But RRA 98 specifically addressed the need to enhance the visibility of this new program and authorized the IRS to spend appropriated funds to do so. The ETA group received their first marketing budget for tax year 1999. Through a series of innovative and attention-getting advertising vehicles, along with the use of the award-winning *Digital Daily* website, the IRS was able to increase the visibility of IRS e-file among taxpayers and potential tax preparer partners. The IRS went so far as to mail out marketing materials for authorized e-file providers to use in their own marketing to supplement the IRS's direct marketing and to build brand identity. The staff at the ETA noted that the marketing campaign has been a big success for the IRS e-file, both in establishing credibility with the preparer community, and in helping to make the benefits of electronic filing more apparent to taxpayers and EROs.

2. Private partners' characteristics and objectives

The multifaceted experiences of the partners were another critical success factor. There were smart, knowledgeable, and committed people involved, both from the IRS and within the industry. The ability to take advantage of innovative procurement processes, coupled with constant legal advice, was also noted as critical to the good outcome of the e-file collaboration. The private-sector partners said that had the IRS used a traditional government request for proposal (RFP) process, few, if any of them, had the expertise or resources to deal with the administrative overhead that a RFP process requires. The private-sector partners were willing to take some risks too as this was an untested approach. Interviews with some of the partners made it clear that they as individuals took risks in their organizations to advocate investment of time, computing resources, and brand identity to enable the new features

Finally, the private-sector participants felt that this was a huge untapped opportunity and that the market conditions were right for expanding electronic filing. As noted earlier, there was also general agreement on the barriers to e-file adoption were. The IRS had been trying on its own to enable some of the features (e.g., electronic payments) that ultimately came to fruition through the collaboration. The tax preparation industry had also been working on some of these product features (e.g., eliminating paper signature documents) at the state level. They further had e-commerce investments that they were able to leverage in providing a more user-friendly face on IRS e-file products for direct taxpayer interaction. As radical as some of the product and program changes were, neither the IRS nor the partners "started from scratch" on a number of the most visible changes like electronic signatures and payments. The partners were extremely willing to work for mutually agreed-upon goals, in some instances blurring the boundaries between the sectors for the benefit of the IRS e-file program.

As much as each side of the collaboration process had different motivations and interests in their participation, there were also some commonalities that were vital to the success of the process. In addition to knowing the IRS e-file program, the partners knew each other and their institutions. Both kinds of knowledge were vital to resolving the myriad issues that arose during the planning and implementation of nonmonetary agreements. At the outset, the RFAs and the list of problems that served as the focus for the collaboration effort was not a surprise to the private-sector partners. The IRS sought help from their value chain partners on the challenges that the partners themselves had been complaining about for years. As a result, all the players knew what was wanted and were committed to achieving the goals of the collaboration. There was also high-level agreement that the ultimate goal of the collaboration was to increase the adoption of IRS e-file, which provided agreed-upon business goals and evaluation criteria.

One somewhat unwritten understanding that later became more explicit was that the IRS did not intend to enter into the marketspace for tax preparation and *e-filing* on the Web. Starting with Commissioner Rossotti and in most corners of the ETA, there was a commitment to devote the IRS's energy to maximizing value through the partnership process. This meant the IRS did not have to develop either the software or customer support capabilities to enable direct filing on the Web. In a classic example of virtual value chain analysis, the IRS decided to leave the distribution of tax preparation and e-filing to its private-sector partners.[2]

3. Barriers

While there were lots of positive stories about the barriers overcome during the collaboration process, some remained nonetheless. Both ETA staff and private-sector partners viewed the paperbound infrastructure and culture of the IRS as problematic. It required major change management to get the buy-in from all the IRS offices that either had or believed they had a decision-making role in e-file.

Protection of information privacy and security were seen as two high-visibility issues that complicated the collaboration and nearly scuttled parts of it. While there was high-level agreement that the IRS and its partners shared responsibilities for mitigating privacy and security risks to preserve public trust in the product, there were disagreements on the tools and techniques needed to mitigate those risks.

The goals set by Congress in RRA 98 were seen by the participants as too high to achieve, although, at the time, no one was willing to say so in public on the record. The reality is that there is no precedent in technology diffusion, other than Internet adoption itself, which supports such a steep adoption curve. Despite the skepticism about the ability to achieve 80% market share of electronic filing in 2007, there was some agreement that the ETA staff were able to use the 80% goal as a catalyst for change within the IRS. So what existed as a barrier for some observers and participants served conversely as an enabler or impetus for success for others.

---

[2] This decision did not really become explicit until the announcement of the private-sector consortium that expanded the availability of free tax preparation and e-filing on the Web for the 2003 filing season, which was after the data was gathered for this study.

VII. THE VALUE CHAIN REVISITED

The collaboration process for the IRS e-file program of 1999 represents a new way of enabling value for customers, distributors, and producers of tax information, products, and services. As noted above, the old model, where the IRS treated tax preparers and software developers as entities to be regulated, was remarkably inefficient and ineffective for all participants in the tax preparation and e-filing process. In general, value chain activities strive to remove inefficiencies while gaining some new economic value for the players. Here we have a case where the producers and the distributors were not partners in any productive way and often worked at cross-purposes with each other. There was a lack of recognition by the IRS that the producers and distributors were critical components of the tax filing value chain and could be leveraged as such. There was a further lack of recognition that the software development and tax preparation industries served as intermediary suppliers between taxpaying consumers and the IRS as producers of the tax filing and paying process. Until the IRS initiated this new collaboration, the distribution channels were mostly overlooked and underappreciated, and as a result, taxpayers got a mediocre product.

The new model of collaboration for IRS e-file, as explained through the virtual value chain, emphasizes the mutual benefit of partnership between the IRS, again the producer, and the tax preparation and related software industries, which are now recognized as distributors for the IRS. The value chain had been there since the inception of the electronic filing program in 1986. It was not until 1999, however, that the IRS started to manage that relationship, recognizing the value to be gained from a more constructive relationship with its distributors. In fact, it was the realization that the software development and tax preparation industries were distributors of electronic filing that provide to be a defining moment that enabled the collaboration to reshape the old model of antagonistic partnership that had existed for years. One important outcome of the new collaboration between the IRS and its private-sector partners was an array of new products features for the e-file program that the IRS did not "pay for" in the traditional sense.

Several events outside and inside the IRS converged to make the virtual value chain a viable framework for reshaping the e-file program. The dimensions of the partnership discussed earlier help to illuminate the significance of these events. At the institutional level, the IRS needed to move away from paper processing of form 1040s and the private sector was testing new business models in the e-commerce marketspace that provided a useable analogue for e-government. The political context supported this change with the passage of RRA 98 and the emphasis on e-file. The 2007 target, while may be not achievable, provided impetus for change and risk taking both by the IRS and its partners. In the larger social context, the public was becoming accustomed to both e-commerce and e-government and doing business electronically in other facets of their lives.

As noted above, in the critical success factors for the new collaboration, both the public- and the private-sector players in the collaboration process took advantage of the other environmental variables that seemed to have aligned at just the right moment. The ETA organization emerged from the IRS with a dramatically different attitude about its partnership with the private sector, as evidenced by the RFA process and the stated recognition of the new marketspace for electronic filing and the private sector's legitimate role there. The private sector was just beginning to recognize this marketspace too, through the development of online tax preparation and e-filing services on the Web, and was open to working with the IRS to gain access to the millions of taxpayers going to *The Digital Daily*. Recognizing the mutual benefit from the new collaboration, consistent with a virtual value chain analysis, both groups of players in the collaboration took significant risks with staff time, reputation, and organizational resistance to change. In particular, both sides took the calculated risk that they could use a nonmonetary and noncontractual set of arrangements to add value to the IRS e-file program. While both the IRS and its partners clearly benefited from this leveraging of the virtual value chain, it was the taxpayers who really benefited. The customers gained a better, more user-friendly, and less expensive IRS e-file product.

VIII.   CONCLUSION

The existence of distributors in government value chains is not unique to the IRS. Many other firms and organizations intermediate relationships and transactions between government and the public (e.g., veteran service organizations help veterans and dependents with benefits offered by the Department of Veterans Affairs). The question is whether the conditions that led to the successes of IRS e-file in leveraging the virtual value chain can also be applied in other public organizations. As seen from the IRS case example, a necessary and seminal condition is to view electronic government applications as a value chain. An understanding of how and where value can be captured in a process is a critical first step. In virtual environments such as electronic government, it is vital to apply value chain analysis so that the new processes can take full advantage of all the components in the process, from leveraging the strengths of suppliers and distributors, to recognition of what constitutes value for all system users.

The earlier discussion of government information and the virtual value chain makes the point that e-government holds the potential to disrupt existing value chains where private or not-for-profit organizations are assisting users of federal information services and products. This chapter did not explore or debate whether the potential disintermediation of third parties between federal agencies and their clients was a good or a bad thing as this is a topic for another piece of research. Instead, this chapter provides readers with an analytic lens through which to view existing federal information product and service delivery mechanisms to see whether e-government solutions might be disruptive. From there, policymakers can debate the merits of such implications.

As noted in "Introduction," the three disciplines of business administration, IS, and PA all contributed to the creation of value in the IRS e-file case study. Yet, these disciplines are often viewed as disparate and not relevant to each other. This is the first barrier to overcome then — creating an environment in the mind of public organizations and researchers where the unique value of electronic processes can be viewed as an opportunity for all to be involved.

REFERENCES

Bozeman, B., *Government Management of Information Mega-technology: Lessons from the Internal Revenue Service's Tax Systems Modernization,* The IBM Endowment for the Business of Government, Arlington, VA, 2002.

Coalition for Networked Information, Access to and Services for Federal Information in the Network Environment, Coalition for Networked Information, 1997.
    Available at: http://www.cni.org/projects/fedinfo/fedinfo.draft.html
    Retrieved on 3/10/2003.

Council for Excellence in Government, *The New E-Government Equation: Ease, Engagement, Privacy and Protection*, Council for Excellence in Government, Washington, D.C., 2003.

Department of Commerce, *A Nation Online: How Americans Are Expanding Their Use of the Internet*, Department of Commerce, Washington, D.C., 2002.

Di Maio, A., It is time for online partners, *Gartner*, 2002
    Available at: http://www.gartner.com/resources/110900/110978/110978.pdf
    Retrieved on 6/9/2003.

Federal Computer Week, 2000 Federal 100 Awards, *Federal Computer Week*, 2000.
    Available at: http://www.fcw.com/events/fed100/2000/intro.asp
    Retrieved on 7/23/2003.

Fletcher, P.D., The Government Paperwork Elimination Act: operating instructions for an electronic government, *International Journal of Public Administration*, 25, 723–736, 2002.

GAO (General Accounting Office), *Tax Administration: Electronic Filing Fall Short of Expectations*, General Accounting Office, Washington, D.C., 1996 (GGD-96–12).

GAO (General Accounting Office), *High-Risk Series*, General Accounting Office, Washington, D.C., 1999 (GAO/HR-99-01).

Hiller, J.S. and Bélanger, F., Privacy strategies for electronic government, in *E-Government 2001*, Abramson, M.A. and Means, G.E., Eds., Rowman & Littlefield, Lanham, MD, 2001.

Internal Revenue Service (IRS), *A Strategy for Growth*, IRS Publication 3187, Internal Revenue Service, Washington, D.C., 2000.

Internal Revenue Servic (IRS), *Handbook for Authorized IRS E-File Providers of Individual Tax Returns*, IRS Publication 1345, Internal Revenue Service, Washington, D.C., 2001 (Rev 1-2001).

Internal Revenue Service (IRS), *Individual Tax Statistics – Filing Season/TPUS* [Text file], Internal Revenue Service, Washington, D.C., 2002
    Available at: http://www.irs.gov/taxstats/article/0,,id = 96629,00.html
    Retrieved on 1/24/2003.

Internal Revenue Service (IRS), *IRS Sets New Tax Filing Season Records*, Internal Revenue Service, Washington, D.C., May 2, 2003
    Available at: *http://www.irs.gov/newsroom/article/0,,id = 109446,00.html*
    Retrieved on 5/30/2003.

IRS Reform and Restructuring Act of 1998, 26 U.S.C. 1 note.

Lacijan, C., and Crockett, A., Making electronic filing a value proposition for tax practicitioners, *Journal of Tax Practice and Procedure*, 2, 25–36, 2000.

Layne, K., and Lee, J., Developing fully functional e-government: a four stage model, *Government Information Quarterly*, 18, 122–136, 2001.

Linder, S.H., and Rosenau, P.V., Matting the terrain of public–private partnership, in *Public–Private Policy Partnerships*, Rosenau, P.V., Ed., MIT Press, Boston, 2000.

National Commission on the Restructuring the Internal Revenue Service, *A Vision for a New IRS*, House of Representatives, Washington, D.C., 1997.

Nielsen/NetRatings, More Than One Third of All Online Users Log on to Government Sites, 2003
    Retrieved on 7/23/2003.
    http://www.nielsen-netratings.com

Office of Management and Budget (OMB), *Management of Federal Information Resources*, OMB Circular No. A-130 (Transmittal Memo No. 4), Office of Management and Budget, Washington, D.C., 2000.

Office of Management and Budget (OMB), *Managing Information Collection and Dissemination*, Office of Management and Budget, Washington, D.C., 2003.

Pardo, T.A., Realizing the Promise of Digital Government: It's More Than Building a Web Site [Internet], 2000
    Available at: http://www.cisp.org/imp/october_2000/10_00pardo.htm
    Retrieved on 5/26/2002.

Porter, M.E., *Competitive Advantage: Creating and Sustaining Performance*, Free Press, New York, 1985.

Porter, M.E. and Millar, V.E., How information gives you competitive advantage, *Harvard Business Review*, 63, 149–160, 1985.

Quick, S., International e-government, *Brand Strategy*, (Issue 167), 29, 2003.

Rayport, J. F. and Sviokla, J.J., Managing in the marketspace, *Harvard Business Review*, 72, 141–150, 1994.

Rayport, J. F. and Sviokla, J.J., Exploiting the virtual value chain, *Harvard Business Review*, 73, 75–85, 1995.

Schwartz, A., Mirror, Mirror on the Web, *Federal Computer Week,* June 9, 2000.

Software Information Industry Association, *Promoting Public–Private Cooperation in eGovernment, Not Competition*, Congressional Internet Caucus, Washington, D.C., 2001.

Stafford, T.F., E-services, *Communications of the ACM*, 46, 27–28, 2003.

United Nations, *Benchmarking E-government: A Global Perspective*, United Nations Division for Public Economics and Public Administration, New York, 2002.

University of Michigan, *ASCI:Federal Government Scores* [WWW], University of Michigan, Ann Arhor, Michgain, 2002.
    Available at: http://www.theacsi.org/government.htm
    Retrieved on 12/20/2002.

Venkatraman, N. and Kambril, A., The check's not in the mail: strategies for electronic integration in tax return filing, *Sloan Management Review*, Winter, 33–43, 1991. Volume 32, 2.

West, D.M., *State and Federal E-Government in the United States, 2003,* Taubman Center for Public Policy, Brown University, Providence, RI, 2003
    Available at: http://www.insidepolitics.org/egovt03us.pdf
    Retrieved on 10/7/2003.

PART V

APPLICATIONS

24

COMPUTER-BASED TRAINING IN THE PUBLIC SECTOR

Genie N. L. Stowers
San Francisco State University

CONTENTS

I. Introduction 392
II. Training today 392
III. Using the computer as a tool to enhance learning... 393
    A. Computer-based training.. 395
    B. Expert systems 395
    C. CD-ROM and related technologies 395
    D. Electronic performance support systems.. 396
    E. Games and simulations.. 397
    F. Virtual reality (VR) 397
    G. Internet and intranet technologies 398
IV. Developing online training courses 401
V. Conclusions 404
References.. 404

ABSTRACT

This chapter focuses on computer-based training in the public sector. It discusses the various technologies involved in computer-based training today and provides a special emphasis on online training (OLT). As technology has changed society and public-sector organizations, there is an increasing need for new types of training in order to support these organizations. Computer-based training is one source of that training, since it can be provided just-in-time and allows participants to have more flexibility in their learning experiences. This chapter reviews these options, including the fast-changing OLT opportunities. The existing evidence suggests most types of computer-based training are just as effective, if not more so, than traditional forms of instruction.

I. INTRODUCTION

This chapter discusses computer-based training and the technologies involved in computer-based training in the public sector today. Special attention will be paid to the newer technologies of online web-based training (WBT) that has such great potential for the public sector.

Speed of change in the economy and society brought about by new telecommunications technologies (Davis and Meyer, 1998; U.S. Department of Commerce, 1998) is reflected in how we are conducting training and how organizations are adapting the ways they learn (Davenport and Prusak, 1998). More and more, organizations are requesting cost-effective training available to them on demand; using computer technology for training purposes is one way to achieve these goals (Negroponte, 1995). As a result, the top training methodologies are likely to shift to those that can take advantage of distributive network technologies and so, can provide the just-in-time (JIT) training[1], anytime, anywhere mode demanded (Bassi et al., 1997). In the near past, CD-ROM technology was the basis of much computer-based training. That is largely being supplanted today by World Wide Web–based training and, even more in the future — by virtual reality (VR) technologies and technologies that can provide JIT, just-for-me (JFM) training opportunities.

Terminology in the field has changed over time with the technology. CAT or computer-assisted training, is often used interchangeably with CBT, or computer-based training meaning, "training delivered, tested or managed by a computer, either mainframe or PC" (Tucker, 1997: 4). E-Learning, online training (OLT), or WBT are terms that refer to training technologies based on the World Wide Web (WWW). TBT, or technology-based training, is a broader term meaning "training or learning which is undertaken using computer and/or communications technologies to enable learning to take place" (Tucker, 1997: 3). In this chapter, CBT will be used to refer to general computer-based training and WBT will refer to web-based training.

II. TRAINING TODAY

Of the increased time spent training employees in computer procedures and software, most (57.1%) hours were actually spent in informal training; the remainder was spent in formal training (U.S. Bureau of Labor Statistics, 1995), like computer-based training (Table 24.1). The role of computer-based training in the 1990s grew in most organizations (ASTD, 1998: 27) and by the turn of the century, online and other computer-based training had grown into a full-blown industry. According to the Bureau of Labor Statistics, 31% of all training time is spent on computer and professional or technical training (ASTD, 1998: 30). In the public sector, *Training Magazine* found that 26% of all formal training was devoted to computer skills (Training, 1998: 64) and 14% of all training was delivered via technology (pp. 65); this was very comparable with the 17% of all training delivered via technology across all industries.

By 2003, 42% of all organizations had been using e-learning techniques for some time, another 17% were beginning implementation, and another 10% were designing or piloting programs (ASTD, 2003, p. 3). Of the courses that are taught via computers, many were

---

[1] Just-in-time training refers to training that is readily available just when it is needed. Just-for-me training is training that provides just the information needed by a particular individual.

Table 24.1 Instructional Methods and Media, 1998

Type of Instruction	Percent Using
Classroom programs — live	88
Workbooks/manuals	73
Videotapes	70
Public seminars	57
Computer-based training via CD-ROM	50
Audiocassettes	39
Noncomputerized self-study programs	35
Case studies	33
Role-plays	33
Internet (WWW)	31
Self-assessment instruments	23
Intranet/organization's internal computer network	21
Satellite/broadcast TV	20
Games or simulations (not computer-based)	19
Videoconferencing (to groups)	17
Teleconferencing (audio only)	11
Outdoor experiential programs	9
Computer-based games or simulations	9
Desktop videoconferencing	4
VR programs	2

Source: From Training, *Training*, October, 58, 1998. With permission.

focused on computer topics but a full 57% across all industries and 52% in public administration were non-computer-based courses. (Training, 1998: 76). Ninety-one percent of organizations offered their employees training in computer literacy and computer applications (ASTD, 1998: 29) — the only two types of courses offered more often were management-supervisory courses (93%) and new employee orientation (94%).

Companies primarily utilized e-learning to train for task-specific skills (50.9% of all companies in a 2003 survey), for information technology end-user applications (49.1%), and for general business skills such as leadership or antisexual harassment information (48.7%). (See Table 24.2).

III. USING THE COMPUTER AS A TOOL TO ENHANCE LEARNING

Today, a variety of computer-based training technologies continue to be used because the emphasis is on interactivity in today's training activities, and computer-based training allows and encourages interactivity. As stated by Scott Brooks, managing director of a health-related e-learning firm, "Training in the new millennium is all about interactivity — simulations, game-based training, experiential learning…did I mention simulations? Effective use of interactivity can direct the learner to hone in on knowledge and skills that improve performance"(Galagan, 2003: 37).

Today's computer-based training technologies include:

■ Computer disk-based instruction
■ Expert systems

Table 24.2　How e-Learning is Used

Use of e-Learning	Percent Using
Task-specific skills	50.9
IT (end user/desktop applications)	49.1
General business skills (leadership/sexual harassment, etc.)	48.7
Regulatory/compliance issues	34.5
Customer service training	30.5
Product updates and rollouts	29.6
Sales force training	29.2
External customers/clients	23.5
IT (network/infrastructure)	19.9
Technical/manufacturing issues	19.5
IT (programming languages)	18.6
Others	16
We are in the initial states of implementing e-learning	12.8
Enterprise transformations	8.4
Supply chain or channel partner training	6.6
Military	5.3
Keeping staff up-to-date on acquisitions	4.9

Source: From American Society for Training and Development, *Learning Circuits,* 2003. With permission.

Available at www.learningcircuits.org/2003/ nov2003/2003trends.htm

- Electronic performance support systems
- CD-ROM and related technologies
- Games and simulations
- Virtual reality (VR)
- Internet and intranet technologies (including off-the-shelf web courses and blended instruction mixing face to face with online instruction, chat, shared whiteboards, voice-over-IP [VOIP], videoconferencing, and live webcasts)

One important trend is that, with additional experience and sophistication, trainers have moved toward blended, or mixed-mode, instruction, utilizing traditional classroom with one or more of a variety of different computer-based technologies. These could involve traditional classroom instruction plus the use of a CD-ROM combined with asynchronous (web content and discussion board) and synchronous (chat) WBT.

Training magazine's Industry Report 1998 reports that 88% of the organizations surveyed used live traditional classroom programs while 31% of the training was delivered via the Internet, or World Wide Web; another 21% was delivered with the same technology over an organization's intranet.

In the past, CD-ROMs were the most commonly used type of training technology (ASTD, 1998; Training, 1998), but these are now being replaced, in many cases, by online systems. The 1998 American Society for Training and Development survey (pp. 36) found that 35% of organizations used CBT methods, 30% used CD-ROM, 22% used multimedia, 7% used electronic performance support system (EPSS), and 3% used intranets. CD-ROMs were initially popular because they moved organizations toward a model of JIT training — training was available when needed rather than when it could be scheduled. Twenty percent of the growth in training time by 2000 was in CD-ROMs and 17% was using intranets.

A. Computer-Based Training

Disk-based tutorials were the first type of computer-based instruction and training and was used extensively for years. Using this methodology, participants would utilize computer tutorials, drilling and practice, or interactive presentation of materials to learn material (Ravet and Layte, 1997). Many studies have found that levels of effective learning with these techniques are at least comparable with those of traditional education (Kulik, 1994; Bowman et al., 1995) and are cost-effective (Bowman et al., 1995). Bassi et al. (1997) also found that this training can be faster (20 to 80% faster) due to "tighter instructional design," the self-paced nature of the course, and the fact that students can bypass material already mastered. A classic usage of the computer disk technology is to drill and practice to learn or develop foreign language skills.

B. Expert Systems

Expert systems are computer programs that capture the knowledge and expertise of human experts and are then designed to perform tasks that emulate human reasoning — like diagnosing illnesses or maintenance problems or making financial forecasts (Schultz, 1988; Jonassen and Wang, 2003). Based on artificial intelligence techniques, they rely upon knowledge engineers to capture the knowledge of experts and convert that knowledge into rule-based systems that perform tasks. Although this technology led to some excitement in the 1980s and the early 1990s, it has, in general, not met those early expectations (Schultz, 1988; Tucker, 1997). As a learning tool in the public sector, expert systems can help students build their knowledge base of a subject (Siegel, 1989) by answering questions with information at their fingertips. In essence, they can act as JIT training tools.

C. CD-ROM and Related Technologies

CD-ROMs are storage media that were initially popular because they allowed enough storage to accommodate space-hungry multimedia ("a combination of at least three of the following media: text, graphics, still pictures, animation, video, audio and data" [Tucker, 1997: 11]) and offer it to a mass market. Another important reality was that the technology needed to use CD-ROMs was readily available throughout many organizations. One survey of local governments indicated that the penetration of CD-ROM technology was very high in 1995: 61.0% of all local jurisdictions and 91.3% of large local jurisdictions reported having the technology (Moulder and Huffman, 1996).

Because they could be used when needed in desktop computer systems, CD-ROMs represented progress toward the JIT model of training, itself increasingly popular as technology advanced. This approach also provided savings in training dollars when personnel did not have to travel to receive training. Partly due to the immediacy possible, CDs are best used for knowledge and awareness training but can also be used to reinforce learning as lessons are consistent and can be repeated (Keegan and Rose, 1997). In fact, some research has indicated a sizeable enhancement of learning when using CD-ROMs incorporating multimedia technology over traditional teaching methods

(McDonald, 1999). However, as training tools, they can be quite expensive to produce (Allen, 1996).

There are other variations of the basic CD-ROM technology, including CD-ROM with interactive audio (possible with newer compression techniques), CD-ROM (XA), which also allows computer code to be stored and loaded at the same time as audio, and interactive CDs (CD-Is), which provide integrated full-motion and full-screen video. One additional twist is the use of digital video disks (DVDs), which allow much more storage capacity (Ravet and Layte, 1997; Tucker, 1997).

While the emphasis on CD-ROM multimedia as a training mode is receding as the World Wide Web becomes more of a viable vehicle for the transmission of multimedia, CD-ROMs continue to represent a large share of the training technologies used today. Two examples of public-sector CD-ROM training efforts are "Ethos" and "Applying Performance Measurement." "Ethos" is a CD-ROM produced by the International City/County Managers Association in 1994. The CD-ROM contains training materials, organized in case studies, on conflict of interest, abuse of power, fraud, waste, and corruption — politics, and whistleblowing, and control of information. Information is presented via a small TV screen icon, which shows a video on each topic and then presents a scenario and questions for each case selected. In addition to the case study and video, definitions and a code of ethics are provided (International City/County Managers Association, 1994).

Another public-sector training effort, "Applying Performance Measurement," was produced in 1995 as a joint effort of the International City/County Managers Association, the American Society for Public Administration, the Urban Institute, and Public Technology, Inc. After a video introduction by a series of experts on performance measurement, this CD-ROM is organized into modules, such as data sources, identifying outcomes, and reporting performance measures. Within each module, content is provided, as well as opportunities for participants to apply their new knowledge, further reinforcing the lesson learned. At any time, participants can go back to earlier lessons or skip ahead if already familiar with one section. The material can be repeated at any time and can be used as further reference when required. (International City/County Managers Association, 1995) This example represents an effective effort at bringing JIT training about a public-sector issue from the experts themselves directly to users when they need it most — when they are attempting to develop their own performance measures.

This technology has already been used effectively to provide computer-based training in the medical and many other fields. DeAmicis (1997) found that, although some differences existed between interactive digital videodisk instruction in nursing skills (intravenous therapy) and traditional classroom skills, these differences were insignificant.

D. Electronic Performance Support Systems

Electronic performance support systems (EPSSs) are an "integrated computer application that uses any combination of expert systems, hypertext, embedded animation, and/or hypermedia to enable a user to perform a task quickly in real time and with a minimum of support by other people" (Cohen, 1998a: 54).

EPSS can contain three levels of support — embedded (intrinsic) support, linked or "extrinsic" support, or external support (Cohen, 1998a). Embedded support includes the built-in capacity of software applications to identify an icon when a mouse over is performed. Extrinsic support is represented by strategies like wizards that help the user to perform particular functions by providing step-by-step instructions, such as the wizards that assist the user in creating new graphs in a spreadsheet package or a new database. Help desk support, a form of external support, is an example of the third type of EPSS (Cronje and Baker, 1996).

As an example of EPSS development in the public sector, the military has developed an EPSS system as a way to provide a "knowledge-based, just-in-time training solution" (Krisak et al., 1997: 1) for maintenance problems. Their system, the Interactive and Distributive Electronic Performance Support System (IDEPSS), includes interactive electronic technical manuals that provide effective and quick support for their personnel. Using traditional training methods, Krisak et al. (1997: 2) estimate that 42% of information on how to fix a problem is forgotten in 20 minutes, 66% after 24 hours, and over 98% after 1 month. When an EPSS is used so that technicians do not have to refer to paper-based technical materials, Krisak et al. (1997) estimate that 50 to 75% of the time needed for the task can be saved.

E. Games and Simulations

Computer-based simulations and game software are programs that allow the user to experience and train in a situation that has some of the characteristics of reality without any of the risks or expense. With simulations, procedures and processes can be taught by computers so that even more complex systems can be approximated.

Simulations can approximate chemistry experiments or can be used to train airline pilots. In the public sector, the military has made extensive use of simulations to train on new technology or on military strategy. In fact, the U.S. Navy has so many simulations available that an online catalog and database exists to list them all (see http://navmsmo. hq.navy.mil/index.cfm); among those simulations listed in the last months of 2003 were mobile weapons systems trainers, a tactical warfare simulation, and an airframe model that allows training and experimentation of one of the Navy's aircrafts. Simulations can also be successfully used in other high-risk situations, such as natural disasters and other emergencies. Benini and Benini (1999) argue for the use of training for workers in areas of armed conflict as they plan for humanitarian relief and train their personnel to act in difficult and dangerous situations. They suggest that simulations help to reduce the complexity and confusion to a manageable level so that workers can understand the steps they need to take to be most effective and to be sure their humanitarian efforts do not cause additional violence.

F. Virtual Reality (VR)

Technologically, the next step beyond games and simulations is VR. Using VR technologies, users participate in what can appear to be a very realistic environment (Tucker, 1997). The traditional form of VR is when "... a user dons special gloves, earphones, and goggles, all of which receive their input from the computer system. In this way, at least three of the five senses are controlled by the computer" (Webopaedia, 2003). VR today can also be a visualization on a personal computer using the mouse or the keyboard (a window into a system) or a projection VR (a view into a system) (Ravet and Layte, 1997). In addition, VR is moving onto the Internet with the Virtual Reality Modeling Language (VRML) language, opening up new opportunities for accessible training using this technology.

According to Tucker (1997: 46), VR is particularly useful when the task requires "a highly refined sense of spatial recognition". VR technologies have great potential for growth in the field of computer-based training. These technologies provide the user a safe and more inexpensive environment in which to learn to complete potentially dangerous or expensive tasks. "According to VR advocates, trainees using simulations could 'learn by doing' in environments nearly identical to actual workplaces. They could master the proper technique and sequence of procedures for a task without diverting expensive equipment from production lines. And they could learn how to operate in hazardous environments without facing the risks of practicing with real equipment" (Hodges, 1998: 46). This can lead to improved ability to learn and retain information, often since participants are doing rather than simply studying (Gunther-Mohr, 1997). VR today is more affordable than in the past, mostly since it is not the total immersive system once considered to be the technology's true potential. It can also be easier to change and update (Gunther-Mohr, 1997).

The public sector is using this technology in many ways:

■ FBI bomb technicians practice bomb disposal techniques using VR (Hodges, 1998).
■ The U.S. Navy uses VR to train shipboard firefighters (Tate et al., 1997).
■ The U.S. Marine Corps uses VR systems to train precision gunners (Hodges, 1998).
■ U.S. naval officers use VR systems to practice ship-handling techniques (Hodges, 1998).
■ VR systems are used to practice airplane maintenance (Hodges, 1998).
■ The National Guard trains members on tank maintenance through VR rather than the expensive "real thing" (Gunther-Mohr, 1997).

Evidence of effectiveness for learning does exist. In one experiment, Tate et al. (1997) determined that Navy firefighters using a VR environment to train to fight shipboard fires showed statistically significant improvements in their performance. Firefighters training in a virtual mode made fewer wrong turns, arrived at the scene faster, and put out the fire faster. Participants also reported increased confidence in their ability to do their jobs.

G. Internet and Intranet Technologies

Today, computer-based training is moving more and more toward WBT or e-learning. WBT represents the third generation of distance education. The first generation was correspondence courses, the second was centered around television and radio as the medium of instruction, and the Internet provides the medium for this third generation (Bullen, 2003). The Internet can provide five levels of training — distribution of the content itself, communications between participants, online reference, testing, and needs and training assessments (Kruse, 1997) in either a synchronous or an asynchronous fashion. EPSS systems can also be built in so that basic levels of support can be provided.

The web-based tools used for OLT have developed to a great extent and they can be used together or separately in an endless set of combinations. Current technologies include videoconferencing (Sorensen, 2000), use of shared whiteboards to work simultaneously on documents, application sharing and viewing, VOIP allowing telephone connections over the Web, and synchronous chat tools in addition to the already existing asynchronous discussion boards (for threaded discussions) (Collins and Barron, 2000). In addition, many organizations today are broadcasting their conferences or lectures over the World Wide Web in live webcasts. (Maiden, 2003).

Much of this can be delivered on an intranet (knowledge management's "killer application" [Cohen, 1998b]) as well as over the Internet itself. Intranets are intraorganizational networks that provide, in the hypertext (HTML) format of the Internet, a full range of organizational information, including OLT modules (Curtin, 1997). Any proprietary data and information on the intranet can be protected by "firewalls," software or hardware that protects the intranet from the outside user and makes the intranet a private space. The availability of bandwidth and user equipment are crucial issues in the use of this technology.

WBT can provide a more effective JIT, JFM training experience for participants in a more cost-effective fashion than other technologies (Younghans-Haug, 1998). Further, the penetration of online services in public-sector agencies is growing every day. Even in 1995, ICMA reported that 46% of local governments had an online service of some sort (Moulder and Huffman, 1996), indicating that enough governments have access to the technology to make Internet-based training possible.

WBT can provide other advantages as well as a significantly different training environment compared with the traditional CBT training (Huang, 1997). These advantages include:

- Flexibility for users in timing and pace of learning (Curtin, 1997; Huang, 1997)
- Training that is available 24 hours a day, 7 days a week so that students can learn at their own time and pace (the JIT, JFM training model) (Keckan, 1997; Kruse, 1997)
- An ability to take advantage of the enormous resources on the World Wide Web and integrate them into training courses (Curtin, 1997; Stowers, 1998)
- Removal of status cues from discussions, resulting in more equitable interactions (Stowers, 1995; Munger, 1997)
- Multimedia and interactive applications, which are more effective since active learning is retained more effectively (Keckan, 1997)
- Automation of course administration (Keckan, 1997)
- More cost-effective training, although WBT is not necessarily less costly or time-consuming (Keckan, 1997; Ravet and Layte, 1997; Stowers, 1998)
- Easy updating of courses (Curtin, 1997; Kruse, 1997)
- Training materials that can be easily and affordably distributed (Kruse, 1997)
- Affordable technology once the basic infrastructure is available (Kruse, 1997)
- High levels of interactivity (Kruse, 1997)

There is a growing body of research on the effects and effectiveness of OLT and education methods as well as user satisfaction with these efforts. Much of this suggests that there are few learning outcome differences between traditional instruction and web-based courses and what does occur generally favors web-based courses; some of these differences can be attributed to the structure and design of the courses themselves (Swan et al., 2000; Maki and Maki, 2003). That is, students do better in web-based courses with more active learning, instantaneous performance feedback, and clear-cut deadlines (Maki and Maki, 2003) as well as in those courses with active discussion and contact with instructors (Swan et al., 2000). Of course, it could be argued that most students would do better in any course with these characteristics. However, Maki and Maki (2002) do suggest that students with higher levels of comprehension skills found greater benefits from web-based courses.

Another important trend is the utilization of multimodal, blended, or mixed-mode instruction, incorporating the best of technology and traditional education modes. Thus

Table 24.3   Variables Associated with Learning and Satisfaction in Web-Based and Lecture Courses

Both Lecture and Web-Based	Lecture Only	Web-Based Only
	Associated with better learning	
More initial knowledge	Specific instructor (varied depending on instructor)	Do not enjoy class discussion
Sophomore or higher		
Humanities or science/ technology major		
Introverted or intellectual		
Lower computer anxiety		
Less use of the World Wide Web at course beginning		
Preference for working independently		
Knowing what to expect on tests		
	Associated with greater satisfaction	
Lower workload	Specific instructor	No variables predicted satisfaction in web-based but not lecture courses
Better scores on exams	Enjoy class discussion	
Expected liking of course		
Preference for working independently		
Knowing what to expect on tests		

Source: Taken From Maki, Ruth H. and Maki, William S. 2003. Prediction of Learning and Satisfaction in Web-Based and Lecture Courses. *Journal of Educational Computing Research* 28 (3): p. 217.

far, multimodal training has proven to be effective in imparting knowledge and in satisfying the learners with their experience (King and Fricker, 2002).

A summary of Maki and Maki's findings is found in Table 24.3, which also suggests that mixed-mode or blended courses provide more favorable environments for learning and satisfaction. There are differences in learner satisfaction across course types as well; much of this could be attributed to student characteristics, suggesting that online education is not right for everyone and should be tailored to the learning styles of various students. Eastmond (2000) also suggests that the presence of online institutional support services also positively influences student satisfaction and success in online courses.

Of course, there are disadvantages to online courses as well. As an OLT module is being designed, it is critical to consider the equipment and bandwidth that target students currently possess and develop only for that level, not above (Rose, 1998). And, while some have assumed that Internet courses would be easy to teach and cheap to produce, that is generally not the case (Stowers, 1998).

Currently, public-sector agencies are already seeing and taking advantage of online technologies for their training purposes. Public health (Polhamus et al., 2000) and medical education (Konstan et al., 1997), and health and safety training (Younghans-Haug, 1998) are just two types of courses currently being provided online. The Defense

Department's Advanced Distributed Learning Network (www.adlnet.org) (Abernathy, 1998) represents access to another type of system. The goal of this network is to provide cost-effective OLT. It attempts to do this by serving a clearinghouse function, developing guidelines, and fostering collaboration and discussion of new techniques.

IV. DEVELOPING ONLINE TRAINING COURSES

There are several steps to developing an effective OLT course (Stowers, 1998). The first and most important is to determine whether or not training materials are appropriate and suited for online delivery. This is a crucial step, as not all material is appropriate for this method of delivery (Porter, 1997). As technology changes, the criteria for determining suitability will also change. According to Porter (1997), these criteria include:

- An appreciative and appropriate audience with needs that can be met by the course in question and who have access to the necessary equipment
- Courses whose content is suitable for a wide audience
- Courses with content as the main focus of the course, to be reinforced with exercises
- Courses with content suitable for viewing
- Courses that can be designed with the appropriate amount of trainer–participant interaction (i.e., material does not have to be taught on a one-on-one basis)
- Courses that can be designed with the technically appropriate information and tools available
- Courses that can be designed while maintaining standards of high quality

The next step is to determine the course delivery system that is appropriate for the course. Today's online courses can take advantage of numerous technologies already noted — chat, discussion boards, streaming audio and video, videoconferencing, shared applications and whiteboards (workspaces), and even telephony. Courses can be delivered via e-mail or listservs, although now that the World Wide Web is more widely available, these are less desirable alternatives. Multiuser environments like MUD, Object Oriented (MOO) or Multi-User Dimensions (or Dungeon) (MUDs) can also be used but, since they were not originally designed for training purposes, these are also not optimal.

The World Wide Web is becoming a more realistic and optimal choice for delivery of interactive course materials, particularly as the technology gains more penetration into organizations and individual homes. Today, there are many options for providing courses on the World Wide Web. Courses may be provided on web pages open to the public, although few courses are offered in that fashion due to potential loss of intellectual property. Instead, most OLT is provided via one of a series of course management tools that provide a secure environment for courses, tools that are multiplying and improving rapidly. Some of these were designed specifically to provide online courses while others were designed for other purposes but are being adjusted for those purposes.

The market for course management tools, or learning management systems (LMSs), has burgeoned, now including numerous systems for online course delivery like Blackboard or WebCT. Most of these systems are web-based, contain some sort of editable template system for content presentation, and contain numerous other features. The features considered important for a web course content provider/course management system are:

- ■ A password-protected and secure environment, providing a protected area for the delivery of course content
- ■ An internal e-mail system
- ■ A threaded discussion or discussion board area
- ■ Ability to control access to the course
- ■ Ability for instructors to automate examinations, which can be automatically graded
- ■ Utilities for tasks like assigning student accounts and passwords and other class-room management tools

With the World Wide Web, other technologies may also be used. Computer conferencing, or asynchronous communication, now takes place on the World Wide Web, where it can be used for interaction between training course participants. Chat, or synchronous communications, can be used to supplement OLT by scheduling time periods for class discussions or interactions with the instructor. Currently, real-time or streaming audio and video can also be used to supplement online courses once users have small software packages called plug-ins (usually available for free on the World Wide Web); these applications are bandwidth-intensive so this must be taken into consideration when using these technologies. Animations can also be used on World Wide Web courses to illustrate points but most of the more advanced courses require the use of another plug-in. White board applications allow users to work from and simultaneously discuss shared information, and users can also share applications and work on them simultaneously. Audio and video streaming allows users to play back audio or videotape to illustrate points, while webcasts allow real-time broadcast of events like conferences or training lectures. Finally, desktop videoconferencing on a one-to-one basis is also available to provide some face-to-face interaction. The use of these applications is limited by the technology available to users as well as the bandwidth they have available.

The next step is to prepare course content. Experienced online instructors (subject matter experts, or SMEs) organize courses into small, coherent, and manageable modules and do so by first developing an outline of the course and then preparing a "storyboard" of the content. Several systems have been developed to organize these course modules, which can be presented on separate web pages within the website or course manage-ment system. The first of these is the ICARE system, which suggests five components or pages per module system (Center for Learning, Instruction, and Performance Technol-ogy, 1997b). The sections include an introduction to the module, a Connect section to present the lecture notes, graphics, video, and other course content, and an Apply section, which assigns some exercise to reinforce the material. These are followed by a Reflect page, which provides discussion questions for the students (to be discussed using some asynchronous conferencing tool), and an Extend page, listing additional resources or materials. Another possibility is the LADR system, which is very similar to ICARE, except that there are only four components. This system includes Lecture, Application, Discussion, and Reflection. The APT system is even simpler, containing only three components — Analyze (the content), Practice, and Talk (Center for Learning, Instruc-tion, and Performance Technology, 1997b).

Whatever the organizational structure chosen, the main components for each module should include the presentation of course content (the "lecture"), an assignment that will engage the student in some way, and an opportunity for discussion or reflection on the module topic. In addition to the introductory material, instructors also develop discussion questions, exercises to reinforce learning, and additional resources to allow further exploration. To create an interactive experience for participants, the enormous resources of the World Wide Web may also be utilized in the course. Web linkages, graphics, video and audio clips, and other resources may all be used in courses to enhance their value — the instructor must simply find and utilize these resources by linking to them (while providing proper citation and respecting others' intellectual property rights) (Brooks, 1997; Khan, 1997).

According to the San Diego State University Center for Learning, Instruction, and Performance Technologies, course materials for an online course should fulfill the following criteria:

- Chunkiness — Materials should be in smaller chunks rather than long paragraphs and papers (Curtin, 1997; Center for Learning, Instruction, and Performance Technology, 1997a, 1997b)
- Readability — Material should include explanatory headings and subheadings, clear colors, fonts, and layout (Curtin, 1997; Center for Learning, Instruction, and Performance Technology, 1997a, 1997b)
- Printability — Since participants will probably print out pages, make sure they are only one long page (Curtin, 1997; Center for Learning, Instruction, and Performance Technology, 1997b)
- Smart structure — The more important material should be near the top of all pages (Center for Learning, Instruction, and Performance Technology, 1997b)
- Flat structure — Material should be organized so that it takes only a few clicks of the mouse for students to go from the top to the bottom of course materials (Center for Learning, Instruction, and Performance Technology, 1997b)
- Rapid display — Graphics and other materials should be kept small enough to limit the time it takes to load (Center for Learning, Instruction, and Performance Technology, 1997b)

After collecting the materials for the websites, it is time to create the actual web pages and website. The steps to completing this will largely depend on the type of web delivery or course management tool used for the course but can be completed using any web authoring tool. Like any website or course materials, the materials should be maintained and kept up to date at all times.

The next and most crucial step is to present or teach the class. Several options for organization exist — students can complete a training course completely at their own pace and speed. Or, some time parameters can be applied and the instructor can attempt to help create a classroom community through discussion and chat. If the latter option is desired, a critical mass of students working and focusing on the same topic is generally required in order to ensure that adequate discussion takes place. Students can then be required to participate during a certain time period or can be given rewards for participation.

To structure the student's time to some degree in this latter model, deadlines may be utilized, with modules going up and then being removed by certain dates to structure the student's experience. The time period in which students may work on individual modules is also an issue to be determined by the trainer. In OLT, the trainer may allow 1 week for varying time limits for various modules, depending on the material.

V. CONCLUSIONS

This chapter has presented an introduction to computer-based training and the technologies involved, with an emphasis on OLT. It is clear that computer-based training is here to stay and is part of the wave of the future.

In the future, there are questions which need to continue to be researched (Simonson, 1997; Ganzel, 1998; Tobin, 1998):

- Are students satisfied with their experience?
- How do learners respond to the computer-based training environment?
- Did participants master the material? Did they retain the material?
- Are participants using their new skills? Are these skills making a difference?

In fact, existing evidence suggests most types of computer-based training are just as effective, if not more so, than traditional forms of instruction. Computer-based training methods can offer effective training using a wide variety of technologies while providing opportunities for the all-important JIT, JFM training and information being demanded today. As technologies rapidly change and influence the organizations of tomorrow, training technologies must change with them, if not move ahead of them. As the economy, the public sector, and organizations themselves change and develop, computer-based training must provide needed support and can help prepare the employees who are working and shaping the public-sector organizations of tomorrow (Negroponte, 1995; Tobin, 1998; U.S. Department of Commerce, 1998).

REFERENCES

Abernathy, D.J., Online with Uncle Sam, *Training and Development*, May, 22, 1998.

Allen, R., The ROI of CBT, *CD-ROM Professional*, October, 34–45, 1996.

Appleton, E.L., 1998 state of the industry report, *Technology Training*, June, 12–18, 1998.

ASTD (American Society for Training and Development), The 1998 ASTD state of the industry report, *Training and Development*, January, 23–43, 1998.

ASTD (American Society for Training and Development), E-learning trends 2003, *Learning Circuits*, November, 2003.
　Available at: www.learningcircuits.org/2003/nov2003/2003trends.htm

Bassi, L.J., Cheney, S., and Van Buren, M., Training industry trends 1997, *Training and Development*, November, 46–59, 1997.

Benini, A.A. and Benini, J.K.B., Computer simulation of humanitarian scenarios: tools for training and field management in relief agencies, *International Journal of Public Administration*, 22, 637–653, 1999.

Bowman, B.J., Grupe, F.H., and Simkin, M.G., Teaching end-user applications with computer-based training: theory and an empirical investigation, *Journal of End User Computing*, Spring, 7(2), 12–18, 1995.

Brooks, D.W., *Web-Teaching: A Guide to Designing Interactive Teaching for the World Wide Web*, Plenum Press, New York, 1997.

Bullen, P.M., The use of the Internet and multimedia technologies in distance education and post-secondary course curricula is increasing worldwide, *CGA Magazine*, July–August, 15–19, 2003.

Center for Learning, Instruction, and Performance Technology, Principles for One-Stop Information and Training, 1997a.
　Available at: clipt.sdsu.edu/posit/tx/db.htm

Center for Learning, Instruction, and Performance Technology, Tools, Templates, and Training, 1997b
　Available at: EdWebiii.sdsu.edu/T3/index.html

Cohen, S., EPSS to go, *Training and Development*, March, 54–56, 1998a.

Cohen, S., Knowledge management's killer app., *Training and Development*, January, 50–57, 1998b.

Collins, D. and Barron, T., A comparison of thin-client synchronous classroom systems, *Learning Circuits*, 1, 2000.
Available at: www.learningcircuits.org

Cronje, J. and Baker, S.J.B., Electronic Performance Support: Appropriate Technology for the Development of Middle Management in Developing Countries, 1996.
Available at: hagar.up.ac.za/catts/epss.html
Last updated on 10/28/1996.

Curtin, C., Getting off to a good start on intranets, *Training and Development*, February, 42–58, 1997.

Davenport, T.H. and Prusak, L., *Working Knowledge: How Organizations Manage What They Know*, Harvard Business School Press, Boston, 1998.

Davis, S. and Meyer, C., *Blur: The Speed of Change in the Connected Economy*, Addison-Wesley, Reading, MA, 1998.

DeAmicis, P.A., Interactive videodisc instruction is an alternative method for learning and performing a critical nursing skill, *Computers in Nursing*, May–June, 155–158, 1997.

Eastmond, D., Enabling student accomplishment online: an overview of factors for success in web-based distance education, *Journal of educational computing research*, 23. 343–358, 2000.

Galagan, P., The future of the profession formerly known as training, $T \pm D$ *(Training and Development)*, 28–38, 57(12), 2003.
Available at http://www.astd.org/virtual_community/td_magazine/2003/PDF/76031226.pdf

Ganzel, R., Online learning's Family Tree, *Training*, August, OL 4–9, 1998.

Gunther-Mohr, C., Virtual reality training takes off, *Training and Development*, June, 47–48, 1997.

Hodges, M., Walking through Virtual Reality, *Computer Graphics World*, 45–52, March, 1998.

Huang, A.H., Online training: a new form of computer-based training, *Journal of Education for Business*, 35–38, 73(2), 1997.

International City/County Managers Association, *Ethos. CD-ROM*, International City/County Managers Association, Washington, D.C., 1994.

International City/County Managers Association, *Applying Performance Measurement. CD-ROM*, American Society for Public Administration, Urban Institute, and Public Technology, Inc., International City/County Managers Association, Washington, D.C., 1995.

Jonassen, D.H. and Wang, S., Using expert systems to build cognitive simulations, *Journal of Educational Computing Research*, 28, 1–13, 2003.

Keckan, M., Computer-based staff training: can you afford not to?, *Nursing Homes*, 46(6), 101–102, June 1997.

Keegan, L. and Rose, S., The good news about desktop learning, *Training and Development*, June, 24–27, 1997.

Khan, B.H., Ed., *Web-Based Instruction*, Educational Technology, Englewood Cliffs, New Jersey, 1997.

King, C.and Fricker, B. Multimodal curriculum delivery in distance education, *Journal of Distance Education*, 17, 102–111, 2002.

Konstan, J.A., Sturm, P., Mcleod, J, and Lichtblau, L., Internet self-assessment in Pharmacology: a model for Internet medical education, *Computers Education*, 29, 63–71, 1997.

Krisak, R.W., Marshall, W., and Lacontora, J.M., The 21st Century Technical Training Environment, 1997.
Available at: www.adlnet.org/InfoExchange/ReviewMessage.cfm?messageid = 265

Kruse, K., Five levels of Internet-based training, *Training and Development*, February, 60–61, 1997.

Kulik, J.A., Meta-analytic studies of findings on computer-based instruction, in *Technology Assessment in Education and Training*, Baker, E.L. and O'Neil, H.F., Jr., Eds., Lawrence Erlbaum Associates, Hillsdale, NJ, 1994, pp. 9–33.

Maiden, B., Virtual classroom starter guide, *Learning Circuits*, October 2003.
Available at: http://www.learningcircuits.org/2003/oct2003/maiden.htm

Maki, R.H. and Maki, W.S., Multimedia comprehension skill predicts differential outcomes of web-based and lecture courses, *Journal of Experimental Psychology: Applied*, 8, 85–98, 2002.

Maki, R.H. and Maki, W.S., Prediction of learning and satisfaction in web-based and lecture courses, *Journal of Educational Computing Research*, 28, 197–219, 2003.

McDonald, D.S., Improved training methods through the use of multimedia technology, *Journal of Computer Information Systems*, 40, 14–25, 1999.

Moulder, E.R. and Huffman, L.A., Connecting to the future: local governments online, in *Municipal Year Book,* International City/County Management Association, Washington, D.C., 1996, pp. 24–30.

Munger, P.D., High-tech training delivery methods: when to use them, *Training and Development*, January, 46–47, 1997.

Negroponte, N., *Being Digital*, Vintage Books, New York, 1995.

Polhamus, B., Farel, A., and Trester, A., Enhancing technology skills of maternal and child health professionals. *Maternal and Child Health Journal*, 4, 271–275, 2000.

Porter, L.R., *Creating the Virtual Classroom: Distance Learning with the Internet*, John Wiley & Sons, New York, 1997.

Ravet, S. and Layte, M., *Technology-Based Training: A Comprehensive Guide to Choosing, Implementing, Managing, and Developing New Technologies in Training*, Gulf Publishing Company, Houston, Texas, 1997.

Rose, R., Detour on the I-Way, *Training*, January, 70–78, 1998.

Schultz, J.B., Artificial intelligence meets training and simulation needs, *Armed Forces Journal*, November, 70, 1988.

Siegel, P., What expert systems can do, *Training and Development Journal*, September, 71–73, 1989.

Simonson, M.R., Evaluating teaching and learning at a distance, in *Teaching and Learning at a Distance: What it Takes to Effectively Design, Deliver, and Evaluate Programs*, Cyrs, T.E., Ed., Jossey-Bass, San Francisco, 1997, pp. 87–94.

Sorensen, K., Videoconferencing for training: two organizations' experiences, *Learning Circuits*, January 1(1), 2000.
   Available at: http://www.learningcircuits.org/jan2000/sorensen.html

Stowers, G., Getting Left behind? Gender differences in computer-mediated communications, *Public Productivity and Management Review*, 19, 143–159, 1995.

Stowers, G., Teaching a Fully Online Public Administration Course, Presented at the Annual Meeting of the Teaching Public Administration Conference, Colorado Springs, Mar. 22–24, 1998.

Swan, K., Shea, P., Fredericksen, E., Pickett, A., Pelz, W., and Maher, G., Building knowledge: building communities consistency, contact and communication in the virtual classroom, *Journal of Educational Computing Research* 23(4), 359–384, 2000.

Tate, D.L., Sibert, L., and King, T., Using virtual environments to train firefighters, *EE Computer Graphics and Applications*, November–December, 23–29, 1997.

Tobin, D.R., *The Knowledge-Enabled Organization: Moving from Training To Learning to Meet Business Goals*, American Management Association, New York, 1998.

Training, Industry Report 1998: who gets trained?, *Training*, October, 55–76, 1998.

Tucker, B., *Handbook of Technology-Based Training*, Gower, Hampshire, U.K., 1997.

U.S. Bureau of Labor Statistics, 1995 Survey of Employer Provided Training-Employee Results, 1995.
   Available at: stats.bls.gov/news.release/sept.nws.htm

U.S. Department of Commerce, The Emerging Digital Economy, 1998.
   Available at:www.ecommerce.gov/emerging.htm

Webopaedia, P.C., Virtual Reality, 2003.
   Available at: http://webopedia.internet.com/TERM/v/virtual_reality.html

Younghans-Haug, C., Comparing Traditional versus WWW-Based Health and Safety Training in the Workplace — Learning Retention, Costs, Trainee Satisfaction, Unpublished Master's project, San Francisco State University Public Administration Program, San Francisco, 1998.

25

ISSUES IN CONTRACTING AND OUTSOURCING INFORMATION TECHNOLOGY

Jay D. White
University of Nebraska–Omaha

Ronnie L. Korosec
University of Central Florida

CONTENTS

I.	Introduction	408
II.	Big bucks, high risks	409
III.	Understanding IT acquisition risks	410
IV.	Mitigating software acquisition risks	412
V.	The outsourcing wave	413
VI.	The pros and cons of outsourcing	415
	A. Choosing a vendor: using "best value" in IT contracts	416
VII.	Some practical advice on outsourcing	419
	A. Federal outsourcing best practices	419
	B. Managing contracts	420
	C. Project and risk management	420
	D. Outsourcing core business processes	421
VIII.	Conclusions	423
	References	423

ABSTRACT

Contracting for information technology (IT) and outsourcing information services in the public sector is fraught with many financial risks and project failures. This chapter provides an overview of some major issues in contracting and outsourcing IT in public organizations. It examines the risks and failures of large-scale IT projects, and addresses some of the things that management can do to deal with risks and failures in contracting and outsourcing deals.

Without action by federal executives, the gap between public expectations and agency performance will continue to expand. Program risks will continue and unique opportunities for improvement will remain unexploited. Many low-value, high-risk information systems projects will continue to be developed unimpeded and undermanaged as leaders blindly respond to crises by purchasing more technology. Most federal managers will continue to operate without the financial and management information they need to truly improve mission performance. Moreover, many federal employees will struggle unsuccessfully, under increasing workloads, to do their jobs better as they are hampered with information systems that simply add on another automated layer of bureaucracy. Given these risks, sustained Congressional attention is vital to reinforce the link between accountability for returns on information-related investments and the satisfaction of real public needs (U.S. GAO, 1994).

I. INTRODUCTION

Ten years ago, the U.S. General Accounting Office (GAO) expressed the above concern for information technology (IT) acquisition and management. The same concerns could have been expressed for IT acquisition and management at the state and local levels of government. Today, while some modest progress has been made in government IT management, more progress is still called for, especially in the direction of seeking information, advice, and assistance from the private sector through contracting for services.

Agencies at all levels of government are increasingly looking to private contractors to provide them with technology and information management services. The reasons for this are political and economic. Politically, reforms such as the National Performance Review (NPR), the Government Performance and Results Act of 1993, and the New Public Management movement have pushed many agencies into providing IT-enabled public services through private contractors under policies of privatization. Economically, some agencies are finding it cheaper to rent than to buy ITs and information management services. The financial costs of hardware and software can be exceedingly expensive and often prohibitive. The human resource costs of finding and retaining highly knowledgeable and skilled personnel to support information systems are also extremely high and often prohibitive, preventing agencies from hiring the best and the brightest IT professionals. A turn to the private sector for technology and services seems inevitable, and the private sector is responding with many increased IT services to government clients. Such firms often call themselves application service providers (ASPs) or integrators and they often promise a lot. Whether they deliver is a matter of their capabilities and an agency's ability to effectively manage contracts.

Contracting for IT services is not unique to the public sector. For the same economic reasons, small to even large businesses have discovered that it can pay to rent technologies and services. This usually begins with ancillary services such as local area networks (LANs), wide area networks (WANs), websites, and help desks, but it can move to core services like financial management, human resource, and database management systems. In the private sector, such contracting for IT services is called outsourcing, a term that is increasingly being used in the public sector under the more general philosophy of privatization.

The purpose of this chapter is to highlight some of the key issues associated with contracting and outsourcing IT services in the public sector. These issues include:

1. The "big bucks and high risks" associated with IT acquisition and development
2. Understanding IT acquisition risks
3. Mitigating software acquisition risks
4. The outsourcing wave
5. The pros and cons of outsourcing;
6. Some practical advice on contracting and outsourcing

II. BIG BUCKS, HIGH RISKS

U.S. GAO reports that federal government spending on IT services almost doubled from fiscal years 1997 to 2001, increasing from $9 billion to more than $17 billion (2003). INPUT (2003a), a market research firm, predicts that federal spending on IT will grow at a compound annual rate of 8.5% from $45.5 billion in 2003 to $68.2 billion in 2007. State and local government IT spending is expected to increase at an average annual rate of 4.6%, from $41.4 billion in 2003 to $47.4 billion in 2006 (Gartner Dataquest, 2002), and the overall market for state and local IT outsourcing is projected to grow from $10.6 billion in 2003 to $23.7 billion in 2008, representing a compound annual growth rate of 17% (INPUT, 2003b). Needless to say, this is a lot of taxpayer dollars. How successful are governments in managing this money? Unfortunately, there is no comprehensive or conclusive answer to this question, but there are indicators and cases suggesting that government investment in IT can be risky.

In 1994 the Standish Group International, a market research firm, issued the classic "Chaos Report." It tells the story of tremendous IT failures across both public and private organizations. The report estimated that companies and governments spent $81 billion on software projects that were cancelled before becoming operational and $59 billion on projects that were completed long after their original start times, often over budget, and with less functionality than promised. Of the companies and agencies surveyed, only 16% reported successful software projects, defined as coming in on time and on budget, with all of the promised functionality. Fifty-three percent were "challenged," meaning that they came in over budget, overtime, with less functionality than promised. Remarkably, 30% of the projects were "impaired," meaning that they were started but not completed. Indeed, no public or private project estimated to cost more than $10 million succeeded. Half of these big dollar projects failed completely. The plug was pulled before going live after considerable start-up expense. The other half of the projects experienced time and cost overruns, and did not provide the desired functionality.

The Standish Group conducted several case studies to uncover some of the reasons for the high failure rate. They focused on the California Department of Motor Vehicles (DMV) as one example of failure. In 1987 the DMV set out to modernize its driver license and registration process through automation. By 1993 this effort was scraped after spending $45 million. The reasons given for the failure were: "no monetary payback, lack of support from executive management, no user involvement, poor planning, poor design specifications, and unclear objectives" (Standish Group, 1994: 11).

Other studies indicate widespread IT acquisition and development failures (IT Cortex, nd, 2003). A 1995 study conducted in the U.K. by OASIG, an interest group concerned with the organizational aspects of IT, concluded that seven out of ten IT projects fail in some respect, and that success rates hover somewhere between 20 and 30%. They conclude, as other studies have, that technology alone is not the source of failure. It is on the human side where failures occur in poor planning, project management, and acquisition practices. In 1997, KPMG Canada conducted a survey of technology development efforts in a wide variety of private- and public-sector organizations. They found that 61% of the projects studied failed by going over budget by substantial margins. This led them to conclude that "unbudgeted IT projects must run into billions of dollars" (IT Cortex, nd, 2003). Given the high dollar cost of IT acquisition and the risks involved in IT application acquisition and development it is important to have an understanding of some of the general risks involved.

III. UNDERSTANDING IT ACQUISITION RISKS

No single piece of research grasps the magnitude of IT failures in the public sector, but the number of horror stories exceeds stories of success in industry trade publications such as *Computer Weekly, Washington Technology, CIO Magazine, Government Computer News*, and *Network World Fusion*. As such, it is important to have some sense of the risks involved in software acquisition.

There is no standard definition of what constitutes an IT failure, but we can get a sense of the shaky ground upon which some federal agencies tread when it comes to IT acquisition by reviewing some U.S. GAO reports. For example, U.S. GAO examined the software acquisition process at the Department of Housing and Urban Development (HUD) and found them to be "immature," "*ad hoc*," "sometimes chaotic," and "not repeatable" (U.S. GAO, 2001a: 8). The report concludes, "These weaknesses can lead to systems that do not meet the information needs of management and staff, do not provide support for needed programs and operations, and cost more and take longer than expected to complete" (p. 8). U.S. GAO considers the Department of Defense to be at risk in its management of ITs and resources in several areas. They found that DOD lacks "institutional information technology investment management practices to effectively minimize the inherent risk in very large, multiyear projects," and "institutionalized systems acquisition processes to allow consistent delivery of promised capabilities, on time and within budget" (U.S. GAO, 2003). Also, in an overview of "Major Management Challenges and Program Risks" over a wide variety of federal agencies, U.S. GAO has observed, "Using our Information Technology Investment Management maturity framework, our evaluations of selected agencies found that while some processes have been put in place to help them effectively manage their planned and ongoing IT investments, more work remains" (U.S. GAO, 2003: 47). Almost all of that work has to do with the ways in which agencies acquire software to conduct the business of government.

Whenever a government agency enters into a contract for the acquisition or development there are always risks involved. In the best of all possible worlds, the client can hope that the resulting system will "go live" on schedule, do exactly what it was promised to do, come in within budget, and be accepted by end users. Unfortunately, a lot can go wrong during the acquisition or development of projects. The following are just some of the risks associated with software acquisition and development.

The potential for failure often starts before the contract is signed. Clients may have only a vague idea of what they want the system to do. This is a dangerous position since contractors can take advantage of the client's ignorance by providing them additional features at a higher final cost, features that might not be worth paying for. As the client becomes more knowledgeable about what the proposed system might do, they face the problem known as "requirements creep." Here the client may begin to ask for additional features as they become aware of what the new technology can do. This can add to the cost of the overall project and extend the project completion time. Strict requirements analysis along with cost analysis helps to mitigate this risk. Another risk to avoid at the start is to automate an existing paperwork process that is inefficient and ineffective. In the end, the client gets a new system that only speeds up an ineffective and inefficient paperwork process. This situation invokes the image of business process reengineering (BPR) which advocates throwing out all of the old ways of doing things and starting with a clean slate.

Yet another risk to avoid at the start is to decide whether it is better to modify an existing application or replace an old application with a new one. Both public and private organizations are often faced with "legacy" systems. These systems have been around for a long time. They support key business functions that cannot be suspended without drastically affecting the day-to-day operations of the organization. Many of them were originally written in COBOL or even assembler language, making them inefficient and ineffective compared with today's state-of-the-art applications written in advanced programming languages. Frequently, these legacy systems have been modified or adapted over time to perform additional functions. This means that their programming code has been altered, rewritten, or added to. Sometimes, the programming code has not been documented, leaving subsequent programmers to wonder what exactly the code does. Often, an application's code has been altered or "stepped on" so many times that the speed of the application slows down or the frequency of system crashes increases. Ultimately there comes a time when it is no longer feasible to modify or patch a legacy system. This usually means a huge investment in a modern system.

Public agencies need to understand the risks associated with commercial off-the-shelf software (COTS) packages. In the 1960s and 1970s most software applications were built from scratch for specific business activities such as payroll, accounts payable, accounts receivable, inventory, etc., usually by in-house staff. As the software industry developed, the vendors began offering generic software programs for a variety of business, as well as government, applications. Since most of the code had already been written for these applications and the vendors were recouping the development costs the cost of COTS began to decline. At the same time, the government software market began to develop as agencies began to realize the benefits of more automation. Unfortunately, government agencies found that software developed for the private sector often needed to be reworked to meet the unique needs of government, usually resulting in significant additional development costs and project delays.

This is also true for software developed for government applications. There is no *a priori* reason to believe that a software application developed for one federal, state, or local government can be easily transported to a different government entity. For example, each state has different procedures for dealing with child support enforcement matters, making it difficult to standardize software applications across states, despite the fact that "deadbeat" parents can be quite mobile. Also, within various states one finds agencies that have managed their own information systems. Usually this means that agencies have acquired hardware platforms and software programs that are incompatible with one another, meaning that data cannot be shared electronically across agencies. While the universal sharing of data across all agencies within a state is unrealistic there are certainly instances in which agencies should share data and private-sector industry trends are moving toward seamless integration of data and technology across all functional environments.

The integration of data across functions using a common set of software applications is exactly what enterprise resource planning (ERP) software packages are designed to do, and the states and federal agencies are moving in this direction. They are looking to replace diverse and often-incompatible legacy systems with web-based ERP systems. Vendors such as SAP, Oracle, and PeopleSoft are lining up to take advantage of this lucrative government market (Terry, 2000). Unfortunately, ERP implementations in both the private and the public sectors are viewed with some skepticism due to a high rate of failure, defined as coming in well over budget, well over time, and with considerable resistance on the part of end users (Robb, 2001).

IV. MITIGATING SOFTWARE ACQUISITION RISKS

Several states, most federal agencies, the OMB, and the U.S. GAO have embraced the "Software Acquisition Capability Maturity Model (SA–CMM)"developed by the Software Engineering Institute at Carnegie Mellon University (SA–CMM, 2002) as the standard by which to manage and judge all government software acquisition activities. The model consists of five levels of maturity that an agency must progress through in order to mitigate the risks associated with software development and acquisition projects, which are:

1. Initial — The acquisition process is characterized as *ad hoc*, and occasionally even chaotic. Few processes are defined and success depends on individual effort. For an organization to mature beyond the initial level, it must install basic management controls to instill self-discipline.
2. Repeatable — Basic acquisition project management processes are established to plan all aspects of the acquisition, manage requirements, track project team and supplier team performance, manage the project's cost and schedule baselines, evaluate the products, and successfully transition a product to its support organization. The project team is basically reacting to circumstances of the acquisition as they arise. The necessary process discipline is in place to repeat earlier successes on projects in similar domains. For an organization to mature beyond the level of self-discipline, it must use well-defined processes as a foundation for improvement.
3. Defined — The acquisition organization's acquisition process is documented and standardized. All projects use an approved, adapted version of the organization's standard acquisition process for acquiring their products. Project and contract management activities are proactive, attempting to anticipate and deal with acquisition circumstances before they arise. Risk management is integrated into all aspects of the project, and the organization provides the training required by personnel involved in the acquisition. For an organization to mature beyond the level of defined processes, it must base decisions on quantitative measures of its processes and products so that objectivity can be attained and rational decisions made.
4. Quantitative — Detailed measures of the acquisition processes and products are collected. The processes and products are quantitatively and qualitatively understood and controlled.
5. Optimizing — Continuous process improvement is empowered by quantitative feedback from the process and from piloting innovative ideas and technologies. Ultimately an organization recognizes that continual improvement (and continual change) is necessary to survive.

This model goes a long way in improving the acquisition of software at some federal agencies, but U.S. GAO (2003) reports that few federal agencies have been able to accomplish all five stages of maturity. Indeed, many agencies are struggling somewhere between the "repeatable" and the "defined" stages.

There is some question about the contemporary relevance of the SA–CMM. It was developed at a time when agencies were designing their own custom software applications in-house with the possible assistance of private vendors. The focus was on software development for improving existing applications as well as developing new applications. Today, most software applications are not developed in-house (or from scratch) by agencies. Most software applications are purchased by agencies from private-sector vendors. Indeed, there is a strong movement in government to simply contract out some or all IT functions. Despite this outsourcing trend, the logic of the SA–CMM stages of maturity still seems relevant, but it must focus now on the contract with the vendor who owns the hardware and software, and provides the information processing services instead of internal efforts to address software development.

While there may be limitations, it is possible to derive specific guidance on IT outsourcing from the SA–CMM model, and others like it. First, public agencies must focus on long-term strategic approaches to managing IT outsourcing agreements (Chen and Perry, 2003). This means that the decision to buy or lease IT goods and services is made with respect to current *and* future needs. Second, managers must remember that IT outsourcing requires more management skills than traditional (government-provided) procurements (Smith et al., 2001). This includes the support and dedication of management in the contracting process. Because vendors do not necessarily understand or uphold the same types of levels of public values that the public sector is responsible for, public managers must maintain an enduring commitment to assure that realistic goals, expectations, and objectives are set early in the partnership. Finally, the success of IT outsourcing depends on the use of performance measurement and service agreements that allow organizations to track, measure, and hold the vendor accountable for expected outcomes. While there is no sure way to completely eliminate risk in IT outsourcing, organizations can improve their prospects for success by developing a better understanding of these core issues.

V. THE OUTSOURCING WAVE

Outsourcing initially appears to be very attractive for a variety of reasons. Imagine not having to own any expensive hardware or software; having software tailored to your own special needs; not having to employ expensive IT specialists; having professionals manning your help desk in their office, not yours; having same-day or next-day professional technicians in your office to solve your problems; having a dysfunctional piece of equipment replaced immediately with a new and usually better one; having immediate access to state-of-the-art software upgrades that enhances the functionality of your systems; having someone else train your people in the use of hardware and software; having someone else manage your data; having a "partner" who looks out for your technology interests and who can guide you through new technology developments that will enhance your organization's performance; and all of this for a low monthly fee with no surprise added expenses.

Sounds impossible? No. Not with client–server technology, network management, telecommunications, the Internet, ERP, data center operations, call centers, application services, and seat management. ASPs are extolling the virtues of outsourcing some if not all of an agency's IT applications. The following are some examples:

■ Northrop Grumman entered into a 6-year, $33.8 million contract in 2002 with the Texas Department of Criminal Justice to manage the department's data center operations (northgrum.com).

■ Unisys entered into a 3-year, $252 million contract renewal in 2002 with the Pennsylvania Office of Administration for the continued operation and maintenance of the state's data center facility (unisys.com).

■ Unisys also has a 7-year, $56 million contract with Minneapolis to provide outsourcing services to support the city's IT infrastructure (unisys.com).

■ Convergys Corp. has a 7-year, $280 million contract to provide all Florida state employees with human resource services, such as benefits and payroll administration, recruiting, and training (convergys.com).

■ Affiliated Computer Systems entered a $234 million contract with the state of Ohio to operate the state's child support collections and disbursement unit (acs-inc. com).

These are just a few examples of the government's growing interest in outsourcing. The trend began a few years ago with "back office" type of applications, like payroll processing, but now governments, like firms, have their eye on outsourcing core functions, but with some skepticism in view of some reports of troubled government outsourcing deals.

In 1999, San Diego County entered into a $644 million 7-year contract with Computer Sciences Corporation (CSC) to outsource its entire local IT functions (High Anxiety, 2000). It was the biggest outsourcing deal ever initiated by a regional government. It covered everything from desktop computer replacements, telecommunications, networking, a new and integrated data center, a consolidated help desk, and an aggressive ERP software rollout. Initially it looked like a good idea for several reasons. It would eliminate the capital cost of owning and maintaining hardware and software. It would take pressure off personnel expenses because IT professionals in government are retiring or moving to the private sector for higher pay and hiring new IT professionals is just too expensive. Overall, it would drastically reduce the county's annual expenditures on IT technology and operations.

While this partnership is not considered a total failure, there have been some difficulties. To start with, the county did not know how many systems it actually owned when it turned ownership over to the vendor. So from the start, the vendor did not know what the actual scope of work would be. By 2002 the vendor exceeded expected IT investment in the county by about $10 million and 300 employees. Relations between the county and the vendor have become strained. The vendor has paid as much as $3.5 million in penalties to the county for a variety of failures such as its inability to get all of the county employees on the same e-mail platform. The promised ERP systems for human resources, payroll, and finance were delayed, and negotiations between the county and the vendor about what these systems would do became strained. As *CIO Magazine* points out, other local government and state government IT executives are keeping a careful eye on San Diego County as they ponder outsourcing possibilities. (You Can't Outsource City Hall, 2002).

In 1999 the state of Connecticut abandoned several years' worth of effort to outsource all of its IT functions. The state's chief information officer (CIO) was in negotiations with Electronic Data Systems (EDS) to manage the state's entire $300 million IT investments for a 7-year $1 billion contract when the deal did not go through due to pressure from labor unions and lack of approval from the legislature (Connecticut Antes Up, 1999). So the CIO did the next best thing. He "outsourced from inside," meaning that 65 separate state information systems were consolidated into one state IT department, servicing all of the state agencies on a "fee for services" basis just as if the state's IT functions had been outsourced to the private sector (Connecticut, 2002).

The U.S. Naval Marine Corp Intranet is the largest outsourcing deal in the history of government (around $8 billion) and it is fully consistent with current federal policies on privatization. Under contract with EDS, awarded in October of 2000, this project entails taking over 3000 independent legacy systems residing on many different computer platforms in many different geographic locations and placing all of the data and about 20 application programs on a single secure intranet. Access to the applications and the data will be made available at hundreds of locations worldwide via ordinary personal computer workstations. EDS will be responsible for all IT purchases, training, maintenance and upgrades, ensuring standardization and interoperability. The Department of the Navy (DON) will specify all information processing and telecommunications requirements that need to be met. EDS will own and maintain all of the hardware and software to meet those requirements. The DON will be renting, not owning, its IT requirements under a special contracting arrangement known as "seat management," which is a fixed price per user for a specified period of time. Under the terms of the contract the DON will monitor EDS's performance. Penalties are built into the contract if EDS does not meet specified performance levels. There are also additional rewards for EDS if they exceed performance levels. While several industry publications hint at some minor problems with this outsourcing agreement, so far it has been largely successful. The reasons for this success appear to be a strong emphasis placed on requirements analysis, project management, and contract compliance measures. Despite the size, complexity, and highly integrated nature of this IT project, it seems to be a success story — largely due to proper management, contract specification, and diligent monitoring on the part of the contracting organization.

VI. THE PROS AND CONS OF OUTSOURCING

The movement to privatize various services has resulted in new challenges for public managers — especially in contracting out IT activities. Services that are contracted are mostly delivered through a network of private agents working for a contractor — although there is a growing supply of public and nonprofit agents who also may fill this need (ICMA, 2002). In the privatization of IT, a contractor becomes the direct provider of goods and services, and the government assumes the secondary role of a monitor who manages and tracks the contractual agreement. This represents a change in roles for governments as they must focus more on the legal specifications of the agreement than on direct service provision (NASPO, NASIRE, 1996). IT goods and services may be purchased or leased from an outside agent. This creates new options and flexibility for governments with "asset specificity" issues (not having the necessary tools, resources, or personnel on an "as needed" basis).

Agents who provide goods and services are ultimately accountable to the rules and regulations set forth by the original organizations that hired them, not necessarily the government entity that has contracted with them. Only when governments carefully specify contractors to uphold public values (in advance) are employees of the agent subject to the laws and regulations applicable to public organizations. In addition, whereas government organizations typically follow a traditional, hierarchical organizational structure, many private organizations operate with much more autonomy. This means that agents of the contractor may not be subject to the same standards and regulations (such as loyalty, ethics, and nonpartisanship) that government workers are held to, and that often, these workers are only expected to be accountable to their direct supervisors — not to the larger scope of government contract administrators or to the constituencies that they may serve.

The very nature of privatization introduces private-sector values into a system that must be accountable to the public. Specifically, because the profit motive drives most activity in the private sector, private contractors are faced with pressure to provide goods and services in a highly cost efficient manner to protect the firm's profits. This can be both a positive and a negative issue. Public managers are ultimately accountable for the expenditure of public funds, the exercise of public authority, and the results of any public action. Choosing agents on a "lowest responsible bidder" basis may result in contracts for which goods and services are provided more cheaply or "efficiently" than government provision could otherwise offer. From an expenditure standpoint, this may be an appealing option to taxpayers and public administrators with limited budgetary resources.

The net results of contracting are varied. The introduction of new agents into the service delivery realm can create opportunities for innovation, cost efficiency, and expanded service delivery. This is mostly due to the increased competition that these providers introduce into environments that may previously have been served by monopolies (governments). The age-old adage of "the more, the merrier" seems to hold true in some respects. Outsourcing is most likely to be successful when the terms and measurements of the service or good are clear and well-defined; where there are several competitors vying for the project; where the contractor has expertise and familiarity with the type and scope of work; and where the contract can be subject to monitoring, renewal, and renegotiation on a regular basis.

When several of these conditions are missing, however, there is a diminished likelihood of success. The end result of these contracts may involve inferior products, agents who shirk responsibilities, and even fraudulent actions. In the 1970s and 1980s, the U.S. Department of Defense learned firsthand that contractors who miss deadlines, overcharge their clients, and provide inferior workmanship can waste millions of taxpayer dollars and result in considerable headaches (Linowes, 1988).

Still, contracting can be an appealing option for governments who do not have the long-term resources, training, or expertise to implement new ITs on an "as needed" basis. Studies indicate that the private sector is much more likely to invest more resources in IT training and development. Despite this, public organizations rate IT equally important as their counterparts in the private sector (Rocheleau and Wu, 2002). When governments can draw from a competitive pool of providers, effectively monitor and track the contractual work, and keep contractors in line, they may find outsourcing to be a useful tool. This is especially relevant in relation to IT hardware and software as both are fairly expensive, evolving constantly, highly complex, and requiring ongoing training for optimal effectiveness. An IT manager in Kansas recently indicated, "If it takes me three months to complete the paperwork for procuring some aspect of our IT system, it will already be considered to be a generation behind by the time I get it . . . ." (Government Performance Project, 1998–2000).

A. Choosing a Vendor: Using "Best Value" in IT Contracts

So how do public managers effectively outsource their IT needs without going broke or being taken advantage of? Increasingly, managers are using "best value" principles to guide their contracting decisions (NASPO, NASIRE, and NASDAGS, 1998). While the definition of "best value" differs from organization to organization, and even from state to state, the common denominator is that the selection of a vendor or contract is made on more than just the "lowest responsible bidder" basis. Best value requires contractors to provide more than just costing information for goods and services. Some common specifications in best value include:

- Total cost of ownership (including operational and replacement costs)
- Performance history of the vendor, complete with references
- Justification of the originality or uniqueness of the good or service
- Verification of the quality of the good or service
- Evidence of delivery standards/timeliness
- Proposed technical components and performance history
- Financial stability of the vendor and any subcontractors it may use
- Cost of necessary related training
- Risk assessment of the proposed IT solution
- Vendor qualifications
- Availability and cost of technical support
- Testing and quality assurance methods
- Compliance to industry standards

Through best value in contracting, public agencies can evaluate the technical merits of the proposals they receive, consider the vendor on more issues than bottom line costs, and gain a better understanding of the long-range expectations about operating, maintaining, and supporting a specific good or service. This is especially true of IT, as the range of IT products and technology may take many different forms, and may be viewed very differently by systems users. Also, it is clear that not every organization has the same understanding of, or necessity for, IT. Consider the case of two states: Virginia and Delaware. A 1998 to 2000 report by the Government Performance Project asked both states about the extent of their use of IT. Virginia indicated that it had created an "e-mall" for procurement staff to make best-value purchases over the Internet from catalogs, and from vendors on master contracts using "e-purchasing cards." They also implemented a "virtual surplus inventory," which flags agencies to let them know about available, inventoried surplus items that may meet their needs, so that they do not need to negotiate new contracts with vendors. Delaware indicated, "there is no formal IT system in place. We do utilize Word or Excel for spreadsheet documentation which works very well" (Government Performance Project, 1998–2000). IT, it seems, is truly in the eye of the beholder.

In addition to these specifications, public organizations should also regularly train agency personnel and vendors on the philosophy, methods, and specific criterion of best value. Sources of reliable data (such as other governments) should be identified for evaluation of best value, and agencies should maintain their own benchmark reports to document, justify, and enhance contracting outcomes. Finally, organizations should design and implement effective performance measurement systems to evaluate vendors, maintain standards, and create incentives for compliance.

Several governments have already realized great success in implementing best-value strategies in IT outsourcing. In New York, all contracts are legally required to start with best value as a minimum requirement. Officials in that state believe this levels the playing field for all vendors, and creates incentives for innovation, quality products, and cost efficiency. Texas has implemented an integrated computer system that assesses vendors and allows citizens to provide feedback on postservice delivery. Vendors can view the feedback and make changes to their systems, in "real time," if necessary, rather than waiting for formal notifications from the contracting organization. Finally, agencies in Hawaii use an integrated monitoring system to evaluate IT vendors. Public managers can consult with other governments for the newest innovations in IT, with corresponding rates and costing information, and can receive updates on potential hardware and software systems directly from vendors. This helps educate personnel and provides them with both long- and short-term forecasting information (Korosec, 2003).

Because IT is very expensive, highly complex, and can often reach beyond the confines of the organization that has purchased and implemented it, it is important to ensure that the contractual agreement is effectively considered, negotiated, monitored, and implemented. An IT manager in Florida has clearly illustrated this point by confirming, "If it isn't in writing, it isn't in the contract — no matter what the vendor promises (wink, wink, nod, nod). And if it isn't in the contract, you aren't going to get it ... " (Korosec and Berman, 2003). At a minimum, any contract proposal should include specific details such as start and stop dates; payment options and deadlines; cancellation procedures; renewal and contract change notices; specifications for upgrades; and (perhaps most importantly) the ability to work with specific IT assets individually, rather than collectively.

Organizations should also request a complete description of the service, property, or equipment they are purchasing; delivery times and means; warranty coverage and conditions; acceptable criteria for delivery; insurance and business continuity requirements; minimum maintenance and upgrade standards; roles and responsibilities for support agreements; roles and responsibilities for installation and training; and indication of software ownership/licensure. They should avoid common contractual pitfalls, such as pressure to enter into long-term or indefinite contracts with vendors as the nature of IT products suggests that new, better, and cheaper products are entering the market on a daily basis. Also, public agencies should "do their homework" and gain an understanding of the going rate for specific applications of IT. In Rhode Island, public managers can consult a master price list for numerous IT goods and services. While many agencies also have established "approved" going rates for IT vendors, they are also encouraged to obtain competitive quotes for almost all projects. This approach provides the public organization with a competitive advantage in that they have the understanding, flexibility, and opportunity to save time and money on IT.

Any IT contractual agreement must safeguard the organization and the resources it manages while working to create optimal outcomes with needed partners. This is true in both the public and the private sectors. One of the most publicized IT contractual failures occurred with Kmart in 2000. In that year, the struggling retailer employed the services of "i2," the well-known IT firm, to create an innovative technology structure to boost sales and jump-start consumer confidence in its fleet of stores. The contract that Kmart negotiated with i2 was estimated to be worth $330 billion. By April 2003, the plan had been scrapped and Kmart was struggling with bankruptcy. What went wrong? Both Kmart and i2 agreed on some basic reasons for the demise of the IT contract. First, Kmart fell prey to a common issue in IT contracts. It simply did not fully understand what it was purchasing (Konicki, 2002).

This leads to the second issue. Kmart requested major modifications to the software because the original package was too expensive for it to maintain. The modifications required additional time, consideration, and logistical support, which in the end were also very expensive. Third, even with new and innovative technology, Kmart could not compete on a major issue — price — with other stores. Finally, after purchasing a complete, integrated system, Kmart did not fully implement all portions of the technology required for success. Because of this, they could not fully realize the potential effect of the larger system. Despite the caveats of contracting for technology and information services, organizations continue to look toward vendors to provide them with new state-of-the-art solutions to increasing complex problems.

VII. SOME PRACTICAL ADVICE ON OUTSOURCING

Since political and economic forces are driving public agencies to embrace more outsourcing, some practical advice is in order.

A. Federal Outsourcing Best Practices

In an effort to enhance the success of outsourcing IT services the U.S. GAO (2001b) has issued a report titled "Information Technology: Leading Commercial Practices for Outsourcing of Services". It contains an overarching framework for outsourcing, consisting of seven phases:

1. Define the operational model
2. Develop the contract
3. Select the providers
4. Transition to the providers
5. Manage providers' performance
6. Ensure services are performed

Each phase is supported by detailed best practices culled from existing IT research and interviews with academic specialists, industry leaders, and government executives, including such things as seeking third-party advice and experience, learning from others engaged in similar sourcing decisions, aligning the sourcing decision with agency strategic goals and business activities, identifying leadership positions, bench marking, cost–benefit analysis, establishing productivity measures, etc. The list of best practices goes on in considerable detail.

Supporting both the framework and its best practices are three important critical success factors: (1) establish executive leadership that is charged with keeping communication among all relevant parties open; (2) keep the partners aligned so that both understand each other's motives, intentions, and expectations; and (3) manage the relationship beyond the structure of the contract to handle changes in business strategies and practices, overcome resistance to change on both sides of the contract, and keep the communication open between client and provider.

Perhaps the most interesting thing about U.S. GAO's recommendations for outsourcing is the way the relationship between the client and provider is defined. The role of the client is to tell the provider what results need to be achieved, manage for results, and possibly transfer people, equipment, and facilities to the provider. The role of the provider is to decide how to accomplish the results. Then the provider is compensated according to performance-based criteria. These roles reflect a clear commitment to privatization, downsizing, and performance management, all of which are a legacy of the past two presidential administrations.

B. Managing Contracts

Since the federal government and virtually all of the states are moving toward outsourcing agreements for IT services, a few words of advice on how to manage contracts are in order. Belarc, Inc., a major vendor of Internet-based products and one of the subcontractors for the NMCI, offers the following advice on managing contracts (Belarc, 2003). They say that before a contract is signed the following should be in place:

- An accurate and complete baseline of existing computer hardware, software, and users. This element is frequently left until after the contract has been awarded, and can result in scope creep (defined above as requirements creep) and other unpleasant surprises.
- Realistic goals and objectives. The setting of goals and objectives is what most customers focus on; however, without an accurate, complete, and up-to-date baseline these goals can be unrealistic from the start.
- An independent performance measurement and review process. The issue is that the service provider supplies IT infrastructure and services and then sends the customer a bill. However, the customer has no independent method of auditing the level of services, systems, software, and networks actually provided.

Although there is a gag order in place on what has been going on with San Diego County's outsourcing agreements, it appears that none of these three critical success factors were well addressed in the initial contract for services. Indeed, the contract has undergone several contentious renegotiations to provide for these provisions (You Can't Outsource City Hall, 2002).

C. Project and Risk Management

Perhaps the two most important things that any government agency can do to effectively manage IT contracts, acquisitions, and outsourcing is proper project management and risk management. Unfortunately, the federal government does neither very well. In February 2003 the Office of Management and Budget identified more that 700 projects totaling $21 billion of the 2004 IT budget request as being at risk because of a lack of adequate project management. At that time they indicated that they would hold up funding 300 of the projects (Frank, 2003). The federal government simply does not do enough project management to alleviate OMB's perceptions of risk. The problem is that the federal government simply does not have enough qualified project managers or staff to oversee IT acquisitions and development efforts.

Until recently, the federal government had not given much attention to project management. Evidence of this is the fact that the Office of Personnel Management does not have a project management job path or Schedule series, and project management competencies are not included in the skill requirements for the Senior Executive Service. The Chief Information Officer Council's Project Management Working Group has recently made several recommendations to OMB concerning project management, including the creation of a federal project management office, the collection and dissemination of best practices in project management, and the establishment of project management standards (Miller, 2003). The report notes that historically there has been a lack of project management knowledge and skills in government, a lack of clear project management skill requirements and measures, a lack of professional identity for project managers, inconsistent project management methods across agencies, and barriers to sharing project management talent within and among agencies.

The Standish Group (1999), which offered the original "Chaos Report" depicting the tremendous IT failures in 1995, has recently formally endorsed project management as a remedy for such failures. They have observed that since 1995 project failure rates are down and success rates are up because of increased attention to project management, and the realization that IT project failure and success is about people and processes, not technology. This is clear from its research showing that the top criteria for the success of an IT project are user involvement, executive support, clear business objectives, experienced project managers, small milestones, firm basic requirements, competent staff, proper planning, and project ownership.

The key to successful IT acquisition and development projects is project managers who are not necessarily IT professionals in the sense that they have a programming or a computer engineering background. They need a broader, more managerial, perspective that includes an understanding of an organization's business vision, goals, processes, constraints, and opportunities. Of course, they also need an understanding of IT fundamentals and capabilities. Such individuals are a scarce commodity not only at the federal level but also within the states and local governments (Ford, 2003). As such, many public agencies are looking to private contractors to outsource their project management efforts.

Risk management should be an integral part of project management. It is a systematic approach to identifying, analyzing, and controlling areas or events with a potential for causing unwanted change. Through risk management, the risks of a project are assessed and systematically managed to reduce risk to an acceptable level. Risk is a measure of the inability to achieve project milestones or objectives within defined cost, schedule, and technical constraints and has two components: (1) the probability of failing to achieve a particular outcome and (2) the consequences of failing to achieve that outcome. Risk management strives to control risk. This includes risk planning, assessing risk areas, developing risk-handling options, monitoring risks to determine how risks have changed, and documenting the overall risks associated with a project. While various local, state, and federal agencies actively practice risk management for a variety of activities not associated with IT, more attention needs to be directed to risk management in IT project management.

D. Outsourcing Core Business Processes

Government is highly dependent on technology and communication for daily operations. In some situations, such as core business processes like arrest warrant systems, mail and e-mail, telephone and Internet access, and financial/accounting systems, the activities are so critical and vital to ongoing operations that they would result in service disruptions, downtime, or larger crises if they were not functioning properly. The effects of these interruptions are often passed along to other entities due to the integrated nature in which business and government operate. For example, the largest commercial bank in Hawaii, the Bank of Hawaii, indicated that 5500 to 6000 of their customers were not able to access accounts or cash checks for several weeks after the terrorist attacks in New York

City on September 11, 2001 due to mail service interruptions and the anthrax scare (www.boh.com/new/20010914.asp). This example illustrates the importance and sensitivity of core business processes, and suggests why extra caution should be taken when outsourcing these areas. Specifically, three issues should be considered when outsourcing core business processes: legal limitations, number and types of providers, and the extent to which the good or service is integrated (or "bundled") with other items (Edwards and Shaoul, 2003).

Although administrators work hard to transfer risk, provide the best value for taxpayers' dollars, and monitor various aspects of the project through contracts, their ability to control the contract workflow is limited to the legal specifications of the original contract. Most contractors and their legal staff are experienced enough to include language that indicates that "acts of God" or "unforeseen circumstances" fall beyond the normal confines of the contractual agreement. This is a huge but useful loophole for vendors. For example, if an IT contractor in Tennessee falls behind schedule because its software developers in New England are snowed in due to a blizzard, or if it meets an unexpected obstacle, such as a network worm or virus that delays the transfer of needed hardware or software, it is easy for the contractor to request an extension of the contractual deadline. Public organizations may fight or complain about these delays, and may even threaten to delay payment to the contractor. When core business processes are at stake, however, these actions may be useless, as they may cause further delays, or (in extreme instances), result in the vendor stopping all work. This could result in a service interruption crisis. Consider the case of a local government that mistakenly shuts off electricity to thousands of citizens in the middle of the winter because of a glitch in a computer software program on its mainframe. Citizens and administrators alike would not want to hear that the problem could not be fixed because the software vendor was snowed in. They would want the problem fixed and the electricity restored immediately, in the best interest of the public. When public organizations are involved in outsourcing, they transfer operations to another entity, yet retain responsibility for the delivery of services. As was noted earlier, vendors are not always accountable to the best interests of the public. Because core business processes are essential activities and may result in outcomes that are devastating to citizens or governments, exceptional care should be taken in negotiating these contracts.

A second concern with outsourcing core business processes involves the number and types of service providers. Having highly trained, available staff to support and maintain technology is a critical factor in minimizing service disruptions or downtime. Governments must find large reputable vendors that are capable of managing the project over a long period. This may be a constraining element, as vendors enter and leave the marketplace frequently, due to economic (i.e., bankruptcy), technological (i.e., training deficiency), or personnel (i.e., hiring freeze) reasons. One study indicated that there were just three major contractors responsible for providing the overwhelming majority of IT contract work for governments (Dunleavy et al., 2001). Again, this raises concerns over the availability of responsible contractors. With limited choices in possible vendors, governments may find that they loose the advantages of competition that contracting is expected to provide. They may also be unable to find alternative providers that can be substituted quickly, in the event that a contractor is not performing according to specifications.

Finally, because of the complex and interrelated nature of IT, many core business strategies are "bundled" with other processes. If one aspect of the process fails, it can create a domino effect along the rest of the supply chain, and spill over into other related processes. Not only can core business be affected under such circumstances, but secondary ones as well. This creates highly complex and inherently more expensive problems for governments to solve.

Since the contractual partnership relies on sharing or transferring risk to the vendor, contracts for core business processes must contain clauses that explicitly illustrate how 'back-up' facilities would be created to limit the exposure governments would face in the event of an IT failure. These back-up mechanisms can be more costly than traditional arrangements, and therefore may not necessarily result in greater cost efficiency for the contracting organization. Governments may find that they are locked into a partnership with an IT vendor for "better or worse" (Edwards and Shaoul, 2003). For these reasons, outsourcing core business strategies is particularly sensitive. Extreme caution should be exercised when negotiating contracts of this nature.

VIII. CONCLUSIONS

IT has been a mostly evolutionary, sometimes revolutionary process, as we move into the 21st century. The dynamic, rapidly diversifying global economy has resulted in increased customer service demands, pressure to compete in new markets, and opportunities to use more sophisticated processes within public organizations. Never before has there been such a focus on IT to facilitate strategic processes, make more informed decisions, simplify and expedite activities, as well as create new opportunities for enhanced services. The highly complex, ever-changing, and integrated nature of most IT ventures indicates why most public and private organizations indicate that they will continue to spend a large portion of their budgets in IT products and services for the foreseeable future.

As public organizations become more aware of their needs and limitations, they are increasingly relying on partnerships with contractors to promote mutually beneficial goals. Although past IT contracting experiences have produced mixed results, public managers are gaining a new understanding on how to mitigate risks and enhance opportunities for success. They are beginning to understand that contractual partnerships must have the enduring commitment and real involvement of management, as well as constant reinforcement and monitoring, to achieve realistic goals and expectations. In addition, public organizations must become better educated in assessing their long- and short-term needs, clearly stating requirements, communicating performance measurement expectations, and proactively managing the specifications of the contract — especially when these issues relate to core business processes. IT outsourcing is not a panacea by any means. However, it can be a useful tool for enhancing organizational efficiency when public managers are properly educated on the pros and cons of outsourcing, work toward a larger definition of "best value" principles, create mutually beneficial partnerships with needed vendors, and carefully safeguard their organizations against possible risks.

REFERENCES

Belarc, Inc., IT as a Utility: Recommendations for Success, 2003 belarc.com

Chen, Y. and Perry, J., Outsourcing for e-government: managing for success, *Public Performance and Management Review*, June 1, 26:404–421, 2003.

Connecticut: Rebuilding a Dynasty or a Dinosaur?, *CIO Magazine*, June 15, 2002.
    Available at: http://www.cio.com/archive/061502/govt_connecticut.html
    Accessed on 5/24/04.

Connecticut Antes Up, *CIO Magazine*, Apr. 1, 1999.
>Available at: http://www.cio.com/archive/040199_conn.html
>Accessed on 5/24/04.

Dunleavy, P., Margetts, H., Bastow, S., and Yared, H., Policy Learning and Public Sector Information Technology: Contractual and E-Government Change, paper presented at the American Political Science Association's Annual Conference, San Francisco, CA, Spring 2001.

Edwards, P. and Shaoul, J., Partnerships: for better, for worse?, *Accounting, Auditing, and Accountability Journal*, March 1, 16, 397–421, 2003.

Ford, C.M., A Growth Industry: Project Management Education Programs, *Government Computer News*, Nov. 11, 2003.
>Available at: http://www.gen.com/vol1_no1/daily-updates/24136-1.html
>Accessed on 5/24/04.

Frank, D., OMB Puts Agencies on Notice: Funding Could Be Held Up if Goals for IT Management Not Met, *Federal Computer Week*, Feb. 10, 2003 FCW.Com
>Available at: http://www.fcw.com/fcw/articles/2003/0210/news-omb-02-10-03.asp
>Accessed on 5/24/04.

Gartner Dataquest, State and Local Government IT Spending, 2002 Gartner.com

Government Performance Project, Alan K. Campbell Public Affairs Institute at the Maxwell School of Citizenship and Public Affairs of Syracuse University, March 1998–2000.

High Anxiety, *CIO Magazine*, September 1, 2000.
>Available at: http://www.cio.com/archive/090100_anxiety.html
>Accessed on 5/24/04.

INPUT, Federal IT Spending to Reach $68 Billion, April 16, 2003a www.input.com

INPUT, State and Local IT Outsourcing to Reach $23 Billion, October 22, 2003b www.input.com

ICMA (International City Management Association), *The Municipal Yearbook*, International City Management Association, Washington, D.C., 2002.

IT Cortex, Failure Rate: Statistics over IT Project Failure Rates nd. IT-Cortex.com, 2003.

Konicki, S., Now in Bankruptcy, Kmart Struggled with Supply Chain, Information Week, January 28, 2002.
>Available at: http//www.informationweek.com/story/IWK20020125S0020
>Accessed on 5/24/04.

Korosec, R., Information Technology Procurement Issues: A Report to the Florida Auditor General, Tallahasse, FL, Spring 2003.

Korosec, R. and Berman, E., A National Survey of Public Administration in U.S. Cities, Fall 2003.

Linowes, D., *Privatization: Toward More Effective Government, A Report of the President's Commission on Privatization*, Illini Books, Urbana-Champaign, IL, 1988.

Miller, J., CIO Council Group Recommends a Federal Project Management Office, *Government Computer News*, November 4, 2003 GCN.Com
>Available at:http://www.gcn.com/vol1_no1/daily-updates/24061-1.html
>Accessed on 5/24/04.

NASPO (National Association of State Purchasing Officials) and NASIRE (National Association of State Information Resource Executives), Buying Smart: State Procurement Reform Saves Millions, September, 1996.

NASPO (National Association of State Purchasing Officials), NASIRE (National Association of State Information Resource Executives), and NASDAGS (National Association of State Directors of Administration and General Services), Buying Smart: A Blueprint for Action, May, 1998.

National Governors Association, Using Information Technology to Transform State Government, March 11, 2003 nga.org

Rocheleau, B. and Wu, L., Public versus private information systems: do they differ in important ways? A review and empirical test, *The American Review of Public Administration*, December, 32(4): 379–397, 2002.

Robb, D., Fed helps ERP make financial turns in tough year, *Washington Technology*, June 4, 2001 Washingtontechnology.com

Smith, L., Campbell, J., Subramanian, A., Bird, D., and Nelson, A., Strategic planning for municipal systems: some lessons from a large U.S. city, *The American Review of Public Administration*, June, 31:139–157, 2001.

SA–CMM (Software Acquisition–Capability Maturity Model), Version 1.03, Technical Report, CMU/SEI_2002_TR_010 ESC_TR_2002_010, Carnegie Mellon University, Pittsburgh, PA, March 2002.

Standish Group, The Chaos Report, 1994
    Standishgroup.com

Standish Group, Chaos: A Recipe for Success, 1999
    Standishgroup.com

Terry, L., Feds, states lean on ERP as e-gov pillar, *Washington Technology*, September 25, 2000
    Washingtontechnology.com

U.S. GAO (U.S. General Accounting Office), *Contracting for Information Technology Services*, Government Printing Office, Washington, D.C., February, 2003 (GAO-03-384R).

U.S. GAO (U.S. General Accounting Office), *Improving the Sourcing Decisions of the Government. Final report of the Commercial Activities Panel*, Government Printing Office, Washington, D. C., April, 2002a (GAO-02-866T).

U.S. GAO (U.S. General Accounting Office), *Information Technology: Inconsistent Software Acquisition Processes at the Defense Logistics Agency Increase Project Risks*, Government Printing Office, Washington, D.C., January 10, 2002b (GAO-02-9).

U.S. GAO (U.S. General Accounting Office), *HUD Information Systems: Immature Software Acquisition Capability Increases Project Risks*, Government Printing Office, Washington, D.C., September 14, 2001a (GAO-01-962).

U.S. GAO (U.S. General Accounting Office), *Information Technology: Leading Commercial Practices for Outsourcing of Services*, Government Printing Office, Washington, D.C., November 30, 2001b (GAO-02-214).

U.S. GAO (U.S. General Accounting Office), *Customs Service Modernization: Serious Management and Technical Weaknesses Must Be Corrected*, Government Printing Office, Washington, D.C., February 26, 1999 (GAO/AIMD-99-41).

U.S. Naval Marine Corp Intranet
    http://www.chips.navy.mil/archives/00_oct/nmci.html

You can't outsource city hall, *CIO Magazine*, June 15, 2002.
    Available at: http://www.cio.com/archive/061502/govt.html
    Accessed on 5/24/04.

26

MANAGEMENT INFORMATION SYSTEMS AND AN INTERDISCIPLINARY BUDGET MODEL

George B. K. de Graan
Road and Hydraulic Engineering Institute

CONTENTS

I.	Introduction	428
II.	Some aspects of information systems	430
III.	The budget model	433
	A. Introduction	433
	B. The economic crisis during the 1930s	435
	C. Issue 1: management information crisis in the U.S. public sector after World War II	435
	1. The management information crisis in the public sector	435
	2. The management information crisis in the private sector	440
	3. State-of-the-art performance budgeting in the public sector in Holland	443
	4. Knowledge: a new economic production factor	444
	D. Issue 2: some developments in theory organization and administration	447
	1. The structuring principles	447
	2. Some causes for the swelling of complexity	448
	3. The introduction of rationalities	448
	4. Some concepts for reducing complexity	449
	E. Issue 3: some aspects of the development of the macroeconomic modeling of the Centraal Planbureau (CPB) in Holland	449
IV.	An illustration of a Dutch budget model of pavement	451
	A. The budget model: a synopsis	451
	1. Effectiveness/outcome	451
	2. Efficiency/productivity/output	451
	3. The link between effectiveness and efficiency	451

B. An illustration of the budget model: costs of maintenance/replacement
    of pavement 451
    1. Introduction 451
    2. The budget model 452
    3. Life cycle time and the distribution of probability 454
    4. Model in formula 455
C. Service level agreement (SLA) 457
D. An MIS and a budget model of pavement 457
V. Some final conclusions 459
References 460

ABSTRACT

In both the public and private sectors in the U.S. and in Europe there has been a continuous flow of new management systems that have been introduced such as performance budgeting; planning, programming, budgeting systems (PPBSs); management by objectives (MBO); zero-base budgeting (ZBB); New Zealand model; new public management; balanced scorecard (BSC); and government governance. All these innovations suffer from the lack of adequate measures of efforts for efficiency and effectives and the retrospective-oriented management information. Traditional accounting in the public sector has been based on cash accounting, modified accounting (kas-en verplichtingenstelsel), and accrual accounting. And in the private sector traditional business accounting concerns accrual accounting and triple accounting. In the private sector in the U.S., there has been a persistent controversy between financial accounting (FA) (balance sheet, loss and profit account) and management accounting (MA) (Daniel, 1960s; Kaplan and Cooper, 1980s). In the public there has hardly been a similar debate. In spite of the disagreement of productivity (efficiency) and effectiveness with traditional accounting (double bookkeeping), the measurement problem of efficiency and effectiveness in the public sector is solved by the selection of double bookkeeping for product costing. By this, one cost system is selected for both FA (double bookkeeping) and MA.

A budget model can be characterized as a Tinbergen type of model for budgeting. Double bookkeeping is no longer the only absolute uniform structuring principle for all the financial transactions in an organization. By styling the causal relationships of the transformation process from inputs to outputs independently of the traditional administration and in a strongly prospective-oriented way, this information can be used to reinforce the strategic planning (effectiveness) and the management control process (efficiency).

A budget model can be described as a quantitative and a qualitative goal to be achieved on the basis of parameters that have been estimated by statistical methods or by experts. Management information systems (MISs) play a vital role in providing relevant information to the different management layers for efficiency and effectiveness. In this context the information pyramid is an adequate instrument to solve the aggregation problem.

I. INTRODUCTION

Many organizations in both the private and public sector need inputs, which are transformed to énd products and services. In order to measure the productivity of the production processes of organizations one needs information about the efficiency of the transformation processes and about the effectiveness of the selected strategies for realizing the goals of these organizations. In this context, missions are formulated and linked to strategies in order to realize the formulated goals.

Efficiency concerns a performance indicator, which indicates to what extent a given output can be produced with the least possible use of resources (inputs).

The effectiveness indicator regards the amount of end products the real service delivered to the public.

Productivity regards the ratio of output to input for a particular activity. The productivity indicator measures the percentage of change from one year to the next one. Productivity generally includes both efficiency and effectiveness.

Information systems play a vital role in providing this information to the different management layers. For organizational planning (strategic and operating planning), budgets are necessary to quantify the costs of these future activities.

In general, budgeting depends on historical data generated by the various accounting subsystems. One can conclude that traditional budgeting concerns a projection of the past to the future. Traditional accounting is generally based on two structuring principles, making changes in equity in the balance sheet transparent and providing an insight into the causes of these changes in the loss and profit account.

During the last four decades information crises have been signaled in the U.S. in both the private and public sector. To style the real world in a better way, budgets should be based on structuring principles of other disciplines and translated into a model. That is why it is recommended that an interdisciplinary approach to organizational planning (strategic and operating levels) be used through budgets. As a consequence of the application of an interdisciplinary budget, efficiency and effectiveness increase. On the other side, the factor complexity grows due to the introduction of more indicators. The problem of matching complexity between the various management layers in micro-organizations has not been solved yet in an adequate way.

The concept of an interdisciplinary budget model is illustrated in the appendix through a new funding model for pavements in Holland. Other examples of a budget model concern a budget model for dikes, banks, bridges, dredges, lock chambers, and dynamic route information systems (DRIPSs).

Generally, the former traditional financial information systems of the infrastructure have been based on historical data. And further on, the information for the different management layers was too aggregate. The former traditional budgets of the financial information systems of the infrastructure in Holland did not make it possible to analyze the cause-and-effect relationships of the various cost drivers and to link these indicators to the goals.

The application of the interdisciplinary budget model resulted in the following main characteristics:

- An improvement in efficiency and effectiveness (strategic planning)
- The transformation process from inputs to outputs regarding the cause-and-effect relationships (cost drivers) has become transparent; based on this insight, budgeting in financial information systems has been improved
- Through the introduction of more performance indicators in the interdisciplinary budget model, the factor complexity increased; until now no general accepted solution can be given for matching complexity in information systems

■ Through the application of the interdisciplinary budget model the transformation processes from inputs to outputs has been made transparent; based on this insight for each cost category of the funding system an expert system could be developed; these expert systems are of great importance for the decision-making process regarding strategic planning and the management control process

In the following paragraphs, first, attention is given to some characteristics and definitions of an information system. Second, the rise of an interdisciplinary budget is explained. And finally the budget model is illustrated for pavements.

II. SOME ASPECTS OF INFORMATION SYSTEMS

In general, organizations need relevant, timely information about the transformational activities/processes from inputs to outputs (end products/services) and about the environment of organizations. This information is necessary in order to ensure that the resources have been transformed efficiently and that the strategies have proved to be effective in realizing the goals of the organizations.

Generally, one can distinguish the following components of organizations that are needed to achieve their objectives/goals:

1. Resource inputs such as money (capital), human resources/people, raw materials and services, knowledge
2. Transformation of activities/processes from input to output, such as production, logistics, marketing, finance, technology (research and development, information systems)
3. Resource outputs (products/services) to customers and clients

In this context, information systems play a vital role in providing information to the different management layers. According to O'Brien (1993: 14–20), the following characteristics of an information system can be distinguished:

An information system is a set of people, procedures and resources that collects, transforms, and disseminates information in an organization.

A system is a group of interrelated components working together toward a common goal by accepting inputs and producing outputs in an organized transformation process. Such a system has three basic interacting components or functions:

■ Inputs
■ Processing
■ Output

If information systems focus on providing information to the management information process, they are called management information systems (MISs).

Regarding the different layers of management in an organization the following information pyramid can be distinguished (Figure 26.1):

■ Strategic management
■ Tactical management

Figure 26.1   Management layers in information systems.

■   Operational management
■   Business operations

According to Alter (1996: 2):

> Information systems are systems that use information technology to capture,
> transmit, store, retrieve, manipulate, or display information used in one or
> more business processes. Firms consist of groups of business processes and
> compete in a business environment. More specifically:
>   Information technology is the hardware and software that make information
> systems possible. Hardware is the devices and other physical things involved
> in processing information, such as computers, workstations, physical things
> networks, and data storage and transmission devices.
> Software is the computer programs that interpret user inputs and tell the
> hardware what to do.
>   An information system is a system that uses information technology to
> capture, transmit, store, retrieve, manipulate, or display information used in
> one or more business processes.

Since World War II the different roles of information systems gradually shifted from data
processing to strategy-based information systems. According to O'Brien (1993: 37), the
following evolution of information systems has taken place:

1. Data processing: 1950s–1960s; in this period information systems focused on
    transaction processing, record keeping and traditional accounting applications.
2. Management reporting: 1960s–1970s; besides data processing in the 1960s there
    has been a trend to provide managerial end user information for managerial
    decision-making processes. This trend can be characterized as the development
    of management information systems (MISs).
3. Decision support: 1970s–1980s; in general one can state that the information
    systems at that time did not provide the relevant information for the managerial
    decision-making processes. In this context the concept of decision support
    systems (DSS) has been developed. The aim of DSS was to provide relevant
    managerial information to support the decision-making process.

4. Strategic and end user support: 1980s–1990s; in the 1980s the following trends can be distinguished in information systems:

End user computing systems: the development of microcomputer processing power, application software packages and telecommunication networks. End users use their own computing resources to support their job requirements instead of waiting for the indirect support of corporate information services departments.

There has been a shift of production of output from corporate service departments to the individual end users.

Executive information systems (EIS): most top executives did not directly use either the reports of informationreporting systems or the analytical modelling capabilities of decision support systems. In order to match the relevant and timely delivery of top corporate executives the EIS has been developed.

Knowledge based systems: artificial intelligence (AI) and expert systems (ES).

According to Alter (1996: 503–506), artificial intelligence and an expert system can be defined as follows:

Artificial intelligence is the field of research related to the demonstration of intelligence by machines. This includes, but is not limited to, the ability to think, see, learn, understand, and use common sense.

An expert system is an information system that supports or automates decision-making in an area where recognized experts do better than nonexperts. Expert systems do this by storing and using expert knowledge about a limited topic, such as authorizing or analysing machine vibrations. These systems produce conclusions based on data they receive. They are used either as interactive advisors or as independent systems for converting data into recommendations or other conclusions.

Many expert systems have been developed to record and disseminate the knowledge of recognized experts.

Expert systems are often called knowledge-based systems because they represent knowledge in an explicit form so that it can be used in a problem-solving process. Knowledge is a combination of instincts, ideas, rules and procedures that guide actions and decisions. In this sense, a person may remember a lot of facts or a database may contain a lot of facts without having much knowledge.

According to Davis et al. (1990: 5–12), accounting products, financial statements, are prepared for:

■ Financial accounting (external information and is concerned principally with the financial strength and performance of the business.
■ Internal management (management accounting). Internal management focuses primarily on (1) organizational planning through the use of budgets and (2) data refined for use in control and decision-making.
■ Management accounting systems uniquely serve management's need to (1) control operations and make responsibility assignments and (2) effectively plan the organization's financial activities through operations budgets.

■ The purpose of management accounting systems is: (1) effective planning and the subsequent analysis of deviations from operating plans, (2) activation and direction of daily operations and (3) problem solving and intelligent decision-making.

It is almost unthinkable in the modern business world to enter a new operational period without a financial plan. Such a plan is commonly referred to as a budget. Budget's reflect management's best estimates of its financial operations during an ensuing accounting period.

The most successful method of budget construction is "bottom-up" approach.

The process of budgeting depends, of course, on historical data generated by the various accounting subsystems.

The end product of the budgeting process is the full range of the pro forma operating statements by which management can see the effect of its operating strategies.

According to Davis et al. (1990: 12–13), a symbiosis has gradually grown between the disciplines of accounting and electronic data processing:

> Beginning with the invention of the "computing machine" by the Englishman Charles Babbage in 1832, and aided by the previous creation of the punched card idea by Joseph Jacquard in France to control weaving patterns on textile looms, the potential for ameliorating the data processing burden was born. The first adaptation of these principles to mass data processing was accomplished by Herman Hollerith in the US Census Bureau around 1890
>
> The shift in emphasis at most managerial levels from data manipulation to data evaluation and control represents another advantage of computerization. The increased accuracy, efficiency, and timeliness of reporting can be most helpful in improving the decision-making activities of management.
>
> Although modern, sophisticated accounting information systems are the products of the marriage of two separate disciplines, accounting and electronic data processing, these disciplines evolved independently of each other and from completely different origins.
>
> Data processing focuses largely on the incredible ability of computers to ingest vast quantities of raw data, to manipulate the data in an almost unlimited variety, and to report the results quickly and accurately.
>
> In contrast, information systems concentrate on the orderly and controlled transformation of raw transaction data into useful information to fulfil the decision-making needs of management. Interest focuses on the origination of the data, the data's authenticity and legitimacy, the controlled steps of the data-to-information process, the protection of the documents and records involved, and the utility of the end product.
>
> The synergistic combination of accounting and EDP has given status to accounting information systems and has concomitantly created a new area of knowledge.

III. THE BUDGET MODEL

A. Introduction

A budget model can be described as quantitative standards on the basis of parameters that have been estimated with statistical methods or have been fixed by experts.

Important differences can be distinguished between the traditional budget and a budget model:

■ A traditional budget in the private or the public sector, on a microlevel, concerns a projection of the past and concerns the quantitative information based on traditional administration. In general, budgets are fixed on the basis of historical costs of the business administration of an organization. In this way, the past is extrapolated to the future. Moreover, information from the administration concerns only one aspect of reality.
■ In contrast, the information in a budget model is independent of traditional administration.
■ The traditional budget has a strong retrospective character; a budget model thereby is prospective oriented, which is why the planning and management control aspects can be reinforced.

Three trends can be distinguished for the development of the budget model:

1. The management information crises in the private and the public sector
2. Some developments in business administration
3. Some aspects of the development of macroeconomic modeling in Holland, resulting in the so-called *budget model*

The evolution in the conceptual thinking about budgets that resulted in the budget model is represented in Figure 26.2.

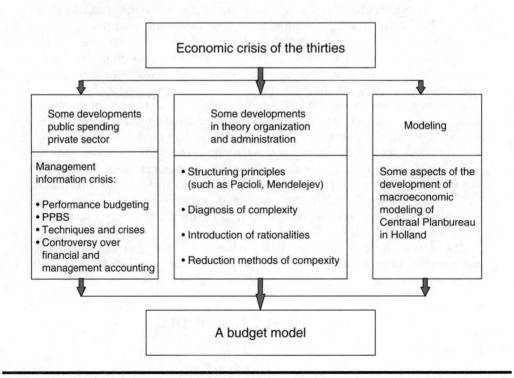

Figure 26.2 The evolution of the budget model.

In this context, attention is paid to issue 1, namely the information crisis in the MISs both in the U.S. and in Holland concerning the private and the public sector.

Issue 2 deals with some developments in theory organization and administration. And issue 3 deals with some aspects of macroeconomic modeling in Holland. Modeling as invented by Tinbergen in the 1930s has been used as a way out of these crises, through the development of a budget model. A budget model can be characterized as a Tinbergen type of model for budgeting.

B. The Economic Crisis During the 1930s

In the 1930s there was a global economic depression and Holland also suffered from this economic collapse. The breakdown of the stock market in 1929 resulted in an international trade declination (−30%) and a decrease of national income (−18%) and an unemployment of about 17.4%. The Dutch government was confronted with this severe economic and social crisis. To diminish unemployment the government could devaluate the Dutch guilder or lower the wages but at that time there was an economic policy crisis due to the lack of macroeconomic insight regarding the economy.

The year 1936 is generally accepted as the beginning of macroeconomic modeling in Holland and the rise of policy analysis. Tinbergen (1940) developed a macroeconomic model for analyzing the business cycle. On the basis of the Tinbergen model, the government decided to devaluate the Dutch guilder in order to diminish the unemployment.

The basis for the crises in the public sector is the great economic depression of the 1930s. Due to this global economic crisis, the influence of central government on economic and social life increased strongly. This development resulted in:

- More public spending, resulting in a management control and management information problem. The main issue concerns were the effectiveness and efficiency of the policy of spending by the government
- More attention to financial accounting (FA) (the SEC principles)
- A separation between management and FA for both the public and the private sector
- More interest for quantitative economic information regarding macroeconomic aspects for macroeconomic policy analysis in order to solve the macroeconomic information crisis

C. Issue 1: Management Information Crisis in the U.S. Public Sector after World War II

1. The management information crisis in the public sector

In the U.S. shortly after World War II a public-sector crisis became manifest due to the rise of the administrative state and the New Deal. In this context interest increased in the efficient performance of government activities. There was a shift from line-item budgeting to performance budgeting. Performance budgeting deals with the problem of *what government does* in contrast to line-item budgeting, which deals with *what government buys*.

In 1949 the Hoover Commission formulated performance budgeting as follows:

> We recommend that the whole budgetary concept of the federal government should be fashioned by the adaptation of a budget based upon functions, activities and projects: this we designate as a performance budget.

A second aspect of this crisis manifested in the late 1950s. As a consequence of disagreement with incremental budgeting (muddling through) the concept of planning, programming, budgeting systems (PPBSs) was developed. The aim of PPBS was to link the goals with the means for continuous improvement of the efficiency and effectiveness of public management.

In the 1970s, 1980s, and 1990s, other new management accounting (MA) concepts were developed, including management by objectives (MBO) and zero-base budgeting (ZBB).

Performance budgeting, PPBS, MBO, ZBB, etc. suffer from the same problem, namely, the lack of adequate measures of efforts for efficiency and effectiveness and retrospective-oriented management information. Furthermore, the basis for this management information is generally based on traditional administration.

Since ZBB no new management model has been introduced in the public sector in the U.S. This management crisis is characterized by Strausmann and Bozeman (1982) as "Shrinking budgets and the shrinkage of a budget theory."

a. Reinventing the government

To improve the efficiency and effectiveness of public management of organizations there has been a trend to introduce more entrepreneurial behavior in the public sector. In this context one can refer to the book of Osborne and Gaebler (1993):

> The fact that government cannot be run just like a business does not mean it cannot become more entrepreneurial, of course. There is a vast continuum between bureaucratic and entrepreneurial behaviour, and government can surely shift its position on that spectrum.

The ten commandments of Osborne and Gaebler are summarized by them as follows:

1. Catalytic government
2. Community-owned government
3. Competitive government
4. Mission-driven government
5. Results-oriented government
6. Customer-driven government
7. Enterprising government
8. Anticipatory government
9. Decentralized government
10. Market-oriented government

According to Nathan (1995), reinventing the government can be described as follows:

> There are 15 million state and local public employees, 13 percent of the national's total work force, accounting for 14 percent of the gross national product in 1993.

The Osborne–Gaebler book can be read at least eight ways of involving competing rationales for the reinvention movement: (1) to empower citizens, (2) to promote mission-driven entrepreneurial leadership in order to "steer rather than row," (3) to enhance competition and deregulate government by cutting red tape, (4) to foster "total quality management," (5) to decentralize government, and as an argument for (6) performance budgeting, (7) civil service reform, and (8) privatization. All these purposes, of course, are not mutually exclusive; some clearly conflict. Nor does the list exhaust the possibilities. Intellectually, the reinvention movement is a grab-bag. Everyone who is interested gets to pick his or her own particular purpose. Anyone can play. Experts in public administration should view the reinvention moment as an opportunity to win acceptance for reforms in public administration, which, as in past periods, involve a delicate balancing of political accountability and professional expertise in American government.

Still, I am optimistic that there is a new mood now that we can take advantage of the advanced reforms to enable leaders in government to be change agents, to convert promises (public policies) into performance. I give credit to David Osborne and Ted Gaebler for creating this new mood. Because of their work, there is a more positive and upbeat tone now about improving government rather than just bashing it.

According to Goodsell (1993) the book of Osborne and Gaebler almost asks, Is public administration obsolete?:

> For those who have not yet been exposed to Osborne and Gaebler's message, let me summarise it. To them, the principal public issue at hand is not what government should do, but how. The current "reinvention" of government that in my eyes is inevitable, constitutes a rejection of the governmental model they say was employed in the Progressive Era and New Deal. This model, according to the authors, is one of in-house program implementation and service delivery by hierarchically organised administrative departments, run by professional managers in accordance with operational rules and fiscal checks. The model was originally adopted, it is said, to rid the country of inept patronage machines. However, in this era of global competition, instant communication, a knowledge-based economy, and niche markets, such "industrial era" bureaucracy is said to produce mediocrity, inflexibility, and an obsession with control.
>
> To replace this model of government, contend Osborne and Gaebler, a new form of governance must be created at all levels of government (and are now being created) that is adaptable, responsive, efficient, and effective. It must be able to produce high quality goods and services, be responsive to customers, be led by persuasion and incentives rather than command, empower clients, and — above all — be entrepreneurial. In sum, I argue, public administration is not obsolete.

Another development concerns the concept of new public management (Thompson and Jones, 1995):

> Some observers may associate these ideas with Osborne and Gaebler (1993), but while these authors have popularised this approach, they did not originate it. Rather, it has grown out of both theory and practice. The new public management is a worldwide phenomenon, evolving as governments in many countries struggle to create more efficient and responsive public agencies (Schick, 1990; Rhodes, 1991; Cothran, 1993).
>
> What is new about the new public management? First, according to Thompson and Jones, many of its core concepts are new. Some, such as process engineering, just-in-time inventory management, activity-based costing (ABC), and the critique of functional specialization are products of the information revolution. Second and most important, is the reliance on the new economics of institutions

and organizations, which deals with issues of institutional design. Thus Thompson and Jones say that the new public management is based on the economics of Kenneth Arrows, William Niskanen, Roger Noll, Charles Schultz, Ronald Coase, Oliver Williamson, and even Abba Lerner's market socialism. Thompson and Jones argue that the new institutional economics gives public managers the tools they need to handle complex problems, which in some ways are tougher than those faced by business. Moreover, they argue that the economics of institutions and organizations has been put to the test and has been found to work. The design of regulatory instruments (ranging from affluent markets and bubbles to outright deregulation of the airlines and interstate motor carriage) in the United States and the privatization and securization of an astonishing array of government-owned assets (and some liabilities) in Europe, Great Britain, Canada, and the antipodes are a few of its success.

According to Moe (1994),

> Gaebler asserts there are ten principles for entrepreneurial government that if fully implemented will effectively result in a government so changed as to merit the description of reinvented. These principles (e.g., "entrepreneurial governments are competitive," "entrepreneurial governments are custom driven") are stated in a theoretical manner (that is, propositions subject to empirical proof or disproof), but rather are offered as statements exhorting the reader to acceptance and action.

A call for a new management paradigm of the public sector is made by Moe:

> This call for a new paradigm has been answered, according to supporters of the reinventing government effort, by the Gore Report. Much of the public administration community leadership early-on joined in saluting this unshackling from the allegedly outdated bureaucratic paradigma and in the adoption of the entrepreneurial paradigm.

b. Improvement of performance indicators

During this period, attention to the application of the concept of government performance measurement increased, according to Epstein (1992):

> This a time of heightened national attention to the idea of government performance measurement and reporting. Recent congressional legislation, as well as several pending bills, may result in a greater level of performance measurement and reporting by federal agencies. Three states recently passed laws requiring performance reporting by state agencies. Accreditation, regulation, and oversight organisations have been taking actions to increase performance measurement and accountability of schools, colleges, and hospitals. The National Academy of Public Administration passed an important resolution on the subject in 1991. The American Society for Public Administration passed a similar resolution in April 1992. Other professional and public interest organisations, such as the National Governors Association, have also been encouraging increased government performance measurement and reporting. The Governmental Accounting Standards Board's (GASB) series of

seven reports on the subject, titled Service efforts and accomplishments reporting: Its time has come.

The GASB research reports are a visible part of a trend encouraging more performance measurement and reporting by governments throughout the country.

c. Decline of budgeting

According to Schick (1990), the measurement of performance is an old practice that is taking on a new lease:

> In the United States, progress in this area can be traced to Ridley–Simon's work in the 1930s, performance budgeting in the 1950s, and program budgeting in the 1960s.

According to Lee (1997), by the year 2000 budgeting will be incomplete:

> States are now more likely to revise effectiveness and productivity measures when funding levels change. Such a development is important in keeping expected program results in balance with available funding. Another trend, and one that has reached its limit of 100 percent saturation, is the use of computers. Effectiveness has gained increasing prominence in budget documents over the five-year period.
>   The executive in budget decision-making was said to rely less in 1995 on effectiveness and productivity analysis. Budget offices reported that legislatures also relied less on productivity analysis in budget decision-making.

Schick concluded:

> On the other hand, a forecaster in 1970 might well have expected state budget offices to be more advanced than they were in 1995 regarding the use of program information and analysis. Indeed, a forecaster from that earlier period is likely to be dismayed by what most likely will be the status of state budgeting in the year 2000. Unless some dramatic unforeseen reform movement materialises in the next five years, the year 2000 will be reached with many states still making limited use of program information and analysis, and with program information being included in documents for only some agencies or none at all. The revolution in budgeting that was foreseen in the name of planning–programming–budgeting in the 1960s, and which has its roots in the early 1900s, almost certainly will be incomplete by the year 2000.

Another new development in the public sector at the end of the 1980s concerned the introduction of a new strategic performance framework in New Zealand (1988). In contrast to the former input-based management system, the innovation focused on achieving strategic objectives (to link the goals with the means in a new performance framework). Another innovating issue concerned the use of management practices such as accrual accounting. According to Poot (1997), the following benefits of the transfer to accrual accounting can be distinguished:

1. Accrual accounting has no disincentives for capital expenditures
2. Accrual accounting shows long-term consequences

3. Accrual accounting makes cash manipulation no longer relevant
4. Accrual accounting provides a basis for cost accounting
5. Accrual accounting provides insight in the development of a net asset
6. Accrual accounting matches costs with benefits

The New Zealand model focuses on strategic direction. The strategic concepts accentuate long-term planning through determining the so-called strategic result areas, such as health and education, for the next 5 to 10 years, and by defining the desired outcomes. For each ministry the so-called key result areas have been determined. The minister has been held responsible for that ministry for achieving the mentioned objectives. The introduction of the management process resulted in making transparent the link between desired outcomes, required outputs and available inputs.

Poot (1997) identified the following main advantages of the New Zealand model:

1. Public management
   ■ More strategic focus
   ■ Clearer objectives and outputs
   ■ Clearer accountability
   ■ Incentives do work
2. Financial management
   ■ Better cash control
   ■ Better cost control
   ■ Better asset management
   ■ Long-term balance sheet focus
   ■ Better management information

According to Pallot (1996) the innovating issues can be summarized as follows:

> In its financial management reforms, the New Zealand government has moved from an initial emphasis on management of individual government departments to a greater concern with collective strategizing and the government as a whole. While very different in its orientation, the more recent phase should not be seen as a repudiation of the former.

In summary, the shift has been from management *in* the public sector (public *management*) to management *of* the public management (*public* management); i.e., from defining management in terms of where it takes place to defining it in terms of the nature of the task. Metcalfe (1993) describes the distinction as one of "locus" to "focus."

In the 1990s strategizing performance management in the private sector has been introduced by Kaplan and Norton (1992, 1993, 1996), with the introduction of the balanced scorecard (BSC). Strategizing performance management in the public sector at the end of the 1980s is not a new concept. Strategizing performances in the public sector has its roots in the 1960s and can be compared with PPBSs.

2. The management information crisis in the private sector

Daniel (1961) pointed out a structural information problem in the beginning of the 1960s. He believes that the information from the traditional accounting systems can be characterized as insufficient for controlling the operating costs. According to him the following causes can be mentioned:

- The design of accounting systems is generally primarily based on the demands of FA
- The cost accounting systems are primarily based on information from the past (historical costs)

To control operating costs there is a need for new management tools.

Another discussion in this period concerned the use of the rate of return on investment (ROI). This macroindicator provides insufficient insight in the cost structure of an organization and provides only information for the short term.

In the 1970s the following developments increased the cost consciousness to control the internal costs of an organization:

- The first energy crisis in the 1970s
- The growth of global competition (i.e., Japan)
- The declining growth of the American economy

A remarkable phenomenon in this period concerns the interest for internal cost allocation in the banking and service industry. In the 1970s two new management concepts have been introduced: MBO and zero-base management. The aim of both systems is to improve the efficiency and effectiveness of an organization.

The 1980s can be characterized by an intense increase in global competition and the introduction of total integrated systems (such as the total quality control and just-in-time). The market has changed from a seller's to a buyer's market and there has been a shortening in the life cycle of products.

These changes in internal and external environment factors have led to a review of the existing accounting systems, such as a revitalization of the allocation of costs. In traditional accounting systems, the indirect costs have generally been allocated by cost drivers of the direct costs. However, with the introduction of ABC, more attention has been directed toward a more precise allocation of the indirect costs. The ABC concept deals with a better relationship between (indirect) costs and the cost drivers.

Generally, the application of the ABC concept concerns traditional business administration. The costs of traditional business administration are strongly retrospective oriented. Indeed, the costs of the future concern a projection of the past.

a. Limitation of traditional accrual accounting: shareholder value

The concept of shareholder value is closely related to Rappaport (1981).The traditional valuation methods of a firm consider historical costs, current costs, etc. Through the concept of the accrual accounting principle, revenues and expenditures are allocated to different periods. But the application of the traditional valuation methods do not result in an unambiguous profit concept. Profit can be influenced by management through the modification of, for instance, the depreciation time, the decision about whether to put an asset on the balance sheet. In the concepts of accrual accounting it has been assumed that the environment of a company is quite stable. But due to changes in the environment (Klaasen et al., 1995), such as shortening of product life cycles, the accrual accounting concept became obsolete. So there was a growing need for a new concept of the valuation of a company. The most important method for the estimation of the valuation of a company concerns the discounted cash flow method. Creation of value can be realized if the company can gain a higher ROI on its activities than the amount to be paid to the providers of capital such as shareholders.

So market value assumes significant importance for the success of the company. And strategic planning, programming, and budgeting phases have to be pinpointed to this value.

b.   The balanced scorecard

Kaplan and Norton (1992) introduced the concept of BSC. The basis of this concept has been laid down in Kaplan and Johnson's (1987) book and in Kaplan's articles on ABC since the mid-1980s (e.g., Kaplan, 1986). In Kaplan and Norton's (1996) book BSC is defined as follows:

> The Balanced Scorecard translates an organisation's mission and strategy into a comprehensive set of performance measures that provides the framework for a strategic measurement and management system. The Balanced Scorecard retains an emphasis on achieving financial objectives, but also includes the performance drivers of these financial objectives. The scorecard measures organisational performance across four balanced perspectives: financial, customers, internal business processes, and learning and growth. The BSC enables companies to track financial results while simultaneously monitoring progress in building the capabilities and acquiring the intangible assets they need for future growth.

The concept of BSC is not new. The concept of PPBSs of the public sector already linked the goals with the means (linking mission and strategy to a comprehensive set of performance indicators).

The fourth perspective of BSC concerns the learning and growth perspective (innovation and learning perspective). This is one of the most important perspectives, because it deals with the management of knowledge in an organization. Kaplan and Norton (1996: 126) describe this as follows:

> The Balanced Scorecard stresses the importance of investing for the future, and not just in traditional areas for investment, such as new equipment and new product research and development. Equipment and R&D investments are certainly important but they are unlikely to be sufficient by themselves. Organisations must also invest in their infrastructure — people, systems, and procedures — if they are to achieve ambitious long-term financial growth objectives.

Kaplan and Norton (1996) also conclude in their book that there exist fewer examples of specific performance measures for the learning and growth perspective:

> We have found that many companies already have excellent starts on specific measures for their financial, customer, innovation, and operating process objectives. But when it comes to specific measures concerning employee skills, strategic information availability, and organisational alignment, companies have devoted virtually no effort for measuring either the outcomes or the drivers of these capabilities. This gap is disappointing since one of the most important goals for adopting the scorecard measurement and management framework is to promote the growth of individual and organisational capabilities.

The problem of the BSC is to balance (to rank) the four perspectives in relation to the different priorities.

3. State-of-the-art performance budgeting in the public sector in Holland

The concept of performance budgeting has been laid down in the Dutch Government Accounts Act of 1976. In the new Governments Accounts Act of the federal government of the Netherlands the concept of PPBS has partly been adopted, namely performance budgeting and long-term budgets.

In view of the experience with PPBS in the U.S., the Dutch government decided to introduce a more simpler concept of planning and control at the central government level.

In general, one can conclude that because of an insufficient theoretical basis for quantifying costs of performance of the central government and an insufficient expression of this concept in the Dutch Accounts Act, such concepts have not been practiced. Performance budgeting, in contrast with the original concept that was laid down in the Dutch Government Accounts Act, has even gradually declined.

A similar occurence has taken place in the counties (provinces) and municipalities; the public sector has about 20 years of experience with performance budgeting.

During this period there have been many critiques on the way this concept has been applied in the public sector. On the basis of an analysis of the budgets of the central government, Hazeu (1980) concluded that the concept of performance budgeting, concerning efficiency indicators, has been applied on a very limited scale. Boorsma and Mol (1983) have characterized this development as a poor show.

In the mid-1980s, Haselbekke (1995) concluded again that only 17% of the budget of the central government was based on the presentation of real performance indicators about efficiency. If one applies a more general definition of performance budgeting, then the percentage rises to 71%. In this context one can conclude that the development of performance indicators of the central government is still a poor show. For the coming years the goal of the Ministry of Finance is to stimulate the development of effectiveness indicators, which represent to what extent the formulated goals of the central government have been realized. To improve the application of performance budgeting the following step-by-step approach has been distinguished by Janssen and Maessen (1996):

- Step 1: from 1994 to 1996 a performance-measurement-oriented approach has been applied; in the budget of 1997 about 90% of the performances have been illustrated
- Step 2: from 1997 until now the development of efficiency indicators has been accentuated in order to make the transformation process from inputs to end products more transparent
- In the coming years the developments of effectiveness indicators shall be emphasized

a. Government governance

A "new" phenomenon in Holland concerns government governance. Kooiman (1993) defines governance as follows:

> By "governance" we mean the patterns that emerge from governing activities of social, political and administrative actors. Governance of a social political system can be seen in terms of a balancing process. It is not something static, but a constant process of coming to grips with the tension between governing needs on the one hand (problem situations or the grasp of opportunities) and governing capacities (creating patterns of solutions or developing strategies) on the other hand.

Holland's Ministry of Finance encourages government governance (Government Governance, 2000). The aim of government governance is to safeguard the realization of policy objectives set by parliament.

In the private sector, firms produce financial statements (balance sheet, loss and profit account, etc.) to inform stakeholders about the present and future financial condition of the firm. By this, top management is held accountable for the performances achieved. Also, profits earned by markets (creating share holder value) are of great importance for surviving. On the other hand, the public sector focuses on policy proposals resulting in a budget. Generally, government governance focuses on control and accountability. The measurement problem of efficiency and effectiveness in Holland is solved by the Ministry of Finance by choosing double bookkeeping.

Government governance is not a new management concept. Since World War II there has been a permanent struggle in the public sector to rationalize the budgetary decision process. In this context, one can refer to performance budgeting, PPBS, the New Zealand model, and the BSC. All these models try to link the goals with the means.

The signaled controversy between FA (balance sheet, loss and profit account, etc.) and MA in the 1960s (Daniel) and 1980s (Kaplan and Cooper) has not been solved.

With the introduction of ABC, Kaplan concluded that one cost system is not enough. The traditional accounting system is not the solution for both FA and MA (MA = Management Information System = MIS). FA should be based on traditional accrual accounting and MA = MIS should be based on the relationship between critical success factors and key performance indicators. The measurement of efficiency and effectiveness in MA = MIS should not be based on traditional accounting but on cause-and-effect relationships. Considering the trend of the management information crisis in the private and the public sector, introduction of the macroconcept of Tinbergen's modeling to individual organizations (microlevel) is recommended. A budget model is an illustration of this innovation.

b. Conclusions

Generally, one can say that in Holland the developments in the public and the private sector have been similar to developments in the U.S., but with a time lag of about 10 years.

The management information crisis in both the private and the public sector still exists and is not confined to a particular period. Despite the introduction of new management concepts, such as performance budgeting, PPBS, MBO, and ZBB, the measurement problem for quantifying the costs of the performance of the internal transformation process from inputs to outputs has not yet been solved in an adequate way. The basis of all these new management concepts is traditional business administration. This information is generally retrospective oriented. Another distortion concerns the application of double bookkeeping based on the concept of a homogeneous mass production. The rise of complexity of the production systems was not reflected adequately in the MISs. Kaplan pointed these inadequacies in the 1980s in his book *The Rise and Fall of Management Accounting*. Nevertheless, the concept of double bookkeeping for the public sector was introduced in the New Zealand model at the end of the 1980s. A similar development took place in the public sector in Holland at the same time. Performance budgeting in the public sector concerns double bookkeeping = FA.

4. Knowledge: a new economic production factor

Has there been a similar trend in the information crisis of the production factor knowledge in the private and public sector in the U.S.?

a. Private sector

i. Disagreement with measurement of productivity and effectiveness of R&D In the mid-1960s a rise can be signaled for managing technology as a new production factor. The traditional factors of production such as land, labor, and capital are no longer considered as the only basis for the economic growth of a nation. Besides the traditional factors of production, production factor technology emerged.

As a consequence of the continuous increase in the R&D costs and expenditures there was a growing need to improve the effectiveness and productivity of research. The traditional indicator of performance measurement of R&D investment is investment as a percentage of sales. This performance indicator should be replaced by the ratio of R&D investment and expenditure. For technically intensive industries the indicator is high and for nonintensive ones it is low.

For improving the effectiveness of R&D, Cook (1966) suggested the introduction of a formal appraisal approach based on experiences at the General Electric Research Development Centre. To make the management of technology more goal oriented, Ansoff and Stewart (1967) recommend the development of a framework for making the technological strategy of the company more transparent. In this context, they refer to the concept of product life cycle (Levitt, 1965).

ii. Human resource accounting A remarkable development in the 1960s concerned the treatment of human resources as a business asset. In traditional accounting, employees are considered an "expense."

In this context one can mention Brummet et al. (1969) and Management Accounting (1969).

Human resource accounting is an information system that supplies information about the production factor wages within a firm. The aim of such a system is to increase effectiveness of the acquisition, replacement, and allocation of this production factor.

In Bulte's opinion it is strange that until now less attention has been given to this important production factor.

According to generally accepted accounting principles, investments in current and fixed assets are mentioned as assets in the balance sheet and deprecation goes to the loss and profit account.

Investments in "human assets," in contrast, are not mentioned in the balance sheet, but go directly to the loss and profit account.

The unequal treatment of "physical assets" in comparison with "human assets" should be corrected. For valuation of human assets in the balance sheet one can think of historical costs, actual costs, opportunity costs, or the "economic value" (earning power).

iii. Global competition In the mid-1960s the U.S. had a dominant global scientific and technological position in comparison with Europe. Western Europe has woken to the threat of U.S. dominance and is developing its institutions in the direction of more effective national and international competition.

At the end of the 1960s, Rhodes (1969) concluded that Europe has not become a second-class industrial power. The lag in technology and production facilities and management skills has been matched by the European companies through invention, imitation, or licensing. In the early 1960s, Europe gave priority to rebuilding and production volume and not to costs or efficiency.

In the 1960s America felt comfortable with its global lead in basic research and technology in comparison with the rest of the world. But gradually, this satisfactory feeling changed to skepticism. Brooks (1972) draws the following conclusion:

> The scientific system and technology is obsolescent. It will be harder and harder to tell who is "ahead" or "behind." The United States will never again enjoy its enormous superiority of the first half of the 1960s, but neither is it about to be overtaken dramatically by Europe or Japan.

iv. Target-budgeting for R&D A very remarkable contribution to the development of indicators for efficiency and effectiveness concerns the results of the "Company of Future" (COF) project, which is a joint effort of European and Japanese companies and universities. COF is sponsored by the European Commission as an ESPRIT project in the Technologies for Business processes domain (TBP) and by various Japanese bodies including JRIA and MITI.

The concept of "Target-budgeting for research & development" (Perlitz et al., 1997) is based on the concept of target-costing. According to the authors, traditional accounting methods of cost accounting are insufficient for quantifying R&D budgets:

> This process cost system is among other things necessary, since the classic systems of cost accounting can only inform insufficiently about project development related costs. Traditional methods of accounting allocate the overheads to the cost centre and apply them in product calculations on the basis of reference figures, which as a rule illustrate the real origin of costs insufficiently.

v. A shift of the measurement problem of performance into the direction of mission and strategy In U.S., Japan, and Europe a never-ending debate exists about global technology innovation. All the nations have had their national debate about global innovation. This issue is of great importance to the survival of their economies and indirectly to their national employment. Global competition is a issue of goal congruence between the national level and the individual companies (multinationals and middle- and small-sized ones). All the global leaders agree that national technology planning is out of the question. It is remarkable that the national debate started already in the 1960s for the U.S., but became a real issue until the 1980s in Europe at a national level.

The lead of the U.S. in the 1960s gradually declined and awakened Europe and Japan into becoming global winners. In this way, they all formulated their national target sectors to become number one. Knowledge management both at the national level and at the individual level of a company has become a significant factor. National knowledge management and knowledge management at the microlevel dominates global survival.

The measurement problem of the performance regarding knowledge management has intensified in the direction of mission and strategy at both a national and a microlevel (companies) into a comprehensive set of performance indicators (how to link the goals with the means in an adequate way). It is remarkable that all the global companies have reengineered their transformation processes from inputs to outputs and have linked these results to their strategic planning. There has been a change from financial control (such as income statements) to strategic control. The strategic priorities of companies are reflected in the BSC.

a.   Knowledge management in the public sector

During the 1970s, knowledge management in the public sector has mainly been concentrated on the application of information technology (IT). The aim of this policy was to improve the productivity in this sector. In this context, research programs have been initiated to develop performance indicators in order to make the production function of the public sector more transparent.

In the 1980s the application of IT was intensified. Another trend in the 1980s concerns the rise of expert systems as a component of a decision support system. In spite of this development, productivity declined. In this period, knowledge transfer has been considered as a way out to narrow the gap between theorists and practitioners of the public sector. In the context of the U.S. debate about global competitiveness, domestic technology transfer has been regarded as an instrument to preserve economic growth. In this context, in the mid-1980s there has been an emphatic call for a U.S. acceleration of technology innovation to match global competitiveness.

In the 1990s another phenomenon concerns the persistent debate about the improvement of performance indicators in favor of efficiency and effectiveness. In this context, information systems have been considered important in the public sector. Another trend in the 1990s is the efforts to restructure the processes and the organization structure of the public sector (reinventing the government) and to make the public sector more entrepreneurial. Reengineering and entrepreneurship have been considered as the new trend of the 1990s to improve productivity in the public sector.

In general, one may conclude that knowledge management has not been generally accepted as a new production factor. Innovation in computer-based technologies and knowledge transfer as components of knowledge management have been dominant. One may conclude that knowledge management in the public sector is a fragmented, oriented approach.

b.   Conclusion

The information crisis in the private and the public sector affected not only the traditional production factors, but also new production factor knowledge. The trend has been similar. Another trend concerns the change from financial control to strategic control, which resulted in a rise of indicators.

D.   Issue 2: Some Developments in Theory Organization and Administration

To gain insight about the real world, it can be necessary to structure this world in a model. By structuring the information in this way, the decision-making process can be made easier.

The systematic structuring of the real world can generally be based on the following principles:

- ■   The use of so-called structuring principles (see "The structuring principles")
- ■   The structuring through the use of different rationalities (see "Some causes for the swelling of complexity" and "The introduction of rationalities")

1.   The structuring principles

A structuring principle can be characterized as an instrument, a key for decoding the complex real world. Some structuring principles concern the sexual system of Linnaeus, the periodic system of Mendelejev, and the bookkeeping system of Pacioli. In Pacioli's double-entry bookkeeping model, all the financial transactions are classified as assets or equities for measuring the wealth of a business at a specific moment (balance sheet) and for analyzing the causes of changes in this wealth (loss and profit account). Through this systematic and chronologic way of structuring, one gets a permanent insight into the total wealth of an organization and in the changes in this wealth.

However, Pacioli's model is no longer the only absolute uniform structuring principle for all the financial transactions in an organization due to the following reasons:

- The consumption and the production organizations have in general different accounting systems; the structuring principle of Pacioli does not fit all financial transactions in all kinds of organizations; the Pacioli's model deals with profit organizations that are generally focused on earning an income through markets; generally, a consumption organization (i.e., public sector) is mainly interested in the allocation of money and not in the acquisition of income
- Besides the traditional balance sheet and the loss and profit account, additional information is becoming more essential (such as the Report of the Executive Board and the Social Report)

2. Some causes for the swelling of complexity

The following causes can be mentioned for the growth of complexity of the real world:

- The rise of the Industrial Revolution and scientific management: the economic and technologic rationalities had a tremendous influence on society; the economic rationality dominated the decision-making process and organizations could be characterized as closed systems
- In response to these developments we see the rise of human relations (i.e., Human Relation School, Human Resources); this leads also to the transformation from closed systems to open systems thinking

With the introduction of the first-generation system theory, the "closed" organizations had to be changed. A more flexible organization was needed to adapt to changes in the internal and the external environment. The changes are generally caused by global competition, which results in a continuous introduction of new products and production technologies. At the moment no generally accepted definition is available for the factor complexity for all circumstances; one should not avoid complexity, because complexity deals with the different aspects of the real world, which have to be controlled.

Through the second-generation system theory, issues as "autopoiesis and double-look learning" are important aspects. In this context metaphors of organizations play an important role. A metaphor concerns a characterization of an organization through a certain symbolic description such as:

- The metaphor organization as a machine
- The metaphor organization as an organism
- The metaphor organization as brains

3. The introduction of rationalities

As a consequence of the introduction of different rationalities in social systems, the need for indicators of all kind of activities to style this real world grew rapidly. The factor complexity increased fast in social systems.

One can say that there is a paradox. The introduction of different rationalities should structure the real world in a better way, but a more intensive use of the different rationalities increased the factor complexity in social systems. If one wants to structure the real world in a realistic way, this image of reality has the tendency to become as complex as reality. In this way, the accountability and controllability of social systems is a paradox.

Complexity concerns a generic phenomenon that manifests in the technical, economic, social, etc. processes. Complexity concerns no absolute concept and at the moment there exists no concept to quantify the factor complexity, just like the measurement of an earthquake on the scale of Richter.

4. *Some concepts for reducing complexity*

To reduce the factor complexity in models some methods have been developed, such as:

■   The Weick/Maruyama model (1979):

   Any system consists of several causal relationships, some direct and some inverse. The crucial factor about these relationships is that their pattern determines the fate of the system. The system is not controlled by any single relationship to understand the system, we must know all the causal relationships and whether they are direct or inverse; we must determine the consequences of the entire pattern of relationships.

■   A cost–benefit analysis that optimizes the number of cost drivers of the traditional allocation process from inputs to outputs. Holland Van der Schroeff (1970) recommended limiting the number of cost drivers (indicators) on the basis of the usefulness of cost information for the organization; this concept has to be applied as per individual case.
■   ABC and the number of cost drivers/indicators: Kaplan and Cooper (mid-1980s) developed the concept of ABC in the U.S.; in their opinion the number of cost drivers should be fixed per individual case and should be based on cost–benefit analysis
■   Babad and Balachandran (1993) have expanded the concept of Kaplan and Cooper using a similar approach; in order to reduce the number of cost drivers/ indicators they recommended applying an algorithm for confronting the costs of the cost drivers and the use of these indicators
■   The number of indicators needed in an organization differs at the different decision-making levels; the need of the number of indicators for top management differs from the need of information at the transaction levels; reason why there has to be a balance between the number of indicators at the macro- and microlevels

The link between the number of indicators between the decision-making process of the micro- and macrolevels can be solved by styling the so-called information pyramid (Starreveld et al., 1991) of an organization, as shown in Figure 26.3.

E.   Issue 3: Some Aspects of the Development of the Macroeconomic Modeling of the Centraal Planbureau (CPB) in Holland

Generally, a model is a simplified representation of the real world. To get a better insight of the complexity of the macroeconomic processes one needs to style the real macroeconomic world through quantitative equations.

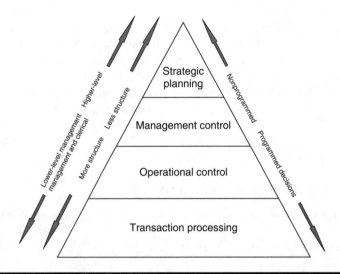

Figure 26.3 The information pyramid of an organization.

The macroeconomic model of Tinbergen (from 1936) is generally considered as a model in which the causal relations between the macroeconomic entities have been quantitatively made transparent. By analyzing the macroeconomic processes in the real world, macroeconomic planning and management control functions are reinforced. The 1936 Tinbergen model (24 equations) is generally considered as the rise of the macroeconomic modeling in Holland by the CPB.

One of the most important critiques of Keynes (1939) on the Tinbergen model was the projection of the past into the future regarding the decision-making process. The figures of the business cycles had been related to trends of many years from the past.

In general four generations of the macroeconomic modeling can be distinguished of the CPB since World War II:

1. The first-generation models (1950s and 1960s/27 equations): in this period the models had a short-term character and have been based on the Keynesian demand structure
2. The second-generation models (Vintaf model/1970s/112 equations): in the macroeconomic Vintaf model of the CPB, special attention has been paid to the supply side of the economy and to a more realistic estimation of the development of the structural employment
3. The third-generation models (Freia-Kompas model/1980s/851 equations): in the Freia-Kompas model, the monetary relations have been specified in more detail
4. the fourth-generation models (FKSEC model/1990s/about 1000 equations): the main issue of the revitalization of the model of the CPB concerned the disaggregation of the supply side into six sectors

It has lasted for about 20 years to make the model of the CPB more representative/specific by introducing the disaggregated supply side and the monetary side in the model. Gradually, the CPB model became more complex. This model expanded since the 1936

Tinbergen model from 24 equations to about 1000 equations in 1996. A real discussion about the control aspects of the macroeconomic model of the CPB has never taken place. The improvement of the macroeconomic model of the CPB is a continuous process.

IV. AN ILLUSTRATION OF A DUTCH BUDGET MODEL OF PAVEMENT

A. The Budget Model: A Synopsis

1. Effectiveness/outcome

The aim of a budget is to link the policymaking of the Ministry of Transport, Public Works and Water Management (Strategic Planning, mission, vision) with the implementation/ realization of this policy for the costs of the Dutch infrastructure. The budget model focuses on the measurement problem of efficiency and effectiveness and on making the interrelationship between these issues transparent. Effectiveness indicators for different goals must be developed for measuring the effectiveness of the ministry's policy. One of the goals of the ministry concerns safety (safety of the road or dikes). The degree of safety can be expressed in a report mark. Politicians and society are interested in the degree of safety of the different products. Should the report mark be a 6 or a 8 for the safety of the dikes or a 7 for the safety of the roads. For all the other goals of the ministry, such as attainability and the environment, similar report marks can be developed. And the overall report mark of all the goals can be characterized as the ROI of the ministry.

At the moment a service level agreement (SLA) project is running to solve this issue adequately.

2. Efficiency/productivity/output

The efficiency problem deals with the development of cost drivers of the transformation process from inputs to outputs (input–output analysis). In this context a good insight into the costs of the life cycle time of the different products is of great importance. The costs of the products are not taken from the traditional (historical) accounting system, but are based on a technical program of requirements. In a program of requirement the functional requirements of the products are described.

3. The link between effectiveness and efficiency

If report marks are given, the necessary quality and costs can be defined for the products. If top-level management modifies the report marks, then the technical and economic consequences can be made transparent, and by this, the level of the budgets of the products. If politicians want to raise the report mark for safety of dikes from 7 to 8, then the consequences of this decision can be clarified in terms of technical and economic consequences.In the scheme below the structure of a Budget Model is represented.

B. An illustration of the Budget Model: Costs of Maintenance/ Replacement of Pavement

1. Introduction

In Holland about 3200 km of pavement has to be maintained for the highways. In this context two main variants of pavement can be distinguished, namely ZOAB and DAB.

Budgetmodel = SERVICE LEVEL AGREEMENTT(SLA) = TARGET COSTING																	
D1				D2					D3/D4								
to link the goals with the means				Programme of requirement=service level					life cycle costing				formulas of model				
goals	core business		varying service level= sensitivity analysis	customer oriented requirements	Functional require ments	faillings	Perfor- mance require ments	Innovation	Activi -ties	life time	cause and effects	distribution of probability	D1 management layer	D2 ditto	D3 ditto	D4 ditto	
	1		2	3	4	5	6	7	8				9				
attainability	Netwerk- and mobility management of high ways and water ways																
safety	Watemanagement of the main water systems																
environment	management of the infrasture																
Comfort	additional functions																
a : from 3 to 9 = efficiency b : 1 = effectiveness c : from 1 to 9 = one integral model																	

ZOAB concerns a special paving by which the drainage is stimulated. By this the safety (such as the number of accidents) on the highway is increased. And DAB concerns the traditional paving with no drainage facilities.

The target costs (budgets) of the Ministry of Public Works and Transport for Pavement (inclusive costs of contraflow/traffic) in million euros are represented below for the following years:

Target budgets for pavements on a national level					
2003	2004	2005	2006	2007	2008
168	203	197	189	317	277

2. The budget model

The budget model is illustrated for the efficiency issue. In a budget model the following steps can be distinguished to quantify the efficiency performance indicator:

1. To develop a technical program of requirement
2. To make the economic product costing process transparent (life time cost cycling)
3. To develop a model on both a national and a regional level

a. Program of requirements

Just to get a good insight into the costs of maintenance of pavements, a technical program of requirements needs to be developed. The aim of this program of requirements is to make the functional technical characteristics transparent, to analyze the technical cause-and-effect relationships of the life cycle time of the pavement, and to develop a technical model in which the technical deterioration process is simulated for the life cycle time of the pavement.

The technical functional specifications of pavement concern the following character-istics:

- Attainability (continuous flow of traffic)
- Traffic safety
- Comfort (such as flooding, unevenness)
- Noise pollution (such as maximum of 60 decibels for ZOAB)
- Environment (harmony with the landscape, no pollution)

Some technical road characteristics are:

- Unevenness
- Cross fall (maximum of new road is 2.5% and the intervention level for maintenance is 1%)
- Nonskid quality
- Plucking (stripping of aggregate of ZOAB)

The technical (behavioral) simulation of the deterioration process of ZOAB is based on the following assumptions:

- The right traffic lane has to be replaced after 8 years
- The integral road has to be replaced after 12 years

Based on the results of test road sections, the life time cycle had to be adjusted to 10 years respectively 16 years.

Based on the insight of the technical cause-and-effect relationships, the significant factor at the end of the technical life time of ZOAB is plucking. A similar significant factor for DAB is tracking. For DAB, the technical intervention time for the right traffic lane is 12 years and for the integral replacement of the road 20 years.

b. Product costing

The aim of product costing is to trace costs to products. In this case the product concerns pavement. Based on an input–output analysis, the activities of the life cycle time of the pavement can be described. These necessary activities are the intellectual capital of the Ministry of Transport and Traffic. The cost driver for the end of the life cycle time can be predicted on the basis of the cause-and-effect relationship. The frequent yearly costs concern the cleaning of the hard shoulder for emergency stop and some small repairs. The cleaning activities have to be done because of the restoration of the raindrain (safety). The investment in pavements can be considered as a durable asset that has a certain life cycle time. The stock of performances has to be valued and allocated to the product pavement.

In this context it is assumed that the road surface of the right lane of the product pavement ZOAB has to be replaced every 10 years. And every 16 years the surface of the whole road has to be replaced. The life cycle time of both ZOAB and DAB is represented in Table 26.1.

c. Cost drivers

Based on the insight of the cause-and-effect relationships, the following cost drivers can be distinguished for pavement (ZOAB and DAB):

- Road surface in square meters of pavement
- Type of pavement: ZOAB and DAB
- Age of pavement: ZOAB (Figure 26.4) and DAB

Table 26.1   The life cycle time for ZOAB and DAB

		Cost per Square Meter of Pavement (in Euros)	
Life Cycle Time (Years)	Activity	ZOAB	DAB
1	Cleaning hard shoulder for emergency stop and small repairs	0.16	0.02
10	Replacement of right lane	12.3	
12	Replacement of right lane		13.26
16	Full replacement of road surface	21.37	
20	Full replacement of DAB bt ZOAB		13.25

- Natural ground
- Traffic volume
- Axle road
- The quality of pavement at the moment of road construction
- Weather influences (such as hot summers and cold winters)

At this moment three cost drivers have been selected for the budget model namely:

1. The road surface in square meter of pavement
2. The type of pavement: ZOAB and DAB
3. The age of pavement: ZOAB and DAB

3. Life cycle time and the distribution of probability

The estimation of the life cycle time is based on the technical intellectual capital of the employees of the Ministry of Transport, Public Works and Water Management. But, in practice the real life cycle times of ZOAB and DAB differ. To compensate for the problem of spreading of different life cycle times, the theory of probability has been introduced.

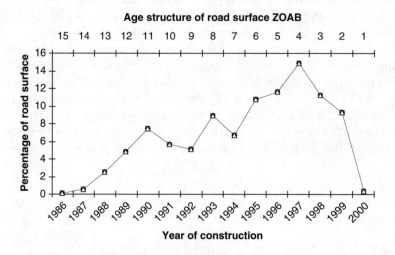

Figure 26.4   Age structure of road surface (ZOAB).

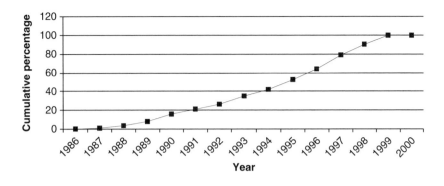

Figure 26.5 Results based on the distribution of probability.

Based on the insight into the age structure of the road sections, the distribution of probability has been made (Figure 26.5). Results are presented in Table 26.2.

4. Model in formula

The last stage of the budget model concerns the development of a formula for quantifying the costs of maintenance/replacement of pavement. The formula is:

$$Y = A \times P \times K$$

where
  Y = costs of maintenance/replacement of pavement
  A = number of net per square meter of pavement differentiated according to age and type of pavement
  P = price per square meter of pavement differentiated according to age and type of pavement
  K = distribution of probability for the total road surface in Holland and differentiated according to the different counties in Holland.

The national budget for the costs of maintenance/replacement of pavement of a budget model is represented in Figure 26.6 based on the following assumptions:

  ■ All the road sections consist of the road surface ZOAB
  ■ The intervention moment for replacement of the road surface is based on the Dienst Weg-en Waterbouw (DWW) criterion of 4% serious plucking

a. Cleaning costs of the hard shoulder for emergency per year

Besides the repetitive costs of replacement of the pavement, the hard shoulder of emergency has to be cleaned on a yearly basis because of prevention requirements. For the year 1999/2000 it is assumed that the total square kilometers (net) can be divided in 7.7 million km^2 of ZOAB and 6.1 million km^2 DAB.
    The yearly cleaning costs are:

  ■ ZOAB: 7.7 km^2 × 10.6 × €0.16 = €1.232 million
  ■ DAB: 6.1 km^2 × 10.6 × €0.02 = €0.122 million

Total: €1.354 million = €1.4 million

Table 26.2 Spreading of Different Life Cycle Times (Bol-de Jong, 2002)

						Age Structure in May 2000			
Year of Construction	Age	Total Road Surface (m²)	Fraction	Percentage	Cumulative Percentage	Age	CritE = 0.04 Fraction (%)	Cumulative percentage	CritE = 0.05 Fraction (%)
1986	15	17150.05	0.000484476	0.05	0.05	1	0.0	0.0	0.0
1987	14	186144.20	0.005258437	0.53	0.57	2	0.0	0.0	0.0
1988	13	896337.42	0.025320876	2.53	3.11	3	0.0	0.0	0.0
1989	12	1699986.94	0.048023387	4.80	7.91	4	0.1	0.1	0.0
1990	11	2641572.93	0.074622502	7.46	15.37	5	1.2	1.2	0.9
1991	10	2020290.64	0.057071732	5.71	21.08	6	2.6	3.8	2.2
1992	9	1806845.87	0.051042073	5.10	26.18	7	3.4	7.3	3.0
1993	8	3158833.63	0.059234738	8.92	35.11	8	3.8	11.1	3.4
1994	7	2380526.99	0.067248145	6.72	41.83	9	4.1	15.2	3.7
1995	6	3827224.03	0.108116278	10.81	52.64	10	4.3	19.5	3.8
1996	5	4105025.21	0.115963958	11.60	64.24	11	4.6	24.0	4.0
1997	4	5265610.73	0.148749649	14.87	79.11	12	5.0	29.1	4.3
1998	3	3982848.92	0.112512567	11.25	90.36	13	5.7	34.8	4.7
1999	2	3278619.33	0.092618596	9.26	99.63	14	7.0	41.8	5.4
2000	1	132130.35	0.003732586	0.37	100.00	15	10.3	52.0	6.6
		35399147.24				16	48.0	100.0	9.4
						17			48.5

C. Service Level Agreement (SLA)

At the moment within the ministry, SLAs are worked out for the different products The aim of this project is to make the effect and cause relationships transparent of changes in the different levels of efficiency of the products in relation to the effectiveness indicators (SLA) and vice versa. The effect of the policy decision to raise the critical success factor of safety of pavement from 7 to 8 can be made transparent to the efficiency cost level of the products (sensitivity analysis). The Dutch SLA of the Ministry of Transport, Public Works and Water Management can be compared with the management model of PPBS in the public sector. The purpose of this management concept in the U.S. in the 1970s was to rationalize the budgeting process of the government by linking the goals with the means. The SLA project of the ministry can be characterized as a version of the balanced scorecard and of the New Zealand model (to link the goals with the means and to solve the measurement problem through the introduction of double bookkeeping).

D. An MIS and a Budget Model of Pavement

McGowan and Lombardo (1986) define an MIS and a DSS as follows:

> Management Information System (MIS) is defined as a computer information system which provides information as a basis for routine, structured decision-making. An example of this type is one in which the output information provides a list of employees eligible for salary increases based on longevity or service to the agency.
> Decision Support sysytem (DSS) is defined as a computer information system which provides information as a basis for nonroutine, semi-structured decision-making. An example of this type of system is one in which the output information provides various policy options for the agency to consider in its dealings with the public and the legislature.

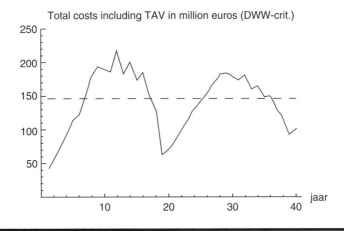

Figure 26.6   National budget for the costs of maintenance/replacement of pavement of a budget model.

continued

	K (DWW)	G (DWW)	Tot	Tot [M€]	Tot incl. TAV [M€]
1.00	1.87	0.72	2.59	38.40	45.70
2.00	2.41	0.94	3.35	49.68	59.12
3.00	3.22	1.19	4.42	65.18	77.57
4.00	3.93	1.52	5.45	80.80	96.15
5.00	4.46	1.96	6.42	96.72	115.09
6.00	4.02	2.60	6.62	105.00	124.95
7.00	3.91	3.64	7.55	125.90	149.83
8.00	4.61	4.57	9.18	154.41	183.75
9.00	4.08	5.32	9.40	163.90	195.05
10.00	4.84	4.71	9.55	160.22	190.66
11.00	4.81	4.59	9.40	157.27	187.15
12.00	5.12	5.63	10.75	183.36	218.19
13.00	3.98	4.96	8.94	154.86	184.29
14.00	3.22	6.08	9.29	169.45	201.64
15.00	1.33	6.09	7.41	146.43	174.25
16.00	1.42	6.58	8.00	158.12	188.16
17.00	1.62	5.00	6.62	126.81	150.90
18.00	1.85	3.95	5.80	107.14	127.50
19.00	2.15	1.27	3.42	53.67	63.87
20.00	2.49	1.43	3.91	61.10	72.71
21.00	2.87	1.73	4.59	72.17	85.88
22.00	3.30	2.05	5.34	84.28	100.29
23.00	3.77	2.40	6.17	97.70	116.27
24.00	4.10	2.80	6.90	110.32	131.29
25.00	4.25	3.27	7.51	122.06	145.26
26.00	3.96	3.81	7.77	130.07	154.78
27.00	3.85	4.44	8.30	142.33	169.37
28.00	4.06	4.89	8.95	154.47	183.82
29.00	3.76	5.11	8.87	155.47	185.01
30.00	3.99	4.73	8.73	150.25	178.80
31.00	3.86	4.62	8.48	146.23	174.01
32.00	3.80	4.96	8.76	152.80	181.83
33.00	3.14	4.58	7.72	136.56	162.51
34.00	2.70	4.95	7.65	138.97	165.37
35.00	1.92	4.78	6.70	125.80	149.71
36.00	2.10	4.73	6.83	126.96	151.09
37.00	2.33	3.80	6.14	109.99	130.89
38.00	2.57	3.18	5.75	99.52	118.43
39.00	2.83	2.07	4.90	79.03	94.05
40.00	3.10	2.32	5.42	87.68	104.33

K = costs of replacement of right traffic lane [road surface in km^2]
G = costs of rehabilitation = total replacement of the road surface [surface in km^2]
Tot = total costs of replacement of road surface [surface in km^2]
Tot[M€] = total costs in millions of €, based on €21,37 per m^2
Total incl. BTW [M€] = total costs in millions of €, based on €21,37 per m^2 and 19%
BTW = Added Tax Value

Figure 26.6 *continued*

According to Hurley and Wallace (1986), a relatively new technology for decision support concerns expert systems:

> The area of expert systems has recently emerged as the leading practical application of Artificial Intelligence (AI) research. Knowledge representation, efficient searching of possibilities, and learning processes are all essential to AI programming.

The intellectual capital of the Ministry of Transport, Public Works and Water Management is specified in the technical and economic programs of requirements of the budget Model. Besides the budget model, the ministry is developing an information system of the infrastructure in which technical information about the assets are stored. The information system is called TISBO = Technical Information System of Facility Management of Construction Works. In this system information can be generated about the number of square meters of the lock chambers, the square meters of the road surface, etc. Based on the TISBO information the budget of the life cycle costs of the products can be calculated through the budget model.

V. SOME FINAL CONCLUSIONS

The following conclusions can be made about a budget model:

- The signaled controversy between FA (balance sheet, loss and profit account, etc.) and MA in the 1960s (Daniel) and 1980s (Kaplan, Cooper) has not been solved as yet. The basis of the measurement of efficiency (and effectiveness) is still based on traditional business administration. The traditional accounting system is not adequate for both FA and MA (MA = Management Information System = MIS). FA should be based on traditional accrual accounting and MA = MIS should be based on cause-and-effect relationships. Nevertheless, the concept of double bookkeeping was introduced in the New Zealand model for the public sector at the end of the 1980s. At the moment in Holland a similar development is taking place in the public sector. Performance budgeting in the public sector concerns traditional accounting. The measurement problem is solved by the introduction of double bookkeeping.
- The new production factor knowledge suffered from a similar information crisis during the last few decades (1970s, 1980s, and 1990s).
- In general the budgets in both the private and the public sector have been historically oriented and based on the two dimensions of bookkeeping (Pacioli). The real world can be styled in a better way through a multidisciplinary approach, i.e., using the structuring principles of other disciplines. In this way budgets become more prospective oriented and contribute to a better performance measurement of strategic planning (effectiveness indicators) and the management control process (efficiency indicators).
- A budget model is a model in which the goals are linked with the means; efficiency is inseparably related to efficiency.
- In the context of government governance the budget model is an instrument to be "In Control" and "accountability" for the stakeholders (account of activities at all management levels, activities are clear, transparent and issued on a timely basis).
- Budget models have advantages because they provide insight into the causal relationships of the transformation process from inputs to outputs.

■ However, some disadvantages are also related to a budget model, such as the increase of the factor complexity.

■ The increase of equations of the Dutch macroeconomic modeling concerned the growth from 24 equations (Tinbergen model of the 1930s) to about 1000 equations of the present macroeconomic model of the CPB (FKSEC, 1992).

■ As a consequence of the introduction of the factor complexity in a MA system, the problem of the controllability of such a system is introduced.

■ Controllability of complexity of models has not yet been solved; especially the use of noneconomic factors in these type of models are of importance.

■ Public-sector accounting can be advanced by using models because it provides a clear structuring of problems.

■ The models can be made independent of traditional accounting; other experience and knowledge can be brought into a budget model; in this way the real world is styled in a budget model in a more adequate way.

■ Considering the trend of the management information crisis in the private and the public sector, it is recommended to introduce the macroconcept of Tinbergen's modeling to individual organizations (microlevel):

■ A budget model is based on the intellectual capital of the Ministry of Transport, Public Works and Water management; the knowledge and experience is laid down in the technical and economical programs of requirements; a budget model can be characterized as an expert system.

REFERENCES

Alter, S., *Information Systems: A Management Perspective*, 2nd ed., The Benjamin/Cummings, Menlo Park, CA, 1996, p. 2.

Ansoff, H.I. and Stewart, J.M., Strategies for a technology-based business, *Harvard Business Review*, 45, 71–83, 1967.

Babad, Y.M. and Balachandran, B.V., Cost driver optimization in activity-based costing, *Accounting Review*, 68, 563–575, 1993.

van den Bol-de Jong, M.E., *Levensduurverdelingen ZOAB*, Delft : Ministerie van Verkeer en Waterstaat, Rijkswaterstaat, Dienst Weg- en Waterbouwkunde, 2002.

Boorsma, P.B. and Mol, N.P., *Privatisering*. – 's-Gravenhage, Stichting Maatschappij en Onderneming, 1983.

Brooks, H., What's happening to the U.S. lead in technology?, *Harvard Business Review*, 50, 110–118, 1972.

Brummet, R.L., Flamholtz, E.G., and Pyle, W.C., Human Resource Accounting in Industry, Personnel Administration, July–August 1969.

Cook, L.G., How to make R & D more productive, *Harvard Business Review*, 44, 145–153, 1966.

Cothran, D.A., Entrepreneurial budgeting: an emerging reform? *Public Administration Review,* 53, 445–454, 1993.

Daniel, R.D., Management information crisis, *Harvard Business Review*, 39, 111–121, 1961.

Davis, J.R., Alderman, C.W., and Robinson, L.A., *Accounting Information Systems*, 3rd ed., John Wiley & Sons, New York, 1990, pp.5–12.

Epstein, P.D., Get ready: the time for performance measurement is finally coming!, *Public Administration Review*, 52, 513–519, 1992.

FKSEC, *A Macro Economic Model for the Netherlands*, Centraal Planbureau,Den Haag, Netherlands, 1992.

Goodsell, C.T., Reinvent government or rediscover it?, Book Reviews, *Public Administration Review*, 53, 85–87, 1993.

Haselbekke, A.G.J., Prestaties van de rijksoverheid, *Openbare uitgaven*, 27, 133–141, 1995.

Hazeu, C.A., Prestatiebegroting op proef: een tussenstand, *Openbare uitgaven*, 12, 298, 1980.

Hurley, M.W. and Wallace, W.A., Expert systems as decision aids for public managers: an assessment of the technology and prototyping as a design strategy, *Public Administration Review*, Special issue, 46, 563–571, 1986.

Jansen, G.S.H. and Maessen, F.C.M.M., Doelmatigheidskengetallen bij de rijksoverheid: een tussenbalans op weg naar transparantie en sturen op resultaat, *Beleidsanalyse*, 25, 3, 20–28, 1996.

Kaplan, R.S., Accounting lag: the obsolescence of cost accounting systems, *California Management Review*, 28, 174–199, 1986.

Kaplan, R.S. and Atkinson, A.A., *Advanced Management Accounting*, 2nd ed., Prentice-Hall, Englewood Cliffs, NJ, 1989.

Kaplan, R.S. and Johnson, H.T., *Relevance Lost: The Rise and Fall of Management Accounting*, Harvard Business School Press, Boston, 1987.

Kaplan, R.S. and Norton, D.P., The balanced scorecard — measures that drive performance, *Harvard Business Review*, 70, 71–79, 1992.

Kaplan, R.S. and Norton, D.P., Putting the balanced scorecard to work, Harvard Business Review, 71, 134–142, 1993.

Keynes, J.M., Professor Tinbergen's method, *The Economic Journal*, 49, 558–568, 1939.

Klaasen, A., Monster, F.H., Sloterdijk, M.O., and Vlotman, F.W. (redactie), *Toepassen van aandeelhouderswaarde*, Kluwer Bedrijfswetenschappen, Deventer, 1995 (Finem-rapporten; 10).

Kooiman, J., *Modern Governance: New Government-Society Interactions*, Sage, London, 1993.

Lee, R.D., Jr., A quarter century of state budgeting practices, *Public Administration Review*, 2, 133–140, 1997.

McGowan, R.P. and Lombardo, G.A., Decision support systems in state government: promises and pitfalls, *Public Administration Review*, 46, 579–583, 1986.

Metcalfe, L., Public management: from imitation to innovation, *Australian Journal of Public Administration*, 52, 292–304, 1993.

Moe, R.C., The "Reinventing Government" exercise: misinterpreting the problem, misjudging the consequences, *Public Administration Review*, 55, 111–122, 1994.

Morgan, G., *Images of Organizations*, Sage, London, 1986.

Nathan, R.P., Reinventing government: what does it mean?, *Public Administration Review*, 55, 213–215, 1995.

O'Brien, J.A., *Management Information Systems: A Managerial End User Perspective*, 2nd ed., Irwin, Homewood, Boston, 1993, pp. 14–20.

Osborne, D. and Gaebler, T., *Reinventing Government*, McGraw-Hill, New York, 1993, p. 121.

Pallot, J., "Newer than New" Public Management: Financial Management and Collective Strategizing in New Zealand, Conference on the New Public Management in International Perspective, St. Gallen, p. 18–19, 1996.

Perlitz, M., Schug, K., and Schrank, R., Target-Budgeting for Research and Development, Modelling Techniques for Business Process Re-engineering and Benchmaking, IFIP TC5 WG5. Seventh International Workshop on Modelling Techniques for Business Process Re-engineering and Benchmarking, 18–19 Apr. 1996, Bordeaux, France, Documeingts, G. and Browne, J., Eds, Chapman, London, pp. 3–15, 1997.

Poot, J.K., Performance budgeting: a perspective on modeling and strategic planning in the public sector in Holland, in *Performance Management in the Public Sector*, Eburon, Delft, 1997, pp. 228–233.

Rhodes, J.B., "The American challenge" challenged, *Harvard Business Review*, September–October, 1969.

Rhodes R.A.W. Ed., The new public management. *Public Administration*, 69, 1–2, 1991.

Schick, A., Budgeting for results: recent developments in five industrialized countries, *Public Administration Review*, 50, 26, 1990.

Starreveld, R.W., Mare, H.B. de, and Joels, E.J., *Bestuurlijke informatieverzorging, (deel I), Algemene grondslagen*, 3e druk, 1991, p. 88.

Strausmann, J. and Bozeman, B., Shrinking budgets and the shrinkage of budget theory, *Public Administration Review*, 42, 509–515, 1982.

The Netherlands Ministry of Finance, *Government governance: corporate governance in the public sector, why and how?*, The Hague, The Netherlands Ministry of Finance, Government Audit Policy Directorate (DAR), 2000.

Thompson, F. and Jones, L.R., Reinventing the Pentagon: How the New Public Management Can Bring Institutional Renewal, 1994, Book Review.

Tinbergen, J., Notes and memoranda on a method of statistical business cycle research. A reply, *The Economic Journal*, 50, 141–154, 1940.

27

ANALYSIS AND COMMUNICATION FOR PUBLIC BUDGETING

Carl Grafton
Auburn University

Anne Permaloff
Auburn University

CONTENTS

I. Introduction 464
II. The key question 464
    A. Reformers and pragmatists 464
    B. Jeffersonian budgeting 465
III. Economics-based budget reforms 466
    A. Classic performance budgeting 466
    B. Program budgeting 468
    C. Program budgeting and the relationships between activities,
       outputs, and outcomes 472
    D. The impact of program budgeting 474
    E. Zero-base budgeting (ZBB) 475
    F. Performance budgeting 475
IV. An example of a contemporary performance budgeting system: Louisiana 479
    A. Contemporary performance budgeting elsewhere in the U.S. 481
V. Software tools 482
VI. Conclusions 484
References 485

ABSTRACT

Today all levels of government are using a variety of budgeting techniques and research methodologies. Relatively inexpensive and common computing tools permit these budgeting and analytical techniques to be used quickly, accurately, and less expensively than would have been the case only a few years ago. Computer tools also permit great improvements in the production and dissemination on the Internet of budgetary information transparent to the public and their legislative and news media representatives. However, important lessons learned in relation to the budgetary techniques need to be applied.

I. INTRODUCTION

For more than a half century public administrators have been trying to substitute economics-based criteria for politics in budget formulation. Today the federal government, states, and localities are using mixtures of budgeting techniques developed since the early 1950s, including classical performance budgeting with its workload emphasis, program budgeting, and contemporary performance budgeting with its quantitative indicators of outputs and outcomes, as well as specific methodologies, such as benefit–cost analysis, regression analysis, interrupted time series analysis, complex time series analysis for forecasting, and pivot tables. Relatively inexpensive and common computing tools permit all of these budgeting and analytical techniques to be used more quickly, accurately, and less expensively than would have been the case only a few years ago.

In addition to benefiting analysis, computer tools permit great improvements in the production and dissemination on the Internet of information transparent to the public and their legislative and news media representatives.

II. THE KEY QUESTION

According to Wildavsky (1985: 1), a budget is a document containing "words and figures that propose expenditures for certain objects and purposes." Writing in 1940 V. O. Key, Jr., identified the basic problem of budgeting: "On what basis shall it be decided to allocate X dollars to activity A instead of activity B?" (p. 1138). Both quotes suggest that the amount of total spending for all governmental objects, purposes, and activities is a matter to be determined as part of the budgetary process. Key also made the point that the budget "represents a judgment upon how scarce means should be allocated to bring the maximum return in social utility" (p. 1138).

Judgments regarding the allocation of scarce means (dollars) among government programs are often the center of intense interest group struggles, i.e., politics. The total size of budgets and how funds are allocated within budgets are frequently the battlegrounds of elections for legislative and executive office at all levels of government. The budgetary wars often continue after new executives and legislators are sworn in, and the conflict rarely ends throughout their terms of office.

For well over half a century critics have argued that government budgets should be formulated in a better way than by brute politics. In particular, reformers have tried to apply the logic of economics to budgeting. Key's description of budgeting as a judgment regarding how scarce resources should be allocated to produce the maximum return in social utility was an early example of this approach. In the same vein, Key quoted economist Arthur Pigou, "Expenditure should be distributed between battleships and poor relief in such wise that the last shilling devoted to each of them yields the same real return" (Key, 1940: 1139). Pigou meant that in a perfect budget there would be no way to redistribute funds to produce a larger total return or societal benefit.

A. Reformers and Pragmatists

Since Key and Pigou wrote and even before, the literature on budget reform has been divided into two camps. On one side are reformers who advocate procedures and techniques that they see as moving budgetary decision-making toward the kind of rational economics-based logic suggested by Key and Pigou. Key had reservations about these reformers, describing them this way, "Toilers in the budgetary field have busied themselves primarily with the organization and procedure for budget preparation, the forms for the submission of requests for funds, the form of the budget document itself, and like questions" (Key, 1940: 1137).

Standing against reformers are pragmatists who argue in the words of Alabama Governor James E. Folsom, Sr., "You can't take the politics out of politics" (Grafton and Permaloff, 1985: 135). Folsom's dictum applied to budget reform means that any attempt to distance budgeting from politics merely changes the venue of politics from one location, such as the legislature, to another place, such as a group of (unelected) budget analysts working for the mayor, governor, or president. Judgments regarding the amounts that should be spent on battleships, poor relief, and thousands of other worthy and sometimes unworthy expenditures are inherently value laden, interest based, and un-quantifiable. It is the job of the executive and legislative branches to balance these political forces to formulate budgets. In an optimistic mood, Key appeared to side with the pragmatists when he suggested that politics constitutes a kind of marketplace with the resulting budgets reflecting, "the social consensus on the relative values of different services" (Key, 1940: 1143). Key argued that until reformers answer basic questions about how political interests are to be resolved, mechanical changes in budget proced-ures and forms will have little effect.

Both pragmatists and economics-based reformers have tended to assume that budget-ary politics and policymaking have been conducted within the confines of a representa-tive democracy. Pragmatists tend to characterize budgetary politics as a struggle among competing interest groups in the executive and legislative branches. The electorate participates only through their interest group memberships and periodically in elections. The image of budgetary policymaking presented by early economics-based reformers is even narrower in scope: executive branch and to a lesser degree legislative staff use analytical tools to develop policy choices that aid executive branch budget formulation and legislative branch budgetary decision-making. To some degree, reformers see analy-sis as counterbalancing the influence of raw politics; few reformers are so naive as to believe that analysis can take the politics out of budgeting.

B. Jeffersonian Budgeting

In recent years a new influence that emphasizes the need for broader participation in budgeting has appeared, especially in state and local governments. It has been acceler-ated or intensified by the financial crises experienced by state governments and many local governments following the September 11, 2001 attack and the subsequent eco-nomic downturn together with private-sector accounting dishonesty exemplified by Enron. This broadening of participation has been greatly facilitated by the placement of budgets for most states and cities on the Internet. Only a few years ago finding a current state budget required considerable effort. Now most jurisdictions make at least summar-ies of their budgets available on the Internet. Citizens and the news media interested in how tax dollars are being spent can find considerable information with little effort. However, most of these documents are still difficult to interpret, and citizens concerned with why services are being cut and taxes increased are asking questions and demanding clear answers. In the private sector, corporate stock holders victimized by deceptive accounting practices are also asking questions and demanding clear answers. What citizens and stock holders both require is often called transparency. They want to be able to read, understand, and trust financial statements. All of this is consistent with the democratic Jeffersonian standard of a well-informed electorate. We could call it Jeffersonian budgeting.

III. ECONOMICS-BASED BUDGET REFORMS

Economics-based budget reforms have appeared in waves, and elements of these reforms remain in budgeting processes for many local and state governments and the federal government. Each wave has taught us lessons about what works and what does not. In particular, we have learned a great deal about the limits and opportunities afforded by economics-based reforms as well as how these reforms can be enhanced by contemporary computer tools. To absorb these lessons we must understand the reasons reforms were introduced.

A. Classic Performance Budgeting

The first reform wave appeared in mature form in the 1950s (U.S. Commission on Organization of the Executive Branch of the Government, 1949; Schick, 1966). This reform was called performance budgeting, not to be confused with the current and broader approach of the same name. We call the 1950s version classic performance budgeting. Classic performance budgeting focuses on spending by discrete government activities, such as training, regulation, highway construction, research, refuse collection, and executive direction (Schick, 1966; Wanat, 1978; Lee et al., 2004: 117). Classic performance budgeting consists of two basic parts: first, cost analyses of all the activities that a government agency performs, and second, forecasts of amounts of those activities that will be needed in the next fiscal year. The budget is generated by multiplying the cost of each unit of an activity by forecasts of the number of units required in the next fiscal year and then adding these projected costs for each activity.

Classic performance budgeting was used for a number of years by the state universities of Indiana. The system saw teaching as the central activity of the institution. Teaching was divided into courses, and the cost of conducting each course was calculated. The largest cost of each course was the instructor's salary or more precisely the percentage of an instructor's salary devoted to a given course. Added to the instructor's salary were administrative costs, library costs (derived by studies of library usage by various kinds of students), heating, and the like (Grafton, 1970). Classic performance budgeting's close ties to cost accounting are readily apparent (Schick, 1966). Once the cost of each course was calculated, the number of each course to be taught in the next biennium (Indiana's budget was biennial) was estimated (McKeown, 1989; Center for State Higher Education Policy and Finance, 1991). By multiplying the cost of each course by the estimated number of such courses to be offered and adding the result, a large portion of the institutional budget could be derived. As a graduate assistant in the 1960s one of the authors was employed in the Purdue University office that managed this system. Initially, this process was done by hand, but later it was computerized.

Schick (1966: 252–253) emphasized that classic performance budgeting was much more useful to executive branch managers than to policymakers in the chief executive's office and the legislature, "Does it really help top officials if they know that it cost $0.07 to wash a pound of laundry or that the average postal employee processes 289 items of mail per hour? These are the main fruits of [classic] performance measurements, and they have an important place in the management of an organization."

> Classic performance budgeting can be useful for internal organizational management.

Ideally, managers are primarily concerned with implementing policy efficiently and effectively. The difference between efficiency and effectiveness is central to understanding budget reform. In general terms, efficiency is the ratio of useful energy delivered by a system (output) to the energy supplied to it (input). For government the result is a ratio of a service delivery measure to all the costs related to producing the service. Internal agency cost data can make a valuable contribution to decisions regarding efficiency but little to effectiveness.

Internal agency cost data provide little assistance to answering questions about effectiveness, i.e., the questions posed by Key and Pigou. In particular, cost data say nothing about whether an activity whose cost is being measured is worthwhile. The state universities of Indiana could measure the cost of a class on basketball coaching and a doctoral-level chemistry seminar, but the relative merits of the two offerings were not assessed. However, if cost data are combined with information about the benefits that an activity yields, the cost data can help policymakers select activities that yield the greatest benefit for the lowest cost.

> Classic performance budgeting by itself provides no information about the effectiveness of government activities.

In addition to its usefulness for managerial purposes, classic performance budgeting can reduce conflict at the policymaking level. It was introduced in Indiana when conflict among the state universities became so intense that legislators and governors became annoyed. Using classical performance budgeting a large portion of the university budgets was generated more or less automatically, and conflict among the universities was drastically reduced. Today, some state university coordinating boards prepare budget submissions using similar but usually less refined classic performance budgeting techniques. Typically, instead of determining costs for each individual course, the costs of producing credit hours are calculated for undergraduates, master's students, and doctoral students.

> Classic performance budgeting can reduce budgetary conflict.

Because classic performance budgeting by itself is not very useful to legislators or even high-level executive branch policymakers, it provides relatively little help to citizens or the news media as they try to make sense of government budgets.

> Classic performance budgeting by itself can provide little useful information to legislators, the news media, and the general public.

B. Program Budgeting

The second wave of economics-based budget reforms grew partly out of the realization that classic performance budgeting failed to address concerns about effectiveness expressed by Key and Pigou. The second-wave reforms, most closely associated with the 1960s and the administrations of Presidents John F. Kennedy and Lyndon B. Johnson, are known as: program budgeting; planning, programming, and budgeting (PPB); or PPB systems (PPBS). A decision-making technique called benefit–cost analysis is usually considered to be part of the second wave of reforms.

Where classic performance budgeting focuses exclusively on internal government activities, such as teaching a class, sorting mail, or inspecting meat, program budgeting and related techniques (PPB and PPBS) concentrate on government outputs and outcomes (see Figure 27.1). For example, in the case of university budgeting the emphasis would shift from the cost of offering a course to the merits of a course, or more, importantly the relative merits of all courses and the relative merits of different ways of offering courses (e.g., at community colleges vs. universities vs. online for the first two years of study), and the possibility that some students might be better off in technical–vocational institutions or by not participating in postsecondary education at all. In other words, program budgeting is intended to address elements of the Key–Pigou question (Dugan and Hernon, 2002).

Program budgeting tries to identify government activities (outputs) carried on to serve specific clients. Axelrod (1995: 40–41) provides the example of meat inspection performed by the state of Wisconsin. The inspection work measured in various ways is the output. The clients are meat consumers. The output might be the number of diseased or spoiled carcases discovered. The result, impact, or outcome of the work could be measured by numbers of cases of illness caused by tainted meat. The best indicator of effective inspection work would be zero cases of illness. Classic performance budgeting statistics would be the number of carcases inspected by each employee, and the average cost of each inspection. Such a statistic reveals nothing about the quality of work done or the effect of inspections on public health (Brown and Pyers, 1988: 736).

In program budgeting and later budgeting reforms, agency activities and outputs are sometimes distinguishable, but more often fuzzy. Activities and outputs are distinguishable if the activities and the measures of the activities do not directly impact clients, e.g., number of meat inspections. What directly impacts meat consumers is the number of diseased or spoiled carcases discovered and kept off the market. With the example of university courses the distinction between activities and outputs is less clear. Individual university courses, the central activity of universities, directly impact students. The focus of original performance budgeting was the cost of each class while the focus of program budgeting is the quality of classes and alternative ways of delivering classes to students. The tendency of program budgeting and later budgeting reforms is to treat agency activities and outputs as one and the same.

Activities or outputs are sometimes called program elements in the terminology of program budgeting. A program is a collection of related activities or program elements. Thus in Axelrod's example, meat inspection is part of an activity or program element called food inspection, which in turn is part of a program called food and trade regulation, which in turn is part of a function called agriculture. Thus functions, programs, subprograms, and activities or program elements form a pyramidal structure. State government as a whole might be divided among a dozen or so functions, each function

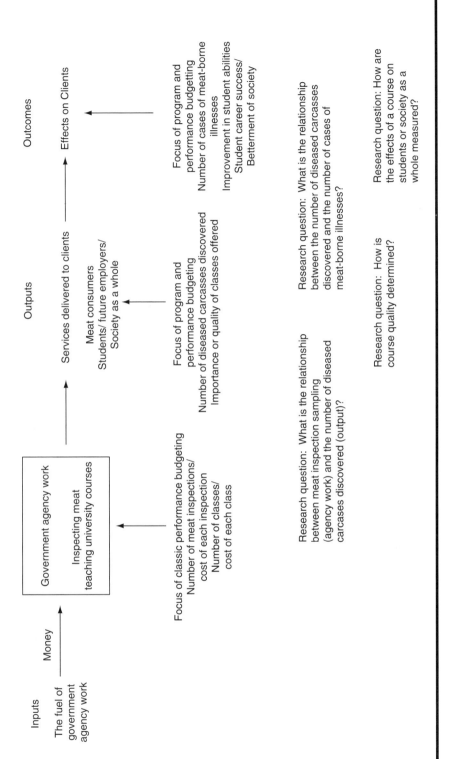

Figure 27.1 Budgeting and budget reform critical connections.

might be divided among a dozen programs, each program into a dozen subprograms, and each subprogram into a dozen activities or program elements. If the number of each division in this example is exactly 12, there are $12 \times 12 \times 12 \times 12$, or 20,736, activities or program elements. This pyramid of functions, programs, subprograms, and activities is called a program structure.

When budget reformers began thinking about determining the costs of related government activities, they realized that existing budget formats were not adequate (Novick, 1954). A particular way of laying out budgetary words and figures is called a format. These words and figures can be arrayed in infinitely varied ways.

In the 1950s virtually all government budgets were structured by organizational unit using the line item or object of expenditure format. Table 27.1 shows a recent example for a state agency called Management Services. The figures are in thousands of dollars. This agency is engaged in a number of activities, but it is impossible to determine from this example how much is being spent on each. Furthermore, it is likely that other agencies are performing activities similar to those of Management Services, making it even more difficult to measure total expenditures for these activities.

The line-item budget is the oldest and simplest budget format. Its primary purpose is expenditure (the inputs in Figure 27.1) control. Its expenditure categories represent what can be thought of as the fuel or inputs of government, not the outputs or activities. A program budget contains expenditure categories structured by outputs or activities.

> Simple line item budgets typically reveal little about what government is producing or what effect it is having on clients.

Program budgeting as it was formulated in the 1960s was extraordinarily ambitious. The program structure was supposed to be arranged by activities performed for particular purposes, usually for specific groups or clients. If the group or clientele in question was, for example, children, the programs might be administered by agencies scattered throughout a state government concerned with education, welfare, health, and criminal justice. Such administrative divisions were to be of no importance in the program budget; this format was meant to span organizational lines to determine how much was being spent throughout government on the related outputs of government (Novick, 1972, 2002; Sallack and Allen, 1987: 39). At the state level we have observed few instances of this original pure form of program budgeting. Most state budgets are still arranged organizationally.

One reason for the scarcity of program budgets tied to functions rather than a government's organizational structure is the enormous amount of time, effort, and expense required to produce what amounts to a second budget. A state budget is a large document,

Table 27.1   Line-Item Budget Example

Component Expenditures	Actuals (FY 2000)	Authorized (FY 2001)	Governor (FY 2002)
Personal services	2114.0	2350.2	2585.9
Travel	19.7	32.2	32.2
Contractual	448.4	312.2	312.2
Supplies	40.1	44.6	44.6
Equipment	62.5	35.0	35.0
Expenditure totals	2684.7	2774.2	3009.9

as are many city and county budgets. Earlier we gave the example of a four-layer program budget, with each layer divided into 12 parts totaling 20,736 activities. Even if each of ten state government functions contains only ten programs, each program ten subprograms, and each subprogram ten activities, we would still have 10,000 activities, and $8 \times 8 \times 8 \times 8$ gives 4,096 activities. Making matters worse, there is no single system for dividing government work into functional and programmatic categories (Grafton and Permaloff, 2000). To a substantial degree, the categories are arbitrary, and they might easily be changed from one governor or president, mayor, or county commission to the next.

The budget of the state of Hawaii is one of the purest examples of program budgeting. The Hawaii government's organizational structure is substantially different from the budget program structure. The reader can confirm this by comparing the two online. Hawaii's (2001) budget begins its discussion of program budgeting by listing its highest-level program (Level I) categories (what Axelrod [1995] calls functions): economic development, employment, transportation facilities and services, environmental protection, wealth, social services, formal education, culture and recreation, public safety, individual rights, and governmentwide support (p. 5). The Hawaii budget then describes its program structure's pyramidal nature, "Within each of these 11 programs is a hierarchical structure of subordinate programs disaggregated into levels to the extent that meaningful resource allocation decisions can be made thereon. In most cases, this has meant a disaggregation to four or five levels" (p. 5).

The bottom of a program structure should consist of activities — where government is accomplishing something for clients (or *to* clients in the case of prisons). What Hawaii's budget lists at the bottom of its program structure is often not at the activity level because it is much too broad. For example, two activities at the bottom of the Hawaii program structure are Business Services and the Foreign Trade Zone. Appropriation figures attached to these broad categories are no more revealing and informative than comparable organizational line-item budget amounts.

A program structure independent of a government's organizational structure is no guarantee that a budget will reveal what government is producing or what effect it is having on clients.

The Hawaii budget fails to reach down to the activity level for all programs and is singularly uninformative regarding activity outputs or outcomes at least as the budget is available on the Internet. Furthermore, even if the Hawaii program structure was fully broken down to the activity level, the reader would know little about the cost of these activities. Even sketchy explanations of activities are absent from the budget. One must move to individual agency web pages to find such explanations, and those explanations are typically unaccompanied by cost or output data or studies regarding outcomes. Thus the Hawaii budget, while having a program structure free of the government's organization structure, does not come close to answering the Key–Pigou question. Also, it does not answer the most basic questions that a citizen or reporter might pose. It is not transparent.

Like Hawaii's program structure, the state of Pennsylvania's original PPBS system was independent of organizational lines. Furthermore, the bottom of the structure consisted of activities with associated costs. But, according to Sallack and Allen (1987: 42), this "system was overly ambitious, and overestimated the capacity of both the executive and legislative branches to devise and manage the date (sic) presented by the system … the state government found it difficult to develop the technology in management information and accounting systems to maintain and administer PPBS." Making matters worse, with program categories scattered over multiple agencies it was impossible to assign accountability to any one agency for the success or failure of a program (p. 43). Sallack and Allen added, "The crossing of the traditional departmental lines for the purpose of budget and decision-making created many problems, including insufficient accountability for program impacts, and difficulty in allocating dollar resources across agencies. From a legislative perspective, the commonwealth program structure often caused confusion in appropriation hearings because of multi-agency responsibility for programs" (p. 43).

> A program structure independent of a government's organizational structure has several important drawbacks: it is expensive to create and administer; it may make it difficult to assign accountability to any one agency for the success or failure of a program or activity; and it may cause confusion in the legislative budgetary process.

Pennsylvania redesigned its program structure so that each program was the responsibility of a single agency. As a consequence of this necessary change Pennsylvania has lost its ability to perform "cross-agency analysis concerning program activity"(Sallack and Allen, 1987: 47). Most other practitioners of program budgeting have followed Pennsylvania's example either by changing back to an organizational focus or by beginning with program structures that adhere to organizational constraints.

C. Program Budgeting and the Relationships between Activities, Outputs, and Outcomes

Even more difficult than establishing a program structure free of a government's organizational structure is understanding the relationships between activities, outputs, and outcomes. Determining the cost of activities (the realm of original performance budgeting) is relatively simple, but moving to outputs and (even more difficult) outcomes is not. Again, referring to Figure 27.1, assuming that inspecting every carcass is impossible because of cost, what sampling techniques insure that diseased carcasses will be found within an acceptable level of risk? And, are there alternative agency work techniques (e.g., irradiation) that can more effectively reduce the number of diseased carcasses discovered? Also, what is the relationship between the number of diseased carcasses discovered and the number of cases of meat-borne illnesses? Answering these questions requires time and effort, and the irradiation example suggests that new technologies can change established answers.

Turning to higher education, the other example in Figure 27.1, what combinations of courses in what combinations of institutions (e.g., community colleges or four-year universities) are best for students? In this context, what does "best" mean? How are course quality and the best mixture of courses to be determined or even defined? Here the clients are not just students but their future employers and society as a whole that potentially benefit from the work of university graduates. Shifting to outcomes, how do we measure the effects of courses on students, student career success (which occurs years after they have left school), and the betterment of society (however that is defined). Unlike the meat inspection example, all of these questions are difficult to define let alone measure.

Even if it is possible to measure the effect of a particular set of government activities on outputs and the effect of outputs on outcomes, it is often difficult to attach a dollar value to the outcomes. For example, how much is it worth to meat consumers and taxpayers to insure to 100% certainty that no one will become mildly ill because of bad meat? In addition, the benefits of government activities are notoriously difficult to measure.

Making matters even more complex, a central question in budgeting is not just what benefits are created at a given cost (a difficult question to answer for most activities), but what effect will changes in funding have on output levels and after that benefit changes. There is no way to determine the relationship between funding levels and outcome benefits without time-consuming and expensive empirical research.

Answering the Key–Pigou question essentially requires that an entire government budget be subjected to an enormous set of benefit–cost analyses. In addition to the complications discussed above, to be fully useable benefit–cost analysis requires that all benefits (and costs) be rendered in dollars. In the case of meat inspection that would mean that we would have to attach a dollar value to lives and to the pain suffered from fatal and nonfatal cases of food poisoning. Since many government programs have lives saved as benefits, there is a substantial literature on how lives are valued in terms of dollars, but there is widespread disagreement within that literature (e.g., Schmid, 1989; Nas, 1996; Boardman et al., 2001). A thorough benefit–cost analysis would probably require the use of several life-valuation methods to determine whether the analysis is sensitive to these differing methods. Attaching at least approximate dollar values to university programs is probably easier at least in so far as the enhanced future earnings of college graduates are concerned.

> An idealized economics-based budgetary process requires that we know the dollar value of outcomes and that we know the marginal benefit of marginal changes in outcomes. These measurements are often impossible to achieve.

Answering the Key–Pigou question throughout a government's budget (federal, state, or local) requires much more than deciding on optimal funding levels for each individual activity. The heart and soul of budgeting is making choices among funding levels for many different activities: funding levels among prison systems, universities, primary and secondary schools, traffic control, highway construction, and so forth. In theory this would require analysts to determine the benefits in dollars to society of each activity and the marginal (additional) benefits to society of marginal (additional) funding for each activity or the marginal negative benefits to society of reductions in funding. Such a governmentwide analysis is impossible even in theory if only because of the benefit valuation problem.

> A rigorous answer to the Key–Pigou question requires comparisons among government activities so that funds can be allocated where they will do the most good. Such comparisons are mostly impossible to make except intuitively and politically.

The best that program budgeting can do is to generate cost data (using original performance budgeting cost analysis) that shed light on the intuitive judgements that chief executive and lawmakers are obliged to make, and to permit citizens in the tradition of Jeffersonian governance to know how their tax dollars are being spent.

D. The Impact of Program Budgeting

Has program budgeting made a difference? In other words, would dollars be distributed differently with and without a program budget? It would be difficult to make this case statistically, and we know of no one who has. We are essentially asking what would have happened if a state or locality that has switched to program budgeting had stayed with traditional pragmatic budgeting using a line-item format. The impact of other factors such as an election campaign immediately before or after the introduction of the new budgeting system, a new chief executive and legislature or council, and an economic downturn or upturn could swamp the effect of a new budget format. Making matters even more difficult is the fact that new approaches to budgeting are often phased in over a period of years or characterized by a long break-in period when many modifications occur; the difference between the end of the old system and the complete installation of the new system may be half a decade. This long phase-in or break-in period also allows such factors as the political and economic environments to play even larger roles than might be the case if there were a sharp break between old and new. The impact of program budgeting will probably never be measured by differences in spending before and after reform.

> Attempts to determine empirically whether changes in budgeting systems have changed the ways dollars are allocated have failed.

A less rigorous standard than one requiring that dollar apportionments be affected requires only that a budget reform such as program budgeting merely affect approaches to decision-making. This is a more manageable problem methodologically. Pettijohn and Grizzle (1997) examined U.S. House Appropriations Committee subcommittee hearings for five federal agencies that had been the focus of earlier studies also attempting to detect the effect of budget formats on decision-making. Pettijohn and Grizzle limited their analysis to 1949 to 1984, years that saw the introduction of classic performance budgeting and PPBS and enactment of the Congressional Budget and Impoundment Control Act of 1974. They analyzed the hearings in terms of the types of questions asked. Following the introduction of classic performance budgeting there was an 8% increase in programmatic themes and an 8.29% drop in line-item expenditure themes (p. 35). PPBS had an even larger impact — an 18.36% increase in programmatic themes and a 13.59% reduction in line-item themes (p. 34).

Similarly, Sallack and Allen (1987) concluded that while Pennsylvania's modified, limited PPBS system was far from its ideal beginnings, it represented a marked improvement over the purely political budgeting of a few decades before. And while a modified, limited PPBS system such as Pennsylvania's falls short of answering the Key–Pigou question, it might go a long way toward informing citizens and the media, who might bring their own values to bear on questions regarding the dollar worth of particular government activities. Limited program budgeting is extremely common. It is found in combination with the traditional line-item format. The most recent reform called performance budgeting (to be discussed later) is also often a part of program budgets.

> Different budgeting systems change legislative decision-making approaches in predictable directions.

E. Zero-Base Budgeting (ZBB)

Like performance budgeting, ZBB has two meanings. The first was related to program budgeting and was rarely if ever written with the capitalized initials ZBB. Some early program budgeting advocates claimed that budgets should be reconsidered every year from the ground up as if there were no base and as if there were a possibility that agency budgets could be eliminated. The base is typically defined as last year's budget plus a little for inflation or minus a little because of an economic downturn. It quickly became apparent that such a total reconsideration of the entire budget was not feasible or even desirable (Merewitz and Sosnick, 1979). For example, in a state budget no one seriously believes that we can or should think about budgets for the prison system, the public universities, or myriad other established programs and agencies as if we were rethinking their very existence every fiscal year. Furthermore, many programs fulfill statutory requirements so that zeroing them out of existence would mean that those statutes would also have to be eliminated.

> Zero base budgeting that seeks to reconsider budgets every year from the ground up as if there was no base has never been a working feature of any budgeting system.

A newer and more reasonable form of zero-base budgeting was abbreviated with the capitalized initials ZBB. This ZBB was originated by Texas Instruments, Inc. executive Peter A. Pyhrr and embraced by Georgia Governor and President Jimmy Carter (Pyhrr, 1970; Sarant, 1978). Pyhrr–Carter ZBB's emphasis was on evaluating the marginal impact of various funding levels for agency activities.

Unlike program budgeting, ZBB was explicitly tied to organization structure. While ZBB had some advantages over program budgeting, it faded quickly from use as soon as its primary advocate, Jimmy Carter, left the presidency in 1981. Establishing a ZBB system involves a great deal of effort, and there is little evidence that it made much of a difference (Schick, 1978). Describing Oregon's ZBB system, McCaffery (1981: 52) wrote, "Agency personnel had to cope with increased paperwork and more forms as a result of detailed summaries at various levels of the process and the redundancy in forms. This resulted in an extremely time-consuming process." McCaffery reported that the Oregon ZBB process encouraged administrators to think about budgetary and policy issues creatively, but this sort of anecdotal evidence was not sufficient to save ZBB (p. 55).

> ZBB was costly and time consuming, and there is little evidence that it was beneficial.

F. Performance Budgeting

Beginning roughly in the late 1980s a new generation of economics-based reformers introduced a loosely related set of techniques they labeled performance budgeting, performance-based budgeting, PBB, or program-based performance budgeting. The overlap in names with those used in the 1950s leads us to label these techniques as contemporary performance budgeting to avoid confusion.

In general, contemporary performance budgeting refers to the inclusion of outcome measures in the budget. Meagan M. Jordan and Merl M. Hackbart distinguish between performance budgeting (defined as we have just done) and performance funding, by which they mean that decisions regarding allocation of dollars are "contingent upon" performance measures (Jordan and Hackbart, 1999). Ideally, contemporary performance budgeting identifies activities (outputs) and studies the effect they are having (outcomes), also an objective of program budgeting. Performance information is then used in executive budget formulation and legislative decision-making. In practice, many local and state governments and the federal government include performance measures in their budgets, but there is little evidence that the presence of the measures is anything but decorative. The reader need only examine budgets on the Internet to determine the validity of this observation.

Jordan and Hackbart's term performance funding seeks to rule out the use of performance measures for ornamentation, but their phrase "contingent upon" is broad and could include the possibility that factors other than performance influence budgetary decisions. Other writers distinguish between the use of performance measures for executive branch management (with no direct impact on the budget) and budgeting. It is notable that much of the sizeable and rapidly growing literature on performance measurement devotes considerably more attention to executive branch management than to budgeting (National Center for Public Productivity, 1997; Poister and Streib, 1999; Berman and Wang, 2000; Ammons et al., 2001; Heinrich, 2002).

The introduction of the new performance budgeting is usually credited to the Government Accounting Standards Board (GASB). In 1985 GASB passed a resolution encouraging state and local governments to experiment with performance indicators for service efforts and accomplishments. The trend toward performance budgeting was endorsed by the U.S. Congress with the passage of the Government Performance and Results Act of 1993 (P.L. 103-62), which requires federal agencies to develop multiyear and annual performance-based plans. There is no attempt to produce a program structure, although if a program structure exists performance budgeting can adapt to it and is probably better for it.

> Performance budgeting does not require a program structure that is independent of a government's organizational structure.

Schedler (1994: 44) describes what he sees as the basic requirements for an effective performance measurement system whether tied to budgeting or just used for management: "(1) objectives must be clear, measurable, and consistent; (2) performance of the administration must be unambiguously defined and measured; (3) costs of production must be able to be determined; and (4) access to information must be available at any time."

Schedler describes some but not all of the practical problems associated with each of his requirements. With regard to the first, he emphasizes that objectives are not likely to be permanent or universally agreed to in a democracy, "Objectives still are, and will be, an issue for continuous political debate in parliament [or Congress, the legislature, county commission, or city council], whose duty it is to scrutinize, reassess, and negotiate issues of policy and governance" (p. 45).

In elaborating on his second requirement for a performance measurement system, Schedler asserts the primacy of the politics–administration dichotomy. The politics–administration dichotomy was a concept developed by Wilson (1941) in 1887. Wilson, observing public administration choked by Jacksonian Spoils politics, suggested that administration should be and could be devoted to the efficient implementation of public policy (developed through the political process in the legislature) without political interference. Wilson's politics–administration dichotomy is the intellectual foundation (together with Max Weber's model of bureaucracy) of scientific public administration and to some degree economics-based budget reforms.

The process of defining and measuring performance, according to Schedler's experience in Switzerland, should be under the complete control of the executive:

> Neither residents of a city nor the parliament is, due to size, able to define clearly, carefully, and accurately two hundred different products or services … as was done in a project directed by the author for the city of Berne. Therefore, product/service plans should be prepared in the administration before parliamentary debate, and the government should present the fully formulated plans for approval by parliament. The objective of performance budgeting is to make the financial consequences of the fully articulated performance plan clear to parliament. The role of parliament is to either adopt or change the proposed product plan but not to become involved in the detailed financial aspects of budgeting. Economic measures should be decided on the basis of cutting product/service plans, goals, targets, and activities, not by cutting budgets. The latter is just the consequence. The change of perspective from debating budgets to debating performance contracts and agreements is a great step toward forging a completely new way of thinking in the public sector (Schedler, 1994: 45)

Schedler's rather lifeless references to the formulation of performance measures fails to mirror the politics of the American experience. For example, in developing its performance measurement system the state of Louisiana has witnessed disagreement among governor's budget office personnel, executive line administrators, and legislators about the content of long- and short-term plans and what performance indicators should be used (Epstein and Campbell, undated: 30). The same point was made in an interview the authors conducted with a state of Illinois governor's budget staff person engaged in trying to install performance measures in a few agencies on a trial basis (Grafton and Permaloff, 1996). Echoing James E. Folsom, she characterized the conflict over the formulation of performance measures as traditional budgetary politics set in a new arena. Instead of fighting directly over the distribution of dollars, agency personnel battled over indicators that would influence the distribution of funds many years in the future. Similarly, Grizzle and Pettijohn (2002: 55) describe conflict among Florida "legislators and between legislators and their own committee staffs" that encouraged executive branch "agencies to provide the legislature with lots of measures for each program, in the hope there will be something in the measurement set that each of the legislative committees will find acceptable." This practice renders problematic the connection between performance and budget incentives or disincentives. Behn (1999: 2) suggests that piling on measures to please everyone is not unique to Florida with his observation that "performance measures are often a hodgepodge collection."

Politics is an inherent part of the development of performance indicators.

Turning to his third point, Schedler asserts that a system of cost accounting is an absolute requirement. Performance cannot be evaluated without knowing how much it costs. Here we return full circle to the original performance budgeting.

> A large number of performance indicators can make it difficult to establish a connection between performance and budget incentives or disincentives.

With regard to his fourth point, Schedler asserts that performance budgeting information must be clearly understandable, "The adequacy and accessibility of information is influenced by the appropriate selection of information parameters, appropriateness of density relative to user capability and need, and by its truth and clarity. The citizen does not want 'data cemeteries' but annual statements that are intelligibly formulated and even clearly illustrated" (p. 47). Here Schedler touches on the Jeffersonian theme central to contemporary performance budgeting.

> Classic performance budgeting data are essential in order to make sense of contemporary performance indicators.

In 1987 GASB listed three "primary users" of performance budgets: citizens, legislators, and creditors (Brown and Pyers, 1988: 736). The authors have yet to see a budget at any level of government that could be characterized as accessible except to sophisticated users such as veteran legislators. In describing a number of jurisdictions' budgets, Behn (1999) found many flaws, "The baseline against which performance is measured (or should be measured) is often unclear" (p. 3); "When a measure goes up, it isn't obvious if this is good or bad" (p. 4); "It isn't obvious whether the performance measure should be an absolute number, a change number, or a percent change number" (p. 4).

Schedler (1994) addresses the ultimate problem of PBB, which was the also the Achilles heel of program budgeting (and ZBB), "there is the problem of sanctions for inefficiency and ineffectiveness: if we *cut* the budget, the agency will often lose incentive and potential to improve; if we *increase* the budget, there is a risk of increasing inefficiency" (Italics in original, p. 44). Unable to come up with an answer to this conundrum, Schedler concludes, "No measurement or evaluation system in the world can replace *leadership, which can be guided and assisted by PM*" (italics in original, p. 44).

Melkers and Willoughby (1998) found that only Florida (2003) and Texas linked budget incentives and disincentives (penalties) to performance results. Melkers and Willoughby (1998) describe Florida's incentives as, "Increased budget, personnel flexibility, retention of unencumbered appropriations, employee bonuses, resources improvements" (p. 70). Florida's disincentives are: "Mandatory quarterly reports on progress, quarterly appearances, elimination or restructuring of program, retention of total positions, restriction or reduction of positions, reduction of managerial strategies" (p. 70). However, what triggers the disincentives is not defined (p. 71), suggesting that the disincentives are not real, as does the welter of Florida performance indicators described earlier. Melkers and Willoughby list Texas incentives as: "Increased funding, exemption from reporting requirements, increased funding transferability, formalized recognition or accolade, awards or bonuses, expanded responsibility or expanded contracting authority." Disincentives are defined as: "Evaluation of outcome variables for remedial plan, reduction, elimination, restriction or withholding of funding, ... transfer of functional responsibility to other entity ... ." (p. 70).

> There is no comprehensive theory establishing a relationship between, on the one hand, budget increases or reductions and, on the other hand, performance.

Tucker (1999) observes as so many others have that, "It is difficult to link actual dollars allocated to specific performance measures ... ."(p. 2). In reviewing performance measurement usage in Great Britain, Canada, Australia, Denmark, and Sweden, Schick (1990: 32) observed, "In practice, none of the governments has forged a tight relationship between resources and results, nor is any likely to try." Schick believed that these governments wanted to avoid explicit connections between results and budgets because failures to meet specific targets would be too publicly visible. Tucker, Schick, and many others have emphasized the internal management virtues of performance measures.

Both outputs and outcomes measures are found in most budgets posted on the Internet. Lee (1997) found that 41% of state budgets contained measures of outcomes. This percentage is undoubtedly higher today. Indeed, it is unusual to see a state or local budget lacking in some sort of outcomes measure. Lee (1997: 136) found that only 24% of state budgets contained outcomes measures for "most agencies." The substantially lower figure for outcomes measures is consistent with the points repeated several times above that outcomes analysis is more difficult (Julnes and Holzer, 2001).

IV. AN EXAMPLE OF A CONTEMPORARY PERFORMANCE BUDGETING SYSTEM: LOUISIANA

Performance budgeting in Louisiana has attracted a great deal of attention and for good reason: it is a model in many ways. The Louisiana performance budgeting system contains two major parts. The first is a 5-year plan that includes each agency's: "mission, goals, strategic objectives, strategies to achieve their objectives, and key performance indicators ..." (Epstein and Campbell, undated, p. 4). The second part is an annual operational plan (OP) that includes: "specific annual objectives for each program, linked to the strategic objectives of the Strategic Plan; and performance indicators for each objective, with specific targets (called performance standards) ... ." (Epstein and Campbell, undated, p. 4).

The Louisiana (2003) budget comes in three basic parts: the budget itself, financial supporting documents, and performance supporting documents. It is noteworthy that nearly as much space is devoted to performance indicators as expenditures. For example, one of the pages of the Department of Economic Development budget contains a number of performance indicators, which are reproduced in slightly reformatted form in Table 27.2.

Greater detail regarding business services including a mission statement can be found in supporting documents at the Louisiana Office of Planning and Budget website (Louisiana, 2003: 1). A list of ten activities follows the mission statement. The Louisiana budget is seen as having a four-level program structure constrained within organizational boundaries. The Department of Economic Development (one of approximately 17 departments depending on how "department" is defined) contains nine offices (called clusters), each office operates a number of programs, and each program comprises a number of activities.

Supporting documents provide greater detail than the Louisiana budget itself. For example, information for the Business Retention and Assistance activity includes the information shown in Table 27.3 (Louisiana, 2003 — Performance: 1–2) The material has been edited by the authors for formatting purposes.

These data are connected to the larger program goals as well as to a long-term plan that appears to have a span greater than the 5 years mentioned by Epstein and Campbell

Table 27.2   Department of Economic Development's Business Services Program

*Objective: through the small and emerging business development initiative, to exceed the
national survival rate of assisted businesses annually*

Performance indicators	FY2002–2003	FY2003–2004
Number of small businesses certified	114	250
Number of certified small and emerging businesses provided assistance	117	220
Percentage by which certified companies 2-year survival rate exceed that of similar companies	10	10

*Objective: through the technology, innovation, and modernization activity, to achieve an
85% satisfaction rating from stakeholders*

Satisfaction level of stakeholders (%)	na[a]	85
Number of technology assistance requests processed	250	250
Number of start-up companies assisted	25	25
Number of Louisiana research universities assisted	5	5

[a]na = not applicable

Table 27.3   Louisiana Business Retention and Assistance Activity

To provide timely and accurate information to assist 300 Louisiana companies in marketing
products and services to new markets outside of Louisiana

Strategic link: relates to program Goal 1: to encourage access to international marketing
opportunities

Louisiana: *Vision 2020* link: relates to Objective 3.1: to increase personal income and the number
and quality of jobs in each region of the state

LaPAS code	Performance Indicator Name	Yearend Performance Standard (FY 2001–2002)	Actual Yearend Performance (FY 2001–2002)	Performance Standard as Initially Appropriated (FY 2001–2002)	Existing Performance Standard (FY 2002–2003)	Performance at Continuation Budget Level (FY 2003–2004)
6998	Number of companies assisted in exporting	100	340	100	100	300
1033	Number of trade opportunities developed	1000	1635	1000	1000	1000
14037	Export sales of companies assisted in millions	na[a]	na[a]	$5	$5	$5

[a]Because this is a new performance indicator for FY 2002–2003, there are no prior year standards
and no actual performance for FY 2001–2002.

(undated). Also, in the first column (LaPAS code) each performance indicator is tied to part of the budget.

The column headed "Performance Indicator Name" is self-explanatory. The remaining columns show estimated or actual performance data. There were 6043 indicators in the Louisiana system as of 1998 to 1999 (Epstein and Campbell, undated: p. 22).

Table 27.3 lists one output measure (number of companies assisted) and two outcomes measures (number of trade opportunities developed and export sales of companies assisted). Most other Louisiana budget entries and supporting documents display similar mixes of outputs and outcomes indicators. However, there is no indication if, or how, relationships between outputs and outcomes have been established. For example, how does the reader know that there is a relationship between number of companies assisted and export sales of companies assisted? Presumably, both statistical and interview data could determine if there is such a relationship. Performance budget supporting documents should include studies of these kinds of relationships performed by government personnel as well as literature citations.

Some Louisiana government personnel interviewed by Epstein and Campbell (undated, p. 4) believe that performance data may have influenced budgeting for new programs and incremental or decremental changes in existing programs, but: "Performance information has reportedly not yet influenced decisions about agencies' 'base budgets'." Nor is there any indication of a logic (discussed several times above) that establishes a relationship between outputs and outcomes and budget changes.

> The need to study the often complex relationships between outputs and outcomes is as great with performance budgeting as it was with program budgeting.

Epstein and Campbell report on the Louisiana Department of Public Safety and Corrections using performance measurement for internal management purposes. Comparisons are made with other states using a technique called benchmarking. This term refers to systematic comparisons of an activity with best practices in other jurisdictions (Ammons, 2002). Much benchmarking data is collected by the National Institute for Corrections (Epstein and Campbell, undated: p. 16). In this way administrators in Louisiana can determine how efficient and effective administrative techniques are compared with other states (Ammons, 1999).

Louisiana interview subjects maintained that outputs and outcomes data were used in legislative budgetary deliberations (Epstein and Campbell, undated: p. 10). According to one interview subject, these data often shed light on the implications of amendments adding or removing funding from particular programs (p. 12). This observation suggests that these data not only change the nature of legislative deliberations in the manner described by Grizzle and Pettijohn (2002), they sometimes affect the allocations of dollars.

A. Contemporary Performance Budgeting Elsewhere in the U.S.

How widely is performance budgeting used and how well does it work? In their survey Willoughby and Melkers (2000) found that 29 states (58%) had implemented performance budgeting systems. However, some respondents commented that "the process is not necessarily comprehensive or complete" (see also, Jordan and Hackbart, 1999).

A respondent from California indicates that PBB implementation has occurred on a pilot basis in only four departments. The reader need only peruse the California (2003) budget on the Internet to confirm that performance budgeting is barely noticeable.

Willoughby and Melkers (2000: 113) observe that: "Overall, budgeters consider that PBB has been at least 'somewhat effective' in improving agency program results, decision-making in government and coordination between agencies and the legislature. Generally, responses reflected a more cautious reaction to PBB than an enthusiastic one. Budgeters view PBB as less effective in reducing duplicative (sic) services and affecting cost savings, and 'not effective at all' in appeasing the public [angry about government spending and taxation] and changing appropriation levels."

Willoughby and Melkers (2000) list 15 states in which legislative or executive budgetary decision-makers respond that performance budgeting has been "effective" or "very effective" in doing at least some of the following: "improving effectiveness of agency programs," "improving decision-making in government," "improving coordination between agencies and the legislature," "reducing duplicative services" (only five states), "affecting cost savings" (only five states), "appeasing the public" (only two states), and "changing appropriation levels" (only two states) (pp. 115–116). The 15 states are: Arizona, Iowa, Kansas, Louisiana, Montana, North Carolina, North Dakota, Utah, Wyoming, Mississippi, Texas, Virginia, Ohio, Virginia, and Delaware.

Jordan and Hackbart (1999) report from a survey of state executive branch budget officials that only 13 states use "some form of performance funding." The reader should keep in mind their distinction between performance budgeting (including performance measures in the budget) and performance funding (decisions regarding allocation of dollars is "contingent upon" performance measures (p. 77). Only five states reported that performance funding was used for all state agencies, not just a few as part of a pilot program. Oddly, given these low figures, 33 states reported that "performance affects funding for the next fiscal year,"(p. 77) although there is no indication by how much or in what areas or any other details.

Overall, the realities of contemporary budgeting suggest that this reform is not producing an answer to the Key–Pigou question. While the reform is increasing the amount, if not always the quality, of information available, transparency has not been achieved so far. Software tools are available that can assist with enhancing transparency for the public and for others.

V. SOFTWARE TOOLS

Particular software tools greatly enhance classic performance budgeting; program budgeting, and performance budgeting; and even simple line-item budgeting. Software tools also make possible the convenient use of analytical techniques such as benefit–cost analysis, regression analysis, and interrupted time series analysis.

The most basic tool for presenting budgetary material to decision-makers and the public is the spreadsheet such as Excel and Quattro Pro found on most PCs as part of an office suite such as those manufactured by Microsoft or Corel. A spreadsheet facilitates mathematical calculations and the presentation of text and numerical data in tabular form. For preparation of even a small budget a spreadsheet is far faster and more reliable than a hand calculator, and it carries the extra advantage of allowing figures to be automatically recalculated. Since budget formulation frequently involves trial-and-error reduction of expenditure proposals to fit smaller revenue amounts, automatic recalculations allow decision-makers to observe the results of cuts as soon as they are made.

A spreadsheet permits pinpoint control of fonts, shadings, styles (e.g., using dollar signs or not, placing negative numbers in parentheses or red). Effects such as these produce a look of professionalism and enhance readability. Spreadsheets also contain a substantial array of plotting capabilities. Every pie chart, scatter plot, and bar chart that we have seen in government budgets could have been and probably was produced using a spreadsheet. Spreadsheet data and graphs can be printed or generated on a web page on a stand-alone basis or they can be incorporated into pages produced in part on a software suite's word processor. Spreadsheet output can also be incorporated in slides produced by presentation software such as Microsoft PowerPoint or Corel Presentations.

The line-item budget in Table 27.1 is an example of the simplest possible spreadsheet application, a two-dimensional worksheet (specific data on one computer page). The two dimensions in Table 27.1 are line-item categories and time. Most budgets have more than two dimensions. In this example, there might also be agency, funding sources, program or activity categories, and geographical areas in which this agency might work. A third dimension such as geography is easily incorporated by adding worksheets (with each sheet representing a specific geographical area). A collection of worksheets is called a workbook. Even more dimensions can be included using a spreadsheet device called a pivot table (Grafton and Permaloff, 2000: 435–437; Grafton and Permaloff, 2003: 194–197). A pivot table can be thought of as a multidimensional shape that can be turned in various directions to view different aspects of a budget. Any combination of budgetary dimensions can be viewed in turn — even three or more dimensions simultaneously (although more than three at a time can become confusing). For example, budget numbers for all activities related to children cross-referenced by agencies administering those activities together with funding sources for those activities could be viewed at once.

Throughout this chapter we have pointed to the importance of policy analysis in budgeting, and the spreadsheet is often the only tool needed for this purpose. An example is a statistical study relating various kinds of meat inspection regimens to numbers of bad carcasses discovered. Spreadsheets include a variety of statistical functions and others can be added using such programs as StatPlus, which comes with a superb tutorial text that teaches not only statistical applications but basic Excel spreadsheet techniques (see Berk and Cary, 2004).

Benefit–cost analysis was also discussed in this chapter, and spreadsheets are ideal tools for this purpose (Grafton and Permaloff, 2000: 439–441; Grafton and Permaloff, 2003: 197–200). A benefit–cost analysis is rarely complete without the presentation of results based on a variety of benefit and cost figures that allow policymakers to gauge the sensitivity of results to varying assumptions. Performed manually, calculations of this sort can be tedious and time-consuming. Done on a spreadsheet with its extensive copying and editing capabilities, multiple benefit–cost computations can be quickly and easily produced.

Regression analysis is a commonly employed policy analysis technique described in many books (Wilkinson et al., 1996; Garson, 2002; Berk and Cary, 2004). This technique is used to study the relationships between, and among, variables. An example is the relationship between primary and secondary school class size and SAT or ACT results. Using the language of statistics class size is the independent variable thought to affect standardized test scores (the dependent variable). If larger class size can be related to poor test scores, a case can be made for increased spending to reduce class size. A spreadsheet is an adequate tool for regression analysis for budgeting.

Interrupted time series analysis is another policy analysis technique that can be useful in budgeting. It is designed to spot statistically significant breaks in time series data that signal that a new policy is having an effect. An example is the sudden release of prison inmates due to budget constraints. The dependent variable might be a measure of crime. Interrupted time series analysis can determine whether the relationship between the inmate release and an increase in crime is statistically significant. The importance of such a finding to subsequent appropriations to prisons is clear. Again, a spreadsheet is adequate for this purpose.

Forecasting is an important element in the budgetary process, especially with regard to expected revenues. Space limitations prevented us from covering this topic, but the spreadsheet and its built-in statistical functions can also be used for this purpose.

Although the spreadsheet may be sufficient for many statistical applications in budgeting, especially sophisticated or voluminous work is better done with a statistics package such as SPSS, SYSTAT, or NCSS (NCSS, 2001; SYSTAT 10.2, 2002; SPSS 12.0, 2003). NCSS includes especially powerful and easy-to-use forecasting features.

VI. CONCLUSIONS

Budget reforms from the 1950s through the 1970s were sometimes oversold with immodest claims of bringing scientific objectivity to an inherently political process. Program budgeting with its attempt to overcome organizational boundaries may represent the peak of ambitious reform. The contemporary performance budgeting literature is oddly atheoretical, but it is considerably more realistic and modest. We have seen no hint that performance budgeting advocates believe that they can answer the Key–Pigou question. Clearly, they cannot.

Organizational boundaries almost guarantee that there will be duplication and gaps in budgets. Logically thought-out program structures free of organizational boundaries are more trouble than they are worth. On the other hand, the emphasis on outputs and outcomes provided by program budgeting and contemporary performance budgeting gives legislators, reporters, and the public a much clearer picture of how funds are spent than was the case a few years ago.

We are no closer to understanding the relative benefits of government activities now than we ever were. This is the heart of Key–Pigou. Benefits are often difficult to measure, and opinions differ on the relative merits of government activities.

We are slowly moving closer to understanding some relationships between outputs and outcomes. Virtually every branch of the applied sciences is engaged in this work as are a host of professional organizations that serve as repositories of information that can be used for benchmarking.

The original (classical) performance budgeting's emphasis on cost is absolutely necessary in contemporary performance budgeting. Determining the cost of activities is well within our capabilities with modern computerized data systems, but it is still virtually impossible for a reporter, legislator, or citizen to determine the cost of any government activity using only the information available on the Internet. This should not be the case. It can be fixed.

With clear cost data available to everyone through the Internet, valid and comparable indicators of inputs and outputs, and rigorous scientific analyses of the thousands of output–outcome relationships in federal, state, and local government using commonly available computer tools, the budgetary process will be improved by greater participation by the news media and the general public.

> Even though flawed, the budgetary reforms produce information which if presented with the appropriate software can improve public and media knowledge of the budgetary process and governmental decision-making.

REFERENCES

Ammons, D.N., A proper mentality for benchmarking, *Public Adm. Rev.*, 59, 105–109, 1999.

Ammons, D.N., Coe, C., and Lombardo, M., Performance-comparison projects in local government: participants perspectives, *Public Adm. Rev.*, 61, 100–110, 2001.

Ammons, D.N., *Tools for Decision Making: A Practical Guide for Local Government*, CQ Press, Washington, D.C., 2002.

Axelrod, D., *Budgeting for Modern Government*, 2nd ed., St. Martins, New York, 1995.

Behn, R.D., Performance measures in state administrative agencies: bureaucratic hoop jumping or management tool?, Remarks prepared for the Annual Conference of the National Association of State Chief Administrators, Salt Lake City, UT, 1999.

Berk, K.N. and Cary, P., *Data Analysis with Microsoft Excel*, Brooks/Cole — Thomson Learning, Belmont, CA, 2004.

Berman, E. and Wang, X., Performance measurement in U.S. counties: capacity for reform, *Public Adm. Rev.*, 60, 409–419, 2000.

Boardman, A.E., Greenberg, D.H., Vining, A.R., and Weimer, D.L., *Cost–Benefit Analysis*, Prentice-Hall, Upper Saddle River, NJ, 2001.

Brown, R.E. and Pyers, J.B., Putting teeth into the efficiency and effectiveness of public services, *Public Adm. Rev.*, 48, 735–742, 1988.

California, 2003–2004 Governor's Budget, California Department of Finance, 2003
  http://www.osp.dgs.ca.gov/On-Line+Publications/Governors+Budget+2003-2004.htm

Center for State Higher Education Policy and Finance, with the assistance of MGT of America, Inc., A Study of the Funding Process for State Colleges and Universities, American Association of State Colleges and Universities, Washington, D.C., 1991.

Dugan, R.E. and Hernon, P., Outcomes assessment: not synonymous with inputs and outputs, *J. Acad. Librarianship*, 28, 376–380, 2002.

Epstein, P.D. and Campbell, W., GASB Sea Research Case Study: State of Louisiana, Undated.

Florida, E-Budget Tutorial, 2003
  http://www.ebudget.state.fl.us/userguide.pdf

Garson, G.D., PA 765 Statistics Notes, 2002
  www2.chass.ncsu.edu/garson/pa765/statnote.htm

Grafton, C., The Coordination of State Universities in Indiana and Illinois, Doctoral dissertation, Purdue University, West Lafayette, IN, 1970.

Grafton, C. and Permaloff, A., *Big Mules and Branchheads: James E. Folsom and Political Power in Alabama*, University of Georgia Press, Athens, GA, 1985.

Grafton, C. and Permaloff, A., The use of analysis by governors' budget offices, *Southeastern Pol. Rev.*, 24, 675–697, 1996.

Grafton, C. and Permaloff, A., Budgetary analysis using computer tools, in *Handbook of Public Information Systems*, Garson, G.D., Ed., Marcel Dekker, New York, 2000, pp. 429–446.

Grafton, C. and Permaloff, A., Computer tools for better public sector management, in *Public Information Technology: Policy and Management Issues*, Garson, G.D., Ed., Idea Group, Hershey, PA, 2003, pp.190–220.

Grizzle, G.A. and Pettijohn, C.D., Implementing performance-based program budgeting: a system-dynamics perspective, *Public Adm. Rev.*, 62, 51–62, 2002.

Hawaii, The Multi-Year Program and Financial Plan and Executive Budget for the Period 2001–2007 (Budget Period: 2001–2003), 2001.

Heinrich, C.J., Outcomes-based performance management in the public sector: implications for government accountability and effectiveness, *Public Adm. Rev.*, 62, 712–724, 2002.

Jordan, M.M. and Hackbart, M.M., Performance budgeting and performance funding in the states: a status assessment, *Public Budg. Finance*, 19, 68–88, 1999.

Julnes, PdeL and Holzer, M., Promoting the utilization of performance measures in public organizations: an empirical study of factors affecting adoption and implementation, *Public Adm. Rev.*, 61, 693–703, 2001.

Key, V.O., Jr., The lack of a budgetary theory, *Am. Pol. Sci. Rev.*, 34, 1137–1144, 1940.

Lee, R.D., Jr., A quarter century of state budgeting practices, *Public Adm. Rev.*, 57, 133–140, 1997.

Lee, R.D., Jr., Johnson, R.W., and Joyce, P.G., *Public Budgeting Systems*, 7th ed., Jones and Bartlett, Sudbury, MA, 2004.

Louisiana, Department of Economic Development, Office of Business Development-Program A: Business Services, Supporting Document, 2003
www.state.la.us/opb/pbb/ebsd.html

McCaffery, J., The transformation of zero based budgeting: program level budgeting in Oregon, *Public Budg. Finance*, 1, 50–55, 1981.

McKeown, M.P., State funding formulas for public institutions of higher education, *J. Public Finance*, 15, 101–112, 1989.

Melkers, J. and Willoughby, K., The state of the states: performance budgeting requirements in 47 out of 50, *Public Adm. Rev.*, 58, 66–73, 1998.

Merewitz, L. and Sosnick, S.H., Public expenditure analysis: some current issues, in *Contemporary Approaches to Public Budgeting*, Kramer, F.A., Ed., Winthrop, Cambridge, MA, 1979, pp. 78–93.

Nas, T.F., *Cost–Benefit Analysis*, Sage, Thousand Oaks, CA, 1996.

National Center for Public Productivity, A Brief Guide for Performance Measurement in Local Government, Rutgers University, New Brunswick, NJ, 1997
http://rutgers.edu/~ncpp/cdgp/Manual.htm

NCSS 2001 (computer software), NCSS Statistical Software, East Kaysville, UT, 2001.

Novick, D., *Which Program Do We Mean in "Program Budgeting?,"* Rand Corporation, Santa Monica, CA, 1954.

Novick, D., *Program Budgeting*, Rand Corporation, Santa Monica, CA, 1972.

Novick, D., What program budgeting is and is not, in *Government Budgeting*, 3rd ed., Hyde, A.C., Ed., Belmont, CA, Wadsworth, 2002, pp. 52–68.

Pettijohn, C.D. and Grizzle, G.A., Structural budget reform: does it affect budget deliberations?, *Public Budg. Acc. Finan. Manage.*, 9, 26–45, 1997.

Poister, T.H. and Streib, G., Performance measurement in municipal government: assessing the state of the practice, *Public Adm. Rev.*, 59, 325–335, 1999.

Pyhrr, P., Zero-base budgeting, *Harv. Bus. Rev.*, 20, 111–121, 1970.

Sallack, D. and Allen, D.N., From impact to output: Pennsylvania's planning–programming budgeting system in transition, *Public Budg. Finance*, 7, 38–50, 1987.

Sarant, P.C., *Zero-Base Budgeting in the Public Sector*, Addison-Wesley, Reading, MA, 1978.

Schedler, K., Performance measurement in a direct democratic environment: local government reforms in Switzerland, *Public Budg. Finance*, 14, 36–53, 1994.

Schick, A., The road to PPB: the stages of budget reform, *Public Adm. Rev.*, 26, 243–258, 1966.

Schick, A., The road from ZBB, *Public Adm. Rev.*, 38, 177–180, 1978.

Schick, A., Budgeting for results: recent developments in five industrialized countries, *Public Adm. Rev.*, 50, 26–34, 1990.

Schmid, A.A., *Benefit–Cost Analysis*, Westview, Boulder, CO, 1989.

SPSS 12.0 (computer software), SPSS, Chicago, 2003.

SYSTAT 10.2 (computer software), Systat Software, Richmond, CA, 2002.

Tucker, L., GASB Sea Research Case Study, State of Texas, Austin, TX, 1999
www3. chass.ncsu.edu/PA540/aypavlic/pgm/Texas.doc

U.S. Commission on Organization of the Executive Branch of the Government, *Budgeting and Accounting*, U.S. Government Printing Office, Washington, D.C., 1949.

Wanat, J., *Introduction to Budgeting*, Duxbury Press, Scituate, MA, 1978.

Wildavsky, A., *The Politics of the Budgetary Process*, 4th ed., Little, Brown, Boston, 1985.

Wilkinson, L., Glank, G., and Gruber, C., *Desktop Data Analysis with SYSTAT*, Prentice-Hall, Upper Saddle River, NJ, 1996.

Willoughby, K.G. and Melkers, J.E., Implementing PBB: conflicting views of success, *Public Budg. Finance*, 20, 105–120, 2000.

Wilson, W., The study of administration, *Pol. Sci. Q.*, 56, 481–506, 1941.

28

PUBLIC FINANCE MANAGEMENT INFORMATION SYSTEMS

John W. Swain
Governors State University

Jay D. White
University of Nebraska–Omaha

CONTENTS

I. Introduction 490
II. Terms 490
III. MIS applied in PFM 491
IV. A conceptual model for more fully integrating PFMIS 494
V. Private-sector adoption of MIS in financial management 494
    A. Why the public sector has not followed the private-sector
       pattern of adoption 495
    B. Integrating PFMIS 498
    C. The integration of PFM and MIS: a brief assessment 501
VI. Conclusion 503
References 503

ABSTRACT

Public finance management (PFM) and management information systems (MIS) represent the convergence of old and new public-sector concerns, i.e., using of information to maximize the utility of resources. MIS promises to make PFM better, primarily through integrating the use of information. This chapter defines key terms, describes the application of MIS to accounting in the public sector, and explains the barriers to the fulfillment of MIS promises. Because of fragmentation of PFM, the best choice for integrating PFM and MIS is a conceptual model that represents the logic of application of MIS to financial management in the private sector. The PFM and MIS integration model starts with operational applications as a precursor to tactical applications and then to applications oriented to strategic decision-making.

The chapter also assesses developments in this area since the publication of the first edition of this book.

I. INTRODUCTION

Public finance management (PFM) and management information systems (MIS) represent the convergence of old and new concerns for public finance management information systems (PFMIS). PFM represents some of the oldest concerns of public organizations and MIS some of the newest ones. PFM and public information systems have a long history. Some of the earliest known public records involve financial matters, primarily tax records (Webber and Wildavsky, 1986: 17, 50, 78, 86, 158). We will proceed by briefly defining terms, discussing the application of MIS in PFM, and presenting a conceptual model for more fully integrating MIS into PFM. Also, we will comment on developments since the initial publication of this chapter.

Since the publication of the first edition of this book, much has happened in the world of information technology (IT). The changes in IT include faster processing, greater storage capacity, the spread of new applications of IT, increased flexibility of communications, and generally declining costs. The applications of IT to PFM have not advanced proportionally with the changes in IT. The changes in PFMIS associated with IT appear to be incremental; they appear to reflect a gradual diffusion of technology and declining costs.

II. TERMS

PFM refers broadly to the activities of public organizations in gathering, deciding on, and using resources, or, in other words, everything conventionally understood as part of, or connected to, public budgeting. Public budgeting involves deciding about revenues and expenditures, i.e., what resources will be collected and how those resources will be used. Specific PFM activities occur within the context of budgeting: accounting; forecasting; auditing; purchasing; various forms of analysis; and the administration or management of revenues, expenditures, cash flow, debt, investments, risk, and economic development (for more details, see Reed and Swain, 1997, especially Chapter 2). We cannot focus on all the processes here; however, we want to point out that they share commonalities, including monetary values, purposive behaviors, quantities, sequential activities, and in many cases processes parallel to those in private-sector organizations. Several other chapters in this book exemplify the mindset involved in PFM processes concerning management decisions about resource utilization.

How MIS relates to PFM can best be understood by covering some basic concepts beginning with the notion of data and moving to the concept of MIS. Data are "facts or observations about physical or business transactions" (O'Brien, 1990: 644). By themselves, data are meaningless until they have been transformed into information through the use of an information system. An information system is

> a set of people, procedures, and resources that collects, transforms, and disseminates information in an organization. Or, a system that accepts data resources as input and processes them into information products as outputs. Also, a system that uses the resources of hardware (machines and media), software (programs and procedures), and people (users and specialists) to

perform input, processing, output, storage, and control activities that transform data resources into information products (O'Brien, 1990: 649).

A variety of information systems can be found in modern public organizations. Accounting systems most directly support PFM systems. Information systems alone are not MIS
unless they support managerial decision-making (O'Brien, 1990: 651). This is a fine but
important distinction. Information systems turn data into information, but they become
MIS only when they create information that is useful for managerial decision-making.
PFMIS relies on information systems to provide relevant financial information in a timely
and accurate way to support financial decision-making in public organizations. Under the
broad rubric of PFMIS, a host of other systems support specific managerial decision-
making in a variety of financial areas, such as revenue forecasting, capital budgeting, and
risk management. All of the more highly specialized systems build on the hierarchy of
data, information systems, and management information.

Information systems are orderly processes for gathering and using information.
Because of its symbolic character, language is peculiarly associated with information
systems, but language also depends on physical technologies (Holden, 1996: 174).
Numeric information systems are prominent in PFM because of the importance of
quantities and the use of analysis. Accounting systems and budgets, both of which
contain words and numbers, are the central information systems in PFM. Budgets show
proposed or approved revenue and expenditure plans in quantitative terms in categories
denoted by words. Accounting systems show information from approved budgets,
revenues, and expenditures. Accounting systems serve as the central repository of PFM
information; other PFM information systems and processes rely on accounting system
information. The fact that accounting systems were the most common MIS predating
digital technology indicates their importance.

III. MIS APPLIED IN PFM

Those responsible for PFM have applied MIS to it because of expected advantages. MIS
promises to make PFM better and enables it to do more. We will look at some of the
general ways in which such promises about MIS may be realized in PFM. A description of
MIS in regard to accounting allows us to see how such matters play out in more specific
terms. Here, because of space limitations, we assume more MIS than PFM background.

Those familiar with MIS should easily recognize why the promises, which include
doing things better and doing more things, would be appealing in the area of PFM. Doing
things better usually encompasses the notions of cheaper, faster, more automatic, over
greater distances, and potentially involving more people. Doing more things usually
centers on capacities based on processing vast amounts of information but also includes
related storage and communication capacities. Although sometimes such promises may
be oversold (see Swain and White, 1992), they have led to the widespread usage of MIS in
PFM (Botner, 1987).

How MIS fits into PFM generally can be seen by looking at the two core PFM
processes of budgeting and accounting, and how MIS affects them. Despite many
variations, budgeting essentially involves deciding about revenues and expenditures for
the operation of public organizations. Operating officials prepare budget proposals;
policymakers make decisions; and operating officials implement those decisions. Similarly, accounting essentially involves dealing with information on things owned and

owed and on budget-related information, including approved and actual revenues and expenditures. More than anything else, accounting in PFM concerns keeping track of budget implementation. Accounting produces financial reports in the same information categories found in an organization's budget.

MIS applications in PFM started off primarily with internally focused applications and later came to involve externally oriented ones. PFM always involved gathering and using information. As MIS gradually enveloped and became integrated into PFM, particular applications succeeded others. Electronic calculation was an early application that occasioned great joy among PFM practitioners because it obviated the need for performing highly repetitive calculative routines for hours or days on end. In addition to simplifying the execution of preexisting routines, the implementation of electronic calculation led to a vastly expanded capacity to conduct analysis. Electronic storage and word processing facilitated printing and thereby the provision of PFM information in greater detail and to more people (Lee et al., 2004: 397–417).

PFMIS has contributed to an increased capacity to communicate. The dimensions of increased communications include the spatial or geographical one, the numbers of persons or points in a system (information devices), speed, and durability. Together the dimensions have radically changed the situation for PFM. First, the geographical expanse is very wide, theoretically worldwide and practically nationwide. Second, as the geographical expanse has increased, so too has the number of persons with whom communications can take place through MIS. Information can be sent out to one or more specific persons and can be made available to any and all interested persons simultaneously and directly through digital communications or indirectly through the mass media. Third, the speed of communication is nearly instantaneous, beyond the initial time spent to prepare information for communication. Fourth, digital communications show remarkable durability at relatively low cost. One can store, manipulate, and distribute digital communications fairly easily and cheaply, beyond the initial investments to gain the capability. Financial offices within public organizations communicated internally first, then they communicated to other offices in their organizations, and now they communicate with outside parties.

The application of MIS to PFM in specific terms can be appreciated by looking at the area of accounting. Very simply (leaving aside the many details concerning the precise information categories that make accounting difficult), accounting involves gathering, processing, and reporting information. The application of MIS to accounting creates significant changes. With respect to gathering, the universal rule prior to electronic MIS was that information was gathered by producing a written document when a transaction occurred. A transaction, according to accounting rules, is a significant financial event. Now, although most of the information in electronic accounting systems is produced in the same manner as earlier, some is gathered by a variety of electronic devices and processes. Such devices and processes include electronically readable meters for water, natural gas, and tolls; coin-counting machines; cash registers; electronically prepared bills; electronic fund transfers for payments (including transactions involving checking accounts and debit and credit cards); electronic purchase orders; and tax returns filed by electronic means. Electronic forms of gathering accounting information can be automated, which makes them labor saving (after the systems are set up and debugged). Such systems gather information much more quickly than before and generally do so with a greater degree of accuracy. In addition, such systems provide for the possibility of centralized or decentralized administration of accounting and related systems. For example, a marine in Twentynine Palms,

California, can place an electronic order for computer peripherals from anywhere and simultaneously create an accounting entry at a site anywhere. This example abstracts from the practical technical considerations of communication channels and protocols and security concerns of such gathering, e.g., codes and digital signatures. Now, instead of a series of events involving writing in some form, accounting entries for specific transactions can be generated by a single input session that can serve all of the information requirements of the accounting system for that transaction.

The processing of accounting information proceeds differently when the information is digital, whether the information is initially communicated in a digital form from a transaction or entered into an electronic system from written records. The electronic processing of accounting information not only proceeds almost instantaneously, as might be imagined, but also essentially reduces the number of steps compared wih paper-based accounting. The instantaneous character of the processing means that accounting information may be available at almost the same time that events are taking place instead of requiring a waiting period of 1 day or more.

Electronic accounting systems are essentially databases that add and subtract by specified categories. Information is entered into electronic accounting systems once, which compares favorably with the two-step process of entering information into paper-based systems. Paper-based accounting systems use a two-stage process for recording information from written transaction information primarily to track and correct errors in entries. The first stage involves writing information from the transaction into a journal that is organized by date, and the second stage involves writing information from a journal into a ledger that is organized by account. A single entry suffices for computer processing because each entry is almost always done correctly and because error-avoiding and error-correcting routines are incorporated into the data entry process. An example of an error-avoiding routine is the requirement that the mathematical value of debits equal the mathematical value of credits for any one entry; an entry that violates this rule is rejected by any standard computerized accounting program. Still, most programs can display accounting information in a journal format (useful for figuring out what happened when) and a ledger format (useful for figuring out what happened with specific accounts). The virtual instantaneousness of the processing of accounting information from the time the data are entered into an accounting program also affects the reporting of accounting information. Formerly, the three writing events in a paper-based accounting system were expensive with regard to labor and were more likely to produce random errors.

The reporting of accounting information, although vital to administrators and policy-makers in public organizations, generally was done infrequently and in limited-information categories because preparing reports was difficult, time-consuming, and therefore costly. Electronic processing with virtually instantaneous results makes reports available as frequently as reasonably desired at low cost (beyond the initial investments in electronic accounting systems). Accounting reports come in two basic formats (still leaving aside all of those pesky information categories): point-in-time reports and period reports, which really report the difference between two specific points in time. The calculating capacity of electronic systems means that a report can be generated on literally anything in an accounting system in either kind of format at any conceivable level of detail or aggregation at any time. Also, accounting reports can be communicated widely through an electronic medium to a wide variety of audiences on a routine or a demand basis. For example, the marines at Twentynine Palms, California, at their headquarters in Quantico, Virginia, and at the Pentagon in Arlington, Virginia, can routinely get a weekly or a monthly electronic report concerning their accounts, including purchases. The same information can be incorporated into routine accounting reports for various levels of the federal establishment, up to and including the White House. Although monthly accounting reports are the norm, an electronic accounting system can disgorge a report tailored to any conceivable kind of concern that is coded into the accounting system at virtually any point in time, e.g., specific marine accounts or federal purchasing of computer peripherals. In addition, electronic media can be used to facilitate widespread dissemination of accounting reports to the public.

Because accounting reports are basically reports of budget implementation, they can be used to facilitate public accountability of public organizations, especially governments. A variety of governments make annual accounting reports readily available to the public either directly or through the news media.

Since the first edition, the use of MIS in accounting in PFM continues to expand. More public organizations have adopted electronic accounting systems. Electronically gathered data are being used more and more in accounting systems, e.g., devices to directly read meters, devices that record and transmit information on meter readings into computer systems, and electronic toll recording devices are a few examples. The electronic accounting systems contain more modules and features than they did formerly. Unfortunately, in the case of nonprofit organizations, many use private-sector or personal accounting programs that are not particularly suitable (a search engine search on "fund accounting" brings up many discussions of how to make inappropriate software work for nonprofit organizations). Those discussions typically reflect a great deal of ignorance of the basic requirements of fund accounting.

IV. A CONCEPTUAL MODEL FOR MORE FULLY INTEGRATING PFMIS

In many public agencies the integration of IT and all of its potential benefits into the financial management functions of the agencies has been haphazard, incremental, and disjointed. Here, we outline a more systematic way of viewing the potential benefits of using IT to enhance the financial management functions of public agencies. Indeed, we offer a conceptual framework for the development of a more fully integrated PFMIS. The model we offer addresses operational, tactical, and strategic financial decision-making. It provides a flexible framework for designing or redesigning PFMIS. Our model is based on the example of MIS applications concerning financial management in private organizations. Public organizations have not adopted the private-organization model as a matter of course because their differences with private organizations are very significant. However, despite differences, we believe that the use of our conceptual model would greatly benefit public organizations.

V. PRIVATE-SECTOR ADOPTION OF MIS IN FINANCIAL MANAGEMENT

In the private sector, the adoption of MIS technology for financial management generally followed the sequential pattern of operational, tactical, and strategic applications. Operational applications concern routine and repetitive tasks. Such routines include calculating prices for invoices, accounting for collecting and spending money, and providing reports. Historically, IT has supported operational concerns through the development of transaction-processing information systems. Before the advent of IT, these operational tasks were performed manually on paper or on a calculating device such as an abacus or a mechanical calculator. A transaction-processing system simply uses IT instead of manual technology to increase the volume, accuracy, and consistency in processing the data of an organization.

At the onset of the use of IT, transaction-processing systems required large and expensive mainframe computers and complicated software programs to handle transactions. As technology improved, the size and cost of the hardware dramatically decreased, and the software programs became easier to use. Consequently, transaction-processing systems are available for virtually all private organizations.

As transaction-processing systems became more sophisticated, managers realized that the systems could be designed to contain data needed to make tactical decisions. Some accounting reports aid in tactical decision-making. A tactical MIS supports managerial decision-making by providing periodic summary reports, periodic exception reports, *ad hoc* reports, and other information that help the managers control their functional responsibilities and allocate resources. Transaction systems focus on tasks; tactical systems focus on decision-making and resource allocation. We can use cash management to show how that works. In cash management, organizations try to use their cash flows to their best advantage. With MIS, an organization can predict, with a high degree of certainty in most cases, the flow of money into and out of its accounts. Knowledge of how much money is available for how long can be used to select the most beneficial array of investment, borrowing, credit-offering, and bill-paying options.

Strategic systems focus on the goals and future directions of an organization. They rely not only on the data provided by operational and tactical systems but also on specialized information and technologies to address current financial conditions, relevant information about the current environment, and forecasts of possible future environmental conditions. Operational and tactical systems provide most of the baseline data about current conditions and the environment. Additional ITs are often used to gather more information about the environment, forecast possible futures, and perform "what if" scenarios about the future.

A. Why the Public Sector Has Not Followed the Private-Sector Pattern of Adoption

Despite the private-sector model of MIS integration in financial management, many public agencies have integrated IT, with all of its potential benefits for financial management functions, in a haphazard, incremental, and disjointed fashion. Although some might attribute this circumstance entirely to the failings of the people involved or not involved (less-than-brilliant people or the lack of an effective chief information officer role), much of the difficulty in following the path of the private sector involves the differences in the substantive character of PFM. Some of the differences are inherent in the well-known political character of public organizations that requires relating to various people through decision-making, which also results in various laws that restrict PFM. As one follows through the consequences of the publicness of public organizations, the difficulties that the situation creates for PFM and the adoption of MIS become clear. In addition, some leaders of public organizations may fail to exercise sufficient concern for maximizing their organization's performance because they are not like private-sector organizations that are subject to the compulsion of market competition (e.g., compete successfully or perish). The logic of private-sector adoption of MIS applications in financial management followed the pattern of transactions to tactics to strategy. In the public sector, this logic, although it certainly applies, is not a relentless situational demand.

Public organizations provide public goods (including services) having characteristics that make it unlikely for a private organization to make a profit by providing such goods. Examples include lighthouses and defense. The policymakers of public organizations decide the level of publicly provided goods. Funding for services often flows from taxes, which are required payments that are not necessarily related to goods or services received by the persons or organizations making the tax payment. Typically, this results in public organizations emphasizing control rather than management or planning in PFM (Schick, 1966). The emphasis on control generally manifests itself through annually approved budgets in which the levels of revenues are set by source (e.g., parking meter revenues) and the levels of expenditures are set by organization unit and by categories of items purchased (e.g., contractual services for the Forest Service). The emphasis on control results in highly fragmented budgets. The emphasis on control and the fragmentation of public budgets carry over into public-sector accounting systems. These accounting systems, although superficially similar to private accounting systems in many ways, are profoundly different in that they exist to exercise control rather than to provide information required in the private sector, that is, the net worth of companies and the profitability of their operations.

The ways that PFM differs from private financial management start with the consequences of budgets. Private organizations have plans, including some that are called budgets, but they respond mostly to the marketplace. If people buy more or less of their products, they produce more or less and even get out of unprofitable lines of business. Public-sector organizations essentially decide what to do in their budgets. Revenues and expenditures are decided on separately, and most revenues, regardless of source, can be directed to any expenditure area. Private firms tend to relate income and expenses closely because they vary together.

Public-sector accounting systems exist to track the implementation of budgets. Although public-sector revenues and expenditures look superficially like private-sector income and expenses, the key differences involve the comparisons made in the two sectors. In the private sector, income and expenses are compared with computed profit and the corresponding impact on the net worth of the organization. In the public sector, revenues are compared with estimated revenues, and expenditures are compared with appropriations (estimated expenditures), to track budget compliance.

Another difference is that public-sector accounting systems are broken up into funds. Funds essentially divide public finances into separate parts to account for different public activities. Funds are used to record finances for various activities, e.g., general fund, motor fuel tax fund, water fund, and pension fund. Each fund effectively uses a separate accounting equation that has to be operated separately, which contrasts with the use of a single equation for accounting and reporting for all private organizations. As a general rule, only the smallest public organizations use only one fund; a village government is likely to have between 5 and 20 funds, while the largest private organizations use one equation, which is like using one fund.

A corollary complicating factor in public-sector accounting is the use of different bases of accounting in different funds and among public organizations. An accounting basis mostly concerns when transactions are recognized and written down. Most private businesses use the accrual basis, i.e., recording a transaction when a legal obligation occurs. Public organizations, on the other hand, use the accrual basis only in some funds, primarily as a result of legal requirements, e.g., local utility operations. Most public revenues are collected from taxes that cannot be recorded on an accrual basis. Payments, revenue or income, can be accrued, i.e., recorded at the time that a bill is submitted for services rendered or goods delivered. Amounts for most taxes are known only when returns are filed because no bills are submitted. Therefore, public organizations can only use a basis known as modified accrual in most funds to account for those revenues. Furthermore, some small public organizations use the cash basis, i.e., recording a transaction when money moves, as in a checking account register, because it is easier. Finally, some public organizations use the encumbrance basis for expenditure accounts, i.e., recording a transaction when a commitment or a decision to spend is made. The use of different bases makes it difficult to relate funds to each other, to understand a public organization's finances, and to compare different public organizations.

Thus, because of budgeting and accounting practices public organizations have fragmented systems of financial management. When MIS is introduced into the various situations, electronic accounting systems and spreadsheet operations are used on highly fragmented information. The electronic accounting systems primarily deal with revenue and expenditure transaction processing. The spreadsheet operations include routine and analytical calculations concerning budgets and other financial management routines. The spreadsheet operations may use accounting system information and may result in inputs into the accounting system or decisions for financial actions.

Although the public sector might look appealing to MIS entrepreneurs, the public sector is highly fragmented with regard to accounting standards. Federal accounting is unique (U.S. GAO, 1998: 43). State and local governments theoretically should follow standards issued by the Governmental Accounting Standards Board but do not always choose to do so. States have many specific differences. Local governments, which are of diverse types, are regulated to some extent in their budget and accounting categories and behaviors by state laws and regulations. In addition, other entities, such as colleges and universities, hospitals, voluntary health and welfare organizations, and nonprofit organizations, all have different accounting standards (Freeman et al., 1988: 13–17). The fragmentation of accounting standards means that the market for MIS financial applications is broken up into a large number of relatively small market niches with little promise of profit for entrepreneurs.

The use of applications can be divided into three groups. First, larger organizations have proprietary accounting systems that initially ran on mainframes but that now run on client–server networks with some degree of integrated applications added on over time. Second, smaller organizations use PC-based software for accounting. Third, both large and small organizations use spreadsheet operations. In few cases has there been anything approaching a complete integration of MIS into PFM because the initial installation of transaction-processing systems for accounting has seldom reflected a concern for other PFM operations. The integration achieved in private-sector MIS financial applications could not be transferred directly to the public sector because of accounting system differences. Also, in many cases, public organizations did not require many possible financial management routines, e.g., cash management for organizations with little cash flow. With the degree of fragmentation of accounting systems within public organizations and the small size of many markets, integrated software did not make sense for small organizations, and software packages designed for larger public organizations have seldom been usable by other public organizations. Public accounting software packages are larger than private software packages and therefore are more expensive to write relative to the amount of data symbolized by the numbers of entries, and require larger amounts of core to process and larger amounts of space for storage. Conversely, all public organizations can use off-the-shelf spreadsheets that run on PCs to handle all sorts of calculative routines. Information for spreadsheets often includes accounting system information that has been exported or that has simply been input into spreadsheets by hand when that is quicker and easier than functional integration.

Since the first edition of this book, we have seen a general increase of PFMIS accounting and accounting-related applications running on PCs rather than other platforms and increases in routines contained in modules associated with accounting software, especially among local governments and nonprofit organizations. Similarly, we see an increased use of routines using spreadsheet software. Currently, the implementation of Governmental Accounting Standards Board Statement No. 34, a major reform in accounting standards, has been capturing much of the attention for PFM among local governments. The federal and state governments appear to be making advances particularly at the operational level, with less development at the tactical level and very little evidence of real development at the strategic level despite regular announcements of great advancements in PFM just around the proverbial next bend, particularly at the federal level.

B. Integrating PFMIS

Integrating MIS into PFM would provide many benefits to public organizations. The benefits would come not only from the labor-saving aspects of MIS but also, and perhaps even more, from comprehensively dealing with PFM. Because that integration cannot arise from the private-sector example or from the logic of public organization operations, the source of inspiration for integration will have to come from the dedication for the public benefit found generously among public-sector practitioners. The starting point has to be a comprehensive conceptualization of PFM. Simply automating routines that are stupid on paper means doing stupid things faster, which is not very smart. Here, we propose a way of thinking about PFMIS that can aid in the integration. We think that the logic of the development of MIS applications for finance in the private sector provides a rational template for thinking about PFMIS. However, it really helps to pay attention to the unique characteristics of PFM. As the first President Bush once said (approximately), "it's the vision thing." That vision involves keeping in mind operational, tactical, and strategic concerns at the same time and sequentially adding MIS routines that make sense for individual public organizations within that vision and their own circumstances. Attempted integration of MIS into PFM without an adequate vision of PFM is pointless; MIS cannot compensate for lack of understanding.

The starting point has to be transaction-processing systems, which means accounting systems in the public sector. That is the key repository of information. Initially, that means revenue and expenditure transaction processing; for situations similar to private-sector operations this can include many of the same processes as found in private-sector MIS systems, e.g., billing information for revenues and expenditures, inventory, and other asset and liability information. Nevertheless, before vaulting onward and upward to greater achievements, public organizations have to get their accounting systems squared away. In many cases, the accounting systems are defective or poorly understood and just stagger along, providing very imperfect information, whether automated or not. Other modules or routines can be added to the initially designed systems in the form of more modules connected to the accounting system. Other routines can run parallel to the accounting system and derive appropriate information from the accounting system. Such additional modules or routines include other transaction-processing systems, such as purchasing information for orders made (accounting for encumbrances or recording purchase orders), expenditure restrictions (apportionment and controls on transfers, reprogramming, and specific expenditure areas), inventory valuation and control, property management, billing, and payroll processing. All of these obviously make perfect sense in some situations. Software vendors specializing in public organization applications that offer electronic accounting systems continue to develop and market modules to add on to those accounting systems (e.g., PeopleSoft and HTE, Inc.).

Much less understood, however, is the fact that many transaction-processing systems make no sense in situations where the operations are unnecessary either because the underlying requirement does not exist (as in no spending restrictions or no inventory to control) or because gains that could be made from automating a process would be insufficient to justify the expense and effort, e.g., adopting payroll routines for two people with fixed salaries or controlling property in a small office. In many cases, the needs of public organizations for MIS can be satisfied by the use of spreadsheets or databases. After the basic accounting system is functioning properly, public organizations can look at implementing more transaction-processing routines and integrating tactical MIS applications.

Tactical systems, ones having to do with resource allocation, necessarily rely on transaction-processing systems for basic financial information about both actual and budgeted resource flows. In almost every case, however, the information within the transaction-processing system, although absolutely necessary, is not sufficient to make allocation decisions. Such systems include ones dealing with budgeting proposals, budget management, cash management, investment programs, debt management, risk management, and short-term forecasting. Budgeting for annual proposals, which has tactical and strategic aspects, necessarily requires price information on proposed objects of expenditures, decisions on changes in operations based on experience, and predictions of levels of service or accomplishments (if only expressed implicitly). Annual budgets may require forecasts based on economic and demographic factors. Also, budgeting frequently involves concern with equity in the acquisition of resources and the provision of services. Although analysis of information in accounting systems, the use of electronic templates of information categories (the same as accounting systems), and electronic calculation of quantities are all useful, the first step in automating is the ability to export and import data files for analysis and calculations. Completely integrated budgeting modules are relatively difficult to operate because of the multiplicity of budget proposals (usually two to five) in different public organizations, their size in terms of having the same number of information categories as the accounting system, the technical requirements for large amounts of storage, and the need for security of electronic files.

Other tactical systems, although much less broad in scope, require information that is not contained in transaction-processing systems and that involves external sources or special circumstances. Information routinely available from external sources is more easily automated, but then the source has to be automated, which primarily means large or sophisticated business operations, at least for the foreseeable future. Here, we need to point out that governments and nonprofit organizations are usually locality based and rely on local vendors and local banks. As long as one external information source is not automated, a public organization cannot automate a function involving that information source. Special circumstances might include when a check will arrive from a revenue source or when a local government allows a 1-day sales tax exemption on selected categories, as did New York City in August 1998. An additional technical complication that can be solved is the use of calendar-related information. Holidays and nonbusiness days can be programmed into automated routines, but they do complicate things. Changes in circumstances are key in dealing with tactical systems because resource allocation decisions are made on the basis of evaluations of costs and benefits that change with circumstances — new products, new risks, new prices, new laws, new policies, new situations in regard to political sentiments, and new economic conditions. For tactical systems, the key requirement for integration is the capacity to make analysis and calculations possible. This capacity can be achieved in two ways. First, modules can be integrated with electronic accounting systems. Such modules would have to incorporate three capabilities: accessing transaction-processing data, accepting external data, and running various calculative routines. Second, data can be exported either electronically or manually from transaction-processing systems and used in a spreadsheet. Currently, most tactical PFM systems involve spreadsheets that use data hand-keyed from automated accounting system reports.

The obvious option of a transaction-processing system with its own fully functional built-in spreadsheet for tactical system applications is not likely because low-cost, easily used off-the-shelf spreadsheet programs are widely available. The software manufacturers are facing a similar difficulty in this area that they initially faced with word processing software, i.e., making their products sufficiently superior to manual systems, except in this case they are competing against full-range spreadsheets that use both manual data input and data electronically exported from their database products with specialized spreadsheets integrated with their database products. Time will tell which path will succeed. At this juncture, manufacturers seem to be forging ahead with successive efforts at integration.

Strategic PFM systems, focusing on goals and future directions, involve a longer time horizon than tactical systems. Such systems focus on budget proposals concerning the extended future, capital budgeting, financial condition analysis, pensions, revenue policy, and economic development. All require that some attention be paid to events that occur beyond the near term. Integrating these concerns into PFM requires some kind of long-term forecasting. One reason that strategic PFMIS systems cannot rely exclusively on data found in operational and tactical systems is the need for a full range of historically relevant data for forecasting purposes so that the informational basis for forecasts is not limited and therefore biased. Another reason is that they involve policy choices benefiting from "what if" modeling, especially the dynamics of changes in variables not recorded in operational and tactical systems. As the budgeters at the federal level cope with the consequences of erroneous long-term forecasts of Medicare and Medicaid entitlement costs and Social Security cost-of-living adjustments, the value of strategic PFMIS becomes more obvious. Another relevant example is the use of capital budgeting analysis to make decisions about physical infrastructure, e.g., military bases, school buildings, and state prisons. In each case, one has to forecast factors external to the PFMIS, e.g., possible military threats, school children, and prisoners, to make long-range resource allocation plans. Once again, data from transaction and tactical systems can be used in strategic systems, but the complete electronic integration of strategic systems is not likely at present because of the same kinds of concerns discussed with respect to tactical systems. Strategic systems, although they include calculations, rely especially on nonroutinized information that can be used in computations also involving the more routine transaction and tactical systems information. The most likely pattern for the foreseeable future is the exporting of data to be used in spreadsheet calculations. Emerging trends, by definition, will probably always be difficult to handle in a standard fashion.

Strategic systems are at once the most difficult to develop and potentially the most valuable because they involve the future. They are equivalent to strategic planning in the private sector. Unfortunately, public-sector entities are mostly bound by territorial or subject matter restrictions and cannot follow the business lines promising the most profits. The boundedness of public organizations makes strategic systems more, rather than less, necessary for the fulfillment of their missions. With public trust and responsibilities in addition to their boundedness, public organizations have to rely on the resources available and have to provide for the apparent public needs within their bounds. Thankfully, strategic systems require a clear vision of the issues facing a public organization and the techniques appropriate for looking at choices concerning the future. Most of the techniques can be accomplished using a spreadsheet and data from transaction and tactical systems and from other sources. The necessary precursors of integration of strategic systems in PFMIS are a strategic vision and a working knowledge of strategic systems, which are most likely to develop and be used in a nonintegrated manner. An integrated PFMIS is not likely to engage public practitioners in strategic processes. They are most likely to use such routines, integrated or not, on the basis of the preexistence of a strategic vision. Efforts in PFMIS should be directed more toward promoting strategic vision than toward the integration of strategic systems into PFMIS.

C. The Integration of PFM and MIS: A Brief Assessment

At the beginning of this chapter we noted that the integration of PFM and MIS appears to be incremental, with a gradual diffusion of IT to support financial management practices. A brief look at what federal, state, and local government agencies have recently been doing to improve PFM through MIS confirms this view.

In 1990 Congress passed the Chief Financial Officers (CFO) Act in an effort to modernize the federal government's financial management practices with the aid of IT. The act designates 24 agencies as CFO Act agencies. On the advice of the Joint Financial Management Improvement Program (an effort of the Office of Management and Budget, Department of the Treasury, the Office of Personnel Management, and the General Accounting Office), core financial systems were defined as consisting of general ledger, funding, payments, receivables, some basic cost functions, acquisitions, grants, and personnel systems. On June 27, 2003, the U.S. General Accounting Office (U.S. GAO) transmitted a report on the Core Financial Management Systems at the 24 agencies to the House of Representatives Committee on Government Reform. That report shows that the agencies are using a mixture of custom-built legacy systems, commercial off-the-shelf software systems (COTS), and enterprise resource planning systems (ERP) to support their core financial management practices (U.S. GAO, 2003).

Legacy systems are almost always a problem for government agencies not just at the federal level. They are usually very old, custom-built, very big, and very costly to replace.

They cannot be shut down because they are vital to the day-to-day business of government. They are also difficult to manage because they were originally written in older programming languages like COBOL and sometimes even assembler language. The code often lacks proper documentation concerning what it does, and the code has often been rewritten or added to increase functionality, usually resulting in inefficient and ineffective system operation, slowing the systems down or causing them to crash frequently. To make matters worse, agencies frequently have several legacy systems built on different hardware platforms using different programming languages. Consequently, the data cannot be shared across programs even when it makes sense to do so. Public agencies at all three levels of government are slowly replacing these legacy systems. The pace is slow because of the cost of the new technology and the tremendous amount of time it takes to move the existing data from the old systems to the new ones. A case in point is the U.S. Naval Marine Corp Intranet, which is a multiyear effort to replace thousands of legacy systems with one integrated information system running on an intranet accessed by over 300,000 workstations (http://www.nmci-isf.com/nmci.htm).

There is a long-standing debate about the efficacy of COTS software in the IT profession (Schiff and Mersha, 2002). Some argue against the use of COTS software, saying that such systems are too generic and do not meet the unique data-processing needs across different types of agencies or other governmental units; e.g., different agencies may use different accounting, purchasing, or inventory systems. Others argue that COTS software is very inexpensive compared with custom software. Although COTS software is inexpensive, it frequently needs to be modified to meet the unique features of an agency. Modifications to COTS software lead to additional expense, including delaying the implementation date, and may not allow users all of the functionality originally expected from the modifications. Sometimes COTS simply cannot be modified to meet the needs of a particular agency.

ERP software packages usually provide an integrated suite of programs that allow data to be shared within and across functional areas in an organization. For example, in 1998 the city of Phoenix, Arizona, initiated an ERP system for its financial management functions, integrating its old legacy system with 400 subsystems, significantly streamlining their financial management practices. Now needed financial reports can be generated in minutes rather than days, weeks, or months (Towns, 2000). In that same year, the state of Georgia's Department of Administrative Services consolidated decades-old legacy systems running on an assortment of antiquated mainframes into a single integrated platform using a common database (Songini, 2000). Consequently, financial reporting has become much more timely, accurate, and easy to do.

Today, vendors like SAP, PeopleSoft, Oracle, and American Management Systems (AMS) are offering ERP software packages for financial and human resource applications that are tailored specifically for federal, state, and local governments, greatly eliminating the need to customize software applications. Some suites include more than 50 modules that span the gamut of back-office business processes from manufacturing and engineering, finance, accounting, and human resources to a host of front-office modules such as customer relations management. Others are industry-specific and less ambitious. Still others allow clients to pick and choose specific modules to meet their needs without the major modifications that come with COTS software.

The GAO report indicates that many of the 24 CFO agencies are taking advantage of ERP software. The Department of Education and the Small Business Administration have adopted Oracle's U.S. "Federal Financials" software. The Office of Personnel Management uses the AMS "Momentum" financial software package. The Departments of Housing and Urban Development, Veterans Affairs, the Nuclear Regulatory Commission, and the Environmental Protection Agency use the AMS "Federal Financial System" software package. The Department of Justice uses AMS and SAP financial software packages. Health and Human Services uses the Arthur Young "Federal Success Software" package. The list goes on, indicating that some of the CFO agencies are picking and choosing financial management modules that integrate data for a variety of financial practices commonly found in government agencies as opposed to private firms, eliminating the need for major costly modifications to the software.

Despite these apparent successes, several major federal agencies are lagging way behind in their efforts to adopt core financial management systems. Three agencies planned to complete their implementation of these systems in 2003. Three agencies have a target of 2004. Ten agencies have targeted implementation dates of 2 to 6 years in the future. One agency, the Department of Defense, has set no target date so far. Some agencies are still in the modeling and requirements specification phase, some are in the analysis and design phase, some in the development phase, and some in the testing phase. Considering the fact that the legislation mandating the implementation of core financial management systems is over 10 years old, much of the federal government is not "up to speed" in modernizing their PFMIS. No one knows for sure where the states and local governments are with respect to modernizing their PFM systems, but reports in industry trade publications such as *Government Computing News*, *Government Technology*, and *Computerworld* suggest some activity on this front. An article in *American City & County* reported in 2000 that state and local spending on IT will reach $52.2 billion in 2003 and that much of that spending is going toward ERP systems (Ferrando, 2000). So there is hope for improvements in public financial management systems in state and local governments as well as at the federal level, yet it will take some time to achieve full modernization.

VI. CONCLUSION

Management of the finances of public organizations can benefit from the integration of MIS. Nonetheless, the key to integration continues to be a conceptual model of transaction, tactical, and strategic systems in PFM rather than complete physical integration of such systems. The complexities of PFM and the requirements of information from outside sources make conceptual integration a more realizable and practical goal than complete physical integration. Quite some time will pass before complete integration is the norm. With regard to PFMIS integration, we are reminded of the answer by the character Jim in the television program *Taxi* to the question, "When will you straighten out?" His reply was, "August." Unfortunately, we do not believe that anyone can speak definitely about when public organizations will realize all of the promise in PFMIS integration.

REFERENCES

Botner, S.B., Microcomputers in state central budget offices, *Public Budgeting & Finance*, 3, 99–108, 1987.

Ferrando, T., ERP systems help with integration, *American City & County*, August 1, 2000.

Freeman, R.J., Shoulders, C.D., and Lynn, E.S., *Governmental and Nonprofit Accounting: Theory and Practice*, 3rd ed., Prentice-Hall, Englewood Cliffs, NJ, 1988.

Holden, M., Jr., *Continuity and Disruption: Essays in Public Administration*, University of Pittsburgh Press, Pittsburgh, 1966, pp. 171–207.

Lee, R.D., Jr., Johnson, R.W., and Joyce, P.G., *Public Budgeting Systems*, 7th ed., Jones and Bartlett, Sudbury, MA, 2004.

O'Brien, J.A., *Management Information Systems: A Managerial End User Perspective*, Irwin, Homewood, IL, 1990.

Reed, B.J. and Swain, J.W., *Public Finance Administration*, 2nd ed., Sage, Thousand Oaks, CA, 1997.

Schick, A., The road to PPB, *Public Administration Review*, 26, 243–258, 1966.

Schiff, A. and Mersha, T., *An Innovative Adaptation of General Purpose Accounting Software for a Municipal Social Service Agency*, Idea Group, Hershey, PA, 2002.

Songini, M., Despite odds, Georgia hits it big with ERP system, *Computerworld*, October 9, 2000.

Swain, J.W. and White, J.D., Information technology for productivity: maybe, maybe not: an assessment, in *Public Productivity Handbook*, Holzer, M., Ed., Marcel Dekker, New York, 1992, pp. 643–663.

Towns, S., Embracing the enterprise in ERP, *Government Technology*, August 2, 2000.

U.S. GAO (U.S. General Accounting Office), *1997 Consolidated Financial Statements of the United States Government*, Government Printing Office, Washington, D.C., 1998 (GAO/AIMD-98-127).

U.S. GAO (U.S. General Accounting Office), *Financial Management Systems: Core Financial Systems at the 24 Chief Financial Officers Act Agencies*, General Accounting Office, June 27, 2003 (GAO-03-903R Core Financial Systems).

Webber, C. & Wildavsky, A., *A History of Taxation and Expenditure in the Western World*, Simon and Schuster, New York, 1986.

29

STATISTICAL ANALYSIS SOFTWARE IN PUBLIC MANAGEMENT

T.R. Carr

Southern Illinois University

CONTENTS

I. Decision-making and statistical software 506
II. Managerial activities 507
III. Statistics and decision-making 508
IV. Guidelines for the use of statistical packages 509
    A. Characteristics and capabilities of statistical software 509
    B. Guidelines for use of statistical analysis software 510
V. Significance levels 511
    A. Significance tests 511
    B. Misinterpretations of significance tests 512
    C. Guidelines for managers 513
VI. Applications of statistical software programs 514
VII. Advantages of statistical software over spreadsheets 515
References 516

ABSTRACT

This chapter examines the role of statistical packages as a management tool in the public sector. With the need for public agencies to engage in policy analysis and program evaluations to justify continuation of current programs or the need for new program initiatives, statistical packages have become an increasingly important management tool. This chapter discusses the use of these packages in improving the quality of information available to decision-makers. The capability of statistical software programs continues to increase with the development of data mining and other analytic techniques. Statistical software, today, has moved from descriptive and inferential statistics to include the capability to link agency databases with an expanded array of analytic techniques designed to exploit the potential of existing data files. Public-sector managers may be vulnerable to numerous pitfalls, such as those that the manager may encounter in the utilization of statistical software programs. Common pitfalls can be avoided if managers evaluate assumptions, examine descriptive statistics, understand statistical significance as it relates to Type I and Type II errors, and examine the values that have guided the analytic effort. While spreadsheets have significant value in terms of managing financial and accounting data, statistical software packages have a utility that extends beyond that of current spreadsheet programs. Statistical software provides the public manager with the potential to integrate data files and to conduct a segmented analysis to answer complex managerial questions.

I.   DECISION-MAKING AND STATISTICAL SOFTWARE

Statistical software packages are important tools for public managers to employ in the decision-making process. These software packages afford the manager the opportunity to record data, engage in analysis, and document the specific procedures and techniques that have been performed. This provides the manager with the valuable ability to audit previous analyses at a future point in time. Managers can thus avoid the need to "reinvent the wheel" when faced with the need to engage in similar policy analysis or program evaluation activities in the future.

Perhaps most importantly, managers have the ability to replicate previous studies. Quantitative analysis is founded on the scientific method and the requirement for replication of investigative efforts (Campbell and Stanley, 1966; Mohr, 1988). Unfortu-nately, replication of research tends to have a relatively low priority for decision-makers due to time and resource costs associated with replication efforts. The use of statistical software allows managers to audit previous studies and to then replicate those studies in future evaluation efforts. For example, a study of citizen satisfaction with local govern-ment services can be replicated with relative ease. In the same manner, managers have the capacity to replicate the evaluation of a variety of public programs through the use of previously developed and documented research tools and data analysis techniques.

Statistical software also allows the manager to engage in sensitivity analysis by asking a variety of "What if?" questions. Judgments and insights may be sharpened by changing assumptions and parameters used in the statistical analysis. The ability of managers to conduct sensitivity analysis is enhanced with a workable knowledge of a statistical software package.

Effective communications of results is an integral component of policy analysis or program evaluation activities. The graphing capabilities of packages such as SPSS and SAS allow results to be presented in a variety of visual formats. This provides managers with the ability to indicate not just the results of an analysis but how those results were obtained. Perhaps one of the greatest strengths of statistical software packages is their ability to extract information from data and to present that information in a format that can be readily communicated to others.

Statistical software provides managers the ability to handle information necessary for a variety of functions, such as evaluation, planning, and control. Consequently, it is helpful to note that a distinction exists between data, information, and intelligence. *Data* is best defined as the raw material that is mined and refined to produce *information* the manager can use and apply in the decision-making process. *Intelligence* can then be defined as the result of combining information from a variety of sources (such as quantitative analysis, organizational goals and mission, political values, and legislative or executive mandates) to arrive at appropriate policy decisions.

This means that statistical software is best viewed in the context of a decision support system (DSS) as opposed to a management information system (MIS) (Thierauf, 1993). A DSS is characterized by flexibility and adaptability appropriate for specific situations. The emphasis tends to center on planning and effectiveness, with models that focus on logic, judgment, and probability. DSS applications have been documented in a wide range of applications (Keffer et al., 2002). Energy applications include such areas as environmental risk, production strategies, and technical choices. Medical applications include decision-tree analysis in the selection of treatment protocols for patients. Military applications include development of models for the "best mix" of various weapons systems in developing requests for proposals in the acquisitions process. Potential applications of DSSs in the field of public policy are both varied and wide-ranging.

DSSs are validated by the "appropriateness" of the analysis that is produced. An MIS is characterized by a structured flow of data, with models that focus on a fixed logic and a standardized general format designed to produce standard reports. MISs tend to focus on exactness and have what might be described as a classical systems approach to input and outputs (Edwards and Finlay, 1997; Heeks, 1998). In terms of the relationship between an MIS and a DSS, a DSS may often utilize data from an MIS to generate information for managers. As a DSS, a statistical software package is related to an organization's MIS but has a unique function concerning data analysis.

II. MANAGERIAL ACTIVITIES

The role of statistical software in the administrative process is influenced by the environment in which it will be used. Understanding this environment is important because it provides a framework for insights into the potential inherent in statistical software as an aid in the decision-making process as well as an awareness of the limitations of their use for public managers. This preliminary discussion has two primary goals. The first is to acknowledge that the use of statistical software in the context of all of the activities in a manager's life is limited. The second is to indicate that statistical software does have an important role in the administrative process and that the effective manager adopts and adapts this software into the wider context of managerial activities (Finlay, 1994; Edwards and Finlay, 1997).

It is important to acknowledge that most managers do not conduct statistical analyses but are consumers of the research and analysis conducted by specialists within the organization (Matlack, 1993). How does technical analysis such as that produced by a statistical software package fit into the decision-making process of managers? Much of the work of executives is *ad hoc* in nature (Buckholtz, 1995). Traditionally, MISs have been applied to tasks that are repetitive and routine in nature. While this type of information is helpful, managers also need access to analysis that is not routine in nature. Managers also display a receptivity to information that is both verbal and visual or graphic in nature. This is where statistical software has the ability to enhance the decision-making process through flexible analysis and the capability to generate high-quality graphs that can clearly communicate information to the manager.

Meltsner (1976) developed a typology for understanding the roles and orientation of policy analysts in the public service. He stated that not all individuals classified as "analysts" possessed the necessary desire and skill to actually engage in analysis. In his typology individuals were divided into categories based on the level of political and technical skills they possessed. Relatively few individuals were classified as "entrepreneurs," individuals with both high political and technical skills. Accordingly, most analysis is produced by "politicians," individuals with high political skills and low technical skills; or "technicians," individuals with low political skills and high technical skills; or "pretenders," individuals with low political and low technical skills. Meltsner's typology provides a cautionary note for managers: know and understand the abilities of the analyst providing the information used in decision-making. The output from statistical software may be impressive, but if it is the product of a "politician" or "pretender," the manager faces significant risks when relying on that analysis for decision-making.

Accuracy and trustworthiness of information enhance the decision-making process. Statistical software allows analysts to present measures of uncertainty, such as standard deviation or confidence intervals, as an integral component of the analysis. This allows managers to understand limitations associated with the data analysis and to evaluate the overall trustworthiness of the analysis.

III. STATISTICS AND DECISION-MAKING

Managers in the public sector are expected to possess the skills necessary to engage in effective decision-making. This means that managers are faced with a need for extensive information but may lack both the quality and the quantity of information that may be required to support the decision-making process. For example, assume that a city manager is considering whether or not to recommend that a new employee training program be implemented in order to improve productivity. The manager needs a wide range of data: demographic information, indicators of employee productivity in the past, information on the costs of implementing the program (in both financial and human resource terms), as well as developing measures of the actual impact of the training program on productivity. Acquiring this type of information in a form suitable for statistical analysis is the challenge faced by this manager. Indeed, managers as a group face similar challenges as they engage in the decision-making process.

Statistics can be defined as the science and art of using quantitative data to make inferences that improve the quality of decision-making. The scientific component involves the mathematics associated with computation and with probability theory. The artistic component refers to the ability of the analyst to apply the scientific component to a real-world situation in which not all of the mathematical assumptions can be met and that is characterized by uncertainty and a persistent degree of "fuzziness."

The steps involved in using statistics for decision-making generally adhere to the following pattern (Matlack, 1993). As these steps are detailed the relationship between the manager as decision-maker and the analyst is revealed.

Formulate the question. All statistical evaluations begin with questions that can be answered. The question to be answered must be directly related to the management issue of interest and have the ability to be operationalized, that is, structured into researchable terms. It is at this point that the decision-maker and the analyst engage in discussions that allow questions to be structured in such a way that the needs of the manager can be met and at the same time be within the capabilities of the analyst.

Design the study. At this phase of the analysis, issues relating to research design are addressed. What kind of data will be gathered, what will be the source of the data, what kind of data collection instrument will be used, what statistical tests will be used, what kinds of comparisons will be made, and to what extent will the results be generalized to the larger setting with confidence are the issues examined by the manager and the analyst.

Data collection. At this phase the research design is implemented and data are collected for analysis.

Data analysis. Statistical software is used at this point to compute the specified statistics and develop a graphic presentation to accompany the analysis. At this stage the results of the analysis are summarized for presentation to the decision-maker.

Make decisions. The manager as decision-maker answers the original question in the context of the statistical analysis that has been conducted. It is at this point that the manager determines the level of confidence in the results of the analysis by formulating a plan for implementing the study.

Implement the decision. This is the point of divergence between traditional academic research and applied research. In applied research the manager makes appropriate decisions concerning the research results: whether or not to spend the resources to implement the program or policy. Applied research implies that a course of action is being considered and that action will or will not be taken. It at this point that budgets and professional reputations are placed at risk.

The application of statistical methods allows managers to reduce but not completely eliminate risks in the decision-making process. The goal is to allow managers the ability to make an informed decision in the context of the results of a specific analysis. Statistical methods are then intended to facilitate disciplined decision-making within the parameters specified in the research process itself. Statistical methods do not lend themselves to the discovery of absolute truths, but rather to the discovery of a sufficient level of confidence that can be applied to the decision-making process.

IV. GUIDELINES FOR THE USE OF STATISTICAL PACKAGES

Statistical software packages such as SPSS and SAS have the potential to serve as a valuable DSS for public administrators. Spreadsheets such as Excel or Lotus 123 have traditionally been characterized as being better tools than statistical packages for such functions as data entry, data editing, and printing (Grafton and Permaloff, 1998). That advantage is not as great as in the past, with the advances made in the more recent releases of SPSS and SAS. Data entry and editing are in the form of a spreadsheet, with columns representing variables and rows representing cases. This structure brings more of an intuitive feel to the process than with the early SPSS/PC versions with their formidable batch processing format. In fact, this ability to clearly and easily label variables and values within statistical software packages exceeds the capacity of spreadsheets even though printing of data files remains somewhat cumbersome.

A. Characteristics and Capabilities of Statistical Software

With SPSS, for example, the analyst can supply a brief eight-character variable name (such as: jobsat), a longer descriptive variable label (such as: "Respondent's reported level of job satisfaction"), value labels to clearly identify the meaning of data entered (such as: 1, low; 2, moderate; 3, high), as well as indicate the level of measurement (nominal, ordinal, or interval/ratio) for future reference.

Data analysis with statistical packages such as SPSS is now menu-driven with the advantages of point and click mouse operations. On the positive side, it is no longer necessary to remember complex syntax commands and formula to obtain output. The software package now performs these routine tasks through the use of the mouse. On the negative side, it is now very easy for a beginning-level analyst to engage in rather sophisticated statistical analysis without fully understanding the options and selections used to create the analysis. Ease of use by definition facilitates potential misapplication of statistical techniques.

As a desktop statistical software package, SPSS is a relatively fast and efficient program. Satisfactory performance can be obtained from any inexpensive "Pentium" class computer. With this type of system an analyst can analyze a virtually unlimited number of variables and cases.

Statistical software such as SPSS can be linked easily with other data formats, such as spreadsheets or databases to either import data for statistical analysis or export data for inclusion into a different format. This means that significant managerial flexibility exists in the use of statistical software packages.

One potentially important capability of a statistical software package is its ability to generate random samples from large databases. Both simple random and stratified random samples can be drawn from large databases with a few clicks of the mouse.

Perhaps the greatest advance in recent versions of statistical software, particularly SPSS, is the nature, quality, and ease with which publication-quality graphs can be created. Data analysis is enhanced through the use of appropriate charts and graphs.

B. Guidelines for Use of Statistical Analysis Software

Finlay (1997) developed a series of guidelines for the use of spreadsheets in managerial decision-making. These guidelines can be applied to the use of statistical software, with only slight modifications.

Statistical software increases in value as the importance of the issue under investigation increases. When a problem or an issue has the potential to consume significant resources of an agency the benefits to management of statistical analysis expand significantly. When the issues are relatively small, the benefit of statistical analysis as a management tool decreases considerably.

As the number of actors involved in the decision-making process increases, the value of statistical analysis also increases. Statistical analysis provides managers with a disciplined framework for asking questions, gathering data, and arriving at decisions. Statistical analysis serves as a mechanism for creating structure for debate over the policy options under consideration and establishing a common framework for evaluating options.

As the complexity of an issue increases, the value of statistical analysis increases. Statistical analysis serves the crucial function of reducing large numbers of variables into a limited number of factors in order to increase comprehension. Statistical analysis has the capability of identifying the underlying structure of a large array of data. This characteristic increases the value of engaging in statistical analysis.

The greater the value placed on analysis within an agency, the greater the value of statistical analysis. Agencies have differing values concerning the analytic process. If an agency lacks a commitment to quantitative analysis, the value of statistical analysis decreases significantly. An agency or manager that understands and values quantitative evaluation will derive a greater benefit from statistical analysis.

The greater the impact of political factors, the less the potential value of statistical analysis. Statistical analysis has a much lower value when policy or management issues are determined or heavily influenced by political pressures than when political values have less influence. Statistical analysis serves to structure the debate surrounding policy or management options in the context of an established framework of analysis. The political process may be contrary to this rational framework, which acts to minimize the utility of statistical analysis.

V. SIGNIFICANCE LEVELS

In the context of applied public administration research, tests of statistical significance provide one criterion against which the validity of findings can be judged. The proper interpretation of statistical significance ought to be a major concern for both analysts and administrators. This is especially true as statistical software packages are widely utilized in program evaluation and policy analysis efforts. Applied research is intended to improve the decision-making process by providing insights and guidance to both administrators and elected officials (Quade, 1982). Consequently, decisions to adopt programs, terminate programs, and the selection of optimum program levels are based on statistical significance tests.

A. Significance Tests

Statistical significance is a measure of the willingness of the analyst to make a type I, or alpha error, which involves the rejection of a true null hypothesis. The .05 alpha level indicates that the analyst is willing to incorrectly reject a true null hypothesis up to 5 out of 100 times. A type II, or beta error, occurs when the analyst fails to reject a false null hypothesis. An inverse relationship exists between the two types of errors. As the probability of making a type I error is decreased (by the selection of a lower alpha level such as .001), the probability of making a type II error is increased. For managers, the selection of a specific level of statistical significance involves the evaluation of the trade-offs between the consequences of a type I and a type II error. The use of significance tests allows analysts to eliminate sampling error in explaining differences observed in sample statistics. These tests are most appropriate when applied to data generated by true experimental research designs.

Selvin (1957) stated that the use of statistical significance tests was not appropriate in nonexperimental research designs due to the difficulty of achieving randomization of uncontrolled variables. Winch and Campbell (1969) differed with Selvin and supported the use of significance tests in nonexperimental research as an important aid in hypothesis testing. Current research practice in public administration reflects a willingness to apply statistical significance test to data generated from nonexperimental designs.

In the social sciences .05 has emerged as a "sacred" alpha level (Skipper et al., 1967; Labovitz, 1968). This alpha level is the product of human cognitive processes and the evolutionary process in the development of inferential statistics (Cowles and Davis, 1982). Before the development of standard deviation, the notion of probable error (PE) was widely used. PE was used to indicate the range, above and below the mean, which contained about half of the observations in a distribution. The standard of 3 PEs was widely used as an appropriate guide to determine chance occurrences. Since 1 PE is about 2/3 of a standard deviation, 3 PEs are approximately 2 standard deviation units. This translates into roughly 95% of the area under the normal curve, which is consistent with the .05 alpha level. Even though the standard deviation replaced PE, a continuity remained with the widespread adoption of the .05 alpha level.

The .05 alpha level is also consistent with the cognitive process of living in a base-10 math system. Being 95% confident seems a reasonable standard. A desire for higher levels of confidence is easily expressed as 99% or 99.9%, which is equivalent to the .01 and .001 alpha levels, respectively. Consequently, the .05 level is easily complimented by .01 and .001 alpha levels. There is something that is not cognitively appealing about other levels of confidence such as 87% or 97.6%. The convention of .05 and its extension to .01 and .001 seem more acceptable to the cognitive process.

Since these three alpha levels are the product of convention and a need to be cognitively consistent with a base-10 math system, they are probably quite arbitrary standards against which differences are to be judged.

Managers should remember that analysts using statistical software tend to rely on conventional alpha levels of .05, .01, and .001 and that these may not be the most appropriate for making informed decisions.

B. Misinterpretations of Significance Tests

Statistical tests are subject to a number of inaccurate interpretations. Managers need to be aware of these misinterpretations as they receive statistical output for use in the decision-making process.

"The hypothesis is proved" misinterpretation. It is not accurate to state that a significance test proves a hypothesis. It is only one step in a process of gathering evidence to assess support for a hypothesis (Winch and Campbell, 1969). It is tempting to interpret significance tests as $P(H|E)$, that is, the probability that the hypothesis is true given the evidence. Yet this is an incorrect interpretation. The correct interpretation is $P(E|H)$, that is, the probability that the evidence would be produced if the null hypothesis of no difference were true. The focus of the test is on the probability of the evidence, not of the hypothesis (Carver, 1978).

"The replicability" misinterpretation. When a significance level is interpreted to indicate the probability that future research will produce the same results, this error is made. In statistical terms, reliability means that the results can be replicated by other investigators. Occasionally, the issue of reliability is introduced as an appropriate interpretation of significance tests (Gold, 1969). The probability of replication is not estimated by significance tests.

"Degree-of-significance" misinterpretation. When a given alpha level is interpreted as providing information on the degree of significance, this error is made (Gowger, 1984). An example is stating that a difference statistically significant at the .05 level is "significant," at the .01 level is "very significant," and at the .001 level is "highly significant." Managers are advised to remember that a difference is either significant or not significant at any given alpha level. Alpha levels measure the probability of differences, not the degree of significance. When this misinterpretation is made, the fact that the probability of a type II error increases as alpha level decreases is ignored.

"The measure of association" misinterpretation. This is similar to the degree of significance error and occurs when a conclusion concerning the strength of a relationship is made by comparing alpha levels. Statements that a relationship significant at the .01 level is "stronger" than one at the .05 level is a misapplication of statistical significance tests. A range of statistical tests exists for measuring strength of relationship after statistical significance is evaluated.

"The substantive significance" misinterpretation. Substantive significance implies that a relationship is important for policy or program evaluation. Statistical significance

in itself is not a complete guide to practical importance. Managers are cautioned to remember that substantive significance is assessed by examining the magnitude of the relationship, the strength of the relationship, and the relevance of the issues to the research questions under investigation. It is possible to find that a statistically insignificant finding may be of substantive importance to decision-makers.

C. Guidelines for Managers

The proper interpretation of statistical tests is essential if the research findings are to be of genuine value to managers. A number of guidelines exist that enhance the ability of managers to use the results of significance tests in applied research efforts.

Evaluate assumptions. Significance tests require that certain assumptions be met for their proper use (such as level of measurement, population distribution, nature of sampling). When these assumptions cannot be met, analysts are often willing to relax assumptions and still use the statistical test. With the relaxation of assumptions, potential threats to the validity of the findings are introduced. The robustness of the test statistic becomes an issue. Robustness is a measure of the ability of a statistic to maintain its validity when assumptions are relaxed. It may be possible to relax one assumption with little impact, but when two or more assumptions are relaxed, a marked decrease in robustness will probably result (Labovitz, 1967).

Statistical power and sample size. The power of a test is the measure of the ability of the test to reject the null hypothesis. Power is a function of the class of the statistic (parametric or non-parametric), sample size, and level of statistical significance. One mechanism to increase statistical power is to increase sample size. If a sample is sufficiently large, small differences become statistically significant. In smaller samples the magnitude of the difference must be greater to achieve statistical significance. Managers are advised to evaluate the impact of sample size on statistical significance.

Use descriptive statistics. Descriptive statistics have the ability to summarize the data and provide an understanding of the underlying structure in the data. A cursory discussion of the mean or standard deviation does not permit a thorough understanding of the distribution of the data. Greater emphasis on a variety of descriptive statistics would probably be useful. Managers are advised to rely on inferential statistics only after the structure of the data are clearly understood.

Evaluate consequences of type I and type II errors. The manager should evaluate the managerial and policy consequences of both rejecting a true null hypothesis and failing to reject a false null hypothesis. This will involve an evaluation of the consequences of acting after having made either error. Alpha levels should be selected after the consequences of making a beta error are evaluated and understood.

Evaluate the magnitude of the relationship. Even if a relationship is statistically significant, the magnitude of the relationship requires evaluation. Relationships that are small in magnitude may be judged as having no real importance for managers.

Evaluate the relevance of academic standards to applied research efforts. Applied research is targeted to a different audience with a different objective than traditional academic research. A study investigating quality of life for publication in an academic journal illuminates our understanding of human values. The same study conducted for a city council may result in changed spending patterns and other policy impacts. Consequently, academic standards may not be relevant.

Managers are advised to remember that the goal of applied research is to improve the quality of decision-making and that the decision to employ significance tests and the selection of alpha levels merit extensive consideration. The guidelines presented in this section help provide a framework for the appropriate application of significance tests.

VI. APPLICATIONS OF STATISTICAL SOFTWARE PROGRAMS

Perhaps one of the greatest reasons for public administrators to acquire and utilize statistical software is that it affords them the opportunity to take full advantage of the large volumes of data that they have collected. During the past two decades, government agencies have created databases containing a wealth of information that can now be analyzed to improve service delivery and program effectiveness.

Applications of statistical software expand as additional analytic techniques are integrated into the software. The increased integration of "data mining" techniques into statistical packages such as SPSS and SAS has increased the capability of public managers to improve decision-making as patterns in existing data are identified. One such example is the adoption of SPSS Clementine data mining module to predict property crimes and reduce the risk of an escalation to violent crimes against individuals. North Carolina's Wachovia Corporation now utilizes a data mining procedure developed by SAS to monitor financial transactions in order to identify potential money laundering activities that might violate the Patriot Act as enacted by Congress (SAS, 2002; Callaghan, 2003).

Applications of statistical software packages continue to expand as managers require more information on program and policy decisions. One such example is activity-based management (ABM) as developed by SAS (Fabian, 2002). ABM involves the integration of financial, operational, and performance data in order to improve planning, budgeting, and operational decision-making. As demands on public-sector managers increase with the expectation of providing more services at a reduced cost, there continues to be an evolution of the capacity of statistical packages to incorporate more analytic techniques. At the same time, statistical analysis packages are being increasing merged with decision support systems as managers ask increasingly complex questions (Babcock, 2001).

Data mining statistical techniques have significant utility to administrators in higher education (Luan, 2002). Administrators can avoid being tied to conventional wisdom and answer with increased confidence questions relating to: Which students will take more credit hours? Which students are likely to complete their degree program? Which alumni are more likely to contribute? What courses or degree programs are more likely to attract students? As these and other questions are answered, administrators can more effectively allocate financial and academic resources in order to achieve their goals.

Perhaps there is no single activity of local government that has the potential to create controversy and an atmosphere of distrust than the real estate property reappraisal process. As property is reappraised, tax bills tend to increase, which contributes to questions relating to the accuracy, equity, and fairness of the newly adjusted property values. Since the actual market value of real estate is unknown until the property actually sells, property must be valued on estimates. Statistical analysis provides local governments with the ability to improve the credibility of these estimates and to increase the level of public confidence in government (Gloudemans and Almy, 2002). The utilization of data profiles, time series trend analysis, and multiple regression to produce cost and market models is central to this application.

Managers in the public sector today find that funding is increasingly tied to measurable, quantifiable results. At the same time, public agencies are collecting and warehousing more and more data that can be utilized in a variety of statistical routines and procedures. Statistical software has the potential to allow managers in improve the quality of decision-making and to increase the level of confidence in those decisions. Some typical applications might include:

- *Public safety*: crime incident analysis, court sentencing analysis
- *Revenue*: property taxation assessment
- *Public health*: epidemiological studies investigating distribution of diseases, Medicare service utilization
- *Fraud*: use of data mining to detect Medicare misuse
- *Environment*: water and air quality analysis
- *Strategic planning*: economic forecasting and analysis, labor force utilization

Given the ability of statistical software packages such as SPSS and SAS to import data from a variety of formats, in-depth analysis can now be achieved without engaging in expensive data conversion tasks.

A basic reason for engaging in statistical analysis is to reduce uncertainty in the decision-making process. Through the use of statistical software managers have a tool within their grasp that will allow them to assess program performance and make appropriate responses.

VII. ADVANTAGES OF STATISTICAL SOFTWARE OVER SPREADSHEETS

Given the fact that spreadsheets provide managers with the ability to conduct statistical analysis, should managers consider adopting a statistical software package to engage in analysis? The answer to this question is yes, because of additional data analysis capabilities possessed by statistical software:

- Statistical software now typically has a greater array of graphs available to illustrate the underlying structure of the data. In addition to traditional bar, scatter, and pie charts, statistical software includes other options such as boxplots, control charts, Pareto charts, etc. to facilitate communication of results to others.
- Statistical software programs provide managers with a wide array of statistical tests, which allow them to asses what is really important. The statistical tests available with spreadsheets may be sufficient for routine analyses but many managerial questions are not "routine" in nature and require statistical analysis from a variety of perspectives.
- Statistical software packages such as SPSS and SAS have significant data management capabilities not found in spreadsheets. Data files can be merged, separated into smaller files, and aggregated with minimal effort. Perhaps the greatest advantage is the ability of software packages to recode data into different values when categories are combined or scales are created. With the ability of software packages to include extensive variable labels and value labels, confusion about the interpretation of numerical data is minimized or eliminated completely.
- Statistical software packages have a greater flexibility in handing missing data than do spreadsheets. Missing data typically fall into a range of responses from non-response, to "don't know," to "not applicable." Statistical software allows

managers to differentiate between these categories and to identify cases with missing data for follow-up analysis if necessary.

■ Statistical software has a greater capability to handle large data files than do spreadsheets. Spreadsheets are typically limited to somewhere around 256 variables, a potentially severe limitation. SPSS, for example, has the capability of handling a virtually unlimited number of variables in the analysis process.

■ Statistical software such as SPSS have built-in statistical glossaries and tutorials to provide the manager with information with the click of a mouse button. This feature saves time and provides essential statistical information quickly and easily.

■ Statistical software has the capacity to expand as data analysis needs expand. This is an important feature in that managers can purchase additional statistical modules only as they are required, a feature that contributes to financial savings. Through the use of add-on modules managers can reduce the financial cost of the software by acquiring only those that are actually necessary for the evaluation effort.

Statistical software will not replace spreadsheets for managers but serves as an effective compliment to them. Spreadsheets are very effective for routine tasks and when relatively limited analysis is required. Statistical software provide managers with a significantly expanded capability to engage in analysis that can reduce uncertainty in the decision-making process.

REFERENCES

Babcock, J., *Best Practices Approach to Government Technology Solutions*, SAS Institute, Cary, NC, 2001.

Buckholtz, T.J., *Information Proficiency: Your Key to the Information Age*, Van Norstrand Reinhold, New York, 1995, pp. 30–51.

Callaghan, D., Law enforcement: analytic detective work, *EWEEK*, September 1, 30–31, 2003.

Campbell, D.T. and Stanley, J.C., *Experimental and Quasi Experimental Designs for Research*, Rand McNally, Chicago, 1966.

Cowles, M. and Davis, C., On the origins of the.05 level of statistical significance, *Am. Psychologist*, 37, 553–558, 1982.

Craver, R., The case against significance testing, Harward Ed. Rev. 48, 378–399, 1978.

Edwards, J.S. and Finlay, P.N., *Decision Making with Computers*, Pitman, Washington, D.C., 1997, pp. 22–25.

Fabian, A., *Activity Based Management in the Public Sector*, SAS White Paper, SAS Institute, Cary, NC, 2002.

Finlay, P.N., *Introducing Decision Support Systems*, Blackwell, Cambridge, MA, 1994, pp. 1–11.

Gloudemans, R. and Almy, R., *More Defensible Values with Statistics*, SPSS, Chicago, 2002.

Gold, D., Statistical tests and substantive significance, *Am. Soc.*, 4, 378–399, 1969.

Gowger, C.D., Statistical significance tests: scientific ritualism or scientific method?, *Soc. Serv. Rev.*, 4, 358–372, 1984.

Grafton, C. and Permaloff, A., The software toolkit approach for public administrators, in *Information Technology and Computer Applications in Public Administration*, Garson, G.D., Ed., Idea Group, Hershey, PA, 1998, pp. 174–195.

Heeks, R., Management information systems in the public sector, in *Information Technology and Computer Applications in Public Administration*, Garson, G.D., Ed., Idea Group, Hershey, PA, 1998, pp. 157–173.

Keefer, D.L., Kirkwood, C.W., and Corner, J.L., Summary of Decision Analysis Applications in the Operations Research Literature, 1990–2001, Technical Report, Department of Supply Chain Management, Arizona State University, Tempe, AZ, 2002.

Labovitz, S., Criteria for selecting a significance level: a note on the sacredness of.05, *Am. Soc.*, 3, 220–222, 1968.

Luan, J., *Data Mining Applications in Higher Education*, SPSS, Chicago, 2002.

Matlack, W.F., *Statistics for Public Managers*, F.E. Peacock, Itasca, IL, 1993, pp. 1–10.

Meltsner, A.J., *Policy Analysts in the Bureaucracy*, University of California Press, Berkely, CA, 1976, pp. 14–59.

Mintzberg, H., The manager's job: folklore and fact, *Harv. Bus. Rev.*, July–August, 49–61, 1975.

Mohr, L.B., *Impact Analysis for Program Evaluation*, Dorsey Press, Chicago, 1988.

Quade, E.S., *Analysis for Public Decisions*, 2nd ed., Elsevier, New York, 1982.

SAS, *SAS White Paper: Anti-Money Laundering Solution*, SAS Institute, Cary, NC, 2002.

Selvin, H.C., A critique of tests of significance in survey research, *Am. Soc. Rev.* 22, 519–527, 1957.

Skipper, J.K., Guenther, A.L., and Nass, G., The sacredness of .05: a note on the uses of statistical levels of significance in social science, *Am. Soc.*, 2, 16–18, 1967.

Thierauf, R.J., *Creative Computer Software for Strategic Thinking and Decision Making*, Quorum Books, Westport, CT, 1993, pp. 131–174.

Winch, cf. and Campbell, D.T., Proof? no. evidence? yes, the significance of tets of significance, *Am. Soc.*, 4, 140–143, 1969.

PART VI

E-GOVERNMENT

30

ENACTING VIRTUAL FORMS OF WORK AND COMMUNITY: MULTIWAVE RESEARCH FINDINGS ACROSS INDIVIDUAL, ORGANIZATIONAL, AND LOCAL COMMUNITY SETTINGS

Thomas Horan
Claremont Graduate University

Kimberly J. Wells
Claremont Graduate University

CONTENTS

I.   Introduction 522
     A.   Telework 524
          1.   Defining the concept 524
          2.   Factors regarding implementation 525
          3.   Minnesota traffic problems 525
          4.   Individual and organizational dimensions 526
     B.   Community network research issues 527
          1.   Digital place design 528
II. Methodology 529
     A.   Phase i: survey of telecommuters 529
     B.   Phase ii: in-depth qualitative interviews 529
     C.   Phase iii: community design studios 530
III. Findings 531
     A.   Individual factors influencing telework 531
          1.   Telecommuter profiles 531
          2.   Productivity perceptions 531
          3.   Understanding individual participation motivation 532

    B. Organizational networks surrounding telework 533
        1. Teleworkers' perspectives 533
        2. Coworker perspectives 534
        3. Management perspectives 535
    C. Community factors influencing networks.. 536
        1. Infrastructure issues 537
        2. Service delivery issues 537
        3. Stakeholders issues 538
IV. Discussion.. 538
    A. Home work environment: telecommuting and beyond 538
    B. Community environment: a service-driven approach 539
V. Research directions 540
VI. Conclusion... 541
Acknowledgments... 541
References... 542

ABSTRACT

This chapter examines how digital technologies are affecting work and community, with a special emphasis on how these technologies are enacted across individual, organizational, and community levels. The specific areas of interest are virtual forms of telework and community technology applications as have been pursued in the state of Minnesota. Three waves of data collection activities were conducted: a survey of teleworkers in public and private organizations, a series of follow-on in-depth interviews with telecommuters and colleagues from these organizations, and focus groups with community leaders on broader planning challenges to integrated community technology services. Findings from these waves revealed the extent to which the success of virtual activities depends on the surrounding activities by local organizational and community networks. In terms of individual teleworking, the survey results found that teleworkers had positive perceptions of their personal productivity, but that they also realized how success was dependent on supportive organizational actions. Follow-up interviewers confirmed this perception, as teleworkers, coworkers, and their managers all noted the need to undertake actions (such as regular face-to-face meetings) that attend to social networking and knowledge-sharing limitations of teleworking. Further, the community focus group findings highlighted the extent to which community success with technology deployment is in significant part due to the extent to which community participants collaborate to develop "action-oriented" forums for deployment. These results provide confirmation that virtual activities do not occur in isolation, but rather should be seen as part of a broader knowledge sharing and building enterprise occurring in organizations and communities.

I. INTRODUCTION

Fulfilling the promise of the digital economy is increasingly understood to depend less on infrastructure investment and more on its strategic use in fostering knowledge. In his 1959 book *Landmarks of Tomorrow* the ever-prescient Peter Drucker predicted the rise of knowledge work and its critical role in the U.S. economy. Indeed, recent surveys indicate high-knowledge industries, such as health care and computer software, accounted for 43% of net employment growth during the 1990s, with continued growth expected despite the recent downturn in the economy (Florida, 2002). Such growth and concurrent changes in work forms have in significant part benefited from the expansion of the electronic infrastructure (Weill and Broadbent, 1998).

In fact, substantial literature suggests that the continuing growth in telecommunications will facilitate remarkable changes in nearly every aspect of life, not only in the work arena, but in individual developments in lifestyle and travel, as well as macrolevel changes in, for example, organizational and community infrastructure systems for delivery of crucial human services (Mitchell, 1999; Horan, 2000). Over the last 4 years, the Hubert H. Humphrey Institute of Public Affairs, University of Minnesota, and the Claremont Information and Technology Institute, Claremont Graduate University, have collaborated on research to examine the realized and potential implications of telecommunications implementation for local communities in Minnesota.

As across the nation, prosperity in Minnesota is increasingly equated with access to knowledge. Access to the appropriate community-level infrastructure is perceived to be a fundamental requirement for accessing digitally based knowledge systems. At the national and international levels, concern regarding implementation of adequate telecommunications capacity has resulted in several major initiatives aimed at bringing information to all walks of life (Bridges.org, 2001). At the local level, communities across the country are wrestling with how to accelerate access (Department of Commerce, 2000). The driving belief behind such efforts is captured in a report written by Minnesota's Citizens League (2000: 1), which declared, "telecommunications networks are the highways of this century and, just as success in communities of the 1950s and 1960s depended upon access to roadways, economic success in the 21st century is dependent upon access to infrastructure-dependent information highways."

This and similar perspectives, however, imply a deterministic model with technology pictured as causative agents of change and eventual systemwide evolution. The implication is that technology and access to it are independent phenomena capable of driving change within social settings. This study, however, is predicated on the basis of an alternative theoretical frame — one in which the technology–change relationship is depicted by an *enacted* model (Orlikowski and Iacono, 2000). Developing this model, Orlikowski and Iacono (2000: 357) argue, "changes associated with the use of technologies are shaped by human actions and choices, while at the same time having consequences that we cannot fully anticipate or plan." Recognition of the embedded nature of technical and social dimensions has historical roots in early organizational studies. For example, Trist (1951) noted changes in mining technology were met with substantial and unanticipated alterations in work outcomes largely related to the then unacknowledged role of the social context. Consequences were unanticipated, and, failed to understand the enacted nature of change, in an unintended direction.

Policy and research initiatives suggest benefits to local communities accrue with improved access to advanced telecommunications infrastructure (Wheeler et al., 2000). Major anticipated benefits include improvement in community-knowledge-enabling capacity and concurrent economic well-being. Knowledge, in particular the personal tacit dimension, is understood to be embedded in and conveyed through social systems. Scholarly literature devoted to understanding knowledge creation and distribution in organizational settings, too, suggests management efforts through infrastructure and technology development alone underappreciate the potential for unintended negative consequences (Sveiby, 1997; Davenport and Prusak, 1998). Specifically, the deterministic model on which such management approaches are based fails to consider the enacted properties of the technology within the social context.

Broadly speaking, the intent of the research described in this chapter has been to contribute toward efforts to identify and understand the infrastructure and public policy issues related to realizing knowledge-enabled communities. By way of focusing the discussion, telework implementation in Minnesota will be used to explore the application of an enacted perspective for understanding the relationship between technological change and systems performance at the organizational level. Findings will then be applied to exploring ways in which an enacted perspective can inform study and design of infrastructure at the community level.

A. Telework

From among a number of technology-enabled programs, telework was chosen as the focus for this study because of the multilayered perspective it offers to the problem of enacted change. While previous literature has focused on the individual, organizational, and community-wide implications of telework, the multiyear research strategy employed here has provided the opportunity to explore both the micro- and the macrolevel in an integral fashion, thus highlighting the embedded nature of technology.

1. Defining the concept

It must first be noted, however, that there are fundamental difficulties in understanding the current and potential long-term effects of anticipated changes with telework implementation, challenges that cross studies and are widely attributed to the problem of defining the concept in a consistent fashion (e.g., National Research Council, 1994; Handy and Mokhtarian, 1995; Ellison, 1999; Bailey and Kurland, 2002; Vega, 2003). As part of a movement toward location-independent work styles, telework falls along what is increasingly conceptualized to be a continuum from the more traditional forms of work predicated upon consistent face-to-face contact to the more virtual forms of organizing, such as teams in which face-to-face interaction is nonexistent (Davenport and Pearlson, 1998). While telework has been used with reference to the entire continuum of forms of location-independent work, initial conceptualizations anticipated the substitution of technology for work-related travel (Nilles, 1998). McCloskey and Igbaria (1998) note that telework has been redefined with successive studies, each study emphasizing varying aspects including:

(1) Work location (e.g., home vs. telecenter)
(2) Employment status (salaried employees vs. contractors)
(3) Implementation strategy (part-time work at home vs. virtual work)
(4) The role of technology (technology dependent vs. technology independent)

The manner in which telework is defined focuses attention on certain combinations of these (four) attributes (Bailey and Kurland, 2002).

In a related vein, while telework and telecommuting are often used interchangeably, researchers tend to view telework as more inclusive, incorporating a range of alternative strategies including mobile work and telecommuting (Nilles, 1998; Ellison, 1999; Vega,

2003). Telecommuting is a narrower range of activities usually limited to employees who choose to conduct some portion of regularly scheduled work from a remote location away from the central workplace, including home or some other remote center (Handy and Mokhtarian, 1995; Nilles, 1998). In terms of the survey summarized below, participants were initially identified as a result of either their own or a coworker/subordinate's participation in formal telecommuting programs. Results, however, revealed most respondents were engaged in multiple forms of virtual work, including off-site work from a client's office. Thus, the broader term telework is employed in this chapter.

2. Factors regarding implementation

Judging from the growing volume of literature devoted to the topic, telework has tremendous appeal in academic, management, and public policy circles. Spurring this interest, or perhaps spurred by it, the implementation of such programs in both private- and public-sector organizations has steadily increased nationwide during the 1990s. The appeal of telework results from the multiple benefits it promises across a wide range of stakeholders, including individual employees, their families, employing organizations, and public agencies. In the corporate world, the establishment of telework is driven by efforts to improve employee productivity, increase worker morale, reduce worker turn-over, and decrease office facility costs (see McCloskey and Igbaria, 1998; Ellison, 1999). Benefits to workers include the reduced expense and stress of commuting and the increased flexibility in work hours, offering potentially more time for fulfilling family obligations (Duxbury et al., 1998; Gillespie and Richardson, 2000). Public policy supports telework for achieving employee and organizational benefits as well as social advantages such as decreased traffic congestion, reductions in environmental pollution, and energy conservation (Niles, 1994; Ellison, 1999; Vega, 2003).

Despite substantial benefits, formal telework programs continue to be relatively underutilized (Mokhtarian and Salomon, 1997; Ellison, 1999; Vega, 2003). Recognizing benefits to be gained, however, steps have been taken in the public sector to encourage its utilization. According to the National Telecommuting Initiative Action Plan (1996), federal government agencies are responsible for implementing telecommuting as part of their overall strategy to improve services and working conditions. The Department of Transportation, for example, has provided project leadership, assistance, or set forth examples for a functioning telework policy.

At the state level, Minnesota has generally mirrored this national trend. Minnesota policy developed in 1996 provides strong support for the implementation of telework programs in public agencies throughout the state (Minnesota Department of Administration, 1997b). Further, the Minnesota Department of Transportation (MnDOT) avidly promotes alternative travel behavior including telecommuting. The department views telework as a means to reduce congestion and improve well-being and productivity among its own employees, as well as in public and private organizations throughout the state (Cahoon, 1996).

3. Minnesota traffic problems

Among macrolevel social concerns, the problem of congestion has largely spurred a policy focus in telework program facilitation (United States Department of Transportation, 1997). The impetus for this study emerged initially from a similar concern. As in urban areas across the U.S., roadway congestion presents a major growing problem to the Minneapolis–Saint Paul region (MnDOT, 2000). Findings from a recent Texas Transportation Institute study placed the twin cities area 16th among 70 of the nation's most congested urban areas (TTI, 2000). Faced with the pressures increased congestion implies, since 1991 MnDOT has joined with other state and county agencies to encourage drive-alone commuters to choose alternative modes of transportation. Efforts encourage multiple solutions, including carpools and telecommuting (MnDOT, 2000).

In promoting a multiple-solutions approach, Minnesota policymakers join scholars in recognizing that remote work alone is unlikely to reverse the congested roadway conditions brought about by diverse changes in lifestyle, organizations, and technology (MnDOT, 2000). Early projections of significantly reduced roadway congestion with telework emerged from theory that argues technology substitutes for travel. Research, however, suggests a more complex relationship and a number of alternative theories. Evincing an enacted perspective of the relationship between technologically enabled change and human behavior, these theories include the possibility of complementary trips and travel stimulation (Mokhtarian and Varma, 1998).

4. Individual and organizational dimensions

As across the U.S., research indicates there was also a steady increase in the implementation of telework programs in Minnesota organizations over the past decade (ITRC, 2000). For example, results from the 1997 statewide Omnibus Survey show percentage of respondents claiming to telecommute at least 1 day per month increased from 18% in 1994 to 24% in 1997 (Jackson, 1999). The U.S. West study, conducted for the Minnesota Chamber of Commerce, also explored the extent of statewide telework implementation (Sundel Research, 1999). Interviews of 200 businesses indicate nearly one third (36%) of respondents allowed employees to engage in work from home and other sites.

While research suggests telework implementation is growing, organizational barriers to participation (e.g., managerial reluctance) continue to constitute an obstacle in realizing the initial exuberant estimates regarding participation levels (Ellison, 1999; Vega, 2003). Program implementation largely rests on social contextual aspects that alternately serve to facilitate or constrain adoption rates. Thus, while public policy may provide general support, organizational acceptance and promotion remains the key factor for the continued expansion of remote work (Baltes et al., 1999).

Among organizational benefits examined in the literature, the most frequently discussed and tested relate to anticipated productivity improvements. A number of studies suggest a link between performance indicators and telework, with teleworkers in general comparatively more productive than on-site employees (Dubrin, 1991; Park et al., 1996). Impressive increases have been cited in research across private- and public-sector organizations (e.g., Dubrin, 1991; Moss and Carey, 1994; Belanger, 1999). As predicted by the enacted change model, the implementation of a telework technology, however, is not without unanticipated and sometimes negative consequences. Some of these have proved to be significant barriers in the individual adoption of telework. Among unintended negative consequences, employee isolation has been particularly remarked upon, beginning with the early literature (Olson and Primps, 1984; Shamir and Salomon, 1985). On the whole, the literature suggests one of the more notable constraints to participation in telework is fear of isolation (e.g., Salomon and Mokhtarian, 1997; Cascio, 2000; Vega, 2003).

Early research and theory suggest isolation through telework has potentially negative implications for individual employees, including reduction in social support (Olson and Primps, 1984; Richter and Meshulam, 1993). While such outcomes may be unfavorable to individual well-being, telework implementation and participation have potentially important implications for both individual employee and organizational knowledge creation and dispersal capacity.

Nonaka and Takeuchi (1995) argue that social context functions to foster and support the dynamic interplay between the explicit and tacit knowledge dimensions in realizing innovation within organizations. Explicit knowledge is consciously accessible; it can be articulated and is frequently acquired through formal education, or explicit instruction, or both (Polanyi, 1967; Sternberg, 1996). Consequently, sharing of explicit knowledge does not require colocation, but can be transmitted via electronic communications (Majchrzak et al., 2000). Embodied or tacit knowledge, on the other hand, is more personal and not so easily transmitted. Theoretically it underlies that knowledge is acquired essentially at an unconscious level, thus the tacit domain generally must be inferred from actions or statements as it can not be or is not easily articulated (Nonaka and Takeuchi, 1995; Sternberg, 1996). It tends to be context specific, increases with experience, and is relevant to the attainment of goals (Nonaka and Takeuchi, 1995; Sternberg, 1996).

Theorizing the implications of telework for knowledge creation, Raghuram (1996) suggests remote work may function to impede the sharing of the tacit component in particular. As ongoing face-to-face social interaction is required for its sharing, the tacit element may not be transmitted within contexts limiting contact between organizational members. And in their early work, Shamir and Salomon (1985) argued isolation from the work group is likely to actively reduce productivity because coworkers play a key role in socialization, which in turn is the foundation for tacit knowledge sharing (Nonaka and Takeuchi, 1995). Accordingly, depending on the strategy used in implementing telework, the consequences for individual and organizational level performance in the knowledge economy could be far-ranging and potentially disadvantageous. Findings from the first and second waves of research (below) explore this very issue.

B. Community Network Research Issues

Access to telework programs varies widely. To the extent such variation is a function of factors associated with the workplace, the home environment, or the community, it can be said that the electronic activity occurs within the context of a multilayered socio-technical network. Recognizing the enacted character of the relationship between technology and its consequences, the research issue addressed here surrounds elucidation of the manner in which community design might best facilitate integrated digital connections in such a fashion as to realize anticipated positive consequences.

Design, in the sense used here is more than just an exercise in academic semantics; design represents a way of seeing that seeks to understand community development as a part of an integrated whole. The frame used here has been adapted from the design process for the built environment offered by Bolan et al. (1999). From this perspective, design "focuses on synthesizing information from many sources in such a way that it converges on a particular situation at hand. A design tends to blend and fuse facts and values — the way things are and the way things turn out to be ... a good design imagines a future circumstance that is both coherent and valued, all the while being explicit about how to resolve the conflicting tradeoffs inherent in all situations" (p. 2).

1. Digital place design

A good design focuses on artifacts, and paralleling enacted theory, designers recognize that physical structures are integrated within a social community. Thus design ideally proceeds with the recognition that changes in one component of the environment will not only affect the built environment but other related system components as well. Further, design focuses attention on the potential of community development to alter not only the physical world but to fundamentally transform community relationships (Bolan et al., 1999). The last point has particular application for integration of the electronic and physical environment. While the intangible nature of telecommunications may suggest there are no implications for community relationships, in reality, its deployment has the potential to fundamentally alter the way people create, share, and exploit information. As information content and applications often reflect important underlying value structures, connectivity has the capability to profoundly change both the relationship and valuation components of the community. Social relations, values, and knowledge overlap (Nonaka and Takeuchi, 1995; Cohen and Prusak, 2001), ultimately therefore design can influence knowledge creating capacity. The goal of design, consequently, is to simultaneously develop a solution of utility while protecting critical community cultures and their embedded stores of knowledge. As Simon (1996) recognized, the design of an artifact focuses attention not only on the integrated solution but also on the values and contexts that surround the solution. This study (in the third wave) investigated this broader context of digital design — that is, not just in the home or workplace, but the home or workplace as embedded within the context of a community.

Previous works by Mitchell (1999), Horan (2000), Wellman (1999), and others have outlined the synergistic relationship between electronic and physical community infrastructure. While it is understood that the local community provides the context, setting, and content for creating vibrant community networks, less is known about the process of knowledge sharing for creating electronic networks within communities. While separate public-sector agencies have differing individual organizational motivations for creating digital networks, a process has to be identified and implemented that unites the disparate talents, expertise, and perspectives of individuals involved in the community effort in a synergistic fashion (Horan, 2000). This synergy provides the foundation for creating new knowledge about individual community contingencies that, appropriately applied, provide for design plans to build upon unique histories and values. The key challenge is to ensure information is strategically targeted in its development and supply and to recognize and stimulate concurrent relationships between community members so as to assure both availability and utility for achieving the ultimate goal of community-wide knowledge creation. To borrow a term from the education literature, the idea is to develop learning communities (Hord, 1997).

The concept of digital place design is envisioned to address these two fundamental challenges, thus providing a process and a system to both meet current needs and allow systems management to adapt to changing environmental demands. The first of these two challenges (the planning process) has been addressed in depth elsewhere (Horan, 2000). Suffice it to say, the community network planning *process* has been undertaken in various settings and the possible actions of various sectors are becoming understood. For example, the e-readiness guide devised by the Computer Systems Policy Project provides benchmarks for action by various community sectors (CSPP, 2001). Several other processes contain similar methods (see Bridges.org, 2001). Not contained in these processes is a contextual understanding of how one can implement a knowledge-sharing system in communities; that will be the focus of third wave of this research.

II. METHODOLOGY

This multiphased project utilized a range of research methods to examine telework and related virtual activity within organizational and community settings. Methods include a survey of teleworkers from two organizations (one public, one private), follow-on in-depth interviews with a subset of these teleworkers and their colleagues (both supervisors and coworkers) and, finally, two focus groups with community representatives regarding broader community network development issues.

A. Phase I: Survey of Telecommuters

The first phase of the research was a survey conducted in 1999. Participants to the study were drawn from two large organizations, one representing private enterprise and the other the public sector. Both had well-established telework programs dating from 1995 (public agency) and 1996 (private firm). Research questions guiding this exploratory work included:

■ What factors are involved in the decision to telecommute?
■ How might telecommuting program implementation impact both individual well-being and organizational effectiveness and productivity?

Data were collected from a total of 797 participants representing a cross section of telecommuting and nontelecommuting employees from each organization. Respondents to the public-agency survey included a census of all formally recognized teleworkers (293), plus a purposive sample of their coworkers. In the private firm, two departments had implemented a formal telework program. Consequently, all 550 employees, including both teleworkers and nonteleworkers, were asked to participate in the study. The response rate was 65% in the public agency and 50% in the private firm.

The structured survey included questions about the nature and type of telework, perceptions on productivity and organizational performance, and (stated) impact on travel behavior. A number of sociodemographic items were also included to assist in developing a telecommuting profile. (For a full description of this survey methodology, see Wells et al., 2001).

B. Phase II: In-depth Qualitative Interviews

In 2000 a second follow-up phase of research was undertaken with the two public and private organizations. In-depth interviews were conducted with approximately 51 teleworkers, their supervisors, and coworkers — these groups were identified through respondents to the first-phase survey. Key research questions were:

- Does telework alter the social and work context significantly for teleworkers and coworkers?
- What were the effects on the employee's and, ultimately, the organizations' knowledge creation capacity?
- Are there telework program implementation strategies that facilitate the maintenance and development of social context?

Following Miles and Huberman (1994) a structured approach was employed for interview development; scripts were developed for each of the three groups. Interviews were detailed and broad in scope. Topics covered with teleworkers included:

1. Characteristics of the respondent (e.g., details of employment history, demographics)
2. Program implementation characteristics (e.g., rationale for implementation, nature of program guidelines, managerial expectations, training)
3. Telework and work outcomes (e.g., work quality, job satisfaction, relationships with coworkers and managers, communications)
4. Questions probing the social context of work (e.g., friendship and peer networks, community involvement and fellowship)
5. Probes related to the challenges of explicit and tacit knowledge dispersal and sharing (e.g., turnover intentions, meeting structure and content, informal information sharing, opportunities for learning through observation, levels of work experience)

The interviews were long; discussions with coworkers lasted between 30 and 45 minutes; with teleworkers and supervisors anywhere between 50 minutes and 1.5 hours. Interviewees were conducted via telephone and taped. Transcripts of the interviews were coded in tandem by three researchers. Analyses were conducted to explore the relationship between telework and a number of factors including organizational social system and learning variables, as well as the potential implication of outcomes for community systems. (For a complete description of this methodology, see Wells et al., 2001 and Wells and Horan, 2004.)

C. Phase III: Community Design Studios

The potential value of community-level networks was examined through two focus groups. These two meetings (dubbed "Design Studio I" [DSI] and "Design Studio II" [DSII]) were held in July and September 2000 at the Humphrey Institute, University of Minnesota. Invited participants included community leaders, experts in telecommunications development, design, telecommunications services, public policy, and so forth. In DSI, participants were invited to ponder and offer insights regarding the problem of identifying possible workable telecommunications services. They were asked to consider the questions:

- What set of telecommunications-related services would help create better communities in Minnesota?
- How do we implement telecommunications infrastructures that achieve envisioned economic benefits while simultaneously preserving community integrity and important underlying values and social structure?
- What local institutions and settings can play a key role in ensuring quality services and access?

During DSII, participants enacted and explored the potential of the design studio — a forum for creating actionable, synergistic knowledge. Before meeting they were provided an agenda with brief guidelines for the design studio. The steps included:

1. Describe the context by identifying key values, existing services, and community goals (provided by the researchers in this case)
2. Using this information, frame the problem through discussion and generative metaphor
3. Identify services to improve and integrate community services and values (again provided by researchers and including distance education, telework, smart travel and telemedicine)
4. Through iterative discussion and reflection, identify implementation challenges and potential community impacts

(A complete description of this design studio group methodology can be found in Wells and Horan, 2001; implications of the findings for creating digital "communities of practice" can be found in Horan and Wells, 2004).

III. FINDINGS

A. Individual Factors Influencing Telework

1. Telecommuter profiles

The survey provided data with which to profile teleworkers and explore potential facilitators or constraints for future telework use. In terms of the responses, of the 797 individuals surveyed, 43% ($n = 343$) engaged in telecommuting while 57% ($n = 454$) did not. Most participant's teleworked from home, with just 5% traveling to a telecenter. In an average week over half (55%) of the entire sample engaged in remote work for 3 to 4 days, 38% 1 to 2 days, while only 7% worked remotely for the entire scheduled work week. Public agency respondents ($M = 2.99$ days, SD $= 3.18$) tended to telecommute more frequently than did those from the private sector ($M = 1.92$ days, SD $= 1.45$).

In agreement with the literature, survey findings suggest person/situation characteristics exist that may predispose one to seek opportunities to work off-site (e.g., Mokhtarian and Salomon, 1997; Vega, 2003). Paralleling findings reported elsewhere, teleworkers in the present sample were more likely to have a high degree of formal education and were also more likely to be married. Departing from previous studies, however, most teleworkers as compared with nonteleworkers in this group were women with children. Results reported in other research suggest teleworkers are more typically male (Vega, 2003). Findings from the current study support literature, which suggests telework may provide a way for career-oriented women to balance the often-conflicting demands resulting from overlapping work and family roles (Duxbury et al., 1998).

2. Productivity perceptions

The survey explored to what extent factors mentioned as motivating implementation of telework in the two organizations might be realized. For example, two variables — commitment and job satisfaction — have been linked to employee turnover. More committed and satisfied employees are less likely to leave their jobs, thus reducing organizational human resource costs (Meyer and Allen, 1991). Both affective commitment and job satisfaction measures were included in the survey. In agreement with the findings from previous studies (e.g., Dubrin, 1991), job satisfaction in both the private and the public organization was higher among teleworkers than in their nonteleworking coworkers. However, in neither sample did teleworkers display any greater commitment to their organizations than did their nonteleworking colleagues.

Survey queries also explored the potential for greater productivity with telework. In one question, teleworkers were asked to rate themselves in terms of work location and work load accomplished. Perhaps not surprisingly, respondents in both organizations tended to believe they were more productive — in terms of greater amounts of work completed — away from the workplace while teleworking. In addition, both teleworkers and their nonteleworking coworkers were asked to rate teleworker productivity levels when working outside the office as (1) less productive, (2) more productive, and (3) equally as productive. Interestingly, teleworkers typically selected *more productive*, while coworkers perceived them to be *equally as productive* when working outside the office as in the office. Thus whether in fact or in perception, results suggest that teleworkers view themselves at least as productive when out as opposed to working in the office, that is, when measured in terms of quantity of work.

3.　*Understanding individual participation motivation*

To understand perceived motivations driving telework participation, survey respondents were also presented with a list of ten of the most frequently reported arguments for engaging in remote work programs. They were asked to choose as many as three for their own circumstances. Among public-sector teleworkers, the number one choice was *I can get more work done away from my usual workplace* (30%), second was *It saves me money* (13%), while the third most frequently chosen response was *I have a long commute* (10%). The same three were chosen among private-organization teleworkers, but in reverse order. Cost savings was still number two (17%), while a long commute moved to number one (23%), and personal productivity fell to third (16%). Note that while 19% of public respondents travel more than 20 miles each way to and from work, over half of the participants from the private firm reported equally long commutes. This notable difference may explain the emphasis placed on commute distance factor by private-sector respondents in the decision to telecommute.

Survey queries explored factors that also might function to prohibit employees from engaging in telework. Again, participants were presented with a list of the ten most commonly reported constraints. Among private-sector respondents, the top three reasons given by nonteleworkers were ordered as follows: *Work tasks require face-to-face interactions with clients* (23%), concerns that he/she would *miss important work-related information* (16%), and he/she *would feel lonely/isolated* (11%). As for public nonteleworkers, the three most commonly chosen constraints included: *Work tasks require face-to-face interaction with clients* (25%), *tasks require face-to-face interaction with coworkers* (20%), and *My manager will not allow me to telecommute* (11%). Recognition of the necessity for face-to-face interaction and perceptions of potential isolation are reflected in prior telework research and, as discussed previously, are often cited as constraining factors. Such findings also suggest implications for the knowledge creating capacity of individual teleworkers and sponsoring organizations; potential results that were explored in follow-up interviews with teleworkers, their supervisors, and coworkers.

B. Organizational Networks Surrounding Telework

During follow-up interviews (i.e., wave two), respondents were queried at great length about their experiences in working from home or a remote satellite office. In general terms, teleworkers in both agencies noted a high level of satisfaction with the program. Most indicated an increased level of productivity, job satisfaction, and improved personal well-being. However, responses from teleworkers, their colleagues, and supervisors suggest telework, and the manner in which it is implemented, may have unintended consequences for workplace functions and processes — particularly for social networks and social learning opportunities.

Through empirical study, social networks (the basis for social capital) have been demonstrated to be important conduits for information sharing between individuals (Cohen and Prusak, 2001). The formal and informal relations upon which such networks are built have clear importance for explicit knowledge-enabling capacities (e.g., Cross et al., 2001). The social environment is also important for tacit knowledge development as its sharing depends on observation within a social context characterized by shared values and collegiality (Von Krogh et al., 2000). Interview results demonstrate the propensity for telework to affect the context for both the explicit and the tacit knowledge dimensions.

1. Teleworkers' perspectives

The private-sector telecommuters had quite different perceptions than their public-sector counterparts due to the different context of the program. For instance, because the (private-sector) program was open to all employees and acceptance nearly guaranteed, enterprise teleworkers did not express as much worry about potential coworker resent-ment. Attenuated coworker tension probably also results from the fact that most firm teleworkers elect to work from home only a part of each workweek, thus there is less perceived potential for work to spill over onto in-office coworkers.

Related to this last observation, few teleworkers in the private organization report the sense of isolation or loneliness agency teleworkers reported. One respondent observed, "I currently telecommute just part time, two to three days per week. I tried to do four to five, and that did not work because I felt too isolated and it was too hard to communicate with coworkers. This is why I only telecommute part time."

In the private organization, five of the nine teleworkers also mentioned the potential for remote work to disrupt social networks and learning opportunities. This seems to be especially the perception and experience of completely virtual employees. For example, one respondent noted, "Maintenance of [work] relationships is very dependent on face-to-face. I wouldn't want to telecommute every day for this reason." When asked *Have you noticed any change in your relationship with coworkers?* another observed, "No because we all do, however, those that telecommute most of the time are now more distant than the rest of the group. Out of site, out of mind, that kind of thing." A third who works 80% from home noted feeling lonely and missing out on important information and ties, noting, "Yesterday I just discovered that a coworker had resigned and the last day is today. This causes me to wonder if 80% telework is too much."

As within the public agency, private-sector teleworkers commented on a number of useful strategies for maintaining social networks. For one, as noted previously, they were required by agreement to be available during core hours (10 a.m. to 2:00 p.m.). And as one teleworker noted, the biggest challenge is "realizing the onus is on me to stay connected." Working out of the office for the majority of the workweek, this teleworker reported increased efforts to send more e-mails and "pick up the phone" more frequently. Another respondent noted, "When I'm on site, it is very important to have face time. I go and have an informal conversation at some point with each team member." Yet another teleworker said, "I try to maintain contact by scheduling lunches, and so on to maintain face-to-face contact with each of my coworkers." A third respondent commented on the critical importance of full attendance, face-to-face unit meetings saying "meetings become important. Aggressive scheduling has to take place to make sure they really take place with all members." One participant related that teleworker guidelines include rules regarding meetings. Teleworkers have to be willing to adjust their own schedules to attend manager's weekly staff meetings. Again, the combined efforts of employees and management seems to be key in maintaining important social network ties.

2. Coworker perspectives

By and large, interviewed coworkers had worked closely with one or more teleworkers for years across both organizations. Private-firm respondents have actually had longer, direct experience, with five reporting direct association for 4 or more years, three from 2 to 3 years, and the last for 1 year. Among agency coworkers, three reported working closely with their teleworking coworkers for at least 5 years, three others for 2 years, and two for 1 year. Most also worked with teleworkers before they began remote work, so they were often able to compare and contrast "before and after" experiences.

Coworker comments overall tended to reveal a positive view of telework, however, they too remarked on the potential for negative outcomes related to social networks and social learning. As in the telework interviews, the more negative experiences seem to relate to full-time, or virtual, telework. For example, when asked *What do you think about telecommuting — is it a good idea, bad idea?* one public agency respondent, who worked in a full time only telework department said, "I do think overall it has had more of a negative than positive effect on our organization and the group as a whole. It has totally alienated everybody as far as you don't see anybody anymore, except rarely. They come in for meetings once in a while so if you want to talk to someone you have to call them. I think the morale is worse and there's no camaraderie anymore." This respondent added, "But it would have been a whole different story if telecommuting were done differently here. There may have been better ways to do it, but employees weren't given the chance to give their input into how it might best be implemented."

Neither agency nor private-firm coworkers seemed to express the resentment their teleworking colleagues feared. The most common source of dissatisfaction on the part of coworkers came from perceptions of slowed responses. One respondent noted, "The people I work with [teleworkers] really, really like it and that makes them good and happy employees and I think that's a good thing. Other than a couple of times I've needed to get hold of a teleworker at home and have not been successful or not gotten an immediate response, it [telecommuting] doesn't impact me at all." Several other coworkers noted a slowed response from telecommuters — in each case the constraint was not perceived as characteristic of telework per se, but rather attributed to individual characteristics of the employee (good vs. bad), technology problems, or information overload.

In contrast, several private-firm coworkers noted that they perceived teleworkers as more accessible than are colocated colleagues. One remarked, "It's easier to reach a telecommuter at home." Another coworker of a field service teleworker noted, "response times are faster as it's more efficient to have the teleworker log on from home." However agreeing with agency respondents, three coworkers did note teleworkers' responses seemed a bit slow.

As previously observed in agency teleworker interviews, the more effective teams and units have developed strategies to foster social learning and strengthen network ties. For example, several report that they engage in both formal and informal meetings. For instance, when asked, *Have you noticed any change in your interpersonal relationship with him/her*, one agency respondent said, "No change. Relationships with telecommuters have remained close because coworkers function as a team. We help each other out a lot and are frequently in contact." Another observed that coworkers and teleworkers both attend meetings in which they discuss difficult cases and possible solutions. These provide opportunities in which "we learn from each other's experiences." Yet another respondent said, "Every two weeks we all try to have 'informal time' when we all get together for lunch, and we catch up there. Everybody's kept 'in the loop' and we find out what's going on with each other."

Finally, in agreement with agency teleworker interviews, a couple of agency respondents noticed and commented on increased incidents of "good citizenship" behavior among teleworking colleagues. These help to facilitate social networks and offset potential resentment. One agency coworker related, "When I went on vacation . . . they [teleworkers] just offered to take my cases and that was very helpful to me since I didn't have to worry about work so much on my vacation. I came back and things were really great."

3. *Management perspectives*

Spontaneous comments from manager interviews served to illustrate an overall awareness of the importance of social learning to agency performance. At the same time, a couple of agency supervisors expressed concern that telework might play a negative role. For example, when asked, *To your knowledge, are there plans underway to expand telework [in the agency] in the future"* one manager said, "Yes, although there has been a hold on telecommuting, because we [department managers] didn't want more than 30% of the staff telecommuting. One of the reasons given for the halt was widespread concern among managers that the more experienced workers would be telecommuting and not available enough in the office. Specifically, our concerns related to the problems this might bring about for informal learning and socialization of new employees."

When queried regarding the potential disadvantages of telework, another agency manager expressed similar concerns saying, "Brainstorming is compromised. Just the interchange that takes place in the office, talking with someone and maybe someone in the next cubicle overhears and says 'oh yes, I had something like that happen' and can we talk about it? In this way they find new solutions for issues." In part to facilitate social learning opportunities in the workplace, this manager had made it a policy to enforce personal attendance at bimonthly staff meetings because "Meetings are often held around the computer so we can see particular problems with a case." In this way, both tacit and explicit learning is facilitated through such group exploration of complex problems.

Asked to comment about communication networks among staff since the implementation of telework, another agency supervisor had this to add: "Teleworkers and coworkers probably communicate a little less, but when telecommuters do come into the office, they communicate with their coworkers more than before telecommuting. This is understandable since telecommuters want to build upon and maintain connections. For this reason I believe more than half time telecommuting would be a problem and lead to a feeling of disconnectedness and not belonging to the group."

The potential for a network divisive "us" vs. "them" perspective across nonteleworkers and their teleworking employees was another concern echoed by agency managers. Illustrating manager comments, interviewers noted coworkers referred to in-office, nonteleworking staff as "us" and teleworkers as "them" across agency interviews. And one of the chief concerns expressed among agency teleworkers was the potentially negative effect their work location had on relationships with coworkers. Such observations and comments imply a common recognition of the possible need for social network maintenance across employees and their supervisors in the agency.

C.   Community Factors Influencing Networks

During a telling interview, one manager suggested problems with network maintenance among his teleworkers was due largely to uneven availability of and access to electronic/digital infrastructure across local communities. The third wave of research activities that occurred in summer and fall 2000, builds upon this observation and explores the problem of access in the wider context of community implications of digital technologies. Below are the findings and directions from the two expert roundtables. While the association between telework and knowledge building in communities may not be immediately obvious, there is a connection. To the extent organizations are embedded within communities, their actions affect the immediate environment and in reciprocal fashion so too does the community context influence organizational capacity. For example, knowledge workers may be attracted to communities with family-friendly employers, bringing in sources of both explicit and tacit knowledge to the organization and community. In this vein, theorists have argued that dense social ties within communities form important knowledge resources (Putnam and Feldstein, 2003). Such social capital becomes important in the knowledge enabling of communities as it provides the conditions necessary (e.g., shared values, trust) for realizing tacit knowledge sharing (Coleman, 1988).

In general, roundtable participants recognized important community benefits from telecommunications infrastructure implementation. Improvements in health care, education systems, and other important services, including telework, were all perceived as achievable across communities but their delivery is perceived as stalled by inadequate or nonexistent infrastructure. Developing such infrastructure was seen as a desirable and critical goal for economic development as, from an enacted conceptual frame, such technologies potentially provide not just conduits for information streams, but also potential platforms for community network development. In this fashion, infrastructure development might potentially stimulate both explicit and tacit components for realization of knowledge-enabled community environments.

Achieving actionable solutions to the problem of inadequate access proved difficult, as illustrated by design studio participants' use of multiple and diverse metaphors/frames used to understand the problem. These frames included, for example, (1) a business problem, (2) a policy quagmire, (3) a problem of achieving and maintaining intracommunity relationships, and (4) a problem of equitable information access. However, this is in part explained by the varying community conditions that confront those who endeavor technological advancements for community gain. That is, contingencies in the environment would likely suggest a particular frame.

Despite this variability in problem definition, observations made in DSI and DSII suggested utility in the service-driven, integrated design approach. This analysis of focus group discussions revealed a plethora of issues and challenges to achieving this "service driven, integrated design approach" to community electronic connectivity and these were grouped into infrastructure, service-delivery, and stakeholder issues (Wells and Horan, 2001). The findings are summarized below.

1. Infrastructure issues

Community planners are often daunted by the prospect of tailoring the "right" telecommunications infrastructure to rapidly changing conditions and technologies. Participants in DSII suggested an all-at-once approach is untenable and, accentuating the enacted vision for the role of technology, argued for a needs-driven strategy focused on delivering valued services. For example, representatives from southwest Minnesota noted that the interest in jobs and economic development was a key driver for developing services in their (rural) region. From this perspective, infrastructure design should begin with assessment to identify which services would best fit community needs. This assessment should expand beyond consideration of current infrastructure and should include description of the context, current economic clusters, institutional structures, and so on.

Particularly in rural areas, the "last mile" has proven an imposing barrier to ubiquitous access. Participants in DSI and DSII noted it is not always practical or possible to achieve infrastructure to each individual dwelling and, accordingly, embedding infrastructure in community centers (such as schools and libraries) might serve as a useful location for community-based electronic services. This suggestion is consistent with the idea that community learning can be an integrated electronic and location-based experience.

2. Service delivery issues

DSII participants acknowledged the challenge of integrating various service streams (e.g., distance learning, telecommuting) and DSI and DSII participants noted the need for leadership to achieve an integrated telecommunications infrastructure design. Participant experiences suggest implementation is especially facilitated through inclusion of community leaders and decision-makers from the very beginning in community design efforts. While this leadership often came from existing institutional players (e.g., state colleges such as Winona State University in Winona), participants concurred on the need to develop an "action oriented forum" that allowed these institutional players to operate outside of their traditional purview and develop a shared understanding of the community needs.

Comments from DSI and DSII suggested creating sources of knowledge and user-focused services may be particularly important for the long-term prosperity and well-being of small and rural regions — especially those that have historically relied on traditional industries. In Minnesota, as elsewhere in the U.S., logging and agriculture, for example, are losing ground to knowledge work industries, including medicine and medical device development. The general theme of these remarks was that the goal should be to provide opportunities for new industries while simultaneously respecting, preserving, and even building upon valued characteristics of existing industries that make communities unique. (For example, the Snowmobile industry in northern Minnesota has used distance learning to enhance the training of its employees).

3.   Stakeholders issues

Participation is a critical prerequisite to achieving an effective design. It is generally held that multiple perspectives aid in the generation of actionable solutions, and participation is acknowledged as an important component in achieving commitment (Sanoff, 2000). In terms of the design studios, their discussion also suggested citizen participation speeds resident education with possible uses of advanced telecommunications systems. In addition, inclusion of local decision-makers helps speed implementation and with more positive consequences.

To realize effective community networks for telecommunications systems, strategic alliances and partnerships were viewed as instrumental. These must be identified and developed early in the process. DSII comments suggested that, lacking strategic partnerships (e.g., providers, intracommunity relations, nodes of access), effective telecommunications infrastructure is difficult to achieve. A number of experts in developing telecommunications noted that it is difficult if not impossible for any single organization (government or private) to be responsible for developing all of a community's information infrastructure resources. Local government might take the lead but partnerships must be actively pursued to provide the necessary ingredients for realizing community e-rich visions (e.g., capital, expertise, resources, and maintenance). Community telecommunications planning efforts should make it *a priori*ty to target a range of partnerships. This was considered by DSII participants to be an "action-based" forum that could make advanced telecommunications a reality in areas that might not be served, such as rural areas. Moreover, participants from previous efforts in Minnesota (e.g., Winona) noted that a range of participants could be involved, such as educational and community institutions.

As noted earlier, a number of problem frames were proffered by participants as instructive for developing telecommunications system design. The unfolding of these multiple perspectives serves to reiterate the critical point in a design perspective: multiple possible frames exist for any problem and the frame depends on the individual/professional lens or perspective used and the context in which it is developed. Multiple actionable solutions are possible in response to these varying frames. This suggests two points brought out in DSI and DSII. First, there is no one best approach to the design of a community telecommunications system. As an enacted perspective might presuppose, the "right" approach depends on the individual community context and the current needs of residents. A needs assessment should drive infrastructure development. Frames are not mutually exclusive but can and should be integrated in the design process such as "reflective practice" (Schön and Rein, 1994). Second, local participation is a necessary prerequisite — the "true" problem often lies somewhere at the convergence point between problem framing and participant knowledge desires.

IV.   DISCUSSION

A.   Home Work Environment: Telecommuting and Beyond

Examination of the overall telework environment suggests advantageous outcomes may be realized at both the micro- and macrolevels through policies supporting teleworking. Concurring with other studies, the wave one and wave two findings from Minnesota suggest there is merit in facilitating telework choice among individuals, for example, to escape from a long commute and improve personal productivity. Results also demonstrate variables important to organizations, such as potentially effectiveness-enhancing productivity and job satisfaction, are achievable through telework implementation. Thus findings provide an argument for continued promotion of telework in both the private and pubic firms included in the study. However, results also suggest outcomes associated with telework are not always clearly advantageous. Interview probes suggest perhaps unintentional negative consequences may result from telework implementation strategies that fail to consider and preserve important opportunities for social learning and social networks.

Results from this study agree with earlier research that shows variables related to the individual as well as organizational factors function to constrain telework. Among public respondents, a number of nontelecommuters reported that their manager would not allow them to telecommute — managerial resistance is an obstacle frequently mentioned in the literature (e.g., Ellison, 1999; Vega, 2003). The realities of the employment environment, such as jobs that require face-to-face interaction with clients or customers, also impose obstacles that will likely continue to effectively limit telework — especially as realization of tacit knowledge intensifies in importance, with innovation increasingly important to the success of workplaces.

Finally, the in-depth interviews noted the blurring of organizational networks across business and home network lines. While a teleworker may be working at home, often his or her "work network" resides in the office place. And, therefore, a range of management policies and practices need to be implemented to gain the advantages of telework while minimizing the potential adverse consequences.

B. Community Environment: A Service-Driven Approach

The design studios revealed the importance of networks within the community setting as well. And, like the private sector, there needs to be consideration for the perceived value of the information being transmitted electronically (vis-à-vis traditional face to face). Electronic services must be perceived to fill a need in order for it to be used — and consequently useful — to community members. Thus, community leaders and planners should begin by embracing an attitude tantamount to a classic marketing perspective and ask a fundamental question, "What is truly a 'service', truly a 'utility' to the customer" (Drucker, 1985). This service-driven perspective is consistent with designing infrastructure appropriate to developing learning communities.

Pulling these streams together and given the current focus on knowledge creation as key to economic success, it seems logical to target systems of learning in community infrastructure design. Schools become obvious access nodes. One of the distinguishing characteristics of a knowledge-driven society is that "access to jobs is gained through a good deal of formal education and the ability to apply theoretical and analytical knowledge. Above all, [knowledge workers] require a habit of continuous learning (Drucker, 1995: 226). One way to ensure effective community knowledge management is to ensure opportunities for learning through strategic implementation of distance education or tele-education services.

Distance learning has been applied successfully at the K-12 level to achieve a number of benefits. Of broad appeal is the use of the Web as a tool to enhance learning opportunities in traditional school settings by promoting inquiry and learning that reaches beyond the limitations of textbooks (Barker, 2000; Cohill and Kavanaugh, 2000). In Blacksburg, Virginia, school networking has proven successful in improving family and community involvement — both of which are related to student performance (Ehrich and Kavanaugh, 2000: 150). Similar efforts are underway in Minnesota at the elementary school level (Minnesota Office of Technology, 1998).

At the higher education level, universities — such as the University of Minnesota — have taken steps to play an important role in the provision of continuous, lifelong learning possibilities. For example, a wide number of courses are offered through the University of Minnesota's Independent and Distance Learning program (Minnesota College of Continuing Education, 2000). Fittingly, scholars such as Noam (1995) have observed that the most powerful learning environments may very well be those that combine the on-demand characteristics of the online learning environment with the strongly tacit characteristics of the local learning environment. And indeed, learning is not limited to the formal education process. These findings have highlighted the importance of learning communities in organizations and communities, and the challenge to using electronic technology to enhance (not detract from) such learning.

V. RESEARCH DIRECTIONS

The enacted view of technology, therefore, nests the employee within the organizational and community context. While the multiwave nature of this study provided streams of findings from each level — and some interactions — clearly a more tightly integrated analysis is needed, including perhaps a quasiexperimental style to assessing the influence of service-driven broadband infrastructure on community learning and knowledge building. While previous studies have persuasively identified the links between high-bandwidth connectivity and local community social networks (e.g., Hampton and Wellman, 2003), the embedded view would expand this analysis to include organizational and community learning dimensions. And, in terms of a design perspective, it would assess these connections in a proactive deliberate manner — that is, examination of how integrated public–private partnerships for enhancing connectivity affects employees, citizens, managers, and community enterprises. This multiwave effort was conducted to explore such connections, but more systematic research on case implementations is clearly needed. Such research would build on the strong foundation first begun in the examination of "civic networks" and recently expanded to include a wider array of community informatics (Gurstein, 2000).

Returning to the earlier waves of this research, one dimension of "community informatics" that could benefit from continued exploration is the emerging role of the teleworker in the workforce as well as in the community. There is more than one approach to telecommuting; this study focused on instances where telecommuters remain part of the "traditional organization," are typically home-based or in a satellite office, and enjoy the benefits of both employer and employee. Studies show, however, that new, small organizations built around networked technology have been established in the last 5 to 10 years, often resulting from outsourced tasks from larger traditional organizations. Their structures and methods and location of working may be fundamentally different from the more traditional organization. Increasingly, the U.S. economy depends on such small entrepreneurial businesses. Small businesses tend to implement telecommuting and other alternative work approaches in an effort to offer benefit packages that are competitive with those offered by large organizations. Thus future research should focus on telecommuting in these nontraditional, small, and home-based organizations and what these forms of work mean for local community (economic) development.

VI. CONCLUSION

In conclusion, knowledge creation and management are increasingly viewed as essential for effective performance of individuals, organizations, and even larger communities. Yet, planning efforts toward planning and management of information-access infrastructures are frequently narrow in their focus. The focus is too heavily on the provision of hardware as a proxy for knowledge without due consideration of the dynamics for achieving knowledge creation. And, a key dynamic for creating knowledge-based communities (whether in the private or the public sphere) is the interaction between the situation and the social interaction of people in that setting. As Nonaka and Takeuchi (1995: 58) maintain, "knowledge is created by that very flow of information, anchored in the beliefs and commitment of its holders."

A similar observation is made by Davenport (1997) in his *Information Ecology* in which he urges an approach to managing information that ensures materials suited to context, need, and the values of end users. Davenport writes, "the status quo approach to information management — invest in new technology, period — just doesn't work. Instead managers need a holistic perspective, one that can weather sudden business shifts and adapt to changeable social realities. This new approach ... emphasizes an organization's entire information environment. It addresses all of a firm's values and beliefs about information (culture); how people actually use information and what they do with it (behavior and work processes); the pitfalls that can interfere with information sharing (politics); and what information systems are already in place" (Davenport, 1997:4).

While Davenport's observations were written about individual organizations, the same statements could be made concerning telecommunications infrastructure planning and management at the level of the community (Horan and Wells, 2005). Providing communities with information-producing infrastructure will not provide the sort of resources needed for effective development unless community members perceive the information to be of value, readily accessible, and of use. While some have suggested that digital information has led to the "death of distance," the reality is that locally based knowledge creation remains a vital part of local economic and community growth.

ACKNOWLEDGMENTS

The authors would like to gratefully acknowledge the support provided by the Minnesota Department of Transportation (MnDOT), the Minnesota Guidestar Program, the ITS Institute at the University of Minnesota, and the U.S. Department of Transportation. The authors would like to especially acknowledge the contributions of Frank Douma, Lee Munnich, and Daryl Anderson to the overall conduct of these studies. The authors also express their appreciation to Hannes Loimer, Laura Olson, and Cynthia Pansing for their contributions to data collection and analyses. More detailed findings on individual research waves (particularly with regard to transportation implications) can be found in Wells and Horan (2001, 2003), Wells et al. (2001), and Horan and Wells (2005) also elaborate on these (wave three) findings in terms of digital communities of practice.

REFERENCES

Bailey, D.E. and Kurland, N.B., A review of telework research: findings, new directions, and lessons for the study of modern work, *Journal of Organizational Behavior*, 23, 383–400, 2002.

Baltes, B.B., Briggs, T.E., Huff, J.W., Wright, J.A., and Neuman, G.A., Flexible and compressed work-week schedules: a meta-analysis of their effects on work related criteria, *Journal of Applied Psychology*, 84, 496–513, 1999.

Barker, B.O., Anytime, anyplace learning, *Forum for Applied Research and Public Policy*, 15, 88–92, 2000.

Belanger, F., Worker's propensity to telecommute: an empirical study, *Information and Management*, 35, 139–153, 1999.

Bolan, R., Pitt, D., Rickey, P., Williams, G., and Wilwerdig, J., *The Epistomology of Design*, Humphrey Institute, University of Minnesota, Minneapolis, MN, 1999.

Bridges.org, Spanning the Digital Divide: Understanding and Tackling the Issues, Washington, D.C., 2001.
Available at: http://www.bridges.org/spanning/pdf/SpanningTheDigitalDivide.pdf

Cahoon, E.H., Mn/DOT Policy Position Statement, Administration No. 93-4A-G-1 Telecommuting Policy, March 4, 1996.

Cascio, W.F., Managing a virtual workplace, *Academy of Management Executive*, 14, 81–90, 2000.

Citizens League, Securing Minnesota's Economic Future: A New Agenda for a New Economy, 2000.
Available at: http://www.citizensleague.net/studies
Accessed on 8/10/2000.

Cohen, D. and Prusak, L., *In Good Company: How Social Capital Makes Organizations Work*, Harvard Business School Press, Boston, 2001.

Cohill, A.M. and Kavanaugh, A.L., Eds., *Community Networks: Lessons from Blacksburg, Virginia*, Artech House, Boston, 2000.

Coleman, J.S., Social capital in the creation of human capital, *American Journal of Sociology*, 94, S95–S120, 1988.

Computer Systems Policy Project (CSPP), *The CSPP Readiness Guide for Living in the Networked World*, Washington, D.C., 2001.
Available at: http://www.cspp.org/projects/readiness/

Cross, R., Rice, R.E., and Parker, A., Information seeking in social context: structural influences and receipt of information benefits, *EE Transactions on Systems, Man, and Cybernetics*, 31, 438–448, 2001.

Davenport, T.H., *Information Ecology: Mastering the Information and Knowledge Environment*, Oxford University Press, Oxford, 1997.

Davenport, T.H. and Pearlson, K., Two cheers for the virtual office, *Sloan Management Review*, 39, 51–65, 1998.

Davenport, T.H. and Prusak, L., *Working Knowledge: How Organizations Manage What They Know*, Harvard Business School Press, Boston, 1998.

Drucker, P.F., *Innovation and Entrepreneurship*, Harper & Row, New York, 1985.

Drucker, P.F., *Managing in a Time of Great Change*, Truman Talley Books/Dutton, New York, 1995.

Dubrin, A.J., Comparison of the job satisfaction and productivity of telecommuters versus in-house employees: a research note on work in progress, *Psychological Reports*, 68, 1223–1234, 1991.

Duxbury, L., Higgins, C., and Neufeld, D., Telework and the balance between work and family, in *The Virtual Workplace*, Igbaria, M. and Tan, M., Eds., Idea Group, Hershey, PA, 1998, pp. 219–255.

Ellison, N.B., Social impacts: new perspectives on telework, *Social Science Computer Review*, 17, 338–356, 1999.

Florida, R., *Rise of the Creative Class*, Basic Books, New York, 2002.

Gillespie, A. and Richardson, R., Teleworking and the city: myths of workplace transcendence and travel reduction, in *Cities in the Telecommunications Age: The Fracturing of Geographies*, Wheeler, J.O., Aoyama, Y., and Warf, B., Eds., Routledge, New York, 2000, pp. 228–245.

Gurstein, M., Ed., *Community Informatics: Enabling Communities with Information and Communications Technologies*, Idea Group, Hershey, PA, 2000.

Hampton, K. and Wellman, B., Neighboring in Netville: how the Internet supports community and social capital in a wired suburb, *City and Community*, 2, 277–311, 2003.

Handy, S.L. and Mokhtarian, P.L., Planning for telecommuting: measurement and policy issues, *Journal of the American Planning Association*, 61, 99–111, 1995.

Hill, J.E., Miller, B.C., Weiner, S.P., and Colihan, J., Influences of the virtual office on aspects of work and work/life balance, *Personnel Psychology*, 51, 667–683, 1998.

Horan, T., *Digital Places: Building Our City of Bits*, The Urban Land Institute, Washington, D.C., 2000.

Horan, T. and Wells, K., Digital communities of practice investigation of actionable knowledge for local information networks, *Knowledge, Technology & Policy*, 2005 (forthcoming).

Hord, S. M., Professional learning communities: what are they and why are they important?, *Issues... about Change*, 6, 1–8, 1997.
Available at: http://www.sedl.org/change/issues/issue61.html

ITRC (International Telework Research Council), Telework America 2000: Research Results, 2000.
Available at: http://www.telecommute.og/twa2000/research_results_key.shtml

Jackson, M.E., *1998 Employee Telecommuting Survey Results*, Minnesota Department of Transportation, Saint Paul, MN, 1999.

Majchrzak, A., Rice, R.E., Malhotra, A, King, N., and Ba, S., Technology adaptation: the case of a computer-supported inter-organizational virtual team, *MIS Quarterly*, 24, 569–600, 2000.

McCloskey, D.W. and Igbaria, M., A review of the empirical research on telecommuting and directions for future research, in *The Virtual Workplace*, Igbaria, M. and Tan, M., Eds., Idea Group, Hershey, PA, 1998, pp. 219–225.

Meyer, J.P. and Allen, N.J., A three-component conceptualization of organizational commitment, *Human Resource Management Review*, 1, 61–89, 1991.

Miles, M.B. and Huberman, A., *Qualitative Data Analysis*, 2nd ed., Sage, Thousand Oaks, London, 1994.

Minnesota College of Continuing Education, *Independent and Distance Learning*, University of Minnesota, Minneapolis, MN, 2000.

Minnesota Department of Administration, *State of Minnesota Telecommuting Program*, Minnesota Department of Administration, St. Paul, Minnesota, 1996.

Minnesota Department of Administration, Telecommuting Pilot Program Assessment, 1997.
Available at: http:www.state.mn.us/ebranch/admin/ipo/telecomm/telecomm.html

Minnesota Department of Transportation (MnDOT), About Minnesota Guidestar: Mission, Vision, Background, Organization, Strategic plan, 2000.
Available at: http://www.dot.state.mn.us/guidestar/aboutus.html

Minnesota Office of Technology, News Release: Five Schools Receive Grants from Virtual School Ventures to Start a Community Web Site, 1998.
Available at: http://www.state.mn.us

Mitchell, W., *E-topia*, MIT Press, Cambridge, MA, 1999.

Mokhtarian, P.L. and Salomon, I., Modeling the desire to telecommute: the importance of attitudinal factors in behavioral models, *Transportation Research A*, 31, 35–50, 1997.

Mokhtarian, P. and Varma, K., The tradeoff between trips and distance traveled in analyzing the emission impacts of center based telecommuting, *Transportation Research D*, 3, 419–428, 1998.

Moss, M.L. and Carey, J., Telecommuting for individuals and organizations, *The Journal of Urban Technology*, Fall, Vol. 2, No. 1, 18–29, 1994.

National Research Council, *Research Recommendations to Facilitate Distributed Work*, National Academy Press, Washington, D.C., 1994.

Niles, J.S., Beyond Telecommuting: A New Paradigm for the Effect of Telecommunications on Travel, September 1994.
Available at: http://www.1b1.gov/ICSD/Niles

Nilles, J., What's Telework?, Jala International, Inc., 1998.
Available at: http://www.jala.com/definitions.htm

Noam, E., Electronics and the dim future of the university, *Science*, 270, 247–249, 1995.

Nonaka, I. and Takeuchi, H., *The Knowledge Creating Company: How Japanese Companies Create the Dynamics of Innovation*, Oxford University Press, Oxford, 1995.

Olson, M.H. and Primps, S.B., Working at home with computers: work and nonwork issues, *Journal of Social Issues*, 40, 97–112, 1984.

Orlikowski, W. and Iacono, S., The truth is not out there: an enacted view of the "Digital Economy," in *Understanding the Digital Economy: Data, Tools, and Research*, Brynjolfsson, E. and Kahin, B., Eds., Massachusetts Institute of Technology, Boston, 2000, pp. 352–380.

Park, G.S., Nilles, J.M., and Baer, W.S., Trends and Factors Influencing Telecommmuting in Southern California, Report DRU-1465-SCTP, Center for Information-Revolution Analysis, Santa Monica, CA, RAND, 1996.

Polanyi, M., *The Tacit Dimension*, Doubleday & Company, Garden City, New York, 1967.

Putnam, R. and Feldstein, L., *Better Together*, Simon & Shuster, New York, 2003.

Raghuram, S., Knowledge creation in the telework context, *International Journal of Technology Management*, 11, 859–870, 1996.

Richter, J. and Meshulam, I., Telework at home: the home and organization perspective, *Human Systems Management*, 12, 193–203, 1993.

Salomon, I. and Mokhtarian, P., Why don't you telecommute?, *Access*, Spring, 10, 27–29, 1997.

Sanoff, H., *Community Participation Methods in Design and Planning*, John Wiley & Sons, New York, 2000.

Schön, D. and Rein, M., *Frame Reflections*, Basic Books, New York, 1994.

Shamir, B. and Salomon, I., Work-at-home and the quality of working life, *Academy of Management Review*, 10, 455–464, 1985.

Simon, H., *Sciences of the Artificial*, MIT Press, Cambridge, MA, 1996.

Sundel Research, Minnesota Telework Study, prepared for Minnesota Chamber of Commerce and U.S. West, March 1999.
Available at: http://www.telework-connections.com/telework-studies.htm
Accessed on 6/24/1999.

Sternberg, R.J., *Successful intelligence: How practical and creative intelligence determine success in life*. Plume, New York, 1996

Sveiby, K.E., *The New Organizational Wealth: Managing and Measuring Knowledge-Based Assets*, Berrett-Koehler, San Francisco, 1997.

Trist, E.L., Some social and psychological consequences of the Longwall method of coal getting, *Human Relations*, 4, 3–38, 1951; Reprinted in *Organizational Theory*, Pugh, D.S., Ed., Penguin Books, New York, 1997.

TTI (Texas Transportation Institute), Mobility Study, 2000.
Available at: http://mobility.tamu.edu

United States Department of Transportation, *Successful Telecommuting Programs in the Public and Private Sector: A Report to Congress*, Washington, D.C., 1997.

Vega, G., *Managing Teleworkers and Telecommuting Strategies*, Praeger, Westport, CT, 2003.

Von Krogh, G., Ichijo, K., and Nonaka, I., *Enabling Knowledge Creation*, Oxford University Press, Oxford, 2000.

Weill, P. and Broadbent, M., *Leveraging the New Infrastructure*, Harvard Business School Press, Cambridge, 1998.

Wellman, B. ed., *Networks in the Global Village*, Westview Press, Boulder, CO, 1999.

Wells, K., Douma, K., Loimer, H., Olson, L., and Pansing, C., Telecommuting Implications for Travel Behavior: Case Studies from Minnesota, Transportation Research Record, No: 1752, 2001.

Wells, K. and Horan, T., Discovering Actionable Knowledge about Community Telecommunications Systems: Concepts and Case Applications of Design Studio Methodology, Proceedings of the Annual Meeting of the Association of Information Systems and Technology, Nov., 2001.

Wells, K. and Horan, T., *Telework and Social Learning*, Paper Presented at Academy of Management, Denver, CO, August 12, 2002.

Wheeler, J., Aoyama, Y., and Warf, B., *Cities in the Telecommunications Age*, Routledge, London, 2000.

31

E-GOVERNMENT: THE URBIS CITIES REVISITED

Alana Northrop
California State University

CONTENTS

I.   Introduction 546
II. Data sets 546
     A.   URBIS 547
     B.   Best of the web 547
     C.   ICMA 548
     D.   Taubman center 548
     E.   Scavo 548
III. Do U.S. cities have a website and how up to date is it? 548
IV. What is on the website? 549
V.   Online transaction features 554
VI. Conclusion 555
References 555

ABSTRACT

In 1975 and 1988 the National Science Foundation funded $1.9 million on studies of information technology (IT) in 42 U.S. cities (URBIS I and II). These are the most studied cities in regard to IT or computer use and were intended to offer us a view of where cities would be moving in the future. But that future has become the past. Moreover, something that represents an IT revolution, with broad ramifications for government and governance, has changed IT in the last 15 years, which is the Internet. This chapter focuses on the URBIS cities and explores their use of e-government, contrasting them with several other data sets: *Government Technology* magazine's Best of the Web (2001, 2002) city winners, ICMA's 2002 city/county survey, the 2002 municipal survey of Brown University's Taubman Center, and Scavo's 2002 survey of city/county websites in each state. Focus is on how up to date the websites are, on common features across websites, on the number of clicks on the home page, and on online transaction features.

I. INTRODUCTION

The most studied U.S. cities in terms of information technology (IT) are the URBIS cities. URBIS was the name given to a $1.9 million set of grants from the National Science Foundation to study IT in U.S. local government in 1975 and 1988. Forty-two cities were selected for the 1975 to 1978 study, which included site visits, interviews with about 40 elected officials and municipal personnel in each city, and 50 to 100 questionnaires for computer users in each city. In 1988 surveys of city employees were again done in those cities. On the basis of these data, numerous books and articles were written that enhanced our knowledge of computer use and relevant management issues across a wide array of information tasks and departments into the 1990s. (A small sample of the writings would include Kraemer et al., 1981; Danziger et al., 1982; Northrop et al., 1982; Danziger and Kraemer, 1986; Northrop et al., 1990.) But since those studies, IT has seen another IT revolution, this time via the Internet, that has also either changed or has the potential of changing the quality and efficiency of public-sector work for both employees and citizens.

E-government is the fastest growing application of IT in the public sector. It is also very new for local governments. Two thirds of city websites are less than 5 years old (Moon, 2002). Hence, our knowledge about e-government is in its infant state. Actually, e-government can refer to government's use of IT in all forms and not just the Web. But in the case of this chapter e-government will refer just to utilizing the Internet and the World Wide Web for delivering government information and services, a definition recognized by the American Society for Public Administration and the United Nations (UN and ASPA, 2001).

In this chapter we revisit the URBIS cities and explore their use of e-government by analyzing the cities' home web pages. The chapter consistently contrasts the web pages of the URBIS cities with the Best of the Web (2001, 2002) city winners. When possible those two data sets are also contrasted with three other national studies on e-government.

II. DATA SETS

The data sets are not perfectly comparable. URBIS and the Best of the Web both focus on cities. ICMA and Scavo include counties as well as cities. Taubman deals with cities but not just the main web page; department- and agency-level web pages are also explored and equally so. Each data set has its own strengths and weaknesses, and none could be argued to perfectly represent e-government in U.S. local government today nor were they all intended to do so. Still, each adds another piece to the e-government story, both present and future, so it was felt the comparison of data sets was useful whenever possible.

It should also be emphasized that this chapter's interest is not simply to describe the current state of e-government in cities but rather to possibly get a feel for where U.S. cities in the future will be going; hence, its emphasis is on the URBIS cities as well as on the Best of the Web winners. Another reason not to focus on the other three data sets is that e-government in those data sets are explored in depth in other professional publications (West, 2001; Scavo, 2003; Moon, ?),[1] unlike the URBIS cities and the Best of the Web

---

[1] At the time of this writing, analysis of the ICMA data were presented in convention papers that are not for quotation. Given the time lag of publication, the analyses will have come out by the time this book is published. Look for articles by Donald F. Norris and M. Jae Moon.

winners. Moreover, some topics are systematically raised only in the current chapter and thus analyses of ICMA, Taubman, and Scavo data do not enlighten us.

Finally, all the data sets are within a year or two of each other, which is important for a study of such a changing IT field.

A. URBIS

The research purpose behind the selection of the city was to prescribe policies for "future cities," rather than simply to describe policy impacts in U.S. cities in the mid-1970s. The study wanted to answer what would happen if cities did X (where X is a policy to decentralize computing, or to automate more, and so forth).

Two conventional approaches to deriving such answers were not chosen. The most conventional approach is an experimental design that was not possible in the governmental setting. The second conventional approach is to sample cities randomly. Such a design was also inadequate because resources limited the sample size to 42 cities,[2] and many policies of interest are rare and would be underrepresented in a random sample. The adopted sample design represented an innovative fusion of designs. By drawing a highly stratified random sample of 42 cities (stratifying simultaneously on six policy variables), the adopted design ensured adequate variation on important policies and substantial statistical independence among these polices (Kraemer et al., 1976).

The URBIS cities are biased toward medium to large cities (see Table 31.1). In fact, no city under 50,000 in population was originally included. Analysis of the websites was done in late April 2003.

B. Best of the Web

Seven cities won the award in 2001 or in 2002. They were New York; Conyers, Georgia; Chicago; Tampa; Honolulu; Dallas; and Indianapolis (Best of the Web, 2001, 2002).

A panel representing the Center for Digital Government and *Government Technology* magazine and other appointed experts chose the cities. There were also county and state winners that were omitted from this study due to their lack of comparability. The

Table 31.1 Population of U.S. Cities and the URBIS Cities

	U.S. (%)	URBIS (%)
Over 1,000,000	1	3
500,000–1,000,000	3	12
250,000–499,000	6	32
100,000–249,999	28	34
50,000–99,999	62	20

---

[2] Albany, NY; Atlanta, GA; Baltimore, MD; Brockton, MA; Burbank, CA; Chesapeake, VA; Cleveland, OH; Costa Mesa, CA; Evansville, In; Fort Lauderdale, Fl; Florissant, MO; Grand Rapids, MI; Hampton, VA; Kansas City, MO; Lancaster, PA; Las Vegas, NV; Lincoln, NB; Little Rock, AK; Long Beach, CA; Louisville, KY; Miami Beach, Fl; Milwaukee, WI; Montgomery, AL; New Orleans, LA; New Rochelle, NY; Newton, MA; Oshkosh, WI; Paterson, NJ; Philadelphia, PA; Portsmouth, VA; Quincy, MA; Riverside, CA; Sacramento, CA; San Francisco, CA; San Jose, CA; Seattle, WA; Spokane, WA; St. Louis, MO; Stockton, CA; Tampa, Fl Tulsa, OK; Warren, MI.

websites were judged on innovation and use of web-based online technology to deliver services, efficiency or time saved, economy or money saved, and ease of use and improved citizen access. Each of these judgmental criteria would seem to be rational standards or goals for e-government. Analysis of the websites was done in late April 2003.

C. ICMA

In 2002 the International City/County Management Association (ICMA) surveyed cities and counties with populations over 2500 on electronic government. Three thousand seven hundred cities and 423 counties responded, which reflects a 53% response rate. The data from this survey were available on the association's website (ICMA, 2002).

D. Taubman Center

In 2001 the Taubman Center at Brown University conducted an e-government survey in the 70 largest metropolitan areas in the U.S. The sample of 1506 websites reflects a 21.5 website average per city, which means department level websites were studied vs. just the central web page for the city. An executive summary of this survey was available on the Taubman Center web page (West, 2001).

E. Scavo

Scavo (2003) of East Carolina University surveyed 145 municipal and county government websites in 1998 and repeated the survey in 2002. The websites were chosen on the basis of a one-fifth stratified sample of local governments in each state, with 114 cites and 31 counties making up the final national sample.

III. DO U.S. CITIES HAVE A WEBSITE AND HOW UP TO DATE IS IT?

According to the ICMA 2002 survey, 74.2% of local governments do have a website. All but one or 98% of the URBIS cities have city websites.[3] It is likely that the lower website percent for ICMA is because the study included cities and counties with very small populations, minimally 2500, whereas URBIS's minimum is 50,000 (Brudney and Selden, 1995). The other three data sets offer us no insight here because they only deal with cities/counties with websites.

Not surprisingly, city websites have become standard for U.S. cities. At first, size of the city and its slack resources seemed to dictate adoption (Brudney and Selden, 1995; Streib and Willoughby, 2002), but time has dampened this. It has gotten easier and cheaper to set up a web page because there are a number of publications that tell local governments how to do so and because help can be found easily on the Web itself (Stark, 2000; Center for Technology in Government, 2001; ICMA InfoPak, 2001.) Thus, we can conclude with a fair amount of confidence that whether to have a city website is no longer a meaningful or that complicated a question.

But how up to date the website is is an issue. As one can see in Table 31.2, there is great variability in how current a city keeps its website. The more current the website is,

---

[3] Little Rock does not have a city website but is part of a metropolitan area website that covers two cities and several towns. Because of this, only 41 cities are used to study the URBIS websites.

Table 31.2   Up-to-Datedness of City Websites[a]

	Twenty-Five URBIS Cities (%)	Five Best of the Web Cities (%)
Updated daily	48	100
Within last week	16	
More than 1 week	4	
Over a month ago	32	

[a] Sixteen or 39% of URBIS cities' sites and two or 29% of Best of the Web cities' sites gave no indication of how current the site was.

the more useful the site is to citizens or tourists (Streib and Willoughby, 2002). For example, websites that list events that have passed discourage use. But websites that do not list weekly events so that the site does not become outdated are also less useful and will be used less by the citizenry or by visitors because they provide no changing information to make more frequent website visits interesting. Why explore a site to get out-of-date and useless information or to get the same old information that has no relation to what to do this weekend or what meeting topics are on the public agenda? "Older" sites also do not reflect well on the professionalism of the city's administration.

Consider that all Best of the Web winners who listed when they update their sites do it daily. But one would not expect less of such winners. Perhaps more interesting, only 48% of URBIS cities update daily, with 32% letting over a month pass between updates; this is among those sites that list such information (39% of the URBIS sites do not give a clue to how current they are). Scavo comments that some of his 145 sites seemed over 2 years old, which is the only other data set to touch on this issue at all.

One conclusion that can be made on the basis of these data is that while cities agree that a website is a no-brainer, the importance they attach to the currency of that website still varies greatly. The opportunities for e-government that come with slack resources and skilled staff (Streib and Willoughby, 2002) may no longer be key to having a website but rather may now apply to the content and currency of the site (Bacher, 2002). Knowledgeable leadership also is said to play an important role in the development of e-government applications (Streib and Willoughby, 2002).

IV.   WHAT IS ON THE WEBSITE?

To answer the above question regarding URBIS and the Best of the Web cities, each website's home page was reviewed, looking for key words or features, such as "calendar" or "government" or photo that appeared from city to city site. Table 31.3 shows the 33 most common key words or features that appear on at least five of the URBIS cities' home pages. (Five was chosen as the cutoff because anything less would represent fewer than 10% of the cities and thus be truly uncommon.) What is initially interesting is how many clickable features appear on a page: an average of 36 and a median of 33 for the URBIS cities, which is really similar to the Best of the Web cities (see Table 31.3).

What is also initially striking is that there is no absolutely common feature for a city web page.[4] No feature is found on every city's web page or even nearly every city's web

---

[4] For an inventory of local government uses of the Internet in 2000 see ICMA (2000).

Table 31.3 Common Items on City Web Pages

Frequency Rating	Item	Forty-One URBIS Cities (%)	Seven Best of the Web Cities (%)
1	News	71	43
1	Search	71	57
2	Government	68	86
2	Mayor	68	57
2	Business	68	71
3	Services	63	43
4	Department	61	43
5	Job/employment	59	71
6	Contact us	56	29
7	Visitors	46	29
8	Map	44	43
8	Recreation and parks	44	71
9	Events	41	43
9	Calendar	41	29
10	City directory	37	43
10	Privacy policy	37	71
11	Police department	27	29
12	Public library	24	14
12	Weather	24	14
13	Fire department	22	29
13	Arts and entertainment	22	29
14	Public meetings	20	29
14	Communities	20	57
14	Neighborhood	20	29
15	Tourism	17	0
15	Link to another website	17	29
15	Taxes	17	43
16	FAQ	15	29
16	Resident information	15	14
16	e-government	15	14
16	Traffic	15	29
17	Photo	12	14
17	Online service	12	29
	Mean number of clicks	36	33
	Median number of clicks	33	30

page (see Table 31.3). "News" (71%), "search" (71%), "government" (68%) "mayor" (68%), and "business" (68%) are the most common on the URBIS cities' sites, using two thirds as the cutoff percent. By the same two-thirds standard the most common features on the Best of the Web city sites are "government" (85%), "business" (71%), "job/employment" (71%), "recreation and parks" (71%), and "privacy policy" (71%). So we venture to say that the number of reasonable features to put on a city's web page is in the low 30s, but what those features are aside from, say, "government" and "business" is highly variable.

Taking a different look at Table 31.3, what do the two groups of cities disagree the most about in terms of what should be featured? The Best of the Web cities highly tout "privacy" (71%) and "communities" (57%) whereas the URBIS cities do not, 37% and 20%, respectively. These are over 30% gaps. If we lower the differences to a 25% gap, we find the Best of the Web cities emphasizing "recreation and parks" (71%) and "taxes" (43%) in contrast to URBIS cities (44% and 17%, respectively). We also see that the URBIS cities emphasize news (71%) and "contact us" (56%) whereas the Best of the Web do not (43% and 29%).

Given that one of the criteria for Best of the Web sites was online services, it is to be expected that they emphasized privacy because this would be of concern for users of such services (Edmiston, 2003; West, 2004). The emphasis on taxes and "recreation and parks" may also be in this vein because the latter listing can allow for class schedules and checking whether a person is registered or not in a class. We will discuss this issue more in the section "Online Transaction Features."

But here it may be enough to suggest that there are so far two operating models of city websites. One is oriented to providing information to citizens; aside from listing "government" and "business" information it also provides news and contact information for citizens. The URBIS cities represent this model (see Table 31.3). Scavo (2003) also describes most U.S. cities as fitting this model today. The other model is more the business or the business end of government model. This type of website is focused on saving citizens time by providing online service payments and must be concerned with privacy issues, as appears to be the case with the Best of the Web cities (see Table 31.3). While the rare business of government model may be celebrated in the Best of the Web cities, it may more clearly reflect the future of e-government because the public demand for e-government as yet is not very great (Holden, 2002). Even in 2000 only 36% of a random sample of Americans had visited a local or state site (West, 2004).

Scavo (2003) found that local government websites were getting more sophisticated and doing so at a fairly rapid pace even though the websites were not as sophisticated as they could be. But getting more sophisticated meant adding more bulletin board items and just barely beginning getting into online service delivery and the ability for citizens to send messages to government personnel. West (2004) found state websites as changing incrementally with few online features but more than cities. What has apparently occurred is that cities have adopted websites per se at a very fast pace. They have moved from no site to almost all having a site and from a few bulletin board features to an increasing number within the last 5 years. A few cities have also considered or are currently offering a little interaction on the site, such as searching records, applying for a permit, and requesting a service.

Marchionini et al. (2003) talked of three categories of e-government services:

1. Access to information apparently like the URBIS cities
2. Transaction services apparently like the Best of the Web cities
3. Citizen participation perhaps more a future dream than any even outpost reality as yet

Moon (2002) takes the progression to five steps, referring to a first step like Marchionini's as information dissemination, then a second step as two-way communication. The URBIS cities seem to fit, making it to the second step. Moon goes on to list a third step, which is service and financial transaction which looks like so many the Best of the Web cities in this page listing online services (see Table 31.3 and Table 31.4). Scavo (2003) provides some evidence that there is a correlation between these steps. Moon's fourth and fifth future steps of e-government are vertical and horizontal integration and political participation.

The last hypothesized political participation steps are speculative and involve an assumption that each successive step is a higher one and an effective, positive, and meaningful goal. Yet, IT's impacts and progressions have been full of surprises. For example, in 1984 the Internet was a somewhat haphazard connection of university computers. Who would have thought the Internet would become a source of individual and business information and a buying and selling outlet? Could anyone have imagined that the Internet would take over the travel industry, cutting out travel agents? So it may really be hard if not impossible to predict where e-government will take us in the future.

At the same time, it is assumed that the Internet is a source of political information that will transform turnout and the way citizens participate in a positive way (London, 1994; Szilagyi, 1994; Edwards, 1995; Sardar, 1996; Pew Research Center, 2000; Moon, 2002; Kakabadse et al., 2003; Marchionini, 2003). But early analyses in the late 1990s and 2000 show only an effect on turnout at the presidential level and not in midterm elections and who knows on local elections (Tolbert and NcNeal, 2003). Also there is some suggestion that the Internet may actually dampen one's political information and have a negative effect on political engagement and democratic community (Putnam, 2000; Sunstein, 2001; Kakabadse et al., 2003). For instance, unlike reading a major newspaper or watching major network television news, a person who gets the majority of his or her

Table 31.4 Online Transaction Features

	ICMA (%)	URBIS Obvious on Home Page	Total[a]	Best of the Web Obvious	Total[a]
Online payment of taxes	4.6%	12.2%	26.8%	14.3%	57.1%
Online payment of utility bills	4.6	2.4	22	14.3	28.6
Online payment of fines/fees	3.9	7.3	29.3	14.3	42.9
Online completion and submission of permit apps	9.3	2.4	12.4	42.9	42.9
Online completion and submission of business licenses	5.1	4.9	7.3	28.6	42.9
Online requests of local government records	28.6	2.4	4.9	42.9	42.9
Online delivery of local government records to requestor	18.4	0	0	14.3	14.3
Online requests for services, such as pothole repairs	30.9	2.4	2.4	42.9	42.9
Online registration for use of recreational facilities, classes	13.1	0	2.4	0	0
Online voter registration	2.1	0	0	0	0
Online property registration, e.g., animal, bicycle	2.5	0	2.4	0	0
Forms that can be downloaded for manual completion	2.5	14.6	31.7	14.3	42.9
Online communication with elected and appointed officials	2.7	0	0	0	0

[a] Total means the sum of the following count: whether the online feature is clearly obvious on the city home page plus whether the online feature does not appear until a citizen clicks on a topic on the home page plus whether it takes two clicks to find an online feature, which would mean it can be found on the second subpage but is not obvious on the home page or on the first subpage.

political information from the Internet via chat rooms and websites may be getting a more biased, less tolerant, and more narrow political view.

Thus, what future cities will put on their web pages may not be an expanded orientation to, or effect on, political participation. In fact, I would hazard that the political setting will have more effect on e-government than vice versa. This hunch is supported by earlier studies of computers and their effect on city government (Dutton and Kraemer, 1977; Danziger et al., 1982). These studies found that automation did not change the political setting but rather reinforced the current political power structure. Others scholars also agree that technology will end up reinforcing the existing social and political structure (Davis, 1999; Margolis and Resnick, 2000; Chadwick, 2001).

Why else would what might appear to be rational expectations about e-government transforming political participation not be an accurate portrayal of the future? Well, for one, political effects, which make rational sense, have been found not always the case in practice. For example, political scientists assumed that independent voters were more likely to be the most thoughtful political actors. Yet, it was found that independent voters are independent not because they are holding off judgment until they research the candidates but because they have so little political knowledge that they cannot even tell the difference between Republicans and Democrats (Campbell et al., 1960). Or consider the expected dramatic Democratic benefits and voter turnout increases expected from the Motor Voter law. No Democratic benefit or turnout effect so far (Knack, 1999). Thus, political scientists have experience with what might be very rational predictions not panning out.

A further reason for not endorsing the political participation step as the future of e-government is it assumes that the Web can seriously drive and transform participation vs. the citizen himself or herself determining such participation. Yet, the citizen has to first come to the Web for political information or online participation and that leaves us with the normal determinants of political participation being initially key: education, income, age, race, and partisanship. Local gadflies might use the Web to keep tabs on and communicate with local government officials, but they are already driven to pay attention and participate. Finally, as of 2001, only 36% of a national random sample had even visited a local government website (West, 2004). So first citizens must come in significant numbers and be transformed politically for there to be a chance for a political participation revolution, which so far appears unlikely.

To answer the question of what is on the website, we again focused on the URBIS and Best of the Web cities. The ICMA data only covered online features, which is discussed in the section "Online Transaction Features."

The Taubman Center analysis evaluated the websites using a 28-feature list. Thus rather than letting the websites dictate the common features, Taubman began with a list and this list emphasized online transaction features. Taubman data show that the most common feature is phone contact information, with 92% of the city government websites (remember the average of 21.5 websites per city) posting the number. Links to other sites is common (67%). The cities in Table 31.3 have a much lower percentage of links, which can probably be attributable to Table 31.3 dealing with city main sites and the Taubman data dealing with department sites that would likely contain a link to the more encompassing main city site. Only 14% of the Taubman sites list a privacy policy, which is much lower than the URBIS and Best of the Web cities. And only 13% have fully online executable services, which is like the URBIS cities. Now we turn to discussing the online executable services discussed in all four data sets and that are considered a higher step in local e-government websites than the information focus, which seems to be the most common.

V.   ONLINE TRANSACTION FEATURES

This step in e-government makes sense given the success of e-commerce generally and government's focus on citizens as customers. And the Best of the Web cities' sites suggest that online transactions will become far more common (see Table 31.4), as does Scavo's (2003) research . West's (2004) research on state government also suggests this but again with more of an incremental change expected.

Several caveats need to be made before we discuss Table 31.4 in detail. In essence, the data in this table can be considered soft and thus should be looked at for grosser patterns only. What makes the data soft is, first, that the ICMA data are based on surveys of chief administrative officers. These officers may not be perfectly knowledgeable about what is on the website. One could either make the case that they would tend to underestimate the online features because they may not be totally up to date on the changing features, or one could make the case that they would tend to overestimate the online features, believing the features are available or "should" be available or at least were planned to be last they knew and probably are online by now. Second, even if forms can be downloaded, it may not be obvious to all site visitors or the forms may not be easy to access. If it takes two or more clicks to get to downloading the right form, not all visitors may find their way or find it in as few clicks. For example, the home page could say "taxes" on it; then when you click on "taxes," you get "business license" as a choice. Click on "business license," and on the next page you see that you can fill out a form. So was submitting a business license online (Table 31.4) obvious on the first web page of the city's site? Probably not for most visitors. In essence, what is obvious to one visitor may not be obvious to another. This caveat particularly applies to the Table 31.4 data on the URBIS and Best of the Web cities. And at the very least raises the issue whether because a city has an online feature, according to the ICMA survey, whether the city really does have it in any practical sense if it is not an obvious and/ or easy to access feature. Third, some of the online features are open for interpretation, such as "online requests for services." This feature is so broad almost anything could fit in it, which might explain why it is the most common feature according to the ICMA data.

All this being said, Table 31.4 can provide us with information when viewed on a gross level. Our initial observation is that online features are still extremely rare. Taubman Center's study also found this. Regarding the first five categories of online transactions, the Best of the Web cities are more on line than URBIS cities, which are more online than the ICMA sample. Our guess is that this makes sense because the Best of the Web cities can be considered the more cutting-edge cities, followed by the URBIS cities, and the ICMA sample may be the most representative of current practice in local government. Still, for now, the ability to pay taxes, fines, or utility bills online is extremely rare, as is the ability to complete permits and business licenses.

The online requests for records and their delivery and the online request for services are very vague categories and perhaps the least trustworthy of the data. Let us say that these look like features that will become more common soon given the ICMA and the Best of the Web cities' experiences or expectations.

Across the three data sets, the most rare online features are voter registration and communication with elected and appointed officials (Table 31.4). Given that these two features would fit with the hypothesized future e-government step of political participation, the race to that step has really not begun and who knows if more than a handful of cities will enter within the next 5 years. This might support our earlier doubt about the political participation step.

VI. CONCLUSION

This chapter has tried to learn about the state, present and near future, of e-government in U.S. cities by focusing on the 42 URBIS cities, the subject of much study over the last quarter century. The URBIS cities' web pages were compared with the 2001 and 2002 Best of the Web winners as well as with results, where possible, of three other national local government studies. Here is what was found.

First, it appears that city websites are now an expected service of city governments, except for the smallest cities in terms of population.

Second, many city websites are not updated very often. Among the URBIS cities, about a third waited for more than a month before any changes were made to the site. Close to half did update daily, and one out of eight updated weekly. All the Best of the Web cities updated daily. We believe that websites are more useful if they contain information that needs daily or weekly updating. Cities that provide such information exhibit a higher presumption of citizen–government interaction and create an atmosphere in which it can take place. We expect that most cities, again maybe exempting very small cities, will increasingly find themselves moving to more frequent website updates.

Third, there was no absolutely common feature on a city web page. But it is common for web pages to contain many features, such as information about the government, weather, jobs, services, events, and traffic. So each city appears to be customizing its web page for its citizenry and visitors. Yet, if the city has a number of online transaction features, it will most likely have a clear privacy policy feature on its home page. Features that could promote political participation appear to be almost totally absent, such as the ability to register to vote or contact an official on line.

Fourth, online transaction features are still very rare across the board except in the cutting-edge Best of the Web cities. But it is likely that the Best of the Web and URBIS cities are indicative of the future trend of city websites. While change may be more incremental than comprehensive with regard to online transactions, it does appear reasonable that the next common step in e-government will be cities offering online transactions in addition to the bulletin features that are the most common today. Budget constraints and privacy concerns are critical to how fast cities can move to this step.

Finally, perhaps an unheralded aid to the progress of e-government may just be getting the word out. City employees need to know about the website and promote it. City publications and tax and utility bills all need to list the web address. Newspaper stories and public service announcements should frequently focus on the existence and features of the website. Just getting the word out can start a dialogue between citizen and government that moves the e-government ball along the road.

REFERENCES

Bacher, G., E-government: for better or worse, *PA Times*, 25, 5, 2002.
Best of the Web, 2001, 2002
    Accessed at www.enterdigitalgov.com

Brudney, J. and Selden, S., The adoption of innovation by smaller local governments: the case of computer technology, *American Review of Public Administration*, 25, 71–86, 1995.

Campbell, A., Converse, P.E., Miller, W.E., and Stokes, D.E., *The American Voter*, University of Chicago Press, Chicago, 1960.

Center for Technology in Government, A World Wide Web Starter Kit, 2001
    Accessed at www.ctg.albany.edu/projects/inettb/startkit.html

Chadwick, A. with C. May, Interaction between States and Citizens in the Age of the Internet: E-Government in the United States, Britain and the European Union, paper presented at the annual meeting of the American Political Science Association, San Francisco, August 30–September 2, 2001.

Danziger, J.N. and Kraemer, K.L., *People and Computers*, Columbia University Press, New York, 1986.

Danziger, J.N., Dutton, W.H., Kling, R., and Kraemer, K.L., *Computers and Politics: High Technology in American Local Governments*, Columbia University Press, New York, 1982.

Davis, R., *The Web of Politics: The Internet's Impact on the American Political System*, Oxford University Press, New York, 1999.

Dutton, W.H. and Kraemer, K.L., Technology and urban management: the power payoffs of computing, *Administration and Society*, 9, 304–340, 1977.

Edmiston, K., State and local e-government: prospects and challenges, *American Review of Public Administration*, 33, 20–45, 2003.

Edwards, A.R., Informatization and views of democracy, in *Orwell in Athens: A Perspective on Informatization and Democracy*, Wim, B.H.J.Van de Donk, Snellen, I.M., and Tops, P.W., Eds., IOS Press, Amsterdam, 1995, pp. 33–49.

Holden, S.H. and Ha, L., Do the facts match the hype?, *PA Times*, 25, 3, 2002.

ICMA, Appendix B: Sample Local Government Uses of the Internet, Local Government Online: Putting the Internet to Work, Item 42550, ICMA, Washington, D.C., 2000.

ICMA, E–Government, ICMA, Washington, D.C., 2001.

ICMA, Electronic Government, ICMA, Washington, D.C., 2002
    Accessed at WWW.icma.org

Kakabadse, A., Kakabadse, N.K., and Kouzmin, A., Reinventing the democratic governance project through information technology? A growing agenda for debate, *Public Administration Review*, 63, 44–60, 2003.

Knack, S., Drivers wanted: motor voter and the election of 1996, *PS*, June, XXXII, 237–243, 1999.

Kraemer, K.L., Danziger, J,N., Dutton, W.H., Mood, A., and Kling, R., A future cities survey research design for policy analysis, *Socio-economic Planning Sciences*, 10, 199–211, 1976.

Kraemer, K.L., Dutton, W.H., and Northrop, A., *The Management of Information Systems*, Columbia University Press, New York, 1981.

London, S., Electronic Democracy: A Literature Survey, paper prepared for the Kettering Foundation, Santa Barbara, CA, 1994.

Marchionini, G. et al., Digital government, *Communications of the ACM*, 46, 24–27, 2003.

Margolis, M. and Resnick, D., *Politics as Usual: The Cyberspace Revolution*, Sage, Thousand Oaks, CA, 2000.

Moon, M.J., The evolution of e-government among municipalities: rhetoric or reality?, *Public Administration Review*, 62, 424–433, 2002.

Northrop, A., Dutton, W., and Kraemer, K. L., The management of computer applications in local government, *Public Administration Review*, 42, 234–243, 1982.

Northrop, A., Kraemer, K.L., Dunkle, D., and King, J., Payoffs from computerization: lessons over time, *Public Administration Review*, 50, 505–514, 1990.

Pew Research Center for the People and the Press, Campaign and Internet Survey, October 10–November 25, N = 1,435, 2000.

Putnam, R., *Bowling Alone: The Collapse and Revival of American Community*, Simon & Schuster, New York, 2000.

Sardar, Z., The future of democracy and human rights, *Futures*, 28, 839–859, 1996.

Scavo, C., World wide web site design and use in public management, in *Public Information Technology: Policy and Management Issues*, Garson, G.D., Ed., Idea Group, Hershey, PA, 2003, pp. 299–330.

Stark, N., Getting Online: A Guide to the Internet for Small Town Leaders, 2000
    Accessed at: www.natat.org/ncsc/Pubs/Getting%20Online/gettingonline.htm

Streib, G.D. and Willoughby, K.G., *The Future of Local Government Administration*, Frederickson, H.G. and Nalbandian, J., Eds., ICMA, Washington, D.C., 2002, pp.199–208.

Sunstein, C., Freedom of expression in the United States: the future, in *The Boundaries of Freedom of Expression and Order in American Democracy*, Hensley, T., Ed., Kent State University Press, Kent, OH, 2001.

Szilagyi, M.N., *How to Save Our Country: A Non-partisan Vision of Change*, Pallsas Press, Tucson, AZ, 1994.

Tolbert, C. and NcNeal, R.S., Unraveling the effects of the Internet on political participation?, *Political Research Quarterly*, 56, 175–185, 2003.

UN and ASPA, Benchmarking E-Government: A Global Perspective-Assessing the UN Member States, 2001
    Accessed at: www.unpan.org/egovernment2.asp

West, D.M., *Urban E-Government: An Assessment of City Government Websites*, Brown University Political Reports, Brown University, Providence, RI, 2001
    Accessed at: www.brown.edu/Departments/Taubman Center/polreports/egovt01city.html

West, D.M., E-government and the transformation of service delivery and citizen attitudes, *Public Administration Review*, 62, 15–27, 2004.

32

AGENCY INTERNETS AND THE CHANGING DYNAMICS OF CONGRESSIONAL OVERSIGHT

Julianne G. Mahler
George Mason University

Priscilla M. Regan
George Mason University

CONTENTS

I.   Introduction 560
II. Online access and requests for congressional casework 561
     A.   Findings and discussion 562
III. Effects on the process of congressional oversight 563
     A.   Findings and discussion 563
IV. Micromanagement 565
     A.   Findings and discussion 566
V.   Implications and conclusions 566
References 568

ABSTRACT

As federal government agencies offer more sophisticated and useful web access to their programs, many have examined citizen use of these services. Other effects of the increasing online access to agency information and services have been less well studied. Here we focus on the effects of the increasing digital capacity of federal agencies on congressional oversight. We explore the impact of expanded online agency offerings on the number and type of requests for casework; on the focus, duration, and number of investigative hearings; and on the detail and specificity with which program legislation is written. This research is based on interviews with committee staff with jurisdiction over two agencies with a strong Internet presence and two with a weak presence.

I. INTRODUCTION

Governments at all levels are rapidly expanding the availability of Internet sites and the range of informational and interactive services at those sites (Mahler and Regan, 2002). In turn, growing numbers of Americans are visiting and using government websites for a variety of purposes, from finding program information to filing forms or offering comments (Larsen and Rainie, 2002). Digital agencies have become more visible to the public and have much lower transaction costs for public use. For example, the federal government website www.regulations.gov allows interested respondents to search out what new regulations are open for comment, lets them search to find what comments have been offered on a regulatory docket, and either provides an address for mailing comments or an e-mail link to submit comments online. Even children (and their parents) are encouraged to visit agency websites and their homework help sections.

A number of researchers have been investigating whether digital agencies are generating new patterns of citizen access and participation, and what the effects of these patterns are on government accountability (Bimber, 1998; Hill and Hughes, 1998; Johnson, 1998; Dawes et al., 1999; Van Wert, 2002; Thomas and Streib, 2003). Here we explore the effects of online agency access on citizen participation and democratic accountability by investigating the implications of digital enhancement in agencies for congressional oversight. Relations with Congress may be affected by public expectations for agency services. Digitally sophisticated websites provide a great deal of agency information. Many websites offer access to detailed program instructions and background reports. In some cases, agencies provide online records of decisions and actions, performance records, research and position papers useful for legislation, and agendas and minutes of meetings. Programs may be offered online, and thereby can be observed in real time. What effects do all these changes in visibility and low-cost information have on oversight?

The implications of agency website enhancement for congressional relations extend in several directions. Higher levels of citizen contacts with agencies may generate higher expectations for agency services and dissatisfaction with what is available, leading to more complaints and calls for casework from members of Congress. A second set of effects could alter the process of oversight. The availability of much greater amounts and variety of information online could influence the number or the focus of hearings. It may be possible for congressional committees to undertake much more detailed investigations based on the ready availability of a rich information base. Finally, the ready access to agency performance data and reports of action could lead to heightened monitoring, restrictions on agency discretion, and a greater degree of micromanagement. These expectations rest on an analysis of congressional oversight, which views Congress as a principal and the bureaus as agents seeking to maximize autonomy and responsiveness to constituencies (Ogul and Rockman, 1990). The costs of information and control are a feature of these choices, and the availability of online information alters these economies in important ways (Figure 32.1).

We investigated these three sets of effects in a series of focused interviews with congressional staff selected to represent committees and subcommittees with responsibility for two agencies with a strong Internet presence and two associated with agencies with a weak online presence. We determined agency Internet presence on the basis of a published report card evaluation of the quality of citizen Internet access (West, 2003) and

Figure 32.1 Hypothesized effects of enhanced agency websites on congressional oversight activties.

our own checklist of available online features and performance. We selected a cabinet-level agency and an independent regulatory agency in each group. The high-ranking agencies under study are the Food and Drug Administration (FDA) and the U.S. Department of Agriculture (USDA). The low-ranking agencies are the Department of Commerce and the Equal Employment Opportunity Commission.

For all the four agencies we interviewed both House and Senate committee staff with oversight responsibility. More than a dozen congressional staff from both the majority and minority were part of our study. We questioned staff about casework, frequency and type of oversight activities, the kinds of information collected for oversight, and perceived links to restrictions on agency discretion in legislative language. Our questions about the effects of enhanced agency websites on oversight were mainly exploratory. As will become evident, interviews with committee staff were not the best way to answer all of our questions. But these results do offer an interesting window into the evolution of oversight in the e-government era. We should note also that because oversight for the Department of Commerce is shared among so many committees, we were not able to cover that department thoroughly.

II. ONLINE ACCESS AND REQUESTS FOR CONGRESSIONAL CASEWORK

How does the greater level of online services affect the casework requests? Though a majority of citizens who access government websites are satisfied with the help they get at the sites, 20 to 25% express dissatisfaction with the sites or services (Larsen and Rainie, 2002) and these citizens may be generating requests for congressional intervention. Have complaints about online services become a visible category of requests for assistance? Johannes (1980: 521) reports that growth in program complexity and in citizen awareness and expectations about programs are the main sources of casework requests. As citizens become aware of federal websites and expect to find information and services at these sites, have complaints to members become more common? Has heightened citizen access to agency information and services created more opportunities for mistakes or misunderstandings in the services offered? Are the expanded information and services themselves more likely to strain agency resources and lead to breakdowns? Do more sophisticated sites generate more or fewer complaints and requests for help than more modest agency websites and services? Casework offers a kind of tacit, informal oversight activity (Johannes, 1980) and a way for Congress to monitor constituency satisfactions. We investigated how these alternative scenarios are beginning to emerge by comparing staff casework requests for agencies with more advanced and less advanced online offerings.

A. Findings and Discussion

In general, our interviews indicated that agency websites have minimal impact on the flow of casework requests from members and district offices. Majority and minority staff in the House and in the Senate agreed that constituents who turn to Congress are usually disgruntled and have a specific question related to their particular case. Although the information on agency websites may be helpful as background information for a constituent letter or phone call, it is usually too general to be of help in resolving a particular case.

In some instances, staff mentioned that they did direct constituents to resources on agency websites for answers to queries that were less specific and immediate than traditional casework concerns. Both majority and minority staff specifically referred to information on implementation of the Farm Bill on the USDA website and information on clinical trials and other drug or treatment information on the FDA and National Institute of Health (NIH) websites. Staff suggested that their casework load may be decreasing, because citizens can get more direct access to previously difficult-to-find information. Staff with oversight responsibility for the FDA in particular indicated that they were receiving many fewer calls than they did before.

Interestingly, these findings do not confirm the effects we expected, as shown in Figure 32.1. Greater citizen use of FDA and USDA websites does not lead to more citizen complaints but enables at least some citizens to find needed information and actually avert casework. It appears in these cases that the higher the quality of the agency website, the more likely was this result. Both the FDA and USDA websites were our highly rated websites. Staff referred citizens to these websites and believed that the information on these websites reduced calls to their offices. No staff indicated that they referred citizens to the Equal Employment Opportunity Commission (EEOC) or Commerce websites or mentioned that agency websites had lessened calls to their offices (Figure 32.2).

An unanticipated finding suggests that interest groups may have a role in building constituency awareness of agency web resources. Staff with oversight responsibility for all the four agencies indicated that information on agency websites was being monitored by interest groups and that these groups were using website information to encourage group members to contact congressional members and committee staff. There is more e-mail correspondence, especially form letters, from constituents and more constituent issue pressure. Staff, especially with oversight for USDA, reported an upsurge in letters related to specific environmental and farm issues.

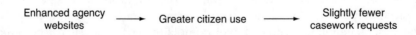

Figure 32.2 Observed effects of enhanced agency websites on casework.

III. EFFECTS ON THE PROCESS OF CONGRESSIONAL OVERSIGHT

A second set of issues emerges surrounding the effects of online agency information on the process of oversight. For agencies with the most enhanced online presence, the capacity of congressional committees to find information they need may be very high and the sheer amount of potentially relevant information may be great. Several questions arise from this circumstance. First, what are the effects of enhanced online presence for the number and duration of hearings and other oversight activities? In an influential article, McCubbins and Schwartz (1984) argue that Congress exercises its oversight duties in at least two ways: by "police patrol," monitoring agency actions in hearings and formal investigations, or by "fire alarm," facilitating complaints by individual citizens and organized interest groups. The latter method is a more indirect but politically efficient oversight method by which members can focus their energies on resolving the problems that matter most to the constituents who elect them, i.e., responding to "fire alarms." Ogul and Rockman (1990) review this and other research that suggests that rich information sources and lower opportunity costs of information for congressional members lead to increased oversight activity. Does this finding hold true for online information as well? How do higher levels of online agency information affect the depth and focus of congressional oversight questioning? We questioned staff to determine if they perceive that the availability of information has led to fewer or shorter hearings. We also wanted to see whether agencies with more online information relevant to program performance are subjected to more detailed or focused questioning. Does access to online information lead to more "police patrol" oversight rather than "fire alarm" oversight? (McCubbins and Schwartz, 1984).

A related issue is the extent to which staff find the online information interpretable and useful for oversight. A major problem in agency policymaking has been the capacity of administrators to interpret performance data for the task of program improvement. Information that the program has not reached its objectives does not necessarily provide an indication of whether or how the agency failed to follow the directives of Congress (Wilson, 1989). Thus we questioned staff about whether they found the information agencies offer online to be useful and relevant for oversight purposes. What information has been used and how has it been interpreted? That information is abundant is not evidence of its usefulness. In fact, information that is too plentiful may cause information overload. Has this occurred? How have staff coped with these pressures?

A. Findings and Discussion

Staff universally agreed that agency websites have not changed the number or types of hearings. As one staffer said, "the drivers for hearings are independent of webpages and agency actions." No staff members in any of the four agencies were able to specify an instance in which an agency website was the original, unique source of an oversight topic. Many did note that websites may help to define an issue, provide an angle for a topic, or point to other related issues.

There was, however, universal agreement that agency websites have resulted in more substantive and more focused hearings, with fewer general questions, less posturing, and less accusation. This finding is consistent with our expectation, as illustrated in Figure 32.3. Several staff mentioned that at the hearings members can quote directly from documents or

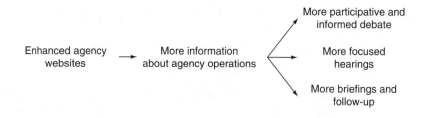

Figure 32.3 **Observed effects of enhanced agency websites on the oversight process.**

letters found on agency websites, ask for clarification about conflicting or ambiguous information, and get agency personnel on the record. Website sources were also thought to provide more analytic information. Agency websites are used extensively in putting together hearing notebooks for committee members with background information and lists of possible questions. In this way, as one staffer said, "web information lets you write questions with more precision and more effective level of detail." Another staff similarly noted that agency websites allow "more choices in where to go with questions and staff can follow up with more questions after the hearings." One staffer noted that the real exploration of issues happens not in hearings, which are typically stage-managed, but in the briefings in which topics are negotiated. These briefings, one staff member linked to the Department of Agriculture noted, are much more frequent than a decade ago. Because of the agency website, staff are aware of more issues more quickly than previously. Staff agreed that in general information on agency websites helps Congress to hold the agencies accountable. This was true for three of the four agencies; the exception was EEOC for which there have not been recent oversight hearings.

Congressional staff, particularly those related to USDA and FDA, concurred that agency websites facilitate other types of oversight. Most often mentioned were more targeted "request letters" that are "better informed, more pointed and more focused." One staff member thought that this minimized "Article I and Article II disputes" and "more time on policy and not on the difficulties of getting information." Both minority and majority staff for the House and the Senate referred to this change, especially staff with oversight of FDA. Staff with oversight of USDA suggested that there might be more meetings with agency personnel and more staff briefings and that this might in part be attributed to information on agency websites. Again, both minority and majority staff for the House and the Senate found this to be the case.

Congressional staff observed that agency websites have significantly enhanced and enlarged information networks. Communication among agency, constituents, and staff is smoother and quicker as participants can so easily access material on agency websites. Websites and e-mails have replaced paper documents and faxes as a means of disseminating information. One staff member described how the Office of Legislative Relations at the FDA communicates by e-mail with links to relevant online announcements and documents, greatly increasing the speed and thoroughness of communication. Stakeholders in the government and outside are linked more closely and fruitfully. This point was highlighted by one majority staff member who noted that agency leadership now plays a particularly important role in deciding what information will be disseminated publicly and so setting the agenda for program debate. Another staffer, in the minority, suggested that agency websites give political appointees more control over information dissemination than was typical when more dispersed and personalized contacts among networks of agency officials, Congress, and constituents were the first source of information. The currency of information is also vastly improved. USDA and FDA scored very high points with staff on this feature, while, not surprisingly, staff had much less to say about communications with EEOC and Commerce.

Although the websites have sped up the process of information gathering, staff did not think that this had changed the nature of congressional oversight or lawmaking. However, their comments did indicate that the speed and volume of information exchange with agencies has actually aided oversight functions. For example, before the Web, USDA published huge handbooks with program information; these are now online and are far easier to access and to search, and they are much more timely. The online documents from the Inspector General's Office of the Department of Commerce were also cited as a means of getting investigative information. The reduction in time spent on gathering information was not seen as insignificant; one staff member said, "the USDA website reduces cost in terms of time and effort from several weeks to a few minutes." Several staff also mentioned that online information gave them "more than a snapshot of what's happening" because policy and management documents were available over a period of time and in a way that allowed one to see other relevant documents. Also, very importantly, one staffer suggested that agency websites "may decrease the influence of the media in raising and defining issues," and others noted that hearings and briefings are less driven by current events and more by long-term monitoring.

The question of information overload drew mixed opinions from staff. All acknowledged that information overload was a potential problem. Some believed that search engines and especially the ability to search large documents for relevant items could overcome any problems. Others noted that overload was more of a challenge for newer staff, who did not have the experience to evaluate the importance or relevance of website information. Two staff members thought that agency websites were a particular advantage for newer staff, who do not have the network of contacts that long-term staff can rely on. In contrast, more experienced staff have the advantage of understanding more about the context of the information.

Staff also acknowledged that the usefulness of agency websites in gathering needed information was likely to depend on party. One majority staff member said, "if you are in the majority, then you don't need the information on websites because you can get it through personal contacts; websites never give you the inside scoop." A minority staff member agreed, but another noted that the information on the agency websites made it possible for minority staff to come up to speed quickly (within a week) even when the majority delayed informing them about an upcoming hearing.

IV. MICROMANAGEMENT

The final set of effects of online agency information on the process of oversight involves the level of detail written into legislation. Because of the complexity of policy issues and the conflict surrounding difficult policy decisions, Congress often gives agencies discretion in developing specific standards and in selecting implementation technologies. Does committee investigation in the presence of plentiful online information lead to micromanagement in oversight or in subsequent legislation? If rich agency websites allow low opportunity costs for at least some of the information collected for oversight purposes, does this encourage or permit congressional interventions at ever more detailed levels of agency operations? By putting program reports online, agencies may open themselves to narrowly focused questions from congressional staff or from citizens through congressional staff.

A. Findings and Discussion

Staff in general agreed that information on agency websites was not leading to micromanagement. However, there were some important nuances as to the effects of websites on the details in legislation. In one case, staff with oversight responsibility for Commerce reported an instance where a Senate bill contained many earmarks; the minority House staff was able to discern from information on an agency website that 28 grants were being awarded on the same topic and were able to have some of these deleted from the legislation. Staff with oversight responsibility for FDA noted cases where documents on the FDA website informed conversations and drafting of legislation. One good example of this was in a recent floor debate over medical devices legislation in which online reports by FDA were circulated to member's legislative aids, leading to an unusually participative and substantive debate, according to staff respondents. In another example we heard about, however, website information documented the absence of effectiveness of a past piece of legislation, and debate turned on the accuracy of the website information.

Our interviews also revealed another unexpected trend. Staff reported that agency websites are particularly useful in tracking implementation of current legislation. Again, this was especially true for the FDA and the USDA, agencies with more advanced and highly rated websites. One staff member noted that based on 10 years of experience with farm legislation there was no change in interactions with agency staff or in the content of the bill, but there was a huge difference in oversight of implementation. "The bulk of the data we use is after we pass the bill and agency websites give us quick access to enormous information." Another staff mentioned that it was easier to monitor implementation of the Farm Bill. Indeed, USDA has put tools up on its website to make it easier for farmers to make informed decisions regarding base acreage; the authorizing committees had encouraged, but not required, USDA to do so and the effect has been that implementation of that part of the bill has gone smoothly. Congress asked FDA to post certain information on its website regarding prescription drug approval to ensure that companies were finishing the trials after the drug was approved. The agency website "provided transparency that was available to everyone." Staff associated with oversight of USDA and FDA also noted that it is easier to keep track of the various stages of the regulatory process on agency websites (Figure 32.4).

V. IMPLICATIONS AND CONCLUSIONS

Our interviews do not reveal a change in what Ogul (1976) distinguishes as manifest or formal oversight as would be exemplified by a change in the number or length of hearings. The interviews do, however, indicate that agency websites make it easier for staff to engage in more subtle or reactive forms of oversight. This is the type of oversight

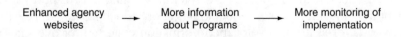

Figure 32.4   Observed effects of enhanced agency websites on micromanagement.

for which it is generally more difficult to gather empirical data. More than half of the staff we interviewed reported that they visited agency websites routinely, if not every day. This was particularly true for staff tracking implementation, rulemaking, and comments on proposed rules. Staff also report more information exchanged through briefings, sparked by information on the websites, and access to analytic information on agency performance.

This increase in more informal oversight may over the long term decrease the need for formal oversight hearings except in periods of divided government. Our interviews clearly revealed that minority staff visited agency websites more frequently than majority staff and were increasingly relying on agency websites as a means of determining what agencies were doing. Previous research indicates that there are more oversight hearings during times of divided government. This research confirms that and may forecast that such hearings will be more targeted and more effective in monitoring agency activities.

In a similar vein, the opportunities for indirect oversight based on paying attention to "fire alarms" (McCubbins and Schwartz, 1984: 166) appear to have been enhanced by the agency websites. Staff report that campaigns organized by interest groups and based on website data are more common since the development of enhanced agency websites. We do not know whether congressional action has followed from these "alarms," but Congress is at least noticing reactions to agency websites as the agencies are required to post certain types of program implementation information. This is occurring for specific agencies, for example the FDA, and also more broadly with various e-government legislation initiatives including the Electronic Freedom of Information Act.

At the same time, our interviews indicate that agency websites make it easier for Congress to engage in what McCubbins and Schwartz (1984) term "police patrol" oversight review. Agency websites lower the opportunity costs of gathering information and provide richer intelligence networks for Congress. Information is more certain or reliable and easier to obtain, which are two conditions fostering police patrol oversight. The police patrol oversight that Aberbach (1990) saw the appropriations subcommittees exercising may in the future become more prevalent throughout Congress. Our inter-views, particularly with staff responsible for those agencies with highly rated websites, indicate that this has already begun to occur. Reports that oversight activities are less driven by events or media revelations and more by intelligence gathered from websites reinforces this conclusion. For example, congressional staff were told that information about DARPA projects to create incentives for nongovernmental intelligence estimates, which they sought for oversight purposes, could be found on DARPA's Internet site. (Graham, 2003)

Finally, our research addresses ongoing discussions regarding the application of principal-agent theory to congressional oversight. Agency websites quite clearly reduce costs of time and effort that the principal needs to expend to achieve control over the agent. But as Ogul and Rockman (1990) argue, there are a number of different entities to whom agencies can be responsible: professional norms, internal constituencies, public interest constituencies, committees, and Congress as a whole. Although information posted on agency websites is available to all these entities, it may privilege some entities more than others. Our interviews suggest that agency websites advantage interest groups and minority staff more than others, especially more than committees. Agency websites may contribute to a weakening of the strength of subgovernments. The interviews lend support to Moe's (1987, 1989) broader institutional theory of bureaucratic control with multiple principals.

REFERENCES

Aberbach, J.D., *Keeping a Watchful Eye: The Politics of Congressional Oversight*, Brookings Institution, Washington, D.C., 1990.

Bimber, B., The Internet and political transformation: populism, community, and accelerated pluralism, *Polity*, 31, 133–160, 1998.

Dawes, S.S., Bloniarz, P.A., Kelly, K.L., and Fletcher, P., Some Assembly Required: Building a Digital Government for the 21st century, 1999
http://www.ctg.albany.edu/resources/rptwplst.html

Graham, B., Poindexter to Leave Pentagon Research Job: Project to Create Futures Market on Events in Middle East Caused Controversy, *Washington Post*, Aug. 1, 2003, pp. A1, 9.

Hill, K.A. and Hughes, J.E, *Cyberpolitics: Citizen Activism in the Age of the Internet*, Rowman & Littlefield, Lanham, MD, 1998.

Johannes, J., The distribution of casework in the U.S. Congress: an uneven burden, *Legislative Studies Quarterly*, 5, 517–544, 1980.

Johnson, S.M., The Internet changes everything: revolutionizing public participation and access to government information through the Internet, *Administrative Law Review*, 50, 277–337, 1998.

Larsen, E. and Rainie, L., The Rise of the E-Citizen: How People Use Government Agencies' Web Sites, Pew Internet and American Life Project, April, 2002.

Mahler, J. and Regan, P.M., Learning to govern online: federal agency Internet use, *American Review of Public Administration*, 32, 326–349, 2002.

McCubbins, M.D. and Schwartz, T., Congressional oversight overlooked: police patrols versus fire alarms, *American Journal of Political Science* 28, 166, 1984.

Moe, T.M., An assessment of the positive theory of 'congressional dominance,' *Legislative Studies Quarterly*, 12, 475–520, 1987.

Moe, T.M., The politics of bureaucratic structure, in *The New Directions in American Politics*, John, E.C. and Paul, E.P., Eds., The Brookings Institution, Washington, D.C., 1989.

Ogul, M.S., *Congress Oversees the Bureaucracy*, University of Pittsburgh Press, Pittsburgh, 1977.

Ogul, M. and Rockman, B., Overseeing oversight: new departures and old problems, *Legislative Studies Quarterly*, 15, 5–24, 1990.

Thomas, J.C. and Streib, G., The new face of government: citizen-initiated contacts in the era of e-government, *Journal of Public Administration Research and Theory*, 13, 83–102, 2003.

Van Wert, J., E-government and performance: a citizen-centered imperative, *The Public Manager*, 31, 16–21, 2002.

West, D.M., State and Federal E-Government in the United States, 2001, (Sept, 2001).
http://insidepolitics.org/egout01us.html

Wilson, J.Q., *Bureaucracy*, Basic Books, New York, 1989.

33

PRIVACY CONSIDERATIONS IN ELECTRONIC JUDICIAL RECORDS: WHEN CONSTITUTIONAL RIGHTS COLLIDE

Charles N. Davis
University of Missouri

CONTENTS

I.   Introduction.. 569
II. The legal principle of open judicial records... 571
III. Electronic access policies.. 573
IV. Conclusion... 579

ABSTRACT

This chapter addresses the growing trend toward electronic judicial records and the policies various states have enacted addressing the issue of privacy. By examining the results of a much-anticipated working group studying issues of e-government and information access, the author examines the challenges posed by electronic records and proposes a more proper balance between the public's right to know and other competing interests.

I. INTRODUCTION

No part of government faces more direct legal compulsion to provide access to its records than the judiciary. Unlike other administrative apparatuses, court records that are not deemed confidential by statute, rule, or court order have historically been open for public inspection, and the U.S. Supreme Court has squarely recognized a federal common law right of access to judicial records,[1] and has hinted broadly at a constitutional right of access as well.[2] That right is not absolute, however; the Court has also stated that "every court has supervisory power over its own records and files."[3] To determine whether access to a judicial record may be denied, the court must employ a balancing test, determining whether the interest in access is outweighed by the interest favoring nondisclosure.[4]

The rapid growth and development of the Internet and related software has revolutionized the way in which governments produce, store, and disseminate information, altering the landscape for judicial records by placing greater weight than ever before on privacy interests in that balancing act. The rise of e-government has seen the personal computer dramatically alter the fundamental nature of the information created through litigation, as records once stored in obscure clerk's offices become digitized and posted on keyword-searchable websites. The growth of e-government in the courtroom thus raises many new and challenging policy issues, particularly on the proper balance to strike between public access and privacy rights. While there has always been inherent tension between the need for public access to certain information and the need to protect private or sensitive information, electronic court records raise the ante considerably by replacing difficult-to-use systems with the ubiquity of Internet access. Twenty-four-hour access to court records by anyone, at any time, heightens concerns about the private nature of information captured in case files.

On the other hand, the movement toward e-government in the judiciary represents a quiet revolution in citizen access and government accountability, part of the growing reality of e-government. Public access to electronic court records provides a convenient way for the public to monitor the judicial system and ensure the fairness and equality of its operations. Public interest is often served by access to judicial records, and remote, anonymous access to court records empowers citizens to better scrutinize the judiciary free from the restraints of time and geography.

Against this backdrop of competing values and goals, courts and legislative bodies across the U.S. have begun the task of implementing policies dictating access to electronic court records.[5] The policies vary widely, but all are influenced to some degree by a seminal 1989 U.S. Supreme Court opinion, *United States Department of Justice v. Reporters Committee for Freedom of the Press*, that forever recast the balance between access and privacy.

This chapter examines the rules that a number of municipal and state governments have adopted in order to move court records online, and discusses the *Reporters Com-*

---

[1] *Nixon v. Warner Communications, Inc.*, 435 U.S. 589, 597 (1978). The right is designed to promote public confidence in the judicial system and diminish the possibilities for injustice, perjury and fraud. See, e.g., *Richmond Newspapers v. Virginia*, 448 U.S. 555, 595 (1980); *Leucadia, Inc. v. Applied Extrusion Technology, Inc.*, 998 F.2d 157, 161 (3d Cir. 1993).

[2] The Supreme Court has not clearly stated that the First Amendment right of access in criminal proceedings extends to judicial records, but a number of lower federal courts have taken that position. See, e.g., *Washington Post v. Robinson*, 935 F.2d 282, 287–88 (D.C. Cir. 1991); In re Search Warrant for Secretarial Area Outside Office of Gunn, 855 F.2d 569, 573 (8th Cir. 1988).

[3] Nixon, supra Note 1, at 598–599.

[4] Id. at 602. See also, *U.S. v. McVeigh*, 119 F.3d 806, 811 (10th Cir. 1997).

[5] At least ten states have drafted or approved rules for access to electronic court records. See Privacy & Electronic Access to Court Records Report and Recommendations Judicial Management Council. Available at http://www.flcourts.org/pubinfo/documents/privact.pdf

mittee decision and how its conceptualization of data privacy has resulted in the triumph of information privacy over the public interest regarding access to information. Using the rules themselves, the chapter explores the dominant strands of privacy doctrine, illustrating the divide between privacy law and privacy policy regarding data protection statutes, freedom of information law exemptions, and other data controls.

II. THE LEGAL PRINCIPLE OF OPEN JUDICIAL RECORDS

Court records are presumptively open to the public for the express purpose of assuring that the public can monitor the integrity of the judicial system. That right is not to complete and unfettered access, but is a rebuttable presumption of openness. In the cases that discuss the right to public access, there is no declaration that access must be provided with state-of-the-art tools. Instead, the message is that where there is a determination that information should be available for review, access to the information should be provided. It must be noted, however, that the right of access to judicial records predates the rise of e-government, and thus cannot be expected to provide much in the way of guidance for electronic access.

The courts generally have recognized a strong presumption in favor of access, holding that only compelling reasons justify denial of access to the case file.[6] Other courts have held that the common law presumption extends to filed documents as well, in the absence of compelling reasons for closure.[7]

In addition to the common law right of access, the U.S. Supreme Court has recognized a limited constitutional right of access under the First Amendment. In *Richmond Newspapers v. Virginia*,[8] the Court held that the First Amendment can be read as protecting a right to attend criminal trials, but the Court has never explicitly extended that right to documents.[9]

Whether common law or constitutional, the right of access to electronic information involves privacy interests that may justify restrictions on access. In recent years, privacy interests have expanded through a series of influential decisions whose catalyst was a 1989 Freedom of Information Act (FOIA) case. Though concerned with a range of records far broader than mere courthouse files, the U.S. Supreme Court's decision in *U.S. Department of Justice v. Reporters Committee for Freedom of the Press* fundamentally altered the jurisprudence concerning claims of privacy under the Freedom of Information Act.[10]

Reporters Committee presented a question crucial to the emergence of electronic access: could an agency invoke privacy concerns to deny access to public records compiled electronically, in large part because they were compiled electronically? The case arose after a reporter filed an FOIA request asking for the FBI's "rap sheet" on a businessman identified by the Pennsylvania Crime Commission as an owner of a business dominated by organized-crime figures. The reporter was investigating because the com-

---

[6] See, e.g., *United States v. Beckham*, 789 F.2d 401, 409–415 (6th Cir. 1986); *F.T.C. v. Standard Financial Management Corp.*, 830 F.2d 404, 408–410 (1st Cir. 1987).

[7] See, e.g., *Pansy v. Borough of Stroudsburg*, 23 F.3d 772, 782 (3d Cir. 1994)

[8] 448 U.S. 555, 575–578 (1980).

[9] Several lower courts have extended Richmond Newspapers to grant a limited First Amendment right to various types of judicial records, both criminal and civil. See, e.g., In re Continental Illinois Securities Litigation, 732 F.2d 1302 (7th Cir. 1984); *Publicker Industries v. Cohen*, 733 F.2d j1059, 1067–1070 (3d Cir. 1984).

[10] 489 U.S. 749 (1989).

pany received defense contracts allegedly in exchange for political contributions to U.S. Rep. Daniel J. Flood.[11]

The FBI refused to release Charles Medico's rap sheet on privacy grounds, and the U.S. District Court for the District of Columbia granted the FBI's motion for summary judgment to dismiss the suit. The court held that the information was protected under the privacy provision of the FOIA's law enforcement exemption.[12] The U.S. Court of Appeals for the D.C. Circuit ruled in favor of the CBS journalist and *Reporters Committee*, reasoning that the government cannot claim a privacy interest in an FBI compilation of law enforcement agency records when those same records would be available as public records from the individual agencies themselves.[13]

The Department of Justice appealed to the Supreme Court, which balanced the individual's right of privacy against the public interest in disclosure and reversed the appellate court ruling, thus allowing the FBI to withhold the information.[14] Writing for the Court, Justice John Paul Stevens said the FOIA's "central purpose is to ensure that the government's activities be opened to the sharp eye of public scrutiny, not that information about private citizens that happens to be in the warehouse of the government be so disclosed."[15] The Court reasoned that because a computerized compilation of an individual's rap sheet does not directly shed light on governmental performance, it falls "outside the ambit of the public interest that the FOIA was enacted to serve."[16]

The Court then turned to the privacy interests raised by e-government. According to the Court, a citizen possesses a protected privacy interest in the criminal history information because "plainly there is a vast difference between the public records that might be found after a diligent search of courthouse files, county archives, and local police stations throughout the country and a computerized summary located in a single clearinghouse of information."[17] Thus, individuals maintain a privacy interest in the "practical obscurity" of records.[18]

Taken literally, this means that public documents that are difficult or time-consuming to locate assume some unspecified, but certainly heightened, level of privacy for no other reason than that they are obscure. And when those hard-to-find documents are assembled electronically, their "practical obscurity" implicates privacy interests in new ways.

The restructuring of the FOIA in *Reporters Committee* through the lens of the "core purpose" test, coupled with the Court's creation of "practical obscurity," has shifted the burden of proof in privacy-related cases. Instead of a presumption of openness, there

---

[11] Flood, who eventually left office in disgrace, was already under investigation for corruption. See id. at 770.

[12] See 5 USC Sec. 552 (b) 7 (C) (1994). The exemption states that the FOIA does not apply to matters that are "(7) records or information compiled for law enforcement purposes, but only to the extent that the production of such law enforcement records or information (C) could reasonably be expected to constitute an unwarranted invasion of personal privacy. Exemption 7 (C) is one of two privacy exceptions to the FOIA. The other exception, Exemption 6, pertains to "personnel and medical files and similar files the disclosure of which would constitute a clearly unwarranted invasion of personal privacy." See id. Sec. 552 (b) 6.

[13] See *Reporters Comm. for Freedom of the Press v. U.S. Dep't of Justice*, 816 F.2d 730, 740 (1987).

[14] See 489 U.S. at 772–773 (citing 425 U.S. at 372.)

[15] See 489 U.S. at 774.

[16] See id. at 775.

[17] Id. at 764.

[18] Id.

now exists a requirement that the requester show that the information sought will reveal — directly — something about governmental operations.[19]

The concept of "practical obscurity" as an interest mitigating toward privacy is seldom discussed in these post–*Reporters Committee* cases, but the notion certainly thrives within the "central purpose" doctrine. The cases present an overall picture of a federal judiciary actively reigning in citizen access to the information collected and compiled by government. The fact that much of that information is compiled, stored, and disseminated through computer networks leads to the logical conclusion that the more the government documents created electronically, the greater the "practical obscurity" of the data. Despite the revolutionary ability of the computer, and of the Internet, to make information more readily available to the citizenry, "practical obscurity" stands ready to limit its vast potential to democratize information.

At the heart of "practical obscurity" is the Court's new categorical approach in cases involving privacy claims. To the *Reporters Committee* Court information is either about individuals or about government; when the two categories blend, the result, in the Court's view, should almost always be nondisclosure. Neither life, nor data, is ever quite so simple. Judicial records are a fine example of that conundrum. The concept of "practical obscurity" embraced by the Court in *Reporters Committee* runs headlong into the far more historical First Amendment right of access to judicial records. The result is a mixed bag of state policies dictating electronic access to an important sector of e-government.

III. ELECTRONIC ACCESS POLICIES

Recognizing the need to reconcile competing privacy and access interests, a variety of national organizations comprising state and municipal court administrators have begun to study the ways in which courts can implement electronic access systems while safeguarding privacy. Several organizations that work in and fund initiatives in the nation's state courts developed a project entitled "Developing a Model Written Policy Governing Access to Court Records."[20] The State Justice Institute (SJI) has funded this project since January 2002, staffed by the National Center for State Courts and the Justice Management Institute, to develop a policy for dissemination to, and review by, the nation's state courts. The SJI-funded project, staffed by NCSC and JMI, has its own project advisory committee, but has provided project updates to the Conference of Chief Justices (CCJ) and Conference of State Court Administrators (COSCA), Joint Court Management Committee, throughout the life of the project.

Within the states themselves, several, including Maryland[21] and New York, have established independent committees to determine the best way for providing electronic

---

[19] See, e.g., Martin E. Halstuk and Charles N. Davis, "The Public Interest Be Damned: Lower Court Treatment of The Reporters Committee "Central Purpose" Reformulation," Administrative Law Review, Vol. 54, No. 3 (fall 2002).

[20] Martha Wade Steketee and Alan Carlson, Developing CCJ/COSCA Guidelines for Public Access to Court Records: A National Project to Assist State Courts (State Justice Institute, National Center for State Courts and the Justice Management Institute, 2002.) Available at http://www.courtaccess.org/model policy.

[21] Report of the Committee on Access to Court Records. Available at http://www.courts.state.md.us/access.

access while preserving privacy.[22] Some states such as New Jersey have actually curtailed their efforts to make records available electronically due to both budgetary constraints and privacy concerns. And while the states' practices and policies on access to electronic court records may differ, they all grapple with the same issues and concerns regarding privacy, cost, and sensitive information. A look at several states' policies reveals the influence of *Reporters Committee* on emerging e-government policy involving access to electronic public records.

Two policy models appear to be emerging in the various guidelines relating to electronic case files. The first position is reflective of pre–*Reporters Committee* ideals that court files are presumptively open under the First Amendment. The essence of this position, which one author has labeled the "public is public" model, lies in the proposition that the medium in which case files are stored does not affect the presumption of openness.[23] Under this model, current means of protecting privacy, such as protective orders and motions to seal, are adequate even in the e-government age. Advocates of this position suggest that litigants do not have the same expectation of privacy in court records that may apply to other information kept by the government.

A second model may properly be described as the "practical obscurity" school of thought, thanks to its reliance (stated or not) on *Reporters Committee* dicta to the effect that unrestricted Internet access to case files inherently compromises privacy by subjecting individuals to scrutiny not linked directly to the central purpose of access, i.e., the monitoring of government itself. While there may be no expectation of privacy in case file information, advocates of this model argue that there is an expectation of practical obscurity that will be eroded through the development of electronic case files.

A look at the federal government's current policy and at several states' approaches to electronic court files underscores the differences between the two models. In 2001, the federal courts issued guidelines for e-filing of court records.[24] The federal guidelines divided civil and criminal files for purposes of policymaking, declaring that the presumption of a right to access for civil filings regardless of medium. Thus, all civil filings and related e-documents are presumtively open, save for a single class of records that might be restricted based on the identity of the individual or the nature of the document being sought.[25]

Criminal files, however, fall squarely into the practical obscurity model. The federal courts recommended that criminal files not be made accessible electronically at all, citing the storage problems of criminal filings and the safety and security problems attendant to them.[26] The committee also cited the danger of defendants and others being intimidated

---

[22] The Center for Democracy and Technology has compiled an excellent 50-state synopsis of state efforts at e-filing, available at http://www.cdt.org/publications/020821courtrecords.shtml

[23] Robert Deyling, Privacy and Access to Electronic Case Files in the Federal Courts, Administrative Office of the United States Courts, Dec. 15, 1999, at 6. Available at http://www.uscourts.gov/privacyn.htm

[24] Report on Privacy and Public Access to Electronic Case Files, Judicial Conference Committee in Court Administration & Case Management, Agenda F-7 (Appendix A). June 26, 2001. Available at http://www.uscourts.gov/press-Releases/att81501.pdf

[25] Id. at A14.

[26] Id. at A-15.

by codefendants with easy access to information about the level of cooperation by other defendants.[27] The federal courts have since relented somewhat, beginning a pilot test of criminal file access in 11 federal courts.[28] If successful, the pilot would be expanded throughout the federal judiciary.

Several states have moved further along the policymaking continuum, falling generally within each of the two policy models.[29] The New Jersey Supreme Court in 1998 became one of the first states to comprehensively address e-government policy with regard to court records. The court created the Public Access Subcommittee in 1996 to develop electronic access policy, and after 2 years of research, the subcommittee concluded that releasing court records over the Internet did not violate privacy rights.[30] Recommendation 5 of the report states, "After carefully considering the privacy concerns ... privacy interests should neither preclude nor limit the public's right to access nonconfidential information in electronic form." The comment to Recommendation 5 further states that the subcommittee acknowledged "the troublesome issues raised by privacy advocates" but rejected "the notion that it is the role of the courts to restrict or suppress access to otherwise public information, gathered and maintained at public expense, based on the possibility that it might be used to the prejudice of individuals in certain cases."[31]

The subcommittee clearly favored the "public is public" model, further finding that requests for information in electronic form should be treated in the same manner as requests for paper copies, and that the judiciary should make available information in the form in which it is used, including data in bulk or batch form.[32] The subcommittee rejected the notion that restricting access to nonconfidential court records is an effective solution to "a societal problem rooted in our information-fueled economy."[33] Instead, the subcommittee declared that the issue at stake was "whether it should attempt to control the 'troublesome' secondary uses of non-confidential information by making such information more difficult for everyone to find, access and compile."[34] This it refused to do. The result is a policy that mandates electronic disclosure of nearly all court files, criminal

---

[27] Id.

[28] Brian Krebs, "Federal Courts to Permit Web Access to Criminal Records," Newsbytes, May 7, 2002, available at http://www.courtaccess.org/federal/documents/federal%20courts%20to%20permit%20web%20access%20To%20criminal%20records.pdf.

[29] More than a dozen states have drafted or are in the process of developing policy for electronic court records. See Privacy & Electronic Access to Court Records Report & Recommendations, Judicial Management Council. Available at http://www.flcourts.org/pubinfo/documents/privacy.pdf.

[30] Supreme Court of New Jersey, Report of the Public Access Subcommittee of the Judiciary Information Systems Policy Committee, at 5 (1998). See also Susan Larson, Public Access to Electronic Court Records and Competing Privacy Interests, Judgelink, at 1. Available at http://www.judgelink.org/Insights/2001/E-Records/.

[31] Id. at 6.

[32] Id. See also Victoria Salzmann, "Are Public Records Really Public? The Collision Between the Right to Privacy and the Release of Public Courts Records Over the Internet," 52 Baylor L. Rev. 355 (2000), at 371.

[33] Supra Note 30, at 69–71.

[34] Id.

and civil, unless protective orders are in place to shield the documents. Vermont's policy has developed along similar lines, as has Washington.[35]

Maryland began developing policy for electronic access to judicial records in 2001, when Chief Judge Robert Bell of the Maryland Court of Appeals appointed a committee to study and make recommendations on electronic dissemination.[36] To date, Maryland's efforts at formulating policy concerning electronic access represent the most thorough and timely review of the issues, and thus merit detailed discussion, in large part because they gave rise to a more formal cooperative between several administrative bodies serving court administrators.

The Maryland effort served as a catalyst for a committee working under the auspices of the National Center for State Courts to develop a model policy for states beginning similar efforts. The model, completed in 2002, was a joint project of the National Center for State Courts and the Justice Management Institute, and featured a public comment period that drew more than 100 comments from interested parties.[37] The guidelines have earned the endorsement of the CCJ and the COSCA and became effective in October 2002, and serve today as the benchmark for current and future access policy development.

The CCJ/COSCA guidelines begin with the proposition that court records are presumptively open, that format should not predicate access, and that while some information might be precluded from public access, such exclusions should be made consistently and not be subject to subjective personal interpretations of potential harm.[38] The guidelines also state that the decision to grant or deny access to court records should not depend on the nature of the request.[39] This is an important policy consideration, for it frustrates the creation of conditional or tiered access policies, in which "approved" requesters enjoy greater access than other, nonprofessional or nonlegal, requesters.

The guidelines document many of the vexing issues surrounding electronic access to court records, some of which must be addressed by policymakers at all levels in the formulation of e-government access policy. While mindful of the many benefits of widespread public access to court records in electronic form, the guidelines are also careful to ensure efficiency on the part of the courts, and to protect individual privacy rights and the interests of businesses in protecting proprietary business information. By beginning with the presumption of openness and then balancing countervailing interests, the guidelines serve as a useful starting point for development of e-government access policy.

From that initial proposition, the guidelines begin to define central terms, such as "court records," "public," "public access," and "judicial proceedings."[40] The definitions are purposefully broad, so as to provide ample room for states to adjust accordingly. For

---

[35] See Vermont Supreme Court, Dissemination of Electronic Case Records, March 6, 2002. Available at http://www.vermontjudiciary.com/Resources/ComReports/pafinalrpt.htm; Washington Supreme Court, General Rules of Application, Judicial Information Systems Committee Rules for Washington, July 1, 1987. Available at http://www.courts.wa.gov/court_rules/?fa = court_rules.display&group = ga&set = jisc&ruleid = gajiscr15

[36] Report of the Committee on Access to Court Records, Maryland Court of Appeals. Available at http://www.courts.state.md.us/access.

[37] Id. at iv–xi.

[38] Steketee & Carlson, CCJ?COSCA Guidelines, supra Note 20, at 1–7.

[39] Id.

[40] Id. at 12–15.

example, the guidelines define "court records" as documents falling within three categories:

1. Documents filed or lodged with the court in proceedings or as part of the case file. Documents in this category include exhibits offered during hearings and trials, and information before the court in making its decision.
2. Information generated by the court, including information from the court administrator and the clerk of court, proceedings before temporary judges or referees ....
3. Information related to the operation of the court. This includes informal policies, memoranda and correspondence, court budget and fiscal records as well as other data that makes the internal policy of the court more transparent.[41]

The guidelines then move from the general presumption of openness to a discussion of the conditions necessary for nondisclosure. First, the guidelines state that when access is denied, the requestor must at least be informed of the existence of the information.[42] In order to facilitate this exchange, the guidelines suggest the use of generic descriptions, captions, or pseudonyms, so that the description of nondisclosable information does not inadvertently disclose the information. This is an area of some contention, as many electronic systems lack the dexterity to process such requests. Where it is possible, however, such masked indicies could help provide the necessary accountability with regard to nondisclosure. Future electronic record-keeping systems should incorporate this goal, or the result will be denials that serve to mask the very existence of information, a scenario to be avoided in all but the most sensitive of information requests.

The next section of the guidelines discusses another contentious issue — that of making access to electronic records conditional upon establishment of identity through tracking users.[43] Traditionally, public records access has been predicated upon the notion that requesters need not disclose their identity or the purpose of their request. The reason for such conditions are obvious: if a right of access exists for all citizens, then the record keeper has no right to ask for such information, which could chill requesters leery of official or nonofficial retribution, tracking, or other responses from the record keeper.

Today's post–September 11 security environment has many policymakers reevaluating nonconditional access, and the guidelines note that such decisions must be made at the local level and thus might vary from jurisdiction to jurisdiction. The guidelines note that the benefits of tracking requesters must be balanced against the inconvenience, intrusiveness, and potential chiling effect of such policies, not to mention the added cost.[44]

The guidelines then turn to the task of suggesting which documents merit what level of electronic access. Section 4.20 of the guidelines begin with the less sensitive documents that should be made remotely accessible almost without exception: indices to cases filed; listings of new cases, including the names of litigants; docket calendars; hearing times and locations; and judgments, orders and decrees.[45] All could be protected,

---

[41] Id. at 14.
[42] Id. at 22.
[43] Id. at 25–26.
[44] Id. 26.
[45] Id. at Sec. 4.20 (a)–(e).

but only by court order; otherwise, the presumption of access would dictate remote electronic access to all such documents.

The guidelines then address the issue of bulk distribution of judicial records and requests for compiled information, the request addressed earlier by the U.S. Supreme Court in *Reporters Committee*. Rather than take a categorical, yes-or-no approach to such data, the guidelines recommend that states recognize the unique time and cost factors inherent in such a request but not reject them out of hand on the basis of time and cost. Instead, the guidelines urge states to consider whether the request is "an appropriate use of public resources,"[46] an amorphous standard but nonetheless an improvement on *Reporters Committee*'s far narrower approach.

In addition, the guidelines allow bulk distribution and compiled information not generally accessible where the information is to be used for "scholarly, journalistic political, governmental, research, evaluation, or statistical purposes,"[47] a vast improvement over the *Reporters Committee* dicta cognizant of the public interest so often attendant to requests for electronic court records.

Finally, the guidelines turn to two broad areas of more sensitive record content. The first involves records relating to children, mental health proceedings, and sterilization proceedings; the second, identifying information of victims, witnesses, informants, and jurors.[48] It is at this point that the guidelines begin to reflect *Reporters Committee* standards, at least with regard to individual privacy interests. Several strands of *Reporters Committee* logic appear in the guidelines, and clearly inform the recommendations.

First, in addressing the identifying data included in electronic court records, the guidelines recommend that states consider whether some categories of information might instead only be accessible at a court facility within the jurisdiction.[49] This clearly harks back to the "practical obscurity" of *Reporters Committee*, in which privacy is maintained thanks to the inefficiencies of paper-based systems.

The guidelines recommend placing such documents in a "restricted access" field, meaning that requesters could ask for access — a definite improvement over blanket exemptions — and states that courts would then be asked to evaluate the risk of injury to individuals, individual privacy rights, trade secrets, and public safety.[50] While recommending that courts employ the least restrictive means neccesary, they do not explicitly recognize the public interest in such records nor do they acknowledge the possibility that privacy interests might be outweighed by such interests.

The "restricted files" approach has much to recommend it, however. As technology advances, courts will be better able to screen identifiers and automate privacy protections, and thus can move greater numbers of records into the public domain as redaction becomes easier. The guidelines suggest, at least halfheartedly, that a subscription-based approach as an alternative to the "restricted files" approach might exist, but the committee saw several problems with that as well, including cost and access to members of the general public.[51]

---

[46] Id. at Sec. 4.40 (b).

[47] Id. at Sec. 4.30(b) &4.40 (c) (1).

[48] Id. at 48–49. These categories include other subsidiary information such as wills, psychological examination records, tax returns and other identifiable financial information.

[49] Id. at 4.50 (a), p. 40.

[50] Id. at 4.70 (a) (1)–(4).

[51] Id. at 4.50.

Overall, though, the CCJ/COSCA guidelines represent the state of play in electronic access issues and highlight all of the critical issues. They recommend a presumption of openness and represent a step forward from the use of exemptions or judicial pronouncements that give short shrift to redaction as a protector of privacy interests. They leave states with ample room to develop more expansive policies. Maryland, in fact, did exactly that, as its committee made no recommendation on subscription access and saw no need to protect privacy interest beyond that afforded by sealed court records and existing statutory provisions elsewhere in state law.[52]

The bottom line is that the CCJ/COSCA guidelines quite rightly leave privacy determinations to the states, and recommend that courts address them on a case-by-case basis. The committee's guidelines are no more than recommendations, but they do signal a commitment toward greater access to electronic court files. The significant step forward from a policy perspective is that records to which access has been prohibited are not forever closed. Indeed, any member of the public may apply for access to such records, initiating a determination of privacy interests to examine whether there are sufficient grounds to continue prohibiting access.[53] The question, then, is whether courts will implement the guidelines in a meaningful fashion or simply revert to the categorical privacy protections of the *Reporters Committee* "practical obscurity" doctrine.

IV. CONCLUSION

Courts are facing the first series of many difficult policy choices with regard to e-government. Much of the discussion over electronic court records to date has focused on privacy issues. Future discussions may well merge privacy interests with security interests. Because new technology eliminates the built-in safeguards that have evolved over time in a paper system, the natural tension between the need for public access to case information and the need to protect certain case information has escalated dramatically.

Many of the arguments in favor of tiered, or conditional, or subscriber-based access to court records focus on the benefits of maintaining some control over the requester, but in their haste to establish prerequisites for access downplay the countervailing value of access itself. Likewise, privacy interests must be balanced against societal interests in access, in accountability, in transparency — values that form the basis of democratic governance.

E-government — particularly electronic court records — forms the intersection in which governmental operations most often collide with the lives of citizens. At the federal, state, and local levels, the courts represent the only venue imbued with First Amendment protections for access. While court administrators have set forth the general parameters for addressing the tension between public access and privacy interests in the context of court records, there remains much room for policy development that better reflects the primary value of transparency within the justice system.

---

[52] Maryland Report, supra Note 21, at Sec. IV 3(a).
[53] Guidelines at Sec. 4.70 (b) (1).

34

INFORMATION TECHNOLOGY AND POLITICAL PARTICIPATION: A COMPARATIVE INSTITUTIONAL APPROACH

Juliet Ann Musso
University of Southern California

Christopher Weare
University of Southern California

CONTENTS

I.   Introduction 582
II. Technological and institutional approaches to participation 583
     A. Democratic participation and the administrative state........................ 585
     B. Methodology 587
III. ENS in a historical perspective 587
     A. Lessons from history.. 587
         1. Vaguely expressed goals and weak sanctions hamper participation
             reforms.. 588
         2. Participatory reforms are not politically neutral 589
         3. Public administrators often resist participatory programs............ 589
         4. Opportunities for participation are exercised differentially......... 589
         5. Benefits from participation are difficult to measure and occur in the
             longer run.. 590
     B. Implementing ENS: the triumph of hope over experience 590
IV. ENS as a technological and institutional innovation.............................. 594
V.   Conclusions 596
Acknowledgments.. 596
References... 596

ABSTRACT

This chapter considers whether new information and communication technologies have significant effects on citizen participation by evaluating the development of a

581

major innovation in electronic governance. We analyze the creation of an electronic system in Los Angeles for providing stakeholders a warning of upcoming political decisions and an opportunity to furnish feedback. We evaluate this innovation not only as a technological innovation that affects citizens' capacity and motivation for participation but also as an alternative institutional means for involving citizens in policymaking and public administration. To place this experiment within this larger institutional perspective, we draw upon the lessons of historical reforms aimed at expanding citizen participation. We find that technology can positively affect individuals' capacity and motivations. Nevertheless, it is not a panacea, because, by itself, technology does not overcome the complex of political, institutional, and behavioral impediments that have limited previous participatory reforms.

I. INTRODUCTION

As with other major innovations in communications technology such as radio and television, the rise of the Internet has spurred significant interest in how this technology may affect the structure and process of political participation. Many have argued that Internet can powerfully advance political communication by providing easier, faster, and cheaper access to information; improving the organization of information; presenting information in more compelling formats; and creating new paths for mobilizing populations (Grossman, 1995; Negroponte, 1995; Morris, 2000). Others have countered that new communication technologies will lead to a potentially detrimental "accelerated pluralism" (Bimber, 1998), and that they reinforce power asymmetries due to the digital divide, and to the ability of elites to control design and use of new technologies. (Davis, 1999; Margolis and Resnick, 2000; Norris, 2000).

This debate on the democratic impacts of the Internet has been heavily influenced by the literature on the relationship between technology and society (Street, 1992). For example, Bimber (2003) argues that the development of new communication technologies introduced a new information regime akin to those created by the advent of the popular press and television. This perspective, not surprisingly, places primary emphasis on technology in the study of technology and politics.

In this chapter we take a different route, treating technology design as one alternative institutional means to increase citizen participation in policymaking and public administration.[1] Efforts to promote greater participation in administrative decision-making, after all, are not new phenomena. Multiple reforms dating back to the rapid growth of the administrative state associated with the New Deal have attempted to forge stronger bonds between citizens and their government. From these reform efforts we glean a number of lessons that enable us to place e-governance reforms in a historical and institutional perspective. Overall, we note a participatory puzzle in previous efforts. While the general

---

[1] In parallel to efforts to increase citizen participation in administrative decision making, there has been significant movement in the U.S. to increase voter turnout and electoral participation. Such reforms include the expansion of the franchise to nonproperty owners, women, African Americans, the young, and the poor. In addition, there has been an expansion of direct elections, most notably the direct election of senators. During the Progressive movement many states adopted efforts of direct ballot-box democracy, including referendums, recalls, and initiatives. More recently, there have been efforts to reduce the costs of voting such as same-day registration, the Motor Voter registration bill, and expansion of write-in ballots. Technology is also playing a role, most notably with the March 2000 Arizona Democratic Primary that was conducted online.

concept of improved citizen participation receives wide support, implementation of programs has typically fallen short of expectations due to goal conflict, political and administrative resistance to reform, and the multiple hurdles in seeking to modify entrenched patterns of political interest and participation.

This chapter employs these lessons to analyze an important experiment in digital government, the creation of an electronic early notification system (ENS) in the city of Los Angeles. In June 1999, Los Angeles voters approved a new city charter that attempted to increase the effectiveness and responsiveness of the city government. The charter's most ambitious provisions created a neighborhood council system, and mandated an ENS that would notify communities "as soon as practical" of pending city decisions and provide them with a "reasonable opportunity to provide input." It was widely understood that this ENS would be an Internet application. The ENS is intended to "level the playing field" of the policymaking process by making government more transparent and responsive.

The ENS demonstrates the promise of Internet-based participatory applications. Most municipal e-government applications have focused on information provision, service delivery, and transaction processing (Musso et al., 1999; Moon, 2002). In contrast, applications that promote citizen input in decision-making or create forums to facilitate democratic discourse have been rare. Importantly, this experiment in Internet-based democratic participation differs significantly from previous Internet initiatives in its level of formality. While other democratic uses of the Internet typically have been voluntary initiatives or demonstrations, the ENS is mandated in Los Angeles' city charter, increasing the potential impact of communications. In addition, it is being created in conjunction with a system of neighborhood councils envisioned to have the interest and organizational capability to employ the ENS to track city actions, disseminate information, mobilize interests, and provide feedback. As such, Los Angeles' new system provides a model of electronic governance that may be emulated by other governmental entities.

Viewing digital governance from a historical and institutional perspective, we find that while technology does affect individuals' capacity and motivations to participate, technology, by itself, does not overcome the political, institutional, and behavioral impediments that limit previous participatory reforms. The chapter proceeds as follows. We first discuss technological and institutional perspectives on participation. We then turn to a comparison of cases, beginning with a summary of major lessons from the history of participatory reforms and continuing with a more detailed review of the Los Angeles case. We then discuss the ENS case from the historical and institutional perspective and offer conclusions.

II. TECHNOLOGICAL AND INSTITUTIONAL APPROACHES TO PARTICIPATION

The burgeoning literature on electronic democracy generally has focused on the analysis of the structure and flows of information (Bimber, 2003). This perspective is natural given that the major thrust of recent innovations such as the Internet has been to improve our ability to manage, manipulate, and communicate information.[2] Moreover, governance can be conceptualized in terms of information processing, involving the aggregation of information concerning political demands and constraints, processing of information in

---

[2] Contrast these results to earlier innovations in computing that more narrowly focused on the manipulation and management of numerical data (e.g., budgets and financial transactions).

decision-making, and dissemination of rules and enforcement actions (Deutsch, 1966; Weare, 2002; Bimber, 2003). Within this framework the literature has explored several avenues by which changing information structure and communication flows can affect political participation, with diverging theoretical and empirical results. These results can usefully be organized employing Verba et al. (1995) typology of factors that determine levels of participation: political capacity, motivation, and recruitment.

New technology is theorized to improve *individual capacity* for political participation by lowering the costs of communication and easing access to the information required for political activity (e.g., candidate positions, policy papers). Studies have shown that e-mail has led to increasing volumes of contacts to Congressional representatives (Davis, 1999; Goldschmidt, 2001). Similarly, Verba et al. (1995: 73) credit technology for increases in citizen contacts with public officials. Whether increased information intensity changes the voices heard by decision-makers, however, remains debated. For example, Congress has reacted defensively to the barrage of e-mails they receive, suggesting that information overload is a problem (Davis, 1999; Goldschmidt, 2001). Others have also argued that increases in informational resources may simply reinforce existing biases in political participation. Observed differences in access to technology and differential predispositions or aptitudes for using new information technologies (ITs) do appear to advantage social and economic elites, who are already the most likely to participate (Norris, 2000; Bimber, 2001).

A number of techno-optimists have argued that multimedia combined with the possibilities for tailoring information more closely to the interests of citizens can *motivate citizens* by making politics more compelling, thus increasing awareness and interest in politics (Grossman, 1995). New technologies also create new communities of interest based on geography or policy interests (Rheingold, 1993; Brainard and Siplon, 2002). Communitarians have argued that this practice in group and community dynamics is critical for building interest in democratic processes. For example, Dahlberg (2001) found online discourse in the Minnesota e-Democracy initiative to encourage respectful listening, facilitate an open and honest exchange, and provide equality of opportunity to all participants. In contrast, analyses of online communities such as Usenet groups have argued that they are dominated by a few individuals and do not support real deliberation (Wilhelm, 1998). Others find that use of the Internet can be just as much of a social isolator as incubator of communities (Nie and Erbring, 2000).

Technology can also *mobilize citizens* by creating new ways in which existing organizations can communicate with existing and potential members and can facilitate the organization of new organizations. A recent example of government-led efforts is the creation of a single portal, www.regulations.gov, through which citizens can comment on rules proposed by federal agencies (Brandon and Carlitz, 2003). Such official efforts remain scarce, supporting scholars who argue that the design and implementation of new technologies will be controlled by existing power elites to sustain their positions (Danziger et al., 1982).

The Internet may also increase mobilization by facilitating collective action and enabling individuals to overcome the problem of free-riding (Macy, 1991; Sell and Wilson, 1991; Cason and Khan, 1999). In a number of case studies Bimber (2003) shows that interest groups have used the Internet to mobilize their members in new ways. Similarly, there are numerous well-known cases in which major protests have been successfully organized on the Web (Norris, 2002). Evidence from new forms of advocacy organizations supported by Internet communications suggests that the Internet does facilitate these intraorganizational communicative needs (Brainard and Siplon, 2002; Norris, 2002). There continues to be debate, though, concerning the extent to which new organizations will benefit from these capabilities, with some contending that existing organized and powerful groups will be best able to take advantage of new technologies (Davis, 1999).

A. Democratic Participation and the Administrative State

In contrast to much of the literature on technology and society, in which the analytic emphasis is a presumed cause–effect relationship between technological change on the one hand, and social or political factors on the other, the starting point for the participation literature is a normative interest in ameliorating institutional failure by engaging the citizenry more directly in governance. These differences in orientation have analytic implications: the participation literature incorporates institutional considerations in a more richly textured fashion than does the technology literature, and it is generally more normative in emphasis.

From the public administration perspective, efforts at digital democratic reform may be framed as variants of the recent "participatory state" movement (Peters, 1996). They are manifestations of the "reassertion of localism" and drive toward citizen participation observed by Box (1998). The resurgence of interest in citizen participation that we observe in recent years is arguably sparked by a sense of "government failure" that comprises both what Box terms a "failure of representation," as well as what one might label a "failure of administration." There is a sense that representatives "shape policy lacking the knowledge necessary for informed choice ... [or] represent the views and interests of a select few rather than the community as a whole" (Box, 1998). This general problem has been aggravated by the forces of modernization and population diversification, which have made urban life more complex, and contributed to an array of "wicked" social and environmental problems that are difficult for a traditional hierarchical government agency to address (Rittel and Webber, 1973). Thus there is a need to address the problems of the Weberian administrative state, wherein implementation by technicians is disconnected from street-level knowledge and coproductive capacities that might facilitate service delivery (Box, 1998; Fung and Wright, 2003).

The participation literature highlights a wide variety of designs for participatory reform, which employ three broad categories of mechanisms: (1) procedural rules, (2) collaborative processes, and (3) devolution of decision-making authority. Procedural rules are employed to assure opportunities for participation by creating check points in the administrative decision-making process at which time citizens are informed of pending actions and given an opportunity to participate. For example, the Administrative Procedures Act mandates federal agencies to advertise pending decisions and allow public comments on proposals. Similarly, sunshine laws require government agencies to make their decisions in public. These check points, however, do not compel governments actively to solicit citizen input.

Collaborative mechanisms are more proactive and include a range of methods for more direct citizen involvement in the policymaking process. These include the community action program boards of the War on Poverty and numerous innovations implemented in the 1970s such as fish bowl planning, public meetings, and citizen review boards. Devolution of decision-making power places the greatest demands on citizen participation and is illustrated by neighborhood councils with formal budget authority over portions of municipal budgets.

Some scholars argue that these institutional options represent a spectrum stretching from weak or thin forms of participation to strong forms of participation (Arnstein, 1969; Barber, 1984). Lower forms of participation such as procedural guarantees and more basic forms of collaboration are argued to often be mere tokenism or efforts to placate citizen groups, while higher forms involve true partnership or devolution of power.

These institutional reforms also might be considered as reflective of a fundamental philosophical tension around the role of the citizen in a democratic society. A critique of American institutions is that liberal representative democracy ("thin democracy" in the words of Barber (1985)) is disempowering because it does not create room for meaningful citizen deliberation. As De Leon (1997) argues, this reflects a historical rift in philosophical visions that oppose the representative model of indirect American democracy with its attendant checks and balances against a Toquevillian participatory or associative democracy.

> De Toqueville undoubtedly posed a much more participatory (i.e. direct) democracy than Madison's "republican" control of factions via pluralism ... Madison chose to redress what he viewed as democracy's shortcomings through external means (e.g., an institutional balance and separation of powers) while by contrast De Toqueville opted for internal (individual civic virtues through personal associations) checks and controls.

Thus the "lower rungs" on the participatory ladder might be considered to emphasize a Madisonian vision in which representation and the authority of bureaucrats is preeminent, while higher forms emphasize Toquevillian concepts of strong or empowered participatory governance.

The goals for participatory reform would depend on the democratic vision informing the program. From a standpoint of Madisonian representative democracy, the criteria have to do with the extent to which voters are informed and mobilized to express their preferences at the polls, thus holding their representatives accountable; whether the interest groups that act as mediating organizations are able to attain information and provide input into the policymaking process; and whether administrative agencies have information regarding the effectiveness of local service delivery. In contrast, proponents of "empowered participatory governance" (Fung and Wright, 2003) argue that deliberation should educate people about the workings of government and their roles as citizens, and build social capital, the norms of trust and reciprocity described by Putnam (2000). It is also thought that properly structured deliberation can help to generate more innovative solutions to public problems (Fung and Wright, 2003), and help people to understand and "work through" intrinsic value conflicts (Yankelovich, 1991). The ability to generate new alternatives and work through conflict implies that community deliberation may also help to promote consensus, or at least, assist people to structure the process by which conflict will be resolved (Mansbridge, 2003). Thus civic engagement has both instrumental goals (results that reflect community preferences) as well as broader constitutive goals: developing a sense of civic identity, increasing political tolerance, educating citizens regarding the norms of citizenship.

In sum, we can enrich our understanding of technological reform by framing electronic forums as part of a broader array of institutional approaches aimed at ameliorating the shortcomings of representative democracy and the administrative state. This in turn requires that a reform program be evaluated with careful attention to the political context for the reform and the goals attendant upon its creation. These goals include promoting an informed citizenry, broadening representation, involving citizens who would otherwise be disenfranchised due to socioeconomic inequalities, and empowering people by creating opportunities to affect government decisions and to self-govern.

B. Methodology

We examine the role of IT in promoting political participation from a comparative institutional perspective by comparing a case analysis of the ENS in Los Angeles to historical efforts at increasing citizen participation. The early notification case study was initiated in September 2001 and is ongoing. The primary sources for the case study include semi-structured interviews (Hammer and Wildavsky, 1993);, field observation, analysis of archival data, and a structured survey of elected neighborhood council board members. In all, we conducted over 100 interviews with major actors at all stages of the implementation process: members of the two charter reform commissions, City Council and Board of Neighborhood Commissioners; staff of the Department of Neighborhood Empowerment; key IT personnel; and representatives from city departments. We observed meetings of the task force on early notification, as well as meetings of the City Council's relevant committees, and the Board of Neighborhood Empowerment. The archival data included reports and internal memos that chart the implementation of the early warning system. The board member survey was conducted during the summer of 2004, and 64% of the target group completed the survey.

We utilize the literature on previous participatory reforms to place the ENS in historical context, and to consider both the promises of technological reform, and the obstacles it must overcome. These cases, listed in Table 34.1, are well known and have been documented and analyzed by a number of scholars (Moynihan, 1965; Langton, 1978; Kweit and Kweit, 1981; Berry et al., 1993). Our discussion of the historical record relies on secondary sources, and takes a thematic approach in comparing previous reform efforts to the ENS along the evaluative dimensions identified above.

III. ENS IN A HISTORICAL PERSPECTIVE

In this section we consider the ENS from a historical perspective. We begin by presenting a number of key findings from previous participatory reforms that provide an analytic lens for evaluating the ENS. We then discuss the implementation of the ENS in greater detail, paying attention to the extent to which it parallels and diverges from previous participatory reforms. In the following section we then employ these historical lessons to analyze the ENS as participatory reform and digital democracy innovation.

A. Lessons from History

Although experiments with participatory reforms have entailed a wide range of institutional reforms and government arenas and have emphasized differing goals, there is surprising consistency regarding their results. Most importantly, program success is difficult to achieve due to a number of significant hurdles including conflict over the goals of participation, political and administrative opposition, and limited public interest. When these programs do succeed, their most important effects tend to evolve over the long run and emphasize constitutive rather than instrumental goals. Five major lessons may be drawn from the history of participatory reforms.

Table 34.1   Characteristics of Selected Participatory Programs

Participatory Program	Goals	Institutional Characteristics
Administrative Procedures Act of 1946	Improve access to agency decision-making; create informed citizenry; fairness and uniformity in administrative procedures	Procedural rules governing providing of opportunities for notification and feedback
1960s War on poverty programs	Empower disenfranchised target populations of legislation; improve representativeness	Federal mandate on local programs required elected community action program boards with mandatory representation from target population; legislation called for "maximum feasible participation"
Expansion of administrative participation programs in 1970s	Address perceived deficiencies in democratic practice; broaden participation; improve representativeness; empowerment	Wide variety of mechanisms including: public meetings; citizen review boards; fishbowl planning; intervener programs; community representatives on policymaking bodies; intervention in environmental review reports
Federal and state sunshine laws	Create informed citizenry; improve transparency of decision-making process	Procedural requirements on public decision-making bodies; advanced notification of meetings; public access to meetings
Neighborhood governance	Address perceived deficiencies in democratic practice; broaden participation; improve representativeness;	Elected boards with staff support; formal role in budgetary decisions; also includes more intense forms of deliberation

1.   Vaguely expressed goals and weak sanctions hamper participation reforms

Legislative mandates have rarely been more explicit than calls for "maximum feasible participation," or "widespread" participation. Such language offers bureaucrats and politicians discretion to avoid political conflict or dilution of power by implementing programs selectively or ignoring mandates altogether (Rosenbaum, 1978a). Noncompliance is made more common by the lack of real sanctions. For example, open meeting laws are often ignored or circumvented by public bodies, and surveys of enforcement activities find that existing sanctions have rarely been applied (Borenstein, 1986; Davis et al., 1998). While the Administrative Procedures Act would appear to be a counterexample in that it provides for court review of agency rules, in practice the same issues arise. Courts may reject rules that are "arbitrary and capricious," thereby constraining agency discretion to ignore or marginalize views and data submitted during the comments phase of the rulemaking. These sanctions, however, have been more the exception than the rule, and they have been primarily employed by organized interests (Noll et al., 1984).

2. Participatory reforms are not politically neutral

While advocates focus on the systemic benefits increased participation can have on democratic governance, stakeholders in particular policy arenas perceive changing patterns of participation as threats. An object lesson is provided by the Economic Opportunity Act of 1964, which called for "maximum feasible participation of residents of the areas and members of the groups being served." This federal mandate on local policymakers set off a political backlash from big city mayors who resisted the prospect that these programs would undermine their control of the political agenda (Moynihan, 1965). The political reaction was attributable to the difficulty of realizing redistribution of power within an urban landscape within which development interests dominate the interests of the poor (Peterson et al., 1987). The fate of the 1970 regulatory participation programs is also telling. Programs to organize consumer interests and provide them with a voice appeared in a wide variety of legislative initiatives. With the rise of the Republicans in the 1980s and a shift in policy toward reducing the burden of government regulation, however, these programs quickly withered from neglect (Berry et al., 1993).

3. Public administrators often resist participatory programs

Participation threatens key administrative values of efficiency and expertise (Rosenbaum, 1978a). Thus, administrators have often sought to limit public participants to more peripheral roles, such as attendance at public meetings, that do not threaten program management (Checkoway and Til, 1978). For example, local efforts to implement the Economic Opportunity Act's mandate received searing criticism for their failure to take citizen participation seriously, and for the mountain of administrative and political obstacles placed in community activists. (Moynihan, 1965; Berry et al., 1993; Arnstein, 2001) They were criticized for disillusioning citizens, generating divisiveness, and were ultimately softened or abandoned. These experiences are argued by Berry et al. (1993) to indicate that purely administrative reforms are prone to failure and successful participation must also involve true political reform.

4. Opportunities for participation are exercised differentially

Although core goals across reforms are broad and representative participation, evaluations find that participation is neither broad nor representative. Evaluations of the federal regulatory participation programs initiated in the 1970s and of contemporary neighborhood governance efforts found that participation was dominated by white middle- to upper-class public interest groups and those who were already politically active (Checkoway and Til, 1978; Rosenbaum, 1978a, 1978b; Cnaan, 1991). Moreover, because the costs of organizing are such an impediment to participation, these programs primarily benefit organized interests (Checkoway and Til, 1978; Berry et al., 1993). For example, while the Administrative Procedures Act set a minimum standard for opening agency actions to public scrutiny, administrative decision-making is nonetheless dominated by iron triangles or close-knit policy networks consisting of organized interest groups, agencies, and Congressional committee staff (Freeman, 1965; Heclo, 1978; Marsh, 1998).

5. Benefits from participation are difficult to measure and occur in the longer run

Evidence that participatory reforms lead to immediate, instrumental effects on policy-making is sparse. Nevertheless, authors have argued that there are important constitutive impacts. For example, Berry et al. (1993) find that neighborhood participation programs increase awareness of policy issues and citizens' sense of political efficacy. In addition, such programs have been found to be training grounds for political leaders. Even early war on poverty participation programs, which were initially criticized as tokenistic, were found to be important stepping stones for a new generation of minority community leaders (Browning et al., 1986).

B. Implementing ENS: The Triumph of Hope over Experience[3]

The roots of the Los Angeles ENS grew from widespread dissatisfaction with a city government that was perceived to be unresponsive and controlled by a tight clique of City Hall insiders. In the San Fernando Valley, where dissatisfaction ran highest, activists were mobilizing support for a movement to secede from the city. Political elites responded by proposing to rewrite Los Angeles' Byzantine, progressive era charter that had created an especially ungovernable institutional structure.[4] The focus of charter reform was to rationalize city government, realigning responsibility and authority within city agencies. Empowering citizens and opening up the decision-making process, while perhaps perceived as a secondary goal by charter designers, was acknowledged to be the selling point for charter reform at the polls. A number of proponents advocated for the creation of neighborhood councils and in conjunction with that, the development of an ENS.

The idea for the ENS came from decidedly low-tech origins. In 1979 St. Paul, Minnesota, which had a well-functioning system of district councils, created a list of key neighborhood representatives and began regularly mailing them notices of proposed actions such as liquor license applications and development proposals. Propelled by the enthusiasm for the Internet that raged in the late 1990s, the mail notification concept borrowed from St. Paul quickly evolved into an electronic system. Politicians and citizen focus groups consulted in the process advocated a heavy emphasis on Internet applications. Councilman Joel Wachs, a leading advocate of neighborhood councils, considered the ENS to be the single most important element in the package of reforms contained in the charter because it was essential to pry open City Hall's secretive and inaccessible policymaking process.

In keeping with historical experiences with participatory reforms, the system was characterized by vague goals, and a lack of sanctions for noncompliance. Resulting from a compromise between reformers and City Hall insiders who were wary about weakening traditional bases of power, the final language was quite broad, leaving standards and

---

[3] For more case detail, see Weare et al. (2002).

[4] There were actually two competing charter reform commissions, one appointed by the City Council and another elected one that was promoted by the mayor. Several progressives and union members successfully ran for the elected commission, defeating the mayor's candidates. The elected commission was the one that introduced the idea of neighborhood councils and the early notification system, and their proposals were included in a compromise plan when the two commissions agreed to work together to present voters with a single charter reform plan.

technologies for notification to the implementing City Council and administrative agencies. It read:

> The Regulations shall establish procedures for receiving input from neighborhood councils prior to decisions by the City Council, City Council Committees and boards and commissions. The procedures shall include, but need not be limited to, notice to neighborhood councils as soon as practical, and a reasonable opportunity to provide input before decisions are made. Notices to be provided include matters to be considered by the City Council, City Council Committees, and City boards or commissions.

The expectations of ENS proponents deflated as the system was designed and implemented. Political resistance to creating a system that would dramatically alter power relationships in the city was immediately evident in the writing of the implementing ordinances. The City Council copied the ENS-related language from the new charter, but eliminated potential sanctions for noncompliance through a provision that "failure of a neighborhood council to receive notice shall not invalidate any action of the City Council, City Council Committees, City boards or commissions or any other City official statement." Although the mandate appears to establish expectations for two-way dialogue between City Hall and neighborhood councils, the developing system more closely resembles the "thin" reforms described above, such as the Administrative Procedures and Open Meeting Acts.

The system was also hampered by administrative resistance and financial constraints. The Information Technology Agency (ITA), responsible for designing the system, was initially allocated no staff funds for system development and was forced to borrow staff from other projects; later implementation was hampered by fiscal constraints resulting from the state budget crisis. The technological capability of city agencies also varied widely, with some cities having little or no experience with the Internet, forcing ITA to cater to the least common denominator with an inexpensive and simple to operate system.

These political and bureaucratic constraints were reinforced by legal and technical path dependencies as the city developed the ENS design. The City Clerk's Office had developed a listserv that distributed through e-mail each day's referral memorandum, a compilation of every piece of business referred to a Council committee, and the City Council agenda and minutes. In addition, a status report on each business item in front of the City Council was posted on the Web in a fully searchable format. The system became a focal point in discussions of how to design the ENS, and the working group in charge of the ENS decided that the first phase of development should focus on extending the listserv to all other city boards and commissions.

More generally, the availability of this technology had the effect of narrowing the focus of ENS development to purely technological issues. The implementation plan for the ENS went through three full drafts. In each revision there was a continued shift from the *who*, *what*, and *when* of early notification to the technology through which it would be disseminated. Thus, the technology presented the city with something that could be accomplished given political and bureaucratic constraints, but at the cost of reducing attention on understanding how agencies would accommodate notification requirements, the types of information that would get noticed, and the amount of notice that was "practical."

Legal precedence had even greater impacts. During the charter reform process, ENS proponents clearly envisioned early notification to provide weeks of lead time. Literature that was circulated set 30- and 45-day notice periods. As the working group searched for a system that it could feasibly implement, it quickly seized on the definitions inherent in California's open meetings law, the Brown Act. This act requires all the public bodies that were covered by the ENS charter provision to post agendas 72 hours before all public meetings. While the working group understood that disseminating agendas 72 hours in advance was a narrow vision of the ENS, the agendas already existing in paper form and the technology for disseminating them electronically also existed.

Despite these formidable political and organizational obstacles, Phase I of the ENS debuted July 2001 with a direct link on the front page of the city's newly redesigned website. The system consists of a web page from which individuals may subscribe to receive official notices via e-mail. There are currently 89 different items available and more than 3000 subscriptions are being served. Although this represented an important technological advance in information dissemination, it was a far cry from the revolutionary system that was envisioned to "level the playing field." Nonetheless, administrators were "very excited" and with ITA conducting training sessions on preparing documents for the Internet (called "NetDocs"), the departments became more cooperative as it appeared that the ENS would not be a tremendous burden. Although still in development, the ENS is arguably one of the most comprehensive systems for public notification among large American cities. In a survey of large American cities, 88% reported having some notification requirements, usually concerning land use decisions.[5] Only 20%, however, notify citizen by e-mail, and no city reported having a system as comprehensive as the one envisioned in the Los Angeles charter.

The system has had some successes. The listserv has increased the volume of information received by interested parties. Before the rollout of the ENS, the City Clerk's online subscription service had been available for several years, but fewer than 800 users subscribed to receive Council agendas. After 2 years of operation over 3500 individuals subscribe to the service, receiving well over 300,000 documents per year, and the range of available information has expanded to include dozens of boards and commission not previously available on the City Clerk's system. Available evidence indicates that this information is being distributed beyond the close-knit circles of City Hall insiders. Some 60% of City Council notices go to e-mail addresses outside of the City Hall, and numerous neighborhood council activists report extensive use of the system.[6] The ENS is also strongly supported by neighborhood council board members. In a survey of elected neighborhood council board members, 88% stated that the system would be important or very important for the success of the neighborhood councils. In addition, the board members support the emphasis on Internet technologies, with 74% preferring the information to be disseminated via e-mail or web pages.

Critics of the ENS have raised concerns that a purely Internet-based system would disadvantage neighborhoods and board members that were not online, but access does not appear to have posed a significant constraint. The vast majority of neighborhood

---

[5] We surveyed 102 large cities concerning their notification and feedback procedures and received responses from 41, for a response rate of 40%.

[6] In addition, the City Planning Department has begun providing e-mail reports to neighborhood councils of the applications for permits and variances that it receives. This service has been enthusiastically welcomed, but it is provided in an *ad hoc* manner not connected with the main ENS service.

council board members, 92%, report going online, and 88% have Internet access at home. While our survey found that board members from more economically disadvantaged areas are somewhat less likely to have home Internet access, in no board did less than two thirds of members have home access, and most preferred electronic forms of notification and response.

The mandate for early notifications has also played a role in a number of policy disputes. In January 2003, the Police Commission voted on a policy change to stop responding to private burglar alarms unless they were independently verified. This decision caught neighborhood councils and even City Council members by surprise. Through an e-mail campaign in part orchestrated by a City Council member's office, neighborhood councils placed pressure on the City Council to review the decision. While opinions were mixed about the wisdom of the policy change, the neighborhood councils widely agreed they had been inadequately notified. Eventually, a task force was formed with representatives from the police department, neighborhood councils, and the alarm industry. It developed a compromise proposal in which police would only stop responding after a number of false alarms at a location. In another instance, an outgoing council member wished to rename a prominent avenue after former mayor Tom Bradley. Several neighborhood councils objected because they had not been given adequate notice and no opportunity to provide input, and again the final decision was delayed to accept neighborhood council input.

While these instances suggest the potential impacts of the ENS system, they cannot be attributed to the technology in isolation. In neither case did the distribution of agendas through the ENS play a major role in disseminating information about the upcoming decisions. In the alarm issue, the Police Commission did mark out an agenda item for its vote on the policy change and one major newspaper reported on the pending vote, but this information generated scant attention. Only after the Police Commission acted did e-mail among neighborhood councils bring the issue to the front burner and mobilize calls for the City Council to review the commission's decision. In the avenue renaming case, reports in the traditional media alerted neighborhood councils of the action contemplated by the City Council. Paradoxically, rather than the technology mobilizing people around issues of concern, it was the perceived failure of the ENS to meet citizen expectations for notification that catalyzed citizen action around these issues.

The city has attempted to engage community leaders, through focus groups and a working group, to help enhance the existing ENS. These sessions, however, have done more to highlight the difficulties of early notification than to generate solutions. The main problem is that the institutional structure of the city is highly fragmented and complex. City services are provided by 32 departments; oversight of city services is shared between a relatively weak mayor, the 15-member City Council, and more than 240 citizen commissioners who are appointed by the mayor. Moreover, many decisions of interest to residents (e.g., when to pave a street or trim trees) do not appear on agendas, and developing rules for when and how agencies should notify neighborhood councils of their coming actions has defied neat categorization. A second problem has been information overload. Neighborhood council members that attempt to survey city activities by reviewing agendas are met with a flood of agendas each week. One reported spending 20 hours a week to identify actions that are of concern to his neighborhood council.

At this time, 4 years since the adoption of the charter and 2 years since the rollout of the first version of the ENS, the project is stalled. The city has made efforts to introduce improvements to the ENS, including proposals to categorize agenda items by geographical and subject matter codes, and to provide reports and other information relevant to issues on the Web. It has also created an electronic template to accept neighborhood council feedback on issues. Budget cuts related to the California state fiscal crisis have delayed the implementation of these initiatives. More importantly, however, the city is stalled on defining what ENS should do. While neighborhood council members want to be notified, they are less certain what they want to be notified about. Policy issues such as the alarm debate have played an important role in testing citizen expectations, but have not led to a means of usefully organizing information about emerging policy issues, much less promoting deliberation among stakeholders and their representatives.

IV. ENS AS A TECHNOLOGICAL AND INSTITUTIONAL INNOVATION

When compared with historical participatory reforms, the case of the ENS suggests more continuity than radical break. Technology does have benefits that lower barriers to participation. Technology does not, however, surmount the complex of behavioral, political, institutional, and implementation barriers that impede efforts to expand the breadth and depth of citizen participation. Considering the ENS within the context of prior participatory reforms makes three lessons clear.

First, the ENS shares the problems of past programs in addressing goal complexity and translating broad and vaguely defined mandates into effective programs. While ENS is arguably highly advanced from an electronic democracy perspective, it falls far short of its original rhetoric. In its current form, the ENS promotes a relatively narrow and Madisonian vision of participation. Like the Administrative Procedures Act and the state sunshine laws, the ENS strives to increase citizen awareness by disseminating information and ensuring that decision-making forums are open to stakeholders. The original vision of the ENS, in contrast, predicted decentralized deliberation on a level playing field and was more akin to the more ambitious Toquevillian participatory reforms.

In the broader implementation of the neighborhood council system, Los Angeles has attempted to develop more structured arenas for decentralized deliberation, such as a participatory budget-making process. These efforts, however, have all relied on traditional face-to-face meetings, such as task forces, focus groups, and group negotiations. This tendency to shun technology despite the initial embrace of the Internet suggests that technology may be better at promoting what Arnstein (1969) would characterize as "lower rungs" on the participatory ladder: informing and consultation. While technology may facilitate deliberation (Price, 2003), future research should explore whether empowered deliberation of the sort described by Fung and Wright is better achieved by face-to-face contact, perhaps aided secondarily by the tools of IT.

Second, the ENS case echoes lessons from the history of participatory reform in its vulnerability to implementation barriers, including political and administrative opposition, financial constraints, and organizational path dependency. Paradoxically, its lack of association with a specific program or interest, which has helped the system be politically and administratively acceptable, has also made it less useful to the citizenry. Unlike such historical reforms as the War on Poverty programs, the ENS has not become associated with a specific program, thereby avoiding political attacks that could ultimately eliminate it. As some scholars have argued, the ability of such institutional reforms to mature free of political controversy are key to long-run success (Berry et al., 1993). At the same time, information provision is arguably most valuable in specific policy arenas in which the range of pertinent information is well defined. The orientation of the ENS toward the entire scope of city activities makes it difficult to parse information about policy issues, requiring significant organizational effort on the part of neighborhood councils to use the system effectively.

Technology and politics literature would characterize the implementation of the ENS as the social shaping of technology in which the design of technology reflects broader power relations in society. The historical cases suggest, in contrast, that such implementation difficulties are not primarily a technological phenomenon but, rather, are common to all changes in governance procedures that can alter power relations. Moreover, technology itself appears to have constrained implementation of the original vision for the ENS. As technology assumed a greater focus in the implementation process, it became a distraction, shifting focus toward the types of information that could feasibly be disseminated electronically, and away from the administrative and political reforms necessary to identify issues of concern to neighborhood stakeholders, and to find a way to circulate information, promote deliberation, and solicit advice.

Third, reforms such as the ENS cannot by themselves overcome entrenched patterns of participation. While the ENS arguably has broadened participation, as discussed above, it is unlikely to have made the pattern of participants more representative by increasing participation of historically disenfranchised groups. The clearest effect of the ENS to date has been its success in strengthening individuals' capacity for participation by reducing the costs of information dissemination, thereby making city agendas much more widely available to interested parties throughout the city. Nevertheless, while hundreds of City Council agendas are disseminated to the public each week, this information remains the domain of an exclusive class of high participators. Even among elected neighborhood council members only 35% had visited the ENS page on the city's website, indicating that the availability of this information does not have significant effects on individual's motivations.

The ENS case also clarifies the limits of information provisions as means to motivate greater participation. Proponents of participation programs emphasize the importance of information provision for making participation compelling and productive and argue that relevant information can be made understandable to nonexperts (Yankelovitch, 1991; Fung and Wright, 2003). In contrast, Los Angeles' experience illustrates that the ability of information dissemination to increase political capacity and motivation is limited by the dual problems of information overload and information processing. The technology has not been developed such that users can filter information to manage hundreds of irrelevant notices. In a city with dozens of agencies operating over 470 square miles, lack of geographic and topical filters vastly complicate information processing. Moreover, city agendas tend to be written in arcane language that often obscures the issues at hand. Even astute political participants rely largely on informal networks of departmental officials and lobbyists to help draw out the important issues from agenda listings. Mere information provision will not "level the playing field" if residents must weed through city agendas while insiders have them predigested and translated by paid staff and lobbyists.

While these three lessons highlight the limitations of reform, there is a glimmer of hope that the ENS may lead to longer-run changes. With only a handful of neighborhood councils submitting feedback on issues of importance to them, it has had little impact on policy decisions. It has, nevertheless, raised expectations concerning government responsiveness, as evidenced by the reaction of citizens to the burglar alarm and street naming controversies. The ENS is also having indirect effects as it is training individuals in the political process and creating incentives to build citywide coalitions to respond to issues. As the historical record suggests, institutional change can have unforeseen effects over the long term.

V. CONCLUSIONS

Counter to the position advanced in technology and politics literature, the Internet is not revolutionary, at least in the short run. The Internet does facilitate access to information and enhances one's ability to organize dispersed individuals, and in so doing, it does positively affect individuals' capacity and motivation for political participation. Nevertheless, as is evident in the history of participatory reforms in the U.S., this technology is being implemented in a complex political context resistant to change. Technology, in itself, cannot overcome the institutional and behavioral constraints that have impeded the success of past reform efforts. In the short run, the informative and communicative advantages afforded by the Internet appear able to facilitate lower forms of democratic participation such as notification, public comment, and "thin" forms of consultation best.

Placed in historical perspective, the ENS case suggests that successful participatory reform requires a combination of institutional restructuring with technological advance. The ENS case suggests that notification requirements, access to information, and the right to provide input will not suffice if government-level institutions continue to resist change and if grassroot organizations do not arise that can manage the new flood of available information. In the long run, the ENS has the promise of becoming a powerful tool for Los Angeles neighborhood councils both as a mechanism by which board members learn about the inner workings of city politics and as a motivational technology that increases expectations for governmental openness and responsiveness.

ACKNOWLEDGMENTS

This research was support by National Science Foundation Information Technology Research Grant #0112899 and the John Randolph Haynes and Dora Haynes Foundation. The authors would like to thank Tony Silbert, Nail Oztas, Kyu-Nahm Jun, Tony Valluzzo, Alicia Kisuse for expert research assistance. All errors are our own.

REFERENCES

Arnstein, S.R., A Ladder of Citizen Participation, *Journal of the American Planning Association*, 35, 216–224, 1969.

Arnstein, S.R., Maximum feasible manipulation, in *Democracy, Bureaucracy, and the Study of Administration*, Stivers, C., Ed., Westview Press, Boulder, CO, 2001.

Barber, B., *Strong Democracy: Participatory Politics for a New Age*, University of California Press, Berkeley, CA, 1984.

Barber, J.D., *The Presidential Character: Predicting Performance in the White House*, Prentice Hall, Englewood Cliffs, NJ, 1985.

Berry, J.M., Portnoy, K.E. et al., *The Rebirth of Urban Democracy*, The Brookings Institution, Washington, D.C., 1993.

Bimber, B., The Internet and political transformation: populism, community, and accelerated pluralism, *Polity*, 31, 133–160, 1998.

Bimber, B., Information and political engagement in America: the search for effects of information technology at the individual level, *Political Research Quarterly*, 54, 53, 2001.

Bimber, B., *Information and American Democracy: Technology in the Evolution of Political Power*, Cambridge University Press, New York, 2003.

Borenstein, D., The Brown Act: how open is local government?, *California Journal*, 17, 316–317, 1986.

Box, R., *Citizen Governance: Leading American Communities into the 21st Century*, Sage, Thousand Oaks, CA, 1998.

Brainard, L.A. and Siplon, P.D., Cyberspace challenges to mainstream non-profit health organizations, *Administration & Society*, 34, 141–175, 2002.

Brandon, B.H. and Carlitz, R.D., Online rulemaking and other tools for strengthening our civil infrastructure, *Administrative Law Review*, 54(4): 1422–1478, 2003.

Browning, R.P., Marshall, D.R. et al., *Protest Is Not Enough: The Struggle of Blacks and Hispanics for Equality in Urban Politics*, University of California Press, Berkeley, CA, 1986.

Cason, T. and Khan, F., A laboratory study of voluntary public goods provision with imperfect monitoring and communication, *Journal of Development Economics*, 58, 533–552, 1999.

Checkoway, B. and Til, J.V., What do we know about citizen participation? A selective review of research, in *Citizen Participation in America*, Langton, S., Ed., D.C. Heath and Company, Lexington, MA, 1978.

Cnaan, R.A., Neighborhood-representing organizations: how democratic are they, *Social Science Review*, 65, 614–634, 1991.

Dahlberg, L., The Internet and democratic discourse, *Information, Communication, and Society*, 4, 615–633, 2001.

Danziger, J.N., Dutton, W.H. et al., *Computers and Politics: High Technology in American Local Governments*, Columbia University Press, New York, 1982.

Davis, R., *The Web of Politics: The Internet's Impact on the American Political System*, Oxford University Press, New York, 1999.

Davis, C.M., Chance, S.F., and Chamberlin, B.F., Guardians of access: local prosecutors and open meeting laws, *Communication Law and Policy*, 3, 35–54, 1998.

DeLeon, P., *Democracy and the Policy Sciences*, State University of New York Press, Albany, NY, 1997.

Deutsch, K.W., *The Nerves of Government: Models of Political Communication and Control*, The Free Press, New York, 1966.

Freeman, J.L., *The Political Process*, Random House, New York, 1965.

Fung, A. and Wright, E.O., Thinking about empowered participatory governance, in *Deepening Democracy: Institutional Innovations in Empowered Participatory Governance*, Fung, A. and Wright, E.O., Eds., Verso, London, 2003.

Goldschmidt, K., Email Overload in Congress: Managing a Communications Crisis, Congress Online Project, Washington, D.C., pp. 1–15, 2001.

Grossman, L.K., *The Electronic Republic: Reshaping Democracy in the Information Age*, Viking, New York, 1995.

Hammer, D. and Wildavsky, A., The semi-structured interview: an (almost) operational guide, in *Craftways: On the Organization of Scholarly Work*, Wildavsky, A., Ed., Transaction, New Brunswick, NJ, 1993.

Heclo, H., Issue networks and the executive establishment, *American Political System*, King, A., Ed., American Enterprise Institute, Washington, D.C., 1978, pp. 87–124.

Kweit, M.G. and Kweit, R.W., *Implementing Citizen Participation in a Bureaucratic Society: A Contingency Approach*, Praeger Scientific, New York, 1981.

Langton, S., Ed., *Citizen Participation in America*, D.C. Heath and Company, Lexington, MA, 1978.

Macy, M.W., Chains of cooperation: threshold effects in collective action, *American Sociological Review*, 56, 730–747, 1991.

Mansbridge, J., Practice-thought-practice, in *Deepening Democracy: Institutional Innovations in Empowered Participatory Governance*, Fung, A. and Wright, E.O., Eds., Verso, London, pp. 175–199, 2003.

Margolis, M. and Resnick, D., *Politics as Usual: The Cyberspace "Revolution,"* Sage, Thousand Oaks, 2000.

Marsh, D., Ed., *Comparing Policy Networks*, Open University Press, McGraw-Hill House, UK, 1998.

Mazmanian, D. and Sabatier, P., *Implementation and Public Policy*, Scott Foresman and Company, Glencoe, IL, 1983.

Moon, M.J., The evolution of e-government among municipalities: rhetoric or reality?, *Public Administration Review*, 62, 424, 2002.

Morris, D., *Vote.com*, Renaissance Books, St. Martin's Press, NY, 2000.

Moynihan, D.P., *Maximum Feasible Misunderstanding: Community Action in the War on Poverty*, Free Press, New York, 1965.

Musso, J.A., Weare, C. et al., Designing web technologies for local governance reform: good management or good democracy, *Political Communications*, 17, 1–19, 1999.

Negroponte, N., *Being Digital*, Knopf, New York, 1995.

Nie, J. and Erbring, L., *Internet and Society: A Preliminary Report*, Stanford Institute for the Quantitative Study of Society, Stanford, CA, 2000.

Noll, R., McCubbins, M.D. et al., Regulating regulation: the political economy of administrative procedures and regulatory instruments, *Law and Contemporary Problems*, 57, 3–38, 1984.

Norris, P., *Democratic Phoenix: Political Activism Worldwide*, Cambridge University Press, New York, 2002.

Peters, B.G., *The Future of Governing*, The University Press of Kansas, Lawrence, KS, 1996.

Peterson, P.E., Wong, K.K. et al., *When Federalism Works*, The Brookings Institution, Washington, D.C., 1987.

Pippa, N.P., Bennett, W.L., and Entman, R.L., Eds., *Digital Divide: Civic Engagement, Information Poverty, and the Internet Worldwide*, Cambridge University Press, NY, 2001.

Price, V., *Electronic Dialogue: A National Experiment in Online Engagement*, Mass Communication and Civic Engagement, 2nd Annual Pre-APSA Conference on Political Communication, Philadelphia, PA, 2003.

Putnam, R.D., *Bowling Alone : The Collapse and Revival of American Community*, Simon & Schuster, New York, 2000.

Rheingold, H., *The Virtual Community: Homesteading on the Electronic Frontier*, Addision-Wesley, Reading, MA, 1993.

Rittel, H. and Webber, M., Dilemmas in a general theory of planning, *Policy Sciences*, 4, 155–169, 1973.

Rosenbaum, W.A., Public involvement as reform and ritual: the development of federal participation programs, in *Citizen Participation in America*, Langton, S., Ed., D.C. Heath and Company, Lexington, MA, 1978a.

Rosenbaum, W.A., Slaying beautiful hypotheses with ugly facts: EPA and public participation, *Journal of Voluntary Action Research*, 3–4, (Summer-Fall), 161–174, 1977.

Sell, J. and Wilson, R., Levels of information and contributions to public goods, *Social Forces*, 70, 107–124, 1991.

Street, J., *Politics and Technology*, Guilford Press, New York, 1992.

Verba, S., Schlozman, K.L. et al., *Voice and Equality: Civic Voluntarism in American Politics*, Harvard University Press, Cambridge, MA, 1995.

Weare, C., The Internet and democracy: the causal links between technology and politics, *International Journal of Public Administration*, 25, 659–692, 2002.

Weare, C., Musso, J.A. et al., *The Early Implementation of Los Angeles' Early Notification System: Finally Getting It Right or the Triumph of Hope over Experience?*. Available at: http://www.usc.edu/schools/sppd/research/hpp/pdf/ens.pdf. Civic Engagement through Neighborhood Empowerment: The L.A. Experiment and Beyond, Los Angeles, CA, January 25, 2002.

Wilhelm, W., Virtual sounding boards: how deliberative is on-line political discussion?, *Information, Communication, and Society*, 1, 313–338, 1998.

Yankelovitch, D., *Coming to Public Judgment: Making Democracy Work in a Complex World*, Syracuse University Press, Syracuse, NY, 1991.

35

E-GOVERNMENT PERFORMANCE-REPORTING REQUIREMENTS

Patrick R. Mullen

U.S. Government Accountability Office

CONTENTS

I. Introduction 600
II. Laws for performance-based management and accountability 601
    A. Timing of performance-reporting requirements in relation to the
       congressional budget process 603
    B. Performance-reporting requirements produce useful information, but
       implementation issues remain 603
III. Performance-based laws require specific reports 603
    A. Paperwork Reduction Acts of 1980 and 1995 604
    B. Computer Security Act of 1987 606
    C. Clinger–Cohen Act of 1996 607
    D. Government Paperwork Elimination Act of 1998 608
    E. Government Information Security Reform Act of 2001 608
    F. E-government Act of 2002 610
IV. Security weaknesses identified in federal IT performance reports 611
V. Some observations about what to include in future IT performance reports 613
VI. Conclusion 614
References 614

ABSTRACT

Electronic government (e-government) is the use of information technology (IT) and the Internet to transform federal agency effectiveness — including efficiency and service quality. Several U.S. laws contain IT and e-government performance-reporting requirements, including the Paperwork Reduction Act (PRA), the Computer Security Act, the Clinger–Cohen Act (CCA), the Government Information Security Reform Act (GISRA), and the e-Government Act (e-GA). For each, the author reviews the legislative history and then focuses on the specific requirements for reporting to Congress, the Office of Management and Budget (OMB), and agency heads. The author concludes that OMB's new Office of Electronic Government needs to evaluate whether performance requirements could be improved through (1) consolidation, thereby providing a more comprehensive discussion of agency IT and e-government issues and (2) addressing broader issues, such as an across-government focus on both national and international IT issues.

I. INTRODUCTION

Electronic government (e-government) uses information technology (IT), especially the Internet, to improve the delivery of government services to the public, as well as businesses and government agencies. E-government has the potential to more directly connect government with the public, thereby opening new opportunities, but also giving rise to new challenges. For example, e-government could enable the public to interact with and receive services from the federal government 24 hours a day, 7 days a week,[1] making service delivery more convenient, dependable, and less costly. The Gartner Group describes e-government as "the continuous optimization of service delivery, constituency participation, and governance by transforming internal and external relationships through technology [IT], the Internet, and new media."[2]

As part of e-government, federal agencies have implemented a wide array of IT applications, including using the Internet to collect and disseminate information and forms; buying and paying for goods and services; submitting bids and proposals; and applying for licenses, grants, and benefits. Although substantial progress has been made, according to the U.S. General Accounting Office (GAO),[3] the full potential of e-government has not yet been reached.

Recognizing the magnitude of modern challenges facing the federal government, Congress has encouraged a more performance-based approach to program management and accountability within the federal government, enacting the Government Performance and Results Act (GPRA) of 1993, perhaps the best-known performance-based law. To be most useful, program managers should consider the reports developed in response to GPRA when they write the performance reports required by specific IT and e-government laws discussed in this chapter.

Some of the first IT performance-based laws, focusing on the importance of using IT to improve government operations, were the Paperwork Reduction Act (PRA) of 1980 (reauthorized in 1995), the Computer Security Act of 1987, and the Clinger–Cohen Act (CCA) of 1996. Congress recognized the growing importance of e-government in 1998 by enacting the Government Paperwork Elimination Act. It requires federal agencies to use IT in order to provide the public, when practicable, the option of submitting, maintaining, and disclosing required information electronically. The e-Government Act (e-GA) of 2002 includes promoting the use of the Internet and other IT to provide government services electronically; strengthening agency information security; and defining how to

---

[1] Seifert, Jeffrey W. A Primer on E-Government: Sectors, Stages, Opportunities, and Challenges of Online Governance (updated January 28, 2003), Congressional Research Service: Washington, DC, 2003.

[2] Gartner Group. Key Issues in e-Government Strategy and Management, Research Notes, Key Issues, May 23, 2000.

[3] See, for example, U.S. General Accounting Office. Electronic Government: Success of the Office Of Management and Budget's 25 Initiatives Depends On Effective Management and Oversight (GAO-03-495T, Mar. 13, 2003). Washington, DC.

manage the federal government's growing IT personnel needs. In addition, this law established an Office of Electronic Government within the Office of Management and Budget (OMB) to provide strong central leadership and full-time commitment to promoting and implementing IT and e-government. This new and relatively small office will face implementation issues to achieve its broad mission. However, one useful task the office can perform is to review the IT and e-government performance laws to see if the numerous reporting requirements can be consolidated, thereby providing a more comprehensive discussion of agency IT and e-government activities than currently exists.

II. LAWS FOR PERFORMANCE-BASED MANAGEMENT AND ACCOUNTABILITY

GPRA — or "the Results Act" — is a key performance-based law for management and accountability. Before enactment of GPRA, policymaking, spending decisions, and oversight had been severely handicapped by a lack of (1) sufficiently precise program goals and (2) program performance and cost information. GPRA sought to remedy that situation by following private-sector best practices, requiring agencies to set multiyear strategic goals and corresponding annual goals, to measure performance toward the achievement of those goals, and to report on progress made. IT managers and those with an interest in expanding use of e-government to better serve the public should read agency GPRA reports in order to gain an overview of strategic goals and performance measures.

In instituting IT performance-based laws, Congress followed private-sector best practices, as with GPRA, enabling agencies to more effectively manage IT requirements. Under IT performance-based laws, agencies are to link technology plans and IT use in program missions and goals in a better manner. To do this, agencies are to:

1. Involve senior executives in IT management decisions
2. Establish senior-level chief information officers (CIOs) who are to evaluate IT programs on the basis of applicable performance measurements
3. Impose much-needed discipline on technology spending
4. Redesign inefficient work processes
5. Use performance measures to assess the contribution of IT to the achievement of mission results

In addition, laws such as the Computer Security Act of 1987, as amended in 1996, address the importance of ensuring and improving the security and privacy of sensitive information in federal computer systems. IT performance-based laws, including purposes, are summarized in Table 35.1.

Implemented together, GPRA and IT performance-based laws provide a powerful framework for developing and fully integrating information about:

1. Agencies' missions and strategic priorities
2. The results-oriented performance goals that flow from those priorities
3. Performance data showing the level of goal achievement
4. Investments in IT in relation to goals achieved, along with reliable and audited financial information about the costs

Table 35.1 IT Performance-Based Laws and Purpose

IT Law	Purpose
Paperwork Reduction Acts of 1980 and 1995	Minimize the public's paperwork burdens; coordinate federal IRM; improve dissemination of public information; ensure the integrity of the federal statistical system
Computer Security Act of 1987	Improve the security and privacy of sensitive information in federal computer systems
Clinger–Cohen Act of 1996	Improve federal programs through improved acquisition, use, and disposal of IT resources
Government Paperwork Elimination Act of 1998	Requires federal agencies to provide the public, when practicable, the option of submitting, maintaining, and disclosing required information electronically
Government Information Security Reform Act of 2001	Direct federal agencies to conduct annual IT security reviews; IGs to perform annual independent evaluations of agency programs and systems and report results to OMB; OMB to (1) report annually to Congress on governmentwide progress and (2) issue guidance to agencies on reporting instructions and quantitative performance measures
e-Government Act of 2002	Promote the use of the Internet and other ITs to provide government services electronically; strengthen agency information security; define how to manage the federal government's growing IT human capital needs; establish an Office of Electronic Government, within OMB, to provide strong central leadership and full-time commitment to promoting and implementing e-government

Source: Analysis of laws.

This framework should promote a more results-oriented management and decision-making process within the Congress, the OMB, and the federal agencies. Reports required by these laws can provide information that is pertinent to a broad range of management-related decisions confronting IT and e-government managers. In addition, these reports help members of Congress with responsibilities for budget, authorization, oversight, and appropriations committees. However, as pointed out by GAO and OMB on several occasions,[4] critical implementation issues remain to be addressed. As discussed below, although the legal framework for more performance-

---

[4] See GAO and OMB websites for recent reports on federal management, performance reporting, and IT and e-government (www.gao.gov and www.omb.gov). There are many GAO and OMB reports on these issues, and examples are cited in notes 3 and 10.

based IT and e-government is in place, key parts are in their first years of implementation; how best to integrate and implement reporting requirements continues to be a work in progress.

A. Timing of Performance-Reporting Requirements in Relation to the Congressional Budget Process

Performance-based laws contain different reporting requirements, which are due at various times during the fiscal year; key dates for the fiscal year and legal sources are given in Table 35.2. These requirements — including GPRA, IT performance-based, and selected financial management — are ones the IT community should be aware of since they may affect IT reporting requirements. In addition, there are IT performance-based reporting requirements that do not have specific reporting dates and are, therefore, not included in Table 35.2, but discussed later. It should also be noted that there are laws, such as the Privacy Act of 1974 (P.L. 93–579), that affect IT and e-government management, but do not have reporting requirements; these laws are therefore not discussed in this chapter.

In addition to the dates for requirements, there are several milestone dates in the congressional budget process, as shown in Table 35.3. Given that the performance-reporting requirements provide information that can be used in the process, it is important to view them in relation to the process. Performance and financial information is most useful to decision-makers when closely linked with the federal government's budget, as well as the appropriations process.

B. Performance-Reporting Requirements Produce Useful Information, but Implementation Issues Remain

The reporting requirements, if effectively implemented, will produce program performance and financial information that has previously not been available to decision-makers and the public. This information will be a valuable resource for Congress to use in carrying out its program authorization, oversight, and appropriations responsibilities, as well as to ensure a more accountable, as well as responsive, government. However, implementation of some of these laws, such as GISRA and the e-GA, are in the early stages. Integration of the resulting information will be critical in effectively implementing the performance-based laws. For example, agencies continue to work on developing results-oriented performance goals in conjunction with the cost accounting systems needed to provide reliable program and cost information. In addition, more attention is being paid to the adequacy of agencies' performance goals, given OMB's use of the Program Assessment Reporting Tool (PART) to evaluate the effectiveness of federal agency programs. Such attention is bringing about changes that improve the adequacy of goals for OMB and federal agency heads.

III. PERFORMANCE-BASED LAWS REQUIRE SPECIFIC REPORTS

This section discusses what performance-based laws are and what information they require in reports to Congress.

A. Paperwork Reduction Acts of 1980 and 1995

The purpose of the Paperwork Reduction Act (PRA), as reauthorized, is to:

1. Minimize the public's paperwork burdens resulting from the collection of information by or for the federal government
2. Coordinate agencies' information resources management (IRM) policies
3. Improve the dissemination of public information
4. Ensure the integrity of the federal statistical system[5]

PRA also requires agencies to indicate, in strategic information management plans, how they are applying IRM to improve the effectiveness of government programs, including improvements in the delivery of services to the public.

Table 35.2 Key Dates and Legal Sources for Selected Performance-Reporting Requirements

Date	Source
October 1	Beginning of fiscal year, Congressional Budget Act, 31 USC Sec. 1102
October 30	Agency heads submit GISRA reports, to the Director of OMB, with the results of each evaluation required under the act; each year, the director of OMB submits to Congress a report summarizing the data received from agencies in that year
October 31	IGs' first semiannual reports to agency heads,[a] Inspector General Act, 5 USC App. 3, Sec. 5
November 30	Agencies submit IGs' first semiannual reports, including agency heads' comments, to Congress,[a] Inspector General Act, 5 USC App. 3, Sec. 5
December 31	Agencies submit federal managers' Financial Integrity Act reports to the president and the Congress, 31 USC Sec. 3512 (d)
January 31	OMB's governmentwide 5-year financial management plan sent to Congress for each succeeding 5-year period, as well as a report on accomplishments for the preceding fiscal year, Chief Financial Officers Act, 31 USC Sec. 3512 (a)
February	OMB must include in the president's annual budget submission to Congress, due no later than the first Monday of February, a report on the net performance benefits achieved due to major capital investments, as well as reports from agencies on their progress in using IT,[b] Information Technology Management Reform Act (Clinger–Cohen Act), 40 USC Sec. 1412
	Beginning with the budget submission for FY 1999 and annually thereafter, the president must include agencies' annual performance plans, 31 USC Sec. 1115 (a), and a governmentwide performance plan for the succeeding fiscal year, 31 USC Sec. 1105 (a) (28), GPRA
	OMB's e-government status report to the Committee on Governmental Affairs, the Senate, and the Committee on Government Reform, the House of Representatives
March 1	Agencies' audited financial statements to OMB, Chief Financial Officers Act and Government Management Reform Act, 31 USC Sec. 3515 (a)

[5] U.S. Congress. *Paperwork Reduction Acts of 1980 and 1995*, P.L. 96–511 and P.L. 104–13.

Table 35.2   Key Dates and Legal Sources for Selected Performance-Reporting Requirements — continued

Date	Source
March 31	Audited consolidated financial statements to the president and the Congress, Government Management Reform Act, 31 USC Sec. 331 (e)
	Beginning March 31, 2000, agencies' annual performance reports to OMB, GPRA, 31 USC Sec. 1116
April 30	Chief financial officers' reports to agency heads and the OMB, Chief Financial Officers Act and Government Management Reform Act, 31 USC Sec. 902 (a) (6)
	IGs' second semiannual reports to agency heads,[a] Inspector General Act, 5 USC App. 3, Sec. 5
May[c]	The director of OMB annually submits to Congress a report summarizing the GISRA data received from agencies in that year
May 30	Agencies submit IG's second semiannual reports, including agency heads' comments, to Congress,[a] Inspector General Act, 5 USC App. 3, Sec. 5
September[d]	OMB's annual information resources management plan for the federal government to Congress, PRA, 44 USC Sec. 3514
September 30	Beginning September 30, 1997, and every 3 years thereafter, agencies' strategic plans to Congress and OMB, covering the succeeding 5 fiscal years, GPRA, 5 USC Sec. 306

[a]The IGs' first semiannual report covers the last 6 months of the preceding fiscal year. The second semiannual report covers the first 6 months of the current fiscal year.

[b]Under the Clinger–Cohen Act, agency CIOs must report annually to the head of the agency, as part of the strategic planning and performance evaluation process, on the progress made in improving resource management capabilities of the agency's personnel.

[c]The act requires an annual report, but does not specify a reporting date; OMB usually submits the report in May.

[d]The act requires an annual report but does not specify a reporting date; OMB usually submits the report in September.

Source: Analysis of laws.

PRA requires OMB, in consultation with agency heads, to set annual governmentwide goals for the reduction — by at least 10% during fiscal years (FYs) 1996 and 1997 and 5% during each of the next 4 fiscal years — of the paperwork burden. PRA also requires OMB, in consultation with agency heads, to set annual agency goals that reduce, to the maximum extent practicable, the paperwork burden imposed on the public. Agencies cannot conduct or sponsor information collection resulting in paperwork, unless the agency has taken a number of specified actions and OMB has approved the collection. OMB may not approve the collection for a period in excess of 3 years. To test alternative paperwork policies and procedures, PRA requires OMB to conduct pilot projects.

PRA also requires OMB, in consultation with certain other agencies, to develop and maintain a governmentwide strategic plan for IRM. In particular, PRA requires agencies to develop and maintain a strategic IRM plan that describes how IRM activities help accomplish agency missions. In addition, PRA requires OMB to (1) keep Congress and congressional committees fully informed of the major activities under the act and (2) report on such activities, at least annually. In this report, OMB is to describe the extent to

Table 35.3   Milestone Dates in the Congressional Budget Process

Milestone Date	Budget Process Milestone
No later than the first Monday in February	President submits budget
February 15	Congressional Budget Office submits report to budget committees
February 25	Committees submit views and estimates to budget committees
April 1	Senate Budget Committee reports concurrent resolution on the budget
April 15	Congress completes action on concurrent resolution on the budget
May 15	Annual appropriation bills may be considered in the House
June 10	House Appropriations Committee reports last annual appropriation bill
June 15	Congress completes action on reconciliation legislation
June 30	House completes action on annual appropriation bills
October 1	Fiscal year begins

Source: Congressional Budget Act of 1974, 2 USC Sec. 631.

which agencies have reduced paperwork burdens on the public, as well as improved the quality and utility of statistical information, public access to government information, and program performance and mission accomplishment through IRM.

B.   Computer Security Act of 1987

The purpose of the Computer Security Act, as amended,[6] is to improve the security, including privacy, of sensitive information in federal computer systems. To control loss and unauthorized modification or disclosure of sensitive information and to prevent computer-related fraud and misuse, the law relies on the National Institute of Standards and Technology (NIST) to develop standards and guidelines for computer systems to be promulgated by the Secretary of Commerce.

Under the law, all operators of federal computer systems, including both federal agencies and their contractors, are required to establish security plans. The Office of Personnel Management (OPM) is required to issue regulations concerning mandatory periodic training related to security awareness and accepted security practices. This training is for all personnel involved in management, use, or operation of federal computer systems that contain sensitive information. The law also establishes a Computer System Security and Privacy Advisory Board within the Department of Commerce. The purpose of the board is to identify emerging managerial, technical, administrative, and physical safeguard issues. The board is to report its findings to the Secretary of Commerce, the Director of OMB, the Director of the National Security Agency, and the appropriate congressional committees.

To date, agencies have developed information security plans and NIST has continued to issue standards and other guidance. However, reports from agency inspectors general

---

[6] U.S. Congress. *Computer Security Act of 1987*, P.L. 100–235, 101 Stat. 1724 (1988), as amended by P.L. 104–106, 110 Stat. 701 (1996).

(IGs) and GAO show that "major agencies," those with chief financial officers (CFOs), have significant information security weaknesses. These weaknesses pose risks — fraud, disruption, and disclosure of sensitive data — to federal operations.

C. Clinger–Cohen Act of 1996

The purpose of the Clinger–Cohen Act of 1996 (CCA) is to improve the productivity, efficiency, and effectiveness of federal programs through the improved acquisition, use, and disposal of IT resources.[7] Among other provisions, the law:

1. Encourages federal agencies to evaluate and adopt best management and acquisition practices used by both private- and public-sector organizations
2. Requires agencies to base decisions about IT investments on quantitative and qualitative factors — associated with the costs, benefits, and risks of those investments — and to use performance data to demonstrate how well the IT investments support improvements to agency programs — through measurements such as reduced costs, improved employee productivity, and higher customer satisfaction
3. Requires executive agencies to appoint executive-level CIOs

CCA also streamlines the IT acquisition process by eliminating the General Services Administration's central acquisition authority. CCA places procurement responsibility directly with federal agencies and encourages the adoption of smaller and better integrated IT procurements.
   CCA requires OMB to:

1. Issue directives to executive agencies concerning capital planning and investment control, revisions to mission-related and administrative processes, and information security
2. Promote and improve the acquisition and use of IT through performance-based and results-based management
3. Use the budget process to analyze, through tracking and evaluation, the risks and results of major agency capital investments in IT systems and to enforce accountability of agency heads
4. Report to Congress on agency progress and accomplishments

CCA amends the PRA, thus requiring executive agency heads to appoint senior-level CIOs, responsible for the agency's IRM activities and reporting directly to the agency head. And CCA requires executive agencies to design and implement an IT acquisitions process, maximizing the value and assessing and managing the risks. CCA also lists specific elements agencies must include in that process and requires integrating it with budget, financial, and program management decisions. Before making significant investments in IT, federal agencies must analyze mission-related and administrative practices, revising them as appropriate. Federal agencies must also benchmark these practices against comparable ones

---

[7]U.S. Congress. *Clinger–Cohen Act of 1996*, P.L. 104–208. *The Omnibus Consolidated Appropriations Act of 1997* (P.L. 104–208), combining both the *Federal Acquisition Reform Act of 1996* (P.L. 104–106, Div. D) and the *Information Technology Management Reform Act of 1996* (P.L. 104–106, Div. E), was renamed the *Clinger–Cohen Act of 1996*.

for public- or private-sector organizations. Finally, federal agencies must also ensure that information security practices are adequate for protecting agency resources.

In addition, CCA requires agencies to assess IT personnel needs and capabilities. In particular, federal agencies must assess, as part of the GPRA strategic planning and performance evaluation process, (1) requirements for agency personnel concerning knowledge and skills in IRM and (2) the extent to which positions and personnel at executive and management levels in the agency meet those requirements. Agencies must develop strategies and plans for hiring, training, and — if any deficiencies are found — professional development. More details on the specific reporting requirements contained in CCA are shown in Table 35.4.

D. Government Paperwork Elimination Act of 1998

The Government Paperwork Elimination Act of 1998, P.L. 105–277,[8] authorizes OMB to provide for acquisition and use of alternative IT by federal agencies. Alternative IT includes (1) electronic submission, maintenance, or disclosure of information as a substitute for paper and (2) electronic signatures in conducting government business through e-government transactions. The law requires that the director of OMB, in conjunction with the National Telecommunications and Information Administration, study the use of electronic signatures in e-government transactions and periodically report to Congress the results of the study.

E. Government Information Security Reform Act of 2001

The purposes of the Government Information Security Reform Act (GISRA) are the following:[9]

1. To provide a comprehensive framework for establishing and ensuring the effectiveness of controls over information resources that support federal operations and assets
2. To recognize the highly networked nature of the federal computing environment, including the need for federal government interoperability, and, in the implementation of improved security management measures, to ensure that opportunities for interoperability are not adversely affected
3. To provide effective governmentwide management and oversight of related security risks, including coordination of information security efforts throughout the civilian, national security, and law enforcement communities
4. To provide for development and maintenance of the minimum controls required to protect federal information and information systems
5. To provide a mechanism for improved oversight of information security programs in federal agencies

The reporting requirements of GISRA are shown in Table 35.5.

---

[8] U.S. Congress. *Government Paperwork Elimination Act of 1998*, P.L. 105–277, which was the omnibus consolidated and emergency appropriations act for the fiscal year ending September 30, 1999.
[9] U.S. Congress. *Government Information Security Reform Act of 2001*, P.L.106–39. GISRA was part of the national defense authorization for fiscal year 2001.

Table 35.4   Reporting Requirements of Clinger–Cohen Act

CCA Section: Who Reports	What Is to Be Reported
5112 (c): Director, OMB	Submit a report (at the same time the president submits his budget request) about (1) the net benefits achieved as a result of major capital investments made by executive agencies in information systems and (2) how the benefits relate to the accomplishment of the goals of the executive agencies
5112 (j): Director, OMB	"Keep Congress fully informed" on improvements in the performance of agency programs and in accomplishing agency missions through the use of the best practices in IRM
5123 (2): Federal agency heads	Submit annual report, to be included with the agency's budget submission to Congress, on the progress in achieving goals for improving the efficiency and effectiveness of agency operations and, as appropriate, the delivery of services to the public through the effective use of IT
5302: Administrator, OFPP[a]	Submit detailed test plans, procedures to be used, and lists of regulations to be waived before federal executive agencies conduct pilot programs to test alternative approaches to IT acquisition
5303: Administrator, OFPP[a]	Submit, not later than 180 days after completion of a pilot program to test alternative approaches to IT acquisition, a report to Congress and OMB on the results, findings, and recommendations derived from the pilot program
5312 (e): Comptroller General, GAO	Monitor the conduct and review the results of acquisitions under "solutions-based contracting pilot programs" and submit to Congress "periodic" reports containing the comptroller general's views on the activities, results, and findings under those pilot programs
5401 (c) (3): Comptroller General, GAO	Review pilot programs to test streamlined procedures for procuring IT products and services through online multiple-award schedules and report to Congress, not later than 3 years after the date on which each pilot program was established, the extent of competition for orders and the effect of streamlined procedures on (1) prices charged and (2) paperwork requirements for multiple-award schedule contracts and orders; in addition, include the effect of the pilot program on small businesses, especially socially and economically disadvantaged ones

[a] *OFPP:* Office of Federal Procurement Policy, within OMB.

Source: Review of CCA.

Table 35.5   Reporting Requirements of GISRA

GISRA Section: Who Reports	What Is to Be Reported
Sec. 3535: each federal agency	Annually, each agency shall have performed an independent evaluation of the information security program and practices of that agency; each evaluation by an agency under this section shall include testing of the effectiveness of information security control techniques for an appropriate subset of the agency's information systems; an assessment must be made (on the basis of the results of the testing) of the compliance with the requirements of this subchapter; and related information security policies, procedures, standards, and guidelines
Sec. 3535: IG or independent evaluator	The IG or the independent evaluator performing an evaluation under this section may use an audit, evaluation, or report relating to programs or practices of the applicable agency
Sec. 3535: each federal agency	Annually, not later than the anniversary of the date of the enactment of this subchapter, the applicable agency head shall submit to the director of OMB the results of (1) each evaluation required under this section, other than an evaluation of a system described under subparagraph (A) or (B) of section 3532 (b) (2), and (2) each audit of an evaluation required under this section of a system, described under subparagraph (A) or (B) of Sec. 3532 (b) (2)
Sec. 3535: Director, OMB	Annually, the director of OMB shall submit to Congress a report summarizing the data received from agencies under subsection (c)
Sec. 3535: Director, CIA, and Secretary of Defense	Evaluations and audits of evaluations of systems, under the authority and control of the Director of Central Intelligence, and evaluations and audits of evaluation of National Foreign Intelligence Programs systems, under the authority and control of the Secretary of Defense, shall be made available only to the appropriate oversight committees of Congress, in accordance with applicable laws

Source: Review of GISRA.

F.   E-Government Act of 2002

The e-Government Act (e-GA) of 2002[10] was passed to enhance the management and promotion of e-government services and processes. To increase citizen access to gov-

---

[10] U.S. Congress. *E-Government Act of 2002*, P.L. 107–347. Title III of the E-Government Act is also referred to as the *Federal Information Security Management Act* (FISMA). FISMA lays out a framework for annual IT security reviews, reporting, and remediation planning.

ernment information and services, the law established a federal CIO in an Office of e-Government within OMB — which oversees IRM, including development and application in the federal government — and established a broad framework of measures that require the use of Internet-based IT. The law also authorizes $45 million for an e-government fund in the U.S. Treasury, to pay for IT projects aimed at linking agencies and facilitating information sharing.

The law is designed to streamline the government's information resources, close security gaps, and create more public-centered websites. In addition, the e-GA

1. Directs OMB to establish an interagency committee on government information and to issue guidelines for agency websites
2. Requires federal courts to establish websites with information about the court and cases being presented
3. Requires federal agencies to adhere to uniform security standards for information
4. Creates an IT interchange program between the private and public sectors
5. Authorizes governmentwide use of share-in-savings contracts, which permit agencies to pay contractors using savings realized through technological improvements
6. Requires federal agencies and OMB to submit reports to Congress (as shown in Table 35.6)

As shown in Table 35.6, there are many reporting requirements affecting federal IT and e-government. The next section discusses what these reports tell Congress about the current state of IT and e-government activities.

IV. SECURITY WEAKNESSES IDENTIFIED IN FEDERAL IT PERFORMANCE REPORTS

OMB identified six common governmentwide weaknesses in its 131-page GISRA report, *Fiscal Year 2002 Report to Congress on Federal Government Information Security Reform.*[11] The report is based primarily on agency and IG performance reports to OMB, along with information provided through plans of action and milestones, and agency IT budget materials. Agency FY 2001 reports established a baseline of agency IT security performance. As a result of reviewing these materials, OMB identified these six IT security weaknesses:

1. Lack of agency senior management attention to IT security
2. Nonexistent IT security performance measures
3. Poor security education and awareness
4. Failure to fully fund and integrate IT security into the capital planning and investment control process
5. Failure to ensure that contractor services are adequately secure
6. Failure to detect, report, and share information on vulnerabilities

As a result of GISRA requirements and OMB performance measures, the federal government is now in a better position to measure progress in improving IT security, and

---

[11]U.S. Office of Management and Budget. *Fiscal Year 2002 Report to Congress on Federal Government Information Security Reform* (GISRA report). The download URL is http://www.whitehouse.gov/omb/inforeg/2002gisra_report.pdf, Washington, D.C., 2003.

Table 35.6   Reporting Requirements of e-GA

e-GA Section: Who reports	What Is to Be Reported
202 (b): Each federal agency	Agencies shall develop performance measures that demonstrate how e-government enables progress toward agency objectives, strategic goals, and statutory mandates; areas of performance measurement that agencies should consider include (1) customer service, (2) agency productivity, and (3) adoption of innovative IT, including the appropriate use of commercial best practices; agencies shall link their performance goals, as appropriate, to key groups, including citizens, businesses, and other governments, and to internal federal government operations
202 (g): Each federal agency	Compile and submit to the OMB Director an annual e-Government status report on (1) the status of the implementation of e-government initiatives by the agency, (2) compliance by the agency with this act, and (3) how e-government initiatives of the agency improve performance in delivering programs to their constituencies
3606 (a) (b): Director, OMB	Not later than March 1 of each year, submit an e-government status report to the Committee on Governmental Affairs, the Senate, and the Committee on Government Reform, the House of Representatives; the report under subsection (a) shall contain (1) a summary of the information reported by agencies under section 202 (f) of the e-Government Act of 2002, (2) the information required to be reported by section 3604 (f), and (3) a description of compliance by the federal government with other goals and provisions of the e-Government Act
1706 (a) (b): Director, OMB	OMB, in cooperation with the National Telecommunications and Information Administration, is to conduct an ongoing study of the use of electronic signatures for (1) paperwork reduction and electronic commerce, (2) individual privacy, and (3) the security and authenticity of transactions; the director shall submit to Congress on a periodic basis a report describing the results of the study carried out

Source: Review of e-GA.

funding for IT security is increasing. For FY 2002, from a total IT investment of about $48 billion, agencies spent almost $2.7 billion for security measures. OMB estimates FY 2003 funding for IT security at $4.2 billion and FY 2004 funding at over $4.7 billion. In particular, OMB points out that spending more does not always improve IT security performance. Rather, the key is effectively incorporating IT security in management and accountability at the project and agency levels.

OMB states that agencies are demonstrating progress, although much work remains. While agencies have applied more rigorous IT security reviews, more threats and vulnerabilities have also materialized. OMB also refers to IT provisions specified in the president's FY 2004 budget:

1. Agencies must establish and maintain an agencywide process for developing and implementing, at the program and system levels, plans of action and milestones to serve as an agency's primary management tool. The FY 2004 budget submission (February 3, 2003) established the goal, for the end of FY 2003 (September 30, 2003), that all agencies shall create a process ensuring that IT security weaknesses, once identified, are tracked and corrected.
2. Many agencies face the same security weaknesses year after year. OMB will continue to assist agencies in prioritizing and reallocating funds to address these problems. By the end of FY 2003, 80% of federal IT systems shall be certified and accredited.
3. While improvements in integrating security into new IT investments are evident, significant problems remain, especially in older systems. By the end of FY 2003, 80% of the federal government's FY 2004 major IT investments shall integrate security, as appropriate, into the investment life cycle.

V. SOME OBSERVATIONS ABOUT WHAT TO INCLUDE IN FUTURE IT PERFORMANCE REPORTS

In addition to reporting on individual agency initiatives, it is important for OMB's future annual reports to include the larger interagency and intergovernmental aspects of IT and e-government activities. Increasingly, the challenges that the federal government faces are interagency and intergovernmental problems that cut across numerous programs, agencies, constituencies, and levels of government. For example, coordination and sharing among agencies, across horizontal organizational barriers, is a critical aspect of implementing effective IT and e-government solutions and developing and deploying major systems development projects. Fountain calls this the development of information capacity,[12] as well as information capital. Both capacity and capital are needed to support congressional and agency actions to address today's IT and e-government challenges and prepare for the future.

Such preparation includes transforming the federal government by maximizing IT performance and ensuring accountability. Although efforts to transform agencies — by improving performance and accountability — are under way, decisive action and sustained attention will be necessary, and more remains to be done. Increased efforts can ensure that the government has the information capacity to deliver on its promises and meet current and emerging needs. Undoubtedly, contributing to these efforts will be OMB's new Office of Electronic Government, created by e-GA (2002). As the author observed,[13] "in an increasingly networked and globalized world, attention will also need to be paid to efforts to build information capacity and networks with state and local governments, nongovernmental organizations, other countries, and international institutions. These efforts will need to be addressed in future agency IT performance reports."

---

[12] Fountain, Jane E. Building The Virtual State: Information Technology and Institutional Change, Brookings Institution Press: Washington, DC, 2001.
[13] Mullen, Patrick R. The Need for Government-wide Information Capacity, Social Science Computer Review: Winter, **2003**.

VI. CONCLUSION

As discussed in this chapter, there are many IT and e-government performance-reporting requirements associated with the federal government's IT utilization and e-government initiatives. The sound application and management of IT and e-government to support strategic program goals is an important part of any serious attempt to improve agency performance, cut costs, and enhance responsiveness to the public. In particular, through performance-reporting requirements, agencies can, and should, be expected to show how IT contributes to reducing operating costs, increasing productivity, and enhancing overall program quality. Agency track records can be established through reports to Congress, OMB, and others. These reports can form the basis for federal agency and congressional decision-making about (1) appropriate levels for continued funding and (2) how to address future national and, increasingly, international IT and e-government needs.

REFERENCES

Fountain, J.E., *Building the Virtual State: Information Technology and Institutional Change*, Brookings Institution Press, Washington, D.C., 2001.

Gartner Group, Key Issues in E-Government Strategy and Management, Research Notes, Key Issues, Gartner Press, Stemford, CT, May 23, 2000.

Mullen, P.R., The need for government-wide information capacity, *Social Science Computer Review*, Winter, 21(4), 456–463, 2003.

Seifert, J.W., *A Primer on E-Government: Sectors, Stages, Opportunities, and Challenges of Online Governance*, Congressional Research Service, Washington, D.C., 2003 (updated January 28, 2003).

U.S. Congress, Computer Security Act of 1987 (P.L. 100–235, 101 Stat. 1724, 1988, amended by P.L. 104–106, 110 Stat. 701, 1996).

U.S. Congress, Clinger–Cohen Act (CCA) of 1996 (P.L. 104–208).

U.S. Congress, e-Government Act (e-GA) of 2002 (P.L. 107–347).

U.S. Congress, Government Information Security Reform Act (GISRA) of 2001 (P.L.106–39).

U.S. Congress, Government Paperwork Elimination Act of 1998 (P.L. 105–277).

U.S. Congress, Government Performance and Results Act (GPRA) of 1993 (P.L. 103–62).

U.S. Congress, Paperwork Reduction Acts (PRA) of 1980 and 1995 (P.L. 96–511 and P.L. 104–13).

U.S. Government Accountablility Office, *Electronic Government: Success of the Office of Management and Budget's 25 Initiatives Depends on Effective Management and Oversight*, Washington, D.C., March 13, 2003, (GAO-03-495T).

U.S. Office of Management and Budget, Fiscal Year 2002 Report to Congress on Federal Government Information Security Reform (GISRA Report), Washington, D.C., 2003.

36

ASSESSING E-GOVERNMENT INNOVATION

Jonathan D. Parks
Raleigh, North Carolina

Shannon H. Schelin
University of North Carolina

CONTENTS

  I. E-government overview 615
 II. Theoretical constructs 616
III. E-government typology 618
 IV. Hypotheses 621
  V. Theoretical justification for hypotheses 621
 VI. Methodology 622
VII. Findings 622
VIII. Correlations 623
 IX. Multiple regression 626
  X. Implications 628
 XI. Conclusion 628
References 629

ABSTRACT

Information technology (IT) has radically changed many aspects of daily life, including interactions with the government. By capitalizing on the Internet revolution, governments can create new channels of communication and new methods for participation via e-government efforts. The changing environment, coupled with citizen and business demands, encourages government involvement in e-government initiatives and related uses of public-sector ITs. This chapter highlights the importance of e-government, offers a theoretical framework for understanding e-government, examines two methodologies for assessing e-government capacity, empirically tests several hypotheses about policy innovation at the local level, and, offers implications and questions for future research.

I. E-GOVERNMENT OVERVIEW

Electronic government (e-government) has become a mainstay in local, state, and federal governments. According to the 2002 International City/County Managers Association e-government survey, over 73% of municipalities with populations larger than 2500 have websites. Additionally, the 2002 Pew Internet and American Life Project indicates that 58% (68 million people) of American Internet users have accessed at least one government website (Rainie, 2002). Citizens are looking for improved ways to interact with the government, and elected officials demand improved services to enhance their legacies.

Although there is widespread interest in the topic, e-government lacks a consistent, widely accepted definition. It is often related to revolutionizing the business of government through the use of information technology (IT), particularly web-based technologies, which improve internal and external processes, efficiencies, and service deliveries. The American Society for Public Administration (ASPA) and United Nation's Division for Public Economics and Public Administration (UNDPEPA) have defined e-government as "utilizing the Internet and the world wide web for delivering government information and services to citizens" (UN and ASPA, 2001: 1). On the basis of this working definition of e-government, this chapter highlights the importance of e-government, offers a theoretical framework for understanding e-government, examines two methodologies for assessing e-government capacity, empirically tests several hypotheses about policy innovation at the local level, and, offers implications and questions for future research.

II. THEORETICAL CONSTRUCTS

E-government has been viewed in a variety of ways. One context for examining e-government centers on recognition that e-government is more than just a shift in communication patterns or mediums. At least potentially, it involves a transformation of the organizational culture of the government. Recent authors argue that governments are mandated by citizen and business demands to operate within new structures and parameters precipitated by IT (Osborne and Gaebler, 1992; Heeks, 1999; Bovens and Zouridis, 2002; Ho, 2002). These new requirements, which fundamentally alter the nature of government, are made possible through the strategic use of IT.

Garson (2000) has divided the theoretical frameworks of e-government into four main areas, decentralization/democratization, critical theory, sociotechnical systems, and global integration theories. The first two suffice to explain basic variations in e-government theory. The decentralization/democratization theory of e-government revolves around the progressive potential of technology and focuses on the positive governmental advances associated with e-government. Critical theory emphasizes the high rate of conflict and failure associated with IT applications and counters the positivist progressivism of decentralization/democratization theory with a realist view of inherent technological limits and contradictions. Each school of thought has its proponents as well as its critics. Taken together, the frameworks provide a useful delineation of the theoretical literature on e-government.

Decentralization/democratization theory is the most commonly held orientation associated with e-government. In fact, articles beginning with Bozeman and Bretschneider's seminal article in 1986 refer to the transformational, progressive nature of technology adoption in the government sector. Others have concluded that e-government and associated IT adoption lead to shifting paradigms, extending beyond the notion of simple progress (Reschenthaler and Thompson, 1996; Ho, 2002). Reschenthaler and Thompson (1996) are among theorists who note the revolutionary potential of IT in government. They contend that the power of e-government technology lies in its ability to even the playing field for all sizes and types of governments. Additionally, they see in e-government the basis for reengineering the business of government, refocusing its work on the needs of the citizens, and returning government to its core functions (Reschenthaler and Thompson, 1996). Other authors have also used the decentralization theory to highlight the transformational components of IT and e-government.

Some authors examine the traditional bureaucratic model of public service delivery (the Weberian model), which highlights specialization, departmentalization, and standardization (Weber, 1947; Ho, 2002). This traditional model has created the "stovepipes" associated with government, those departmental silos that resist functioning across agency boundaries. The main promise of the Weberian model is to ensure that all citizens are treated equitably with the utmost efficiency. However, in the 1990s, the reinventing government movement sought to alter the core focus of government, moving from departmentalization and centralization to citizen-centric decentralization (Osborne and Gaebler, 1992), much in contrast to the Weberian model.

According to Ho (2002), the e-government paradigm, which emphasizes coordinated network building, external collaboration, and customer services, is slowly replacing the traditional bureaucratic paradigm and its focus on standardization, hierarchy, departmentalization, and operational cost efficiency. The new paradigm mirrors many of the tenets of the reinventing government movement, including user control and customization, flexibility in service delivery, horizontal and vertical integration culminating in "one-stop" shopping, and innovative leadership focused on the end user (Osborne and Gaebler, 1992; Ho, 2002). This paradigm shift is precipitated by the advent of the Internet, which provides government the ability to use technology to impact customers directly, instead of simply reengineering internal processes (Scavo and Shi, 1999).

A core concept of e-government, which falls under the decentralization orientation, is the idea of using technology as a linkage between citizens and government. According to the work of Milward and Snyder (1996), the governmental use of ITs to engage and interact with the public further enhances the value of technology adoption, which in turn leads to greater e-government penetration. IT can be substituted for other governmental institutions to link citizens to government services. This linkage causes both the citizens and the government to become reliant on IT functions, increasing the penetration and adoption rates of e-government.

As governments, federal, state, and local, become more involved in IT and gain recognition for their e-government efforts, other jurisdictions, not currently engaged in e-government, will increasingly become interested in and adept at this form of IT usage (Norris, 1999). That is, the decentralization theory predicts that e-government's diffusion will snowball as its benefits to citizens and to the agencies themselves is demonstrated.

Technology and e-government adoption rates are a key interest of decentralization proponents. In fact, the argument is virtually tautological — in order to define the factors that increase e-government penetration and adoption, one must believe in the positive potential of the concept. In terms of IT adoption and implementation, the greater the number of governments planning for and using ITs and e-government approaches, the more legitimacy the technology gains (Fletcher, 1999). It is evident from the proliferation of e-government activities at the federal and state levels that the widespread benefits of using IT to provide more timely, seamless government services is a legitimate, even preferred, method of action. Citizen and business demands for e-government applications have extended to the local government level and as more local governments begin using e-technologies, the legitimacy of the applications will further increase (Norris et al., 2001).

By adopting new technologies, governments may be able to respond to the changing environment with improved service delivery, increased efficiency, and reduced costs (West, 2000). The use of e-government applications allows governments to more readily engage citizens and businesses in a virtual world that is thought to be more responsive and accountable to the needs of the customer.

Support for e-government is allied with the decentralization theory, which offers optimistic prospects for the future of virtual governance. However, the stark reality of public technology and e-government failures has been repeatedly noted in news media. The concerns associated with privacy, security, and the digital divide are common threads under critical theory, which offers a critical approach to evaluating e-government. Proponents of this view of e-government are traditionally concerned with the dehumanizing and isolating aspects of IT. Recent concerns about the "digital divide," the technology gap that exists between certain subpopulations in the U.S., highlight the problems of fairly implementing technology as a mode of communication and service delivery (see Fisher, 1998 for more discussion).

Bovens and Zouridis (2002) highlight the critical theory framework of e-government by examining the inherent problems associated with the application of IT and the shift toward an e-government paradigm in real-world settings. They contend that the emerging emphasis on ITs as the medium for citizen interaction with government fundamentally alters the role of the bureaucrat. The traditional Weberian model uses street-level bureaucrats to interact with citizens and to determine the proper services and service levels to assist these citizens (Lipsky, 1980). However, as technology becomes more integrated into government agencies, computer programs are often used to interface with clients, determine eligibilities, and decide on proper levels of service (Boven and Zouridis, 2002). As a result of this new computer-based assessment trend, street-level bureaucrats are losing their discretionary power. Bovens and Zouridis (2002) do not judge the new, nondiscretionary technology models, but rather, use the paradigm shift to focus on the risks of arbitrariness and associated threats to the legitimacy of governmental actions at the street level.

III. E-GOVERNMENT TYPOLOGY

Although several typologies have been developed to explain the progression of e-government (Layne and Lee, 2001; Moon, 2002), the UN and ASPA definition of the stages of e-government maintains continuity with the working definition set forth at the outset of this chapter. It is also important to note that the stages are a continuum in which governments can be within the same stage with very different functionalities and service offerings.

According to the UN and ASPA (2001), there are five main stages of e-government. The lack of an organizational website is not defined by a stage, but may be considered Stage Zero. Stage 1 is the emerging web presence, which involves static information presented as a type of online brochure (UN and ASPA, 2001: 16). The main goal of the emerging web stage is to provide an online mechanism for communicating key general information about the government to interested citizens and entities. The website lacks information about services and is not organized in a citizen-focused manner. Typically, the government has used a "go it alone" approach, which visually represents the "stovepipes" that exist within agencies — there is little coordination across agencies and levels of government in Stage 1 websites.

In Stage 2, enhanced web presence, the role of the website becomes associated with information on services, although it is still organized by departments rather than by user groups. Enhanced web presence sites typically have e-mail as a means of two-way communication. However, rarely are there available forms for download. Stage 2 offers limited communication and greater information about the services of the government, but it does not meet the citizen-centric approach that has been advocated for e-government (UN and ASPA, 2001: 17).

Stage 3, interactive web presence, begins to move into the citizen-centric realm of e-government (UN and ASPA, 2001: 18). Typically, the information is portrayed by intuitive groupings that cross agency lines. For example, the website might use a portal as the single point of entry into various departments and service areas. The portal would offer major groupings like business, new resident, seniors, children, or other standard groups. Then, the end user would select the grouping that applies and be launched into a new section of the portal where the most common services requested for the group are located. The services would not be listed by departmental areas, but rather by functional areas. Stage 3 sites have downloadable forms with online submissions, e-mail contact for various governmental employees, and links to other government websites.

Stage 4, transactional web presence, offers the ability to conduct secure online transactions (UN and ASPA, 2001: 19). This stage is also organized by user needs and contains dynamic information. The website may offer a variety of transactions, including paying for services, paying bills, and paying taxes. Transactional web presence includes online submission of forms, many downloads, e-mail contact, and several links to other governments. The use of digital signatures also falls under Stage 4.

The final stage, Stage 5, involves seamless government. Although this stage represents an ideal, there is no real example of its application. Stage 5 involves a cross-agency, intergovernmental approach that only displays one front, regardless of service area (UN and ASPA, 2001: 20). For example, a seamless website would offer local, state, and federal government services via the state portal without the end user recognizing what level of government provides the service. A Stage 5 site would offer vertical and horizontal integration and would require true organizational transformation with respect to administrative boundaries (UN and ASPA, 2001: 20).

With a working knowledge of the typology associated with e-government, it is easy to assess the current status of the concept. Much of the literature indicates that Stage 2, enhanced web presence, is the typical placement of an American local government on the continuum. Alexander and Grubbs (1998: 3) note:

> Few sites capitalized on the interactive nature of the Internet to conduct public discussions, maintain bulletin boards, or provide data and information available for download.

In his analysis of the 2000 ICMA e-government survey, Moon (2002) finds that a majority of municipalities with populations over 10,000 are not offering transactional websites. Furthermore, based on the 2002 ICMA e-government survey, only 62 (1.7%) municipalities offer online payment of taxes, 113 (3.1%) offer online payment of utility bills, and 91 (2.5%) offer online payment of fines and fees. The percentages for counties are only slightly higher, with 69 (16.3%) offering online payment of taxes, 17 (4.0%) offering online payment of utility bills, and 21 (5.0%) offering online payment of fines and fees.

The state and federal governments offer more robust transactional services, which is to be expected based on IT diffusion patterns.

A different dimension of e-government typology is the orientation of the website. There are three primary orientations identified by Ho (2002) in his analysis of city websites. These orientations are designed to demonstrate the shift from the Weberian bureaucratic model to the e-government paradigm. The first orientation involves administration-oriented websites. These sites are organized along departmental lines and represent the traditional bureaucratic paradigm (p. 437). The second orientation is information-oriented, which offers the one-stop shop concept via the home page of the government unit (p. 437). This design crosses departmental lines in order to provide comprehensive information in a centralized location. The final orientation is user-oriented. This design attempts to categorize information in intuitive groupings that enable end users to quickly select their grouping and retrieve only the information that pertains to them (p. 437). As in information orientation, the user-oriented site crosses departmental boundaries in order to provide a specialized one-stop shop. Ho's analysis of the 55 largest municipalities' websites indicates that a majority have moved toward varying degrees of user orientation (p. 438). Again, this finding is consistent with the main predictor of early IT adoption, population size (Bozeman and Bretschneider, 1986; Scavo and Shi, 2000; Moon, 2002).

There are alternative approaches to defining the e-government typology, which are more readily associated with the critical theory orientation. This typology uses various levels of communication, applications of technology, and citizen participation in demo-cratic forums to define its stages. West's (2003) methodology has gained wide acceptance as of late. This framework focuses on the evaluation of a government's website as an indicator of the adoption rate of e-government. West uses his methodology to evaluate state government websites, large municipal government websites, and national govern-ment websites. From these assessments, he constructs a rankings list that indicates those governments that are leaders in e-government adoption.

While other frameworks evaluate the quality of e-government offerings, West simply measures the presence or absence of the offerings to form his ratings. The core of his framework rests on a combination of traditional measures, such as e-mail contact listings, making payments via credit card, and the number of online services accessible through the website, and newer, emerging issues. Some of these emerging issues are indicators of privacy protection and security assurance, level of accessibility compliance with the World Wide Web Consortium (W3C) accessibility standards, and levels of readability of content on these websites using the Flesch-Kincaid test.

Kaylor et al. (2001) believe that much of the current literature on evaluation of e-government offerings focuses on developing a set of "best practice" benchmarks by which governments can compare themselves instead of evaluating the implementa-tion of e-government services. The Kaylor methodology seeks to develop such a framework by identifying core services offered by local governments and measuring the degree to which these services are made available to citizens in the context of e-government. Using a four-point progression scale with accompanying operational definitions, Kaylor evaluates local government websites to develop "e-scores," which are then used to produce a rankings list of e-government adoption among local govern-ments.

IV. HYPOTHESES

Given the recent interest in e-government, several research initiatives have been undertaken to assess the value of e-government, determine the predictors of adoption, and offer prescriptive recommendations on the advancement of e-government. However, little research on the factors contributing to innovation diffusion at the local level is available. As such, it is the goal of this study to provide valuable insight into the factors that allow e-government policy innovation to occur. The various independent variables included in this study are grounded in policy literature, particularly innovation and group theories, as well as existing e-government research.

The hypotheses included in this study are:

1. Population size will positively influence e-government capacity
2. Growth rate of jurisdictions will positively influence e-government capacity
3. Mean per capita income will positively influence e-government capacity
4. The level of jurisdictional IT professionalism, measured as presence of IT departments with five or more full-time employees, will positively influence e-government capacity

These issues are particularly relevant to public administration research and application. The need to understand the influence of various political, social, and economic factors in predicting innovation adoption is critical to improving the reach and scope of e-government. This study seeks to highlight the importance of such research by providing empirical evidence as to the impact of theoretically based factors in e-government adoption.

V. THEORETICAL JUSTIFICATION FOR HYPOTHESES

The first hypothesis, population size will influence e-government capacity, has been widely noted in e-government literature. In particular, Ho (2002) and Moon (2002) have noted the size of population as the main predictor of e-government adoption.

The growth rate of municipalities is also predicted to influence the e-government capacity scores of jurisdictions. As growth rates increase, the tax base of local governments increase. Accordingly, those jurisdictions with high growth rates traditionally have higher levels of wealth than jurisdictions with lower levels of growth. According to Walker (1969), size, wealth, and urbanization are predictors of state innovation, which can be extended to the municipal level without much conjecture. On the basis of extant literature, we can conclude that the growth rate of municipalities will have a positive and strong influence on e-government capacity. In addition, according to Walker (1969), per capita income will also have a positive and strong influence on e-government capacity.

The fourth hypothesis, e-government capacity will be influenced by jurisdictional IT professionalism, is derived from research conducted in the e-government arena. Both McNeal et al. (2002) and Moon (2002) have found that the form of government, in particular council-manager, can have a positive impact on e-government capacity score. In North Carolina all counties are governed by professional managers and elected boards, so this measure was not used.

However, the professionalism of the IT department is another important factor to consider when assessing e-government capacity. In fact, public-sector literature repeatedly notes the problems associated with untrained and poorly skilled technology staff. A survey of local government IT managers reveals that many technology staff, particularly web masters, are administrative staff who have been promoted (Schelin, 2003). Furthermore, the 2002 ICMA e-government survey indicates that lack of technology/web staff and expertise are two of the leading challenges to successful e-government implementation. The importance of high-quality technology staff cannot be overlooked when assessing those factors that contribute to the success or failure of technology projects. Various public- and private-sector scholars have noted the importance of highly qualified technology staff on project success.

According to Norris (2003), the importance of "well-trained, capable technical personnel" cannot be understated when assessing critical success factors. By having technical personnel to provide assistance with planning and implementation, as well as to assist in end user support, IT projects will face lower hurdles from the onset. Staff and their skill sets are mentioned throughout the literature (see Hartman and Ashrafi, 2002). Furthermore, Poon and Wagner (2001) rate appropriate technology staff as one of the ten most critical success factors for technology projects. Aforementioned research indicates that jurisdictions with professional IT departments with five or more full-time employees are expected to have higher e-government capacities.

VI. METHODOLOGY

The objective of this study is to determine the factors that contribute to innovation adoption, measured as e-government capacity, in counties in North Carolina. This study involves the application of two methodologies by Darrell West and Charles Kaylor to twenty North Carolina counties' websites. In addition, demographics, such as population and growth rate information, for the counties are included from the 2000 census.

The two methodologies of interest attack the measurement of e-government adoption by local governments from different vantage points. The West methodology focuses on the presence or absence of various e-government offerings, as shown in Figure 36.1.

The Kaylor methodology identifies core services (Figure 36.2) of local governments and measures the degree to which these services are offered in an e-government capacity.

In this study, the authors modified the original Kaylor methodology to avoid measuring some services that are not traditionally the responsibility of county government in North Carolina. The items removed include payments for utilities, parking permits, sidewalk dining permits, a parking referee as a customer service, utility start/stop requests, bicycle licensing, dog licensing, and taxi licensing. Removing these services from evaluation provides a more accurate assessment of e-government adoption by counties in North Carolina.

VII. FINDINGS

Twenty North Carolina counties were selected at random for analysis. In terms of demographics, the counties are representative of the remaining 80 counties in the state. Thirty percent of the counties surveyed have populations under 30,000, while 25% have populations of 30,000 to 60,000. Twenty percent of the counties have 60,000 to 90,000

Measure	Points awarded
• Audio clips • Databases • Digital signatures • E-mail contact • E-mail updates • Foreign language • No advertisements • No premium fees • No restricted areas • No user fees • Payment via credit cards • PDA access • Personalization allowed • Posting of comments allowed • Privacy policy • Publications • Readability below 10th grade • Security policy • Video clips • W3C accessibility standards compliance	0 points if absent 4 points if present
• Online services	1 point for each service up to 20 services

Figure 36.1   West methodology measures.

residents, while another 10% have 90,000 to 120,000. Finally, 10% of the counties have between 120,000 and 150,000 citizens and 5% have over 150,000.

In terms of growth rate from 1990 to 2000, again the selected counties are representative of the state. Fifteen percent of the counties had a growth rate of 10% or less, while 35% had a growth rate between 11 and 20%. Another 25% of the counties had a growth rate between 21 and 30%, while 10% of the counties had a growth rate of 31 to 40%. Finally, 15% of the counties had a growth rate of 41% or higher for 1990 to 2000.

Moving beyond the demographics of the counties, the following data provide descriptive statistics on the dependent variable indices. The median number of e-government applications offered by the counties included in this study is two. The most common applications offered include access to electronic records (51.6%), geographic information systems (47.4%), and online requests for service (31.6%). In general, the North Carolina counties are slightly below the average local government in terms of their e-government capacity, based on a comparison of the selected counties with the total population of the ICMA data set.

VIII.   CORRELATIONS

In terms of the influence of various independent variables on the current status of e-government in the North Carolina counties, correlation has been used to determine which variables should be included in the regression equation for prediction.

The first independent variable, population size, is expected to have a positive relationship with both the West and Kaylor e-government capacity scores. Both Ho (2002) and Moon (2002) have indicated that population size is the number one predictor of e-government adoption and sophistication. As shown in Table 36.1, population size has a strong correlation with both the West and Kaylor e-government capacity scores. Accordingly, population size will be included in the regression model.

The second independent variable, growth rate, is expected to have a positive relationship with e-government capacity. Historically, increased levels of wealth, generated

Service measured	Points awarded
Audio/Video • Audio of council meetings • Live traffic cameras • Streaming video of council meetings • Video or still-image tours • Video walk-through directions	**0 points**—absent **1 point**—information about the topic exists on the web site **2 point**—a link to relevant contact (phone number or email) exists on the web site **3 points**—downloadable forms are available on the web site **4 points**—the transaction/interaction can take place completely online
Applications • Affirmative Action form • Bidder application • Job application	Same as above
Customer Service • Action request • Code enforcement • Information request • Parking referee* • Payment histories • Schedules • Utility start/stop requests*	Same as above
Communication • Emergency management • Incident closure • Road closure	Same as above
Documents • Budget report • Country charter • Country code • Downloadable forms • Minutes from council/public meetings	Same as above
e-Procurement • Accepting bids online	Same as above
Images • As-built • Document management service • GIS • Plat maps	Same as above
Licenses • Bicycle licensing* • Business license • Dog licensing* • Taxi licensing*	Same as above
Miscellaneous • Conversation forums • Online surveys • Property assessments • Scheduling e-meetings • Zoning	Same as above

Figure 36.2 Core services of local governments.

Service measured	Points awarded
Payments • Fines • Permits • Registrations • Taxes • Utilities*	Same as above
Permits • Building • Parking* • Right-of-way • Sidewalk dining* • Street vendor • Temporary-use	Same as above
Registration • Classes • Facilities • Visitors	Same as above

• Denotes items not considered in this evaluation

Figure 36.2 continued

from an influx of taxable revenue, have contributed to innovation adoption (Walker, 1969). However, as shown in Table 36.2, growth rate has a statistically significant correlation with only the West e-government capacity score. This situation may be a function of the items counted in the West methodology. For instance, the presence of a website may be more important as the growth rate increases, but actual e-government offerings, as measured by the Kaylor methodology, are not predicted by growth rate.

Table 36.1 Bivariate Correlation: Population Size and e-Government Capacity

	Population Size	
	e-Government Capacity (West)	e-Government Capacity (Kaylor)
Correlation coefficient	.637**	.505*
Significance (2-tailed)	.003	.023
N	20	20

**Correlation is significant at the .01 level (2-tailed).
*Correlation is significant at the .05 level (2-tailed).

Table 36.2 Bivariate Correlation: Growth Rate and e-Government Capacity

	Growth Rate	
	e-Government Capacity (West)	e-Government Capacity (Kaylor)
Correlation coefficient	.540*	.321
Significance (2-tailed)	.014	.167
N	20	20

*Correlation is significant at the .05 level (2-tailed).

Table 36.3 Bivariate Correlation: Per Capita Income and e-government Capacity

	Per Capita Income	
	e-Government Capacity (West)	e-Government Capacity (Kaylor)
Correlation coefficient	.571**	.392
Significance (2-tailed)	.009	.087
N	20	20

**Correlation is significant at the .01 level (2-tailed).

Table 36.4 Bivariate Correlation: IT Professionalism and e-government Capacity

	IT Professionalism	
	e-Government Capacity (West)	e-Government Capacity (Kaylor)
Correlation coefficient	.560*	.328
Significance (2-tailed)	.013	.170
N	20	20

*Correlation is significant at the.05 level (2-tailed).

Regardless, growth rate is included in the regression equation, due to its correlation with one of the capacity scores.

The third independent variable, per capita county income, is expected to have a positive relationship with e-government capacity. Historically, increased levels of wealth, generated from an influx of taxable revenue, have contributed to innovation adoption (Walker, 1969). However, as shown in Table 36.3, per capita income has a statistically significant correlation with only the West e-government capacity score. Regardless, income is included in the regression equation, due to its correlation with one of the capacity scores.

Organizational IT professionalism is the fourth independent variable. Contemporary research indicates that jurisdictions with highly skilled IT staff have higher rates of innovation. The positive correlation between professionalism and e-government is replicated in the West e-government capacity score, as shown in Table 36.4. Again, the lack of congruence between the West and Kaylor methodologies offers some cause for concern. Perhaps the more professional IT departments score higher on specific West items, such as privacy and security policies, while the actual impact on e-government offerings is limited. Regardless, the measure of professionalism is included in the regression equation.

IX. MULTIPLE REGRESSION

As previously noted, the purpose of the bivariate correlations was to determine which variables to include in the regression equation for prediction of e-government capacity. All four of the hypothesized variables were determined to be significantly correlated to warrant inclusion in the model. Table 36.5 demonstrates the results of the multiple regression analysis with the West methodology capacity score as the dependent variable.

The regression indicates that population size, growth rate, per capita income, and organizational IT professionalism, taken as a whole, account for 71.1% of the variance in the West methodology scores. This finding indicates that the model is sufficient for predicting e-government capacity scores within the West methodology. However, as

Table 36.5 Multiple Regression for West Methodology (Model 1)

Model Summary[a]				
R	R²	Adjusted R²	Standard Error of the Estimate	Durbin-Watson
.711[b]	.505	.374	5.85539	.856

Coefficients[a]							
	Unstandardized Coefficients		Standardized Coefficients			Collinearity Statistics	
	B	Standard Error	Beta	t	Significance	Tolerance	VIF
(Constant)	28.134	12.498		2.251	.040		
POPULAT	2.672E−05	0.000	0.476	1.580	.135	0.363	2.758
GROWTH	10.773	15.519	0.183	0.694	.498	0.474	2.110
INCOME	−5.714E−05	0.000	−0.047	−0.136	.893	0.281	3.556
5 + FTE	3.855	3.565	0.245	1.081	.297	0.642	1.557

[a]Dependent variable: WEST_SC.
[b]Predictors: (constant), FTE_O5, POPULAT, POPCHANG, INCOME

Table 36.6 Multiple Regression for Kaylor Methodology (Model 1)

Model Summary[a]				
R	R²	Adjusted R²	Standard Error of the Estimate	Durbin-Watson
.531[b]	.282	.09	17.86145	1.328

Coefficients[a]							
	Unstandardized Coefficients		Standardized Coefficients			Collinearity Statistics	
	B	Standard Error	Beta	t	Significance	Tolerance	VIF
Constant	59.343	38.125		1.557	.140		
POPULAT	7.254E−05	0.000	0.511	1.406	.180	0.363	2.758
POPCHANG	6.146	47.340	0.041	0.130	.898	0.474	2.110
INCOME	0.000	0.001	−0.122	−0.296	.771	0.281	3.556
FTE_O5	6.652	10.876	0.167	0.612	.550	0.642	1.557

[a]Dependent variable: KAYLOR_S.
[b]Predictors: (Constant), FTE_O5, POPULAT, POPCHANG, INCOME.

illustrated in Table 36.5, none of the variables that demonstrated correlation with the West methodology score prove to be influential in the overall regression model.

Table 36.6 demonstrates the regression model using the Kaylor methodology score as the dependent variable, with the independent variables of population size, growth rate, per capita income, and organizational IT professionalism.

In terms of the Kaylor methodology, the model explains 53.1% of the variance of the e-government capacity scores. Again, Table 36.6 indicates that no individual variables are influential in the overall regression model. Clearly, more research is needed to develop a more complete predictive model.

X. IMPLICATIONS

This study on e-government innovation in North Carolina counties highlights the importance of e-government, offers a theoretical framework for understanding e-government, empirically tests several hypotheses about policy innovation at the local level, and offers implications and questions for future research. The review of extant literature, coupled with the cursory summary of recent legislation, clearly identifies the political salience of e-government. However, as evidenced by the empirical analysis, the theoretical underpinnings of innovation diffusion, the premise of this chapter, do not accurately predict the adoption of e-government by local jurisdictions. Traditional predictive measures, such as per capita income and growth rate, are not significant predictors in the area of e-government when used within a regression model. Clearly, these findings warrant more in-depth research to determine if the promises of e-government, including increased access for citizens and greater responsiveness, are holding true.

Other factors not considered in this study may be able to account for more of the variance in e-government adoption. Three specific variables should be investigated on the basis of case study research. The first variable for future research is the presence of a policy entrepreneur for e-government. One of this study's authors has conducted several case studies on U.S. local governments and the most common finding is the presence of an elected official or high-ranking staff member who desires an e-government presence. Although this finding is not surprising, very little research on this issue has been undertaken.

The second issue for future research involves the role of technical staff in e-government initiatives. In the aforementioned case study work, the author has found that highly skilled IT staff members often create and implement e-government applications based on creativity of the solution instead of applicability of the end product. This type of development, based on the "wow factor" of the technology, is contrary to the promises of e-government.

The final aspect that may slow down e-government adoption is the existence of slack resources in the local government. Although virtually all governments are currently facing significant budgetary constraints, many e-government applications were deployed in the late 1990s, during times of economic prosperity. Although growth rate did not significantly predict e-government capacity scores, better measures, such as increased revenue to expenditure ratios, may offer insight into e-government adoption. Regardless of which factors prove to be significant, it is clear that understanding and anticipating e-government requires further research.

XI. CONCLUSION

IT has fundamentally altered the way we interact in today's society. The role of the Internet continues to increase in society as connectivity becomes more readily available to disparate geographical and demographic sectors of the U.S. E-government offers an opportunity to create new channels of communication and new methods for participation. Success of existing e-government efforts provides increased legitimacy for further IT adoption (Norris, 1999). The changing information environment and the movement toward the knowledge economy, juxtaposed against citizen and business demands, mandates that government become involved in e-government initiatives and related uses of ITs (Ho, 2002).

Although e-government has been offered as a panacea for the ills of the public sector, it has not yet achieved the massive reform and reorientation promised by its proponents. In fact, the e-government movement, similar to other management movements such as total quality management (TQM), new public management, and the reinventing government efforts, has not been successful in altering the core structures of government or avoiding its associated failures (Scavo and Shi, 2000). Leading observers such as Fountain (2001) continue to emphasize the formidable obstacles to higher types of e-government posted by the inertia of sunk investment in existing governmental structures and their associated vested interests.

The structural inertia that afflicts most governments, as well as a propensity toward risk aversion, means that governments are slow to adopt and implement new technologies. Given the documented lag time for technology adoption in the public sector, public-sector realization of the power of the Internet and e-government must be seen as nascent at best. By understanding the theoretical premises that underlie e-government and public IT, programs and processes can be designed to assist government in reaping the benefits associated with the strategic use of IT and e-government.

REFERENCES

Alexander, J.H. and Grubbs, J.W., Wired government: information technology, external public organizations, and cyberdemocracy, *Public Administration and Management: An Interactive Journal*, 3, 1998. Available at: http://www.pamij.com/

Bovens, M. and Stavros, Z., From street level to system level bureaucracies: How information and communication technology is transforming administrative discretion and constitutional control, *Public Administration Review*, 62, 174–185, 2002.

Bozeman, B. and Bretschneider, S., Public management information systems: theory and prescription, *Public Administration Review*, 46 (special edition), 475–487, 1986.

Fisher, D., Rumoring theory and the Internet: a framework for analyzing the grass roots, *Social Science Computer Review*, 16, 158–168, 1998.

Fletcher, P.D., Strategic planning for information technology management in state governments, in *Information Technology and Computer Applications in Public Administration: Issues and Trends*, Garson, G.D., Ed., Idea Group, Hershey, PA, 1999, pp. 81–97.

Fountain, J., Building the Virtual State: Information Technology and Institutional Change, Brookings Institution, Washington, D.C., 2001.

Garson, G.D., Information systems, politics, and government: leading theoretical perspectives, in *Handbook of Public Information Systems*, Garson, G.D., Ed., Marcel Dekker, New York, 2000, pp. 591–605.

Hartman, F. and Rafi A., Project management in the information systems and information technologies industries, *Project Management Journal*, 33, 5–15, 2002.

Heeks, R., Reinventing government in the information age, in *Reinventing Government in the Information Age*, Heeks, R., Ed., Routledge, New York, 1999, pp. 9–21.

Ho, A. Tat-Kei, Reinventing local government and the e-government initiative, *Public Administration Review*, 62, 434–444, 2002.

Kaylor, C., Deshazo, R., and Van Eck, D., Gauging e-government: a report on implementing services among American cities, *Government Information Quarterly*, 18, 2001, pp. 293–307. Available at: http://www.pewinternet.org/reports/pdfs/PIP_Govt_Website_Rpt.pdf

Layne, K. and Lee, J., Developing fully functional e-government: a four-stage model, *Government Information Quarterly*, 18, 122–136, 2001.

Lipsky, M., *Street Level Bureaucracy: Dilemmas of the Individual in Public Services*, Russell, Sage Foundation, New York, 1980.

McNeal, R.S., Carolina J.T., Karen, M. and Lisa J.D., Innovating in digital government in the American states, *Social Science Quarterly*, 84, 52–70, 2003.

Milward, H.B. and Snyder, L.O., Electronic government: linking citizens to public organizations through technology, *Journal of Public Administration Research and Theory*, 6, 261–276, 1996.

Moon, M.J., The evolution of e-government among municipalities: rhetoric or reality?, *Public Administration Review*, 62, 424–433, 2002.

Norris, D.F., Leading edge information technologies and their adoption: lessons from U.S. cities, in *Information Technology and Computer Applications in Public Administration: Issues and Trends*, Garson, G.D., Ed., Idea Group, Hershey, PA, 1999, pp. 137–156.

Norris, D.F., Fletcher P.D., and Holden, S.H., Is Your Local Government Plugged in?, Highlights of the 2000 Electronic Government Survey, prepared for International City and County Managers Association and Public Technologies, Incorporated, 2001.
Available at: http://icma.org/download/catIS/grp120/cgp224/E-Gov2000.pdf

Norris, D.F., Leading-edge information technologies and American local governments, in *Public Information Technology: Policy and Management Issues*, Garson, G.D., Ed., Idea Group Press, Hershey, PA, 2003, pp. 139–169.

Osborne, D. and Gaebler, T., *Reinventing Government: How Entrepreneurial Spirit Is Transforming the Public Sector*, Addison-Wesley, Reading, MA, 1992.

Poon, P. and Wagner, C., Critical success factors revisited: success and failure cases of information systems for senior executives, *Decision Support Systems* 30, 393–418, 2001.

Raine, L., The Rise of the E-Citizen: How People Use Government Agencies' Web Sites, Pew Internet and American Life Project, 2002.

Reschenthaler, G.B. and Thompson, F. The information revolution and the new public management, *Public Administration Research Theory*, 6, 125–143, 1996.

Scavo, C. and Shi, Y., World Wide Web site design and use in public management, in *Information Technology and Computer Applications in Public Administration: Issues and Trends*, Garson, G.D., Ed., Idea Group, Hershey, PA, 1999, pp. 246–266.

Scavo, C. and Shi, Y., The role of information technology in the reinventing government paradigm — normative predicates and practical challenges, *Social Science Computer Review*, 18, 166–178, 2000.

Schelin, S., Training for digital government, in *Digital Government: Principles and Best Practices*, Garson, G.D., Ed., Idea Group Press, Hershey, PA, 2003, pp. 263–275.

UN and ASPA, Benchmarking E-Government: A Global Perspective — Assessing the UN Member States, 2001.
Available at: http://www.unpan.org/egovernment2.asp

Walker, J.L., The diffusion of innovations among American states, *American Political Science Review*, 63, 880–899, 1969.

Weber, M., *Max Weber: The Theory of Social and Economic Organization*, Translated by A.M. Henderson & T. Parsons, The Free Press, New York, 1947.

West, D.M., Assessing E-Government: The Internet, Democracy, and Service Delivery by State and Federal Government, Taubman Center for Public Policy, Brown University, Providence, RI, 2000.
Available at: http://www.brown.edu/Departments/Taubman_Center/polreports/egovtreport00.html

West, D.M., City, State, Federal, and Global E-Government Survey Reports, Taubman Center for Public Policy, Brown University, Providence, RI, 2003.

37

E-DEMOCRACY AND THE U.K. PARLIAMENT

Stephen Coleman
Oxford Internet Institute

CONTENTS

I.   Introduction 631
II. Research questions and methodology 632
III. Inclusive consultation or "the usual suspects" 633
IV. Creating and connecting online networks 635
V.   Representative–represented interaction 636
VI. Evidential quality 638
VII. Conclusions from the case studies 639
VIII. Toward an e-parliament 640
References 642

ABSTRACT

Representative institutions are slowly adapting to the digital world. In 1996 the U.K. Parliament established its own website. Although a highly informative resource, of particular value to journalists and those familiar with the parliamentary system, the site is designed to promulgate official knowledge rather than facilitate interactive communication between citizens and legislators.

I.   INTRODUCTION

The first experiments in using the Internet to enable the public to contribute to the U.K. Parliament began in 1998. Between then and 2002 ten online consultations have been run by or on behalf of parliament. Instead of simply creating a web forum and inviting the public to have its say, rather like an online phone-in program, these consultations have been designed to recruit participants with experience or expertise in relation to specific policy issues. The consultations have been designed to:

- Gather informed evidence from the public to help parliamentarians understand policy issues
- Recruit citizens whose evidence might be unheard or neglected in the usual course of parliamentary evidence taking
- Enable participants to interact and learn from with one another over an extended period of asynchronous discussion
- Enable participants to raise aspects of policies under discussion that might not otherwise have been considered
- Enable legislators to participate in online discussion, raising questions and responding to citizens' comments, as time permits
- Derive a fair, independent summary of views raised that can constitute official evidence to parliament

II. RESEARCH QUESTIONS AND METHODOLOGY

The purpose of the research was to test a number of assumptions about the nature and value of online deliberation. Ambitious normative aspirations have been associated with the potential of online public talk. It has been argued that the online environment could provide space for inclusive public discourse, which is a substantive prerequisite of democracy (Blumler and Coleman, 2001; Levine, 2001; Lenihan, 2002); that there is scope for generating and connecting online networks of interest and practice, which would otherwise remain dispersed and disempowered by distance (Rheingold, 1994; Powazek, 2002); and that online interaction between representatives and represented can enrich mutual understanding and enhance public trust in representative democracy (Bimber, 1999; Coleman, 2003).

Critics of these claims argue, on the basis of political theory and empirical observation, that most online talk is bound to fall short of the normative standards set by deliberative theorists. Theoretical objections to deliberative democracy are based on Lippmannesque assumptions about the scale and complexity of meaningful public deliberation being more than most citizens can be expected to cope with. Femia (1996) rejects what he sees as the idealistic assumptions of deliberative democrats; Peters (1999) regards public communication itself to be overrated in relation to more passive habits of listening.

Emprical observers of online public discussions have found that these tend to bear little relation to the rational norms of deliberative democracy. Hill and Hughes (1998: 130), who conducted research on political chat rooms, concluded, "Chat rooms are a difficult format for thoughtful discussion. The short line space and the fast pace require people to make snap comments, not thoughtful ones". Davis (1999: 177) found, on the basis of his study of political Usenet groups, that "In Usenet political discussions, people talk past one another, when they are not verbally attacking each other. The emphasis is not problem solving, but discussion dominance. Such behavior does not resemble deliberation and it does not encourage participation, particularly by the less politically interested." Wilhelm (2000: 102) concluded from his research, "The sorts of virtual political forum that were analyzed do not provide viable sounding boards for signaling and thematizing issues to be processed by the political system." These are strangely noncontextualized accounts of online discussion. Chat rooms and political party discussion lists during election campaigns are hardly appropriate places to seek the discursive characteristics of democratic deliberation. The environment and structure of communication has a significant effect on its content; synchronous chat rooms and peer-generated Usenet groups are no more indicative of the scope for online public deliberation than loud, prejudiced, and banal political arguments in crowded pubs are indicative of the breadth of offline political discussion.

On the basis of these claims and counterclaims, there are four hypotheses that were tested:

- H1 — online consultations provide a space for inclusive public deliberation.
- H2 — online consultations generate and connect networks of interest or practice.
- H3 — online interaction between representatives and the represented leads to greater trust between them.
- H4 — most online discussion is uninformed and of poor quality.

Two out of the ten U.K. parliamentary online consultations were used as case studies: the Womenspeak consultation on domestic violence and the consultation on the draft Communications Bill. Both were set up, moderated, and summarized by the Hansard Society, an independent, nonpartisan body. Womenspeak was commissioned by the All-Party Domestic Violence Group and was conducted in March 2000. The consultation on the draft Communications Bill occurred in May 2002, when a joint committee of MPs and peers was established to consider and report on this important piece of draft legislation. Prelegislative scrutiny is a post-1997 innovation introduced by the Modernisation Select Committee with a view to enabling parliamentarians to examine draft legislation before the ink is dry on the final bill. The joint committee introduced two important innovations into its proceedings:

- The public was able to see and hear all of its evidence sessions, which were webcast live on parliament's own site, http://www.parliamentlive.tv, and broadcast on BBC Parliament the following weekend.
- In order to gather a wider range of views on the draft bill, the committee commissioned an online forum, under the auspices of the Hansard Society and the Parliamentary Office of Science and Technology, to accompany its formal evidence taking.

The two consultations examined here contrasted in their purposes: the first was designed to enable women survivors of domestic violence to submit experiential testimony to a group of parliamentarians interested in developing policy; the second allowed the public to submit and discuss evidence for consideration by a committee of MPs and peers as part of the process of prelegislative scrutiny.

Demographic profiles of participants in both consultations were produced by examining user registration forms. All messages in both consultations were analyzed by a team of trained coders, using a frame designed to plot variables related to the four research hypotheses. A postconsultation survey was sent to participants in both consultations and face-to-face interviews were conducted with participating MPs (Allan, 2002; White, 2002) and peers.

III. INCLUSIVE CONSULTATION OR "THE USUAL SUSPECTS"

Identifying survivors of domestic violence and persuading them to participate in an online parliamentary consultation is far from simple. The Hansard Society recruited the participants for this consultation in partnership with Women's Aid, which has access to confidential numbers for a national network of refuges and outreach organizations. The Hansard Society's consultation outreach worker was able to locate local refuges, as well as women's groups and disability groups. In October and November 1999, 5 months before the consultation began, it was announced via flyers in Women's Aid newsletters. Other recruitment was conducted at a number of regional meetings across the U.K. Most of the registration for the consultation was conducted face-to-face or by post. The use of the Internet as a medium for this sensitive consultation topic was the source of two problems: accessibility and security.

Many women who were enthusiastic about participating had no access to or familiarity with the Internet. Fifty-two percent of participants had no knowledge of using the Internet before they took part. Most of the participants were able to go online using computers in refuges. This had several advantages: the personal and often distressing stories they had to tell could be recounted in friendly and familiar surroundings; there were trained workers to help them if they needed personal support during or after posting their messages; IT help was close at hand — 60% of the women reported needing help in getting to the consultation website, and most of the time that was provided by refuge workers.

A second problem concerned security. Had the participants been invited to attend parliament to tell their stories and express their views, few would have gone. Parliament is an intimidating place and most women would not want their names recorded as witnesses. Many of the women thinking of participating in this consultation expressed concerns about the confidentiality of the online medium. This was particularly the case when they were sharing homes or computers with their abusers. In the consultation, participants were given pseudonyms, assured that their real names (which were registered for purposes of authentication) would remain private and that the content of the online discussion would only be made available to other participants and the Hansard Society. According to the postconsultation survey, 85% of the participants felt that the website was a safe and secure place.

The Womenspeak forum recorded an average of 1574 hits per day. On average, 78 users visited the forum each weekday and 111 during weekends. Seventy-three percent of the participants visited the site at least six times; 18% visited at least ten times. The average visitor session lasted 16 minutes and 31 seconds. One hundred ninety-nine women registered and participated online, submitting 960 messages between them. Participants came from throughout England and Wales, with a typical demographic spread of different ages and ethnic backgrounds. Ten percent of the participants described themselves as being disabled; 6% were registered disabled.

Recruitment of participants for the draft Communications Bill consultation was much easier. The clerks of the joint committee were able to provide the Hansard Society with a list of potential participants, including organizations from which the committee would like to have heard evidence had there been more time. In addition, the Hansard Society, as an independent body, sought to recruit participants who were unknown to parliamentarians and could bring some very different perspectives to the consultation.

The consultation website recorded 1949 hits per day, the average duration of which were 17 minutes and 12 seconds. An average of 85 people visited the site each weekday and 55 during weekends. Three hundred seventy-three people registered for this consultation, but only 136 posted messages to the consultation forum. Two hundred twenty-two messages were posted in all. Unlike the domestic violence consultation, where the emphasis was on sharing experiences, discussion, and mutual support, in this consultation there was a clear focus on influencing policy; most of those who registered were either more interested in what others had to say or else felt that they would not be able to influence policy. Typical comments from registered nonposters in the postconsultation survey were "I preferred to watch the debate develop and take note of the points raised" and "I did not submit a personal message mainly because I did not feel I knew enough about the topic, and time reasons."

How politically engaged were these consultees? In the postconsultation surveys, participants were asked whether they had ever contacted an MP and whether they were members of political parties. Fifty-eight percent of Womenspeak participants had never been in contact with an MP; for the Communications Bill consultation only 38% had never contacted an MP. Ninety-six percent of Womenspeak participants and 78% of the participants in the Communications Bill consultation were not members of political parties. So, for a majority of the participants there was no involvement in a political party, which is the usual point of entry to the policy process. And for a majority of Womenspeak participants and over a third of Communications Bill participants these online consultations constituted their first ever encounters with MPs.

Was it the case that participants in these consultations, while registering as individuals, were in fact representing interest groups? According to the postconsultation survey, 94% of the Womenspeak participants and 82% of the Communications Bill participants had no organizational affiliation related to the subject of the consultations.

The majority of participants in both consultations lived outside of London: 77.5% for Womenspeak and 63% for the Communications Bill consultation. In the case of Womenspeak, which included many low-income participants and single mothers, the opportunity to take part in a parliamentary inquiry without traveling to London was a significant benefit. Although one might have expected Communications Bill consultees to be more able to visit parliament in person, according to the postconsultation survey only 17% of registered participants ever attended parliament to see the committee in session. (Twenty-seven percent watched at least one webcast of the committee in session and 66% visited the committee's website.) This suggests that interactions, which would not otherwise have taken place, were facilitated by the creation of a space for online consultation.

IV. CREATING AND CONNECTING ONLINE NETWORKS

The Womenspeak consultation lasted for 1 month. Many participants found the experience of interacting online with other survivors of domestic violence to be empowering. As the month went on, they began to use the forum to create an online community of mutual support, as well as engaging in a parliamentary consultation. Comments posted in the forum toward the end of the consultation indicated the extent to which a virtual community was being built:

> It was brilliant; I felt really close to the participants during the consultation as if I were part of a giant support network.

> I am just glad that you found out about this site before it closes at the end of next week. I hope you will see over the next week that none of us are alone. Love Sharon.

> Emails, while enabling us to keep in touch, will not serve the purpose of contact the way this message board has. They will not enable the free flow

of ideas and support that we have become used to. Thank you all for sharing your fears, frustrations and hopes for the future with me. Stay strong and stay safe.

Through this site I have built up so much strength by reading all your stories and I wish the best to every one out there and a big thank you to all that have worked tirelessly to get this site working every day. Let's hope this isn't the last.

Thank you to everyone involved in this discussion. Thank you to all of you who have become friends to me. I never imagined feeling this sad at the end of this. I will miss you all and hope it is not to long until we are in touch again. Take care and stay safe.

A majority of women (60%) reported in the postconsultation survey that the consultation helped them deal with their own experiences of domestic violence. As a result of networking online, some participants made contacts with one another in the offline world. In the postconsultation survey, 24% of participants reported making new contacts and 92% reported learning something new as a result of reading other participants' messages. Several of the participants were eager to continue the virtual network beyond the life of the parliamentary consultation and subsequently set up their own website in which survivors' stories and views could be exchanged:

I have been surfing since my last post and have found a free message board. If it's suitable I will begin setting it up straight away. It runs on the same principle as this with registered passwords and we may be able to use the same ones we have now. I am really excited at the possibility that we could have the new one ready to go to when this one closes. I don't want us to lose any time to support each other and I am sure everyone feels the same as I do.

I am sending my details to Jeanine [the moderator]. I am asking her to give my email address to you. I live in Manchester but I would love to meet up, I'm only a train away. We will all definitely have to keep in touch. Thanks for being a pal this past month.

In the case of the Communications Bill consultation there were fewer signs of community building, related to the markedly lower level of online interaction between contributors to this forum. Nonetheless, in the postconsultation survey, 72% of participants (including majorities of both message posters and nonposters) claimed to have learned something new from reading messages from other participants.

There was a significant contrast in the extent of interaction in the two consultations: in the Womenspeak forum over four fifths (82%) of all messages were replies to previous messages; in the Communications Bill forum fewer than one in ten (8%) messages were replies to previous messages. This reflects the sociable, networking character of the former consultation, as opposed to the more advocative nature of the latter forum.

V. REPRESENTATIVE–REPRESENTED INTERACTION

In the Womenspeak consultation forum, 31 messages (3.2% of all) were contributed by 6 MPs. In the Communications Bill consultation forum, 8 messages (3.6% of all messages) were contributed by 4 MPs and peers.

Despite the emphasis on community building in the Womenspeak forum, three quarters of the participants reported that a major reason for taking part was the opportunity to interact with MPs. In the postconsultation survey, however, 68% of Womenspeak participants stated that they did not consider that the MPs who took part were interested in what they had to say and almost four out of ten (39%) were not satisfied with the contributions from MPs. Nonetheless, perhaps surprisingly, 94% of participants considered that the online consultation was a worthwhile exercise and 93% said that they would like to take part in future online consultations of this kind. This suggests that participants measured success in terms of group networking more than political interaction.

In the case of the Communications Bill consultation, a majority (53%) of participants were satisfied with the degree of involvement in the forum by members of the committee. One in four participants considered that the committee was interested in what they had to say; fewer than 3% disagreed, and the majority were unsure. But 72% considered the online consultation to have been worthwhile, 91% were in favor of there being more online parliamentary consultations and 87% said that they would definitely be prepared to participate in future online consultations — with the other 13% saying that they would possibly do so.

These are mixed messages. Clearly, there was some concern among both groups of consultees about the extent of parliamentarians' interest in what they had to say. If an objective of online consultations is to increase public trust in politicians as good listeners, the exercises reported here do not provide grounds for optimism.

The parliamentarians who participated in the Womenspeak consultation expressed enthusiasm about its expansive, deliberative nature of collecting evidence:

> If you meet with a group in the constituency for 5–10 minutes you don't always have sufficient time to listen to all the problems. This was a unique experience because you were able to listen to a dialogue for an extensive period of time. (Linda Gilroy, MP)

But the length of the process proved difficult to integrate into already crowded schedules:

> I knew I had to do it because I had been asked to. But I had other commitments which I had to make time for as well. And my brief is actually Health . . . I guess it was worthwhile, but it was hard to find time to do it. It coincided with other commitments. (Caroline Spelman, MP)

> With the Internet format, people are used to immediate responses, but it does take time to change legislation. In that sense it isn't an equal participation; a lot of women had this as their number one priority, whereas MPs work on a huge amount of other issues. And with the time you have it is not realistic to expect MPs to read all the contributions. (Julia Drown, MP)

Members of the committee examining the draft Communications Bill, from all parties, were enthusiastic about the exercise:

> The online consultation worked exceptionally well, and proved its worth as a vital tool in the democratic process. I am sure future committees will find it as invaluable as we did. The responses were of a very high quality, and gave us a

real sense of public opinion across a wide range of issues. We should promote future fora as aggressively as possible to maximise participation. (Lord Puttnam, Chair of the Committee)

It helped us change the questions we were asking the witnesses and made us focus on areas we would not necessarily have thought of. It tended either to reinforce something that we already knew or it changed questions that we would not otherwise have asked. (Brian White, MP)

It opens it up to a wider range of people to feed in ideas and opinions into the parliamentary process. The fact that we were able to get ideas and opinions from the regions, particularly input on the importance of regional broadcasting, meant that the exercise was not restricted to Whitehall and Westminster. It allowed us to get on the road, electronically. The alternative would have been to hold a series of public meetings around the country. In my view, it was an advantage to the credibility of the committee and its work. One benefit of this consultation is reinforcing policies that are already well known and throwing up the concerns that may not previously have arisen. The argument against it is that you have to have the facility to participate in an online forum. (Lord McNally)

We thought it worked very well — it clearly was popular, we had very substantial response, we had very good information and we incorporated some of the points that came out from the online forum in our recommendations. (Lord Crickhowell)

VI. EVIDENTIAL QUALITY

The purpose of parliament consulting the experience and expertise of the public is to derive evidence that can inform and improve policy and legislation. Parliamentary inquiries have traditionally selected witnesses who are acknowledged experts, questioned them formally, minuted their evidence verbatim, and used evidence so received to support their recommendations. From a parliamentary perspective, online consultations should fulfil the same purpose: the accumulation of high-quality evidence. Critics of online deliberation argue that empirically, citizens' behavior in online discussions is rarely characterized by the lofty ideals of deliberative democracy, and theoretically, that most policy issues are too complex and time-consuming for the public to give them serious consideration, especially given the potentially overwhelming scale of mass public debate.

Assessing the quality of public deliberation is particularly problematic, involving sensitive normative standards. Nonetheless, attempts have been made to design methodologies for measuring the quality of stated opinions (Kuhn, 1991; Price and Neijens, 1997; Muhlberger, 2000; Wayatt et al., 2000; Capella et al., 2002). Three characteristics of deliberative quality were analyzed in this study: the extent to which messages were supported by external information, the frequency of message posting, and the level of interaction between messages and previous messages. Normatively, one might expect a deliberative discourse to include widespread use of external information sources; non-domination by a minority of frequent posters, to the exclusion of other, less articulate or sociable prospective participants; and high levels of interaction between agenda-setting messages and responses.

In submitting messages, participants could draw upon information from a number of external sources, including books, reports, newspaper articles, and websites, or upon self-referential information derived from personal experience. The use of external sources is commonly associated with the rational validation of evidence. In the Womenspeak consultation, one in three messages (32%) cited external sources of information. The fact that two thirds of the messages did not go beyond personal testimony or opinion reflects the highly subjective nature of the experience of domestic violence. In the case of the Communications Bill consultation, nearly half of all messages (48%) referred to an external source, but fewer than one in ten (7%) drew upon personal, anecdotal experience. Insofar as rational argumentation is dependent upon external sources of support, beyond subjective experience, feelings, or opinion, the majority of messages submitted to both consultations fell short of this standard, although a significant proportion of messages to both consultations were informed by external sources.

In the Womenspeak consultation, most participants (52%) submitted only one message; 90% submitted fewer than ten messages; but 21% of all messages were submitted by just two participants and a third were submitted by just 11% of the participants. Frequent posters were much more likely to be agenda setters than one-time posters: 18% of messages to the consultation were classified as "seeds" (they started a new discussion thread); of these, most were submitted by the minority of participants who were frequent posters. In the Communications Bill consultation 82% of participants submitted only one message. There were very few frequent posters (4%) and these contributed fewer than one in ten messages.

Rafaeli (1988) defines interactivity as "the extent to which messages in a sequence relate to each other, and especially the extent to which later messages recount the relatedness of earlier messages". Eighty-two percent of messages to Womenspeak responded in some way to a previous message in the forum. The extent of dialogue and information exchange in this forum was striking. In the Communications Bill consultation only 14% of messages were responses to preceding messages. Participants in this forum were less interested in discussing others' ideas than in stating their own. The largest number of responses in the forum were to messages submitted by MPs.

Unlike the online discussions and chats analyzed by Hill and Hughes, Davis and Wilhelm, the connection of these forums to constitutional legitimacy helped to generate a relatively high quality of deliberation. This is not surprising: public talk is intimately and dialectically related to broader relationships of power and place. It would be a mistake to assume from limited studies of informal, partisan online forums that all, or even most, online political discussion would be similarly banal and nondeliberative.

VII. CONCLUSIONS FROM THE CASE STUDIES

An obvious conclusion from these studies is that not all online consultations are alike. Womenspeak was a relatively informal consultation designed to collect experiential evidence. The Communications Bill consultation was more closely connected to the legislative process and was part of a multimedia strategy for making this process more accessible to interested citizens. It would be a mistake to expect all online parliamentary consultations to perform the same functions or deliver the same results.

The first research hypothesis, that online consultations provide a space for inclusive public deliberation, is supported by the findings of both studies. Most participants in both of the consultations were not "the usual suspects": party members, lobbyists, or people who lived in or around the Westminster village. The voices heard in these consultation forums would probably not otherwise have been heard by parliamentarians. But there is no evidence that the Internet, as a medium, is intrinsically inclusive. Public participation had to be actively promoted. In particular, the success of the Womenspeak consultation depended on extensive outreach work, not least to overcome problems associated with the use of the Internet as a democratic tool.

The second hypothesis, that online consultations generate and connect networks of interest or practice, is strongly supported by evidence from the Womenspeak consultation, where participants bonded so closely that several of them went on to set up their own community website. In both consultations a majority of participants claimed to have learned something from other contributors, but, whereas in the Womenspeak consultation, the overwhelming majority of messages were responses to earlier messages, in the Communications Bill consultation there was little interaction between participants.

The third hypothesis, that online interaction between representatives and represented leads to greater trust between them, is not supported by the findings from these studies. In the case of Womenspeak, many of the participants were dissatisfied with the contributions from MPs and were unconvinced at the end of the consultation that MPs had been interested in what they had to say. Participants in the Communications Bill consultation were more divided over these questions, but, on balance, most considered that the committee had been interested in what they had to say and that members of the committee had participated in a satisfactory way.

The fourth, critical hypothesis, that most online discussion is uninformed and of poor quality, is not supported by the findings from this study, although these findings are based on elementary indicators of discursive quality. Significant proportions of messages to both consultations referred to external information; frequent posters did not dominate the discussion to the exclusion of others; and, in the case of the Womenspeak consultation, there was a high level of interactivity.

VIII.   TOWARD AN E-PARLIAMENT

British parliamentarians have been enthusiastic about the potentiality of the Internet as a democratic tool. Robin Cook, MP, the Leader of the House of Commons, stated:

> There is a connection waiting to be made between the decline in democratic participation and the explosion in new ways of communicating. We need not accept the paradox that gives us more ways than ever to speak, and leaves the public with a wider feeling than ever before that their voices are not being heard. The new technologies can strengthen our democracy, by giving us greater opportunities than ever before for better transparency and a more responsive relationship between government and electors. (Cook, 2002)

The House of Commons Information select committee has produced a comprehensive report entitled *Digital Technology: Working for Parliament and the Public*, setting out a number of recommendations for the conduct of future online consultations:

■   The purpose and terms of the consultation should be made clear at the outset, both to those initiating the consultation and those participating in it. Consultations may range from a simple invitation to submit views to a more deliberative and interactive debate including senior decision-makers.

- It must be made clear to participants that they are not being asked to make policy but to inform the thinking of legislators.
- Efforts need to be made to recruit participants, whether individuals or organizations, who can impart experience and expertise.
- Special efforts are needed to make online consultations socially inclusive: these may include training in the necessary ICT skills and directions to public Internet access for participants.
- Contributions to consultations need to be interpreted or summarized by an independent body or staff.
- A good consultation exercise will bring value to both decision-makers and consultees. This can be tested through effective evaluation procedures, which should be built into each consultation proposal. These should be both quantitative and qualitative. Of particular value would be follow-up with a selection of both consultees and decision-makers to assess the value of the consultation to them. The results of any evaluation should be produced in good time and made available to all participants
- Participants should receive feedback on the outcomes of the consultations.

In each case, the consultee should be given clear information on what they can expect, perhaps in the form of a "consultation contract" (House of Commons Information Committee, 2002).

As parliaments, and other representative institutions, move from experimentation to routine use of online interactivity as a way of improving communication with the public and improving the quality and legitimacy of legislation, principles of the kind set out by the Information Committee will need to be debated and expanded. To ensure effective and credible practical implementation, there are six practical considerations that need to be addressed by parliaments running e-consultations. First, the *purpose* of the consultation needs to be clear from the outset. The expectations and boundaries of the process need to be agreed and then set out explicitly. Politicians and other policymakers need to be committed to the value and impact of the process and need to sign up to an agreed level of active involvement. Second, attention needs to be given to the *design* of the consultation. Appropriate channels and software must be selected for the facilitation of the discussion. Most existing software is not well designed for deliberative communication: it is difficult to "thread" discussions, navigate around them, or summarize content. The discussion interface needs to be attractive and simple to use. Third, a process of *recruitment* is required to ensure that the right mix of "voices" are signed up to participate. Recruitment should seek to be as inclusive as possible, seeking out potential participants from hard-to-reach groups across both the digital and the broader socio-economic divides. All consultation processes should begin with extensive outreach, using a range of media, not just online. Fourth, democratic consultation requires fair, transparent, and inclusive *moderation* Moderators should be independent and trusted. The training and accreditation of moderators should be encouraged. Fifth, in lengthy online discussions there is a need for regular *summation* of what has been said, otherwise it becomes very time-consuming for late-joiners to enter the discussion. Credible, trusted summaries are vital for policymakers who might not have time to read all contributions, but require a sense not only of what was said, but also the underlying narrative that emerges from the discussion. New techniques in "conversation mapping" and "discourse visualization" are especially valuable in this respect. Sixth and crucial, online consultations will only be taken seriously if they have *impacts and outcomes*. A link must be demonstrated between the initial purpose for engaging the public and the consequence of their participation. Such linkage provides democratic legitimacy for consultative processes. There should be a preconsultation commitment to minimal levels of response from parliamentarians (or other promoters) and these should include time limits for responses to be made. Ultimately, as in most areas of political behavior, unless a connection between collective action and beneficial output can be demonstrated, the strong likelihood is that public interest and enthusiasm would eventually wane.

REFERENCES

Allan, R., Interview with Richard Allan, MP, July 30, 2002.

Bimber, B., The Internet and citizen communication with government: does the medium matter?, *Political Communication*, 16, 409–428, 1999.

Blair, T., Speech to labour MPs, May 8, 1997.

Blumler, J.G. and Coleman, S., *Realising Democracy Online: A Civic Commons in Cyberspace*, IPPR/ Citizens Online, 2001.

Capella, J.N., Price, V., and Lilach N., Argument repertoire as a reliable and valid measure of opinion quality: electronic dialogue during campaign 2000, *Political Communication*, 19, 73–93, 2002.

Coleman, S., Ed., *The E-Connected World: Risks and Opportunities*, McGill University Press, Montreal, 2003.

Cook, R., MP, Speech to Yougov conference, April 10, 2002.

Davis, R., *The Web of Politics : The Internet's Impact on the American Political System*, Oxford University Press, New York. 1999.

Femia, J., Complexity and deliberative democracy, *Inquiry*, 39, 359–397, 1996.

Hill, K.A. and Hughes, J.E., *Cyberpolitics: Citizen Activism in the Age of the Internet*, Rowman & Littlefield, Lanham, MD, 1998.

House of Commons Information Committee, *Digital Technology: Working for Parliament and the Public*, HC 1065, 2002, p. 15.

Kuhn, D., *The Skills of Argument*, Cambridge University Press, Cambridge, New York, 1991.

Lenihan, D., *Realigning Governance: From E-Government to E-Democracy*, Crossing Boundaries, Ottawa, 2002.

Levine, P., Civic renewal and the commons of cyberspace, *National Civic Review*, 90, 205–212, 2001.

Muhlberger, P., Defining and Measuring Deliberative Participation and Potential: A Theoretical Analysis and Operationalization, paper presented at the International Society of Political Psychology Twenty-Third Annual Scientific Meeting, Seattle, 2000.

Peters, J.D., *The Idea of Public Journalism*, Glasser, T.D., Ed., Guilford Press, New York, 1999.

Powazek, D.M., *Design for Community: The Art of Connecting Real People in Virtual Places*, New Riders, Indianapolis, IN, 2002.

Price, V. and Neijens, Opinion quality in public opinion research, *International Journal of Public Opinion Research*, 9, 336–360, 1997.

Rafaeli, S., *Annual Review of Communication Research: Advancing Communication Science*, Hawkins, R.P., Wiemann, J.M., and Pingree, S., Eds., Vol. 16, Sage, Beverly Hills, CA, 1988.

Rheingold, H., *The Virtual Community : Homesteading on the Electronic Frontier*, Harper Perennial, New York, 1994.

Wayatt, R.O., Katz, E., and Kim, J., Bridging the spheres: political and personal conversation in public and private places, *Journal of Communication*, 50, 71–92, 2000.

White, B., Interview with BrianWhite, MP, August 5, 2002.

Wilhelm, A.G., *Democracy in the Digital Age: Challenges to Political Life in Cyberspace*, Routledge, NY, 2000, p. 102.

38

EMERGING ELECTRONIC INFRASTRUCTURES: EXPLORING DEMOCRATIC COMPONENTS

Åke Grönlund
Örebro University

CONTENTS

I. Introduction — perspectives on electronic government.................................. 644
II. European e-gov origins... 645
III. Research method — theoretical framework 647
    A. Case study design 649
    B. Four case studies 649
        1. Bollnäs — municipal community network..................................... 650
        2. Kista — management democracy.. 651
        3. Älvsjö — citizen panel 653
        4. Kalix — annual consultation 655
IV. Conclusion.. 657
References... 659

ABSTRACT

The concepts of electronic government (e-gov) and electronic democracy have common roots in that the electronic government must rest on, and support, democratic principles. This chapter discusses how the components of a democratic society are treated as they are built into the emerging electronic infrastructures dealing with services and dialogues pertinent to the functioning of the public sector and tries to find emerging patterns.

It also opens a discussion on the nature of the emerging infrastructures by reviewing four implementations of local "e-democracy" and putting them into the context of the global e-gov development, in particular the EU development of "eEurope." The cases presented here represent different models of democracy, models that are only partially explicit. The development is governed more by gradual implementation of ICT tools than a general political agenda. This means local actors have great influence and hence e-democracy is not deterministic, it can come in many shapes.

I. INTRODUCTION — PERSPECTIVES ON ELECTRONIC GOVERNMENT

Electronic Government (e-gov) refers certainly to more use of IT, but more importantly to attempts to achieve more strategic use of IT in the public sector. History shows that uses are emerging rather than strategy-based (Norris, 1999; Grönlund, 2000), and that by now use is so comprehensive and so diverse that strategies are badly lacking in order to get some kind of return on the investment. Typically, so far electronic services have been set up at additional costs (G8, 1999; West, 2000), leaving operations much as they were rather than achieving savings or better services by improved logistics.

E-gov is about changes in two related but distinct fields. First, it is about changes in the internal government operations that come about as IT is used for automation, cooperation, integration among government agencies, and as tools assisting in decision-making processes. While such IT use has been going on for a couple of decades, the current spark of interest in the field is because now external operations are also transformed as information and services increasingly become available on the Internet. This has meant that government agencies begin trying to organize their operations based on the premise that citizens and companies will increasingly manage their interactions with the public sector on a self-service basis.

The term "government" covers several aspects of managing a country, ranging from the very form of government, over strategic management to daily operations. Definitions of e-gov generally also cover all these areas, and hence most typically contain not only goals of more efficient operations but also of better quality of services and increased and better-quality citizen participation in democratic processes. Sometimes, the term governance is more appropriate, as it incorporates the concept of other organizations than public-sector ones engaged in delivering public services by means of outsourcing, partnerships or value-added services.

There is a need for defining an e-gov context in terms of a public-sector model. In simple terms, and at a general level where national differences do not matter, a democratic government is organized as shown in Figure 38.1.

Often, an overly simplified view of a democratic system is propagated, where the relationships of the model are presented as straightforward; citizens elect officials, who then go to work in a formal political system containing certain institutions and rules. Their work produces results in the form of directives to the administration, which with blind obedience — without any influence on the political decisions — executes the decisions.

In practice, the system is of course much more complex. The political impact administrations can exert by having the expertise necessary to prepare decisions in complicated matters is often acknowledged (Watson et al., 1999; Snellen, 2001). Citizens act in many other ways than by casting votes; for example, they organize in many ways, and they lobby. This is not the place for indulging in all the various aspects of this or for discussing different variations of democratic systems. For now, let us just observe that there are a number of relations, and that each node in the system influences both the others by a number of relationships, given that all nodes are interrelated. The details of these relations are always under discussion and borders are changing slightly. Currently, however, they are in a process of profound change in many countries, for several reasons including globalization, economic constraints, changing demographics, and the availability of IT. We will briefly discuss the cases from this point of view in the section "Conclusion."

"E-democracy" (teledemocracy, IT democracy, and so on) is a term usually, and vaguely, used to mean information technology (IT) applied to enhance public participa-

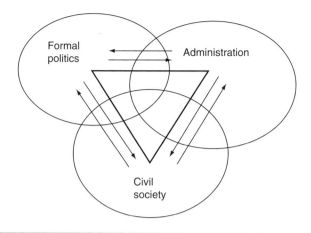

Figure 38.1   Basic elements and relations in a democratic government system. Arrows indicate influence, and circles indicate domains of control. Domain intersections indicate "transaction zones" where control is negotiated by means such as lobbying and media on the left-hand side, intermediary service deliverers on the right-hand side, and professional interaction in government boards and committees on the top (adapted from Molin et al., 1975: 16).

tion in democratic processes. E-democracy projects are usually found at local levels of government, but there are also efforts at the national level (e.g., Macintosh et al., 2001; Hansard, 2002). In this chapter, following the above discussion, the idea is rather that "e-democracy" should be assessed in terms of its defining processes, not to which extent IT artefacts are used. This means that the term e-democracy is only a convenient shorthand for IT use in democratic processes. While many, if not most, contemporary studies focus on the IT artefacts used, there are early studies that have highlighted the infrastructure dimensions that we address in this chapter (e.g., Snellen, 1995; Taylor et al., 1995).

We are interested in knowing to what extent "e-democracy" projects lead to lasting change, i.e., if changes in communication patterns are established. This amounts to asking, *are new/changed information infrastructures within the field of democratic decision-making constructed?* In this chapter, this question is answered in two ways. First, by examining four cases representing four different ways of implementing e-democracy, which have different implications for democracy as they inscribe different behavior. Second, by putting the findings into the wider context of the European development toward electronic government and the model of government just presented.

II.   EUROPEAN E-GOV ORIGINS

There are several lines of development behind the idea of electronic government. IT itself is obviously one, but there are also political initiatives and agendas. We shall look at the development in a European Union perspective, as the European agenda is currently about to reshape government practices across Europe, and electronic government practices and principles are part of this process.

The European project "Information Society" started as a reaction to the U.S. National Information Infrastructure Initiative, NII, 1993 (NIST, 1996) and Reinventing Government

(NPR, 2000[1]). The White Paper of 1993, *Growth, Competitiveness and Employment: The Challenges and Courses for Entering into the XXIst Century* is a milestone. The basic idea was to develop an IT infrastructure across Europe as a precondition for growth, European competitiveness, new markets, and more jobs.

The European Council formed an expert group that was to suggest measures to be taken to achieve that vision. The group published in 1994 the so-called *Bangemann Report: Europe and the Global Information Society: Recommendations to the European Council* (High-Level Group, 1994). This report made IT officially a part of the EU strategy. The report emphasizes the importance of competitiveness of European companies. Telecommunications deregulation was one important point for that purpose. Moreover, ten initiatives to demonstrate the potential of IT were suggested, such as teleworking, distance education, electronic services to small- and medium-size enterprises, etc.

The 1996 *The Information Society: From Corfu to Dublin — The new emerging priorities* marked a second phase in the project. The earlier measures to support business competitiveness were complemented by focusing on improvement of the European knowledge base by investing in education and research, social and security issues.

In 1999 a new initiative was presented by the European Commission, *eEurope. An Information Society for All*. The "e" was apparently incorporated as a response to the e-commerce boom during the last years of the 1900s. This initiative mentions ten high-priority areas. Among traditional areas (since the *Bangemann Report*) like cheap Internet access for all and electronic services in education and health care, there is now also "Government Online" (European Communities, 2000).

In early 2000, the European Council stated that the EU strategic goal for the first decade of the 21st century was "to become the most competitive and dynamic knowledge-based economy in the world capable of sustainable economic growth with more and better jobs and greater social cohesion" (Matthews, 2000). A rapid growth of the information society was seen as an important foundation for achieving this.

The commission presented the *eEurope Action Plan* in June 2000 (European Commission, 2000). The plan has a more open attitude toward Internet technology compared with the the *Bangemann Report*. This action plan urges the member states and the commission to commit to working to achieve:

- A cheaper (for the users) and more secure and trustworthy Internet
- Increased user competence
- Increased Internet use

This was to be achieved by 2002. The arguably most important incentive is to reduce the gap with the U.S.; as of early 2001, only 22% of the European households had Internet access, while the corresponding U.S. figure was around 50% (Anttiroiko, 2001). There is also an even larger gap between northern and southern Europe, with Sweden having more than 50% and Spain around 13% access.For the eEurope subproject "Government Online", goals that were to be achieved by 2002 are:

- Easy access to important public-sector information
- Consultation via Internet on major political initiatives
- Broad citizen access to basic interaction technologies

---

[1] http://www.npr.gov/converse/conversa.html

The *Bangemann Report* mirrors mainly the large industry interests represented in the group: deregulation, security, propriety rights, technical innovation, and infrastructure. A social dimension on the information society entered later. The digital divide was brought to attention, and was seen as dividing different groups of citizens, different age groups, and different regions. There are some reports on social aspects, for instance the Green Paper *Living and Working in the Information Society: People First* (European Commission, 1996) and *Building a European Information Society for Us All* (European Commission, 1997), where inclusion of different social groups and general risks with the information society are discussed.

Still, it seems fair to say that the social dimension is so far subordinated to the technical dimension and — currently on top of the agenda — the urge to achieve more use (Anttiroiko, 2001).

At the local level, however, there are a number of ongoing developments where social perspectives are promoted. One such is the ambitious Swedish Official Committee on Democracy, initiated as a measure to tackle a perceived problem of decreasing legitimacy of the democratic system, which presented its final report, the Official Report on Democracy (ORD), in 2000 (ORD, 2000). It painted a picture of the current situation, and encouraged developments for the future.

The ORD concluded that there was currently too much focus on information and services, and too little on the individual's political role as a citizen. Most e-democracy pilots, it was found, were "aiming at increasing information supply. Projects aiming at active participation and influence in democratic processes are few and have so far had limited ambitions" (ORD, 2000: 101, author's translation). The ORD claimed there was need for real change, meaning not only experiments but also continuity and integration into the standard procedures (ORD, 2000: 106).

The ORD pointed out that democracy is not an unambiguous concept, and saw a need for analyzing conflicts between different democratic ideals. It clearly marked a preference for "strong," participatory, democracy, and discussed how IT should be used to promote deliberation rather than polling: "A too widespread routine use of IT for quick polling may create situations where basic democratic demands are not fulfilled. There is a risk that the time necessary for finding knowledge and for discussion and deliberation is lost." (ORD, 2000: 107). Instead, IT should be used for implementing strong democracy in practice, where not only information supply and "comments" but also interactive dialogues would be an important part.

The above quotes reflect a basic taxonomy of democratic models using three categories, strong, quick, and thin,[2] which are traced back to Barber (1984, the "strong" and "quick" models) and Premfors (2000, the "thin" model) (Table 38.1).

We will not discuss the merits of either model here, only use them as a background to our investigations into the four cases, the obvious reason being the choices made by the ORD.

III. RESEARCH METHOD — THEORETICAL FRAMEWORK

As most e-democracy projects are still at the experimental or at least embryonic stage, it is hard to find any project with flourishing participation and radically changed citizen —

---

[2] There are many labels for different views on democracy. As can be seen from Table 38.1, the "quick" category incorporates what is often referred to as "direct" democracy: popular votes which politicians are bound by.

Table 38.1 Dimensions of Democracy (Åström, 1999, Author's Translation)

	Quick Democracy	Strong Democracy	Thin Democracy
Goal	Sovereignty of the people	Autonomy	Individual freedom
Base for legitimacy	Majority decision	Public debate	Accountability
Citizen role	Decision maker	Opinion former	Voter
Representatives' mandate	Bound	Interactive	Open
Focus of IT use	Decision	Discussion	Information

decision-maker relations. This is not surprising — projects aimed at changing an established tradition will face resistance. And even if they are pursued effectively, measurable results take a long time to show. Until this happens, a good way to look for places where more permanent changes are likely to occur is where the input, particularly in terms of the strength and commitment of the main actors involved, is the greatest, assuming that those cities that put the most effort into making changes last are most likely those where this will eventually happen.

Earlier research on participatory democracy projects (e.g., Schuler, 1996; Becker and Slaton, 2000) pointed to such factors as important for success. Further, and more importantly, the theoretical framework of the actor-network theory (ANT) pointed us in this direction. ANT sees technological development as a result of the strengthening and weakening of different actor networks. Different actors try to impose different behavior patterns by inscribing them in features of the materials used, a process called translation (Walsham, 1997). Often ANT studies concern inscriptions into computer artefacts, which then become delegates, acting on behalf of the actors who managed to inscribe certain behavior into the artefacts. Technology in ANT terms, however, has a wider definition, "technology is society made durable" (Latour, 1991), and thus also institutional arrangements as well as social conventions are important candidate delegates, objects for inscriptions: "roundtable discussions, public declarations, texts, technical objects, embodied skills, currencies — the options are endless" (Callon, 1991: 143).

Inscriptions get stronger the more they are supported by a sizable network, close alignment to the surrounding actor network, and an inscription that is strong in itself, for instance because it is inscribed into a medium that is hard or expensive to make changes in. The very definition of actor networks implies that there is no such thing as a "final" inscription. Inscriptions can be more or less strong, but they can never totally determine behavior (Monteiro and Hanseth, 1997). Rather the *irreversibility* of a development should be thought of in terms of degree (Walsham, 1997). Irreversibility, the impossibility of returning to a situation where translation was just one of several options, is achieved by alignment of interests, which are eventually stabilized and eventually inscribed into technology (Holmström, 2000: 69). But all along this path, it is not clear what the eventual inscriptions will be; they are constantly under "negotiation."

For this study, then, we were interested in finding strong inscriptions, i.e., such that have come some way down the road toward irreversibility. We used the ANT concepts mentioned above in three steps: first, to select cases to study, second, to analyze the four cases we eventually ended up with, and third, to compare the local inscriptions with the global development, in particular in a EU perspective. In this chapter, we have played down the microlevel ANT analysis for the purpose of leaving room for a more general discussion about how these cases relate to the more general e-gov development.

A. Case Study Design

To select cities and boroughs, we checked the cities that had democracy-related projects of different kinds. One group of cities included those that Ranerup (1999) found most advanced. Another group was those that received funding from the Swedish government within the "Time for democracy" program launched by the Ministry of Justice as a result of the ORD, and those that participated in EU projects where democratic processes were at least one item on the agenda.

As we wanted to find sustainable working models, we studied those projects because we were more interested in projects that had come some way toward implementation rather than new projects, no matter how innovative.

Looking for projects with a primary focus on the interaction between citizens and politicians and making innovative use of IT, we eventually found a few active projects, four of which are discussed below. The feature that these projects have in common is that they would not have been possible without IT use, and they are not only using IT in innovative ways, but they do so on the basis of a more or less clear, if not necessarily explicitly defined, management/democracy model.

Two towns (Bollnäs and Kalix) and two boroughs (Älvsjö and Kista, both within the city of Stockholm) were studied. Data were collected from websites, project documentation, independent evaluation reports, and personal interviews with key individuals. Some interviews were made over the phone, but we also visited the cities/boroughs for interviews and on-site inspection. The studies have in most cases taken place over a period of one and a half year. Kista has been studied for more than 4 years. Early work was done by the author during the fall of 2000 and the spring of 2001, for a book in Swedish about these cases (Grönlund, 2001b). This book was discussed with representatives from the cities studied. During the winter of 2001 to 2002, Ph.D. students were assigned the task of revisiting the cases. Their reports (referred to explicitly below) have been discussed at internal seminars, and have been used to bring the description and analysis up to date. Finally, the content of this chapter has been presented to, and discussed with, representatives for the towns and districts at a conference in June 2002.

B. Four Case Studies

The interest for "e-democracy" in Sweden has so far focused on the local level. The preconditions for IT use for democratic purposes are quite good in Sweden. The penetration of Internet use in the population has passed 50% and is over 70% in the ages 30 to 44 (IT-kommissionen, 2002: 15). All municipalities have a website, even the very small ones with as few as 3000 inhabitants.

In the service area, there are several good examples of useful systems, mostly at national government agencies (Grönlund, 2001a). The status is less impressive for specifically democratic activities of which the website is a part. Only about 15% of the municipalities have an online debate forum, and only a few of those have more than ten postings per month (Ranerup, 1999). These figures appear rather average in an international perspective (Musso et al., 1999; Aurigi, 2000).

A nationwide website comparison in 2001 found that service processes were much more developed than democratic processes on the city websites. Also, "Generally, the cities are far better at informing and 'teaching' about democratic processes than letting the citizens actively exert democracy through the web site." (SKTF, 2001: 9). International experiences give a similar picture; so far, it seems Internet use has not led to much participation (e.g., Harrison and Stephen, 1999).

But online discussion forums are just one component of democratic processes. The electronic tools have to be put into a context of some efforts to improve democratic processes. The cases presented below are examples of municipalities where there have been strong efforts to build a positive context for democratic development, and where IT is innovatively used as a part of those efforts.

1. Bollnäs — municipal community network[3]

Bollnäs is a small town of around 25,000 inhabitants in central Sweden, some 250 km north of Stockholm. Bollnäs' e-democracy activities demonstrate a number of innovations in democratic procedures. The inhabitants can make written propositions to the Town Council, the Executive Board, and to all the town committees. As of spring 2001, some 20 proposals had come in this way. The meetings of the council, the board, and the committees are open to the public. A cooperation group involving representation from the local associations of the several villages within the jurisdiction of the town of Bollnäs has been established.

E-democracy activities are part of a long-term plan for achieving participatory democracy, including plans for electronic voting and citizen panels. There are a number of activities. Citizens can e-mail directly to the two municipal commissioners, with a guaranteed answer. On the website, there is "the Dialogue," an open forum running since 1998, containing discussions in several predefined categories. Meetings of the City Council are video broadcast live on the Web. Viewers can send questions via e-mail during the break halfway through the meeting, which are answered after the break. In the following sections, we concentrate on electronic discussions, as they are the most IT-dependent activity.

All operations are conceived and run by the municipality itself, both the technical system and the processes in which they are used, as it has been considered important to develop knowledge in-house.

The municipal commissioners are the champions of e-democratic activities. They are also the active politicians on the discussion forums. However, the administration has over time become very much engaged in the activities, as questions from the public relating to administrative issues are routinely forwarded to civil servants. Indeed, during an observation period from January through April 2001, 23% of the postings came from civil servants while only 7% came from politicians (70% came from citizens), indicating that dialogues were more about municipal services than political issues (Öhrvall, 2002).

Some discussions in the Dialogue have attracted "a large number of participants," which in practice so far means a couple of hundred people, the all-time high so far being 500.

There have been problems, of course. Öhrvall (2002) found that discussions were shallow and that postings were often statements not supported by argument. The commissioners also feel they should be more active in asking questions to citizens instead of just responding to incoming questions, which is so far the normal mode of operation.

---

[3] This section is based on several conversations with Municipal Commissioner Stefan Permickels, public presentations by Permickels and Olle Nilsson Sträng (also Commissioner and Chair of the Municipal Executive Committee), a meeting with the Bollnäs project group including the webmaster and the leading opposition politician.

Some discussions have not turned out well. One example is a discussion about taxes, which ended inconclusively. The problem of formulating problems in ways suitable for electronic discussion is seen as a crucial success factor.

As a response to these problems and shortcomings of the electronic discussions, there have been discussions about how to improve them. The current most prominent idea is to arrange for more deliberative discussions using the model of a "citizen jury" (Becker and Slaton, 2000), that is a small group of people selected to represent the population on some important criteria, which is consulted intensively during a limited time on a specific issue, using not only the citizens as discussion partners, but also contributing expert knowledge in various forms. This is partly a response to the wish for more deliberative discussions in the open forums, partly a step toward electronic voting — plans and financing for such a project are already in place.

What is striking, and possibly worrying, from a Swedish political perspective, is that the political parties are largely invisible in the discussion forums. All communication, when politicians are involved, is between the commissioners, or members of the party in office, and the citizens. This is not customary in Swedish political debates, where typically all parties are represented. One explanation, offered by one politician, is that they do not want to unnecessarily disturb the debate; after all, it is a forum for citizens so it is better to participate as a listener.

It is very clear that there are two individuals who are the most prominent actors in Bollnäs — the two municipal commissioners. They are the main actors in the discussion forums, and they are championing the e-activities. They have engaged other actors for support, including civil servants to whom incoming questions are forwarded routinely. Other politicians have also been enrolled, but mainly as listeners. Although politicians from the opposition generally endorse the activities, they clearly play a minor role. There have been no major changes during the period the e-democracy activities have been online. Technical features and routines have been improved, and disturbances have been dealt with, but no major design change has yet occurred. Thus the actor network has been extended to consolidate the original design.

2. *Kista — management democracy*[4]

Kista, a borough within the city of Stockholm, is interesting because the management has what might be labeled a business-like view of their web. Over the past half-decade, the IT manager and a couple of civil servants at the district management office have been championing web development. The web is developed in close cooperation with local businesses. One expression of this is that the Kista web has two addresses, www.kista. stockholm.se and www.kista.com.

The "Kista Portal" opened on January 1, 1997, coinciding with the establishment of the district committee as part of a decentralization of the political power in Stockholm. The portal currently attracts some 6000 unique visits per month. Initially, the web development engaged local business in developing a broad set of services. Over the past couple of years, contents relating to democratic procedures have been developed. Minutes from the district council are published on the Web since 1998, and interactive features such as discussion forums, chat, and "question of the month" have been

---

[4] This section is based on contacts with the Kista District Management over sevaral years, discussions with, and information from, IT manager Leif Rydén, webmaster Gail Watt and reseacher/consultant Olov Forsgren, studies of the Kista website, and discussions with a user panel during 1999.

included since April 2000. Since 2000, these services have been given more focus by clustering them in a designated web department for "e-democracy," where different topics can be discussed, politicians are available for real-time chat during certain hours in conjunction with the "Politicians' corner," an event at the Borough Hall where politicians are (physically) available to citizens for open discussions. Also, the meetings of the district committee are video broadcast live on the Web.

The e-democracy department currently attracts some 1500 unique visits per month. During the first year of operation, it attracted some 300 postings to the discussion forums, 25 per month on an average. This is considerable compared with other Swedish cities, but according to the moderator, discussions tend to halt when sensitive topics are brought up (Andersson, 2002).

In February 2002, the e-democracy activities were again given more attention by the opening of the "Kista e-parliament." This is an effort to create a larger and more permanent forum that could be addressed as a sort of citizen panel, i.e., with members who have agreed to participate on a more regular and deliberative basis in the local development. The e-parliament is an activity within Cybervote (IST-1999-20338, http://www.eucybervote.org), an EU project aimed at developing and using secure voting technology, and also at putting some pressure on the process of changing legislation in EU member states toward allowing electronic voting.

The Kista web has thus developed rapidly over some 5 years. The small initiator team has enrolled several important networks of actors: first, local businesses, then the city administration, and most recently local politicians. But this work method has entailed both some criticism and some solutions that are problematic from a democratic point of view.

Internal criticism from local politicians is that the civil servants have proceeded too quickly, sometimes without having properly anchored their moves in the political assembly. Partly due to that criticism, a small informal "citizen panel," including local politicians, was established by the IT manager during 1999 both for soliciting comments on the site's usability and content and for making it more known among politicians. From that time, the web champions have actively recruited local politicians to participate in the electronic discussion forums. A result of this is that one third of the members of the borough council have now been active in the forum "talk to your politicians," contributing to making it by far the most active forum. It has also been arranged for people in the administration and in the political organization to answer incoming questions within normal routines.

The web targets not just Kista inhabitants, but also people spending time in Kista. Kista is a district with many commuters. Many of those living in Kista work elsewhere, and because Kista is a highly industrialized area with a lot of high-tech industries, a lot of people also commute to Kista to work. This is a reason why the enrollment of local business has been a high-priority concern.

This is also a reason why the team developing the e-democracy department feel that participation should be open not just for inhabitants but also for people working and studying in Kista, as these people are also part of the life and development of the district. Hence, they should be allowed to participate in discussion forums as well as in opinion polls.

This opinion, controversial from a democracy point of view because geography-based citizenship is the requirement for participation, appears practical from the point of view of a local management striving also to attract companies and other organizations to the district without necessarily restricting recruitment to the Kista inhabitants.

Although it is too early to make any assessment of how this policy has turned out from a democratic point of view, it should at least be considered as one possible main development for the future. First, Kista is not alone; the same approach has been taken by at least one other major Stockholm borough. More generally, local management, political as well as administrative, in most cities and boroughs share the problem of attracting companies, and thus workplaces and services. Therefore, there are strong incentives to use this kind of "management democracy," referred to as "consumer democracy" by Bellamy and Taylor (1998).

In terms of actors, the Kista project started in a different way than Bollnäs, through the initiative of actors in the administrative system rather than in the political one. The IT manager and a small group of local technical and administrative managers have extended the town web to also include democratic activities. These have first been organized administratively and only later, at a pace necessary to make them work, anchored in the local political community. Political support has been solicited by means of several techniques, involving politicians in a "panel" and in answering mail questions from the public, attracting EU projects, and close cooperation with the central Stockholm agencies in development projects. This small network of initiators has gradually inscribed its ideas in different technical tools — a growing and more elaborate website, discussion forums, and most recently voting technology. Although support has been gained from several parties, only a small group of initiators are still the active core of the network.

3. Älvsjö — citizen panel[5]

Like Kista, Älvsjö is a borough within the city of Stockholm with some independence and with a district council reflecting the political representation in the Stockholm City Hall. The Älvsjö e-democracy project started in 1997. At that time some town staff visited York, U.K., to study their work using citizen panels. Inspired by this work, Älvsjö managers translated their method into one using electronic questionnaires and online discussions.

Like Bollnäs and Kista, Älvsjö district administration views the e-democracy work as a process leading to new methods of working rather than a project. The e-activities are seen as tools to improve citizen contacts and citizen influence over local development processes: "at the end of the day, e-democracy will have to be assessed compared to the other methods" (Molander, 2001).

The Älvsjö e-democracy efforts have been championed by civil servants. The politicians endorsed the activities at the outset, but have not taken active part as champions during the first years of operation. Only in the early summer of 2001 a group of politicians representing all parties was set up to handle the democracy issues.

There is no external financing. Like in Bollnäs, a technical consultant was originally employed, but the ideas and design have come from the Älvsjö administration. Like the Bollnäs management, they make a point of doing so as the development of new methods is considered important internal work.

The Älvsjö e-democracy has several components. The web page "e-democracy" has three main parts: the Citizen Panel, the Agora, and the Citizen Proposal.

---

[5] This section is based on interiews with, and public presentations by, Crister Molander, until summer 2001 Development Manager in Älvsjö, and studies of the Älvsjö Web.

The Citizen Panel, set up in spring 2000, comprises 500 individuals, selected to represent the population by age, sex, and address (there are two geographical areas in Älvsjö that are distinctively different socioeconomically).

The panel is approached by questionnaires. Both the questions and the answers (aggregated, plus anonymized comments) are published on the Web for public discussion.

The Agora is a discussion forum with several predefined topics. The activity in the different groups varies depending on if a hot issue is discussed or not, but it is high compared with the Swedish average.

The Citizen Proposal: as in Bollnäs and Kista, Älvsjö inhabitants are allowed to make suggestions to the district committee. Proposals can be made by e-mail or by any other means.

A fourth component, so far only seen in Älvsjö and Norrmalm, another Stockholm borough, is that the searchability of the Älvsjö administrative system has been increased by a search tool covering all formal documents relating to the district committees' activities. Citizens can also subscribe to these documents by using a technical tool named Insight (Insyn), developed and used in the district of Norrmalm.

The e-democracy activities have been received positively by the citizens. The city of Stockholm makes annual reviews of the activities in the boroughs, and in the 2001 review, Älvsjö scored best by far.

Although the activities have been going on for a number of years, it is hard to make a more conclusive evaluation. New activities start continuously, and old ones are reshaped. Clearly, administrative routines have changed. Citizen proposals and panel responses are routinely fed into the local planning processes. Citizen proposals are considered frequent, as there is at least one at every (monthly) committee meeting.

There have been some problems, however. It turned out to be very expensive to put the panel together in the first place, so dropouts have been replaced gradually, reducing representativity. Although people have been eager to become enrolled in the panel, response rates have been only 60 to 65%. There have also been technical problems.

More important is the lack of a clear and appropriate organizational home for the e-democracy activities. After the active year of 2000, 2001 meant a lower level of activities. During 2000 three questionnaires were distributed to the panel, during 2001 none. The most important reason was that the new political group assigned with the task of reviewing the democratic procedures started a reassessment of the work (Nolte, 2002), the result of which is not yet clear.

In an interview in spring 2001, one of the initiators indicated problems with the political commitment: "If you ask questions you must be ready to be changed by the answers you get. Eventually, activities like these lead to a point where this readiness is put to the test" (Molander, 2001). As a response to this problem, a group comprising politicians was formed. As of early 2002 the discussions in the group have come some way, although a clear policy on how to use different media in a complementary and efficient manner has still not been developed.

In a Swedish context, it is worrying that the political parties do not have an important role in the development. There is a small group of recently enrolled politicians, but little involvement of the party organizations (Nolte, 2002). The value of the e-activities is therefore questioned.

In terms of actors, the above story shows how a small group of initiators on the administrative side has managed to enroll the local administration to routinely run the activities. They have also tried to enroll political actors to assume the overall responsibility for the e-democracy activities. After considerable delay and decline of the activities, in 2001 a formal political steering committee was set up. A main problem of this committee is that the larger network that it would naturally try to enroll at the next stage, the local party organizations, is very small and inactive. Because of this, the network so far enrolled can be labeled a managerial network rather than one of the political system.

4. Kalix — annual consultation[6]

Kalix (www.kalix.se) is a town of about 18,000 inhabitants in the far north of Sweden. The town won a prize for "e-democracy town of the year" in 2001, very much because of their "Consultations," two of which have so far been conducted. The first, in September 2000, concerned the remodeling of the town center. It got a lot of attention in the press, in Sweden and internationally. A second consultation dealing with tax levels was held in October 2001, and there are plans to make it an annual event.

The context of the consultations includes a series of efforts to renew town politics. In 1998, 73 years of Social Democratic rule was replaced by a coalition of all the other seven parties, led by the Greens. A democracy program was formulated, including open committee meetings, citizen proposal right, and an effort to make better use of IT in democratic processes.

Starting 1998, the work in the Town Hall has been changed by the implementation of a network organization, which means people in different departments working with similar issues are cooperating. The thrust is to enable the political will to influence work in the Town Hall at an earlier stage.

Hence, when the first consultation took place it was one ingredient in a broad program for renewal of work procedures and making them more open to the public. The consultation was implemented with the help of a consultant company, Votia, whose business idea is defined as *consultations*. The general design includes the following:

Information to the citizens was largely provided on the Web, and also in traditional meetings and in the local press. In the first consultation, on city planning, the questions were rather open and did not suggest specific solutions. There were no elaborate alternatives to vote for or against, and the political parties had not yet committed to any policies. There was also no discussion about costs. Questions were sent by ordinary mail to inhabitants.

On the contrary, the second consultation was more like a traditional public vote. People could choose among three specific alternatives — raised taxes, lowered taxes, or taxes kept at current level. Follow-up questions asked were (1) if a surplus should be used for investment, for reducing debt, or for extending activities, and (2) which activities should be given priority in case of a surplus and priority for extended activities.

There were ample opportunities for debate, on the Internet by means of chat and mail, and in person at public physical meetings. The first consultation was open to every Kalix inhabitant aged 12 or above, whereas the second was open only to those entitled to vote in regular elections (minimum age is 18 years).

---

[6] This section is based on public presentations by, and discussions with, Kalix Municipal Commissioner Peter Eriksson, CIO Eivor Ekholm-Bryngelson, Municipal Secretary Ingegerd Sandlund, and Votia CEO Katja Lepola, Consultation statistics from Votia Empowerment, and printed material distributed for the Consultation.

Voting could take place from a computer in the home, at work, or in public places such as libraries, homes for the elderly, and Internet cafés in the villages. Everyone received a password that could only be used once.

The first consultation attracted a turnout of 7%. Eighty-six percent of those participated via the Internet, which seemed to indicate that the Internet option was an important factor, as it was the main channel for participation. This view is somewhat moderated by the figures from the second consultation. This time, 51% of those entitled to vote participated. Participation via the Internet was higher in number (1994 people) but lower measured as a share of the total (28%) than in the first consultation.

The interpretation of Kalix management is that the prompt action following the result of the first consultation showed the inhabitants that the political management was serious about consultations (Andersson, 2002). From the point of view of democratic theory, however, this outcome illustrates one dilemma of the "strong" democracy (Barber, 1984; Åström, 1999) — an active minority achieves an influence far beyond their number. After all, participation was only 7%. Whether this should be seen as a problem of representativity or a call for those who did not participate to do so next time is a matter of interpretation. There are no guidelines in the literature on "strong," "participatory," etc. democracy to indicate how much participation is "enough." As a matter of fact, the literature is not at all helpful for those who want to find ways to measure participation in a way that makes it comparable to other democratic activities, such as turnout in elections.

The Kalix politicians went for a positive interpretation. They compared the participation with the typical participation in city planning issues, which is around ten people. Judging from the much higher participation in 2001, many inhabitants seem to have interpreted the outcome of the first consultation as a call for them to participate. Also, the second consultation was promptly followed by a decision in the political assembly. On the other hand, this time there was already a publicly stated opinion among the political majority that this was indeed their view. Consequently, there was some debate after the consultation on whether the "will of the people" was somewhat pushed in a specific direction. This illustrates a classical problem of popular votes: how to inform without unduly directing the public opinion?

In terms of actor networks, the Kalix story so far shows a quick and quite dramatic expansion. It started as a project of the new political majority, largely driven by one party, the Greens, and in particular by one person, the party leader. Early on, the administrative staff was enrolled by means of changed procedures in the City Hall. As the first consultation was successful in terms of turnout, possible opposition by the political minority, and indeed by at least one party within the majority coalition, was neutralized — there was really no way they could oppose something that was generally lauded both within and outside of Kalix. By acting rapidly on the outcome of the first consultation, popular credibility was won. Enquiries showed that even those who did not participate thought it was a good idea; also the turnout in the second consultation was dramatically increased. This means the initiators today have a local network that can be considered very strong as it not only has a lot of supporters, but also has neutralized the potential opposition. It seems that only some mistake made by themselves could discredit the consultation model and thus make the actor network crumble.

IV. CONCLUSION

In this chapter, I have briefly reviewed four implementations of information infrastructures for e-democracy. The cities studied should be seen as precursors in the quest for making good use of IT in local democratic practices. We have seen that not only is implementation still an issue, but also that the cases represent different models of democracy (e.g., representative panels, self-selected participants in electronic discussions, popular votes), models that are only partially explicit not least because some have developed out of the administration rather than by political design. We have seen that e-democracy is not determined by technology, it can come in many shapes.

We found conflicts between local e-democracy and global e-government developments. It appears unlikely that the methods can come much further — locally as well as in terms of becoming role models for others on a more general scale — without a more well-defined relation between the e-democratic activities and policy, as institutions will have to be reshaped. This restructuring is a fundamental one, involving a rethinking of the government model as such. I will conclude by briefly discussing some forces currently at play in this remodeling as seen in the cases presented above.

In the development of democracy there is generally an ongoing struggle between two perspectives, both beneficial for democracy but neither sufficient (Goldkuhl and Röstlinger, 2001). The *top-down perspective* is about implementing political decisions in activities directed toward the citizens: *politics as design*. The *bottom-up perspective*, sometimes called user democracy or consumer democracy (Bellamy and Taylor, 1998), is about interaction between users and suppliers leading to user influence over service design and content: *politics as evolution*. Real user influence over service design also means real influence over politics.

Today's governments, even those not called "electronic" use IT in more or less every activity. This means that most political decisions are dependent on existing IT systems to be implementable. These systems constitute an existing (information) infrastructure, which is not easy to change rapidly. IT systems are shaped by political decisions, and also by the implementation procedures through which the civil servants' knowledge of the organization and the services, and their interaction with users, is revealed. IT systems do not come from manufacturers as plug-and-play governments, they are completed by local rules and professional knowledge.

These two perspectives exist together in local government activities, and they partially conflict. From an administrative perspective it would be easier if a higher degree of standardization could be achieved, and to be sure IT can be a powerful tool for the manager who wants to reinforce standards. On the other hand, a local government ambition is to be able to adapt IT systems to local preferences, and users are one important part of realizing this ambition.

Historically, most countries in Europe have embraced the idea of central planning, but there are signs of change. Today, many decisions are delegated to local government. Also, partly as a consequence, cities and regions are now cooperating horizontally across national borders within a EU context. Indeed, the Internet itself has grown evolutionary.

Inspecting the two perspectives for what values they reflect reveals major differences. In the design perspective, values of justice, rule of law, equality, common good, etc. are emphasized. In the evolutionary perspective, the most prominent values are citizen influence, diversity, individualization, local self-determination, etc. Neither set of

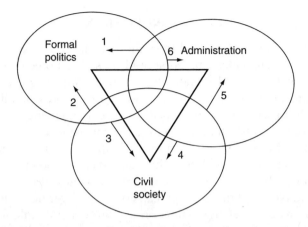

Figure 38.2   The government model under change — different actors affect the development in the transaction zones.

values can be discarded, but the balance between them can change, and this is what e-government can contribute to in any direction, by design or mistake.

Returning to the scenario presented in the "Introduction," we can see different forces stretching the spheres of influence of the political system, the administrative one, and the civil society (Figure 38.2). There is indeed a possibility that a kind of user democracy is developed within the political decision-making system. We have seen in the cases presented above that small groups of self-elected citizens can achieve considerable influence over politicians (e.g., in Bollnäs), and that civil servants in fact design the political interaction processes (Kista, Älvsjö). If this becomes the predominant model, in fact "users" of political processes will change politics rather than the majority of citizens who do not participate, or some group of people representing this majority on some predefined criteria.

In Figure 38.2, we see a development formed by the influence of different, partially conflicting, forces — actors:

The increasing use of IT in administrative processes — a more comprehensive electronic information infrastructure — restricts the action space of the political sphere as this infrastructure becomes increasingly hard to change (and, indeed, understand). This means the influence of the administrative system is increased at the expense of the political one (Arrow 1). This is a general development, but is clearly visible in the Kista case, where extensive IT use was implemented by the administration without political discussion about the implications for the role of government.

The civil society cultures, in the electronic world, for instance, manifested in virtual communities of different kinds, contain strong social elements but less of the character-istics of formal politics ("citizen" and "member" are not synonyms, for instance). To the extent that electronic tools and techniques from such cultures become used in formal politics (as we have seen above in Bollnäs, Kista, and Älvsjö) it will become less formal and thus more open to the influence of active minorities (Arrow 2).

The official e-democracy initiatives, as indeed municipal practice as we saw in the literature review, generally endorse information rather than participation. "Participation" then most often means "everybody should know about … ." rather than something that involves citizen influence. These efforts can be seen as a means to reinforce the current procedures of formal politics by complementing them with increased direct communication with citizens (Arrow 3). Probably also the second Kalix consultation should be seen as a measure designed to reinforce the politicians' position rather than the citizens', as the agenda was set by the politicians and the alternatives were fixed.

We saw that in Kista andÄlvsjö, the local e-democracy projects were virtually controlled by the civil servants due to their control of the IT system. Politicians did not control the development, but had to adjust to the development at a later stage when important traits of the information infrastructure were already implemented. This means the action space of the political system has been reduced and that of the administration has been increased (Arrow 4).

Increasing IT use in the civil society includes efforts to affect services in practice by individuals, by using electronic communication to influence individual administrative decision-makers or simply by acquiring a better understanding of how the administration works by using the electronic information and tools provided. This includes new pressures on the administration, which can no longer hide behind an information monopoly, and hence increases the influence of civil society at the administration's expense (Arrow 5).

Initiatives like the eEurope electronic government strive for more administrative control over, and efficiency within and among, the many activities of the public sector by formalizing them to the point of being implementable in electronic tools. This means that the action space of civil society actors diminishes as their interactions with government are more formalized (Arrow 5); it also means that the political system's control over the administration is strengthened as political initiatives are more directly expressed in computer code and hence can be more easily inspected and evaluated (Arrow 6). We saw this in the Kalix case, where Town Hall procedures were reorganized to be more responsive to the politicians' requests.

We thus can see from the cases we have reviewed here, that there is no single development in terms of the relative strengths of the "influence" arrows in Figure 38.2. Although very interesting, we must note that they represent a tiny minority of municipalities, in Sweden as well as globally. We should see them as food for discussion about possible futures rather than emerging trends. They are indeed actors in the ongoing development, but rather weak such in a global perspective.

REFERENCES

Andersson, L., Report from Kalix and Kista, Memorandum, Örebro University, Democrit, 2002.

Anttiroiko, A-V., Toward the European information society, *Communications of the ACM*, January, 44(12), 2001.

Åström, J., "Digital demokrati?" Idéer och strategier i lokal IT-politik" (Digital democracy? ideas and strategies in local IT policy), in *IT i demokratins tjänst*, SOU, Fakta info direkt, Stockholm, 1999, p. 117.

Aurigi, A., Digital city or 'urban simulator'?, in *Digital Cities. Technologies, Experiences, and Future Perspectives*, Ishida, T. and Isbister, K., Eds., Springer-Verlag, Berlin, 2000, pp. s. 33–44.

Barber, B., *Strong Democracy*, University of California Press, Berkeley, 1984.

Becker, T. and Slaton, C., *The Future of Teledemocracy*, Praeger, London, 2000.

Bellamy, C. and Taylor, J.A., *Governing in the Information Age*, Open University Press, Buckingham, 1998.

Callon, M., Techno-economic networks and irreversibility, in *A Sociology of Monsters. Essays on Power, Technology and Domination*, Law, J., Ed., Routledge, London, 1991, pp 132–161.

European Commission, Green Paper – Living and Working in the Information Society: People First, *COM*, 96, 389, 1996
http://europa.eu.int/comm/off/green/index_en.htm

European Commission, Building the European Information Society for Us All, Final Policy Report of the High-Level Expert Group, Employment and Social Affairs, European Commission, 1997 (manuscript completed in April 1997).

European Commission, eEurope 2002. An Information Society for All, action plan prepared by the Council and the European Commission for the Feira European Council, 19–20 June 2000
http://europa.eu.int/comm/information_society/eeurope/actionplan/index_en.htm

European Communities, Government Online, 2000
http://europa.eu.int/comm/information_society/eeurope/objectives/10areas_en.htm

G8, Government On-Line Project, Final Project Report, April 1999
http://www.open.gov.uk/govoline/golintro.htm

Goldkuhl, G. and Röstlinger, A., IT som möjliggörare och hinder – i samspel mellan politik och verksamhet i kommuner (IT as enabler and obstacle), I Åke Grönlund & Agenta Ranerup (red), Elektronisk förvaltning, elektronisk demokrati, Studentlitteratur, 2001.

Grönlund, Å., Electronic Service Management – Local Government as a Service Provider, Proceedings of E-government in Europe, Access Conferences International, St. James's Court Hotel, London, Mar. 30–31, 2000.

Grönlund, Å, *Electronic Government – Design, Appications and Management*, Idea Group, Hershey, PA, 2001a.

Grönlund, Å, *IT, demokratin och medborgarnas deltagande (IT, Democracy, and the Citizens' Participation)*, Vinnova and Teldok, Stockholm, 2001b.

Hansard, Hansard Society – Promoting Effective Parliamentary Democracy, 2002.
Publications list at http://www.hansardsociety.org.uk/publications.htm

Harrison, T.M. and Stephen, T., Researching and creating community networks, in *Doing Internet Research. Critical Issues and Methods for Examining the Net*, Jones, S., Ed., Sage, London, 1999, pp. s. 221–241.

High-Level Group, Europe and the Global Information Society: Recommendations to the European Council, The Bangemann Report, ISPO, High-Level Group on the Information Society, Bryssel, May 26, 1994
http://www.ispo.cec.be/infosoc/backg/bangeman.html

Holmström, J., Information Systems and Organization as Multipurpose Network, Ph.D. thesis, Informatics, Umeå University, Umeå, Sweden, 2000.

IT-kommissionen, Who Uses Internet and for What?, IT-kommissionen Report, January 2002 (in Swedish).

Latour, B., Technology is society made durable, in *A Sociology of Monsters: Essays on Power, Technology and Domination*, Law, J., Ed., Routledge and Kegan Paul, London, 1991, pp. 196–233.

Macintosh, A., Davenport, E., Malina, A., and Whyte, A., Technology to support participatory democracy, in *Electronic Government – Design, Applications, and Management*, Grönlund, Å., Ed., Idea Group, Hershey, PA, 2001.

Matthews, C., The EU's Lisbon Summit: Gearing Up for the Knowledge Economy, ebizChronicle.com, 2000
http://www.ebizchronicle.com/columns/march/chrismatthrew_eeurope.htm

Christopher Matthews är Press Officer and Editor of Eurecom, European Commission (New York).

Molander, C., E-Democracy Methods, presentation at the Workshop, Umeå University, Umeå, Sweden, Feb. 15, 2001.

Molin, B., Månsson, L., and Strömberg, L., *Offentlig förvaltning*, Bonniers, 1975.

Monteiro, E. and Hanseth, O., Inscribing behavior in information infrastructure standards, *Accounting, Management and Information Technologies*, 7, 183–211, 1997.

Musso, J.A., Weare, C., and Hale, M.C., Designing Web Technologies for Local Governance Reform: Good Management or Good Democracy, 1999
http://www.usc.edu/dept/LAS/SC2/junior_ publications.html

NIST (National Institute of Standards and Technology), United States National Information Infrastructure Virtual Library, 1996
http://nii.nist.gov/

Nolte, F., IT, Demokrati och det politiska uppdraget (IT, Democracy, and the Political Mission), HumanIT, May 2002, 189–206.

Norris, D.F., Leading edge information technologies and their adaption: lessons from U.S. cities, in *Information Technology and Computer Applications in Public Administration: Issues and Trends*, Garson, G.D., Ed., Idea Group, Hershey, PA, 1999.

Öhrvall, R., *Det digitala torget – en studie av kommunala debattforum på Internet (The Digital Agora – A Study of Municipal Debate Forums on the Internet)*, Political Science Dept., Uppsala University, East Orange, NJ, 2002
http://dm.statsvet.uu.se

ORD, *A Sustainable Democracy – Policy for Rule by the People in the 2000s*, SOU, Fritzes, Stockholm, 2000 (in Swedish).

Premfors, R., *Den starka demokratin (The Strong Democracy)*, Atlas, Stockholm, 2000.

Ranerup, A., Internet-enabled applications for local government democratisation. Contradictions of the Swedish experience, in *Reinventing Government in the Information Age. International Practice in IT-Enabled Public Sector Reform*, Heeks, R., Ed., Routledge, London, 1999, pp. 77–193.

Schuler, D., *New Community Networks – Wired for Change*, Addison-Wesley, Reading, MA, 1996.

SKTF, Om demokratiska processer och offentlig service på Sveriges kommuners webbplatser (On Democratic Processes and Public Service at the Web Sites of Swedish Cities), April 2001
http://www.sktf.se/media/rapporter/2001/rapport_2_2001.pdf

Snellen, I.Th.M., Channeling democratic influences through bureaucracies, in *Orwell in Athens – A Perspective on Informatization and Democracy*, van de Donk, W.B.H.J., Snellen, I.Th.M., and Tops, P.W., Eds., IOS Press, Amsterdam, 1995, pp. 51–60.

Snellen, I., ICT:s, bureaucracies, and the future of democracy, *Communications of the ACM*, January, 44(1), 45–48, 2001.

Taylor, J.A., Bardzki, B., and Wilson, C., Laying down the infrastructure for innovations in teledemocracy: the case of Scotland, in *Orwell in Athens – A Perspective on Informatization and Democracy*, van de Donk, W.B.H.J., Snellen, I.Th.M., and Tops, P.W., Eds., IOS Press, Amsterdam, 1995, pp. 61–78.

Walsham, G., Actor-network theory and IS research: current status and future prospects, in *Information Systems and Qualitative Research*, Lee, A.S., Libenau, J., DeGross, J.I., Eds., Chapman & Hall, New York, 1997, pp. 466–480.

Watson, R., Akselsen, S., Evjemo, B., and Aasaether, N., Teledemocracy in local government, *Communications of the ACM*, December, 42(12), 58–63, 1999.

West, D.M., Assessing E-Government: The Internet, Democracy, and Service, Delivery by State and Federal Governments, 2000
http://www.insidepolitics.org/egovtreport00.html

PART VII

CONCLUSION

39

INFORMATION SYSTEMS, POLITICS, AND GOVERNMENT: LEADING THEORETICAL PERSPECTIVES

G. David Garson

North Carolina State University

CONTENTS

I.	Introduction	666
II.	Democratization/empowerment theory	667
III.	Critical theory	671
IV.	Sociotechnical systems theory	675
V.	Global integration theory	679
VI.	Conclusion	682
References		683

ABSTRACT

This chapter focuses on recent theorists who have addressed the core concern of social science theory: the modeling of long-term trends to postdict the past and predict the future of the impact of information and communication technology (ICT) on society. Such theories are pertinent to many fields and are central to public administrationists' concern for policy development and pragmatic efforts to reconcile the potential of ICT with societal needs as we enter the 21st century. The theorists discussed in this chapter are grouped in four broad camps. The decentralization/democratization school emphasizes the progressive potential of ICT in government, business, education, the home, and almost all spheres of life. The critical theory school emphasizes the internal contradictions of information systems and promulgates a cautionary counter to the enthusiasm of the decentralization/democratization theorists. The third school discussed in this chapter is one of the oldest and best established, that of sociotechnical systems theory, which combines elements of the first two, but at the expense of predictive theory. The fourth school, the global integrationist school, transcends the optimism/pessimism duality of the first two schools and is critical of both while still laying the basis for predictive theory. Theorists and writers in this school focus on the globality of worldwide information networks as a transformative socioeconomic force.

I. INTRODUCTION

Since the printing of the first edition, notions of information technology (IT) theory have broadened to see more and more preference for the phrase information and communications technology (ICT) theory. This shift de-emphasizes the focus on the computer as a decision-making tool and places greater emphasis on networking and the instantaneity of information transfer. Perhaps the most notable theoretical development since 1999 has been the putting forward of "technology enactment" theory by Fountain (2001). While claiming to be wholly novel, this may be seen as an elaboration of sociotechnical systems theory, one of the four categories that formed the framework of this chapter in its first edition, hence not requiring alteration in the second edition. In another change from the first edition, I have replaced the former second category of theories, dystopian theory, with the broader label of critical theory, to reflect the ongoing development of critiques of mainstream democratization/empowerment theories of ICT.

For some writers, combining "theory" in the same breath as "information systems" is almost an oxymoron. For instance, in the first edition Messmer et al. (2000) quote Selnow (1998: 19), who writes, "the information age is marked by an extraordinary richness of sources that makes analysis increasingly difficult." Messmer et al. (2000) go on to note the difficulties complexity creates for theory construction. Theory construction in the field of information systems is difficult not only due to the complexity of causal forces at work at technical, social, political, economic, and other levels, but also due to the relative novelty of computing itself. In a field noted for astonishingly rapid transformation, everything is a "moving target." The ability to form reliable long-range forecasts is the illusory holy grail of information and communication technology (ICT), possession of which might confer literal riches. Only a few claim to have this ability as an intuitive art, and even rarer are claims to be able to make such forecasts based on a theoretical model. Nonetheless, theory of this type is directly relevant to public administration because strategic information policy ultimately rests on assumptions about the meaning of the long-term evolution of the interaction of ICT with social structures.

The heart of social science theory is the modeling of long-term trends to postdict the past and predict the future. There are, of course, many other aspects of ICT theory, starting with theories about what constitutes "information," typologies and levels of information, success factors in information systems implementation, and so on. However, this chapter focuses on recent theorists who have addressed the core concern: seeking to model long-term change regarding the impact of information systems on society. These theorists are grouped in four broad camps.[1] The democratization/empowerment school emphasizes the progressive potential of ICT in government, business, education, the home, and almost all spheres of life. The critical theory school emphasizes the internal contradictions of information systems and promulgates a cautionary counter to the

---

[1] As in all intellectual history, grouping of authors into perspectives partakes of the arbitrary as nearly all authors articulate complex, even contradictory views and acknowledge points made by those with whom they disagree. The purpose here is not to ascribe labels to particular authors but rather to highlight the fundamental views and differences of the four schools of thought.

enthusiasm of the first school. The third school discussed in this chapter is one of the oldest and best established, that of sociotechnical systems theory, which combines elements of the first two, but, as we shall see, at the expense of predictive theory. The fourth school, the global integrationist school, transcends the optimism/pessimism duality of the first two schools and is critical of both while still laying the basis for predictive theory. Theorists and writers in this school focus on the globality of worldwide information networks as a transformative socioeconomic force.

II. DEMOCRATIZATION/EMPOWERMENT THEORY

The leading theoretical perspective on the impact of ICT in organizational life, public administration included, may be called the democratization/empowerment theory. For democratization theorists, in the wake of the information revolution comes decentralization because ICT allows dramatic broadening of the span of control, and democratization because knowledge, which is a critical basis of power, is also dispersed by ICT. Citizens gain control over their lives because of the power of vastly increased information, education becomes more accessible and appropriate when delivered online, firms and markets become more efficient due to financial networking, and global communication leads to greater global harmony and understanding (cf. Rheingold, 1994; Negroponte, 1995; Schuler, 1996; Cohill and Kavanaugh, 1997). In Negroponte's terms, the new digital world is seen as one that transcends all spatial, temporal, and material constraints and as such represents a societal transformation as or more profound and beneficial than the industrial revolution.

This optimistic view of the social impacts of computing has a long history. Vannevar Bush, science advisor to Franklin Delano Roosevelt, was one of the early utopians. His article "As we may think" (Bush,1945) envisioned a desk-sized "memex" that would give access to vast archives of books. Douglas Engelbart headed Stanford University's project "to augment the human intellect" in the 1960s, studying how time-shared computers could be linked to enhance analysis and decision-making. Also in the 1960s, McLuhan (1964) popularized computer technology and telecommunications as forces that were creating a "global village," uniting everyone, everywhere, to everything. When Toffler (1980) wrote about how telecommunications was creating an "infosphere," the utopian vision of computing as a mind-expanding, empowering force was well established. The vision of a "democratic information society" or "electronic democracy" has been set forth for three decades by many other writers (Sackman and Nie, 1970; Hiltz and Turoff, 1978; Becker and Scarce, 1984; see also Caporael, 1984; McCullough, 1991; for a European view, see Frosini, 1987).

Many authors see in the new ICT the means to revitalize American democracy, which has suffered from declining voter interest and participation in the last few decades. Abramson et al. (1988), for instance, emphasized both the communitarian and the pluralist impact of ICT. It is communitarian, they said, because it provides through electronic discussion groups a way to arrive at community consensus on policy issues. It is pluralist in impact, they argued, because it provides networking tools for citizens to organize around mutual interests to influence public policy. These arguments are all part of a broader argument that democracy rests on social capital, which has been declining in the face of technologies such as passive television (Putnam, 1993, 1995a, 1995b), but which may be rebuilt through new interactive information media (Calabrese and Borchert, 1996). Numerous studies emphasize the capacity of the Internet in particular to promote political organizing and mobilization, even when organizers have few resources by traditional standards (Bonchek, 1995; Grossman, 1995; Witting and Schmitz, 1996; Gurak, 1997; Bimber, 1998; Tsagarousianou et al., 1998).

At the individual level, Stefik (1996) is among those who have cast ICT as a profoundly liberating force for personal growth. Stefik, himself a computer scientist, envisions a world in which personal capacities are magnified many times over by smart computational agents that do everything from filtering e-mail to managing team collaboration to carrying out customized research. With the Internet as yellow pages, library, school, counselor, broker, entertainer, and mall, technology brings into reality the ancient aspirations of humankind — hence the title of his work, *Internet Dreams*. The digital world is seen as no less than the culmination of human history, making manifest yearnings from the collective unconscious of the species.

At the organizational level, democratization/empowerment theory has been applied not only to the private but also to the public sector, as discussed below. Democratization/empowerment theory contends that ICT is a revolutionary force, overturning the bureaucratic forms associated with the industrial revolution — forms associated with Frederick Taylor and "scientific management," Max Weber and "ideal-typical bureaucracy," and Henry Ford and the assembly-line as a prototype of the organization of work. Authors associated with this perspective believe ICT is destined to overturn traditional bureaucracy, the Fordist pattern of work organization, and the autocratic control of nations. Such authors include Piore and Sable (1984), Zuboff (1988), Kenney and Florida (1993), Heckscher and Donnellon (1994), and Stefik (1996), to name a few.

That the information revolution of the computer era has reduced information costs drastically is the starting point of an argument made by Reschenthaler and Thompson (1996) about the impact of ICT specifically on public administration. They theorize that the effects of reduced information costs are:

1. Increased efficacy of market mechanisms vis-à-vis governmental services or regulation
2. Increased efficacy of decentralized allocation of resources and after-the-fact control vis-à-vis centralized and before-the-fact controls (e.g., pushing decision-making as low in the organization as possible)
3. Increased efficacy of job-oriented process structures vis-à-vis broad functional structures (e.g., multidisciplinary teams working holistically rather than functional departments working sequentially)

For instance, they argue that information explosion in the financial sector lessens the need for governmental financial regulations to protect investors, that advances in information processing allow such things as pollution rights or airport landing rights to be securitized and bought and sold on the market, and that technology-based improvements in costing and pricing transportation and telecommunications services justified the deregulation of these industries. More generally, Reschenthaler and Thompson argue that ICT erodes economies of scale in administration, production, and marketing, giving even smaller organizations first-class management tools in each of these functional domains. Put another way, they see the technological tide pushing administrators, public ones included, toward increased span of control, reduced layers of management, and delegation of more power to computer-equipped frontline employees.

Reschenthaler and Thompson point to New Zealand's "new public management" as an illustration of the desirable reduction of public administration's scope to as small a core as possible, linking appropriations to performance, in turn monitored through new ICT. They conclude with the argument that as the bureaucratic revolution spawned the discipline of public administration, so now the information revolution requires its radical reorientation toward governmental restructuring (cutting back to core functions), reinvention through a customer-oriented product–market strategy, actual devolution to market mechanisms, reengineering (creating new processes rather than incrementally adjusting existing bureaucratic ones), rethinking (creating an adaptive information culture throughout the organization), and realigning (assuring that organizational structure matches the new information culture).

The paradigm shift seen in public administration by Reschenthaler and Thompson, while representing a sea change (their term), still falls short of those theorists who see the birthing of "virtual society." Agres et al. (1998), for instance, present a conceptual research framework centered on the forces that are creating virtual societies, by which is meant societies in which most transactions (work, consumption, entertainment, education, etc.) are accessible without the need of face-to-face interaction. They identify four "driving forces" leading to virtual society:

1. Global economies are moving toward electronic transactions in all functional areas, including accounts receivable and payable, inventory management, tax filings, communications, and even many aspects of production and delivery of goods and services.
2. Governmental policies and politics increasingly see subsidy and promotion of a "wired nation" as strategically necessary to stay globally competitive in the 21st century.
3. Likewise, the public and private sectors, and citizens themselves, increasingly see an enlightened population as a national goal, based on personal career goals and necessities, with ICT education starting early in childhood.
4. Technology inherently promotes virtual society, continually making it more likely and more attractive through such developments as improved networking, videoconferencing, groupware, and Internet technology, as well as lower costs.

The organizational implications seen by the authors are transformation from traditional, centralized hierarchies to networked, decentralized structures that have fewer layers of control (are flatter), that empower employees at lower organizational levels, and that embrace interlocking virtual alliances and partnerships with other organizations. Simultaneously, at the family level, telework, distance education, and virtual forms of entertainment will increase. Similar predictions are found by Targowski (1997), whose futuristic view foresees a national electronic village, virtual business, online government, virtual schools, and universities, and an integrated "TeleCity."

These organizational implications are supported by other recent writers. Zuboff (1988), for instance, has tied decentralization trends in information processing closely with human resource development, viewing the former as providing a revolutionary opportunity for the latter. Likewise Tapscott and Caston (1992) argued that workgroup computing, distributed processing, and interorganizational networking (airline links to travel agents) are making the centralization–decentralization pendulum swing obsolete in modern organizations. Instant availability of information, they say, is turning hierarchical organization into a liability. Rather, in a competitive world, strategic advantage goes to firms and agencies that can take advantage of multidisciplinary problem-oriented teams who can exploit technological opportunities as they occur.

Many others have discerned similar trends. Blanchard and Horan (1998: 303), for instance, surveyed a California community and found citizen interest in developing virtual communities around education, community activities, and government and politics in at least two out of three ,respondents. They interpret this as an indication that technology may be leading people into an era that reverses the decline of social capital as represented by lower levels of civic interest. Passive television viewing may be replaced by interactive Internet building of virtual communities, which in turn will, it is argued, reinvigorate democratic society. This argument dovetails with that of Putnam (1995a, 1995b) and others that rebuilding social capital through increased civic involvement is an essential prerequisite to improving the performance of governments and other social institutions.

Democratization/empowerment theory holds that ICT is democratizing governmental and organizational life. Braman (1994), for instance, develops the theory of state autopoiesis (self-making), contending that modern information networks for the first time create a ubiquitous capacity for nonhierarchical dispersion of intelligence. The emergence of the Internet as the primary communication technology of the nation will, Braman says, alter substantially the forms of power on which the state has traditionally rested. The dispersion of intelligence limits the capacity of elites to define issues through propaganda and to influence public opinion, increases the bargaining power of nonelites, and provides greater opportunity for resistance to implementation of governmental policies. Likewise, in the first edition, Shi and Scavo (2000) write, "a well-designed online public information system can significantly improve our democratic life" by increasing voter information, improving political communications, and promoting a high level of citizen participation in government. Some, like Naisbitt (1981), have even envisioned the possibility that ICT will someday allow representative democracy to be replaced by a direct democracy of citizens indicating policy and candidate preferences through electronic networks. In this extreme view, Congress's main duty would become to oversee the electronic decision process and the president's primary responsibility would be only to find superior candidates to fill top government jobs (Rubens, 1983; Cohen, 1984). Perhaps the most extreme view of all is expressed in Mann's (1998) *Tomorrow's Global Community: How the Information Deluge Is Transforming Business and Government*, which optimistically foresees the emergence of a virtual global community consisting of a wide array of private partnerships eventually replacing the nation-state itself.

At a macrolevel, Northrop and Kraemer (2000) have demonstrated the close link between computerization in a society and its level of socioeconomic development. Broad diffusion of computing is associated not only with advanced industrialization, but also with provision of mass education, the permeation of all forms of "information society," such as widespread use of telephones and television, and with provision of open access to information. Some go so far as to argue that information society requires information openness, for which democratization is a prerequisite (Kedzie, 1995).[2] In policy terms, technological competitiveness is seen as the "new frontier" in world competition, with the prospect that the gap between the technological "haves" and technologically undeveloped nations will grow (Inman and Burton, 1990). The clear implication is that

---

[2] This perspective was articulated in November 1998, by Vice President Al Gore, a strong advocate of ICT investment. Speaking at an international economic summit dealing with the Asian economic crisis, Gore angered his Malaysian hosts by stating bluntly that economic progress depended on democratization and acceptance of reform.

nations that wish to compete must democratize as well as computerize, and that democratization and computerization are mutually reinforcing processes.

III. CRITICAL THEORY

Democratization/empowerment theory has many critics. Even without embracing critical theory countertheories, empirical social scientists have questioned the optimism of democratization theory. The mantra of the business model for large-scale ICT initiatives, first under Clinton–Gore's National Performance Review (NPR) and now under the Bush–OMB President's Management Agenda, is that ICT can be used to leverage organizational changes and restructuring and reengineering government processes. Heintz and Bretschneider (2000) studied the use of IT in relation to restructuring in public organizations, asking if adoption of IT affected organizational structures, communications, and decision-making? They found that there is little empirical relationship between ICT adoption and subsequent agency restructuring in the public sector. In the cases where restructuring occurs, managers reported only minimal effects on performance. While ICT may improve performance directly it did not appear that ICT changes public organizational structure. At a societal level, essayists in Alexander and Pal (1998) critiqued digital democracy theory and noted that the Internet could increase levels of civic disinterest and accelerate social fragmentation and the decline of social capital.

There seems to be more evidence for ICT as a control strategy in public organizations than as a restructuring strategy, for example, Henman and Adler (2003) found that in the case of Social Security Administration, computerization has generally increased management control over both staff and claimants, contrary to the ICT empowerment theory. Similarly, Hood (2000) found that ICT is unlikely to change organizational control patterns, except insofar as different cultures use ICT differently. A common variant of the control theory for ICT is "amplification theory" — the view that ICT is neither democratizing nor the opposite, but rather serves to reinforce the prevailing power structure of organizations and societies. Agre (2002), for instance, presents the amplification model as one in which an institution's participants appropriate technology to enhance preexisting organizational goals and relationships. Agre's research found amplification theory to be a better explanatory model than technological determinism, arguing that the Internet is rapidly amplifying existing political relationships, not overthrowing them. This research is in line with other research of the 1970s, including the noted work of Kraemer and associates, which consisted of a study of local governments that found that ICT decisions tended to amplify the political power of the dominant coalition within the organization (Danziger et al., 1982; Kraemer and Dedrick, 1998).

Critical theories of ICT are often traced back to the Luddites, English workmen in early-19th-century Leicestershire who destroyed labor-saving machinery in a protest against the adverse social effects of technology, as described in Sale (1996). In terms of information systems, even more inspiration can probably be credited to the vision expressed by George Orwell in his dystopian novel, *1984.* Writers have long raised fears that ICT would lead to the pervasive invasion of privacy by all-seeing bureaucrats, reminiscent of the totalitarian government of Orwell's novel (cf. Bovard and Bouvard, 1975; Wicklein, 1979; Donner, 1981; Reinecke, 1984).

Critical theory holds that ICT confers on governments (and corporations) unprecedented abilities to oversee the everyday lives of everyone and to increase control, with the poorer and less educated increasingly marginalized from the informational basis of power. In extreme form, critical theory raises the fear that society is moving toward a system of technological apartheid. For instance, Burnham (1983) painted a picture of a high-tech city of the future in which a privileged class ruled through computerized business, education, entertainment, and security, while a poverty-stricken underclass was unable to even enter the high-tech world without computer-enforced work passes. While stopping short of technological determinism, literature of this school heavily emphasizes the powerful market and political forces that bring informational inequality about, as in books by Haywood (1995), Stoll (1995), Schiller (1996), Wresch (1996), Perelman (1998), as well as a whole cottage industry of similar books inventorying the dysfunctions of computerization (e.g., Kroker and Weinstein, 1994; Rushkoff, 1996; Rawlins, 1997; Rochlin, 1997).

At the level of the individual psyche, critical thought emphasizes the alienating effects of computing technology. Early work held that ICT diverts people into "fraudulent" computer–human interactions (Weizenbaum, 1976). Conomikes (1967) even predicted that computing would crush *esprit de corps* in organizations, creating an underclass of dispirited workers devoid of dedication to the organization. This genre further held that computerization tends to abstract human problems to a depersonalized level so that social workers become insensitive to client needs, doctors become insensitive to patient needs, and so on. Thus, for instance, in the military arena Beusmans and Wieckert (1989: 946) wrote, "computer simulations of warfare distance users from the consequences of their actions." Several other works have since appeared, focusing on the dehumanizing effects of computing, including Talbott (1995) and Slouka (1996).

"Deindividuation" is seen as the process of alienation of the individual from social norms. Kiesler et al. (1991), for instance, found that computer-mediated communication removed the contextual salience of social norms, weakening conformity to them. Likewise, Loch and Conger (1996) linked computer use to deindividuation and degradation of social norms pertaining to computer use. More broadly, if social order rests on cultural enchantment, computer use is said to lead to disenchantment in the Weberian sense.

At the level of the individual in the workplace, the critical argument is that ICT reinforces and exacerbates existing inequalities (cf. Kolleck, 1993: 458). Writers have long raised the fear that technical experts would gain power at the expense of elected officials or even over corporate CEOs simply because such experts had control over the means of information (Downs, 1967). Tepas (1972: 101, 103) argued that "The innovations of the industrial revolution often led to dull jobs that were mindless, boring, monotonous, and/or fatiguing" and now again in our own times "the misapplication of computer systems in the current technological revolution is also leading us to dull jobs" and "underutilization of workers, monotonous duties, fear of job loss, and/or frequent shortages of trained technical staff."

In the dystopian argument, adverse impacts on lower-level workers are believed to be the greatest. For instance, Vallas (1998: 353) has shown how, in the context of a paper mill, the introduction of automation "led managers to institute credential barriers that restricted manual workers' opportunities, eventually enabling engineers to gain exclusive control over analytic functions as their own 'natural' domain … reproducing social inequalities even when new technologies render them unnecessary." This is a major theme of Perelman (1998). Thomas (1994) similarly found that technological change was at least as much determined by power considerations in a desire to further increase inequality in the workplace (the "power-process model"). More generally, critical theorists argue that democratization/empowerment theorists grossly underestimate the self-serving boundary-policing roles and capacities of organizational elites when techno-logical challenges arise (Abbott, 1995).

The work of Thomas and Vallas is in a long tradition of scholarship that argues that new technology multiplies elite privileges, frequently at the expense of the less educated (Curtis, 1988; Derber and Schwartz, 1991; Burris, 1993; Reich, 1993; Aronowitz and DiFazio, 1995; Rifkin, 1995; Michaelson, 1996). Sometimes this argument is extended to make the case not only for technology reinforcing workplace and income inequality, but also for its leading to disemployment or unstable chronic underemployment of those at the bottom of technology's social ladder (Reich, 1992; Aronowitz and DiFazio, 1995; Rifkin, 1995). For lower-level employees who remain in stable employment, the critical theorists argue that work is not enriched as democratization/empowerment theorists argue, but rather pace and load is increased while discretion is not.

At the level of political movements, dystopians place emphasis on the social inequal-ity inherent in the expensiveness of high tech. Fisher (1998) has recently looked at the use of Internet technology by grassroot social movements, for instance. On the one hand, he finds support for the argument that such movements magnify their power through the Internet, e-mail, and the like — an argument frequently made by democratization/empowerment theorists like Reschenthaler and Thompson, who cite examples like the use of high tech by Chinese dissidents in the Tiananmen Square crisis. On the other hand, Fisher's central conclusion is that advanced ICT increases the gap between the haves and have-nots within the U.S. and dramatically more so when considered on a global basis. Moreover, Fisher notes, future potential increases in Internet costs and regulation may well exacerbate inequalities in power based on ICT. Similarly, Novotny (1998: 178), surveying Internet use in the 1996 campaign, concluded, "Not only does the Internet and its World Wide Web appear to be a promise as yet unfilled for many parts of society, but it seems to be exacerbating seemingly intractable racial, class, and regional inequalities."

Historically speaking, writers like Mosco (1998: 58) draw analogies to radio, which, in its early days was also touted as a two-way technological revolution destined to bring radical democratization through creation of virtual communities in the ether — but which, in fact, saw the market forces of commercialism become overwhelmingly dom-inant, leaving the vision of democratic community and amateur radio a socially periph-eral curiosity. Mosco acknowledges such examples as the Tiananmen dissidents but aligns his own work (Mosco, 1996) with the critics who conclude, "it is just a matter of time ... before a handful of transnational companies takes near complete control of the [Information] Highway and its product. The early warning signs, such as Internet adver-tising, shopping, banking, access fees, tightening security controls...point to the inev-itable victory of the market over democratic communication" (Mosco, 1998: 60), though he calls on community groups to make efforts to organize for social change via the Web. For Mosco, however, the world of information haves and have-nots is far more likely than the digital global village.

At the international level, critical theory arguments go well beyond a focus on seemingly insurmountable cross-national inequalities in the cost of ICT. Wresch (1998), for instance, notes that maintaining web pages in Africa often exceeds the total income of an African faculty member. A broader case can be made that the rise of ICT is associated with the decline in power of the nation-state (Mathews, 1997). The rapid movements of speculative capital, made possible by the computerization of international finance, for instance, in 1998 dramatically laid bare the relative powerlessness of Asian nations to control their own economies, with disastrous results. Computerization is part and parcel of the globalization of economic enterprise, with great enhancements in the ability to shift information, resources, human talent, and money from one part of the globe to another, with diminished effective oversight by any form of government. John Kenneth Galbraith's concept of social order based on the "countervailing powers" of business, government, and labor, is now seen as a mid-20th-century relic, replaced in the information age by the monism of global corporations, benevolent at times and iniquitous at others. Castells (1996, 1997, 1998) has presented a grand theory, backed by an enormous diversity of historical and empirical research, which interprets the modern era in terms of the dialectic between "informational capitalism" based on networked international corporations on the one hand, and social movements and regional efforts to assert unique cultural identities on the other. The overall thrust of the argument is dystopian. Castells (1998: 70) writes, "The rise of informationalism in this end of millenium is intertwined with rising inequality and social exclusion throughout the world". International inequalities grow, particularly at the extremes, and groups are systematically denied the resources for meaningful survival of their cultural identity. "Black holes of information capitalism" appear, from which there is no empirically evident means to escape poverty and deidentification. The political dynamics of the age are not class-based or even nationalist, as a century ago, but rather involve the conflict of one set of informational capitalists against another (e.g., the U.S. vs. the Pacific Rim vs. the European Union), against the new international criminal economy, and against regional pockets of resistance to free trade acceptance of the full impact of informational capitalism on cultural identity.

Castell's theory is not far from those of Marxist and critical thinkers collected in McChesney et al. (1998), where the argument is made that the contradictions of capitalism are revealed in the growing tension between the democratic potential of info-tech and economic demands for profit. Castells predicts that in the context of global corporations structured on ICT, nation-states may turn away from regulatory/distributive politics as it becomes clear that form of politics lies in areas of diminished control.[3]

Like Castells, Huntington (1997) argues that the rise of ICT is associated at the state level with a reversion to arenas more under the influence of the state, namely traditional cultural politics. As Northrop and Kraemer (2000) summarize Huntington's views, nations "become more parochial as they seek solace in cultural traditions." In developing countries, ICT has thus become widely seen as a new resurrection of economic imperialism and a threat to the cultural identity of emerging nations (Kyem, 1999). Analysts of the left, such as Stallabrass (1995), argue that the information revolution is associated with stagnating wages due to intensified global competition, with consequent alienation from politics as ordinary people become preoccupied with their own needs and increased insecurities.

As Singapore demonstrates, and Northrop and Kraemer (2000) acknowledge, it is entirely possible to "leap into the Information Age" while suppressing civil liberties,

---

[3] See also Feenberg and Hannay (1995) for more on critical social theory and ICT. See also Kember (2003) for a feminist perspective that builds on Castell's theory, but that more optimistically sees information culture leading to a postmodern synthesis characterized by an ethics of the posthuman subject mobilized in the tension between cold war and post–cold war politics, psychological and biological machines, centralized and decentralized control, top-down and bottom-up processing, autonomous and autopoietic organisms, cloning and transgenesis, species-self and other species.

freedom of the press, and democratization. Critical theory emphasizes that the boundaries of information openness can be controlled from the top-down and can be circumscribed in ways inconsistent with democratization/empowerment visions of the future "information society."

Coyne and Wiszniewski (1999) have conveniently highlighted the five common themes of critical theories of IT:

1. Although computer networks provide an opportunity for access, restore an informed and active citizenry, and overcome social barriers, in reality there is a digital divide that inhibits equal access, which means that ICT, including the Internet, is dominated by and is primarily in the service of economically advantaged groups and nations.
2. The presentation of ICT is characterized by deception: the claims of egalitarian access and the necessity, inevitability, and desirability of growth in ICT conceal other agendas associated with the growth of big business, globalization, control, and the preparation of a yet more compliant consumer culture.
3. Computer simulation (in the form of virtual reality, game playing, virtual communities, computerized theme parks, and so on) functions to present the unreal as real, and to mask the true reality of everyday existence in a consumer culture.
4. ICT systems function to set the terms of discourse and to undercut dissent by concealing domination under the legitimating cloak of metanarratives of logic, order, rule, and objective reasoning, whereas they are unmasked by critical theory to be shown to be a form of symbolic hegemony by the powerful.
5. ICT cannot be analyzed in isolation from the social system of consumers, advertisers, developers, designers, manufacturers, educators, mass media, and lawmakers, because the function of ICT is not primarily technological at all, but rather to perpetuate the dominant social system.

Coyne and Wiszniewski advance hermeneutics as an alternative to critical theory, interpreting ICT in terms of power rather than domination, providing a more open-ended context for the discussion of ethics in an information society (see Coyne, 1995, 1999).

IV. SOCIOTECHNICAL SYSTEMS THEORY

Democratization/empowerment theory and critical theory display alternative normative perspectives on where the world of ICT should or should not be going. Each can be a form of technological determinism, assuming that technology itself is taking us in the direction pointed. A third branch of information systems theory, to be contrasted next, is possibilistic and nonnormative.

The focus of sociotechnical systems theory is on (1) the rejection of technological determinism and (2) a view of information systems as being determined by social choices and demands, ignoring of which leads to ICT implementation failures. In this genre, Stewart and Williams (1998: 281) share findings of the European Commission–sponsored study, "Forecasting the Applications and Environment of Technology to the Year 2010 and Beyond" (FAME 2010+), faulting both democratization/empowerment theory and critical theory as "simplified analysis" that "can have very damaging effects on the ability to generate useful policy." Technological determinism can lead the pessimistic toward resistance to change, while leading the optimistic toward undue emphasis on technology as the only meaningful focus for policy support and intervention, neglecting psychological, social, political, and cultural elements in sociotechnical systems. The technocratic focus on technology alone to the neglect of such a broader perspective is traced by the FAME 2010+ study as critical to understanding the relative slowness of electronic market-places to emerge in retail, for digital education to displace traditional teaching, and for telework to create virtual organizations at the expense of traditional structures.

Sociotechnical systems advocates believe that introduction of new technologies invariably changes the social system, and changes in the social system invariably impact technical systems (Whyte, 1997). If there is a normative implication, it is that interdependence of social and technical systems means that ICT success is most likely where end users as well as technical experts have been involved in the design as well as implementation phases of introducing new technologies. Sociotechnical systems analysts reject top-down imposition of technology on people, assuming people must adapt to technology; rather, they seek to adapt technology to human relationships and patterns of interaction (Trist and Murray, 1990). Sociotechnical systems management was originally an action-oriented methodology used by researchers and practitioners who sought to apply behavioral principles to information system (IS) implementation. The sociotechnical perspective emphasizes that what is technically optimal may not be sociotechnically optimal. Sociotechnical management seeks to improve both organizational effectiveness and the quality of working life through a design process that integrates technical and social concerns. Four common attributes of sociotechnical management are:

1. Reliance on small "action groups" in a bottom-up, user-oriented process of design specification, experiments sanctioned by higher management; a team approach
2. Skills development as an organizational objective (as opposed to acceptance of deskilling); encouragement of and use of autonomous work groups when possible
3. Structuring the reward system to encourage participation in productivity planning and implementation; encouragement of self-inspection; provision of feedback on performance
4. Introduction of new technologies under a facilitative (as opposed to command-driven) leadership

These and other sociotechnical management principles have been outlined by writers such as Trist (1973), Blackler and Oborne (1987), Chisholm (1988), and Trist et al. (1997).

A recent version of sociotechnical theory is the "technology enactment theory" put forward by Fountain (2001) in her book, *Building the Virtual State*. Though Fountain advances her theory as wholly novel, Grafton (2003) has observed, it is a restatement and updating of the sociotechnical viewpoint. Technology enactment theory holds that technological possibilities are enacted into technological realities in ways strongly affected by organizational, political, and cultural environments, with nondeterministic results, which cannot be predicted from technological considerations alone. This view contrasts sharply with simplistic versions of technological determinism. However, those who see technology as a powerful wave of force in its own right, sweeping over and inundating old cultural, social, and organizational processes, do not go so far as to believe technology brings things about in a magical manner free from the touch of human hands. Neither the technological determinist nor the sociotechnical theory perspective is this naive. Rather, the real argument is a relative one, with sociotechnical theory (and its technology enactment version) holding that contextual factors are relatively more powerful than are technological determinants in typical information systems outcomes in the public sector in general.

There are reasons for assuming technology enactment theory to be true. Large-scale public-sector IT projects often fail, and neglect of human factors is commonly found to be at the root of the problem (cf. Garson, 1995). The relative importance of human factors over narrowly technological factors is the central thrust of sociotechnical theory (Emery and Trist, 1965; see also Emery, 1969; Trist, 1981; Mumford, 1987) — one of the foundational theories in the study of public-sector IT, but one not attributed by Fountain. Likewise, the work of Ken Kraemer and associates on the URBIS studies (e.g., Kraemer and King, 1986) has long focused on the relative importance of political factors over narrowly technological factors in public information systems, another highly influential body of work not attributed by Fountain but closely relevant to her theory of technology enactment. In general, technology enactment theory is simply the common wisdom of the bulk of social science literature on information systems implementation as it has existed for over 40 years.

Common wisdom or not, there is an argument to be made on the other side. Technological determinism is Aristotelian social science. In Aristotle's teleological metaphysics everything has an inherent essence or *telos*. The *telos* is, in modern terms, the DNA or plan that determines how each thing is destined to unfold and what it is to become. The *telos* is both the essence of something and its goal or destiny. The *telos* of the acorn, for instance, is to become the mighty oak. The *telos* is both descriptive (it is what is apt to happen) and normative (it is what should happen). While it is true that under classical determinism, teleological understanding of things referred to sequential, mechanistically predetermined design, in modern times teleologists who focus on technology are apt to understand the *telos* of technology as a spontaneously self-organizing phenomenon of a nonlinear, dynamic nature. Technological determinists believe this nature usually will prevail over social, political, and cultural circumstances, though the dynamics by which it prevails may be nonlinear.

Part of the problem of pitting sociotechnical theory against technological teleology is that one is pitting a small-scale theory against a large-scale theory. Consider the case of video recording. One may focus on the fact that the Beta format, which was technologically superior to video home system (VHS), nonetheless was beaten into extinction by the politics of the marketplace. In this, one might say technological determinants lost out to nontechnological determinants and enactment theory is upheld. On a larger scale, however, video recording technology by nature (*telos*) had the capacity to bring convenient entertainment into the home on a mass scale, overcoming the reservations and resistance of powerful motion picture interests who saw it as a threat. In this, one may say that the technological *telos* triumphed over nontechnological determinants. Whether technological teleology or technology enactment theory was "right" in the case of video recording depends on the scale of analysis. In general, technological determinism takes the large-scale, long-term viewpoint.

With regard to the case of the International Trade Data System (ITDS), a case study pivotal to Fountain's work, Fountain of necessity took a relatively short-term view, covering developments from 1994 to 1999. The International Trade Data System was an attempt to integrate networked data pertaining to trade, uniting many federal agencies. It arose from a need to do something about the fact that in a global digital economy, old government methods were failing to keep track of the volume of trade. The ITDS was promoted by the NPR under Al Gore, during the Clinton administration, and its full acceptance required significant change by vested interests in the U.S. Customs Service. The debate between technological determinism and technology enactment theory in the ITDS case revolves around a question of relative importance: between the technology-oriented logic envisioned by a rather sweeping NPR vision vs. the relatively parochial political, economic, and cultural contextual interests of the Customs Service.

From a theoretical point of view, examining the ITDS case for a few more years reveals that most of the aspects Fountain cites as exemplifying how the technological imperative loses to bureaucratic enactment (abandonment of a multiagency approach, abandonment of a one-stop web portal, disregard of non-Customs priorities in exports and enforcement, lack of international integration) appear in fact not to be losses at all, but *are* being implemented, contrary to the impression a reader might receive based on an account ending in 1999 (see Garson, 2003).

What emerges from the ITDS case is not a rejection of technological determinism and an upholding of sociotechnical theory. Rather we see that it is true that (1) what determinists might call the technological telos and what Fountain calls "objective technology" exerts a very powerful force for organizational change, creating pressures to enact those functions that advance national interests, and (2) enactment does involve interagency conflicts over the manner of implementation, its timetable, and its priority relative to other projects competing for limited funds. No doubt there are other cases that might be found in which narrow agency interests clearly defeat technological changes that, from a public interest viewpoint, would otherwise make sense, and thus constitute cases supporting sociotechnical theory and discrepant with technological determinism. The ITDS case, however, was not one of these cases.

Others have taken up themes developed by Fountain. Gascó (2003), for instance, develops "new institutionalism" theory, explicitly following Fountain, arguing that technology creates perceived win–win situations for all actors, prompting organizational change, but the direction of change may be positive or negative, depending on technological, managerial, and political variables. "Governance theory" likewise is a loose, currently popular constellation of ideas in the sociotechnical tradition, holding that the process of governing transcends the institutions of government and that the enhancement of democratic governance rests in part on leveraging ICT choices in creative ways that are not technologically determined.

A weakness of sociotechnical systems theory is that its emphasis on the importance of complex social factors in the making of technical choices leaves the analyst with a normative prescription for policy but great uncertainty in forecasting stages of development, whether toward democratization/empowerment, organizational and societal inequality, or global integration. In any policy area, the sociotechnical systems writer will have much to say about the importance of taking a diverse complex of factors into account and may even have a methodology for doing so, but the writer is apt to come close to those, noted at the outset of this chapter, who find the complexity of ICT an intellectual barrier to predictive theory, instead dictating uncertainty. Martin (1995), for instance, is among those who reject exaggerated democratization/empowerment claims and instead concentrates on ICT as a social process, reflected in the shifting of old paradigms to new uncertainties. Likewise, Falk (1998) writes, "The Web is an example of a sociotechnical network ... each actor entering the Web draws upon both external and existing Web resources to construct new 'actor worlds' which jostle for positing and legitimacy with preexisting actor worlds within the Web. It is difficult to predict with any confidence the likely result of this interplay."

Some versions of sociotechnical perspectives emphasize the power of ICT decision-making at the agency or the community organization level. This flows from the focus of sociotechnical theory on the importance of complex local factors and the decision-making free will of local actors to implement ("enact") ICT in any number of directions. The local perspective is apparent, for instance, in Howley (1998: 407), who writes, referring to democratization/empowerment theorists, "Despite the hyperbole of some enthusiasts, community networking is no guarantee that the gap between information haves and have-nots will close. Moreover, the regeneration of community spirit, the rekindling of civic life, and the revitalization of the local economy is far from certain even in a 'wired' community." Howley goes on to advocate grassroot community involvement in information access planning as the only approach with any hope of impacting inequality in information societies. Likewise, Falk (1998), while recognizing the globalization associated with ICT, sees integration arising not so much from government action (he sees governments as merely additional actors jostling for influence) as does global integrationist theory, discussed below, but rather from transnational community building on the Web by "robust social organization," through such organizations as Communications for a Sustainable Future, his own Environmental Education Information and Resource Clearinghouse, and innumerable social organizations like them (Falk, 1998: 292).

Sociotechnical systems theory raises a powerful critique of democratization/empowerment theory and of critical theory. It generates sage advice about the centrality of social and political processes to seemingly technical arenas, and it comes armed with an impressive practical methodology for helping organizations adapt to technological change. Ultimately, however, it is middle-range theory, focusing on organizational behavior in the face of new technology. It does not seek to articulate a theory of the long-term development of ICT, or of its impact on government and society.

V. GLOBAL INTEGRATION THEORY

A final general perspective on the development of ICT combines a critical theory pessimism about the likely outcomes of unregulated ICT development with relative optimism, not in the benign nature of market forces as with democratization/empowerment theory, but in the possibilities for global intergovernmental integration of ICT with socioeconomic policy. Global integration theory is, like sociotechnical systems theory, possibilistic rather than deterministic, but unlike sociotechnical approaches it is still normative in its prescriptions. An example of this perspective is the work of Ferguson (1998), who sees the convergence of mass media, telecommunications, and ICT, combined with worldwide market liberalization and deregulation, leading to increased opportunities for improvements in employment, education, health, welfare, the environment, science, minority empowerment, and political participation. Ferguson reviewed current multilateral information initiatives, such as the World Bank Information for Development Program, the UNESCO Intergovernmental Informatics Program, the UN/World Bank Africa's Information Society Initiative, and others. His conclusion was that such initiatives at present are very limited and he issued a call for a stronger mode of international policymaking and perhaps regulation of information and communication technology to achieve equitable ends which market forces would otherwise negate. Ferguson (1998: 267) concluded, "Without international communications policy and regulatory debate, the world will continue to divide into the information rich and the information poor."

Ferguson's work is part of a sizeable body of literature that argues that market forces alone will not lead to equality of information opportunity but rather may be expected to reflect existing socioeconomic inequalities if left to the market. Authors who have made this argument, usually recommending proactive government information policy as a remedy, include Pavlik and Thalhimer (1994), King and Kraemer (1995), and Calabrese and Borchert (1996), and Seneviratne (2000). In the same vein, Riedel et al. (1998: 385), in a case study of a computer outreach project, found that in addressing information inequality, even government efforts to provide access were likely only to reinforce inequality unless affirmative efforts, beyond mere access, were made to give priority to information have-nots. The calls for affirmative governmental action dovetail with studies that detail the conflict of global information forces with diverse national laws — a conflict that forces government action in its own right (Kahin and Nesson, 1997).

To take a negative example, lack of effective government efforts in promotion of networking has demonstrable adverse effects. This was illustrated by the Russian economy after the dissolution of the Soviet Union. When Russia attempted to convert to a market economy following the fall of Communism in the early 1990s, privatization created an overwhelming volume of stock. However, Russia lacked automated systems for handling stock exchanges and other economic transactions taken for granted in the West. Through neglect, inefficiency, and a restrictive security-centered national policy, telecommunications links were woefully inadequate. Data communications were largely reserved for the military and communication outside a local area was in most cases essentially impossible. All of this constituted a staggering obstacle to reviving the Russian economy (Parady, 1991). Though a dramatic case, most modern industrial countries are being forced in one way or another to face up to the question of the role of government under global information economies (cf. Carnoy et al., 1993).

The global integrationist perspective approaches evangelical urgency, as in the work of Hedley (1999: 86–87), who concluded his study of global information system inequalities with the remark "to the extent that apartheid and cultural imperialism, that is, processes of exclusion, continue to gain in ascendancy, there is diminishing likelihood of the inclusive global village option... At stake is the very survival of our species." This was echoed by Nelson Mandela, speaking at the Telecom95 conference in Geneva, "Nevertheless, one gulf will not be easily bridged — that is the division between the information rich and the information poor. Justice and equity demand that we find ways of overcoming it. If more than half the world is denied access to means of communication, the people of developing countries will not be fully part of the modern world" (quoted in Pfister, 1999: 88). Indeed, evangelical overtones of liberation theology pervade even the work of Feenberg (1995), a leading scholar of the philosophy of technology (discussed below).

The global integrationist perspective is not at all limited to advocates for developing nations or the poor, nor is there agreement within the global integrationist camp on liberal vs. conservative policy. No less an economic authority than international financier George Soros was recently quoted in *Newsweek* as agreeing with the dystopians that new global financial mechanisms, made possible by new global information systems, can have dysfunctional effects that tear at the fabric of the world economy. "It is difficult to escape the conclusion," Soros (1998: 82) wrote, "that the international financial system itself is the main culprit in the meltdown process." He went on to observe that, "I think that financial markets, particularly the global markets, need greater supervision." That is,

Soros preaches the gospel of global integration, foreseeing a future in which as-yet unspecified transnational organizations will bring discipline to multinational financial firms by limiting their ability to leverage instant economic information through the global reallocation of investments.

Likewise, Winn (2000) has noted that the acceleration in the growth of the global information economy caused by advances in IT is challenging the ability of financial markets to adapt, and the growth of global networked information systems creates threats to the safety and soundness of financial markets because information and transactions can flow more quickly and easily across borders, destabilizing markets in more than one country. The logical corollary is that nations should act aggressively to protect their sovereignty in the information age. This view is reflected, for instance, in the writings of Golden (1998), a military officer, in which he argues for the development of a national information policy focusing on exploiting American advantages as a strategic broker of global protocols for technological competition and the principles for military integration.

Many other writers also see a real-world emergence of technological global integrationism as a public policy priority. Bellamy (2000), for instance, concluded, "a crossnational consensus about the significance for government of information-age technologies is emerging among countries of the developed world." She cited as evidence of this emerging consensus various ICT plans promulgated by the European Union's Information Society Initiative, the G7 Government Online Project, the International Council for Information Technology in Government Administration, and country-specific information plans in the U.K., Australia, and the U.S. Additional European and American governmental ICT planning efforts are detailed in Garson (1995: chaps. 7 and 8).

Underlying the form of optimism found in global integration theory is a rejection of technological determinism, whether utopian or dystopian. Ultimately, what binds global integration theory together is a belief that humankind has the potential to transcend the thought patterns of the workplace and even of nationality to embrace global thinking. This is apparent, for instance, in the work of Lyman (1996), who views the present state of cyberspace as one transcending its origins in command-and-control technology. Rather, Lyman (1996: 10) argues, "the most urgent agenda of an information policy may be the creation of a public culture for cyberspace, one that fulfills the criterion for public art, reassociating cyberspace with common rituals and concerns." The creation of a global culture is made possible and desirable by technology. Like Ferguson and others of this perspective, however, Lyman does not make the argument that possibility will lead to forecastable probability. That is, global integration theory remains possibilistic, not deterministic.

Similarly, Schroeder (1996) noted that what Max Weber called the "disenchantment" of the individual from the world, due to the replacement of mysticism by impersonal scientific explanation, impels people to "re-enchant" their lives. Schroeder argued that computer-generated worlds hold a compelling attraction for such people. This "social dynamic," as he titled his book, is one which is said to be destined to flower in a cyberculture fusing scientific means and imaginative ends, creating a global cultural force of the type contemplated by Lyman as well.

More recently Feenberg (1991), a leader in the philosophy of technology, has put the argument about alienation and technological bondage of the individual in more positive terms: the human mind, he theorizes, can only assume a "free relation" to technology when technology is designed to operate democratically. Without democratization, technological rationality no longer conforms to social rationality. Feenberg (1995: 2) subsequently wrote, "The philosophy of technology is adjusting gradually to the emergence of technical politics. Until recently it polarized around two contrary positions: we were obliged to choose between uncritical acceptance of the claims made for technology or the uncompromising rejection of its dystopian powers." That is, Feenberg's stance is generally consistent with the global integrationist perspective, rejecting both the market-forces optimism of democratization/empowerment theory and the technological determinism of critical theory while calling for political action to achieve through government the objectives other theorists believe will come through the marketplace.

Summers (1999) summarized the global integrationist viewpoint in a distinguished lecture on economics and government, in which he held that "there is more potential for increased international economic integration than is usually recognized" (p. 6) because "continuing improvements in technology, increasing skill levels in developing countries, the spread of cross-border organizations — all of these are operating to increase global integration" (p. 12). Summers acknowledges global integration brings great benefits, but he emphasizes the same technology-driven global integration also inevitably circumscribes governments' ability to correct market failures. He writes, "just at the time that integration may be increasing the desire for policies that insure citizens, it may also be making important income generators more mobile, thus reducing the capacity for insurance and redistribution." He goes on to argue that those favoring international integration have an obligation to press for more effective international efforts to insure that the public interest in correcting market failures is defended, as is the democratic structure under which citizens live in a balanced economy managed by their elected representatives. Technology-driven global integration is seen as a fundamental threat to national sovereignty, but Summers also believes thoughtful national and international policies may yet protect democratic governance.

VI. CONCLUSION

Schools of thought rarely emerge without a powerful theoretical basis. Each of the four perspectives outlined in this chapter is rooted in its own dimension of strength. For democratization/empowerment theory, that dimension is the market-driven spread of ICT with consequent great socioeconomic opportunities providing a basis for the broadly optimistic perspective of this approach.. For critical theory, strength lies in its understanding that ICT is a tool, and that tools tend not so much to change social relations as to reinforce existing patterns, notably patterns of inequality within and among nations. The strength of sociotechnical theory is its understanding of technological change as a profoundly human and political one, requiring a holistic rather than technocratic approach to organizational adaptation to new technologies. Finally, the strengths of the global integrationist approach are its rejection of both the optimistic and pessimistic versions of technological determinism, its global perspective, and the fact that its call for proactive government information policies conforms so closely to the real-world politics and processes of various national and international governmental bodies.

For social scientists, the purpose of theory is to pose plausible predictions of the future as the basis for research agendas. Democratization/empowerment theory predicts a future of pluralistic use of ICT based on ever-greater acceptance of the market forces associated with it. The research agenda for public administration associated with this approach is focused on documenting the evolution of pluralism in the varieties of ICT use in government, relating the new capacities born of ICT to greater reliance on market mechanisms in performing government functions, to democratization of organizational hierarchies, and to individual transformation and development of social capital through virtual communication, education, and work.

Critical theory predicts a future of widening informational inequality and consequently of widening organizational and political inequality. The research agenda for public administration associated with this approach is focused on documenting the social inequalities of the "information revolution" by class, race, gender, and state of national economic development, relating the new capacities of ICT to national strategies for maintaining economic superiority, elite strategies for reinforcing boundary-maintaining functions within organizations, and to individual alienation through virtual communication, education, and work.

Sociotechnical theory is, as we have seen, middle-range theory focused at the organizational level. It predicts organizational success and comparative advantage when ICT implementation is holistic rather than technocratic. Its research agenda for public administration is therefore implementation-focused, seeking to establish the correlation between implementation success and the integration of social, political, and economic factors with technological ones.

Finally, global integrationist theory predicts a future, naturally, of global integration. Its research agenda for public administration is focused on national and international public policies toward ICT, looking at the interrelationship among use of the marketplace to foster technological development, national strategies for comparative advantage, and global issues of public interest in the era of multinational corporations. At the organizational level, global integrationist theory focuses attention on what was once framed as the question of whether "What is good for General Motors is good for the country," as asserted by an erstwhile head of that corporation. At the individual level, the research agenda of global integrationist theory focuses on the impact on the worker in a global economy, with changed demands and possibilities in not only work and remuneration, but in education and culture as well, as global integration wrought by ICT impinges on every aspect of the ordinary life of individuals.

In conclusion, one might be tempted to observe that each of the four theoretical perspectives discussed in this chapter represents a portion of the truth, implying the need to meld all perspectives into one. Before succumbing to this temptation, it is well to remember the purpose of theory in the first place is to generate hypotheses to be investigated through the research agendas that flow from them. If this is the purpose, then perhaps it is useful to have multiple strong theories rather than a unitary muddled one that carries us back to the view, noted at the beginning of this chapter, which holds that ICT is so complex that predictive theory is an impossibility. Those who hold that technology is complex and situational, defying generalization, are in an intellectually safe position, rarely criticized, yet in conclusion I must ask whether those who have articulated strong theories have not contributed more to the scientific process in the end?

REFERENCES

Abbott, A., Things of boundaries, *Social Research*, 62, 857–882, 1995.
Abramson, J.B., Arterton, F.C., and Orren, G.R., *The Electronic Commonwealth: The Impact of New Media Technologies on Democratic Politics*, Basic Books, New York, 1988.

Adler, P., *Machines as the Measure of Man: Science, Technology, and Ideologies of Western Dominance*, Cornell University Press, Ithaca, NY, 1989.

Adler, P., The 'learning bureaucracy': new united motor manufacturing, Inc., *Research in Organizational Behavior*, 15, 111–194, 1991.

Agres, C., Edberg, D., and Igbaria, M., Transformation to virtual societies: forces and issues, *The Information Society*, 2, 71–82, 1998.

Agre, P.E., Real-time politics: the Internet and the political process, *The Information Society*, 18, 311–331, 2002.

Alexander, C.J. and Pal, L.A., Eds., *Digital Democracy: Policy and Politics in the Wired World*, Oxford University Press, New York, 1998.

Aronowitz, S. and DiFazio, W., *The Jobless Future*, University of Minnesota Press, Minneapolis, MN, 1995.

Becker, T. and Scarce, R., Teledemocracy Emergent: State of the Art and Science, American Political Science Association 1984 Annual Meeting, Washington, D.C., Aug. 30–Sept. 2, 1984.

Bellamy, C., The politics of public sector information systems, in *Handbook of Public Information Systems*, Garson, G.D., Ed., Marcel Dekker, New York, 2000.

Beusmans, J. and Wieckert, K., Computing, research, and war: if knowledge is power, where is responsibility?, *Communications of the ACM*, 32, 939–951, 1989.

Bimber, B., The Internet and political mobilization: research note on the 1996 election season, *Social Science Computer Review*, 16, 391–401, 1998.

Blackler, F. and Oborne, D., Eds., *Information Technology and People: Designing for the Future*, British Psychological Society, Letchworth, U.K., 1987.

Blanchard, A. and Horan, T., Virtual communities and social capital, *Social Science Computer Review*, 16, 393–307, 1998.

Bonchek, M., A Grassroots in Cyberspace: Using Computer Networks to Facilitate Political Participation, paper presented to the Midwest Political Science Association, Annual Meeting, Chicago, 1995.

Bovard, M.G. and Bouvard, J., Computerized information and effective protection of individual rights, *Society*, 12, 62–68, 1975.

Braman, S., The autopoietic state: communication and democratic potential in the Net, *Journal of the American Society for Information Science*, 45, 358–368, 1994.

Burnham, D., *The Rise of the Computer State*, Pantheon Books, New York, 1983.

Burris, B., *Technocracy at Work*, State University of New York Press, Albany, NY, 1993.

Bush, V., As We May Think, *The Atlantic Monthly*, 1945. Reprinted in *Computer-Supported Cooperative Work: A book of readings*, Greif, I., Ed., Morgan-Kaufman, San Mateo, CA, 1988.

Calabrese, A. and Borchert, M., Prospects for electronic democracy in the United States: rethinking communications and social policy, *Media, Culture, and Society*, 18, 249–268, 1996.

Caporael, L., Computers, prophecy, and experience: a historical perspective, *Journal of Social Issues*, 40, 15–29, 1984.

Carnoy, M., Castells, M., Cohen, S.S., and Cardoso, F., Eds., *The New Global Economy in the Information Age: Reflections on Our Changing World*, Pennsylvania State University Press, University Park, PA, 1993.

Castells, M., *The Information Age: Economy, Society, and Culture, Vol. 1: The Rise of the Network Society*, Blackwell, Oxford, 1996.

Castells, M., *The Information Age: Economy, Society, and Culture, Vol. 2: The Power of Identity*, Blackwell, Oxford, 1997.

Castells, M., *The Information Age: Economy, Society, and Culture, Vol. 3: The End of the Millenium*, Blackwell, Oxford, 1998.

Chisholm, R.F., Introducing advanced information technology into public organizations, *Public Productivity Review*, 11, 39–56, 1988.

Cohen, C., Electronic democracy, *PC World*, 2, 21–22, 1984.

Cohill, A.M. and Kavanaugh, A.L., Eds., *Community Networks: Lessons from Blacksburg*, Artech House, Virginia, Boston, 1997.

Conomikes, G., Computers are creating personnel problems, *Personnel Journal*, 46, 52–53, 1967.

Coyne, R.D., *Designing Information Technology in the Postmodern Age: From Method to Metaphor*, MIT Press, Cambridge, MA, 1995.

Coyne, R.D., *Technoromanticism: Digital Narrative, Holism, and the Romance of the Real*, MIT Press, Cambridge, MA, 1999.

Coyne, R. and Wiszniewski, D., Technical Deceits: Critical Theory, Hermeneutics and the Ethics of Information Technology, Proceedings of the Second International Workshop on Philosophy of Design and Information Technology: Ethics in Information Technology Design, 9–10 December, Saint-Ferréol, Toulouse, France, pp. 35–44, 1999.
Available at: http://www.caad.ed.ac.uk/~richard/FullPublications/TechnicalDeceits.pdf Retrieved on 11/24/2003.

Curtis, T., The information society: a computer-generated caste system?, in *The Political Economy of Information*, Mosco V. and Wasko, J., Eds., University of Wisconsin Press, Madison, WI, pp. 95–107, 1988.

Danziger, J.N., Dutton, W.H., Kling, R., and Kraemer, K.L., *Computers and Politics: High Technology in American Local Governments*, Columbia University Press, New York, 1982.

Derber, C. and Schwartz, W., New mandarins or new proletariat? Professional power at work, *Research in the Sociology of Organizations*, 8, 71–96, 1991.

Donner, F.J., *The Age of Surveillance*, Random House, New York, 1981.

Downs, A., A realistic look at the final payoffs from urban data systems, *Public Administration Review*, 77, 204–210, 1967.

Emery, F.E., Ed., *Systems Thinking*, Penguin Books, New York, 1969.

Emery, F.E. and Trist, E.L., The causal texture of organizational environments, *Human Relations*, (18), 21–32, 1965.

Falk, J., The meaning of the Web, *The Information Society*, 14, 285–293, 1998.

Feenberg, A., *Critical Theory of Technology*, Oxford University Press, Oxford, 1991.

Feenberg, A., *Alternative Modernity: The Technical Turn in Philosophy and Social Theory*, University of California Press., Berkeley, CA, 1995.

Feenberg, A. and Hannay, A., Eds., *Technology and the Politics of Knowledge*, Indiana University Press, Bloomington, IN, 1995.

Ferguson, K., World information flows and the impact of new technology, *Social Science Computer Review*, 16, 252–267, 1998.

Fisher, D.R., Rumoring theory and the Internet: a framework for analyzing the grass roots, *Social Science Computer Review*, 16, 158–168, 1998.

Frosini, V., Social implications of the computer revolution: advantages and disadvantages, *Informatica e Diritto*, 13, 7–23, 1987.

Garson, G.D., *Computer Technology and Social Issues*, Idea Group, Hershey, PA, 1995.

Garson, G.D., Technological teleology and the theory of technology enactment: the case of the International Trade Data System, *Social Science Computer Review*, 21, 2003.

Gascó, M., New technologies and institutional change in public administration, *Social Science Computer Review*, 21, 6–14, 2003.

Golden, J.R., *Economics and National Strategy in the Information Age : Global Networks, Technology Policy, and Cooperative Competition*, Praeger, New York, 1998.

Grafton, C., "Shadow Theories" in Fountain's theory of technology enactment, *Social Science Computer Review*, 21, 2003.

Grossman, L.K., *The Electronic Republic: Reshaping Democracy in the Information Age*, Viking, New York, 1995.

Gurak, L., *Persuasion and Privacy in Cyberspace*, Yale University Press, New Haven, CT, 1997.

Haywood, T., *Info-rich–Info-poor : Access and Exchange in the Global Information Society*, K. G. Saur, Munich, Germany, 1995.

Heckscher, C. and Donnellon, A., Eds., *The Post-bureaucratic Organization: New Perspectives on Organizational Change*, Sage, Thousand Oaks, CA, 1994.

Hedley, R.A., The information age: apartheid, cultural imperialism, or global village?, *Social Science Computer Review*, 17, 78–87, 1999.

Heintz, T. and Bretschneider, S., IT and restructuring organizations: do IT related structural changes improve organizational performance?, *Journal of Public Administration Research and Theory*, 10, 801–830, 2000.

Henman, P. and Adler, M., Information technology and the governance of social security, *Critical Social Policy*, 23, 139–164, 2003.

Hiltz, R.S. and Turoff, M., *The Network Nation: Human Communication via the Computer*, Addison-Wesley, Reading, MA, 1978.

Hood, C., Where the state of the art meets the art of the state: traditional public-bureaucracy controls in the information age, *International Review of Public Administration* (South Korea), 5, 1–12, 2000.

Howley, K., Equity, access, and participation in community networks, *Social Science Computer Review*, 16, 402–410, 1998.

Huntington, S.P., The West: unique, not universal, *Foreign Affairs*, 75, 28–46, 1996.

Inman, B.R. and Burton, D.F., Jr., Technology and competitiveness: the new policy frontier, *Foreign Affairs*, 69, 116–134, 1990.

Kahin, B. and Nesson, C., Eds., *Borders in Cyberspace: Information Policy and the Global Information Infrastructure*, MIT Press, Cambridge, MA, 1997. (Publication of the Harvard Information Infrastructure Project.)

Kedzie, C.R., *Democracy and Network Interconnectivity*, RAND, Santa Monica, CA, 1995.

Kember, S., *Cyberfeminism and Artificial Life*, Routledge, London, 2003.

Kenney, M. and Florida, R., *Beyond Mass Production: The Japanese System and its Transfer to the U.S.*, Oxford University Press, New York, 1993.

Kiesler, S., Siegel, J., and McGuire, T.W., Social psychological aspects of computer-mediated communication, in *Computerization and Controversy: Value Conflicts and Social Choices*, Dunlop, C. and Kling, R., Eds., Academic Press, San Diego, CA, 1991, pp. 330–349.

King, J.L. and Kraemer, K.L., Information infrastructure, national policy, and global competitiveness, *Information Infrastructure and Policy*, 4, 5–28, 1995.

Kolleck, B., Computer information and human knowledge: new thinking and old critique, in *Technology in People Services: Research, Theory, and Applications*, Leiderman, M., Guzetta, C., Struminger, L., and Monnickendam, M., Eds., Haworth Press, New York, 1993, pp. 455–464.

Kraemer, K.L. and Dedrick. J., Computing and public organizations, *Journal of Public Administration Research and Theory*, 7, 89–112, 1997.

Kraemer, K.L. and King, J.L., Computing and public organizations, *Public Administration Review*, (46), 488–496, 1986.

Kroker, A. and Weinstein, M.A., *Data Trash: The Theory of the Virtual Class*, St. Martin's Press, New York, 1994.

Kyem, P.A.K., Examining the discourse about the transfer of GIS technology to traditionally non-Western societies, *Social Science Computer Review*, 17, 1999 (Forthcoming).

Loch, K.D. and Conger, S., Evaluating ethical decisions and computer use, *Communications of the ACM*, 39, 48–60, 1996.

Lyman, P., What is a digital library?, *Daedalus*, 125, 1–33, 1996.

Mann, J., *Tomorrow's Global Community: How the Information Deluge is Transforming Business and Government*, Bainbridge Books, 1998.

Martin, W.J., *The Global Information Society*, Ashgate, Brookfield, VT, 1995.

Mathews, J.T., Power shift, *Foreign Affairs*, 76, 50–66, 1997.

McChesney, R.W., Wood, E.M., and Foster, J.B., Eds., *Capitalism and the Information Age : The Political Economy of the Global Communication Revolution*, Monthly Review Press, New York, 1998.

McCullough, M.F., Democratic questions for the computer age, *Computers in Human Services*, 8, 9–18, 1991.

McLuhan, M., *Understanding the Media*, McGraw-Hill, New York, 1964.

Messmer, J., Carreiro, D., and Metivier-Carreiro, K.A., Cyber-communication: congressional use of information technologies, in *Handbook of Public Information Systems*, Garson, G.D., Ed., Marcel Dekker, NewYork, 2000.

Michaelson, K.L., Information, community, and access, *Social Science Computer Review*, 14, 57–59, 1996.

Mosco, V., *The Political Economy of Communication: Rethinking and Renewal*, Sage, London, 1996.

Mosco, V., Myth-ink links: power and community on the information highway, *The Information Society*, 14, 57–62, 1998.

Mumford, E., Sociotechnical systems design: evolving theory and practice, in *Computers and Democracy*, Bjerknes, G., Ehn, P., and Kyng, M., Eds., Aldershot, Avebury, U.K., pp. 59–76, 1987.

Naisbitt, J.M., *Megatrends: Ten New Directions Transforming Our Lives*, Warner Books, New York, 1982.

Negroponte, N., *Being Digital*, Knopf, New York, 1995.

Northrop, A. and Kraemer, K.L., The information age: which nations will benefit?, in *Handbook of Public Information Systems*, Garson, G.D., Ed., Marcel Dekker, New York, 2000.

Novotny, P., The World Wide Web and multimedia in the 1996 presidential election, *Social Science Computer Review*, 16, 169–184, 1998.

Parady, J.E., Free market at last: but the lack of a technology infrastructure presents an awesome obstacle, *InformationWeek*, (July 15), 60, 1991.

Pavlik, J.V. and Thalhimer, M.A., Roundtable: sizing up prospects for a national information service, in *The People's Right to Know: Media, Democracy and the Information Highway*, Williams, F. and Pavlik, J.V., Eds., Hillsdale, Erlbaum, NJ, 1994, pp. 69–104.

Perelman, M., *Class Warfare in the Information Age*, St. Martin's Press, New York, 1998.

Pfister, R., Africa's right to information: a review of past developments and future prospects, *Social Science Computer Review*, 17, 88–106, 1999.

Piore, M.J. and Sabel, C.F. *The Second Industrial Divide: Possibilities for Prosperity*, Basic Books, New York, 1984.

Putnam, R.D., with Leonardi, R. and Nanetti, R.Y., *Making Democracy Work: Civic Traditions in Modern Italy*, Princeton University Press, Princeton, NJ, 1993.

Putnam, R.D., Bowling alone: America's declining social capital, *Journal of Democracy*, 6, 65–78, 1995a.

Putnam, R.D., Tuning in, tuning out: the strange disappearance of social capital in America, *Political Science and Politics*, 28, 664–683, 1995b.

Rawlins, G.J.E., *Moths to the Flame: The Seductions of Computer Culture*, MIT Press, Cambridge, MA,. 1997.

Reich, R., *The Work of Nations*, Oxford University Press, Oxford, 1992.

Reinecke, I., *Electronic Illusions: A Skeptic's View of Our High Tech Future*, Penguin, New York, 1984.

Reschenthaler, G.B. and Thompson, F., The information revolution and the new public management, *Journal of Public Administration Research and Theory*, 6, 125–143, 1996.

Rheingold, H., *The Virtual Community: Homesteading on the Electronic Frontier*, Addison-Wesley, Reading, MA, 1994.

Riedel, E., Dresel, L., Wagoner, M.J., Sullivan, J.L., and Borgida, E., Electronic communities: accessing equality of access in a rural Minnesota community, *Social Science Computer Review*, 16, 370–390, 1998.

Rifkin, J., *The End of Work: The Decline of the Global Labor Force and the Dawn of the Post-market Era*, Putnam, New York, 1995.

Rochlin, G.I., *Trapped in the Net: The Unanticipated Consequences of Computerization*, Princeton University Press, Princeton, NJ, 1997.

Rubens, J., Retooling American democracy, *Futurist*, 17, 59–64, 1983.

Rushkoff, D., *Media Virus! Hidden Agendas in Popular Culture*, Ballantine Books, New York, 1996.

Sackman, H. and Nie, N., Eds., *The Information Utility and Social Choice*, AFIPS Press, Montvale, NJ, 1970.

Sale, K., *Rebels Against the Future: The Luddites and Their War on the Industrial Revolution — Lessons for the Computer Age*, Perseus Press, New York, 1996.

Schiller, H., *Information Inequality: The Deepening Social Crisis in America*, Doubleday, New York, 1996.

Schroeder, R., *Possible Worlds: The Social Dynamic of Virtual Reality Technology*, Westview Press, Boulder, CO, 1996.

Schuler, D., *New Community Networks: Wired for Change*, ACM, New York, 1996.

Selnow, G.W., Electronic whistle-stops: the impact of the Internet on American politics, in *Political Communication Series*, Praeger, Westport, CT, 1998.

Seneviratne, S.J., Is technological progress social progress?, in pp, 71–84 *Handbook of Public Information Systems*, Garson, G.D., Ed., Marcel Dekker, New York, 2000.

Shi, Y. and Scavo, C., Citizen participation and direct democracy through computer networking, in *Handbook of Public Information Systems*, Garson, G.D., Ed., Marcel Dekker, New York, 2000.

Slouka, M., *War of the Worlds: Cyberspace and the High-Tech Assault on Reality*, Basic Books, New York, 1996.

Soros, G., The Crisis of Global Capitalism, *Newsweek*, Dec. 7, 1998, pp. 78–86.

Stallabrass, J., Empowering technology: the exploration of cyberspace, *New Left Review*, 211, 3–32, 1995.

Stefik, M., *Internet Dreams: Archetypes, Myths, and Metaphor*, MIT Press, Cambridge, MA, 1996.

Stewart, J. and Williams, R., The coevolution of society and multimedia technology, *Social Science Computer Review*, 16, 268–282, 1998.

Stoll, C., *Silicon Snake-Oil: Second Thoughts on the Information Highway*, Doubleday, New York, 1995.

Summers, L.H., Distinguished lecture on economics in government: reflections on managing global integration, *Journal of Economic Perspectives*, 13, 3–18, 1999.

Talbott, S.L., *The Future Does Not Compute: Transcending the Machines in Our Midst*, O'Reilly and Associates, Sebastopol, CA, 1995.

Tapscott, D. and Caston, A., *Paradigm Shift*, McGraw-Hill, New York, 1992.

Targowski, A.S., Global information infrastructure: the birth, vision, and architecture, in *Global Information Technology Management Series*, Idea Group, Hershey, PA, 1998.

Tepas, D., Introductory remarks. Behavior research methods and instrumentation, (4), 42–43, 1972.

Thomas, R., *What Machines Can't Do: Politics and Technology in the Industrial Enterprise*, University of California Press, Berkeley, CA, 1994.

Toffler, A., *The Third Wave*, William Morrow/Bantam Books, New York, 1980.

Trist, E.L., *Organizations and Technical Change*, Tavistock Institute of Human Relations, London, 1973.

Trist, E.L., The Evolution of Sociotechnical Systems: A Conceptual Framework and an Action Research Program, Ontario Quality of Working Life Center, Occasional Paper No. 2, Toronto, June, 1981.

Trist, E.L., Emery, F., Murray, H., and Trist, B., Eds., *The Social Engagement of Social Science: A Tavistock Anthology, Vol. 23: The Socio-ecological Perspective*, University of Pennsylvania Press, Philadelphia, PA, 1997.

Trist, E. and Murray, H., *The Social Engagement of Social Science: A Tavistock Anthology, Vol. 2: The Socio-technical Perspective*, University of Pennsylvania Press, Philadelphia, PA, 1990.

Tsagarousianiu, R., Tambini, D., and Bryan, C., *Boice and Equality: Civic Voluntarism in American Politics*, Harvard University Press, Cambridge, MA, 1998.

Vallas, S., Manufacturing knowledge: technology, culture, and social inequality at work, *Social Science Computer Review*, 16, 353–369, 1998.

Weizenbaum, J., *Computer Power and Human Reason: From Judgment to Calculation*, W. H. Freeman, San Francisco, 1976.

Whyte, W.F., Socio-technical systems, in *Creative Problem Solving in the Field: Reflections on a Career*, Whyte, W.F., Ed., Walnut Creek, Altamira, CA, 1997, pp. 57–62.

Wicklein, J., *Electronic Nightmare*, Viking, New York, 1979.

Winn, J.K., Catalytic impact of information technology on the new international financial architecture, *The International Lawyer*, 34, 2000
http://www.law.washington.edu/faculty/winn/Publications/Catalytic%20Impact%20of%20Information.htm
Retrieved on 11/24/2003.

Wittig, M.A. and Schmitz, J., Electronic grassroots organizing, *Journal of Social Issues*, 52, 53–69, 1996.

Wresch, W., *Disconnected: Haves and Have-Nots in the Information Age*, Rutgers University Press, New Brunswick, NJ, 1996.

Wresch, W., Information access in Africa: problems with every channel, *The Information Society*, 14, 295–300, 1998.

Zuboff, S., *In the Age of the Smart Machine: The Future of Work and Power*, Basic Books, New York, 1988.

INDEX

A
Access to IT, 174
Actor-Network Theory (ANT), 648
Agency website enhancement, 560
American Enterprise Institute (AEI), 261
American Society of Public Administration, 5, 108
Application of Internet taxes, 289–290
Application service providers (ASPs), 408
Army Enterprise Infostructure Transformation (AEIT), 230
ARPANET, 28–30
Artificial intelligence, 432
Atrium model, 232–233f

B
Balanced scorecard, 442
Bangemann report, 646–647
Best of the Web, 547
Bifurcated governance, 110–111
Bounded rationality, 356
Budget model, 428, 433–435, 452–456
Budgeting, 464
Business Systems Modernization (BSM), program, 378

C
California Voter Foundation, 262
CAN–SPAM, 40
Case Studies
   E-government in Florida, 335
   Georgia's consumer services, 353
   IT and the New York state legislation, 321
   Nonmonetary agreements in the IRS E-file program, 369
Casework, 327–329, 332–333
CCJ/COSCA guidelines, 576
CD-ROM, 392, 395–396
Center for Responsive Politics, 262
Centraal Planbeaureau in Holland, 449
Chief Financial Officers Act (COFA), 30
Classic performance budgeting, *see* Economics-based budget reforms

Clinger–Cohen Act (CCA), 12–13, 16, 22, 33, 145–146, 607, 609; *see also* E-government
   Executive Order 13011, 34
Collaboration, 321–325, 328, 330–332
Commercial off-the-shelf Software (COTS), 411
Communication Decency Act (CDA), 33
Communication technology, 582
Computer-based information system (CBIS), 146
Computer-based training, 7, 392, 395
   CD-ROM, 395
   expert systems, 395
   games, 397
   in public sector, 7, 391
   online courses, 401
   virtual reality, 397
Computer Fraud and Abuse Act (CFAA), 30
Computer networking, 255, 266, 275
   citizen participation, 265
Computer Security Act, 601, 606
Contract
   contract management, 47–48
   contract mechanism, 47
Controlling the Assault of Non-solicited Pornography Act (CAN-SPAM), 40
Copyrights, 190, 197
Cosmopolitanism, 108–109, 111–113, 116–117, 123
   concepts of, 113
Criminal justice sharing efforts, 66
   local-local efforts, 66
   pull strategies, 66
   push strategies, 66
   query, 66
   state-local efforts, 66
Critical theory, 671
   amplification theory, 671
Cyber security, 203
   computer misuse, 206, 208
      abuse of authority, 206
      direct penetration, 207

Cyber security, (*continued*)
 direct probing, 206
 human error, 206
 malicious software, 207
 subversion of security mechanism, 207
 secure system construction, 211
 cost of security, 215
 economy of mechanism, 212
 fail-safe defaults, 212
 least privilege, 211
 open design, 213
 security policy, 209
Cyber Security Research and Development Act
 (CSRDA), 39

D
Data sharing, 143
 initiatives, 149
 XML, 151
 research, 147
Decision making, 508
Decision support system, 128, 507
De-escalation process, 98–100
Democratic theory, 248–250
Democratization/empowerment theory,
 667–671
Department of Management Services (DMS),
 337
Depository Library Program, 27
Digital agencies, 560
Digital Daily, 377, 382, 385
Digital divide, 173–175, 182–183
 control variables, 177
 gender, 176
 geographic location, 176
 race, 175
Digital government
 initiatives and change processes, 12, 87
Digital government efforts, 157
Digital infrastructure, 174
Digital place design, 528–529
Digital sunlight, 262
Double taxation, 286, 296
Dual use technologies, 229
Dystopian theory, 257

E
E-activism, 244
Early Notification System (ENS)
 history, 587
 technological and institutional implication,
 594
Economic crisis of 1930, 434
Economic Opportunity Act, 589

Economics-based budget reforms, 466
 classic performance budgeting, 466–467
 performance budgeting, 475–479
 program budgeting, 468–473
 software tools, 482–484
E-democracy, 264, 269, 631, 643, 645–647
E-Europe Action Plan, 646
Effectiveness indicator, 429
E-file, 370–371, 375–380
E-governance, 108–110, 113, 123
E-government, 8, 83, 108, 149, 237, 336, 370,
 374, 545, 570, 599, 615, 643
 dysfunctions, 85
 Electronic Government Act 2002, 39
 initiatives, 87
 IT performance-based Laws, 602t
 Clinger–Cohen Act 1996, 602t, 607
 Computer Security Act of 1987, 602t, 606
 Government Information Security Reform
 Act of 2001, 602t, 608
 Government Paperwork Elimination Act of
 1998, 602t, 608
 Paperwork Reduction Acts of 1980 and
 1995, 602t, 604
 programs, 86
 public management model, 85
 strategy, 37
 theory of locals and cosmopolitans, 108, 113
 cosmopolitan, 112, 117
 locals, 111, 120
 typology, 618
E-government Act, 600–601, 610–611, 615–616
E-learning, 394
Electronic access, 573
 practical obscurity, 572–573
Electronic-based innovation, 248
Electronic bulletin board communication, 113
Electronic data, 143
Electronic Early Notification System (ENS),
 583
 as technological innovation, 594
 case analysis of, 587
 implementation of, 590–593
 limitations of, 594–595
Electronic infrastructure, 693
Electronic judicial records, 569
 access policies, 573
 legal principles, 571
Electronic Performance Support Systems
 (EPSS), 394, 396–398
Electronic Tax Administration (ETA), 377
 organization 370, 371, 385
E-mail, 257, 261, 263–265, 269–270, 276, 278
Enterprise resource planning (ERP), 94

Enterprise-wide projects, 98
E-parliament, 640
E-readiness guide, 529
E-rulemaking, 237–240, 242–244, 246–248, 250
    challenges, 240, 243
    data collection, 240
    IT tools, 242
Escalation of commitment, 95; *see also*
        Information Technology
Ethnography, 115, 116
Ethnomethodological technique, 108
Expert systems, 393, 395–396, 432

F
Fair Activities Inventory Reform Act (FAIR), 35
Federal Acquisition Streamlining Act (FASA), 32
Federal Advisory Committee Act (FACA), 29
Federal Information Security Management Act
        (FISMA), 39
Federal State Intergovernmental sharing, 70, 74
Federal Voting Rights Act, 268

G
Games, 397
Games and simulation, 397
Gateway number, 326
Geographic information system (GIS), 20, 24,
        60, 65
Global integration theory, 679–682
Global Internet Tax Freedom Act, 282
Global positioning system (GPS), 225
Global supply-chain integration systems, 94
Goods and Service Tax (GST), 286, 287
Governance, 157
    diffusion of the web, 162
    interactivity, 160
    measurement, 158
    openness, 157
    performance, 163–164
    transparency, 159
Governance and WWW, 155
Government effectiveness, 155
Government governance, 443–444
Government Information Locator Service
        (GILS), 32
Government Information Security Reform Act
        (GISRA), 608–610
Government Paperwork Elimination Act, 608
Government performance, 156–157, 162–164
Government Performance and Results Act
        (GPRA), 31, 601
Governmental Management Information
        Sciences (GMIS), organization, 64
Gross domestic product, 303

H
High-Performance Computing Act, 31
Homeland security, 150
Human resource accounting, 445

I
ICMA, 548
I-fighters, 232
Informal sharing, 59, 67, 74–75, 77
Information, 104, 143–151, 506
Information acquisition, 258
Information age war, 224
Information and communication technology
        (ICT), 3, 10, 27, 83–84
Information and Technology Act, 31
Information asymmetry, 97
Information ecology, 541
Information Quality Act, 36
Information revolution, 301
Information society, 645
Information technology (IT), 11, 93, 127, 143,
        407, 581, 666
    Brainbench report, 13
    de-escalation theory, 95
    escalation theory, 94–95
    failure to commitment, 100
    informative, 135, 138, 138f
    introduction, 12, 582
        growth in public sector, 12
        IT failures, 16, 93
        IT management, 14, 22
        software application, 13
    instruction system application use, 17
    methodology and data collection, 16
    outsourcing, 407, 413, 419
        choosing a vendor, 416
        Project and Risk Management, 420
        pros and cons, 415
    projects
        de-escalating, 94–95, 102
        escalating, 94–95, 98–103
    public budgeting, 463
        classic performance budgeting, 466
        performance budgeting, 475
        program budgeting, 468
        zero-based budgeting, 475
    strategic, 135
    transactional, 135, 138
    training, 17
        applications, 19
        CCA concepts, 22–23
        Microcomputing in MPA curricula, 18,
            20–21
Information and militaries, 219, 221, 231

Information and militaries, (*continued*)
  Gold Standards, 229
  U.S. model of IT-enabled military, 226
Information sharing, 143
  introduction, 143
  paperwork reduction, 144
  research, 147
Information systems, 59, 145, 204–205, 427, 665
  budget model, 434
  informal sharing, 74
  information sharing, 61, 66, 68, 70, 143
  introduction, 60, 428
  management layers, 431
  methodology, 63
  providers, 67
  public vs. private, 145, 435, 428
  sharing relationships, 75, 76
Information Technology Agency, 591
Intellectual property, 186–190, 192, 200
  history, 186
  types, 188, 201
    copyrights, 190, 197
    patents, 188, 196
    trade secrets, 190, 195
    trademarks, 189
  risks, 190
  violations, 192–194
Interdisciplinary budget model, 428–429
  applications of, 429–430
Internal Revenue Service (IRS), 385
Internet, 309, 398
  findings, 303, 313
  hypothesis, 307–308
Internet Access Tax, 291; *see also* Internet
    taxes
Internet Sales Tax, 292; *see also* Internet taxes
Internet Tax Freedom Act, 282
Internet tax policy, 281, 284, 287, 289, 296
  analysis, 289
  Australia, 285
  Canada, 287
  Europe, 284
  U.S. 287
Internet taxes, 282–283, 288–291, 296–297
Internet technology, 310–311, 394, 398
Internet use, 309
Interorganizational information sharing
  barriers to state–local sharing, 61
Intranet, 394, 398–399
IPI, 268
IRS e-file program, 370, 375, 378–379, 383–385
IRS Restructuring and Reform Act (RRA) 1998,
    35
IRS systems, 100

IT Contracts, *see also* Information Technology
  Best Value in, 416–419
    Project and risk management, 420–421
IT Failure, 93, 410
  causes of, 410–412
  de-escalation of commitment, 98
    conditions for de-escalation, 98
  escalation of commitment, 95
    escalation process, 97
    project determinants, 96
  implications, 102
  introduction, 94
  re-escalation of commitment, 99
    re-escalation cycle, 100
    threats, 99
IT investment, 127–131, 133–139
  and organizational performance, 127
  framework, 135, 138
  introduction, 128
  its impact on organizational performance,
    129
    guidelines, 139
  literature, 130
IT management, 336, 338–340, 344
IT performance, 129f, 134 *see* E-government
IT performance-based laws, 602t
IT services
  contracting for, 408

J
Jeffersonian budgeting, 465–466

K
Kaylor methodology, 627
Kraemer and Dutton's analysis, 323

L
Large-scale IT Failure, 93
Large-scale systems, 94
Legislative Retrieval System (LRS), 329–332
Limited rights, 191
Local Area Networks (LAN), 204, 408
Local Government Information Systems
    Association (LOGIS), system, 64
Localism, 108–109, 111–113, 116–117,
    121–123

M
Mailing lists, 263–264, 270
Management by Objectives (MBO), 436
  data processing, 431
  decision support, 431
  management reporting, 431
  strategic and end user support, 432

Management information system (MIS), 428, 457, 459, 489, 491, 507
Marketspace, 372, 375, 383–384
Microcomputing, 17–22
  microcomputing in MPA curricula, 18t
Micromanagement, 565
Militaries, 219
  atrium model, 233
  global diffusion, 227
  middle eastern, 228
  U.S. Model of IT-enabled military, 226
Minnesota e-democracy project, 264, 274
MPA, 12–14, 17–21
Multi-user dimensions, 401

N
NASPAA, 12–14, 16–18, 24
National Performance Review, 31
National Telecommunication Information Administration (NTIA), 175
NATO, 222–224
NetDocs, 592
Network Enterprise Technology Command, 230
Network Security, 205, 271

O
Office of Consumer Affairs (OCA), 354
Online public information system, 270
Online transaction, 552, 554
Organizational Networks, 44–49
  influence of changing technology, 44
  management challenges, 45–46
  organizational performance, 127
  performance management, 46
    information needs, 47
    performance investment program, 55
    performance measurement systems, 48–49
Organization for Economic Cooperation and Development (OECD), 284
Orientations, 108–113, 116, 123
  cosmopolitan, 108–120, 123
  local, 108–118, 120, 122–123
Outsourcing, 413
  federal outsourcing, 419
  managing contracts, 420
  outsourcing core business processes, 421
  project and risk management, 420
  pros and cons, 415

P
Paperwork Reduction Act, 144–145, 604
Patents, 186–193, 196, 200
People First, 344, 347

Performance-based laws, 601, 603; see also Performance-based laws
Performance budgeting, 475
Performance indicator, 429
Performance investment program (PIP), 55–56
Performance management, 44, 46–47, 49–51, 54
Performance measurement systems, 48, 49
  input, 50
  integrating, 498–501
  outcome, 51
  output, 50
  process, 50
Policy formulation, 321–322, 329–333
Political information, 258
Primary centrism, 117
Privacy Act 29–30, 34
Productivity, 429
  productivity indicator, 429
Program Assessment Reporting Tool (PART), 603
Program budgeting, 468; see also Classic performance budgeting
  impact, 474
Project, 93–104
  business systems modernization, 101
  termination of, 100, 102
Project vote smart, 261
Public Finance Management (PFM), 490
Public Finance Management Information System (PFMIS), 498
Public information system, 3, 257, 269–271, 274, 276
  applications, 7
  organizational research, 4
  policy issues, 5
Public vs. private information systems, 145
  differences, 146
  Public Finance management, 489, 491
Public web-sites, 119
Public sector performance measures, 128
  efficiency, 111
  productivity, 112

R
Real world
  structuring principles of, 447–448
Re-escalation, 99
  cycle, 100
  of commitment, 99
  repeated failure, 100
Request for proposal (RFP), 382
Restricted access, 578
Restricted rights, 191–192
Revolution in military affairs, 227

Right of publicity, 187
Rulemaking process, 238, 240–249

S
Scavo, 548
Secure system, 204–205, 208, 211, 214–216
Security and privacy, 161
Security policy, 208–211, 214
Self-justification theory, 96
Self-presentation theory, 96
Semi-Automatic Ground Environment (SAGE), 28
Service level agreement, 457
Service marks, 189
Simulations, 397–398
Sociotechnical systems theory, 675–679
Software Acquisition Capability Maturity Model (SA-CMM), 412–413
Software safety, 205
Special works, 190
Spirit of community, 273–274
State Technology Office (STO), 341
State-local systems, 61
Statistical software, 505
    applications of, 514–515
    relation with managerial activities, 507–508
    role in decision making, 506–507
    significance tests, 511–512
    SPSS, SAS, 505
Streamlined Sales Tax Project, 288
Structural equation model, 167, 168
    advantages, 515
    in decision making, 506, 508
    use, 509
Sunshine Act, 29
System, 430

T
TANF program, 70–71
Taubman Center, 548
Technology Assessment Act 29
Technology enactment theory, 666
Telecommunications Act of 1996, 32
Telenet, 29
Telework, 524–527, 531
    community design studies, 530
    Community network, 527
    factors affecting, 531–532
    telecommuters, 529, 531, 533
        digital place design, 528
Theory Net, 29
Trade display properties, 194–195
Trade dress, 189
Trade secrets, 190, 195

Trademarks, 186–191, 193–194, 200
Training CAT, 392
    CBT, 392, 394–399
    disadvantages, 400–401
    JFM, 392, 399, 404
    Just-in-time (JIT), training, 392, 394–396, 399
    online training (OLT), 391
        disadvantages, 400–401
        opportunities, 391
    WBT, 392, 398–399
Transparency, 157–164, 167t
Trojan Horse, 207, 210, 212

U
Unlimited rights, 191–192, 199
URBIS, 546–547, 549–555
Usenet, 632–633
U.S. RMA model, 228

V
Value Added Tax (VAT), 284
Value chain analysis, 384, 385
Virtual communities, 109–110
Virtual cosmopolitans, 117–120
Virtual locals and Cosmopolitans, 108, 110, 117, 120
Virtual reality, 392, 394, 397
Virtual society, 669
Virtual value chain, 371–372, 374, 383, 385
Voice-over-IP, 394
Voter Integrity Project, 267
Voting Rights Act (1965), 265n

W
Web-based training, 392, 400
Web operations
    organizational interactivity, 159
    organizational transparency, 159
Webcasts, 394, 399, 402
Weberian model, 617
Website Attribute Evaluation System (WAES), 158
Website density, 158
Website diffusion, 158
Website interactivity, 158
Website openness, 158
Website transparency, 158, 167b
Websites, 199, 260, 548–549, 562
Websites orientations, 620
Weick/Maruyama model, 449
West Methodology measures, 623
Womenspeak, 633–640
World Bank governance indicators, 165–166
World Trade Organization (WTO), 264, 282

World Wide Web (WWW), 30, 60, 155, 257, 259–263, 266, 272, 336, 392, 402

XY
XML (Extensible Markup Language), 60, 151

Z
Zero-base budgeting (ZBB), 475